Women's Lives

Multicultural Perspectives

Fourth Edition

Gwyn Kirk

Margo Okazawa-Rey

McGraw Hill

Boston   Burr Ridge, IL   Dubuque, IA   Madison, WI   New York   San Francisco   St. Louis
Bangkok   Bogotá   Caracas   Kuala Lumpur   Lisbon   London   Madrid   Mexico City
Milan   Montreal   New Delhi   Santiago   Seoul   Singapore   Sydney   Taipei   Toronto

The McGraw·Hill Companies

Higher Education

WOMEN'S LIVES: MULTICULTURAL PERSPECTIVES
Published by McGraw-Hill, a business unit of The McGraw-Hill Companies, Inc., 1221 Avenue of the Americas, New York, NY, 10020. Copyright © 2007, 2004, 2001, 1998 by The McGraw-Hill Companies, Inc. All rights reserved. No part of this publication may be reproduced or distributed in any form or by any means, or stored in a database or retrieval system, without the prior written consent of The McGraw-Hill Companies, Inc., including, but not limited to, in any network or other electronic storage or transmission, or broadcast for distance learning.

Some ancillaries, including electronic and print components, may not be available to customers outside the United States.

This book is printed on acid-free paper.

2 3 4 5 6 7 8 9 0 FGR/FGR 0 9 8 7 6

ISBN-13: 978-0-07-352941-7
ISBN-10:   0-07-352941-9

Vice President and Editor-in-Chief: *Emily Barrosse*
Publisher: *Phillip A. Butcher*
Sponsoring Editor: *Sherith H. Pankratz*
Development Editor: *Kate Scheinman*
Freelance Permissions Coordinator: *Karyn Morrison*
Senior Marketing Manager: *Daniel M. Loch*
Managing Editor: *Jean Dal Porto*
Project Manager: *Catherine R. Iammartino*

Art Director: *Jeanne Schreiber*
Art Editor: *Ayelet Arbel*
Design Manager: *Laurie Entringer*
Senior Photo Research Coordinator: *Alexandra Ambrose*
Photo Researcher: *Judy Mason*
Senior Media Project Manager: *Nancy Garcia*
Production Supervisor: *Jason I. Huls*
Composition: *9/11 Palatino, by Techbooks*
Printing: *45 # New Era Matte, Quebecor World*

Cover credit: Linda Colsh, *May Day, May Day,* 1996. art apron; H36 × W32 inches (92 × 82 cm). Courtesy of the artist.
Credits: The credits section for this book begins on page C-1 and is considered an extension of the copyright page.

Library of Congress Cataloging-in-Publication Data

Kirk, Gwyn.
    Women's lives : multicultural perspectives / Gwyn Kirk, Margo Okazawa-Rey.—4th ed.
        p. cm.
    Includes bibliographical references (p.) and indexes.
    ISBN-13: (invalid) 978-0-07-352941-7 (softcover : alk. paper)
    ISBN-10: (invalid) 0-07-352941-9 (softcover : alk. paper)
    1. Women—United States—Social conditions. 2. Women—United States—Economic conditions. 3. Feminism—United States. I. Okazawa-Rey, Margo. II. Title.
HQ1421.K573 2007
305.420973—dc22   2006043347

The Internet addresses listed in the text were accurate at the time of publication. The inclusion of a Web site does not indicate an endorsement by the authors or McGraw-Hill, and McGraw-Hill does not guarantee the accuracy of the information presented at these sites.

www.mhhe.com

About the Cover

"May Day, May Day", 1996. By Linda Colsh.

Excerpt from the Artist's Statement

My apron is a distress signal: stop violence against women. Although most venues choose to hang this apron right side up, my intention is for this apron to hang upside down, because a flag flying upside down and sending a "May Day" message is a sign of distress.

While men sometimes wear them, the apron has become identified with women. The apron protects.

With the motif of upraised hands, I invite the viewer to stop and think about the hand as a symbol. One hand raised, palm forward, is clearly "STOP"; two hands raised, palms forward, is "I am unarmed; I am surrendering"; the back of the hand is a threat. Many hands are a crowd and to be among the others gives safety and comfort.

To those who connect us to the past,
our mothers,
who birthed us, raised us,
taught us, inspired us, and took no nonsense from us
Edwina Davies, Kazuko Okazawa, Willa Mae Wells
and to those who connect us to the future
Charlotte Elizabeth Andrews-Briscoe
Gabrielle Raya Clancy-Humphrey
Jesse Simon Cool
Issac Kana Fukumura-White
Akani Kazuo Ai-Lee James
Ayize Kimani Ming Lee James
Hansoo Lim
Uma Talpade Mohanty
Camille Celestina Stovall-Ceja
Aya Sato Venet

Brief Contents

Contents

CHAPTER TWO

◆◆◆

Identities and Social Locations: Who Am I? Who Are My People?   61

◆ **PART TWO** ◆

OUR BODIES, OURSELVES

CHAPTER THREE

◆◆◆

Women's Bodies and Beauty Ideals   121

READINGS

CHAPTER FOUR

Women's Sexuality   165

Stereotypes, Contradictions, and Double Standards   165

What Is Women's Autonomous Sexuality?   167

Challenging Binaries   169

Theorizing Sexuality   171

The Erotic as Power   173

Activism and Sexuality   173

Questions for Reflection   174

Finding Out More on the Web   174

Taking Action   174

READINGS

CHAPTER FIVE

◆◆◆

Women's Health   203

CHAPTER SIX

◆◆◆

Violence Against Women   249

◆ **PART THREE** ◆

MAKING A HOME, MAKING A LIVING

CHAPTER SEVEN
◆◆◆

Relationships, Families, and Households   291

CHAPTER EIGHT

◆◆◆

Work, Wages, and Welfare   339

CHAPTER NINE

◆◆◆

Living in a Global Economy   387

READINGS

◆ PART FOUR ◆

SECURITY AND SUSTAINABILITY

CHAPTER TEN

◆◆◆

Women, Crime, and Criminalization   439

CHAPTER ELEVEN

♦♦♦

Women and the Military, War, and Peace   483

CHAPTER TWELVE

◆◆◆

Women and the Environment   533

Theoretical and Activist Perspectives   535

Environmentalism   535

Deep Ecology and Bioregionalism   536

Ecofeminism   537

Environmental Justice   538

Connectedness and Sustainability   540

Questions for Reflection   542

Finding Out More on the Web   542

Taking Action   543

READINGS

◆ PART FIVE ◆

ACTIVISM AND CHANGE

CHAPTER THIRTEEN

◆◆◆

Creating Change: Theory, Vision, and Action   569

Preface

An introductory course is perhaps the most challenging women's studies course to conceptualize and teach. Depending on their overall goals for the course, instructors must make difficult choices about what to include and what to leave out. Students come into the course for a variety of reasons and with a range of expectations and prior knowledge, and most will not major in women's studies. The course may fulfill a distribution requirement for them, or it may be a way of taking one women's studies course during their undergraduate education out of a personal interest to broaden their knowledge of women's lives. For women's studies majors, the course plays a very different role, offering a foundation for their area of study.

Women's studies programs continue to build their reputations in terms of academic rigor and scholarly standards. Women's studies scholarship is on the cutting edge of many academic disciplines, especially in arts and humanities, and social sciences. At the same time, women's studies occupies a marginal position within academia, challenging male-dominated knowledge and pedagogy, with all the tensions this entails. Women's studies faculty and our allies within academic institutions necessarily live with these tensions personally and professionally. Outside the academy, economic changes and government policies have made many women's lives more difficult in the United States—a loss of factory and office work as jobs continue to be moved overseas or become automated; government failure to introduce a health-care system that will benefit everyone or to introduce an adequate system of child care; cuts in welfare programs; greater restriction of government support to immigrants and their families; and a dramatic increase in the number of women now incarcerated compared with fifteen years ago.

The political climate for women's studies on campuses and in the wider society is undoubtedly becoming more challenging as conservative viewpoints are normalized through political rhetoric, the narrow range of public debate, changes in law and policy, and the "disappearing" of information. A National Council for Research on Women report itemized actions of Bush Administration officials to delete, bury, and alter information that directly affects women's lives from government Web sites and publications (National Council for Research on Women 2004). The Department of Labor removed 25 reports from its Women's Bureau Web site, and deleted or distorted important information on many issues from pay equity to reproductive health care. The Department of Education "archived" its guidelines on sexual harassment in schools. The National Cancer Institute posted information, long discredited by researchers, suggesting a link between abortion and breast cancer (National Women's Law Center 2004). At the same time, a questioning of academic freedom on campuses is making many teachers' lives more difficult. Moreover, the erosion of hard-won gains for women, amply born out by data presented in this book, means that women's studies teachers are often in the unfortunate position of bearing "bad news."

This text started out as two separate readers that we used in our classes at Antioch College (Gwyn Kirk) and San Francisco State University (Margo Okazawa-Rey) over ten years ago. Since then, we have learned a lot about teaching an introductory women's studies course and the book has grown and developed as a result, becoming clearer and maintaining its usefulness, we hope, especially in these more difficult times.

What We Want in an Introductory Women's Studies Book

Several key issues concern us as teachers. We want to present a broad range of women's experiences to our students in terms of class, race, culture, nation, disability, age, and sexual orientation. We assume that hierarchies based on these factors create systems of disadvantage as well as systems of privilege and that women's multiple positions along these dimensions shape our life experiences in important and unique ways. Although the national discourse on race, for example, is still dominated by a Black/White paradigm, we want teaching materials that do justice to the diversity and complexity of race and ethnicity in this country. We also want materials that address the location of the United States in the global economic and political system. Students need to understand the economic forces that affect the availability of jobs in this country and elsewhere. They also need to understand the significance of U.S. dominance abroad in terms of language and popular culture, the power of the dollar and U.S.-based corporations, and the prevalence of the U.S. military.

In our introductory courses, we both included some discussion of theory because a basic understanding of various theoretical frameworks is a powerful tool not only for women's studies courses but also for other courses students take. Another shared concern is women's activism. As women's studies has become more established and professionalized, it has tended to grow away from its roots in the women's liberation movement, a trend that troubles us. As we talked about our own lives, it was clear that we both value our involvements in political movements. This activism teaches us a great deal and provides us with vital communities where we can learn, grow, and make a contribution on issues we care about. Currently, there are many women's activist and advocacy projects across the country, but many students do not know about them. In our teaching, we make it a point to include examples of women's activism and urge students to think of themselves as people who can make a difference in their own lives and in the world around them. Much of the information that students learn in women's studies concerning the difficulties and oppression of women's lives can be discouraging. Knowing about women's activism can be empowering, even in the face of sometimes daunting realities. This knowledge reinforces the idea that current inequalities and problems are not fixed but have the potential to be changed.

Linking Individual Experiences to National and International Trends and Issues

We are both trained in sociology. We have noticed that students coming into our classes are much more familiar with psychological explanations for behavior and experience than they are with structural explanations. They invariably enjoy first-person accounts of women's experiences, but a series of stories, even wonderfully insightful stories, leaves us unsatisfied. In class, we provide a context for the various issues students study. Taking a story about a woman with cancer, for example, we add details about how many women in the United States have cancer, possible explanations for this, the effects of age, race, and class on treatment and likelihood of recovery. The overview essay for each chapter provides some broader context for the selected readings. We've included readings that reflect the complexity of women's identities, where the authors wrote, for example, about being African American and bisexual in an integrated way. In the first edition we added a section on crime and criminalization in response to the great increase in women caught up in the criminal justice system in the past fifteen years, and added a chapter on women and the environment.

Challenges for the Twenty-First Century: Security and Sustainability

We are concerned about the challenges facing women and men in the twenty-first century: challenges regarding work and livelihood, personal and family relationships, violence on many levels, and the fragile physical environment. These issues pose major questions concerning the distribution of resources, personal and social values, and the definition of security. How is our society going to provide for its people in the years to come? What are the effects of the increasing polarization between rich and poor in the United States and between rich and poor countries of the world? Genuine security—at personal, community-wide, national, and planetary levels—is a key issue for the future, and, similarly, sustainability. These themes of security and sustainability provide a wider framework for the book.

As teachers, we are concerned with students' knowledge and understanding, and beyond that, with their aspirations, hopes, and values. One of our goals for this book is to provide a series of lenses that will help students understand their own lives and the lives of others. The second goal is that, through this understanding, they will be able to participate in some way in the creation of a secure and sustainable future.

New to the Fourth Edition

In the second edition we added two new chapters, one on sexuality and another on violence against women. We paid more attention to the role of women in politics, in both feminist movements and electoral politics. And we made explicit acknowledgment of the fact that women's studies students include a growing number of men.

The third edition paid more explicit attention to the role of media representations and popular culture in the creation of knowledge. We introduced a section at the end of each overview essay, titled "Finding Out More on the Web" to encourage student exploration of Internet sources. We also included cartoons and photos, and provided an Instructor's Manual.

This fourth edition relies on the analyses, principles, and style of earlier editions, with the following important additions and changes:

- Updated statistics throughout, and new readings on identity, gay marriage, religion, reproductive justice, men's opposition to violence against women, work, the global sex trade, privatization of water, criminalization, military wives, environmental effects on health, and women's political activism.

- A strong emphasis on media representations, popular culture, and advertising.

- More readings that make connections to the global level.

- Brief biographical notes for authors and first publication dates for readings to create a context for the readings.

- Updated and expanded citations to relevant literature as a starting point for student research.

- New diagrams, boxes, cartoons, and photos.

- Completely revised password-protected Instructor's Manual available on our companion Web site: **www.mhhe.com/kirk4**

A number of considerations—sometimes competing and contradictory—influenced these decisions. We are committed to including established writers and lesser-known writers, and writers from a range of racial and ethnic backgrounds and with differences in ability, age, class, culture, nation of birth, and sexuality. As before, we have looked for writers who, implicitly or explicitly, integrate several levels of analysis (micro, meso, macro, and global) in their work. Teachers invariably want more theory, more history, and more research-based pieces. The students we have talked with, including our own, love first-person pieces as this kind of writing helps to draw them into the more theoretical discussions. In the second edition we included more articles that give historical or theoretical accounts as a complement to first-person writings recognizing that if teachers do not assign the book, students will never see it. As we searched for materials, however, we found much more theoretical work by White women than by women of color. We assume this is because there are far fewer women of color in the academy, because White women scholars and writers have greater access to publishers, and because prevailing ideas about what theory is and what form it should take tend to exclude work by women of color. This can give the misleading impression that, aside from a few notable exceptions, women of color are not theorists. This raises the whole issue of what theory is and who can theorize, questions we take up in the first chapter. We have tried hard not to reproduce this bias in our selection, but we note this problem here to make this aspect of our process visible. We include personal essays and narratives that make theoretical points, what Gloria Anzaldúa (2002, p. 578) calls "autohistoria-teoria"—a genre of writing about one's personal and collective history that may use fictive elements and that also theorizes.

This new edition represents our best effort to balance these considerations, as we sought to provide information, analysis, and inspiration concerning the myriad daily experiences, opportunities, limitations, oppressions, hopes, joys, and satisfactions that make up U.S. women's lives. As before, our focus is on women in the United States, paying attention also to the many complex ways that U.S. women are tied to and part of the wider world.

Acknowledgments

Many people—especially our students, teachers, colleagues, and friends—made it possible for us to complete the first edition of this book. We are grateful to everyone at Mayfield who worked to put our manuscript between covers: Franklin Graham, our editor, whose confidence in our ideas never wavered and whose light hand on the steering wheel and clear sense of direction got us into print; also Julianna Scott Fein, production editor; the production team; and Jamie Fuller, copyeditor extraordinaire.

For the second edition, we were fortunate to have the support of Hamilton College as Jane Watson Irwin Co-Chairs in Women's Studies (1999–2001). Women's studies colleagues, other faculty members, and librarians welcomed and supported us. Again, we acknowledge the Mayfield team: Serina Beauparlant, our editor; Julianna Scott Fein, production editor; the production team; and Margaret Moore, a wonderful copyeditor.

The third edition benefited from support of the Women's Leadership Institute at Mills College, and the DataCenter, an Oakland-based nonprofit, providing research and training to grassroots social justice organizations across the country. We acknowledge the encouragement and skills of our editors, Beth Kaufman and Sherith Pankratz, and the work of the entire team: Jean Mailander, Jen Mills, Karyn Morrison, Amy Shaffer, and April Wells-Hayes.

As before, this fourth edition builds on the accumulated work, help, and support of many people who continue to sustain us. Particular thanks go to Onnesha Roychoudhuri, Suad Joseph and Benjamin D'Harlingue, and Asian Communities for Reproductive Justice who wrote specifically for this edition. Thanks also to Judith Arcana, Sharon Gormley, Michiko Hase, Aileen Hernandez, Gala King, Martha Matsuoka, Judith Raiskin, and Penny Rosenwasser for providing leads to new material, information, and insights. We thank the feminist scholars and activists whose work we have reprinted and all those whose research and writing not only have informed our work but have shaped the field of women's studies. We appreciate the independent bookstores and small presses that keep going due to dedicated staff and loyal readers, especially our "local"—Modern Times in San Francisco. We also rely on other feminist publishing "institutions": *The Women's Review of Books*, *Ms.*, scholarly journals, and WMST-L, ably "mastered" by Joan Korenman. We benefit enormously from discussions on this list and suggestions for readings and classroom activities generously shared by women's studies teachers.

The United States continues to gain more brilliant young feminist writers, teachers, organizers, and artists—some of whose work is included here. Many seasoned feminists are passing on. We honor and remember four courageous trailblazers and internationally recognized public figures who died while this manuscript was in preparation: Gloria Anzaldúa, cultural theorist and creative writer extraordinaire; Shirley Chisholm, first African American woman elected to Congress and the first woman to seek nomination as a presidential candidate; Andrea Dworkin, passionate feminist theorist, novelist, and organizer; and Susan Sontag, who was an innovative essayist, fiction writer, and a leading commentator on modern culture. We are among the many people who found inspiration in the way they sought to live their lives according to their principles, values, and visions.

This is our second edition with McGraw-Hill. We greatly appreciate the encouragement, enthusiasm, and skills of our editors, Kate Scheinman and Sherith Pankratz, and the work of the entire book team: Cathy Iammartino, Jason Huls, Alex Ambrose, and Laurie Entringer. Once again we benefited from the insights and advice of outside reviewers:

Piya Chatterjee, University of California–Riverside
Susan S. Lanser, Brandeis University
Naydi Nazario, University of North Carolina, Wilmington
Cara L. Okopny, University of South Florida
Cecilia Rio, Towson University
Gwendolyn T. Sorell, Texas Tech University
Nancy Tolson, Illinois State University

Lastly, we acknowledge the importance of our friendship, deepening over these past thirteen years, that provides a firm foundation for our shared understandings and our work together. We continue to be inspired by the cultural work of Sweet Honey in the Rock, a national living treasure whose blend of music and politics touches the head, heart, and hands, and also by the "sociological imagination"— C. Wright Mills' concept—that draws on the need for complex social analysis in order to make change.

To everyone, very many thanks.

— Gwyn Kirk and Margo Okazawa-Rey

We have chosen each other
and the edge of each other's battles
the war is the same
if we lose
someday women's blood will congeal
upon a dead planet
if we win
there is no telling
we seek beyond history
for a new and more possible meeting.

— AUDRE LORDE

The Framework of This Book

To study alongside men, to have access to the same curriculum, and to be admitted to male professions were goals that dominated women's education in the United States for several generations, from the early nineteenth century on. In the late 1960s and early 1970s, however, the gendered nature of knowledge itself—with its focus on White, male, and middle-class perspectives that are assumed to be universal—was called into question by feminists.

The Focus and Challenge of Women's Studies

The early 1970s saw the start of many women's studies programs across the country, building on the insights and energies of the women's liberation movement. Early courses had titles like "Women's Liberation," "The Power of Patriarchy," or "Sexist Oppression and Women's Empowerment." Texts often included mimeographed articles from feminist newsletters and pamphlets, as there was so little appropriate material in books. By contrast, women's studies is now an established field of study with an extensive body of literature and more than seven hundred programs with Web sites worldwide, over five hundred of them in U.S. universities and colleges, including master's and Ph.D. programs. Women's studies graduates are employed in many fields, including law, business, publishing, health, social and human services, and education and library work (Luebke and Reilly 1995). Students report that women's studies courses are informative and empowering; they provide a perspective on one's own life and on other college courses in ways that are often life changing (Luebke and Reilly 1995; Musil 1992).

Women's studies seeks new ways of understanding—more comprehensive than those offered by traditional academic disciplines. It started as a critique of earlier scholarship that typically ignored women's lives or treated women in stereotypical ways. Women's studies sought to provide missing information, new theoretical perspectives, and new ways of teaching that bridge academic learning and life experience. Most women studies teachers do not use what Brazilian educator Paulo Friere called the "banking method" of education, common in many fields, whereby teachers deposit information—historical facts, dates, definitions—and students withdraw it in quizzes and exams. This method may work well for some subjects. It is less appropriate for women's studies where students come into class with experience, knowledge, opinions, and theories about many of the topics discussed. You are familiar with perspectives on issues that are circulating in the media, for example. You may know where your spiritual community stands on matters you care about. In a women's studies class, you are encouraged to share and reflect on your own experiences and to relate the readings and discussions to your own life. Women's studies focuses on critical reading and critical thinking, which is a new way of learning for many students, especially those just starting college. It requires you to synthesize information, and integrate diverse points of view, all significant academic and workplace skills.

Women's studies courses provide data that are often absent in the rest of the curriculum. You may be challenged by this and pushed to rethink some of your assumptions about gender, your own experiences of schooling, family, and relationships, and your positions on a number of complex issues. This kind of study often evokes strong emotional reactions, as your own life may be deeply affected by issues under discussion. These aspects of women's studies have given rise to criticisms that it is too "touchy-feely," more like therapy than serious study, or that it is an extended gripe session against men. We discuss these criticisms later in this introduction. Women's studies also often generates anger in students at the many forms of women's oppression, at other students' ignorance or lack of concern for this, at being female in a male-dominated world, and at the daunting nature of the issues and problems faced by women (Boxer 1998; Howe 2000).

In the first part of each chapter we present data and theoretical perspectives, drawing from several academic fields, government reports, journalists' accounts, personal narratives, and the work of nonprofit research and advocacy organizations. Our goal is to provide some historical and contemporary context for the articles that follow. We have selected particular articles to help you think through issues that matter in women's lives, many of them complex and contentious. Be warned. This can be challenging, intellectually and emotionally. The biggest assets are curiosity, careful reading, and an open mind as you digest and evaluate the material. Weigh arguments carefully—the familiar and the unfamiliar—before deciding where you stand on an issue, and why. College is a time when many previously taken-for-granted assumptions are questioned, examined, embraced, or discarded. This is part of the growth that education provides. You do not have to agree with everything in this book, of course, but whether you do or you don't, you should be able to support your opinions.

The data we present show significant gains and some serious setbacks for women as a whole over the past thirty years or so. Some of the information and analysis here is very discouraging. At the same time, important change has taken place—including the very existence of women's studies and the wealth of women's writing and organizing that we draw on in this collection.

The Framework for This Book: Collective Action for a Sustainable Future

This book is concerned with women in the United States and the rich diversity of their life experiences. We have selected readings that reflect this diversity. As writers and editors, a big challenge for us has been to choose effective writings and salient facts from the vast wealth of materials available. There has been a groundswell of women's writing and publishing in the past thirty-five years, as well as a proliferation of popular and scholarly books and journals on issues of interest to women's studies students. When opinion polls, academic studies, government data, public debates, and grassroots research, available in print and through electronic media, are added to this, it is easy to be swamped with information and opposing viewpoints.

In making our selections, we have filtered this wealth of material according to a number of principles—our particular road map.

An Activist Approach

We argue that women and men in the United States face a range of serious problems in the years ahead if we are to sustain our lives, the lives of our children, and the lives of our children's children. Although some women have benefited from greater opportunities for education and wage earning, many are now working harder, or working longer hours, than their mothers did, under pressure to keep a job and to juggle their work lives with family responsibilities. In the 1980s and 1990s, a range of economic changes and government policies made many women's lives more difficult. Examples include a loss of factory and office work as jobs were moved overseas or became automated; government failure to introduce an adequate system of child care or a health-care system that would benefit everyone; cuts in welfare; greater restriction of government support to immigrants and their families; and a dramatic increase in the number of women now incarcerated compared with the number from twenty years ago. While the U.S. military budget consumes a massive 46 percent of federal income tax (for the fiscal year 2005), according to the War Resisters League (2005), and some states spend more public money on incarceration than on higher education, thousands of people are homeless, inner-city schools lack basic resources, and funding for Head Start and other preschool programs is cut back. Individual women and men are personally affected by such changes and policies as they negotiate intimate relationships and family life.

We see collective action for progressive social change as a major goal of scholarly work, and thus, in the face of these economic and political trends, we take a deliberately activist approach in this book. We mention many practical projects and organizations to give students a sense of how much activist work is going on that is often not visible in the mainstream media. Throughout our discussion we emphasize the diversity of women's experiences. These differences have often divided women. We assume no easy "sisterhood" across lines of race, class, nation, age, or sexual orientation, for example, but we do believe that alliances built firmly on the recognition and understanding of such differences make collective action possible.

A Sustainable and Secure Future

We see sustainability and security as central issues for the twenty-first century. These involve questions about the distribution of wealth, both within the United States and between the rich and poor countries of the world, and about the direction of future economic development. Another concern is the rapid deterioration of the physical environment on our overburdened planet. In many chapters, security is an underlying theme. This includes the individual security of knowing who we are; having sturdy family relationships; living in freedom from threats, violence, or coercion; having adequate income or livelihood; and enjoying health and well-being. It also involves security for the community, the nation, and the planet, and includes issues like crime, the role of the military, and the crucial importance of the physical environment. Throughout the book we emphasize severe structural inequalities between people: women and men, White people and people of color, older people and young people, people from the United States and other nations, for example. We see these inequalities as a major threat to long-term security because they create literal and metaphorical walls, gates, and fences that separate people and maintain hierarchies among us. We also argue that a more sustainable future means rethinking materialism and consumerism and finding new ways to distribute wealth so that everyone has the basics of life. These issues affect not only women, of course, and are not solely the responsibility of women, but women are actively involved in community organizing and movements for economic and environmental justice in the United States and many other countries, often in greater numbers than men.

The United States in a Global Context

This is not a book about global feminism. Its focus is on the United States, but we also comment on the wider global context. We recognize the racial and ethnic diversity of this country; many people in the United States were not born here and come with hopes for a better future, but they also may have no illusions about inequalities in the United States. We argue that people in the United States need to understand the significance of this country's preeminence in the world, manifested culturally, through the dominance of the English language and in widespread distribution of U.S. movies, news media, TV shows, pop music, books, and magazines; economically, through the power of the dollar as an international currency and the impact of U.S.-based corporations abroad; and militarily, through the global reach of U.S. foreign policy, troops, bases, and weapons. We need to understand the significance of the globalization of the economy for people in the United States as well as throughout the world. We must understand the connections between domestic policy issues like health care, child care, and welfare, and foreign policy issues such as military expenditures and foreign aid.

Linking the Personal and the Global

Throughout the book we use the terms **micro level** (personal or individual), **meso level** (community, neighborhood, or school, for example), **macro level** (national), and **global level.** To understand people's experiences or the complexity of a particular issue, it is necessary to look at all of these levels and how they interconnect. For instance, a personal relationship between two people might be thought to operate on a micro level. However, both partners bring all of themselves to the relationship. Thus, in addition to micro-level factors such as appearance, generosity, or their determination not to repeat the mistakes of their parents' relationships, there are meso-level factors—such as their connections to people of other faiths or races—and macro-level factors—such as the obvious or hidden ways in which men or White people are privileged in this society. As editors we have made these connections in our overview essays and looked for writings that make these links between levels of analysis.

A Matrix of Oppression and Resistance

Underlying our analysis is the concept of oppression, which we see as a group phenomenon, regardless of whether individuals in a group think they are oppressed or want to be in dominant positions. Men, as a group, are advantaged by sexism, for example, whereas women, as a group, are disadvantaged. Every form of oppression—for instance, **sexism,** **racism, classism, heterosexism, anti-Semitism, able-bodyism**—is rooted in our **social institutions,** such as the family, education, religion, government, law, and the media. Oppression, then, is systemic, and it is systematic. It is used consistently by one group of people—those who are dominant in this society—to rule, control, and exploit (to varying degrees) another group—those who are subordinate—for the benefit of the dominant group.

Oppression works through systems of inequality, as well as the dominance of certain values, beliefs, and assumptions about people and how society should be organized. These are institutional and ideological controls. Members of dominant groups generally have built-in economic, political, and cultural benefits and power, regardless of whether they are aware of, or even want, these benefits. This process of accruing benefits and power from institutional inequalities is often referred to as **privilege.** Those most privileged are often those least likely to be aware of it or to recognize it (McIntosh 1988). Oppression works on personal (micro), community (meso), national (macro), and global levels.

Oppression involves **prejudice,** which we define as unreasonable, unfair, and hostile attitudes toward people, and **discrimination,** differential treatment favoring those who are in positions of dominance. But oppression reaches beyond individual bigotry or good intentions: It is promoted by the **ideologies** and practices of every institution we encounter and are part of and cannot be fully changed without fundamental changes in these institutions. Our definition of oppression assumes that everyone is socialized to participate in oppressive practices, thereby helping to maintain them. People may be involved as direct perpetrators or passive beneficiaries, or they may direct **internalized oppression** at members of their own group. Oppression results in appropriation and the loss—both voluntary and involuntary—of voice, identity, and agency of oppressed peoples.

It is important to think about oppression as an intricate system, at times blatantly obvious and at others subtly nuanced, rather than an either/or dichotomy of privileged/disadvantaged or oppressor/oppressed. We use the term **matrix of oppression and resistance** to describe the interconnection and interrelatedness of various forms of oppression. People can be privileged in some respects (race or gender, for example) and disadvantaged in others (class or sexual orientation, for example). Even negative ascriptions may be the source of people's resistance based on shared identity.

Feminisms: Tangling with the "F" Word

Whether or not you consider yourself a feminist as a matter of personal identity, in women's studies you will study feminist perspectives and theories because these seek to understand and explain gender. In a nutshell, *feminism* concerns the liberation of women and girls from discrimination based on gender. The goal of feminist theory and practice is women's self-determination. For some feminists this means securing equal rights for women within existing institutions—from marriage and the family to government policy and law. For others it means fundamentally changing these institutions. We focus on feminist theories in Chapter 1 and discuss a range of feminist perspectives throughout the book. Brief summaries for reference are provided in the glossary. Gender subordination is linked to discrimination based on other systems of inequality such as race, class, sexuality, and national origin, and we emphasize these links through selected readings and in our introduction to each chapter.

Feminism is a term with a great deal of baggage. For some it is positive and empowering. For others it conjures up negative images of "ugly" women in overalls and flannel shirts, women who do not wear makeup or shave their legs or underarms and who are said to be lesbians, man-haters, or "ball-busters." Many women do not want to be associated with the label "feminist." They may agree that women deserve higher pay, sexual freedom, or greater opportunity, but they are careful to start their comments with a disclaimer: "I'm not a feminist, but. . . ."

In the past ten to fifteen years, virtually every major U.S. publication has published a "feminism has gone too far" or "feminism is dead" piece. Some lamented the difficulties of being White and male; others blamed women's dissatisfactions on "too much equality"; and still others equated feminism with a "victim" mentality (e.g., Fox-Genovese 1994; Lehrman 1993; Paglia 1990; Roiphe 1993; Wolf 1993). An *Esquire* magazine article talked approvingly of

"do me feminism" and quoted a woman academic who claimed that there are a lot of "homely girls" in women's studies (Quindlen 1994). According to Erica Jong (1998), *Time* magazine published "no less than 119 articles" criticizing feminism during the last twenty-five years. Its June 29, 1998, cover story, "Is Feminism Dead?" argued that feminism has become "a whole lot of stylish fluff"(p. 56).

When women talk of violence—battering, incest, rape, sexual abuse, and harassment—or racism, or living in poverty, or aging without health insurance, detractors describe them as "victim" feminists or, perhaps worse, "feminazis"—antisex, no fun, whining critics who are out to destroy men and the male establishment. This is part of what Pulitzer Prize–winning writer Susan Faludi (1991) meant when she wrote of a backlash against feminism and women's rights and an erosion of the gains made for and by women in the past thirty-five years or so. In our society, women are socialized to care for men and to spare their feelings, but recognizing and discussing institutional inequalities between women as a group and men as a group are very different from "man-bashing." This garbled, trivializing media framework contributes to the many myths and misunderstandings about women's studies on the part of students and scholars in other fields. We consider three of these myths here.

Myth 1: Women's Studies Is Ideological

Some people assume that women's studies is not "real" scholarship but, instead, is feminist propaganda. Yet feminist inquiry, analysis, and activism have arisen from real problems experienced by real women, from well-documented inequalities and discrimination. For instance, data recorded for more than one hundred years show that U.S. women's wages, on average, have never risen above 75 percent of what men earn on average— that is, on average, women earn seventy-five cents for every dollar earned by men. And women of color fare much worse in this respect than White women. As we mentioned earlier, women's studies arose out of feminist organizing, and it values scholarly work that is relevant to activist concerns. Women's studies courses and projects seek to link intellectual, experiential, and emotional forms of connected knowing with the goal of improving women's lives. Women's studies is a rigorous

Girls display their banner at a demonstration protesting war against Iraq, San Francisco, February 16, 2003.

endeavor, but its conception of rigor differs from that of much traditional scholarship, which values abstract, in-depth knowledge, narrowly defined. By contrast, women's studies scholarship places a high value on breadth and connectiveness; this kind of rigor requires broad understandings grounded in a range of experiences and the ability to make connections between knowledge and insights from different fields of study. Knowledge is never neutral, and in women's studies this is made explicit.

To some students and scholars, feminism is something to believe in because it provides a perspective that makes sense of the world and is personally empowering. But students who blithely blame everything on "rich White men" or "the patriarchy" without taking the trouble to read and think critically are anti-intellectual and inadvertently reinforce the notion that women's studies is anti-intellectual.

Myth 2: Women's Studies Is a White, Middle-Class Thing

Some White middle-class feminists have made, and still make, untenable claims about all women based on their own, necessarily partial, experience. Since the writings of Aphra Behn in the early 1600s, however, there have been White women who have thought about race and class as well as gender. Some White feminists worked against slavery in the nineteenth century, organized against the Ku Klux Klan,

THE INCREDIBLE SHRINKING WOMAN

and participated in the civil rights movement of the 1950s and 1960s. Indeed, the 1970s revitalization of feminism in the United States came out of civil rights organizing. In the past thirty years or so, some White feminists have linked race and gender in their teaching, research, and activism (e.g., Frankenberg 1993; McIntosh 1988; Pratt 1984; Rich 1986c; Segrest 1994). Many notable scholars, writers, and activists of color also identify as feminists, among them, Betty Burkes, the Combahee River Collective, Sandra Cisneros, bell hooks, Audre Lorde, Elizabeth Martínez, and Chandra Talpade Mohanty included in this anthology. Accounts of the diverse beginnings of 1960s and 1970s women's movement also explode this myth (e.g., Allen 1986; Baxandall 2001; Baxandall and Gordon 2000; Guy Sheftall 1995; Moraga and Anzaldúa 1981; Omolade 1994; Roth 2003; Springer 2005; Thompson 2002). African American writer bell hooks (2000) argues that "there should be billboards; ads in magazines; ads on buses, subways, trains; television commercials spreading the word, letting the world know more about feminism," because "feminism is for everybody" (p. x).

Myth 3: Women's Studies Is Narrowly Concerned with Women's Issues

Although women's studies aims to focus on women's experiences—in all their diversity—we do not see this as catering to narrow "special interests." On the contrary, feminist analyses provide a series of lenses to examine many topics and academic disciplines, including psychology, sociology, anthropology, political science, law, international relations, economic development, environmental studies, ethnic studies, national income accounting, human biology, philosophies of science, and physics. Feminist scholarship is on the cutting edge of many academic fields, especially literature, history, philosophy, and film and media studies. It also raises crucial questions about teaching and learning, research design and methodologies, and theories of knowledge. Far from narrow, women's studies is concerned with thinking critically about the world in all its complexity.

It is important to acknowledge that women's studies students include a growing number of men. We are mindful that our readership includes male students, and in places we pose questions and give specific suggestions to them. There are many ways that men can contribute to and support wider opportunities for women—as sons, brothers, fathers, partners, friends, coworkers, supervisors, labor organizers, spiritual leaders, teachers, doctors, lawyers, police officers, judges, legislators. Sociologist Michael Kimmel calls for pro-feminist men to be cheerleaders, allies, and foot soldiers; "and we must be so in front of other men, risking our own fears of rejection, our own membership in the club of masculinity, confronting our own fears of other men" (in Kimmel and Messner 1998, p. 68). The questions at the end of each chapter and suggestions for taking action provide pointers in this direction. There is a long history of men's support for women's equality in the United States (see, for example, Digby 1998; Kimmel and Mosmiller 1992; and Movement for a New Society 1983), and a training in women's studies can provide a powerful impetus for this. Clearly, the changes we discuss in this book cannot be achieved by women alone without male allies. But we also assume that masculinity is socially constructed and highly constrained in our society and that there is something for men in this whole project, beyond being allies to women (Readings 2 and 37; Johnson 2005). We believe that those in dominant positions (on any social dimension, be it gender, race, class, age, ability, and so forth) are also limited by oppressive structures. Despite the obvious benefits, privilege separates people and makes us ignorant of important truths. To be able to look others in the eye openly and completely, to join together to create a secure and sustainable future for everyone, we have to work to end systems of inequality. This repudiation of privilege, we believe, is not a sacrifice but rather the possibility of entering into genuine community, where we can all be more truly human.

Scope of the Book

This book is concerned with the project of theorizing about the oppressive conditions facing women today and the long-term work of transforming those conditions. In Part 1 (Chapters 1 and 2), we discuss the creation of knowledge and the significance of identity and social location for understanding ourselves, our communities, and the world we live in. Part 2 (Chapters 3–6) explores women's experiences of self in terms of our bodies, sexuality, health, and gender violence. In Part 3 (Chapters 7–9), we look at what is involved in making a home and making a living, and the significance of living in a global economy. In Part 4 (Chapters 10–12), we discuss women's experiences of crime and criminalization, the military, and the environment. We end, in Part 5 (Chapter 13), with a discussion of social change and focus on the importance of theories, visions, and action for creating change. Our overall argument is that to improve the lives of women in the United States also means redefining security and directing ourselves, our communities, this society, and the wider world toward a more sustainable future.

1

◆◆◆

Theories and Theorizing:
Integrative Frameworks
for Understanding

Why are girls in the United States generally bet-ter at creative writing than at math? Has this always been so? Is this difference inevitable? Is rape about sexuality? Power? Both? Or neither? What is pornography? Is it the same as erotica? Do lesbians really want to be men? Why do so many marriages end in divorce? Why are so many children in the United States brought up in poverty? Why are more women going to jail than ever before?

People often say that facts speak for themselves. On the contrary, we argue that facts are always open to interpretation. They are "made to speak" according to your particular point of view. This is why we open this book about U.S. women's lives with a chapter on theory and theory making. How you think about women's situations and experiences affects what you see and what you understand by what you see. This chapter may seem abstract in the beginning, and you may want to return to it as you work with the material in the book. It would also be a good idea to review it at the end of your course. In this chapter we look at theory and

theory making in general terms and give a brief account of feminist theoretical perspectives in preparation for understanding and interpreting women's experiences and issues presented in the rest of the book. In this discussion we will consider these questions: What is a theory? Who creates theory, and how is it created? What is the purpose of theory?

Definition of a Theory

Consider the following assertion about poverty that many people in our society make: Poor people are poor because they are lazy. Think about the following questions:

1. What is the purpose of this statement?
2. What are the underlying assumptions on which it is based?
3. Who came up with this idea, under what circumstances, and when?

4. How did this idea become popular?

5. If the statement were true, what would it imply about action that should be taken?

6. What would you need to know to decide whether this statement is really true?

The statement above is a theory. It is one explanation of poverty. It is built on a set of assumptions, or certain factors taken for granted. For example, this theory assumes there are well-paying jobs for all who want to work and that everyone meets the necessary requirements for those jobs, such as education, skills, or a means of providing for child care. These factors are proposed as facts or truths. This explanation of poverty takes a moral perspective. A psychological explanation of poverty may argue that people are poor because they have low self-esteem, lack self-confidence, and take on self-defeating behaviors. A sociological explanation might conclude that structures in our society, such as the educational and economic systems, are organized to exclude certain groups from being able to live above the poverty line. Each theory explicitly or implicitly suggests how to address the problem, which could then lead to appropriate action. If the problem is defined in terms of laziness, a step to ending poverty might be to punish people who are poor; if it is defined in psychological terms, assertiveness training or counseling might be suggested; and if it is defined in terms of structural inequality, ending discrimination would be the answer.

Theories, Theorizing, and Ways of Knowing

Virtually everyone thinks up explanations for their experiences; that is, they create theory. For instance, we analyze the causes of poverty in our communities, the impact of immigration on the state we live in, or the experience of date rape. Theories generated by ordinary people, however, are usually not regarded as worthy of consideration beyond their own spheres of influence, among friends or coworkers, for example. Historically, Western, university-educated men from the upper classes and their theories, which are supported by societal institutions such as education and government, have had the greatest impact on how human beings and social phenomena are explained and understood. Their considerable influence has compelled many people simply to accept what is presented to them as conventional wisdom. In the following sections, we discuss how certain kinds of theories have been legitimized in this society and suggest another way of theorizing and developing knowledge that engages ordinary people.

Dominant Perspectives

From the perspective of the **dominant culture**—the values, symbols, means of expression, language, and interests of the people in power in this society—only certain types of theories have authority. Generally, the authoritativeness of a theory about human beings and society is evaluated primarily along two dimensions. One is its degree of formality, which is determined according to how closely its development followed a particular way of theorizing, the so-called scientific method, the basics of which most of us learned in high school science classes. The second is the scope and generality of the theory.

Although in practice there are several variations of the scientific method, key elements must be present for a theory to fit in this category. The scientific method, originally devised by natural scientists, rests on the presumption of **objectivity,** "an attitude, philosophy, or claim . . . independent of the individual mind [through emotional detachment and social distance] . . . verified by a socially agreed-upon procedure such as those developed in science, mathematics, or history" (Kohl 1992, p. 84). Objectivity is seen as both a place to begin the process of theorizing and the outcome of that process. It has been long argued that "if done properly, [science] is the epitome of objectivity" (Tuana 1989, p. xi). Therefore, theories developed correctly using the scientific method are held out as value-free and neutral. The method is also empirical. That is, for something to be a fact, it must be physically observable and countable or measurable. This proposition is extended to include the notion that something is either true or not true, fact or not fact. Last, the experimental method, commonly used in science, "attempts to understand a whole by examining its parts, asking how something works rather than why it works, and derives abstract formulas to predict future results" (Duff 1993, p. 51). In summary, these elements add up to research methods that

> generally require a distancing of the researcher from her or his subjects of study; . . . absence of emotions from the research process; ethics and values are deemed inappropriate in the research process, either as the reason for scientific inquiry or as part of the research process itself; . . . adversarial debates, whether written or oral, become the preferred method of ascertaining truth: the arguments that can withstand the greatest assault and survive intact become the strongest truth.
> *(Collins 1990, p. 205)*

The scientific method was adopted by theorists in the social sciences as a way to validate and legitimate social scientific knowledge beginning in the late nineteenth century, as disciplines such as psychology and sociology were being developed. Since that time, academic disciplines like education, nursing, and social work have also adopted it as the primary method with which to develop new knowledge in their fields.

The second dimension for evaluating and judging theory is concerned with its scope and generality. The range is from the most specific explanation with the narrowest scope and most limited generality to the other end of the continuum, the general theory, which is the most abstract and is assumed to have the most general application. Many general theories have been promoted and accepted as being universally applicable. One of them, **biological determinism,** holds that a group's biological or genetic makeup shapes its social, political, and economic destiny. In mainstream society, biology is often assumed to be the basis of women's and men's different roles, especially women's ability to bear children. Most social scientists and feminist theorists see behavior as socially constructed and learned through childhood socialization, everyday experience, education, and the media, as argued by sociologist Judith Lorber (Reading 1). They explain differences in women's and men's roles in these terms and argue that variations in gender roles from one society to another provide strong evidence for a **social constructionist** view.

Alternative Perspectives

Evaluating and judging theories according to the scientific method has come under heavy criticism from feminist theorists who typically have been viewed as outsiders to traditional academic circles (e.g., Bleier 1984; Collins 1990; Duran 1998; and Shiva 1988). These theorists have seen the fallacies, biases, and harmful outcomes of that way of creating knowledge. The primary criticisms are that knowledge created by the scientific method is not value-free, neutral, or generalizable to the extent it is claimed to be. Science, as with other academic disciplines, is "a cultural institution and as such is structured by the political, social, and economic values of the culture within which it is practiced" (Tuana 1989, p. xi). As biologist Ruth Hubbard (1989) argues:

> To be believed, scientific facts must fit the worldview of the times. Therefore, at times of tension and upheaval . . . some researchers always try to prove that differences in the social, political, and economic status of women and men, blacks and whites, poor people and rich people, are inevitable because they are the results of people's inborn qualities and traits. Such scientists have tried to "prove" that blacks are innately less intelligent than whites, or that women are innately weaker, more nurturing, less good at math than men.
> *(p. 121)*

Rather than being neutral, all knowledge is socially constructed, value-laden, and biased and reflects and serves the interests of the culture that produced it, in this case the dominant culture.

The problem is not that theories are value-laden or biased, but that the values and biases of many theories are hidden under the cloak of "scientific objectivity." Moreover, 'there is the assumption that "if the science is 'good,' in a professional sense [following closely the rules of scientific method], it will also be good for society" (Hubbard 1989, p. 121). Many theories are applied by scholars, policy makers, and commentators not only to the United States but also to the rest of the world, often without acknowledgment that they primarily serve the interests of the dominant group in the United States. They use these theories to justify the inequalities in our society as well as differences and inequalities between the United States and other societies. Despite claims to the contrary, general theories created by mainstream scholars serve a political purpose in addition to whatever other purpose they are intended to serve. And, as sociologist Patricia Hill Collins (1990) asserts, "Because elite white men and their representatives control structures of knowledge validation, white male interests pervade thematic content of traditional scholarship" (p. 201).

We further argue that theorizing is a political project, regardless of whether this is acknowledged. Social theories—explaining the behavior of human beings and society—may serve to support the existing social order or can be used to challenge it. For women and men of color, White women, poor people, members of oppressed groups, and people with privilege who are interested in progressive social change, the political work of theorizing is to generate knowledge that challenges conventional wisdom and those formal theories that do not explain their real lived experiences, provide satisfactory solutions to their difficulties, or lead to their liberation. Director of the Center for Women's Global Leadership, Rutgers University, Charlotte Bunch (1987) has recommended an effective four-step way to think about theory: describing what exists, analyzing why that reality exists, determining what should exist, and hypothesizing how to change what is to what should be.

The Role of Values

"Determining what should exist," the third part of Charlotte Bunch's model, is clearly a matter of values and beliefs. It involves being able to envision a world free from discrimination and oppression, if only vaguely. Feminism is concerned with values by definition: the liberation of women and girls from discrimination based on gender, race, class, sexuality, and so on. Values do not come from facts or from the analysis of a situation but rather from people's beliefs in principles like fairness, equality, or justice. We may learn such principles from our families and communities, or through organized religion or a more personal sense of spirituality. We may think of them in terms of fundamental human rights (e.g., Agosín 2001; Bunch and Carillo 1991; Bunch and Reilly 1994; Kerr 1993). Whatever the source, feminist work invariably involves values

whether stated explicitly or implied. In Reading 5, JeeYeun Lee describes a woman's studies class she took as an undergraduate: "For the first time I found people who articulated those murky half-formed feelings that I could previously only express . . . as 'But that's not fair!'" Notice the value positions in all the readings in this chapter and throughout this book. Several writers draw on spirituality (bell hooks, Reading 33), progressive secularism (Melanie Kaye/Kantrowitz, Reading 11), or an explicitly faith-based perspective that informs their view of the world and their sense of life purpose (Christina Leaño, Reading 78). Others show how religious traditions and values restrict and oppress women (Readings 22, 39, and 46). At the individual and community level, spirituality is a source of comfort, connection, inspiration, and meaning for many women. They play a key role in teaching their children spiritual beliefs and practices and are respected for this in their families and communities. The world's major religions are all patriarchal, although this plays out in different ways in different traditions. Sacred texts are often open to divergent interpretations and are sometimes much more supportive of women than organized religious practice. At the institutional level, organized religions have a mixed record, at best, in supporting women's agency and empowerment. Religious leaders and representatives of international women's organizations who met in Chiang Mai, Thailand, in 2004, called for a commitment to women's human rights on the part of all religions (Reading 83).

Theoretical Frameworks for Understanding Women's Lives

As an interdisciplinary field of study, women's studies incorporates theoretical insights from several academic disciplines, including anthropology, cultural studies, economics, history, literature, philosophy, politics, psychology, and sociology. In turn, feminist scholarship has made significant contributions to these disciplines.

Women's studies also draws on feminist theories that primarily seek to understand and explain women's experiences. Many of these theories were developed in the context of women's organizing for change—for the abolition of slavery, for women's suffrage, for labor rights, the civil rights of people of color, women's rights, and gay/lesbian/bisexual/transgender rights. Feminist theories have been concerned with fundamental questions: Why are women in a subordinate position in our society and, indeed, worldwide? What are the origins of this subordination, and how is it perpetuated? How can it be changed?

We argue for a theoretical framework that allows us to see the diversity of women's lives and the fundamental structures of power, inequality, and opportunity that shape our experiences. The readings in this chapter all contribute to this understanding. Judith Lorber (Reading 1) argues that gender differences are not natural or biological but learned from infancy. Gender differences are maintained by key social institutions such as education, marriage, popular culture, news media, religion, government, and law. The implication of her argument is that our society's gender arrangements are not fixed or inevitable but can be changed.

Sociologist Jackie Stacey (1993) notes that the concept of **patriarchy,** meaning "the systematic organization of male supremacy" (p. 53), is one that many feminist theorists have found useful. Sociologist Allan Johnson discusses this concept in Reading 2, arguing that patriarchy is not just a collection of individuals but a system whose core value is control and domination. Everyone is involved and implicated in this system, but we can choose *how* we participate. This emphasis on a wider system is crucial. Without it, as Johnson shows, our thinking and discussion get reduced to the personal level and bogged down in accusations, defensiveness, and hurt feelings.

An important strand in feminist thinking— **liberal feminism**—grew out of one of the most significant strands of U.S. political thought, liberalism, a theory about individual rights, freedom, choice, and privacy with roots in seventeenth-century European political thought (e.g., the writings of John Locke). Liberalism has been a major part of U.S. political discourse since the inception of the nation, although political and legal rights were originally limited to White men who owned land and property. Liberal feminists explain the oppression of women in terms of unequal access to existing political, economic, and social institutions (e.g., Eisenstein 1981; Friedan 1963; and Steinem 1983). They are concerned with women's rights being equal to those of men and that women have equal access to

opportunities within existing economic and social structures. From the mid-nineteenth century onward, much feminist organizing—for example, for the vote, equal pay, and women's access to education and the professions—has been based on this view. Many people hold liberal feminist opinions though they may not realize it. Despite the disclaimer "I'm not a feminist . . . ," the comment "but I *do* believe in equal pay" is a liberal feminist position. Women's right to legal abortion in the United States, established in 1973, is grounded in this tradition, as a right to privacy. Liberal feminism can be criticized because it accepts existing institutions as they are, only seeking equal access for women within them. This objective should not be underestimated, however, given the strength of patriarchy as a system of power. Many gains for women over the past thirty-five years are increasingly under attack. The right to abortion, for example, has been steadily whittled away, and is increasingly contested (see Chapter 5).

In Reading 3, the Combahee River Collective, a group of Black feminists active in the Boston area in the 1970s, provide an integrated analysis of interlocking systems of oppression based on race, class, gender, sexuality, and so forth. They note that "Black, other Third World, and working women have been involved in the feminist movement from its start," but that their participation has been obscured by external forces like the media, and internal racism and elitism. "What we believe"—the values part of their thinking—is explicit: Black women have inherent value; "our liberation is a necessity not as an adjunct to somebody else's but because of our need as human persons for autonomy." This statement comes out of a three-year process (1974–77) of meeting, thinking, sharing perspectives, working in various social movements and organizations, reflecting on this activism, clarifying a shared analysis over time. Starting with an emphasis on race and gender, the group went on to critique **capitalism** and **imperialism** in the statement reprinted here.

The Combahee River Collective identified themselves as **socialists** who believed that "work must be organized for the collective benefit of those who do the work and create the products, and not for the profit of the bosses." This links to another significant strand of feminist thought, **socialist feminism,** that grew out of Marxist theories of the economy and concern for the emancipation of workers as a class from economic exploitation and drudgery. Feminist activists and writers who draw from this tradition see the oppression of women in terms of two interconnected systems, patriarchy and capitalism, and they are particularly concerned with the economic-class aspects of women's lives (Eisenstein 1979; Hartmann 1981; Hennessy and Ingraham 1997; Radical Women 2001; Roberts and Mizuta 1993; Smith 2005). Zillah Eisenstein (1998) notes that "the language of socialism" seems foreign nowadays in the United States, due to the collapse of the former Soviet Union and the discrediting of the political philosophy of socialism along with it. She argues that an anticapitalist, feminist politics is currently of great relevance given the increasing integration of the world economic system, though "whether those politics are named socialist feminism remains to be seen" (p. 219). The Combahee River Collective's "A Black Feminist Statement" also includes an anti-imperialist strand, reflecting the fact that, many U.S. feminists of color, as well as some White feminists, have supported liberation movements in Africa, Asia, and Central America.

The thinking of Collective members also overlapped with a third key strand of feminist theory, **radical feminism.** On this view, male domination manifests itself in women's sexuality, gender roles, and family relationships, and it is carried over into the male-dominated world of work, government, religion, and law (Bell and Klein 1996; Daly 1976; Echols 1989; Harne and Miller 1996; Koedt, Levine, and Rapone 1973; Rhodes 2005). For radical feminists, women's liberation requires the eradication of patriarchy and the creation of alternative ways of living. Lesbians have been particularly influential in developing this strand of feminist thought and creating alternative women's institutions, including women's health projects, publishing companies, bookstores, coffeehouses, recording studios, and music festivals (Shugar 1995). The Combahee River Collective found White radical feminism too focused on male domination at the expense of oppressions based on race and class. Collective members also found lesbian **separatism,** advocated by some White lesbians, too limiting theoretically and in practice. These writers argued that the most profound politics "come directly out of our own identity." Their emphasis on **identity politics**

meant that they saw no role for White heterosexual men in the transformation they envisioned, though they did challenge White women to contribute by working on their racism.

In the late 1960s and 1970s, many prominent U.S. feminist activists and writers were White, middle-class, heterosexual women who generalized from their own experiences. They focused on their subordination as women without paying attention to their privilege on other dimensions, notably race, class, and sexual orientation. These limitations were roundly criticized by women of color (hooks 1984a; Moraga and Anzaldua 1981; Smith 1981; Trujillo 1998), working-class women (Kadi 1996; Steedman 1986), women from outside the United States (Mohanty, Russo, and Torres 1991), women with disabilities (Fiduccia and Saxton 1997), and lesbians and bisexual women (Harne and Miller 1996; Lorde 1984; Pharr 1988; Rich 1986a).

These activists and writers, like the Combahee River Collective, were developing feminist perspectives that integrated gender with other systems of inequality based on race, class, sexuality, ability, and nation—approaches that have become known by the shorthand term, **intersectionality.** For African American women, especially, this idea has a long history. Public speakers and writers in the nineteenth century, such as Maria Stewart, Sojourner Truth, and Frances E. W. Harper explicitly linked oppression based on race and gender, at least from the 1830s onward (Guy-Sheftall 1995). Writing in 1892, Anna Julia Cooper commented: "The colored woman of today occupies . . . a unique position in this country. . . . She is confronted by both a woman question and a race problem, and is as yet an unknown or unacknowledged factor in both" (quoted in Guy-Sheftall 1995, p. 45). Linda Burnham, Director of Women of Color Resource Center, notes that

> numerous Black feminist theorists have advanced the view that Black women's experience as women is indivisible from their experiences as African Americans. They are always "both/and," so analyses that claim to examine gender while neglecting a critical stance towards race and class inevitably do so at the expense of African American women's experiences.
>
> *(Burnham 2001, p. 1)*

Burnham (2001, p. 1) acknowledges "the invaluable work of university-based theorists" but argues that too many people "assume that the core concepts of Black feminism were born in the academy." She traces the development of Black feminist thinking in the late 1960s and early 1970s from "the emergence of gender consciousness among Black women activists in the Student Non-Violence Coordinating Committee (SNCC)" through to organizations such as the Third World Women's Alliance and the Combahee River Collective. Her purpose is to show "the struggle for social transformation as a powerful generator of theoretical insight" (Burnham 2001, p. 4).

An integrative perspective that emphasizes intersectionality is not only the prerogative of women of color, though White women have been slower to develop this kind of analysis (e.g., Frankenberg 1993; Segrest 1994; and Spelman 1988). Writer, organizer, and educator Minnie Bruce Pratt explores what this means for her, as a White woman, "raised small-town middle-class, Christian, in the Deep South" (Reading 4).

In Reading 6, antiracist, feminist educator and scholar Chandra Talpade Mohanty writes about intersectionality as a South Asian woman studying and working in the United States. She notes that "racism and sexism became the analytic and political lenses through which I was able to anchor myself here." She made a significant shift in her sense of self when she began to think of herself as a student of color rather than a foreign student. These new understandings also challenged her to rethink her place in Indian society. Mohanty is explicit in her values: opposing social injustice, opposing Hindu fundamentalism, and opposing the role of the World Bank and International Monetary Fund in "restructuring" the Indian economy. She draws on a **postcolonial** theoretical framework, extending analysis of gender, race, and class to include the negative effects of Western colonialism; "the 'post' in postcolonialism does not indicate that colonialism is over, but, rather, that colonial legacies continue to exist" (Mack-Canty 2004, 164). Mohanty describes her genealogy—the tracing of her complex identity as a South Asian in the United States and a nonresident Indian—as "interested, partial, and deliberate." "The stories I recall, the ones I retell and claim as my own, determine the choices and decisions I make in the present and the future."

Often overlapping with postcolonial approaches, **postmodern feminisms,** developed by academic feminists in the 1980s and '90s, emphasize the particularity of women's experiences in specific cultural and historical contexts. Indeed, some feminists have asked whether it is meaningful to talk of women as a group, when there are so many differences among women (Weedon 1987). Denise Riley (1988) argues that the category "woman" has not meant the same thing throughout history and that its specific meaning should be investigated in different historical contexts, not assumed. An emphasis on difference also raises the question as to whether women can engage in effective collective action, something which 1970s feminists usually took for granted. Like members of the Combahee River Collective, Chandra Talpade Mohanty also commits herself to activist projects. Indeed, her wider goal is to envision and contribute to a **transnational multicultural feminism,** a theory and practice that is "noncolonized," and anchored in equality and respect. This would avoid false universalisms and involve ethical and caring dialogue across differences, divisions, and conflicts.

Theoretical perspectives are developed in response to particular circumstances and with reference to previous theories. Linda Burnham comments:

> As people engage in developing strategies to influence and shift power relations, they also— if the political movement is broad and vibrant enough—progressively deepen their process of reflection, reaching more profound and comprehensive understandings of the social dynamics and institutions that shape their lives.   *(Burnham 2001, p. 4)*

Theories are refined and adapted as understanding grows and as events shed new light on issues or problems. Theory is never finished but is continuously evolving. The rich period of feminist activism from the late 1960s to the late 1980s, often referred to as **second-wave feminism,** grew out of the civil rights movement of the 1950s and 1960s, and also built on the work of suffragists and women's rights advocates active from the mid-nineteenth century to the 1920s (**first-wave feminism**). The mainstream media has given great visibility to White, middle-class, second-wave leaders like Betty Friedan and Gloria Steinem, and often characterized the entire movement as White and middle-class. Feminist scholars are writing more detailed and nuanced histories, showing the significant involvement of women of color and White working-class women in feminist organizing (e.g., Cole and Guy-Sheftall 2003; Omolade 1994; Springer 2005; Thompson 2002). In the 1990s, the mainstream media consistently depicted facile stereotypes of feminism and feminists that have deterred many younger women from using the term, even though they often support feminist ideas. Some may think of themselves as **third-wave feminists,** challenging the second-wave feminism of their mothers' generation as no longer relevant and emphasizing personal voice, ambiguity, contradiction, and multiple identities (Baumgardner and Richards 2000; Dicker and Piepmeier 2003; Findlen 1995; Heywood and Drake 1997; Walker 1995; Zita 1997). JeeYeun Lee (Reading 5) and Gwendolyn Pough (Reading 10) exemplify this approach and argue for inclusive forms of feminism. Lee calls for "recognition of the constructed racial nature of *all* experiences of gender"; that "heterosexual norms do not oppress solely lesbians, bisexuals and gay men, but affect all of our choices and non-choices"; that "issues posed by differently abled women question our basic assumptions about body image, health care, sexuality and work"; and so forth.

The wave metaphor suggests both continuity and discontinuity with the past as women shape theoretical understandings for their generation, circumstances, and historical period. Note that these shorthand labels—first wave, second wave—make complex, powerful transformative movements, with their divergent and overlapping strands, seem much neater, more unitary, and more static than they are in reality.

"Socially Lived" Theorizing

As discussed earlier, traditional scholarship primarily validates knowledge that is produced using some form of the scientific method, by White men and others who form an elite group of scholars or subscribe to their views and approaches. We argue that theorizing is not the sole domain of elites. Feminist legal scholar Catharine MacKinnon (1991) talks about "articulating the theory of women's practice—resistance, visions, consciousness, injuries, notions of community, experiences of inequality. By practic[e],

I mean socially lived" (p. 20). The writings included in this chapter all exemplify socially lived theorizing. For members of the Combahee River Collective this came through their activist work. For JeeYeun Lee it was a college course that provided "a language with which I could start to explain my experiences and link them to larger societal structures of oppression and complicity." Another example is provided by Abra Fortune Chernik (Reading 16), who discusses her personal struggle with an eating disorder and the process of understanding and overcoming it. In Reading 34, Marcy Jane Knopf-Newman describes the film *Rachel's Daughters,* in which women ask "whatdunit?" as they research and theorize possible environmental causes of breast cancer in their communities.

To recap, our framework for theory making is based on the following assumptions:

- All knowledge is socially constructed; there is no value-free or neutral knowledge.

- Everyone has the capacity to be a creator of knowledge.

- What one knows comes out of a specific historical and cultural context, whether one is an insider or an outsider to that context.

- It is the responsibility of everyone to reflect on, evaluate, and judge the world around us, and our places in that world, as an essential element of theorizing.

- Knowledge should be used for the purposes of helping to liberate oppressed people and to transform the current social and economic structures of inequality into a sustainable world for all people.

As Catharine MacKinnon (1991) remarks, "It is common to say that something is good in theory but not in practice. I always want to say, then it is not such a good theory, is it?" (p. 1).

In writing about the Holocaust—the mass murder primarily of Jewish people but also of Roma people, people with disabilities, and gay people in Europe during World War II—philosopher Alan Rosenberg (1988) makes an important distinction between knowing and understanding something. According to Rosenberg, knowing is having the facts about a particular event or condition. We know the Holocaust happened: Eight million people were murdered, and countless others were tortured, raped, and otherwise devastated; the Nazis, under the leadership of Adolf Hitler, were the perpetrators; others, both inside and outside Germany, including the United States initially, were unable or refused to help; the result was the slaughter of six million Jewish people. Traditional educational practices, epitomized by the scientific method, teach us primarily to know. For Rosenberg, knowing is the first step to understanding, a much deeper process that, in the case of the Holocaust, involves not only comprehending its significance and longer-term effects but also trying to discover how to prevent similar injustices in the future.

> Knowing . . . refers to factual information or the process by which it is gathered. Understanding refers to systematically grasping the significance of an event in such a way that it becomes integrated into one's moral and intellectual life. Facts can be absorbed without their having any impact on the way we understand ourselves or the world we live in; facts in themselves do not make a difference. It is the understanding of them that makes a difference.
>
> *(Rosenberg 1988, p. 382)*

Recognizing theory making as a political project helps us understand, in the way Rosenberg describes it, the conditions facing women in particular, as well as men in subordinate positions. So, how do we begin to understand?

Feminist activists of the 1960s and the '70s women's liberation movement popularized the slogan "The personal is political" to validate individual women's personal experiences as a starting point for recognizing and understanding discrimination against women as a group. This promoted the practice of "starting from one's own experiences" as a legitimate way to theorize and create new knowledge. This practice was also useful in counteracting the dominant view of theorizing that personal experience, along with emotions and values, contaminates the "purity" of the scientific method. As a first step, starting from what we know the most about—our experiences, thoughts, and feelings, our **subjectivity**—is extremely helpful. It also contains problems. On the one hand, there is self-centeredness, as reflected in comments such as "I can know only my experience," "I can speak only for myself," and "What does all this have to do with

me?" On the other hand, a naive generalization like "As a woman, I assume that all women have experienced the same things I have" also limits the extent to which we can understand diverse women's experiences.

As mentioned earlier in our brief discussion of feminist theories, different social and historical situations give rise to very different experiences and theories about those experiences, hence the importance of **situated knowledge** (Belenky, Clinchy, Goldberger, and Tarnle 1986; Collins 1990) or **standpoint theory** (Harding 2004; Hartsock 1983). What we know as the direct result of our experience, is understood in a specific historical and cultural context, and cannot be generalized. For instance, the experience of being a single mother as a poor teenager in a rural community in the 1990s would be very different from that of being a single mother as an established professional in a big city in the twenty-first century. One could not apply her experience to the other, and neither could speak authoritatively about being a single mother in the 1960s.

The task of socially lived theorizing involves several important challenges. We are faced with the self-centeredness of pure subjectivity, "in which knowledge and meaning [are] lodged in oneself and one's own experiences" (Maher and Tetreault 1994, p. 94). We must also negotiate the problem of **cultural relativism.** Situated knowledge is authoritative because it is someone's or some group's real experience. As a result, others may think they have no basis upon which to question or challenge it, and no right to do so. Thus, the White supremacist views of Ku Klux Klan members might be considered equally as valid as those held by antiracist activists, or a New York judge could justify sentencing a Chinese immigrant man to a mere five years' probation for killing his wife on the basis of "cultural difference" (Yen 1989).

Given these major challenges arising out of subjectivity and cultural relativism, how can we generate knowledge and understanding that reflects the perspectives and interests of a broad range of people, communities, and life circumstances, that is visionary, not just reactive, and that could lead to social change? Socially lived theorizing requires a methodology that includes collective dialogue and **praxis**—reflection and action on the world to transform it. Paulo Freire (1989), Brazilian founder of the

popular education movement, calls this methodology **conscientization,** or gaining a "critical consciousness," and describes it as "learning to perceive social, political, and economic contradictions . . . and to take action against the oppressive elements of this reality" (p. 19).

"Learning to perceive social, political, and economic contradictions" is a tall order for many of us who have been formally educated by what Freire calls the "banking method," whereby teachers deposit knowledge—dates, historical facts, formulas for problem solving, for example—into the minds of students and expect them to be able to withdraw this information at a given time, such as during exams, quizzes, and class presentations. During our schooling most of us are not often asked such questions as, What are the assumptions in the statement you are making? How do you know what you know? Why do you think so? What are the implications of your position? Many of us may have sat in class listening to a teacher or other students and have kept quiet when we knew what was being said did not match our experience. When we put forward our ideas and observations, they might have been dismissed as silly, naive, or too idealistic. We were expected to back up our experience with facts. We were encouraged to accept facts and ideas as they were given to us and to accept social conditions as they are. Indeed, we may often have accepted things as they are without thinking about them, or simply not noticed injustices happening around us. Most likely, too, we have had

little opportunity to engage in honest dialogue with others — both people like ourselves and those from different backgrounds—about important issues.

Having honest dialogues and asking critical questions move us beyond excessive subjectivity because we are compelled to see and understand many different sides of the same subject. Creating theory for social change—something that will advance human development and create a better world for all—gives us a basis for evaluating facts and experiences. This in turn provides a framework for deciding where to draw the line on cultural relativism. Through ongoing, detailed discussion and conscientious listening to others, we can generate a carefully thought-out set of principles that lead to greater understanding of issues and of acceptable actions in a given situation.

Many assume that the scientific method involves authoritativeness and rigor. We believe this alternative way of theorizing redefines rigor by demanding the engagement of our intellectual, emotional, and spiritual selves. It compels us to think systematically and critically, requires us to face the challenges of talking about our differences, and obligates us to consider the real implications and consequences of our theories. Knowledge created in this way helps us "to systematically grasp . . . the significance of an event in such a way that it becomes integrated into [our] moral and intellectual life," also a form of rigor (Rosenberg 1988, p. 382).

Media Representations and the Creation of Knowledge

A major source of our understanding of our own lives is our ability to reflect on our experiences. We learn about people from other groups through our, often limited, interactions with them and through many kinds of media representations. It is a truism to say that we live in a media-saturated culture with constant access to the Internet, TV and radio stations broadcasting 24 hours a day, daily newspapers, weekly magazines, new movies coming out all the time, and so on. This list shows the plurality of media sources (singular: medium). From opinion polls to academic research, media studies evaluate the role of media in creating opinions, attitudes, and knowledge. The line between information and entertainment is blurred as TV shows take up serious issues and news reporting focuses on the flip, titillating, and controversial. The repetition of images on television also shapes our view of events and of history (Morrow 1999). The mainstream media are owned and controlled by mega-corporations like Disney/ABC and Time Warner/Turner. One of the media's main functions is to round up an audience for advertisers, and advertisers exert considerable influence concerning media content, especially in television. From time to time they threaten to pull advertising if they think the content of a show will "turn off" their intended audience, and editors and directors are usually forced to tow the line.

Onnesha Roychouduri (Reading 7) contrasts her earlier belief that reading the *New York Times* made her well informed with her current skepticism about news reporting after working as a fact-checker and writer for a political magazine. She notes:

> The daily news is composed of articles by writers who string together the handful of facts they have obtained in their research. They call it a "story" for good reason. Every day they are expected to produce a cohesive article on an issue. There are bound to be mistakes and oversights. But we rarely stop to consider this because the end product is so seductively authoritative.

Media scholars, critics, and some leading journalists are increasingly concerned about the "unasked" and "unanswered" questions in much contemporary journalism (e.g., Alterman 2003; Borjesson 2002; Cohen 2005; Hamilton 2004), and often attribute this to corporate media ownership, characterized by Robert McChesney (2004) as "hyper-commercialism."

As consumers of media, we develop sophisticated skills in "reading" media texts, whether they are ads, sitcoms, or documentaries. Media audiences bring their experiences, values, and beliefs to what they watch, read, and hear, just as students bring their experiences, beliefs, and ideas into the classroom. The more we know about particular people, the more we are able to judge the accuracy of media portrayals and to notice whether they reproduce myths and stereotypes, and romanticize or exoticize people, as discussed by Diane Raymond (Reading 25).

Women have been marginalized in media portrayals, as have people of color and working-class people. "Blatantly stereotypical images dominated the earlier years of mass media" (Croteau and Hoynes 1997, p. 147). More recently, there has been "a wider diversity of images and roles for women" (p. 147), though still with serious distortions. Women on television, for example, are still mainly shown in the context of entertainment, sport, home, and family. Media analyst and radio reporter Laura Flanders (1997) notes that in the news media, women and girls are usually represented in "human interest" stories. Media representations serve to reinforce ideological notions of women's roles, women's bodies, and sexuality, while also giving complex and sometimes contradictory messages. A study undertaken by the Project for Excellence in Journalism (2005) found that "despite rising numbers of women in the workforce and in journalism schools, the news . . . still largely comes from a male perspective." This study examined 16,800 news stories across 45 news outlets during 20 randomly selected days in a nine-month period, and found that "more than three quarters of all stories contain male sources, while only a third of stories contain even a single female source." Women are more likely to be included if the reporter is female, or in "lifestyle" pieces as opposed to "hard" news, business, or sports. Women are least likely to be quoted in stories about foreign affairs, giving the impression that there are no women with expertise in this area. *The Nation* columnist Katha Pollitt noted that White men's voices are assumed to be authoritative and neutral: " . . . a woman's opinion about Iraq or the budget is seen as a woman's

How to Watch TV News

1. **In encountering a news show, you must come with a firm idea of what is important.** TV news is highly selective. Your values and beliefs are essential in judging what it is that really matters in the reporting of an event.

2. **In preparing to watch a TV news show, keep in mind that it is called a "show."** A TV news show is a successful business enterprise as well as a form of entertainment and a public service.

3. **Never underestimate the power of commercials.** They tell a great deal about our society. Note contradictory messages as you compare commercials and the news.

4. **Learn something about the economic and political interests of those who run TV stations.** This is relevant to judging what they say and don't say.

5. **Pay special attention to the language of newscasts.** Film footage and visual imagery claims our attention on TV news shows, but it is what newscasters *say* that frames the pictures and tells us how to interpret them.

(Adapted from Postman and Powers 1992, pp. 160–68.)

opinion. The same for a black person . . . " (quoted in Zimmerman 2003, p. 5).

Given the central importance of advertising, media representations, and popular culture in shaping knowledge and opinions, we include several articles on these topics in relation to feminist identity and hip hop culture (Reading 10), the influence of advertising on girls' confidence and self esteem (Reading 15), queer representation in TV sitcoms (Reading 25), community-based research into the causes of breast cancer (Reading 32), media reactions to men dealing with date rape on a college campus (Reading 37), women in the global sex trade (Reading 56), newspaper reports on Muslim Americans and Arab Americans (Reading 62), and the increasing militarization of U.S. culture (Reading 65).

To summarize, in this chapter we argue that facts are always open to interpretation and that everyone makes theory in trying to understand their experiences. Feminist theories that seek to explain women's lives involve clear value positions and constitute a critique of the dominant view that sees theory as "objective" or "value-free." Socially lived theorizing is essential for women's studies. It creates knowledge that reflects the points of view and interests of a broad range of people. It is visionary and can lead to social change. Socially lived theorizing requires collective dialogue, careful listening to other people's theories, and sophisticated skills in "reading" media texts so that we do not draw stereotypical notions of others into our theory making.

◆◆◆

Questions for Reflection

In attempting to understand any theoretical perspective, we find the following questions helpful:

1. What does the theory aim to explain?

2. How does it do this? What are the basic arguments and assumptions?

3. What does the theory focus on? What does it ignore?

4. What is the cultural and historical context giving rise to the theory?

5. Do you find this perspective useful? If so, why?

6. Are you convinced by the arguments? Why or why not?

7. What kinds of research questions does this perspective generate?

8. What kinds of actions and projects follow from this perspective?

As you read and discuss the readings in this chapter, think about these questions:

1. How do you explain poverty?

2. How do you explain inequality between women and men in this country? Between White people and people of color in this country?

3. How do you think change happens? How is knowledge related to social change?

4. How do people with privilege contribute to eliminating the systems of privilege that benefit them? Why might they want to do this?

5. Think about people and events that have affected the development of your thinking. How did this happen?

6. Have spiritual beliefs and religious institutions influenced your values and perspectives? If so, how?

◆◆◆

Finding Out More on the Web

1. In the Combahee River Collective's "A Black Feminist Statement," the writers mention Dr. Kenneth Edelin, Joan Little, and Inéz García. Who were these people? Why were they significant?

2. Explore the Web site of a women's organization. What can you learn about the organization's theoretical framework? How does this perspective inform its activities? Here are a few examples to get you started:

   Center for Women's Global Leadership: **www.cwgl.rutgers.edu**

   Global Women's Strike: **www.globalwomenstrike.net**

   National Organization for Women: **www.now.org**

   Third Wave Foundation: **www.thirdwavefoundation.org**

   Women of Color Resource Center: **www.coloredgirls.org**

3. Compare editorial perspectives and news coverage of an issue you care about in progressive magazines, Web logs, foreign newspapers online, or WomenseNews (**www.womensenews.org**) with those of mainstream U.S reporting.

◆◆◆

Taking Action

1. Analyze what happens when you get into an argument with a friend, classmate, or teacher about an issue that matters to you. Are you both using the same assumptions? Do you understand the other person's argument? Do you have compatible understandings of the issue? Can you explain your position more clearly or do you need to rethink it? Are facts enough to convince someone who is skeptical of your views?

2. Pay attention to the theoretical ideas incorporated into TV news reports. When the presenter says, "Now for the stories behind the headlines," whose stories are these? Who is telling them? What, if anything, is missing from these accounts? What else do you need to know in order to have a full explanation?

3. Look critically at media representations of people in your group and other groups. How are they portrayed? What is left out of these representations? What stereotypes do they reinforce?

4. Read a novel like Gerd Brantenberg's *Egalia's Daughters* or Marge Piercy's *Woman on the Edge of Time* that redefines gender roles and stereotypes.

 O N E

◆◆◆

The Social Construction of Gender (1991)

Judith Lorber

Judith Lorber is Professor Emerita of Sociology and Women's Studies at Broooklyn College and The Graduate School, City University of New York, and the author of numerous books and articles on gender, feminism, and women's health. In 1996 she received the American Sociological Association Jessie Bernard Career Award for her contribution to feminist scholarship.

Talking about gender for most people is the equivalent of fish talking about water. Gender is so much the routine ground of everyday activities that questioning its taken-for-granted assumptions and presuppositions is like thinking about whether the sun will come up. Gender is so pervasive that in our society we assume it is bred into our genes. Most people find it hard to believe that gender is constantly created and recreated out of human interaction, out of social life, and is the texture and order of that social life. Yet gender, like culture, is a human production that depends on everyone constantly "doing gender" (West and Zimmerman 1987).

And everyone "does gender" without thinking about it. Today, on the subway, I saw a well-dressed man with a year-old child in a stroller. Yesterday, on a bus, I saw a man with a tiny baby in a carrier on his chest. Seeing men taking care of small children in public is increasingly common—at least in New York City. But both men were quite obviously stared at—and smiled at, approvingly. Everyone was doing gender—the men who were changing the role of fathers and the other passengers, who were applauding them silently. But there was more gendering going on that probably fewer people

noticed. The baby was wearing a white crocheted cap and white clothes. You couldn't tell if it was a boy or a girl. The child in the stroller was wearing a dark blue T-shirt and dark print pants. As they started to leave the train, the father put a Yankee baseball cap on the child's head. Ah, a boy, I thought. Then I noticed the gleam of tiny earrings in the child's ears, and as they got off, I saw the little flowered sneakers and lace-trimmed socks. Not a boy after all. Gender done.

Gender is such a familiar part of daily life that it usually takes a deliberate disruption of our expectations of how women and men are supposed to act to pay attention to how it is produced. Gender signs and signals are so ubiquitous that we usually fail to note them—unless they are missing or ambiguous. Then we are uncomfortable until we have successfully placed the other person in a gender status; otherwise, we feel socially dislocated. In our society, in addition to man and woman, the status can be *transvestite* (a person who dresses in opposite-gender clothes) and *transsexual* (a person who has had sex-change surgery). Transvestites and transsexuals construct their gender status by dressing, speaking, walking, gesturing in the ways prescribed for women or men—whichever they want to be taken for—and so does any "normal" person.

For the individual, gender construction starts with assignment to a sex category on the basis of what the genitalia look like at birth. Then babies are dressed or adorned in a way that displays the category because parents don't want to be constantly asked whether their baby is a girl or a boy. A sex category becomes a gender status through naming, dress, and the use of other gender markers. Once a child's gender is evident, others treat those in one gender differently from those in the other, and the children respond to the different treatment by feeling different and behaving differently. As soon as they can talk, they start to refer to themselves as members of their gender. Sex doesn't come into play again until puberty, but by that time, sexual feelings and desires and practices have been shaped by gendered norms and expectations. Adolescent boys and girls approach and avoid each other in an elaborately scripted and gendered mating dance. Parenting is gendered, with different expectations for mothers and for fathers, and people of different genders work at different kinds of jobs. The work adults do as mothers and fathers and as low-level workers and high-level bosses, shapes women's and men's life experiences, and these experiences produce different feelings, consciousness, relationships, skills—ways of being that we call feminine or masculine. All of these processes constitute the social construction of gender.

Gendered roles change—today fathers are taking care of little children, girls and boys are wearing unisex clothing and getting the same education, women and men are working at the same jobs. Although many traditional social groups are quite strict about maintaining gender differences, in other social groups they seem to be blurring. Then why the one-year-old's earrings? Why is it still so important to mark a child as a girl or a boy, to make sure she is not taken for a boy or he for a girl? What would happen if they were? They would, quite literally, have changed places in their social world.

To explain why gendering is done from birth, constantly and by everyone, we have to look not only at the way individuals experience gender but at gender as a social institution. As a social institution, gender is one of the major ways that human beings organize their lives. Human society depends on a predictable division of labor, a designated allocation of scarce goods, assigned responsibility for children and others who cannot care for themselves, common values and their systematic transmission to new members, legitimate leadership, music, art, stories, games, and other symbolic productions. One way of choosing people for the different tasks of society is on the basis of their talents, motivations, and competence—their demonstrated achievements. The other way is on the basis of gender, race, ethnicity—ascribed membership in a category of people. Although societies vary in the extent to which they use one or the other of these ways of allocating people to work and to carry out other responsibilities, every society uses gender and age grades. Every society classifies people as "girl and boy children," "girls and boys ready to be married," and "fully adult women and men," constructs similarities among them and differences between them, and assigns them to different roles and responsibilities. Personality characteristics, feelings, motivations, and ambitions flow from these different life experiences so that the members of these different groups become different kinds of people. The process of gendering and its outcome are legitimated by religion, law, science, and the society's entire set of values.

Gender as Process, Stratification, and Structure

As a social institution, gender is a process of creating distinguishable social statuses for the assignment of rights and responsibilities. As part of a stratification system that ranks these statuses unequally, gender is a major building block in the social structures built on these unequal statuses.

As a *process*, gender creates the social differences that define "woman" and "man." In social interaction throughout their lives, individuals learn what is expected, see what is expected, act and react in expected ways, and thus simultaneously construct and maintain the gender order: "The very injunction to be given gender takes place through discursive routes: to be a good mother, to be a heterosexually desirable object, to be a fit worker, in sum, to signify a multiplicity of guarantees in response to a variety of different demands all at once" (J. Butler 1990, 145). Members of a social group neither make up gender as they go along nor exactly replicate in rote fashion what was done before. In almost every encounter, human beings produce gender, behaving in the ways they learned were appropriate for their gender status, or resisting or rebelling against these norms. Resistance and rebellion have altered gender norms, but so far they have rarely eroded the statuses.

Gendered patterns of interaction acquire additional layers of gendered sexuality, parenting, and work behaviors in childhood, adolescence, and adulthood. Gendered norms and expectations are enforced through informal sanctions of gender-inappropriate behavior by peers and by formal punishment or threat of punishment by those in authority should behavior deviate too far from socially imposed standards for women and men.

Everyday gendered interactions build gender into the family, the work process, and other organizations and institutions, which in turn reinforce gender expectations for individuals. Because gender is a process, there is room not only for modification and variation by individuals and small groups but also for institutionalized change (J. W. Scott 1988, 7).

As part of a *stratification* system, gender ranks men above women of the same race and class. Women and men could be different but equal. In practice, the process of creating difference depends to a great extent on differential evaluation. As Nancy Jay (1981) says: "That which is defined, separated out, isolated from all else is A and pure. Not-A is necessarily impure, a random catchall, to which nothing is external except A and the principle of order that separates it from Not-A" (45). From the individual's point of view, whichever gender is A, the other is Not-A; gender boundaries tell the individual who is like him or her, and all the rest are unlike. From society's point of view, however, one gender is usually the touchstone, the normal, the dominant, and the other is different, deviant, and subordinate. In Western society, "man" is A, "woman" is Not-A. (Consider what a society would be like where woman was A and man Not-A.)

The further dichotomization by race and class constructs the gradations of a heterogeneous society's stratification scheme. Thus, in the United States, white is A, African American is Not-A; middle class is A, working class is Not-A, and "African-American women occupy a position whereby the inferior half of a series of these dichotomies converge" (P. H. Collins 1989, 70). The dominant categories are the hegemonic ideals, taken so for granted as the way things should be that white is not ordinarily thought of as a race, middle class as a class, or men as a gender. The characteristics of these categories define the Other as that which lacks the valuable qualities the dominants exhibit.

In a gender-stratified society, what men do is usually valued more highly than what women do because men do it, even when their activities are very similar or the same. In different regions of southern India, for example, harvesting rice is

men's work, shared work, or women's work: "Wherever a task is done by women it is considered easy, and where it is done by [men] it is considered difficult" (Mencher 1988, 104). . . . Conversely, because they are the superior group, white men do not have to do the "dirty work," such as housework; the most inferior group does it, usually poor women of color (Palmer 1989). . . .

Societies vary in the extent of the inequality in social status of their women and men members, but where there is inequality, the status "woman" (and its attendant behavior and role allocations) is usually held in lesser esteem than the status "man." Since gender is also intertwined with a society's other constructed statuses of differential evaluation—race, religion, occupation, class, country of origin, and so on—men and women members of the favored groups command more power, more prestige, and more property than the members of the disfavored groups. Within many social groups, however, men are advantaged over women. The more economic resources, such as education and job opportunities, are available to a group, the more they tend to be monopolized by men. In poorer groups that have few resources (such as working-class African Americans in the United States), women and men are more nearly equal, and the women may even outstrip the men in education and occupational status (Almquist 1987).

As a *structure*, gender divides work in the home and in economic production, legitimates those in authority, and organizes sexuality and emotional life (Connell 1987, pp. 91–142). As primary parents, women significantly influence children's psychological development and emotional attachments, in the process reproducing gender. Emergent sexuality is shaped by heterosexual, homosexual, bisexual, and sadomasochistic patterns that are gendered—different for girls and boys, and for women and men—so that sexual statuses reflect gender statuses.

When gender is a major component of structured inequality, the devalued genders have less power, prestige, and economic rewards than the valued genders. In countries that discourage gender discrimination, many major roles are still gendered; women still do most of the domestic labor and child rearing, even while doing full-time paid work; women and men are segregated on the job and each does work considered "appropriate"; women's work is usually paid less than men's work. Men dominate the positions of authority and leadership in government, the military, and the law; cultural productions, religions, and sports reflect men's interests. . . .

Gender inequality—the devaluation of "women" and the social domination of "men"—has social functions and social history. It is not the result of sex, procreation, physiology, anatomy, hormones, or genetic predispositions. It is produced and maintained by identifiable social processes and built into the general social structure and individual identities deliberately and purposefully. The social order as we know it in Western societies is organized around racial, ethnic, class, and gender inequality. I contend, therefore, that the continuing purpose of gender as a modern social institution is to construct women as a group to be the subordinates of men as a group.

The Paradox of Human Nature

To say that sex, sexuality, and gender are all socially constructed is not to minimize their social power. These categorical imperatives govern our lives in the most profound and pervasive ways, through the social experiences and social practices of what Dorothy Smith calls the "everday/evernight world" (1990, 31–57). The paradox of human nature is that it is *always* a manifestation of cultural meanings, social relationships, and power politics; "not biology, but culture, becomes destiny" (J. Butler 1990, 8). Gendered people emerge not from physiology or sexual orientation but from the exigencies of the social order, mostly, from the need for a reliable division of the work of food production and the social (not physical) reproduction of new members. The moral imperatives of religion and cultural representations guard the boundary lines among genders and ensure that what is demanded, what is permitted, and what is tabooed for the people in each gender is well known and followed by most (C. Davies 1982). Political power, control of scarce resources, and, if necessary, violence uphold the gendered social order in the face of resistance and rebellion. Most people, however, voluntarily go along with their society's prescriptions for those of their gender status, because the norms and expectations get built into their sense of worth and identity as

[the way we] think, the way we see and hear and speak, the way we fantasy, and the way we feel.

There is no core or bedrock in human nature below these endlessly looping processes of the social production of sex and gender, self and other, identity and psyche, each of which is a "complex cultural construction" (J. Butler 1990, 36). *For humans, the social is the natural.* Therefore, "in its feminist senses, gender cannot mean simply the cultural appropriation of biological sexual difference. Sexual difference is itself a fundamental—and scientifically contested—construction. Both 'sex' and 'gender' are woven of multiple, asymmetrical strands of difference, charged with multifaceted dramatic narratives of domination and struggle" (Haraway 1990, 140).

REFERENCES

Almquist, Elizabeth M. 1987. "Labor market gendered inequality in minority groups," *Gender & Society* 1:400–14.

Butler, Judith. 1990. *Gender Trouble: Feminism and the Subversion of Identity.* New York and London: Routledge.

Collins, Patricia Hill. 1989. "The social construction of black feminist thought," *Signs* 14:745–73.

Connell, R. [Robert] W. 1987. *Gender and Power: Society, the Person, and Sexual Politics.* Stanford, Calif.: Stanford University Press.

Davies, Christie. 1982. "Sexual taboos and social boundaries," *American Journal of Sociology* 87:1032–63.

Haraway, Donna. 1990. "Investment strategies for the evolving portfolio of primate female," in Jacobus, Mary Evelyn Fox Keller, and Sally Shuttleworth (eds.). 1990. *Body/politics: Women and the Discourse of Science.* New York and London: Routledge.

Jay, Nancy. 1981. "Gender and dichotomy," *Feminist Studies* 7:38–56.

Mencher, Joan. 1988. "Women's work and poverty: Women's contribution to household maintenance in South India," in Daisy Dwyer and Judith Bruce (eds.) *A Home Divided: Women and Income in the Third World.* Stanford, Calif.: Stanford University Press.

Palmer, Phyllis. 1989. *Domesticity and Dirt: Housewives and Domestic Servants in the United States, 1920–1945.* Philadelphia: Temple University Press.

Scott, Joan Wallach. 1988. *Gender and the Politics of History.* New York: Columbia University Press.

Smith, Dorothy E. 1990. *The Conceptual Practices of Power: A Feminist Sociology of Knowledge.* Toronto: University of Toronto Press.

West, Candace, and Don Zimmerman. 1987. "Doing gender," *Gender & Society* 1:125–51.

T W O

◆◆◆

Patriarchy, the System (1997)

An It, Not a He, a Them, or an Us

Allan G. Johnson

Allan G. Johnson is a sociologist, author, and public speaker with thirty years of teaching experience exploring the issues of privilege, oppression, and social inequality. http://www.agjohnson.us.

"When you say patriarchy," a man complained from the rear of the audience, "I know what you *really* mean—me!" A lot of people hear "men" whenever someone says "patriarchy," so that criticism of male privilege and the oppression of women is taken to mean that all men—each and every one of them—are oppressive people. It's enough to prompt many men to take it personally, bristling at what they often see as a way to make them feel guilty. And some women feel free to blame individual men for patriarchy simply because they're men. Some of the time, men feel defensive because they identify with patriarchy and its values and don't want to face the consequences these produce or the prospect of giving up male privilege. But defensiveness can also reflect a common confusion about the difference between patriarchy as a kind of society and the people who participate in it. If we're ever going to work toward real change, it's a confusion we'll have to clear up.

To do this, we have to realize that we're stuck in a model of social life that views everything as beginning and ending with individuals. Looking at things in this way, the tendency is to think that if bad things happen in the world, it's only because there are bad people who have entered into some kind of conspiracy. Racism exists, then, because white people are racist bigots who hate members of racial and ethnic minorities and want to do them harm. The oppression of women happens because men want and like to dominate women and act out hostility toward them. There is poverty and class oppression because people in the upper classes are greedy, heartless, and cruel. The flip side of this individualistic model of guilt and blame is that

race, gender, and class oppression are actually not oppression at all, but merely the sum of individual failings on the part of blacks, women, and the poor, who lack the right stuff to compete successfully with whites, men, and others who know how to make something of themselves.

What this kind of thinking ignores is that we are all participating in something larger than ourselves or any collection of us. On some level, most people are familiar with the idea that social life involves us in something larger than ourselves, but few seem to know what to do with that idea. Blaming everything on "the system" strikes a deep chord in many people. But it also touches on a basic misunderstanding of social life, because blaming "the system" (presumably society) for our problems, doesn't take the next step to understanding what that might mean. What exactly *is* a system, for example, and how could it run our lives? Do *we* have anything to do with shaping *it,* and if so, how? How, for example, do we participate in patriarchy, and how does that link us to the consequences? How is what we think of as "normal" life related to male privilege, women's oppression, and the hierarchical, control-obsessed world in which everyone's lives are embedded?

Without asking such questions, we can't understand gender fully and we avoid taking responsibility either for ourselves or for patriarchy. Instead, "the system" serves as a vague, unarticulated catchall, a dumping ground for social problems, a scapegoat that can never be held to account and that, for all the power we think it has, can't talk back or actually *do* anything.

A powerful example of this is found in the work of Sam Keen and Robert Bly, whose influential books on gender were part of the mythopoetic men's movement, which attracted a wide following, especially during the 1990s. Although younger readers probably won't have heard of it, the movement is still important to understand because it expresses views of gender inequality that are still widely used to reject feminism and defend male privilege.

Both Keen and Bly blame much of men's misery on industrialization and urbanization.[1] The solutions they offer, however, amount to little more than personal transformation and adaptation, not changing society itself. So, the system is invoked in contradictory ways. On the one hand, it's portrayed as a formidable source of all our woes, a great monster that "runs us all." On the other hand, it's ignored as a nebulous blob that we think we don't have to include in any solutions.

But we can't have it both ways. If society is a powerful force in social life, as it surely is, then we have to understand it and how we are connected to it. To do this, we have to change how we think about it, because how we think affects the kinds of questions we ask. The questions we ask in turn shape the kinds of answers and solutions we'll come up with.

If we see patriarchy as nothing more than men's and women's individual personalities, motivations, and behavior, for example, then it probably won't even occur to us to ask about larger contexts—such as institutions like the family, religion, and the economy—and how people's lives are shaped in relation to them. From this kind of individualistic perspective, we might ask why a particular man raped, harassed, or beat a woman. We wouldn't ask, however, what kind of society would promote persistent *patterns* of such behavior in everyday life, from wife-beating jokes to the routine inclusion of sexual coercion and violence in mainstream movies. We'd be quick to explain rape and battery as the acts of sick or angry men, but we'd rarely take seriously the question of what kind of society would produce so much male anger and pathology or direct it toward sexual violence rather than something else. We'd rarely ask how gender violence might serve other more "normalized" ends such as male control and domination. We might ask why a man would like pornography that objectifies, exploits, and promotes violence against women, or debate whether the Constitution protects an individual's right to produce and distribute it. But it'd be hard to stir up interest in asking what kind of society would give violent and degrading visions of women's bodies and human sexuality such a prominent and pervasive place in its culture to begin with.

In short, the tendency in this society is to ignore and take for granted what we can least afford to overlook in trying to understand and change the world. Rather than ask how social systems produce social problems such as men's violence against women, we obsess over legal debate and titillating but irrelevant case histories soon to become made-for-television movies. If the goal is to change the world, this won't help us. We need to see and deal with the social roots that generate and nurture the social problems that are reflected in and manifested through the behavior of individuals. We can't do this without realizing that we all participate in something larger than ourselves, something we didn't create but that we have the power to affect through the choices we make about *how* to participate.

Some readers have objected to "participate" as a way to describe women's relation to patriarchy. This is based on the idea that participation is something voluntary, freely chosen, entered into as equals, and it therefore makes little sense to suggest that women can participate in their own oppression. But that is not my meaning here, nor is it a necessary interpretation of the word. To *participate* is simply to have a *part* in what goes on, to do something (or *not*) and to have the choice affect the consequences, regardless of whether it is conscious or unconscious, coerced or not. Of course, the *terms* of women's participation differ dramatically from those that shape men's, but it is participation, nonetheless.

This concept is similar to the participation of workers in the system of capitalism. They do not participate as equals to the capitalists who employ them or on terms they would choose if they could. Nevertheless, without them, capitalism cannot function as a system that oppresses them.

The importance of participation can be seen in the great variety of ways that women and working-class people respond to oppression—all the forms that fighting back or giving in can take. To argue that women or workers do not participate is to render them powerless and irrelevant to patriarchy's and capitalism's past and future, for it is only as participants that people can affect anything. . . .

The something larger we all participate in is patriarchy, which is more than a collection of individuals (such as "men"). It is a system, which means it can't be reduced to the people who participate in it. If you go to work in a corporation, for example, you know the minute you walk in the door that you've entered "something" that shapes your experience and behavior, something that isn't just you and the other people you work with. You can feel yourself stepping into a set of relationships and shared understandings about who's who and what's supposed to happen and why, and all of this limits you in many ways. And when you leave at the end of the day you can feel yourself released from the constraints imposed by your participation in that system. You can feel the expectations drop away and your focus shift to other systems such as family or a neighborhood bar that shape your experience in different ways.

To understand a system like a corporation, we have to look at more than people like you, because all of you aren't the corporation, even though you make it run. If the corporation were just a collection of people, then whatever happened to the corporation would by definition also happen to them, and vice versa. But clearly this isn't so. A corporation can go bankrupt or cease to exist altogether without any of the people who work there going bankrupt or disappearing. Or everyone who works for a corporation could quit, but that wouldn't necessarily mean the end of the corporation, only the arrival of a new set of participants. We can't understand a system, then, just by looking at the people who participate in it, for it is something larger and has to be understood as such.

Even more so, we cannot understand the world and our lives in it without looking at the dynamic relationship between individual people and social systems. Nor can we understand the countless details—from sexual violence to patterns of conversation to unequal distributions of power—that make up the reality of male privilege and the oppression of women.

As the accompanying figure shows, this relationship has two parts. The arrow on the right side represents the idea that as we participate in social systems, we are shaped as individuals. Through the process of *socialization*, we learn how to participate in social life—from families, schools, religion, and the mass media, through the examples set by parents, peers, coaches, teachers, and public figures—a continuing stream of ideas and images of people and the world and who we are in relation to them.

Through all of this, we develop a sense of personal identity—including gender—and how this positions us in relation to other people, especially in terms of inequalities of power. As I grew up watching movies and television, for example, the message was clear that men are the most important people on the planet because they're the ones who supposedly do the most important things as defined by patriarchal culture. They're the strong ones who build, the heroes who fight the good fight, the geniuses, writers and artists, the bold leaders, and even the evil—but always interesting—villains. Even God is gendered male.

Among the many consequences of such messages is to encourage in men a sense of entitlement in relation to women—to be tended to and taken care of, deferred to and supported no matter how badly they behave. In the typical episode of the television sitcom, *Everybody Loves Raymond,* for example, Ray Barone routinely behaves toward his wife, Debra, in ways that are insensitive, sexist, adolescent, and downright stupid, but by the end of each half hour we always find out why she puts up with it year after year—for some reason that's never made clear, she just loves the guy. This sends the message that it's reasonable for a heterosexual man to expect to "have" an intelligent and beautiful woman who will love him and stay with him in spite of his behaving badly toward her a great deal of the time.

Invariably, some of what we learn through socialization turns out not to be true and then we may have to deal with that. I say "may" because powerful forces encourage us to keep ourselves in a state of denial, to rationalize what we've learned in order to keep it safe from scrutiny, if only to protect our sense of who we are and ensure our being accepted by other people, including family and friends. In the end, the default is to adopt the dominant version of reality and act as though it's the only one there is.

In addition to socialization, participation in social systems shapes our behavior through *paths of least resistance,* a concept that refers to the conscious and unconscious choices we make from one moment to the next. When a man hears other men tell sexist jokes, for example, there are many things he *could* do, but they vary in how much social resistance they're

We make social systems happen.

System

Individuals

As we participate in social systems, we are shaped by *socialization* and by *paths of least resistance.*

likely to provoke. He could laugh along with them, for example, or remain silent or ignore them or object. And, of course, there are millions of other things he could do—sing, dance, go to sleep, scratch his nose, and so on. Most of these possibilities won't even occur to him, which is one of the ways that social systems limit our options. But of those that do occur to him, usually one will risk less resistance than all the rest. The path of least resistance is to go along, and unless he's willing to deal with greater resistance, that's the choice he's most likely to make.

Our daily lives consist of an endless stream of such choices as we navigate among various possibilities in relation to the path of least resistance in each social situation. Most of the time, we make choices unconsciously without realizing what we're doing. It's just what seems most comfortable to us, most familiar, and safest. The more aware we are of what's going on, however, the more likely it is that we can make conscious, informed choices, and therein lies our potential to make a difference.

This brings us to the arrow on the left side of the figure, which represents the fact that human beings are the ones who make social systems happen. A classroom, for example, doesn't happen as a social system unless and until students and teachers come together and, through their choices from moment to moment, *make* it happen in one way or another. Because people make systems happen, then people can also make systems happen differently. And when systems happen differently, the consequences are different as well. In other words, when people step off the path of least resistance, they have the potential not simply to change other people, but to alter the way the system itself happens. Given that systems shape people's behavior, this kind of change has enormous potential. When a man objects to a sexist joke, for example, it can shake other men's perception of what's socially acceptable and what's not so that the next time they're in this kind of situation, their perception of the social environment itself—not just of other people as individuals, whom they may or may not know personally—may shift in a new direction that makes old paths (such as telling sexist jokes) more difficult to choose because of the increased risk of social resistance.

The model in the figure represents a basic sociological view of the world at every level of human experience, from the global capitalist economy to sexual relationships. Patriarchy fits this model as a social system in which women and men participate. As such, it is more than a collection of women and men and can't be understood simply by understanding *them*. We are not patriarchy, no more than people who believe in Allah *are* Islam or Canadians *are* Canada. Patriarchy is a kind of society organized around certain kinds of social relationships and ideas that shape paths of least resistance. As individuals, we participate in it. Paradoxically, our participation both shapes our lives and gives us the opportunity to be part of changing or perpetuating it. But *we are not it*, which means patriarchy can exist without men having "oppressive personalities" or actively conspiring with one another to defend male privilege.

To demonstrate that gender privilege and oppression exist, we don't have to show that men are villains, that women are good-hearted victims, that women don't participate in their own oppression, or that men never oppose it. If a society is oppressive, then people who grow up and live in it will tend to accept, identify with, and participate in it as "normal" and unremarkable life. That's the path of least resistance in any system. It's hard not to follow it, given how we depend on society and its rewards and punishments that hinge on going along with the status quo. When privilege and oppression are woven into the fabric of everyday life, we don't need to go out of our way to be overtly oppressive for a system of privilege to produce oppressive consequences, for, as Edmund Burke tells us, evil requires only that good people do nothing.

"The System"

In general, a system is any collection of interrelated parts or elements that we can think of as a whole. A car engine, for example, is a collection of parts that fit together in certain ways to produce a "whole" that is identified by a culture as serving a particular purpose. A language is also a collection of parts—letters of the alphabet, words, punctuation marks, and rules of grammar and syntax—that fit together in certain ways to form something we can identify as a whole. And societies include a variety of interrelated aspects that we can think of as a whole. All of these are systems that differ in what they include and how those elements are organized.

The crucial thing to understand about patriarchy or any other social system is that it's something people participate in. It's an arrangement of shared understandings and relationships that connect people to one another and something larger than themselves. In some ways, we're like players who participate in a game. Monopoly, for example, consists of a set of ideas about things such as the meaning of property and rent, the value of competition and accumulating wealth, and various rules about rolling dice, moving around a board, buying, selling, and developing property, collecting rents, winning, and losing. It has positions—player, banker, and so on—that people occupy. It has material elements such as the board, houses and hotels, dice, property deeds, money, and "pieces" that represent each player's movements on the board. As such, the game is something we can think of as a social system whose elements cohere with a unity and wholeness that distinguish it from other games and from non-games.[2] Most important, we can describe it as a system without ever talking about the personal characteristics or motivations of the individual people who actually play it at any given moment.

If we watch people play Monopoly, we notice certain routine patterns of feeling and behavior that reflect paths of least resistance inherent in the game itself. If someone lands on a property I own, for example, I collect the rent (if I happen to notice); and if they can't pay, I take their assets and force them from the game. The game encourages me to feel good about this, not necessarily because *I'm* greedy and merciless, but because the game is about winning, and this is what winning consists of in Monopoly. Since everyone else is also trying to win by driving me out of the game, each step I take toward winning protects me and alleviates some anxiety about landing on a property whose rent *I* can't pay.

Because these patterns are shaped by the game far more than by the individual players, we can find ourselves behaving in ways that might seem disturbing in other situations. When I'm not playing Monopoly, I behave quite differently, even though I'm still the same person. This is why I don't play Monopoly anymore—I don't like the way it encourages me to feel and behave in the name of "fun," especially toward people I care about. The reason we behave differently outside the game doesn't lie in our personalities but in the *game's* paths of least resistance, which define certain behavior and values as appropriate and expected. When we see ourselves as Monopoly players, we

feel limited by the rules and goals the game defines, and experience it as something external to us and beyond our control.

It's important to note how rarely it occurs to people to simply change the rules. The relationships, terms, and goals that organize the game aren't presented to us as ours to judge or alter. The more attached we feel to the game and the more closely we identify ourselves as players, the more likely we are to feel helpless in relation to it. If you're about to drive someone into bankruptcy, you can excuse yourself by saying, "I've got to take your money, those are the rules," but only if you ignore the fact that you could choose not to play or could suggest a change in the rules. Then again, if you can't imagine life without the game, you won't see many alternatives to doing what's expected.

If we try to explain patterns of social behavior only in terms of individual people's personalities and motives—people do greedy things, for example, because they *are* greedy—then we ignore how behavior is shaped by paths of least resistance found in the systems people participate in. The "profit motive" associated with capitalism, for example, is typically seen as a psychological motive that explains capitalism as a system: Capitalism exists because there are people who want to make a profit. But this puts the cart before the horse by avoiding the question of where wanting to make a profit comes from in the first place. We need to ask what kind of world makes such wants possible and encourages people to organize their lives around them, for although we may pursue profit as we play Monopoly or participate in real-world capitalism, the psychological profit motive doesn't originate with us. We aren't born with it. It doesn't exist in many cultures and was unknown for most of human history. The profit motive is a historically developed aspect of market systems in general and capitalism in particular that shapes the values, behavior, and personal motives of those who participate in it.

To argue that managers lay off workers, for example, simply because managers are heartless or cruel ignores the fact that success under capitalism often depends on this kind of competitive, profit-maximizing, "heartless" behavior. Most managers probably know in their hearts that the practice of routinely discarding people in the name of profit and expedience is hurtful and unfair. This is why they feel so bad about having to be the ones to carry it out, and protect their feelings by inventing euphemisms such as "downsizing" and "outplacement." And yet they participate in a system that produces these cruel results anyway, not because of cruel personalities or malice toward workers, but because a capitalist system makes this a path of least resistance and exacts real costs from those who stray from it.

To use the game analogy, it's a mistake to assume that we can understand players' behavior without paying attention to the game they're playing. We create even more trouble by thinking we can understand the *game* without ever looking at it as something more than what goes on inside the people who play it. One way to see this is to realize that systems often work in ways that don't reflect people's experience and motivations. . . .

In spite of all the good reasons to not use individual models to explain social life, doing so constitutes a path of least resistance because personal experience and motivation are what we know best. As a result, we tend to see something like patriarchy as the result of poor socialization through which men learn to act dominant and masculine and women learn to act subordinate and feminine. While there is certainly some truth to this, it doesn't work as an explanation of patterns like privilege and oppression. It's no better than trying to explain war as simply the result of training men to be war-like, without looking at economic systems that equip armies at huge profits and political systems that organize and hurl armies at one another. It's like trying to understand what happens during Monopoly games without ever talking about the game itself and the kind of society in which it would exist. Of course, soldiers and Monopoly players do what they do because they've learned the rules, but this doesn't tell us much about the rules themselves and why they exist to be learned in the first place. Socialization is merely a process, a mechanism for training people to participate in social systems. Although it tells us how people learn to participate, it doesn't illuminate the systems themselves. As such, it can tell us something about the *how* of a system like patriarchy, but very little about the *what* and the *why*.

Without some sense of how systems work and how people participate in them, we can't do much about either. Robert Bly and others in the mythopoetic men's movement, for example, want to change cultural definitions of masculinity and femininity. They want men to become "spiritual warriors" in touch with the "deep masculine," who feel good about themselves as men and who don't need to rely on coercion and violence. And they want the "old men"—the fathers—to initiate the young men into this new way of being. However, because the concept of a patriarchal system has no place in Bly's analysis, changing cultural definitions will have no affect on that system. In other words, masculinity will be transformed without confronting the control-driven system of patriarchal power relations and male competition and all the ways they are embedded in social institutions.

Where, then, will we find these old men who are prepared to give up their male privilege and adopt, promote, and welcome young men into ways of seeing men (and women) that contradict the prevailing patriarchal order that gives those same old men the most to lose? And where will we find young men willing to follow their lead? Quite simply, we won't, except among a relative few who adopt "new masculinities" as personal styles. . . .

Either way, the individualistic model offers little hope of changing patriarchy because patriarchy is more than how people think, feel, and behave. As such, patriarchy isn't simply about the psychic wounding of sons by their fathers, or the dangers and failures of heterosexual intimacy, or boys' feelings about their mothers, or how men treat women and one another. It *includes* all of these by producing them as symptoms that help perpetuate the system, but these aren't what patriarchy *is*. It is a way of organizing social life through which such wounding, failure, and mistreatment can occur. If fathers neglect their sons, it is because fathers move in a world that makes pursuit of goals other than deeply committed fatherhood a path of least resistance. If heterosexual intimacy is prone to fail, it is because patriarchy is organized in ways that set women and men fundamentally at odds with one another in spite of all the good reasons they otherwise have to get along and thrive together. And men's use of coercion and violence against women is a pervasive pattern only because force and violence are supported in patriarchal society, because women are designated as desirable and legitimate objects of male control, and because in a society organized around control, force and violence *work*.

We can't find a way out of patriarchy or imagine something different without a clear sense of what patriarchy is and what it's got to do with us. Thus far, the alternative has been to reduce our understanding of gender to an intellectual gumbo of personal problems, tendencies, and motivations. Presumably, these will be solved through education, better communication skills, consciousness raising, "heroic journeys," and other forms of individual transformation. Since this isn't how social systems actually change, the result is widespread frustration and cycles of blame and denial. . . .

We need to see more clearly what patriarchy is about as a system. This includes cultural ideas about men and women, the web of relationships that structure social life, and the unequal distribution of power, rewards and resources that underlies privilege and oppression. We need to see new ways to participate by forging alternative paths of least resistance; for the system doesn't simply "run us" like hapless puppets. It may be larger than us, it may not *be* us, but it doesn't happen except *through* us. And that's where we have power to do something about it and about ourselves in relation to it.

Patriarchy

The key to understanding any system is to identify its various aspects and how they're arranged to form a whole. . . .

Patriarchy's defining elements are its male-dominated, male-identified, male-centered, and control-obsessed character, but this is just the beginning. At its core, patriarchy is based in part on a set of symbols and ideas that make up a culture embodied by everything from the content of everyday conversation to literature and film. Patriarchal culture includes ideas about the nature of things, including women, men, and humanity, with manhood and masculinity most closely associated with being human and womanhood and femininity relegated to the marginal position of "other." It's about how social life is and how it's supposed to be, about what's expected of people and about how they feel. It's about standards of feminine beauty and masculine toughness, images of feminine vulnerability and masculine protectiveness, of older men coupled with younger women, of elderly women alone. It's about defining women and men as opposites, about the "naturalness" of male aggression, competition, and dominance and of female caring, cooperation, and subordination. It's about the valuing of masculinity and maleness and the devaluing of femininity and femaleness. It's about the primary importance of a husband's career and the secondary status of a wife's, about child care as a priority in women's lives and its secondary importance in men's. It's about the social acceptability of anger, rage, and toughness in men but not in women, and of caring, tenderness, and vulnerability in women but not in men.

Above all, patriarchal culture is about the core value of control and domination in almost every area of human existence. From the expression of emotion to economics to the natural environment, gaining and exercising control is a continuing goal. Because of this, the concept of power takes on a narrow definition in terms of "power over"—the ability to control others, events, resources, or one's self in spite of resistance—rather than alternatives such as the ability to cooperate, to give freely of oneself, or to feel and act in harmony with nature. To have power over and to be prepared to use it are culturally defined as good and desirable (and characteristically "masculine"), and to lack such power or to be reluctant to use it is seen as weak if not contemptible (and characteristically "feminine"). This is a major reason that patriarchies with the means to do so are often so quick to go to war. Studies of the (mostly) men who formulate U.S. military strategy, for example, show that it is almost impossible to lose standing by advocating an excessive use of force in international relations (such as the U.S. response to terrorism and the 2003 invasion of Iraq). But anyone—especially a man—who advocates restraint in the use of force, runs the serious risk of being perceived as less than manly and, therefore, lacking credibility.

The main use of any culture is to provide symbols and ideas out of which to construct a sense of what is real. As such, language mirrors social reality in sometimes startling ways. In contemporary usage, for example, the words *crone, witch, bitch,* and *virgin* describe women as threatening, evil, or heterosexually inexperienced and thus incomplete. In prepatriarchal times, however, these words evoked far different images. The crone was the old woman whose life experience gave her insight, wisdom, respect, and the power to enrich people's lives. The witch was the wise-woman healer, the knower of herbs, the midwife, the link joining body, spirit, and Earth. The bitch was Artemis-Diana, goddess of the hunt, most often associated with the dogs who accompanied her. And the virgin was merely a woman who was unattached, unclaimed, and unowned by any man and therefore independent and autonomous. Notice how each word has been transformed from a positive cultural image of female power, independence, and dignity to an insult or a shadow of its former self so that few words remain to identify women in ways both positive and powerful.

Going deeper into patriarchal culture, we find a complex web of ideas that define reality and what's considered good and desirable. To see the world through patriarchal eyes is to believe that women and men are profoundly different in their basic natures, that hierarchy is the only alternative to chaos, and that men were made in the image of a masculine God with whom they enjoy a special relationship. It is to take as obvious the idea that there are two and only two distinct genders; that patriarchal heterosexuality is "natural" and same-sex attraction is not; that because men neither bear nor breast-feed children, they cannot feel a compelling bodily connection to them; that on some level every woman, whether heterosexual or lesbian, wants a "real man" who knows how to "take charge of things," including her; that females can't be trusted, especially when they're menstruating or accusing men of sexual abuse. In spite of all the media hype to the contrary, to embrace patriarchy still is to believe that mothers should stay home and that fathers should work outside the home, regardless of men's and women's actual abilities or needs. It is to buy into the notion that women are weak and men are strong, that women and children need men to support and protect them, all in spite of the fact that in many ways men are not the physically stronger sex, that women perform a huge share of hard physical labor in many societies (often larger than men's), that women's physical endurance tends to be greater than men's over the long haul, that women tend to be more capable of enduring pain and emotional stress.[3] And yet, as Elizabeth Janeway notes, such evidence means little in the face of a patriarchal culture that dictates how things *ought* to be and, like all cultural mythology, "will not be argued down by facts. It may seem to be making straightforward statements, but actually these conceal another mood, the imperative. Myth exists in a state of tension. It is not really describing a situation, but trying by means of this description *to bring about* what it declares to exist.[4]

To live in a patriarchal culture is to learn what's expected of men and women—to learn the rules that regulate punishment and reward based on how individuals behave and appear. These rules range from laws that require men to fight in wars not of their own choosing to customary expectations that mothers will provide child care. Or that when a woman shows sexual interest in a man or merely smiles or acts friendly, she gives up her right to say no and to control her own body. And to live under patriarchy is to take into ourselves ways of feeling—the hostile contempt for femaleness that forms the core of misogyny and presumptions of male superiority, the ridicule men direct at other men who show signs of vulnerability or weakness, or the fear and insecurity that every woman must deal with when she exercises the right to move freely in the world, especially at night and by herself in public places.

Such ideas make up the symbolic sea we swim in and the air we breathe. They are the primary well from which springs how we think about ourselves, other people, and the world. As such, they provide a taken-for-granted everyday reality, the setting for our interactions with other people that continually fashion and refashion a sense of what the world is about and who we are in relation to it. This doesn't mean that the ideas underlying patriarchy determine what we think, feel, and do, but it does mean they define what we'll have to deal with as we participate in it.

The prominent place of misogyny in patriarchal culture, for example, doesn't mean that every man and woman consciously hates all things female. But it does mean that to the extent that we don't feel such hatred, it's *in spite of* paths of least resistance contained in our culture. Complete freedom from such feelings and judgments is all but impossible. It is certainly possible for heterosexual men to love women without mentally fragmenting them into breasts, buttocks, genitals, and other variously desirable parts. It is possible for women to feel good about their bodies, to not judge themselves as being too fat, to not abuse themselves to one degree or another in pursuit of impossible male-identified standards of beauty and sexual attractiveness. All of this is possible, but to live in patriarchy is to breathe in misogynist images of women as objectified sexual property valued primarily for their usefulness to men. This finds its way into everyone who grows up breathing and swimming in it, and once inside of us it remains, however unaware of it we may be. So, when we hear or express sexist jokes and other forms of misogyny, we may not recognize it, and even if we do, we may say nothing rather than risk other people thinking we're "too sensitive" or, especially in the case of men, "not one of the guys." In either case, we are involved, if only by our silence.

The symbols and ideas that make up patriarchal culture are important to understand because they have such powerful effects on the structure of social life. By *structure,* I mean the ways privilege and oppression are organized through social relationships and unequal distributions of power, rewards, opportunities, and resources. This appears in countless patterns of everyday life in family and work, religion and politics, community and education. It is found in family divisions of labor that exempt fathers from most domestic work even when both parents work outside the home and in the concentration of women in lower-level pink-collar jobs and male predominance almost everywhere else. It is in the unequal distribution of income and all that goes with it, from access to health care to the availability of leisure time. It is in patterns of male violence and harassment that can turn a simple walk in the park or a typical day at work or a lovers' quarrel into a life-threatening nightmare. More than anything, the structure of patriarchy is found in the unequal distribution of power that makes male privilege possible, in patterns of male dominance in every facet of human life, from everyday conversation to global politics. By its nature, patriarchy puts issues of power, dominance, and control at the center of human existence, not only in relationships between men and women, but among men as they compete and struggle to gain status, maintain control, and protect themselves from what other men might do to them. . . .

The System in Us in the System

One way to see how people connect with systems is to think of us as occupying social positions that locate us in relation to people in other positions. We connect to families, for example, through positions such as "mother," "daughter," and "cousin"; to economic systems through positions such as "vice president," "secretary," or "unemployed"; to political systems through positions such as "citizen," "registered voter," and "mayor"; to religious systems through positions such as "believer" and "clergy." How we perceive the people who occupy such positions and what we expect of them depend on cultural ideas—such as the belief that mothers are naturally better than fathers at child care. Such ideas are powerful because we use them to construct a sense of who we and other people are. When a woman marries, for example, how people (including her) perceive and think about her changes as cultural ideas about what it means to be a wife come into play—ideas about how wives feel about their husbands, what's most important to wives, what's expected of them, and what they may expect of others.

From this perspective, *who* we and other people think we are has a lot to do with *where* we are in relation to social systems and all the positions we occupy in them. We wouldn't exist as social beings if it weren't for our participation in one social system or another. It's hard to imagine just who we'd be and what our existence would consist of if we took away all our connections to the symbols, ideas, and relationships that make up social systems. Take away language and all that it allows us to imagine and think, starting with our names. Take away all the positions that we occupy and the roles that go with them—from daughter and son to occupation and nationality—and with these all the complex ways our lives are connected to other people. Not much would be left over that we'd recognize as ourselves.

We can think of a society as a network of interconnected systems within systems, each made up of social positions and their relations to one another. To say, then, that I'm white, male, college educated, nondisabled, and a writer, sociologist, U.S. citizen, heterosexual, middle-aged, husband, father, grandfather, brother, and son identifies me in relation to positions which are themselves related to positions in various social systems, from the entire world to the family of my birth. In another sense, the day-to-day reality of a society only exists through what people actually do as they participate in it. Patriarchal culture, for example, places a high value on control and maleness. By themselves, these are just abstractions. But when men and women actually talk and men interrupt women more than women interrupt men, or men ignore topics introduced by women in favor of their own or in other ways control conversation, or when men use their authority to harass women in the workplace, then the reality of patriarchy as a kind of society and people's sense of themselves as female and male within it actually happen in a concrete way.

In this sense, like all social systems, patriarchy exists only through people's lives. . . . This has two important implications for how we understand patriarchy. First, to some extent people experience patriarchy as external to them. But this doesn't mean that it's a distinct and separate thing, like a house in which we live. Instead, by participating in patriarchy we are *of* patriarchy and it is *of* us. Both exist *through* the other and neither can exist without the other. Second, patriarchy isn't static. It's an ongoing *process* that's continuously shaped and reshaped. Since the thing we're participating in is patriarchal, we tend to behave in ways that create a patriarchal world from one moment to the next. But we have some freedom to break the rules and construct everyday life in different ways, which means that the paths we choose to follow can do as much to change patriarchy as they can to perpetuate it.

We're involved in patriarchy and its consequences because we occupy social positions in it, which is all it takes. Because patriarchy is, by definition, a system of inequality organized around gender categories, we can no more avoid being involved in it than we can avoid being female or male. *All* men and *all* women are therefore involved

in this oppressive system, and none us can control *whether* we participate, only *how*. As Harry Brod argues, this is especially important in relation to men and male privilege:

> We need to be clear that there is no such thing as giving up one's privilege to be "outside" the system. One is always *in* the system. The only question is whether one is part of the system in a way which challenges or strengthens the status quo. Privilege is not something I *take* and which I therefore have the option of *not* taking. It is something that society *gives* me, and unless I change the institutions which give it to me, they will continue to give it, and I will continue to *have* it, however noble and egalitarian my intentions.[5]

NOTES

1. Sam Keen, *Fire in the Belly: On Being a Man* (New York: Bantam, 1991), 207; Robert Bly, *Iron John: A Book about Men* (Reading, MA: Addison-Wesley, 1990).

2. Although the game analogy is useful, social systems are quite unlike a game in important ways. The rules and other understandings on which social life is based are far more complex, ambiguous, and contradictory than those of a typical game and much more open to negotiation and "making it up" as we go along.

3. See, for example, Rosalyn Baxandall, Linda Gordon, and Susan Reverby, eds., *America's Working Women: A Documentary History—1600 to the Present* (New York: Vintage Press, 1976); Ashley Montagu, *The Natural Superiority of Women* (New York: Collier, 1974); Robin Morgan, ed., *Sisterhood Is Global* (New York: Feminist Press, 1996); and Marilyn Waring, *If Women Counted: A New Feminist Economics* (San Francisco: HarperCollins, 1990).

4. Elizabeth Janeway, *Man's World, Woman's Place: A Study in Social Mythology* (New York: Dell, 1971), 37.

5. Harry Brod, "Work Clothes and Leisure Suits: The Class Basis and Bias of the Men's Movement," in *Men's Lives*, edited by Michael S. Kimmel and Michael A. Messner (New York: Macmillan, 1989), 280.

THREE

A Black Feminist Statement (1977)

Combahee River Collective

Active in the mid to late seventies, the **Combahee River Collective** was a Black feminist group in Boston whose name came from the guerrilla action led by **Harriet Tubman** that freed more than 750 slaves and is the only military campaign in U.S. history planned and led by a woman.

We are a collective of Black feminists who have been meeting together since 1974. During that time we have been involved in the process of defining and clarifying our politics, while at the same time doing political work within our own group and in coalition with other progressive organizations and movements. The most general statement of our politics at the present time would be that we are actively committed to struggling against racial, sexual, heterosexual, and class oppression and see as our particular task the development of integrated analysis and practice based upon the fact that the major systems of oppression are interlocking. The synthesis of these oppressions creates the conditions of our lives. As Black women we see Black feminism as the logical political movement to combat the manifold and simultaneous oppressions that all women of color face.

We will discuss four major topics in the paper that follows: (1) the genesis of contemporary Black feminism; (2) what we believe, i.e., the specific province of our politics; (3) the problems in organizing Black feminists, including a brief herstory of our collective; and (4) Black feminist issues and practice.

1. The Genesis of Contemporary Black Feminism

Before looking at the recent development of Black feminism we would like to affirm that we find our origins in the historical reality of Afro-American women's continuous life-and-death struggle for survival and liberation. Black women's extremely negative relationship to the American political system (a system of white male rule) has always been determined by our membership in two oppressed racial and sexual castes. As Angela Davis points out in "Reflections on the Black Woman's Role in the Community of Slaves," Black women have always embodied, if only in their physical manifestation, an adversary stance to white male rule and have actively resisted its inroads upon them and their communities in both dramatic and subtle ways. There have always been Black women activists—some known, like Sojourner Truth, Harriet Tubman, Frances E. W. Harper, Ida B. Wells Barnett, and Mary Church Terrell, and thousands upon thousands unknown—who had a shared awareness of how their sexual identity combined with their racial identity to make their whole life situation and the focus of their political struggles unique. Contemporary Black feminism is the outgrowth of countless generations of personal sacrifice, militancy, and work by our mothers and sisters.

A Black feminist presence has evolved most obviously in connection with the second wave of the American women's movement beginning in the late 1960s. Black, other Third World, and working women have been involved in the feminist movement from its start, but both outside reactionary forces and racism and elitism within the movement itself have served to obscure our participation. In 1973 Black feminists, primarily located in New York, felt the necessity of forming a separate Black feminist group. This became the National Black Feminist Organization (NBFO).

Black feminist politics also have an obvious connection to movements for Black liberation, particularly those of the 1960s and 1970s. Many of us were active in those movements (civil rights, Black nationalism, the Black Panthers), and all of our lives were greatly affected and changed by their ideology, their goals, and the tactics used to achieve their goals. It was our experience and disillusionment within these liberation movements, as well as experience on the periphery of the white male left, that led to the need to develop a politics that was antiracist, unlike those of white women, and antisexist, unlike those of Black and white men.

There is also undeniably a personal genesis for Black feminism, that is, the political realization that comes from the seemingly personal experiences of individual Black women's lives. Black feminists and many more Black women who do not define themselves as feminists have all experienced sexual oppression as a constant factor in our day-to-day existence. As children we realized that we were different from boys and that we were treated differently. For example, we were told in the same breath to be quiet both for the sake of being "ladylike" and to make us less objectionable in the eyes of white people. As we grew older we became aware of the threat of physical and sexual abuse by men. However, we had no way of conceptualizing what was so apparent to us, what we *knew* was really happening.

Black feminists often talk about their feelings of craziness before becoming conscious of the concepts of sexual politics, patriarchal rule, and most importantly, feminism, the political analysis and practice that we women use to struggle against our oppression. The fact that racial politics and indeed racism are pervasive factors in our lives did not allow us, and still does not allow most Black women, to look more deeply into our own experiences and, from that sharing and growing consciousness, to build a politics that will change our lives and inevitably end our oppression. Our development must also be tied to the contemporary economic and political position of Black people. The post–World War II generation of Black youth was the first to be able to minimally partake of certain educational and employment options, previously closed completely to Black people. Although our economic position is still at the very bottom of the American capitalistic economy, a handful of us have been able to gain certain tools as a result of tokenism in education and employment which potentially enable us to more effectively fight our oppression.

A combined antiracist and antisexist position drew us together initially, and as we developed politically we addressed ourselves to heterosexism and economic oppression under capitalism.

2. What We Believe

Above all else, our politics initially sprang from the shared belief that Black women are inherently valuable, that our liberation is a necessity not as an adjunct to somebody else's but because of our need as human persons for autonomy. This may seem so obvious as to sound simplistic, but it is apparent that no other ostensibly progressive movement has ever considered our specific oppression as a priority or worked seriously for the ending of that oppression. Merely naming the pejorative stereotypes attributed to Black women (e.g. mammy, matriarch, Sapphire, whore, bulldagger), let alone cataloguing the cruel, often murderous, treatment we receive, indicates how little value has been placed upon our lives during four centuries of bondage in the Western Hemisphere. We realize that the only people who care enough about us to work consistently for our liberation are us. Our politics evolve from a healthy love for ourselves, our sisters and our community which allows us to continue our struggle and work.

This focusing upon our own oppression is embodied in the concept of identity politics. We believe that the most profound and potentially the most radical politics come directly out of our own identity, as opposed to working to end somebody else's oppression. In the case of Black women this is a particularly repugnant, dangerous, threatening, and therefore revolutionary concept because it is obvious from looking at all the political movements that have preceded us that anyone is more worthy of liberation than ourselves. We reject pedestals, queenhood, and walking ten paces behind. To be recognized as human, levelly human, is enough.

We believe that sexual politics under patriarchy is as pervasive in Black women's lives as are the politics of class and race. We also often find it difficult to separate race from class from sex oppression because in our lives they are most often experienced simultaneously. We know that there is such a thing as racial-sexual oppression which is neither solely racial nor solely sexual, e.g., the history of rape of Black women by white men as a weapon of political repression.

Although we are feminists and lesbians, we feel solidarity with progressive Black men and do not advocate the fractionalization that white women who are separatists demand. Our situation as Black people necessitates that we have solidarity around the fact of race, which white women of course do not need to have with white men, unless it is their negative solidarity as racial oppressors. We struggle together with Black men against racism, while we also struggle with Black men about sexism.

We realize that the liberation of all oppressed peoples necessitates the destruction of the political-economic systems of capitalism and imperialism as well as patriarchy. We are socialists because we believe the work must be organized for the collective benefit of those who do the work and create the products, and not for the profit of the bosses. Material resources must be equally distributed among those who create these resources. We are not convinced, however, that a socialist revolution that is not also a feminist and antiracist revolution will guarantee our liberation. We have arrived at the necessity for developing an understanding of class relationships that takes into account the specific class position of Black women who are generally marginal in the labor force, while at this particular time some of us are temporarily viewed as doubly desirable tokens at white-collar and professional levels. We need to articulate the real class situation of persons who are not merely raceless, sexless workers, but for whom racial and sexual oppression are significant determinants in their working/economic lives. Although we are in essential agreement with Marx's theory as it applied to the very specific economic relationships he analyzed, we know that his analysis must be extended further in order for us to understand our specific economic situation as Black women.

A political contribution which we feel we have already made is the expansion of the feminist principle that the personal is political. In our consciousness-raising sessions, for example, we have in many ways gone beyond white women's revelations because we are dealing with the implications of race and class as well as sex. Even our Black women's style of talking/testifying in Black language about what we have experienced has a resonance that is both cultural and political. We have spent a great deal of energy delving into the cultural and experiential nature of our oppression out of necessity because none of these matters has ever been looked at before. No one before has ever examined the multilayered texture of Black women's lives. An example of this kind of revelation/conceptualization

occurred at a meeting as we discussed the ways in which our early intellectual interests had been attacked by our peers, particularly Black males. We discovered that all of us, because we were "smart" had also been considered "ugly," i.e., "smart-ugly." "Smart-ugly" crystallized the way in which most of us had been forced to develop our intellects at great cost to our "social" lives. The sanctions in the Black and white communities against Black women thinkers are comparatively much higher than for white women, particularly ones from the educated middle and upper classes.

As we have already stated, we reject the stance of lesbian separatism because it is not a viable political analysis or strategy for us. It leaves out far too much and far too many people, particularly Black men, women, and children. We have a great deal of criticism and loathing for what men have been socialized to be in this society: what they support, how they act, and how they oppress. But we do not have the misguided notion that it is their maleness, per se—i.e., their biological maleness—that makes them what they are. As Black women we find any type of biological determinism a particularly dangerous and reactionary basis upon which to build a politic. We must also question whether lesbian separatism is an adequate and progressive political analysis and strategy, even for those who practice it, since it so completely denies any but the sexual sources of women's oppression, negating the facts of class and race.

3. Problems in Organizing Black Feminists

During our years together as a Black feminist collective we have experienced success and defeat, joy and pain, victory and failure. We have found that it is very difficult to organize around Black feminist issues, difficult even to announce in certain contexts that we *are* Black feminists. We have tried to think about the reasons for our difficulties, particularly since the white women's movement continues to be strong and to grow in many directions. In this section we will discuss some of the general reasons for the organizing problems we face and also talk specifically about the stages in organizing our own collective.

The major source of difficulty in our political work is that we are not just trying to fight oppression on one front or even two, but instead to address a whole range of oppressions. We do not have racial, sexual, heterosexual, or class privilege to rely upon, nor do we have even the minimal access to resources and power that groups who possess any one of these types of privilege have.

The psychological toll of being a Black woman and the difficulties this presents in reaching political consciousness and doing political work can never be underestimated. There is a very low value placed upon Black women's psyches in this society, which is both racist and sexist. As an early group member once said, "We are all damaged people merely by virtue of being Black women." We are dispossessed psychologically and on every other level, and yet we feel the necessity to struggle to change the condition of all Black women. In "A Black Feminist's Search for Sisterhood," Michele Wallace arrives at this conclusion:

> We exist as women who are Black who are feminists, each stranded for the moment, working independently because there is not yet an environment in this society remotely congenial to our struggle—because, being on the bottom, we would have to do what no one else has done: we would have to fight the world.[1]

Wallace is pessimistic but realistic in her assessment of Black feminists' position, particularly in her allusion to the nearly classic isolation most of us face. We might use our position at the bottom, however, to make a clear leap into revolutionary action. If Black women were free, it would mean that everyone else would have to be free since our freedom would necessitate the destruction of all the systems of oppression.

Feminism is, nevertheless, very threatening to the majority of Black people because it calls into question some of the most basic assumptions about our existence, i.e., that sex should be a determinant of power relationships. Here is the way male and female voices were defined in a Black nationalist pamphlet from the early 1970s.

> We understand that it is and has been traditional that the man is the head of the house. He is the leader of the house/nation because his knowledge of the world is broader, his

awareness is greater, his understanding is fuller and his application of this information is wiser . . . After all, it is only reasonable that the man be the head of the house because he is able to defend and protect the development of his home . . . Women cannot do the same things as men—they are made by nature to function differently. Equality of men and women is something that cannot happen even in the abstract world. Men are not equal to other men, i.e. ability, experience or even understanding. The value of men and women can be seen as in the value of gold and silver—they are not equal but both have great value. We must realize that men and women are a complement to each other because there is no house/family without a man and his wife. Both are essential to the development of any life.[2]

The material conditions of most Black women would hardly lead them to upset both economic and sexual arrangements that seem to represent some stability in their lives. Many Black women have a good understanding of both sexism and racism, but because of the everyday constrictions of their lives cannot risk struggling against them both.

The reaction of Black men to feminism has been notoriously negative. They are, of course, even more threatened than Black women by the possibility that Black feminists might organize around our own needs. They realize that they might not only lose valuable and hard-working allies in their struggles but that they might also be forced to change their habitually sexist ways of interacting with and oppressing Black women. Accusations that Black feminism divides the Black struggle are powerful deterrents to the growth of an autonomous Black women's movement.

Still, hundreds of women have been active at different times during the three-year existence of our group. And every Black woman who came, came out of a strongly-felt need for some level of possibility that did not previously exist in her life.

When we first started meeting early in 1974 after the NBFO first eastern regional conference, we did not have a strategy for organizing, or even a focus. We just wanted to see what we had. After a period of months of not meeting, we began to meet again late in the year and started doing an intense variety of consciousness-raising. The overwhelming feeling that we had is that after years and years we had finally found each other. Although we were not doing political work as a group, individuals continued their involvement in Lesbian politics, sterilization abuse and abortion rights work, Third World Women's International Women's Day activities, and support activity for the trials of Dr. Kenneth Edelin, Joan Little, and Inéz García. During our first summer, when membership had dropped off considerably, those of us remaining devoted serious discussion to the possibility of opening a refuge for battered women in a Black community. (There was no refuge in Boston at that time.) We also decided around that time to become an independent collective since we had serious disagreements with NBFO's bourgeois-feminist stance and their lack of a clear political focus.

We also were contacted at that time by socialist feminists, with whom we had worked on abortion rights activities, who wanted to encourage us to attend the National Socialist Feminist Conference in Yellow Springs. One of our members did attend and despite the narrowness of the ideology that was promoted at that particular conference, we became more aware of the need for us to understand our own economic situation and to make our own economic analysis.

In the fall, when some members returned, we experienced several months of comparative inactivity and internal disagreements which were first conceptualized as a Lesbian-straight split but which were also the result of class and political differences. During the summer those of us who were still meeting had determined the need to do political work and to move beyond consciousness-raising and serving exclusively as an emotional support group. At the beginning of 1976, when some of the women who had not wanted to do political work and who also had voiced disagreements stopped attending of their own accord, we again looked for a focus. We decided at that time, with the addition of new members, to become a study group. We had always shared our reading with each other, and some of us had written papers on Black feminism for group discussion a few months before this decision was made. We began functioning as a study group and also began discussing the possibility of starting a Black feminist

publication. We had a retreat in the late spring which provided a time for both political discussion and working out interpersonal issues. Currently we are planning to gather together a collection of Black feminist writing. We feel that it is absolutely essential to demonstrate the reality of our politics to other Black women and believe that we can do this through writing and distributing our work. The fact that individual Black feminists are living in isolation all over the country, that our own numbers are small, and that we have some skills in writing, printing, and publishing makes us want to carry out these kinds of projects as a means of organizing Black feminists as we continue to do political work in coalition with other groups.

4. Black Feminist Issues and Projects

During our time together we have identified and worked on many issues of particular relevance to Black women. The inclusiveness of our politics makes us concerned with any situation that impinges upon the lives of women, Third World and working people. We are of course particularly committed to working on those struggles in which race, sex and class are simultaneous factors in oppression. We might, for example, become involved in workplace organizing at a factory that employs Third World women or picket a hospital that is cutting back on already inadequate health care to a Third World community, or set up a rape crisis center in a Black neighborhood. Organizing around welfare and daycare concerns might also be a focus. The work to be done and the countless issues that this work represents merely reflect the pervasiveness of our oppression.

Issues and projects that collective members have already worked on are sterilization abuse, abortion rights, battered women, rape and health care. We have also done many workshops and educationals on Black feminism on college campuses, at women's conferences, and most recently for high school women.

One issue that is of major concern to us and that we have begun to publicly address is racism in the white women's movement. As Black feminists we are made constantly and painfully aware of how little effort white women have made to understand

and combat their racism, which requires among other things that they have a more than superficial comprehension of race, color, and Black history and culture. Eliminating racism in the white women's movement is by definition work for white women to do, but we will continue to speak to and demand accountability on this issue.

In the practice of our politics we do not believe that the end always justifies the means. Many reactionary and destructive acts have been done in the name of achieving "correct" political goals. As feminists we do not want to mess over people in the name of politics. We believe in collective process and a nonhierarchical distribution of power within our own group and in our vision of a revolutionary society. We are committed to a continual examination of our politics as they develop through criticism and self-criticism as an essential aspect of our practice. In her introduc-tion to *Sisterhood Is Powerful*, Robin Morgan writes:

> I haven't the faintest notion what possible revolutionary role white heterosexual men could fulfill, since they are the very embodi-ment of reactionary-vested-interest-power.

As Black feminists and Lesbians we know that we have a very definite revolutionary task to perform and we are ready for the lifetime of work and struggle before us.

NOTES

1. Michele Wallace, "A Black Feminist's Search for Sis-terhood," *The Village Voice*, 28 July 1975, pp. 6–7.
2. Mumininas of Committee for Unified Newark, *Mwanamke Mwananchi (The Nationalist Woman)*, Newark, N.J., © 1971, pp. 4–5.

F O U R

◆◆◆

"Who Am I If I'm Not My Father's Daughter?" (1984)

Minnie Bruce Pratt

Minnie Bruce Pratt has taught creative writing, women's studies, and LGTB studies. She is the author of many autobiographical essays and five books of poetry. She received the 2003 Lambda Literary Award for her poetry collection *The Dirt She Ate*.

As a white woman, raised small-town middle-class, Christian, in the Deep South, I was taught to be a *judge*, of moral responsibility and punishment only in relation to *my* ethical system; was taught to be a *preacher*, to point out wrongs and tell others what to do; was taught to be a *martyr*, to take all the respon-sibility for change and the glory, to expect others to do nothing; was taught to be a *peacemaker*, to medi-tate, negotiate between opposing sides because *I* knew the right way. When I speak, or speak up, about anti-Semitism and racism, I struggle not to speak with intonations, the gestures, the assump-tion of these roles, and not to speak out of any role of ought-to; I ask that you try not to place me in that role. I am trying to speak today to women like myself, out of need: as a woman who loves other women passionately and wants us to be able to be together as friends in this unjust world.

But where does the need come from, if by skin color, ethnicity, birth culture, we are women who are in a position of material advantage, where we gain at the expense of others, of other women? A place where *we* can have a degree of safety, comfort, familiarity, just by staying put. Where is our *need* to change what we were born into? What do we have to gain?

When I try to think of this, I think of my father, of how, when I was about eight years old, he took me up the front marble steps of the courthouse in my town. He took me inside, up the worn wooden steps, stooped under the feet of the folks who had gone up and down to be judged, or to gawk at oth-ers being judged, up past the courtroom where my grandfather had leaned back in his chair and judged for more than 40 years, up to the attic, to some narrow steps that went to the roof, to the clock tower with a walled ledge.

What I would have seen at the top: on the streets around the courthouse square: the Methodist church, the limestone building with the county health department, board of education, welfare department (my mother worked there), the yellow brick Baptist church, the Gulf station, the pool hall (no women allowed), Cleveland's grocery, Ward's shoe store; then all in a line, connected: the bank, the post office, Dr. Nicholson's office, one door for whites, one for blacks, then separate: the Presbyterian church, the newspaper office, the yellow brick jail, same brick as the Baptist church, and as the courthouse.

What I could not have seen from the top: the sawmill, or Four Points where the white mill folks lived, or the houses of blacks in Veneer Mill quarters.

This is what I would and would not have seen, or so I think, for I never got to the top. When he told me to go up the steps in front of him, I tried to, crawling on hands and knees, but I was terribly afraid. I couldn't—or wouldn't—do it. He let me crawl down: he was disgusted with me, I thought. I think now that he wanted to show me a place he had climbed to as a boy, a view that had been his father's, and his, and would be mine. But I was *not* him. I had not learned to take that height, that being set apart as my own: a white girl, not a boy.

And yet I know I have been shaped by my relation to those buildings, and to the people in the buildings, by ideas of who should be working in the board of education, of who should be in the bank handling money, of who should have the guns and the keys to the jail, of who should be *in* the jail; I have been shaped by what I didn't see, or didn't notice, on those streets.

Each of us carries around with us those growing-up places, the institutions, a sort of backdrop, a stage-set. So often we act out the present against a backdrop of the past, within a frame of perception that is so familiar, so safe that it is terrifying to risk changing it even when we know our perceptions are distorted, limited, constricted by that old view.

So this is one gain for me as I change: I learn a way of looking at the world that is more accurate, complex, multilayered, multidimensioned, more truthful: to see the world of overlapping circles, like movement on the millpond after a fish has jumped, instead of the courthouse square with me in the middle. I feel the *need* to look differently because

I've learned that what is presented to me as an accurate view of the world is frequently a lie: so that to look through an anthology of women's studies that has little or no work by women of color is to be up on that ledge above the town and be thinking that I see the town, without realizing how many lives have been pushed out of sight, beside unpaved roads. I'm learning that what I think that I *know* is an accurate view of the world is frequently a lie: as when I was in a discussion about the Women's Pentagon Action with several women, four of us Christian-raised, one Jewish. In describing the march through Arlington Cemetery, one of the four mentioned the rows of crosses. I had marched for a long time through that cemetery; I nodded to myself, visualized rows of crosses. No, said the Jewish woman, they were headstones, with crosses or Stars of David engraved above the names. We four objected; we had all seen crosses. The Jewish woman had some photographs of the march through the cemetery, laid them on the table. We saw rows and rows of rectangular gravestones, and in the foreground, clearly visible, one inscribed with a name and a Star of David.

So I gain truth when I expand my constricted eye, an eye that has only let in what I have been taught to see. But there have been other constrictions: the fear around my heart when I must deal with the *fact* of folk who exist, with their own lives, in other places besides the narrow circle I was raised in. I have learned that my fear of these folks is kin to a terror that has been in my birth culture for years, for centuries, the terror of people who have set themselves apart and *above*, who have wronged others and feel they are about to be found out and punished. It is the terror that in my culture has been expressed in lies about dirty Jews who kill for blood, sly Arab hordes who murder, brutal Indians who massacre, animal blacks who rise in rebellion in the middle of the night and slaughter. It is the terror that has *caused* the slaughter of all these peoples. It is the terror that was my father with his stack of John Birch newspapers, his belief in a Communist-Jewish-Black conspiracy. It is the desperate terror, the knowledge that something is *wrong*, and tries to end fear by attack.

I get afraid when I am trying to understand myself in relation to folks different from me, when there are discussions, conflicts about anti-Semitism and racism among women, criticisms, criticisms of *me;* when, for instance, in a group discussion about race and class, I say I feel we have talked too much about race, not enough about class, and a woman of color asks me in anger and pain if I don't think her skin has something to do with class; when, for instance, I say carelessly to a Jewish friend that there were no Jews where I grew up, she begins to ask me: How do I know? Do I hear what I'm saying? and I get afraid; when I feel my racing heart, breath, the tightening of my skin around me, literally defenses to protect my narrow circle, I try to say to myself: yes, that fear is there, but I will try to be at the edge between my fear and the outside, on the edge at my skin, listening, asking what new thing will I hear, will I see, will I let myself feel, beyond the fear. I try to say to myself: that to acknowledge the complexity of another's existence is not to deny my own. I try to say: when I acknowledge what my people, what those who are like me, have done to people with less power and less safety in the world, I can make a place for things to be different, a place where I can feel grief, sorrow, not to be sorry *for* the others, but to mourn, to expand my circle of self, follow my need to loosen the constrictions of fear, be a break in the cycle of fear and attack.

To be caught within the narrow circle of the self is not just a fearful thing, it is a *lonely* thing. When I could not climb the steps that day with my father, maybe I knew on some level that my place was with women, not with men, that I did not want his view of the world. Certainly, I have felt this more and more strongly since my coming out as a lesbian. Yet so much has separated me from other women, ways in which my culture set me apart by race, by ethnicity, by class. I understood abruptly one day how lonely this made me when a friend, a black woman, spoke to me casually in our shared office: and I heard how she said my name: the lingering accent, so much like how my name is said at home. Yet I knew enough of her history and mine to know how much separated us: the chasm of murders, rapes, lynchings, the years of daily humiliations done by my people to hers. I went and stood in the hallway and cried, thinking of how she said my name like home, and how divided our lives were.

It is a pain I come to over and over again when, for instance, I realize how *habitually* I think of my culture, my ethics, my morality, as the culmination of history, as the logical extension of what has gone before; the kind of thinking represented by my use, in the past, of the word *Judeo-Christian,* as if Jewish history and lives have existed only to culminate in Christian culture, the kind of thinking that the U.S. government is using now to promote Armageddon in the Middle East; the kind of thinking that I did until recently about Indian lives and culture in my region, as if Indian peoples have existed only in museums since white folks came in the 1500s; the kind of thinking that separates me from women in cultures different from mine, makes their experience less central, less important than mine. It is painful to keep understanding this separation, within myself and in the world. Yet I have felt that the need to be with other women can be the breaking through the shell around me, painful, but a coming through into a new place, where with understanding and change, the loneliness won't be necessary.

If we have these things to gain, and more, by struggling against racism and anti-Semitism in ourselves, what keeps us from doing so, at any one moment, what keeps us from action? In part, I know I hesitate because I have struggled painfully, for years, to make this new place for myself with other women, and I hesitate to disrupt it.

In part I hesitate because the process of uncovering my complicity is so painful: it is the stripping down, layer after layer, of my identity: skin, blood, heart: to find out how much of what I am has been shaped by my skin and family, to find out which of my thoughts and actions I need to change, which I need to keep as my own. Sometimes I fear that stripping away the layers will bring me to nothing, that the only values that I and my culture have are based on negativity, exclusion, fear.

Often I have thought: *what* of who I am is worth saving? worth taking into the future? But I have learned that as the process of shaping identity was long, so the process of change is long. I know that change speeds up the more able I am to put into material shape what I have learned from struggling with anti-Semitism and racism, to begin to act for change can widen perception, loosen fear, ease loneliness. I know that we can choose to act in ways that get us closer to the longed-for but unrealized world, a world where we each are able to live, but not by trying to make someone less than us, not by someone else's blood or pain.

FIVE

Beyond Bean Counting (1995)

JeeYeun Lee

JeeYeun Lee is an activist, artist, teacher and writer living in Chicago. Her writing has been published in *Q & A: Queer in Asian America* and *Queer Studies: A Lesbian, Gay, Bisexual, & Transgender Anthology*. Her paid work has included social service management, teaching, research, training, fund raising, desktop publishing, editing, and sewing.

I came out as a woman, an Asian American and a bisexual within a relatively short span of time, and ever since then I have been guilty of the crime of bean counting. . . . Every time I am in a room of people gathered for any reason, I automatically count those whom I can identify as women, men, people of color, Asian Americans, mixed-race people, whites, gays and lesbians, bisexuals, heterosexuals, people with disabilities. . . .

Such is the nature of feminism in the 1990s: an uneasy balancing act between the imperatives of outreach and inclusion on the one hand, and the risk of tokenism and further marginalization on the other. This dynamic has indelibly shaped my personal experiences with feminism, starting from my very first encounter with organized feminism. This encounter happened to be, literally, Feminist Studies 101 at the university I attended. The content of the class was divided into topics such as family, work, sexuality and so forth, and for each topic we studied what various feminist paradigms said about it: "liberal feminism," "socialist feminism," "radical feminism" and "feminism and women of color."

Taking this class was an exhilarating, empowering and very uneasy experience. For the first time, I found people who articulated those murky half-formed feelings that I could previously only express incoherently as "But that's not fair!" People who agreed, sympathized, related their own experiences, theorized, helped me form what I had always known. In seventh grade, a teacher made us do a mock debate, and I ended up arguing with Neil Coleman about whether women or men were better

cooks. He said more men were professional chefs, therefore men were better. I responded that more women cooked in daily life, therefore women were better. He said it was quality that mattered, not quantity, and left me standing there with nothing to say. I knew there was something wrong with his argument, something wrong with the whole issue as it was framed, and felt extremely betrayed at being made to consent to the inferiority of my gender, losing in front of the whole class. I could never defend myself when arguments like this came up, invariably with boys who were good at debates and used to winning. They left me seething with resentment at their manipulations and frustrated at my speechlessness. So to come to a class that addressed these issues directly and gave me the words for all those pent-up feelings and frustrations was a tremendously affirming and empowering experience.

At the same time, it was an intensely uncomfortable experience. I knew "women of color" was supposed to include Asian American women, but I could not find any in the class readings. Were there no Asian American feminists? Were there none who could write in English? Did there even exist older Asian American women who were second or third generation? Were we Asian American students in the class the first to think about feminism? A class about women, I thought, was a class about me, so I looked for myself everywhere and found nothing. Nothing about Asian American families, immigrant women's work patterns, issues of sexuality and body image for Asian women, violence against Asian American women, Asian American women in the seventies feminist movement, nothing anywhere. I wasn't fully conscious then that I was searching for this, but this absence came out in certain feelings. First of all, I felt jealous of African American and Chicana feminists. Their work was present at least to some degree in the readings: They had research and theories, they were eloquent and they *existed*. Black and Chicana women in the class could claim them as role models, voices, communities—I had no one to claim as my own. My emerging identification as a woman of color was displaced through the writings of black and Chicana women, and I had to read myself, create my politics, through theirs; even now, to a certain extent, I feel more familiar with their issues than those of Asian American women. Second, I felt guilty. Although it was never expressed outright, I felt that there was some pressure on me to represent Asian American issues, and I could not. I felt estranged from the Asian American groups on campus and Asian American politics and activism in general, and guilty about this ignorance and alienation.

Now mind you, I'm still grateful for this class. Feminism was my avenue to politics: It politicized me; it raised my consciousness about issues of oppression, power and resistance in general. I learned a language with which I could start to explain my experiences and link them to larger societal structures of oppression and complicity. It also gave me ways that I could resist and actively fight back. I became interested in Asian American politics, people of color politics, gay/lesbian/bisexual politics and other struggles because of this exposure to feminism. But there is no excuse for this nearly complete exclusion of Asian/Pacific American women from the class. Marginalization is not simply a politically correct buzzword, it is a material reality that affects people's lives—in this case, my own. I would have been turned off from feminism altogether had it not been for later classes that dealt specifically with women of color. And I would like to name names here: I went to Stanford University, a bastion of privilege that pretends to be on the cutting edge of "multiculturalism." Just under twenty-five percent of the undergraduate population is Asian/Pacific American, but there was no mention of Asian/Pacific American women in Feminist Studies 101. All the classes I took on women of color were taught by graduate students and visiting professors. There was, at that time, only one woman of color on the feminist studies faculty. I regret that I realized the political import of these facts only after I left Stanford.

I understand that feminists in academia are caught between a rock and a hard place—not too many of us hold positions of decision-making power in universities. And I must acknowledge my gratitude for their struggles in helping to establish feminist studies programs and produce theories and research about women, all of which create vital opportunities and affirmation. But other women's organizations that are not constrained by such explicit forces are also lily-white. This obviously differs from group to group, and I think many of them are very conscientious about outreach to historically marginalized women. But, for instance, in 1992 and 1993, at the meetings I attended of the Women's Action Coalition (WAC) in New York City, out of approximately two hundred women usually fewer than twenty women of color were present.

But this is not a diatribe against feminism in general. I want to emphasize that the feminism that I and other young women come to today is one that is at least sensitive to issues of exclusion. If perhaps twenty years ago charges of racism, classism and homophobia were not taken seriously, today they are the cause of extreme anguish and soul-searching. I am profoundly grateful to older feminists of color and their white allies who struggled to bring U.S. feminist movements to this point. At the same time, I think that this current sensitivity often breeds tokenism, guilt, suspicion and self-righteousness that have very material repercussions on women's groups. I have found these uneasy dynamics in all the women's groups I've come across, addressed to varying degrees. At one extreme, I have seen groups that deny the marginalizing affects of their practices, believing that issues of inclusion really have nothing to do with their specific agendas. At the other extreme, I have seen groups ripped apart by accusations of political correctness, immobilized by guilt, knowing they should address a certain issue but not knowing how to begin, and still wondering why "women of color just don't come to our meetings." And tokenism is alive and well in the nineties. Those of us who have been aware of our tokenization often become suspicious and tired of educating others, wondering if we are invested enough to continue to do so, wondering if the overall goal is worth it.

In this age when "political correctness" has been appropriated by conservative forces as a derogatory term, it is extremely difficult to honestly discuss and confront any ideas and practices that perpetuate dominant norms—and none of us is innocent of such collusion. Many times, our response is to become defensive, shutting down to constructive critiques and actions, or to individualize our collusion as solely a personal fault, as if working on our individual racist or classist attitudes would some-how make things better. It appears that we all have a lot of work to do still.

And I mean *all*. Issues of exclusion are not the sole province of white feminists. I learned this very vividly at a 1993 retreat organized by the Asian Pacifica Lesbian Network. It has become somewhat common lately to speak of "Asian and Pacific Islanders" or "Asian/Pacific Americans" or, as in this case, "Asian Pacifica." This is meant to be in-clusive, to recognize some issues held in common by people from Asia and people from the Pacific Islands. Two women of Native Hawaiian descent and some Asian American allies confronted the group at this retreat to ask for more than lip service in the organization's name: If the group was seri-ously committed to being an inclusive coalition, we needed to educate ourselves about and actively advocate Pacific Islander issues. And because I don't want to relegate them to a footnote, I will mention here a few of these issues: the demand for sover-eignty for Native Hawaiians, whose government was illegally overthrown by the U.S. in 1893; fight-ing stereotypes of women and men that are differ-ent from those Asian people; decrying U.S. imperialist possession and occupation of the is-lands of Guam, the Virgin Islands, American Samoa, the Marshall Islands, Micronesia, the North-ern Mariana Islands and several others.

This was a retreat where one would suppose everyone had so much in common—after all, we were all queer API women, right? Any such myth was effectively destroyed by the realities of our experiences and issues: We were women of differ-ent ethnic backgrounds, with very different issues among East Asians, South Asians, Southeast Asians and Pacific Islanders; women of mixed race and heritage; women who identified as lesbians and those who identified as bisexuals; women who were immigrants, refugees, illegal aliens or second generation or more; older women, physically chal-lenged women, women adopted by white families, women from the Midwest. Such tangible differ-ences brought home the fact that no simplistic iden-tity politics is *ever* possible, that we had to conceive of ourselves as a coalition first and foremost; as one woman on a panel said, our identity as queer API women must be a *coalitional* identity. Initially, I thought that I had finally found a home where I could relax and let down my guard. This was true

to a certain degree, but I discovered that this was the home where I would have to work the hardest because I cared the most. I would have to be com-mitted to push myself and push others to deal with all of our differences, so that we *could* be safe for each other. And in this difficult work of coalition, one positive action was taken at the retreat: We changed the name of the organization to include "bisexual," thus becoming the Asian Pacifica Lesbian and Bisexual Network, a name that people started using immediately.

All this is to say that I and other young women have found most feminist movements today to be at this point, where there is at least a stated emphasis on inclusion and outreach with the accompanying risk of tokenism. I firmly believe that it is always the margins that push us further in our politics. Women of color do not struggle in feminist movements sim-ply to add cultural diversity, to add the viewpoints of different kinds of women. Women of color femi-nist theories challenge the fundamental premises of feminism, such as the very definition of "women," and call for recognition of the constructed racial nature of *all* experiences of gender. In the same way, heterosexist norms do not oppress solely lesbians, bisexuals and gay men, but affect all of our choices and non-choices; issues posed by differently abled women question our basic assumptions about body image, health care, sexuality and work; ecofemi-nists challenge our fundamental ideas about living on and with the earth, about our interactions with animals, plants, food, agriculture and industry. Many feminists seem to find the issues of class the most difficult to address; we are always faced with the fundamental inequalities inherent to late-twentieth-century multinational capitalism and our unavoidable implication in its structures. Such an overwhelming array of problems can numb and im-mobilize us, or make us concentrate our energies too narrowly. I don't think that we have to address everything fully at the same time, but we *must* be fully aware of the limitations of our specific agen-das. Progressive activists cannot afford to do the masters' work for them by continuing to carry out oppressive assumptions and exclusions.

These days, whenever someone says the word "women" to me, my mind goes blank. What "women"? What is this "women" thing you're talk-ing about? Does that mean me? Does that mean my mother, my roommates, the white woman next door, the checkout clerk at the supermarket, my aunts in Korea, half of the world's population? I ask people to specify and specify, until I can figure out exactly what they're talking about, and I try to remember to apply the same standards to myself, to deny myself the slightest possibility of romanticization. Sisterhood may be global, but who is in that

sisterhood? None of us can afford to assume anything about anybody else. This thing called "feminism" takes a great deal of hard work, and I think this is one of the primary hallmarks of young feminists' activism today: We realize that coming together and working together are by no means natural or easy.

S I X

◆◆◆

Genealogies of Community, Home, and Nation (1993/2003)

Chandra Talpade Mohanty

Chandra Talpade Mohanty is a professor of women's studies at Syracuse University. Her widely acclaimed scholarly work, most recently *Feminism Without Borders: Decolonizing Theory, Practicing Solidarity,* focuses on transnational feminist theory, cultural studies, and antiracist education.

. . . At a time when globalization (and monoculturalism) is the primary economic and cultural practice to capture and hold hostage the material resources and economic and political choices of vast numbers of the world's population, what are the concrete challenges for feminists of varied genealogies working together? Within the context of the history of feminist struggle in the United States, the 1980s were a period of euphoria and hope for feminists of color, gay and lesbian, and antiracist, white feminists. Excavating subjugated knowledges and histories in order to craft decolonized, oppositional racial and sexual identities and political strategies that posed direct challenges to the gender, class, race, and sexual regimes of the capitalist U.S. nation-state anchored the practice of antiracist, multicultural feminisms.

At the start of this century, however, I believe the challenges are somewhat different. Globalization, or the unfettered mobility of capital and the accompanying erosion and reconstitution of local and national economic and political resources and of democratic processes, the post–cold war U.S. imperialist state, and the trajectories of identity-based social movements in the 1980s and 1990s constitute the ground for transnational feminist engagement

in the twenty-first century. Multicultural feminism that is radical, antiracist, and nonheterosexist thus needs to take on a hegemonic capitalist regime and conceive of itself as also crossing national and regional borders. Questions of "home," "belonging," "nation," and "community" thus become profoundly complicated.

One concrete task that feminist educators, artists, scholars, and activists face is that of historicizing and denaturalizing the ideas, beliefs, and values of global capital such that underlying exploitative social relations and structures are made visible. This means being attentive not only to the grand narrative or "myth" of capitalism as "democracy" but also to the mythologies that feminists of various races, nations, classes, and sexualities have inherited about one another. I believe one of the greatest challenges we (feminists) face is this task of recognizing and undoing the ways in which we colonize and objectify our different histories and cultures, thus colluding with hegemonic processes of domination and rule. Dialogue across differences is thus fraught with tension, competitiveness, and pain. Just as radical or critical multiculturalism cannot be the mere sum or coexistence of different cultures in a profoundly unequal, colonized world, multicultural feminism cannot assume the existence of a dialogue among feminists from different communities without specifying a just and ethical basis for such a dialogue.

Undoing ingrained racial and sexual mythologies within feminist communities requires, in Jacqui Alexander's words, that we "become fluent in each other's histories." It also requires seeking "unlikely coalitions" (Davis 1998, 299)[1] and, I would add, clarifying the ethics and meaning of dialogue. What are the conditions, the knowledges, and the attitudes that make a noncolonized dialogue possible? How can we craft a dialogue anchored in equality, respect, and dignity for all peoples? In other words, I want to suggest that one of the most crucial challenges for a critical multicultural feminism is working out how to engage in ethical and caring dialogues (and revolutionary struggles) across the divisions, conflicts, and individualist identity formations that interweave feminist communities in the United States. Defining genealogies is one crucial element in creating such a dialogue.

Just as the very meaning and basis for dialogue across difference and power needs to be analyzed and carefully crafted, the way we define genealogies also poses a challenge. Genealogies that not only specify and illuminate historical and cultural differences but also envision and enact common political and intellectual projects across these differences constitute a crucial element of the work of building critical multicultural feminism.

To this end I offer a personal, anecdotal meditation on the politics of gender and race in the construction of South Asian identity in North America. My location in the United States is symptomatic of large numbers of migrants, nomads, immigrants, workers across the globe for whom notions of home, identity, geography, and history are infinitely complicated in the twenty-first century. . . .

Emotional and Political Geographies of Belonging

On a TWA flight on my way back to the United States from a conference in the Netherlands, the white professional man sitting next to me asks which school I go to and when I plan to go home—all in the same breath. I put on my most professorial demeanor (somewhat hard in crumpled blue jeans and cotton T-shirt) and inform him that I teach at a small liberal arts college in upstate New York and that I have lived in the United States for over twenty years. At this point, my work is in the United States, not in India. (This is no longer entirely true—my work is also with feminists and grassroots activists in India, but he

doesn't need to know this.) Being "mistaken" for a graduate student seems endemic to my existence in this country: few Third World women are granted professional (i.e., adult) and/or permanent (one is always a student) status in the United States, even if we exhibit clear characteristics of adulthood such as gray hair and facial lines. The man ventures a further question: what do I teach? On hearing "women's studies," he becomes quiet and we spend the next eight hours in polite silence. He has decided that I do not fit into any of his categories, but what can you expect from a feminist (an Asian one) anyway? I feel vindicated and a little superior, even though I know he doesn't really feel "put in his place." Why should he? He claims a number of advantages in this situation: white skin, maleness, and citizenship privileges. Judging by his enthusiasm for expensive "ethnic food" in Amsterdam, and his J. Crew clothes, I figured class difference (economic or cultural) wasn't exactly a concern in our interaction. We both appeared to have similar social access as "professionals."

I have been asked the "home" question (when are you going home?) periodically for twenty years now. Leaving aside the subtly racist implications of the question (go home, you don't belong), I am still not satisfied with my response. What is home? The place I was born? Where I grew up? Where my parents live? Where I live and work as an adult? Where I locate my community, my people? Who are "my people"? Is home a geographical space, a historical space, an emotional, sensory space? Home is always so crucial to immigrants and migrants—I even write about it in scholarly texts (perhaps to avoid addressing it, as an issue that is also very personal?). What interests me is the meaning of home for immigrants and migrants. I am convinced that this question—how one understands and defines home—is a profoundly political one.

Since settled notions of territory, community, geography, and history don't work for us, what does it really mean to be "South Asian" in the United States? Obviously, I was not South Asian in India: I was Indian. What else could one be but "Indian" at a time when a successful national independence struggle had given birth to a socialist democratic nation-state? This was the beginning of the decolonization of the Third World. Regional geography (South Asia) appeared less relevant as a mark of identification than citizenship in a postcolonial independent nation on the cusp of economic and political autonomy. However, in North America, identification as South Asian (in addition to Indian, in my case) takes on its own logic. "South Asian" refers to folks of Indian, Pakistani, Sri Lankan, Bangladeshi, Kashmiri, and Burmese origin. Identifying as South Asian rather than Indian adds numbers and hence power within the U.S. state. Besides, regional differences among those from different South Asian countries are often less relevant than the commonalities based on our experiences and histories of immigration, treatment, and location in the United States.

Let me reflect a bit on the way I identify myself, and the way the U.S. state and its institutions categorize me. Perhaps thinking through the various labels will lead me to the question of home and identity. In 1977, I arrived in the United States on a F1 visa (a student visa). At that time, my definition of myself—a graduate student in education at the University of Illinois—and the "official" definition of me (a student allowed into the country on a F1 visa) obviously coincided. Then I was called a "foreign student" and expected to go "home" (to India, even though my parents were in Nigeria at the time) after getting my Ph.D. This is the assumed trajectory for a number of Indians, especially the postindependence (my) generation, who come to the United States for graduate study.

However, this was not to be my trajectory. I quickly discovered that being a foreign student, and a woman at that, meant being either dismissed as irrelevant (the quiet Asian woman stereotype), or treated in racist ways (my teachers asked if I understood English and if they should speak slower and louder so that I could keep up—this in spite of my inheritance of the Queen's English and British colonialism) or celebrated and exoticized ("You are so smart! Your accent is even better than that of Americans"—a little Anglophilia at work here, even though all my Indian colleagues insist we speak English the Indian way).

The most significant transition I made at that time was the one from "foreign student" to "student of color." Once I was able to "read" my experiences in terms of race, and to read race and racism as they are written into the social and political fabric of the United States, practices of racism and sexism became the analytic and political lenses through which I was able to anchor myself here. Of course, none of this happened in isolation: friends, colleagues, comrades, classes, books, films, arguments, and dialogues were constitutive of my political education as a woman of color in the United States.

In the late 1970s and early 1980s feminism was gaining momentum on American campuses: it was in the air, in the classrooms, on the streets. However, what attracted me wasn't feminism as the mainstream media and white women's studies departments defined it. Instead, it was a very specific kind of feminism, the feminism of U.S. women of color and Third World women, that spoke to me. In thinking through the links among gender, race, and class in their U.S. manifestations, I was for the first time able to think through my own gendered, classed, postcolonial history. In the early 1980s, reading Audre Lorde, Nawal el Sadaawi, Angela Davis, Cherrie Moraga, bell hooks, Gloria Joseph, Paula Gunn Allen, Barbara Smith, Merle Woo, and Mitsuye Yamada, among others, generated a sort of recognition that was intangible but very inspiring. A number of actions, decisions, and organizing efforts at that time led me to a sense of home and community in relation to women of color in the United States: home, not as a comfortable, stable, inherited, and familiar space but instead as an imaginative, politically charged space in which the familiarity and sense of affection and commitment lay in shared collective analysis of social injustice, as well as a vision of radical transformation. Political solidarity and a sense of family could be melded together imaginatively to create a strategic space I could call "home." Politically, intellectually, and emotionally I owe an enormous debt to feminists of color—especially to the sisters who have sustained me over the years. . . .

For me, engagement as a feminist of color in the United States made possible an intellectual and political genealogy of being Indian that was radically challenging as well as profoundly activist. Notions of home and community began to be located within a deeply political space where racialization and gender and class relations and histories became the prism through which I understood, however partially, what it could mean to be South Asian in North America. Interestingly, this recognition also forced me to reexamine the meanings attached to home and community in India.

What I chose to claim, and continue to claim, is a history of anticolonialist, feminist struggle in India. The stories I recall, the ones that I retell and claim as my own, determine the choices and decisions I make in the present and the future. I did not want to accept a history of Hindu chauvinist (bourgeois) upward mobility (even though this characterizes a section of my extended family). We all choose partial, interested stories/histories—perhaps not as deliberately as I am making it sound here, but, consciously or unconsciously, these choices about our past(s) often determine the logic of our present.

Having always kept my distance from conservative, upwardly mobile Indian immigrants, to whom the South Asian world in the United States was divided into green card holders and non-green card holders, the only South Asian links I allowed and cultivated were with South Asians with whom I shared a political vision. This considerably limited my community. Racist and sexist experiences in graduate school and after made it imperative that I understand the United States in terms of its history of racism, imperialism, and patriarchal relations, specifically in relation to Third World immigrants. After all, we were then into the Reagan-Bush years, when the neoconservative backlash made it impossible to ignore the rise of racist, antifeminist, and homophobic attitudes, practices, and institutions. Any purely culturalist or nostalgic sentimental definition of being "Indian" or "South Asian" was inadequate. Such a definition fueled the "model minority" myth. And this subsequently constituted us as "outsiders/foreigners" or as interest groups that sought or had obtained the American dream.

In the 1980s, the labels changed: I went from being a "foreign student" to being a "resident alien." I have always thought that this designation was a stroke of inspiration on the part of the U.S. state, since it accurately names the experience and status of immigrants, especially immigrants of color. The flip side of "resident alien" is "illegal alien," another inspired designation. One can be either a resident or illegal immigrant, but one is always an alien. There is no confusion here, no melting pot

ideology or narratives of assimilation: one's status as an "alien" is primary. Being legal requires identity papers. (It is useful to recall that the "passport"—and by extensions the concept of nation-states and the sanctity of their borders— came into being after World War I.)

One must be stamped as legitimate (that is, not gay or lesbian and not communist) by the Immigration and Naturalization Service. The INS is one of the central disciplinary arms of the U.S. government. It polices the borders and controls all border crossings, especially those into the United States. In fact, the INS is also one of the primary forces that institutionalizes race differences in the public arena, thus regulating notions of home, legitimacy, and economic access to the "American dream" for many of us. For instance, carrying a green card documenting resident alien status in the United States is clearly very different from carrying an American passport, which is proof of U.S. citizenship. The former allows one to enter the United States with few hassles; the latter often allows one to breeze through the borders and ports of entry of other countries, especially countries that happen to be trading partners (much of Western Europe and Japan, among others) or in an unequal relationship with the United States (much of the noncommunist Third World). At a time when notions of a capitalist free-market economy is seen (falsely) as synonymous with the values attached to democracy, an American passport can open many doors. However, just carrying an American passport is no insurance against racism and unequal and unjust treatment within the United States.

A comparison of the racialization of South Asian immigrants to second-generation South Asian Americans suggests one significant difference between these two generations: experiencing racism as a phenomenon specific to the United States, versus growing up in the ever-present shadow of racism in the case of South Asians born in the United States. This difference in experience would suggest that the psychic effects of racism would also be different for these two constituencies. In addition, questions of home, identity, and history take on very different meanings for South Asians born in North America. But this comparison requires a whole other reflection that is beyond the scope of this chapter.

Home/Nation/Community: The Politics of Being Nri (Nonresident Indian)

Rather obstinately, I refused to give up my Indian passport and chose to remain a resident alien in the United States for many years.[2] This leads me to reflect on the complicated meanings attached to holding Indian citizenship while making a life for myself in the United States. In India, what does it mean to have a green card or U.S. passport, to be an expatriate? What does it mean to visit Mumbai (Bombay) every two to four years and still call it home? Why does speaking in Marathi (my mother tongue) become a measure and confirmation of home? What are the politics of being a part of the majority and the "absent elite" in India, while being a minority and a racialized "other" in the United States? And do feminist politics, or advocating feminism, have the same meanings and urgencies in these different geographical and political contexts?

Some of these questions hit me smack in the face during a visit to India in December 1992, after the infamous destruction of the Babri Masjid in Ayodhya by Hindu fundamentalists on 6 December 1992. (Horrifically, these deadly clashes between Hindus and Muslims took a new turn in March 2002, with Muslims burning a train full of Hindus returning from Ayodhya, inaugurating yet another continuing bloodbath.) In my earlier, rather infrequent visits (once every four or five years was all I could afford), my green card designated me as an object of envy, privilege, and status within my extended family. Of course, the same green card has always been viewed with suspicion by leftist and feminist friends, who (quite understandably) demand evidence of my ongoing commitment to a socialist and democratic India. During my 1992 visit, however, with emotions running high within my family, my green card marked me as an outsider who couldn't possibly understand the "Muslim problem" in India. I was made aware of being an "outsider" in two profoundly troubling shouting matches with my uncles, who voiced the most hostile sentiments against Muslims. Arguing that India was created as a secular state and that democracy had everything to do with equality for all groups (majority and minority) got me nowhere. The very

fundamentals of democratic citizenship in India were/are being undermined and redefined as "Hindu."

Mumbai was one of the cities hardest hit with waves of communal violence following the events of Ayodhya. The mobilization of Hindu fundamentalists, even paramilitary organizations, over the last century and especially since the mid-1940s, had brought Mumbai to a juncture at which the most violently racist discourse about Muslims seemed to be woven into the fabric of acceptable daily life. Racism was normalized in the popular imagination such that it became almost impossible to raise questions in public about the ethics or injustice of racial/ethnic/religious discrimination. I could not assume a distanced posture toward religion anymore. Too many injustices were being committed in my name.

Although born into a Hindu family, I have always considered myself a nonpracticing Hindu—religion had always felt rather repressive when I was growing up. I enjoyed the rituals but resisted the authoritarian hierarchies of organized Hinduism. However, the Hinduism touted by fundamentalist organizations like the RSS (Rashtriya Swayamsevak Sangh, a paramilitary Hindu fundamentalist organization founded in the 1930s) and the Shiv Sena (a Maharashtrian chauvinist, fundamentalist, fascist political organization that has amassed a significant voice in Mumbai politics and government) was one that even I, in my ignorance, recognized as reactionary and distorted. But this discourse was real—hate-filled rhetoric against Muslims appeared to be the mark of a "loyal Hindu." It was heart-wrenching to see my hometown become a war zone, with streets set on fire and a daily death count to rival any major territorial border war. The smells and textures of my beloved Mumbai, of home, which had always comforted and nurtured me, were violently disrupted. The scent of fish drying on the lines at the fishing village in Danda was submerged in the smell of burning straw and grass as whole *bastis* (*chawls*) were burned to the ground. The very topography, language, and relationships that constituted "home" were exploding. What does community mean in this context?

December 1992 both clarified as well as complicated for me the meanings attached to being an

Indian citizen, a Hindu, an educated woman feminist, and a permanent resident in the United States in ways that I have yet to resolve. After all, it is often moments of crisis that make us pay careful attention to questions of identity. Sharp polarizations force one to make choices (not in order to take sides, but in order to accept responsibility) and to clarify one's own analytic, political, and emotional topographies.

I learned that combating the rise of Hindu fundamentalism was a necessary ethical imperative for all socialists, feminists, and Hindus of conscience. Secularism, if it meant absence of religion, was no longer a viable position. From a feminist perspective, it became clear that the battle for women's minds and hearts was very much center stage in the Hindu fundamentalist rhetoric and social position of women. (Two journals, the *Economic and Political Weekly of India* and *Manushi,* are good sources for this work.)

Religious fundamentalist constructions of women embody the nexus of morality, sexuality, and nation — a nexus of great importance for feminists. As in Christian, Islamic, and Jewish fundamentalist discourses, the construction of femininity and masculinity, especially in relation to the idea of the nation, are central to Hindu fundamentalist rhetoric and mobilizations. Women are not only mobilized in the "service" of the nation, but they also become the ground on which discourses of morality and nationalism are written. For instance, the RSS mobilizes primarily middle-class women in the name of a family-oriented Hindu nation, much as the Christian Right does in the United States. But discourses of morality and nation are also embodied in the normative policing of women's sexuality (witness the surveillance and control of women's dress in the name of morality by the contemporary Iranian state and Taliban-ruled Afghanistan). Thus, one of the central challenges Indian feminists face at this time is how to rethink the relationship of nationalism and feminism in the context of religious identities. In addition to the fundamentalist mobilization that is tearing the country apart, the recent incursions of the International Monetary Fund and the World Bank, with their structural adjustment programs that are supposed to "discipline" the Indian economy, are redefining the meaning of postcoloniality and of democracy in India. Categories such as gender, race, caste/class are profoundly and

visibly unstable at such times of crisis. These categories must thus be analyzed in relation to contemporary reconstructions of womanhood and manhood in a *global* arena increasingly dominated by religious fundamentalist movements, the IMF, the World Bank, and the relentless economic and ideological colonization of much of the world by multinationals based in the United States, Japan, and Europe. In all these global economic and cultural/ideological processes, women occupy a crucial position.

In India, unlike most countries, the sex ratio has declined since the early 1900s. According to the 1991 census, the ratio was 929 women to 1,000 men, one of the lowest sex ratios in the world. Women produce 70 to 80 percent of all the food in India and have always been the hardest hit by environmental degradation and poverty. The contradictions between civil law and Hindu and Muslim personal laws affect women but rarely men. Horrific stories about the deliberate genocide of female infants as a result of sex determination procedures such as amniocentesis and recent incidents of *sati* (self-immolation by women on the funeral pyres of their husbands) have even hit the mainstream American media. Gender and religious (racial) discrimination are thus urgent, life-threatening issues for women in India. Over the last decade or so, a politically conscious Indian citizenship has necessitated taking such fundamentally feminist issues seriously. In fact, these are the very same issues South Asian feminists in the United States need to address. My responsibility to combat and organize against the regressive and violent repercussions of Hindu fundamentalist mobilizations in India extends to my life in North America. After all, much of the money that sustains the fundamentalist movement is raised and funneled through organizations in the United States.

On Race, Color, and Politics: Being South Asian in North America

It is a number of years since I wrote the bulk of this chapter,[3] and as I reread it, I am struck by the presence of the journeys and border-crossings that weave into and anchor my thinking about genealogies. The very crossing of regional, national, cultural, and geographical borders seems to enable me to reflect on questions of identity, community, and politics. In the past years I have journeyed to and lived among peoples in San Diego, California; Albuquerque, New Mexico; London, England; and Cuttack, India. My appearance as a brown woman with short, dark, graying hair remained the same, but in each of these living spaces I learned something slightly different about being South Asian in North America; about being a brown woman in the midst of other brown women with different histories and genealogies.

I want to conclude with a brief reflection on my journeys to California and New Mexico, since they complicate further the question of being South Asian in North America. A rather obvious fact, which had not been experientially visible to me earlier, is that the color line differs depending on one's geographical location in the United States. Having lived on the East Coast for many years, my designation as "brown," "Asian," "South Asian," "Third World," and "immigrant" has everything to do with definitions of "blackness" (understood specifically as African American). However, San Diego, with its histories of immigration and racial struggle, its shared border with Mexico, its predominantly brown (Chicano and Asian-American) color line, and its virulent anti-immigrant culture unsettled my East Coast definitions of race and racialization. I could pass as Latina until I spoke my "Indian" English, and then being South Asian became a question of (in)visibility and foreignness. Being South Asian here was synonymous with being alien, non-American.

Similarly, in New Mexico, where the normative meanings of race and color find expression in the relations between Native American, Chicano, and Anglo communities, being South Asian was a matter of being simultaneously visible and invisible as a brown woman. Here, too, my brownness and facial structure marked me visibly as sometimes Latina, sometimes Native American (evidenced by being hailed numerous times in the street as both). Even being Asian, as in being from a part of the world called "Asia," had less meaning in New Mexico, especially since "Asian" was synonymous with "East Asian": the "South" always fell out. Thus, while I could share some experiences with Latinas and Native American women, for instance, the experience of being an "alien"—an outsider within, a woman outside the purview of normalized U.S. citizenship—my South Asian genealogy also set me apart. Shifting the color line by crossing the geogra-

phy and history of the American West and Southwest thus foregrounded questions about being South Asian in a space where, first, my brownness was not read against blackness, and second Asian was already definitively cast as East Asian. In this context, what is the relation of South Asian to Asian American (read: East Asian American)? And why does it continue to feel more appropriate, experientially and strategically, to call myself a woman of color or Third World woman? Geographies have never coincided with the politics of race. And claiming racial identities based on history, social location, and experience is always a matter of collective analysis and politics. Thus, while geographical spaces provide historical and cultural anchors (Marathi, Mumbai, and India are fundamental to my sense of myself), it is the deeper values and strategic approach to questions of economic and social justice and collective anticapitalist struggle that constitute my feminism. Perhaps this is why journeys across the borders of regions and nations always provoke reflections of home, identity, and politics for me: there is no clear or obvious fit between geography, race, and politics for someone like me. I am always called on to define and redefine these relationships—"race," "Asianness," and "brownness" are not embedded in me, whereas histories of colonialism, racism, sexism, and nationalism, as well as of privilege (class and status) are involved in my relation to white people and people of color in the United States.

Let me now circle back to the place I began: defining genealogies as a crucial aspect of crafting critical multicultural feminist practice and the meanings I have come to give to home, community, and identity. By exploring the relationship between being a South Asian immigrant in America and an expatriate Indian citizen (NRI) in India, I have tried, however partially and anecdotally, to clarify the complexities of home and community for this particular feminist of color/South Asian in North America. The genealogy I have created for myself here is partial and deliberate. It is a genealogy that I find emotionally and politically enabling—it is part of the genealogy that underlies my self-identification as an educator involved in a pedagogy of liberation. Of course, my history and experiences are in fact messier and not at all as linear as this narrative makes them sound. But then the very process of constructing a narrative for oneself—of telling a story—imposes a certain linearity and coherence that is never entirely there. That is the lesson, perhaps, especially for us immigrants and migrants: that home, community, and identity all fit somewhere between the histories and experiences we inherit and the political choices we make through alliances, solidarities, and friendships.

One very concrete effect of my creating this particular space for myself has been my involvement in two grassroots organizations, one in India and the other in the United States. The former, an organization called Awareness, is based in Orissa and works to empower the rural poor. The group's focus is political education (similar to Paolo Friere's notion of "conscientization"), and its members have also begun very consciously to organize rural women. The U.S. organization I worked with is Grassroots Leadership of North Carolina. It is a multiracial group of organizers (largely African American and white) working to build a poor and working people's movement in the American South. While the geographical, historical, and political contexts are different in the case of these two organizations, my involvement in them is very similar, as is my sense that there are clear connections to be made between the work of the two organizations. In addition, I think that the issues, analyses, and strategies for organizing for social justice are also quite similar. This particular commitment to work with grassroots organizers in the two places I call home is not accidental. It is very

much the result of the genealogy I have traced here. After all, it took me over a decade to make these commitments to grassroots work in both spaces. In part, I have defined what it means to be South Asian by educating myself about, and reflecting on, the histories and experiences of African American, Latina, West Indian, African, European American, and other constituencies in North America. Such definitions and understandings do provide a genealogy, but a genealogy that is always relational and fluid as well as urgent and necessary.

NOTES

1. Davis, Angela, and Elizabeth Martinez. 1998. "Coalition Building Among People of Color: A Discussion with Angela Davis and Elizabeth Martinez." In *The Angela Davis Reader,* edited by Joy James. Boston: Blackwell.

2. I became a U.S. citizen in 1998, in order to adopt my daughter Uma Talpade Mohanty from Mumbai. Now I no longer hold an Indian passport, although of course my designation as NRI (Nonresident Indian) remains the same.

3. An earlier version of this chapter, entitled "Defining Genealogies: Feminist Reflections on Being South Asian in North America," was published in Women of South Asian Descent Collective (1993). This chapter is dedicated to the memory of Lanubai and Gauribai Vijaykar, my maternal grandaunts, who were single, educated, financially independent, and tall (over six feet), at a time when it was against the grain to be any one of these things; and to Audre Lorde, teacher, sister, friend, whose words and presence continue to challenge me.

SEVEN

◆◆◆

Constructing News, Creating Worldviews (2005)

Onnesha Roychoudhuri

Onnesha Roychoudhuri, recipient of a 2000 National Foundation for the Advancement of the Arts award in short fiction, is a recent graduate of Bard College. Her articles have appeared in *Mother Jones.com, Alternet,* and other online publications.

It was 1991. Operation Desert Storm was in full swing. I was 9 years old, and I had no idea why U.S. soldiers were in the Middle East, could hardly

name the countries that composed the Middle East. I remember watching the evening news with my mother. On the couch, as we ate eggplant parmesan, the local North Carolina anchor interviewed a mother whose son was in Iraq. The camera bobbed along as the crew followed her across the campus of UNC Chapel Hill, while she tied yellow ribbons to trees and lampposts. I didn't really know what patriotism was, but I could sense it, and I was swept up in the righteous passion of this woman whose son was risking his life for our country. The camera cut to candlelight vigils in other cities. People were holding hands and singing to American troops overseas. To this day, when I think of Operation Desert Storm, I think of yellow grosgrain ribbon and the song I sang in the shower, gripped by the emotion of a country united, a country at war. "Stand tall, stand proud/voices that care are crying out loud/and when you close your eyes tonight/feel in your heart how our love burns bright."

Fast forward to 2000. At a college in the middle of the woods in upstate New York, I am drinking cheap red wine and watching TV as the presidential election wraps up. Most of the campus has come out to watch Al Gore thrash George Bush. I had just turned 18 but had not registered to vote. I felt a bit guilty but didn't think it mattered much. From what I had heard, it was obvious that Gore was going to win and that this was who *should* win. But he didn't. When the final figures came in, silence fell in the room. No amount of cheap wine could bring back the upbeat confidence that most of us had before we knew the result. Our hopes were dashed. But I realized that night that I didn't know what it meant. I didn't really know what issues were at stake. I didn't even know if I should have been rooting for Gore, or why.

After the election, I was mortified that I hadn't voted. While before it seemed the world of politics was vastly separate, almost alien, from my own, I saw, for the first time, where I *could have* mattered, could have had a hand in shaping the outcome. I had to confess to myself the main reason I hadn't registered was because I thought I didn't know enough about the issues. I thought the decision was better left in the hands of those who were informed and knew what was at stake. But who were those people, anyway? I thought of my fellow students gathered on election night. Truth be told, I wouldn't have trusted the majority of them with my pet hamster, let alone the direction our country should go in for the next four years. And that was just a group of people in a room. Imagine how many people I would disagree with throughout the country. I made a conscious decision to become informed. I started to read the *New York Times* every morning. Almost every morning. Well, sometimes I just read the headlines when I was in a hurry. But I felt informed. Could at least cite a statistic here and there in my politics classes. It didn't seem to take many nuggets

of information to sound like you knew what you were talking about.

When I graduated, I found myself with a degree in political science and a passion for writing. I started an internship at a political magazine in San Francisco. I spent four months combing through articles and checking facts. It was, much of the time, mind-numbing (Do you, in fact, have a beard?). But at other times, I felt on the cutting edge of investigative journalism (When did you first report that the death was not only a murder, but also, allegedly, at the hands of a military officer?). Every time I fact-checked an article, I discovered, at best, typographical errors and misleading information. At worst, I uncovered outright falsities that needed substantial rewriting to make the article accurate and consistent. It was a simultaneously disturbing and gratifying endeavor. On the one hand, I couldn't believe the errors that some of these published authors were making; on the other, it made me think that if they could get published, I could too.

After four months of fact-checking, I was upgraded to the status of "fellow" (oh, the many pseudonyms the working world has created for exploiting inexpensive labor). I was no longer working for the print magazine, but the online site. The job description was a dream come true: I was to read the news daily and write about what was going on in the world from my standpoint. I was a contributor to the magazine's weblog or "blog," a fascinating media species that takes a critical look at what is in the news, oftentimes focusing on issues that aren't being adequately covered by the mainstream media. Every day, I would come into work and spend hours reading the major newspapers from the *L.A. Times* and the *New York Times*, the BBC to the *Christian Science Monitor*. I also read other major blogs that provided critical news analysis, each comparing different stories, and commenting on the issues. Often these blogs drew on news sources from around the world—comparing an issue as reported by American news media with that of a foreign press. The first week, I found myself searching for something new to write about. What could I add to the mix? How could I possibly know more about an issue than these journalists, these people who write with such authority?

A few days into the job, after writing repeats and summaries of news articles I'd read, I came across a small item in a major news source. It was a brief article that addressed an upcoming legal case against a firm called Custer Battles that had U.S. government contracts in Iraq. Two former employees had brought a "whistleblower" suit against the company because they claimed to have evidence that it was swindling the government out of millions of dollars. According to this short piece, the government didn't appear eager to take part in the case, but it didn't explain why. As I searched the Web further, the most I uncovered was a quote from the lawyer representing the two former employees suing Custer Battles.

So, I did a "google" search using the lawyer's name: Alan Grayson. Then I found his phone number (also online). Drinking coffee until I could muster my most professional "journalist voice," I gave him a call and asked him what was going on. He ended up providing me with documents that showed the U.S. government was aware of Custer Battles' overcharging—had known all along and done nothing to stop it. So that explained the reluctance to take part in the court case: the government was guilty of letting taxpayers' funds go down the drain. After doing a little further research and calling the lawyers defending Custer Battles to get their side of the story ("no comment"), I wrote up a piece on what was at stake in the pending case. It appeared online and Alan Grayson e-mailed to thank me for writing something that, finally, looked more deeply into an issue he clearly found important. I began to get phone calls and e-mails from other journalists too. They were calling me because they thought I was an expert on the issues. I felt fantastically devious. If only they knew that I was a recent college graduate merely fronting as a "journalist."

After that experience, I look at the news very differently now. When I read an article on any issue, I look for quotes from both sides. What is at stake, and for whom? What serves whose interests? What questions remain unanswered? What questions remain unasked? I realized that I used to let the authoritative tone of the news writers lull me into a false sense of security. Indeed, I had written an article and been called an expert. But, while I had obtained some important information, I was no "expert." I'd assumed that the newspapers I read were staffed with journalists who asked all the relevant questions, and gave a pretty good approximation of what was going on. Not so. Just as I had learned from my time fact-checking that all writers

make mistakes, so reading the news I realized that many writers fail to explore the full depths of a story, or rely on too few details, often giving a very partial view of events.

To some extent, there is no way around this. Journalists are subject to the faults and shortcomings that are part and parcel of being human. On top of the pressures of deadlines, they are also limited by their editor's views. Every journalist develops a sixth sense for what their editor is likely to publish. The editors, in turn, base what they are willing to publish on what they think their readers, and oftentimes the businesses that fund the publication, want to hear. It is a complex and circular logic that can very easily elbow out important and pertinent information about what's going on in the world. But we rarely stop to consider this because the end product is so seductively authoritative.

As I began to develop a "beat," my journey into journalism became ever murkier. I followed the legal issues surrounding the war on terror—specifically the detainees who were being held in Guantanamo Bay, Cuba, without charges, by the Bush administration. In February 2005, *Newsweek* magazine published an article reporting that a detainee's Koran had allegedly been flushed down a toilet by a guard. A spokesman for the administration immediately stated that the allegations were being looked into, but they couldn't locate the document that *Newsweek* cited to support this story. In the meantime, riots had broken out in Afghanistan. Some articles exploring the events tied the riots in with the *Newsweek* article, leading readers to assume that the false information in the *Newsweek* article had led directly to the riots in Afghanistan. Reading other articles, and scanning the pertinent blogs, I found that, while the *Newsweek* allegations had certainly played a part in instigating the riots, Afghanistan's own president, Hamid Karzai, publicly stated that many of the riots were being stirred up in opposition to the upcoming parliamentary elections. Even the senior U.S. military commander in Afghanistan, Lt. Gen. Karl Eikenberry, thought "the violence that we saw . . . was not at all tied to the article in the magazine."

If I had read just one article on the issue, depending on which it had been, I would have radically different opinions of what was going on with U.S. media, Afghanistan, Guantanamo detainees, and this administration. By reading different media sources and a range of blogs, I was able to see important discrepancies. The specific document that *Newsweek* cited was not located but the International Committee for the Red Cross came forward and stated that their 2002 and 2003 reports to the Pentagon cited allegations of abuse of the Koran in Guantanamo.

After four months, my fellowship came to an end. While I never felt comfortable calling myself a "journalist," I left the job with the understanding that every one of us has the capability to be a journalist, to become an "expert," by asking the right questions. Anyone who asks, "What's going on?" or, "Why is this happening?" possesses the spirit of journalism. After investing some time reading different news sources, as well as finding out which "bloggers" I trust to give me to-the-point information on the issues that I am most concerned with, I've found that staying informed, even after leaving the world of journalism, is an attainable endeavor.

Living in this affluent society, most Americans have access to a wealth of information via the Internet. Many of us take a substantial amount of time online to compare prices and features when looking for a new VCR, or stereo. Why should our view of world events, our country, and our elected representatives bear any less scrutiny or comparative exploration? Of course, investigating snazzy electronics results in a piece of machinery you can enjoy. The value of a handful of informative news sources is much more nebulous. What do you do with this information? In a country where the voter turnout rate rarely bobs above 50 percent, it is clear that many people experience a significant disconnect between their knowledge of politics and their ability to impact it. But the benefit of becoming more informed is that it leads you to see more clearly where

you *can* effect change. We, as the public, carry significant clout in our capacity to hold leaders to account for their actions. But we cannot do this unless we first follow their actions and know what's at stake.

Those in power rely on us to take them at their word rather than judge them by their actions when it comes time to vote. Having spent close to a year making a living by reading the news and working to get at the full story behind many issues, I've learnt that if it is within a politician's interest to deceive us, they will oftentimes do it. At the same time, journalists do not always cover the full story or explore all sides. The daily news is composed of articles by writers who string together the handful of facts they have obtained in their research. They call a news item a "story" for good reason. By reading information from different news sources, by finding trusted news analysis that looks critically at the coverage of the issues, you can start to construct something resembling a more whole "story." Find your niche—which newspapers, which blogs, look at the issues you care about? Which ones ask the questions you want to ask?

I look back to the time I sang patriotic songs as a child without understanding why I was singing. I have since learned that if we sing our support of something, it is our responsibility to understand what it is. With the amount of information at our disposal, it is as much of a decision to remain uninformed as it is to stay informed. What you choose to read, the information that you rely on, is what will shape your decisions. No one can hand us the truth. We have to construct it using our own brains, and our own volition. And the difference between us and an expert is oftentimes a matter of a handful of questions and a few phone calls.

2

◆◆◆

Identities and Social Locations: Who Am I? Who Are My People?

Our identity is a specific marker of how we define ourselves at any particular moment in life. Discovering and claiming our unique identity is a process of growth, change, and renewal throughout our lifetime. One's identity may seem tangible and fixed at any given point. Over the life span, however, identity is more fluid. For example, an able-bodied woman who suddenly finds herself confined to a wheelchair after an automobile accident, an assimilated Jewish woman who begins the journey of recovering her Jewish heritage, an immigrant woman from a traditional Guatemalan family "coming out" as a lesbian in the United States, or a young, middle-class college student, away from her sheltered home environment for the first time and becoming politicized by an environmental justice organization on campus, will probably find herself redefining who she is, what she values, and what "home" and "community" mean to her.

Identity formation is the result of a complex interplay among a range of factors: individual decisions and choices, particular life events, community recognition and expectations, societal categorization, classification and socialization, and key national or international events. It is an ongoing process that involves several key questions:

Who am I? Who do I want to be?

Who do others think I am and want me to be?

Who and what do societal and community institutions, such as schools, religious institutions, the media, and the law, say I am?

Where/what/who are my "home" and "community"?

Which social group(s) do I want to affiliate with?

Who decides the answers to these questions, and on what basis?

The *American Heritage Dictionary* (1993) defines *identity* as

> the collective aspect of the set of characteristics by which a thing is definitely known or recognizable;
>
> a set of behavioral or personal characteristics by which an individual is recognizable as a member of a group;
>
> the distinct personality of an individual regarded as a persisting entity;
>
> individuality.

The same dictionary defines *to identify* as "to associate or affiliate (oneself) closely with a person or group; to establish an identification with another or others."

These definitions point to the connections between us as individuals and how we are perceived by other people and classified by societal institutions. They also involve a sense of individual agency and choice regarding affiliations with others. Gender, race, ethnicity, class, nationality, sexual orientation, age, religion, dis/ability, and language are all significant social categories by which people are recognized by others. Indeed, on the basis of these categories alone, others often think they know who we are and how we should behave. Personal decisions about our affiliations and loyalties to specific groups are also shaped by these categories. For example, in many communities of color, women struggle over the question of race versus gender. Is race a more important factor than gender in shaping their lives? If a Latina speaks out publicly about sexism within the Latino community, is she betraying her people? This separation of categories, mirrored by our segregated social lives, tends to set up false dichotomies in which people often feel that they have to choose one aspect of their identity over another. It also presents particular difficulties for mixed-race, bisexual, or transgender people who do not fit neatly into such narrow categories, and reinforces the need for an intersectional framework as we argued in Chapter 1.

In order to understand the complexity and richness of women's experiences, we must examine them from the micro, meso, macro, and global levels of social relations. Each level involves the standards—beliefs, behaviors, customs, and worldview—that people value. But it is important to emphasize that in a society marked by serious social and economic inequality, such as the United States, oppressed peoples rarely see their values reflected in the dominant culture. Indeed, this absence is an important aspect of their oppression. For example, writing about her family, whom she describes as "the ungrateful poor," Dorothy Allison (Reading 9) states: "My family's lives were not on television, not in books, not even comic books. There was a myth of the poor in this country; but it did not include us, no matter how hard I tried to squeeze us in."

Critically analyzing the issue of identity at all of these levels will allow us to see that identity is much more than an individual decision or choice about who we are in the world. Rather, it is a set of complex and often contradictory and conflicting psychological, physical, geographical, political, cultural, historical, and spiritual factors.

Being Myself: The Micro Level

At the micro level, individuals usually feel the most comfortable as themselves. Here one can say, for example, "I am a woman, heterosexual, middle class, Buddhist, with a movement disability; but I am also much more than those categories," or, like Gwendolyn Pough (Reading 10), a feminist who loves hip-hop culture. At this level we define ourselves and structure our daily activities according to our own preferences. At the micro level we can best feel and experience the process of identity formation, which includes naming specific forces and events that shape our identities. At this level we also seem to have more control of the process, although there are always interconnections between events and experiences at this level and the other levels.

Critical life events, such as entering kindergarten, losing a parent through death, or divorce, or the onset of puberty, may all serve as catalysts for a shift in how we think about ourselves. A five-year-old Vietnamese American child may experience the first challenge to her sense of identity when her kindergarten teacher admonishes her to speak only in English. A White, middle-class professional woman who thinks of herself as "a person" and a "competent attorney" may begin to see the significance of gender and "the glass ceiling" for women when she witnesses younger, less experienced male colleagues in her law office passing her by for promotions. A woman who has been raped who attends her first meeting of a campus group organizing against date rape feels the power of connection with other rape survivors and their allies. An eighty-year-old woman, whose partner of fifty years has just died, must face the loss of her life-time companion, friend, and lover. Such experiences shape each person's ongoing formulation of self, whether or not the process is conscious, deliberate, reflective, or even voluntary.

Identity formation is a lifelong endeavor that includes discovery of the new; recovery of the old, forgotten, or appropriated; and synthesis of the new and old, as illustrated by several writers in this chapter who reflect on how their sense of identity has developed over the course of their lives. At especially important junctures during the process, individuals mark an identity change in tangible ways. An African American woman may change her name from the anglicized Susan to Aisha, with roots in African culture. A Chinese immigrant woman, on the other hand, may adopt an anglicized name, exchanging Nu Lu for Yvonne Lu as part of becoming a U.S. citizen. Another way of marking and effecting a shift in identity is by altering your physical appearance: changing your wardrobe or makeup; cutting your hair very short, wearing it natural rather than permed or pressed, dyeing it purple, or letting the gray show after years of using hair coloring. More permanent changes might include having a tattoo, having your body pierced, having a face lift or tummy tuck, or, for Asian American women, having eye surgery to "Europeanize" your eyes. Transsexuals—female to male and male to female—have surgery to make their physical appearance congruent with their internal sense of self. Other markers of a change in identity include redecorating your home, setting up home for the first time, or physically relocating to another neighborhood, another city, or another part of the country in search of a new home.

For many people, home is where we grow up until we become independent, by going to college, for example, or getting married; where our parents, siblings, and maybe grandparents are; where our needs for safety, security, and material comfort are met. In reality, what we think of as home is often a complicated and contradictory place where some things we need are present and others are not. Some people's homes are comfortable and secure in a material sense but are also places of emotional or physical violence and cruelty. Some children grow up in homes that provide emotional comfort and a sense

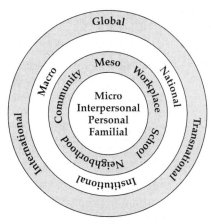

Figure 2.1 Levels of Analysis and Interaction

of belonging, but as they grow older and their values diverge from those of their parents, home may become a source of discomfort and alienation.

Regardless of such experiences—perhaps because of them—most people continue to seek places of comfort and solace and others with whom they feel they belong and with whom they share common values and interests. Home may be a geographic, social, emotional, and spiritual space where we hope to find safety, security, familiarity, continuity, acceptance, and understanding, and where we can feel and be our best, whole selves. Home may be in several places at once or in different places at different times of our lives. Some women may have a difficult time finding a home, a place that feels comfortable and familiar, even if they know what it is. Finally, this process may involve not only searching outside ourselves but also piecing together in some coherent way the scattered parts of our identities—an inward as well as an outward journey.

Community Recognition, Expectations, and Interactions: The Meso Level

It is at the meso level—at school, in the workplace, in the neighborhood, or on the street—that people most frequently ask "Who are you?" or "Where are you from?" in an attempt to categorize us and determine their relationship to us, as exemplified in the story,

"Hanaan's House" (Reading 12). Moreover, it is here that people experience the complexities, conflicts, and contradictions of multiple identities, which we consider later.

The single most visible signifier of identity is physical appearance. How we look to others affects their perceptions, judgments, and treatment of us. Questions such as "Where do you come from?" and questioning behaviors, such as feeling the texture of your hair or asking if you speak a particular language, are commonly used to interrogate people whose physical appearances especially, but also behaviors, do not match the characteristics designated as belonging to established categories. At root, we are being asked, "Are you one of us or not?" These questioners usually expect simple and straightforward answers, assuming that everyone will fit existing social categories, which are conceived of as undifferentiated and unambiguous. Among people with disabilities, for example, people wanting to identify each other may expect to hear details of another's disability rather than the fact that the person being questioned also identifies equally strongly as, say, a woman who is White, working class, and bisexual.

Community, like home, may be geographic and emotional, or both, and provides a way for people to express group affiliations. "Where are you from?" is a commonplace question in the United States among strangers, a way to break the ice and start a conversation, expecting answers like "I'm from Tallahassee, Florida," or "I'm from the Bronx." Community might also be an organized group like Alcoholics Anonymous, a religious group, or a political organization like the African American civil rights organization, the National Association for the Advancement of Colored People (NAACP). Community may be cultural or religious as discussed by Melanie Kaye/Kantrowitz (Reading 11) and Christina Leaño (Reading 78), or something more abstract, as in "the women's community" or "the queer community," where there is presumed to be an identifiable group. In these examples there is an assumption of shared values, interests, culture, or language sometimes thought of as essential qualities that define group membership and belonging. This can lead to **essentialism,** where complex identities get reduced to specific qualities deemed to be essential for membership of a particular group: being Muslim or gay, for example.

At the community level, individual identities and needs meet group standards, expectations, obligations, responsibilities, and demands. You compare yourself with others and are subtly compared. Others size up your clothing, accent, personal style, and knowledge of the group's history and culture. You may be challenged directly, "You say you're Latina. How come you don't speak Spanish?" "You say you're working class. What are you doing in a professional job?" These experiences may both affirm our identities and create or highlight inconsistencies and contradictions in who we believe we are, how we are viewed by others, our role and status in the community, and our sense of belonging.

Some individuals experience **marginality** if they can move in two or more worlds and, in part, be accepted as insiders (Stonequist 1961). Examples include bisexuals, mixed-race people, and immigrants, who all live in at least two cultures. Margaret, a White, working-class woman, for instance, leaves her friends behind after high school graduation as she goes off to an elite university. Though excited and eager to be in a new setting, she often feels alienated at college because her culture, upbringing, and level of economic security differ from those of the many upper-middle-class and upper-class students. During the winter break she returns to her hometown, where she discovers a gulf between herself and her old friends who remained at home and took full-time jobs. She notices that she is now speaking a slightly different language from them and that her interests and preoccupations are different from theirs. Margaret has a foot in both worlds. She has become sufficiently acculturated at college to begin to know that community as an insider, and she has retained her old community of friends, but she is not entirely at ease or wholly accepted by either community. Her identity is complex, composed of several parts.

Dorothy Allison (Reading 9) describes her experience of marginality in high school and in college. First-generation immigrants invariably experience marginality, as described by Chandra Talpade Mohanty (Reading 6) and Shailja Patel (Reading 47). The positive effect of marginality—also mentioned by writers in this chapter—is the ability to see both cultures more clearly than people who are embedded in any one context. This gives bicultural people a broader range of vision and allows them to see the complexity and contradictions of both cultural settings. It also helps them to be cultural interpreters and bridge builders, especially at the micro and meso levels (Chiawei O'Hearn 1998; Kich 1992; Okazawa-Rey 1994; Root 1996; Walker 2001).

Social Categories, Classifications, and Structural Inequality: Macro and Global Levels

Classifying and labeling human beings, often according to real or assumed physical, biological, or genetic differences, is a way to distinguish who is included and who is excluded from a group, to ascribe particular characteristics, to prescribe social roles, and to assign status, power, and privilege. People are to know their places. Thus social categories such as gender, race, and class are used to establish and maintain a particular kind of social order. The classifications and their specific features, meanings, and significance are socially constructed through history, politics, and culture. The specific meanings and significance were often imputed to justify the conquest, colonization, domination, and exploitation of entire groups of people, and although the specifics may have changed over time, this system of categorizing and classifying remains intact. For example, Native American people were described as brutal, uncivilized, and ungovernable savages in the writings of early colonizers on this continent. This justified the near-genocide of Native Americans by White settlers, public officials, and the U.S. military, as well as the breaking of treaties between the U.S. government and Native American tribes (Zinn 1995). Today, Native Americans are no longer called savages but are often thought of as a vanishing species, or a nonexistent people, already wiped out, thereby rationalizing their neglect by the dominant culture and erasing their long-standing and continuing resistance. Frederica Y. Daly speaks to the oppression of Native American people, as well as their success in retaining traditional values and the cultural revival they have undertaken (Reading 8). Andy Smith (Reading 39) also provides a perspective on Native American history and contemporary life that is pertinent here. Note how this macro-level process of classification and labeling has affected Arabs, Arab Americans, and "people who look like Muslims," especially after the attacks of

September 11, 2001 (Amani Elkassabani, Reading 12). Dorothy Allison points out that a "horror of class stratification, racism, and prejudice is that some people begin to believe that the security of their families and community depends on the oppression of others, that for some to have good lives others must have lives that are mean and horrible" (Reading 9).

These social categories are at the foundation of the structural inequalities present in our society. In each category there is one group of people deemed superior, legitimate, dominant, and privileged while others are relegated—whether explicitly or implicitly—to the position of inferior, illegitimate, subordinate, and disadvantaged.

Category	Dominant	Subordinate
Gender	Men	Women, transgender people
Race	White	Peoples of color
Class	Middle and upper class	Poor, working class
Nation	U.S./global North	Global South
Ethnicity	European	All other ethnicities
Sexual orientation	Heterosexual	Lesbian, gay, bisexual, transgender
Religion	Christian	All other religions
Physical ability	Able-bodied	Persons with disabilities
Age	Youth	Elderly persons
Language	English	All other languages

People are not simply in a dominant or a subordinate position, however. Many people are privileged on one or more dimensions, and at the same time subordinated on other dimensions. Self-awareness involves recognizing and understanding the significance of our identities, which are often complex and contradictory. For White people descended from European immigrants to this country, the advantages of being White are not always fully recognized or acknowledged. In Reading 14, Mary C. Waters describes how, at the macro level, this country's racial hierarchy benefits European Americans who can choose to claim an ethnic identity as, for example, Irish Americans or Italian Americans. These symbolic identities are individualistic, she argues, and do not have serious social costs for the individual compared with racial and ethnic identities of people of color in the United States. As a result, White people in the United States tend to think of all identities as equal: "I'm Italian American, you're Polish American. I'm Irish American, you're African American." This assumed equivalence ignores the very big differences between an individualist symbolic identity and a socially enforced and imposed racial identity. In Reading 11, Melanie Kaye/Kantrowitz writes about the complex social location of Jews in the United States, and her conviction that privilege can and should be deployed to bring about equality and justice. In Reading 4, Minnie Bruce Pratt writes about becoming more aware of her advantaged position and describes her fear of losing her familiar place as she becomes conscious of how her White privilege affects people of color. She sees the positive side of this process—"I gain truth when I expand my constricted eye"—and asks what White women have to gain by changing systems of inequality. Melanie Bush (2004), an educator and administrator at Brooklyn College (CUNY), explores White students' perceptions of identity, privilege, democracy, and intergroup relations. She identifies "cracks in the wall of whiteness"—circumstances that can foster understanding about systemic, racialized patterns of inequality—and argues that such understanding can provide a springboard for change.

Maintaining Systems of Structural Inequality

Maintaining systems of inequality requires the objectification and dehumanization of subordinated peoples. Appropriating their identities is a particularly effective method of doing this, for it defines who the subordinated group/person is or ought to be. This happens in several ways:

Using the values, characteristics, features of the dominant group as the supposedly neutral standard against which all others should be evaluated. For example, men are generally physically larger and stronger than women. Many of the clinical trials for new pharmaceutical drugs have been conducted using men's bodies and activities as the standard. The results, however, are applied equally to both men and women. Women are often prescribed the same dosage of a medication as men are even though their physical makeup is not the same. Thus women, as a distinct group, do not exist in this research.

Using terms that distinguish the subordinate from the dominant group. Terms such as "non-White" and "minority" connote a relationship to another group, White in the former case and majority in the latter. A non-White person is the negative of the White person; a minority person is less than a majority person. Neither has an identity on her or his own terms.

Stereotyping. Stereotyping involves making a simple generalization about a group and claiming that all members of the group conform to it. Stereotypes are behavioral and psychological attributes; they are commonly held beliefs about groups rather than individual beliefs about individuals; and they persist in spite of contradictory evidence. Lesbians hate men. Latinas are dominated by macho Latinos. Women with physical disabilities are asexual. Fat women are good-humored but not healthy. As philosopher Judith Andre (1988) asserts, "A 'stereotype' is pejorative; there is always something objectionable in the beliefs and images to which the word refers" (p. 260).

Exoticizing and romanticizing. These two forms of appropriation are particularly insidious because on the surface there is an appearance of appreciation. For example, Asian American women are described as personifying the "mysterious orient," Native American women as "earth mothers" and the epitome of spirituality, and Black women as perpetual towers of strength. In all three cases, seemingly positive traits and cultural practices are identified and exalted. This "positive" stereotyping prevents people from seeing the truth and complexity of who these women are.

Another aspect of romanticization may be **cultural appropriation,** where, for example, White people wear cowrie shells, beaded hairstyles, cornrows and dreadlocks, or claim to have been Native American in a former life (Smith 1991). Joanna Kadi (1996) sees cultural appropriation as reinforcing imperialist attitudes and a form of cultural genocide.

She urges people to think carefully about their right to wear "exotic" clothing or to play musical instruments from other cultures. Our intentions, our knowledge of those cultures, and authentic connections with people from different groups are all part of moving from cultural appropriation to what Kadi calls "ethical cultural connections."

Images that are circulated and popularized about a group may also contribute to their "exoticization" or romanticization. How are various groups of women typically depicted in this society? The fundamental problem with the representation of women, as with all oppressed peoples, is that "they do not have central control over the production of images about themselves" (McCarthy and Crichlow 1993, p. xvii). The four processes of identity appropriation described above are used to project images of women that generally demean, dehumanize, denigrate, and otherwise violate their basic humanity.

In the face of structural inequalities, the issue of identity and representation can literally and metaphorically be a matter of life and death for members of subordinated groups for several reasons. They are reduced to the position of the "other"—that is, fundamentally unlike "us"—made invisible, misunderstood, misrepresented, and often feared. Equally significant, designating a group as "other" justifies its exploitation, its exclusion from whatever benefits the society may offer, and the violence and, in extreme cases, genocide committed against it. Therefore, at the macro and global levels, identity is a matter of collective well-being and survival. Individual members of subordinate groups tend to be judged by those in dominant positions according to negative stereotypes. If any young African American women, for example, are poor single mothers, they merely reinforce the stereotype the dominant group holds about them. When young African American women hold advanced degrees and are economically well off, they are regarded as exceptional by those in the dominant group, who rarely let disconfirming evidence push them to rethink their stereotypes.

Given the significance of identity appropriation as an aspect of oppression, it is not surprising that many liberation struggles have included projects and efforts aimed at changing identities and taking control of the process of positive identity formation and representation. Before liberation struggles, oppressed people often use the same terminology to name themselves as the dominant group uses to label them. One crucial aspect of liberation struggles is to get rid of pejorative labels and use names that express, in their own terms, who people are in all their humanity. Thus the name a group uses for itself gradually takes on more of an insider perspective that fits the evolving consciousness growing out of the political movement.

As with individual identity, naming ourselves collectively is an important act of empowerment. One example of this is the evolution of the names African Americans have used to identify themselves, moving from Colored, to Negro, to Black, to Afro-American, and African American. Similarly, Chinese Americans gradually rejected the derogatory label "Chink," preferring to be called Orientals and now Chinese Americans or Asian Americans. These terms are used unevenly, sometimes according to the age and political orientation of the person or the geographic region, where one usage may be more popular than another. Among the very diverse group of people connected historically, culturally, and linguistically to Spain, Portugal, and their former colonies (parts of the United States, Mexico, the Caribbean, and Central and South America), some use more inclusive terms such as Latino or Hispanic; others prefer more specific names such as Chicano, Puerto Rican, Nicaraguan, Cuban, and so on. Elizabeth Martínez discusses the significance of this terminology in Reading 13.

Colonization, Immigration, and the U.S. Landscape of Race and Class

Global-level factors affecting people's identities include colonization and immigration. Popular folklore would have us believe that the United States has welcomed "the tired, huddled masses yearning to breathe free" (Young 1997). This ideology that the United States is "a land of immigrants" obscures several important issues excluded from much mainstream debate about immigration: Not all Americans came to this country voluntarily. Native American peoples and Mexicans were already here on this continent, but the former experienced near-genocide and the latter were made foreigners in their own land. African peoples were captured, enslaved, and forcibly imported to this country to be laborers. All were brutally exploited and violated—physically, psychologically, culturally, and spiritually—to serve the interests of those in power. The relationships between these groups and this nation and their experiences in the United States are fundamentally different from the experiences of those who chose to immigrate here, though this is not to negate the hardships the latter may have faced. These differences profoundly shaped the social, cultural, political, and economic realities faced by these groups throughout history and continue to do so today.

Robert Blauner (1972) makes a useful analytical distinction between colonized minorities, whose original presence in this nation was involuntary, and all of whom are people of color, and immigrant minorities, whose presence was voluntary. According to Blauner, colonized minorities faced insurmountable structural inequalities, based primarily on race, that have prevented their full participation in social, economic, political, and cultural arenas of U.S. life. Early in the history of this country, for example, the Naturalization Law of 1790 (which was repealed as recently as 1952) prohibited peoples of color from becoming U.S. citizens, and the Slave Codes restricted every aspect of life for enslaved African peoples. These laws made race into an indelible line that separated "insiders" from "outsiders." White people were designated insiders and granted many privileges while all others were confined to systematic disadvantage. As Mary C. Waters points out in Reading 14, the stories that White Americans learn of how their grandparents and great-grandparents triumphed in the United States "are usually told in terms of their individual efforts." The role of labor unions, community organizations, and political parties, as well as the crucial importance of racism, is usually left out of these accounts, which emphasize individual effort and hard work.

Studies of U.S. immigration "reveal discrimination and unequal positioning of different ethnic groups" (Yans-McLaughlin 1990, p. 6), challenging the myth of equal opportunity for all. According to political scientist Lawrence Fuchs (1990), "Freedom and opportunity for poor immigrant Whites in the seventeenth and eighteenth centuries were connected fundamentally with the spread of slavery" (p. 294). It was then that European immigrants, such as Irish, Polish, and Italian people—who were differentiated in a hierarchy based on skin color, culture, and history in Europe—began to learn to be White (Roediger 1991). Whiteness in the United States was constructed in relation to blackness (Morrison 1992). Acclaimed novelist and essayist James Baldwin (1984) comments: "no one was white before he/she came to America" and that "it took generations, and a vast amount of coercion, before this became a white country." Thus the common belief among descendants of European immigrants that the successful **assimilation** of their foremothers and forefathers against great odds is evidence that everyone can "pull themselves up by the bootstraps" if they work hard enough does not take into account the racialization of immigration that favored White people. In Reading 11, Melanie Kaye/Kantrowitz discusses Jewish assimilation in the United States, and notes that despite its benefits, this process has been accompanied by extreme cultural loss—of language, history, literature, music, cultural diversity, and experience of rich Jewish traditions.

On coming to the United States, immigrants are drawn into the racial landscape of this country. In media debates and official statistics, this is still dominated by a Black/White polarization. Demographically, the situation is much more complex and diverse, but is usually still characterized in binary terms: people of color or White people. Immigrants generally identify themselves according to nationality—for example, as Cambodian or Guatemalan. Once in the United States they learn the significance of racial divisions in this country and may adopt the term *people of color* as an aspect of their identity here. Chandra Talpade Mohanty notes her transition from "foreign student" to "student of color" in the United States. "Racist and sexist experiences in graduate school and after made it imperative that I understand the U.S. in terms of its history of racism, imperialism and patriarchal relations, specifically in relation to Third World immigrants" (Reading 6).

This emphasis on race tends to mask differences based on class, an important distinction among immigrant groups. For example, the Chinese and Japanese people who came in the nineteenth century and early twentieth century to work on plantations in Hawaii, as loggers in Oregon, or building roads and railroads in several western states were poor and from rural areas of China and Japan. The 1965 immigration law made

A Timeline of Key U.S. Immigration Law and Policy*

U.S. immigration laws and policies seek to balance a concern for national security with the fact that immigrants contribute greatly to the U.S. economy. Tens of millions of newcomers have made their way to the United States throughout the nation's history, and the United States has resettled more refugees on a permanent basis than any other industrialized country. Immigration law changes in response to economic shifts, political concerns, and perceived threats to national security.

1790   The Naturalization Law of 1790, which was not repealed until 1952, limited naturalization to "free white persons" who had resided in the United States for at least two years. Slave Codes restricted every aspect of life for enslaved African peoples.

1875   The Immigration Act of 1875 denied admission to individuals considered "undesirable," including revolutionaries, prostitutes, and those carrying "loathsome or dangerous contagious diseases."

1882   The Chinese Exclusion Act, one of the most racist immigration laws in U.S. history, was adopted and subsequently upheld by the U.S. Supreme Court; variations were enforced until 1943. The act was a response to fear of the large numbers of Chinese laborers brought to the United States to lay railroads and work in mines.

1917   Congress banned immigration from Asia except Japan and the Philippines.

1921   The Immigration Act of 1921 set an overall cap on the number of immigrants admitted each year and established a nationalities quota system that strongly favored northern Europeans at the expense of immigrants from southern and eastern Europe and Asia.

1924   The Immigration Act of 1924 based immigration quotas on the ethnic composition of the U.S. population in 1920; it also prohibited Japanese immigration.

1945   President Harry Truman issued a directive after World War II allowing for the admission of 40,000 refugees.

1946   The War Brides Act permitted 120,000 foreign wives and children to join their husbands in the United States.

1948   The Displaced Persons Act of 1948 permitted entry to an additional 400,000 refugees and displaced persons as a result of World War II.

1952   The Immigration and Nationality Act of 1952 was a response to U.S. fear of communism and barred the admission of anyone who might engage in acts "prejudicial to the public interest, or that endanger the welfare or safety of the United States." It allowed immigration for all nationalities, however, and established family connections as a criterion for immigrant eligibility.

1953   The Refugee Relief Act of 1953 admitted 200,000 people, including Hungarians fleeing communism and Chinese emigrating after the Chinese revolution.

1965   The Immigration Act of 1965 established an annual quota of 120,000 immigrants from the Eastern Hemisphere, which increased the number of Asian immigrants, especially middle-class and upper-middle-class people.

1980   The Refugee Act of 1980 codified into U.S. law the 1951 United Nations Convention Relating to the Status of Refugees and its 1967 Protocol; it defines a refugee as a person outside her

---

* Thanks to Wendy A. Young for providing material.

or his country of nationality who has a well-founded fear of persecution on account of race, religion, nationality, political opinion, or membership in a particular social group.

1986   The Immigration Reform and Control Act of 1986 was intended to control the growth of illegal immigrants through an "amnesty" program to legalize undocumented people resident in the United States before January 1, 1982, and imposing sanctions against employers who knowingly employ undocumented workers.

1990   The Immigration Act of 1990 affirmed family reunification as the basis for most immigration cases; redefined employment-based immigration; created a new system to diversify the nationalities immigrating to the United States, ostensibly to compensate for the domination of Asian and Latin American immigration since 1965; and created new mechanisms to provide refuge to those fleeing civil strife, environmental disasters, or political upheaval in their homelands.

1996   The Illegal Immigration Reform and Immigrant Responsibility Act targeted legal and illegal immigration. It provided for increased border controls and penalties for document fraud; changes in employer sanctions; restrictions on immigrant eligibility for public benefits, including benefits for those lawfully in the United States; and drastic streamlining of the asylum system.

   The Personal Responsibility and Work Opportunity Reconciliation Act mainly dealt with changes in the welfare system and made legal immigrants ineligible for various kinds of federal assistance. In 1997, Congress restored benefits for some immigrants

already in the country when this law took effect. There is a five-year waiting period before noncitizens can receive Medicaid or Temporary Assistance for Needy Families.

2001   Uniting and Strengthening America by Providing Appropriate Tools Required to Obstruct Terrorism Act (known as the USA Patriot Act) was signed into law on October 26, 2001, following the attacks on the World Trade Center and the Pentagon on September 11. It significantly enhances the government's powers of detention, search, and surveillance. It permits the detention of noncitizens if the attorney general has "reasonable grounds to believe" that they endanger national security. It permits the definition of domestic groups as terrorist organizations; authorizes the interception of "wire, oral, and electronic communication relating to terrorism"; makes it easier for the FBI to get access to records about a person that are maintained by a business; and expands the use of secret searches. It requires financial institutions to monitor daily transactions and academic institutions to share information about students.

The "pull" factors drawing immigrants to the United States include the possibility of better-paying jobs, better education—especially for children—and greater personal freedom. "Push" factors include poverty, wars, political upheaval, authoritarian regimes, and fewer personal freedoms in the countries they have left. Immigration will continue to be a thorny issue in the United States as the goals of global economic restructuring, filling the country's need for workers, and providing opportunities for family members to live together are set against the fears of those who see continued immigration as a threat to the country's prosperity and security and to the dominance of European Americans.

way for "the second wave" of Asian immigration (Takaki 1987). It set preferences for professionals, highly skilled workers, and members of the middle and upper-middle classes, making this group "the most highly skilled of any immigrant group our country has ever had" (quoted in Takaki 1987, p. 420). The first wave of Vietnamese refugees who immigrated between the mid-1970s and 1980 were from the middle and upper classes, including many professionals; by contrast, the second wave of immigrants from Vietnam was composed of poor and rural people. The class backgrounds of immigrants affect not only their sense of themselves and their expectations but also how they can succeed as strangers in a foreign land. For example, a poor woman who arrives with no literacy skills in her own language will have a more difficult time learning to become literate in English than one who has formal schooling in her country of origin that may have included basic English.

Multiple Identities, Social Location, and Contradictions

The social features of one's identity incorporate individual, community, societal, and global factors. **Social location** is a way of expressing the core of a person's existence in the social and political world. It places us in particular relationships to others, to the dominant culture of the United States, and to the rest of the world. It determines the kinds of power and privilege we have access to and can exercise, as well as situations in which we have less power and privilege.

Because social location is where all the aspects of one's identity meet, our experience of our own complex identities is sometimes contradictory, conflictual, and paradoxical. We live with multiple identities that can be both enriching and contradictory and that push us to confront questions of loyalty to individuals and groups. This is discussed by Chandra Talpade Mohanty (Reading 6), Dorothy Allison (Reading 9), Melanie Kaye/Kantrowitz (Reading 11), and in the short story, "Hanaan's House" (Reading 12).

It is also through the complexity of social location that we are forced to differentiate our inclinations, behaviors, self-definition, and politics from how we are classified by larger societal institutions. An inclination toward bisexuality, for example, does not mean that one will necessarily act on that inclination. Defining oneself as working class does not necessarily lead to activity in progressive politics based on a class consciousness.

Social location is also where we meet others socially and politically. Who are we in relation to people who are both like us and different from us? How do we negotiate the inequalities in power and privilege? How do we both accept and appreciate who we and others are, and grow and change to meet the challenges of a multicultural world? In the readings that follow, the writers note significant changes in the way they think about themselves over time. Some mention difficulties in coming to terms with who they are and the complexities of their contradictory positions. They also write about the empowerment that comes from a deepening understanding of identity, enabling them to claim their place in the world.

Questions for Reflection

As you read and discuss the readings in this chapter, think about these questions:

1. Where do you come from? Who are you? How has your identity changed? How do you figure out your identity?

2. Which parts of your identity do you emphasize? Which do you underplay? Why?

3. Who are your "people"? Where or what are your "home" and "community"?

4. How many generations have your family members been in the United States? What was their first relationship to it? Under what conditions did they become a part of the United States?

5. What do you know of your family's culture and history before it became a part of the United States?

6. What is your social location?

7. Which of the social dimensions of your identity provide power and privilege? Which provide less power and disadvantage?

♦♦♦

Finding Out More on the Web

1. Find out about women who are very different from you (in terms of culture, class, race/ethnicity, nationality, or religion) and how they think about their identities.

2. Research identity-based organizations. Why did they form? Who are their members? What are their purposes and goals? Did/do they have a vision of justice and equality?

3. Mary C. Waters mentions the "one drop rule." What is it? Why is it significant?

♦♦♦

Taking Action

1. Think about all aspects of your own identity. How do you identify yourself? Take some action to affirm an aspect of your identity.

2. Talk to your parents or grandparents about your family history. How have they constructed their cultural and racial/ethnic identities?

EIGHT

Perspectives of Native American Women on Race and Gender (1994)

Frederica Y. Daly

Frederica Y. Daly taught psychology at Howard University, the State University of New York, and the University of New Mexico. She also practiced as a clinical psychologist for many years. In retirement she writes poetry and is engaged in genealogical research into her African and Indian ancestries.

... Native Americans constitute well over five hundred recognized tribes, which speak more than two hundred (mostly living) languages. Their variety and vital cultures notwithstanding, the official U.S. policy unreflectively, and simply, transforms them from Indians to "Americans" (Wilkinson 1987). Some consideration will be given to their unifying traditions, not the least of which are their common history of surviving genocide and their strong, shared commitment to their heritage.

Any discussion of Indian people requires a brief review of the history of the violent decimation of their populations as well as the massive expropriation of their land and water holdings, accomplished with rare exception with the approval of American governments at every level. To ignore these experiences prevents us from understanding the basis for their radical and profound desire for self-determination, a condition they enjoyed fully before the European incursions began. . . .

Historical Overview

Indian history, since the European invasion in the early sixteenth century, is replete with incidents of exploitation, land swindle, enslavement, and murder by the European settlers. The narration includes well-documented, government-initiated, biological warfare, which included giving Indians clothing infected with smallpox, diphtheria, and other diseases to which Indians were vulnerable. Starvation strategies were employed, with forced removal from their lands and the consequent loss of access to basic natural resources, [for] example, the Cherokee and Choctaw experiences in the famous "trail of tears."

Wilkinson as well as Deloria and Lytle (1983) assert that Indian history is best understood when presented within a historical framework established by four major, somewhat overlapping, periods. The events dominate federal policy about Indians, subsequent Indian law, and many of the formational forces described in Indian sociology, anthropology, and culture.

Period 1: 1532–1828

This period is described by Europeans as one of "discovery" and is characterized by the conquest of Indians and the making of treaties. The early settlers did not have laws or policies governing their relationships with the indigenous tribes until the sixteenth-century theologian Francisco de Vitorio advised the king of Spain in 1532 that the tribes should be recognized "as legitimate entities capable of dealing with the European nations by treaty." As

a result, writes Deloria, treaty making became a "feasible method of gaining a foothold on the continent without alarming the natives" (1970, 3). Deloria explains further that inherent in this decision was the fact that it encouraged respect for the tribes as societies of people and, thus, became the workable tool for defining intergroup relationships. By 1778 the U.S. government entered into its first treaty, with the Delaware Indians, at which point the tribe became, and remains, the basic unit in federal Indian law. . . .

Period 2: 1828–87

The second period, beginning . . . a few decades before the Civil War, witnessed massive removal of Indians from their ancestral lands and subsequent relocation, primarily because of their resistance to mainstream assimilation and the "missionary efforts" of the various Christian sects.

Early in his presidency Andrew Jackson proposed voluntary removal of the Indians. When none of the tribes responded, the Indian Removal Act of 1830 was passed. The act resulted in the removal of the tribes from the Ohio and Mississippi valleys to the plains of the West. "Nearly sixteen thousand Cherokees walked from Georgia to Eastern Oklahoma . . . the Choctaws surrendered more than ten million acres and moved west" (Deloria and Lytle 1983, 7). Soldiers, teachers, and missionaries were sent to reservations for policing and proselytizing purposes, activities by no means mutually exclusive and which represented the full benefit of the act as far as the tribes were concerned. Meanwhile, discovery of gold (especially "strikes" on or near Indian land) in the West, coupled with the extension of the railroad, once again raised the "Indian Problem." But at this point, with nowhere else to be moved, Indian tribes were even more in jeopardy, setting the basis for the third significant period.

Period 3: 1887–1928

During the final years of the nineteenth century, offering land allotments seemed to provide a workable technique for assimilating Indian families into the mainstream. The Dawes Act of 1887 proposed the formula for allotment. "A period of twenty-five years was established during which the Indian owner [of a specified, allotted piece of reservation property] was expected to learn proper methods of self-sufficiency, e.g., business or farming. At the end of that period, the land, free of restrictions against sale, was to be delivered to the allottee" (Deloria and Lytle 1983, 9). At the same time, the Indian received title to the land and citizenship in the state.

The Dawes Act and its aftermath constitute one of the most sordid narratives in American history involving tribal peoples. Through assimilation, swindling, and other forms of exploitation, more than ninety million acres of allotted land were transferred to non-Indian owners. Furthermore, much of the original land that remained for the Indians was in the "Great American Desert," unsuitable for farming and unattractive for any other kind of development. During this same period, off-reservation boarding schools began to be instituted, some in former army barracks, to assist in the overall program of assimilation, and the Dawes Act also made parcels of reservation land available to whites for settlement. The plan to assimilate the Indian and thereby eradicate the internal tribal nations caused immense misery and enormous economic loss. But as we know, it failed. Phyllis Old Dog Cross, a nurse of the North Dakota Mandan Tribe, mordantly puts it, "We are not vanishing" (1987, 29).

Period 4: 1928–Present

The fourth period is identified by Wilkinson especially as beginning just before the Depression in 1928. It is characterized by reestablishment of tribes as separate "sovereignties" involving moves toward formalized self-government and self-determination, and cessation, during World War II, of federal assistance to the tribes.

Prucha (1985) reminds us that, with the increased belief in the sciences in the 1920s and the accompanying beliefs that the sciences could solve human problems, attitudes toward Indians hardened. At this point the professional anthropologist began to be sent and be seen on the reservations to study and live with the people, alongside the missionaries. The changing attitudes continued into the 1930s with the Roosevelt administration. It was during this period that John Collier became commissioner of Indian Affairs, and the reforms of the Indian Reorganization Act of 1934 invalidated

the land allotment policies of the Dawes Act, effectively halting the transfer of Indian land to non-Indians. As Deloria indicates, the Reorganization Act provided immense benefits, including the establishment and reorganization of tribal councils and tribal courts.

After about a decade of progress, the budgetary demands of World War II resulted in deep reductions in domestic programs, including assistance to the tribes. John Collier resigned in 1945 under attack from critics and amid growing demands in Washington to cancel federal support for Indians. . . .

Deloria writes that Senator Watkins of Utah was "firmly convinced that if the Indians were freed from federal restrictions, they would soon prosper by learning in the school of life those lessons that a cynical federal bureaucracy had not been able to instill in them" (1970, 18). He was able to implement his convictions during the Eisenhower administration into the infamous Termination Act of 1953, in consequence of which several tribes in at least five states were eliminated. In effect, as far as the government was concerned, the tribes no longer existed and could make no claims on the government. Contrary to its original intent as a means of releasing the tribes from their status as federal wards under BIA [Bureau of Indian Affairs] control, the Termination Act did just the opposite, causing more loss of land, further erosion of tribal power, and literally terrorizing most of the tribes with intimidation, uncertainty, and, worst of all, fear of the loss of tribal standing.

Deloria quotes HR Doc. 363 in which, in 1970, President Nixon asserted, "Because termination is morally and legally unacceptable, because it produces bad practical results, and because the mere threat of termination tends to discourage greater self-sufficiency among Indian groups, I am asking the Congress to pass a new concurrent resolution which would expressly renounce, repudiate, and repeal the termination policy" (1970, 20). This firm repudiation by Nixon of the termination policy earned him the esteem of many Indian people, in much the same way that presidents Kennedy and Johnson are esteemed by many African Americans for establishing programs designed to improve their socioeconomic conditions.

From the Nixon administration through the Carter administration, tribal affairs were marked by strong federal support and a variety of programs aimed at encouraging tribal self-determination. The Indian Child Welfare Act of 1978, which gave preference to Indians in adoptions involving Indian children and authorized establishment of social services on and near reservations, was one of the major accomplishments of this period.

Prucha believes that the tribes' continued need for federal programs is an obstacle to their sovereignty . . . (1985, 97). Deloria insists that Indians are citizens and residents of the United States and of the individual states in which they live and, as such, "are entitled to the full benefits and privileges that are offered to all citizens" (246). . . .

Contemporary Native American Women and Sexism

I have just presented a very abbreviated statement of the general, post-European influx historical experiences of Indians in America, drawing from the research and insights of lawyers and social scientists. Without this introduction it would be difficult to understand Native American women and their contemporary experiences of sexism and racism.

Although many tribes were matrilineal, Indian women were seldom mentioned prominently in the personal journals or formal records of the early settlers or in the narratives of the westward movement. They were excluded from treaty-making sessions with federal government agents, and later ethnologists and anthropologists who reported on Indian women frequently presented distorted accounts of their lives, usually based on interviews with Christianized women, who said what they believed would be compatible with the European worldview. Helen Carr, in her essay in Brodzki and Schenck's *Life-Lines: Theorizing Women's Autobiographies,* offers some caveats about the authenticity of contemporary autobiographies of Indian women, when they are written in the Euro-American autobiographical tradition. She cautions that, in reading the autobiographies collected by early anthropologists, we need to be "aware that they have been structured, consciously or unconsciously, to serve particular 'white' purposes and to give credence to particular white views" (1988, 132).

Ruby Leavitt, writing in Gornick and Moran's *Women in Sexist Society,* states: "Certainly the status of women is higher in the matrilineal than the patri-

lineal societies. Where women own property and pass it on to their daughters or sisters, they are far more influential and secure. Where their economic role is important and well defined . . . they are not nearly so subject to male domination, and they have much more freedom of movement and action" (1972, 397).

We do not learn from social scientists observing Indian communities that women also were the traders in many tribes. With this history of matrilinealism and economic responsibilities, it is not surprising that some Indian women deny the existence of an oppressed, nonparticipatory tribal female role. Yet just as other North American women, they are concerned with child-care needs, access to abortion, violence against women, and the effects of alcoholism on the family, all symptomatic of sexism experiences. They are also aware of these symptoms as prevalent throughout our society in the United States; they do not view them as specifically Indian related.

Bea Medicine, Lakota activist, anthropologist, and poet *as quoted* in the preface of *American Indian Women—Telling Their Lives,* states "Indian women do not need liberation, they have always been liberated within their tribal structure" (1984, viii). Her view is the more common one I have encountered in my readings and in conversations with Native American women. In the middle 1970s, Native American women who were in New York City to protest a U.S. treaty violation, in a meeting to which they had invited non-Indian women, were adamant that they did not need the "luxury of feminism." Their focus, along with that of Indian men, concerned the more primary needs of survival.

The poet Carol Sanchez writes in *A Gathering of Spirit,* "We still have Women's societies, and there are at least thirty active woman-centered Mother rite cultures existing and practicing their everyday life in that manner on this continent" (1984, 164). These groups are characterized by their "keeping of the culture" activities.

Medicine and Sanchez concur about the deemphasis of the importance of gender roles in some tribes as reflected in the "Gia" concept. *Gia* is the word in the Pueblo Tewa language which signifies the earth. It is also used to connote nurturance and biological motherhood. The tribal core welfare role, which can be assumed by a male or a female, is defined by the tribe in this Gia context. To be a nurturing male is to be the object of much respect and esteem, although one does not act nurturing to gain group approval. Swentzell and Naranjo, educational consultant and sociologist, respectively, and coauthors, write, "The male in the gia role is a person who guides, advises, cares, and universally loves and encompasses all." The authors describe the role, saying, "The core gia was a strong, stable individual who served as the central focus for a large number of the pueblo's members . . . [for example], 'she' coordinated large group activities such as marriages, feast days, gathering and preparing of food products, even house building and plastering" (1986, 37). With increasing tribal governmental concerns the role of core group Gia has lessened, "so that children are no longer raised by the core group members" (39). Interestingly, the Gia concept is being used currently by social ecologists. For them it parallels the notion of Mother Earth and corresponds with the increasingly widespread understanding of the earth as a living organism.

Charles Lange, in *Cochiti—A New Mexico Pueblo, Past and Present*, says: "Among the Cochiti, the woman is boss; the high offices are held by men, but in the households and in the councils of the clans, woman is supreme. . . . She has been arbiter of destinies of the tribe for centuries" (1959, 367). The important role performed by the "Women's Society," Lange continues, includes "the ceremonial grinding of corn to make prayer meal" (283). Compatible with women's having spiritual role assignments is the fact that in some tribes the gods are women—for example, in the matrifocal Cherokee and Pueblo nations, Corn Mother is a sacred figure.

A Cheyenne saying reflects the tribe's profound regard for women: "A nation is not conquered until the hearts of its women are on the ground. Then it is done, no matter how brave its warriors, nor how strong its weapons" (Kutz 1988, 143–58). Historically, in some tribes women were warriors and participated in raiding parties. The Apache medicine woman and warrior Lozen lived such a role and was the last of the women warriors (Kutz 1988, 143–58). Paula Gunn Allen, in *The Sacred Hoop* (1986), notes that "traditional tribal lifestyles are more often gynocratic . . . women are not merely doomed victims of Western progress; they are also the carriers of the dream. . . . Since the first attempts at colonization . . . the invaders have exerted every

effort to remove Indian women from every position of authority, to obliterate all records pertaining to gynocratic social systems and to ensure that no Americans . . . would remember that gynocracy was the primary social order of Indian America" (2–3). Later she alludes to the regeneration of these earlier roles: "Women migrating to the cities are regaining self-sufficiency and positions of influence they had held in earlier centuries" (31). "Women's traditions," she says, "are about continuity and men's are about change, life maintenance/risk, death and transformation" (82).

When Indian women deny having experienced sexism they seem mainly to be referring to their continuing historical roles within their tribes, in which they are seen as *the keepers of the culture*. There exists a general consensus that the powerful role of tribal women, both traditionally and contemporarily, is not paralleled in the non-Indian society. Additionally, they allude to the women serving in various tribes as council members, and they point to such prominent, well-known leaders as Wilma Mankiller, chief of the Oklahoma Cherokee Nation; Verna Williamson, former governor of Isleta Pueblo; and Virginia Klinekole, former president of the Mescalero Apache Tribal Council.

Contemporary Native American Women and Racism

The relentless system of racism, in both its overt and covert manifestations, impacts the lives of Indian women; most are very clear about their experiences of it, and they recognize it for what it is. Although many are reticent about discussing these experiences, a growing number of Native American women writers are giving voice to their encounters with racism.

Elizabeth Cook-Lynn, a poet and teacher with combined Crow, Creek, and Sioux heritage, writes about an editor who questioned her about why Native American poetry is so incredibly sad. Cook-Lynn describes her reaction . . . : "Now I recognize it as a tactless question asked out of astonishing ignorance. It reflects the general attitude that American Indians should have been happy to have been robbed of their land and murdered" (1987, 60–61).

In the same anthology Linda Hogan, from the Chickasaw Tribe in Oklahoma, writes with concern about the absence of information about Native American people throughout the curricula in our educational systems: "The closest I came to learning what I needed was a course in Labor Literature, and the lesson there was in knowing there were writers who lived similar lives to ours. . . . This is one of the ways that higher education perpetuates racism and classism. By ignoring our lives and work, by creating standards for only their own work" (1987, 243). Earlier she had written that "the significance of intermarriage between Indian and white or between Indian and black [has not] been explored . . . but the fact remains that great numbers of apparently white or black Americans carry notable degrees of Indian blood" (216). And in Brant's *A Gathering of Spirit* Carol Sanchez says, "To be Indian is to be considered 'colorful,' spiritual, connected to the earth, simplistic, and disappointing if not dressed in buckskin and feathers" (1984, 163).

These Indian women talk openly about symptoms of these social pathologies, [for] example, experiencing academic elitism or the demeaning attitudes of employees in federal and private, nonprofit Indian agencies. Or they tell of being accepted in U.S. society in proportion to the lightness of skin color. The few who deny having had experiences with racism mention the equality bestowed upon them through the tribal sovereignty of the Indian nations. In reality the tribes are not sovereign. They are controlled nearly completely by the U.S. Department of Interior, the federal agency that, ironically, also oversees animal life on public lands.

Rayna Green, a member of the Cherokee nation, in her book *That's What She Said* (1984), makes a strong, clear statement about racism and sexism: "The desperate lives of Indian women are worn by poverty, the abuse of men, the silence and blindness of whites. . . . The root of their problem appears attributable to the callousness and sexism of the Indian men and white society equally. They are tightly bound indeed in the double bind of race and gender. Wasted lives and battered women are part of the Indian turf" (10). It is not surprising to find some Indian men reflecting the attitudes of the white majority in relating to Indian women. This is the psychological phenomenon found in oppressed people, labeled as identification with the oppressor.

Mary Tallmountain, the Native Alaskan poet, writes in *I Tell You Now* (1987) that she refused to attend school in Oregon because her schoolmates mocked her "Indianness": "But, I know who I am. Marginal person, misfit, mutant; nevertheless, I am of this country, these people" (12). Linda Hogan describes the same experience, saying, "Those who are privileged would like for us to believe that we are in some way defective, that we are not smart enough, not good enough" (237). She recalls an experience with her former employer, an orthodontist, whom she says, "believed I was inferior because I worked for less than his wife's clothing budget or their liquor bill . . . and who, when I received money to attend night school and was proud, accused me of being a welfare leech and said I should be ashamed" (242). In her poem "Those Who Thunder," Linda translated the experience into verse:

> *Those who are timid are sagging in the soul,*
> *And those poor who will inherit the earth*
> *already work it*
> *So take shelter you*
> *because we are thundering and beating on floors*
> *And this is how walls have fallen in other cities.*
>
> *(242)*

In the United States we do not know one another, except from the stereotypes presented in the media. As a result, there is the tendency to view people of a differing group vicariously, through the eyes of media interpreters.

Louise Erdrich and Michael Dorris, both Indian and both university professors and eminent writers, reported in Bill Moyers's *World of Ideas* (1989): "We had one guy come to dinner, and we cleaned our house and made a nice dinner, and he looks and says, kind of depressed, 'Do you always eat on the table?'" (465). They used the example to demonstrate how people "imagine" (as distinguished from "know") Indians on the basis of movie portrayals, usually as figures partially dressed or dressed in the fashion of the nineteenth century and typically eating while seated on the ground. It is difficult to form accurate perceptions of the people and worldview of another group. Carol Sanchez seems to challenge us to do just that when she asks us not to dismiss Native Americans and then asks, "How many Indians do you know?" (163). . . .

Sanchez charges non-Indians with the wish to have Indians act like whites, so they will be more acceptable to whites, another example of accommodation, assimilation. She is describing the attitude cited by the young child-care worker who said to me, "They like our food, our drum music, our jewelry, why don't they like us!?" Activist Winona La Duke, of the Ojibwa Tribe and by profession an economist, asserts in her offering in *A Gathering of Spirit:* "As far as the crises of water contamination, radiation, and death to the natural world and her children are concerned, respectable racism is as alive today as it was a century ago . . . a certain level of racism and ignorance has gained acceptance . . . in fact respectability . . . we either pick your bananas or act as a mascot for your football team . . . in this way, enlightened people are racist. They are arrogant toward all of nature, arrogant toward the children of nature, and ultimately arrogant toward all of life" (65–66). . . .

Continuing Tensions

That since the sixteenth century the history of Native Americans is one of racist oppression has become an integral part of contemporary historical understanding. Indian women are speaking with increasing frequency and force about their experiences of the double jeopardy of racism and sexism. I wish now to consider three factors that continue to contribute to serious tensions within the tribes and between the tribes and the so-called dominant culture. . . .

Tensions within the Indian Community

Indian People who wish to retain their identity and culture by continuing reservation life have constantly to struggle with choices regarding adaptation to the dominant culture. They realize that extremism in either direction will result in destruction of their ways of life. Those who resist any adaptation will be made to do so involuntarily, and those who accept "white men's ways" completely and without modification by that very fact forgo their heritage. For well over a century, governmental policy favored assimilation and the concomitant dissolution of Indian tribal existence. Real estate value and greed for precious natural resources were crucial motivating factors throughout the period. Indians simply were in the way of the invaders' efforts to amass money. . . .

At the Flathead reservation in Montana, attempts are under way to "revive the traditional Salish culture and preserve the rugged land from development" (Shaffer 1990, 54). Attempts to protect the Indian land for future generations are buttressed by the traditional, nearly universal Indian belief that we do not own the land, that we are simply caretakers of it and will pass it on to future generations. Thus, how the land is used can become an issue of deep tension between strict traditionalists and those who want to assimilate contemporary economic development thinking into tribal life and institutions. Likewise, nearly universally held precepts include the prevailing rights of the tribe over individual rights and the discouragement of aggression and competitiveness, which are seen as threats to tribal harmony and survival. Phyllis Old Dog Cross, a Sioux and a nurse, speaking at a health conference in Denver in 1987, stated: "The need not to appear aggressive and competitive within the group is still seen among contemporary Indians . . . even quite acculturated Indians tend to be very unobtrusive. . . . [If not,] they receive strong criticism . . . also anything that would seem to precipitate anger, resentment, jealousy was . . . discouraged, for it is believed that tribal group harmony is threatened" (1987, 20).

Acknowledging their need for self-sufficiency as reductions in federal funding continue, the tribes are searching intensively for economic solutions. Some have introduced organized gambling onto the reservations and the leasing of land to business corporations; others are considering storage on reservation land of toxic wastes from federal facilities. Many of these measures are resisted, especially by traditionalists within the tribes, who see them as culturally destructive.

Erosion of Tribal Life: Cultural Marginality

Cultural marginality is increasingly experienced by Indian people because of the confusion resulting from ambiguities about what defines Indian identity, individually and tribally. The questions "Who is an Indian?" and "What is a tribe?" no longer permit neat unequivocal answers.

Different tribes have different attitudes toward people of mixed heritage. In some a person with white blood may be accepted, while a person with some African-American blood may or may not be identified as Indian. Indian women, if they marry non-Indians, may or may not be identified within their tribes as Indians. To be a member of a tribe, a person must meet that tribe's requirements. Many tribes require proof of a person's being one-sixteenth or one-quarter or more of Indian descent to receive tribal affiliation. . . .

A group or an individual may qualify as an Indian for some federal purposes but not for others. A June 1977 statement by the U.S. Department of Labor on American Indian Women reads: "For their 1970 Census, the Bureau included in their questionnaire the category 'American Indian,' persons who indicated their race as Indian. . . . In the Eastern U.S., there are certain groups with mixed white, Negro, and Indian ancestry. In U.S. censuses prior to 1950, these groups had been variously classified by the enumerators, sometimes as Negro and sometimes as Indian, regardless of the respondent's preferred racial identity." LeAnne Howe, writing in Paula Gunn Allen's *Spider Woman's Granddaughters,* says, "Half-breeds live on the edge of both races . . . you're torn between wanting to kill everyone in the room or buying them all another round of drinks" (1989, 220).

Paula Gunn Allen, of the Laguna Pueblo tribe and a professor of literature, in her essay in *I Tell You Now,* writes: "Of course I always knew I was an Indian. I was told over and over, 'Never forget that you're an Indian.' My mother said it. Nor did she say, 'Remember you're part Indian'" (1987, 144).

Conflicts between Tribal and Other Governmental Laws

The Bureau of Indian Affairs, which has specific oversight responsibilities for the reservations, has played, at best, an ambivalent role, according to its very numerous critics. There have been many rumors of mishandled funds, especially of failure of funds to reach the reservations. It is the source of endless satire by Indian humorists, who, at their kindest, refer to it as the "Boss the Indian Around" department. By federal mandate the BIA is charged with coordinating the federal programs for the reservations. Originally, it was a section of the War Department, but for the last century and a half it has operated as part of the Department of the Interior.

Continuing skirmishes occur over violations of reservation land and water rights. Consequently,

the tribes continue to appeal to the Supreme Court and to the United Nations for assistance in redressing federal treaty violations. When these cases are made public, they become fodder for those who continue to push for the assimilation of Indians into the dominant society as well as for the ever-present cadre of racial bigots.

Federal law and policy have too often been paternalistic, detrimental, and contrary to the best interests of the Indian people. Further, the federal dollar dominance of the tribes has a controlling interest on Indian life. Levitan and Johnston conclude that "for Indians, far more than for any other group, socioeconomic status is a federal responsibility, and the success or failure of federal programs determines the quality of Indian lives" (1975, 10).

To receive eligibility for government services requires that the person live on or near a reservation, trust, or restricted land or be a member of a tribe recognized by the federal government. To be an Indian in America can mean living under tribal laws and traditions, under state law, and under federal laws. The situation can become extremely complex and irksome, for example, when taxes are considered. The maze and snarl of legalese over such questions as whether the Navajo tribe can tax reservation mineral developments without losing its "trust status" and accompanying federal benefits would defeat, and does, the most ardent experts of jurisprudence. And the whole question of income tax for the Indian person living on a reservation and working in a nearby community requires expertise that borders on the ridiculous.

University of New Mexico law professor Fred Ragsdale, describing the relationship of reservation Indians with the federal government, compares it to playing blackjack: "Indians play with their own money. They can't get up and walk away. And the house gets to change the rules any time it wants" (1985, 1).

The outlawing of certain Indian religious practices occurred without challenge until the 1920s, when the laws and policies prohibiting dancing and ceremonies were viewed as cultural attacks. With the passage of the Indian Civil Rights Act in 1964, Indians have been able to present court challenges to discrimination based on their religious practices. Members of the North American Church use peyote, a psychoactive drug, in their ceremonies. Many consider their religion threatened by the . . . Supreme

Court ruling that removes First Amendment protection of traditional worship practiced by Native Americans.

The negative impact of the 1966 Bennett freeze, a federally attempted solution to the bitter Navajo-Hopi land dispute, continues to cause pain to the Hopi, who use this 1.5-million-acre land mass for grazing, and to the Navajo, many of whom have resided on this land for generations. Sue Ann Presley, a *Washington Post* reporter, describes the area as being among the poorest in the nation and notes that the people living there are prohibited by law from participating in federal antipoverty programs. She reports that 90 percent of the homes have neither electricity nor indoor plumbing, and home repairs are not permitted. She quotes Navajo chair, Peterson Zah: "There are many Navajos who want to live in what we call the traditional way. But that does not mean they want to live with inadequate sewers, unpaved roads, no running water or electricity and under the watchful eye of the Hopi Tribe" (1993, B1). The forced removal of some of the Navajos from this area to border town housing caused a tremendous increase in the number of people who sought mental health treatment for depression and other disorders, according to the clinical observations of Tuba City, Arizona, psychologist Martin Topper. . . .

Conclusions

. . . Studies showing the impact of the privileged culture and dominant race on the development of Native Americans deserve continued exposure and extended development. We need medical research that investigates the health conditions and illnesses of minorities, including Native American women, whose general health status has to be among the worst in America. . . .

The development of new theories must include appropriate, representative definitions of the total population, free of gender bias and not derived disproportionately from the observation of middle-class white men and women. Curriculum offerings with accurate and comprehensive historical data about gender-specific Native American experiences are needed. . . .

As a country, we have failed to acknowledge our despicable treatment of the Indians. . . . It is hoped that the Indian quest for self-determination and proper respect will be realized, and with it will come our healing as a nation as well. There exists a tremendous need to help the U.S. public begin to understand the real significance of Indian history. . . .

REFERENCES

Allen, P. G. 1986. *The Sacred Hoop*. Boston: Beacon Press.

———. 1987. "The Autobiography of a Confluence." In *I Tell You Now*, ed. B. Swann and A. Krupat. Lincoln: University of Nebraska Press, 141–54.

———. ed. 1989. *Spider Woman's Granddaughters*. Boston: Beacon Press.

Bataille, G., and K. Sands. 1984. *American Indian Women—Telling Their Lives*. Lincoln: University of Nebraska Press.

Bergman, R. 1971. "Navajo Peyote Use: Its Apparent Safety." *American Journal of Psychiatry* 128:6.

Canby, W. C. 1981. *American Indian Law*. St. Paul, Minn.: West Publishing.

Carr, H. 1988. "In Other Words: Native American Women's Autobiography." In *Life-Lines: Theorizing Women's Autobiographies*, ed. Bella Brodzki and Celeste Schenck. Ithaca, N.Y.: Cornell University Press, 131–53.

Cook-Lynn, E. 1987. "You May Consider Speaking about Your Art." In *I Tell You Now*, ed. B. Swann and A. Krupat. Lincoln: University of Nebraska Press, 55–63.

Deloria, V. 1970. *We Talk, You Listen*. New York: Dell Publishing.

Deloria, V., and C. Lytle. 1983. *American Indians, American Justice*. Austin: University of Texas Press.

Erdrich, L., and M. Dorris. 1989. "Interview." In *Bill Moyers: A World of Ideas*, ed. B. S. Flowers. New York: Doubleday, 460–69.

Gornick, V., and B. Moran, eds. 1972. *Women in Sexist Society*. New York: Signet.

Green, R. 1984. *That's What She Said*. Bloomington: University of Indiana Press.

Hogan, L. 1987. "The Two Lives." In *I Tell You Now*, ed. B. Swann and A. Krupat. Lincoln: University of Nebraska Press, 231–49.

Howe, L. 1989. "An American in New York." In *Spider Woman's Granddaughters*, ed. P. G. Allen. Boston: Beacon Press, 212–20.

Kutz, J. 1988. *Mysteries and Miracles of New Mexico*. Corrales, N.M.: Rhombus Publishing.

La Duke, W. 1988. "They Always Come Back." In *A Gathering of Spirit*, ed. B. Brant. Ithaca, N.Y.: Firebrand Books, 62–67.

Lange, C. 1959. *Cochiti—A New Mexico Pueblo, Past and Present*. Austin: University of Texas Press.

Levitan, S., and W. Johnston. 1975. *Indian Giving*. Baltimore: Johns Hopkins University Press.

Old Dog Cross, P. 1987. "What Would You Want a Caregiver to Know about You?" *The Value of Many Voices Conference Proceedings*, 29–32.

Presley, S. 18 July 1993. "Restrictions Force Deprivations on Navajos." *The Washington Post*, G1–G2.

Prucha, F. 1985. *The Indians in American Society*. Berkeley: University of California Press.

Ragsdale, F. 1985. Quoted in Sherry Robinson's "Indian Laws Complicate Development." *Albuquerque Journal*, 1.

Sanchez, Carol. 1984. "Sex, Class and Race Intersections: Visions of Women of Color." In *A Gathering of Spirit*, ed. B. Brant. Ithaca, N.Y.: Firebrand Books.

Shaffer, P. January/February 1990. "A Tree Grows in Montana." *Utne Reader*, 54–63.

Swentzell, R., and T. Naranjo. 1986. "Nurturing the Gia." *El Palacio* (Summer–Fall): 35–39.

Tallmountain, M. 1987. "You Can Go Home Again: A Sequence." In *I Tell You Now*, ed. B. Swann and A. Krupat. Lincoln: University of Nebraska Press, 1–13.

Wilkinson, C. 1987. *American Indians, Time, and the Law*. New Haven, Conn.: Yale University Press.

N I N E

◆◆◆

A Question of Class (1993)

Dorothy Allison

Dorothy Allison authored the critically acclaimed novel, *Bastard Out of Carolina*. A member of the board of PEN International, her 1995 collection of essays, *Skin: Talking About Sex, Class and Literature*, won the American Library Association Gay and Lesbian Book Award.

. . . My people were not remarkable. We were ordinary, but even so we were mythical. We were the *they* everyone talks about, the ungrateful poor. I grew up trying to run away from the fate that destroyed so many of the people I loved, and having learned the habit of hiding, I found that I also had learned to hide from myself. I did not know who I was, only that I did not want to be *they*, the ones who are destroyed or dismissed to make the real people, the important people, feel safer. By the time I understood that I was queer, that habit of hiding was deeply set in me, so deeply that it was not a choice but an instinct. Hide, hide to survive, I thought, knowing that if I told the truth about my life, my family, my sexual desire, my real history, then I would move over into that unknown territory, the land of *they*, would never have the chance to name my own life, to understand it or claim it.

Why are you so afraid? my lovers and friends have asked me the many times when I have suddenly seemed to become a stranger, someone who would not speak to them, would not do the things they believed I should do, simple things like applying for a job, or a grant, or some award they were sure I could acquire easily. Entitlement, I have told them, is a matter of feeling like *we*, not *they*. But it has been hard for me to explain, to make them understand. You think you have a right to things, a place in the world, I try to say. You have a sense of entitlement I don't have, a sense of your own importance. I have explained what I know over and over again, in every possible way I can, but I have never been able to make clear the degree of my fear, the extent to which I feel myself denied, not only that I am queer in a world that hates queers but that I was born poor into a world that despises the poor. The need to explain is part of why I write fiction. I know that some things must be felt to be understood, that despair can never be adequately analyzed; it must be lived. . . .

I have known I was a lesbian since I was a teenager, and I have spent a good twenty years making peace with the effects of incest and physical abuse. But what may be the central fact of my life is that I was born in 1949 in Greenville, South Carolina, the bastard daughter of a poor white woman from a desperately poor family, a girl who had left the seventh grade the year before, who worked as a waitress and was just a month past fifteen when she had me. That fact, the inescapable impact of being born in a condition of poverty that this society finds shameful, contemptible, and somehow deserved, has dominated me to such an extent that I have spent my life trying to overcome or deny it. I have learned with great difficulty that the vast majority of people pretend that poverty is a voluntary condition, that the poor are different, less than fully human, or at least less sensitive to hopelessness, despair, and suffering.

The first time I read [Jewish writer] Melanie Kaye/Kantrowitz's poems, I experienced a frisson of recognition. It was not that my people had been "burned off the map" or murdered as hers had. No, we had been erased, encouraged to destroy ourselves, made invisible because we did not fit the myths of the middle class. Even now, past forty and stubbornly proud of my family, I feel the draw of that mythology, that romanticized, edited version of the poor. I find myself looking back and wondering what was real, what true. Within my family, so much was lied about, joked about, denied or told with deliberate indirection, an undercurrent of humiliation, or a brief pursed grimace that belies everything that has been said—everything, the very nature of truth and lies, reality and myth. What was real? The poverty depicted in books and movies was romantic, a kind of backdrop for the story of how it was escaped. The reality of self-hatred and violence was either absent or caricatured. The poverty I knew was dreary, deadening, shameful. My family was ashamed of being poor, of feeling hopeless. What was there to work for, to save money for, to fight for or struggle against? We had generations before us to teach us that nothing ever changed, and that those who did try to escape failed.

My mama had eleven brothers and sisters, of whom I can name only six. No one is left alive to tell me the names of the others. It was my grandmother who told me about my real daddy, a shiftless pretty man who was supposed to have married, had six children, and sold cut-rate life insurance to colored people out in the country. My mama married when I was a year old, but her husband died just after my little sister was born a year later. When I was five, Mama married the man she lived with until she died. Within the first year of their marriage Mama miscarried, and while we waited out in the hospital

parking lot, my stepfather molested me for the first time, something he continued to do until I was past thirteen. When I was eight or so, Mama took us away to a motel after my stepfather beat me so badly it caused a family scandal, but we returned after two weeks. Mama told me that she really had no choice; she could not support us alone. When I was eleven I told one of my cousins that my stepfather was molesting me. Mama packed up my sisters and me and took us away for a few days, but again, my stepfather swore he would stop, and again we went back after a few weeks. I stopped talking for a while, and I have only vague memories of the next two years.

My stepfather worked as a route salesman, my mama as a waitress, laundry worker, cook, or fruit packer. I could never understand how, since they both worked so hard and such long hours, we never had enough money, but it was a fact that was true also of my mama's brothers and sisters, who worked in the mills or the furnace industry. In fact, my parents did better than anyone else in the family, but eventually my stepfather was fired and we hit bottom—nightmarish months of marshals at the door, repossessed furniture, and rubber checks. My parents worked out a scheme so that it appeared my stepfather had abandoned us, but instead he went down to Florida, got a new job, and rented us a house. In the dead of night, he returned with a U-Haul trailer, packed us up, and moved us south.

The night we left South Carolina for Florida, my mama leaned over the back seat of her old Pontiac and promised us girls, "It'll be better there." I don't know if we believed her, but I remember crossing Georgia in the early morning, watching the red clay hills and swaying gray blankets of moss recede through the back window. I kept looking back at the trailer behind us, ridiculously small to contain everything we owned. Mama had, after all, packed nothing that wasn't fully paid off, which meant she had only two things of worth, her washing and sewing machines, both of them tied securely to the trailer walls. Through the whole trip, I fantasized an accident that would burst that trailer, scattering old clothes and cracked dishes on the tarmac.

I was only thirteen. I wanted us to start over completely, to begin again as new people with nothing of the past left over. I wanted to run away completely from who we had been seen to be, who we had been. That desire is one I have seen in other members of my family, to run away. It is the first thing I think of when trouble comes, the geographic solution. Change your name, leave town, disappear, and make yourself over. What hides behind that solution is the conviction that the life you have lived, the person you are, are valueless, better off abandoned, that running away is easier than trying to change anything, that change itself is not possible, that death is easier than this life. Sometimes I think it is that conviction—more seductive than alcoholism or violence and more subtle than sexual hatred or gender injustice—that has dominated my life, and made real change so painful and difficult.

Moving to central Florida did not fix our lives. It did not stop my stepfather's violence, heal my shame, or make my mother happy. Once there our lives became dominated by my mother's illness and medical bills. She had a hysterectomy when I was about eight and endured a series of hospitalizations for ulcers and a chronic back problem. Through most of my adolescence she superstitiously refused to allow anyone to mention the word cancer. (Years later when she called me to tell me that she was recovering from an emergency mastectomy, there was bitter fatalism in her voice. The second mastectomy followed five years after the first, and five years after that there was a brief bout with cancer of the lymph system which went into remission after prolonged chemotherapy. She died at the age of fifty-six with liver, lung, and brain cancer.) When she was not sick, Mama, and my stepfather, went on working, struggling to pay off what seemed an insurmountable load of debts.

By the time I was fourteen, my sisters and I had found ways to discourage most of our stepfather's sexual advances. We were not close but we united against our stepfather. Our efforts were helped along when he was referred to a psychotherapist after losing his temper at work, and was prescribed psychotropic drugs that made him sullen but less violent. We were growing up quickly, my sisters moving toward dropping out of school, while I got good grades and took every scholarship exam I could find. I was the first person in my family to graduate from high school, and the fact that I went on to college was nothing short of astonishing.

Everyone imagines her life is normal, and I did not know my life was not everyone's. It was not until I was an adolescent in central Florida that I began to realize just how different we were. The people we met there had not been shaped by the rigid class structure that dominated the South Carolina Piedmont. The first time I looked around my junior high classroom and realized that I did not know who those people were—not only as individuals but as categories, who their people were and how they saw themselves—I realized also that they did not know me. In Greenville, everyone knew my family, knew we were trash, and that meant we were supposed to be poor, supposed to have grim low-paid jobs, have babies in our teens, and never finish school. But central Florida in the 1960s was full of runaways and immigrants, and our mostly white working-class suburban school sorted us out, not by income and family background, but by intelligence and aptitude tests. Suddenly I was boosted into the college-bound track, and while there was plenty of contempt for my inept social skills, pitiful wardrobe, and slow drawling accent, there was also something I had never experienced before, a protective anonymity, and a kind of grudging respect and curiosity about who I might become. Because they did not see poverty and hopelessness as a foregone conclusion for my life, I could begin to imagine other futures for myself.

Moving into that new world and meeting those new people meant that I began to see my family from a new vantage point. I also experienced a new level of fear, a fear of losing what before had never been imaginable. My family's lives were not on television, not in books, not even comic books. There was a myth of the poor in this country, but it did not include us, no matter how hard I tried to squeeze us in. There was an idea of the good poor—hard-working, ragged but clean, and intrinsically noble. I understood that we were the bad poor, the ungrateful: men who drank and couldn't keep a job; women, invariably pregnant before marriage, who quickly became worn, fat, and old from working too many hours and bearing too many children; and children with runny noses, watery eyes, and bad attitudes. My cousins quit school, stole cars, used drugs, and took dead-end jobs pumping gas or waiting tables. We were not noble, not grateful, not even hopeful. We knew ourselves despised.

But in that new country, we were unknown. The myth settled over us and glamorized us. I saw it in the eyes of my teachers, the Lions' Club representative who paid for my new glasses, and the lady from the Junior League who told me about the scholarship I had won. Better, far better, to be one of the mythical poor than to be part of the *they* I had known before. *Don't let me lose this chance*, I prayed, and lived in fear that I might suddenly be seen again as what I knew I really was.

As an adolescent, I thought that the way my family escaped South Carolina was like a bad movie. We fled like runaway serfs and the sheriff who would have arrested my stepfather seemed like a border guard. Even now, I am certain that if we had remained in South Carolina, I would have been trapped by my family's heritage of poverty, jail, and illegitimate children—that even being smart, stubborn, and a lesbian would have made no difference. My grandmother died when I was twenty and after Mama went home for the funeral, I had a series of dreams in which we still lived up in Greenville, just down the road from where Granny had died. In the dreams I had two children and only one eye, lived in a trailer, and worked at the textile mill. Most of my time was taken up with deciding when I would finally kill my children and myself. The dreams were so vivid, I became convinced they were about the life I was meant to have had, and I began to work even harder to put as much distance as I could between my family and me. I copied the dress, mannerisms, attitudes, and ambitions of the girls I met in college, changing or hiding my own tastes, interests, and desires. I kept my lesbianism a secret, forming a relationship with an effeminate male friend that served to shelter and disguise us both. I explained to friends that I went home so rarely because my stepfather and I fought too much for me to be comfortable in his house. But that was only part of the reason I avoided home, the easiest reason. The truth was that I feared the person I might become in my mama's house.

It is hard to explain how deliberately and thoroughly I ran away from my own life. I did not forget where I came from, but I gritted my teeth and hid it. When I could not get enough scholarship money to pay for graduate school, I spent a year of blind rage working as a salad girl, substitute teacher, and maid. I finally managed to get a job by agreeing to take any city assignment where the Social Security Administration needed a clerk. Once I had a job and my own place far away from anyone in my family, I became sexually and politically active, joining the Women's Center support staff and falling in love with a series of middle-class women who thought my accent and stories thoroughly charming. The stories I told about my family, about South Carolina, about being poor itself, were all lies, carefully edited to seem droll or funny. I knew damn well that no one would want to hear the truth about poverty, the hopelessness and fear, the feeling that nothing you do will make any difference, and the raging resentment that burns beneath the jokes. Even when my lovers and I formed an alternative lesbian family, sharing all our resources, I kept the truth about my background and who I knew myself to be a carefully obscured mystery. I worked as hard as I could to make myself a new person, an emotionally healthy radical lesbian activist, and I believed completely that by remaking myself I was helping to remake the world.

For a decade, I did not go home for more than a few days at a time.

It is sometimes hard to make clear how much I have loved my family, that every impulse to hold them in contempt has sparked in me a countersurge of stubborn pride. . . . I have had to fight broad generalizations from every possible theoretical viewpoint. Traditional feminist theory has had a limited understanding of class differences or of how sexuality and self are shaped by both desire and denial. The ideology implies that we are all sisters who should turn our anger and suspicion only on the world outside the lesbian community. It is so simple to say the patriarchy did it, that poverty and social contempt are products of the world of the fathers. How often I felt a need to collapse my sexual history into what I was willing to share of my class background, to pretend that both my life as a lesbian and my life as a working-class escapee were constructed by the patriarchy. The difficulty is that I can't ascribe everything that has been problematic or difficult about my life simply and easily to the patriarchy, or even to the invisible and much-denied class structure of our society. . . .

One of the things I am trying to understand is how we internalize the myths of our society even as we hate and resist them. Perhaps this will be more understandable if I discuss specifically how some of these myths have shaped my life and how I have been able to talk about and change my own understanding of my family. I have felt a powerful temptation to write about my family as a kind of moral tale with us as the heroes and the middle and upper classes as the villains. It would be within the romantic myth, for example, to pretend that we were the kind of noble Southern whites portrayed in the movies, mill workers for generations until driven out of the mills by alcoholism and a family propensity to rebellion and union talk. But that would be a lie. The truth is that no one in my family ever joined a union. Taken as far as it can go, the myth of the poor would make my family over into union organizers or people broken by the failure of the unions. The reality of my family is far more complicated and lacks the cardboard nobility of the myth.

As far as my family was concerned, union or-ganizers, like preachers, were of a different class, suspect and hated as much as they might be ad-mired for what they were supposed to be trying to achieve. Serious belief in anything—any political ideology, any religious system, or any theory of life's meaning and purpose—was seen as unrealistic. It was an attitude that bothered me a lot when I started reading the socially conscious novels I found in the paperback racks when I was eleven or so. I particularly loved Sinclair Lewis's novels and wanted to imagine my own family as part of the working man's struggle. But it didn't seem to be that simple.

"We were not joiners," my Aunt Dot told me with a grin when I asked her about the union. My cousin Butch laughed at that, told me the union charged dues and said, "Hell, we can't even be per-suaded to toss money in the collection plate. An't gonna give it to no fat union man." It shamed me that the only thing my family wholeheartedly be-lieved in was luck, and the waywardness of fate. They held the dogged conviction that the admirable and wise thing to do was to try and keep a sense of humor, not to whine or cower, and to trust that luck might someday turn as good as it had been bad—and with just as much reason. Becoming a political activist with an almost religious fervor was the thing I did that most outraged my family and the Southern working-class community they were part of.

Similarly, it was not my sexuality, my lesbianism, that was seen by my family as most rebellious; for most of my life, no one but my mama took my sex-ual preference very seriously. It was the way I thought about work, ambition, and self-respect that seemed incomprehensible to my aunts and cousins. They were waitresses, laundry workers, and counter girls. I was the one who went to work as a maid,

something I never told any of them. They would have been angry if they had known, though the fact that some work was contemptible was itself a diffi-cult notion. They believed that work was just work, necessary, that you did what you had to do to sur-vive. They did not believe so much in taking pride in doing your job as they did in stubbornly endur-ing hard work and hard times when you really didn't have much choice about what work you did. But at the same time they did believe that there were some forms of work, including maid's work, that were only for black people, not white, and while I did not share that belief, I knew how intrinsic it was to how my family saw the world. Sometimes I felt as if I straddled cultures and belonged on nei-ther side. I would grind my teeth at what I knew was my family's unquestioning racism but still take pride in their pragmatic endurance, but more and more as I grew older what I truly felt was a deep es-trangement from the way they saw the world, and gradually a sense of shame that would have been completely incomprehensible to them.

"Long as there's lunch counters, you can always find work," I was told by both my mother and my aunts, and they'd add, "I can always get me a little extra with a smile." It was obvious that there was supposed to be nothing shameful about it, that needy smile across a lunch counter, that rueful grin when you didn't have rent, or the half-provocative, half-begging way my mama could cajole the man at the store to give her a little credit. But I hated it, hated the need for it and the shame that would follow every time I did it myself. It was begging as far as I was concerned, a quasi-prostitution that I despised even while I continued to use it (after all, I needed the money). But my mother, aunts, and cousins had not been ashamed, and my shame and resentment pushed me even further away from them.

"Just use that smile," my girl cousins used to joke, and I hated what I knew they meant. After col-lege, when I began to support myself and study feminist theory, I did not become more understand-ing of the women of my family but more contemp-tuous. I told myself that prostitution is a skilled profession and my cousins were never more than amateurs. There was a certain truth in this, though like all cruel judgments made from the outside, it ignored the conditions that made it true. The women in my family, my mother included, had sugar daddies, not johns, men who slipped them money because they needed it so badly. From their point of view they were nice to those men because the men were nice to them, and it was never so direct or crass an arrangement that they would set a price on their favors. They would never have described what they did as prostitution, and nothing made them angrier than the suggestion that the men who helped them out did it just for their favors. They worked for a living, they swore, but this was different.

I always wondered if my mother had hated her sugar daddy, or if not *him* then her need for what he offered her, but it did not seem to me in memory that she had. Her sugar daddy had been an old man, half-crippled, hesitant and needy, and he treated my mama with enormous consideration and, yes, respect. The relationship between them was painful because it was based on the fact that she and my stepfather could not make enough money to support the family. Mama could not refuse her sugar daddy's money, but at the same time he made no assumptions about that money buying anything she was not already offering. The truth was, I think, that she genuinely liked him, and only partly because he treated her so well.

Even now, I am not sure whether or not there was a sexual exchange between them. Mama was a pretty woman and she was kind to him, a kindness he obviously did not get from anyone else in his life, and he took extreme care not to cause her any problems with my stepfather. As a teenager with an adolescent's contempt for moral failings and sexual complexity of any kind, I had been convinced that Mama's relationship with that old man was contemptible and also that I would never do such a thing. The first time a lover of mine gave me money, and I took it, everything in my head shifted. The amount she gave me was not much to her, but it was a lot to me and I needed it. I could not refuse it, but I hated myself for taking it and I hated her for giving it to me. Worse, she had much less grace about my need than my mama's sugar daddy had displayed toward her. All that bitter contempt I had felt for my needy cousins and aunts raged through me and burned out the love I had felt. I ended the relationship quickly, unable to forgive myself for *selling* what I believed should only be offered freely—not sex but love itself.

When the women in my family talked about how hard they worked, the men would spit to the side and shake their heads. Men took real jobs—hard, dangerous, physically daunting work. They went to jail, not just the hard-eyed, careless boys who scared me with their brutal hands and cold eyes, but their gentler, softer brothers. It was another family thing, what people expected of my mama's family, my people. "His daddy's that one was sent off to jail in Georgia, and his uncle's another. Like as not, he's just the same," you'd hear people say of boys so young they still had their milk teeth. We were always driving down to the county farm to see somebody, some uncle, cousin, or nameless male relation. Shaven-headed, sullen and stunned, they wept on Mama's shoulder or begged my aunts to help. "I didn't do nothing, Mama," they'd say and it might have been true, but if even we didn't believe them, who would? No one told the truth, not even about how their lives were destroyed. . . .

By 1975, I was earning a meager living as a photographer's assistant in Tallahassee, Florida, but the real work of my life was my lesbian feminist activism, the work I did with the local Women's Center and the committee to found a Feminist Studies Department at Florida State University. Part of my role as I saw it was to be a kind of evangelical lesbian feminist, and to help develop a political analysis of this woman-hating society. I did not talk about class, more than by giving lip service to how we all needed to think about it, the same way I thought we all needed to think about racism. I was a serious and determined person, living in a lesbian collective, studying each new book that purported to address feminist issues and completely driven by what I saw as a need to revolutionize the world. . . .

The idea of writing fiction or essays seemed frivolous when there was so much work to be done, but everything changed when I found myself confronting emotions and ideas that could not be explained away or postponed for a feminist holiday. The way it happened was simple and completely unexpected. One week I was asked to speak to two completely divergent groups: an Episcopalian Sunday School class and a juvenile detention center. The Episcopalians were all white, well-dressed, highly articulate, nominally polite, and obsessed with getting me to tell them (without their having to ask directly) just what it was that two women did together in bed. The delinquents were all women, eighty percent black and Hispanic, dressed in green uniform dresses or blue jeans and work shirts, profane, rude, fearless, witty, and just as determined to get me to talk about what it was that two women did together in bed.

I tried to have fun with the Episcopalians, teasing them about their fears and insecurities, and being as bluntly honest as I could about my sexual practices. The Sunday School teacher, a man who had assured me of his liberal inclinations, kept blushing and stammering as the questions about my growing up and coming out became more detailed. When the meeting was over, I stepped out into the sunshine angry at the contemptuous attitude implied by all their questions, and though I did not know why, also so deeply depressed that I couldn't even cry. The delinquents were different. Shameless, they had me blushing within the first few minutes, yelling out questions that were partly curious and partly a way of boasting about what they already knew.

"You butch or femme?" "You ever fuck boys?" "You ever want to?" "You want to have children?" "What's your girlfriend like?" I finally broke up when one very tall confident girl leaned way over and called out, "Hey girlfriend! I'm getting out of here next weekend. What you doing that night?" I laughed so hard I almost choked. I laughed until we were all howling and giggling together. Even getting frisked as I left didn't ruin my mood. I was still grinning when I climbed into the waterbed with my lover that night, grinning right up to the moment when she wrapped her arms around me and I burst into tears.

It is hard to describe the way I felt that night, the shock of recognition and the painful way my thoughts turned. That night I understood suddenly everything that happened to my cousins and me, understood it from a wholly new and agonizing perspective, one that made clear how brutal I had been to both my family and myself. I understood all over again how we had been robbed and dismissed, and why I had worked so hard not to think about it. I had learned as a child that what could not be changed had to go unspoken, and worse, that those who cannot change their own lives have every reason to be ashamed of that fact and to hide it. I had accepted that shame and believed in it, but why? What had I or my cousins really done to deserve the contempt directed at us? Why had I always believed us contemptible by nature? I wanted to talk to someone about all the things I was thinking that night, but I could not. Among the women I knew there was no one who would have understood what I was thinking, no other working-class women in the women's collective where I was living. I began to suspect that we shared no common language to speak those bitter truths.

In the days after that I found myself . . . thrown back into my childhood, into all the fears and convictions I had tried to escape. Once again I felt myself at the mercy of the important people who knew how to dress and talk, and would always be given the benefit of the doubt while I and my family would not.

I felt as if I was at the mercy of an outrage so old I could not have traced all the ways it shaped my life. I understood again that some are given no quarter, no chance, that all their courage, humor, and love for each other is just a joke to the ones who make the rules, and I hated the rule makers. Finally I also realized that part of my grief came from the fact that I no longer knew who I was or where I belonged. I had run away from my family, refused to go home to visit, and tried in every way to make myself a new person. How could I be working-class with a college degree? As a lesbian activist? I thought about the guards at the detention center, and the way they had looked at me. They had not stared at me with the same picture-window emptiness they turned on the girls who came to hear me, girls who were closer to the life I had been meant to live than I could bear to examine. The contempt in their eyes was contempt for me as a lesbian, different and the same, but still contempt. . . .

In the late 1970s, the compartmentalized life I had created burst open. It began when I started to write and work out what I really thought about my family. . . . I went home again. I went home to my mother and my sisters, to visit, talk, argue, and begin to understand.

Once home I saw that, as far as my family was concerned, lesbians were lesbians whether they wore suitcoats or leather jackets. Moreover, in all that time when I had not made peace with myself, my family had managed to make a kind of peace with me. My girlfriends were treated like slightly odd versions of my sisters' husbands, while I was simply the daughter who had always been difficult but was still a part of their lives. The result was that I started trying to confront what had made me unable to really talk to my sisters for so many years. I discovered that they no longer knew who I was either, and it took time and lots of listening to each other to rediscover my sense of family, and my love for them.

It is only as the child of my class and my unique family background that I have been able to put together what is for me a meaningful politics, gained a sense of why I believe in activism, why self-revelation is so important for lesbians, reexamining the way we are seen and the way we see ourselves. There is no all-purpose feminist analysis that explains away all the complicated ways our sexuality and core identity are shaped, the way we see ourselves as parts of both our birth families and the extended family of friends and lovers we invariably create within the lesbian community. For me the bottom line has simply become the need to resist that omnipresent fear, that urge to hide and disappear, to disguise my life, my desires, and the truth about how little any of us understand—even as we try to make the world a more just and human place for us all. Most of all I have tried to understand the politics of *they*, why human beings fear and stigmatize the different while secretly dreading that they might be one of the different themselves. Class, race, sexuality, gender, all the categories by which we categorize and dismiss each other need to be examined from the inside.

The horror of class stratification, racism, and prejudice is that some people begin to believe that the security of their families and community depends on the oppression of others, that for some to have good lives others must have lives that are mean and horrible. It is a belief that dominates this culture; it is what made the poor whites of the South so determinedly racist and the middle class so contemptuous of the poor. It is a myth that allows some to imagine that they build their lives on the ruin of others, a secret core of shame for the middle class, a goad and a spur to the marginal working class, and cause enough for the homeless and poor to feel no constraints on hatred or violence. The power of the myth is made even more apparent when we examine how within the lesbian and feminist communities, where so much attention has been paid to the politics of marginalization, there is still so much exclusion and fear, so many of us who do not feel safe even within our chosen communities.

I grew up poor, hated, the victim of physical, emotional, and sexual violence, and I know that suffering does not ennoble. It destroys. To resist destruction, self-hatred, or lifelong hopelessness, we have to throw off the conditioning of being despised, the fear of becoming that *they* that is talked about so dismissively, to refuse lying myths and easy moralities, to see ourselves as human, flawed and extraordinary. All of us—extraordinary.

TEN

◆◆◆

Love Feminism but Where's My Hip Hop? (2002)
Shaping a Black Feminist Identity
Gwendolyn D. Pough

Gwendolyn D. Pough is a professor of Women's Studies and Writing at Syracuse University. Her teaching, research, and writing focus on Black women writers and theorizing Black feminisms.

The very idea that someone can attribute coming into Black feminist consciousness to the masculine spaces of rap music and hip-hop culture must seem outrageous to some people. When you add

the abstract concept of love into the mix, it might become a little bit more astonishing. Even though third-wave Black feminists such as Joan Morgan, Eisa Davis, Tara Roberts, dream hampton and Eisa Nefertari Ulen have begun to make a case for a Black feminist identity and agenda tied to hip-hop culture, the linking of hip hop and feminism is still a bit much for some to bear.[1] And although Black feminist diva bell hooks has started the much-needed dialogue on love, feminism and the revolutionary potential such a combination would grant, there are not a whole lot of feminists openly checking for the L-word. Given the history of oppression women have suffered at the hands of patriarchs who no doubt claimed to love them, it is not hard to imagine why love would be thought of as suspect. But, nevertheless, I feel the need to explore the connections between love, hip hop and my coming to voice as a third-wave Black feminist.

. . . LL Cool J's soulful rap ballad "I Need Love" (1987) was the first rap love song I heard, and it would not be the last. Rap and rap artists' never-ending quest to "keep it real" is not limited to real-life struggles on American streets. Some rappers show an interesting dedication to exploring aspects of love and the struggles of building and maintaining intimate relationships between Black men and women. Although this reeks of heterosexism—as do many rap love songs—it also points to the very real nature of the relationship between Black men and women and most men and women of color. When you call someone your sister or brother, or comrade in the struggle against racism, a bond is created. In that bond there is love. Rap music therefore offers space for public dialogues about love, romance and struggle in a variety of combinations.

This kind of public dialogue is found in the answer/dis raps of the 1980s, which gave rise to women rap stars Roxanne Shanté and Salt-N-Pepa. These women paved the way for other women rappers by recording very successful songs, which were responses to the hit records of the men who were their contemporaries. Shanté gave the woman pursued in UTFO's "Roxanne, Roxanne" a voice and ultimately let it be known that women would no longer suffer insults and degradation in silence. Salt-N-Pepa's "The Show Stoppa (Is Stupid Fresh)" was a direct refutation to Doug E. Fresh and Slick Rick's "The Show"—a song in which women are portrayed as objects of conquest.

As a Black woman coming of age during the hip-hop era, I saw the answers that Shanté and Salt-N-Pepa put to wax as more than just temporary jams to get the body moving. They let me know I could have a voice as well. They offered the strong public presence of Black womanhood that I had seen in my mother and her friends but had not witnessed in my generation in such a public forum. Before I ever read bell hooks's *Talking Back: Thinking Feminist, Thinking Black*, I heard Shanté and Salt-N-Pepa rapping and

securing a strong public voice for women's issues in general and young Black women's issues specifically. Their talking back and speaking out against unwanted advances that could easily be read as sexual harassment gave me a model for dealing with similar issues as I braved inner-city streets. In addition, their talking back changed the way I looked at romance and courtship as well as the voice I could have in those socially scripted spaces. I no longer thought I had to simply smile and keep walking when brothers made catcalls or lewd comments as I walked down the street. I felt perfectly fine and justified in rolling my eyes and telling them how rude they were or that they would never "get the digits" behaving in such a manner. I began to make up rhymes about these street encounters that sought to disrupt the men's behavior by offering a woman's response. One rhyme in particular was a direct reflection on a street corner encounter with a rude guy who also claimed to be an MC. I rapped:

> *I was on my way to the jam, you see.*
> *Saw a fly guy, you know he was sweatin' me.*
> *Told him my name was MC Gwenny Dee.*
> *He looked at me, laughed and asked sarcastically,*
> *Gwenny Dee, hmm, can you rhyme?*
> *I said not only can I rhyme, I'm a one of a kind.*
> *He said, How can this be, you're a girl?*
> *And a female can't make it in an MC's world.*
> *I said, please tell me what you're talking about*
> *when you say females can't turn it out,*
> *when you say that the best MCs are the men*
> *and chances for a female are zero to ten*
> *Well, I'm here to say, whether you like it or you don't.*
> *So, fellas listen up, 'cause I'm sure you won't:*
> *Females make the best MCs, you know.*
> *So just step on back cause we run the show.*
> *Your gear and your gold make you look fly,*
> *but you rap wack enough to make me cry.*
> *And that's true, you know why,*
> *'cause I don't lie, as a matter of fact, I'm really too fly.*
> *Got to the party everyone was chillin'.*
> *Looked on the stand saw dude justa illin'*
> *Trying like a dummy to rock hard, with a rhyme he*
>   *stole off a Hallmark card.*

My own clearly old-school flow and rapping skills aside, this is how I began to use rap to talk back in ways very similar to the women rappers I listened to on the radio. I wrote this rhyme when I was a fifteen-year-old aspiring rapper. The rhymes I wrote and the developing prominence of female MCs on the radio prompted me to look for a DJ and a crew so that I could start my rap career. With very few women rappers to serve as role models, the success of these answer/dis songs let me know that women could make it in the rap arena. They also inspired the kinds of raps I wrote—raps that were pro-woman and critiqued the inequities of gender that my young mind saw. I am not arguing that I had a strong and carefully theorized critique of gender as a fifteen-year-old B-girl. However, strong and successful women rappers and the space that hip hop provided gave me a chance to develop a critique that I now know to be the beginnings of my current Black feminist consciousness.

Even though I had no idea what feminism was at the time, I had seen strong Black women all my life. My mother was a single parent and she worked hard to make sure that my sisters and I had the things we needed. She did not call herself a feminist. But she left an abusive husband and told any other Black man who could not act right where the door could hit him. Having this strong female presence in my own home not withstanding, there was something particularly inspiring about seeing that presence personified in my own generation. Hip hop gave me that.

Another way that hip hop helped me to develop a feminist consciousness was the exposure it gave me to sexual harassment and the attitude it gave me to deal with it. The thing that stands out very clearly about that time for me was being the only girl in someone's basement as we took turns on the microphone. At different times I warded off advances from fellow male MCs and even the DJ. It seemed like every one of them wanted to at least try and get me to have sex with him. When none of their advances worked, they eventually stopped. DJ Ronnie Ron, however, took offense to my performance of the rap I've included here. He thought the rhyme was aimed at him, because he too had tried to get with me and failed. So he put on an instrumental cut, grabbed the mike and proceeded to freestyle a dis rap just for me. I stopped working with him, and after a few other failed attempts at finding a DJ, I stopped writing rhymes.

As I reflect back on that time, I realize now that there was something about writing rhymes and saying them on the mike—hearing my voice loud, strong and clear—that made me feel strong. After I gave up the dream of becoming a rapper, the acts of writing and performing still give me a surge of strength. The only difference is that now I'm writing feminist critiques of rap and performing them at academic conferences and other venues. I also use rap to teach other young women of color about feminism.

As a woman born in 1970, who was nine years old when the first rap record hit the airwaves (The Sugarhill Gang's "Rapper's Delight"), I grew up on rap music. Reading Tricia Rose's discussion of the evolution of hip-hop culture through the changes in clothing commodified by rappers and hip-hop audiences reminds me of my own evolution: from a teenage B-girl wearing Lee jeans, Adidas sneakers with fat laces, LeTigre shirts, gold chunk jewelry, and a gold tooth to an "Around the Way Girl" college freshman sporting a leather jacket, baggy jeans, sweat hood and Fendi/Gucci/fake Louis Vuitton.[2]

Once I was in college, however, my relationship with hip hop changed when I stopped consuming the female identities put forth by male rappers as the girl of their dreams. As I had once been willing to be LL Cool J's "Around the Way Girl" (1989), I began taking issue with the very notion of Apache's "Gangsta Bitch" (1992). While I still consumed the music, I began to question the lyrics and constructed identities. Although both of these songs sought to give "props" to the girls in the hood, I found myself struggling with the image that Apache put forth. It was then that I realized it wasn't the "bitch" that bothered me. It was the things he applauded that did. Things like the gangsta bitch fighting other women and helping him to sell drugs to other people in the hood that bothered me. These things did not fit in with the feminist identity that I was developing.

Like many of the academics and Black popular critics now writing about rap, I have a love for hip-hop culture and rap music. This love prompts me to critique and explore rap in more meaningful ways. I am no longer the teenaged girl who spent Friday nights listening to Mr. Magic's "Rap Attack" and writing rhymes, Saturdays reading her mama's Harlequin or Silhouette romance novels and Sundays writing rhymes and short stories. . . .

Although I still listen to rap music and read a romance novel every time I get a chance, Black feminist/womanist theories and politics inform my listening and reading. Whenever I can, I go back to my undergraduate university to work with the youth participating in the summer Pre-College Academy. These high school students are from the North Jersey area, and I see it as a way to give back.

I do it to spread feminist consciousness to new up-and-coming feminists. Young women growing up today are not privy to the same kind of prowoman rap that I listened to via Salt-N-Pepa, Queen Latifah, Yo-Yo, and MC Lyte. Even though I like Lil' Kim and Foxy Brown, I know that younger women of color need the critical tools to unpack some of the messages they get from these artists.

One student during the summer of 2000 was obsessed with fancy cars. She asked me, "Ay, yo, what you pushing, Miss Pough?" After telling the student that I drove a Ford Escort, she kind of frowned, pushed up her nose and said, "Oh, that's cute." This student's fascination with fancy cars and her desire to one day "push" one was not a problem in and of itself. There is nothing wrong with desiring nice things, especially when those things are out of reach and they give one something to work for. The problem occurs when students like this young lady have these desires absent of a critique of materialism and the harsh realities that go along with it. It is one thing to desire nice things and quite another to put drugs in one's purse because "the police won't check or suspect you" and a drug dealer boyfriend can buy you nice things in return for drug smuggling. It is one thing to want a nice car and quite another to think that the only way you will get one is to use your body sexually.

Parents and educators alike admonish rap because of lyrics that use profanity and glamorize sex and violence. Parents do not want their children listening to it, and educators do not see the educational value in it. I believe that the value resides in the critique. This means that we need to create spaces—both inside and outside of the classroom—for young women especially to make the kinds of connections to larger societal issues that they do not make in the clubs on the dance floors. For me, a critical look at hip hop that is based not only on a love for the music and the culture but on a love of the people that are influenced by it, is what I want to inform my Black feminist consciousness and ultimately my action.

June Jordan's poignant essay "Where Is the Love" haunts me. Jordan discusses the need for a self-love and self-respect that would create and foster the ability to love and respect others. As I think about hip hop and the images of niggas and bitches that inhibit this kind of self-love and self-respect, I am faced with a multitude of questions. I am concerned particularly with rap and the love that hate produced—love that

is fostered by a racist and sexist society. This is the kind of love that grows *despite* oppression but holds unique characteristics *because of* oppression. In many ways it is a continuation of the way Black men and women were forced to express love during slavery and segregation, when Black people were not allowed to love one another freely. Family members could be taken away at any moment. The legacy of slavery—it has yet to be dealt with properly—is the legacy that haunts Black people specifically and the rest of the country in general.

This legacy stands behind the war zone in which Morgan attributes Black men and women today living and trying to love. This legacy prompts me to value love as the connecting factor between hip hop and my identity as a Black feminist. Love has been and continues to be a struggle for Black people in the United States. Yet Black people have found ways to love each other and to be together anyway, despite separations and sales of partners during slavery. During the days of segregation and Jim Crow, Black people—especially parents—had to practice tough love to ensure that loved ones would live to see another day and not become the victim of Klan violence.

While the hip-hop generation has the legacy of African-American history to build on and strands of these kinds of love still persist, the hip-hop generation also has its own demons. Life for young Black Americans is different, and the very nature of relationships within hip-hop culture is necessarily going to be expressed differently. What continues to fascinate me is that despite all the historical baggage and contemporary struggles, young Black people are still trying to find ways to love, just as their ancestors did. A recognition of the plight that Black men and women are up against, along with a realization that in spite of it all living and loving go hand in hand, is central to any brand of feminism that is going to work for young Black women.

A new direction for Black feminism would aid in the critique and exploration of the dialogue across the sexes found in rap music and hip-hop culture. Black feminists such as dream hampton, Tara Roberts, Joan Morgan and Eisa Davis have begun to explore the relationship between love and hip hop. Rap music provides a new direction for Black feminist criticism. It is not just about counting the bitches and hoes in each rap song. It is about exploring the nature of Black male and female relationships. These new Black feminists acknowledge that sexism exists in rap music. But they also recognize that sexism exists in America. Rap music and Black popular culture are not produced in a cultural and political vacuum. The systems of oppression that plague the larger society plague subcultures of society as well. Black feminists are looking for ways to speak out against sexism and racism while starting a dialogue with Black men right on the front lines of the battlefield against oppression.

On these front lines I will be fighting and hollering out, "Love feminism but where's my hip hop?"

NOTES

1. Coker, Cheo, dream hampton, and Tara Roberts. "A Hip-Hop Nation Divided," *Essence Magazine* August 1994: 62–64, 112–115.

Davis, Eisa. 2000. "if we've gotta live underground and everybody's got cancer/will poetry be enuf?: A Letter

to Ntozake Shange" In *Step into a World: A Global Anthology of the New Black Literature*, ed. Kevin Powell, 380–384. New York: John Wiley & Sons.

_____. "Sexism and the Art of Feminist Hip-Hop Maintenance." *To Be Real: Telling the Truth and Changing the Face of Feminism*. ed. Rebecca Walker. New York: Anchor, 1995. 127–142.

Morgan, Joan. *When Chickenheads Come Home to Roost: My Life as a Hip-Hop Feminist*. New York: Simon & Schuster, 1999.

Roberts, Tara and Eisa Nefertari Ulen. "Sisters Spin the talk on Hip Hop: Can the Music Be Saved," *MS Magazine* February/March 2000. 70–74.

Ulen, Eisa Nefertari. 2000. "What happened to Your Generation's Promise of 'Love and Revolution'?: A Letter to Angela Davis." In *Step into a World: A Global Anthology of the New Black Literature*. ed. Kevin Powell, 401–403. New York: John Wiley & Sons.

2. Rose, Tricia. *Black Noise: Rap Music and Black Culture in Contemporary America*. Hanover: Wesleyan UP, 1994.

ELEVEN

◆◆◆

Jews in the U.S. (1994/5755)
The Rising Costs of Whiteness

Melanie Kaye/Kantrowitz

Melanie Kaye/Kantrowitz has taught writing, Women's Studies, and Jewish Studies. She is also a long-time activist for social justice, was founding director of Jews for Economic and Racial Justice, and former Director of Queens College/CUNY Worker Education Extension Center. Her published work includes *The Issue is Power: Essays on women, Jews, violence, and resistance.*

Before America No One Was White

In 1990 I had returned to New York City to do antiracist work with other Jews, when a friend sent me an essay by James Baldwin. "No one was white before he/she came to America," Baldwin had written:

It took generations, and a vast amount of coercion, before this became a white country. . . . It is probable that it is the Jewish community—

or more accurately, perhaps, its remnants—that in America has paid the highest and most extraordinary price for becoming white. For the Jews came here from countries where they were not white, and they came here in part because they were not white, and incontestably—in the eyes of the Black American (and not only in those eyes) American Jews have opted to become white. . . .[1]

Everything I think about Jews, whiteness, racism, and contemporary U.S. society begins with this passage. What does it mean: *Jews opted to become white.* Did we opt? Did it work? Was it an illusion? Could we have opted otherwise? Can we still?

Rachel Rubin, a college student who's been interning at Jews for Racial and Economic Justice, where I'm the director, casually mentions: when she was eight, a cross was burned on her lawn in Athens, Georgia. I remember the house I moved into Down East Maine in 1979. On the bedroom door someone had painted a swastika in what looked like blood. I think about any cross-country drive I've ever taken, radio droning hymn after Christian hymn, 2000 miles of heartland.

On the other hand, I remember the last time I was stopped by cops. It was in San Francisco. I was getting a ride home after a conference on Jews and multiculturalism. In the car with me were two other white Jews. My heart flew into my throat, as always, but they took a quick look at the three of us and waved us on— *We're looking for a car like this, sorry.* I remember all the stories I've heard from friends, people of color, in which a quick look is not followed by a friendly wave and an apology. Some of these stories are about life and death....

Where is *Jewish* in the race/class/gender grid? Does it belong? Is it irrelevant? Where do those crosses and swastikas fit in?

Race or Religion?

"Race or religion?" is how the question is usually posed, as though this doublet exhausts the possibilities. Christians—religiously observant or not— usually operate from the common self-definition of Christianity, a religion any individual can embrace through belief, detached from race, peoplehood, and culture.

But I have come to understand this detachment as false. Do white Christians feel kinship with African American Christians? White slave-owners, for example, with their slaves? White Klansmen with their black neighbors? Do white Christians feel akin to Christians converted by colonialists all over the globe? Doesn't Christianity really, for most white Christians, imply *white?* And for those white Christians, does *white* really include *Jewish?* Think of the massive Christian evasion of a simple fact: Jesus Christ was not, was never, a Christian. He was a Jew. What did he look like, Jesus of Nazareth, 2000 years ago? Blond, blue-eyed?

Of course Jewish is not a race,[2] for Jews come in all races. Though white-identified Jews may skirt the issue, Jews are a multiracial people. There are Ethiopian, Indian, Chinese Jews. And there are people of every race who choose Judaism,

were adopted, or born into it from mixed parents. The dominant conception of "Jewish"—European, Yiddish-speaking—is in fact a subset, Ashkenazi. Estimated at 85–97% of Jews in the U.S. today, Ashkenazi Jews are those whose religious practice and diaspora path can be traced through Germany.[3] The huge wave of Jewish immigration from Eastern Europe was Ashkenazi (as was the earlier, much smaller, highly assimilated community of German Jews, who looked with dread upon the arrival of— from their perspective—an impoverished, Yiddish-babbling, superstitious horde). Ashkenazi Jews also migrated to the far points of the globe—to South America, Australia, Africa, Asia. They may be very fair or very dark.

Sephardic Jews are those whose mother tongue is/was Ladino (Judeo-Español) and whose religious practice and diaspora path can be traced at some point through the Iberian Peninsula (Spain and Portugal), where they flourished, unghettoized, contributing along with Muslims to Spanish culture, until the Inquisition (read, *torture*) forced conversion or expulsion from Spain of all non-Christians. Sephardim migrated to, and lived for generations and even centuries, in Holland, Germany, Italy, France, Greece, the Middle East, and the Americas. The first Jews in the New World were Sephardim: 1492 marks not only Columbus's voyage but also the expulsion of the Jews from Spain. Some Sephardi consider themselves the aristocrats of the Jews, and look with contempt upon the Ashkenazi history of ghettoization and persecution. They may also be quite fair or quite dark.

Mizrachi Jews are those who lived in the Arab world and Turkey (basically, what was once the Ottoman Empire), as minorities in Muslim rather than Christian culture. Their mother tongue often is/was Judeo-Arabic. *Mizrachi* means "Eastern," commonly translated as "Oriental," and is used by and about Israelis, often interchangeably with *Sephardi.* Spanish Sephardim sometimes resent the blurring of distinctions between themselves and Mizrachim, reacting with pride in their history and with Eurocentric bias against non-Europeans, referring to themselves as "true" or "pure" Sephardim.[4] The confusion between the categories is only partly due to Ashkenazi ignorance/ arrogance, lumping all non-Ashkenazi together. Partly it's the result of Jewish history: some Jews never left the Middle East, and some returned after the expulsion from Spain, including to Palestine. Some kept Ladino, some did not. I imagine there was intermarriage. Mizrachim, though they may also range from fair to dark, are usually defined as people of color.

The point is, categories of white and color don't correspond neatly to Jewish reality. (What does correspond is Ashkenazi cultural hegemony: in the U.S., where they are dominant by numbers, and in Israel, where Sephardi/Mizrachi Jews make up about two-thirds of the Jewish population and strongly contest this hegemony.) Jewish wanderings have created a people whose experience eludes conventional categories of race, nationality, ethnicity, geography, language—even religion. Cataclysm and assimilation have depleted our store of common knowledge.

No, Jews are not a single race. Yet there is confusion here, and subtext. Confusion because we have so often been racialized, hated *as if* we were a race. Ethnic studies scholars have labored to document the process of racialization, the fact that race is not biological, but a socio-historically specific phenomenon. Observing Jewish history, Nancy Ordover has noted, offers an opportunity to break down this process of racialization, because by leaving Europe, Jews "changed" our "race," even as our skin pigment remained the same.[5]

> For the Jews came here from countries where they were not white, and they came here in part because they were not white. . . .

Confusion, too, because to say someone *looks Jewish* is to say something both absurd (Jews look a million different ways) and commonsense communicative.

When I was growing up in Flatbush (in Brooklyn, NY), every girl with a certain kind of nose—sometimes named explicitly as a Jewish nose, sometimes only as "too big"—wanted a nose job, and if her parents could pay for it, often she got one. I want to be graphic about the euphemism "nose job." A nose job breaks the nose, bruises the face and eye area like a grotesque beating. It hurts. It takes weeks to heal.

What was wrong with the original nose, the Jewish one? Noses were discussed ardently in Flatbush, this or that friend looking forward to her day of transformation.[6] My aunts lavished on

me the following exquisite praise: *look at her, a nose like a shiksa* (gentile woman). This hurt my feelings. Before I knew what a *shiksa* was, I knew I wasn't it, and, with that fabulous integrity of children, I wanted to look like who I was. But later I learned my nose's value, and would tell gentiles this story so they'd notice my nose.

A Jewish nose, I conclude, identifies its owner as a Jew. Nose jobs are performed so that a Jewish woman does not look like a Jew.

Tell me again Jewish is just a religion.

Yet Nazi racial definitions have an "only a religion" response. Even earlier, the lure of emancipation (in Europe) and assimilation (in the U.S.) led Jews to define Judaism as narrowly as possible, as religion only: "a Jew at home, a man in the streets,"[7] a private matter, taken care of behind closed doors, like bathing.

Judaism, the religion, does provide continuity and connection to Jews around the globe. There is something powerful even for atheists about entering a synagogue across the continent or the ocean, and hearing the familiar service.

But to be a Jew, one need not follow religious practice; one need not believe in god—not even to become a rabbi, an element of Judaism of which I am especially fond.[8] Religion is only one strand of being Jewish. It is ironic that it is precisely this century's depletion of Jews and of Jewish identity, with profound linguistic and cultural losses—continuing as Yiddish[9] and Ladino speakers age and die—that makes imaginable a Jewishness that is *only a religion*—only now, when so much else has been lost. But to reduce *Jewishness* to *Judaism* is to forget the complex indivisible swirl of religion/culture/language/history that *was* Jewishness until, in the 18th century, Emancipation began to offer some Jews the possibility of escaping from a linguistically/culturally/economically isolated ghetto into the European "Enlightenment." To equate Jewishness with religion is to forget how even the contemporary, often attenuated version of this Jewish cultural swirl is passed down *in the family*, almost like genetic code.

Confusion and subtext. *Jewish* is often trivialized as something you choose, a preference, like tea over coffee. In contrast with visible racial identity, presumptions of choice—as with gayness—are seen as minimizing one's claim to attention, sympathy, and remedy. As a counter to bigotry, *I was born like this* strategically asserts a kind of victim-status, modeled on race, gender, and disability: if you can't help yourself, maybe you're entitled to some help from others. . . .

What happens if, instead, I assert my right to choose and not suffer for it. To say, *I choose:* my lesbianism and my Jewishness.[10] Choose to come out, be visible, embrace both. I could live loveless or sexless or in the closet. I could have kept the name *Kaye,* and never once at Christmas—in response to the interminable "what are you doing for . . . ? have you finished your shopping?"—never once answer, "I don't celebrate Christmas. I'm a Jew." I could lie about my lover's gender. I could wear skirts uncomfortably. I could bleach my hair again, as I did when I was fifteen. I could monitor my speech, weeding out the offensive accent, as I was taught at City College, along with all the other first and second generation immigrants' children in the four speech classes required for graduation, to teach us not to sound like ourselves. I could remain silent when queer or anti-Semitic jokes are told, when someone says "you know how *they* are." I could endure the pain in the gut, the hot shame. I could scrunch up much, much smaller.

In the U.S., *Christian,* like *white,* is an unmarked category in need of marking.[11] Christianness, a majority, dominant culture, is not only about religious practice and belief, any more than Jewishness is. As *racism* names the system that normalizes, honors and rewards whiteness, we need a word for what normalizes, honors and rewards Christianity. Jews designate the assumption of Christianity-as-norm, the erasure of Jews, as "anti-Semitic." In fact, the erasure and marginalization of non-Christians is not just denigrating to Jews. We need a catchier term than *Christian hegemony,* to help make visible the cultural war against all non-Christians.

Christianism? Awkward, stark, and kind of crude—maybe a sign that something's being pushed. *Sexism* once sounded stark and kind of crude. Such a term would help contextualize Jewish experience as an experience of marginality shared with other non-Christians. Especially in this time of rising Christian fundamentalism, as school prayer attracts support from "moderates," this contextualization is critical for progressive Jews, compelling us to seek allies among Muslims and other religious minorities.

I also want to contextualize Jews in a theoretical framework outside the usual bipolar frame of black/white—to go beyond dualism; to distinguish race from class, and both from culture; to understand "whiteness" as the gleaming conferral of normality, success, even survival; to acknowledge who owns what in whose neighborhood; to witness how money does and does not "whiten."

> For in the eyes of the Black American (and not only in those eyes) American Jews have opted to become white. . . .

To begin to break out of a polarity that has no place for Jews, I survey the range of color in the U.S. People of color, a unity sought and sometimes forged, include a vast diversity of culture and history, forms of oppression and persecution. Contemporary white supremacists hate them all, but define some as shrewd, evil, inscrutable, sexually exotic, and perverse, and others as intellectually inferior, immoral, bestial, violent, and sexually rapacious. If it is possible to generalize, we can say that the peoples defined as shrewd and evil tend to be better off economically—or at least perceived as better off economically—than those defined as inferior and violent, who tend to remain in large numbers stuck at the bottom of the economic ladder (and are assumed by the dominant culture, to be stuck there), denied access to decent jobs and opportunities, systematically disadvantaged and excluded by the educational system.

In other words, among the creeping fearsome dark ones are, on one hand, those who exploit, cheat, and hoard money they don't deserve, and, on the other, those (usually darker) who, not having money, threaten to rob and pillage hard-working tax-paying white Christians. In this construct, welfare fits as a form of robbery, the women's form; the men are busy mugging. Immigrant-bashing—whether street violence or political movements like "English-only" . . .—becomes a "natural" response to "robbery."

It is easier now to see where Jews fit: we are so good with money. Our "darkness" may not show, and this ability to pass confers protection and a host of privileges. But we are the model money-grubbing money-hoarding scapegoats for an increasingly punitive economic system. Jews, Japanese, Koreans, Arabs, Indians, and Pakistanis—let's face it: *interlopers* are blamed for economic disaster; for controlling the economy or making money on the backs of the poor; for raising the price of oil; for stealing or eliminating jobs by importing goods or exporting production.

At the same time, those defined as inferior and violent are blamed for urban crime and chaos, for drugs, for the skyrocketing costs and failures of social programs. This blame then justifies the oppression and impoverishment of those brought here in chains and the peoples indigenous to this continent. Add in the darker, poorer immigrants from Latin America and the Caribbean, and recent immigrants from China and Southeast Asia. Media codes like "inner-city crime" and "teen gangs" distort and condense a vast canvas of poverty, vulnerability, and exploitation into an echoing story of some young men's violent response to these conditions. Thus those who are significantly endangered come to be defined as inherently dangerous.

That is, one group is blamed for capitalism's crimes; the other for capitalism's fallout. Do I need to point out who escapes all blame?

When a community is scapegoated, members of that community are most conscious of how they feel humiliated, alienated, and endangered. But the other function of scapegoating is at least as pernicious. It is to protect the problem which scapegoats are drafted to conceal: the vicious system of profit and exploitation, of plenty and scarcity existing side by side.

The Cost of Whiteness

Aryan ideology aside, Jews are often defined as white, though this wipes out the many Jews who are by anyone's definition people of color, and neglects the role of context: many Jews who look white in New York City look quite the opposite in the South and Midwest. Radicals often exclude the category *Jewish* from discussion, or subsume us into *white*, unless we are by *their* definition also people of color, in which case they subsume us as *people of color*.

The truth is, Jews complicate things. *Jewish* is both a distinct category and an overlapping one. Just as homophobia is distinct from sexism yet has everything to do with sexism, anti-Semitism in this country is distinct from racism yet has everything

to do with racism. It's not that a Jew like myself should "count" as a person of color, though I think sometimes Jews do argue this because the alternative seems to be erasure. But that means we need another alternative. The problem is a polarization of white and color that excludes us. We need a more complex vision of the structure of racism, one that attends to the sick logic of white supremacists. We need a more complex understanding of the process of "whitening."

> It is probable that it is the Jewish community—or more accurately, perhaps, its remnants—that in America has paid the highest and more extraordinary price for becoming white.

Every time I read this passage, at the word "remnants," my hand moves to the hollow at the base of my throat, to help me breathe. *Remnants.*

What have we paid?

How many of us speak or read Yiddish or Ladino or Hebrew? How many of us have studied Jewish history or literature, recognize the terms that describe Jewish experience, are familiar with the Jewish calendar, can sing more than three or four Jewish songs, know *something* beyond matzoh balls or stuffed grape leaves? Many of us—especially secular Jews, but also those raised in some suburban synagogues where spirituality took a back seat to capital construction, where Jewish pride seemed like another name for elitism—many of us have lost our culture, our sense of community. Only anti-Semitism reminds us who we are, and we have nothing to fight back with—no pride and no knowledge—only a feeble, embarrassed sense that hatred and bigotry are wrong. I have even heard Jews, especially, "progressives," justify anti-Semitism: maybe we really are "like that," rich and greedy, taking over, too loud, too pushy, snatching up more than our share, ugly and parasitical, Jewish American Princesses, Jewish landlords, Jewish bosses, emphasis on *Jewish*. Maybe we really deserve to be hated. . . .

Do we even know the history of which we, Jewish radicals, are a part? As Trotsky's master biographer Isaac Deutscher explained "the non-Jewish Jew" to the World Jewish Congress in 1958:

> The Jewish heretic who transcends Jewry belongs to a Jewish tradition. . . . Spinoza, Heine, Marx, Rosa Luxemburg, Trotsky, and

Freud . . . all went beyond the boundaries of Jewry. They all found Jewry too narrow, too archaic, and too constricting. . . . Yet I think that in some ways they were very Jewish indeed. . . . as Jews they dwelt on the border-lines of various civilizations, religions, and national cultures.[12]

. . . It is frustrating that those Jews best equipped to grasp what it means to choose *not to be white*—not to blend, pass, or mute one's differences—are the Hasidim (ultra-orthodox).[13] But because they are also separatist, and by ideology and theology do not value encounters with diversity, the Hasidim have rarely forged alliances around diversity and against bigotry. Instead, they tend to protect their individual communities and to blame urban chaos on their neighbors, often people of color, with law-and-order rhetoric and actions both racist and quin-tessentially American.[14]

The response of other Jews toward the Hasidim is instructive. Embarrassment, exposure, shame, rage; *why do they have to be so blatant?*—including *so blatantly Jewish* and *so blatantly racist*—as opposed to the discreet liberal norm of moving out of the neighborhood or sending the kids to private schools faintly integrated by race but starkly segregated by class. And somewhere, for Jews who care about Jewish identity, the Hasidim also represent a kind of courage: they dare to walk around look-ing Jewish.

Progressive Jews need to reconstruct an authenti-cally American progressive Jewish identity, choosing from the vast storehouse of history/culture/religion which pieces we want to reclaim, which will enable us to be out as Jews with our own brand of Jewish courage. It's not that most Jews in the U.S. will en-dure the same unsheddable visual vulnerability as most people of color, though buttons and t-shirts, the *kipah* (skullcap worn by observant men)) and the *magen david* (Star of David—"Jewish star") may draw us into street visibility. But Jews, like all other people, make political choices. With whose interests will we identify and stake our future? With the dominant and privileged few—white, Christian, and rich, ensuring that poverty remains part of the American landscape, leaving bigotry unchallenged, to feed on the local minority of choice?

. . . Many Jews who work against racism and on various progressive issues do this work as progres-sives, as women, as workers, as queers, as whites, as people of color. We are invisible *as Jews*, while Jewish political conservatives are highly visible. We relinquish to the Jewish right wing the claim to represent the Jewish community, though the sheer number of Jews involved with progressive politics is stunning. We abandon Jewish culture to the reli-gious orthodox: we think they are the "real Jews" and we are not. We neglect the powerful tradition of Jewish radicalism, a potential source of instruction, inspiration, and courage. Committed as progres-sives to the survival of people's culture, we stand, unseeing and uncaring, at the edge of a chasm opened by assimilation and infinitely deepened by the Holocaust. We facilitate the dwindling of the Jewish community—*to remnants.*

Is It Coming Again?

How can I concern myself with progressive coali-tions and alliances when everyone—including progressives—hates Jews? When I speak in the Jewish community, people say this to me all the time. And they have a point. Look at the July 1994 bomb-ing of the Jewish Community Center in Buenos Aires. The center had housed libraries, cemetery records, archives of 100 years of Yiddish theater, Yiddish newspapers, services of all kinds. Among the 95 killed, the hundreds wounded, were workers at the Center, students doing research in the library, and poor people in need of the services dispensed on Mondays, when the bombing took place. One of the oldest Jewish communities in South America was devastated. . . .

At a recent Jews for Racial and Economic Justice meeting, in a discussion which begins with the Buenos Aires bombing, we talk about how anti-Semitism is often used as a counterweight to pro-gressive values, and how this use makes it hard to establish or sometimes even to feel solidarity with other Jews. We are often so busy reminding the mainstream Jewish community that Palestinians are killed all the time. . . .

Several people note the difference between New York City and the rest of the country; here Jews are hardly a minority, and most benefit from the privileges of white skin, while "in the Diaspora" at least one person present has been confronted with the question, *where are your borns?* Another says, "People are always asking me, *what are you? They don't know I'm Jewish, but they know I'm something.*". . . Someone remarks that in the South and Northwest, Jews and people of color join to fight white supremacist groups as a matter of course. We agree that focusing on the seriousness and connectedness of right wing activity—racist, anti-Semitic, homophobic, and anti-abortion—helps us reach out to other Jews.

I am writing this at Rosh Hashonah, the Jewish New Year opening year 5755 of the Jewish calendar. We call the ten days following Rosh Hashonah *Yamim Noraim,* the Days of Awe, the most solemn time of our year, culminating in Yom Kippur, the Day of Atonement. If a Jew steps foot inside a synagogue once a year, Yom Kippur is the day. I am thinking about the danger, in this time of increased attacks on Jews, of stepping inside visibly Jewish spaces packed with Jews. At this time of heightened danger I feel intensely, paradoxically, the need to be among Jews in a Jewish space.

Elsewhere I have written, "to be a Jew is to tangle with history."[15] In the U.S. people tend to be both ahistorical and insulated from the impact of international events. From this tunnel perspective, Jews have it good. What are we worried about? And we *do* have it good. And we do worry. Jews have a history of nearly 6000 recorded years of repeated cycles of calm, then chaos: periods of relative safety and prosperity disrupted by persecution, brutal oppression, murder, and expulsion or exile for the surviving remnant to a strange land where the cycle begins again. Grace Paley reports her immigrant mother's succinct comment on Hitler's rise to power: "It's coming again."[16]

In the U.S. much of the bias against Jews has been mitigated by the development of some institutionalized Jewish power. This should be a cause for celebration. Instead it makes us nervous. Jewish success is often used against us, as evidence of our excessive control, power, and greed, evidence which could at any moment topple us from the calm and, for many Jews, prosperous phase of the cycle into danger and chaos.

Besides, Jewish success—like any other U.S. success—has been achieved inside a severe class structure, and Jews, like many other ethnic and racial minorities, have benefitted in concrete ways from racism against African Americans. Karen Sacks' brilliant investigation, "How Did Jews Become White Folks?" describes how "federal programs which were themselves designed to assist demobilized Gls and young families systematically discriminated against African Americans," and functioned as "affirmative action . . . [which] aimed at and disproportionately helped male, Euro-origin Gls."[17] Thus she convincingly explains post-World War II Jewish upward mobility.

History. In 1492 the Inquisition forced thousands of us to convert to Christianity or flee Spain and Portugal. Some of us ended up in the Americas and were forced to convert anyway. But many of us maintained our Jewishness secretly. . . .

Passing. I get to choose when to disclose I'm a Jew. It doesn't show, at least not blatantly or automatically. If I need to, I can hide. Clearly, this applies to some Jews and not others, a benefit something like that "enjoyed" by the conventionally feminine-looking lesbian vis-à-vis the stone butch; or by the lighter skin, English-speaking Chicana. In other words, Jews benefit from not looking Jewish.[18] That many Jews walk safely down the streets of North America because our Jewishness is not visible is a fact, but not necessarily a comforting one. Many of us would prefer to be both visible and safe. Sometimes it's hard to find each other (why confirmed atheists like me, when we live rurally or outside large Jewish communities—join synagogues; how else would we find the Jews?). Passing/invisibility has a double edge.

Yet any time I feel whiny about passing's double edge, I picture myself in a car, any car, with a cop pulling up alongside. I think of all the times I didn't get followed around stores with someone assuming I was about to rip them off, even when I *was* about to rip them off.

I also think of my father changing his name from Kantrowitz to Kaye before I was born, pressured by the exigencies of being a Jew in the forties, even in New York. "It was easier," he'd explain, "people always called me Mr. K. anyway, they couldn't pronounce or remember it." (But when have you heard of a Gloucester, a Leicester, a McLoughlin changing his name?) When he died, in 1982, I took back Kantrowitz. I just didn't like the name going out of the world, and a certain incident weighed on me: a white gentile lesbian who knew my writing exclaimed upon meeting me, "Oh! I expected you to be tall and blond." I knew if my name were Melanie Kantrowitz, no one would ever expect me to be tall and blond.

But I have recognized in some situations exactly how I need to stiffen my spine to say (and then spell, though it is perfectly phonetic) *Kantrowitz. Kantrowitz. Kantrowitz.* And sometimes when I just don't have the *koyekh* (strength), I say *Kaye*, and feel grimly close to my dead ghetto-raised father.

To Discover Water

My father. *My father loved all things Jewish,* I wrote after he died in a poem I called *Kaddish,* which is the Jewish prayer for the dead.[19] My father who changed his name. My father *who loved the sound of Yiddish but would not speak it.* And my mother: hates bagels, hates matzoh balls, never went to *shul,* is careful to distinguish herself from *those others,* has spent her lifetime hating her nose, her Jewish nose. Yet says, repeatedly, *scratch a goy* (non-Jew) *you'll find an anti-Semite.*

My grandparents immigrated from Russia and Poland early in this century. My father, a teenager in Brownsville (a poor Jewish ghetto in Brooklyn) during the Depression, joined the Young Communist League; as an adult his major hero remained his friend Aaron, a communist who had spoken on street corners and died fighting in the second World War. My mother had circulated petitions against the Korean War, walking up to people on the streets of Flatbush during peak McCarthy period, and she had been spat on.

. . . This was my Jewish upbringing, as much as the candles we lit for Hanukkah, or the seders where bread and matzoh shared the table. My father had been raised observant, my mother, not. But to us breaking religious observance was progressive, the opposite of superstitious. When we ate on Yom Kippur, it never occurred to me that this was un-Jewish. I knew I was a Jew. I knew Hitler had been evil. I knew Negroes—we said then—had been slaves and that was evil too. I knew prejudice was wrong, stupid. I knew Jews believed in freedom and justice (the screaming arguments at extended family gatherings never challenged my belief that we, the un-prejudiced, were the "real" Jews). My parents' attachment to Adlai Stevenson was such that I grew up sort of assuming he was Jewish,

while a photograph of FDR hung on our living room wall, surrounded by reverence, god in modern drag. When Eisenhower-Nixon ran against Stevenson in 1952, I noticed Nixon's dark, wavy hair, like my father's, and said, "He looks like Daddy." "Nothing like him, *nothing,* how could you think such a thing," my mother snapped. She then explained in detail how Nixon got elected to congress only by redbaiting Helen Gahagan Douglas (the liberal Congresswoman). I was seven years old.

I remember my mother crying when the Rosenbergs were executed, and I was terrified, because I knew they were good people, like my parents, with children the same age as my sister and me. *Who would take care of their children?* Soon we would get our first TV, so my mother (and I) could watch the McCarthy hearings. I knew the whole fate of humanity hinged on these hearings, as surely as I knew McCarthy and his people had killed the Rosenbergs. It literally did not occur to me that real people, people I might meet, people who had children and went to work, hated the Rosenbergs or liked McCarthy. Not did it occur to me that there were people who thought unions were bad, people who did not know you never cross a picket line, did not know prejudice was wrong and stupid. I could not even conceive of someone voting for Eisenhower: *how had he won?*

That this set of principles was Jewish never occurred to me. Around me was Flatbush, a swirling Jewish ghetto/community of first and second generation immigrants, including Holocaust survivors; . . . there were clerks, trade unionists, salespeople, plumbers, small business people, radio and TV repairmen, people like my parents (small shopkeepers) "in the middle," apartment dwellers where the kids shared a room, and fathers worked 60–70 hours a week; and people poorer than us, who lived in apartments where kitchen smells lingered on the stairs, someone slept in the living room, and summers the kids swam in underwear instead of bathing suits. There were teachers and even doctors who were rich and lived in what we called "private houses" in the outreaches of the neighborhood at the point where not everyone was Jewish.

But where I lived, everyone was, or almost. Jewish was the air I breathed, nothing I articulated, everything I took for granted.

Not-Jewish meant, for the most part, Catholic. Catholics were plentiful and scary: if you married them they would demand your children, and the pope could tell you what not to read. My high school, Erasmus Hall, the oldest and largest in the country, in theory integrated, was so severely tracked that the mostly Jews, Italians, and African Americans who attended rarely had classes together. As for WASPs, I knew they were the majority somewhere, but where? I knew *Jones* and *Smith* were someone's idea of an ordinary dime-a-dozen name, but I never met one: my idea of the commonest name on earth was *Susan Goldberg*.

I was 17 and a high school graduate before I met privileged WASPs, and that was in the Civil Rights Movement in Harlem. Before Harlem, I barely thought consciously about either whiteness or Jewishness (though I straightened my hair and performed unspeakable obscenities on my eyebrows). In Harlem the world divided up into white and black and there was no question what I was. I barely registered the large proportion of Jews among white people working in the Civil Rights Movement.[20] Nor in years of activism on the left did I note the extent of Jewish participation as something to take pride in, or understand that my rebellion against traditionalism had been enacted simultaneously by thousands of young Jews. Not until the early seventies when I moved to Oregon and encountered white Christian anti-Semites, did I even understand that to them I was not white: I was a Jew.

In 1972, I had just moved to Portland, Oregon, and was attending a feminist conference, talking with a woman while we waited for the elevator. I have forgotten the context for what she said: that she did not like Jews. Jews were loud and pushy and aggressive. This was the first time I had heard someone say this outright. I was stunned, didn't know what to say—"no, they're not?"—and I couldn't believe she didn't know that I was Jewish. My voice came out loud and flat: "I'm Jewish." To this day I can't remember how she responded or what I did next.

In Portland, I heard for the first time the habitual use of *Christian* interchangeably with *virtuous: Act like a Christian.* Even among leftists, it was tricky: liberation theology was sometimes a contemporary version of *Christian* equals *good*. As for feminists, the one thing they knew about Jews was that Jewish men thank god every morning for not

making them a woman (this prayer exists, but is hardly a core ritual). . . .

And *my* Jewishness? I had never articulated it. I began to think about it.

That first year in Portland, I read Hannah Arendt's *Eichmann in Jerusalem,* and realized something I had somehow up to this point managed not to notice: I would have been killed. My family, everyone I grew up around, practically, would have been killed. Random family tidbits clicked into place: my grandparents' families *had* been killed. . . .

What is clear is this: the more outside of a Jewish ambience I was, the more conscious I became of Jewishness. Like Marshall McLuhan's perhaps apocryphal remark: *I don't know who discovered water, but I'm sure it wasn't a fish.* Inside a Jewish environment, where I could take for granted a somewhat shared culture, an expectation about Jewsih survival, where my body type and appearance were familiar, my voice ordinary, my laughter not too loud but hearty and normal, above all, normal . . . in this environment, I did not know what it meant to be a Jew, only what it meant to be a *mentsh*. I did not know that *mentsh* was a Jewish word in a Jewish language.

To Create Solidarity

The more conscious I became, the more I thought and talked and came to write about it and act visibly and politically as a Jew, the more I encountered both blankness and kinship, anti-Semitism and solidarity—the more I came to locate myself in a tradition of Jewish women.

Initially I felt most connected to women like myself, with thick dark eyebrows, sturdy legs, full mouths, big teeth, wild hair, skin full of oil glands for the desert. Secular, Ashkenazi, from Eastern Europe. English modelled on Yiddish inflection. Laughter explosive and frequent. We interrupt. We argue. We take for granted that the work of this lifetime is to seek justice; that if you're not a *mentsh,* you're a *shanda* (shame).

Emma Goldman lectured frequently in Yiddish. Clara Lemlich, at sixteen, cut short the speechifying at the famous Cooper Union garment workers meeting by calling for a strike vote (it passed). Rose Schneiderman first spoke the demand for bread *and* roses adopted by second wave feminism (could feminists have noticed *this* as Jewish, along with that obscure prayer?). Pauline Newman, Mary Dreier, Lillian Wald were open lesbians and important labor activists and social reform advocates. Anzia Yezierska wrote in Yiddish-inflected English about the struggles of immigrant women for education, independence and love. Lil Moed and Naomi Kies devoted their lives to the struggle for Palestinian rights and peace between Israel and Palestine. Grace Paley and Vera Williams create wildly original stories and continue to slog along in the trenches of social justice.[21]

But the list goes on, to encompass the women *not* "like me"—rabbis and theologians whose critiques of traditional Judaism, or fights to include women in a transformed Judaism, have made it possible for a secularist like myself to go to *shul*. Scholars Judith Plaskow and Susannah Heschel demand the presence of women in the Jewish religion. Rabbi Julie Greenberg reinterprets Jewish practice and, as a single mother and a lesbian, raises her three joyfully-chosen children. Rabbi Susan Talve leads her St. Louis congregation into justice-seeking partnership with an African American church. Poet/translator Marcia Falk creates highly evolved feminist blessings and prayers, using traditional imagery but taking back the source of divinity, the power to bless.[22]

. . . And what is this new Jewish tradition we are creating and which, in turn, creates us? I once heard Judith Plaskow respond to someone's discomfort with new prayers reformed to eliminate male god language—"Those aren't the prayers I grew up with," the woman said, "I don't feel comfortable with them." And Plaskow responded, "We're not the generation that gets to feel comfortable. We're the generation that gets to create a tradition so the next generation grows up in it, and for them it will be the authentic tradition, and they will feel comfortable." No, we are not the generation that gets to feel comfortable. But we are the generation that sometimes gets to feel whole.

On the evening of Election Day, 1992, I was driving down from Seattle to Portland, Oregon, where Measure 9, the most vitriolic of the homophobic hate measures, was on the ballot. Measure 9 would have sanctioned discrimination explicitly and violence implicitly; would have banned from public libraries and schools books that deal positively with gay and lesbian experience; would have

blocked funding of any public institutions that aided gays and lesbians—for example, AIDS counselling.

. . . As I pulled into my friend's neighborhood, Northeast Portland, a neighborhood mixed by income and by race—not especially gay—I saw signs on every lawn—NO ON 9. I started to cry, and I realized I had no concept of allies. Even though the friend I was going to stay with was heterosexual, and I knew she'd been working very hard on this issue, I had still somewhere assumed that no one would stand with us—that we would be fighting alone. And I knew this came from my history as a Jew.

I had heard about the escalation of violence against Oregon lesbians and gays. But I still was not prepared for what I found. I saw antigay propaganda that copied actual Nazi cartoons which showed Jews controlling the economy, substituting gays instead. Powell's Bookstore, which had been featuring displays of books endangered by 9, had received bomb threats, as had individuals working against 9. House and car windows had been smashed, cars tampered with. Physical attacks on lesbians and gays had skyrocketed, and in Salem a black lesbian and a white gay man had been murdered. . . .

I heard bits and pieces of this struggle: how some people in Portland or Salem didn't want to bother organizing rurally, how some white people did not understand the need to build coalitions with communities of color. Yet despite some reluctance and ignorance, a vast broad coalition was created. People told me not about the ease of creating this coalition but about the clarity and desperation and drive. . . . Out of something ugly and outrageous has come something astonishing and inspiring, a model for the rest of the country, for the continued struggle against hatred—for survival.

A model for Jews as well. Oregon's Jews stood unanimously against Measure 9: every synagogue, every community organization and institution, every rabbi. . . . Here is an excerpt from the Oregon Jews' statement, deeply informed by Jewish history, and by Jewish recognition of the intolerably high cost and inevitable slippage of any safety based on "whiteness":

[The Holocaust] began with laws exactly like Ballot Measure 9. Those laws first declared groups of people to be sub-human, then legalized and finally mandated discrimination against them. Comparisons to the Holocaust must be limited. But clearly, this is the start of hatred and persecution that must stop now.

At the victory rally the night after the election, all the coalition partners spoke to celebrate, warn, rage, and comfort. There were representatives from the Jewish community, African American community, Native American community, labor. . . . Two voices especially stand out in my memory. One was a Chicano organizer from the Farmworkers Union, who said, "In this, we were there for you. Now we're organizing our strike, and I need to ask you to be there for us." The other voice was a white lesbian activist, who answered the farmworker: *"Su lucha es mi lucha." Your struggle is my struggle.*

I may be secular, but I know holiness when I hear it. One of its names is solidarity, the opposite of "whiteness." The more you claim it, honor it, and fight for it, the less it costs.

NOTES

I thank Esther Kaplan, Roni Natov, and Nancy Ordover for substantial critical feedback. Sections of this essay are drawn from earlier writings published in *The Issue Is Power: Essays on Women, Jews, Violence and Resistance* (San Francisco: Aunt Lute, 1992).

1. "On Being 'White'. . . and Other Lies," *Essence* (April, 1984).

2. On the other hand, Karen Sacks, "How Did Jews Become White Folks?" in *Race,* eds., Steven Gregory and Roger Sanjek (New Brunswick: Rutgers University Press, 1994), points to "a 1987 Supreme Court ruling that Jews and Arabs could use civil rights laws to gain redress for discrimination against them . . . on the grounds that they are not racial whites."

3. *Ashkenazi* comes from the word for Germany; *Sephardi,* from Spain.

4. For Sephardi in the former Ottoman Empire, see Interview with Chaya Shalom in *The Tribe of Dina: A Jewish Women's Anthology,* eds., Melanie Kaye/Kantrowitz and Irena Klepfisz (Boston: Beacon Press, 1989: 1st pub., *Sinister Wisdom,* 1986), pp. 214–226.

5. Nancy Ordover, oral critique, December, 1994.

6. See Aisha Berger's poem, "Nose is a country . . . I am the second generation," in *The Tribe of Dina.* pp. 134–138. One of Berger's many illuminating images: "this unruly semitic landmass on my face." The era of Jewish nose jobs is not over, though Barbra Streisand broke the spell that mirrored Jewish noses as inherently ugly.

7. First expressed by Moses Mendelssohn (1729–86), the central figure in the German Jewish *Haskalah* (Enlightenment), as the ideal of Jewish assimilation.

8. One is, however, hard put to be a Jew without Jewish community. Even in religious practice, the unit of prayer is not the individual but the *minyan,* at least ten adult Jews, the Jewish quorum—in Orthodox Judaism, ten men.

9. There is painful irony in the fact that Yiddish, the beloved *mame-losbn* of Jewish socialists, is dwindling to a living language only for the ultra-orthodox Hasidim.

10. In this discussion I am indebted to Nancy Ordover, "Visibility, Alliance, and the Practice of Memory." *Socialist Review.* 25, no. 1 (1995): 119–134.

11. Ruth Frankenberg's *White Women/Race Matters* (Minneapolis: University of Minnesota, 1993) offers useful insight on whiteness as an unmarked racial category. But Frankenberg misses opportunities to note the significance of *Jewish* as a category, although she and a disproportionate number of the white anti-racist activists she interviewed are Jews.

12. Isaac Deutscher, "The Non-Jewish Jew," in *The Non-Jewish Jew and Other Essays* (London: Oxford University Press, 1968). pp. 26–27.

13. In appearance, immediately identifiable as Jews because of distinct dress (black hats and coats for the men, arms and legs fully covered for the women) and hair (*peyes*—unshorn sideburns—for the men; hair cropped and covered by a *sheytl*—wig—or headscarf for the women), the Hasidim are magnets for anti-Semitism. Similarly, anti-Semitic graffiti, vandalism, and bombing of synagogues demonstrate that identifiable Jewish places are also vulnerable.

14. Though the Hasidim are vulnerable as individuals to acts of bigotry and violence, in New York City the Hasidic communities (Lubovitcher, in Crown Heights, and Satmar, in Williamsburg) wield influence. This is not a function of numbers; the Hasidim comprise a tiny percent of the world's Jews. Nor is it a function of wealth; indeed, a great many families in the Hasidic communities are poor, partly due to family size (as in all fundamentalist religions, the use of birth control is prohibited). Hasidic influence is a function of social organization: Hasidic leaders can deliver votes in an election and bodies in a demonstration. . . . Here is a lesson for progressive Jews about the need for *progressive* Jewish visibility and organization.

15. In "The Issue Is Power: Some Notes on Jewish Women and Therapy," *The Issue Is Power: Essays on Women, Jews, Violence and Resistance* (San Francisco: Aunt Lute, 1992).

16. Grace Paley, "Now and Then." *Tikkun* (May/June 1989), p. 76. In particular, European medieval and Renaissance history from a Jewish perspective reads like a disaster chronicle: expelled from here, massacred there, forced conversions someplace else. Occasionally there is a bright spot: "Jews return to Worms" (from which they had been expelled the year before); "Jews allowed to

settle in England" (from which they had been expelled some centuries earlier). The late nineteenth and early twentieth century, especially in Eastern Europe, presents a similar wave of persecution, dwarfed only by the magnitude of what followed. Grievous official and unofficial oppression of Jews was a common feature of modern pre-Holocaust Europe.

17. Karen Sacks, in *Race*, eds. Steven Gregory and Roger Sanjek.

18. Jews who could pass as gentile, because they looked less Jewish and could speak the dominant language fluently, were more likely to survive the various swings of anti-Semitism. Thus to tell a survivor of the European Holocaust "you don't look Jewish" is to probe a painful truth—had the person looked more Jewish, s/he would probably be dead.

19. "Kaddish," in *Nice Jewish Girls: A Lesbian Anthology*, ed., Evelyn Torton Beck (Boston: Beacon Press, 1989), pp. 107–11; first published in *Sinister Wisdom* 25 (1984).

20. See Melanie Kaye/Kantrowitz, "Stayed on Freedom: Memories of a Jew in the Civil Rights Movement." in *Narrow Bridge: Jews and Multiculturalism*, ed. Maria Brettschneider (New Brunswick: Rutgers, University Press, 1996).

21. See *The Tribe of Dina*, tribute to Naomi Kies: interviews with Lil Moed and Grace Paley.

22. Judith Plaskow, *Standing Again At Sinai* (San Francisco: HarperSanFrancisco, 1990); Susannah Heschel, *On Being a Jewish Feminist* (New York: Schocken, 1983); Marcia Falk, *The Book of Blessings: Re-Creation of Jewish Prayer* (San Francisco: HarperSanFrancisco, 1994); for Julie Greenberg, "Seeking a Feminist Judaism," and Susan Talve, "Sarika." see *The Tribe of Dina*.

T W E L V E

◆◆◆

Hanaan's House (2005)

Amani Elkassabani

Egyptian-born **Amani Elkassabani** is a high school literature and composition teacher in Maryland. An award-winning writer of short fiction and creative prose, she is a member of the International Women's Writing Guild and the Radius of Arab Women Writers and Friends.

It was the American dream and it was coming true for Hanaan. "We bought a house," she told Maha that afternoon when the two of them met to shop at the Arabic grocery store near their apartment building. Maha congratulated her friend, kissing her once on each cheek, and Hanaan could smell the pungent aroma so distinctive of the mastic gum Maha chewed between meals.

"*Mabruk*!" said Maha. "Where is it?"

"Twenty minutes from D.C.," said Hanaan, her hazel eyes and honey complexion set off by her black headscarf. She had a fleshy nose and cheeks that took the shape of apricots when she smiled. Those who knew her described her as having a baby face, and those who met her for the first time expressed disbelief that she was married and had a child. Hanaan hadn't worked since

Dina, now five years old, was born; but her husband Hisham had secured a job with a law firm in northwest Washington. They had looked for a place close to the District to cut Hisham's commute and they did not want to leave Maryland where Hanaan had grown up, so rather than settle, as many of her friends had, in the predominantly Arab neighborhoods of northern Virginia or the Pakistani community to the northeast of Washington, they bought a house in one of the Maryland suburbs west of the District. "In Brentwood Park," continued Hanaan.

Maha had removed the cellophane from an amber square of mastic gum and popped it in her mouth. Hanaan had always found the gum too bitter for her liking. "You're not serious," said Maha.

Hanaan nodded. "You should see the house. It's got a garage and four bedrooms. It even has a decent sized-backyard."

Maha's brown eyes widened and the smile faded from her lips. "But Brentwood Park? Why *there*?"

"It's not just the house. The schools there are the best and you know Dina's starting kindergarten in the fall. Besides, it's a very safe neighborhood."

"Safe? For who? Muslims? Have you forgotten what happened to Dar-ul-Huda?" It was Maha's habit to ask a series of questions when she wanted to make a point. Her last question awakened a vivid memory of the day the two women, along with several of their neighbors, removed garbage that had been strewn across the lawn of the mosque near their apartment building and cleaned animal feces and rotten eggs from its doors and windows. It had taken longer to replant the azalea bushes that had been uprooted and to remove the words *DIRTY ARABS* and *MUSLIMS WILL DIE* that had been spray-painted across the white cinderblock of the mosque's entrance. And only weeks later did Hanaan feel comfortable enough to wear a scarf again in public instead of the beret she had used to cover her long black hair after the 9/11 attackers were described in newspapers and on television as Muslim extremists.

"I remember. I thought about it every time we looked for a house out there," replied Hanaan.

"And what about now? What they're doing. Taking away our rights, treating our men like criminals." Hanaan had heard Hisham talk about a new law that would require males from Muslim countries to be questioned and fingerprinted; she knew that Maha feared for her cousin, whose legal status was in jeopardy.

"Maha, the people in Brentwood Park are just people. They didn't attack our mosque; they didn't pass that law."

"It's enough that they send money to Israel." Maha pointed to Hanaan's scarf and continued, "Then they see you dressed like that, and they think you're a terrorist. They'll watch you all the time."

"Maha, I'm not trying to prove anything to anybody. I found a house I liked and bought it. We move next week."

Maha eyed the cans of fava beans and the large jar of sesame paste Hanaan had put in her shopping basket. "You'd better stock up," she told Hanaan, placing a bag of pita bread in Hanaan's basket. "The stores out there probably only sell bagels."

When Hanaan returned to her apartment, she found a note saying that Hisham had taken Dina to the playground. It was a warm day in May and earlier that morning Hisham had promised Hanaan time alone so that she could finish packing. She sorted through the magazines on her bookshelf, de-

ciding which, if any, were worth keeping. She leafed through an old issue of *Aramco World* that featured an article about the rise of Islam accompanied by a map of the Middle East. As she studied the arrows originating in Arabia and traveling across North Africa and Asia, she remembered seeing a similar map in her fifth-grade history book. On the facing page of her book was an account of Muhammad's political and religious life, including a paragraph that described how he had murdered hundreds of Jewish men and enslaved their women and children after the Battle of the Trench. She remembered showing it to her father, who had said the story left out that those Jews had betrayed Muhammad and that the book was probably written by Jews to make people hate Muslims. It wasn't until later that Hanaan began to understand how people she had never met could hate her because of who she was. The next year, when her class read *The Diary of Anne Frank,* her father said that Hanaan was only learning one side of a much bigger story. "Do you know what the Jews did to Palestinians?" he had asked her. Without waiting for an answer, he explained that Palestinian men and women were dragged into the street in the middle of the night, forced to watch their homes reduced to rubble, and sent to live in refugee camps. "The Jews," he had said, "wanted to take our land too."

In June of 1967, war broke out between Egypt and Israel. Hanaan's parents fled Ismailia with their infant daughter and drove into the Western Desert, where they stayed with Hanaan's grandparents until they could return home. The cease-fire did not end the tensions between the two countries and the next year, Hanaan's parents left Egypt. When she got older, Hanaan learned how her mother had fed Hanaan in the dark in the midst of the shelling that shook the ground like an earthquake and rocked her to sleep as explosions lit up the sky like fireworks. They were not, said her mother, the same kind of fireworks that had lit up the sky fifteen years before when Egypt was liberated from British rule. That was a time to rejoice, said her mother. The 1967 War was a time to mourn. They had come to America in search of a better life—leaving behind their apartment, personal things, friends and family—but they took with them their sympathy for the many who were suffering and their contempt for those who had made them suffer. Years later her parents shook their heads in disbelief when they saw men who had once been enemies grasp hands as friends. It did not matter, her father said, that a treaty declared peace between Egypt and Israel. Zionist Jews wanted only one thing: to confiscate the lands of neighboring Arab countries. It wouldn't be long before they tried to take Egypt again.

As Hanaan grew older, she found logical reasons to reject much of what her parents taught her, but she never completely forgot it. She had experienced moments of doubt about moving into an area with such a high Jewish population. She was feeling it now as she sat on the floor, magazine in hand, fingers tracing the outline of a place that seemed to exist within her. At this precise moment, she thought, a woman who dressed like her and spoke her language and touched her forehead to the floor when she prayed was mourning the loss of a son or a brother who had fought to regain his home. She felt at once guilty and grateful that she possessed a home of her own in Brentwood Park. Grateful won out, so she set the magazine in a box with others she would take with her and continued packing until the phone rang.

It was Maha calling to ask Hisham for legal advice about Maha's cousin. Apparently, Maha's cousin had decided to evade the Immigration and Naturalization Service, which had set a deadline for foreign nationals of Egypt, as well as 24 other predominantly Muslim countries to register their status with the U.S. government. Three years ago, Maha's cousin had entered the U.S. legally, but he had since overstayed his visa, deciding to risk deportation rather than return home to an uncertain future. Somehow, he had obtained a social security card, found work, and now he was a tax-paying member of society with a permanent residency application pending. Massive backlogs had delayed the processing of his paperwork, and until he got his green card, he faced the daily threat of being sent back to Egypt, especially if he were to appear before an INS judge. Hanaan told Maha not to worry, that she'd talk to Hisham and call her back.

Later that evening, Hisham furrowed his brow and smoothed down his black mustache as Hanaan retold the story of Maha's cousin. "If he doesn't register," Hisham finally said, "he'll probably get deported anyway." He sighed and dialed Maha's number. "Tell him to go in," he advised her, saying that obeying the law might gain him favor with the judge and that he could not be deported without a hearing. After Hisham hung up the phone, he turned to Hanaan and said, "Guys like him aren't who they want. How many terrorists are going to waltz into a government office and let themselves be questioned and fingerprinted?"

On the last Saturday in May, Hanaan and Hisham met the movers in Brentwood Park and carefully presided over the unloading of their belongings. Dina had spent the night with Hanaan's parents, who had offered to bring their granddaughter in from Baltimore the next day along with some things Hanaan didn't want to surrender to the movers. The house sat on a quiet cul-de-sac. It was a two-story brick colonial with a modest yard and flowerbeds along the front walkway. The backyard, level with few trees, was enclosed by a low fence. Beyond the fence, along a row of cypress trees, ran a narrow sidewalk that led into a clearing where Hanaan could see playground equipment.

At first Hanaan had been elated, thinking how lucky she was to live near a park. But then the realtor told her the equipment belonged to a synagogue and, for a moment, Hanaan had felt strangely out of place. The house had appealed to her for reasons she could not logically explain. Maybe it was the way the sunlight poured into the kitchen from a skylight or perhaps it was her visions of family gathered in the dining room. She imagined a glow and crackle in the fireplace on cold winter nights and pictured Dina sitting in her lap as she read her a book in the family room. Her parents, who would finally have their own room if they chose to visit, would disapprove, she thought. Maha, who had once criticized Hanaan for buying lingerie made in Israel and cautioned her against befriending Jews, would not understand. But it was she—not her parents, not Maha—who would inhabit the house. And neither the synagogue next door nor the catechisms vilifying Jews she had learned as a child seemed like good enough reasons to abandon the dream of owning the home she had fallen in love with. Not even the memory of foul words spray-painted on her mosque or the pictures in yesterday's *Washington Post* of Arab men lined up outside an INS building were powerful enough to destroy her faith in the American dream.

Hanaan unpacked the last of the boxes marked FRAGILE and stacked dishes in one of the many cherry cabinets that lined the wall of her kitchen.

Kicking aside the crumpled newspaper that littered the floor, she made her way to the center of the kitchen where she could better survey the contents of her cupboards and drawers. She was not entirely satisfied with the placement of her coffee mugs, which she had moved twice that morning already. She arranged her things by trial and error. Occasionally, her pots and pans and towels and linens fell into their cupboards and closets so naturally that she thought she had a knack for settling in. But now, thought Hanaan, it was no use to rearrange the mugs. Eventually all her things would find their proper places. So instead of emptying the cupboard completely and starting over, she took the mug she had gotten as a souvenir when she visited New York on a college trip, placed a tea bag inside it, and put a kettle of water on the stove. She hadn't used the mug in months and examined, as if for the first time, a series of painted vignettes of the city that decorated the outside of the mug. The vignettes included the Empire State Building, Times Square, and the Statue of Liberty. When she saw the twin towers in a World Trade Center vignette, Hanaan shuddered and set the mug down on the counter. Suddenly, she didn't feel like having tea anymore.

She gazed out a window at her backyard and visualized the flowerbeds of pansies and marigolds she would put in. Maybe she'd even plant a small vegetable garden in the corner that got good sunlight. She pulled on a plum-colored scarf and a loose-fitting button down shirt that extended well beyond the seat of her blue jeans and went to get a closer look at the yard. With arms crossed, she trotted barefoot out toward the fence and at the same time a procession of couples coming from the synagogue ambled down the sidewalk, returning, she guessed, from Saturday services. She glanced from the grass to the people passing by and back again, trying not to stare, not to scrutinize them even though she wanted to look directly at their faces, hoping to catch a glimpse of something she could point to that made them alien to her, something concrete that would justify Maha's warning to stay away from them. The women wore formal dresses and hats, making it difficult to see their faces. A few of them wore gloves, and Hanaan thought of her own mother, who not only wore gloves, but also covered her face, whenever she left the house. The men she saw

wore suits and yarmulkes, mostly black. The boys and young men wore multi-colored ones and held them in place with silver barrettes. Again, she thought of her father, whom she couldn't remember seeing without a skullcap over his graying hair. Some couples were pushing infants in strollers, others held their toddlers' hands as they proceeded along the sidewalk just beyond her backyard. Most of the passersby conversed with each other, some looked straight ahead, a few looked in her direction and were expressionless; one woman smiled, and Hanaan smiled back.

She must have counted seven or eight families by the time the stream of worshippers tapered off and she had gone back into the kitchen. Her new neighbors, she thought, and suddenly she missed Maha and the smell of mastic gum on her breath. She searched for the tin Maha had given her as she was packing and found it buried in her pantry behind some boxes of instant pudding. Hanaan unwrapped a piece of gum, put it into her mouth, and let the saliva soften it before she started chewing. The medicinal juices washed over her tongue and for the first time she resisted the urge to spit out the gum. Putting her things in their proper places suddenly seemed much easier than making a place for herself in Brentwood Park.

By the time the doorbell rang that afternoon, Hanaan had cleared the newspaper from the kitchen floor. Maybe Hisham, who had gone to pick up some picture hanging nails from the hardware store, forgot his key, she thought as she opened the front door. A woman Hanaan did not recognize stood holding a covered dish. She had a fair complexion and blue eyes and Hanaan could see just the ends of her blond curls beneath the blue bandana she had tied around her hair. She wore a blue tank top, denim shorts, and brown sandals. Hanaan stepped back and quietly studied the woman's face, listening as the woman said she lived two doors down. "I saw your moving van this morning and I wanted to welcome you," she said.

Hanaan hesitated. The woman cleared her throat and Hanaan thought she had better say something to break the silence. "I'm sorry. I wasn't expecting anybody."

"I can come back later," said the woman, turning to leave. Hanaan did not know what to say next; she only knew she did not want the woman to go away.

"No, it's okay," said Hanaan, smiling. "Besides, I need an excuse to take a break."

"I'm Karen Sultan and this is Joel." She put one hand on the shoulder of the boy clinging to her leg and Hanaan noticed that, unlike his mother, he had brown eyes fringed with long black lashes.

"Hanaan Zakariah. Please, come in." The two women walked into the kitchen and Karen set the dish on the counter. Hanaan recalled the day she had moved into Maha's neighborhood. Maha's mother had brought over a tray of stuffed cabbage leaves and a roasted chicken when she introduced herself to Hanaan's mother. Maha had come too and given Hanaan three small pieces of chocolate wrapped in silver foil. The two of them ran into Hanaan's room and rummaged through the half-empty boxes looking for toys to play with while Maha's mother helped Hanaan's mother unpack.

"You really didn't have to bring anything," said Hanaan.

"I just brought a little of what I had."

Hanaan could see a mound of yellowish grain-like pasta mixed with pieces of chicken, carrots, and zucchini through the glass lid. "You just happened to have couscous?" she asked.

"We have it every Saturday after services. David loves it and it's the one thing I learned to make from scratch when we were engaged."

Hanaan pictured the boxes of dried couscous she picked up from the Arab grocery and imagined Karen pushing pasta dough through a sieve. "You *make* your own couscous."

"Only when David's mother comes over." They laughed. "It's still the best way to impress her." She gestured toward the dish. "This came out of a box."

"Mine does too," chuckled Hanaan.

Karen asked where Hanaan was from and Hanaan told her that her parents had emigrated from Egypt, but she had grown up in Baltimore. Karen exclaimed that she and David were married in Rabat and spent their honeymoon in Sharm el-Shaikh. "It's where I got this," she said, holding up a gold cartouche bearing a column of hieroglyphs.

Hanaan saw that Joel was still clinging to Karen's leg. "I have a daughter about your age," she said.

Karen beamed and said, "Hear that, Joel? You'll finally have someone to play with!" Hanaan saw Joel grin even as he hid his face in his mother's shorts. Karen explained that her older daughter Jenny had a best friend named Sarah

who lived next door, but most of the neighborhood children were either too young or too old to make good playmates for Joel. "We'll have to get the kids together once you're moved in," said Karen. Hanaan agreed.

Hisham returned from the hardware store and saw two plates of vegetable couscous with chicken on the table. When Hanaan told him that a neighbor brought it over, he said, "And you were worried you wouldn't find a friend out here."

"We're hardly friends. She does have a son Dina's age and an older daughter. She seems nice enough."

The evening, Hanaan got a call from Maha. Her cousin had gone to Annapolis to register with the INS but didn't come home. The judge had ordered him detained and set a July date for the deportation hearing. "It was awful, the way they shackled his feet and hands and led him off to jail," said Maha between sobs. Hanaan tried to console her, and she composed herself long enough to ask, "How can they do this to him? Treat him like a criminal when all he was doing was obey the law? What about his rights? What about his freedom?" Hanaan admitted that the whole thing was horrible, and stayed on the line until she was sure Maha had stopped crying.

The next morning, Hanaan's parents pulled into the driveway, and Dina, full of energy, was the first to emerge from the car. Her auburn curls were tied back into a neat ponytail with a pink ribbon that matched her pink shorts and t-shirt. Hanaan squatted to hug Dina then stood up holding her, planting kisses on her cheeks. Hisham, who had come out to meet them, gathered Dina in his arms and Hanaan embraced her parents. They lingered in the yard and three boys who had been tossing a football in a neighboring yard paused to look at them. Hanaan was sure they had seen her in her headscarf earlier that day; she had been hauling empty boxes to the curb when her parents drove up. The boys had continued tossing the football as Hanaan made half a dozen trips to the curb. But perhaps seeing a man wearing a long garment and a woman with her face covered surprised them. It wasn't their stares that bothered Hanaan. She got them often enough, especially after last September when she ventured out. What bothered her was that the stares now came from people in her neighborhood and she felt uncomfortable in her own front yard. "Let's go inside," said Hanaan.

After she gave her parents a tour of the house, Hanaan could see that her parents were happy for her. "There are so many Jews," said her father. "We drove by three synagogues on the way here."

"There were Jews in Baltimore too," said Hanaan.

"But we didn't live next door to them."

"Baba, this place has everything we wanted and it's so close to Hisham's office. The realtor told us the schools were excellent. And, Mama, look at the backyard. I can finally have a garden."

"There's a synagogue in your backyard!" cried her mother.

"Mama, it's house of worship."

"Remember what they did to our mosque?"

"That was nearly a year ago. And the people in this neighborhood aren't responsible for that."

"They are all the same. Once an enemy, always an enemy."

Hanaan sighed and crossed to the window, where she could see the boys tossing the football. They were lucky, she thought, and though she didn't say so, she felt safe for the first time in months.

Soon after they occupied the house, Hanaan had unpacked all but a few things. The closets were smaller than she had thought so she decided to keep her winter clothes boxed up until the weather turned cold. The rest of the boxes contained things she didn't immediately need but knew she wanted to hang on to—papyrus paintings of Pharonic deities she bought on her last trip to Egypt, Eid decorations she would use later that year, Dina's old toys she could not bring herself to throw away.

Hisham's new job required that he spend long hours at the office, which meant that Hanaan and Dina were left to find ways to fill up their days. Hanaan occupied herself with settling in, dusting the dining room table and hanging curtains; cleaning out the fireplace and placing pillar candles inside it—just for now, she thought, until winter came and she could make a real fire. But the summer days seemed to stretch out interminably. In between phone calls to Maha, browsing through interior design magazines, and making lists of everything she wanted for the house, Hanaan's daily routine left

her with time to become familiar with her surroundings. Karen Sultan, who had lived in Brentwood Park for nine years, was eager for Joel to meet Dina, and Hanaan was eager to know more about the neighborhood.

The visits started as casual encounters. While Hanaan planted flowers in her yard, Karen strolled over and struck up conversations. Hanaan was always surprised at how easy it was to talk to Karen. When Karen learned that Dina and Joel would be in the same kindergarten class that September, she was thrilled for them because Mrs. Shepherd would be their teacher. "Jenny had Mrs. Shepherd, too," Karen said, "and she loved her." Having an older daughter gave Karen the advantage of knowing which teachers at Valley View Elementary School were good and which were merely mediocre. The more Dina and Joel played together, the more often Hanaan and Karen saw each other. When their children weren't jumping on Joel's trampoline, they were running through Dina's yard. Soon Karen was inviting Hanaan and Dina to accompany them on outings—trips to a puppet theater, story time at the library. Sometimes the four of them rode the Red Line into D.C. and spent the afternoons strolling through the Smithsonian; other times they walked to the neighborhood swim club where Dina and Joel splashed in the kiddy pool. Karen's older daughter, Jenny, divided her time between her mother's outings and Sarah Levin's house. Occasionally, Hanaan saw Sarah at Karen's house, but the nine-year old never stopped running around long enough to meet Hanaan. It seemed to Hanaan that Jenny and Sarah, who were inseparable, were oblivious to Dina and Joel and were perfectly content to invent games that did not require the participation of a little brother and his new friend.

While Hanaan sometimes longed for the old neighborhood—the trips she and Maha took to the Arab grocer, the familiar streets and the comforting sights of seeing other women in headscarves instead of being the only one—she admitted that since moving to Brentwood Park a month before, she believed she had fit in better than she first hoped. Hanaan and Karen exchanged recipes and gardening tips; they talked about their children's loose baby teeth and fears of the dark; they shared memories of time spent on the shores of the southern Sinai peninsula and hopes that they one day might return. At times they made oblique references to terrorism and hatred and how so many things had changed since 9/11, but they stopped short of talking about any specific event. Hanaan had come to enjoy Karen's company, not just because they had children who got along, but because Karen never asked Hanaan about her faith or her politics, and Hanaan never felt as though she had to explain either one.

Hanaan wanted to tell Maha about Karen, but every time she tried, Maha told her to be careful. "They're always watching you," she would say. "They're watching all of us now. That's how they got my cousin." The deportation hearing for Maha's cousin was only a few days away and Maha was growing increasingly distraught.

On the morning of July 4, Hanaan rose to the sound of rain on her rooftop. Gray clouds darkened her usually sun-drenched kitchen. When Hanaan went out to retrieve the paper, she saw that nearly every house on the street, including hers, had a flag flying from its front porch. She mused that flags, which used to appear only once or twice a year on days like today or Veteran's Day, now remained in view week after week, month after month, a daily reminder of Americans' love for America and the values that it embodied. She recalled the days following 9/11 when red, white, and blue ribbons fluttered from nearly every car she passed, and flags were displayed on overpasses and outside homes and businesses. Even the Arab grocer near Hanaan's old apartment had hung one inside his window. Hanaan remembered seeing one of his most loyal customers spit on the flag and say she refused to set foot in his store until he removed it. The grocer told her that he did not want any bricks thrown through his window like those that had sailed through his brother's store across town.

The rain fell steadily all morning and Hanaan feared that she, Dina, and Hisham would get drenched if they ventured out to see the fireworks. But when the downpour became heavier that afternoon, Hanaan began to wonder whether there would be any fireworks at all. Dina had grown restless from having spent the morning inside and begged to be taken to Joel's house. When Hanaan stepped into Karen's foyer, she was nearly toppled by Sarah Levin, who was chasing Joel's older sister, Jenny. "She's spending the night," said Karen. "Her parents are out of town and I agreed to watch her. Jenny's loving it." Dina sat down beside Joel, who was sprawled on the floor surrounded coloring books, and surveyed his crayons before reaching for a purple one. Hanaan was amazed how the two younger children could sit so still while Jenny and Sarah raced around the house, running from the den to the kitchen to the staircase that led to Jenny's room. "Jenny, Sarah, come say hi to Dina's mom," insisted Karen. The two girls paused at the foot of the stairs.

"Hi," said Jenny.

"Sarah, this [is] Dina's mom, Mrs. Zakariah. This is Sarah, Jenny's friend." It was the first time Sarah and Hanaan had been introduced.

"Hi, Sarah," said Hanaan.

Sarah was silent, studying Hanaan's scarf and long-sleeved shirt.

"Mrs. Zakariah is from Egypt," said Karen.

Sarah looked at Hanaan with penetrating blue eyes and said, "That makes us enemies."

The girl spoke so casually that Hanaan nearly didn't believe she had heard the child correctly. "What did you say?"

"We're enemies. Because you're Egyptian and we're Hebrew." She giggled and darted off again, racing Jenny upstairs.

Hanaan felt an electric shock travel through her. She tried to contain her horror, but Karen must have seen the color drain from Hanaan's face. Karen's voice cracked as she called after Sarah, saying "No, no, Sarah. We're all friends!" She cleared her throat and there was silence. Hanaan felt a knot in her stomach and her mouth went dry. All at once the intolerance that stemmed from childhood fear and ignorance surfaced and she thought herself naïve for having ignored Maha's warnings and rejected her parents' beliefs. A nine-year old girl who had never met Hanaan had placed her squarely in the category of an enemy. In a single moment, the girl had articulated centuries of theological and political history. Hanaan could almost hear the conversations at Sarah's house, her parents telling her who her enemies had once been, who they were now. And she thought of her own mother's words on the day she moved to Brentwood Park: Once an enemy, always an enemy.

Hanaan swallowed and turned to Karen. "No, we're not all friends. As much as I'd like to believe it."

"Trust me, her parents would be mortified if they knew what she said." But Hanaan was not reassured.

Hanaan returned home and sat by the fireplace with her head in her hands. Even though the room was dark, lighting the candles in the fireplace didn't seem worth the trouble. She knew that a film of dust had accumulated on the dining room table, but she didn't bother to clean it. She finally admitted to herself what she had known all along—the American dream was more than just owning a house and flying a flag from the front porch. She would be safe in Brentwood Park; Dina would attend the best schools, she would continue her friendship with Karen, but Maha was right. There would always be people who were suspicious and fearful of her because of who she was, especially now. Moving into Brentwood Park didn't change that. It only made Hanaan more aware of it.

When Hisham sat down beside her, she leaned her head on his shoulder. She told him what had happened and said, "Maybe I was wrong about this house, this neighborhood."

"She's just a kid. She probably didn't even know what she was saying."

"But she said it with such certainty, without even having to think about it."

That evening, Judith Levin called Hanaan to apologize. "I just want you to know how sorry I am for what Sarah said. She has a very vivid imagination," the mother explained. "When you showed up at Karen's house, you were a ready-made enemy."

"I don't understand."

"Sarah was just incorporating what she heard in synagogue into her game." It struck Hanaan as odd that within fifty yards of where she slept, children were learning who thier historical enemies were and whether she liked it or not, she somehow fit that description. "But I took this opportunity to explain to Sarah that what happened 3000 years ago is very different from how things are today," continued Judith. "I want you to know that we are not raising our children to hate other people."

Judith insisted that Hanaan visit her when they got back in town, and Hanaan promised she would, if only for Karen, whom Hanaan knew must have explained the whole matter to Judith.

The rain continued to fall, but it didn't stop Hanaan from driving to Baltimore to be with Maha, who sounded awful when she called Hanaan to tell her that her cousin was going to be deported. In Brentwood Park, the storm had caused the fireworks to be postponed until the following night. As she traveled up 95 North, Hanaan searched the sky for some sign of celebration, but all she saw was darkness.

THIRTEEN

◆◆◆

A Word about the Great Terminology Question (1998)

Elizabeth Martínez

Elizabeth Martínez is a Chicana writer, teacher, and organizer. A long-time activist, she was involved in the Black and Chicano movements for civil rights. She cofounded and currently chairs the Institute for MultiRacial Justice to help build alliances among communities of color.

When you have a name like Martínez, sooner or later someone will ask the Great Terminology Question. Say that you prefer to be called a Chicana, not Mexican American, and you'll have to explain it at some length. Say that you prefer to be called Latina rather than Hispanic, and prepare for an even longer discussion. Say you are indigenous, and you'd better make another pot of coffee for a long night's debate. So it goes in this land of many identities, with new ones emerging all the time.

On one hand, there are real grounds for confusion. The term "Chicano" or "Chicana" eludes simple definition because it stands for a mix that is both racial and cultural. It refers to a people who are

neither strictly Mexican nor strictly Yankee—as well as both. Go to Mexico and you will quickly realize that most people there do not see Chicanos as Mexican. You may even hear the term "brown gringo." Live in the United States, and you will quickly discover that the dominant population doesn't see Chicanos as real Americans.

Confusion, ignorance and impassioned controversy about terminology make it necessary, then, to begin . . . with such basic questions as: what is a Chicana or Chicano? (And remember, Spanish is a gendered language, hence Chicana/Chicano.)

For starters, we combine at least three roots: indigenous (from pre-Columbian times), European (from the Spanish and Portuguese invasions) and African (from the many slaves brought to the Americas, including some 200,000 to Mexico alone). A smattering of Chinese should be added, which goes back to the sixteenth century; Mexico City had a Chinatown by the mid-1500s, some historians say. Another *mestizaje*, or mixing took place—this time with Native Americans of various nations, pueblos and tribes living in what is now the Southwest—when Spanish and Mexican colonizers moved north. Later our Chicano ancestors acquired yet another dimension through intermarriage with Anglos.

The question arises: is the term "Chicano" the same as "Mexican American" or "Mexican-American"? Yes, except in the sense of political self-definition. "Chicano/a" once implied lower-class status and was at times derogatory. During the 1960s and 1970s, in an era of strong pressure for progressive change, the term became an outcry of pride in one's peoplehood and rejection of assimilation as one's goal. Today the term "Chicano/a" refuses to go away, especially among youth, and you will still hear jokes like "A Chicano is a Mexican American who doesn't want to have blue eyes" or "who doesn't eat white bread" or whatever. (Some believe the word itself, by the way, comes from "Mexica"—pronounced "Meshica"—which was the early name for the Aztecs.)

People ask: are Chicanos different from Latinos?

At the risk of impassioned debate, let me say: we are one type of Latino. In the United States today, Latinos and Latinas include men and women whose background links them to some 20 countries, including Mexico. Many of us prefer "Latino" to "Hispanic," which obliterates our indigenous and African heritage, and recognizes only the European, the colonizer. (Brazilians, of course, reject "Hispanic" strongly because *their* European heritage is Portuguese, not Spanish.) "Hispanic" also carries the disadvantage of being a term that did not emerge from the community itself but was imposed by the dominant society through its census bureau and other bureaucracies, during the Nixon administration of the 1970s.

Today most of the people who say "Hispanic" do so without realizing its racist implications, simply because they see and hear it everywhere. Some who insist on using the term point out that "Latino" is no better than "Hispanic" because it also implies Eurocentricity. Many of us ultimately prefer to call ourselves "La Raza" or simply "Raza," meaning "The People," which dates back many years in the community. (Again we find complications in actual usage: some feel that Raza refers to people of Mexican and perhaps also Central American origin, and doesn't include Latinos from other areas.)

We are thus left with no all-embracing term acceptable to everyone. In the end, the most common, popular identification is by specific nationality: Puerto Rican, Mexican, Guatemalan, Colombian and so forth. But those of us who seek to build continental unity stubbornly cling to some broadly inclusive way of defining ourselves. In my own case, that means embracing both "Chicana" and "Latina."

At the heart of the terminology debate is the historical experience of Raza. Invasion, military occupation and racist control mechanisms all influence the evolution of words describing people who have lived through such trauma. The collective memory of every Latino people includes direct or indirect (neo-)colonialism, primarily by Spain or Portugal and later by the United States.

Among Latinos, Mexicans in what we now call the Southwest have experienced U.S. colonialism the longest and most directly, with Puerto Ricans not far behind. Almost one-third of today's United States was the home of Mexicans as early as the 1500s, until Anglos seized it militarily in 1848 and treated its population as conquered subjects. (The Mexicans, of course, themselves occupied lands that had been

seized from Native Americans.) Such oppression totally violated the Treaty of Guadalupe Hidalgo, which ended the 1846–48 [Mexican-American] war and promised respect for the civil and property rights of Mexicans remaining in the Southwest. The imposition of U.S. rule involved taking over millions of acres of Mexican-held land by trickery and violence. Colonization also brought the imposition of Anglo values and institutions at the expense of Mexican culture, including language. Hundreds of Mexicans were lynched as a form of control.

In the early 1900s, while colonization continued, the original Mexican population of the Southwest was greatly increased by an immigration that continues today. This combination of centuries-old roots with relatively recent ones gives the Mexican-American people a rich and varied cultural heritage. It means that Chicanos are not by origin an immigrant people in the United States (except compared with the Native Americans); their roots go back four centuries. Yet they also include immigrants. Too many Americans see only the recent arrivals, remaining blind to those earlier roots and what they signify.

We cannot understand all that history simply in terms of victimization: popular resistance is its other face. Raza resistance, which took the form of organized armed struggle in the Southwest during the last century, continues today in many forms. These include rejecting the colonized mentality, that pernicious, destructive process of internalizing a belief in the master's superiority and our inferiority.

The intensity of the terminology debate comes as no surprise, then, for it echoes people's struggles for non-racist—indeed, anti-racist—ways of defining themselves. Identity continues to be a major concern of youth in particular, with reason. But an obsession with self-definition can become a trap if that is all we think about, all we debate. If liberatory terminology becomes an end in itself and our only end, it ceases to be a tool of liberation. Terms can be useful, even vital tools, but the house of La Raza that is waiting to be built needs many kinds.

FOURTEEN

Optional Ethnicities (1996)

For Whites Only?

Mary C. Waters

Mary C. Waters is chair of Harvard University Sociology Department. A 1993 Guggenheim Fellow, her research is in the areas of immigration, race, and ethnicity.

. . . What does it mean to talk about ethnicity as an option for an individual? To argue that an individual has some degree of choice in their ethnic identity flies in the face of the commonsense notion of ethnicity many of us believe in—that one's ethnic identity is a fixed characteristic, reflective of blood ties and given at birth. However, social scientists who study ethnicity have long concluded that while ethnicity is based in a *belief* in a common ancestry, ethnicity is primarily a *social* phenomenon, not a biological one (Alba 1985, 1990; Barth 1969; Weber [1921] 1968, p. 389). The belief that members of an ethnic group have that they share a common ancestry may not be a fact. There is a great deal of change in ethnic identities across generations through intermarriage, changing allegiances, and changing social categories. There is also a much larger amount of change in the identities of individuals over their life than is commonly believed. While most people are aware of the phenomenon known as "passing"—people raised as one race who change at some point and claim a different race as their identity—there are similar life course changes in ethnicity that happen all the time and are not given the same degree of attention as "racial passing."

White Americans of European ancestry can be described as having a great deal of choice in terms of their ethnic identities. The two major types of options White Americans can exercise are (1) the option of whether to claim any specific ancestry, or to just be "White" or American (Lieberson [1985] called these people "unhyphenated Whites"), and (2) the choice of which of their European ancestries to choose to include in their description of their own identities. In both cases, the option of choosing how to present yourself on surveys and in everyday social interactions exists for Whites because of social changes and societal conditions that have created a great deal of social mobility, immigrant assimilation, and political and economic power for Whites in the United States. Specifically, the option of being able to not claim any ethnic identity exists for Whites of European background in the United States because they are the majority group—in terms of holding political and social power, as well as being a numerical majority. The option of choosing among different ethnicities in their family backgrounds exists because the degree of discrimination and social distance attached to specific European backgrounds has diminished over time.

The Ethnic Miracle

When European immigration to the United States was sharply curtailed in the late 1920s, a process was set in motion whereby the European ethnic groups already in the United States were for all intents and purposes cut off from any new arrivals. As a result, the composition of the ethnic groups began to age generationally. The proportion of each ethnic group made up of immigrants or the first generation began to gradually decline, and the proportion made up of the children, grandchildren, and eventually great-grandchildren began to increase. Consequently, by 1990 most European-origin ethnic groups in the United States were composed of a very small number of immigrants, and a very large proportion of people whose link to their ethnic origins in Europe was increasingly remote.

This generational change was accompanied by unprecedented social and economic changes. The very success of the assimilation process these groups experienced makes it difficult to imagine how much the question of the immigrants' eventual assimilation was an open one at the turn of the century. At the peak of immigration from southern and central Europe, there was widespread discrimination and hostility against the newcomers by established Americans. Italians, Poles, Greeks, and Jews were called derogatory names, attacked by nativist mobs, and derided in the press. Intermarriage across ethnic lines was very uncommon—castelike in the words of some sociologists (Pagnini and Morgan 1990). The immigrants and their children were residentially segregated, occupationally specialized, and generally poor.

After several generations in the United States, the situation has changed a great deal. The success and social mobility of the grandchildren and great-grandchildren of that massive wave of immigrants from Europe has been called "The Ethnic Miracle" (Greeley 1976). These Whites have moved away from the inner-city ethnic ghettos to White middle-class suburban homes. They are doctors, lawyers, entertainers, academics, governors, and Supreme Court justices. But contrary to what some social science theorists and some politicians predicted or hoped for, these middle-class Americans have not completely given up ethnic identity. Instead, they have maintained some connection with their immigrant ancestors' identities—becoming Irish American doctors, Italian American Supreme Court justices, and Greek American presidential candidates. In the tradition of cultural pluralism, successful middle-class Americans in the late twentieth century maintain some degree of identity with their ethnic backgrounds. They have remained "hyphenated Americans." So, while social mobility and declining discrimination have created the option of not identifying with any European ancestry, most White Americans continue to report some ethnic background.

With the growth in intermarriage among people of European ethnic origins, increasingly these people are of mixed ethnic ancestry. This gives them the option of which ethnicity to identify with. The U.S. census has asked a question on ethnic ancestry in the 1980 and 1990 censuses. In 1980, 52 percent of the American public responded with a single ethnic ancestry, 31 percent gave multiple ethnic origins (up to three were coded, but some individuals wrote in more than three), and only 6 percent said they were American only, while the remaining 11 percent gave no response. In 1990 about 90 percent of the population gave some response to the ancestry question, with only 5 percent giving American as a response and only 1.4 percent reporting an uncodeable response such as "don't know" (McKenney and Cresce 1992; U.S. Bureau of the Census 1992).

Several researchers have examined the pattern of responses of people to the census ancestry question. These analyses have shown a pattern of flux and inconsistency in ethnic ancestry reporting. For instance, Lieberson and Waters (1986, 1988, p. 93) have found that parents simplify children's ancestries when reporting them to the census. For instance, among the offspring in situations where one parent reports a specific single White ethnic origin and the other parent reports a different single White origin, about 40 percent of the children are not described as the logical combination of the parents' ancestries. For example, only about 60 percent of the children of English-German marriages are labeled as English-German or German-English. About 15 percent of the children of these parents are simplified to just English, and another 15 percent are reported as just German. The remainder of the children are either not given an ancestry or are described as American (Lieberson and Waters 1986, 1993).

In addition to these intergenerational changes, researchers have found changes in reporting ancestry that occur at the time of marriage or upon leaving home. At the ages of eighteen to twenty-two, when many young Americans leave home for the first time, the number of people reporting a single as opposed to a multiple ancestry goes up. Thus while parents simplify children's ancestries when they leave home, children themselves tend to report less complexity in their ancestries when they leave their parents' homes and begin reporting their ancestries themselves (Lieberson and Waters 1986, 1988; Waters 1990).

These individual changes are reflected in variability over time in the aggregate numbers of groups determined by the census and surveys. Farley (1991) compared the consistency of the overall counts of different ancestry groups in the 1979 Current Population Survey, the 1980 census, and the 1986 National Content Test (a pretest for the 1990 census). He found much less consistency in the numbers for northern European ancestry groups whose immigration peaks were early in the nineteenth century—the English, Dutch, Germans, and other northern European groups. In other words, each of these different surveys and the census yielded a different estimate of the number of people having this ancestry. The 1990 census also showed a great deal of flux and inconsistency in some ancestry groups. The number of people reporting English as an ancestry went down considerably from 1980, while the number reporting German ancestry went up. The number of Cajuns grew dramatically. This has led officials at the Census Bureau to assume that the examples used in the instructions strongly influence the responses people give. (Cajun was one of the examples of an ancestry given in 1990 but not in 1980, and German was the first example given. English was an example in the 1980 instructions, but not in 1990.)

All of these studies point to the socially variable nature of ethnic identity—and the lack of equivalence between ethnic ancestry and identity. If merely adding a category to the instructions to the question increases the number of people claiming that ancestry, what does that mean about the level of importance of that identity for people answering the census? Clearly, identity and ancestry for Whites in the United States, who increasingly are from mixed backgrounds, involve some change and choice.

Symbolic Ethnicities for White Americans

What do these ethnic identities mean to people, and why do they cling to them rather than just abandoning the tie and calling themselves American? My own field research with suburban Whites in California and Pennsylvania found that later-generation descendants of European origin maintain what are called "symbolic ethnicities." Symbolic ethnicity is a term coined by Herbert Gans (1979) to refer to ethnicity that is individualistic in nature and without real social cost for the individual. These symbolic identifications are essentially leisure-time activities, rooted in nuclear family traditions and reinforced by the voluntary enjoyable aspects of being ethnic (Waters 1990). Richard Alba (1990) also found later-generation Whites in Albany, New York, who chose to keep a tie with an ethnic identity because of the enjoyable and voluntary aspects to those identities, along with the feelings of specialness they entailed. An example of symbolic ethnicity is individuals who identify as Irish, for example, on occasions such as Saint Patrick's Day, on family holidays, or for vacations. They do not usually belong to Irish American organizations, live in Irish neighborhoods, work in Irish jobs, or marry other Irish people. The symbolic meaning of being Irish American can be constructed by individuals from mass media images, family traditions, or other intermittent social activities. In other words, for later-generation White ethnics, ethnicity is not something that influences their lives unless they want it to. In the

world of work and school and neighborhood, individuals do not have to admit to being ethnic unless they choose to. And for an increasing number of European-origin individuals whose parents and grandparents have intermarried, the ethnicity they claim is largely a matter of personal choice as they sort through all of the possible combinations of groups in their genealogies.

Individuals can choose those aspects of being Italian, for instance, that appeal to them, and discard those that do not. Or a person whose father is Italian, and mother part Polish and part French, might choose among the three ethnicities and present herself as a Polish American. For instance, a nineteen-year-old college student, interviewed in California in 1986, told me he would have answered Irish on the 1980 census form that asked about ethnic ancestry. These are his reasons:

Q: Why would you have answered that?
A: Well, my Dad's name is Kerrigan and my mom's name is O'Leary, and I do have some German in me, but if you figure it out, I am about 75 percent Irish, so I usually say I am Irish.
Q: You usually don't say German when people ask?
A: No, no, I never say I am German. My dad just likes being Irish. . . . I don't know I just never think of myself as being German.
Q: So your dad's father is the one who immigrated?
A: Yes. On his side is Irish for generations. And then my grandmother's name is Dubois, which is French, partly German, partly French, and then the rest of the family is all Irish. So it is only the maternal grandmother who messes up the line.

(Waters 1990, p. 10)

Thus in the course of a few questions, this man labeled himself Irish, admitted to being part German but not identifying with it, and then as an afterthought added that he was also part French. This is not an unusual case. With just a little probing, many people will describe a variety of ancestries in their family background, but do not consider these ancestries to be a salient part of their own identities. Thus the 1990 census ancestry question, which estimated that 30 percent of the population is of mixed ancestry, most surely underestimates the degree of mixing among the population. My research, and the research of Richard Alba (1990), shows that many people have already sorted through what they know of their ethnic ancestries and simplified their responses before they ever answer a census or survey question (Waters 1990).

But note that this freedom to include or exclude ancestries in your identification to yourself and others would not be the same for those defined racially in our society. They are constrained to identify with the part of their ancestry that has been socially defined as the "essential" part. African Americans, for example, have been highly socially constrained to identify as Blacks, without other options available to them, even when they know that their forebears included many people of American Indian or European background. Up until the mid-twentieth century, many state governments had specific laws defining one as Black if as little as one-thirty-second of one's ancestors were defined as Black (Davis 1991; Dominguez 1986; Spickard 1989). Even now when the one drop rule has been dropped from our legal codes, there are still strong societal pressures on African Americans to identify in a particular way. Certain ancestries take precedence over others in the societal rules on descent and ancestry reckoning. If one believes one is part English and part German and identifies in a survey as German, one is not in danger of being accused of trying to "pass" as non-English and of being "redefined" English by the interviewer. But if one were part African and part German, one's self identification as German would be highly suspect and probably not accepted if one "looked" Black according to the prevailing social norms.

This is reflected in the ways the census collects race and ethnic identity. While the ethnic ancestry question used in 1980 and 1990 is given to all Americans in the sample regardless of race and allows multiple responses that combine races, the primary source of information on people defined racially in the United States is the census race question or the Hispanic question. Both of these questions require a person to make a choice about an identity. Individuals are not allowed to respond that they are both Black and White, or Japanese and Asian Indian on the race question even if they know that is their background. In fact, people who disobey the instructions to the census race question and check off two races are assigned to the first checked race in the list by the Census Bureau.

In responding to the ancestry question, the comparative latitude that White respondents have does not mean that Whites pick and choose ethnicities out of thin air. For the most part, people choose an identity that corresponds with some element of their family tree. However, there are many anecdotal instances of people adopting ethnicities when they marry or move to a strongly identified neighborhood or community. For instance, Micaela di Leonardo (1984) reported instances of non-Italian women who married into Italian American families and "became Italian." Karen Leonard (1992) describes a community of Mexican American women who married Punjabi immigrants in California. Some of the Punjabi immigrants and their descendants were said to have "become Mexican" when they joined their wives' kin group and social worlds. Alternatively she describes the community acknowledging that Mexican women made the best curry, as they adapted to life with Indian-origin men.

But what do these identities mean to individuals? Surely an identity that is optional in a number of ways—not legally defined on a passport or birth certificate, not socially consequential in terms of societal discrimination in terms of housing or job access, and not economically limiting in terms of blocking opportunities for social mobility—cannot be the same as an identity that results from and is nurtured by societal exclusion and rejection. The choice to have a symbolic ethnicity is an attractive and widespread one despite its lack of demonstrable content, because having a symbolic ethnicity combines individuality with feelings of community. People reported to me that they liked having an ethnic identity because it gave them a uniqueness and feeling of being special. They often contrasted their own specialness by virtue of their ethnic identities with "bland" Americanness. Being ethnic makes people feel unique and special and not just "vanilla" as one of my respondents put it. For instance, one woman describes the benefits she feels from being Czech American:

> I work in an office and a lot of people in there always talk about their background. It's weird because it is a big office and people are of all different backgrounds. People are this or that. It is interesting I think to find out. Especially when it is something you do not hear a lot about. Something that is not common like Lithuania or something. That's the good part about being Czech. People think it is something different.   *(Waters 1990, p. 154)*

Because "American" is largely understood by Americans to be a political identity and allegiance, and not an ethnic one, the idea of being "American" does not give people the same sense of belonging that their hyphenated American identity does. When I asked people about their dual identities—American and Irish or Italian or whatever—they usually responded in a way that showed how they conceived of the relationship between the two identities. Being an American was their primary identity; but it was so primary that they rarely, if ever, thought about it—most commonly only when they left the country. Being Irish American, on the other hand, was a way they had of differentiating themselves from others whom they interacted with from day to day—in many cases from spouses or in-laws. Certain of their traits—being emotional, having a sense of humor, talking with their hands—were understood as stemming from their ethnicity. Yet when asked about their identity as Americans, that identity was both removed from their day-to-day consciousness and understood in terms of loyalty and patriotism. Although they may not think they behave or think in a certain way because they are American, being American is something they are both proud of and committed to.

Symbolic ethnicity is the best of all worlds for these respondents. These White ethnics can claim to be unique and special, while simultaneously finding the community and conformity with others that they also crave. But that "community" is of a type that will not interfere with a person's individuality. It is not as if these people belong to ethnic voluntary organizations or gather as a group in churches or neighborhoods or union halls. They work and reside within the mainstream of American middle-class life, yet they retain the interesting benefits—the "specialness"—of ethnic allegiance, without any of its drawbacks.

It has been suggested by several researchers that this positive value attached to ethnic ancestry, which became popular in the ethnic revival of the 1970s, is the result of assimilation having proceeded to an advanced stage for descendants of White Europeans (Alba 1985; Crispino 1980; Steinberg 1981). Ironically, people celebrate and embrace their ethnic backgrounds precisely because assimilation has proceeded to the point where such identification does not have that much influence on their day-to-day life. Rather than choosing the "least ethnic" and most bland ethnicities, Whites desire the "most ethnic" ones, like the once-stigmatized "Italian," because it is perceived as bringing the most psychic benefits. For instance, when an Italian father is married to an English or a Scottish or a German mother, the likelihood

is that the child will be reported to the census with the father's Italian ancestry, rather than the northern European ancestries, which would have been predicted to have a higher social status. Italian is a good ancestry to have, people told me, because they have good food and a warm family life. This change in the social meaning of being Italian American is quite dramatic, given that Italians were subject to discrimination, exclusion, and extreme negative stereotyping in the early part of the twentieth century.

Race Relations and Symbolic Ethnicity

However much symbolic ethnicity is without cost for the individual, there is a cost associated with symbolic ethnicity for the society. That is because symbolic ethnicities of the type described here are confined to White Americans of European origin. Black Americans, Hispanic Americans, Asian Americans, and American Indians do not have the option of a symbolic ethnicity at present in the United States. For all of the ways in which ethnicity does not matter for White Americans, it does matter for non-Whites. Who your ancestors are does affect your choice of spouse, where you live, what job you have, who your friends are, and what your chances are for success in American society, if those ancestors happen not to be from Europe. The reality is that White ethnics have a lot more choice and room to maneuver than they themselves think they do. The situation is very different for members of racial minorities, whose lives are strongly influenced by their race or national origin regardless of how much they may choose not to identify themselves in terms of their ancestries.

When White Americans learn the stories of how their grandparents and great-grandparents triumphed in the United States over adversity, they are usually told in terms of their individual efforts and triumphs. The important role of labor unions and other organized political and economic actors in their social and economic successes are left out of the story in favor of a generational story of individual Americans rising up against communitarian, Old World intolerance and New World resistance. As a result, the "individualized" voluntary, cultural view of ethnicity for Whites is what is remembered.

One important implication of these identities is that they tend to be very individualistic. There is a tendency to view valuing diversity in a pluralist environment as equating all groups. The symbolic ethnic tends to think that all groups are equal; everyone has a background that is their right to celebrate and pass on to their children. This leads to the conclusion that all identities are equal and all identities in some sense are interchangeable—"I'm Italian American, you're Polish American. I'm Irish American, you're African American." The important thing is to treat people as individuals and all equally. However, this assumption ignores the very big difference between an individualistic symbolic ethnic identity and a socially enforced and imposed racial identity.

My favorite example of how this type of thinking can lead to some severe misunderstandings between people of different backgrounds is from the *Dear Abby* advice column. A few years back a person wrote in who had asked an acquaintance of Asian background where his family was from. His acquaintance answered that this was a rude question and he would not reply. The bewildered White asked Abby why it was rude, since he thought it was a sign of respect to wonder where people were from, and he certainly would not mind anyone asking HIM about where his family was from. Abby asked her readers to write in to say whether it was rude to ask about a person's ethnic background. She reported that she got a large response, that most non-Whites thought it was a sign of disrespect, and Whites thought it was flattering:

Dear Abby,
I am 100 percent American and because I am of Asian ancestry I am often asked "What are you?" It's not the personal nature of this question that bothers me, it's the question itself. This query seems to question my very humanity. "What am I? Why I am a person like everyone else!"

Signed, A REAL AMERICAN

Dear Abby,
Why do people resent being asked what they are? The Irish are so proud of being Irish, they tell you before you even ask. Tip O'Neill has never tried to hide his Irish ancestry.

Signed, JIMMY

In this exchange, JIMMY cannot understand why Asians are not as happy to be asked about their ethnicity as he is, because he understands his ethnicity and theirs to be separate but equal. Everyone has to come from somewhere—his family from Ireland,

another's family from Asia—each has a history and each should be proud of it. But the reason he cannot understand the perspective of the Asian American is that all ethnicities are not equal; all are not symbolic, costless, and voluntary. When White Americans equate their own symbolic ethnicities with the socially enforced identities of non-White Americans, they obscure the fact that the experiences of Whites and non-Whites have been qualitatively different in the United States and that the current identities of individuals partly reflect that unequal history. . . .

Institutional Responses

Our society asks a lot of young people [on college campuses]. We ask young people to do something that no one else does as successfully on such a wide scale—that is to live together with people from very different backgrounds, to respect one another, to appreciate one another, and to enjoy and learn from one another. The successes that occur every day in this endeavor are many, and they are too often overlooked. However, the problems and tensions are also real, and they will not vanish on their own. We tend to see pluralism working in the United States in much the same way some people expect capitalism to work. If you put together people with various interests and abilities and resources, the "invisible hand" of capitalism is supposed to make all the parts work together in an economy for the common good.

. . . There is a lot to be said for the idea that bringing people who belong to different ethnic or racial groups together in institutions with no interference will have good consequences. Students from different backgrounds will make friends if they share a dorm room or corridor, and there is no need for the institution to do any more than provide the locale. But like capitalism, the invisible hand of pluralism does not do well when power relations and externalities are ignored. When you bring together individuals from groups that are differently valued in the wider society and provide no guidance, there will be problems. In these cases the "invisible hand" of pluralist relations does not work, and tensions and disagreements can arise without any particular individual or group of individuals being "to blame." On college campuses in the 1990s some of the tensions between students are of this sort. They arise from honest misunderstandings, lack of a common background, and very different experiences of what race and ethnicity mean to the individual.

The implications of symbolic ethnicities for thinking about race relations are subtle but consequential. If your understanding of your own ethnicity and its relationship to society and politics is one of individual choice, it becomes harder to understand the need for programs like affirmative action, which recognize the ongoing need for group struggle and group recognition, in order to bring about social change. It also is hard for a White college student to understand the need that minority students feel to band together against discrimination. It also is easy, on the individual level, to expect everyone else to be able to turn their ethnicity on and off at will, the way you are able to, without understanding that ongoing discrimination and societal attention to minority status makes that impossible for individuals from minority groups to do. The paradox of symbolic ethnicity is that it depends upon the ultimate goal of a pluralist society, and at the same time makes it more difficult to achieve that ultimate goal. It is dependent upon the concept that all ethnicities mean the same thing, that enjoying the traditions of one's heritage is an option available to a group or an individual, but that such a heritage should not have any social costs associated with it.

As the Asian Americans who wrote to *Dear Abby* make clear, there are many societal issues and involuntary ascriptions associated with non-White identities. The developments necessary for this to change are not individual but societal in nature. Social mobility and declining racial and ethnic sensitivity are closely associated. The legacy and the present reality of discrimination on the basis of race or ethnicity must be overcome before the ideal of the pluralist society, where all heritages are treated equally and are equally available for individuals to choose or discard at will, is realized.

REFERENCES

Alba, Richard D. 1985. *Italian Americans: Into the Twilight of Ethnicity.* Englewood Cliffs, NJ: Prentice-Hall.

———. 1990. *Ethnic Identity: The Transformation of White America.* New Haven, CT: Yale University Press.

Barth, Frederik. 1969. *Ethnic Groups and Boundaries.* Boston: Little, Brown.

Crispino, James. 1980. *The Assimilation of Ethnic Groups: The Italian Case.* Staten Island, NY: Center for Migration Studies.

Davis, Floyd James. 1991. *Who Is Black? One Nation's Definition.* University Park: Pennsylvania State University Press.

di Leonardo, Micaela. 1984. *The Varieties of Ethnic Experience: Kinship, Class and Gender among Italian Americans.* Ithaca, NY: Cornell University Press.

Dominguez, Virginia. 1986. *White by Definition: Social Classification in Creole Louisiana.* New Brunswick, NJ: Rutgers University Press.

Farley, Reynolds. 1991. "The New Census Question about Ancestry: What Did It Tell Us?" *Demography* 28:411–29.

Gans, Herbert. 1979. "Symbolic Ethnicity: The Future of Ethnic Groups and Cultures in America." *Ethnic and Racial Studies* 2:1–20.

Greeley, Andrew M. 1976. "The Ethnic Miracle." *Public Interest* 45 (Fall): 20–36.

Leonard, Karen. 1992. *Making Ethnic Choices: California's Punjabi Mexican Americans.* Philadelphia: Temple University Press.

Lieberson, Stanley. 1985. "Unhyphenated Whites in the United States." *Ethnic and Racial Studies* 8:159–80.

Lieberson, Stanley, and Mary Waters. 1986. "Ethnic Groups in Flux: The Changing Ethnic Responses of American Whites." *Annals of the American Academy of Political and Social Science* 487:79–91.

———. 1988. *From Many Strands: Ethnic and Racial Groups in Contemporary America.* New York: Russell Sage.

———. 1993. "The Ethnic Responses of Whites: What Causes Their Instability, Simplification, and Inconsistency?" *Social Forces* 72(2): 421–50.

McKenney, Nampeo R., and Arthur R. Cresce. 1992. "Measurement of Ethnicity in the United States: Experiences of the U.S. Census Bureau." Paper presented at the Joint Canada–United States Conference on the Measurement of Ethnicity, Ottawa, Canada, April 1–3.

Pagnini, Deanna L., and S. Philip Morgan. 1990. "Intermarriage and Social Distance among U.S. Immigrants at the Turn of the Century." *American Journal of Sociology* 96(2): 405–32.

Spickard, Paul R. 1989. *Mixed Blood.* Madison: University of Wisconsin Press.

Steinberg, Stephen. 1981. *The Ethnic Myth: Race, Ethnicity, and Class in America.* Boston: Beacon Press.

U.S. Bureau of the Census. 1992. *Census of Population and Housing, 1990: Detailed Ancestry Groups for States.* Supplementary Reports CP-S-1-2. Washington, DC: U.S. Government Printing Office.

Waters, Mary C. 1990. *Ethnic Options: Choosing Identities in America.* Berkeley and Los Angeles: University of California Press.

Weber, Max. 1921. *Economy and Society: An Outline of Interpretive Sociology,* edited by Guenther Roth and Claus Wittich, translated by Ephraim Fischoff. New York: Bedminster Press.

3

♦♦♦

Women's Bodies and Beauty Ideals

Our bodies grow and develop from the first moments of life. They provide us with a living, physical basis for our identity where all aspects of our selves are literally embodied. The life cycle—from birth to youth to maturity to dying—plays itself out through our bodies, minds, and emotions as we experience these life stages.

Body Image and the Beauty Ideal

Through our bodies we feel pain, and we experience sexuality, healing, and the complex physical, hormonal, neurological, and emotional changes that come with menstruation and menopause, pregnancy, and aging. Many of us develop and experience physical strength, agility, concentration, and coordination through exercise, dance, sports, martial arts, and outdoor activities. We show our dexterity in such things as handling tools, from kitchen knives to hammers and saws, or in fixing cars. We experience our bodies' suppleness through yoga.

Pregnancy and childbirth provide intense understanding of our elasticity, strength, and stamina and the wonder of being able to sustain another body developing inside us. We have an awareness of our bodily rhythms throughout the day or through the menstrual cycle—the ups and downs of mental and physical energy, tiredness, stiffness, and cramps—and of bodily changes that are part of growing older.

The dominant culture often reduces women to bodies, valuing us only as sex objects or as bearers of children. Postmenopausal women, for example, are sometimes thought of as no longer "real" women, but as "empty shells," their lifework over. This chapter is concerned with how women think and feel about our bodies, the impact of idealized images of beauty, and the ways gender and sexuality are both grounded in our bodies and socially constructed. Something as intimate and personal as how we feel about our bodies is thus also profoundly cultural and political.

Although there are physiological, financial, and technological limits to how much we can shape them, up to a point our bodies are malleable and we can change how we look, who we are, or who we appear to be. We make choices about clothing, hair, makeup, tattoos or piercing, as well as gestures and mannerisms. We may diet or exercise, use skin-lightening creams or tanning salons, have a nose job or tummy tuck, and consciously adopt particular postures and body language. We may have surgeries to counteract disabilities; our bodies may be altered by mastectomy due to breast cancer; we may need to use reading glasses, wheelchairs, or hearing aids. Transsexual people may choose to have surgery to make their physical appearance congruent with their internal sense of self. Others may deliberately defy cultural boundaries by looking as androgynous as possible or by changing their appearance in **gender-bending** ways. As in the previous chapter, the four levels of analysis—micro, meso, macro, and global—are helpful in understanding the range of factors that shape women's bodies. Thus, individual, micro-level choices about our bodies should also be seen within the context of a system that is White-supremacist, patriarchal, and capitalist.

The Beauty Ideal

Starting in childhood with dolls like Barbie, women and girls in the United States are bombarded with images showing what we should look like and how to achieve this look. Movies, TV programs, posters, billboards, magazine articles, and ads all portray images of the "ideal" woman. She is young and tall, with long legs, small breasts and hips, smooth skin, and well-groomed hair. Her body is trim, toned, and very lean. In some years, cleavage is the desired trait; in others, it may be fuller lips; but the basic formula holds. Thus, Naomi Wolf (1991) comments that "450 full-time American fashion models who constitute the elite corps [are] deployed in a way that keeps 150 million women in line" (p. 41). In most of these images, the women are White. Where women of color are used, they are often light-skinned and conform to this same body type.

By contrast, in real life, women come in all shapes, sizes, and skin tones. Many of us have rounded—even sagging—breasts and stomachs. We may have varicose veins, scars, stretch marks, warts, wrinkles, or blemishes, and definitely body hair. Our bodies reflect our lives, as Lani Ka'ahumanu writes in her poem "My Body Is a Map

of My Life" (Reading 19). Many women are short and stocky and will never look tall and willowy no matter how many diets and exercise routines they follow. The ideal standard of beauty is one that even the models themselves cannot achieve. Magazine ads and feature photos are airbrushed and enhanced photographically using computer-based image processing to get rid of imperfections and promote the illusion of flawlessness (Dziemianowicz 1992). Not only do these images show no blemishes; they rarely even show pores. Because this ideal of beauty is all around us, it is not surprising that many women and girls—including models and film stars—think there is something wrong with their bodies and work hard, even obsessively, to eliminate, or at least reduce, their "flaws" (Edut 2000; Lakoff and Scherr 1984; Naidus 1993).

As girls and teenagers, many of us learn to inspect our bodies critically and to loathe ourselves. Girls aged eight or nine are on self-imposed diets; many teenage girls think they are overweight; and by college age one in eight young women in the United States is bulimic, imagining herself to be much fatter than she actually is (Bordo 1993; Fraser 1997; Russell 1995; Thompson 1994). Psychologist D. M. Garner (1997) found that body dissatisfaction in the United States is increasing at a faster rate than ever before, especially among younger women. He reports that 89 percent of the 3,452 female respondents wanted to lose weight. Liz Dittrich (1997) found no ethnic differences in body-image dissatisfaction levels among her diverse sample of 234 women attending a junior college. Myers et al. (1998) argue that heterosexual beauty mandates also affect lesbians to the extent that they continue to worry about their weight. These negative attitudes are increasingly common at a global level as U.S. images of women are distributed worldwide. In Korea and Japan, for example, dieting has increased due to changes in beauty standards linked to an influx of foreign (read Western, especially U.S.) TV programs and advertising (Efon 1997).

In *The Body Project*, social historian Joan Brumberg (1997) argues that U.S. girls' self-scrutiny and anxiety about their bodies has intensified during the course of the last hundred years. Her analysis is based on the diaries of girls aged thirteen to eighteen, from the mid-nineteenth century to the 1990s. She notes a range of "body projects" including hair care and styling, skin care, external constraints on body shape (like corsets and now "bodyshapers"), internal constrains (diets and exercise), orthodontia, and shaving. Greater personal freedom, earlier menarche, and earlier sexual activity, as well as the availability of running water, mirrors, bathroom scales, contact lenses, women's razors, and a myriad "beauty products," have all contributed to many U.S. girls thinking of their bodies as their primary project. Striving to achieve and then maintain a perfect body is an ongoing project that takes time, energy, money, and determination. Laura Fraser (1997) describes women's attempts to be thin as a third job, in addition to being a desirable woman, wife, and mother and to working for a living.

The Beauty Business

Ideal standards of beauty are reinforced by, and a necessary part of, the multi-billion-dollar beauty industry that sees women's bodies only in terms of a series of problems in need of correction. These notions of ideal beauty are very effective ways for men—as well as women—to compare and judge women and to keep them on the treadmill of "body management." Allan Johnson comments: "To live in patriarchy is to breathe in misogynist images of women as objectified sexual property valued primarily for their usefulness to men" (Reading 2).

The beauty business creates needs by playing on our insecurities about our bodies and selling us creams, lotions, sprays, and handy roll-ons to improve our complexions, deodorize body scents, curl, color, condition, and straighten hair, or get rid of unwanted body hair altogether. Americans spend more than $10 billion a year on diet drugs, exercise tapes, diet books, diet meals, weight-loss classes, diet doctors, diet surgery, and "fat farms" even though research reveals that most diets don't work. We buy exercise equipment and pay for fitness classes or join a gym. We buy magazines that continually urge us to improve ourselves:

> Work off those extra pounds! Be a successful eater
>
> Sculpt your dream abs
>
> Get tank-top ready with beautiful arms
>
> Learn to dress thin

Women's magazines suggest that anyone who is comfortable with her body must be lazy or undisciplined, "letting herself go" rather than "making the best of herself." In Reading 15, Jean Kilbourne analyzes magazines that "target" girls and young women, and shows how advertising images can severely undermine their self-confidence and sense of agency.

Despite the fact that genes, metabolism, shape, and size set limits on the possibilities for drastic bodily changes, surgery and hormone therapies are pushing back the boundaries of what once was possible, defying natural processes. Liposuction, for example, described in ads as body "sculpting," is designed to remove unwanted body fat from people of normal weight and is one of the fastest-growing operations in the country. It is the most common cosmetic surgery procedure. The average surgeon's fee for liposuction is $2,220, not including anesthesia, operating-room facilities, or other related expenses (American Society of Plastic Surgeons 2005). Ads emphasize the benefits of slimmer knees and thighs or smoother hips, but like any surgery, liposuction has risks: the chance of injuries to capillaries, nerves, and skin or the possibility of infection. Despite "problems ranging from pulmonary embolisms (which killed about a dozen patients during the early 1980s) to uneven skin tone and texture, it has been judged hugely successful by doctors and patients alike" (Haiken 1997, p. 290). Such risks, taken together with greater public awareness and discussion of the dangers of silicon breast implants, for example, have not stopped women—and some men—from wanting surgical procedures to achieve their desired body profiles.

After liposuction, in 2004 the most common cosmetic surgeries were breast augmentation, eyelid surgery, nose reshaping, and facelifts. Nearly 335,000 women elected to have breast augmentation surgery, 60 percent of them between the ages of 19 and 34, and 3 percent under age 18. This represented a 24 percent increase in breast augmentation surgeries from 2000 to 2004, and an increase in those under 18—some of whom were given cosmetic surgery as a graduation gift (Kreimer 2004). Analyzed by race, data show that cosmetic surgeries increased by 24 percent on average for Latinos, African Americans, and Asian Americans for the same time period. WomenseNews writer Sandy Kobrin (2004) also reported an increase in labiaplasty, "the surgical reshaping of female external genital structures." Doctors who perform this surgery say that most women who get it are "pressured by men

Italian fashion designer Valentino and two supermodels who helped make his collection a success.

who want them to conform to an idea of beauty most often seen in the porn industry" (Kobrin 2004; Jeffreys 2005). Botox injections showed a 280 percent increase from 2000 to 2004 (American Society of Plastic Surgeons 2005).

Commodification and Co-option

Women's bodies and body parts are used as commodities, as things, in many ways in patriarchal societies. A particularly transparent and egregious example concerns enslaved African women.

Her head and her heart were separated from her back and her hands and divided from her womb and vagina. Her back and muscle were pressed into field labour where she was forced to work with men and work like men. Her hands were demanded to nurse and nurture the white man and his family. . . . Her vagina, used for his sexual pleasure, was the gateway to the womb, which was his place of capital investment—the capital investment being the sex act and the resulting child the accumulated surplus, worth money on the slave market.

(Omolade 1983: 354)

Like Rosemarie Garland Thomson (Reading 21), Nancy Mairs (1990) emphasizes the separation of body and mind as a fundamental element of Western thought, where the body is considered inferior to the mind. "I *have* a body, you are likely to say if you talk about embodiment at all; you don't say, I *am* a body" (p. 84). Further, we learn to see ourselves as disconnected parts: ankles, thighs, hips, bottoms, breasts, upper arms, noses, and chins, all in need of improvement; and this **objectification** and **commodification** of women by the advertising media paves the way for women's dismemberment (literal and figurative) in pornography. While women's bodies are used in ads to sell "beauty" products, they are also used to sell virtually everything else—soft drinks, beer, tires, cars, fax machines, chain saws, or gun holsters. The underlying message in a Diet Coke ad is: If someone as beautiful as this drinks Diet Coke, you should, too. You can look like this if you drink Diet Coke. The smiling women draped over cars or caressing fax machines in ads have nothing to do with the product; they are merely tools to draw men's attention and increase sales.

Ads are costly to produce and carefully thought out, with great attention to every detail: the style of the product, its name, color, the shape of the packaging, and the text and layout of the ads (Kilbourne 1999, 2000, and Reading 15). Ad designers make it their business to know women's interests and worries, which they use, co-opt, and undermine. The Nike slogan "Just Do It!" appeals to women's sense of independence and self-directedness while co-opting it for the consumption of products. Another slogan, "Running Like a Girl," takes the commonplace put-down and turns it into a compliment. Over thirty years ago, Virginia Slims pioneered this kind of co-option with "You've Come a Long Way, Baby," to advertise a new brand of cigarettes designed specifically for women. The use of the word "Slims" is no accident, as many women smoke to control their weight. The smoking rate of girls is now higher than that of boys, with weight control as a key motivation. Wendy Chapkis (1986) notes that 1970s feminists' insistence that a woman is beautiful just as she naturally appears has also been co-opted by the cosmetics industry and "re-written in a commercial translation as the Natural Look. The horrible irony of this is, of course, that only a handful of women have the Natural Look naturally" (p. 8).

Whites Only? Forever Young? Always Able?

These ideal notions of beauty are racist, ageist, and ableist. Even though White women are held to unreasonable beauty standards, they see beauty all around them defined as White. Women of color, by contrast, rarely see themselves reflected in mainstream images of beauty. Veronica Chambers (1995) criticizes White women who do not acknowledge or understand that this may make women of color hate their looks. For example, Naomi Wolf (1991) discusses how expectations of beauty affect women in the paid workforce but

does not refer to African American women. Chambers criticizes Wolf for

> failing to give voice to the many ways that black women are instructed to look as "white" as possible, especially with regard to their hair. She doesn't mention the African American flight attendant who brought a famous suit against her employers, who had fired her because she wore braids. She doesn't mention how often braids, dreads and even Afros are strictly prohibited in many workplaces, forcing black women to straighten their hair and wear styles that are more "mainstream."   *(p. 27)*

More recent research and writing focuses on how African American women think about their bodies (e.g., Bennett and Dickerson 2001; Harris and Johnson 2001; Lovejoy 2001; Rooks 1996) and how Black women's bodies have been portrayed in U.S. culture (Wallace-Saunders 2002). Rejecting White beauty ideals has been a key part of African American movements for racial justice, including the rejection of "oppressed hair."

White standards of beauty together with internalized racism are responsible for a hierarchy of value based on skin color among some people of color in the United States. Reading 17, "The Coming of Maureen Peal," an excerpt from Nobel laureate Toni Morrison's novel *The Bluest Eye* shows the affirmation and validation given to a light-skinned African American girl, Maureen Peal, by her teachers, other adults, and her peers. Judith Ortiz Cofer discusses how her light skin, which she describes as *leche con café*, was praised in her Puerto Rican community, but that White people in the United States saw her as dark (Reading 18).

The ideal standard of beauty emphasizes youth and associates youth with sexuality, especially for women. Gray-haired men are often thought distinguished or wise. Women are urged to look young and are thought old at least a decade before men of the same age. The phrase "old woman" is used negatively in mainstream culture. Many middle-aged women do not like others to know their age or are flattered to be told that they look younger than they are. A combination of beauty products, diet, exercise, surgery, and wealth has made movie stars in their sixties and seventies, like Raquel Welch, Sophia Loren, and Jane Fonda, look much younger than their years. These women reinforce ageist standards of beauty as well as selling thousands of copies of their exercise videos and other products. Oprah Winfrey's accounts of her struggles with diet, exercise, and weight losses and gains have also become best-sellers.

Books, tapes, and magazine articles advise women in their sixties and seventies about fitness, nutrition, and sexuality, with an emphasis on "successful aging," new interests, productive lives, and personal growth. Although these images are positive, they assume that older women have the money for dancing lessons, vacations, and retirement financial planning, for example, and give no suggestion that many older women live in poverty and poor health. Eleanor Palo Stoller and Rose Campbell Gibson (1994) note that U.S. culture reflects mixed images of older people—as wise, understanding, generous, happy, knowledgeable, and patriotic, but also as forgetful, lonely, dependent, demanding, complaining, senile, selfish, and inflexible. Not all middle-aged or older women mourn the passing of their youth. Many in their fifties, sixties, or older feel that they have really come into themselves, into their own voice, with newfound confidence and purpose (Bird 1995; Brice 2003). They find that these years may be a time of self-definition and autonomy when they can resist earlier pressures to conform to dominant beauty standards or to set a good example. At the same time, older women must come to terms with their changing looks, physical limitations, and loss of independence and loved ones (see e.g., Bolen 2003; Furman 1997; Jacobs 1993; Macdonald 1983; Walker 1999). Writer Meridel Le Sueur (1982) used the word "ripening" to describe the growth of her work over five decades, and her satisfaction with her fulfilling life—a positive way of thinking about aging with an emphasis on "generativity, rather than decline" (Browne 1998, p. 68). Elders are highly respected among many cultural groups including Native Americans, African Americans, Asian Americans, and Latinos, by contrast with White U.S. society. In these cultures gray hair, for example, is a mark of honor associated with experience and wisdom, which, if they are lucky, young people may live long enough to share. Women's Studies researchers Margaret Morganroth Gullette (2004) and Margaret Cruickshank (2003) both emphasize the social construction of aging. Cruickshank (2003, ix) argues "that aging in America is shaped more by . . . beliefs,

customs, and traditions than by bodily changes" and that "awareness of social constructions and resistance to them is crucial for women's comfortable aging." She critiques the field of gerontology for its acceptance of a medical model of aging and proposes a new approach, gerastology, that emphasizes longevity, life changes, older women's needs, and research conducted by old women. Colette Browne (1998) faults feminist theorists who, typically, do not focus on older women or the process of aging. She urges "a feminist age analysis that can document the strengths of older women, who . . . are trivialized and ignored by patriarchal society" (p. 109).

In addition to being racist and ageist, this ideal standard of beauty is profoundly ableist. Even if one is not born with a disability, everyone ages and dies. Aging is a fact of life that cannot be prevented, despite face creams, hair dyes, surgeries, or hormone treatments. Most people have less physical energy, poorer eyesight and hearing, or weaker immune systems as they age. Philosopher Susan Wendell (1992) writes that "aging is disabling. Recognizing this helps us to see that disabled people are not 'other,' but that they are really 'us.' Unless we die suddenly, we are all disabled eventually" (p. 66). Ynestra King (1993a) notes:

> The common ground for the person—the human body—is a place of shifting sand that can fail us at any time. It can change shape and properties without warning; this is an essential truth of embodied existence. Of all the ways of becoming "other" in our society, disability is the only one that can happen to anyone, in an instant, transforming that person's life and identity forever. *(p. 75)*

In *Aché: A Journal for Lesbians of African Descent*, Aisha (1991) writes:

> I personally feel that we all have challenges, some are visible and some are hidden, mine just happens to be physical but yours is still there! . . . Get in touch with the ways in which you are challenged by being able to share openly my challenge . . . and not become frightened by FEAR (False Evidence Appearing Real) superiority and bigotry. *(p. 28)*

Thanks to untiring campaigning on the part of people with disabilities and their nondisabled allies, the U.S. government passed the Americans with Disabilities Act (ADA) in 1990, the only piece of legislation quite like it in the world, though its provisions are not consistently observed or enforced. Under this act, a person with a disability is defined as having "a physical or mental impairment that substantially limits one or more . . . major life activities." About 50 million people (roughly 19 percent of the U.S. population) have some form of disability, including movement and orthopedic problems, poor physical or mental health that is disabling in some way, blindness, deafness, and learning disabilities (U.S. Department of Labor 2005). Despite their numbers, people with disabilities are largely absent from the mainstream media, often portrayed as pitiful victims—helpless and passive—or as freaks. In the readings that follow, Cheryl Marie Wade (her photo is on page 120) breaks this stereotype (Reading 20). In Reading 21, Rosemarie Garland Thomson theorizes about female and disabled bodies based on Aristotle's construction of "the generic type" (read male) and "monstrosities," or deviations from this type (read female and disabled). This dualism is foundational in Western thought, as mentioned in the previous chapter. Disability rights activists and theorists are claiming space in academic discourse, public policy, and on the streets (see e.g., Clare 1999; Fine and Asch 1988; Fries 1997; Hall 2002; Linton 1999; Mairs 1990, 1996; Rousso 2001; Smith and Hutchison 2004; Wendell 1996). Many people with disabilities argue that they are more handicapped by the mental limitations of nondisabled people than by their own minds and bodies.

Resisting Beauty Stereotypes

Many women flout dominant beauty standards: by not using makeup, for example, by wearing sensible shoes and practical clothes, or by showing hairy legs and underarms. Some breast cancer survivors who have had one or both breasts removed have chosen to go without artificial breasts or have had their mastectomy scars tattooed. Some women challenge conventional standards by gender-bending, pushing a boyish look beyond the dictates of current mainstream fashion into a more genuinely androgynous area. Others do not buy into this ideal but may need to make concessions at times, such as wearing appropriate clothes, hairstyles, and makeup for work or family gatherings.

Beauty standards are always cultural constructions and vary among different groups, hence the importance of a meso-level analysis. For instance, in African American communities, very thin, boyish-looking women are not necessarily thought beautiful. Queen T'isha notes:

> Racism and sexism as practiced in America includes body hostilities. I didn't grow up with the belief that fat women were to be despised. The women in my family were fat, smart, sexy, employed, wanted, married, and the rulers of their households.
> *(Quoted in Edison and Notkin 1994, p. 106)*

Extreme thinness may be associated with poverty, malnutrition, and illnesses such as cancer or AIDS, which eat the body away from the inside. Women who are large, fleshy, and rounded embody strength, sexiness, comfort, and nurturance. American Jewish culture has the word *zaftig*, a positive term for voluptuous women (St. Paige 1999), though Ophira Edut (2001, p.24), who describes herself as a "Jewish chick with a big booty," struggles to feel good about her curves. Many African American women say, "I don't want to be no skinny minny!" and Judith Ortiz Cofer (Reading 18) notes that "a fuller figure" was admired in her Puerto Rican community.

Large women challenge many stereotypes and taken-for-granted assumptions: that they are undisciplined, depressed, sexless, unwanted, or unhealthy; and that they have only themselves to blame for letting themselves go. Elise Matthesen argues,

> We have a right to take up space. We have a right to stretch out, to be big, bold, to be "too much to handle." To challenge the rest of the world to grow up, get on with it, and become big enough themselves to "handle" us. . . .
> *(Quoted in Edison and Notkin 1994, p. 107)*

And Dora Dewey-McCracken confounds common assumptions about fatness with regard to health:

> I've been diabetic since I was nineteen. . . . All my life I gained and lost at least sixty pounds each year. . . . I tried all diets, eating disorders, and fasts, only to gain the fat back, and more each time. I'm the fattest I've ever been, and yet my diabetic blood work is the best it's ever

been. My doctor once told me, "As long as your disease is controlled and your blood chemistry is good, your fat is just a social issue." I'm extremely lucky to have this doctor; with most doctors, fat-phobia is the rule, not the exception. They see the fat and their brains turn off.

(Quoted in Edison and Notkin 1994, p. 104)

There are many ways to be a woman—a spectrum of looks and behaviors, ranging from the conventionally feminine at one end to being able to pass for a man at the other, with various femme/butch combinations in between. Lesbians in the 1950s and '60s who identified as butch or femme adopted dress and hairstyles accordingly. Joan Nestle (1992) argues that this was not a replication of heterosexual gender polarization but rather "a lesbian-specific way of deconstructing gender that radically reclaims women's erotic energy" (p. 14). Many 1970s lesbian feminists saw idealized notions of beauty as oppressive to women and also critiqued butch-femme roles as inherently patriarchal. They adopted flannel shirts, overalls, and short hair, as a rejection of conventional womanly looks. Silva Tenenbein (1998) comments that in mainstream culture women have power in their physical beauty. "I want to reverse the beauty-is-power equation. For dykes it's not beauty which makes us powerful but power that makes us beautiful . . . our passion, our strength, and our courage to choose to be 'other' . . . our adamant refusal to be deflected from what we want" (pp. 159, 160). Current fashion includes practical boots and shoes and leather jackets for women, and fashion ads portray androgynous women, suggesting bisexuality or lesbianism. Lesbian and gay characters are turning up in films and TV shows, and magazines, including *Vanity Fair,* have done issues on "lesbian chic." As women, and men too, push the boundaries of gender and sexual categories, this is represented in the media and also co-opted (Reading 25; Hamer and Budge 1994 Walters 2001).

Numerous women's organizations and projects across the country are working on these issues. Self-help books (e.g., Erdman 1995; Newman 1991) and publications like *Radiance: The Magazine for Large Women* are a source of information and positive attitudes. Organizations that challenge sexist media images include the Body Image Task Force (Santa Cruz, Calif.), Challenging Media Images of Women

(Framingham, Mass.), Media Watch, and Media Action Alliance (Circle Pines, Minn.). Those challenging fat oppression include the Boston Area Fat Liberation (Cambridge, Mass.), the Council on Size and Weight Discrimination (Mount Marion, N.Y.), Largess—the Network for Size Esteem (New Haven, Conn.), and the National Association to Advance Fat Acceptance (Sacramento, Calif.). The Gray Panthers (Washington, D.C.) and OWL, the Older Women's League (Washington, D.C.), both have many local chapters that advocate for older women around a range of issues, including prejudice and discrimination based on age and looks. In several towns and cities, groups of Raging Grannies bring public visibility to progressive issues (Roy 2004). Senior Action in a Gay Environment (New York) and the National Pacific/Asian Resource Center on Aging (Seattle, Wash.) support particular groups. Centers for independent living in many cities work with women with disabilities, as do projects like the Disabled Women's Theater Project (New York), the Disability Project (St. Louis, MO), and dance groups for women with disabilities.

Social historian Joan Jacobs Brumberg (1997) argues that girls should be encouraged to be physically active and taught from an early age that their power is in other things than their appearance. They need to be informed, to know what they want, and to be able to articulate it. She comments that it is an important political/personal mental-health decision not to let a preoccupation with the perfect body rule one's life.

Women are pressured to discipline their bodies in many ways in patriarchal cultures, as this chapter shows. Some feminist theorists think of sport and martial arts in terms of "body discipline" and, hence, as negative. However, more and more girls and women are learning to use their bodies in "unladylike" ways, to train hard, to grunt, and to sweat, and are finding strength and self-esteem through sports, yoga, martial arts, and strenuous outdoor activities such as mountain-biking, skiing, white-water rafting, and so on. Women's sports are televised more than they were in the past, and many high schools and colleges have improved facilities for women's athletics, due to pressure from students and teachers and to Title IX ("title nine") of the 1972 Education Act that requires educational institutions receiving federal funding to provide equal opportunities for male and female students (see e.g., Bolin and Granskog 2003; Cahn 1995; Heywood 1998; Heywood and Dworkin 2003; Sandoz and Winana 1999). However, women athletes still face a chilly climate, including homophobia that is used against strong women generally, and keeps some lesbian athletes "in the closet" (Griffin 1998; Lenskyj 2003).

Feminist Theorizing about Body Image and Beauty Ideals

Explanations of women's dissatisfaction with their bodies have been linked to psychological factors like low self-esteem; depression; childhood teasing, disappointment, and trauma; and family structure and dynamics (Bloom, Chesney-Lind, and Owen 1994; Chernin 1985). Women who diet obsessively, for example, may do it as a way of maintaining control over their bodies, in contrast to the many pressures they experience in other areas of their lives from parents, teachers, and peers. Abra Fortune Chernik (Reading 16) confirms this: "I felt powerful as an anorexic. Controlling my body yielded an illusion of control over my life." Part of her recovery was to face the many ways she had denied herself contact with family and friends, and the social and educational opportunities of college life, so as to avoid eating or to maintain her exercise regime. She comments that she needed to go beyond psychological explanations "to understand why society would reward my starvation and encourage my vanishing," and concludes: "Gaining weight and getting my head out of the toilet bowl was the most political act I have ever committed." Chernik reunites her body/self when she writes of "the body that hosts my life" and "our bodies are our homes." She both reflects on her experience of anorexia and also theorizes about it. This is an excellent example of how women develop theory from our lived experience by raising broader questions—analyzing our micro-level experiences and also seeking to understand the meso- and macro-level contexts that affect us.

The constant promotion of an ideal body image is a very effective way of oppressing women and girls, taking up time, money, and attention that could be devoted to other aspects of life, like education or self-development, or to wider issues such as the need for affordable health care, child care, elder care, and jobs with decent pay and benefits. Striving for a better body keeps us in check. Although ideals of beauty—and fashions in clothes, makeup, hairstyles, and body shape—are not new, sociologist Sharlene Hesse-Biber (1996) notes that they have become increasingly stringent and elusive. Over the past thirty-five years or so, numerous women in the United States have made significant gains toward greater equality with men in education and admission to professions and manual trades with higher pay scales. But, as Faludi (1991) notes in her analysis of backlash against women's progress, as women have gained more independence socially and economically, body standards have become harder to achieve.

Anthropologist Mary Douglas (1966) advanced the insight that the body is a symbolic medium of culture and that one can "see the powers and dangers credited to social structure reproduced in small on the human body" (p. 115). Philosopher Susan Bordo (1993) discusses the contradictory ideals and directives girls and women receive about femininity from contemporary culture that may affect their attitudes to food and eating. She argues that the **gendered division of labor,** under which women have the main responsibility for home and nurturing and men are mainly active in the public sphere, has barely changed despite women's entry into jobs and professions once closed to them. Women are supposed to nurture and care for men—their fathers, brothers, boyfriends, husbands, lovers, bosses, colleagues, and sons. Thus women learn to feed others—emotionally and literally—rather than themselves.

Bordo (1993) notes that women who aspire to be successful professionally "must also learn to embody the 'masculine' language and values of that arena—self control, determination, cool, emotional discipline, mastery, and so on" (p. 171). The boyish body ideals of fashion ads suggest a new freedom from the limitations of reproductive femininity, but when placed next to solid, muscular male models, these ultra-slim women look fragile and powerless. Part of their allure, it seems, is in this relative powerlessness, in their image as little girls who will never grow up to be true equals. Bordo (1993) analyzes the prevalence of hysteria among middle-class, U.S. women in the nineteenth century, agoraphobia in the 1950s and '60s, and anorexia in the 1980s and '90s. She shows that women may attempt to resist assigned gender roles "paradoxically, by pursuing conventional feminine behavior . . . to excess" (p. 179).

She suggests that a conception of power as a "network of practices, institutions, and technologies that sustain positions of dominance and subordination" (p. 167) is helpful in understanding why women would willingly accept norms and practices that limit them.

Much research into body image and eating disorders in the 1980s and '90s involved White middle-class women. Becky Thompson (1994) broke new ground in her qualitative research with a small, but diverse, group of women. She argues that struggles with food and appetite for women of color, White lesbians, and working-class women may not be about wanting to be thin. Her respondents' compulsive eating, she argues, is a response to the stress of living with physical and psychic atrocities such as sexism, racism, classism, heterosexism, and physical, emotional, and sexual abuse. Food can be a significant source of comfort and pleasure, numbing bad feelings, anxiety, and anger. Food is available, inexpensive, and socially acceptable, and it is a safer way to buffer pain than drugs or alcohol. Thompson sees the women she interviewed as courageous survivors dealing with trauma. She argues that freedom from eating problems depends on long-term psychological work at a personal level as well as macro-level political change to transform systems of oppression. Columnists Lynn Ginsburg and Mary Taylor (2002) argue that obsessive dieting and eating disorders are also often a symptom of spiritual emptiness and ask: "What are you hungry for?"

Meg Lovejoy (2001) discusses significant differences between African American women and White women in terms of body image and apparent satisfaction with their weight and looks. She suggests that African American women's more positive body image "may stem from a number of healthy sources, such as their resistance to negative societal images of Black women, the supports they receive from within the Black community, and a feminine gender role that affords greater agency" (p. 255). She quotes a study of Black and White high school girls (Parker et al. 1995), which found that the Black girls were

> more flexible and fluid than their white counterparts in their concepts of beauty, and they expressed far greater satisfaction with their body shape. The white girls described their ideal girl in terms of a set of uniform and fixed physical attributes (e.g., tall, thin, blonde hair, high

cheekbones) encapsulated by the word *perfect*. By contrast, the African American girls de-emphasized external beauty, instead describing their ideal girl in terms of various personality traits, style, attitude, and ability to project a sense of pride and confidence.   *(p. 250)*

Lovejoy (2001) notes that African American women are "typically raised to be strong, independent, and self-reliant" (p. 254) compared with middle-class White women. She argues that African American women do have eating problems—compulsive eating and obesity—that "exact a serious toll on Black women's physical and psychological well-being" (p. 249). Lovejoy (2001) follows Thompson (1994) and earlier work by African American health advocates and theorists (e.g., Avery 1900; hooks 1993; White 1991) in emphasizing Black women's eating problems as a way of coping with multiple oppressions.

Compared with men, most women in the United States have little structural power in terms of money, professional status, inherited wealth, or political influence. Women who are considered beautiful, though, have this personal power, which may help them "catch" a man but is no guarantee that he will stay. Robin Lakoff and Raquel Scherr (1984) argue that this power is more illusory than real when compared with material wealth and political clout. Moreover, beauty, as conventionally defined, does not last. To the extent that beautiful women have personal power, they will probably lose it as they age.

Body Politics

The body is central to patriarchal oppression of women and is a crucial site of resistance, as we argue here. We develop this discussion in the next three chapters: with a focus on sexuality (Chapter 4), on health (Chapter 5), and on violence against women (Chapter 6). In Chapter 2, we noted the significance of marking and effecting shifts in identity by changing physical appearance.

The body is where everything is played out: our choices and desires, as well as the societal forces that shape our lives. Institutions such as the mass media, technology, law, government, and religion all have a profound influence on who we are, who we become, and how we imagine ourselves. Retaining control of our bodily lives is an important aspect of women's autonomy and liberation.

Questions for Reflection

As you read and discuss the readings that follow, consider these questions:

1. How do you feel about your own body?

2. Do you think that makeup, piercing, tattooing, dieting, and body building make women look beautiful? Sexy? Are looking beautiful and looking sexy the same thing?

3. What makes you feel good about your body? About yourself? Are they different?

4. What images of women do you consider positive? Where do you find them?

5. What are positive images of aging? How can aging be celebrated in women's lives?

6. Why is there currently no significant political movement against the ideal of bodily perfection?

7. How would you organize activities among your peers, on your campus, or in your home community to draw attention to the issue of body image for women and to challenge common stereotypes?

8. How can women with disabilities and nondisabled women work together on the issue of body image?

9. How can young women and older women work together on this issue?

10. How much did you eat while reading this section? How much exercise did you do?

Finding Out More on the Web

1. Research the work of organizations cited in this chapter. How are they working to challenge sexist media images of women, fat oppression, or negative images of older women?

2. Mobility International USA is involved with disability rights activists internationally (www.miusa.org). How are women organizing for disability rights? What are they learning from each other? What strategies are they using to improve the lives of women with disabilities?

3. Cheryl Marie Wade mentions Tiergarten in her poem (Reading 20). Where is that and why is it significant? In her dedication she refers to Sharon Kowalski and Karen Thompson. Who were they and why are they significant?

Taking Action

1. Make it your daily practice to affirm your body. What do/can you do to feel good about your body and yourself?

2. Write a letter to a TV station or magazine that shows positive (or negative) images of women and let them know what you think. Send examples of sexist ads to *Bitch*

magazine or *Ms.* Magazine's "No Comment" section; participate in the Third Wave Foundation's "I Spy Sexism" campaign or Mind on the Media's GirlCaught campaign.

3. Find out more about how your body works, for example, by reading *Our Bodies, Ourselves for the New Century.*

4. Learn about the body concerns of women from a different group than your own.

5. Attend a meeting of an organization concerned with body issues.

FIFTEEN

"The More You Subtract, the More You Add" (1999)
Cutting Girls Down to Size

Jean Kilbourne

Award-winning public speaker, writer, and documentary film maker, **Jean Kilbourne** is internationally recognized for her critiques of tobacco and alcohol advertising as well as images of women in advertising. She is the recipient of the 2000 Distinguished Publication Award from the Association for Women in Psychology.

. . . Adolescents are new and inexperienced consumers—and such prime targets. They are in the process of learning their values and roles and developing their self-concepts. Most teenagers are sensitive to peer pressure and find it difficult to resist or even to question the dominant cultural messages perpetuated and reinforced by the media. Mass communication has made possible a kind of national peer pressure that erodes private and individual values and standards, as well as community values and standards. As Margaret Mead once said, today our children are not brought up by parents, they are brought up by the mass media.[1]

Advertisers are aware of their role and do not hesitate to take advantage of the insecurities and anxieties of young people, usually in the guise of offering solutions. A cigarette provides a symbol of independence. A pair of designer jeans or sneakers convey status. The right perfume or beer resolves doubts about femininity or masculinity. All young people are vulnerable to these messages and adolescence is a difficult time for most people, perhaps especially these days. . . . But there is a particular kind of suffering in our culture that afflicts girls.

. . . Girls who were active, confident, feisty at the ages of eight and nine and ten often become hesitant, insecure, self-doubting at eleven. Their self-esteem plummets. As Carol Gilligan, Mary Pipher and other social critics and psychologists have pointed out . . . , adolescent girls in America are afflicted with a range of problems, including low self-esteem, eating disorders, binge drinking, date rape and other dating violence, teen pregnancy, and a rise in cigarette smoking.[2] . . .

It is important to understand that these problems go way beyond individual psychological development and pathology. Even girls who are raised in loving homes by supportive parents grow up in a toxic cultural environment, at risk for self-mutilation, eating disorders, and addictions. The culture, both reflected and reinforced by advertising, urges girls to adopt a false self, to bury alive their real selves, to become "feminine," which means to be nice and kind and sweet, to compete with other girls for the attention of boys, and to value romantic relationships with boys above all else. Girls are put into a terrible double bind. They are supposed to repress their power, their anger, their exuberance and be simply "nice," although they also eventually must compete with men in the business world and be successful. They must be overtly sexy and attractive but essentially passive and virginal. It is not surprising that most girls experience this time as painful and confusing, especially if they are unconscious of these conflicting demands.

Of course, it is impossible to speak accurately of girls as a monolithic group. The socialization that emphasizes passivity and compliance does not apply to many African-American and Jewish girls, who are often encouraged to be assertive and outspoken, and working-class girls are usually not expected to be stars in the business world. Far from protecting these girls from eating disorders and other problems, these differences more often mean that the problems remain hidden or undiagnosed and the girls are even less likely to get help. Eating problems affect girls from African-American, Asian, Native American, Hispanic, and Latino families and from every socioeconomic background.[3] The racism and classism that these girls experience exacerbate their problems. Sexism is by no means the only trauma they face. . . .

Girls try to make sense of the contradictory expectations of themselves in a culture dominated by advertising. Advertising is one of the most potent messengers in a culture that can be toxic for girls' self-esteem. Indeed, if we looked only at advertising images, this would be a bleak world for females. Girls are extremely desirable to advertisers because they are new consumers, are beginning to have significant disposable income, and are developing brand loyalty that might last a lifetime. . . .

Seventeen, a magazine aimed at girls about twelve to fifteen, sells these girls to advertisers in an ad that says, "She's the one you want. She's the one we've got." The copy continues, "She pursues beauty and fashion at every turn" and concludes with, "It's more than a magazine. It's her life." In another similar ad, *Seventeen* refers to itself as a girl's "Bible." Many girls read magazines like this and take the advice seriously. Regardless of the intent of the advertisers, what are the messages that girls are getting? . . .

Primarily girls are told by advertisers that what is most important about them is their perfume, their clothing, their bodies, their beauty. Their "essence" is their underwear. "He says the first thing he noticed about you is your great personality," says an ad featuring a very young woman in tight jeans. The copy continues, "He lies." "If this is your idea of a great catch," says an ad for a cosmetic kit from a teen magazine featuring a cute boy, "this is your tackle box." Even very little girls are offered makeup and toys like Special Night Barbie, which shows them how to dress up for a night out. Girls of all ages get the message that they must be flawlessly beautiful and, above all these days, they must be thin.

Even more destructively, they get the message that this is possible, that, with enough effort and self-sacrifice, they can achieve this ideal. Thus many girls spend enormous amounts of time and energy attempting to achieve something that is not only trivial but also completely unattainable. The glossy images of flawlessly beautiful and extremely thin women that surround us would not have the impact they do if we did not live in a culture that encourages us to believe we can and should remake our bodies into perfect commodities. These images play into the American belief of transformation and ever-new possibilities, no longer via hard work but via the purchase of the right products. . . .

Women are especially vulnerable because our bodies have been objectified and commodified for so long. And young women are the most vulnerable, especially those who have experienced early deprivation, sexual abuse, family violence, or other trauma. Cultivating a thinner body offers some hope of control and success to a young woman with a poor self-image and overwhelming personal problems that have no easy solutions.

Although troubled young women are especially vulnerable, these messages affect all girls. A researcher at Brigham and Women's Hospital in Boston found that the more frequently girls read magazines, the more likely they were to diet and to feel that magazines influence their ideal body shape.[4] Nearly half reported wanting to lose weight because of a magazine picture (but only 29 percent were actually overweight). Studies at Stanford University and the University of Massachusetts found that about 70 percent of college women say they feel worse about their own looks after reading women's magazines.[5] Another study, this one of 350 young men and women, found that a preoccupation with one's appearance takes a toll on mental health.[6]

Women scored much higher than men on what the researchers called "self-objectification." This tendency to view one's body from the outside in—regarding physical attractiveness, sex appeal, measurements, and weight as more central to one's physical identity than health, strength, energy level, coordination, or fitness—has many harmful effects, including diminished mental performance, increased feelings of shame and anxiety, depression, sexual dysfunction, and the development of eating disorders.

These images of women seem to affect men most strikingly by influencing how they judge the real women in their lives. Male college students who viewed just one episode of *Charlie's Angels,* the hit television show of the 1970s that featured three beautiful women, were harsher in their evaluations of the attractiveness of potential dates than were males who had not seen the episode.[7] In another study, male college students shown centerfolds from *Playboy* and *Penthouse* were more likely to find their own girlfriends less sexually attractive.

Adolescent girls are especially vulnerable to the obsession with thinness, for many reasons. One is the ominous peer pressure on young people. Adolescence is a time of such self-consciousness and terror of shame and humiliation. Boys are shamed for being too small, too "weak," too soft, too sensitive. And girls are shamed for being too sexual, too loud, too boisterous, too big (in any sense of the word), having too hearty an appetite. Many young women have told me that their boyfriends wanted them to lose weight. One said that her boyfriend had threatened to leave her if she didn't lose five pounds. "Why don't you leave him," I asked, "and lose 160?"

The situation is very different for men. The double standard is reflected in an ad for a low-fat pizza: "He eats a brownie . . . you eat a rice cake. He eats a juicy burger . . . you eat a low fat entree. He eats pizza . . . you eat pizza. Finally, life is fair." Although some men develop eating problems, the predominant cultural message remains that a hearty appetite and a large size is desirable in a man, but not so in a woman. . . .

Normal physiological changes during adolescence result in increased body fat for women. If these normal changes are considered undesirable by the culture (and by parents and peers), this can lead to chronic anxiety and concern about weight control in young women. A ten-year-old girl wrote to *New Moon,* a feminist magazine for girls, "I was at the beach and was in my bathing suit. I have kind of fat legs, and my uncle told me I had fat legs in front of all my cousins and my cousins' friends. I was so embarrassed, I went up to my room and shut the door. When I went downstairs again, everyone started teasing me."[8] Young women are even encouraged to worry about small fluctuations in their weight. "Sometimes what you wear to dinner may depend on what you eat for breakfast," says an ad for cereal that pictures a slinky black dress. In truth, daily and weekly and monthly fluctuations in weight are perfectly normal.

The obsession starts early. Some studies have found that from 40 to 80 percent of fourth-grade girls are dieting.[9] Today at least one-third of twelve- to thirteen-year-old girls are actively trying to lose weight, by dieting, vomiting, using laxatives, or taking diet pills.[10] One survey found that 63 percent of high-school girls were on diets, compared with only 16 percent of men.[11] And a survey in Massachusetts found that the single largest group of high-school students considering or attempting suicide are girls who feel they are overweight.[12] Imagine. Girls made to feel so terrible about themselves that they would rather be dead than fat. This wouldn't be happening, of course, if it weren't for our last "socially acceptable" prejudice—weightism.[13] Fat children are ostracized and ridiculed from the moment they enter school, and fat adults, women in particular, are subjected to public contempt and scorn. This strikes terror into the hearts of all women, many of whom, unfortunately, identify with the oppressor and become vicious to themselves and each other.

No wonder it is hard to find a woman, especially a young woman, in America today who has a truly healthy attitude toward her body and toward food. Just as the disease of alcoholism is the extreme end of a continuum that includes a wide range of alcohol use and abuse, so are bulimia and anorexia the extreme results of an obsession with eating and weight control that grips many young women with serious and potentially very dangerous results. Although eating problems are often thought to result from vanity, the truth is that they, like other addictions and compulsive behavior, usually have deeper roots—not only genetic predisposition and biochemical vulnerabilities, but also childhood sexual abuse.[14]

Advertising doesn't cause eating problems, of course, any more than it causes alcoholism. Anorexia in particular is a disease with a complicated etiology, and media images probably don't play a major role. However, these images certainly contribute to the body-hatred so many young women feel and to some of the resulting eating problems, which range from bulimia to compulsive overeating to simply being obsessed with controlling one's appetite. Advertising does promote abusive and abnormal attitudes about eating, drinking, and thinness. It thus provides fertile soil for these obsessions to take root in and creates a climate of denial in which these diseases flourish.

The influence of the media is strikingly illustrated in a . . . study that found a sharp rise in eating disorders among young women in Fiji soon after the introduction of television to the culture.[15] Before television was available, there was little talk of dieting in Fiji. "You've gained weight" was a traditional compliment and "going thin" the sign of a problem. In 1995 television came to the island. Within three years, the number of teenagers at risk for eating disorders more than doubled, 74 percent of the teens in the study said they felt "too big or too fat," and 62 percent said they had dieted in the past month. Of course, this doesn't prove a direct causal link between television and eating disorders. Fiji is a culture in transition in many ways. However, it seems more than coincidental that the Fiji girls who were heavy viewers of television were 50 percent more likely to describe themselves as fat and 30 percent more likely to diet than those girls who watched television less frequently. As Ellen Goodman says, "The big success story of our entertainment industry is our ability to export insecurity: We can make any woman anywhere feel perfectly rotten about her shape."[16]

Being obsessed about one's weight is made to seem normal and even appealing in ads for unrelated products, such as a scotch ad that features a very thin and pretty young woman looking in a mirror while her boyfriend observes her. The copy, addressed to him, says, "Listen, if you can handle 'Honey, do I look fat?' you can handle this." These two are so intimate that she can share her deepest fears with him—and he can respond by chuckling at her adorable vulnerability and knocking back

another scotch. And everyone who sees the ad gets the message that it is perfectly normal for all young women, including thin and attractive ones, to worry about their weight. . . .

Not all of this is intentional on the part of the advertisers, of course. A great deal of it *is* based on research and *is* intended to arouse anxiety and affect women's self-esteem. But some of it reflects the unconscious attitudes and beliefs of the individual advertisers, as well as what Carl Jung referred to as the "collective unconscious." Advertisers are members of the culture too and have been as thoroughly conditioned as anyone else. The magazines and the ads deliberately *create* and intensify anxiety about weight because it is so profitable. On a deeper level, however, they *reflect* cultural concerns and conflicts about women's power. Real freedom for women would change the very basis of our male-dominated society. It is not surprising that many men (and women, to be sure) fear this.

"The more you subtract, the more you add," says an ad that ran in several women's and teen magazines in 1997. Surprisingly, it is an ad for clothing, not for a diet product. Overtly, it is a statement about minimalism in fashion. However, the fact that the girl in the ad is very young and very thin reinforces another message, a message that an adolescent girl constantly gets from advertising and throughout the popular culture, the message that she should diminish herself, she should be *less* than she is.

On the most obvious and familiar level, this refers to her body. However, the loss, the subtraction, the cutting down to size also refers to her sense of her self, her sexuality, her need for authentic connection, and her longing for power and freedom. I certainly don't think that the creators of this particular ad had all this in mind. They're simply selling expensive clothing in an unoriginal way, by using a very young and very thin woman—and an unfortunate tagline. It wouldn't be important at all were there not so many other ads that reinforce this message and did it not coincide with a cultural crisis taking place now for adolescent girls.

"We cut Judy down to size," says an ad for a health club. "Soon, you'll both be taking up less space," says an ad for a collapsible treadmill, referring both to the product and to the young woman exercising on it. *The obsession with thinness is most deeply about cutting girls and women down to size. It is only a symbol, albeit a very powerful and destructive* one, of tremendous fear of female power. Powerful women are seen by many people (women as well as men) as inherently destructive and dangerous. Some argue that it is men's awareness of just how powerful women can be that has created the attempts to keep women small.[17] Indeed, thinness as an ideal has always accompanied periods of greater freedom for women—as soon as we got the vote, boyish flapper bodies came into vogue. No wonder there is such pressure on young women today to be thin, to shrink, to be like little girls, not to take up too much space, literally or figuratively.

At the same time there is relentless pressure on women to be small, there is also pressure on us to succeed, to achieve, to "have it all." We can be successful as long as we stay "feminine" (i.e., powerless enough not to be truly threatening). One way to do this is to present an image of fragility, to look like a waif. This demonstrates that one is both in control and still very "feminine." One of the many double binds tormenting young women today is the need to be both sophisticated and accomplished, yet also delicate and childlike. Again, this applies mostly to middle- to upper-class white women.

The changing roles and greater opportunities for women promised by the women's movement are trivialized, reduced to the private search for the slimmest body. In one commercial, three skinny young women dance and sing about the "taste of freedom." They are feeling free because they can now eat bread, thanks to a low-calorie version. A commercial for a fast-food chain features a very slim young woman who announces, "I have a license to eat." The salad bar and lighter fare have given her freedom to eat (as if eating for women were a privilege rather than a need). "Free yourself," says ad after ad for diet products. . . .

Most of us know by now about the damage done to girls by the tyranny of the ideal image, weightism, and the obsession with thinness. But girls get other messages too that "cut them down to size" more subtly. In ad after ad girls are urged to be "barely there"—beautiful but silent. Of course, girls are not just influenced by images of other girls. They are even more powerfully attuned to images of women, because they learn from these images what is expected of them, what they are to become. And they see these images again and again in the magazines they read, even those magazines designed for teenagers, and in the commercials they watch.

"Make a statement without saying a word," says an ad for perfume. And indeed this is one of the primary messages of the culture to adolescent girls. "The silence of a look can reveal more than words," says another perfume ad, this one featuring a woman lying on her back. "More than words can say," says yet another perfume ad, and a clothing ad says, "Classic is speaking your mind (without saying a word)." An ad for lipstick says, "Watch your mouth, young lady," while one for nail polish says, "Let your fingers do the talking," and one for hairspray promises "hair that speaks volumes." In another ad, a young woman's turtleneck is pulled over her mouth. And an ad for a movie soundtrack features a chilling image of a young woman with her lips sewn together.

It is not only the girls themselves who see these images, of course. Their parents and teachers and doctors see them and they influence their sense of how girls should be. A 1999 study done at the University of Michigan found that, beginning in preschool, girls are told to be quiet much more often than boys.[18] Although boys were much noisier than girls, the girls were told to speak softly or to use a "nicer" voice about three times more often. Girls were encouraged to be quiet, small, and physically constrained. The researcher concluded that one of the consequences of this socialization is that girls grow into women afraid to speak up for themselves or to use their voices to protect themselves from a variety of dangers. . . .

"Score high on nonverbal skills," says a clothing ad featuring a young African-American woman, while an ad for mascara tells young women to "make up your own language." And an Italian ad features a very thin young woman in an elegant coat sitting on a window seat. The copy says, "This woman is silent. This coat talks." Girls, seeing these images of women, are encouraged to be silent, mysterious, not to talk too much or too loudly. In many different ways, they are told "the more you subtract, the more you add." In this kind of climate, a Buffalo jeans ad featuring a young woman screaming, "I don't have to scream for attention but I do," can seem like an improvement—until we notice that she's really getting attention by unbuttoning her blouse to her navel. This is typical of the mixed messages so many ads and other forms of the media give girls. The young woman seems fierce and powerful, but she's really exposed, vulnerable.

The January 1998 cover of *Seventeen* highlights an article, "Do you talk too much?" On the back cover is an ad for Express mascara, which promises "high voltage volume instantly!" As if the way that girls can express themselves and turn up the volume is via their mascara. Is this harmless wordplay, or is it a sophisticated and clever marketing ploy based on research about the silencing of girls, deliberately designed to attract them with the promise of at least some form of self-expression? Advertisers certainly spend a lot of money on psychological research and focus groups. I would expect these groups to reveal, among other things, that teenage girls are angry but reticent. Certainly the cumulative effect of these images and words urging girls to express themselves only through their bodies and through products is serious and harmful.

Many ads feature girls and young women in very passive poses, limp, doll-like, sometimes acting like little girls, playing with dolls and wearing bows in their hair. One ad uses a pacifier to sell lipstick and another the image of a baby to sell Baby-Doll Blush Highlight. "Lolita seems to be a comeback kid," says a fashion layout featuring a woman wearing a ridiculous hairstyle and a baby-doll dress, standing with shoulders slumped and feet apart. In women's and teen magazines it is virtually impossible to tell the fashion layouts from the ads. Indeed, they exist to support each other.

As Erving Goffman pointed out in *Gender Advertisements,* we learn a great deal about the disparate power of males and females simply through the body language and poses of advertising.[19] Women, especially young women, are generally subservient to men in ads, through both size and position. . . .

Girls are often shown as playful clowns in ads, perpetuating the attitude that girls and women are childish and cannot be taken seriously, whereas even very young men are generally portrayed as secure, powerful, and serious. People in control of their lives stand upright, alert, and ready to meet the world. In contrast, females often appear off-balance, insecure, and weak. Often our body parts are bent, conveying unpreparedness, submissiveness, and appeasement. We exhibit what Goffman terms "licensed withdrawal"—seeming to be psychologically removed, disoriented, defenseless, spaced out.

Females touch people and things delicately, we caress, whereas males grip, clench, and grasp. We cover our faces with our hair or our hands, conveying shame or embarrassment. And, no matter what happens, we keep on smiling. "Just smiling the bothers away," as one ad says. This ad is particularly disturbing because the model is a young African-American woman, a member of a group that has long been encouraged to just keep smiling, no matter what. She's even wearing a kerchief, like Aunt Jemima. The cultural fear of angry women is intensified dramatically when the women are African-American. . . .

. . . As girls come of age sexually, the culture gives them impossibly contradictory messages. As the *Seventeen* ad says, "She wants to be outrageous. And accepted." Advertising slogans such as "because innocence is sexier than you think," "Purity, yes. Innocence never," and "nothing so sensual was ever so innocent" place them in a double bind. "Only something so pure could inspire such unspeakable passion," declares an ad for Jovan musk that features a white flower. Somehow girls are supposed to be both innocent and seductive, virginal and experienced, all at the same time. As they quickly learn, this is tricky.

Females have long been divided into virgins and whores, of course. What is new is that girls are now supposed to embody both within themselves. This is symbolic of the central contradiction of the culture—we must work hard and produce and achieve success and yet, at the same time, we are encouraged to live impulsively, spend a lot of money, and be constantly and immediately gratified. This tension is reflected in our attitudes toward many things, including sex and eating. Girls are promised fulfillment both through being thin and through eating rich foods, just as they are promised fulfillment through being innocent and virginal and through wild and impulsive sex. . . .

The emphasis for girls and women is always on being desirable, not on experiencing desire. Girls who want to be sexually *active* instead of simply being the objects of male desire are given only one model to follow, that of exploitive male sexuality. It seems that advertisers can't conceive of a kind of power that isn't manipulative and exploitive or a way that women can be actively sexual without being like traditional men.

Women who are "powerful" in advertising are uncommitted. They treat men like sex objects: "If I want a man to see my bra, I take him home," says an androgynous young woman. They are elusive and distant: "She is the first woman who refused to take your phone calls," says one ad. As if it were a good thing to be rude and inconsiderate. Why should any of us, male or female, be interested in someone who won't take our phone calls, who either cares so little for us or is so manipulative?

Mostly though, girls are not supposed to have sexual agency. They are supposed to be passive, swept away, overpowered. "See where it takes you," says a perfume ad featuring a couple passionately embracing. "Unleash your fantasies," says another. "A force of nature." This contributes to the strange and damaging concept of the "good girl" as the one who is swept away, unprepared for sex, versus the "bad girl" as the one who plans for sex, uses contraception, and is generally responsible. A young woman can manage to have sex and yet in some sense maintain her virginity by being "out of control," drunk, or deep in denial about the entire experience.

No wonder most teenage pregnancies occur when one or both parties is drunk. Alcohol and other mind-altering drugs permit sexual activity at the same time that they allow denial. One is almost literally not there. The next day one has an excuse. I was drunk, I was swept away. I did not choose this experience.

In adolescence girls are told that they have to give up much of what they *know* about relationships and intimacy if they want to attract men. Most tragically, they are told they have to give up each other. The truth is that one of the most powerful antidotes to destructive cultural messages is close and supportive female friendships. But girls are often encouraged by the culture to sacrifice their relationships with each other and to enter into hostile competition for the attention of boys and men. "What the bitch who's about to steal your man wears," says one ad. And many ads feature young women fighting or glaring at each other.

Of course, some girls do resist and rebel. Some are encouraged (by someone—a loving parent, a supportive teacher) to see the cultural contradictions clearly and to break free in a healthy and positive way. Others rebel in ways that damage themselves. A young woman seems to have only two choices: She can bury her sexual self, be a "good girl," give in to what Carol Gilligan terms "the tyranny of nice and kind" (and numb the pain by overeating or starving or cutting herself or drinking heavily).[20] Or she can become a rebel—flaunt her sexuality, seduce inappropriate partners, smoke, drink flamboyantly, use other drugs. Both of these responses are self-destructive, but they begin as an attempt to survive, not to self-destruct. . . .

There are few healthy alternatives for girls who want to truly rebel against restrictive gender roles and stereotypes. The recent emphasis on girl power has led to some real advances for girls and young women, especially in the arenas of music and sports. But it is as often co-opted and trivialized. . . . Magazines like *New Moon, Hues,* and *Teen Voices* offer a real alternative to the glitzy, boy-crazy, appearance-obsessed teen magazines on the newsstands, but they have to struggle for funds since they take no advertising. There are some good zines and Websites for girls on the Internet but there are also countless sites that degrade and endanger them. And Barbie continues to rake in two billion dollars a year . . . while a doll called "Happy to be me," similar to Barbie but much more realistic and down to earth, was available for a couple of years in the mid-1990s . . . and then vanished from sight.[21] Of course, Barbie's makers have succumbed to pressure somewhat and have remade her with a thicker waist, smaller breasts, and slimmer hips. As a result, according to Anthony Cortese, she has already lost her waitressing job at Hooter's and her boyfriend Ken has told her that he wants to start seeing other dolls.[22]

Girls who want to escape the stereotypes are viewed with glee by advertisers, who rush to offer them, as always, power via products. The emphasis in the ads is always on their sexuality, which is exploited to sell them makeup and clothes and shoes. . . . A demon woman sells a perfume called Hypnotic Poison. A trio of extremely thin African-American women brandish hair appliances and products as if they were weapons—and the brand is 911. A cosmetics company has a line of products called "Bad Gal." In one ad, eyeliner is shown in cartoon version as a girl, who is holding a dog saying, "grrrr," surely a reference to "grrrls," a symbol these days of "girl power" (as in cybergrrrl.com, the popular Website for girls and young women). Unfortunately, girl power doesn't mean much if girls don't have the tools to achieve it. Without reproductive freedom and freedom from violence, girl power is nothing but a marketing slogan. . . .

Of course, the readers and viewers of these ads don't take them literally. But we do take them in—another grain of sand in a slowly accumulating and vast sandpile. If we entirely enter the world of ads, imagine them to be real for a moment, we find that the sandpile has completely closed us in, and there's only one escape route—buy something.... "Hey girls, you've got the power of control" says an ad for ... hairspray. "The possibilities are endless" (clothing). "Never lose control" (hairspray again). "You never had this much control when you were on your own" (hair gel). "Exceptional character" (a watch). "An enlightening experience" (face powder). "Inner strength" (vitamins). "Only Victoria's Secret could make control so sensual" (girdles). "Stronger longer" (shampoo). Of course, the empowerment, the enlightenment, is as impossible to get through products as is anything else—love, security, romance, passion. On one level, we know this. On another, we keep buying and hoping—and buying.

Other ads go further and offer products as a way to rebel, to be a real individual. "Live outside the lines," says a clothing ad featuring a young woman walking out of a men's room. This kind of rebellion isn't going to rock the world. And, no surprise, the young woman is very thin and conventionally pretty. Another pretty young woman sells a brand of jeans called "Revolt." "Don't just change ... revolt," says the copy, but the young woman is passive, slight, her eyes averted.

"Think for yourself," says yet another hollow-cheeked young woman, demonstrating her individuality via an expensive and fashionable sweater. "Be amazing" (cosmetics). "Inside every woman is a star" (clothing). "If you're going to create electricity, use it" (watches). "If you let your spirit out, where would it go" (perfume). These women are all perfect examples of conventional "femininity," as is the young woman in a Halston perfume ad that says, "And when she was bad she wore Halston." What kind of "bad" is this? ...

NOTES

1. In a speech at Richland College, Dallas, Texas, on February 124, 1977.

2. Gilligan, C. 1982. *In a different voice*. Cambridge, MA: Harvard University Press; Pipher, M. 1994. *Reviving Ophelia: Saving the selves of adolescent girls*. New York: Putnam; Sadker, M and D. Sadker. 1994. *Failing at Fairness: How our schools cheat girls*. New York: Simon and Schuster.

3. Steiner-Adair, C., and A. Purcell. 1996. Approaches to mainstreaming eating disorders prevention. *Eating Disorders*, vol. 4, no. 4: 294–309.

4. Field, A.E., L. Cheung, A.M. Wolf, D.B. Herzog, S.L. Gortmaker, and G.A. Colditz. 1999. Exposure to the mass media and weight concerns among girls. *Pediatrics*, vol. 103, no. 3: 36–41.

5. Then, D. 1992. Women's magazines: Messages they convey about looks, men and careers. Paper presented at the annual convention of the American Psychological Association, Washington, DC; also Richins, M.L. 1991. Social comparison and idealized images of advertising. *Journal of Consumer Research*, 18: 71–83.

6. Fredrickson, B.L. 1998. *Journal of Personality and Social Psychology*, vol. 75. no. 1. Reported in *Media Report to Women*, 5.

7. Strasburger, V.C. 1989, Adolescent sexuality and the media. *Pediatric Clinics of North America*, vol. 36, no. 3, 747–73.

8. E-mail correspondence with Heather S. Henderson, editor-in-chief of *HUES* magazine, New Moon Publishing, March 22, 1999.

9. Stein, J. 1986 (October 29). Why girls as young as 9 fear fat and go on diets to lose weight. *Los Angeles Times*, 1, 10.

10. Rodriguez, C. 1998 (November 27). Even in middle school, girls are thinking thin. *Boston Globe*, B1, B9.

11. Rothblum, E.D. 1994. "I'll die for the revolution but don't ask me to diet": Feminism and the continuing stigmatization of obesity. In *Feminist Perspectives on Eating Disorders*, edited by P. Fallon, M.A. Katzman, and S.C. Wooley. New York: Guildford Press: 53–76.

12. Overlan, L. 1996 (July 2). "Overweight" girls at risk. *Newton Tab*, 15.

13. Steiner-Adair, C., and A. Purcell. 1996. Approaches to mainstreaming eating disorders prevention. *Eating Disorders*, vol. 4, no. 4: 294–309.

14. Smith K.A., C.G. Fairburn, and P.J. Cowen. 1999. Symptomatic relapse in bulimia nervosa following acute tryptophan depletion. *Journal of the American Medical Association*, vol. 56: 171–76. Also, Hsu, L.K. 1990. *Eating Disorders*. New York: Guildford Press; Jonas, J.M. 1989. Eating disorders and alcohol and other drug abuse. Is there an association? *Alcohol Health & Research World*, vol. 13, no. 3: 267–71; Krahn, D.D. 1991. Relationship of eating disorders and substance abuse. *Journal of Substance Abuse*, vol. 3, no. 2: 239–53; Thompson, B.W. 1994. *A hunger so wide and so deep*. Minneapolis: University of Minnesota Press.

15. Becker, A.E., and R.A. Burwell. 1999. *Acculturation and disordered eating in Fiji*. Poster presented at the American Psychiatric Association Annual Meeting, Washington, DC, May 19, 1999.

16. Goodman, E. 1999 (May 27). The culture of thin bites Fiji teens. *Boston Globe*, A23.

17. Faludi, S. 1991. *Backlash*. New York: Crown; also Kilbourne, J. 1986. The child as sex object: Images of children in the media. In *The Educator's Guide to Preventing*

Child Sexual Abuse, edited by M. Nelson and K. Clark. Santa Cruz, CA: Network Publications.

18. Martin, K.A. 1998. Becoming a gendered body: Practices of preschools. *American Sociological Review,* vol. 63, no. 4: 494–511.

19. Goffman, E. 1978. *Gender Advertisements.* Cambridge, MA: Harvard University Press.

20. Brown, L.M., and C. Gilligan. 1992. *Meeting at the crossroads: Women's psychology and girls' development.* New York: Ballantine, 53.

21. Goldsmith, J. 1999 (February 10). A $2 billion doll celebrates her 40th without a wrinkle. *Boston Globe,* D3.

22. Cortese, A. 1999. *Provocateur: Women and minorities in advertising.* Lanham, MD: Rowman and Littlefield, 57.

S I X T E E N

The Body Politic (1995)

Abra Fortune Chernik

> **Abra Fortune Chernik** is a writer who speaks frequently about eating disorders in schools and to women's organizations. She has optioned her first screenplay, *Portrait of an Invisible Girl.*

My body possesses solidness and curve, like the ocean. My weight mingles with Earth's pull, drawing me onto the sand. I have not always sent waves into the world. I flew off once, for five years, and swirled madly like a cracking brown leaf in the salty autumn wind. I wafted, dried out, apathetic.

I had no weight in the world during my years of anorexia. Curled up inside my thinness, a refugee in a cocoon of hunger, I lost the capacity to care about myself or others. I starved my body and twitched in place as those around me danced in the energy of shared existence and progressed in their lives. When I graduated from college crowned with academic honors, professors praised my potential. I wanted only to vanish.

It took three months of hospitalization and two years of outpatient psychotherapy for me to learn to nourish myself and to live in a body that expresses strength and honesty in its shape. I accepted my right and my obligation to take up room with my figure, voice and spirit. I remembered how to tumble forward and touch the world that holds me. I chose the ocean as my guide.

Who disputes the ocean's fullness?

Growing up in New York City, I did not care about the feminist movement. Although I attended an all-girls high school, we read mostly male authors and studied the history of men. Embracing mainstream culture without question, I learned about womanhood from fashion magazines, Madison Avenue and Hollywood. I dismissed feminist alternatives as foreign and offensive, swathed as they were in stereotypes that threatened my adolescent need for conformity.

Puberty hit late; I did not complain. I enjoyed living in the lanky body of a tall child and insisted on the title of "girl." If anyone referred to me as a "young woman," I would cry out, horrified, "Do not call me the *W* word!" But at sixteen years old, I could no longer deny my fate. My stomach and breasts rounded. Curly black hair sprouted in the most embarrassing places. Hips swelled from a once-flat plane. Interpreting maturation as an unacceptable lapse into fleshiness, I resolved to eradicate the physical symptoms of my impending womanhood.

Magazine articles, television commercials, lunchroom conversation, gymnastics coaches and write-ups on models had saturated me with diet savvy. Once I decided to lose weight, I quickly turned expert. I dropped hot chocolate from my regular breakfast order at the Skyline Diner. I replaced lunches of peanut butter and Marshmallow Fluff sandwiches with small platters of cottage cheese and cantaloupe. I eliminated dinner altogether and blunted my appetite with Tab, Camel Lights, and Carefree bubble gum. When furious craving overwhelmed my resolve and I swallowed an extra something, I would flee to the nearest bathroom to purge my mistake.

Within three months, I had returned my body to its preadolescent proportions and had manipulated my monthly period into drying up. Over the next five years, I devoted my life to losing my weight. I came to resent the body in which I lived, the body that threatened to develop, the body whose hunger I despised but could not extinguish. If I neglected a workout or added a pound or ate a bite too many, I would stare in the mirror and drown myself in a tidal wave of criticism. Hatred of my body generalized to hatred of myself as a person, and self-referential labels such as "pig," "failure" and "glutton" allowed me to believe that I deserved punishment. My self-hatred became fuel for the self-mutilating behaviors of the eating disorder.

As my body shrank, so did my world. I starved away my power and vision, my energy and inclinations. Obsessed with dieting, I allowed relationships, passions and identity to wither. I pulled back from the world, off of the beach, out of the sand. The waves of my existence ceased to roll beyond the inside of my skin.

And society applauded my shrinking. Pound after pound the applause continued, like the pounding ocean outside the door of my beach house.

The word "anorexia" literally means "loss of appetite." But as an anorexic, I felt hunger thrashing inside my body. I denied my appetite, ignored it, but never lost it. Sometimes the pangs twisted so sharply, I feared they would consume the meat of my heart. On desperate nights I rose in a flannel nightgown and allowed myself to eat an unplanned something.

No matter how much I ate, I could not soothe the pangs. Standing in the kitchen at midnight, spotlighted by the blue-white light of the open refrigerator, I would frantically feed my neglected appetite: the Chinese food I had not touched at dinner; ice cream and whipped cream; microwaved bread; cereal and chocolate milk; doughnuts and bananas. Then, solid sadness inside my gut, swelling agitation, a too-big meal I would not digest. In the bathroom I would rip off my shirt, tie up my hair, and prepare to execute the desperate ritual, again. I would ram the back of my throat with a toothbrush handle, crying, impatient, until the food rushed up. I would vomit until the toilet filled and I emptied, until I forgave myself, until I felt ready to try my life again. Standing up from my position over the toilet, wiping my mouth, I would believe that I was safe. Looking in the mirror through puffy eyes in a

tumescent face, I would promise to take care of myself. Kept awake by the fast, confused beating of my heart and the ache in my chest, I would swear I did not miss the world outside. Lost within myself, I almost died.

By the time I entered the hospital, a mess of protruding bones defined my body, and the bones of my emaciated life rattled me crazy. I carried a pillow around because it hurt to sit down, and I shivered with cold in sultry July. Clumps of brittle hair clogged the drain when I showered, and blackened eyes appeared to sink into my head. My vision of reality wrinkled and my disposition turned mercurial as I slipped into starvation psychosis, a condition associated with severe malnutrition. People told me that I resembled a concentration camp prisoner, a chemotherapy patient, a famine victim or a fashion model.

In the hospital, I examined my eating disorder under the lenses of various therapies. I dissected my childhood, my family structure, my intimate relationships, my belief systems. I participated in experiential therapies of movement, art and psychodrama. I learned to use words instead of eating patterns to communicate my feelings. And still I refused to gain more than a minimal amount of weight.

I felt powerful as an anorexic. Controlling my body yielded an illusion of control over my life; I received incessant praise for my figure despite my sickly mien, and my frailty manipulated family and friends into protecting me from conflict. I had reduced my world to a plate of steamed carrots, and over this tiny kingdom I proudly crowned myself queen.

I sat cross-legged on my hospital bed for nearly two months before I earned an afternoon pass to go to the mall with my mother. The privilege came just in time; I felt unbearably large and desperately wanted a new outfit under which to hide gained weight. At the mall, I searched for two hours before finally discovering, in the maternity section at Macy's, a shirt large enough to cover what I perceived as my enormous body.

With an hour left on my pass, I spotted a sign on a shop window: "Body Fat Testing, $3.00." I suggested to my mother that we split up for ten minutes; she headed to Barnes & Noble, and I snuck into the fitness store.

I sat down in front of a machine hooked up to a computer, and a burly young body builder fired questions at me:

"Age?"

"Twenty-one."

"Height?"

"Five nine."

"Weight?"

"Ninety-nine."

The young man punched my statistics into his keyboard and pinched my arm with clippers wired to the testing machine. In a moment, the computer spit out my results. "Only ten percent body fat! Unbelievably healthy. The average for a woman your age is twenty-five percent. Fantastic! You're this week's blue ribbon winner."

I stared at him in disbelief. *Winner? Healthy? Fantastic?* I glanced around at the other customers in the store, some of whom had congregated to watch my testing, and I felt embarrassed by his praise. And then I felt furious. Furious at this man and at the society that programmed him for their ignorant approbation of my illness and my suffering.

"I am dying of anorexia," I whispered. "Don't congratulate me."

I spent my remaining month in the hospital supplementing psychotherapy with an independent examination of eating disorders from a social and political point of view. I needed to understand why society would reward my starvation and encourage my vanishing. In the bathroom, a mirror on the open door behind me reflected my backside in a mirror over the sink. Vertebrae poked at my skin, ribs hung like wings over chiseled hip bones, the two sides of my buttocks did not touch. I had not seen this view of myself before.

In writing, I recorded instances in which my eating disorder had tangled the progress of my life and thwarted my relationships. I filled three and a half Mead marble notebooks. Five years' worth of: *I wouldn't sit with Daddy when he was alone in the hospital because I needed to go jogging; I told Derek not to visit me because I couldn't throw up when he was there; I almost failed my comprehensive exams because I was so hungry; I spent my year at Oxford with my head in the toilet bowl; I wouldn't eat the dinner my friends cooked me for my nineteenth birthday because I knew they had used oil in the recipe; I told my family not to come to my college graduation because I didn't want to miss a day at the* *gym or have to eat a restaurant meal.* And on and on for hundreds of pages.

This honest account of my life dissolved the illusion of anorexic power. I saw myself naked in the truth of my pain, my loneliness, my obsessions, my craziness, my selfishness, my defeat. I also recognized the social and political implications of consuming myself with the trivialities of calories and weight. At college, I had watched as classmates involved themselves in extracurricular clubs, volunteer work, politics and applications for jobs and graduate schools. Obsessed with exercising and exhausted by starvation, I did not even consider joining in such pursuits. Despite my love of writing and painting and literature, despite ranking at the top of my class, I wanted only to teach aerobics. Despite my adolescent days as a loud-mouthed, rambunctious class leader, I had grown into a silent, hungry young woman.

And society preferred me this way: hungry, fragile, crazy. *Winner! Healthy! Fantastic!* I began reading feminist literature to further understand the disempowerment of women in our culture. I digested the connection between a nation of starving, self-obsessed women and the continued success of the patriarchy. I also cultivated an awareness of alternative models of womanhood. In the stillness of the hospital library, new voices in my life rose from printed pages to echo my rage and provide the conception of my feminist consciousness.

I had been willing to accept self-sabotage, but now I refused to sacrifice myself to a society that profited from my pain. I finally understood that my eating disorder symbolized more than "personal psychodynamic trauma." Gazing in the mirror at my emaciated body, I observed a woman held up by her culture as the physical ideal because she was starving, self-obsessed and powerless, a woman called beautiful because she threatened no one except herself. Despite my intelligence, my education, and my supposed Manhattan sophistication, I had believed all of the lies; I had almost given my life in order to achieve the sickly impotence that this culture aggressively links with female happiness, love and success. And everything I had to offer to the world, every tumbling wave, every thought and every passion, nearly died inside me.

As long as society resists female power, fashion will call healthy women physically flawed. As long as society accepts the physical, sexual and economic abuse of women, popular culture will prefer women who resemble little girls. Sitting in the hospital the summer after my college graduation, I grasped the absurdity of a nation of adult women dying to grow small.

Armed with this insight, I loosened the grip of the starvation disease on my body. I determined to re-create myself based on an image of a woman warrior. I remembered my ocean, and I took my first bite.

Gaining weight and getting my head out of the toilet bowl was the most political act I have ever committed.

I left the hospital and returned home to Fire Island. Living at the shore in those wintry days of my new life, I wrapped myself in feminism as I hunted seashells and role models. I wanted to feel proud of my womanhood. I longed to accept and honor my body's fullness.

During the process of my healing, I had hoped that I would be able to skip the memory of anorexia like a cold pebble into the dark winter sea. I had dreamed that in relinquishing my obsessive chase after a smaller body, I would be able to come home to rejoin those whom I had left in order to starve, rejoin them to live together as healthy, powerful women. But as my body has grown full, I have sensed a hollowness in the lives of women all around me that I had not noticed when I myself stood hollow. I have made it home only to find myself alone.

Out in the world again, I hear the furious thumping dance of body hatred echoing every place I go. Friends who once appeared wonderfully carefree in ordering late-night french fries turn out not to eat breakfast or lunch. Smart, talented, creative women talk about dieting and overeating and hating the beach because they look terrible in bathing suits. Famous women give interviews insulting their bodies and bragging about bicycling twenty-four miles the day they gave birth.

I had looked forward to rejoining society after my years of anorexic exile. Ironically, in order to preserve my health, my recovery has included the development of a consciousness that actively challenges the images and ideas that define this culture. Walking down Madison Avenue and passing emaciated women, I say to myself, *those women are sick.* When smacked with a diet commercial, I remind myself, *I don't do that anymore.* I decline invitations to movies that feature anorexic actors, I will not participate in discussions about dieting, and I refuse to

shop in stores that cater to women with eating-disordered figures.

Though I am critical of diet culture, I find it nearly impossible to escape. Eating disorders have woven their way into the fabric of my society. On television, in print, on food packaging, in casual conversation and in windows of clothing stores populated by ridiculously gaunt mannequins, messages to lose my weight and control my appetite challenge my recovered fullness. Finally at home in my body, I recognize myself as an island in a sea of eating disorder, a sea populated predominantly by young women.

A perversion of nature by society has resulted in a phenomenon whereby women feel safer when starving than when eating. Losing our weight boosts self-esteem, while nourishing our bodies evokes feelings of self-doubt and self-loathing.

When our bodies take up more space than a size eight (as most of our bodies do), we say, *too big.* When our appetites demand more than a Lean Cuisine, we say, *too much.* When we want a piece of a friend's birthday cake, we say, *too bad.* Don't eat too much, don't talk too loudly, don't take up too much space, don't take from the world. Be pleasant or crazy, but don't seem hungry. Remember, a new study shows that men prefer women who eat salad for dinner over women who eat burgers and fries.

So we keep on shrinking, starving away our wildness, our power, our truth.

Hiding our curves under long T-shirts at the beach, sitting silently and fidgeting while others eat dessert, sneaking back into the kitchen late at night to binge and hating ourselves the next day, skipping breakfast, existing on diet soda and cigarettes, adding up calories and subtracting everything else. We accept what is horribly wrong in our lives and fight what is beautiful and right.

Over the past three years, feminism has taught me to honor the fullness of my womanhood and the solidness of the body that hosts my life. In feminist circles I have found mentors, strong women who live with power, passion and purpose. And yet, even in groups of feminists, my love and acceptance of my body remains unusual.

Eating disorders affect us all on both a personal and a political level. The majority of my peers—including my feminist peers—still measure their beauty against anorexic ideals. Even among feminists, body hatred and chronic dieting continue to consume lives. Friends of anorexics beg them to please start eating; then these friends go home and continue their own diets. Who can deny that the millions of young women caught in the net of disordered eating will frustrate the potential of the next wave of feminism?

Sometimes my empathy dissolves into frustration and rage at our situation. For the first time in history, young women have the opportunity to create a world in our image. But many of us concentrate instead on re-creating the shape of our thighs.

As young feminists, we must place unconditional acceptance of our bodies at the top of our political agenda. We must claim our bodies as our own to love and honor in their infinite shapes and sizes.

Fat, thin, soft, hard, puckered, smooth, our bodies are our homes. By nourishing our bodies, we care for and love ourselves on the most basic level. When we deny ourselves physical food, we go hungry emotionally, psychologically, spiritually and politically. We must challenge ourselves to eat and digest, and allow society to call us too big. We will understand their message to mean too powerful.

Time goes by quickly. One day we will blink and open our eyes as old women. If we spend all our energy keeping our bodies small, what will we have to show for our lives when we reach the end? I hope we have more than a group of fashionably skinny figures.

SEVENTEEN

◆◆◆

The Coming of Maureen Peal (1970)

Toni Morrison

Toni Morrison Internationally acclaimed novelist, editor, and critic, Toni Morrison is Professor in the Humanities at Princeton University. A member of the American Academy of Arts and Letters, she has won a Pulitzer Prize and the Nobel Prize for Literature. The chapter reprinted here is from her first novel, *The Bluest Eye*.

Winter tightened our heads with a band of cold and melted our eyes. We put pepper in the feet of our stockings, Vaseline on our faces, and stared through dark icebox mornings at four stewed prunes, slippery lumps of oatmeal, and cocoa with a roof of skin.

But mostly we waited for spring, when there could be gardens.

By the time this winter had stiffened itself into a hateful knot that nothing could loosen, something did loosen it, or rather someone. A someone who splintered the knot into silver threads that tangled us, netted us, made us long for the dull chafe of the previous boredom.

This disrupter of seasons was a new girl in school named Maureen Peal. A high-yellow dream child with long brown hair braided into two lynch ropes that hung down her back. She was rich, at least by our standards, as rich as the richest of the

white girls, swaddled in comfort and care. The quality of her clothes threatened to derange Frieda and me. Patent-leather shoes with buckles, a cheaper version of which we got only at Easter and which had disintegrated by the end of May. Fluffy sweaters the color of lemon drops tucked into skirts with pleats so orderly they astounded us. Brightly colored knee socks with white borders, a brown velvet coat trimmed in white rabbit fur, and a matching muff. There was a hint of spring in her sloe green eyes, something summery in her complexion, and a rich autumn ripeness in her walk.

She enchanted the entire school. When teachers called on her, they smiled encouragingly. Black boys didn't trip her in the halls; white boys didn't stone her, white girls didn't suck their teeth when she was assigned to be their work partners; black girls stepped aside when she wanted to use the sink in the girls' toilet, and their eyes genuflected under sliding lids. She never had to search for anybody to eat with in the cafeteria—they flocked to the table of her choice, where she opened fastidious lunches, shaming our jelly-stained bread with egg-salad sandwiches cut into four dainty squares, pink-frosted cupcakes, sticks of celery and carrots, proud, dark apples. She even bought and liked white milk.

Frieda and I were bemused, irritated, and fascinated by her. We looked hard for flaws to restore our equilibrium, but had to be content at first with uglying up her name, changing Maureen Peal to Meringue Pie. Later a minor epiphany was ours when we discovered that she had a dog tooth—a charming one to be sure—but a dog tooth nonetheless. And when we found out that she had been born with six fingers on each hand and that there was a little bump where each extra one had been removed, we smiled. They were small triumphs, but we took what we could get—snickering behind her back and calling her Six-finger-dog-tooth-meringue-pie. But we had to do it alone, for none of the other girls would cooperate with our hostility. They adored her.

When she was assigned a locker next to mine, I could indulge my jealousy four times a day. My sister and I both suspected that we were secretly prepared to be her friend, if she would let us, but I knew it would be a dangerous friendship, for when my eye traced the white border patterns of those Kelly-green knee socks, and felt the pull and slack of my brown stockings, I wanted to kick her. And when I thought of the unearned haughtiness in her eyes, I plotted accidental slammings of locker doors on her hand.

As locker friends, however, we got to know each other a little, and I was even able to hold a sensible conversation with her without visualizing her fall off a cliff, or giggling my way into what I thought was a clever insult.

One day, while I waited at the locker for Frieda, she joined me.

"Hi."

"Hi."

"Waiting for your sister?"

"Uh-huh."

"Which way do you go home?"

"Down Twenty-first Street to Broadway."

"Why don't you go down Twenty-second Street?"

"'Cause I live on Twenty-first Street."

"Oh. I can walk that way, I guess. Partly, anyway."

"Free country."

Frieda came toward us, her brown stockings straining at the knees because she had tucked the toe under to hide a hole in the foot.

"Maureen's gonna walk part way with us."

Frieda and I exchanged glances, her eyes begging my restraint, mine promising nothing.

It was a false spring day, which, like Maureen, had pierced the shell of a deadening winter. There were puddles, mud, and an inviting warmth that deluded us. The kind of day on which we draped our coats over our heads, left our galoshes in school, and came down with croup the following day. We always responded to the slightest change in weather, the most minute shifts in time of day. Long before seeds were stirring, Frieda and I were scruffing and poking at the earth, swallowing air, drinking rain. . . .

As we emerged from the school with Maureen, we began to molt immediately. We put our head scarves in our coat pockets, and our coats on our heads. I was wondering how to maneuver Maureen's fur muff into a gutter when a commotion in the playground distracted us. A group of boys was circling and holding at bay a victim, Pecola Breedlove.

Bay Boy, Woodrow Cain, Buddy Wilson, Junie Bug—like a necklace of semiprecious stones they surrounded her. Heady with the smell of their own musk, thrilled by the easy power of a majority, they gaily harassed her.

"Black e mo. Black e mo. Yadaddsleepsnekked. Black e mo black e moya dadd sleeps nekked. Black e mo . . ."

They had extemporized a verse made up of two insults about matters over which the victim had no control: the color of her skin and speculations on the sleeping habits of an adult, wildly fitting in its incoherence. That they themselves were black, or that their own father had similarly relaxed habits, was irrelevant. It was their contempt for their own blackness that gave the first insult its teeth. They seemed to have taken all of their smoothly cultivated ignorance, their exquisitely learned self-hatred, their elaborately designed hopelessness and sucked it all up into a fiery cone of scorn that had burned for ages in the hollows of their minds—cooled—and spilled over lips of outrage, consuming whatever was in its path. They danced a macabre ballet around the victim, whom, for their own sake, they were prepared to sacrifice to the flaming pit.

Black e mo Black e mo Ya daddy sleeps nekked.
Stch ta ta stch ta ta
stach ta ta ta ta ta

Pecola edged around the circle crying. She had dropped her notebook, and covered her eyes with her hands.

We watched, afraid they might notice us and turn their energies our way. Then Frieda, with set lips and Mama's eyes, snatched her coat from her head and threw it on the ground. She ran toward them and brought her books down on Woodrow Cain's head. The circle broke. Woodrow Cain grabbed his head.

"Hey, girl!"

"You cut that out, you hear?" I had never heard Frieda's voice so loud and clear.

Maybe because Frieda was taller than he was, maybe because he saw her eyes, maybe because he had lost interest in the game, or maybe because he had a crush on Frieda, in any case Woodrow looked frightened just long enough to give her more courage.

"Leave her 'lone, or I'm gone tell everybody what you did!"

Woodrow did not answer; he just walled his eyes.

Bay Boy piped up, "Go on, gal. Ain't nobody bothering you."

"You shut up, Bullet Head." I had found my tongue.

"Who you calling Bullet Head?"

"I'm calling you Bullet Head, Bullet Head."

Frieda took Pecola's hand. "Come on."

"You want a fat lip?" Bay Boy drew back his fist at me.

"Yeah. Gimme one of yours."

"You gone get one."

Maureen appeared at my elbow, and the boys seemed reluctant to continue under her springtime eyes so wide with interest. They buckled in confusion, not willing to beat up three girls under her watchful gaze: So they listened to a budding male instinct that told them to pretend we were unworthy of their attention.

"Come on, man."

"Yeah. Come on. We ain't got time to fool with them."

Grumbling a few disinterested epithets, they moved away.

I picked up Pecola's notebook and Frieda's coat, and the four of us left the playground.

"Old Bullet Head, he's always picking on girls."

Frieda agreed with me. "Miss Forrester said he was incorrigival."

"Really?" I didn't know what that meant, but it had enough of a doom sound in it to be true of Bay Boy.

While Frieda and I clucked on about the near fight, Maureen, suddenly animated, put her velvet-sleeved arm through Pecola's and began to behave as though they were the closest of friends.

"I just moved here. My name is Maureen Peal. What's yours?"

"Pecola."

"Pecola? Wasn't that the name of the girl in *Imitation of Life?*"

"I don't know. What is that?"

"The picture show, you know. Where this mulatto girl hates her mother 'cause she is black and ugly but then cries at the funeral. It was real sad. Everybody cries in it. Claudette Colbert too."

"Oh." Pecola's voice was no more than a sigh.

"Anyway, her name was Pecola too. She was so pretty. When it comes back, I'm going to see it again. My mother has seen it four times."

Frieda and I walked behind them, surprised at Maureen's friendliness to Pecola, but pleased. Maybe she wasn't so bad, after all. Frieda had put her coat back on her head, and the two of us, so draped, trotted along enjoying the warm breeze and Frieda's heroics.

"You're in my gym class, aren't you?" Maureen asked Pecola.

"Yes."

"Miss Erkmeister's legs sure are bow. I bet she thinks they're cute. How come she gets to wear real shorts, and we have to wear those old bloomers? I want to die every time I put them on."

Pecola smiled but did not look at Maureen.

"Hey." Maureen stopped short. "There's an Isaley's. Want some ice cream? I have money."

She unzipped a hidden pocket in her muff and pulled out a multifolded dollar bill. I forgave her those knee socks.

"My uncle sued Isaley's," Maureen said to the three of us. "He sued the Isaley's in Akron. They said he was disorderly and that that was why they wouldn't serve him, but a friend of his, a policeman, came in and beared the witness, so the suit went through."

"What's a suit?"

"It's when you can beat them up if you want to and won't anybody do nothing. Our family does it all the time. We believe in suits."

At the entrance to Isaley's, Maureen turned to Frieda and me, asking, "You all going to buy some ice cream?"

We looked at each other. "No," Frieda said.

Maureen disappeared into the store with Pecola.

Frieda looked placidly down the street; I opened my mouth, but quickly closed it. It was extremely important that the world not know that I fully expected Maureen to buy us some ice cream, that for the past 120 seconds I had been selecting the flavor, that I had begun to like Maureen, and that neither of us had a penny.

We supposed Maureen was being nice to Pecola because of the boys, and were embarrassed to be caught—even by each other—thinking that she would treat us, or that we deserved it as much as Pecola did.

The girls came out. Pecola with two dips of orange-pineapple, Maureen with black raspberry.

"You should have got some," she said. "They had all kinds. Don't eat down to the tip of the cone," she advised Pecola.

"Why?"

"Because there's a fly in there."

"How you know?"

"Oh, not really. A girl told me she found one in the bottom of hers once, and ever since then she throws that part away."

"Oh."

We passed the Dreamland Theatre, and Betty Grable smiled down at us.

"Don't you just love her?" Maureen asked.

"Uh-huh," said Pecola.

I differed. "Hedy Lamarr is better."

Maureen agreed. "Ooooo yes. My mother told me that a girl named Audrey, she went to the beauty parlor where we lived before, and asked the lady to fix her hair like Hedy Lamarr's, and the lady said, 'Yeah, when you grow some hair like Hedy Lamarr's.'" She laughed long and sweet.

"Sounds crazy," said Frieda.

"She sure is. Do you know she doesn't even menstrate yet, and she's sixteen. Do you, yet?"

"Yes." Pecola glanced at us.

"So do I." Maureen made no attempt to disguise her pride. "Two months ago I started. My girl friend in Toledo, where we lived before, said when she started she was scared to death. Thought she had killed herself."

"Do you know what it's for?" Pecola asked the question as though hoping to provide the answer herself.

"For babies." Maureen raised two pencil-stroke eyebrows at the obviousness of the question. "Babies need blood when they are inside you, and if you are having a baby, then you don't menstrate. But when you're not having a baby, then you don't have to save the blood, so it comes out."

"How do babies get the blood?" asked Pecola.

"Through the like-line. You know. Where your belly button is. That is where the like-line grows from and pumps the blood to the baby."

"Well, if the belly buttons are to grow like-lines to give the baby blood, and only girls have babies, how come boys have belly buttons?"

Maureen hesitated. "I don't know," she admitted. "But boys have all sorts of things they don't need." Her tinkling laughter was somehow stronger than our nervous ones. She curled her tongue around the edge of the cone, scooping up a dollop of purple that made my eyes water. We were waiting for a stop light to change. Maureen kept scooping the ice cream from around the cone's edge with her tongue; she didn't bite the edge as I would have done. Her tongue circled the cone. Pecola had finished hers; Maureen evidently liked her things to last. While I was thinking about her ice cream, she must have been thinking about her last remark, for she said to Pecola, "Did you ever see a naked man?"

Pecola blinked, then looked away. "No. Where would I see a naked man?"

"I don't know. I just asked."

"I wouldn't even look at him, even if I did see him. That's dirty. Who wants to see a naked man?" Pecola was agitated. "Nobody's father would be naked in front of his own daughter. Not unless he was dirty too."

"I didn't say 'father.' I just said 'a naked man.'"

"Well . . ."

"How come you said 'father'?" Maureen wanted to know.

"Who else would she see, dog tooth?" I was glad to have a chance to show anger. Not only because of the ice cream, but because we had seen our own father naked and didn't care to be reminded of it and feel the shame brought on by the absence of shame. He had been walking down the hall from the bathroom into his bedroom and passed the open door of our room. We had lain there wide-eyed. He stopped and looked in, trying to see in the dark room whether we were really asleep—or was it his imagination that opened eyes were looking at him? Apparently he convinced himself that we were sleeping. He moved away, confident that his little girls would not lie open-eyed like that, staring, staring. When he had moved on, the dark took only him away, not his nakedness. That stayed in the room with us. Friendly-like.

"I'm not talking to you," said Maureen. "Besides, I don't care if she sees her father naked. She can look at him all day if she wants to. Who cares?"

"You do," said Frieda. "That's all you talk about."

"It is not."

"It is so. Boys, babies, and somebody's naked daddy. You must be boy-crazy."

"You better be quiet."

"Who's gonna make me?" Frieda put her hand on her hip and jutted her face toward Maureen.

"You all ready made. Mammy made."

"You stop talking about my mama."

"Well, you stop talking about my daddy."

"Who said anything about your old daddy?"

"You did."

"Well, you started it."

"I wasn't even talking to you. I was talking to Pecola."

"Yeah. About seeing her naked daddy."

"So what if she did see him?"

Pecola shouted, "I never saw my daddy naked. Never."

"You did too," Maureen snapped. "Bay Boy said so."

"I did not."

"You did."

"I did not."

"Did. Your own daddy, too!"

Pecola tucked her head in—a funny, sad, helpless movement. A kind of hunching of the shoulders, pulling in of the neck, as though she wanted to cover her ears.

"You stop talking about her daddy," I said.

"What do I care about her old black daddy?" asked Maureen.

"Black? Who you calling black?"

"You!"

"You think you so cute!" I swung at her and missed, hitting Pecola in the face. Furious at my clumsiness, I threw my notebook at her, but it caught her in the small of her velvet back, for she had turned and was flying across the street against traffic.

Safe on the other side, she screamed at us, "I *am* cute! And you ugly! Black and ugly black e mos. I *am* cute!"

She ran down the street, the green knee socks making her legs look like wild dandelion stems that had somehow lost their heads. The weight of her remark stunned us, and it was a second or two before Frieda and I collected ourselves enough to shout, "Six-finger-dog-tooth-meringue-pie!" We chanted this most powerful of our arsenal of insults as long as we could see the green stems and rabbit fur.

Grown people frowned at the three girls on the curbside, two with their coats draped over their heads, the collars framing the eyebrows like nuns' habits, black garters showing where they bit the tops of brown stockings that barely covered the knees, angry faces knotted like dark cauliflowers.

Pecola stood a little apart from us, her eyes hinged in the direction in which Maureen had fled. She seemed to fold into herself, like a pleated wing. Her pain antagonized me. I wanted to open her up, crisp her edges, ram a stick down that hunched and curving spine, force her to stand erect and spit the misery out on the streets. But she held it in where it could lap up into her eyes.

Frieda snatched her coat from her head. "Come on, Claudia. 'Bye, Pecola."

We walked quickly at first, and then slower, pausing every now and then to fasten garters, tie shoe-laces, scratch, or examine old scars. We were sinking under the wisdom, accuracy, and relevance of Maureen's last words. If she was cute—and if anything could be believed, she *was*—then we were not. And what did that mean? We were lesser. Nicer, brighter, but still lesser. Dolls we could destroy, but we could not destroy the honey voices of parents and aunts, the obedience in the eyes of our peers, the slippery light in the eyes of our teachers when they encountered the Maureen Peals of the world. What was the secret? What did we lack? Why was it important? And so what? Guileless and without vanity, we were still in love with ourselves then. We felt comfortable in our skins, enjoyed the news that our senses released to us, admired our dirt, cultivated our scars, and could not comprehend this unworthiness. Jealousy we understood and thought natural—a desire to have what somebody else had; but envy was a strange, new feeling for us. And all the time we knew that Maureen Peal was not the Enemy and not worthy of such intense hatred. The *Thing* to fear was the *Thing* that made *her* beautiful, and not us.

EIGHTEEN

The Story of My Body (1993)

Judith Ortiz Cofer

Judith Ortiz Cofer is a professor of English and Creative Writing at the University of Georgia. A widely published poet and novelist, she received the 2003 Americas Award for her novel *The Meaning of Consuelo*. She is also the recipient of fellowships and grants from the Rockefeller Foundation and the National Endowment for the Arts.

Migration is the story of my body.

— Victor Hernandez Cruz

1. Skin

I was born a white girl in Puerto Rico, but became a brown girl when I came to live in the United States. My Puerto Rican relatives called me tall; at the American school, some of my rougher classmates called me "skinny-bones" and "the shrimp," because I was the smallest member of my classes. . . . I reached my full stature of five feet even in sixth grade.

I started out life as a pretty baby and learned to be a pretty girl from a pretty mother. Then at ten years of age I suffered one of the worst cases of chicken pox I have ever heard of. My entire body, including the inside of my ears and in between my toes, was covered with pustules that, in a fit of panic at my appearance, I scratched off of my face, leaving permanent scars. A cruel school nurse told me I would always have them—tiny cuts that looked as if a mad cat had plunged its claws deep into my skin. I grew my hair long and hid behind it for the first years of my adolescence. This was when I learned to be invisible.

2. Color

In the animal world it indicates danger: The most colorful creatures are often the most poisonous. Color is also a way to attract and seduce a mate. In the human world, color triggers many more complex and often deadly reactions. As a Puerto Rican girl born of "white" parents, I spent the first years of my life hearing people refer to me as *blanca*, white. My mother insisted that I protect myself from the intense island sun because I was more prone to sunburn than some of my darker, *trigueño* playmates. People were always commenting within my hearing about how my black hair contrasted so nicely with my "pale" skin. I did not think of the color of my skin consciously, except when I heard the adults talking about complexion. It seems to me that the subject is much more common in the conversation of mixed-race peoples than in mainstream U.S. society, where it is a touchy and sometimes even embarrassing topic to discuss, except in a political context. In Puerto Rico I heard many conversations about skin color. A pregnant woman could say, "I hope my baby doesn't turn out *prieto* (slang for dark or black) like my husband's grandmother, although she was a good-looking *negra* in her time." I am a combination of both, being olive-skinned—lighter than my mother yet darker than my fair-skinned father. In America, I am a person of color, obviously a Latina. On the island I have been called everything from a *paloma blanca*, after the song (by a black suitor), to *la gringa*.

My first experience of color prejudice occurred in a supermarket in Paterson, New Jersey. It was Christmastime and I was eight or nine years old. There was a display of toys in the store where I went two or three times a day to buy things for my mother who never made lists but sent for milk, cigarettes, a can of this or that, as she remembered from hour to hour. I enjoyed being trusted with money and walking half a city block to the new, modern grocery store. It was owned by three good-looking Italian brothers. I liked the younger one with the crew-cut blond hair. The two older ones watched me and the other Puerto Rican kids as if they thought we were going to steal something. The oldest one would sometimes even try to hurry me with my purchases, although part of my pleasure in these expeditions came from looking at everything in the well-stocked aisles. I was also teaching myself to read English by sounding out the labels on packages: L&M cigarettes, Borden's homogenized milk, Red Devil potted ham, Nestlé's chocolate mix, Quaker oats, Bustelo coffee, Wonder bread, Colgate toothpaste, Ivory soap, and Goya (makers of products used in Puerto Rican dishes) everything—these are some of the brand names that taught me nouns. Several times this man had come up to me wearing his bloodstained butcher's apron and, towering over me, had asked in a harsh voice whether there was something he could help me find. On the way out I would glance at the younger brother who ran one of the registers and he would often smile and wink at me.

It was the mean brother who first referred to me as "colored." It was a few days before Christmas and my parents had already told my brother and me that since we were in *los estados* now, we would get our presents on December twenty-fifth instead of *Los Reyes, Three Kings Day*, when gifts are exchanged in Puerto Rico. We were to give them a wish list that they would take to Santa Claus, who apparently lived in the Macy's store downtown—at least that's where we had caught a glimpse of him when we went shopping. Since my parents were timid about entering the fancy store, we did not approach the huge man in the red suit. I was not interested in sitting on a stranger's lap anyway. But I did covet Susie, the talking schoolteacher doll that was displayed in the center aisle of the Italian brothers' supermarket. She talked when you pulled a string on her back. Susie had a limited repertoire of three sentences: I think she could say: "Hello, I'm Susie Schoolteacher; two plus two is four," and one other thing I cannot remember. The day the older brother chased me away, I was reaching to touch Susie's blond curls. I had been told many times, as most children have, not to touch anything in a store that I was not buying. But I had been looking at Susie for weeks. In my mind, she was my doll. After all, I had put her on my Christmas wish list. The moment is frozen in my mind as if there were a photograph of it on file. It was not a turning point, a disaster, or an earthshaking revelation. It was simply the first time I considered—if naively—the meaning of skin color in human relations.

I reached to touch Susie's hair. It seems to me that I had to get on tiptoe since the toys were stacked on a table and she sat like a princess on top of the fancy box she came in. Then I heard the booming "Hey, kid, what do you think you're doing!"

spoken very loudly from the meat counter. I felt caught although I knew I was not doing anything criminal. I remember not looking at the man, but standing there feeling humiliated because I knew everyone in the store must have heard him yell at me. I felt him approach and when I knew he was behind me, I turned around to face the bloody butcher's apron. His large chest was at my eye level. He blocked my way. I started to run out of the place, but even as I reached the door I heard him shout after me: "Don't come in here unless you gonna buy something. You PR kids put your dirty hands on stuff. You always look dirty. But maybe dirty brown is your natural color." I heard him laugh and someone else too in the back. Outside in the sunlight I looked at my hands. My nails needed a little cleaning as they always did since I liked to paint with watercolors, but I took a bath every night. I thought the man was dirtier than I was in his stained apron. He was also always sweaty—it showed in big yellow circles under his shirt sleeves. I sat on the front steps of the apartment building where we lived and looked closely at my hands, which showed the only skin I could see, since it was bitter cold and I was wearing my quilted play coat, dungarees, and a knitted navy cap of my father's. I was not pink like my friend Charlene and her sister Kathy who had blue eyes and light-brown hair. My skin is the color of the coffee my grandmother made, which was half milk, *leche con café* rather than *café con leche*. My mother is the opposite mix. She has a lot of café in her color. I could not understand how my skin looked like dirt to the supermarket man.

I went in and washed my hands thoroughly with soap and hot water, and, borrowing my mother's nail file, I cleaned the crusted watercolors from underneath my nails. I was pleased with the results. My skin was the same color as before, but I knew I was clean. Clean enough to run my fingers through Susie's fine gold hair when she came home to me.

3. Size

My mother is barely four feet eleven inches in height, which is average for women in her family. When I grew to five feet by age twelve, she was amazed and began to use the word tall to describe me, as in: "Since you are tall, this dress will look good on you." As with the color of my skin, I didn't consciously think about my height or size until other people made an issue of it. It is around the preadolescent years that in America the games children play for fun become fierce competitions where everyone is out to "prove" they are better than others. It was in the playground and sports fields that my size-related problems began. No matter how familiar the story is, every child who is the last chosen for a team knows the torment of waiting to be called up. At the Paterson, New Jersey, public schools that I attended, the volleyball or softball game was the metaphor for the battlefield of life to the inner city kids—the black kids vs. the Puerto Rican kids, the whites vs. the blacks vs. the Puerto Rican kids; and I was 4F, skinny, short, bespectacled, and apparently impervious to the blood thirst that drove many of my classmates to play ball as if their lives depended on it. Perhaps they did. I would rather be reading a book than sweating, grunting, and running the risk of pain and injury. I simply did not see the point in competitive sports. My main form of exercise then was walking to the library, many city blocks away from my barrio.

Still, I wanted to be wanted. I wanted to be chosen for the teams. Physical education was compulsory, a class where you were actually given a grade. On my mainly all-A report card, the C for compassion I always received from the P.E. teachers shamed me the same as a bad grade in a real class. Invariably, my father would say: "How can you make a low grade *for playing games?*" He did not understand. Even if I had managed to make a hit (it never happened), or get the ball over that ridiculously high net, I already had a reputation as a "shrimp," a hopeless nonathlete. It was an area where the girls who didn't like me for one reason or another—mainly because I did better than they on academic subjects—could lord it over me; the playing field was the place where even the smallest girl could make me feel powerless and inferior. I instinctively understood the politics even then; how the *not* choosing me until the teacher forced one of the team captains to call my name was a coup of sorts—there you little show-off, tomorrow you can beat us in spelling and geography, but this afternoon you are the loser. Or perhaps those were only my own bitter thoughts as I sat or stood in the sidelines while the big girls were grabbed like fish and I,

the little brown tadpole, was ignored until Teacher looked over in my general direction and shouted, "Call Ortiz," or worse, "Somebody's *got* to take her."

No wonder I read Wonder Woman comics and had Legion of Super Heroes daydreams. Although I wanted to think of myself as "intellectual," my body was demanding that I notice it. I saw the little swelling around my once-flat nipples; the fine hairs growing in secret places; but my knees were still bigger than my thighs and I always wore long or half-sleeve blouses to hide my bony upper arms. I wanted flesh on my bones—a thick layer of it. I saw a new product advertised on TV. Wate-On. They showed skinny men and women before and after taking the stuff, and it was a transformation like the 97-pound weakling turned into Charles Atlas ads that I saw on the back cover of my comic books. The Wate-On was very expensive. I tried to explain my need for it in Spanish to my mother, but it didn't translate very well, even to my ears—and she said with a tone of finality, eat more of my good food and you'll get fat—anybody can get fat. Right. Except me. I was going to have to join a circus someday as "Skinny Bones," the woman without flesh.

Wonder Woman was stacked. She had a cleavage framed by the spread wings of a golden eagle and a muscular body that has become fashionable with women only recently. But since I wanted a body that would serve me in P.E., hers was my ideal. The breasts were an indulgence I allowed myself. Perhaps the daydreams of bigger girls were more glamorous, since our ambitions are filtered through our needs, but I wanted first a powerful body. I daydreamed of leaping up above the gray landscape of the city to where the sky was clear and blue, and in anger and self-pity I fantasized about scooping my enemies up by their hair from the playing fields and dumping them on a barren asteroid. I would put the P.E. teachers each on their own rock in space too where they would be the loneliest people in the universe since I knew they had no "inner resources," no imagination, and in outer space, there would be no air for them to fill their deflated volleyballs with. In my mind all P.E. teachers have blended into one large spiky-haired woman with a whistle on a string around her neck and a volleyball under one arm. My Wonder Woman fantasies of revenge were a source of comfort to me in my early career as a shrimp.

I was saved from more years of P.E. torment by the fact that in my sophomore year of high school I transferred to a school where the midget, Gladys, was the focal point of interest for the people who must rank according to size. Because her height was considered a handicap, there was an unspoken rule about mentioning size around Gladys, but of course there was no need to say anything. Gladys knew her place: front-row center in class photographs. I gladly moved to the left or to the right of her, as far as I could without leaving the picture completely.

4. Looks

Many photographs were taken of me as a baby by my mother to send to my father who was stationed overseas during the first two years of my life. With the army in Panama when I was born, he later joined the navy and traveled often on tours of duty. I was a healthy, pretty baby. Recently I read that people are drawn to big-eyed round-faced creatures, like puppies, kittens, and certain other mammals and marsupials, koalas for example, and, of course, infants. I was all eyes, since my head and body, even as I grew older, remained thin and small-boned. As a young child I got a lot of attention from my relatives and many other people we met in our barrio. My mother's beauty may have had something to do with how much attention we got from strangers in stores and on the street. I can imagine it. In the pictures I have seen of us together, she is a stunning young woman by Latino standards: long, curly black hair and round curves in a compact frame. From her I learned how to move, smile, and talk like an attractive woman. I remember going into a bodega for our groceries and being given candy by the proprietor as a reward for being *bonita*, pretty.

I can see in the photographs and I also remember that I was dressed in the pretty clothes, the stiff, frilly dresses, with layers of crinolines underneath, the glossy patent leather shoes, and, on special occasions, the skull-hugging little hats and the white gloves that were popular in the late fifties and early sixties. My mother was proud of my looks, although I was a bit too thin. She could

dress me up like a doll and take me by the hand to visit relatives, or go to the Spanish mass at the Catholic church, and show me off. How was I to know that she and the others who called me pretty were representatives of an aesthetic that would not apply when I went out into the mainstream world of school?

In my Paterson, New Jersey, public schools there were still quite a few white children, although the demographics of the city were changing rapidly. The original waves of Italian and Irish immigrants, silk-mill workers and laborers in the cloth industries, had been "assimilated." Their children were now the middle-class parents of my peers. Many of them moved their children to the Catholic schools that proliferated enough to have leagues of basketball teams. The names I recall hearing still ring in my ears: Don Bosco High vs. St. Mary's High, St. Joseph's vs. St. John's. Later I too would be transferred to the safer environment of a Catholic school. But I started school at Public School Number 11. I came there from Puerto Rico, thinking myself a pretty girl, and found that the hierarchy for popularity was as follows: pretty white girl, pretty Jewish girl, pretty Puerto Rican girl, pretty black girl. Drop the last two categories; teachers were too busy to have more than one favorite per class, and it was simply understood that if there was a big part in the school play, or any competition where the main qualification was "presentability" (such as escorting a school visitor to or from the principal's office), the classroom's public address speaker would be requesting the pretty and/or nice-looking white boy or girl. By the time I was in the sixth grade, I was sometimes called by the principal to represent my class because I dressed neatly (I knew this from a progress report sent to my mother, which I translated for her), and because all the "presentable" white girls had moved to the Catholic schools (I later surmised this part). But I was still not one of the popular girls with the boys. I remember one incident where I stepped out into the playground in my baggy gym shorts and one Puerto Rican boy said to the other: "What do you think?" The other one answered: "Her face is okay, but look at the toothpick legs." The next best thing to a compliment I got was when my favorite male teacher, while handing out the class pictures, commented that with my long neck and delicate features I resembled the movie star

Audrey Hepburn. But the Puerto Rican boys had learned to respond to a fuller figure: long necks and a perfect little nose were not what they looked for in a girl. That is when I decided I was a "brain." I did not settle into the role easily. I was nearly devastated by what the chicken-pox episode had done to my self-image. But I looked into the mirror less often after I was told that I would always have scars on my face, and I hid behind my long black hair and my books.

After the problems at the public school got to the point where even nonconfrontational little me got beaten up several times, my parents enrolled me at St. Joseph's High School. I was then a minority of one among the Italian and Irish kids. But I found several good friends there—other girls who took their studies seriously. We did our homework together and talked about the Jackies. The Jackies were two popular girls, one blonde and the other red-haired, who had women's bodies. Their curves showed even in the blue jumper uniforms with straps that we all wore. The blond Jackie would often let one of the straps fall off her shoulder, and although she, like all of us, wore a white blouse underneath, all the boys stared at her arm. My friends and I talked about this and practiced letting our straps fall off our shoulders. But it wasn't the same without breasts or hips.

My final two and a half years of high school were spent in Augusta, Georgia, where my parents moved our family in search of a more peaceful environment. There we became part of a little community of our army-connected relatives and friends. School was yet another matter. I was enrolled in a huge school of nearly two thousand students that had just that year been forced to integrate. There were two black girls and there was me. I did extremely well academically. As to my social life, it was, for the most part, uneventful—yet it is in my memory blighted by one incident. In my junior year, I became wildly infatuated with a pretty white boy. I'll call him Ted. Oh, he was pretty: yellow hair that fell over his forehead, a smile to die for, and he was a great dancer. I watched him at Teen Town, the youth center at the base where all the military brats gathered on Saturday nights. My father had retired from the military and we had all our base privileges—one other reason we had moved to Augusta. Ted looked like an angel to me. I worked on him for a year before he asked me out. This meant maneuvering to be within the periphery of his vision at every possible occasion. I took the long way to my classes in school just to pass by his locker, I went to football games that I detested, and I danced (I too was a good dancer) in front of him at Teen Town—this took some fancy footwork since it involved subtly moving my partner toward the right spot on the dance floor. When Ted finally approached me, "A Million to One" was playing on the jukebox, and when he took me into his arms, the odds suddenly turned in my favor. He asked me to go to a school dance the following Saturday. I said yes, breathlessly, I said yes but there were obstacles to surmount at home. My father did not allow me to date casually. I was allowed to go to major events like a prom or a concert with a boy who had been properly screened. There was such a boy in my life, a neighbor who wanted to be a Baptist missionary and was practicing his anthropological skills on my family. If I was desperate to go somewhere and needed a date, I'd resort to Gary. This is the type of religious nut that Gary was: When the school bus did not show up one day, he put his hands over his face and prayed to Christ to get us a way to get to school. Within ten minutes a mother in a station wagon on her way to town stopped to ask why we weren't in school. Gary informed her that the Lord had sent her just in time to get us there for roll call. He assumed that I was impressed. Gary was even good-looking in a bland sort of way, but he kissed me with his lips tightly pressed together. I think Gary probably ended up marrying a native woman from wherever he may have gone to preach the Gospel according to Paul. She probably believes that all white men pray to God for transportation and kiss with their mouths closed. But it was Ted's mouth, his whole beautiful self that concerned me in those days. I knew my father would say no to our date, but I planned to run away from home if necessary. I told my mother how important this date was. I cajoled and pleaded with her from Sunday to Wednesday. She listened to my arguments, and must have heard the note of desperation in my voice. She said very gently to me: "You better be ready for disappointment." I did not ask what she meant. I did not want her fears for me to taint my happiness. I asked her to tell my father about my date. Thursday at breakfast my father looked at me across the table with his eyebrows together. My mother looked at him with her mouth set in a straight line. I looked down at my bowl of cereal. Nobody said anything. Friday I tried on every dress in my closet. Ted would be picking me up at six on Saturday: dinner and then the sock hop at school. Friday night I was in my room doing my nails or something else in preparation for Saturday (I know I groomed myself nonstop all week) when the telephone rang. I ran to get it. It was Ted. His voice sounded funny when he said my name, so funny that I felt compelled to ask: "Is something wrong?" Ted blurted it all out without a preamble. His father had asked who he was going out with. Ted had told him my name. "Ortiz? That's Spanish, isn't it?" the father had asked. Ted had told him yes, then shown him my picture in the yearbook. Ted's father had shaken his head. No. Ted would not be taking me out. Ted's father had known Puerto Ricans in the army. He had lived in New York City while studying architecture and had seen how the *spics* lived. Like rats. Ted repeated his father's words to me as if I should understand *his predicament* when I heard why he was breaking our date. I don't remember what I said before hanging up. I do recall the darkness of my room that sleepless night, and the heaviness of my blanket in which I wrapped myself like a shroud. And I remember my parents' respect for my pain and their gentleness toward me that weekend. My mother did not say "I warned you," and I was grateful for her understanding silence.

In college, I suddenly became an "exotic" woman to the men who had survived the popularity wars in high school, who were now practicing to be worldly: They had to act liberal in their politics, in their lifestyles, and in the women they went out with. I dated heavily for a while, then married young. I had discovered that I needed stability more than social life. I had brains for sure, and some talent in writing. These facts were a constant in my life. My skin color, my size, and my appearance were variables—things that were judged according to my current self-image, the aesthetic values of the times, the places I was in, and the people I met. My studies, later my writing, the respect of people who saw me as an individual person they cared about, these were the criteria for my sense of self-worth that I would concentrate on in my adult life.

◆◆◆

NINETEEN

My Body Is a Map of My Life (1994)

Lani Ka'ahumanu

Lani Ka'ahumanu is an author, educator, and poet. A social justice activist and organizer since the '60s, she serves on the editorial boards of the *International Journal of Sexuality and Gender Studies* and the *Journal of Bisexuality*. Her published work includes *Bi Any Other Name: Bisexual People Speak Out*, edited with Loraine Hutchins.

There is a ritual I do when I remove my clothes
    with someone whether it's to sunbathe, sauna,
    massage, or to make love.

I tell the stories of my scars.

Besides the pearly stretch marks that texture my
    arms, legs, breasts and belly from two preg-
nancies and a weight gain there are scars:
a flat wide 7 inch gall bladder scar running
along my right rib line, a thin peniculectomy
scar line from hip to hip and one around my
belly button.

MY BODY IS A MAP OF MY LIFE
A PATCHWORK QUILT
THAT IS WARM AND SOFT AND STRONG.

I didn't always appreciate my body. I used to be
    ashamed and embarrassed. I had a difficult
    time baring myself with or even without
    other people around. I would avoid looking
    at myself, I mean really looking beyond the
    self-hate, beyond the media image that I
    should be, that I could be if only . . . There

was no real sense other than I wasn't good enough. I was constantly comparing myself with others. The more I denied this closet character the more control it had over my life. It was a drag. I wanted to be free; so I practiced. I practiced being nude dancing, walking, sitting, laying, playing all while looking in the mirror at myself from every possible angle.

It wasn't easy but as the months and years passed I became more comfortable and accepting. You could even say I developed a nonchalant attitude when in the nude. I began to feel at home in my body and in the growing sense of well-being SCAR WOMAN emerged from the closet. All imperfections exposed, I claimed the unique, distinctive markings, making them perfect in the showing.

MY BODY IS A MAP OF MY LIFE
A PATCHWORK QUILT
THAT IS WARM AND SOFT AND STRONG.

T W E N T Y

◆◆◆

I Am Not One of the* (1987)

Cheryl Marie Wade

Cheryl Marie Wade is an activist, poet, essayist, and award-winning writer-performer. Her videos include *Body Talk, Vital Signs: Crip Culture Talks Back, Self-Advocacy: Freedom, Equality and Justice for All,* and *Here: A Poetry Performance.*

I am not one of the physically challenged—

I'm a sock in the eye with gnarled fist
I'm a French kiss with cleft tongue
I'm orthopedic shoes sewn on a last of your fears

I am not one of the differently abled—

I'm an epitaph for a million imperfect babies left
    untreated
I'm an ikon carved from bones in a mass grave at
    Tiergarten, Germany
I'm withered legs hidden with a blanket

I am not one of the able disabled—

I'm a black panther with green eyes and scars like
    a picket fence
I'm pink lace panties teasing a stub of milk white
    thigh
I'm the Evil Eye
I'm the first cell divided
I'm mud that talks
I'm Eve   I'm Kali
I'm The Mountain That Never Moves
I've been forever   I'll be here forever
I'm the Gimp
I'm the Cripple
I'm the Crazy Lady

I'm The Woman With Juice

————

*This poem is dedicated "to all my disabled sisters, to the activists in the streets and on the stages, to the millions of Sharon Kowalskis without a Karen Thompson, to all my sisters and brothers in the pits, closets, and institutions of enlightened societies everywhere."

TWENTY-ONE

Feminist Theory, the Body, and the Disabled Figure (2002)

Rosemarie Garland Thomson

Rosemarie Garland Thomson is a professor of Women's Studies at Emory University. Author of *Extraordinary Bodies: Figuring Physical Disability in American Literature and Culture*, her scholarly and professional activities are devoted to developing the field of disability studies in the humanities and women's studies.

The Female Body and the Disabled Body

Many parallels exist between the social meanings attributed to female bodies and those assigned to disabled bodies. Both the female and the disabled body are cast within cultural discourse as deviant and inferior; both are excluded from full participation in public as well as economic life; both are defined in opposition to a valued norm which is assumed to possess natural corporeal superiority. Indeed, the discursive equation of femaleness with disability is common, sometimes in the service of denigrating women and sometimes with the goal of defending them. Examples abound, from Freud's understanding femaleness in terms of castration to late nineteenth-century physicians' defining menstruation as a disabling and restricting "eternal wound" to Thorstein Veblen's describing women in 1900 as literally disabled by feminine roles and costuming. Feminists today even often invoke negative images of disability to describe the oppression of women, as does Jane Flax—to cite a common example—in her assertion that women are "mutilated and deformed" by sexist ideology and practices.[1]

Perhaps, however, the founding association of femaleness with disability occurs in the fourth book of *Generation of Animals*, Aristotle's inaugural discourse of the normal and the abnormal in which he refines the Platonic concept of antinomies so that bodily variety translates into the hierarchies of the typical and the aberrant. "[A]nyone who does not take after his parents," Aristotle asserts, "is really in

a way a monstrosity, since in these cases Nature has in a way strayed from the generic type. The first beginning of this deviation is when a female is formed instead of a male." Here the philosopher whom we might consider the founding father of Western taxonomy projects idealism onto corporeality to produce a definitive, seemingly neutral "generic type" along with its particularized antithesis, the "monstrosity," whose departure from such a "type" constitutes a profound "deviation.". . . Aristotle's choreography of bodies thus conjoins the "monstrosity"—whom we would today term "congenitally disabled"—and the female on a course leading away from the definitive norm. In Book Two, Aristotle also affirms his connection of disabled and female bodies by stating that "the female is as it were a deformed male" or—as it appears in other translations—"a mutilated male."[2]

More significant than his simple conflation of disability and femaleness is that Aristotle reveals here the source from which all otherness arises: the concept of a normative, "generic type" against which all corporeal variation is measured and found to be different, derivative, inferior, and insufficient. Not only does this definition of the female as a "mutilated male" inform later versions of woman as a diminished man, but it arranges somatic diversity into a hierarchy of value that assigns plenitude to some bodies and lack to others based on their configurations. Furthermore, by focusing on defining femaleness as deviant rather than the maleness he assumes to be essential, Aristotle also initiates the discursive practice of marking what is deemed aberrant while concealing the position of privilege by asserting its normativeness. Thus we witness perhaps the originary operation of the logic which has become so familiar in discussions of gender, race, or disability: male, white, or able-bodied superiority is naturalized, remaining undisputed and obscured by the ostensible problem of female, black, or disabled deviance. What this passage makes clearest, however, is that without the monstrous body to demarcate the borders of the generic, without the female body to distinguish the shape of the male, and without the pathological to give form to the normal, these taxonomies of bodily value that underwrite political, social, and economic arrangements would collapse.

Considering this persistent intertwining of disability with femaleness in Western discourse provides a fruitful context for explorations of social identity and the body. As Aristotle's pronouncement suggests, the social category of disability turns upon the significance accorded bodily functioning and configuration, just as the social category woman does. Placing disability studies in a feminist context allows feminist theory's . . . inquiries into gender as a category, the body's role in identity and selfhood, and the complexity of social power relations to be brought to bear on an analysis of disability. Moreover, applying feminist theory to disability analyses infuses it with feminism's politicized insistence on the relationship between the meanings attributed to bodies by cultural representations and the consequences of those meanings in the world. In viewing disability through a feminist lens, I hope at the same time to suggest how the category of disability might be inserted into feminist theory so that the bodily configurations and functioning we call "disability" will be included in all feminist examinations of culture and representation. This brief exploration aims then at beginning the work of altering the terms of both feminist and disability discourses.

Feminist Theory and Disability Discourse

Contemporary feminist theory has proved to be porous, diffuse, and—perhaps most significant— self-critical. . . . Most recently, the debate between viewing gender in terms of minimizing differences in order to achieve equality and elaborating difference in order to valorize the feminine has been complicated by an interrogation of gender construction itself and the recognition of multiple axes of identity, both of which profoundly challenge the very notion of "woman" as any kind of unified identity category. Such simultaneous insistence on a politics of location, coupled with the relentless questioning of identity and subjectivity as cultural constructs, along with the maintenance of a resolutely political

critique comprise the theoretical milieu in which I want to place disability.

Thus, the strands of feminist thought coinciding most harmoniously with disability concerns are those which go beyond a narrow focus on gender alone and avoid the exclusion of other forms of social inflection; they undertake a broad sociopolitical critique of systemic, inequitable power relations based on binary social categories grounded in the body. In its largest sense, feminism becomes a theoretical perspective and methodology that examines gender as a discursive, ideological, and material category that interacts with but does not subordinate either other social identities or the particularities of embodiment, history, and location that inform subjectivity. Briefly put, feminism's often conflicting and always complex dual aims of politicizing the materiality of bodies while rewriting the category of woman are exactly the kinds of interrogations that should be brought to bear upon disability.[3]

I want to extend in a fresh juxtaposition, then, the association of disability and femaleness with which I began this essay. Rather than simply conflating the disabled body with the female body, however, I want to theorize disability in the ways that feminism has theorized gender. Both feminism and the interrogation of disability I am undertaking challenge existing social relations; both resist interpretations of certain bodily configurations and functioning as deviant; both question the ways that particularity or difference is invested with meaning; both examine the enforcement of universalizing norms; both interrogate the politics of appearance; both explore the politics of naming; both participate in positive identity politics. Nevertheless, feminism has formulated the terms and probed the logic of these concerns much more thoroughly than has disability studies, at this point.[4]

Eve Sedgwick's distinction, for example, between a "minoritizing" and a "universalizing" view of difference can be applied usefully to disability discourse. One minoritizes difference, . . . by imagining its significance and concerns as limited to a narrow, specific, relatively fixed population or arena of inquiry. In contrast, a universalizing view sees issues surrounding a particularized form of difference as having "continuing, determinative importance in the lives of people across the spectrum of [identities].[5] . . .

I would advocate for disability studies to be seen as a universalizing discourse. . . . Such a conceptualization makes possible, among other things, recognizing that disability (or gender or homosexuality) is a category that structures a wide range of thought, language, and perception not explicitly articulated as "disability" (or gender or homosexuality). Universalizing, then, names the impulse behind the attempt here to show how the unarticulated concept of disability informs such national ideologies as American liberal individualism and sentimentalism, as well as explorations of African-American and lesbian identities. Such semantics emerging from feminist theory can be enlisted to dislodge the persistent assumption that disability is a self-evident condition of bodily inadequacy and private misfortune whose politics concern only a limited minority—just as femaleness so easily seemed before feminism.

A universalizing disability discourse which draws on feminism's confrontation with the gender system requires asserting the body as a cultural text which is interpreted, inscribed with meaning, indeed *made,* within social relations of power. Such a perspective advocates political equality by denaturalizing disability's assumed inferiority, casting its configurations and functions as difference rather than lack. But while this broad constructionist perspective does the vital cultural work of destigmatizing gender or racial differences as well as the corporeal traits we call disability, it also threatens to obscure the material and historical effects of those differences and to destablize the very social categories we analyze and, in many cases, claim as significant in our own and others' lives. . . .

. . . The kind of legally mandated access to public spaces and institutions which began for women in the nineteenth century and has accelerated since the 1960s was only fully launched for disabled people by the Americans with Disabilities Act of 1990, a broad civil rights bill that is only beginning to be implemented. And while race and gender are accepted generally as differences rather than deviances in the political moves toward equality, disability is still most often seen as bodily inadequacy or misfortune to be compensated for through a pity, rather than a civil rights, model. So, on the one hand, it is important to employ the constructionist argument to denaturalize the assumption that disability is bodily insufficiency and to

assert instead than disability arises from the interaction of embodied differences with an unaccommodating physical and social environment. But, on the other hand, the particular, historical materiality of the disabled body that demands both accommodation and recognition must be preserved as well. Consequently, the embodied difference that using a wheelchair or being deaf makes should be claimed, but without casting that difference as lack.[6]

Both constructionism and essentialism, then, become theoretical strategies—framings of the body—invoked when useful to achieve specific ends in the political arena, to liberate psychologically subjects whose bodies have been narrated to them as defective, or to facilitate imagined communities from which a positive identity politics can emerge. Thus, a strategic constructionism destigmatizes the disabled body, locates difference relationally, denaturalizes normalcy, and challenges appearance hierarchies. A strategic essentialism, by contrast, validates experience and consciousness, imagines community, authorizes history, and facilitates self-naming. The identity "disabled" operates, then, as a pragmatic narrative, what Susan Bordo calls "a life-enhancing fiction," grounded in the materiality of a particular embodiment and perspective embedded in specific social and historical contexts.[7]

Imagining Feminist Disability Discourse

But if the category "disabled" is a useful fiction, the disabled body set in a world structured for the normative, privileged body is not. Disability, perhaps more than other forms of alterity, demands a reckoning with the messiness of bodily variegation, with literal individuation run amok. Because the embodiment we think of as disability exists not so much as a set of observable predictable traits—like racialized or gendered physical features—but rather as *any* departure from an unstated corporeal norm, disability foregrounds embodiment's specificity. In other words, the concept of disability unites a highly marked, heterogeneous collection of embodiments whose only commonality is being considered abnormal. As a departure from a norm made neutral by an environment created to accommodate it, disability becomes intense, extravagant, and problematic embodiment. It is the unorthodox made flesh. Occupying the province of the extraordinary, disability refuses to be normalized, neutralized, or homogenized. More important yet, in an era governed by the abstract principle of universal equality, disability signals the body that cannot be universalized. Unified only by exclusion, disability confounds any notion of a generalizable, constant corporeal subject by flaunting the vagaries of an embodiment shaped by history, defined by particularity, and at odds with its environment. The cripple before the stairs, the blind before the printed page, the deaf before the radio, the amputee before the typewriter, and the dwarf before the counter—all testify with their particular bodies to the fact that the myriad structures and practices of material, daily life enforce the cultural expectation of a certain standard, universal subject before whom all others appear inferior.

Indeed, the identity category of disability can pressure feminist theory to acknowledge bodily particularity and history. Perhaps feminism's most useful concept for doing so is standpoint theory, which recognizes the local and complex quality of embodiment. Emphasizing the multiplicity of all women's identities, history, and embodiment, this theory of positionality recognizes that individual material situations structure the subjectivity from which particular women can speak and perceive with authority. In incorporating postmodernism's challenge of the unsituated, objective Enlightenment viewpoint, feminist standpoint theory has reformulated a monologic notion of gender identity into a more complex conception of identity as a dynamic matrix of interrelated, often contradictory, experiences, strategies, styles, and attributions mediated by culture and one's specific history, forming a network that cannot be separated meaningfully into discrete entities or ordered into a hierarchy. Acknowledging identity's particular and complex nature allows inflections other than the usual trinity of race, class, and gender to emerge. Standpoint theory and the feminist practice of explicitly situating oneself when speaking make way for complicating inflections such as disabilities or, more broadly, the category of corporeal configuration—as in such attributions as fat, disfigured, abnormal, ugly, or deformed—to be inserted into our considerations of identity and subjectivity. Such a dismantling of the unitary category woman has enabled

feminist theory to encompass—although not without contention—such feminist differentiations as Patricia Hill Collins's "black feminist thought," for instance, or my own explorations of a "feminist disability studies."[8] . . .

I am suggesting, then, that a feminist political praxis for women with disabilities needs strategically to focus at times on the specificity and perhaps the ineluctability of the flesh and to find clarity in the identity it occasions. For example, in one of the inaugural explorations of the politics of self-naming, Nancy Mairs claims the appellation "cripple" because it demands that others acknowledge the singularity of her embodiment. "People . . . wince at the word 'cripple,'" Mairs contends. Even though she retains what has been a derogatory term, she insists on determining its significance herself: "Perhaps I want them to wince. I want them to see me as a tough customer, one to whom the fates/gods/viruses have not been kind, but who can face the brutal truth of her existence squarely. As a cripple, I swagger." Here Mairs is not so much rehabilitating the term of otherness as a celebration or as an attempt to reverse its contemptuous connotation; rather, she wants to call attention less to her oppression and more to the material reality of her crippledness, to her bodily difference her experience of it. For Mairs, the social constructionist argument risks neutralizing the difference of her pain and her struggle with an environment built for a body other than hers.[9]

The confrontation with bodily difference that disability provokes also places some disabled women at odds with several mainstream feminist assumptions that do not take into account disabled women's material situations. For example, while feminism quite legitimately decries the sexual objectification of women, disabled women often encounter what Harlan Hahn has called "asexual objectification," the assumption that sexuality is inappropriate in disabled people. One woman who uses a wheelchair and is at the same time quite beautiful reports, for example, that people often respond to her as if this combination of traits were a remarkable and lamentable contradiction. The judgment that the disabled woman's body is asexual and unfeminine creates what Michelle Fine and Adrienne Asch term "rolelessness," a kind of social invisibility and cancellation of femininity which sometimes prompts disabled women to claim an essential femininity which the culture denies them.

For example, Cheryl Marie Wade insists upon a harmony between her disability and her womanly sexuality in a poem characterizing herself as "The Woman With Juice"[10] [see Reading 20]. As Mairs's exploration of self-naming and Wade's assertion of sexuality suggest, a feminist disability politics would uphold the right for women to define their corporeal differences and their relationship to womanhood for themselves rather than acceding to received interpretations of their embodiment.

Wade's poem of self-definition echoes Mairs by maintaining firmly that she is "not one of the physically challenged," but rather she claims, "I'm the Gimp/I'm the Cripple/I'm the Crazy Lady." Affirming her body as at once sexual and different, she asserts, "I'm a French kiss with cleft tongue." Resisting the cultural tendency to erase not only her sexuality but the depreciated materiality of her embodiment, she characterizes herself as "a sock in the eye with gnarled first." This image of the disabled body as a visual assault, as a shocking spectacle to the normative eye, captures a defining aspect of disabled experience. Whereas feminists claim that women are objects of the male gaze which demarcates their subjectivity, Wade's image of her body as "a sock in the eye" subtly reminds us that the disabled body is the object not of the appropriating gaze but of the stare. If the male gaze informs the normative female self as a sexual spectacle, then the stare sculpts the disabled subject as a grotesque spectacle. The stare is the gaze intensified, framing her body as an icon of deviance. Indeed, as Wade's poem suggests, the stare is the material gesture that creates disability as an oppressive social relationship. And as every person with a visible disability knows intimately, managing, deflecting, resisting, or renouncing that stare is the daily business of life.

In addition to having to prove their sexuality, disabled women must sometimes defend as well against the assessment that their bodies are unfit for motherhood or that they are the infantilized objects upon which others exercise their virtue. Whereas motherhood is often seen as compulsory for women, disabled women are often denied access or discouraged from entrance to the arena of reproduction that some feminist thinkers have found oppressive. The controversial feminist ethic of care also has been criticized by feminist disability scholars as potentially threatening to symmetrical, reciprocal relations among disabled and nondisabled women as well as for suggesting that care is the sole responsibility of women. . . .

Perhaps more problematic yet, feminist abortion rationale seldom questions the prejudicial assumption that "defective" fetuses destined to become disabled people should be eliminated.[11] The concerns of older women, who are often disabled, tend also to be ignored by younger feminists, as well. One of the most pervasive feminist assumptions that undermines some disabled women's struggle is the ideology of autonomy and independence emanating from liberal feminism and the broader impulse toward female empowerment. By tacitly incorporating the liberal premise that levels individual particularities and differences in order to posit an abstract, disembodied subject of democracy, feminist practice often leaves no space for the needs and accommodations that disabled women's bodies require.[12] The angry and disappointed words prominent disability rights activist Judy Heumann spoke to me reflect an alienation not unlike that between some black women and some white feminists: "When I come into a room full of feminists, all they see is a wheelchair."[13] These conflicts testify that feminists, like everyone else, including disabled people themselves, have been acculturated to stigmatize those whose bodies are deemed aberrant.

Femininity and Disability

So while I want to insist on disabled women's particularity and identity even while questioning its sources and its production, I also want to suggest nevertheless that a firm boundary between "disabled" and "nondisabled" women cannot be meaningfully drawn—just as any absolute distinction between sex and gender must be problematized. Femininity and disability are inextricably entangled in Western culture, as Aristotle's equation of women and disabled men illustrates. Not only has the female body been represented as deviant, but historically the practices of femininity have configured female bodies in ways that duplicate the parameters of disability. Feminizing conventions such as Chinese foot binding, African scarification, clitoridectomy, and Euroamerican corseting were (and are) socially accepted, encouraged, even compulsory, forms of female disablement that ironically constitute feminine social enablement, increasing a woman's value and status as a woman at a given moment in a particular society. Similarly, such conditions as anorexia, hysteria, and agoraphobia are in a sense standard feminine scripts writ large enough to become disabling conditions, blurring the line between normal feminine behavior and pathology.[14]

Feminine beauty's disciplinary regime often obscures the seemingly self-evident categories of the "normal" and the "pathological" as well. For example, the nineteenth-century Euroamerican prescription for upper-class feminine beauty precisely paralleled the symptoms of tuberculosis just as the cult of thinness promoted by the fashion industry approaches the appearance of disease. In another instance, the iconography and language of contemporary cosmetic surgery presented in women's magazines persistently casts the unreconstructed female body as having "abnormalities" that can be "corrected" by surgical procedures which "improve" one's appearance by producing "natural looking" noses, thighs, breasts, chins, and so on. This discourse casts women's unmodified bodies as unnatural and abnormal while the surgically altered bodies become normal and natural. Although cosmetic surgery is in one sense only the logical extension of beauty practices such as make-up, perms, relaxers, skin lighteners, and hair removal, it differs profoundly from these basically decorative forms of self-reconstruction because, like clitoridectomies and scarification, it involves mutilation, pain, and wounding that is definitive of many disabilities.

While all of these practices cannot, of course, be equated, each nevertheless transforms an infinitely plastic body in ways similar to the ways disability alters the body. The difference is that these changes are imagined to be choices that will sculpt the female body so it conforms to a feminine ideal. Disabilities, despite their affinities with beautifiction procedures, are imagined, in contrast, to be random transformations that move the body away from ideal forms. Within the visual economy in which appearance has come to be the primary index of value for women, feminizing practices normalize the female body, while disabilities abnormalize it. Feminization prompts the gaze, while disability prompts the stare. Feminization alterations increase a woman's cultural capital, while disabilities reduce it.[15]

But as Aristotle's equation of femaleness with mutilated males suggests, the normalized female body is abnormal in reference to the universally human male body. The normative female body—the figure of the beautiful woman—is a narrowly prescribed version of what the ideal male figure is not. If he is to be strong, active, hirsute, hard, and so on, then she must be his opposite—weak, passive, hairless, soft, and so on. The normative female body, then, occupies a dual and paradoxical cultural role: it is the negative term opposing the male body, but it is also simultaneously the privileged term in reference to the abnormalized female body.

For example, the nineteenth-century obsession with scientific quantification actually produced a detailed description of absolute beauty, laid out by Havelock Ellis, which posited a Darwinian ranking of beauty, determined entirely by corporeal characteristics and ranging from the "beautiful" European woman to what was considered to be her grotesque opposite, the African woman. Moreover, scientific discourse conceived this anatomical scale of beauty as simultaneously one of pathology. The further a female body departed from absolute beauty, the more "abnormal" it became as a female body. The markers of this indubitable pathology were traits such as dark skin and physical disability, or behaviors like prostitution, which were often linked to bodily characteristics. Within this scheme, all women are seen as deviant in their femaleness, but some women are imagined as doubly deviant. So the simple dichotomy of objectified feminine body and masculine subject is complicated, then, by other sets of binary oppositions that further clarify the original terms. Indeed, the unfeminine, unbeautiful body mutually constitutes the very shape of the feminine body. This other figure of woman has been identified variously in history and discourse as black, fat, lesbian, sexually appetitive, disabled, ugly, and so on. What is important for this study, however, is that her deviance and subsequent devaluation are always attributed to some visible bodily characteristic—a mark that can operate as an emblem of her difference—just as beauty has always been located in the body of the feminine woman. As one manifestation of the unbeautiful woman, the third term that disrupts a tidy pair of antinomies, the figure of the disabled woman tends to complicate discourses announcing themselves as trafficking in oppositional paradigms.

As this discussion of normalized and abnormalized female bodies suggests, it is the cultural figure of the disabled woman, rather than the actual woman with a disability, that this essay focuses upon. Within the politics of representation I have explored here, the figure of the disabled woman is best apprehended as a product of a conceptual triangulation. She is a cultural third term, a figure constituted by the originary binary pair of the masculine figure and the feminine figure. Thus, the disabled female figure occupies an intragender position; that is, she is not only defined against the masculine figure, but she is imagined as the antithesis of the normative woman as well. But because representation structures reality, the cultural figures that haunt the days of the living often must, like Virginia Woolf's Angel of the House, be wrestled to the floor before even modest self-definition, let alone political action, can proceed.

NOTES

1. See Patricia Vertinsky, "Exercise, Physical Capability, and the Eternally Wounded Woman in Late Nineteenth-Century North America," *Journal of Sport History* 14, 1 (1987): 7–27, p. 7; Thorstein Veblen, *The Theory of the Leisure Class* (Boston: Houghton Mifflin, 1973); Jane Flax, *Thinking Fragments: Psychoanalysis, Feminism, and Postmodernism in the Contemporary West* (Berkeley: University of California Press, 1990), p. 136.

2. Aristotle, *Generation of Animals*, trans. A. L. Peck, (Cambridge: Harvard University Press, 1944) Book IV, 401 and Book II, 175.

3. See Susan Bordo, *Unbearable Weight: Feminism, Western Culture, and the Body* (Berkeley: University of California Press, 1993); Rosemary Hennessy, *Materialist Feminism and the Politics of Discourse* (New York: Routledge, 1993); Jennifer Wicke, "Celebrity Material: Materialist Feminism and the Culture of Celebrity," *South Atlantic Quarterly* 93, 4 (Fall 1994): 751–78; Judith Grant, *Fundamental Feminism;* Linda Nicholson, ed., *Feminism/Postmodernism* (New York: Routledge, 1990).

4. Most theorists of disability either naturalize disability while protesting exclusion and oppression of disabled people or they adopt a strict social constructionist perspective in order to claim equality, while asserting difference for the purposes of establishing identity.

5. Eve Kosofsky Sedgwick, *Epistemology of the Closet* (Berkeley: University of California Press, 1990), p. 1.

6. See Joseph Shapiro, *No Pity: People with Disabilities Forging a New Civil Rights Movement* (New York: Times Books/Random House, 1993); Claire Liachowitz, *Disability as a Social Construct;* and Richard Scotch, *From Good Will to Civil Rights.*

7. Diana Fuss in *Essentially Speaking* examines this tension between constructionist and essentialist conceptions of identity, concluding that to deconstruct identity is not to deny categories, but rather to expose the fictionality of them even while claiming them for political purposes and to establish community and affinity. Benedict Anderson's concept of "imagined communities" is useful here to suggest the strategic aspect of such communities for political and psychological purposes; see *Imagined Communities: Reflections on the Origin and Spread of Nationalism* (New York: Verso, 1991).

8. See Collins, *Black Feminist Thought,* and Rosemarie Garland Thomson, "Redrawing the Boundaries of Feminist Disability Studies," *Feminist Studies* 20 (Fall 1994): 583–95.

9. Nancy Mairs, "On Being a Cripple," *Plaintext: Essays* (Tucson: University of Arizona Press, 1986), p. 90.

10. Michelle Fine and Adrienne Asch, "Disabled Women: Sexism without the Pedestal," *Women and Disability: The Double Handicap,* eds., Mary Jo Deegan and Nancy A. Brooks (New Brunswick, NJ: Transaction Books, 1985), 6–22, 12. Cheryl Marie Wade, MS II (3): 57.

11. For discussions of disability in relation to abortion and reproductive rights, see Ruth Hubbard, "Who Should and Should Not Inhabit the World," in Ruth Hubbard, ed., *The Politics of Women's Biology* (New Brunswick, NJ: Rutgers University Press, 1990); Marsha Saxton, "Born and Unborn: The Implications of Reproductive Technologies for People with Disabilities," in Rita Arditti, Renate Duell Klein, and Shelley Minden, eds., *Test-Tube Women: What Future for Motherhood?* (Boston: Pandora, 1984), 298–312; and Anne Finger, "Claiming All of Our Bodies: Reproductive Rights and Disability," in Arditti et al., ed., *Test-Tube Women,* pp. 281–96; Fine and Asch, eds., *Women with Disabilities,* esp. ch. 12 and 13; and Deborah Kaplan, "Disabled Women," in Alison Jaggar, ed., *Living with Contradictions: Controversies in Feminist Social Ethics* (Boulder: Westview Press, 1994).

12. Susan Bordo argues in a similar vein that the feminist search for equality has caused a flight from gender and, hence, from the body, that often masquerades as "professionalism." Disabled women's inability to erase the claims of their bodies or to be able to fit the standardized image of the "professional" often alienates them from feminists who enter the workplace on such terms. See Bordo, *Unbearable Weight,* 229–33, for a discussion of this point; also see Fine and Asch, eds., *Women with Disabilities,* 26–31.

13. Personal conversation, Society for Disability Studies Annual Meeting, June, 1991, Denver, CO.

14. The philosopher Iris Marion Young argues for the construction of femininity as disability, for example, by asserting that the cultural objectification of women is manifest in their tendency to be inhibited in using their bodies as

unselfconscious agents of physical capability. "Women in a sexist society are physically handicapped," concludes Young in the essay that focuses on the phenomenon of "Throwing Like a Girl" (*Throwing Like a Girl*, 153).

15. Mary Russo's *The Female Grotesque: Risk, Excess, and Modernity* (New York: Routledge, 1994) observes what she calls "the normalization of feminism" which involves "strategies of reassurance" that encourage feminists to focus on standard forms of femininity and avoid the female sites she calls "the grotesque," which I might term the "abnormal."

4

◆◆◆

Women's Sexuality

The body is the place where biological sex, socially constructed gender, and sexuality come together. Sexual attitudes and behaviors vary considerably from society to society and across historical time periods (Caplan 1987; Lancaster and di Leonardo 1997). Sexuality is not instinctive but learned from our families, our peers, sex education in school, popular culture, negotiations with partners, and listening to our own bodies. Much is learned from what is not said as well as what is made explicit. In this society, sexuality is a source of intimacy and pleasure, vulnerability and danger. Over the course of our lives, women's sexuality may take different forms and take on different degrees of significance. There is a heavy emphasis on sexuality in advertising, news reporting, and popular culture. At the same time, there is a dearth of accurate information about women's sexuality, and there are many constraints on it.

This chapter focuses on women's experiences of sexuality, the meso- and macro-level forces that shape these experiences, and the ways that women are defining sexuality for themselves. As you read this chapter, think also about the social construction of male sexuality.

Stereotypes, Contradictions, and Double Standards

In advertising images and popular culture, sexuality is the prerogative of the young, slender, and able-bodied. Many of these images portray White women. Melba Wilson (1993) notes that racism and sexism converge in mainstream stereotypes of women of color as "exotic creatures of passion" (p. 66). Contemporary "pornographic images of black women show us as picturesque, removed from self and deserving of—even asking for—enslavement" (p. 76). She argues that this imagery is based in the historical abuse of Black women by White slave masters. Asian and Asian American women are stereotyped as "Suzie Wong" or as "exotic flowers," passive, accommodating, and focused on serving men. The film *Slaying the Dragon* (1988; distributed by Women Make Movies) provides an excellent critique of this stereotype. Sociologist Patricia Hill Collins (2004, p. 30) argues that ideas of pure White womanhood, developed as part of European national identity, "required a corresponding set of ideas about hot-blooded Latinas, exotic Suzy Wongs, wanton jezebels." She continues:

> Civilized nation-states required uncivilized and backward colonies for their national identity to have meaning, and the status of women in both places was central to this endeavor. In this context, Black women became icons of hypersexuality.

This powerful stereotype continues to this day, and is constantly reinforced in media representations.

By contrast, women with disabilities and older women of all racial groups are stereotyped as sexless. According to the late Barbara Waxman Fiduccia, an advocate for reproductive rights for people with disabilities, and Marsha Saxton, a teacher of disability studies, women with disabilities have been kept socially isolated and discouraged from expressing their sexuality. In their "Disability Feminism: A Manifesto" (1997), they write: "We want our sexuality accepted and supported with accurate information" (p. 60). Lillian Gonzales Brown, of the Institute on Disability Culture (Honolulu, Hawaii), notes the influence of the disability rights movement on changing attitudes for people with disabilities. There has been a shift from feeling shame, then wanting to assimilate, to disability pride. In workshops on sexuality for women with disabilities, she urges participants to explore their sexuality and to see themselves as sexual beings (L. G. Brown, personal communication, October 1996; see also Kaufman, Silverberg, and Odette 2003).

Ads that use women's bodies to sell products also sell ideas of women's sexuality. As sex objects, women are commonly portrayed as child-like or doll-like playthings. These images flow from and reinforce macro-level patriarchal constructions of sexuality and gender based on the following assumptions: Heterosexuality is prescribed or natural for women and men, men are the initiators in heterosexual encounters, and men's sexuality is assumed to be assertive and in need of regular release. Women are expected to be modest and virtuous, to look beautiful, and, simultaneously, to lure men and to fend them off. Traditionally, a woman has been expected to remain a virgin until marriage, untouched except by her husband, and this attitude is still strong in many communities in the United States and around the world. Men's sexual activity is assumed and accepted; after all, "Boys will be boys." Girls may easily get a "bad reputation" and be condemned as "sluts." Writers Leonora Tanenbaum (2000) and Emily White (2002) found many reasons that girls are labeled this way: they may be early developers, victims of rape, outsiders to the community, or targets of revenge. Some may be sexually active but many are not. In response to the "nice girl" stereotype some young women have reclaimed "slut" as a positive identification that emphasizes independence and sexual agency while others have written of their own sexual experimentation (e.g., Johnson 2002; Walker 1995; Wolf 1997).

This fundamental contradiction between encouraging men's sexuality and expecting women to be chaste results in the construction of two categories of women: "good" women and "bad" women, virgins and whores—the women men marry and the women they fool around with. This double standard controls women's sexuality and autonomy, and serves to divide women from each other. This is significant at the micro, meso, and macro levels. Growing up in a Mexican American community, Sandra Cisneros (Reading 22) writes that *la Virgen de Guadalupe* was the model held up to girls. The boys "were fornicating like rabbits while the Church ignored them and pointed us women towards our destiny—marriage and motherhood. The other alternative was *puta*hood," being defined a whore. Writer and literature professor Gloria Wade-Gayles (1993) learned the same double standard, but women in her Memphis neighborhood also divided men into two categories: good men who care for their wives and families, and "dogs" who "only want one thing." This latter category included White men who cruised through the neighborhood "in search of black women who, they assumed, were naturally sensuous, sexually superior, and easy" (p. 84).

Traditional cultural limitations on women's sexuality and sexual expression can divide women in immigrant communities in the United States, as described by human rights activist Surina A. Khan

(Reading 26) and by psychologist Shamita das Dasgupta and pediatrician Sayantani DasGupta (1996). Das Dasgupta and DasGupta write,

> As Asian women of two different generations, we attest to the politically divisive and psychologically unbearable situation in which we have been placed. As daughters, we are faced with the choice of rejecting our community and culture or destroying our sexual selves. As mothers, we can be exiled as destroyers of community culture or be our daughters' prison guards.   *(p. 240)*

They understand the Asian Indian community's control of women's sexuality as an attempt to resist cultural erasure in the United States and as a response to the racism of this society, as well as a result of patriarchal control within their own community. They endorse Indian women's activism (against violence against women, and for gay, lesbian, and bisexual rights) as a way of creating a progressive South Asian space to "define our private selves as public and discover our collective power" (p. 241).

It is important to note that many girls and women experience sexual coercion and abuse—in childhood, as adults, or both (see Chapter 6). Some struggle for many years with the devastating effects of sexual abuse on their confidence, trust, sexuality, and sense of themselves in the world. In Reading 36 Aurora Levins Morales refers to her childhood experience of sexual abuse and her path toward reclaiming "the wounded erotic." At the core of that process, she writes, is "blazing and untarnished aliveness."

What Is Women's Autonomous Sexuality?

In the 1960s and '70s there was much talk of a sexual revolution in the United States, partly made possible by the availability of contraceptive pills for the first time. Women "on the pill" could be sexually active with men without the same fear of pregnancy as in the past. In practice, many feminists argued that this "revolution" was very much on men's terms (Segal 1994), but more recently there has been increasing discussion of women's own sexual needs and preferences (Boston Women's Health Book Collective 2005; Cox 1999; Ehrenreich, Hess, and

Jacobs 1986; Ensler 1998; hooks 1993; Johnson 2002; Muscio 1999; Rose 2003). Women's health advocate Rebecca Chalker (1995) describes this process as a "real woman-friendly sexual revolution in progress" (p. 52). Women's magazines have provided one forum for this discourse, as well as women's erotica (e.g., Blank 2001; Bright 2000; Bruce 2001; Slugocki and Wilson 2000) and images of pop stars like Beyonce and Britney Spears, who revel in their sexuality in public. Eve Ensler, a playwright and screenwriter, has performed her Obie-winning show, *The Vagina Monologues,* in many parts of the country. She notes that, for many women, the word *vagina* is associated with shame, embarrassment, and silencing, even violation.

> And as more women say the word, saying it becomes less of a big deal; it becomes part of our language, part of our lives. Our vaginas become integrated and respected and sacred. They become part of our bodies, connected to our minds, fueling our spirits. And the shame leaves and the violation stops.
>
> *(Ensler 1998, p. xxiv)*

Starting in 1998, students, staff, and faculty from hundreds of U.S. colleges and universities have performed Ensler's script as part of the V-Day College Initiative, a nationwide project to celebrate women and to oppose sexual violence.

Shere Hite is one of the few popular U.S. researchers to conduct extensive surveys of men's and women's sexual experiences and preferences. The following questions, from one of her surveys, were written for women, but they are also relevant for men:

> Is sex important to you? What part does it play in your life?
>
> Who sets the pace and style of sex—you or your partner or both? Who decides when it's over?
>
> Do you think your genital area and vagina are ugly or beautiful?
>
> If you are sexually active, do you ever fake orgasms? Why?
>
> What are your best sex experiences? What would you like to try that you never have?
>
> What is it about sex that gives you the greatest pleasure? Displeasure?

Have you chosen to be celibate at any point? What was/is that like for you?

In the best of all possible worlds, what would sexuality be like?

Do you know as much as you'd like to know, about your own body? Orgasm? Conception and pregnancy? Safe sex?

Do your partners know about your sexual desires and your body? If not, do you ask for it or act yourself to get it?

(Hite 1994, pp. 17–22)

To discover what is sexually empowering for us, ideally women need a safe place and freedom from worries about being attractive and the risk of pregnancy or sexually transmitted infections. In addition, we need information on safer sex, access to reliable contraception, open discussion with sexual partners, the ability to critique popular culture, and better policies and procedures regarding sexual offenses.

For many teens sex is a "rite of passage," an essential part of growing up. How "sex" is defined can vary; for example, many sexually active heterosexual teens do not count oral sex as sex. Magazine editor Susannah Indigo (2000) interviewed girls about their experience with sex play including masturbation, phone sex, and oral sex, which they jokingly referred to as "outercourse," as opposed to "real sex" or intercourse. Some young people who pledge virginity-before-marriage do not necessarily rule out sex play. Lee Che Leong (2004, p. 37), Director of the Teen Health Initiative at the New York Civil Liberties Union, comments that "The ranks of those 'saving themselves' by being blowjob queens are increasing as oral sex is on the rise" among teens of all racial groups.

Leong also discusses the effects of federal funding criteria on sex education programs. To qualify for funding, a program must teach that "abstinence from sexual activity is the only certain way to avoid out-of-wedlock pregnancy, sexually transmitted diseases and other associated health problems"; that "a mutually faithful monogamous relationship in the context of marriage is the expected standard of human sexual activity"; and that "sexual activity outside of the context of marriage is likely to have harmful psychological and physical effects" (Department of Health and Human Services, quoted by Leong 2004, pp. 36, 37).

Thirty-five percent of U.S. sex education programs teach abstinence only; 51 percent teach abstinence as the preferred option; and 14 percent teach about abstinence as one option in a broader sex education program (Alan Guttmacher Institute 2004, p. 17).

This discussion relates to the question of sexual agency. Is sex play and "hooking up" for casual sex empowering for women? Are women valued only for their sexual skills? Are they allowing themselves to be used by the men or is the issue more complicated? Psychologist Lynn Phillips (2000) found young women "flirting with danger" and struggling to negotiate and make sense of power differences around sexuality, and in some cases, sexual abuse and violation. Journalist Paula Kamen (2000) argues that outercourse is an important part of women's pleasure. She sees young women choosing to be in sexual relationships—or not—very much on their own terms. For some this means identifying as queer, bisexual, or lesbian.

Feminists have engaged in heated argument about women's sexuality and the possibility of genuine sexual agency in patriarchal cultures (Jaggar 1994; Snitow, Stansell, and Thompson 1983; Vance 1984). Philosopher Marilyn Frye (1992) notes that "the word 'virgin' did not originally mean a woman whose vagina was untouched by any penis, but a free woman, one not betrothed, not married, not bound to, not possessed by any man. It meant a female who is sexually and hence socially her own person" (p. 133). Frye argues that radical feminist lesbians have created ways of living out this kind of virginity. Is this also possible for heterosexual women? As Frye puts it: "Can you fuck without losing your virginity?"(p. 136). She concludes that this is unlikely, but concedes it may be possible if women are willing to be wild and undomesticated—sexually, socially, and politically.

In Reading 23, Naomi Wolf notes that "all over the country, millions of feminists have a secret indulgence. By day they fight gender injustice; by night they sleep with men. . . . Is sleeping with a man, 'sleeping with the enemy'?" She resolves this question by advocating what she calls "radical heterosexuality." To achieve this, women would need financial independence, marriage would have to be very different, and both women and men would have to give up their "gender benefits." Psychologist Lynne Segal (1994) and sociologist Pepper Schwartz (1994) describe how some heterosexual couples are negotiating sex to make it more egalitarian. Schwartz notes that in U.S. culture there is a commonly held feeling that "male leadership and control is inherently erotic," that role differences between women and men and "the mystery of not knowing each other" make for a more exciting sex life (p. 70).

But only some men, Schwartz writes, "perhaps those with strong mothers, or with a great respect for competence and intelligence, find equality compelling and sexy" (p. 78). And not all women "refuse to be an instrument in male orchestration" (p. 78). She comments that passion is a Western ideal for marriage, although research shows that passion decreases over the length of a relationship. A long-term **peer marriage,** which is intentionally egalitarian, she notes, may be better at providing romance and

respect than providing passion—unless, presumably, the notion of passion is reconstructed.

Challenging Binaries

Our society constructs sex in strictly binary terms: female or male. Geneticist and professor of biology Anne Fausto-Sterling (1993; 2000) shows how intersexual people challenge these categories in a fundamental way. Their social, surgical, and hormonal treatment—which makes them a specific gender and pressures them to stick with it— shows how important this dichotomy is (also see Colligan 2004). Sexuality, too, has been defined in binary terms. According to Jonathan Katz (1995), a historian of sexuality, the concept of heterosexuality developed in parallel with the concept of homosexuality, and both date from the end of the nineteenth century. The word *heterosexuality* was first used in the 1890s, an obscure medical term applied to nonprocreative sex—that is, sex for pleasure. At the time, this was considered a deviant idea, showing "abnormal or perverted appetite toward the opposite sex" (p. 86). Webster's dictionary did not include the word *heterosexuality* until 1934, and it gradually came into common usage in the United States as a "stable sign of normal sex" (p. 40). As with other dominant dimensions of systems of power such as Whiteness, wealth, and, masculinity, heterosexuality has been much less scrutinized than homosexuality. Sociologist Chrys Ingraham (2004) explores the nature of heterosexuality as a dominant institution with cultural, economic, social, and political aspects.

Lesbians and gay men have long challenged the legitimacy and "normalcy" of heterosexuality (Allen 1986; Boswell 1994; Cavin 1985; Duberman, Vicinus, and Chauncey 1989; Faderman 1981; Grahn 1984; History Project 1998). Bisexual people have argued for greater fluidity in sexual desire and behaviors, what Kathleen Bennett (1992) calls "a both/and option for an either/or world" (see also Anderlini-D'Onofrio 2003; Hutchins and Ka'ahumanu 1991; Ochs and Rowley 2005; Storr 1999; Weise 1992). Lisa Orlando (1991) notes that stereotypes about bisexuality have grown out of the fact that bisexuals are poised between what "appear as two mutually exclusive sexual cultures" and from a common assumption "that homosexual and heterosexual desires exclude each other." Eridani (1992) argues that many women are probably bisexual and do not fit into a gay/straight categorization. She suggests that sexual orientation, meaning a "deeply rooted sense . . . that serious relationships are possible only with persons of the opposite sex or the same sex" (p. 174), is itself a masculinist perspective. In Reading 24, the late June Jordan writes "bisexuality invalidates either/or formulation," and urges bisexuality and sexual freedom as part of a wider struggle for freedom and justice. Riki Anne Wilchins (1997) notes the limited notion of the erotic entailed in hetero-homo dualism: "an entire Geography of the Absent—body parts that aren't named, acts one mustn't do, genders one can't perform—because they are outside the binary box" (p. 167).

Those who refuse to tailor their looks and actions to conventional categories—for example, butch lesbians, cross-dressers, drag queens, and queers, described by socialist activist Leslie Feinberg (1996) as "transgender warriors"—are involved in something profoundly challenging and transgressive. Drag, for example, has a long history in Euro-American culture (Bullough and Bullough 1993; Ekins 1997; Garber 1992; Lorber 1994). It plays with the idea of appearance as an illusion; mimics and parodies conventions; and raises questions as to who the person really is in terms of both outside appearance and inner identity. During the 1980s and '90s, younger people reclaimed the word *queer*, which for many older lesbians and gay men was a hateful and oppressive term (Bernstein and Silberman 1996). This is a broader definition of queerness, with an emphasis on experimentation and playfulness, and includes all who challenge heteronormativity (Gage, Richards, and Wilmot 2002; Nestle, Howell, and Wilchins 2002; Rodríguez 2003). What was defined thirty-five years ago as a gay/lesbian movement has grown enormously in size, complexity, and visibility. The most inclusive current term may be LGBTQQ—lesbian, gay, bisexual, transgender, queer, and questioning. In the past decade or so, TV shows have included gay and lesbian characters, as discussed by Diane Raymond (Reading 25; also Walters 2001). Raymond argues there are many ways to "read" these shows depending on viewers' own perspectives, and that, ironically, these queer representations may reinforce the "normalcy" of heterosexism.

Writing about transgender politics, Leslie Feinberg describes herself:

> I am a human being who unnerves some people. As they look at me, they see a kaleidoscope of characteristics they associate with both males and females. I appear to be a tangled knot of gender contradictions. . . . I'm a female who is more masculine than those prominently portrayed in mass culture. . . . My life only comes into focus when the word *transgender* is added to the equation.
>
> *(Reading 27)*

Leslie Feinberg (1998) and Kate Bornstein (1995, 1998) point out that transgender people are creating a broader space for everyone to express their gender and their sexuality (see also Boylan 2003; Halberstam 2005). Philosopher and queer theorist Judith Butler (1990) considers "the binary framework for both sex and gender" to be "regulatory fictions" that consolidate and naturalize the power of masculine and heterosexist oppression (p. 33). Her conception of gender as performative allows and requires us to think of gender and sexuality more fluidly than rigid categories permit. It also opens the possibility that, under less repressive circumstances, people would have a much wider repertoire of behaviors than most currently do. At the same time, Butler notes that people "who fail to do their gender right" by standards held to be appropriate in specific contexts and at particular times, may be punished for it, through name calling, discrimination, hate, and outright violence (p. 140).

Writer Phyllis Burke (1996) argues that transsexuals who choose sexual reassignment surgery both challenge binary gender categories and reinforce them. Sociologist Judith Lorber (1994) notes that "it is Western culture's preoccupation with genitalia as the markers of both sexuality and gender and the concept of these social statuses as fixed for life that produces the problem and the surgical solution for those who cannot tolerate the personal ambiguities Western cultures deny" (p. 86). Transsexuals do not change their sex completely. Their chromosomes remain the same, and they rely on hormone treatments to alter their body shape, hair distribution, and the development of secondary sex characteristics like breasts or beards. Female-to-male transsexuals, for example, do not produce sperm. Lorber argues that they change *gender,* and have to construct a new gender identity, but that they do not disrupt "the deep genderedness of the modern Western world" (p. 96). Whether transgenderism as a movement can deal with structural inequalities of power between men and women raises the question of how personal freedoms, played out through the construction of sexuality and the body, are connected to other political issues and other progressive groups in society, as discussed by June Jordan (Reading 24). Transgender activists who are making these connections include Leslie Feinberg (1998) and Riki Anne Wilchins (1997, 2002).

Theorizing Sexuality

Medical anthropologist Carole Vance (1984) sums up the contradictions of sexuality for women:

> Sexuality is simultaneously a domain of restriction, repression, and danger as well as a domain of exploration, pleasure, and agency. To focus only on pleasure and gratification ignores the patriarchal structure in which women act, yet to speak only of sexual violence and oppression ignores women's experience with sexual agency and choice.   *(p. 1)*

In her now classic essay, award-winning poet and writer Adrienne Rich (1986a) discusses how social institutions like law, religion, philosophy, official kinship, and popular culture support what she terms compulsory heterosexuality. She argues that patriarchy *demands* heterosexuality to keep women serving masculinist interests. For Rich, what needs to be explained is not why women identify as lesbians, but how and why so many women are heterosexual, since, typically, we first experience the intimacy of emotional caring and physical nurture with women—our mothers or other female caregivers. In many cultural settings, women and girls spend time together, care for and depend on one another, and enjoy each other's friendship—often passionately. Why would women ever redirect that search? Rich asks. As you read this chapter, consider Rich's question: What are "the societal forces which wrench women's emotional and erotic energies away from themselves and other women and

from human-identified values" (p. 35), which teach us systematically to see men as appropriate partners?

Many feminists have focused on sexual violence—both theoretically and through active participation in rape crisis centers and shelters for battered women—and understand that sexuality can be a source of profound vulnerability for women. Activist and writer Andrea Dworkin (1987), for example, has argued that intercourse is inherently repressive for women, partly for anatomical reasons, but more because of unequal power relations between women and men. As a way of repudiating the eroticization of inequality, some feminists have argued that women's sexuality should be based on sexual acts that are safe, loving, and intimate, in the context of a caring, monogamous relationship. Others have seen this as a new—feminist—restriction on women's freedom of expression (Duggan and Hunter 1995; Jaggar 1994; Johnson 2002; Leidholdt and Raymond 1990). Gayle Rubin (1984) noted two strains of feminist thought concerning sexuality: one criticizing "restrictions on women's sexual behavior," denouncing "the high costs imposed on women for being sexually active," and calling for "a sexual liberation that would work for women as well as for men"; the other considering "sexual liberation to be inherently a mere extension of male privilege" (p. 301). Heated debate about sexuality, power, and violence continues, especially with regard to issues like prostitution/sex work and pornography (see e.g., Califia 2000; Cornell 2000; Dworkin 1993; Feminist Anti-Censorship Task Force 1992; Jeffreys 1997; Johnson 2002; Kempadoo and Doezema 1998; Nagel 1997; Queen 2002; Russell 1993; Stan 1995; Strossen 2000; Whisnant and Stark 2004).

After the Stonewall Riots (New York) in 1969, a gay rights movement flourished, drawing on feminist ideas as well as "strands of sex research that did not treat homosexuality as pathological, and on an urban gay subculture that had been expanding since the end of World War II" (Lancaster and di Leonardo 1997, p. 3).

> With varying degrees of success and through struggles that continue today, gay and lesbian activists have publicly championed all that is positive, pleasurable and creative in same-sex desire while opposing the obvious sources of

antigay oppression: police harassment, social stigma, religious bigotry, psychiatric persecution, and sodomy laws. In the process, these concrete struggles have revealed the less obvious heteronormative premises deeply embedded in law, science, philosophy, official kinship, and vernacular culture.

(Lancaster and di Leonardo 1997, p. 3).

This gay and lesbian activism, together with gay men's theorizing and feminist theorizing about sexuality led to the development of queer theory and queer studies (Alcoff 1988; Fuss 1991; Jeffreys 2003; Stein 1997; Sullivan 2003), which take sexuality as the main category of analysis. Queer theorist Eve Sedgwick's (1990) Axiom #2 states: "The study of sexuality is not coextensive with the study of gender; correspondingly, antihomophobic inquiry is not coextensive with feminist inquiry" (p. 27). Though not identical, feminism and antihomophobic work often overlap, as exemplified in writer and activist Suzanne Pharr's (1988) analysis of homophobia as a

weapon of sexism and her comment that "as long as the word lesbian can strike fear in any woman's heart, then work on behalf of women can be stopped; the only successful work against sexism must include work against homophobia" (p. 26). Note the unfortunate use of the term *homophobia,* meaning fear of homosexuals, rather than *heterosexism,* the system of heterosexuality as a place of institutional privilege.

Lisa Orlando (1991) hypothesizes that desire involves "some kind of interaction between a more or less shapeless biological 'drive' and a combination of individual experiences and larger social forces." She notes that the very notion of sexual identity is specific to our culture and time in history.

Economic changes such as industrialization, the development of the factory system, and the spread of wage labor had a profound impact on family life. Gradually, families stopped producing the goods they needed and supported themselves through wage labor. Children, who had been an economic advantage to their families by contributing to household production, became a liability and an expense. The U.S. birthrate dropped dramatically during the twentieth century as a result. Further, developments like the contraceptive pill, alternative insemination, in vitro fertilization, and other reproductive technologies have made possible the separation of intercourse and procreation. Heterosexual women can be sexually active without becoming pregnant, and any woman can become pregnant without having intercourse. Historian John D'Emilio (1984) argues that these trends create conditions "that allow some men and women to organize a personal life around their erotic/emotional attraction to their own sex" (p. 104). They have "made possible the formation of urban communities of lesbians and gay men, and more recently, of a politics based on a sexual identity" (p. 104). On this analysis, sexual identity has a basis in macro-level circumstances as much as personal factors (D'Emilio and Freedman 1997), although cultural acceptance of lesbians and gay men does not always follow economic possibilities, in White communities or communities of color (Anzaldúa 1987; Eng and Hom 1998; Leong 1996; Rodríguez 2003; Smith 1998; Trujillo 1991). D'Emilio (1984) accepts that there have been same-sex partnerships for generations, as claimed by Adrienne Rich (1986a) and many other authors and researchers cited above. He complicates this claim, however, by differentiating homosexual *behavior* from homosexual *identity*, and argues that only under certain economic conditions are homosexual identity and community possible. Clare Hemmings (2002) notes that such communities both generate and require supportive locations to survive and flourish, in her discussion of Northampton (Mass.) and San Francisco as cities that support gay, lesbian, and bisexual communities.

This links to the experience of Surina A. Khan (Reading 26), a Pakistani American woman who struggled to reconcile the various parts of her identity. Despite the fact that images of same-sex couples have been part of the history of South Asia for hundreds of years, she notes that most people from South Asia do not have words for homosexuality and regard it as a Western phenomenon. This apparent paradox is exactly what D'Emilio's distinction between behavior and identity helps to explain. Further, it may be useful to think of four distinctive categories: inclination, behavior, identity, and politics. One may have sexual inclinations

but may decide not to act on them. One may engage in certain sexual behaviors but not adopt a bisexual or gay identity. One may identify as a lesbian or transgendered woman but not act on that identity in a political way.

The Erotic as Power

The issue of sexuality is part of our wider concern with security in the sense that sexuality can be a source of restriction and vulnerability—hence insecurity—for women. This is true for women whose sexual activities and identities fit patriarchal norms and expectations, and also for those who challenge or repudiate them. Like beauty—however it is defined—sexuality can be a source of power, affirmation, and self-definition for women. Many women are exploring their sexuality, claiming the right to sexual pleasure on their own terms, and challenging the limitations of conventional expressions of sexuality. Sexuality is a key element in personal relationships, of course, and we explore this in Chapter 7.

Black lesbian poet and activist Audre Lorde discusses the power of the erotic in the broadest way (Reading 28). She sees the erotic as "our most profoundly creative source." She notes that women have been "taught to separate the erotic . . . from most vital areas of our lives other than sex." By contrast, she writes: "When I speak of the erotic . . . I speak of it as an assertion of the life-force of women: of that creative energy empowered, the knowledge and use of which we are now reclaiming in our language, our history, our dancing, our loving, our work, our lives." Lorde sees the distortion and suppression of the erotic as one of the ways that women are oppressed, and concludes: "Recognizing the power of the erotic in our lives can give us the energy to pursue genuine change within our world."

Activism and Sexuality

A number of online educational and activist organizations provide information for young people about sexuality and health (e.g., Go Ask Alice, Scarleteen, Teenwire, and Youth Resource). Many informal networks, local groups, and national organizations support and advocate for lesbians, bisexual and transgendered women, and gay men, especially in urban areas. Some are primarily social groupings; others are support groups that provide information, encouragement, and social connections. Still others focus on particular issues like women's health, HIV/AIDS, parenting, community or police violence, religious bigotry, or the situation of gays in the military. Others run journals, magazines, newsletters, bookstores, presses, churches, bars, coffeehouses, bands, sports teams, and theater companies; support political candidates for local, state, or national office; oppose city and state ordinances designed to limit lesbian, gay, bisexual, and transgender (LGBT) rights; or raise funds for LGBT organizations. These various networks and organizations span a broad political spectrum. Some are overtly feminist; others are more closely aligned with queer politics. Examples include Queer Nation, and Lesbian Avengers—national networks with local participating groups, BiNet USA (Arlington, VA), the Boston Bisexual Women's Network, the Detroit Women's Coffeehouse, Old Lesbians Organizing for Change (Houston, Texas), Trikone: Lesbian, Gay, Bisexual and Transgendered South Asians (San Francisco), New York Association for Gender Rights Advocacy, the National Gay and Lesbian Taskforce (Washington, D.C.), the National Latino/a LGBT Organization (Washington, D.C.), Gender Education and Advocacy (www.gender.org), and the International Gay and Lesbian Human Rights Commission (New York and San Francisco). In addition, lesbians and bisexual women are active in antiracist organizing, rape crisis centers, shelters for battered women, labor unions, antimilitarist organizations, and women's studies programs where they link their knowledge and experiences of oppression based on sexuality with other oppressions.

◆◆◆

Questions for Reflection

As you read and discuss the readings that follow, consider the questions raised by Shere Hite, listed on pages 167–168.

◆◆◆

Finding Out More on the Web

1. Research an organization mentioned in this chapter. What are its goals, strategies, and activities?

2. Review the information about sexuality and health given on one of the online sites mentioned in this chapter.

3. The World Wide Web is a significant new tool in the commodification of women. Type "Philippine women" or "Asian women" into your search engine and see what comes up. Also look at www.asianwomenonline.com—where Asian women are reclaiming cyberspace and breaking stereotypical portrayals.

4. Research the history of transgender activism in the United States.

◆◆◆

Taking Action

1. Write in your journal or have a candid conversation with a friend about your ideas about sexuality. How do you recognize the power of the erotic as Audre Lorde describes it?

2. Analyze the way women's magazines and men's magazines discuss women's sexuality.

3. Look critically at the way women's sexuality is portrayed in movies, on TV, and in ads. What is being represented?

4. However you define your sexuality, participate in campus or community events to commemorate National Coming-Out Day (usually in October) or Gay Pride (usually in June).

TWENTY-TWO

◆◆◆

Guadalupe the Sex Goddess (1996)

Sandra Cisneros

Sandra Cisneros has worked as a creative writing teacher and is an award-winning fiction and poetry writer. Her first book, *House on Mango Street*, has sold over two million copies. Her writing has earned her numerous honorary degrees and fellowships, including a 1995 MacArthur Foundation Fellowship.

In high school I marveled at how white women strutted around the locker room, nude as pearls, as unashamed of their brilliant bodies as the Nike of Samothrace. Maybe they were hiding terrible secrets like bulimia or anorexia, but, to my naive eye then, I thought of them as women comfortable in their skin.

You could always tell us Latinas. We hid when we undressed, modestly facing a wall, or, in my case, dressing in a bathroom stall. We were the ones who still used bulky sanitary pads instead of tampons, thinking ourselves morally superior to our white classmates. *My mama said you can't use tampons till after you're married.* All Latina mamas said this, yet how come none of us thought to ask our mothers why they didn't use tampons *after* getting married?

Womanhood was full of mysteries. I was as ignorant about my own body as any female ancestor who hid behind a sheet with a hole in the center when husband or doctor called. Religion and our culture, our culture and religion, helped to create that blur, a vagueness about what went on "down there." So ashamed was I about my own "down there" that until I was an adult I had no idea I had another orifice called the vagina; I thought my period would arrive via the urethra or perhaps through the walls of my skin.

No wonder, then, it was too terrible to think about a doctor—a man!—looking at you down there when you could never bring yourself to look yourself. *¡Ay, nunca!* How could I acknowledge my sexuality, let alone enjoy sex, with so much guilt? In the guise of modesty my culture locked me in a double chastity belt of ignorance and *vergüenza*, shame.

I had never seen my mother nude. I had never taken a good look at myself either. Privacy for self-exploration belonged to the wealthy. In my home a private space was practically impossible; aside from the doors that opened to the street, the only room with a lock was the bathroom, and how could anyone who shared a bathroom with eight other people stay in there for more than a few minutes? Before college, no one in my family had a room of their own except me, a narrow closet just big enough for my twin bed and an oversized blond dresser we'd bought in the bargain basement of *el Sears*. The dresser was as long as a coffin and blocked the door from shutting completely. I had my own room, but I never had the luxury of shutting the door.

I didn't even see my own sex until a nurse at the Emma Goldman Clinic showed it to me—*Would you like to see your cervix? Your os is dilating. You must be ovulating. Here's a mirror; take a look.* When had anyone ever suggested I take a look or allowed me a speculum to take home and investigate myself at leisure!

I'd only been to one other birth control facility prior to the Emma Goldman Clinic, the university medical center in grad school. I was 21 in a strange town far from home for the first time. I was afraid and I was ashamed to seek out a gynecologist, but I was more afraid of becoming pregnant. Still, I agonized about going for weeks. Perhaps the anonymity and distance from my family allowed me finally to take control of my life. I remember wanting to be fearless like the white women around me, to be able to have sex when I wanted, but I was too afraid to explain to a would-be lover how I'd only had one other man in my life and we'd practiced withdrawal. Would he laugh at me? How could I look anyone in the face and explain why I couldn't go see a gynecologist?

One night, a classmate I liked too much took me home with him. I meant all along to say something about how I wasn't on anything, but I never quite found my voice, never the right moment to cry out—*Stop, this is dangerous to my brilliant career!* Too afraid to sound stupid, afraid to ask him to take responsibility too, I said nothing, and I let him take me like that with nothing protecting me from motherhood but luck. The days that followed were torture, but fortunately on Mother's Day my period arrived, and I celebrated my nonmaternity by making an appointment with the family planning center.

When I see pregnant teens, I can't help but think that could've been me. In high school I would've thrown myself into love the way some warriors throw themselves into fighting. I was ready to sacrifice everything in the name of love, to do anything, even risk my own life, but thankfully there were no takers. I was enrolled at an all-girls' school. I think if I had met a boy who would have me, I would've had sex in a minute, convinced this was love. I have always had enough imagination to fall in love all by myself, then and now.

I tell you this story because I am overwhelmed by the silence regarding Latinas and our bodies. If I, as a graduate student, was shy about talking to anyone about my body and sex, imagine how difficult it must be for a young girl in middle school or high school living in a home with no lock on the bedroom door, perhaps with no door, or maybe with no bedroom, no information other than misinformation from the girlfriends and the boyfriend. So much guilt, so much silence, and such a yearning to be loved; no wonder young women find themselves having sex while they are still children, having sex without sexual protection, too ashamed to confide their feelings and fears to anyone.

What a culture of denial. Don't get pregnant! But no one tells you how not to. This is why I was angry for so many years every time I saw a *la Virgen de Guadalupe*, my culture's role model for brown women like me. She was damn dangerous, an ideal so lofty and unrealistic it was laughable. Did boys have to aspire to be Jesus? I never saw any evidence of it. They were fornicating like rabbits while the Church ignored them and pointed us women toward our destiny—marriage and motherhood. The other alternative was *puta*hood.

In my neighborhood I knew only real women, neither saints nor whores, naive and vulnerable *huerquitas* like me who wanted desperately to fall in love, with the heart and soul. And yes, with the *panocha* too.

As far as I could see, *la Lupe* was nothing but a Goody Two-shoes meant to doom me to a life of unhappiness. Thanks, but no thanks. Motherhood and/or marriage were anathema to my career. But being a bad girl, that was something I could use as a writer, a Molotov cocktail to toss at my papa and *el Papa*, who had their own plans for me.

Discovering sex was like discovering writing. It was powerful in a way I couldn't explain. Like writing, you had to go beyond the guilt and shame to get to anything good. Like writing, it could take you to deep and mysterious subterranean levels. With each new depth I found out things about myself I didn't know I knew. And, like writing, for a slip of a moment it could be spiritual, the cosmos pivoting on a pin, could empty and fill you all at once like a Ganges, a Piazzolla tango, a tulip bending in the wind. I was no one, I was nothing, and I was everything in the universe little and large—twig, cloud, sky. How had this incredible energy been denied me!

When I look at *la Virgen de Guadalupe* now, she is not the Lupe of my childhood, no longer the one in my grandparents' house in Tepeyac, nor is she the one of the Roman Catholic Church, the one I bolted the door against in my teens and twenties. Like every woman who matters to me, I have had to search for her in the rubble of history. And I have found her. She is Guadalupe the sex goddess, a goddess who makes me feel good about my sexual power, my sexual energy, who reminds me that I must, as Clarissa Pinkola Estés so aptly put it, "[speak] from the vulva . . . speak the most basic, honest truth," and write from my *panocha*.

In my research of Guadalupe's pre-Columbian antecedents, the she before the Church desexed her, I found Tonantzin, and inside Tonantzin a pantheon of other mother goddesses. I discovered Tlazolteotl, the goddess of fertility and sex, also referred to as Totzin. Our Beginnings, or Tzinteotl, goddess of the rump. *Putas,* nymphos, and other loose women were known as "women of the sex goddess." Tlazolteotl was the patron of sexual passion, and though she had the power to stir you to sin, she could also forgive you and cleanse you of your sexual transgressions via her priests who heard confession. In this aspect of confessor Tlazolteotl was known as Tlaelcuani, the filth eater. Maybe you've seen her; she's the one whose image is sold in the tourist markets even now, a statue of a woman squatting in childbirth, her face grimacing in pain. Tlazolteotl, then, is a duality of maternity *and* sexuality. In other words, she is a sexy mama.

To me, *la Virgen de Guadalupe* is also Coatlicue, the creative/destructive goddess. When I think of the Coatlicue statue in the National Museum of Anthropology in Mexico City, so terrible it was unearthed and then reburied because it was too frightening to look at, I think of a woman enraged, a woman as tempest, a woman *bien berrinchuda,* and I like that. *La Lupe* as *cabrona.* Not silent and passive, but silently gathering force.

Most days, I too feel like the creative/destructive goddess Coatlicue, especially the days I'm writing, capable of fabricating pretty tales with pretty words, as well as doing demolition work with a volley of *palabrotas* if I want to. I am the Coatlicue-Lupe whose square column of a body I see in so many Indian women, in my mother, and in myself each time I check out my thick-waisted, flat-assed torso in the mirror.

Coatlicue, Tlazolteotl, Tonantzin, *la Virgen de Guadalupe.* They are each telescoped one into the other, into who I am. And this is where *la Lupe* intrigues me—not the Lupe of 1531 who appeared to Juan Diego, but the one of the 1990s who has shaped who we are as Chicanas/*mexicanas* today, the one inside each Chicana and *mexicana.* Perhaps it's the Tlazolteotl-Lupe in me whose *malcriada* spirit inspires me to leap into the swimming pool naked or dance on a table with a skirt on my head. Maybe it's my Coatlicue-Lupe attitude that makes it possible for my mother to tell me, "No wonder men

can't stand you." Who knows? What I do know is this: I am obsessed with becoming a woman comfortable in her skin.

I can't attribute my religious conversion to a flash of lightning on the road to Laredo or anything like that. Instead, there have been several lessons learned subtly over a period of time. A grave depression and near suicide in my thirty-third year and its subsequent retrospection. Vietnamese Buddhist monk Thich Nhat Hanh's writing that has brought out the Buddha-Lupe in me. My weekly peace vigil for my friend Jasna in Sarajevo. The writings of Gloria Anzaldúa. A crucial trip back to Tepeyac in 1985 with Cherríe Moraga and Norma Alarcón. Drives across Texas, talking with other Chicanas. And research for stories that would force me back inside the Church from where I'd fled.

My *Virgin de Guadalupe* is not the mother of God. She is God. She is a face for a god without a face, an *indigena* for a god without ethnicity, a female deity for a god who is genderless, but I also understand that for her to approach me, for me to finally open the door and accept her, she had to be a woman like me.

Once watching a porn film, I saw a sight that terrified me. It was the film star's *panocha*—a tidy, elliptical opening, pink and shiny like a rabbit's ear. To make matters worse, it was shaved and looked especially childlike and unsexual. I think what startled me most was the realization that my own sex has no resemblance to this woman's. My sex, dark as an orchid, rubbery and blue-purple as *pulpo,* an octopus, does not look nice and tidy, but otherworldly. I do not have little rosette nipples. My nipples are big and brown like the Mexican coins of my childhood.

When I see *la Virgen de Guadalupe* I want to lift her dress as I did my dolls, and look to see if she comes with *chones* and does her *panocha* look like mine, and does she have dark nipples too? Yes, I am certain she does. She is not neuter like Barbie. She gave birth. She has a womb. *Blessed art thou and blessed is the fruit of thy womb....* Blessed art thou, Lupe, and, therefore, blessed am I.

◆◆◆

Radical Heterosexuality (1992)

Naomi Wolf

Naomi Wolf's first book, *The Beauty Myth*, was an international bestseller. Her later books deal with women, media and politics, young women's sexuality, and mothering; her essays have appeared in *The New Republic*, *The Wall Street Journal*, *Glamour*, and *The New York Times*. She is co-founder of The Woodhull Institute for Ethical Leadership, an organization for young women leaders.

All over the country, millions of feminists have a secret indulgence. By day they fight gender injustice; by night they sleep with men. Is this a dual life? A core contradiction? Is sleeping with a man "sleeping with the enemy"? And is razor burn from kissing inherently oppressive?

It's time to say you *can* hate sexism and love men. As the feminist movement grows more mature and our understanding of our enemies more nuanced, three terms assumed to be in contradiction—radical feminist heterosexuality—can and must be brought together.

Rules of the Relationship

But how? Andrea Dworkin and Catharine MacKinnon have pointed out that sexism limits women to such a degree that it's questionable whether the decision to live with a man can ever truly be free. If you want to use their sound, if depressing, reasoning to a brighter end, turn the thesis around: radical heterosexuality demands substituting choice for dependency.

Radical heterosexuality requires that the woman be able to support herself. This is not to belittle women who must depend financially on men; it is to recognize that when our daughters are raised with the skills that would let them leave abusers, they need not call financial dependence love.

Radical heterosexuality needs alternative institutions. As the child of a good lifetime union, I believe in them. But when I think of pledging my heart and body to a man—even the best and kindest man—within the existing institution of marriage, I feel faint. The more you learn about its legal structure, the less likely you are to call the caterers.

In the nineteenth century, when a judge ruled that a husband could not imprison and rape his wife, the London *Times* bemoaned, "One fine morning last month, marriage in England was suddenly abolished." The phrase "rule of thumb" descends from English common law that said a man could legally beat his wife with a switch "no thicker than his thumb."

If these nightmarish echoes were confined to history, I might feel more nuptial; but look at our own time. Do I want the blessing of an institution that doesn't provide adequate protection from marital rape? That gives a woman less protection from assault by her husband than by a stranger? That assigns men 70 percent of contested child custodies?

Of course I do not fear any such brutality from the man I want to marry (no bride does). But marriage means that his respectful treatment of me and our children becomes, despite our intentions, a kindness rather than a legally grounded right.

We need a heterosexual version of the marriages that gay and lesbian activists are seeking: a commitment untainted by centuries of inequality; a ritual that invites the community to rejoice in the making of a new freely chosen family.

The radical heterosexual man must yield the automatic benefits conferred by gender. I had a lover once who did not want to give up playing sports in a club that had a separate door for women. It must be tempting to imagine you can have both—great squash courts *and* the bed of a liberated woman—but in the mess hall of gender relations, there is *no such thing as a free lunch*.

Radical heterosexual women too must give up gender benefits (such as they are). I know scores of women—independent, autonomous—who avoid assuming any of the risk for a romantic or sexual approach.

I have watched myself stand complacently by while my partner wrestles with a stuck window, an intractable computer printer, maps, or locks. Sisters, I am not proud of this, and I'm working on it. But people are lazy—or at least I am—and it's easy to rationalize that the person with the penis is the one who should get out of a warm bed to fix the snow on the TV screen. After all, it's the very least owed to me *personally* in compensation for centuries of virtual enslavement.

Radical heterosexuals must try to stay conscious—at all times, I'm afraid—of their gender imprinting, and how it plays out in their erotic melodramas. My own psyche is a flagrant *son et lumière* of political incorrectness. Three of my boyfriends had motorcycles; I am easy pickings for the silent and dysfunctional. My roving eye is so taken by the oil-stained persona of the labor organizer that myopic intellectuals have gained access to my favors merely by sporting a Trotsky button.

We feminists are hard on each other for admitting to weakness. Gloria Steinem caught flak . . . for acknowledging in *Revolution from Within* that she was drawn to a man because he could do the things with money and power that we are taught men must do. And some were appalled when Simone de Beauvoir's letters revealed how she coddled Sartre.

But the antifeminist erotic template is *in* us. We would not be citizens of this culture if swooning damsels and abandoned vixens had not been beamed at us from our first solid food to our first vote. We can't fight it until we admit to it. And we can't identify it until we drag it, its taffeta billowing and its bosom heaving, into the light of day.

I have done embarrassing, reactionary, abject deeds out of love and sexual passion. . . . Only when we reveal our conditioning can we tell how much of our self-abasement is neurotic femininity, and how much is the flawed but impressive human apparatus of love.

In the Bedroom

Those are the conditions for the radical heterosexual couple. What might this new creation look like in bed? It will look like something we have no words or images for—the eroticization of consent, the equal primacy of female and male desire.

We will need to tell some secrets—to map our desire for the male body and admit to our fascination with the rhythms and forces of male arousal, its uncanny counterintuitive spell.

We will also need to face our creature qualities. Animality has for so long been used against us—bitch, fox, *Penthouse* pet—that we struggle for the merit badges of higher rationality, ambivalent about our animal nature.

The truth is that heterosexual women believe that men, on some level, are animals; as they believe that we are animals. But what does "animal" mean?

Racism and sexism have long used animal metaphors to distance and degrade the Other. Let us redefine "animal" to make room for that otherness between the genders, an otherness fierce and worthy of respect. Let us define animal as an inchoate kinship, a comradeship, that finds a language beyond our species.

I want the love of two unlikes: the look of astonishment a woman has at the sight of a male back bending. These manifestations of difference confirm in heterosexuals the beauty that similarity confirms in the lesbian or gay imagination. Difference and animality do not have to mean hierarchy.

Men We Love

What must the men be like? Obviously, they're not going to be just anyone. *Esquire* runs infantile disquisitions on "Women We Love" (suggesting, Lucky Girls!). Well, I think that the men who are loved by feminists are lucky. Here's how they qualify to join this fortunate club.

Men We Love understand that, no matter how similar our backgrounds, we are engaged in a cross-cultural . . . relationship. They know that we know much about their world and they but little of ours. They accept what white people must accept in relationships with people of other ethnicities: to know that they do not know.

Men We Love don't hold a baby as if it is a still-squirming, unidentifiable catch from the sea.

Men We Love don't tell women what to feel about sexism. . . . They do not presume that there is a line in the sand called "enlightened male," and that all they need is a paperback copy of Djuna

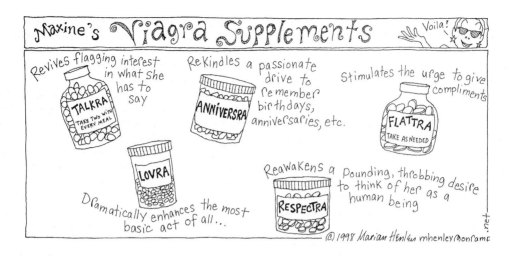

Barnes and good digital technique. They understand that unlearning gender oppressiveness means untying the very core of how we become female and male. They know this pursuit takes a lifetime at the minimum.

Sadly, men in our lives sometimes come through on personal feminism but balk at it intellectually. A year ago, I had a bruising debate with my father and brother about the patriarchal nature of traditional religious and literary canons. I almost seized them by their collars, howling "Read Mary Daly! Read Toni Morrison! Take Feminism 101. *No,* I *can't* explain it to you between the entrée and dessert!"

By spring, my dad, bless his heart, had asked for a bibliography, and last week my brother sent me *Standing Again at Sinai,* a Jewish-feminist classic. Men We Love are willing, sooner or later, to read the Books We Love.

Men We Love accept that successful training in manhood makes them blind to phenomena that are fact to women. Recently, I walked down a New York City avenue with a woman friend, X, and a man friend, Y. I pointed out to Y the leers, hisses, and invitations to sit on faces. Each woman saw clearly what the other woman saw, but Y was baffled. Sexual harassers have superb timing. A passerby makes kissy-noises with his tongue while Y is scrutinizing the menu of the nearest bistro. "There, there! Look! Listen!" we cried. "What? Where? Who?" wailed poor Y, valiantly, uselessly spinning.

What if, hard as they try to see, they cannot hear? Once I was at lunch with a renowned male crusader for the First Amendment. Another Alpha male was present, and the venue was the Supreme Court lunchroom—two power factors that automatically press the "mute" button on the male ability to detect a female voice on the audioscope. The two men began to rev their motors; soon they were off and racing in a policy-wonk grand prix. I tried, once or twice, to ask questions. But the free-speech champions couldn't hear me over the testosterone roar.

Men We Love undertake half the care and cost of contraception. They realize that it's not fair to wallow in the fun without sharing the responsibility. When stocking up for long weekends, they brave the amused glances when they ask, "Do you have this in unscented?"

Men We Love know that just because we can be irrational doesn't mean we're insane. When we burst into premenstrual tears—having just realized the cosmic fragility of creation—they comfort us. Not until we feel better do they dare remind us gently that we had this same revelation exactly 28 days ago.

Men We Love must make a leap of imagination to believe in the female experience. They do not call women nags or paranoid when we embark on the arduous, often boring, nonnegotiable daily chore of drawing attention to sexism. They treat it like adults taking driving lessons: if irked in the short term at being treated like babies, they're grateful in the long term that someone is willing to teach them patiently how to move through the world without harming the pedestrians. Men We Love don't drive without their gender glasses on.

A Place for Them

It's not simple gender that pits Us against Them. In the fight against sexism, it's those who are for us versus those who are against us—of either gender. . . .

It is time to direct our anger more acutely at the Men We Hate—like George Bush—and give the Men We Love something useful to do. Not to take over meetings, or to set agendas; not to whine, "Why can't feminists teach us how to be free?" but to add their bodies, their hearts, and their numbers, to support us.

I meet many young men who are brought to feminism by love for a woman who has been raped, or by watching their single mothers struggle against great odds, or by simple common sense. Their most frequent question is "What can I do to help?"

Imagine a rear battalion of committed "Men Against Violence Against Women" (or Men for Choice, or what have you)—of all races, ages, and classes. Wouldn't that be a fine sight to fix in the eyes of a five-year-old boy?

Finally, the place to make room for radical feminist heterosexuality is within our heads. If the movement that I dearly love has a flaw, it is a tendency toward orthodoxies about other women's pleasures and needs. This impulse is historically understandable: in the past, we needed to define ourselves against men if we were to define ourselves against men if we were to define ourselves at all. But today, the most revolutionary choice we can make is to affirm other women's choices, whether lesbian or straight, bisexual or celibate.

NOW President Patricia Ireland speaks for me even though our sexual lives are not identical. Simone de Beauvoir speaks for me even though our sexual lives are not identical. Audre Lorde speaks for me even though our sexual lives are not identical. Is it the chromosomes of your lovers that establish you as a feminist? Or is it the life you make out of the love you make?

T W E N T Y - F O U R

◆◆◆

A New Politics of Sexuality (1992)

June Jordan

In her distinguished career as a scholar, poet, and essayist, the late **June Jordan** (1936–2002) taught at many academic institutions including Yale University, Sarah Lawrence College, and the University of California at Berkeley. Founder and director of Poetry for the People, Jordan published prodigiously including essays in *The New York Times*, *Ms.*, *Essence*, and the *American Poetry Review*, and received numerous awards.

. . . I believe the Politics of Sexuality is the most ancient and probably the most profound arena for human conflict. Increasingly, it seems clear to me that deeper and more pervasive than any other oppression, than any other bitterly contested human domain, is the oppression of sexuality, the

exploitation of the human domain of sexuality for power.

When I say sexuality, I mean gender: I mean male subjugation of human beings because they are female. When I say sexuality, I mean heterosexual institutionalization of rights and privileges denied to homosexual men and women. When I say sexuality I mean gay or lesbian contempt for bisexual modes of human relationship.

The Politics of Sexuality therefore subsumes all of the different ways in which some of us seek to dictate to others of us what we should do, what we should desire, what we should dream about, and how we should behave ourselves, generally. From China to Iran, from Nigeria to Czechoslovakia, from Chile to California, the politics of sexuality— enforced by traditions of state-sanctioned violence plus religion and the law—reduces to male domination of women, heterosexist tyranny, and, among those of us who are in any case deemed despicable or deviant by the powerful, we find intolerance for those who choose a different, a more complicated—for example, an interracial or bisexual—mode of rebellion and freedom.

We must move out from the shadows of our collective subjugation—as people of color/as women/as gay/as lesbian/as bisexual human beings.

I can voice my ideas without hesitation or fear because I am speaking, finally, about myself. I am Black and I am female and I am a mother and I am bisexual and I am a nationalist and I am an anti-nationalist. And I mean to be fully and freely all that I am! . . .

Recently, I have come upon gratuitous and appalling pseudoliberal pronouncements on sexuality. Too often, these utterances fall out of the mouths of men and women who first disclaim any sentiment remotely related to homophobia, but who then proceed to issue outrageous opinions like the following:

- That it is blasphemous to compare the oppression of gay, lesbian, or bisexual people to the oppression, say, of black people, or of the Palestinians.

- That the bottom line about gay or lesbian or bisexual identity is that you can conceal it whenever necessary and, so, therefore, why don't you do just that? Why don't you keep your deviant sexuality in the closet and let the rest of us—we who suffer oppression for reasons of our ineradicable and always visible components of our personhood such as race or gender—get on with our more necessary, our more beleaguered struggle to survive?

Well, number one: I believe I have worked as hard as I could, and then harder than that, on behalf of equality and justice—for African-Americans, for the Palestinian people, and for people of color everywhere.

And no, I do not believe it is blasphemous to compare oppressions of sexuality to oppressions of race and ethnicity: Freedom is indivisible or it is nothing at all besides sloganeering and temporary, short-sighted, and short-lived advancement for a few. Freedom is indivisible, and either we are working for freedom or you are working for the sake of your self-interests and I am working for mine.

If you can finally go to the bathroom wherever you find one, if you can finally order a cup of coffee and drink it wherever coffee is available, but you cannot follow your heart—you cannot respect the response of your own honest body in the world—then how much of what kind of freedom does any one of us possess?

Or, conversely, if your heart and your honest body can be controlled by the state, or controlled by community taboo, are you not then, and in that case, no more than a slave ruled by outside force?

What tyranny could exceed a tyranny that dictates to the human heart, and that attempts to dictate the public career of an honest human body? . . .

Last spring, at Berkeley, some students asked me to speak at a rally against racism. And I did. There were four or five hundred people massed on Sproul Plaza, standing together against that evil. And, on the next day, on that same plaza, there was a rally for bisexual and gay and lesbian rights, and students asked me to speak at that rally. And I did. There were fewer than seventy-five people stranded, pitiful, on that public space. And I said then what I say today: That was disgraceful! There should have been just one rally. One rally: freedom is indivisible.

As for the second, nefarious pronouncement on sexuality that now enjoys mass-media currency: the idiot notion of keeping yourself in the closet—that is very much the same thing as the suggestion that black folks and Asian-Americans and Mexican-Americans should assimilate and become as "white" as possible—in our walk/talk/music/food/values—or else. Or else? Or else we should, deservedly, perish.

Sure enough, we have plenty of exposure to white everything, so why would we opt to remain our African/Asian/Mexican selves? The answer is that suicide is absolute, and if you think you will survive by hiding who you really are, you are sadly misled: there is no such thing as partial or intermittent suicide. You can only survive if you—who you really are—do survive.

Likewise, we who are not men and we who are not heterosexist—we, sure enough, have plenty of exposure to male-dominated/heterosexist this and that.

But a struggle to survive cannot lead to suicide: suicide is the opposite of survival. And so we must not conceal/assimilate/integrate into the would-be dominant culture and political system that despises us. Our survival requires that we alter our environment so that we can live and so that we can hold each other's hands and so that we can kiss each other on the streets, and in the daylight of our existence, without terror and without violent and sometimes fatal reactions from the busybodies of America.

Finally, I need to speak on bisexuality. I do believe that the analogy is interracial or multiracial identity. I do believe that the analogy for bisexuality is a multicultural, multi-ethnic, multiracial world view. Bisexuality follows from such a perspective and leads to it, as well.

Just as there are many men and women in the United States whose parents have given them more than one racial, more than one ethnic identity and cultural heritage to honor; and just as these men and women must deny no given part of themselves except at the risk of self-deception and the insanities that must issue from that; and just as these men and women embody the principle of equality among races and ethnic communities; and just as these men and women falter and anguish and choose and then falter again and then anguish and then choose yet again how they will honor the irreducible complexity of their God-given human being—even so, there are many men and women, especially young men and women, who seek to embrace the complexity of their total, always changing social and political circumstance.

They seek to embrace our increasing global complexity on the basis of the heart and on the basis of an honest human body. Not according to ideology. Not according to group pressure. Not according to anybody's concept of "correct."

This is a New Politics of Sexuality. And even as I despair of identity politics—because identity is given and principles of justice/equality/freedom cut across given gender and given racial definitions of being, and because I will call you my brother, I will call you my sister, on the basis of what you *do* for justice, what you *do* for equality and what you *do* for freedom and *not* on the basis of who you are, even so I look with admiration and respect upon the new, bisexual politics of sexuality.

This emerging movement politicizes the so-called middle ground: Bisexuality invalidates either/or formulation, either/or analysis. Bisexuality means I am free and I am as likely to want and to love a woman as I am likely to want and to love a man, and what about that? Isn't that what freedom implies?

If you are free, you are not predictable and you are not controllable. To my mind, that is the keenly positive, politicizing significance of bisexual affirmation:

To insist upon complexity, to insist upon the validity of all of the components of social/sexual complexity, to insist upon the equal validity of all of the components of social/sexual complexity.

This seems to me a unifying, 1990s mandate for revolutionary Americans planning to make it into the twenty-first century on the basis of the heart, on the basis of an honest human body, consecrated to every struggle for justice, every struggle for equality, every struggle for freedom.

T W E N T Y - F I V E

◆◆◆

Popular Culture and Queer Representation (2003)
A Critical Perspective

Diane Raymond

Diane Raymond is Professor of Philosophy and Women's Studies and Dean of the College of Arts and Sciences at Simmons College. Her teaching, research, and writing focus on feminist theory, critical race theory, and applied ethics and cultural studies, and include *Sexual Politics and Popular Culture*.

"Queer" is a category in flux. Once a term of homophobic abuse, recently the term has been reappropriated as a marker for some gay, lesbian, bisexual, transgender (glbt), and other marginalized sexual identities. In addition, "queer theory" has emerged in academic scholarship to identify a body of knowledge connected to but not identical with lesbian/gay studies. The term is itself open-ended, and its advocates argue that its fluidity is to be embraced rather than "fixed." Though there is no consensus on the term's meaning (and who is included and who excluded), there is general agreement that the "queer" is politically radical, rejects binary categories (like heterosexual/homosexual), embraces more fluid categories, and tends to be "universalizing" rather than "minoritizing," to use literary theorist Eve Kosofsky Sedgwick's (1990) distinction. That is, queer theory reads queerness throughout the culture and not simply as a fixed, clearly demarcated category. . . .

Queer theory emerged as one of the many oppositional discourses of the 1960s and 1970s, including postcolonial, feminist, and multicultural theory. . . . Regardless of their specific differences, these marginalized views sought to move the "margins" to the "center": "This way of seeing affirmed otherness and difference, and the importance of attending to marginalized, minority, and oppositional groups and voices previously excluded from the cultural dialogue" (Kellner, 1995, p. 24). In addition, these theoretical perspectives tended . . . to reject any strict dichotomy between high and low culture and to reject any vision of popular culture that constructed it as monolithic and viewers as passive dupes. The relationship between viewers and cultural artifacts, including popular media, was, according to these postmodern views, more complex, culturally mediated, and open to a mix of possible "readings."

I want to look at three recurring patterns or tropes that I have identified in situation comedies. The first pattern—the increased appearance of glbt major or supporting characters—acknowledges the very real changes that have occurred in the constitution of the characters populating television's worlds. The remaining two tropes—that of the "gay pretender" and that of the "straight-mistaken-for-gay"—have less to do with the actual diversity of characters we see and more with how gayness itself is understood and metaphorized. All three offer the potential for subverting heterosexist norms and assumptions. I shall argue, however, that how these shows resolve tensions often results in a "reinscription" of heterosexuality and a "containment" of queer sexuality, that is, that the resolution these programs offer enables viewers to distance themselves from the queer and thereby to return to their comfortable positions as part of the dominant culture. Such a dynamic enables power to mask itself, making it all the harder to pin down and question. Thus, . . . my approach suggests how what might seem to be "queer" can come to be normalized in mainstream culture. . . .

I must insist here that my conclusions can be tentative at best and are meant to suggest more complex ways of reading rather than determinative readings themselves. . . . Further, given the truism that no social group is homogeneous and that even a single individual occupies multiple subject positions, I in no way mean to imply that my readings here are "queer," generalizable to any particular group or sort of person, or noncontroversial. To put the point more simply, there is no "correct" queer reading, no one queer reading, and no unchanging queer perspective. . . .

Despite the occasional mention of a drama, my focus here is on comedy, the arena where images of glbt people appear most frequently. To attempt to explain in any persuasive way why such is the case would take me far from my topic. But I might briefly conjecture two possible explanations. First, as traditional family comedies—along with the traditional family—began to disappear, space opened up for "alternative" sorts of narratives, including those of nontraditional "families." . . . For example, the oldest son in *Party of Five* becomes a surrogate father *and* mother to his younger siblings; married characters on popular shows like *Mary Tyler Moore* get divorced; in some cases married characters are never seen with their spouses; and holidays like Thanksgiving, traditionally constructed as times for "family," get reconstructed on shows like *Friends*. These shifts in roles and viewer expectations clearly allowed for the appearance of nonheterosexual characters in major and supporting roles; cultural shifts linked to an increasingly visible gay and lesbian movement no doubt helped to buttress such changes. Finally, situation comedies—however "realistic" they might be—do not claim, like dramas, to be offering us "real life." That lack of seriousness may allow these programs to play with themes under cover of humor where those themes might be too volatile or even too didactic for another sort of audience. Such play and flexibility may also help to account for what may be a wider variety of possible readings. . . .

The Queering of Television

Until very recently, it was not unusual for glbt activists and scholars to bemoan their virtual absence in popular media, particularly television. For example, in 1995, Larry Gross used the term "symbolic annihilation" (p. 62) to describe the invisibility of gays and lesbians in mass media. . . .

Media critics pointed out that those rare depictions of glbt people tended both to dichotomize anyone glbt as victim or villain and to reinforce demeaning stereotypes and caricatures: gay men as effeminate and lesbians as unattractive man-haters, for example. According to Gross (1995), "Hardly ever shown in the media are just plain gay folks, used in roles which do not center on their deviance as a threat to the moral order which must be countered through ridicule or physical violence" (p. 65). . . .

Today's even casual television viewers, however, would find such critiques oddly out-of-date. Network programs are now full of gay/queer characters. . . . Forty-two million people watched the coming-out episode on *Ellen* on April 30, 1997, making it the highest-ranked show on television that year except for the Academy Awards. Though some argue that Ellen DeGeneres's sexuality led to the cancellation of her show in 1998, the queering of prime-time television since that time is without dispute.[1]

A . . . *Boston Globe* article notes there are at least two dozen gay television characters scattered throughout prime-time shows (Rothaus, 2000). Where once soap operas floated gay characters only to have them die of AIDS or leave town mysteriously, *All My Children* has introduced a new plot line in which a character who has grown up on the show comes out as a lesbian. According to the actress who plays the character, the story-line—about how an almost obsessively heterosexual mother deals with her daughter's lesbianism—is meant to be "accessible to everyone" (Rothaus, 2000) and, . . . makes a "concerted effort to show that a gay relationship is just like any other" (Rothaus, 2000). *Will and Grace,* two of whose four major characters are openly gay, is one of the most popular shows on television. Indeed, one might argue that television is light years ahead of mainstream film, whose "gay" characters still seem to be confined to psychopathic murderers (e.g., *Basic Instinct, The Talented Mr. Ripley, Silence of the Lambs, Braveheart, JFK,*

American Beauty, etc.) or lonely, asexual best friends (e.g., *Silkwood, As Good as it Gets,* etc.);[2] for the most part, one needs to turn to independent films to see the "just plain gay folks" Gross seeks.

. . . Given that the majority viewing audience is heterosexual, programming sympathetic to glbt communities must appeal to mainstream liberal viewers who today most likely know someone gay in the workplace, the family, or among friends. Thus, where once glbt viewers had to resort to oppositional or subversive readings . . . —are Cagney and Lacey really lovers? Can one find a queer resonance in the films of Rock Hudson? and so forth—such readings seem quaint and tame by today's television standards when gayness is much discussed, gay sexual practices are the subject of comedic banter, and a range of appealing characters are openly gay or lesbian.

Albeit somewhat one-dimensional, these gay or lesbian television characters are attractive and professional—Will Truman is a lawyer, and the lesbians on *Friends* and the now-defunct but highly popular *Mad About You* are doctors, accountants, and mothers. They include younger characters—*Buffy the Vampire Slayer* has featured two teenaged girls in a budding lesbian relationship, and *Dawson's Creek* featured a main character's coming out in its story line. They are occasionally people of color—*Spin City* includes an African American gay man as part of the political team. Viewers have seen lesbian weddings, lesbian and gay parenting arrangements, gay therapists, gay seniors, and the angst and humor of coming out. Such "main-streaming" seems likely to change popular perceptions and misperceptions about homosexuality. As Mohr (1997) points out, "Without demonization, it is hard, perhaps impossible, to conceptualize homosexuality as a vampire-like corruptive contagion, a disease that spreads itself to the pure and innocent by mere proximity" (p. 333).

Though there is no question that the majority of the viewing audience for these shows is heterosexual, these portrayals engage with viewers who see themselves as hip, nonjudgmental, mostly urban, and gay-friendly. *Will and Grace* is full of campy in-jokes (many referring back to popular culture itself) and sexual innuendo, and as viewers we are asked to feel superior to Jack's mother who fails to realize that he is gay. *Saturday Night Live* pokes fun at a Batman-and-Robin-like team of superheroes, the

Ambiguously Gay Duo, in animated sketches full of phallic imagery and less-than-subtle references to anal intercourse. Smithers is clearly smitten with (and even has erotic dreams about) Mr. Burns in *The Simpsons* and in one episode gay director John Waters is the voice of an antique dealer Homer idolizes until he discovers that the dealer is gay. We are amused that Jaimie's impossible-to-please mother-in-law in *Mad About You* prefers her lesbian daughter's lover to Jaimie. The stars of *Xena* discuss without defensiveness in mainstream periodicals the "lesbian subtext" of that long-running series. It is now homophobes, not gays and lesbians, who are vilified or ignored, and often the test of a character (e.g., the gay plotline in *Dawson's Creek*) comes down to how well he or she deals with a friend or family member's coming out.

This "queering" of television goes well beyond the presence of glbt characters. A . . . *New York Times* article references the growing number of gay television writers who are influencing shows even where there are no gay characters. The article suggests that "a gay sensibility has infiltrated American comedy, even when flying beneath the radar in an ostensibly heterosexual situation" (Kirby, 2001, p. 23). This phenomenon . . . allows for multiple readings of a character or situation, those readings dependent on the subject position of the viewer. Thus, *Frasier*'s two brothers, but for the fact that they sleep with women, are stereotypically gay in their tastes and preferences; knowing more about Puccini than basketball, these brothers evidence a gay sensibility striking to all but the most naïve. Indeed, much of the humor emerges from their macho-cop father's vain attempts to make his sons more "butch." Further, Niles and Frasier's shared memories of the childhood trauma they experienced as a result of being fussy, intelligent, artistic, and averse to athletics resonate with the experiences of many glbt people who did not as youths conform to the dominant culture's gender codes.

These more subtle gestures may, as Danae Clark (1993) suggests in her discussion of advertising campaigns, serve a dual function: They avoid alienating gay audiences at the same time that they mask the gay content and retain majority viewers. Finally, in a number of cases, actors playing heterosexual characters are known to viewing audiences to be gay, lesbian, or bisexual. For example, David Hyde Pierce, who plays Frasier's brother Niles Crane, is openly gay; knowledgeable viewers, then, can play with multiple levels of reading performances such as Pierce's, even where the ostensible plot line involves, for example, his long-term obsession with Daphne, his father's live-in physical therapist. . . .

Though cultural studies critics have tended to look for so-called subversive moments in television and film as opportunities for resistant readings, my approach here adopts a different orientation to suggest how moments of apparently subversive potential are undermined and ultimately contained. . . .

Queering Theory and Representation

Ideology . . . constructs viewing positions and identities. Sexuality, at least in modern times, is one component of that ideology, a component whose regulation occurs both formally and informally. In a culture grounded in what Adrienne Rich (1980) has termed "compulsory heterosexuality," popular culture will tend to portray heterosexuality as if it were natural and inevitable and to position alternative forms of sexuality as "other." Compulsory heterosexuality (or what some have called "heteronormativity") functions to underline the fact that heterosexuality is an institution, a practice, with its own set of expectations, norms, and principles of conduct. If, however, heterosexuality is not a naturalized, innate state of being, then its existence is more fragile than is obvious at first glance. Given that fragility, heterosexuality cannot be taken as a given or presumed; in a culture framed by homophobia and heterosexism, institutions both formal and informal—police behavior, boundaries, expectations, and values—a dynamic blend of incentives and disincentives function to channel desire in "appropriate" ways and to make invisible those practices falling outside its discursive domain.

Heterosexuality and homophobia organize the structures in which we are immersed, structures so pervasive as to become almost invisible. Sociologist Pierre Bourdieu (1990) has employed the notion of *habitus* to describe how what is constructed can come to seem inevitable and natural. Like the fish that does not feel the weight of the water, human beings live in a world of "social games embodied and turned into second nature" (p. 63). . . .

The mechanisms that serve to construct and regulate sexuality may not be obvious or even intentional; indeed, as Foucault (1990) puts it, "Power is tolerable only on condition that it mask a substantial part of itself. Its success is proportional to its ability to hide its own mechanisms" (p. 86). If ideology generally effaces itself, then even the very producers of popular culture—whatever their explicit political leanings, sexuality, or agenda—are immersed in that ideology. Further, power's ability to mask itself may mean that, ironically, the mechanisms of power produce pleasure. We don't have to go far to find such examples—Gothic romances, pornography, certain clothing styles, exercise regimens, gendered toys for children, and so forth—all function to produce pleasure as they disguise the ways that they reinforce norms relating to sexuality and, less obviously, race, age, and class. The question becomes, then, not whether queer (or straight) viewers find pleasure in the proliferation of these television images . . . but rather how one might read and understand such pleasure. Pleasure itself is never innocent or neutral and there is a danger in valorizing pleasure without looking at its context. Given that, I want to ask how the new representations of gays and lesbians circulate in culture.

If the homo/hetero schema is "written into the cultural organization of Western societies" (Epstein, 1987, p. 133), then the question of the homosexual/heterosexual matrix rather than the question of personal identity becomes primary. Such a perspective would suggest that what is at stake is less the question how many gay/queer characters populate television or even how sympathetically they are portrayed but rather about the ways desire and meaning are structured, even in the absence of such images. Thus, identity must be thought of as always in relation, never fixed or stable. As Fuss, Sedgwick, Butler, and others have noted, heterosexuality is a parasitic notion, dependent on that-what-it-is-not, namely, homosexuality. "Each is haunted by the other" (Fuss, 1991, p. 4), and the homosexual comes to represent the "terrifying [sexual] other" of the heterosexual. Yet popular television programming seems to belie this theoretical claim, bombarding us with images of gayness and far less threatening homosexuals who suggest the possibility of new normative understandings of sexual difference.

First, one should note that the appearance of *difference* per se is not necessarily subversive. . . . That heterosexuals now can, like tourists, visit glbt culture does not in itself guarantee social change. Further, capitalist systems need difference to create desire and to sell commodities. Kellner (1995) notes:

> Difference sells. Capitalism must constantly multiply markets, styles, fads, and artifacts to keep absorbing consumers into its practices and lifestyles. The mere valorization of "difference" as a mark of opposition can simply help market new styles and artifacts if the difference in question and its effects are not adequately appraised. *(p. 40)*

[If] Stuart and Elizabeth Ewen (1992) are right that "novelty and disposability make up the backbone of the market" (p. 193), then the static is the enemy of popular media. Difference can also serve to provide one with a sense of uniqueness or individuality. As Jonathan Rutherford has quipped, "It's no longer about keeping up with the Joneses, it's about being different from them" (quoted in hooks, 1995, p. 157). Further, the promotion of gayness as a "lifestyle" tends to attach it to commodities rather than practices as an expression of the self. *Will and Grace's* bitchy attention to fashion, weight, career, and popular media is exemplary in this respect.

In addition, Torres (1993) points to the ways visits from "real lesbians" may help to deflect the viewer's attention from the possibility that ongoing characters may harbor same-sex feelings. Especially in shows that feature all, or mostly, female troupes like *Kate and Allie, Designing Women, Cagney and Lacey,* and *Golden Girls,* for example, the introduction of lesbian and gay characters may serve to reassure viewers that the same-sex groupings are purely platonic. Cultural unease with lesbianism may be tied to cultural unease with feminism, but it may also emerge from lesbianism's own murky boundaries. Obviously, my case would be much easier to make if these characters reflected negative or insulting stereotypes; yet, I have already suggested that the characters we see exhibit a range of personality types, interests, values, and flaws. But I want to look more closely for a moment at a dynamic in *Will and Grace* that may help to clarify how the subversive potential in these images is ultimately policed and contained.

It's Not Just the Numbers . . .

The dynamic I want to explore pervades this show, and its repetition suggests a certain ambivalence over sexuality, queer sexuality in particular. To illustrate this phenomenon more concretely, let's look at the montage that opens the show. In these brief scenes, we see the show's four main characters in a variety of poses and places. Yet, strikingly, we never see the two gay men together and the only times we see the women together occur when they are with at least one of the men. Instead, we are treated to a number of opposite-sex couplings. We see, in the first clip, Will and Grace dancing a tango, a dance which has come to epitomize sexual heat and romance. We see Jack and Karen frequently together in other scenes, including one where they bounce off each other's chests and another where they hug. In episodes of the show, we frequently see Will and Grace in bed together and, though Grace recently had and lost a boyfriend, Will's relationships are rare and end almost as soon as they begin. Will and Grace's behavior mirrors that of a traditional heterosexual husband and wife, and Karen is quick to point to Grace's neurotic attachment to Will (indeed, she often refers to Will as Grace's gay husband). Grace becomes the supremely neurotic fag hag par excellence who identifies with gay culture, surrounds herself with gay men, and is never guilty of even the mildest expression of homophobia. Will and Grace are comfortable physically with one another, they finish each other's sentences, and, though they briefly lived apart (across the hall from one another!), they soon came back together as roommates. Do we, like Grace, hope someday that the two will be united, that Will can be converted to the heterosexual partner that Grace desperately wants? Further, Jack's flamboyance and his stereotypical nature may suggest that Will is somehow less gay and therefore recuperable to heterosexuality.

As already noted, there is no question that the new glbt characters we see on television are an attractive group both morally and physically. In some cases, for example, *ER* and *Buffy,* shows

allow a long-standing character to play with a same-sex attraction, even if the feelings/relationships are temporary. The famous "kisses"—one thinks back to the *Roseanne* show for one of the first—and the more recent kisses on *Friends* and *Ally McBeal*—occur during sweeps weeks and are unabashed strategies to increase the viewing audience. The fact that these episodes earn viewer warnings is noteworthy in itself. But even more noteworthy, it seems to me, is the fact that these episodes result in no change in diegesis or character evolution. These kisses come and go as if they were a dream; they are never incorporated into a character's understanding of his/her identity and sexuality, and the possibility of bisexuality, a more fluid sexual identity, or even a recurrence is rarely if ever entertained.

Indeed, fluidity seems to pose such a threat that its possibility is rarely if ever acknowledged. Thus, when "real" gay or lesbian characters tell their stories, their narratives tend almost always to reinscribe gayness as innate, and those who are gay as having no choice. Thus, we hear that Will has always loved Grace, but that he has never had any sexual feelings of any kind for her. When she is devastated to learn that he has had sex with another woman, he insists that it was merely to have the experience and that he had no real interest in the woman. The idea that Will's best friend Jack might have been attracted to a woman is so obviously ludicrous that the very idea earns a huge laugh. The noteworthy absence of bisexuals in these comedies suggests that the fluidity of a bisexual sexual identity may be too disruptive for such programming. . . .

Finally, an important strategy for learning to read popular texts like television sitcoms is to look for those moments where a moral voice seems to speak. Because these shows . . . are meant to be light and entertaining, they cannot afford to be overly didactic. But there is no question that moral ideology permeates these shows. In some cases, it is certain characters who seem to represent the voice of moral authority. In *Will and Grace* that character seems to be Grace, who, despite her ditziness, often seems to be the moral voice of the show. . . . Grace's total absence of any vestiges of homophobia makes her a kind of model for the heterosexual viewer. . . . Grace is a dependable friend, a creative and dedicated professional, and enemy of oppression. In one episode, Grace is horrified to discover that Jack is not out to his mother. She urges him to come out and emphasizes the importance of being honest about his identity. In another episode . . . Grace refuses to speak to Will because he is willing to date someone who is in the closet. Grace repeatedly pushes on this issue and accuses Will of hypocrisy and self-loathing. The fact that the heterosexual woman on the show is the one to insist on being openly gay is itself worth noting. Even more striking, however, is the fact that the narrative vilifies those glbt people who, for a variety of powerful reasons, decide not to come out. Never acknowledging any costs to being openly gay, the moral message seems to be that all secrets are bad and the decision to stay in the closet is just another secret that one is never justified in keeping. Questions of power and subordination are thereby erased in the effort to homogenize all lies and secrets. Indeed, once Jack does tell his mother that he is gay, she immediately responds, "I have a secret too." The momentum switches away from Jack's confession and its possible implications to her announcement that the man who is Jack's biological father is not who he thinks he is.

Pretending to Be Gay . . .

My second theme, the trope of the gay pretender, has been a staple of situation comedies ever since Jack Tripper in *Three's Company* posed as gay so that his uptight landlord would let him live with two attractive women. . . . Martin, Frasier's dad, poses as gay in order to avoid having to date a woman he's not interested in. Kate and Allie, in that long-defunct series, pose as lesbians in order to curry favor (and a new lease) from their lesbian landladies. In *Three Sisters*, one sister's ex-husband convinced her that he was gay in order to get a quickie divorce. Klinger in *M.A.S.H.* was, we assume as viewers, a heterosexual man posing as gay or transvestite in order to secure a release from the military. Finally, . . . the soap opera *Days of Our Lives* introduced a new plotline where Jack "outs" himself to Greta so as not to hurt her feelings and confess that he is not attracted to her.

Readers no doubt will be able to come up with examples of their own, and the ease with which we are able to produce these examples suggests how common this trope is. How might one explain its recurrence? On the one hand, one reading suggests that these examples of gender and sexuality play may be consistent with a progressive queer agenda that suggests either that we're all queer or that there's a little queer in each of us. Sedgwick labels this approach to sexuality a "universalizing discourse," meaning that it views queerness/sexuality as nonbinary and more amorphous than is traditionally believed. . . . What makes for the humor in these situations is, at least partly, the fact that the viewer knows that the character's heterosexuality is never in doubt. Such certainty enables these characters to play with gay stereotypes without seeming to be homophobic—in *Frasier*, for example, Martin suddenly becomes limp-wristed, interested in décor, and able to express his emotions. Certain mannerisms come to be coded as gay even though the character expressing them is not. The character we "know" is straight is positioned against the character we "know" is gay (interestingly, this trope seems to be rarely used with female characters; does this suggest that lesbians have fewer identifiable mannerisms?) and the comedy of errors and misreadings ensues.

Yet there is never any suggestion whatsoever of any temptation or questioning on the part of the "straight" character; that firmness of resolve serves once again not only to reinforce a strict binary of gay/straight but also to suggest that solid and impermeable boundaries frame one's sexuality. Thus, potentially oppositional discourses are subverted by naturalizing them within terms that make sense in the context of the dominant perspective.

In addition, the "gay pretender" trope implicitly creates a fantasy world where not only do gays and lesbians not experience cultural ostracism and legal discrimination; they also enjoy *more* power than heterosexuals. In addition, it is striking that sex and sexuality seem to be foregrounded in these dynamics. They are landlords who favor "their own kind"; they are released from the burdens of heterosexual dating and romance (and, indeed from having to tell the truth!); they do not have to serve in the military; and they are simply able to have more fun, as Karen in *Will and Grace* discovers, when posing as a lesbian enables her to offer make-up tips and kiss cute women. This inversion results in humor and unanticipated consequences but it may also serve to mask the ways that power operates and to make the mechanisms of power even more covert.

I'm Not Gay but My Boyfriend Is . . .

Finally, the "straight-mistaken-for-gay" trope is common throughout comedy. This trope represents an almost total inversion of the tendency in earlier television audiences to ignore telltale signs of gayness in a television character or actor. To the less naïve viewer today, the flamboyance and campiness of a Liberace, Flip Wilson, or PeeWee Herman suggest a gay sensibility too obvious to be overlooked. But today's situation comedies manipulate signs of gayness to create humor and playfulness. For example, in a now-classic *Seinfeld* episode, Jerry and George are mistakenly identified as a gay couple by a college reporter who then outs them in her school newspaper. The refrain "not that there's anything wrong with it" serves in part to mock standard liberal attitudes toward homosexuality. . . . In *Third Rock From the Sun*, John Lithgow attempts to "come out" as an alien and is instead assumed to be coming out as gay. *Friends* often hints at the ways Chandler's affect positions him as gay. . . . Indeed, part of the humor in these episodes is that the heterosexual character's mannerisms come to be recoded as queer. Further, this trope suggests the ways that virtually any behavior can be reread as gay once the viewer's perspective is framed by that lens.

The "straight-mistaken-for-gay" trope, like the gay pretender, derives much of its humor from the audience's knowledge that the character(s) in question is/are *not* in fact gay. Such an epistemological advantage sets the audience member apart from the mistaken character and provides the audience member not only with a certain degree of distance but also with reinscribed boundaries between the gay and the straight. . . .

Queer theory embraces a kind of intellectual tension: where, on the one hand, the viewer insists that sexuality and the domain of the sexual are cultural inventions and not essential, on the other hand, it deploys sexuality as a (if not *the*) significant determinant of cultural and individual identity.

If Doty (1993) is right that queerness should "challenge and confuse our understanding and uses of sexual and gender categories" (p. xvii), then the sorts of examples I've been describing and analyzing here represent failures.

Marginalized identities are not just oppressed by power; they are also, as Foucault points out, constructed by those very same power relations. Thus, there is no doubt that these new representations of glbt characters and of heterosexuality will give birth to new meanings and new signifiers attached to queer sexuality. But we must wait for that next episode.

NOTES

1. Indeed, fall 2001 premiered a new show starring DeGeneres, who plays an out lesbian who returns to her hometown. Unlike her earlier show, where it took years and much publicity for her to out herself, in this new show she is already out in the first episode and her sexuality is treated casually by her family and those she meets.

2. Unless the film deals explicitly with "gay issues" like AIDS (*Philadelphia, Long Time Companion,* etc.) or homophobic violence (e.g., *Boys Don't Cry*).

REFERENCES

Bourdieu, P. (1990). *In other words: Essays towards a reflexive sociology.* Cambridge, UK: Polity.

Butler, J. (1990). *Gender trouble: Feminism and the subversion of identity.* New York: Routledge.

Clark, D. (1993). Commodity lesbianism. In H. Abelove, M. Aina Barale, & D. M. Haperin (Eds.), *The lesbian and gay studies reader* (pp. 186–201). New York: Routledge.

Doty, A. (1993). *Making things perfectly queer: Interpreting mass culture.* Minneapolis: University of Minnesota Press.

Epstein, S. G. (1987). Gay politics, ethnic identity: The limits of social constructionism. *Socialist Review, 93/94.*

Ewen, S., & Ewen, E. (1992). *Channels of desire: Mass images and the shaping of American consciousness.* Minneapolis: University of Minnesota Press.

Foucault, M. (1990). *The history of sexuality* (Vol. 1, R. Hurley, Trans.). New York: Vintage Books.

Fuss, D. (1991). *Inside/out: Lesbian theories, gay theories.* New York: Routledge.

Gross, L. (1995). Out of the mainstream: Sexual minorities and the mass media. In G. Dines & J. M. Humez (Eds.), *Gender, race and class in media: A text-reader* (pp. 61–69). Thousand Oaks, CA: Sage.

hooks, b. (1995). *Killing rage: Ending racism.* New York: Henry Holt.

Kellner, D. (1995). *Media culture: Cultural studies, identity, and politics between the modern and the postmodern.* London: Routledge.

Kirby, D. (2001, June 17). The boys in the writers' room. *New York Times*, pp. 23, 33.

Mohr, R. (1997). A gay and straight agenda. In J. Corvino (Ed.), *Same sex: Debating the ethics, science, and culture of homosexuality* (pp. 331–344). Lanham, MD: Rowman & Littlefield.

Rich, A. (1980, Summer). Compulsory heterosexuality and lesbian existence. *Signs,* 5(4), 631–660.

Rothaus, S. (2000, December 30). Better reception for gay TV characters. *Boston Globe*, p. D26.

Sedgwick, E. K. (1990). *Epistemology of the closet.* Berkeley: University of California Press.

Torres, S. (1993). Television/feminism: *Heartbeat* and prime time lesbianism. In H. Abelove, M. Aina Barale, & D. M. Halperin (Eds.), *The lesbian and gay studies reader* (pp. 176–185). New York: Routledge.

T W E N T Y - S I X

◆◆◆

The All-American Queer Pakistani Girl (1997)

Surina A. Khan

Surina Khan was born in Pakistan and came to the United States as a child. A writer, researcher, and advocate, she served as Executive Director of the International Gay and Lesbian Human Rights Commission for several years. Currently, Ms. Khan is Senior Program Officer at the Women's Foundation of California.

I don't know if my grandmother is dead or alive. I can't remember the last time I saw her—it must have been at least ten years ago, when I was in Pakistan for a visit. She was my only living grandparent, and her health was beginning to fail. Every once in a while, I think she's probably dead and no one bothered to tell me.

I'm completely out of touch with my Pakistani life. I can hardly speak Urdu, my first language; I certainly can't read or write it. I have no idea how many cousins I have. I know my father comes from a large family—eleven brothers and sisters—but I don't know all their names. I've never read the Koran, and I don't have faith in Islam.

As a kid, I remember being constantly reminded that I was different—by my accent, my brown skin color, my mother's traditional clothing, and the smell of the food we ate. And so I con-

sciously Americanized myself. I spent my early childhood perfecting my American accent, my adolescence affirming my American identity to others, and my late teens rejecting my Pakistani heritage. Now, at the age of twenty-seven, I'm feeling the void I created for myself.

Sometimes I think of what my life would be like if my parents hadn't moved to Connecticut in 1973, when I was five. Most of my family has since moved back to Pakistan, and up until seven years ago, when I came out, I went back somewhat regularly. But I never liked going back. It made me feel stifled, constrained. People were always talking about getting married. First it was, "You're almost old enough to start thinking about finding a nice husband," then, "When are you getting married?" Now I imagine they'd say, with disappointment, "You'll be an old maid."

My family is more liberal than most of Pakistani society. By American standards that translates into conservative (my mother raised money for George Bush). But I was brought up in a family that valued education, independence, integrity, and love. I never had to worry about getting pressured into an arranged marriage, even though several of my first cousins were—sometimes to each other. Once I went to a wedding in which the bride and groom saw each other for the first time when someone passed them a mirror after their wedding ceremony and they both looked into it at once. That's when I started thinking my family was "modern."

Unfortunately they live in a fundamentalist culture that won't tolerate me. I can't even bring myself to visit Pakistan. The last time I went back was seven years ago, for my father's funeral, and sometimes I wonder if the next time will be for my mother's funeral. She asks me to come visit every time I talk to her. I used to tell her I was too busy, that I couldn't get away. But three years ago I finally answered her truthfully. I told her that I didn't like the idea of traveling to a country that lashed lesbians one hundred times in public. More important, I didn't feel comfortable visiting when she and I had not talked about anything important in my life since I had come out to her.

Pakistan has always been my parents' answer to everything. When they found out my sisters were smoking pot in the late 1970s, they shipped all of us back. "You need to get in touch with the Pakistani culture," my mother would say. When my oldest sister got hooked on transcendental meditation and started walking around the house in a trance, my father packed her up and put her on a plane back to the homeland. She's been there ever since. Being the youngest of six, I wised up quickly. I waited to drop my bomb until after I had moved out of the house and was financially independent. If I had come out while I was still living in my parents' home, you can bet I'd have been on the next flight to Islamabad.

When I came out to my mother, she suggested I go back to Pakistan for a few months. "Just get away from it all," she begged. "You need some time. Clear your head." But I knew better. And when I insisted that I was queer and was going to move to Washington, D.C., to live with my girlfriend, Robin (now my ex-girlfriend, much to my mother's delight), she tried another scare tactic: "You and your lover better watch out. There's a large Pakistani community in D.C., and they'll find out about you. They'll break your legs, mutilate your face." That pretty much did it for me. My mother had just validated all my fears associated with Pakistan. I cut all ties with the community, including my family. *Pakistan* became synonymous with *homophobia.*

My mother disowned me when I didn't heed her advice. But a year later, when Robin and I broke up, my mother came back into my life. It was partly motivated by wishful thinking on her part. I do give her credit, though, not only for nurturing the strength in me to live by my convictions with integrity and honesty but also for eventually trying to understand me. I'll never forget the day I took her to see a lawyer friend of mine. She was on the verge of settling a lawsuit started by my father before he died and was unhappy with her lawyer. I took her to see Maggie Cassella, a lawyer/comedian based in Hartford, Connecticut, where I was again living. "I presume this woman's a lesbian," my mother said in the car on the way to Maggie's office. "Yes, she is," I replied, thinking, *Oh, no, here it comes again.* But my mother took me by surprise. "Well, the men aren't helping me; I might as well go to the dykes." I didn't think she even knew the word *dyke.* Now, *that* was a moment.

Her changing attitude about my lesbian identity was instilling in me a desire to reclaim my Pakistani identity. The best way to do this, I decided, would be to seek out other Pakistani lesbians. I barely knew any Pakistanis aside from my family, and I sure as hell didn't know, or even know of, any Pakistani lesbians. I was just naive enough to think I was the only one.

It wasn't easy for me even to arrive at the concept of a Pakistani lesbian. Having rejected my culture from a young age, I identified only as a lesbian when I came out, and in my zeal to be all-American, I threw myself into the American queer liberation movement. I did not realize that there is an active South Asian gay and lesbian community in the United States—and that many of us are here precisely because we're able to be queer and out in the Western world.

South Asian culture is rampant with homophobia—so much so that most people in South Asia literally don't have words for homosexuality, which is viewed as a Western phenomenon despite the fact that images of gays and lesbians have been a part of the subcontinent's history for thousands of years. In the temples of Khajuraho and Konarak in India, there are images of same-gender couples—male and female—in intimate positions. One temple carving depicts two women caressing each other, while another shows four women engaged in sexual play. There are also references to homosexuality in the *Kāma-sūtra*, the ancient Indian text on the diversities of sex. Babar, the founder of the Mughal dynasty in India, is said to have been gay, as was Abu Nawas, a famous Islamic poet. The fact is that homosexuality is as native to South Asia as is heterosexuality. But since the culture pressures South Asian women to reject our sexual identity, many South Asian queers living in the United States reject South Asian culture in turn. As a result, we are often isolated from one another.

Despite the odds, I started my search for queer people from South Asia—and I found them, all across America, Canada, and England. Connecting with this network and talking with other queer South Asians has begun to fill the void I've been feeling. But just as it took me years to reject my Pakistani heritage, it will likely take me as long, if not longer, to reintegrate my culture into my life as it is now.

I'm not ready to go back to Pakistan. But I am ready to start examining the hostility I feel toward a part of myself I thought I had discarded long ago.

TWENTY-SEVEN

◆◆◆

We Are All Works in Progress (1998)

Leslie Feinberg

Leslie Feinberg is a novelist, historian, and transgender activist. Her most recent book is *Transgender Liberation: A movement whose time has come.* Her acclaimed novel, *Stone Butch Blues,* won the Lambda literary award. Feinberg has also received an American Library Association Award for Gay and Lesbian Literature.

The sight of pink-blue gender-coded infant outfits may grate on your nerves. Or you may be a woman or a man who feels at home in those categories. Trans liberation defends you both.

Each person should have the right to *choose* between pink or blue tinted gender categories, as well as all the other hues of the palette. At this moment in time, that right is denied to us. But together, we could make it a reality. . . .

I am a human being who would rather not be addressed as Ms. or Mr., ma'am or sir. I prefer to use gender-neutral pronouns like *sie* (pronounced like *"see"*) and *hir* (pronounced like *"here"*) to describe myself. I am a person who faces almost insurmountable difficulty when instructed to check off an "F" or an "M" box on identification papers.

I'm not at odds with the fact that I was born female-bodied. Nor do I identify as an intermediate sex. I simply do not fit the prevalent Western concepts of what a woman or man "should" look like. And that reality has dramatically directed the course of my life.

I'll give you a graphic example. From December 1995 to December 1996, I was dying of endocarditis—a bacterial infection that lodges and proliferates in the valves of the heart. A simple blood culture would have immediately exposed the root cause of my raging fevers. Eight weeks of 'round-the-clock intravenous antibiotic drips would have eradicated every last seedling of bacterium in the canals of my heart. Yet I experienced such hatred from some health practitioners that I very nearly died.

I remember late one night in December my lover and I arrived at a hospital emergency room during a snowstorm. My fever was 104 degrees and rising. My blood pressure was pounding dangerously high. The staff immediately hooked me up to monitors and worked to bring down my fever. The doctor in charge began physically examining me. When he determined that my anatomy was female, he flashed me a mean-spirited smirk. While keeping his eyes fixed on me, he approached one of the nurses, seated at a desk, and began rubbing her neck and shoulders. He talked to her about sex for a few minutes. After his pointed demonstration of "normal sexuality," he told me to get dressed and then he stormed out of the room. Still delirious, I struggled to put on my clothes and make sense of what was happening.

The doctor returned after I was dressed. He ordered me to leave the hospital and never return. I refused. I told him I wouldn't leave until he could tell me why my fever was so high. He said, "You have a fever because you are a very troubled person."

This doctor's prejudices, directed at me during a moment of catastrophic illness, could have killed me. The death certificate would have read: Endocarditis. By all rights it should have read: Bigotry.

As my partner and I sat bundled up in a cold car outside the emergency room, still reverberating from the doctor's hatred, I thought about how many people have been turned away from medical care when they were desperately ill—some because an apartheid "whites only" sign hung over the emergency room entrance, or some because their visible Kaposi's sarcoma lesions kept personnel far from their beds. I remembered how a blemish that wouldn't heal drove my mother to visit her doctor repeatedly during the 1950s. I recalled the doctor finally wrote a prescription for Valium because he decided she was a hysterical woman. When my mother finally got to specialists, they told her the cancer had already reached her brain.

Bigotry exacts its toll in flesh and blood. And left unchecked and unchallenged, prejudices create a poisonous climate for us all. Each of us has a stake in the demand that every human being has a right to a job, to shelter, to health care, to dignity, to respect.

I am very grateful to have this chance to open up a conversation with you about why it is so vital to also defend the right of individuals to express and define their sex and gender, and to control their own bodies. For me, it's a life-and-death question. But I also believe that this discussion will have great meaning for you. All your life you've heard such dogma about what it means to be a "real" woman or a "real" man. And chances are you've choked on some of it. You've balked at the idea that being a woman means having to be thin as a rail, emotionally nurturing, and an airhead when it comes to balancing her checkbook. You know in your guts that being a man has nothing to do with rippling

muscles, innate courage, or knowing how to handle a chain saw. These are really caricatures. Yet these images have been drilled into us through popular culture and education over the years. And subtler, equally insidious messages lurk in the interstices of these grosser concepts. These ideas of what a "real" woman or man should be straightjacket the freedom of individual self-expression. These gender messages play on and on in a continuous loop in our brains, like commercials that can't be muted.

But in my lifetime I've also seen social upheavals challenge this sex and gender doctrine. As a child who grew up during the McCarthyite, Father-Knows-Best 1950s, and who came of age during the second wave of women's liberation in the United States, I've seen transformations in the ways people think and talk about what it means to be a woman or a man.

Today the gains of the 1970s women's liberation movement are under siege by right-wing propagandists. But many today who are too young to remember what life was like before the women's movement need to know that this was a tremendously progressive development that won significant economic and social reforms. And this struggle by women and their allies swung human consciousness forward like a pendulum.

The movement replaced the common usage of vulgar and diminutive words to describe females with the word *woman* and infused that word with strength and pride. Women, many of them formerly isolated, were drawn together into consciousness-raising groups. Their discussions—about the root of women's oppression and how to eradicate it—resonated far beyond the rooms in which they took place. The women's liberation movement sparked a mass conversation about the systematic degradation, violence, and discrimination that women faced in this society. And this consciousness-raising changed many of the ways women and men thought about themselves and their relation to each other. In retrospect, however, we must not forget that these widespread discussions were not just organized to *talk* about oppression. They were a giant dialogue about how to take action to fight institutionalized anti-woman attitudes, rape and battering, the illegality of abortion, employment and education discrimination, and other ways women were socially and economically devalued.

This was a big step forward for humanity. And even the period of political reaction that followed has not been able to overturn all the gains made by that important social movement.

Now another movement is sweeping onto the stage of history: Trans liberation. We are again raising questions about the societal treatment of people based on their sex and gender expression. This discussion will make new contributions to human consciousness. And trans communities, like the women's movement, are carrying out these mass conversations with the goal of creating a movement capable of fighting for justice—of righting the wrongs.

We are a movement of masculine females and feminine males, cross-dressers, transsexual men and women, intersexuals born on the anatomical sweep between female and male, gender-blenders, many other sex and gender-variant people, and our significant others. All told, we expand understanding of how many ways there are to be a human being.

Our lives are proof that sex and gender are much more complex than a delivery room doctor's glance at genitals can determine, more variegated than pink or blue birth caps. We are oppressed for not fitting those narrow social norms. We are fighting back.

Our struggle will also help expose some of the harmful myths about what it means to be a woman or a man that have compartmentalized and distorted your life, as well as mine. Trans liberation has meaning for you—no matter how you define or express your sex or your gender.

If you are a trans person, you face horrendous social punishments—from institutionalization to gang rape, from beatings to denial of child visitation. This oppression is faced, in varying degrees, by all who march under the banner of trans liberation. This brutalization and degradation strips us of what we could achieve with our individual lifetimes.

And if you do not identify as transgender or transsexual or intersexual, your life is diminished by our oppression as well. Your own choices as a man or a woman are sharply curtailed. Your individual journey to express yourself is shunted into

one of two deeply carved ruts, and the social baggage you are handed is already packed.

So the defense of each individual's right to control their own body, and to explore the path of self-expression, enhances your own freedom to discover more about yourself and your potentialities. This movement will give you more room to breathe—to be yourself. To discover on a deeper level what it means to be your self.

Together, I believe we can forge a coalition that can fight on behalf of your oppression as well as mine. Together, we can raise each other's grievances and win the kind of significant change we all long for. But the foundation of unity is understanding. So let me begin by telling you a little bit about myself.

I am a human being who unnerves some people. As they look at me, they see a kaleidoscope of characteristics they associate with both males and females. I appear to be a tangled knot of gender contradictions. So they feverishly press the question on me: woman or man? Those are the only two words most people have as tools to shape their question.

"Which sex are you?" I understand their question. It sounds so simple. And I'd like to offer them a simple resolution. But merely answering woman or man will not bring relief to the questioner. As long as people try to bring me into focus using only those two lenses, I will always appear to be an enigma.

The truth is I'm no mystery. I'm a female who is more masculine than those prominently portrayed in mass culture. Millions of females and millions of males in this country do not fit the cramped compartments of gender that we have been taught are "natural" and "normal." For many of us, the words *woman* or *man, ma'am* or *sir, she* or *he*—in and of themselves—do not total up the sum of our identities or of our oppressions. Speaking for myself, my life only comes into focus when the word *transgender* is added to the equation.

Simply answering whether I was born female or male will not solve the conundrum. Before I can even begin to respond to the question of my own birth sex, I feel it's important to challenge the assumptions that the answer is always as simple as either-or. I believe we need to take a critical look at the assumption that is built into the seemingly innocent question: "What a beautiful baby—is it a boy or a girl?"

The human anatomical spectrum can't be understood, let alone appreciated, as long as female or male are considered to be all that exists. "Is it a boy or a girl?" Those are the only two categories allowed on birth certificates.

But this either-or leaves no room for intersexual people, born between the poles of female and male. Human anatomy continues to burst the confines of the contemporary concept that nature delivers all babies on two unrelated conveyor belts. So, are the birth certificates changed to reflect human anatomy? No, the U.S. medical establishment hormonally molds and shapes and surgically hacks away at the exquisite complexities of intersexual infants until they neatly fit one category or the other.

A surgeon decides whether a clitoris is "too large" or a penis is "too small." That's a highly subjective decision for anyone to make about another person's body. Especially when the person making the arbitrary decision is scrubbed up for surgery! And what is the criterion for a penis being "too small"? Too small for successful heterosexual intercourse. Intersexual infants are already being tailored for their sexuality, as well as their sex. The infants have no say over what happens to their bodies. Clearly the struggle against genital mutilation must begin here, within the borders of the United States.

But the question asked of all new parents: "Is it a boy or a girl?" is not such a simple question when transsexuality is taken into account, either. Legions of out-and-proud transsexual men and women demonstrate that individuals have a deep, developed, and valid sense of their own sex that does not always correspond to the cursory decision made by a delivery-room obstetrician. Nor is transsexuality a recent phenomenon. People have undergone social sex reassignment and surgical and hormonal sex changes throughout the breadth of oral and recorded human history.

Having offered this view of the complexities and limitations of birth classification, I have no hesitancy in saying I was born female. But that answer doesn't clear up the confusion that drives some people to ask me, "Are you a man or a woman?" The problem is that they are trying to understand my gender expression by determining my sex—and therein lies the rub! Just as most of us grew up with only the concepts of *woman* and *man*, the terms *feminine* and *masculine* are the only two tools most people have to talk about the complexities of gender expression.

That pink-blue dogma assumes that biology steers our social destiny. We have been taught that being born female or male will determine how we will dress and walk, whether we will prefer our hair shortly cropped or long and flowing, whether we will be emotionally nurturing or repressed. According to this way of thinking, masculine females are trying to look "like men," and feminine males are trying to act "like women."

But those of us who transgress those gender assumptions also shatter their inflexibility.

So, why do I sometimes describe myself as a masculine female? Isn't each of those concepts very limiting? Yes. But placing the two words together is incendiary, exploding the belief that gender expression is linked to birth sex like horse and carriage. It is the social contradiction missing from Dick-and-Jane textbook education.

I actually chafe at describing myself as masculine. For one thing, masculinity is such an expansive territory, encompassing boundaries of nationality, race, and class. Most importantly, individuals blaze their own trails across this landscape.

And it's hard for me to label the intricate matrix of my gender as simply masculine. To me, branding individual self-expression as simply feminine or masculine is like asking poets: Do you write in English or Spanish? The question leaves out the possibilities that the poetry is woven in Cantonese or Ladino, Swahili or Arabic. The question deals only with the system of language that the poet has been taught. It ignores the words each writer hauls up, hand over hand, from a common well. The music words make when finding themselves next to each other for the first time. The silences echoing in the space between ideas. The powerful winds of passion and belief that move the poet to write.

That is why I do not hold the view that gender is simply a social construct—one of two languages that we learn by rote from early age. To me, gender is the poetry each of us makes out of the language we are taught. When I walk through the anthology of the world, I see individuals express their gender in exquisitely complex and ever-changing ways, despite the laws of pentameter.

So how can gender expression be mandated by edict and enforced by law? Isn't that like trying to handcuff a pool of mercury? It's true that human self-expression is diverse and is often expressed in ambiguous or contradictory ways. And what degree of gender expression is considered "acceptable" can depend on your social situation, your race and nationality, your class, and whether you live in an urban or rural environment.

But no one can deny that rigid gender education begins early on in life—from pink and blue color-coding of infant outfits to gender-labeling toys and games. And those who overstep these arbitrary borders are punished. Severely. When the steel handcuffs tighten, it is human bones that crack. No one knows how many trans lives have been lost to police brutality and street-corner bashing. The lives of trans people are so depreciated in this society that many murders go unreported. And those of us who have survived are deeply scarred by daily run-ins with hate, discrimination, and violence.

Trans people are still literally social outlaws. And that's why I am willing at times, publicly, to reduce the totality of my self-expression to descriptions like masculine female, butch, bulldagger, drag king, cross-dresser. These terms describe outlaw status. And I hold my head up proudly in that police lineup. The word *outlaw* is not hyperbolic. I have been locked up in jail by cops because I was wearing a suit and tie. Was my clothing really a crime? Is it a "man's" suit if I am wearing it? At what point—from field to rack—is fiber assigned a sex?

The reality of why I was arrested was as cold as the cell's cement floor: I am considered a masculine female. That's a *gender* violation. My feminine drag queen sisters were in nearby cells, busted for wearing "women's" clothing. The cells that we were thrown into had the same design of bars and concrete. But when we—gay drag kings and drag queens—were thrown into them, the cops referred to the cells as bull's tanks and queen's tanks. The cells were named after our crimes: gender transgression. Actual statutes against cross-dressing and cross-gendered behavior still exist in written laws today. But even where the laws are not written down, police, judges, and prison guards are empowered to carry out merciless punishment for sex and gender "difference."

I believe we need to sharpen our view of how repression by the police, courts, and prisons, as well as all forms of racism and bigotry, operates as gears in the machinery of the economic and social system that governs our lives. As all those who have the least to lose from changing this system get together and examine these social questions, we can separate the wheat of truths from the chaff of old lies. Historic tasks are revealed that beckon us to take a stand and to take action.

That moment is now. And so this conversation with you takes place with the momentum of struggle behind it.

What will it take to put a halt to "legal" and extralegal violence against trans people? How can we strike the unjust and absurd laws mandating dress and behavior for females and males from the books? How can we weed out all the forms of transphobic and gender-phobic discrimination?

Where does the struggle for sex and gender liberation fit in relation to other movements for economic and social equality? How can we reach a point where we appreciate each other's differences, not just tolerate them? How can we tear down the electrified barbed wire that has been placed between us to keep us separated, fearful and pitted against each other? How can we forge a movement that can bring about profound and lasting change—a movement capable of transforming society?

These questions can only be answered when we begin to organize together, ready to struggle on each other's behalf. Understanding each other will compel us as honest, caring people to fight each other's oppression as though it was our own.

TWENTY-EIGHT

Uses of the Erotic (1984)

The Erotic as Power

Audre Lorde

> **Audre Lorde** (1934–1992) was an acclaimed lesbian writer, activist, and educator. She held many teaching positions and toured the world as a lecturer, founding a sisterhood in South Africa and the St. Croix Women's Coalition. She published ten volumes of poetry, numerous essays, and won awards and honors, including being named New York State's Poet Laureate. She co-founded Kitchen Table: Women of Color Press.

There are many kinds of power, used and unused, acknowledged or otherwise. The erotic is a resource within each of us that lies in a deeply female and spiritual plane, firmly rooted in the power of our unexpressed or unrecognized feeling. In order to perpetuate itself, every oppression must corrupt or distort those various sources of power within the culture of the oppressed that can provide energy for change. For women, this has meant a suppression of the erotic as a considered source of power and information within our lives.

We have been taught to suspect this resource, vilified, abused, and devalued within western society. On the one hand, the superficially erotic has been encouraged as a sign of female inferiority; on the other hand, women have been made to suffer and to feel both contemptible and suspect by virtue of its existence.

It is a short step from there to the false belief that only by the suppression of the erotic within our lives and consciousness can women be truly strong. But that strength is illusory, for it is fashioned within the context of male models of power.

As women, we have come to distrust that power which rises from our deepest and nonrational knowledge. We have been warned against it all our lives by the male world, which values this depth of feeling enough to keep women around in order to exercise it in the service of men, but which fears this same depth too much to examine the pos-

sibilities of it within themselves. So women are maintained at a distant/inferior position to be psychically milked, much the same way ants maintain colonies of aphids to provide a life-giving substance for their masters.

But the erotic offers a well of replenishing and provocative force to the woman who does not fear its revelation, nor succumb to the belief that sensation is enough.

The erotic has often been misnamed by men and used against women. It has been made into the confused, the trivial, the psychotic, the plasticized sensation. For this reason, we have often turned away from the exploration and consideration of the erotic as a source of power and information, confusing it with its opposite, the pornographic. But pornography is a direct denial of the power of the erotic, for it represents the suppression of true feeling. Pornography emphasizes sensation without feeling.

The erotic is a measure between the beginnings of our sense of self and the chaos of our strongest feelings. It is an internal sense of satisfaction to which, once we have experienced it, we know we can aspire. For having experienced the fullness of this depth of feeling and recognizing its power, in honor and self-respect we can require no less of ourselves.

It is never easy to demand the most from ourselves, from our lives, from our work. To encourage excellence is to go beyond the encouraged mediocrity of our society. To go beyond the encouraged mediocrity of our society is to encourage excellence. But giving in to the fear of feeling and working to capacity is a luxury only the unintentional can afford, and the unintentional are those who do not wish to guide their own destinies.

This internal requirement toward excellence which we learn from the erotic must not be misconstrued as demanding the impossible from ourselves nor from others. Such a demand incapacitates everyone in the process. For the erotic is not a question only of what we do; it is a question of how acutely and fully we can feel in the doing. Once we know the extent to which we are capable of feeling that sense of satisfaction and completion, we can then observe which of our various life endeavors bring us closest to that fullness.

The aim of each thing which we do is to make our lives and the lives of our children richer and more possible. Within the celebration of the erotic in all our endeavors, my work becomes a conscious decision—a longed-for bed which I enter gratefully and from which I rise up empowered.

Of course, women so empowered are dangerous. So we are taught to separate the erotic demand from most vital areas of our lives other than sex. And the lack of concern for the erotic root and satisfactions of our work is felt in our disaffection from so much of what we do. For instance, how often do we truly love our work even at its most difficult?

The principal horror of any system which defines the good in terms of profit rather than in terms of human need, or which defines human need to the exclusion of the psychic and emotional components of that need—the principal horror of such a system is that it robs our work of its erotic value, its erotic power and life appeal and fulfillment. Such a system reduces work to a travesty of necessities, a duty by which we earn bread or oblivion for ourselves and those we love. But this is tantamount to blinding a painter and then telling her to improve her work, and to enjoy the act of painting. It is not only next to impossible, it is also profoundly cruel.

As women, we need to examine the ways in which our world can be truly different. I am speaking here of the necessity for reassessing the quality of all the aspects of our lives and of our work, and of how we move toward and through them.

The very word *erotic* comes from the Greek word *eros,* the personification of love in all its aspects—born of Chaos, and personifying creative power and harmony. When I speak of the erotic, then, I speak of it as an assertion of the lifeforce of women; of that creative energy empowered, the knowledge and use of which we are now reclaiming in our language, our history, our dancing, our loving, our work, our lives.

There are frequent attempts to equate pornography and eroticism, two diametrically opposed uses of the sexual. Because of these attempts, it has become fashionable to separate the spiritual (psychic and emotional) from the political, to see them as contradictory or antithetical. "What do you mean, a poetic revolutionary, a meditating gunrunner?" In the same way, we have attempted to separate the spiritual and the erotic, thereby reducing the spiritual to a world of flattened affect, a world of the ascetic who aspires to feel nothing. But nothing is farther from the truth. For the ascetic position is one of the highest fear, the gravest immobility. The severe abstinence of the ascetic becomes the ruling obsession. And it is one not of self-discipline but of self-abnegation.

The dichotomy between the spiritual and the political is also false, resulting from an incomplete attention to our erotic knowledge. For the bridge which connects them is formed by the erotic—the sensual—those physical, emotional, and psychic expressions of what is deepest and strongest and richest within each of us, being shared: the passions of love, in its deepest meanings.

Beyond the superficial, the considered phrase, "It feels right to me," acknowledges the strength of the erotic into a true knowledge, for what that means is the first and most powerful guiding light toward any understanding. And understanding is a handmaiden which can only wait upon, or clarify, that knowledge, deeply born. The erotic is the nurturer or nursemaid of all our deepest knowledge.

The erotic functions for me in several ways, and the first is in providing the power which comes from sharing deeply any pursuit with another person. The sharing of joy, whether physical, emotional, psychic, or intellectual, forms a bridge between the sharers which can be the basis for understanding much of what is not shared between them, and lessens the threat of their difference.

Another important way in which the erotic connection functions is the open and fearless underlining of my capacity for joy. In the way my body stretches to music and opens into response, hearkening to its deepest rhythms, so every level upon which I sense also opens to the erotically satisfying experience, whether it is dancing, building a bookcase, writing a poem, examining an idea.

That self-connection shared is a measure of the joy which I know myself to be capable of feeling, a reminder of my capacity for feeling. And that deep and irreplaceable knowledge of my capacity for joy comes to demand from all of my life that it be lived within the knowledge that such satisfaction is possible, and does not have to be called *marriage,* nor *god,* nor *an afterlife.*

This is one reason why the erotic is so feared, and so often relegated to the bedroom alone, when it is recognized at all. For once we begin to feel deeply all the aspects of our lives, we begin to demand from ourselves and from our life-pursuits that they feel in accordance with that joy which we know ourselves to be capable of. Our erotic knowledge empowers us, becomes a lens through which we scrutinize all aspects of our existence, forcing us to evaluate those aspects honestly in terms of their relative meaning within our lives. And this is a grave responsibility, projected from within each of us, not to settle for the convenient, the shoddy, the conventionally expected, nor the merely safe.

During World War II, we bought sealed plastic packets of white, uncolored margarine, with a tiny, intense pellet of yellow coloring perched like a topaz just inside the clear skin of the bag. We would leave the margarine out for a while to soften, and then we would pinch the little pellet to break it inside the bag, releasing the rich yellowness into the soft pale mass of margarine. Then taking it carefully between our fingers, we would knead it gently back and forth, over and over, until the color had spread throughout the whole pound bag of margarine, thoroughly coloring it.

I find the erotic such a kernel within myself. When released from its intense and constrained pellet, it flows through and colors my life with a kind of energy that heightens and sensitizes and strengthens all my experience.

We have been raised to fear the *yes* within ourselves, our deepest cravings. But, once recognized, those which do not enhance our future lose their power and can be altered. The fear of our desires keeps them suspect and indiscriminately powerful, for to suppress any truth is to give it strength beyond endurance. The fear that we cannot grow beyond whatever distortions we may find within ourselves keeps us docile and loyal and obedient, externally defined, and leads us to accept many facets of our oppression as women.

When we live outside ourselves, and by that I mean on external directives only rather than from our internal knowledge and needs, when we live away from those erotic guides from within ourselves, then our lives are limited by external and alien forms, and we conform to the needs of a structure that is not based on human need, let alone an individual's. But when we begin to live from within outward, in touch with the power of the erotic within ourselves, and allowing that power to inform and illuminate our actions upon the world around us, then we begin to be responsible to ourselves in the deepest sense. For as we begin to recognize our deepest feelings, we begin to give up, of necessity, being satisfied with suffering and self-negation, and with the numbness which so often seems like their only alternative in our society. Our acts against oppression become integral with self, motivated and empowered from within.

In touch with the erotic, I become less willing to accept powerlessness, or those other supplied states of being which are not native to me, such as resignation, despair, self-effacement, depression, self-denial.

And yes, there is a hierarchy. There is a difference between painting a back fence and writing a poem, but only one of quantity. And there is, for me, no difference between writing a good poem and moving into sunlight against the body of a woman I love.

This brings me to the last consideration of the erotic. To share the power of each other's feelings is different from using another's feelings as we would use a kleenex. When we look the other way from our experience, erotic or otherwise, we use rather than share the feelings of those others who participate in the experience with us. And use without consent of the used is abuse.

In order to be utilized, our erotic feelings must be recognized. The need for sharing deep feeling is a human need. But within the european-american tradition, this need is satisfied by certain proscribed erotic comings-together. These occasions are almost always characterized by a simultaneous looking away, a pretense of calling them something else, whether a religion, a fit, mob violence, or even playing doctor. And this misnaming of the need and the deed give rise to that distortion which results in pornography and obscenity—the abuse of feeling.

When we look away from the importance of the erotic in the development and sustenance of our power, or when we look away from ourselves as we satisfy our erotic needs in concert with others, we use each other as objects of satisfaction rather than share our joy in the satisfying, rather than make connection with our similarities and our differences. To refuse to be conscious of what we are feeling at any time, however comfortable that might seem, is to deny a large part of the experience, and to allow ourselves to be reduced to the pornographic, the abused, and the absurd.

The erotic cannot be felt secondhand. As a Black lesbian feminist, I have a particular feeling, knowledge, and understanding for those sisters with whom I have danced hard, played, or even fought. This deep participation has often been the forerunner for joint concerted actions not possible before.

But this erotic charge is not easily shared by women who continue to operate under an exclusively european-american male tradition. I know it was not available to me when I was trying to adapt my consciousness to this mode of living and sensation.

Only now, I find more and more women-identified women brave enough to risk sharing the erotic's electrical charge without having to look away, and without distorting the enormously powerful and creative nature of that exchange. Recognizing the power of the erotic within our lives can give us the energy to pursue genuine change within our world, rather than merely settling for a shift of characters in the same weary drama.

For not only do we touch our most profoundly creative source, but we do that which is female and self-affirming in the face of a racist, patriarchal, and anti-erotic society.

5

◆◆◆

Women's Health

Health, healing, and learning about our bodies are all issues of major concern to women, helping us to take care of ourselves and others. In times gone by, women made teas, tinctures, oils, and salves and gave baths and massages to heal sickness and alleviate pain (Ehrenreich and English 1972). Some women still study the medicinal properties of plants and treat many complaints with herbal remedies (Gladstar 1993; Perrone, Stockel, and Krueger 1989; Potts 1988). Healthy processes like pregnancy, childbirth, and menopause have become increasingly medicalized from the mid-nineteenth century onward. Many women come into contact with the medical system, not through illness, but through pregnancy, or because we want to control our fertility. Health is a complex mix of physical, mental, emotional, and spiritual well-being, but Western medicine separates these connected aspects into distinct specialisms with different practitioners. The professionalization of health care over many decades has given doctors—mostly White men trained in university-based medical schools—authority in medical matters. Our subjective experiences of health and

illness are negotiated with medical experts and, increasingly, meditated through technologies like mammograms or ultrasound. Women's health varies greatly depending on individual factors like diet, exercise, smoking, stress, or violence, as well as macro-level factors such as race and class. This chapter discusses reproductive health, illness, the U.S. medical industry, and ways to move beyond an over-reliance on drugs and surgery to a more balanced conception of health care and wellness.

Reproductive Health, Reproductive Rights

The ability to become pregnant and have a baby is one of the most fundamental aspects of women's lives. Having a child is a profound experience, usually with far-reaching consequences for the mother. A woman becomes pregnant for many reasons: she wants to have a child; she wants to experience pregnancy and childbirth; she wants to be recognized as a grown woman; she believes it will make her a "real" woman; she hopes it will keep her relationship together or make her partner happy. Some women plan to be pregnant; others get pregnant by accident, still others as a result of being raped. This deeply personal experience is also a public issue. The government has an interest in the numbers of children born, who their parents are, and whether they are married, whether they are teens, poor, or recent immigrants. This interest is reinforced by, and also influences, dominant notions of what kinds of women should be mothers. For some women—especially teenagers, lesbians, and mothers receiving welfare—there may be a serious tension between the personal event of pregnancy and societal attitudes to it. African American women have consistently tried to be self-determining in their reproductive lives despite having been used as breeders by slaveholders and despite subsequent systematic state interventions to control their fertility (Darling and Tyson 1999; Dula 1996; Roberts 1997; Ross 1993; Silliman et al. 2004; Taylor 1997). These include state-sponsored sterilization programs, chemical contraceptives like Depo-Provera and Norplant, and now the chemical sterilizing agent, Quinacrine. Law professor and legal scholar Dorothy Roberts (1997) refers to this phenomenon as nothing less than "killing the black body."

An important indicator of infant and maternal health comes from data on infant mortality, the number of infants who die before their first birthday. Infant mortality for babies born in 2002, for example, showed the typical pattern in the United States. Asian and Pacific Islanders have the lowest rate (4.8 deaths per 1,000 live births), White infants (5.8), Puerto Rican (8.2), American Indian (8.6), and African American (13.8) (Mathews, Menacker and MacDorman 2004).* Infant mortality rates have

---

* Official statistics are a key source of information but are limited for discussion of diversity, as they are usually analyzed according to three main categories only: White, Black, and Hispanic. "Hispanic" includes Puerto Ricans, Cubans, Mexican Americans, and people from Central and South America. Some reports give a separate category for Native Americans and Native Alaskans, or for Asians and Pacific Islanders, another very heterogeneous group for whom there are few data at a national level. Data on many social issues are not usually analyzed by class, another serious limitation. We have tried to be as inclusive as possible; sometimes this is limited by the availability of adequate data.

steadily decreased over the past sixty-five years, but Black infants continue to die at more than twice the rate of White infants. Mortality rates were higher for infants whose mothers did not have prenatal care in the first trimester, did not complete high school, were unmarried, were teenagers or older than forty, or smoked during pregnancy. Rates of first-trimester care are lower for Native American, Mexican American, and African American women, compared with White women and Asian American women.

Controlling Fertility

Women's reproductive years span roughly half our lifetimes, from our teens to our forties. But, typically, women want only two children. Many women in the United States want to control their fertility—to limit the number of children they have, to avoid pregnancy with a particular partner, to postpone pregnancy until they are older, or to avoid it altogether. Women also want the freedom to bear children. To do this we need sex education that is accurate and culturally appropriate; affordable and reliable birth control; safe, legal, affordable abortion; prenatal care and care through childbirth; health care for infants and children; and alternative insemination. In addition we need an adequate income, good general health care, and widespread cultural acceptance that we have a right to control our lives in this way.

Once a woman learns that she is pregnant, the decision to have a child or to have an abortion depends on a broad range of factors, including her age, personal circumstances, economic situation, whether or not she already has children, her level of overall health, cultural attitude to abortion, and the circumstances that led her to become pregnant (Arcana 1994 and Reading 31; Lunneborg 1992; Ross 1993; Townsend and Perkins 1992). As argued by Marsha Saxton in Reading 30, women with disabilities must also fight for the right to have children in the face of a dominant view that they are nonsexual beings who could not cope with being mothers (see also Finger 1990; Prilleltensky 2003; Wilkerson 2002).

Birth Control Barrier methods like condoms and diaphragms have been used for many years. In the 1960s the intrauterine device (IUD), often called the coil, was introduced despite severe unwanted

NON SEQUITOR

side effects for some women, such as heavy bleeding, pain, and cramps. The pill, introduced around the same time—and the most popular form of contraception today for women under 30—was the first chemical contraceptive to be taken every day. It affects the whole body continuously, as do newer methods like Depo-Provera (an injectable contraceptive that is effective for three months) and Norplant (implanted under the skin and effective for up to five years). Poor African American and Native American women and Latinas are much more likely than White women to be encouraged to use these long-acting contraceptives. Official policy seeks to limit their pregnancies and assumes that these women would be unreliable using other methods, thereby continuing the long connection between birth control and eugenics (Roberts 1997; Ross 1993; Smith 2002). The Black Women's Health Network, the National Latina Health Organization, and other women's health advocates have called for the withdrawal of Depo-Provera as unsafe and also called attention to the fact that many women using Norplant had difficulty finding anyone to remove it. These methods compound many of the health problems that affect poor women of color, including hypertension, diabetes, and stress. By the mid-1990s, doctors were taking out more implants than they put in, as many women had experienced severe side effects. In 1999 American Home Products Corporation, which sells Norplant, agreed to offer cash settlements to 36,000 women who filed suit claiming that they had not been adequately warned about possible negative effects of using Norplant (Morrow 1999a). These included excessive

menstrual bleeding, headaches, nausea, dizziness, and depression.

Other birth-control methods include the female condom, a loosely fitting, polyurethane (not latex) pouch with a semiflexible plastic ring at each end that lines the vagina and fits over the vulva. It provides protection from sexually transmitted infections (STIs) as well as pregnancy, but is not as effective as the male condom. Emergency contraception (EC) that prevents fertilization is available on prescription under the trade name Plan B, and can be used in the event of unprotected sex or if another form of contraception fails. This is a chemical method that involves taking oral contraceptives within 72 hours of unprotected sex, the sooner the better. It must be prescribed by a doctor, a big disadvantage if one has unprotected sex on Friday night and cannot get to the doctor's office before Monday. In December 2003, the FDA's Advisory Committee on Reproductive Health Drugs and Nonprescription Drugs voted overwhelmingly to make Plan B available over the counter but as of November 2005 the FDA had not approved this change. A popular over-the-counter contraceptive, the Today Sponge, came back on the market in 2003 but does not offer the same degree of protection as oral contraceptives (Zernike 2003).

Pharmaceutical companies have all but abandoned the field of contraceptive research in this country. Of the nine major companies that were involved in the 1960s and '70s, only two remain. This is due to a decline in funding from the government, international sources, and private foundations, as well as political opposition.

Abortion Attitudes toward abortion have varied greatly over time and from one society to another. Historically, the Catholic Church, for example, held the view that the soul did not enter the fetus for at least forty days after conception and allowed abortion up to that point. In 1869, however, Pope Pius IX declared that life begins at conception, and thus all abortion became murder in the eyes of the Church. In the United States up until the mid-nineteenth century, women were allowed to seek an abortion in the early part of pregnancy before they felt the fetus moving, a subjectively determined time, referred to as the quickening. After the Civil War more restrictive abortion laws were passed, partly to increase population and partly to shift authority over women's reproductive lives to the then developing medical profession. By 1900 the only legal ground for an abortion was to save the life of the mother. Many women were forced to bring unwanted pregnancies to term in poverty, illness, or appalling personal circumstances. Thousands died trying to abort themselves or at the hands of "backstreet" abortionists. Some upper- and middle-class women found doctors to perform safe abortions for a high price, though they and the doctors risked prosecution if they were found out, as described by Grace Paley (1998) in her short article, "The Illegal Days" (also see Joffe 1995; Miller 1993; Reagan 1997; Solinger 1994, 2000). Women with knowledge of herbs or medicine helped other women. The Janes organized a clandestine feminist abortion service in the Chicago area in the early 1970s (Arcana 2005; Kamen 2000; Kaplan 1995).

In 1973 the landmark case *Roe v. Wade* made abortion legal. It defined freedom of choice as a right to privacy, protected by the U.S. Constitution. It recognized that no one except the woman herself has the right to decide whether to have an abortion. Ever since this legislation was enacted, it has been contested. This began in 1977 with the Hyde Amendment that withdrew state funding for abortion for poor women. Subsequent measures included rules requiring waiting periods and parental consent for teens (see Erlich 2003). Throughout the 1990s, anti-choice organizations staged violent protests at abortion clinics, bombed clinics, harassed patients, and killed doctors known to perform abortions as part of their practice (Baird-Windle and Bader 2001; Jaggar 1994). Women's health advocates have struggled to keep clinics open and lobbied for the Freedom of Access to Clinic Entrances

Act 1994, which reduced harassment outside clinics. These legal restrictions, together with severe harassment, have reduced the number of abortion providers, and, by 2000, 87 percent of U.S. counties and 97 percent of rural counties had no abortion provider (Henshaw 2003). Fewer doctors are being trained to carry out the procedure, and many have stopped performing abortions because of the risks to themselves and their families.

In 2001, 16 of every 1,000 women of reproductive age (15 to 44) had abortions, the lowest rate since 1975 (Centers for Disease Control and Prevention 2004). Factors assumed to be responsible for this decline include reduced access to abortion, an increased willingness to use contraception, and negative attitudes toward abortion. Most women who had an abortion in 2001 were 25 or younger, White, and unmarried; and 59 percent of the procedures were done in the first two months of pregnancy and 88 percent before thirteen weeks. Women's complex thoughts and feelings about abortion, about the profound responsibility of choosing to end a life, have been downplayed or ignored by pro-abortion activists as they focus on keeping abortion legal. In Reading 31, Judith Arcana argues that abortion is a motherhood issue, a decision a woman makes because she believes it is the best for herself and her baby. Like anti-choice activists, she calls a fetus a baby. Unlike them, Arcana passionately defends a woman's right to abortion. She argues that the semantics of *"fetus or embryo"* used by pro-choice organizers skirts the central moral issue and has cost them potential support. It has conceded the space for anti-choice activists to excoriate women who have abortions as heartless and irresponsible monsters. She calls for women to speak about our abortions "in open recognition of our joy or sadness, our regret or relief—in conscious acceptance of the responsibility for our choice" (see also Arcana 2005; Jacob 2002).

During the 1990s, the National Organization for Women, the Fund for a Feminist Majority, the National Abortion Rights Action League, and others campaigned for RU-486 (the "abortion pill," also called Mifepristone) to be made available in this country as it was in France. In September 2000, the U.S. Food and Drug Administration approved this drug for use under very specific conditions. It can only be dispensed by physicians; women need to make a follow-up doctors' visit two weeks after taking the drug; it can only be used very early in pregnancy, not more than seven weeks since the last period began.

White feminists made abortion the centerpiece of reproductive rights activism in the 1980s and '90s. According to the Black Women's Health Project (1995), when faced with an unintended pregnancy, the percentage of Black women who choose abortion is about equal to that of White women. However, women of color have generally seen abortion as only one piece in a wider reproductive-health agenda that includes health care for women and children and the freedom to have children (see e.g., Nelson 2003; Ross et al. 2002; Silliman et al. 2004). Abortion advocates originally campaigned for women's *right* to abortion but predominately White women's organizations moved to a "softer" pro-choice framework. Rights apply to everyone; choice is only meaningful for those with resources. Thus, a pro-choice framework creates a hierarchy among women based on resources which are linked to race and class. Some women of color health organizations have developed the concept of **reproductive justice** that relates health and reproductive rights to broader issues of social and economic justice, as elaborated by Asian Communities for Reproductive Justice (Reading 32; Silliman et al. 2004; Smith 2005a). This offers a way of thinking about wellness for individuals, communities, and the wider society in terms of the eradication of systems of inequality, oppression, and injustice, drawing on micro, meso, and macro levels of analysis. Meanwhile, a whole generation of women has grown up, taking abortion rights for granted despite the wide and growing gap between legality and access. In April 2004, more than one million people from all walks of life, many of them young women, participated in the March for Women's Lives, in Washington, D.C., the largest protest march in U.S. history. They demanded broad reproductive freedoms, and opposed other aspects of President Bush's agenda including the war in Iraq and the Executive Order that forbids clinics receiving U.S. international aid from even mentioning abortion (Silliman et al. 2004). According to national pollster Celinda Lake (2005) 56 percent of respondents polled nationwide favored keeping abortion legal in all or most cases, and 62 percent felt that the government should not interfere with a woman's access to abortion.

For the past thirty years, well-funded anti-abortion groups have worked strategically to undermine and overturn the right to abortion. They have used public education, mainstream media, protests and direct action—including clinic bombings and killing doctors as mentioned above—claiming the moral high ground and arguing that "the fetus is a life; hence abortion should be criminalized" (Smith 2005a, p. 121). They have financed and elected anti-choice political candidates at city, state, and congressional levels. Republican Congresspersons have introduced bills session after session to whittle away at the legality of abortion and elevate the unborn child, even as a "nonviable fetus," to the status of "personhood" with rights equal to or greater than those of the mother. In January 2005, on the 32nd anniversary of *Roe v. Wade*, the president assured abortion-rights opponents, "This movement will not fail" (*Associated Press* 2005). If the Supreme Court overturns *Roe v. Wade*, legal jurisdiction will revert to the states, many of which are poised to ban abortion or to re-criminalize it. This issue is central to women's autonomy and will continue to be highly contentious (see e.g., Feldt 2004; Nelson 2003; Petchesky 1990; Silliman et al. 2004; Smith 2005a; Solinger 1998, 2005). Scholar and activist Andrea Smith (2005a) seeks to move beyond pro-choice versus pro-life, and argues that "the major flaw in the pro-life position is NOT the claim that the fetus is a life, but the conclusion it draws from this assertion: that because the fetus is a life, abortion should be criminalized" (Smith 2005a, p. 121).

Sterilization   Sterilization abuse, rather than the right to abortion, has been a concern of poor women, especially women of color, for many years. Sterilization, without women's full knowledge or under duress, has been a common practice in the United States for poor Latina, African American, and Native American women. Dorothy Roberts (1997) notes that sterilization was a key tool in repressing the fertility of women of color in the 1930s, '40s, and '50s. Discussing sterilization of women of color in the 1960s, she comments:

> It is amazing how effective governments— especially our own—are at making sterilization and contraceptives available to women of color, despite their inability to reach these women with prenatal care, drug treatment, and other health services.   *(p. 95)*

By 1982, 24 percent of African American women, 35 percent of Puerto Rican women, and 42 percent of Native American women had been sterilized, compared with 15 percent of White women (Black Women's Health Project 1995; also see Davis 1983a; Jaimes and Halsey 1986; Lopez 1997; Nelson 2003; Silliman et al. 2004; Smith 2002). Currently, sterilization is federally funded under the Medicaid program and is free on demand to poor women. Quinacrine, a chemical sterilizing agent, is the newest method and has dangerous side effects.

Teen Pregnancy U.S. teenagers are having sex at younger ages, despite the risk of contracting sexually transmitted infections and HIV. Teen pregnancies, however, have declined from an all-time high in 1991 to a record low: 84 pregnancies per 1,000 women aged 15–19 in 2000; and 42 births per 1,000 women aged 15–19 in 2003 (Martin et al. 2003). This is apparently because of increased condom use, the adoption of injectable and implant contraceptives (Depo-Provera and Norplant), and changing teenage sexual activity. Analyzed by race and ethnicity, teen birthrates were highest for Mexican American, African American, Native American, and Puerto Rican teenagers. In many cases the fathers of these babies are considerably older than the young women. Babies born to teens present a tremendous responsibility for young women and their families. Many community programs seek to prevent teen pregnancy, although sex education in schools and programs to distribute condoms, to prevent the spread of HIV/AIDS as much as pregnancy, have run into opposition from some parents, school boards, and conservative religious groups. The United States has the highest rate of teen pregnancy of all industrialized countries.

Sexually Transmitted Infections (STIs) Sexually transmitted infections affect some 15 million people each year, more than half of them aged 15–24 (Centers for Disease Control and Prevention 2000). The term STI refers to more than twenty-five diseases, including herpes, genital warts, pubic lice ("crabs"), chlamydia, gonorrhea, syphilis, and HIV. With the exception of syphilis, all STIs are increasing at an alarming rate. One reason for this is that women often do not have any symptoms or, if they do, the symptoms are mistaken for something else. Sexually transmitted infection can affect how a woman feels about her body and her partner and can lead to pelvic inflammatory disease or infertility. Knowing about safer sexual practices is important in reducing the risk of sexually transmitted infections, including HIV/AIDS. But knowing is not enough. Psychologists Nicola Gavey, Kathryn McPhillips, and Marion Doherty (2001) researched women's attitudes to condom use and their ability to influence sexual partners to use condoms. They found that power dynamics between men and women, women's assumptions about assertiveness and what it means to be a "good lover," together with their ideals of giving and sharing, may be in conflict with their desire for safer sex. It is important to note that condoms (male or female) are the only form of birth control that also give some protection against sexually transmitted infections.

Toxic Hazards Toxic workplaces are a serious health hazard especially for women of color. Some companies have kept women out of the most hazardous work—often the highest paid among blue-collar jobs—or required that they be sterilized first, to avoid being sued if these workers later give birth to babies with disabilities (Daniels 1993). Women working in computer manufacturing, chicken processing, the dairy industry, and housecleaning are all exposed to chemicals as part of their work, as are manicurists and farm workers. Reading 34 discusses the film *Rachel's Daughters: Searching for the Causes of Breast Cancer*, named in honor of environmental researcher Rachel Carson (1962) whose groundbreaking book, *Silent Spring*, linked cancer with chemical exposure. The film features women who research possible environmental causes of breast cancer in their communities. We take up this issue of environmental contamination and health again in Chapter 12.

Medicalization of Reproductive Life

Childbirth Before there were male gynecologists, midwives helped women through pregnancy and childbirth (Ehrenreich and English 1972, 2005). As medicine became professionalized in the nineteenth century, gynecology and obstetrics developed as an area of medical specialization. Doctors eroded the position of midwives and ignored or scorned their knowledge as "old wives' tales." Largely for the convenience of the doctor, women began to give birth lying on their backs, perhaps the hardest position in which to deliver a child. Forceps and various pain-killing medications were widely used. From the 1950s onward cesarean sections (C-sections) became more common, often for the doctors' convenience or from fear of malpractice suits. In 2002, 26.1 percent of births in the United States were C-sections, the highest rate in the world (Martin et al. 2003). The past thirty years have seen a further extension of this medicalization process as doctors monitor pregnancy from the earliest stages with a battery of techniques such as amniocentesis, sonograms, and ultrasound. Although this technology allows medical practitioners, and through them, pregnant women, to know details about the health and condition of the fetus, as well as its sex, it also changes women's experiences of pregnancy and childbirth and can erode their knowledge of and confidence in their bodily processes. In Reading 29, Joy Harjo describes changes in Native American women's experiences of childbirth over three generations—her mother, her daughter, and herself. These included variations in their life circumstances, medical technology, and their treatment by hospital staff as Native American women. She notes the routine way she was offered the option of being sterilized and told that "the moment of birth was the best time to do it."

Reproductive Technologies   Technologies such as in vitro fertilization (IVF), in which a woman's eggs are fertilized by sperm outside her body and the fertilized embryo is then implanted into her womb, are an important development. They push the medicalization of pregnancy and childbirth one step further and hold out the hope that infertile couples or postmenopausal women will be able to have children. Bearing a child as a surrogate mother under contract to an infertile couple is one way a relatively poor young woman, usually White, can earn $10,000 or so, plus medical expenses, for nine months' work. Fertility clinics also need ovum donors and seek to harvest the eggs of young, college-educated women from a range of specified racial and ethnic groups. Infertility treatments so far have had a spectacularly low success rate and are very expensive. They are aimed at middle- and upper-middle-class women as a way of widening individual choice. Infertility may stem from a range of causes such as sexually transmitted infections, the effects of IUDs, delayed childbearing, and

occupational and environmental factors. Infertility rates were lower in the 1990s than in previous decades, but this issue has a higher profile nowadays because of technological developments.

These reproductive technologies open up an array of economic, legal, and moral questions (Donchin and Purdy 1999; Ginsburg and Rapp 1995; Hubbard 1990; Ragone and Twine 2000; Teays and Purdy 2001). Are they liberating for women? for which women? and at what costs? Some feminists have argued that women's biology and the ability to reproduce have been used to justify their social and economic subordination. In her now classic radical feminist text, Shulamith Firestone (1970), for example, was convinced that women's liberation requires freedom from biological reproduction and looked forward to developments in reproductive technology that would make it possible for a fetus to develop outside the womb. This is in stark contrast to sociologist Barbara Katz Rothman (1986) and the myriad women who believe that, if women lose their ability to reproduce, we lose a "quintessential female experience" (p. 111). Other feminist critics of reproductive technologies have focused on their invasiveness and consumers' lack of power over and knowledge about these methods, as compared with that of medical experts or "medocrats" (Arditti, Klein, and Minden 1984; Corea 1985, 1987; Lublin 1998; Morgan and Michaels 1999; Petchesky 1997; Stanworth 1987).

Menopause   This natural life process is increasingly treated as a disease rather than as a series of complex bodily and emotional changes. Many middle-aged women have been advised to take hormone-replacement therapy (HRT) to control the symptoms of menopause such as hot flashes, insomnia, and vaginal dryness (Klein and Dumble 1994; Komesaroff, Rothfield, and Daly 1997). A major study of 46,355 women conducted by the National Cancer Institute confirmed that long-term use of hormone replacement after menopause can increase the risk of breast cancer (Grady 2000).

Executive Director of National Women's Health Network, Cindy Pearson, "uses science to challenge science," opposing the biomedical "definition of older women's bodies as deficient" and proving that what is "lost" through menopause "does not need to be replaced in order for a woman to live out the rest of her life healthfully" (*NWSAction* 2004, p. 39; also see Worcester 2004).

Women and Illness

There is a rich and growing literature on women's experiences of illness, healing, and recovery, particularly in relation to breast cancer, chronic fatigue immune deficiency syndrome (CFIDS), and multiple sclerosis (e.g., Duff 1993; Griffin 1999; Lorde 1996; Mairs 1996; Rosenblum 1997; Sigler, Love, and Yood 1999). Counselor and writer Kat Duff (1993) notes that our society's "concepts of physical and psychological health have become one-sidedly identified with the heroic qualities most valued in our culture: youth, activity, productivity, independence, strength, confidence, and optimism" (p. 37). Illness challenges us to rethink our definition of self, our value and worth, in this ablist society, as these authors attest.

In general, women in the United States live longer than men. Women's average life expectancy is 80 years, compared to 74 years for men. On average, African American women die younger than White women (at age 75) but live longer than African American men, who have a life expectancy of 68 years (National Center for Health Statistics 2004, Table 27). Asian Americans of both sexes live longer than White people. Like men, women in the United States are most likely to die from heart disease or cancer, followed by strokes, diabetes, respiratory diseases, pneumonia, and accidents. Older women suffer higher rates of disabling diseases such as arthritis, Alzheimer's, diabetes, cataracts, deafness, broken bones, digestive conditions, and osteoporosis than do men. Women under 45 mostly use reproductive health services. Women over 45 use hospitals less than men do, reflecting a basic health difference between the sexes: Men are more likely to have fatal diseases, whereas women have chronic conditions that worsen with age.

Effects of Gender, Race, and Class on Health and Illness

Taken as a whole, the health of African American women, Native American women, and Latinas is significantly worse than that of White women and Asian American women (Ross et al. 2002). A number of macro-level factors affect women's health, the treatments that doctors prescribe, and our ability to pay. White, middle-class, educated women, for example, are more likely to know about

The World's Deadliest Disease Is Poverty

- Over ten million children worldwide die each year before their fifth birthday, mainly from malnutrition, malaria, acute respiratory infections, measles, diarrhea and HIV/AIDs.

- Most of these conditions can be prevented or cured with improvements in sanitation, clean water supply, better housing, an adequate food supply, and general hygiene. The majority of deaths from infectious diseases can be prevented with existing, cost-effective measures including childhood vaccinations, bed nets and other malariaprevention treatments, oral rehydration therapy, and antibiotics.

- Poor nutrition and underweight affects an estimated 27 percent of all children under 5. This puts them at increased risk for infections like diarrhea and pneumonia. Underweight remains a pervasive problem in developing countries where poverty is a strong underlying determinant, contributing to household food insecurity, mothers' inadequate nutrition, unhealthy environments, and poor health care.

- Diseases linked to high blood pressure, cholesterol, tobacco, alcohol, and obesity have been most common in industrialized countries. They are now becoming more prevalent in countries of the Global South, reflecting changes in living patterns, including diet, physical activity, the availability of tobacco and alcohol, and cultural upheavals.

Source: World Health Organization 2005.

mammograms as a screening procedure for the early detection of breast cancer and that they are recommended for women over 40. They are more likely to have insurance to cover mammograms and to be registered with a doctor who encourages having them. Late diagnosis of breast cancer is directly related to higher mortality rates. Among cancer

patients, White women also get what the literature refers to as "more aggressive treatment" compared to African American women, who are often not told about all relevant treatment options, not given the full range of tests, and not always prescribed the most effective medications. The incidence of breast cancer increases with age, though African American women are more likely than White women to get it at younger ages. Fewer African American women get cancer, but their mortality rate is 28 percent higher. Breast cancer affects one woman in nine nationwide, though there are much higher incidences in certain geographic areas. Science researchers Rita Arditti and Tatiana Schreiber (1998) argue that environmental factors are significant in explaining this discrepancy. The higher incidence is linked to race and class, as poor women, especially women of color, often live in areas with poor physical environment (also see Reading 34).

More African American women die in their twenties as a result of HIV/AIDS, maternal mortality, drug use, and homicide compared to White women. Tuberculosis, an infectious disease associated with poverty and poor living conditions, was prevalent in the late nineteenth century and all but eradicated in the United States during the twentieth century. Compared with the general population, Native Americans are four times as likely to have tuberculosis. Twice as many Native American women die young (age 15 to 24) compared to White women the same age. Frederica Daly (Reading 8) gives detailed historical, legal, and economic background for her brief discussion of Native American health, which is among the worst in the country. Hypertension, a major risk factor for heart disease and stroke, is much more prevalent among African American

women than it is among White women. Public health researchers Nancy Krieger and Stephen Sidney (1996) attribute this difference, in part, to stress related to racism. Obesity is a risk factor for heart disease, diabetes, and strokes, and it particularly affects African American women (Avery 1990; hooks 1993; Lovejoy 2001; White 1991) as mentioned in Chapter 3. Scholars and advocates see overeating as a way that some Black women cope with the stress of racism and poverty.

Gender has also been a significant factor in diagnosing women with HIV/AIDS (Goldstein and Manlowe 1997). In 1993, for the first time, U.S. women's deaths from HIV/AIDS rose more than men's (Hammonds 1995). Women have not been diagnosed as early as men because their symptoms are not so clear-cut and doctors were less likely to look for symptoms of HIV/AIDS in women. Also, because there were fewer women in clinical research trials, they did not receive the better treatment received by men who participated in such trials. Primary care internist Barbara Ogur (1996) has pointed out that negative stereotypes of HIV-positive women (as drug users and women with multiple sex partners) have affected their visibility and care. In 2003, women were 27 percent of those diagnosed with HIV/AIDS in the United States. Far more women than men contract HIV through heterosexual contact (79 percent compared to 17 percent). Among women, Latinas and African American women have the highest HIV/AIDS rates (Centers for Disease Control and Prevention 2003).

Women of all race and class groups who are beaten by their partners or suffer emotional violence or sexual abuse are subject to a significant health hazard (see Chapter 6).

Mental and Emotional Health

Many more women have some sort of mental illness compared to men, especially depression. Men are most likely to be diagnosed with alcohol- and drug-related conditions. There are many problems with diagnostic categories, however, and a great deal of room for interpretation based on individual and cultural factors. For example, the American Psychological Association did not drop homosexuality from its list of mental disorders until 1973. Lesbianism was thought to be caused by dominant mothers and weak fathers or, conversely, by girls' having exclusively male role models. Those who "came out" in the 1950s and '60s risked being sent to psychotherapists or mental institutions for a "cure." Since the 1980s, young women who do not conform to traditional gender roles may be diagnosed with "gender identity disorder" (Scholinski 1997).

Hopelessness and anger at one's life circumstances—which may include childhood sexual abuse, rape, domestic violence, racism, heterosexism, poverty, homelessness, or simply dull routines, heavy responsibilities, and lack of opportunity—are not irrational reactions. Women's symptoms can seem vague to doctors, who may not really try to find out what is troubling them. Even when understood by doctors, such traumas and difficulties are not easy to cure. Patients in mental hospitals represent a relatively small proportion of those who are suffering mentally and emotionally. In general, women are admitted to mental hospitals as inpatients in roughly the same numbers as men.

One reason why more women are classified as having mental illness may be that the proportion of women seeking help for personal or emotional problems is twice as high as it is for men. However, one cannot infer from this that everyone who "seeks help" is doing so voluntarily; sometimes seeing a counselor or therapist is required by a social service agency or is a condition of probation. Voluntarily seeking help for emotional problems is linked to one's ability to pay, finding a suitable therapist, and cultural attitudes toward this kind of treatment.

Many people of all classes and racial groups attempt to deal with the pain and difficulty of their lives through drugs and alcohol. Frederica Daly (1994) notes that rates of alcoholism, homicide, and suicide among Native Americans are significantly higher than the national rates. In the United States, drug addiction is often thought of as a crime rather than as a health issue. We discuss it further under the topic of crime and criminalization in Chapter 10, but we also see it as a symptom of stress brought on by the pressures of life, often caused by social and economic inequality. There are far fewer drug-treatment programs than required, and fewer for women than for men.

A number of feminist writers have argued that contemporary approaches to mental distress, as illness, can be harmful to women (Chesler 1972; Ehrenreich and English 2005; Lerman 1996; Russell 1995; Showalter 1987; Ussher 1991). Philosopher Denise Russell (1995) briefly traces the history of definitions of madness from medieval Europe, where it was thought of as a combination of error and sin. During the seventeenth century, economic crises and rising unemployment in Europe prompted local officials to build houses of confinement for beggars, drunks, vagabonds, and other poor people and petty criminals, as well as for those who were thought mad. Through the eighteenth and nineteenth centuries, psychiatry gradually developed as a new medical specialty and asylums in Europe and the United States were headed by doctors, who theorized that much mental distress experienced by women was due to their reproductive capacities and sexuality. Hysteria, thought to be due to a disturbance of the womb, became a catchall category to describe women's mental illness. (The English word *hysterical* comes from the Greek word *hysterikos,* meaning "of the womb.") Writer/literary critic Elaine Showalter (1987) and psychologist/psychotherapist Phyllis Chesler (1972) show how definitions of madness have been used to suppress women's agency, creativity, education, and political involvement. Nineteenth-century White upper- and middle-class women who wanted to write, paint, travel, or speak out in public on issues of the day were assumed by their husbands—and by psychiatrists—to be insane. Charlotte Perkins Gilman's powerful fictional work *The Yellow Wallpaper,* for example, describes this experience and was written as a result of having lived through it. More recently, depression and premenstrual syndrome (PMS) have replaced "hysteria" as stock phrases used in describing mental illness in women.

Feminist writers offer scathing critiques of the alleged objectivity of much contemporary mental health theorizing and of the value judgments and blatant sexism involved in many diagnostic categories like depression, behavioral disorders, and personality disorders that affect women more than men. Symptoms for these disorders are often very general, vague, and overlapping, and, according to Russell (1995), there is little agreement among practitioners as to what conditions are indicated by the symptoms. She questions the assumption that there is a biological or neurological basis for mental distress and argues that drug therapies based on this assumption have very mixed results in practice. Rather, she points to many external factors affecting women's mental equilibrium, including childhood sexual abuse, domestic violence, restricted educational or economic opportunities, and pressure to look beautiful, to be thin, to be compliant wives and long-suffering mothers, any of which could reasonably make women depressed or "crazy." Women have written powerful fiction and autobiographical accounts of mental illness and medical treatments (e.g., Danquah 1998; Kaysen 1994; Millet 1990; Plath 1971; Shannonhonse 2003; Slater 1998). In Reading 33, cultural critic bell hooks shows the serious long-term effects of racism and internalized oppression on African Americans' mental and spiritual health. She notes that slave narratives often emphasized the importance of Black people's capacity to repress feelings as a key to survival, and that this ingrained habit has been passed on through family experiences for several generations. As a result, she argues, "many black females have learned to deny our inner needs while we develop the capacity to cope and confront in public life."

Health and Aging

The health of women in middle age and later life is partly linked to how healthy they were when they were younger. The effects of stress, poor nutrition, smoking, or not getting enough exercise build up over time. Exposure to toxic chemicals, the physical and emotional toll of pregnancies, accidents, injuries, and caring for others all affect our health as we grow older.

Older women often have to accept the fact that they need support and care. They have to face their changed looks, physical limitations, and the loss of independence and loved ones, which calls on their emotional and spiritual resources, including patience, forbearance, courage, optimism, and religious faith (see, for example, Doress-Worters and Siegal 1994). Older women's health is also adversely affected by caring for their sick partners when they themselves are old and sick. Shevy Healey (1997) argues that confronting ageism in society, as well as individual women's negative feelings about aging, is a must for women's mental health. We note additional feminist work on women and aging in Chapter 3 that is also relevant here (Browne 1998; Cruikshank 2003; Gullette 2004).

Over three million women in the United States provide personal assistance to family members who are sick or disabled, and over ten million women provide care to people outside their own households, usually their elderly parents and their husbands' elderly parents. This caretaking of elders may go on for as much as fifteen years and often overlaps with the women's other responsibilities—holding jobs, taking care of growing children, and managing homes. This regimen can be very trying; it involves physical and emotional stress and added expense and can seriously affect the quality of life and health for women in their middle years, who may have to give up opportunities for education, professional development, social life, or leisure-time activities. These women may be reluctant and resentful at times but accept their situation as part of what it means to be a good wife or daughter. It is important to recognize that women who care for others need support and respite themselves.

The Medical Industry

Since the seventeenth century, Western thought has consistently viewed organic, bodily processes as separate from those of the mind. The Western medical model separates physical, mental, emotional, and spiritual states of well-being and focuses on illness and disease rather than on the wholeness of people's lives, often treating symptoms rather than causes. For example, though stressors generated by racism are a strong influence in the hypertension that disproportionately affects African Americans, the medical response is to treat the symptoms with medication, rather than to involve doctors, patients, and the wider society in combating racism. Similarly, many women are prescribed antidepressants rather than being empowered and supported in changing their life circumstances. This Western medical model also contributes to fantasies of immortality to be achieved by life-prolonging surgeries and drug treatments, as well as expensive cosmetic surgeries.

Because medical care is provided on a fee-paying basis in the United States, the medical industry has many of the characteristics of any business venture (see the discussion of the global economy in Chapter 9). The emphasis is on high-tech treatments, particularly drug therapies and surgery, as these are the most profitable for drug companies and manufacturers of medical equipment. Most people have benefited from vaccines and antibiotics, and the use of drugs and surgery may improve the lives of cancer patients, give relief from constant arthritic pain, or restore good vision to elderly people with cataracts. However, this overall emphasis has severely skewed the range of treatments available. It has led to an over-production of intensive care equipment, for example, while some people, have little access to the most rudimentary medical services. This emphasis has also shaped public policy through the testing and use of new drugs, the routine use of mammograms in breast cancer screening, sonograms and amniocentesis in pregnancy, and the prevalence of hysterectomies and births by cesarean section.

Paying for Medical Care

The United States is the only industrialized country without a national health care system. Current provisions comprise a patchwork of government programs for those who are eligible with employment-based insurance for some workers. Many children, students, people with disabilities, self-employed, and unemployed people fall through the cracks.

Although 70 percent of people in the United States do have some kind of private medical insurance, this often covers only emergencies and hospitalization. Only 7 to 8 percent of participants in group plans are fully covered for hospital maternity charges. Fewer African American women and Latinas initiate prenatal care in the first trimester of pregnancy, at least in part because they lack insurance coverage; by contrast, 80 percent of White women seek early prenatal care. Women's Wellness programs are currently a profitable screening service provided by hospitals, though many insurance policies do not cover them, and they are not always culturally sensitive for all women's needs, especially women of color, women with disabilities, and lesbians. Many large-group insurance plans do not routinely cover any kind of contraception.

For most people who have private medical insurance (62 percent), this is employment-related. The figures for men and women with private coverage are very similar. Twenty-five percent of the population receive coverage through Medicaid or Medicare. More women than men are covered this way, reflecting Medicaid eligibility criteria that focus on mothers and children, and the greater numbers of women among the elderly who rely on Medicare. Cuts in Medicaid and Medicare during the 1990s meant that some people lost medical coverage altogether or in part. In 2002, 15.2 percent of the U.S. population (aged 18 to 64) was uninsured (Mills and Bhandari 2003). Those without health insurance for the entire year are more likely to be young (18 to 34 years), people of color—especially Latino/as—or immigrants. Access to health insurance is also directly related to income, educational attainment, and employment. People without health insurance tend to be concentrated in small businesses with low rates of unionization or are working part-time or on a temporary basis. States with large immigrant populations have the highest proportion of uninsured people: Arizona, California, Louisiana, New Mexico, and Texas (Mills and Bhandari 2003). Since the mid-1990s, changes in government policy have sought to bar undocumented people and some legal immigrants from public health-care services, including emergency care. There is sufficient confusion about eligibility to deter some eligible immigrant women from seeking services.

Other Barriers and Biases in Medical Services and Research

Other barriers to people's use of medical services, include fear of treatment, transportation difficulties, long waiting times, not being able to take time off work or losing pay for doing so, childcare responsibilities, language and cultural differences, and residential segregation, which may mean that there are few medical facilities in some communities. Most inner cities have large teaching hospitals that treat local people, predominantly people of color, in their emergency rooms, but this treatment may be slanted toward the educational needs of the hospital's medical students rather than to the health needs of the patients. African Americans tend to be diagnosed or seek treatment later than Whites for many diseases, which may reduce the effectiveness of treatment and their ability to survive. Once under medical treatment, they receive what official reports describe as "less aggressive" treatment than White people, as mentioned earlier.

Federal law now requires that White women and people of color be included in health research, but it will take time before this makes a big difference to the state of medical knowledge. Heart disease, which affects both men and women, was thought of as a man's disease for many years. As a result, it was studied much more than breast cancer (Dickersin and Schnaper 1996). Preliminary testing of antidepressant medications—prescribed mainly to women—was done only on men, despite evidence suggesting a difference in the drugs' effects between men and women. Research into health problems that men and women share was done on men and made to seem universal, not accounting for specific factors that might affect women differently. For example, the NIH-sponsored five-year Physicians Health Study concerning the effects of aspirin on heart disease used a sample of 22,071 men and no women, even though heart disease is also the number-one killer of women (Nechas and Foley 1994). There has been very little research concerning women and AIDS, the long-term effects of birth control pills, or new safe, reliable forms of contraception. Too little is known about the health needs of women of color, lesbians, transgendered women, older women, and women with disabilities (Gill 1996; Krieger and Fee 1996).

Health as Wellness

Requirements for Good Health

The United Nations World Health Organization defines health as "a state of complete physical, mental and social well-being and not merely the absence of disease or infirmity" (WHO 1946). Many aspects of life are not under our control. For example, living in damp housing or near a busy freeway or polluted industrial area, working in hazardous factories and mines, being exposed to toxic pesticides in agricultural work, doing repetitive tasks all day, and sitting in the same position for long periods of time are all aspects of daily life that can compromise one's health. The many newspaper and magazine articles that focus on individual lifestyle factors—diet, cigarette smoking, weight, exercise, and a positive attitude to coping with stress—urge us to take more personal responsibility for our health. Although this is valuable advice, lifestyle is only part of the story.

Health requires clean water and air, access to nutritious food, adequate housing, safety, healthy working conditions, and emotional and material supports. Thus, seemingly unconnected issues like poverty, racism, and sexism are also health issues.

Feminist Approaches to Wellness

Women's health has been a central concern for activists for the past thirty-five years or more (Avery 1990; Morgen 2002; Norsigian 1996; Nowrojee and Silliman 1997; Ross et al. 2002; Silliman et al. 2004; White 1990). Because many women's health needs are not met under the current system, especially those of African American women, Native American women and Latinas, feminist health practitioners and advocates urge a fundamental shift in emphasis toward a more holistic system of health care that recognizes that physical, emotional, and mental health are intimately connected and which emphasizes self-education, prevention, self-help, alternative therapies, a restructuring of medical financing, and a wider provision of basic facilities and appropriate services.

Self-Education and Preventive Care Preventing illness through self-education has low priority in the United States, and beyond basic dietary guidelines, immunization for infants, and minimal sex education for teens, it has generally been left to interested practitioners, organizations like the American Cancer Society, or community health-care projects. It involves learning to listen to our bodies and becoming more conscious of what they can tell us; learning to eat well and to heal common ailments with home remedies; taking regular exercise; getting enough sleep; quitting smoking; doing breast self-exams; and practicing safer sex. Self-education and preventive care also include various types of self-help, such as programs dealing with substance abuse or codependence. Many of these, like Alcoholics Anonymous, Al-Anon, Narcotics Anonymous, and other twelve-step programs, have been successful in helping people change negative habits and attitudes, though they usually do not address macro-level factors like institutionalized racism, sexism, and heterosexism. A self-help approach also means taking a greater degree of personal responsibility for one's health and being able to make informed decisions about possible remedies and treatments, rather than simply consuming services. Finally, preventive care encompasses creative activities, like dancing, music, poetry, sports, and homemaking, that give us joy and make us feel alive.

Complementary and Alternative Therapies Therapies such as acupuncture, ayurvedic health care, herbalism, homeopathy, chiropractic care, and many kinds of massage may be highly beneficial for a range of complaints. They are considered "alternative" from the perspective of contemporary Western medicine with its emphasis on drugs and surgery, but are rooted in much older systems of knowledge. Many of these therapies have been practiced for centuries in various parts of the world—including pre-industrial Europe and pre-conquest America. Acupuncture, ayurvedic care, and Shiatsu massage, for example, are available in Asian American communities. Native American, Latino, Caribbean, and African American communities also include practitioners who know the medicinal properties of plants and long-standing traditions of herbal medicines. Many alternative therapies have been scorned as "unscientific" and "unproven" by the U.S.

medical establishment but are being used more widely, sometimes in conjunction with Western medicine. Most are not covered by medical insurance.

Reform of Health-Care Financing Many advocates for women's health argue for a fundamental change in the way health care is paid for. In May 1993, for example, the Women's Convergence for National Health Care, attended by over five hundred women from twenty states, called for a universal health-care plan to provide equal access, comprehensive benefits, freedom to choose doctors and other caregivers, health education and prevention, reproductive health, public accountability, and progressive, fair financing (Baker 1993). Participants argued that universal health care is a major component of a social justice agenda. Current national and state proposals for "single payer" or universal health care incorporate these points (e.g., www.healthcareforall.org; www.healthcare-now. org; www.pnhp.org).

Feminist Health Projects Such projects have been active since the early 1970s. Examples include courses in women's health; informal self-health groups like the Bloomington Women's Health Collective (Bloomington, Ind.); women's health centers (e.g., in Concord, N.H., and Burlington, Vt.); campaigns for reproductive rights (e.g., NARAL Pro-Choice America and regional affiliates) or public funding for breast cancer research and treatment (e.g., Women's Community Cancer Project, Cambridge, Mass.); community health campaigns (e.g., Boston Health Access Project); and national organizations like Black Women's Health Imperative (Washington, D.C.), Lesbian Health Fund (San Francisco); the National Asian Women's Health Organization (San Francisco), the National Latina Health Organization (Oakland, Calif.), the National Women's Health Network (Washington, D.C.), and the Native American Women's Health and Education Resource Center (Lake Andes, S. Dak.). The Boston Women's Health Book Collective's ground-breaking book *Our Bodies, Ourselves* first started as mimeographed notes for a course in women's health and was later developed for publication. It has become an essential resource on women's health and sexuality for women of all ages.

◆◆◆

Questions for Reflection

As you read and discuss this chapter, consider these questions:

1. How do you know when you're healthy? Sick?
2. How can you learn more about your own body and your health?
3. What is a health crisis? For an individual person? At the community or national level?
4. Who should pay for health care? How? Why do you think this?
5. How does an individual, a family, or a society construct definitions of illness?
6. What are the main health issues for women in your family, your community, or on your campus?
7. What theoretical frameworks and activist projects are associated with reproductive rights and reproductive justice? What are the strengths and weaknesses of these perspectives?

◆◆◆

Finding Out More on the Web

1. Find out about the history of *Roe v. Wade*. How and why did this piece of legislation gain support? What was the cultural and historical context? Who were some of the key players who helped to make it happen? What is its status now?
2. Find out more about the positions, arguments, and activities of anti-choice organizations (e.g., the Army of God, the Christian Coalition, Focus on the Family, Operation Rescue) and pro-choice organizations (e.g., Choice USA, Fund for a Feminist Majority, Planned Parenthood, NARAL Pro-Choice America). What do you think about what you learned here? Do you have any concerns that are not included?
3. Research one of the women's health organizations mentioned in this chapter. What are its goals, strategies, and activities?

◆◆◆

Taking Action

1. List all the steps you take to care for yourself and any additional ones you could take.
2. Find out more about what your family and community consider effective self-care practices.
3. Find out where women can go to keep healthy or get quality health care in your community.

◆◆◆

Three Generations of Native American Women's Birth Experience (1991)

Joy Harjo

Poet, musician, editor, and teacher **Joy Harjo** has published many award-winning poetry collections, most recently *How We Became Human: New and Selected Poems.* She is the Joseph M. Russo Professor in Creative Writing at the University of New Mexico and the recipient of numerous fellowships and awards including the American Indian Distinguished Achievement in the Arts Award, and the William Carlos Williams Award of the Poetry Society of America. She performs her poetry and plays saxophone with her band, Poetic Justice.

It was still dark when I awakened in the stuffed back room of my mother-in-law's small rented house with what felt like hard cramps. At 17 years of age I had read everything I could from the Tahlequah Public Library about pregnancy and giving birth. But nothing prepared me for what was coming. I awakened my child's father and then ironed him a shirt before we walked the four blocks to the Indian hospital because we had no car and no money for a taxi. He had been working with another Cherokee artist silk-screening signs for specials at the supermarket and making $5 a day, and had to leave me alone at the hospital because he had to go to work. We didn't awaken his mother. She had to get up soon enough to fix breakfast for her daughter and granddaughter before leaving for her job at the nursing home. I knew my life was balanced at the edge of great, precarious change and I felt alone and cheated. Where was the circle of women to acknowledge and honor this birth?

It was still dark as we walked through the cold morning, under oaks that symbolized the stubbornness and endurance of the Cherokee people who had made Tahlequah their capital in the new lands. I looked for handholds in the misty gray sky, for a voice announcing this impending miracle. I wanted to change everything; I wanted to go back to a place before childhood, before our tribe's removal to Oklahoma. What kind of life was I bringing this child into? I was a poor, mixed-blood woman heavy with a child who would suffer the struggle of poverty, the legacy of loss. For the second time in my life I felt the sharp tug of my own birth cord, still connected to my mother. I believe it never pulls away, until death, and even then it becomes a streak in the sky symbolizing that most important warrior road. In my teens I had fought my mother's weaknesses with all my might, and here I was at 17, becoming as my mother, who was in Tulsa, cooking breakfasts and preparing for the lunch shift at a factory cafeteria as I walked to the hospital to give birth. I should be with her; instead, I was far from her house, in the house of a mother-in-law who later would try to use witchcraft to destroy me.

After my son's father left me I was prepped for birth. This meant my pubic area was shaved completely and then I endured the humiliation of an enema, all at the hands of strangers. I was left alone in a room painted government green. An overwhelming antiseptic smell emphasized the sterility of the hospital, a hospital built because of the U.S. government's treaty and responsibility to provide health care to Indian people.

I intellectually understood the stages of labor, the place of transition, of birth—but it was difficult to bear the actuality of it, and to bear it alone. Yet in some ways I wasn't alone, for history surrounded me. It is with the birth of children that history is given form and voice. Birth is one of the most sacred acts we take part in and witness in our lives. But sacredness seemed to be far from my lonely labor room in the Indian hospital. I heard a woman screaming in the next room with her pain, and I wanted to comfort her. The nurse used her as a bad example to the rest of us who were struggling to keep our suffering silent.

The doctor was a military man who had signed on this watch not for the love of healing or out of awe at the miracle of birth, but to fulfill a contract for medical school payments. I was another statistic to him; he touched me as if he were moving equipment from one place to another. During my last visit I was given the option of being sterilized. He explained to me that the moment of birth was the best time to do it. I was handed the form but chose not to sign it, and am amazed now that I didn't think too much of it at the time. Later I would learn that many Indian women who weren't fluent in English signed, thinking it was a form giving consent for the doctor to deliver their babies. Others were sterilized without even the formality of signing. My light skin had probably saved me from such a fate. It wouldn't be the first time in my life.

When my son was finally born I had been deadened with a needle in my spine. He was shown to me—the incredible miracle nothing prepared me for—then taken from me in the name of medical progress. I fell asleep with the weight of chemicals and awoke yearning for the child I had suffered for, had anticipated in the months proceeding from his unexpected genesis when I was still 16 and a student at Indian school. I was not allowed to sit up or walk because of the possibility of paralysis (one of the drug's side effects), and when I finally got to hold him, the nurse stood guard as if I would hurt him. I felt enmeshed in a system in which the wisdom that had carried my people from generation to generation was ignored. In that place I felt ashamed I was an Indian woman. But I was also proud of what my body had accomplished despite the rape by the bureaucracy's machinery, and I got us out of there as soon as possible. My son would flourish on beans and fry bread, and on the dreams and stories we fed him.

My daughter was born four years later, while I was an art student at the University of New Mexico. Since my son's birth I had waitressed, cleaned hospital rooms, filled cars with gas (while wearing a mini-skirt), worked as a nursing assistant, and led dance classes at a health spa. I knew I didn't want to cook and waitress all my life, as my mother had done. I had watched the varicose veins grow branches on her legs, and as they grew, her zest for dancing and sports dissolved into utter tiredness. She had been born with a caul over her face, the sign of a gifted visionary.

My earliest memories are of my mother writing songs on an ancient Underwood typewriter after she had washed and waxed the kitchen floor on her hands and knees. She too had wanted something different for her life. She had left an impoverished existence at age 17, bound for the big city of Tulsa. She was shamed in a time in which to be even part Indian was to be an outcast in the great U.S. system. Half her relatives were Cherokee fullbloods from near Jay, Oklahoma, who for the most part had nothing to do with white people. The other half were musically inclined "white trash" addicted to country-western music and Holy Roller fervor. She thought she could disappear in the city; no one would know her family, where she came from. She had dreams of singing and had once been offered a job singing on the radio but turned it down because she was shy. Later one of her songs would be stolen before she could copyright it and would make someone else rich. She would quit writing songs. She and my father would divorce, and she would be forced to work for money to feed and clothe four children, all born within two years of each other.

As a child growing up in Oklahoma, I liked to be told the story of my birth. I would beg for it while my mother cleaned and ironed. "You almost killed me," she would say. "We almost died." That I could kill my mother filled me with remorse and shame. And I imagined the push-pull of my life, which is a legacy I deal with even now when I am twice as old as my mother was at my birth. I loved to hear the story of my warrior fight for my breath. The way it was told, it had been my decision to live. When I got older, I realized we were both nearly casualties of the system, the same system flourishing in the Indian hospital where later my son Phil would be born.

My parents felt lucky to have insurance, to be able to have their children in the hospital. My father came from a fairly prominent Muscogee Creek family. *His* mother was a full-blood who in the early 1920s got her degree in art. She was a painter. She gave birth to him in a private hospital in Oklahoma City; at least that's what I think he told me before he died at age 53. It was something of which they were proud.

This experience was much different from my mother's own birth. She and five of her six brothers were born at home, with no medical assistance. The only time a doctor was called was when someone was dying. When she was born her mother named her Wynema, a Cherokee name my mother says means beautiful woman, and Jewell, for a can of shortening stored in the room where she was born.

I wanted something different for my life, for my son, and for my daughter, who later was born in a university hospital in Albuquerque. It was a bright summer morning when she was ready to begin her journey. I still had no car, but I had enough money saved for a taxi for a ride to the hospital. She was born "naturally," without drugs. I could look out of the hospital window while I was in labor at the bluest sky in the world. I had support. Her father was present in the delivery room—though after her birth he disappeared on a drinking binge. I understood his despair, but did not agree with the painful means to describe it. A few days later Rainy Dawn was presented to the sun at her father's pueblo and given a name so that she will always be recognized as a part of the people, as a child of the sun.

That's not to say that my experience in the hospital reached perfection. The clang of metal against metal in the delivery room had the effect of a tuning fork reverberating fear in my pelvis. After giving birth I held my daughter, but they took her from me for "processing." I refused to lie down to be wheeled to my room after giving birth; I wanted to walk out of there to find my daughter. We reached a compromise and I rode in a wheelchair. When we reached the room I stood up and walked to the nursery and demanded my daughter. I knew she needed me. That began my war with the nursery staff, who deemed me unknowledgeable because I was Indian and poor. Once again I felt the brushfire of shame, but I'd learned to put it out much more quickly, and I demanded early release so I could take care of my baby without the judgment of strangers.

I wanted something different for Rainy, and as she grew up I worked hard to prove that I could make "something" of my life. I obtained two degrees as a single mother. I wrote poetry, screenplays, became a professor, and tried to live a life that would be a positive influence for both of my children. My work in this life has to do with reclaiming the memory stolen from our peoples when we were dispossessed from our lands east of the Mississippi; it has to do with restoring us. I am proud of our history, a history so powerful that it both destroyed my father and guarded him. It's a

history that claims my mother as she lives not far from the place her mother was born, names her as she cooks in the cafeteria of a small college in Oklahoma.

When my daughter told me she was pregnant, I wasn't surprised. I had known it before she did, or at least before she would admit it to me. I felt despair, as if nothing had changed or ever would. She had run away from Indian school with her boyfriend and they had been living in the streets of Gallup, a border town notorious for the suicides and deaths of Indian peoples. I brought her and her boyfriend with me because it was the only way I could bring her home. At age 16, she was fighting me just as I had so fiercely fought my mother. She was making the same mistakes. I felt as if everything I had accomplished had been in vain. Yet I felt strangely empowered, too, at this repetition of history, this continuance, by a new possibility of life and love, and I steadfastly stood by my daughter.

I had a university job, so I had insurance that covered my daughter. She saw an obstetrician in town who was reputed to be one of the best. She had the choice of a birthing room. She had the finest care. Despite this, I once again battled with a system in which physicians are taught the art of healing by dissecting cadavers. My daughter went into labor a month early. We both knew intuitively the baby was ready, but how to explain that to a system in which numbers and statistics provide the base of understanding? My daughter would have her labor interrupted; her blood pressure would rise because of the drug given to her to stop the labor. She would be given an unneeded amniocentesis and would have her labor induced—after having it artificially stopped! I was warned that if I took her out of the hospital so her labor could occur naturally my insurance would cover nothing.

My daughter's induced labor was unnatural and difficult, monitored by machines, not by touch. I was shocked. I felt as if I'd come full circle, as if I were watching my mother's labor and the struggle of my own birth. But I was there in the hospital room with her, as neither my mother had been for me, nor her mother for her. My daughter and I went through the labor and birth together.

And when Krista Rae was born she was born to her family. Her father was there for her, as were both her grandmothers and my friend who had flown in to be with us. Her paternal great-grandparents and aunts and uncles had also arrived from the Navajo Reservation to honor her. Something *had* changed.

Four days later, I took my granddaughter to the Saguaro forest before dawn and gave her the name I had dreamed for her just before her birth. Her name looks like clouds of mist settling around a sacred mountain as it begins to speak. A female ancestor approaches on a horse. We are all together.

THIRTY

Reproductive Rights (1995)
A Disability Rights Issue

Marsha Saxton

> **Marsha Saxton** teaches Disability Studies at the University of California, Berkeley, and works as a principal investigator at the World Institute on Disability, in Oakland, California, with special interests in women's issues, genetic technologies and Personal Assistance Services. She has published many articles about disability rights, women's health, and genetic screening issues, as well as a literary anthology of disabled women's writing. She has been a board member of the Boston Women's Health Book Collective, and served on the Council for Responsible Genetics, and the National Institutes of Health Ethical, Legal Social Implications Working Group of the Human Genome Initiative.

In recent years, the women's movement has broadened its definition of "reproductive rights" to include not only abortion, but all aspects of sexuality, procreation, and parenthood. . . .

Some women may take for granted birth control, reproductive health care, and sex education, forgetting that people with different life experiences based on class, race, or physical or mental ability may not have access to these fundamental aspects of reproductive freedom. But for people with disabilities, *all* the reproductive rights are still at stake.

For centuries, the oppression of people with disabilities has denied us "choice": choice about who should be regarded as "a sexual being," who should have babies, which babies should be born, which babies should be allowed to live after they're born, who should raise these babies into adulthood. These choices were made, for the most part, by others.

People with disabilities are beginning to demand a say in these decisions now that the Americans with Disabilities Act (ADA) has forced the public to perceive our issues as civil rights issues. In the decades to come, we hope to see a transformation in the public's perception of disability and of people with disabilities. The issue of reproductive rights can serve as a catalyst for this transformation.

The stereotype of asexuality is slowly lifting. There are now a few disabled characters in the popular literature and media who are portrayed as sexual beings participating in intimate activities. (Some of these movie personalities, such as actress Marlee Maitlin, themselves are deaf or have physical disabilities. However, most disabled characters on TV or in the movies are still played by non-disabled actors.)

New and complex issues are emerging in regard to disability and procreation. Many relate to new developments in reproductive technologies. Others reflect changing social values. What follows is a discussion of how these new issues affect people with disabilities.

Reproductive Health Care

Because of patronizing attitudes about disabled people, many medical practitioners and health care facilities do not consider offering reproductive health care services to their patients who have disabilities. Many people with disabilities or with chronic illness, because of the "preexisting condition" exclusion in most health insurance, have been denied access to *any* health care, not only reproductive health care. There are few medical or nursing schools that offer any training on the reproductive health of people with disabilities. Only in the last five years has there been any research on the effects of various birth control methods for people with different kinds of disabilities or chronic illness, and these studies are limited, often focusing only on spinal cord injury. Even people with the more common disabling conditions like diabetes, arthritis, or multiple sclerosis have little or no information about whether they should or shouldn't use particular methods of birth control.

In Chicago, a group of disabled women have created a "disability accessible" gynecological clinic through the Chicago Rehabilitation Institute and the Prentice Women's Hospital, staffed with practitioners who have been trained to serve disabled women. The Health Resource Center for Women with Disabilities is unique. One day a week, it offers accessible core gyn services for women with disabilities and now serves more than 200 women. The staff includes nurse practitioners and midwives; and a nurse who has a disability has been hired. The clinic program plans to expand its resources to include a project director to monitor clinic services and to oversee a library with health-related videos and publications. It will also add an 800 telephone number staffed by a woman with a disability to respond to questions about accessible health care services. The center has initiated research directed at documenting the medical experiences of women with disabilities and improving services for traditionally underserved populations, including developmentally disabled, learning disabled, and mentally retarded women.

Sex Education

Disabled children and adults need information about dating, sex, menstruation, pregnancy, birth control, AIDS, and other sexually transmitted diseases. Attitudes have changed, and increasingly, parents and educators are recognizing that disabled children need sex education. But this is not the norm. Disabled children are still often overprotected by adults who don't know how to teach them about "the facts of life." Questions such as the following tend to provoke confusion: how can blind children be given information about gender anatomy? How should retarded children be told about AIDS? How can deaf children, children who

use wheelchairs, or any child who may have felt the stigma of disability be encouraged to interact positively with non-disabled and disabled peers and to learn positive sexual self-esteem? Many disabled adults never received important information about sex. They are vulnerable to confusing or dangerous misinformation and serious difficulties with their own sexuality, difficulties that result not from actual physical limitations but simply from exclusion from information and experience.

Marriage Disincentives

In the United States, people with disabilities who receive certain kinds of Social Security or Medicaid benefits are discouraged from getting married by threat of reduced or eliminated benefits. These "marriage disincentives" (like "employment disincentives," which discourage disabled people from employment by threat of reduced medical coverage) reveal the serious disability discrimination fundamentally built into our disability policies. If an SSI (Supplemental Security Income) recipient marries, his or her spouse's earnings are considered income, thus reducing the recipient's benefits, jeopardizing essential medical and personal care attendant services, and often placing enormous financial burden on the couple to finance prohibitively expensive services or equipment. The current law has the effect of forcing people with disabilities to accept "living together" as temporary sweethearts rather than an adult, community-sanctioned marriage. . . . While the outward rationale for the law is to save taxpayer money on people who could be supported by a spouse (based on the assumption that two can live as cheaply as one), social scientists and disability rights activists suspect that drafters of these marriage disincentive laws were also intending to thwart marriage and potential procreation for disabled people.

"Reproducing Ourselves"

The very idea of disabled persons as parents scares some people and exposes discriminatory attitudes that might otherwise remain hidden. Acceptance of disabled people as parents simply requires the larger community's acceptance of us as human beings. By denying our rights to be mothers and fathers, it is not only our competence to care for our young, but our very existence, our desire to "reproduce ourselves," that is forbidden.

In late 1991, TV news anchor Bree Walker, who has a genetic disability and who was pregnant, became the brunt of a call-in radio talk show when the host Jane Norris asked listeners, "Should disabled people have children?" Callers aired their opinions about whether Walker should have her baby or, as Norris posed the question, "Is it 'fair' to bring a child with a disability into the world?" The incident became the focal point of the disabled women's community's challenge to the idea that people with disabilities should not be born.

Qualifications for Parenthood

The Earls are a married Michigan couple, both severely disabled with cerebral palsy. They had a baby, Natalie, and sought assistance from the Michigan Home Help Program in providing physical care for the infant. Their desire to raise their own child and to demonstrate their competence as loving parents was thwarted by state regulations that bar the personal care assistant (PCA) of a disabled client from touching the client's child during paid work hours. One result of this regulation seems to be that disabled people who rely on the PCA program for help in daily living cannot have children.

Of course, people with disabilities must take seriously the responsibilities of adult sexuality and the potential for pregnancy and parenthood. We must also educate ourselves, the disability community, and our families and friends about what it means to be a parent and be disabled. And we must be prepared to take on the discriminatory policies of a variety of institutions: medical, social services, legal, and media. But we must also do battle within ourselves. We must overcome the voices we've internalized that say, "You can't possibly do this, you can't be good parents, and you don't deserve the benefits or the assistance required to raise your own children."

In Berkeley, California, an agency called Through the Looking Glass offers the first program specifically designed to assist parents with disabilities in skills development, community resources, and peer support. [www.lookingglass.org]

Custody Struggles

Tiffany Callo is a young woman who wanted to raise her newborn son. Because of her cerebral palsy, the California Department of Social Services challenged her ability to care for the child. Armed with lawyers and court orders, the department refused to allow her to demonstrate her parenting skills in an appropriate environment that would enable her to show the creative approaches she had developed to handle the baby. *Newsweek* reporter Jay Mathews picked up her story, and Callo became a spokesperson for the cause of mothers with disabilities who fight for the right to raise their own children. Social service and child protection agency professionals need training and awareness to allow them to perceive the *abilities* of disabled parents, not only the stereotyped limitations.

Adoption

A large number of children adopted or waiting for adoption are disabled. Many disabled adults were adopted or placed in foster homes. It is still largely the case that adoption agencies do not consider disabled people as prospective parents for either disabled or non-disabled children. We need to challenge this stereotype that people with disabilities cannot be good adoptive parents. A few adoption agencies are changing policies, allowing disabled people to adopt, and in some cases even encouraging disabled adults to adopt children with disabilities. For example, Adoption Resource Associates in Watertown, Massachusetts, has taken a special interest in prospective disabled parents and makes specific mention in their brochure that they do not discriminate on the basis of disability in their placement services.

Sterilization Abuse

Consider this story of a woman with a psychiatric disability: "When I was twenty, I got pregnant by my boyfriend at the state mental school. Of course, there was no birth control for patients. We weren't allowed to have sex, but it went on all the time, even between patients and attendants. A doctor forced my mother to sign a paper giving me an abortion, even though I wanted to give up the baby for adoption. When I woke up, I found out I had had a hysterectomy. Maybe I couldn't take care of the baby then, but nobody even asked me what I wanted to do, or what I hoped for when I got older."

When a guardian or medical professional decides that people labeled retarded, mentally ill, or with other disabilities should not be parents, sterilization without consent may occur. Often, guardians or other decision makers who intervene on behalf of these disabled people have little exposure to the Independent Living Movement, or other community disability resources. As disabled people, we need to be empowered to make our own decisions regarding sexuality and procreation.

Abortion

Women with disabilities have reported significant difficulties with regard to abortion. These include being pressured to undergo an abortion because it is assumed that a disabled woman could not be a good parent, or, conversely, being denied access to abortion because a guardian decides the woman was incapable of making her own reproductive choices. Sometimes, after birth, a disabled woman's child is taken away from her. Women with disabilities experience the same kinds of abortion access difficulties as non-disabled women, but these difficulties are often magnified by disability discrimination.

Prenatal Screening

Scientific advances in the field of genetics have created technologies that can detect an increasing number of genetic conditions in the womb. While the general public seems to regard this medical technology as a wonderful advance and a way to reduce the incidence of disability and improve the quality of life, people with disabilities often have a very different view. As revealed in the Bree Walker case mentioned above, the unchallenged assumption often accompanying the use of these screening tests is that the lives of people with genetically related disabilities (such as muscular dystrophy, Down syndrome, cystic fibrosis, sickle cell anemia, and spina bifida) are simply not worth living and are a burden that families and society would rather not endure. The options to abort a fetus who might die early in life, or to abort in order to preclude the birth of a child with severe disabilities, are framed as "reproductive

options." But in this era of health care cost containment, the notion of controlling costs by eliminating births of disabled babies may become a requirement, rather than an option. Then it ceases to be reproductive freedom and becomes quality control of babies—eugenics. The availability of these tests reinforces these notions, and the tests are actually marketed to women and to health care providers on this basis. Women are increasingly pressured to abort a fetus identified as disabled. Real choice must include the right to bear children with disabilities.

We in the disabled community must voice our ideas about selective abortion and attest to the true value of our lives. Only when a valid picture of the quality of our lives is available can prospective parents make choices about the use of tests for genetic disabilities in fetuses.

The Reproductive Rights Movement

The women's movement has begun to reach out to women with disabilities as a group. Women's organizations have begun to understand and challenge their own discriminatory attitudes and behaviors. More and more events in the women's movement are beginning to be wheelchair accessible and interpreted for the hearing impaired. But we have a long way to go to make the women's community fully welcoming of disabled people. This is a good time to get involved and share our thinking and energies. To be fully integrated into society, we must get involved and take leadership in all movements, and the movement for reproductive health care and real choice is an especially important one for people with disabilities to take on.

As disabled people, we have unique perspectives to share. Our views can enlighten everyone about the fundamental issues of sexuality and reproduction. We have gained much knowledge and experience with medical intervention, asking for and effectively managing help, dealing with bureaucracy, and fighting for access and power. Other controversial issues to which we can contribute our thinking include surrogate motherhood, population concerns, birthing technologies, artificial insemination, and *in vitro* fertilization.

The movement for reproductive rights needs to include people with disabilities as much as disabled people need to be included in the movement.

◆◆◆

THIRTY-ONE

Abortion Is a Motherhood Issue (1991, updated 1994 and 2005)

Judith Arcana

Judith Arcana holds a Doctorate in Literature, a Masters degree in Women's Studies, and a Preceptorship in Urban Medicine. She is a scholar, teacher, and writer whose work appears widely; two of her books focus on motherhood, and a third, *What If Your Mother*, focuses on abortion.

Before I write about the relationship between abortion and mothering, I will first offer a brief history of my uterus and myself—our credentials, so to speak, in terms of that relationship. I came to woman's consciousness through my body, through coming to know and appreciate what my mother and aunts had often called, in the years of my growing up, "female plumbing."

I can picture my youthful cervix as I write. I remember when it was not yet thirty, still smooth and shiny pink all the time, a relatively innocent little volcano, periodically discharging the bloody contents of my uterus, or slowly oozing the thick clear mucous of ovulation. Occasionally it might erupt in some nasty raw eversions or erosions; as it got older, once or twice it stuck out the tiny red tongue of a polyp in the face of my flashlit plastic speculum.

But now, at fifty, it's one of the cauliflower ears of the cervical world, battered by our mutual experience. It's not such a rosy pink these days; it's on the pale side, showing a bit of blue vein on occasion, and that slick cone has gone all bumpy. Motherhood has left its mark on my cervix, just as it has on the rest of me. I can't see into the uterus, but I know it too has altered over the years, and is in the process of making the big change. It doesn't realize its fallopian tubes have been short circuited by sterilization, so it's still doing its periodic building—however erratically—making thick wet red nests, only to drain them away into cotton pads.

Motherhood has left its mark on more of me than just my cervix. I've published two books about the subject (*Our Mothers' Daughters* and *Every Mother's Son*), along with various articles, some essays, and a few poems. I've led dozens of workshops and made many speeches about mothering, from the points of view of both daughter and mother. I've taught classes about the mother/daughter and mother/son relationships, and have carried on from a variety of pulpits about the culture-wide practice of mother-blaming in our time. Then too, I spent years raising my son. I have given a great deal of thought to motherhood issues.

Abortion is a motherhood issue. Abortion is neither a separate subject, nor a subject in a different category. What I mean to emphasize here is that abortion, along with contraception, miscarriage and adoption—including both the giving out and taking in of children—to say nothing of sterilization and current reproductive biotechnology, are all usually separated from discussions of mothering, even when those discussions are carried on in the voices and writings of women of consciousness.

Sometimes that separation is a matter of convenience, because we just can't talk about everything all at once. Sometimes the separation is deliberately—that is, strategically—used by people in favor of legal abortion to fend off attacks from anti-abortion people, who make the same separation in some ways but not in others, and do so out of their own strategic choices as well as their ignorance or closed-mindedness. Sometimes, though, the separation occurs because we have lost sight of the fact that abortion is not only about women getting pregnant, but also about babies growing inside of women's bodies. When that happens, we forget that abortion is, in the ordinary motherhood-type way, the concern of women who are taking responsibility for the lives of their children.

Conception *is* the beginning of maternity, no matter what the religious leaders, legislators, lawyers, scientists or doctors might decide. Women have always known this. When the pregnancy is deliberate, or accepted, we say *baby*. When the pregnancy is an accident, or rejected, we say *fetus* or *embryo*, a mass of cells and tissue. We have sometimes allowed ourselves to be cajoled or forced into accepting a priest's or a government's ruling about "quickening" or, these days, "viability." And when we're on the defensive against those who would deny us the right to make this choice for ourselves and our children, we have sometimes been quiet about language—but we never didn't know that being pregnant meant having a baby growing inside of our bodies.

Choosing to abort a child is like choosing to send it to one school and not another, choosing whether or not to allow it to sleep with you in your bed, choosing whether—or when—to tell it you are a lesbian, choosing whether or not to send it to Hebrew school, to catechism, to Quaker meeting. In magnitude, perhaps this choice is most similar to choosing whether to have it institutionalized or keep it at home when its mental or physical disability is an enormous burden; certainly, deciding whether or not to give it to adoptive parents, an orphanage, or foster care is a similar decision for a mother. Choosing to abort a child is a profoundly made life choice for that child, a choice made by a woman or girl who is already a mother, however ignorant, angry, sad, hopeful or frightened she may be. And whatever our religious teachings and spiritual commitments, we have never not known that choosing to abort our babies is a dreadful responsibility. We have accepted that responsibility—many of us have even accepted eternal damnation—because we believe that the choice we are making is the best one for ourselves and our babies.

I began to think this way when I was a medic in an abortion clinic. I helped women abort in the same period in which I became a mother. In fact, in one five-year period of my life, from when I was 27 to when I was 32, I racked up almost all of my major uterine experiences, with menarche and menopause the only outstanding exceptions thus far. In those five years, I learned and practiced abortion with a small group of women, got pregnant, gave birth to a child, nursed it for fourteen months, got pregnant and had a miscarriage, got pregnant and had an abortion, and then had myself sterilized. In those times, I was a young woman being empowered and enlightened by the second wave of twentieth century women's movement in the United States, and my education about motherhood is born of that extraordinary good fortune. Abortion work was the crucible of much of my consciousness as a woman, and many of my choices as a mother.

My education took place in the Abortion Counseling Service of the Chicago Women's Liberation Union, now called "Jane" in the oral and written history of the women's health movement in the U.S.A. The abortion service worked with over eleven thousand women in less than four years. I learned then that abortion is a simple procedure, especially when done early, in an atmosphere of comfort, by women who care for and about the health and emotional well-being of pregnant women—just like home birth. Through the service, I encountered hundreds of women, the youngest eleven years old, the oldest over fifty, who made the choice to abort. These women were of various races and classes, of many religious and philosophical persuasions. Not one of them—even those who were themselves children—took her decision lightly or carelessly. Every woman who chooses to abort a pregnancy is justified in her decision. Every woman who has an abortion knows what it means, and lives in that meaning the best way she can. Abortion is a matter of life and death, we used to say in the Service; we all knew that.

Long ago and far away, time out of mind, all the peoples of the earth understood that matters of life and death belonged in the hands of the mothers. Mothers gave life and death as their wisdom decreed; this was as it should be. Mawu in Africa, Kali in India, Sussistanako in North America, the Morrigan in the British Isles, Asherah in the Middle East, Pele in the Pacific islands, all the Great Mothers, were respected in their choices, decisions made for the good of the child, the mother, the clan, the tribe, the nation. The Great Mothers of song and ritual—and the human mothers too—understood well that death, like birth, is part of life.

Women, supported by the custom of their societies, took responsibility for their choices, accepting the necessity of the decision to end a just-begun life. They considered the conditions surrounding the mother, and the probability of her child's life being a strong one, including joy, good work, health, maturity, and usefulness. In their considerations then, as now, women sometimes judged that that probability was too slight, uncertain, or simply absent. Their choices, like our own when we abort, were never made in a vacuum; even in our time, in this woman-hating, mother-blaming society, there is always the decision made on balance, weighing both the potential years of the child's life and the mother's struggle to nurture it against great odds.

Surely we too need rituals, songs and dreams and talking in the women's circle, so that we can tell our babies and ourselves that this is not their time, that they would not flourish if they came to us now, that we cannot do right, cannot do enough for them, cannot mother them as they ought to be mothered.

We need to speak of our abortions, not in the atmosphere of guilt and shame created by the spiritual and emotional terrorism of the contemporary anti-abortion movement, but in open recognition of our joy or sadness, our regret or relief—in conscious acceptance of the responsibility for our choice.

THIRTY-TWO

Reproductive Justice: Vision, Analysis and Action for a Stronger Movement (2005)

Asian Communities for Reproductive Justice

Founded in 1989, **Asian Communities for Reproductive Justice** (Oakland, California) has been at the forefront of building a reproductive justice movement that places the reproductive health and rights of Asian women and girls within a social justice framework.

We believe reproductive justice is the complete physical, mental, spiritual, political, economic, and social well being of women and girls, and that it will be achieved when women and girls have the economic, social, and political power and resources to make healthy decisions about our bodies, sexuality, and reproduction for ourselves, our families and our communities. For this to become a reality, we need to make change on the individual, community, institutional, and societal levels.

Oppression and Reproduction

The fight for women's emancipation has been inextricably linked to control over reproduction. The reproductive health and reproductive rights agendas have largely focused on individual rights and solutions rather than structural societal changes. Many women at the margins of the movement have championed the need for greater analysis of oppressions in discussions of reproduction. As Dorothy Roberts stated, "Reproduction is not just a matter of individual choice. Reproductive health policy affects the status of entire groups. It reflects which

people are valued in our society; who is deemed worthy to bear children and capable of making decisions for themselves. Reproductive decisions are made within a social context, including inequalities of wealth and power."[1] The focus on individualism neglects the broader societal context in which Asian and Pacific Islander (API) women live.

Repeatedly, economic, social, and institutional policies have severely affected women's choice to determine reproduction. The regulation and control of API women and girls' bodies, sexuality, and reproduction have played a key role in colonization and racial oppression, and in controlling API communities in the United States. Historically, the nation's immigrant exclusion laws targeted people from Asia and served as a form of population control. As early as 1870, in an attempt to limit the size of the Asian population in California, the state legislature passed a law that prohibited the immigration of Asian women, and in 1875 the United States Congress passed the Page Law to forbid entry of mostly "Chinese, Japanese and Mongolian" women. Current policies restricting immigration and access to social services also significantly prevent API women from truly being able to make reproductive choices.

In focusing on a narrow abortion agenda or even a broader reproductive health agenda, the mainstream reproductive health and reproductive rights movement typically neglects critical circumstances that many Asian and Pacific Islander women face. For example. API women who are immigrants or those with limited English proficiency have little power to negotiate interactions with reproductive health providers. Many queer API women face homophobia that deters them from accessing reproductive care. Reproductive health programs and service providers often focus on women as individuals and may adopt a paternalistic approach that oppresses and regulates women's reproduction. Although there is, currently, a movement to incorporate "cultural competence" and language access in health services, these interventions usually do not address power differentials in the patient-provider relationship. They do not empower API women to be partners with medical practitioners in making decisions. Also they usually do not incorporate or respect traditional health practices that API women value such as homeopathic medicine, herbal healing, or acupuncture. Moreover, numerous Asian cultures promote societal, community, and family decision-making that is incompatible with an individualistic approach to reproductive rights. API women often have to navigate social taboos and traditions within their cultures in making reproductive decisions, so that "choice" is not necessarily theirs to make.

Creation of the Women of Color Reproductive Justice Movement

In response to the limitations of mainstream frameworks in addressing their reality, women of color in the United States and internationally have advocated for a broader reproductive justice analysis that addresses race, class, gender, sexuality, ability, generation, and immigration status.

Although some historians have tended to erase the contributions of women of color to the movement, women of color have been actively organizing for reproductive justice for many years. In the past two decades, this race and ethnic-based organizing has gained visibility and increasing success. The National Black Women's Health Project was formed in 1984 as the first women-of-color reproductive health organization, building a foundation for organizations representing the major ethnic groups. The Mother's Milk Project on the Akwesasne Reservation in New York was created in 1985, followed by the National Latina Health Organization in 1986. The Native American Women's Health Education and Resource Center was launched in 1988, and Asian Pacific Islanders for Choice (forerunner to ACRJ) in 1989. Since then, women of color have organized numerous conferences, collaborated with each other, and formed alliances with civil rights and women's rights organizations.

In November 1994, a Black women's caucus first coined the term *reproductive justice*, naming themselves "Women of African Descent for Reproductive Justice" at the Illinois Pro-Choice Alliance Conference. According to Loretta Ross, one of the caucus participants, "We were dissatisfied with the pro-choice language, feeling that it did not adequately encompass our twinned goals: To protect the right to have—and not to have—children. Nor did the language of choice accurately portray the many barriers African American women faced when trying to make reproductive decisions. We began exploring the use of the human rights framework in our reproductive rights activism in the United States, as many grassroots activists do globally. We sought a way to partner reproductive rights to social justice and came up with the term 'reproductive justice'."[2] Later, the SisterSong Women of Color Reproductive Health Collective was formed by 16 women-of-color organizations in 1997, with a focus on grassroots mobilization and public policy. In April 2004, SisterSong coordinated thousands of women in a "Women of Color for Reproductive Justice" contingent as part of the March for Women's Lives in Washington, DC.

Attacking Reproductive Oppression: Asian Communities for Reproductive Justice (ACRJ)

At ACRJ we work towards a vision of the world where Asian women and girls have self-determination, power, and resources to make the decisions they need. Our Reproductive Justice Agenda illustrates our vision, solutions, and values for attacking the root causes of reproductive oppression (see Figure 1). In this Agenda we articulate our analysis based on the experiences, issues, and research carried out for and by Asian women and girls to develop a model that is at the nexus of the intersections of gender, race, class,

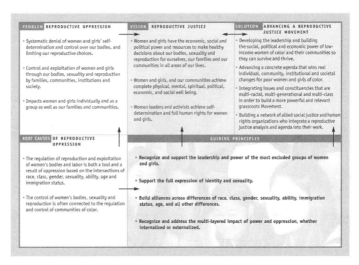

FIGURE 1. ACRJ's Reproductive Justice Agenda

sexuality, ability, generation, and immigration status. In our organizing work, we use popular education and community-based participatory research to develop the leadership of Asian women and girls to plan campaigns for specific and measurable gains at the local and state level. For instance, we worked in collaboration with environmental justice groups to shut down a toxic medical waste incinerator in Oakland, California, and have been working to pass and enforce state legislation that ensures comprehensive sex education in public high schools. And finally, we build and strengthen women of color and mainstream alliances for reproductive justice. We recognize the importance of broader inclusion and leadership of the most excluded groups of women. These include low-income women, queer women, women with disabilities, young women, immigrant and refugee women. Many are women of color; some white women are also excluded on account of their class position, sexuality, language competence, and so on. We believe that organized communities, particularly the most marginalized groups mentioned above, are key agents of change, and we focus on improving social conditions and changing power and access to resources on all levels. Figure 1 summarizes our approach.

ACRJ's Reproductive Justice Agenda (RJA) places reproductive justice at the center of the most

critical social and economic justice issues facing our communities such as domestic safety, labor rights, environmental justice, queer rights, and immigrant rights. For example, under conditions of reproductive justice, we will live in homes free from sexual and physical violence; we will live and work without fear of sexual harassment; we will have safe work and home environments protected from corporate exploitation and environmental toxins; we will be free from hatred due to sexual identity; we will be valued for all the forms of work we do; we will earn equitable and livable wages; we will eat healthy and affordable food; we will have comprehensive health care for ourselves and our families. Moreover, the government and private institutions will support our decisions whether or not to have a child and we will receive the necessary support for our choices. In addition we will receive an education that honors and teaches the contributions of women, people of color, working class communities, and queer communities.

As illustrated in the Reproductive Justice Agenda, women's bodies, reproduction and sexuality are often used as the excuse and the target for unequal treatment in the attempt to control our communities. For example, some blame environmental degradation on the relatively high birth rates among women of color, both in the United States and in the Global South. We believe that by challenging

FIGURE 2. Intersectionality of Reproductive Justice with Social Justice Issues

FIGURE 3. Intersectionality of ACRJ's Reproductive Justice Work with Social Justice Issues

patriarchal social relations and addressing the intersection of racism, sexism, xenophobia, homophobia, and class oppression within a women of color context, we will be able to build the collective social, economic, and political power of all women and girls to make choices that protect and contribute to our reproductive health and overall well being. From this vision, we have developed key strategies and projects. From the perspective of a Reproductive Justice framework, the key problem for women is lack of power, resources and control. At ACRJ we organize to gain power and to make change on the grassroots, community, statewide, and national levels (see Figure 2).

Translating Vision into Action: ACRJ's Impact

Efforts to advance reproductive justice cannot be achieved by vision and analysis alone. In our work with Asian women and girls, we have translated our vision for reproductive justice into action.

Since 1998, ACRJ has instituted a youth organizing program that involves over 250 low-income Asian young women across California. ACRJ-trained youth leaders have won two campaigns, the School Safety Campaign and the Healthy Communities Campaign, protecting the reproductive

health of Asian women. The School Safety Campaign resulted in six school-wide sexual harassment policy changes as well as a district-wide task force on school safety for girls in Long Beach (Calif.). In collaboration with environmental justice groups, the Healthy Communities Campaign increased the visibility of reproductive health issues related to toxic emissions and culminated in victory when one of the most toxic medical waste incinerators in the nation was forced to close in 2002. ACRJ has partnered with the ACLU of Northern California to pass and enforce state legislation that simplifies sex education guidelines and ensures that public school sex education is comprehensive, accurate, and free of bias. Also, in response to the wide body of evidence that shows the health hazards of beauty products, ACRJ has established POLISH, the Participatory Research, Organizing, and Leadership Initiative for Safety and Health. POLISH participants are currently researching the degree to which Asian women and girls and nail salon workers are exposed to toxic chemicals through both personal use and professional occupation. The results will fill major gaps in information, and the project will increase Asian girls' and women's capacity to identify reproductive justice problems and intervene in their community's health. Figure 3 illustrates how ACRJ's work fits into a Reproductive Justice Agenda.

The ultimate goal of our work is to build self-determination for individuals and communities. We believe that translating the vision of our Reproductive Justice Agenda into action will yield social change on all levels. For example,

1. An individual woman or girl will acquire skills, leadership ability, and commitment to furthering reproductive justice;

2. A community will change its norms to support women and girls as community leaders;

3. An institution such as a church, school/school district, business/workplace, or legislative body will make changes to stop reproductive

oppression and protect reproductive justice for women and girls; and

4. Women and girls will gain complete self-determination.

NOTES

1. Roberts, Dorothy. "Race, Reproduction, and the Meaning of Liberty: Building A Social Justice Vision of Reproductive Freedom." Delivered 18 April 2000 at a Public Forum Presented by The Othmer Institute.

2. Ross, Loretta. "Revisions to the ACRJ Reproductive Justice paper." E-mail to the author. 3 August 2005.

THIRTY-THREE

◆◆◆

Living to Love (1993)

bell hooks

bell hooks describes herself as a "black woman intellectual" and "revolutionary activist." She is an educator, a prolific writer, and popular public speaker whose work focuses on gender, race, culture, and media representations.

Love heals. We recover ourselves in the act and art of loving. A favorite passage from the biblical Gospel of John that touches my spirit declares: "Anyone who does not love is still in death."

Many black women feel that we live lives in which there is little or no love. This is one of our private truths that is rarely a subject for public discussion. To name this reality evokes such intense pain that black women can rarely talk about it fully with one another.

It has not been simple for black people living in this culture to know love. Defining love in *The Road Less Traveled* as "the will to extend one's self for the purpose of nurturing one's own or another's personal growth," M. Scott Peck shares the prophetic insight that love is both an "intention and an action." We show love via the union of feeling and action. Using this definition of love, and applying it to black experience, it is easy to see how many black

folks historically could only experience themselves as frustrated lovers, since the conditions of slavery and racial apartheid made it extremely difficult to nurture one's own or another's spiritual growth. Notice, that I say, difficult, not impossible. Yet, it does need to be acknowledged that oppression and exploitation pervert, distort and impede our ability to love.

Given the politics of black life in this white-supremacist society, it makes sense that internalized racism and self-hate stand in the way of love. Systems of domination exploit folks best when they deprive us of our capacity to experience our own agency and alter our ability to care and to love ourselves and others. Black folks have been deeply and profoundly "hurt," as we used to say down home, "hurt to our hearts," and the deep psychological pain we have endured and still endure affects our capacity to feel and therefore our capacity to love. We are a wounded people. Wounded in that part of ourselves that would know love, that would be loving. The choice to love has always been a gesture of resistance for African Americans. And many of us have made that choice only to find ourselves unable to give or to receive love.

Slavery's Impact on Love

Our collective difficulties with the art and act of loving began in the context of slavery. It should not shock us that a people who were forced to witness their young being sold away; their loved ones, companions, and comrades beaten beyond all recognition; a people who knew unrelenting poverty, deprivation, loss, unending grief, and the forced separation of family and kin; would emerge from the context of slavery wary of this thing called love. They knew firsthand that the conditions of slavery distorted and perverted the possibility that they would know love or be able to sustain such knowing.

Though black folks may have emerged from slavery eager to experience intimacy, commitment, and passion outside the realm of bondage, they must also have been in many ways psychologically unprepared to practice fully the art of loving. No wonder then that many black folks established domestic households that mirrored the brutal arrangements they had known in slavery. Using a hierarchical model of family life, they created domestic spaces where there were tensions around power, tensions that often led black men to severely whip black women, to punish them for perceived wrongdoing, that led adults to beat children to assert domination and control. In both cases, black people were using the same harsh and brutal methods against one another that had been used by white slave owners against them when they were enslaved. . . . We know that slavery's end did not mean that black people who were suddenly free to love now knew the way to love one another well.

Slave narratives often emphasize time and time again that black people's survival was often determined by their capacity to repress feelings. In his 1845 narrative, Frederick Douglass recalled that he had been unable to experience grief when hearing of his mother's death since they had been denied sustained contact. Slavery socialized black people to contain and repress a range of emotions. Witnessing one another being daily subjected to all manner of physical abuse, the pain of over-work, the pain of brutal punishment, the pain of near-starvation, enslaved black people could rarely show sympathy or solidarity with one another just as that moment when sympathy and solace was most needed. They rightly feared reprisal. It was only in carefully cultivated spaces of social resistance, that slaves could give vent to repressed feelings. Hence, they learned to check the impulse to give care when it was most needed and learned to wait for a "safe" moment when feelings could be expressed. What form could love take in such a context, in a world where black folks never knew how long they might be together? Practicing love in the slave context could make one vulnerable to unbearable emotional pain. It was often easier for slaves to care for one another while being very mindful of the transitory nature of their intimacies. The social world of slavery encouraged black people to develop notions of intimacy connected to expedient practical reality. A slave who could not repress and contain emotion might not survive.

Repressed Emotions: A Key to Survival

The practice of repressing feelings as a survival strategy continued to be an aspect of black life long after slavery ended. Since white supremacy and racism did not end with the Emancipation Proclamation, black folks felt it was still necessary to keep certain emotional barriers intact. And, in the worldview of many black people, it became a positive attribute to be able to contain feelings. Over time, the ability to mask, hide and contain feelings came to be viewed by many black people as a sign of strong character. To show one's emotions was seen as foolish. Traditionally in Southern black homes, children were often taught at an early age that it was important to repress feelings. Often, when children were severely whipped, we were told not to cry. Showing one's emotions could lead to further punishment. Parents would say in the midst of painful punishments: "Don't even let me see a tear." Or if one dared to cry, they threatened further punishment by saying: "If you don't stop that crying, I'll give you something to cry about."

How was this behavior any different from that of the slave owner whipping the slave by denying access to comfort and consolation, denying even a space to express pain? And if many black folks were taught at an early age not only to repress emotions but to see giving expressions to feeling as a sign of weakness, then how would they learn to be fully open to love? Many black folks have passed down from generation to generation the assumption that to let one's self go, to fully surrender emotionally, endangers survival. They feel that to love weakens one's capacity to develop a stoic and strong character.

"Did You Ever Love Us?"

When I was growing up, it was apparent to me that outside the context of religion and romance, love was viewed by grown-ups as a luxury. Struggling to survive, to make ends meet, was more important than loving. In that context, the folks who seemed most devoted to the art and act of loving were the old ones, our grandmothers and great grandmothers, our granddaddys and great granddaddys, the Papas and Big Mamas. They gave us acceptance, unconditional care, attention and, most importantly, they affirmed our need to experience pleasure and joy. They were affectionate. They were physically demonstrative. Our parents and their struggling-to-get-ahead generation often behaved as though love was a waste of time, a feeling or an action that got in the way of them dealing with the more meaningful issues of life.

When teaching Toni Morrison's novel *Sula*, I am never surprised to see black female students nodding their heads in recognition when reading a passage where Hannah, a grown black woman, asks her mother, Eva: "Did you ever love us?" Eva responds with hostility and says: "You settin' here with your healthy-ass self and ax me did I love you? Them big old eyes in your head would a been two holes of maggots if I hadn't." Hannah is not satisfied with this answer for she knows that Eva has responded fully to her children's material needs. She wants to know if there was another level of affection, of feeling and action. She says to Eva: "Did you ever, you know, play with us?" Again Eva responds by acting as though the question is completely ridiculous:

> Play? Wasn't nobody playin' in 1895. Just 'cause you got it good now you think it was always this good? 1895 was a killer girl. Things was bad. Niggers was dying like flies. . . . What would I look like leapin' round that little old room playin' with youngins with three beets to my name?

Eva's responses suggest that finding the means for material survival was not only the most important gesture of care, but that it precluded all other gestures. This is a way of thinking that many black people share. It makes care for material well-being synonymous with the practice of loving. The reality is, of course, that even in a context of material privilege, love may be absent. Concurrently, within the context of poverty, where one must struggle to make ends meet, one might keep a spirit of love alive by making a space for playful engagement, the expression of creativity, for individuals to receive care and attention in relation to their emotional well-being, a kind of care that attends to hearts and minds as well as stomachs. As contemporary black people commit ourselves to collective recovery, we must recognize that attending to our emotional well-being is just as important as taking care of our material needs.

It seems appropriate that this dialogue on love in *Sula* takes place between two black women, between mother and daughter, for their interchange symbolizes a legacy that will be passed on through the generations. In fact, Eva does not nurture Hannah's spiritual growth, and Hannah does not nurture the spiritual growth of her daughter, Sula. Yet, Eva does embody a certain model of "strong" black womanhood that is practically deified in black life. It is precisely her capacity to repress emotions and do whatever is needed for the continuation of material life that is depicted as the source of her strength. . . .

If We Would Know Love

Love needs to be present in every black female's life, in all of our houses. It is the absence of love that has made it so difficult for us to . . . live fully. When we love ourselves we want to live fully. Whenever people talk about black women's lives, the emphasis is rarely on transforming society so that we can live fully, it is almost always about applauding how well we have "survived" despite harsh circumstances or how we can survive in the future. When we love ourselves, we know that we must do more than survive. We must have the means to live fully. To live fully, black women can no longer deny our need to know love.

If we would know love, we must first learn how to respond to inner emotional needs. This may mean undoing years of socialization where we have been taught that such needs are unimportant. Let me give an example. In her recently published book, *The Habit of Surviving: Black Women's Strategies for Life*, Kesho

Scott opens the book sharing an incident from her life that she feels taught her important survival skills:

> Thirteen years tall, I stood in the living room doorway. My clothes were wet. My hair was mangled. I was in tears, in shock, and in need of my mother's warm arms. Slowly, she looked me up and down, stood up from the couch and walked towards me, her body clenched in criticism. Putting her hands on her hips and planting herself, her shadow falling over my face, she asked in a voice of barely suppressed rage, "What happened?" I flinched as if struck by the unexpected anger and answered, "They put my head in the toilet. They say I can't swim with them." "They" were eight white girls at my high school. I reached out to hold her, but she roughly brushed my hands aside and said, "Like hell! Get your coat. Let's go."

. . . [Kesho] asserts: "My mother taught me a powerful and enduring lesson that day. She taught me that I would have to fight back against racial and sexual injustice." Obviously, this is an important survival strategy for black women. But Kesho was also learning an unhealthy message at the same time. She was made to feel that she did not deserve comfort after a traumatic painful experience, that indeed she was "out-of-line" to even be seeking emotional solace, and that her individual needs were not as important as the collective struggle to resist racism and sexism. Imagine how different this story would read if we were told that as soon as Kesho walked into the room, obviously suffering distress, her mother had comforted her, helped repair the damage to her appearance, and then shared with her the necessity of confronting (maybe not just then, it would depend on her psychological state whether she could emotionally handle a confrontation) the racist white students who had assaulted her. Then Kesho would have known, at age thirteen, that her emotional well-being was just as important as the collective struggle to end racism and sexism—that indeed these two experiences were linked.

Many black females have learned to deny our inner needs while we develop our capacity to cope and confront in public life. This is why we can often appear to be functioning well on jobs but be utterly dysfunctional in private. . . . I see this chaos and disorder as a reflection of the inner psyche, of the absence of well-being. Yet until black females believe, and hopefully learn when we are little girls, that our emotional well-being matters, we cannot attend to our needs. Often we replace recognition of inner emotional needs with the longing to control. When we deny our real needs, we tend to feel fragile, vulnerable, emotionally unstable and untogether. Black females often work hard to cover up these conditions.

Let us return to the mother in Kesho's story. What if the sight of her wounded and hurt daughter called to mind the mother's deep unaddressed inner wounds? What if she was critical, harsh, or just downright mean, because she did not want to break down, cry, and stop being the "strong black woman?" And yet, if she cried, her daughter might have felt her pain was shared, that it was fine to name that you are in pain, that we do not have to keep the hurt bottled up inside us. What the mother did was what many of us have witnessed our mothers doing in similar circumstances—she took control. She was domineering, even her physical posture dominated. Clearly, this mother wanted her black female presence to have more "power" than that of the white girls.

A fictional model of black mothering that shows us a mother able to respond fully to her daughters when they are in pain is depicted in Ntozake Shange's novel *Sassafrass, Cypress and Indigo.* Throughout this novel, Shange's black female characters are strengthened in their capacity to self-actualize by a loving mother. Even though she does not always agree with their choices she respects them and offers them solace. Here is part of a letter she writes to Sassafrass who is "in trouble" and wants to come home. The letter begins with the exclamation: "Of course you can come home! What do you think you could do to yourself that I wouldn't love my girl?" First giving love and acceptance, Hilda later chastises, then expresses love again:

> You and Cypress like to drive me crazy with all this experimental living. You girls need to stop chasing the coon by his tail. And I know you know what I'm talking about . . . Mark my words. You just come on home and we'll straighten out whatever it is that's crooked in your thinking. There's lots to do to keep busy. And nobody around to talk foolish talk or

experiment with. Something can't happen every day. You get up. You eat, go to work, come back, eat again, enjoy some leisure, and go back to bed. Now, that's plenty for most folks. I keep asking myself where did I go wrong? Yet I know in my heart I'm not wrong. I'm right. The world's going crazy and trying to take my children with it. Okay. Now I'm through with all that. I love you very much. But you're getting to be a grown woman and I know that too. You come back to Charleston and find the rest of yourself. Love, Mama.

Loving What We See

The art and practice of loving begins with our capacity to recognize and affirm ourselves. That is why so many self-help books encourage us to look at ourselves in the mirror and talk to the image we see there. Recently, I noticed that what I do with the image I see in the mirror is very unloving. I inspect it. From the moment I get out of bed and look at myself in the mirror, I am evaluating. The point of the evaluation is not to provide self-affirmation but to critique. Now this was a common practice in our household. When the six of us girls made our way downstairs to the world inhabited by father, mother and brother, we entered the world of "critique." We were looked over and told all that was wrong. Rarely did one hear a positive evaluation.

Replacing negative critique with positive recognition has made me feel more empowered as I go about my day. Affirming ourselves is the first step in the direction of cultivating the practice of being inwardly loving. I choose to use the phrase "inwardly loving" over self-love, because the very notion of "self" is so inextricably bound up with how we are seen by and in relation to others. Within a racist/sexist society, the larger culture will not socialize black women to know and acknowledge that our inner lives are important. Decolonized black women must name that reality in accord with others among us who understand as well that it is vital to nurture the inner life. As we examine our inner life, we get in touch with the world of emotions and feelings. Allowing ourselves to feel, we affirm our right to be inwardly

loving. Once I know what I feel, I can also get in touch with those needs I can satisfy or name those needs that can only be satisfied in communion or contact with others.

Where is the love when a black woman looks at herself and says: "I see inside me somebody who is ugly, too dark, too fat, too afraid—somebody nobody would love, 'cause I don't even like what I see;" or maybe: "I see inside me somebody who is so hurt, who is just like a ball of pain and I don't want to look at her 'cause I can't do nothing about that pain." The love is absent. To make it present, the individual has to first choose to see herself, to just look at that inner self without blame or censure. And once she names what she sees, she might think about whether that inner self deserves or needs love.

I have never heard a black woman suggest during confessional moments in a support group that she does not need love. She may be in denial about that need but it doesn't take much self-interrogation to break through this denial. If you ask most black women straight-up if they need love—the answer is likely to be yes. To give love to our inner selves we must first give attention, recognition and acceptance. Having let ourselves know that we will not be punished for acknowledging who we are or what we feel can name the problems we see. I find it helpful to interview myself, and I encourage my sisters to do the same. Sometimes it's hard for me to get immediately in touch with what I feel, but if I ask myself a question, an answer usually emerges.

Sometimes when we look at ourselves, and see our inner turmoil and pain, we do not know how to address it. That's when we need to seek help. I call loved ones sometimes and say, "I have these feelings that I don't understand or know how to address, can you help me?" There are many black females who cannot imagine asking for help, who see this as a sign of weakness. This is another negative debilitating world view we should unlearn. It is a sign of personal power to be able to ask for help when you need it. And we find that asking for what we need when we need it is an experience that enhances rather than diminishes personal power. Try it and see. Often we wait until a crisis situation has happened when we are compelled by circumstances to seek the help of others. Yet, crisis can often be avoided if we seek help when we recognize that we are no longer able to function well in a given situation. For black women who are addicted to being controlling, asking for help can be a loving practice of surrender, reminding us that we do not always have to be in charge. Practicing being inwardly loving, we learn not only what our souls need but we begin to understand better the needs of everyone around us as well.

Black women who are *choosing* for the first time (note the emphasis on choosing) to practice the art and act of loving should devote time and energy showing love to other black people, both people we know and strangers. Within white-supremacist capitalist patriarchy, black people do not get enough love. And it's always exciting for those of us who are undergoing a process of decolonization to see other black people in our midst respond to loving care. Just the other day T. told me that she makes a point of going into a local store and saying warm greetings to an older black man who works there. Recently, he wanted to know her name and then thanked her for the care that she gives to him. A few years ago when she was mired in self-hate, she would not have had the "will" to give him care. Now, she extends to him the level of care that she longs to receive from other black people when she is out in the world.

When I was growing up, I received "unconditional love" from black women who showed me by their actions that love did not have to be earned. They let me know that I deserved love; their care nurtured my spiritual growth.

Many black people, and black women in particular, have become so accustomed to not being loved that we protect ourselves from having to acknowledge the pain such deprivation brings by acting like only white folks or other silly people sit around wanting to be loved. When I told a group of black women that I wanted there to be a world where I can feel love, feel myself giving and receiving love, every time I walk outside my house, they laughed. For such a world to exist, racism and all other forms of domination need to change. To the extent that I commit my life to working to end domination, I help transform the world so that it is that loving place I want it to be.

Love Heals

Nikki Giovanni's "Woman Poem" has always meant a lot to me because it was one of the first pieces of writing that called out black women's self-hatred. Published in the anthology, *The Black Woman*, edited by Toni Cade Bambara, this poem ends with the lines: "face me whose whole life is tied up to unhappiness cause it's the only for real thing i know." Giovanni not only names in this poem that black women are socialized to be caretakers, to deny our inner needs, she also names the extent to which self-hate can make us turn against those who are caring toward us. The black female narrator says: "how dare you care about me—you ain't got no good sense—cause i ain't shit you must be lower than that to care." This poem was written in 1968. Here we are, decades later, and black women are still struggling to break through denial to name the hurt in our lives and find ways to heal. Learning how to love is a way to heal.

I am empowered by the idea of love as the will to extend oneself to nurture one's own or another's spiritual growth because it affirms that love is an action, that it is akin to work. For black people it's an important definition because the focus is not on material well-being. And while we know that material needs must be met, collectively we need to focus our attention on emotional needs as well. There is that lovely biblical passage in "Proverbs" that reminds us: "Better a dinner of herbs, where love is, than a stalled ox and hatred therewith."

When we as black women experience fully the transformative power of love in our lives, we will bear witness publicly in a way that will fundamentally challenge existing social structures. We will be more fully empowered to address the genocide that daily takes the lives of black people—men, women and children. When we know what love is, when we love, we are able to search our memories and see the past with new eyes; we are able to transform the present and dream the future. Such is love's power. Love heals.

THIRTY-FOUR

Public Eyes (2004)
Investigating the Causes of Breast Cancer

Marcy Jane Knopf-Newman

Marcy Jane Knopf-Newman is a professor of English at Boise State University with interests in gender and race, and expertise in Middle East Studies and multiethnic literatures of the United States. Her most recent book is *Beyond Slash, Burn, and Poison: Transforming breast cancer stories into action*.

"Whatdunit?"

Allie Light and Irving Saraf's documentary *Rachel's Daughters: Searching for the Causes of Breast Cancer* (1997) opens with a series of vehicles driving through a central California desert landscape accented with sparse wildflowers set against a vivid blue sky visible beyond the hills. The environment seems pure until a power line, which rests unobtrusively at the top of the camera's frame, enters the viewer's consciousness. The audience soon realizes that these cars are en route to a funeral. We see women crying, hugging as they gently place flowers on a casket. Though we do not know it yet, the body of a young woman lies inside that coffin. Throughout this opening sequence, we hear the voice of poet and ecologist Sandra Steingraber, setting the narrative in motion,

> We are a generation who was born and came of adult age during the most toxic and environmentally unregulated decade ever known. Whose baby food was contaminated with traces of DDT, PCBs, and DES. Our neighborhoods were sprayed with pesticides and filled with toxic waste. Most of these chemicals did not even exist before World War II. We are the generation whose early idealism opened the original generation gap. We didn't know that this gap would come to mean premature and early death in our thirties, forties, and fifties. We didn't know that the "in" generation was destined to become the cancer generation. We

didn't know that so many of our mothers would bury us.

Steingraber's voice-over gives the first hints as to whatdunit? That is, what killed her? We may not know who died, but we have an idea what killed her. It also links the film to Rachel Carson in crucial ways. The audience who listens to these words—while witnessing people grieving over a death—will hear resonances with Carson's *Silent Spring*. Indeed, the film *Rachel's Daughters* is as much a daughter of *Silent Spring* as the women with breast cancer featured in the film are daughters of Rachel. They are Rachel's daughters because they inherited the environment laden with toxic chemicals that her generation exploited. They are Rachel's daughters because they pursue the research questions about the causes of cancer that Carson put into the public sphere with her landmark book. And they are Rachel's daughters because they show us how their narratives and the supporting scientific evidence can lead to change.

Perhaps the most famous claim Carson made public in *Silent Spring* was about the carcinogenic "biocide" DDT (dichloro-diphenyl-trichloro-ethane). Concerned that there was no safe dose since no long-term scientific studies proved otherwise, she alluded to future irreparable damage that could occur if no one researched the potential dangers. Ironically, she posits, "since so many people came into extremely intimate contact with DDT and suffered no immediate ill effects the chemical must certainly be *innocent* of harm" (Carson 1962, 21; emphasis mine). Such an entrenched belief system—that these "elixirs of death" would be considered innocent until proven guilty—struck her as tragic. With the unregulated use of DDT, she anticipated higher cancer rates and worried about the effect on future generations. The film suggests that the woman buried at the beginning of *Rachel's Daughters* may have died as a result of exposure to the contaminants Carson worked tirelessly to limit.

Thirty-five years after the publication of *Silent Spring*, Light and Saraf created a film that revisits and revives Carson's central questions through the lens of breast cancer. That they merge her work with this specific type of cancer is significant: Carson herself was dying of the disease while writing this last book, although the public was not aware of that fact.[1] In the spirit of Carson's life and work, *Rachel's Daughters* awakens viewers who are versed in breast cancer literature, science, or medicine to a paradigm shift. The film unravels three mythologies persistent in public discourse about cancer. First, the film represents a diverse body of U.S. women with breast cancer: working-class and middle-class; African American, Chinese American, Native American, white, Latina; lesbian and heterosexual; women diagnosed in their twenties, thirties, forties, and fifties; and women from the south, the east, the north and the west. Second, it minimizes the use of barren war metaphors. Third, rather than wonder "why me?"—which usually encourages women to blame themselves—the women in the film set out on a journey to discover answers to the more complex and productive questions why? and what causes the disease? Decentering the expected breast cancer discourse leads the film's protagonists and creators to investigate environmental links to the disease and discover why women are diagnosed and dying from breast cancer at alarming rates.

Propelling the film's narrative structure is a new mode of inquiry—one that blends investigative journalism with hard-boiled detective work. In the second scene of the documentary, each of the women with breast cancer gets labeled as an "investigator" or "detective" as they take on the role of private eyes who probe into what caused their breast cancer. There are eight such women, but I hone in on one in particular, Jennifer Mendoza, a thirty-two year old Latina nanny. Although her role in the documentary is the smallest of the group, her presence functions as the film's emotional core. Precisely halfway through *Rachel's Daughters,* we learn that the body in the casket in the opening scene was Jennifer's. Thus she embodies the warning that Carson sounded in the fable that begins *Silent Spring.* Jennifer's body becomes a testament to the need for laws regulating substances that *indicate* harm. For she believes that exposure to DDT led to her cancer, and by extension, to cancer in the farm-worker community she grew up in. Her premature

death feels like déjà vu; just like Carson, Jennifer dies of breast cancer while making the public aware of the dangers pesticides pose. Unlike Carson, Jennifer displays her deteriorating health before the camera. Light and Saraf situate Jennifer's death in ways that interrupt the film's narrative and motivate us—citizens and scientists alike—to intervene with a strategy and an argument for preventing breast cancer. The brevity of Jennifer's life and appearance on screen serves as a cautionary tale to propel viewers into action, action that promotes collaboration among women with cancer, scientists, and activists; action that includes and highlights poor women and women of color; action that investigates the environmental and the biological.

Just the Facts, Mam(m)

Typically detective narratives intimate a crime has taken place. Of course, *Rachel's Daughters* begins with death, though we do not yet know who has died nor how or why she died. Certainly something is out of synch; the natural order of the life cycle is suspended here because we are told mothers are burying their daughters. But a murder did not bring these women to the graveyard. Or dit it? Janette Sherman provocatively posits this question while wondering why those who pollute the environment are not held responsible: "Dr. John Gofman said: 'I am aware of no instance in the civilian economy where we take it as a premise that injury and murder of members of the public are to be regarded as beneficent acts.' Yes, *murder* is the word he used. Think about it! If you or I cause harm, and are told we are causing harm, and don't stop, and it results in the death of a person, wouldn't we be put in prison before we could blink an eye? Why have corporations been allowed to escape punishment for the harm they have caused?" (Sherman 2000, 218). Gofman's provocative use of the term "murder" does not prove a direct cause-and-effect relationship between pollution and cancer. His hyperbolic language certainly implies wrongdoing and projects blame while he suggests that producers of toxic substances should be held accountable for the damage their products cause. Gofman's discourse positions the political nature of breast cancer—especially in one strand of dominant rhetoric that blames women's lifestyle choices rather than investigating larger systemic causes of the disease. For many farmworker families there is no agency in where one lives or what one does for a living. Therefore, blaming women with cancer for "choices" they make within the context of Jennifer's community is not attuned to the complex way that race and class factor into this equation. And this is one gesture the film makes: rather than pointing fingers at women's dietary or reproductive choices, it looks for answers in larger social, political, and institutional forces.

If the first scene of *Rachel's Daughters* suggests that a crime has occurred, the second scene shows us the detectives collecting theories about how and why it happened. Nancy Evans, a fifty-something white woman who is the lead detective, invites her cohorts to tell their stories: "we have come here today as women living with breast cancer to find out why, not just why me? or why us? but why so many of us have this disease." They first convene in a San Francisco house to share their individual cancer stories, each of which doubles as a clue: how they found out about their diagnosis, about their mothers' breast cancer, what course of treatment they chose, and how their physicians minimized their concerns. The camera pans the room following the women tightly as they speak while capturing knowing glances from their peers. Interspersed within each verbal telling of the story are images that the camera uses to reinforce theories of causation the speaker reports. For instance, Essie Mormon, a forty-something African American woman, shares with the group the story of her diagnosis and her theory of its cause: "I was raised in rural Mississippi where DDT was used to kill the bugs and stuff on plants. I remember the stuff flying around in the air like fog. I said to one of the doctors, 'I wonder if this exposure to DDT could be a cause of this breast cancer.' And the doctor said to me in this greater-than-thou attitude: 'Well, I don't think so.'". . . As in Essie's case, in each of these narratives is a doctor who did not believe they had breast cancer or whom they had to fight to get a biopsy or mammogram. Personal narrative underscores the larger purpose of the film—to detect what causes breast cancer—but personal experiences also generate their research questions. They work collaboratively to collect facts from their stories and from scientists to postulate whatdunit? Each woman extrapolates from her story to decide what larger systemic questions she will investigate as they divide the detective work: pesticides, hormones (birth control, hormone replacement therapy [HRT]), genetics, electromagnetic fields (EMFs), polychlorinated biphenyls (PCBs), and radiation.

The new way the film approaches cancer is made clear by the way the women discuss it: there is no mistaking these women for scientists or reporters. They are novices. And this is part of the film's argument: their personal concerns guide their questions, and their emotions affect the way they arrive at conclusions. Their inexperience as scientists makes them, perhaps, more susceptible to an emotional perspective or to be easily persuaded. The documentary style, however, also follows some elements of the generic formula guiding hard-boiled detective stories, which legitimates the use of sentiment in this context. Heta Pyrhönen outlines the traditional plot of this subgenre, which hinges on "the story of the investigation, with a focus on what will happen next" (Pyrhönen 1999, 21). In other words, the crime does not take center stage. Because the primary subject is the detective and not the crime, Pyrhönen argues that "this subgenre evokes a more emotional form of reader participation than does the 'whodunit'" (Pyrhönen 1999, 22). Of course, in traditional detective films and novels, the successful investigator is devoid of emotions. Indeed, when s/he begins to feel or become personally involved in a crime, s/he begins to make mistakes; feelings cloud his/her objectivity and judgment. But in *Rachel's Daughters* the reverse is true.

As the emotional core of the documentary, Jennifer Mendoza's presence in the film elicits viewer participation. Unlike all the other investigators, she speaks of her illness in the present tense, and she wears a cap on her head because she is still bald from chemotherapy. Likely because she has less distance from cancer, she cannot speak about it without tearing up. And, as audience members watch her tell the story of her disease, it becomes increasingly difficult not to cry along with her:

> I was first diagnosed with breast cancer in 1993 at the age of twenty-eight. And I had known that I had breast cancer for five years, but nobody believed me. And I didn't want to believe that I had it either, so I kept letting doctors say

"oh, you're too young." Eventually I found a surgeon who would do a biopsy, and it turned out that I did have a tumor. And my breast wasn't healing well and they found another tumor. And I did the strongest chemotherapy and a year and a half later I was diagnosed with cancer—with metastatic breast cancer—and now it's in my liver and my bones and I also had a brain tumor and that was pretty devastating. I never anticipated that I wouldn't get cancer again, but I always thought that I'd have a little more time.

As she speaks about her chemotherapy treatment, the camera cuts away to a close-up shot to a clear fluid dripping from an IV tube. Taken in concert with all of the environmental hazards shown during the narratives, this shot turns the drug into a suspect as well. Images of chemotherapy in this context juxtaposed with stories of a childhood surrounded by pesticides paints a bleak picture of a life sandwiched between chemicals treating cancer and chemicals that possibly caused cancer—and, significantly, a life in which few choices could be made to limit exposure to those substances. Racism, sexism, and classism converge as Jennifer's intuitive sense about her body gets silenced by medical professionals. Zillah Eisenstein blends all of these concerns about power: "breast cancer is more socially, economically, and racially constructed than it is genetically inherited. This means understanding a range of social factors: an increased number of women being exposed to toxicity in the workplace, shifting discourses about women's health, so-called science narratives with their masculinist and racialized assumptions, and global capital with its petro/chemical-pharmaceutical empire and postindustrial-medical complex" (Eisenstein 2001, 85–86).

In this sociopolitical context, Eisenstein offers a way of seeing how these often unarticulated factors contribute to increased exposure to carcinogenic substances for the most disenfranchised populations. Racism, sexism, and classism collide here in a couple of important ways. First, few studies focus on Latina women's health, let alone breast cancer incidence and mortality rates. Second, little attention is paid to the labor and health conditions of people like migrant farmworkers. Third, the way women's breasts get fetishized in U.S. culture privileges white women's bodies as valuable—if only to serve heterosexual male fantasies—in such a way that erases brown women's bodies. All of these elements play a role in the health care setting: the way Jennifer's concerns about her body were trivialized and silenced indicates that these dominant cultural ideologies seep into medical institutions as well.

The ways in which Latina bodies are devalued by agribusiness in the context of farmworker communities compels Jennifer to uncover the possible cause of breast cancer in her body and in her community. She knows who she wants to interview, in part, because she already has a strong suspicion of what caused her breast cancer at such an early age. As she volunteers, the film cuts from the first group meeting to follow Jennifer climbing a staircase into an office building as she explains her rationale for selecting her subject: "I'm interested in interviewing Marion Moses because she's an expert on the link between cancer and pesticides. She's been very active in the migrant farm community, and prior to my generation everyone was a migrant farmworker in my family. Down below my house they grew pesticide-laden soybeans, and I drank the water that ran off into the creek." Embedded in her story is the hypothesis that pesticides may cause cancer. Woven into her theory is the tangled web of racism, classism, and sexism that controlled both her home and her family's work environments.

Although Jennifer's story already puts forth a compelling and plausible theory about the link between breast cancer and pesticides, her visit with epidemiologist Marion Moses provides the audience with some facts that support her theories.[2] Both women sit down together, side by side, facing the camera, suggesting a collaborative dialogue; the camera angle encompasses both of them, indicating this process of inquiry. Jennifer poses questions that allow Moses to validate her intuitive sense of her body and illness in ways that the medical professionals she dealt with did not. The investigation commences when Jennifer asks a question reminiscent of Carson: "For those of us born in the sixties, how much DDT do we have in our bodies?" To respond, Moses historicizes DDT as a post–World War II product. While she relates this narrative, black-and-white archival footage shows farmers spraying cows with DDT, factory machines mixing the chemicals, and military planes preparing to spray urban and rural landscapes alike. The wartime marching band music in the background accents this propaganda footage. These film images document and allude to answers. Gradually Moses's narrating voice fades out to be replaced with a vintage newsreel voice who promises: "Today's target for this B–25 is Rockford, Illinois. A peacetime mission to spread five hundred gallons of DDT, the army's miracle insecticide, over the city stricken with an infantile paralysis epidemic. By spraying the city, authorities will test the theory that insects are carriers of the dread germ. A farmer turns to an instrument of peace, becomes an instrument of science, and may become the means of saving countless lives." This deep, male radio-announcer voice serves as an ironic reminder of the military's practices, practices intended to *protect* American citizens but that possibly harmed them instead. Those words and images sit uncomfortably in the mind of the viewer as Moses corroborates Jennifer's theories about what caused the cancer in her body. Moses links the current and historical situation to Rachel Carson, who called these chemicals "elixirs of death." The audience watches black-and-white footage of Carson serenely walking through the woods with her binoculars in hand as Moses reveals that she now calls these toxins "the Rachel Carson chemicals."

In this one-on-one interview, Moses teaches the audience that everyone has DDE, the substance DDT becomes once it breaks down in our bodies. This is due, in part, to postwar spraying described in the newsreel; after widespread government use, pesticides like DDT become popular agricultural tools. The danger for women is in the way DDT enters mammalian bodies and mimics the female hormone estrogen. With this information, Moses offers the audience its first important clue: DDT and similar chemicals become foreign invaders, mimic estrogen, and interfere with the body's hormone production: "Some of them are called xeno, xenoestrogens. Xeno means foreign; it's a Greek word, so it means chemicals that are foreign to the body. Our body works, our ovaries and the uterus and the testes, and all of our endocrine functions work because they are very finely tuned. Well, these chemicals—these environmental chemicals—can throw that out of balance. It's called disruption. And so they're called

endocrine disruptors."[3] To demonstrate how ubiquitous these chemicals are, Moses shows Jennifer pesticides currently on the market that behave like estrogen if they come into contact with our bodies. People store many pesticides similar to DDT in their homes: kelthane (more commonly known as insect or vegetable dust), methoxychlor, lindane. These are all chlorinated hydrocarbons that act like female hormones.[4] These products do not label their carcinogenic potential for consumers. Although DDT may not be on the U.S. market any longer, other chemicals interfere with our bodies in the same fashion, most notably PCBs, which, according to Moses, exist in "snow, wind, the arctic snow, wildlife, people's tissue, newborn babies, everywhere they've looked to test for these chemicals."

In what may appear to be a non sequitur, Jennifer pursues a concern about diet by asking, "what does it mean to eat low on the food chain?" Moses's answer, "Not eating things that come from animals," seems at the outset to support the dominant discourse suggesting women need to be responsible for their health by changing their diet. Implicit in this imperative is that she is to blame if she does not watch her diet with an eye toward "preventing" breast cancer.[5] This issue is significant, however, because when we eat, we do not just eat the food on our plates. Moses elaborates, "If everything is contaminated—if the seas are contaminated, if the lakes are contaminated, if the water where you lived is contaminated—everything has to go somewhere. In my work with farmworkers, you'll never convince me that any level of a cancer-causing pesticide is safe. People like Jennifer and farmworker children, I think, are paying the price." Identifying the risk of eating explains that when we eat meat, chicken, or fish we also take in the food eaten by those animals. If their food—other animals and plants—is contaminated, we incorporate all of their contaminated materials into our blood and tissue in addition to the contaminants we take in on our own. Light and Saraf splice in images of a damaged planet that we see as Moses explains the hazards of pollution on the animals that we consume. They juxtapose images of fish swimming near the ocean's floor in what appears to be clean water, a dark trash-filled wave crashing against the shore, and a helicopter spraying pesticides on a farm as workers harvest the crop. We all ingest pollution in same way, but, returning to Jennifer's initial concerns,

Moses concludes by exposing the need for further studies on farmworkers and their families whose proximity to pesticides on a daily basis warrants further investigation.

The narrative frame of *Rachel's Daughters* asks viewers to participate in piecing together the clues as the investigation unfolds. The questions that arise in Jennifer's session with Moses may not be answered definitively, but they lead citizens and scientists in the direction of pursuing research that combines the study of the environment with an examination of power that structures unequal relations between agribusiness and farmworkers. Each meeting between the investigators and scientists builds on the previous one in ways that illustrate the complex landscape of studying cancer. For it is not just what a woman eats, or where she lives, or where she works that predicts a future cancer diagnosis. Nor will her blood relatives' history of breast cancer indicate a woman's chance of developing the disease. Light and Saraf make this clear by constructing a tight argument that demonstrates the role of the environment in increased breast cancer incidence and mortality. If one were to gather the story of breast cancer from the mass media, one might believe that the answers to "curing" the disease lie entirely in genetics. Steingraber also challenges the perception that diet alone explains the increased incidence rates when she echoes Moses's caution about eating high on the food chain. Steingraber depicts this cumulative effect that can create problems in the breast: "If you've got herbicides in your drinking water and you're spraying some on your lawn, and you're getting a little in your diet. Those can all add up to something that's quite significant. And nobody's looking at that right now." Like Moses, she points to an area for further research. To support her claim, Steingraber tells her cancer story. In her home state of Illinois, some studies implicate the triazine family of herbicides in breast cancer in animals and humans. Regardless of whether or not pesticides get phased out, the nature of their chemical composition means that the substances we've already used remain in our soil, drinking water, fog, and rain. Her evocative words describe how contaminants saturate the soil and run off into the drinking water and evaporate into the rain: "A woman can be diagnosed with breast cancer, leave her doctor's office,

stand in the rain at the bus stop, and there'll be breast carcinogens falling on her." While she illustrates this scenario, the camera turns to Essie opening her umbrella to walk to her first interview. Thus the film forces viewers to witness the shift not only from the visual image of a tractor in Illinois to Essie at a bus stop in the rain, but also from the abstract theories about chemical carcinogens to a real person in the documentary with whom viewers come to identify.

Forecasting breast cancer risk gets further complicated, however, depending upon the age of the woman. Menarche and menopause play a crucial role in this scenario, as epidemiologist Devra Lee Davis points out: "when you get to be an adolescent your breast is starting to actually grow. During the time the breast is growing it's getting hit with more DDT. Finally, you get close to the change of life, and your ovaries are no longer producing as much estrogen as they were. But guess what's in your fat in your body? All that DDT that you've been exposed to in your life and all the other xenoestrogens." These hormonal factors become important because one of the proven "vulnerability factors," as Davis refers to them, for breast cancer is a woman's lifetime exposure to estrogen. Davis backs up her scientific theories by reciting some of the mortality statistics of women who die from the disease in industrialized countries. To appeal to our sentiment, she concludes by saying, "These numbers, these statistics are human beings with the tears removed." This statement hits home as the film cuts abruptly to a weakened, emaciated, gaunt Jennifer speaking from a hospital bed.

Light and Saraf's gesture of moving from the findings that the investigators weave together about the pesticides, fat, and hormones to the startling reality of cancer mortality is crucial. It represents the way in which this film will not allow statistics to become abstract. It demonstrates how the film refuses to allow these stories to be perceived as merely anecdotal. The detective narrative is interrupted when the film cuts to the startling scene of Jennifer's hospitalization for neutropenia, which makes us add up all the clues about the suspect DDT. From her bed, she tells the audience that her neutropenic fever originated as an "illness created by a broken-down immune system from chemotherapy." In other words, the chemotherapy agents compromised her immune system to the extent that her body could not fight off invasion by germs. In what would be her last words in the film, a bald and trembling Jennifer who tries to keep from crying says, "I guess I just want to say this all needs to change. This is just too much torture." Her words and presence serve as a reminder for the audience that current treatments do not suffice. To underscore this point, the film splices in earlier footage of a healthy-looking Jennifer with a full head of dark, curly hair, eating a piece of chocolate cake at the Women and Cancer walk in Golden Gate Park where she first met the film's directors. The movement between images from her past and present emphasize the tragedy of a thirty-two-year-old woman living through and dying from breast cancer that metastasized to her liver, brain, and bones.

Jennifer appears one more time in the documentary when her father takes her home to die. At that point the tragically short dates of her life—1964–1996—flash over a smiling photograph of a prepubescent, innocent child. The placement of her death—precisely halfway through the film—amplifies the sentimental tone as it becomes obvious that the funeral at the beginning of the documentary was hers. The film flashes back to scenes from the drive through central California and the funeral; this time we are placed in the perspective of a passenger in one of the cars driving toward the cemetery. Now when we see the funeral scene we are a part of it; we are more attuned to the fact that parents are burying their children. This is not merely a statistical fact. It's personal. And Jennifer's harrowing story and her death sensitize viewers to this by tugging at their emotions as she says goodbye to the directors and the other detectives from the back of her father's van. Something is out of order. This sentiment and fact guides and fragments the film's narrative time. It does so in part to remind the audience of the mystery these women try to unravel. But it also serves to tell a very different story about breast cancer. In this documentary, women are not "cured"; "survival" is as cunning as the cancer cells. Jennifer's life is cut short just as her death interrupts the film's narrative and charges it with an affective sentiment that has the potential to propel viewers into action.

The specter of DDT as a murder suspect—evidenced in the death of Jennifer—shows up in other interviews throughout the remainder of the film. Although the detectives explore a variety of suspicious toxins, DDT remains the one that turns up the most often. For instance, it comes up in discussions of cancer clusters in suburban Long Island, which is one of the places Carson followed while writing her manuscript; it also shows up in inner-city tenements inhabited primarily by African Americans (Lear 1997). But one aspect of pesticide use that was not explicitly on Carson's radar screen was the way that poor people and people of color were and are exposed to harmful chemicals at greater rates and for longer periods of time.

Perhaps because Jennifer's death leaves such an indelible mark on the other investigators, Essie adds to this mix an aspect of how environmental racism taints perceptions of breast cancer incidence and mortality. She wonders why epidemiologists study the farm owners rather than the migrant workers who live and work in and around the pesticides: "I read that some of the studies that were supposed to be done on farmworkers, that they did them on the farm owners." Complicating the issue of race and class is that of nation and language; Marion Moses's research reports that two-thirds of migrant workers are foreign born: "92 percent Mexican, 4 percent other Latinos, 3 percent Asian, and 1 percent Caribbean" (Moses 1993, 162). Moreover, this sometimes hidden distinction is significant, as Rachel, one of the film's investigators, concurs that scientists conduct less research on the workers even though they are the most exposed: ". . . research that has been done on pesticide exposures has been done on growers, people who own the farms, and much less so on workers. And they don't speak English. But if we want to get at the answers those are the people we need to be studying." Nancy echoes Carson when she states, "Absolutely, and they are the most exposed. Really the pesticides are just creating bigger pests that become resistant to the chemicals." The detectives pose these questions to each other as they realize there are far more questions than answers.

The clues the investigators piece together may not yet reveal a unified, airtight case about the suspect pollutants. But the documentary offers some clear directions to guide research. For one function of the documentary, according to Paula Rabinowitz, is "to induce feeling, thought, and action" (Rabinowitz 1994, 8). It should be clear at this juncture that Light and Saraf infuse all of the above elements into their film. . . . The scientific and personal narratives in the film underscore the direction science should follow: that is, in the footsteps of Rachel Carson. Midway through the film, Steingraber accentuates the powerful meaning of the documentary's title. "I consider myself a daughter of Rachel," she says in response to the criticism leveled against Carson by her critics, who could not understand why a woman without biological children would want to protect the environment for future generations. As she speaks, more black-and-white footage of Carson walking through the Maine woods and writing on her porch illuminates the screen. These silent images give way to one of Carson's only television interviews with *CBS Reports.* The camera remains close-up on her face as she says, "We have to remember the children born today are exposed to these chemicals from birth. Perhaps even before birth. Now what is going to happen then in adult life?" This segment supports Steingraber's awareness of the extent to which Carson worked hard to make her science useful to the public: "I often think of her while she was in radiation treatment trying to piece together scientific evidence, to try to make it a compelling narrative for the rest of us." Those words could be used to think about how this film and the scientists, survivors, and activists represented in it construct stories about breast cancer that are provocative enough to move viewers to action. For just as Carson intended *Silent Spring* to capture her audience's attention as concerned citizens—enough to motivate them to act—this film anticipates that viewers will become Rachel's daughters by taking on the role of detective and pushing scientists to be accountable to the public. . . .

Guilty Until Proven Innocent: The Precautionary Principle

In the documentary's final scene, the remaining detectives convene on a beach with a vibrant green, grassy hill in the background. They discuss how scary it feels to walk away from this investigation without solving the mystery. Their frustration and fear are understandable, but as a political

tool this film can potentially help set the research agenda by changing the types of questions we ask about breast cancer. For instance, Rachel says, "part of the problem is that the field of science is such a competitive field that there is little incentive for scientists to actually try and work together. I mean we're told it's genetics or it's the environment. Well, the reality is it's probably both." Indeed. This film demonstrates how powerful multidisciplinary scientific collaboration can be by editing together a diversity of scientific voices. If all of the people studying cancer worked together as do the detectives in the documentary, it might be possible to achieve results that answer some of these lingering questions.

The investigation ends with another possibly lethal interruption, yet another sign that we remain far from a sure-fire treatment or "cure." Two investigators divulge that their breast cancer has recurred: Pamela, an African American woman in her forties, and Susan, a white woman in her fifties. Uttering the last words of the film, Susan says, "I'm alive now, but behind me there are four women who have died and behind each of them there are four more women." Susan's provocative remark is particularly striking because ten of the women featured in *Rachel's Daughters* are now dead. Whether viewers know about these more recent deaths or not, her pronouncement sits indelibly in the audience's mind because these numbers become embodied as women wearing black dresses and veils draped over their heads cover the mountain behind the group. A statistic appears written over their image: "180,000 women are diagnosed each day. 44,000 of those women die." These women comprise a racially and ethnically diverse group. The juxtaposition of text and veiled women dressed in the color of mourning is a warning for what will happen if we do not tend to the environmental causes of cancer. But it is also a provocative form of protest. For although these women are not members of the international feminist peace network known as Women in Black, both groups practice a similar political strategy.[6] Women in Black renders visible the suffering of those who can no longer speak, oftentimes because they are dead. The presence of the women wearing black in this film, a group also called Women in Black, serves as an intervention: mothers can avoid burying their daughters if viewers become actively engaged in the push for environmental research about breast cancer. In other words, viewers must continue the work begun by Rachel Carson.

It should be remembered that Carson herself, while dying of breast cancer, worked through a daunting set of questions that seemed unanswerable at the time. To trace the complex history and science behind post–World War II chemicals, she also had to collaborate with activists and scientists from a variety of subspecialty fields. That collective effort grew into *Silent Spring*. And although there is no tangible solution to the mystery that Jennifer and her cohorts attempt to solve in the film, their labor produces some important outcomes. The detective process does not lead them to definitive answers, but it does show us a new way to look at cancer—or any public health issue, for that matter—and it leaves us with a new way of approaching research and activism. Therefore, the solution to the crime is not whodunit or whatdunit, but what can we collaboratively, collectively do about it? The film answers by asking the audience to take up where it left off. Concluding the film with Women in Black alerts us to the fact that Jennifer and the other women in the film who have since died are at risk of becoming a statistic if we do not act.

When activists, scientists, and policy makers gather together, the potential for new methodologies is remarkable. This was the case when Marion Moses worked with Cesar Chavez to create a union for farmworkers in Delano, California, she explains: "the signing of the table grape contracts was delayed by at least a year because the workers refused to compromise the issue of worker and consumer health and safety in regard to pesticide use" (Moses 1973, 848). Placing a set of social and economic concerns together on the table ultimately helped health care systemically—as opposed to sick care—for migrant farm laborers as well as those who would eat the food products they cultivated. More recently, one can witness a new attitude toward pesticide use in the statement that grew out of the 1998 Wingspread Conference: . . . "When an activity raises threats of harm to human health or the environment, precautionary measures should be taken even if some cause and effect relationships are not fully established scientifically. In this context the proponent of an activity, rather than the public, should bear the burden of proof" (Raffensperger 1998). This statement, otherwise known as the precautionary principle, asks

that chemicals not be treated as innocent until proven guilty.[7] Rather, it implies, harm could be prevented if suspicious toxins or pollutants were studied *before* they were put on the market. Instead of asking people who are sick with illnesses like cancer to testify before Congress and actively work to hold industry accountable for their harm, the precautionary principle makes the corporate entity producing the substance take responsibility for showing their safety. One of the organizations that educates the public about the need for institutionalizing this practice is the Silent Spring Institute, which Light and Saraf feature towards the end of the documentary. This institute pays homage to Carson in name and practice by bringing together activists and scientists to study the cause of breast cancer on Cape Cod. By highlighting this collaborative organization, the film presents a model that could be reproduced in other contexts like farmworker communities to study the links between public health and pesticides.

Rachel's Daughters and the scientists presented in it all allude to the potential held in one of Carson's initial, bold proposals of testing a product's harm prior to placing it on the market for public consumption. As the film makes clear, however, such practices would not necessarily produce positive results unless every nation embraced it. For once harmful chemicals enter the atmosphere, they travel across national boundaries in the air, water, and soil. Zillah Eisenstein imagines what a world would look like if everyone agreed to place public health before profit:

> Agricultural pesticides would be largely eliminated. Foods would not be packaged in carcinogenic plastics. Cows would not be injected with hormones such as rBST to increase milk production. . . . These types of choices are not part of a natural landscape but rather are specifically derivative of a corporate-consumer mentality set on efficiency, productivity, and profitability. This mental set draws the parameters for a particular kind of science. It makes it harder to get grant money for interdisciplinary research, which attempts to look at the multiple factors defining chemical risk.
>
> (*Eisenstein 2001, 89*)

While in some ways Eisenstein speaks of a U.S.-specific context, her concern is decidedly global. For she reminds readers that although DDT was outlawed in the U.S. in 1972, as a result of the work Carson initiated, "it remains in use as a cheap and effective control for malaria in most poor countries. As late as 1991, the U.S. exported at least 4.1 million pounds of pesticides banned or suspended from use here, including tons of DDT" (Eisenstein 2001, 89). Exporting DDT to the Third World while banning it in the United States does not reduce cancer incidence and mortality rates. What it does suggest is that corporations manufacturing toxic chemicals continue to operate with economic concerns overriding concerns about the ways in which exporting pesticides reproduces racism, classism, and sexism on a global scale. This confirms the need for activists to pressure companies to incorporate—not only in rhetoric but in practice—the precautionary principle.

Cognizant of the imperative for a world free from such carcinogenic substances, the United Nations included precautionary principle language in its treaty on persistent organic pollutants, signed by over 122 countries including the United States, at the 2001 Stockholm Convention. Steingraber alerts us to its significance: "The treaty is a strong one. It immediately abolishes from worldwide production and use eight toxic pesticides and severely restricts the use of two others. Beginning in 2025, it prohibits the use of PCBs in electrical transformers. . . . Dioxins and furans are to be reduced immediately and eventually eliminated "where feasible," and "DDT is allowed only on a limited basis and strictly for malaria control" (Steingraber 2001, 286). *Rachel's Daughters* leads viewers along with its detectives to reach the conclusion that the precautionary principle is a logical preventative tool for cancer as well as for other public health concerns. The argument conveyed through the personal and scientific narratives in the documentary make it obvious that if such practices had been implemented soon after the publication of *Silent Spring* in 1962, many of these cancer stories either might not exist or they might have had less morbid endings. Through the union of affectively charged stories and scientific hypotheses and studies, *Rachel's Daughters* presents not only a paradigm shift that embeds the environment in every layer of cancer research, but it also asks us to think in dramatically different terms: that new chemical substances are guilty until proven innocent.

NOTES

I would like to thank Leslie Durham, Kate McCullough, Jacky O'Connor, Michelle Payne, and Tara Penry for their helpful comments on various drafts. I would also like to express my gratitude to Allie Light and Marion Moses who generously provided me with materials used in this article.

1. See Linda Lear's *Rachel Carson* and Sandra Steingraber's *Living Downstream*.

2. Marion Moses's epidemiological work is importantly aimed at Spanish- and English-speaking audiences as she publishes her work in both languages. She has also created a bilingual video for training and education on the dangers of pesticides.

3. See Theo Colborn, Dianne Dumanoski, and John Peterson Myers' *Our Stolen Future* for a study of the myriad ways that endocrine disrupters affect (1) the immune system by making the body less resistant to disease, (2) human intelligence by increasing learning disabilities, (3) reproduction by lowering sperm counts, and (4) puberty by creating earlier menarche.

4. On pesticides that mimic female hormones, see Marion Moses's *Designer Poisons*.

5. See Bob Arnot's *The Breast Cancer Prevention Diet*.

6. Women in Black began in 1988 as a coalition of women who gathered in the West Bank to protest Israel's occupation. Since then this loosely organized group has convened in the United States, England, Italy, Spain, Azerbaijan, and the former Yugoslavia to stand in silent vigil on behalf of those who have been killed, tortured, or raped as a result of wartime atrocities.

7. See Dan Fagin and Marianne Lavelle's *Toxic Deception*.

REFERENCES

Arnot, B. 1999. *The Breast Cancer Prevention Diet: The Powerful Food, Supplements, and Drugs That Can Combat Breast Cancer*. Boston: Little, Brown.

Carson, R. 1962. *Silent Spring*. Boston: Houghton Mifflin.

Colborn, T., D. Dumanoski, J. Peterson Myers. 1996. *Our Stolen Future: Are We Threatening Our Fertility, Intelligence, and Survival? A Scientific Detective Story*. New York: Dutton.

Eisenstein, Z. 2001. *Man-Made Breast Cancers*. Ithaca: Cornell University Press.

Fagin, D., and M. Lavelle. 1999. *Toxic Deception: How the Chemical Industry Manipulates Science, Bends the Law, and Endangers Your Health*. Monroe: Common Courage Press.

Lear, L. 1997. *Rachel Carson: Witness for Nature*. New York: Henry Holt.

Moses, M. 1973. "'Viva la Causa!'" *American Journal of Nursing* 73: 842–48.

——. 1992. *Harvest of Sorrow: Farm Workers and Pesticides.* San Francisco: Pesticide Education Center.

——. 1993. "Farmworkers and Pesticides." In *Confronting Environmental Racism: Voices from the Grassroots,* ed. R. D. Bullard. Boston: South End Press.

——. 1995. *Designer Poisons: How to Protect Your Health and Home from Toxic Pesticides.* San Francisco: Pesticide Education Center.

Pyrhönen, H. 1999. *Mayhem and Murder: Narrative and Moral Problems in the Detective Story.* Toronto: University of Toronto Press.

Rabinowitz, P. 1994. *They Must Be Represented: The Politics of Documentary.* New York: Verso.

Rachel's Daughters: Searching for the Causes of Breast Cancer. 1997. Directed by Allie Light and Irving Saraf. 107 minutes. New York: Women Make Movies.

Raffensperger, C. 1998. "Wingspread Conference on the Precautionary Principle." *http://www.sehn.org/wing.html.*

Sherman, J. D. 2000. *Life's Delicate Balance: Guide to Causes and Prevention of Breast Cancer.* New York: Taylor and Francis.

Steingraber, S. 1997. *Living Downstream: An Ecologist Looks at Cancer and the Environment.* Reading, Mass.: Addison-Wesley.

——. 2001. *Having Faith: An Ecologist's Journey to Motherhood.* Cambridge: Perseus.

SAN FRANCISCO COMMISSION ON THE STATUS OF WOMEN
The sexiest thing you can say to a woman is, "Is this okay with you?"
Make sure she wants you as much as you want her - ask her first. There's a fine line between sexual pressure and sexual violence. And words can be a powerful way to prevent both. To find out more or help end the abuse in a relationship, call (415)647-7273 or (415)864-4722.
RESPECT IS WHAT'S SEXY

6

♦♦♦

Violence Against Women

Gender violence affects women in all societies, all socioeconomic classes, all racial/ethnic groups, and it can occur throughout the life cycle (Heise, Pitanguy, and Germain 1994). Lori Heise (1989) comments: "This is not random violence; the risk factor is being female" (p. 13). In the United States, this includes the interpersonal violence of battering, rape, child sexual abuse, stalking, hassles on the street, obscene phone calls, sexual harassment at school or workplace. Underlying these incidents and experiences are systemic inequalities, also a kind of violence, that maintain women's second-class status—culturally, economically, and politically. This chapter focuses on violence against women in this country and the many efforts to stop it. This is a key issue and we refer to it in other chapters also with regard to relationships and family (Chapter 7), as a workplace issue (Chapter 8), regarding women in prison (Chapter 10), and in connection with the military (Chapter 11). We recognize that this is a tough issue for women and

for many men. It may bring up memories or push you to rethink your own experiences. If this happens, support yourself by talking to a friend, a professor, members of your campus Women's Center or anti-rape group, or go to your campus counseling center.

Since the 1970s, women in many communities have broken the silence about sexual violence, the limits it places on all our lives, ways to heal from it, and how to stop it (e.g., Bart and O'Brien 1993; Bass and Davis 1988; Brownmiller 1975; Frieze 2004; NiCarthy 1987, 2004; White 1985; and Zambrano 1985). Women have written fiction, such as Dorothy Allison's *Bastard Out of Carolina* (1992), also filmed for HBO, short stories (Koppelman 2004), and personal narratives (e.g., Francisco 1999; Pierce-Baker 1998; Raine 1998). In Reading 35, Grace Caroline Bridges writes about a girl's experience of sexual abuse. Barbara Harman (1996) describes how a woman in an abusive relationship is always second-guessing and responding to an

249

abusive partner in her attempts to avoid further violence:

> Don't raise your voice. Don't talk back. Don't say no to sex. Like whatever he does. Don't ask him to do anything he has not already done. Get up when he gets up. Go to bed when he goes to bed. Wait. Do what he wants to do. Never contradict him. Laugh at what he thinks is funny. Never ask for his time, attention, his money. Have your own money, but give it to him if he wants it. Never go out alone but do not expect him to go with you. If he is angry in the car, walk home. Be his friend except when he needs an enemy. Defend his family except when he hates them. Understand everything.
>
> *(p. 287)*

What Counts as Violence Against Women?

Most women tolerate a certain amount of what could be defined as sexual violence as part of daily life. We experience hassles on the street, in parks, or in cafés and bars. We put up with sexist comments from bosses or coworkers. We sometimes make compromises as part of maintaining intimate relationships, including going along with sex when we do not really want it, or tolerating "joking," put-downs, threats, and inconsiderate behavior. We may define some of these experiences as violence, and others not, and different women may define violence differently.

Researchers and writers do not use terms like *sexual assault, sexual abuse, battering,* or *domestic violence* in a standardized way. Differences of definition and terminology have led to marked discrepancies in reporting and have contributed to considerable confusion about these issues, which should be borne in mind throughout this chapter.

The United Nations Declaration on Violence Against Women (General Assembly resolution 48/104) of December 20, 1993, defines such violence as "any act of gender-based violence that results in, or is likely to result in, physical, sexual or psychological harm or suffering to women, including threats of such acts, coercion or arbitrary deprivation of liberty whether occurring in public or private life" (Heise, Pitanguy, and Germaine 1994, p. 46). This includes physical acts like battering,

rape, child sexual abuse, stalking, and inappropriate touching in the case of sexual harassment in the workplace. It includes verbal and psychological violence against intimate partners like yelling, intimidation, and humiliation; inappropriate personal remarks made to coworkers or students; and offensive sexist "jokes." It also includes forced isolation, denial of support, and threats of violence or injury to women in the family. This broad definition implicitly recognizes that men as a group have power over women—the women they are close to and those they encounter in public places. Women may be physically smaller or weaker, they may be economically dependent on their partner, or they may need their boss's support to keep their jobs or to get a promotion or a pay raise. Thus, macro-level inequalities are present in violence at the micro level. An important element of this male power is that it is sexualized. This is a given in interactions between intimate partners. It is also often true of interactions that are violent or that border on violence between men and women who are not intimate but who are friends, coworkers, teachers and students, or complete strangers (see Figure 6.1).

Many researchers and commentators do not use such a broad definition of violence against women. They focus on specific physical acts that can be measured. Emotional violence and the fear of threats are impossible to quantify precisely. It is much easier to bring charges of violence if one can show clear evidence of physical coercion or harm. Indeed, the legal system demands demonstrable damage or there is nothing to claim. The problem with this kind of quantification is that one cannot see the wider social and political context within which violence occurs.

The definition of violence against women can also be expanded beyond the United Nations definition quoted earlier. Psychologist Hussein Bulhan (1985), for example, proposes the following:

> Violence is any relation, process, or condition by which an individual or a group violates the physical, social, and/or psychological integrity of another person or group. From this perspective, violence inhibits human growth, negates inherent potential, limits productive living, and causes death.
> *(p. 135)*

This would include colonization, poverty, racism, lack of access to education, health care and medical

FIGURE 6.1 The Dynamics of Domestic Violence: Power and Control Wheel. (*Source:* Asian Women's Shelter, adapted from Domestic Abuse Intervention Project, Duluth, MN. Used with permission.)

insurance, negative media representations, as well as environmental catastrophes. These factors can affect men as well as women. But women as a group are poorer than men; women's rights may be limited with regard to reproductive freedom; and women are systematically objectified and commodified in the media. We argue that these macro-level factors jeopardize women's security and should be part of this discussion of violence even though they may not always have an explicitly sexual dimension. Andrea Smith, Native American scholar and cofounder of INCITE! Women of Color Against Violence, shows how sexual violence was integral to European colonization of North America (Smith 2005b).

Gender Violence Worldwide, Throughout the Life Cycle

PHASE	TYPE OF VIOLENCE
Prebirth	Sex-selective abortion (e.g., in China, India, Republic of Korea); battering during pregnancy (emotional and physical effects on the woman; effects on birth outcome); coerced pregnancy (for example, mass rape in war).
Infancy	Female infanticide; emotional and physical abuse; differential access to food and medical care for girl infants.
Girlhood	Child marriage; genital mutilation; sexual abuse by family members and strangers; differential access to food and medical care; child prostitution.
Adolescence	Dating and courtship violence (for example, acid throwing in Bangladesh, date rape in the United States); economically coerced sex (African secondary school girls having to take up with "sugar daddies" to afford school fees); sexual abuse in the workplace; rape; sexual harassment; forced prostitution; trafficking in women.
Reproductive age	Abuse of women by intimate male partners; marital rape; dowry abuse and murders; partner homicide; psychological abuse; sexual abuse in the workplace; sexual harassment; rape; abuse of women with disabilities.
Elderly	Abuse of widows; elder abuse (in the United States, the only country where data are now available, elder abuse affects mostly women).

Source: Heise, Pitanguy, and Germain (1994), p. 5.

Reading 39 gives graphic examples of the dehumanization of Native American women by White settlers, a dimension of U.S. history that is rarely taught in U.S. schools. Some activists and writers use the word *rape*—for example, rape by the economic or legal system—to refer to macro-level violence. We caution against this as it reduces the power of the term to refer to sexual violation.

At micro and meso levels, women as well as men can be violent. Women may abuse children, other family members, their peers, and people who work for them. Writer and cultural critic bell hooks (1984b) notes that women "may employ abusive measures to maintain authority in interactions with groups over whom they exercise power" (p. 119). Research shows that, in general, women hit children more than men do, but they also spend much more time with children and often shoulder the major responsibilities for raising children, especially as single parents. Women may contribute to the dynamic of a violent relationship. They may provoke an argument or hit their partner first. Occasionally women kill abusive partners in self-defense, seemingly the only way out

of situations in which they believe they would be killed if they did not defend themselves (Jones 1980; Richie 1996). In 2000, 4 percent of all male murder victims were killed by their wives or girlfriends compared to 33 percent of all female murder victims who were killed by their husbands or boyfriends (Rennison 2003). Indeed, the vast majority of gender violence is violence against women. The chance of being victimized by an intimate is significantly greater for a woman (85 percent) than for a man (15 percent) (Rennison 2003). We use the term "violence against women" here rather than "gender violence" because it makes this inequality explicit.

The Incidence of Violence Against Women

Domestic violence, rape, sexual abuse, and child sexual abuse are all illegal in the United States. The incidence of such violence is difficult to estimate accurately because of discrepancies in definition and terminology, limited research, and underre-

porting. We have included the most up-to-date sources we could find on this topic, recognizing the limitations of available data. According to the Family Violence Prevention Fund (1998), "Every year, as many as 4 million American women are physically abused by men who promised to love them" (p. 1). The U.S. Department of Justice (1997) reported that 37 percent of all women who sought care in hospital emergency rooms for violence-related injuries in 1997 were injured by a current or former spouse, boyfriend, or girlfriend. Abuse-related injuries include bruises, cuts, burns and scalds, concussion, broken bones, penetrating injuries from knives, miscarriages, permanent injuries such as damage to joints, partial loss of hearing or vision, and physical disfigurement. There are also serious mental health effects of isolation, humiliation, and ongoing threats of violence. As mentioned earlier, many writers and researchers do not take account of psychological and emotional dimensions of domestic violence because they are difficult to measure. They define it as physical assault only, which gives the impression that quantifiable acts of violence—kicking, punching, or using a weapon—tell the whole story.

One in five high school girls surveyed reported that she had been physically or sexually abused; the majority of these incidents occurred at home and happened more than once (Commonwealth Fund 1997). Girls aged 16 to 19 experience one of the highest rates of violence by an intimate partner (Rennison 2003). In 1999, 18 percent of public high school girls in Massachusetts reported having ever been physically or sexually assaulted by someone they were dating (Goode 2001). June Larkin and Katherine Popaleni's (1997) interviews with young women reveal how young men use criticism, intimidation, surveillance, threats, and force to establish and maintain control over their girlfriends. Laura O'Toole and Jessica Schiffman (1997) note that young women are vulnerable to abuse because they may feel that involvement in a personal relationship is necessary to fit in; they may be flattered by a dating partner who demands time and attention; and they lack experience negotiating affection and sexual behavior.

The legal definition of rape turns on force and nonconsent. Consent to sexual intercourse is not meaningful if given under the influence of alcohol, drugs, or prescription medication. Like domestic violence, rape is not always reported, and the true scope of the problem is difficult to estimate. Between 1992 and 2000, 63 percent of completed rapes and 65 percent of attempted rapes were not reported to the police (Rennison 2002). Rape is defined as forced sexual intercourse—vaginal, anal, or oral penetration. Sexual assault includes attacks involving unwanted sexual contact; it may involve force and include grabbing or fondling, also verbal threats. The groups most at risk for sexual assault are 16- to 19-year-olds, then 20- to 24-year-olds. In contrast to popular ideas about rape committed by a stranger in a dark alley, 76 percent of women who reported that they had been raped or physically assaulted since the age of 18 said that their partner or date committed the assault (National Institute of Justice and Centers for Disease Control and Prevention 1998). An early-1990s survey found that 13 percent of adult women are victims of forcible rape: one woman in seven (National Victim Center 1992). A 1998 survey reported that 18 percent of women had experienced a completed rape or attempted rape at some time in their lives (National Institute of Justice and Centers for Disease Control and Prevention 1998).

A study of acquaintance rape on campuses in the mid-1980s found that one in nine college women had been raped and that eight out of ten victims knew their attacker, although as few as 5 percent reported the crime (Koss 1988). One in twelve college men responding to the same survey admitted that they had committed acts that met legal definitions of rape (Koss, Dinero, and Seibel 1988). The FBI's Uniform Crime Report (compiled from over 16,000 law enforcement agencies covering 96 percent of the nation's population) estimated that one in four U.S. college women is a victim of rape or attempted rape, and this estimate is still widely used by academics, activists, and journalists. Skeptics counter that such figures are highly inflated and that many women who claim to have been raped blame their dates for their own poor judgement in having sex (Paglia 1990; Roiphe 1993). Police consultant Rana Sampson (2002) reports that most rapes of college women are not date rapes, but rapes by acquaintances maybe at a party or while studying together in a dorm room. Ninety percent of college women who are victims of rape or attempted rape know their assailant, usually a classmate, friend, boyfriend, or ex-boyfriend (in that order)

(Fisher, Cullen, and Turner 2000). College athletes are disproportionately reported to campus officers for acquaintance rape, and fraternities have been at the center of controversy for rapes and attempted rapes at fraternity house parties. Psychologists Stephen Humphrey and Arnold Kahn (2000) distinguished between fraternities and athletic teams that are high risk and low risk for rape, and found that college women correctly identified them, based on the type of parties they held. Under the 1990 Student Right-to-Know and Campus Security Act (updated as the 1998 Jeanne Cleau Disclosure of Campus Security Policy and Campus Crime Statistics Act), all colleges and universities that receive federal funding must spell out rape victims' rights and publish information on prevention programs. In Reading 37, John Stoltenberg, cofounder of Men Against Pornography, records a conversation with Duke University students in Men Acting for Change, a campus group working to confront sexual violence.

Female students are most at risk of acquaintance rape in the first few weeks of college. They often do not report a rape because of confusion, guilt, or fear, or because they feel betrayed; they may be ashamed to tell parents or college counselors; and they may not identify the experience as rape. However, the reporting of rape increased significantly on U.S. college campuses during the 1990s. The psychological effects of rape can be devastating, traumatic, and long-lasting. They include feelings of humiliation, helplessness, anger, self-doubt, self-hate, and fear; and a student may become depressed and withdrawn and do poorly in school.

Effects of Race, Class, Nation, Sexuality, and Disability

Although these forms of violence occur across the board, women's experiences are complicated by race, class, sexual orientation, and disability.

Research   The Bureau of Justice Statistics (1995) notes that domestic violence is consistent across racial and ethnic lines. Jody Raphael and Richard Tolman (1997) found that past and current victims of domestic violence were overrepresented among women on welfare and families with extremely low incomes. Callie Marie Rennison (2002) found that, in 1999, African American women aged 20 to

24 experienced more intimate violence than White women of the same age. Estimates that are based on official reports of violence are limited by the fact that many cases are not reported. Those that rely on research are limited by the scope of studies undertaken. Children and adolescents, prostituted women, homeless women, women with mental disabilities, institutionalized women, very poor women, and women in neighborhoods with high crime rates are rarely included in surveys. Women and girls with physical and mental disabilities are particularly vulnerable to physical, emotional, and sexual abuse from partners, caregivers, and service providers (Abramson et al. 2000; Young et al. 1997). The few studies that exist suggest that women with disabilities are between four and ten times as likely to be sexually assaulted as other women.

Reporting   Violence between intimate partners is illegal in this country, but it is seriously underreported because of confusion, shame, self-blame, loyalty to the abuser, lack of information, or fear of repercussions, including loss of a man's income. Women may not believe that reporting violence to the police will do any good. Women of color, poor women, and prostituted women often have very negative experiences with the police. Women of color may decide not to report domestic violence or rape to avoid bringing more trouble on husbands, partners, friends, and acquaintances who already suffer discrimination based on race, as mentioned by Lora Jo Foo (Reading 38) and Andy Smith (Reading 39). In many communities of color the police are perceived not as helpful but, rather, as abusive, harassing, and violent. Women as well as men "bear the brunt of police indifference and abuse" and "men are frequently targeted for false arrest" (M. Smith 1997). Their community may expect women of color to maintain silence about sexual assault, to protect "family honor and community integrity" (Crenshaw 1993, p. 5). Melba Wilson (1993) discusses the conflicting pressures operating here and urges Black women to hold men accountable for sexual abuse of children. Older women may not report acts of violence committed by spouses, adult children, caregivers, relatives, and neighbors, because they fear being rejected, losing their caregiver, being placed in a nursing home, or losing their property—particularly their home or independent

access to money. Immigrant women who are dependent on an abusive partner for their legal status may fear repercussions from the INS (now U.S. Citizenship and Immigration Service) if they report violence, as discussed by Lora Jo Foo in Reading 38. In a very different subculture, some women have been reluctant to speak about abuse in lesbian relationships, not wanting to feed negative stereotypes of lesbians in the wider society (see e.g., Kaschak 2002; Renzetti 1992; Ristock 2002).

Responses of the Police, Support Services, Medical and Legal Systems   The response to reports of violence against women and the provision of services have greatly expanded over the last thirty-five years as this issue has become recognized publicly. Police officers, judges, doctors, nurses, and emergency-room staff may undergo professional training, although much more still needs to be done in this regard. During slavery times, the rape of Black women in the United States was legal and commonplace. They were chattel, the property of their masters, and available for anything and everything. Currently, negative stereotypes about women of color, poor White women, prostituted women, and lesbians all perpetuate the idea, in the wider society, that these women are not worthy of respect. They are less likely to be taken seriously when they report acts of violence. Law professor Kimberlé Crenshaw (1993) notes an early-1990s study of sentences given to convicted rapists in Dallas: "The average sentence given to the rapist of a Black woman was two years . . . to the rapist of a Latina . . . five years, and . . . to the rapist of a white woman . . . ten years. Interviews with jurors reveal that the low conviction rate of men accused of raping Black women is based on ongoing sexual stereotypes about Black women" (p. 4) as we mentioned in Chapter 4.

Similar pressures that keep lesbians and many heterosexual women of color from reporting acts of violence also keep them from talking openly about this issue within their own communities. African American feminist academics Johnnetta Cole and Beverly Guy-Sheftall (2003) decided to share their personal experiences as part of an extended discussion with other prominent African American thinkers and writers regarding violence against women in African American families and communities. They took this step in service of greater equality for African American women, to show

how the dehumanization of racism distorts and limits ideas of manhood and womanhood for many African Americans, and to honor those seeking to transform interpersonal and family relationships. Sociologist Patricia Hill Collins (2004) analyzes the micro-, meso-, and macro-level forces that affect African American's experiences of sexuality as well as violence. All three authors comment on the difficulty of "airing dirty linen in public" and the possibility that their work will be used to reinforce racist stereotypes. They decided to take this risk in order to strengthen relationships between African American men and women (also see Reading 33).

Explanations of Violence Against Women

Most explanations of violence against women are social theories. Before discussing some of these, we note the resurfacing of a biological explanation of rape. Randy Thornhill and Craig Palmer (2000) argue that rape evolved historically as a form of male reproductive behavior. These authors base their claims on studies of animal species from the scorpion fly to primates. As with other sociobiological theories, they make huge leaps between animal behavior and human life, they are not grounded in an analysis of social systems, and their claims are not borne out by the experience of women who have suffered acts of violence.

As in other chapters, we focus on social theories and separate micro- and macro-level explanations.

Micro-level Explanations

Whatever form it takes, violence against women is always experienced at the personal or micro level. Family violence, rape, and child sexual abuse are often explained in terms of an individual mental health problem, innate sexual craving, or personal dysfunction on the part of perpetrators. By contrast, Jean Grossholtz (1983), a professor of political science and women's studies, argues that research on rapists and batterers shows them to be "ordinary men, indistinguishable from nonrapists and non-batterers" (p. 59). Another micro-level explanation for domestic violence is that the partners have an "unhealthy" relationship.

Three psychological syndromes have been advanced to explain violence against women: battered woman syndrome, rape trauma syndrome, and false memory syndrome.

Battered Woman Syndrome Psychologist Lenore Walker (1979, 1984) put forward the notion of a "battered woman syndrome." She noted a pattern of behavior that she termed "learned helplessness," whereby women who are repeatedly battered "learn" it is impossible to escape. After an episode of violence, they are seduced back by the batterer with declarations of love and promises that he will change. These calm, loving episodes alternate with periods of accelerating violence, isolating the woman further and tying her closer to him. Attorneys have used a "battered woman syndrome" defense for women who kill violent partners by arguing that their clients' judgment was affected "in such a way as to make them honestly believe that they were in imminent danger and that the use of force was their only means of escape" (Gordon 1997, p. 25).

Rape Trauma Syndrome This term is used by mental health and legal professionals to refer to women's coping strategies following rape. The focus is on women's reactions and responses rather than on the actions of the perpetrators or the prevalence of sexual violence in our society. Rape trauma syndrome has been used to explain women's apparently "counterintuitive" reactions—such as not reporting a rape for days or even months, not remembering parts of the assault, appearing too calm, or expressing anger at their treatment by police, hospital staff, or the legal system—in terms of pathology (Stefan 1994, p. 1274). Women diagnosed with rape trauma syndrome—who are generally White and middle class—are given psychiatric treatment with the goal of recovery and resolution. Expert testimony concerning rape trauma syndrome in rape trials improves the chances that a perpetrator will be convicted but at the cost of representing the woman as a pathetic victim. Susan Stefan (1994), an attorney and law professor, argues that the creation of this syndrome has depoliticized the issue of rape.

False Memory Syndrome Childhood sexual abuse by parents, older siblings, stepparents, and other family members, is another aspect of family life that has gradually become a public issue through the efforts of survivors, counselors, and feminist advocates (Reading 35). Many abused children block out memories of what happened to them, and these may not surface again until their adult years, perhaps through flashbacks, nightmares, panic attacks, or pain (Petersen 1991; White 1988). They then gradually piece together fragments of their experience that have been suppressed. Those who have been abused as children often experience confusion, shame, fear, or fear of being crazy. They may spend years thinking they were to blame. They may have feelings of not being worth much, or conversely, they may feel special. The child is invariably told that this special secret must never be spoken about. Healing from the effects of childhood sexual abuse takes time, courage, and support (Bass and Davis 1988; Haines 1999; Herman 1992; Petersen 1991; E.C. White 1985; L. White 1988; Wilson 1993), and many families do not want to open up this can of worms. False memory syndrome (FMS) has been invoked by parents who believe they "have been falsely accused [of incest] as a result of their adult children discovering 'memories' in the course of therapy" (Wasserman 1992, p. 18) and by lawyers acting on their behalf. According to FMS, the incest survivor is someone with impaired cognitive functioning. Memory is complex cognitively, and there are well-regarded psychologists on both sides of this issue.

These syndromes were developed for legal or therapeutic purposes. As explanations of violence against women, they are all inadequate. They pathologize women who suffer acts of violence as helpless victims. As legal defenses in cases involving acts of violence, they are also highly problematic. A battered-woman-syndrome defense for women who have killed abusive partners represents battered women as impaired, rather than as "rational actors responding to perceived danger" (Gordon 1997, p. 25). Attorneys have tried to get courts to accept that the law of self-defense applies to battered women, but without much success. These syndromes all blame the victim for her situation. The advice that police departments often give to women for their safety also assumes that we bring assaults on ourselves: Do not go out alone late at night; do not wear "provocative" clothing; always walk purposefully; do not make eye contact with men on the street; park your car in a lighted area; have your keys ready in your hand before you leave the building; look into the back seat before getting in your car, and so on. This advice is well intentioned and may be helpful. However, it assumes that women are responsible for acts of violence against them, either directly "asking for it" by their dress or behavior or indirectly encouraging it by not being sufficiently cautious.

Macro-level Explanations

Micro-level explanations of violence against women can be compelling if one focuses on specific personal interactions, but by themselves they cannot explain such a universal and systemic phenomenon. It is essential to analyze this issue at the meso and macro levels to understand it fully and to generate effective strategies to stop it.

Macro-level explanations focus on the cultural legitimation of male violence and the economic, political, and legal systems that marginalize, discriminate against, and disempower women.

Hussein Bulhan (1985) uses a very broad definition of violence that emphasizes the structural nature of violence. It rests on several assumptions:

> Violence is not an isolated physical act or a discrete random event. It is a relation, process, and condition undermining, exploiting, and curtailing the well-being of the victim. These violations are not just moral or ethical, but also physical, social, and/or psychological. They involve demonstrable assault on or injury of and damage to the victim. Violence in any of the three domains—physical, social, or psychological—has significant repercussions in the other two domains. Violence occurs not only between individuals, but also between groups and societies. Intention is less important than consequence in most forms of violence. Any relation, process, or condition imposed by someone that injures the health and well-being of others is by definition violent. *(p. 135)*

Applying these ideas to violence against women may make it easier to see this violence in terms of inequalities of power under patriarchy, as argued by Allan Johnson (Reading 2, Chapter 1). In Reading 39, Andy Smith shows the links between patriarchy and White supremacy in her discussion of sexual violence and American Indian genocide.

Macro-level factors such as sexism, heterosexism, racism, economic opportunities, working conditions, unemployment, poverty, or loss of status and cultural roots that may accompany immigration also affect personal and family relationships from the outside. Lora Jo Foo (Reading 38) mentions the severe cultural and economic disruptions and dislocations experienced by first-generation immigrants, which undoubtedly contribute to the incidence of domestic violence in these communities. Immigrants are often at the bottom of the job hierarchy; they may not speak or read English; the U.S. legal and political system is unfamiliar; and parents may have to rely on their children to negotiate and interpret the world outside home and family. This is not to excuse those who abuse their partners or children but, rather, to provide a wider context for understanding violence. Indeed, family violence is embedded in institutional roles and relationships, supported by cultural standards and expectations—meso- and macro-level factors.

The Cultural Legitimation of Male Violence   This includes cultural beliefs in male superiority and male control of women's behavior and of the family, which are supported by social institutions such as education, law, religion, and popular culture. War toys, competitive games, violent and aggressive sports, video games, and violence on TV and in movies are integral to children's socialization, especially that of boys. Popular culture, news media, and advertising all reinforce these cultural attitudes and contribute to the objectification and commodification of women. Jean Kilbourne discusses this in relation to advertising (Reading 15). The music business, MTV, TV shows, and feature films all contribute to a culture of violence against women. At the meso level too, in various communities, cultural attitudes and religious beliefs support domestic violence as a husband's prerogative to "discipline" his wife. The old idea that a wife is the property of her husband still lingers in custom and in law (see Naomi Wolf, Reading 23, Chapter 4). Wives are supposed to agree to sex, for example, as part of their wifely duty. Rape in marriage was made a crime in the United States as recently as 1993, but in thirty-three states there are varying exemptions from prosecuting husbands for rape, which indicates that rape in marriage is still treated as a lesser crime than other forms of rape (National

Clearinghouse on Marital and Date Rape 1998). Examples of exemptions are when a wife is mentally or physically impaired, unconscious, or asleep (Bergen 1996, 1999). Another example of male control is street harassment, where women may be "touched, harassed, commented upon in a stream of constant small-scale assaults" (Benard and Schlaffer 1997, p. 395). The public street is defined as male space where women without male escorts are considered "fair game." Cheryl Benard and Edith Schlaffer note that women need to "plan our routes and our timing as if we are passing through a mine field" (p. 395).

The cultural legitimation of male superiority involves patterns of male and female socialization in the family and in schools, and the social construction of masculinity and of male sexuality (see Kimmel 1993; 2000, chap. 11; Kimmel and Messner 1995; Lefkowitz 1997; Messner 1992). In a White-supremacist society, men of color may be attracted to a construction of masculinity that derives from White patriarchal attitudes and behavior. Discussing violence against women in African American communities, bell hooks (1994) writes:

> Black males, utterly disenfranchised in almost every arena of life in the United States, often find that the assertion of sexist domination is their only expressive access to the patriarchal power they are told all men should possess as their gendered birthright.   *(p. 110)*

Economic Systems That Disempower Women Women as a group earn less than men as a group. It may be difficult for a woman to leave a violent marriage or relationship if she is financially dependent on her partner. In the workplace, women may find it difficult to speak up about sexual harassment. Sociologist Michael Kimmel (1993) notes that sexual harassment "fuses two levels of power: the power of employers over employees and the power of men over women. Thus what may be said or intended as a man to a woman is also experienced in the context of superior and subordinate" (p. 130). We return to these issues in Chapter 8.

Legal Systems That Discriminate Against Women This includes inadequate laws and practices concerning violence against women, and insensitive treatment of women by police and the courts.

Martha Mahoney (1994) emphasizes the narrowness of legal categories and procedures in dealing with violence against women. For instance, the "statute of limitations," a limit on the time period allowed for bringing a lawsuit for damages or criminal charges against a perpetrator, stops some women from using the law for redress in cases of rape or childhood sexual abuse. In the latter case, they may be in their twenties, and years past the time limit, before they recognize that they were abused as children and gain the personal strength to confront the perpetrator publicly. Jean Grossholtz (1983) argues that violence against women has not "simply been overlooked by the criminal justice system" (p. 67), but that this is part of the way patriarchal power compels women "through fear and endangerment, to submit to self-depreciation, heterosexuality, and male dominance in all spheres of life" (pp. 67–68).

Political Systems That Marginalize Women's Concerns Women are still a small minority in elected office in the United States, especially at the congressional level. Violence against women is often not taken seriously by policy makers or legislators. Compared to male voters, more women are concerned about violence against women. More women also favor meaningful gun control, an end to the international trade in arms, reductions in military spending, and disarmament, believing that such changes would greatly increase their security and the well-being of their communities (Ducat 2004; Gallagher 1993). We take up the issue of women in electoral politics in Chapter 13.

The levels of violence mentioned earlier are interconnected and reinforce each other. Debra Borkovitz (1995) argues that it is necessary to transform prevailing ideas of *domination,* whether of racism, imperialism, male violence against women, or same-sex battering. Similarly, bell hooks (1984b) argues that violence against women should be seen as part of a general pattern of violence between the powerful and the powerless stemming from the "philosophical notion of hierarchical rule and coercive authority that is the root cause of violence against women, of adult violence against children, of all violence between those who dominate and those who are dominated" (p. 118). She argues that feminists should oppose

all forms of coercive domination rather than concentrating solely on male violence against women. Kimberlé Crenshaw (1993) points out that the anti-violence movement must be an anti-oppression movement.

Ending Violence Against Women

Violence against women has engaged the attention, anger, and activist efforts of scholars, policy makers, and organizers around the world. Historian Linda Gordon (1988, 1997) notes that U.S. feminists challenged wife-beating as part of antidrinking campaigns in the late nineteenth century, then again in the 1930s in campaigns for child custody and welfare for single mothers so that they could leave abusive men. Extremely important feminist work in the 1960s and '70s broke through the prevailing silence on this subject, as mentioned in Chapter 1 (Brownmiller 1975; Griffin 1971; Russell 1975). Feminists reframed and politicized the issue of rape, exposing the myth that rape is about sex—a crime of "frustrated attraction, victim provocation, or uncontrollable biological urges, perpetrated only by an aberrant fringe" (Caputi and Russell 1990, p. 34). Rather, rape is about power and control—a "direct expression of sexual politics and an assertion of masculinist norms that reinforce and preserve the gender status quo" (Caputi and Russell 1990, p. 34). Feminist writers and organizers insisted that no woman deserves to be abused, or brings it on herself, or "asks for it."

The Importance of a Political Movement

Educator and organizer Judith Herman, M.D. (1992) argues that changing public consciousness about a traumatic issue like violence against women takes a concerted political movement. In her study of trauma and recovery connected to violence, she writes that perpetrators of violence "ask bystanders to do nothing, simply to ignore the atrocity"; whereas "victims demand action, engagement, and remembering" (pp. 7–8). Feminist writers and workers in shelters and rape crisis projects often use the term *survivor* to refer to women who are coping with acts of violence, rather than calling them victims. Herman's use of the term *victim* in the following discussion is perhaps unfortunate, but her comments on the processes of denial and silencing that often surround violence against women are very insightful.

> In order to escape accountability for his crimes, the perpetrator does everything in his power to promote forgetting. Secrecy and silence are the perpetrator's first line of defense. If secrecy fails, the perpetrator attacks the credibility of his victim. If he cannot silence her absolutely, he tries to make sure that no one listens. To this end, he marshals an impressive array of arguments, from the most blatant denial to the most sophisticated . . . rationalization. After every atrocity one can expect to hear the same predictable apologies: it never happened; the victim lies; the victim exaggerates; the victim brought it upon herself; and in any case it is time to forget the past and move on. The more powerful the perpetrator, the greater is his prerogative to name and define reality, and the more completely his arguments prevail.   *(p. 8)*

Herman argues that to cut through the power of the perpetrators' arguments "requires a social context that affirms and protects the victim and that joins victim and witness in a common alliance" (p. 9). For the individual victim of violence, relationships with family, friends, and lovers create this context. For the wider society, "the social context is created by political movements that give voice to the disempowered," (p. 9), a key example being feminist movements.

Philosopher Nadya Burton (1998) criticizes second-wave feminists for using oversimplistic rhetoric in their attempts to get the issue of violence on the public agenda. They also emphasized fear, passivity, and victimhood in discussing violence against women. While acknowledging the damage suffered as a result of violence, it is also important to see women as resistors and survivors, people who cope with violation, who are not defined by it, and who thrive despite it. As Martha Mahoney (1994) comments, it is easy to see this issue in terms of victimization and, hence, to obliterate women's agency.

Feminist theorizing about the systemic nature of violence against women under patriarchy led to concerted efforts to provide supports for women who experienced such violence, to educate the wider society on the issue, and to change public policy.

Providing Support for Victims/Survivors

The first shelter for battered women in the United States opened in 1974. Now there are over 2,500 shelters and service programs nationwide, stretched to capacity. More shelters are needed, and those that exist need to be more accessible—physically and culturally—to women with disabilities, women of color, immigrant women, and lesbians. Shelters that emphasize culturally relevant perspectives and services include the Asian Women's Shelter (San Francisco); Baitul Salaam (a Muslim organization in Atlanta); Black, Indian, Hispanic and Asian Women in Action—BIHA (Minneapolis); Casa Myrna Vasquez (Boston); the Farmworker Women's Leadership Project (Pomona, Calif.); Hermanas Unidas (Washington, D.C.); the Korean American Family Service Center (New York); Sakhi, a South Asian project (New York); and Uzuri (Minneapolis). They include an analysis and understanding of cultural factors, religious beliefs, economic issues, and language barriers facing their clients, in a way that many shelters organized by White women have not done (Bhattacharjee 1997; Tan 1997) as mentioned in Readings 38 and 39. Domestic violence is not restricted to heterosexual relationships; it occurs between lesbians, bisexual, and transgender women (Girshick 2002; Kaschak 2002; Lobel 1984; Renzetti 1992; Ristock 2002; Wingspan Domestic Violence Project 1998).

Similarly, rape crisis centers operate in many cities throughout the country. Volunteers and paid staff answer emergency calls to crisis hotlines, give information, and refer women who have been raped to counseling, medical, and legal services. They may accompany a woman to the police or a doctor or advocate for her in court proceedings. Rape crisis centers often conduct public education and self-defense training for women, and many have peer counselors who are rape survivors. Over the years, some rape crisis projects that mainly served White women have become multicultural by broadening their perspectives to include antiracist work. Other organizations focus their efforts on the needs of women of color, lesbians, bisexual women, and transgender women.

Students and women's organizations continue to organize "Take Back the Night" marches and rallies on campuses and in their neighborhoods where women and men speak out about their experiences of sexual violence, some of them for the first time in a public setting. College women reporting rapes have often been blamed for putting themselves in compromising situations, especially if they have been drinking. Often, the men involved have been protected and punished lightly if at all, especially if they are university athletes. Some administrators have been concerned about the effects of alcohol and drug use and the role of fraternity parties in campus rapes (Sanday 1990). Others seem more concerned to protect their college's reputation. Campus materials and workshops on date rape for incoming students emphasize girls' and boys' different socialization and attitudes toward dating. Notable among the efforts to deal with this issue is Antioch College's sexual offense policy, which expects students to talk through a sexual encounter step by step, giving verbal consent at each step (Gold and Villari 2000), and the work of Students Active for Ending Rape (New York).

Men's projects that work on violence against women are making a crucial contribution to creating change on this issue. Examples include the National Organization for Men Against Sexism (Louisville, Colo.), Emerge (Cambridge, Mass.), Men Can Stop Rape (Washington, D.C.), and MOVE (Men Overcoming Violence; San Francisco). Men's campus groups speak to male students, offer educational programs in men-only settings, show films, bring speakers to campus, and participate in campus or community events. Examples include Haverford Men Against Sexism and Rape, Men Educating Men on the Prevention of Sexual Assault (William and Mary), Men Against Rape and Sexism (University of Minnesota), Men Against Rape (Tulane), Men Against Rape and Sexual Violence (Yale), Western Men against Violence (Western Washington University), and Men Acting for Change (Duke; Reading 37).

Finally, an organization working specifically with survivors of child sexual abuse is Generation Five (San Francisco), which has the goal of eliminating this devastating problem within five generations. In Reading 36, Aurora Levins Morales describes her journey to reclaim her sexuality and sense of integrity after experiencing sexual abuse as a child.

Public and Professional Education

Compared with a generation ago, there is now considerable public information and awareness about violence against women, including public service announcements, bumper stickers, and ads on billboards, buses, and TV. Increasingly, employers and labor unions recognize that domestic violence can interfere with a woman's ability to get, perform, or keep a job. Some corporations and labor unions have developed education and training programs on domestic violence for managers and workers. Others contribute financially to shelters.

There is a growing body of research as well as much theoretical, therapeutic, and political writing on this subject (Bart and O'Brien 1993; Bass and Davis 1988; Bohmer and Parrot 1993; Buchwald, Fletcher, and Roth 2005; Fineman and Mykitiuk 1994; Herman 1992; Jones 1994b; Koss et al. 1994; NiCarthy 1987, 2004; Russell 1990; White 1985; Zambrano 1985). Public exhibitions like The Clothesline Project (East Dennis, Mass.) also make powerful statements. Another development has been the growth of professional education on violence against women for doctors, nurses, emergency-room staff, and other health-care providers, as well as social workers and teachers. Greater knowledge and understanding are also imperative for police officers, judges, and legislators. National-level organizations like the Family Violence Prevention Fund (Washington, D.C.; San Francisco), INCITE! Women of Color Against Violence, the National Coalition Against Domestic Violence (Washington, D.C.), National Domestic Violence Hotline (www.ndvh.org), National Latino Alliance for the Elimination of Domestic Violence (Arlington, Va.), the National Resource Center on Domestic Violence (Harrisburg, Pa.), the Network for Battered Lesbians and Bisexual Women (Boston), Rape Abuse and Incest National Network (Washington, D.C.), and V-Day (New York) provide visibility, public education, research, and expertise to local organizations, the news media, and policy makers at state and federal levels.

Policy and Legislative Initiatives

Thirty-five years ago there were no laws concerning domestic violence. Now there is a growing, if uneven, body of law, mainly at the state level, including protection orders that prohibit the abuser from coming near or contacting the woman and her children. The rape laws have also been reformed because of pressure from feminists and rape survivors. This has been a piecemeal process and also varies from state to state. Nowadays, rape laws no longer require the corroboration of a victim's testimony; women are no longer required to have resisted their attackers; and the sexual histories of rape victims are no longer subject for cross-examination, unless shown to be relevant.

On the federal level, the Violence Against Women Act (VAWA) was signed into law as part of the Violent Crime and Law Enforcement Act of 1994. It authorized $1.6 billion to be spent over six years to address and prevent violence against women. In 2000, VAWA was reauthorized with funds for the National Domestic Violence Hotline, battered women's shelters and community initiatives, training for judges and court personnel, improvements in arrest policies, and legal advocacy programs for victims. It also included additional provisions to deal with violence against women with disabilities and for elder abuse, neglect, and exploitation. In 2005, the House and Senate passed VAWA reauthorization bills.

Contradictions in Seeking State Support to End Violence Against Women

An increase in government funding and increasing professionalization of work involving violence against women may be seen as major successes. A negative aspect of this development is the fact that shelters and rape crisis centers have come under closer official scrutiny, especially regarding workers' qualifications. Although there is still a vital role for volunteers, many leadership positions require a master's degree in social work (MSW) or a counseling qualification. This is linked to the current emphasis on individual services and therapeutic remedies compared to the more political approach of the 1970s and '80s. Yet, as hard as women work to help particular individuals, there are always many more—seemingly an endless stream of women needing help. This can lead to burnout among workers who well understand the continuing strength of meso- and macro-level factors that support violence against women.

There is an inherent contradiction in looking to the government—the State—to solve this problem.

The State is involved in the oppression of women. For example, it supports and requires the maintenance of the nuclear family and the gendered division of labor. As Jean Grossholtz noted more than twenty years ago, "Shelters are radical forces in the midst of social service agencies and radical threats to the ongoing political economy of violence. . . . A battered women's shelter cannot take the maintenance of the nuclear family or sex-role stereotypes as its goal" (1983, p. 67). The State condones and legitimizes violence against women through laws, judges' decisions, and police treatment that discriminate against victims of violence, despite some improvements in the ways courts and the police deal with violence against women and despite federal funding for their education and training under VAWA.

In their capacity as government employees, U.S. prison guards rape and abuse women (Amnesty International USA 2000; Kurshan 1996). Border patrols along the U.S.-Mexico border have assaulted undocumented women entering the United States (Light 1996; Martinez 1998), and INS guards have abused women at an immigrant detention center near Miami (Sachs 2000).

Military personnel also commit acts of violence against women (Guenter-Schlesinger 1999; Morris 1999). They are socialized into a highly masculinist military culture and are trained to dehumanize "the enemy" to be able to kill in time of war (Reardon 1985). Rape in war is a violation against women of the enemy group or country and, through them, an act of aggression, hostility, and humiliation against their husbands, sons, fathers, and brothers.

Examples include the rape of American Indian women by U.S. troops in the nineteenth century (Reading 39), the rape of Vietnamese women by U.S. troops during the Vietnam War (Enloe 1988), and the mass rape and forced impregnation of Muslim and Croatian women by Serbian soldiers in Bosnia-Herzegovina in the early 1990s (Eve Ensler, Reading 40; also MacKinnon 1993, 1998; Pitter and Stilmayer 1993; Tax 1993). In April 2000, participants at The Color of Violence conference, held at the University of California, Santa Cruz, called for a re-politicization of work regarding violence against women and set up a new organization, INCITE! Women of Color Against Violence. In the opening keynote, activist, writer, and scholar

Angela Davis (2001) expressed a core contradiction in current anti-violence work that looks to the state for solutions:

> Given the racist and patriarchal patterns of the state, it is difficult to envision the state as the holder of solutions to the problem of violence against women. However, as the anti-violence movement has been institutionalized and professionalized, the state plays an increasingly dominant role in the way we conceptualize and create strategies to minimize violence against women. One of the major tasks of this conference, and of the anti-violence movement as a whole, is to address this contradiction, especially as it presents itself to poor communities of color.   *(p. 13)*

Reporting on the conference, Andrea Smith (2001) argues for the need to address personal violence and state violence at the same time: to ensure safety for women affected by violence, but without strengthening the criminal justice system that is "brutally oppressive toward communities of color" (p. 66). The conference endorsed a very broad definition of violence against women, echoing Hussein Bulhan (1985), that includes colonization, indigenous people's land rights, and the criminalization of communities of color. In Reading 39, Andy Smith gives examples of alternative approaches currently being pursued in Native American communities in contrast to mainstream anti-violence organizations that are calling for longer prison sentences for batterers and rapists. Lora Jo Foo also notes the importance of community-based peer education to transform family relationships in Asian communities (Reading 38).

Women's Rights as Human Rights

In December 1979, the United Nations adopted the Convention on the Elimination of All Forms of Discrimination Against Women (CEDAW), which includes violence against women. One hundred sixty-five countries have ratified CEDAW and adopted it as national policy, though often with many reservations so that implementation has been much more limited. More than twenty-five years later, U.S. women's organizations are still lobbying for the United States to ratify CEDAW.

Lori Heise (1989) notes that "sex-specific violence has not been treated with the same seriousness as other human rights abuses" (p. 13). Defining violence against women as a human rights issue has been a successful strategy to get this issue onto the international agenda (Agosín 2001; Beasley and Thomas 1994; Bunch and Carillo 1991; Kerr 1993). In June 1993, women from many countries organized the Global Tribunal on Violations of Women's Human Rights to coincide with the Non-Governmental Organization (NGO) Forum of the U.N. World Conference on Human Rights, held in Vienna (Bunch and Reilly 1994). In 1994 the U.N. Commission on Human Rights created a new position—the Special Rapporteur on Violence Against Women, Its Causes and Consequences—based in Geneva, Switzerland. The Center for Women's Global Leadership (Rutgers University) sponsors an annual 16 Days of Activism Against Gender Violence (Nov. 25 to Dec. 10). V-Day and Communities Against Violence Network (Washington, D.C.) are other U.S.-based organizations working on an international level.

As this chapter makes clear, there is an urgent need for many changes at micro, meso, macro, and global levels for women to be secure from violence including:

- the socialization and education of all children to respect and value each other;

- changes in the social construction of femininity and masculinity, and the abolition of cultural attitudes and systems of inequality that support male superiority;

- an end to the objectification and commodification of women;

- changes in women's work and wages, and support for community-based economic development to give women economic security and independence;

- changes in the law, court decisions, police practices, and the political system so that women's human rights are central; and

- continued collaboration among all who are working to end violence, and challenges to those who are not.

Questions for Reflection

In reading and discussing this chapter, consider these questions:

1. What beliefs about rape are really myths? How would your life be different if rape and the threat of rape did not exist?

2. How do the intersections of gender, race, class, nation, sexuality, and so forth, affect violence against women?

3. How do boys in your community learn to respect women? To disrespect women?

4. How has abuse or violence affected your life? Your family? Your community?

5. What kinds of masculinity would help to create personal security for women and for men?

6. What are men's roles and responsibilities in ending violence against women?

Finding Out More on the Web

1. Research how the Web is used to support and reinforce beliefs about violence against women.

2. Research U.S. and international organizations working to end violence against women. What are their goals, strategies, and activities? What theoretical frameworks shape their work? Try to find culturally diverse women's organizations, student organizations, and organizations of men against rape.

3. Eve Ensler wrote "My Vagina Was My Village" based on an interview with one woman among thousands who were raped as a systematic tactic of war in Bosnia in 1993. Find out more about this—and about other examples of rape in war.

Taking Action

1. Talk about this issue with your peers, and initiate public discussion on your campus or in your community. Find out about your college's policy on sexual assault and how it is enforced (or not). Find out about rape crisis centers, shelters, and support groups in your area so that you can support someone who is coping with sexual assault.

2. Volunteer with a rape crisis project on campus or at a shelter for victims of domestic violence. Men students: Work with other men on this issue.

3. Support a campus or community event concerned with violence against women.

THIRTY-FIVE

Lisa's Ritual, Age 10 (1990)

Grace Caroline Bridges

Grace Caroline Bridges is a psychotherapist in private practice. Her poems have appeared in several literary reviews and anthologies.

Afterwards when he has finished
lots of mouthwash helps
to get rid of her father's cigarette taste.
She runs a hot bath
 to soak away the pain
  like red dye leaking from her
   school dress in the washtub.

She doesn't cry.
When the bathwater cools she adds more hot.
She brushes her teeth for a long time.

Then she finds the corner of her room,
curls against it. There the wall is
hard and smooth
as teacher's new chalk, white
as a clean bedsheet. Smells
fresh. Isn't sweaty, hairy, doesn't stick
to skin. Doesn't hurt much
when she presses her small backbone
into it. The wall is steady

while she falls away:
 first the hands lost
arms dissolving feet gone
 the legs dis- jointed
  body cracking down
   the center like a fault
    she falls inside
     slides down like
dust like kitchen dirt
     slips off
the dustpan into
      noplace
a place where
nothing happens,
nothing ever happened.

When she feels the cool
wall against her cheek
she doesn't want to
come back. Doesn't want to
think about it.
The wall is quiet, waiting.
It is tall like a promise
only better.

THIRTY-SIX

Radical Pleasure (1998)
Sex and the End of Victimhood

Aurora Levins Morales

Aurora Levins Morales is a feminist historian, writer, and activist, who is both Puerto Rican and Jewish. Published work includes poetry, essays, and two books: *Getting Home Alive* and *Remedios*. Her poetry is aired regularly on the Pacifica Radio program *Flashpoints*.

1

I am a person who was sexually abused and tortured as a child. I no longer define myself in terms of my survival of this experience, but what I learned from surviving it is central to my political and spiritual practice. The people who abused me consciously and deliberately manipulated me in an attempt to break down my sense of integrity so they could make me into an accomplice to my own torture and that of others. They deliberately and consciously interfered with my sexuality as one method of accomplishing this. We are so vulnerable in our pleasures and desires. The fact they could induce physical pleasure in me against my will allowed them to shame me. It allowed them to persuade me that my sexuality was untrustworthy and belonged to others. It allowed them to persuade me that my desires were dangerous and were one of the causes of my having been abused. My sexuality has stuttered ever since, flaring and subsiding in ways I have not known how to manage, ricocheting from intense excitement to absolute numbness, from reckless trust to impenetrable guardedness. This place of wounded eroticism is one that is honored in survivor culture, evidence of blows inflicted and then denied by our abusers. When the skeptical ask us "Where are your scars?" we can point to the unsteady rhythms of fascination and disgust, obsession and revulsion through which we experience sex as evidence of what we know to be true.

2

"So why choose to reclaim sex?" This is the final question in a five-hour interview of me by my friend Staci Haines. We have been talking about the seductiveness of the victim role; about the thin satisfactions that come from a permanent attitude of outrage. About how having to resist too much, too young, locks us into rigid stances of resistance that interfere with intimacy, which ultimately requires vulnerability and surrender. About the seductiveness of an identity built on righteous indignation, and how close that stance actually lies to rampant self-pity. So when she asks me "Why reclaim sex?" I answer in layers.

Of course because it is part of aliveness. But among the many topics we've ranged over in our hours of conversation, the one that grabs me now is the need and obligation to leave victimhood behind. Staci and I share a somewhat taboo belief that as survivors we have an obligation to think about the healing of the perpetrators who are, after all, our kin—victims who survived in body but were unable to remain spiritually intact. So what comes

to mind is the high price we pay when we settle for being wronged. Victimhood absolves us from having to decide to have good lives. It allows us to stay small and wounded instead of spacious, powerful and whole. We don't have to face up to our own responsibility for taking charge of things, for changing the world and ourselves. We can place our choices about being vulnerable and intimate and effective in the hands of our abusers. We can stay powerless and send them the bill.

But deciding not to heal fully, not to reclaim that place of intimate harm and make it flourish, is also unjust. By making the damage done to us permanent and irreversible, we lock both ourselves and the perpetrators away from any hope of healing. We saddle them with an even bigger spiritual debt than they have already incurred, and sometimes the reason is revenge, as if our full recovery would let them off the hook and we must punish them by seeing to it that our victimhood is never diminished or challenged. But when we refuse healing for the sake of that rage, we are remaking ourselves in the image of those who hurt us, becoming the embodiment of the wound, forsaking both ourselves and the abandoned children who grew up to torment us.

3

The path of reclaiming the wounded erotic is neither placid nor boring. It is full of dizzying precipices, heady moments of release, crushing assaults of shame. But at its core is the real fire we are all after, that blazing and untarnished aliveness that lies within everything of value and spirit that we do. Right here in our bodies, in our defense of our right to experience joy, in the refusal to abandon the place where we have been most completely invaded and colonized, in our determination to make the bombed and defoliated lands flower again and bear fruit, here where we have been most shamed is one of the most radical and sacred places from which to transform the world. To shamelessly insist that our bodies are for our own delight and connection with others clearly defies the predatory appropriations of incestuous relatives and rapists; but it also defies the poisoning of our food and water and air with chemicals that give us cancer and enrich the already obscenely wealthy, the theft of our lives in harsh labor, our bodies used up to fill bank accounts already bloated, the massive abduction of our young people to be hurled at each other as weapons for the defense and expansion of those bank accounts—all the ways in which our deep pleasure in living has been cut off so as not to interfere with the profitability of our bodies. Because the closer I come to that bright, hot center of pleasure and trust, the less I can tolerate its captivity, and the less afraid I am to be powerful, in a world that is in desperate need of unrepentant joy.

◆◆◆

THIRTY-SEVEN

"I Am Not a Rapist!" (1998)
Why College Guys Are Confronting Sexual Violence

John Stoltenberg

Feminist activist and author, **John Stoltenberg** was a founder of "Men Against Pornography" in New York City. His books include *Refusing To Be a Man*, and *The End of Manhood: Parables of sex and selfhood*. He is the managing editor of *AARP The Magazine*.

What follows is an emotionally charged conversation among members of a Duke University student organization called Men Acting for Change (MAC), one of many new men's groups at colleges and universities across the United States and Canada. Besides meeting regularly to talk personally, MAC members present programs about gender and sexuality, focusing on sexual violence and homophobia, to fraternities and other campus groups.

MAC came to national prominence in the United States when members appeared in a segment about pornography on the ABC newsmagazine program *20/20*. On January 28, 1993, millions of viewers heard these college-age males speak graphically about the negative effects of pornography, including *Playboy*, on their sex lives and their relationships with women.

A year earlier, Kate Wenner, an ABC producer, asked to pick my brains about how to do a pornography story that hadn't been done before. Over an amiable lunch at a café near Lincoln Center, I suggested she report how pornography has become a primary form of sex education for young men. She liked the idea and tracked down MAC. The resulting broadcast included footage of frank conversations among both female and male Duke students and was perhaps the most astute coverage of pornography's interpersonal effects yet to appear on network television.

After that *20/20* segment aired, MAC members were invited to appear on *Oprah, Donahue, Jerry Springer, Maury Povich*, and *Montel Williams*, but they declined to have their stories sensationalized. Meanwhile *Playboy* went ballistic and, in an apparent attempt at damage control, ridiculed them in print as "the pointy-headed, wet-behind-the-scrotum boys at Duke."

In January 1994, curious to know what makes MAC tick, I traveled to Durham, North Carolina, to attend the third annual Student Conference on Campus Sexual Violence, to be held at Duke. The brochure promised "focus on student activism and involvement in the anti-rape movement" and quoted Jason Schultz, a conference organizer and *20/20* participant: "Through our work against rape, we take control of our future and generate the skills and perspectives that we need to help make it a better, safer place for both women and men." The afternoon before the conference opened, Jason arranged a private conversation in his home among five MAC members. They understood that I would sit in, ask questions, and try to get an edited transcript of their conversation published where it could contribute to more accurate understanding of the student movement against sexual violence.

As I listened, I realized that these young men had taken the meaning of sexual violence to heart in some intensely personal and generationally specific new ways. Everyone in the group knew friends who had been sexually assaulted. At one point I asked them to estimate how many. One said that one in five of his friends had told him this. Another said fifty. Another said that among his twenty to twenty-five friends who had been sexually assaulted, he also knew the perpetrator in half the cases.

At another point one told something he had never before shared with his fellow MAC members: he himself had been sexually molested in his youth. That dramatic moment was generationally specific too, I realized. Such a disclosure would never have occurred among college-age males even a decade before. The vocabulary and sense of social safety would simply not have existed.

I came to understand that what these college-age males had to say is historically unprecedented: they had each become aware, through personal experience, of their own stake in confronting sexual violence.

There is a newsworthy story here, I thought to myself, a trend to be watched. An extraordinary new student-based social-change movement has begun; yet no major news-gathering medium has thought to listen in to the generationally specific experience represented by these five members of MAC.[1] Although they spoke as individuals and from particular viewpoints—the group was a mix of straight, bi, and gay; white and black—they also seemed at times to speak on behalf of many more male agemates than themselves. Quite matter-of-factly, without any prompting, they each described an experience now so common that it may define their generation more profoundly than any war ever has: how it feels to be perceived by female peers as a potential rapist.

Ever since the women's movement began to bring sexual violence to light in the early 1970s, the extent of rape and the extent of women's fears of it have been trivialized, refuted, and ridiculed by mainstream media. Today the aspirations of campus activists to radical gender egalitarianism and eroticized equality are similarly distorted in the popular press. For example, in the early 1990s students at Antioch College developed a comprehensive, nine-page policy spelling out the meaning of consent in sexual contact and conduct; defining and prohibiting a list of offenses that included rape, sexual assault, "sexual imposition," and nondisclosure of a known HIV-positive

status; and detailing fair hearing procedures and remedies in case of violation. This path-breaking, gender-neutral, ethically acute initiative was widely sneered at by media commentators who had never read it, never talked to the students who drafted and implemented it. During the 1960s and early 1970s, many "with it" magazine and book editors reveled in the ribald romance of covering the radical student antiwar movement in depth and at length. By contrast, today's middle-age male media decision makers act as if their journalistic radar screens got stuck in time along with the anachronistic sexual politics of their youth. Nostalgic for the 1960s "sexual revolution" days before feminism made "no" even an option for women—when, in the hustle of the time, "Girls say yes to [sex with] boys who say no [to the military]"—today's middle-age male media decision makers package smug blather about "date-rape hysteria" (a *New York* magazine cover story) or "sexual correctness" (a *Newsweek* cover story) or "do-me feminism" (an *Esquire* cover story) and sign up execrably researched diatribes about "morning-after misgivings" (Katie Roiphe) or "the new Victorianism" (Rene Denfield). Today's middle-age male media decision makers just don't get it.

What this conversation reveals, however, is that a significant subset of young males have started to get it. Typical of a brand-new kind of self-selected peer group, they voice values that do not much resemble the sexual politics of most men their fathers' age. Within their transcient, education-centered communities, the social and relational meaning of sexual violence to young women has become apparent to them as an everyday, lived reality. Never before have so many young males struggled to take this reality on board in their moral map of the world, and never before have so many known that others are doing so also.

In the student antiwar movement of the 1960s, many young women of conscience organized politically in behalf of young men whose bodies were then regarded as most at risk—deployable as cannon fodder in an immoral military operation. Today, more and more young men of conscience have begun to understand their vital role in the student movement against sexual violence, and this time it is they who have put their lives on the line in behalf of the women whose bodies are most at risk.

For older menfolk—especially those who hold jobs in academia and are therefore in a position to offer material support and substantive resources—this movement presents a classic challenge for teachers: to listen to and learn from students.

When student antiwar activists of the 1960s brought new ideals and values into their subsequent work, family, and civic lives, the cultural and political impact of that movement was felt throughout the larger society for decades. As I write, the president of the United States [President Clinton] is a man who in his student days protested the Vietnam War. Who would have guessed back then that the fledgling youth counterculture, vibrantly antimilitarist, would not only help halt a war but one day inform this nation's governance at the highest level?

Today, too, it is easy not to reckon the profound cultural and political shift portended by the values and ideals of young people in the burgeoning campus antirape movement. But who knows? One day this country could elect a president who in her or his student days protested, and helped end, men's war against women.

Q: Why did you get involved in Men Acting for Change?

Warren Hedges *(30, Ph.D. candidate in English)*[2]: I got involved because of women I was close to and things they had survived. When I walk on campus at night and a woman in front of me sees I'm a man walking behind her, her shoulders tense up and she starts walking more quickly. Her keys come out of her pocket in case she needs them to defend herself from me. It wouldn't do any good to try and convince her I'm a nice guy or "enlightened." I'm perceived as something that doesn't fit with what I want to be, and the only way to change that is by changing the broader social structure—laws and economic relations and things like that.

In our culture having a penis is supposed to be a package deal: You're supposed to have specific desires (for women) and pursue them in specific ways (aggressively, competitively), identify with men instead of women, have specific—and usually boring—sexual practices. There's this broad cultural discourse saying, "This is who you should be if you happen to have this particular organ." I can't create a space where I can express myself and be more upfront about my desires and my identifications and my practices and so forth without trying to change the larger social structures.

Andy Moose *(21, pre-law English major):* My reason for doing this came through a slow process, especially with MAC meetings, of having the space to really reflect about how I felt about a lot of emotional and personal issues that I hadn't spent much time as a man thinking about before. I'm in a fraternity and have seen a lot of abuses that go on within that system. I want to stay in there and work to improve the situation so that my fraternity brothers get to that process as well. I've felt it could help them, and also stop a lot of the abuses that were going on to other friends. It's personal for me, rather than seeing a great deal of violence and wanting to work towards stopping that. That's a major concern, but the bigger driving force for me is the personal gains that I see possible for people in working with these issues.

Carlton Leftwich *(25, premed):* I'm twenty-five years old and I have come to the realization that I've never had a healthy relationship with a woman. There's a lot of issues here that make me reflect on my opinion of women and how I treat them, how I deal with them, and how I could develop a healthy relationship with one. Healthy to me is looking at them and not saying, "Oh, that's a *woman's* point of view"—making everything that she says or feels inferior. I'd like to get on an even keel when discussing something with a woman and not just look at her and say, "She's a totally different king of thing."

Erick Fink *(22, psych major and women's studies minor):* I took this intro to women's studies class and it hit me that this feminist stuff made a lot of sense. Like, even though you've never raped anyone or even thought about it, other men are doing that in your name and they're hurting people that you love in your name. All the pressure that men feel to act a certain way and do a certain thing and fit a certain mold— maybe it *used* to work, but it's not working now. And now I'm here, and I'm going to try to do something about it. I feel like I and people with penises have something to gain from the

women's movement, a lot to gain: being able to be exactly who you are without having to be "a man" in the traditional sense.

I've felt very limited by patriarchy. My sense of masculinity mostly came from where everybody else's does, TV—"If you do this, chicks will dig you." That was what was masculine for me—how to attract the opposite sex. But I didn't want to be this macho guy. It's not that I didn't want to be; I just wasn't.

Carlton: I never could identify with what straight was—this rugby-playing kind of rough-and-tumble guy, always having to prove that I was macho—so I just automatically thought that I had to be gay, because I was very sensitive and I loved classical music. I was not a quote unquote normal young man, because I never liked football. And I always heard, "Well, all guys like football— if you don't play football you're a sissy."

Jason Schultz *(22, public policy major and women's studies minor):* In high school I was one of the top ten in my class academically. The other nine were all girls. They were brilliant and they taught me—about math, physics, English. Learning from female peers really had a big influence. The culture tells you women are bimbos, don't know anything, and are ditzes, sex objects; but my reality was different. I had good relationships with women who were intellectual and spoke their mind and wouldn't let me get away with shit—in a very loving way. Not "Get the fuck out" but "You better change or *I'm* going to get the fuck out." When I got to college, the intelligent, assertive, self-confident women started calling themselves feminists, and these were the people I loved to hang out with—"Oh, sure I'll go to your meeting. Oh, that sounds like an interesting class"—and I started to get involved. But for me there was a piece missing. I went through fraternity rush, didn't find any men that I really liked to hang out with, and felt really stupid. Women in women's studies classes were focusing on women's experience, women's perspective—which made a lot of sense, because it's left out of traditional academia—but nothing was speaking to me on a first-person level. At that time there were a couple other men on campus who wanted the same thing, and it was framed as men interested in confronting sexual violence. It was this group that I felt could look at the other component, the part that I needed to match—not to feel isolated as much as I was sometimes, not to feel like I had to speak for men.

Q: How have you personally been affected by sexual violence?

Jason: My first year in college, a good friend of mine, a female friend, was avoiding me. We weren't communicating; we didn't have the intimacy I enjoyed so much. And I'm like, "What's up with you? what's bugging you? did you flunk some test or something?" I knew that she had gone out with this guy, and I knew who he was, and she told me the story in brief detail: She was raped. And she was like, "That's why I don't feel comfortable around you—it's because I don't know who to trust anymore." I didn't blame her at all. I was pissed at him. I was *really* pissed at him. It made me angry that this guy had ruined a friendship of mine with somebody I cared about. Then when I saw this men-concerned-with-sexual-violence thing, it came together.

As a man doing this kind of work you get stories and stories—it's just exponential. I probably know fifty survivors personally—most of them through campus.

Warren: The first person who told me she had survived a rape—here on campus by another Duke student on Valentine's Day—was during my first year in graduate school. For me it was a real hard lesson learning that just me being sensitive is not enough. This sort of thing was happening to women and it was going to change the way they reacted to all or most men, especially initially. And that prompted me to get involved with this program in Durham with men who batter their wives.

Once it became known on campus that I was concerned about these issues, and once I had a chance to speak at a Take Back the Night march, the number of stories I heard from women just seemed to multiply. One reason MAC has been so important to me is that I feel I've got an emotional support network now—not just feeling utterly overwhelmed by the number of stories that seemed to come flooding in. Probably one in five friends told me—attempted rapes and assaults, but usually rape.

Carlton: When I was growing up I was abused sexually. I just internalized everything and left it there. It was through MAC I could come in con-

tact with people who had a rape encounter and see how they handled it, how they were surviving it, without actually having to admit that I was someone who had been raped also. That was really difficult for me. But to see women have the courage to pick up their lives and keep on going—it's really empowering. I can feel for women a lot more now that I know that it was something that I had no control over and that it wasn't my fault. I can understand that helplessness and that dirty feeling, the pain and sorrow.

Most guys are like, "Well, how do you rape a male?" There are a lot of ways to rape a male. And I would say to any other male survivor, "Don't be ashamed." Even if it happened ten, fifteen, twenty years ago, it still happened, and you're going to have to deal with it. You're going to have to address those feelings. It's not going to be easy, but try and hook up with a group of guys that can really feel for you and care about you. And by caring for women—I guess I took that assumption, that these guys care about women—then they're obviously going to care about my plight and respect me.

Erick: For the women I know that have been sexually assaulted or raped—I'd say twenty to twenty-five percent—it sticks with them; it changes their lives.

Carlton: Your sense of security is gone, and once you lose your sense of security you're never going to get it back.

Erick: There's an awful lot of fear out there—like if there's a woman sitting in a room with me alone, and we're sitting there talking, there's the chance that she is fearful of me.

Carlton: Sometimes I just want to shout, "I'm not going to hurt you!"

Jason: Holding up a sign: "not a rapist"?

Carlton: Yeah.

Andy: My first experience of sexual violence was from the other side, knowing the male who was being accused. During freshman year at Duke, I was faced with a rape case that was going to the Judi [Judicial] Board. This was a huge shock for me—becoming aware of the size of the problem and the frequency with which these acts were going on. It was something I was completely unaware of in high school. Having a very dear personal friend share with me that they were assaulted, coupled with knowing someone accused of the rape—those two things at the same time forced me to try to understand how this could happen. I couldn't just say, "Well, it's obvious these people are incredibly violent," because I wasn't seeing that. How could this happen around me every day and these people don't show me any signs of violent tendencies? How could this be happening with such frequency?

As you begin to get involved, a lot more people, a shocking number, tell you things. It takes you aback, the numbers—between twenty and twenty-five good friends, very close. Mostly women, ninety-some percent. I had one male friend share like that. And there were a number of stories where the male was someone I knew, probably a fourth of them. Actually more than that—probably half.

Talking with other people in MAC and doing programs on sexual violence helped me, because I felt I could do something. In a very basic way that feels good, to fight a situation that before you felt really helpless in. I have a little bit more understanding of how the event could happen—so it's not so much burning hatred towards that individual. I'm not so quick just to discard that person and say, "OK, he raped this woman so now I'm just going to not communicate with him any longer." I don't want to do that. There's definitely resentment and anger, a great deal of anger, and I try to suppress that as much as I can, because when you have these sorts of numbers around you, it's vital that you don't hate and cut that person off just because—. I mean, you become very lonely, obviously.

Q: How do you reach other men?

Jason: Standing up to them never seems to work. It seems to push them farther away, make them reactive. It's a balance of making them feel like I care what they say and being willing to sit down and listen to them for a long time, but then be willing to challenge them. Not saying, "Oh, you're a sexist pig—get the fuck outta here," but when the opportunity is there to say, "What you're saying really bothers me" or "I'd really like to talk to you about this because I'm learning where this is coming from."

Carlton: Don't make men feel like a minority. There are a lot of men out there who really want to understand themselves and their feelings a lot more, and you can really turn somebody off with that raw anger that seems to be associated with feminists. That's intimidating to men. I know it is to me.

Andy: A lot of the successes that I've been a part of talking with fraternity men came from catching them off guard. The minute some discussion on sexual violence comes up they become defensive. When they've gotten in these discussions with women or with non-Greek men, oftentimes it's led to an argument, they didn't feel very good about it, they don't want to talk about it, and so they don't deal with it. If there's something being discussed about a Greek function, they immediately assume that the fraternity men are going to be blamed, and they're going to defend themselves as not being a rapist or whatever. So a lot of the successes have come from surprise, when they realize there's a real conversation that's going to happen and it's not going to become some heated argument—because a lot of men haven't really thought about it much at all, and people really enjoy having an opportunity to reflect about their opinions, to recognize, "Wow, you know, I've thought about this and it really helped."

Erick: I was talking to a good friend and he said, "You know what I think date rape is? I think this woman has sex with this guy and the next morning she decides she shouldn't have done it, so she just screams rape." And I'm like, "Well, you know, I remember not long ago I felt the same way. But if you really think about it, things like that can happen. On a date maybe with somebody that you might know very well or have been seeing for a long time, you could get violent with that person, couldn't you?" And he said, "Uh, I don't know." And I'm like, "Well, have you ever gotten so angry or so frustrated with your girlfriend that you could just—" And he's like, "Sure, I guess so." And there was a relation there, where I could see how he was feeling, and he could see how I was feeling too. I think if he had said that to a woman, she would be very offended—and rightfully so.

Andy: You have to have discussions for the potential rapist, but also focus on how people contribute to an environment or make it easier for a rape to happen. A lot of times they don't recognize how they in a much more subtle way contribute or make these sorts of things easier to happen, by a comment or a particular action in a situation.

Warren: Or by no action.

Andy: Right, exactly, because so quickly they say, "Well, *I'm* not a rapist." They don't think about what environment you're establishing when you're having a party or you're making some joke or you don't say anything in a particular situation. It's better to have dialogue about those issues.

Jason: A lot of men don't hear what feminists are actually saying when it's coming from women. Their words are so devalued, and we value men's words more. My experience has been that it takes some patience, because if somebody said something sexist like "Oh, she deserved to be raped, look at how she's dressed," there's an instinct to want to confront that. But what seems to be more beneficial is to ask questions, maybe let the story weave itself a little more, find a deeper belief system, and figure out what

about that issue to confront. I think with some men you can definitely do that.

Warren: My formative experience thinking about male violence was working with men who beat their wives. They were ordered by the courts to attend. The men couldn't leave the program angry because they might go home and beat their partner. That was a real constraint on my need to be vindictive and self-righteous. There was a counselor who put it very well when he said, "Dealing with abusive men is like judo; you gotta grab ahold of their energy and move them someplace they don't expect to end up."

NOTES

1. I tried for two years to get this conversation into print. Among the publications that passed on it are *Cosmopolitan, Details, Elle, Glamour, Mademoiselle, Ms., On the Issues, Rolling Stone,* and the *Village Voice.*

2. Ages and academic concentrations are given as of the date of this conversation.

THIRTY-EIGHT

◆◆◆

Domestic Violence and Asian American Women (2002)

Lora Jo Foo

Lora Jo Foo is a former garment sweatshop worker turned union organizer turned labor lawyer. She is cofounder of the California-based Sweatshop Watch and the National Asian Pacific American Women's Forum.

. . . Asian American women in abusive relationships face different challenges than white women who speak English and are American citizens, for whom most shelter and outreach programs are designed. Asian American women, the majority of whom are foreign-born immigrants with different languages and cultures, experience numerous institutional barriers to seeking safety. The categories of safety-related challenges particular to Asian American women—ill-equipped shelter programs, language

barriers, laws that discriminate against immigrants, cultural values that lead to violent behavior, and barriers to safety for Asian American lesbians—are described below.

Lack of Culturally and Linguistically Accessible Services

1. Limited and Inadequate Shelter Space Shelter space in general is limited, but those with the capacity to serve Asian women's language needs and who make their facilities culturally supportive for immigrant women are in extremely short supply. In Massachusetts, out of 35 women's shelters, only two have Asians on staff. Some shelters do not accept non-English-speaking women at all. The Asian Women's Shelter (AWS) in San Francisco has the capacity to help non-English-speakers but is forced to turn away 600 individuals each year. This number represents 75% of the women who contact the clinic. Moreover, mainstream women's shelters are not designed for women with more than one or two kids.[1] Hmong women in the St. Paul/Minneapolis area who have larger than average families were not able to make use of most shelters until Asian Women United designed a shelter to accommodate larger families. Asian Health Services, an Oakland community health clinic, believes that these institutional barriers are so formidable that only 2 out of 10 Asian American women patients who experience abuse actually find refuge in a shelter. This ratio is low compared to the mainstream population.

2. Lack of Accurate Interpretation   Police who respond to domestic violence calls are seldom bilingual and often do not bring interpreters with them. They seek to communicate with someone who speaks English and that is often the husband. As a result, in many cases the Asian woman's story goes unheard. In some instances, children, family, and friends have inappropriately been asked to interpret. When those close to the situation have judgmental attitudes and/or fear retaliation by the abuser, they often engage in victim-blaming and are unable to accurately or completely convey the woman's perspective. An example of the tragic results of inadequate translation occurred in the state of Washington. A battered woman's estranged husband threatened her with a gun, with the intention to kill her. Because of the lack of adequate translation, the abuser was never prosecuted because the police did not obtain statements from the victim and two witnesses with sufficient detail for the prosecutor to proceed. A year after the incident, the abuser killed his wife.

In addition, many Asian women come from countries where police and other institutions do not respond to domestic disputes, which contributes to the lack of reporting. Moreover, the U.S. criminal justice system is viewed as discriminatory toward immigrants, people of color, and other minorities, and this also creates negative perceptions that prevent women from seeking police protection when necessary.

3. Lack of Services for Batterers   In most parts of the U.S., linguistically and culturally accessible intervention programs for batterers from the Asian community do not exist. Court sentences for batterers that require mandatory participation in such programs are rendered meaningless if no such program exists in the batterer's native tongue.[2]

Laws That Trap Asian Women in Violent Domestic Situations

1. Anti-Immigrant Legislation   Anti-immigration legislation poses the most difficult barrier to Asian immigrant women seeking safety. Prior to 1986, a U.S.-citizen husband could petition for and obtain lawful permanent residence status (a green card) for his immigrant wife immediately after marriage. However, in 1986 Congress enacted the Immigration Marriage Fraud Amendments (IMFA) that created a new conditional residence status requiring that an immigrant spouse must stay married to a citizen spouse for two years. At the end of two years, the partners must file a joint application to adjust the conditional status to permanent status. As a result, some immigrant women were trapped in violent domestic situations, unable to leave out of fear that their husbands would become unwilling to cooperate in jointly filing the application, thereby rendering them undocumented and thus subject to deportation at the end of the two years.

In 1990, Congress enacted the Battered Spouse Waiver to remedy the unintended consequences of the 1986 law after powerful documentation of the physical, emotional, and economic abuses suffered by battered immigrant women was brought to light. The Battered Spouse Waiver allowed a battered immigrant woman to leave her U.S.-citizen husband and "self-petition" for lawful permanent residence without the cooperation of her husband. In 1994, Congress enacted the Violence Against Women Act (VAWA) to provide broader protections to immigrant women, allowing any woman, documented or undocumented, married to a citizen or green-card-holder to self-petition if she is a victim of domestic violence. When VAWA was reauthorized by Congress in 2000, other barriers to the self-petition process were removed. These included allowing divorced spouses to self-petition, allowing abused wives living abroad to self-petition if married to employees of the government or U.S. military, and eliminating the requirement to show extreme hardship to her or her children if deported to her home country.[3]

2. Limitations of the Battered Spouse Waiver and VAWA   The Battered Spouse Waiver and VAWA have been on the books for twelve and eight years, respectively. However, because of lack of education and outreach, many monolingual women are unaware of these legal protections. Many women are under the impression that their batterers have complete control over their immigration status and continue to live in dangerous and violent domestic situations. In addition, there are not enough attorneys trained in immigration law, family law, and domestic violence law to deal with the most complicated VAWA cases, especially those involving undocumented women. Even when a woman self-petitions, she may not get the relief she seeks.

An attorney from the Asian Law Caucus in San Francisco found that Asian immigrant women have difficulty meeting the documentation requirements for self-petitioning. For example, in order to self-petition for permanent residence status after leaving an abusive husband, immigrant women must document the abuse through either police reports or protective orders, record of time spent at a shelter, or affidavits from friends. The extreme isolation of many Asian immigrant women, their lack of awareness of the availability of shelter programs or police protection, and the language barriers to obtaining assistance from them, make it difficult for them to use these channels to document the abuse. In addition, because the crime of domestic violence is a deportable offense, some Asian immigrant women hesitate to report their batterers to law enforcement. These women often must use only their own declarations and rely on the discretion of INS officers. But an advocate who tracks VAWA cases nationally notes that the INS has a great deal of discretion in hearing a case, and even if the woman's declaration is legally sufficient, many INS officers in local district offices are not sympathetic to the plight of battered immigrant women.

3. Restrictions Created by Welfare Reform   Welfare reform has resulted in serious financial barriers to Asian immigrant women seeking safety. Recognizing that welfare programs serve as an essential bridge to safety for women fleeing domestic abuse, Congress created exceptions for battered immigrant women. For example, a battered immigrant woman, even if she is undocumented, is eligible for public benefits when she has a pending VAWA or family-sponsored petition. . . . Congress also created the Family Violence Option (FVO), which allows states to exempt a battered woman from TANF [Temporary Assistance for Needy Families] work requirements if meeting these requirements would make it more difficult for the woman to escape an abusive situation. FVO also permits the clock on the five-year lifetime cap to stop running until the woman is safe. Under FVO, a state can waive the paternity establishment and child support requirements. However, the widespread, erroneous impressions among both caseworkers and battered women themselves that "immigrants aren't entitled to any benefits anymore" have kept battered women from applying and caseworkers from accepting applications. . . .

Welfare reform has also resulted in shelters mistakenly believing that it is unlawful to provide services to undocumented women and thus increasingly denying services to battered immigrant women. In fact, emergency medical care and shelters continue to be available to everyone, regardless of immigration status. Some shelters also believe that their funding streams preclude them from serving immigrant women when in fact federal domestic violence funding carries no such restrictions. Given the limited number of beds, some shelters have chosen to provide services only where there is a guarantee of public benefits reimbursement and to deny these services to immigrant women whose eligibility for public benefits is in doubt. One Asian women's shelter director suspects that instead of fund-raising to increase language capacity and transitional programs specifically needed by immigrant women, these shelters justify discriminating against Asian immigrant women by simply stating that their programs cannot serve their needs.

Cultural Norms and Values That Lead to Violent Behavior

1. Acceptance of Violence Against Women

A survey conducted by the Boston Asian Task Force revealed that 20–25% of the respondents from the Cambodian, Chinese, Korean, South Asian, and Vietnamese communities surveyed thought that violence against a woman was justifiable in certain domestic disputes. The report also found that a higher number of Asian men than women condone family violence. Among Korean respondents, 29% (the highest percentage among the five ethnic groups surveyed) felt that a battered woman should not tell anyone. In general, Cambodian and Vietnamese respondents believe that a battered woman should not leave or divorce her husband. South Asian respondents felt that the woman in marriage becomes her husband's property and thus she cannot turn to her family and/or parents to ask them to intervene. Older Chinese respondents were more tolerant of the use of violence in certain situations, and younger Chinese were less likely to see leaving and divorce as viable options for battered women. Response patterns were similar between the foreign-born and U.S.-born. Moreover, these attitudes permeate all sectors of a community, including those who are supposed to protect battered women. One legal advocate who represents battered women in Hawai'i was dismayed to hear female interpreters at an immigrant social service agency siding with a particularly violent batterer on the grounds that his estranged wife was pregnant by another man.

In the home countries of many Asian women, extended families often exert collective pressure to prevent abuse of wives. However, migration to the U.S. broke up extended families and changed social practices to the detriment of women who often rank lowest in the family structure. In some communities this has resulted in the perversion of extended families from protector to perpetrator. NARIKA, a South Asian domestic violence resource center in Berkeley, has reported that there are cases where entire families, extended and joint, get involved in abusing a woman, with some members holding her down while others do the hitting. Therefore, conventional legal restraints, such as protective orders against the lone male abuser, are of limited use when there are multiple perpetrators including in-laws and other women in the family.

2. Cultural Emphasis on Preserving Family

The notion of having to preserve the family and "save face" often makes Asian women more hesitant to leave and break up the family. Women in abusive marriages are frequently blamed for not behaving or told to tolerate the abuse in order to save face for the entire family or clan. Because certain Asian communities are small and close-knit, victim advocates from the communities often face harassment and threats from the abuser and the family for helping women leave the relationship and upsetting the social order. Also, this pronounced belief in the sanctity of the family even in the face of violent victimization, combined with a cultural antipathy toward divorce, makes it more difficult for white shelter workers and advocates to provide support and understanding to Asian women. As the Boston-based Asian Task Force against Domestic Violence notes, "One of the biggest and most important challenges to addressing family violence within Asian communities is reconciling the differences between Western ideals of independence and individualism with Asian ideals of interdependence and group harmony."

In addition, the traditional Asian gender roles of male providers and female homemakers are often disrupted by the American economy that requires both partners to work outside the home. While this has been liberating for some Asian women, women's economic independence is seen as a threat to social orders that privilege men and has, in some communities, contributed to a rise in domestic violence.

3. Transforming Culture

Culture is not static, fixed, and unchangeable. Norms, values, and beliefs are constructed in the interchanges between and among people within cultural groups and are constantly evolving. As Asian immigrants, it can be threatening in light of changes forced by relocating to the United States, to think that cultures must also be changed from within. Who will we be then? Will we disappear as a distinct social group? There are aspects of Asian cultures that are worthy of saving and passing on. There are others that must be transformed in order to honor basic human rights—in this case, the right of women to be free from domestic violence (Perilla 1999). In Asian American communities, for example, the emphasis on preservation of the family is worthy but must be transformed so that it is achieved not by pressuring women into staying in violent situations, but by changing the cultural and social cues that sanction men's use of violence to control women. Thus, a number of Asian women's shelters and outreach groups frame their organizing work as "work to perpetuate the core values of each Asian community that are positive and to eliminate those parts that are no longer useful or healthy."

Battered Queer Asian American Women

Domestic violence is equally prevalent in queer Asian women's relationships. However, there is little research and data on same-gender relationship violence and what does exist tends to underreport the incidents involving queer Asian women. There are several causes for this underreporting. In 1998 national and local focus groups held by the Family Violence Prevention Fund and the San Francisco-based Asian Women's Shelter, queer Asian women divulged that they did not feel safe reporting relationship violence to the police or authorities. They feared that disclosing oneself as a lesbian being abused by another lesbian may subject them to further abuse at hands of the police. Many were hesitant to access service providers due to sexism, racism, homophobia, language and cultural barriers, and fear of disbelief among service providers. Queer Asian women often do not feel safe even speaking to friends. They may also hesitate to report their abusive partner because they do not want to further isolate a woman who is already marginalized by society or subject her to a homophobic, racist legal system and its consequences.

Even when abused queer Asian women seek help, they find that the vast majority of domestic violence agencies are not able to meet their needs. . . . The mainstream domestic violence movement understands violence as a patriarchal phenomenon, deriving from sexism, with men using violence to control women. . . . Women can be survivors and batterers. The typical response of mainstream domestic violence agencies is to ostracize the batterer. But banishing the abuser from a small, marginalized queer Asian community is akin to cutting her off from her only family members. Agencies do not have programs that assist both the batterer and survivor. The San Francisco shelter is the only program with a Queer Asian Women Services project.

The Organizations

The Shelter Programs

Since the first shelter program for Asian American women and children started in Los Angeles in 1981, six other Asian women's shelters have emerged

across the country along with over a dozen outreach, education and hotline programs for Asian women.[4] The majority of these were started by and for South Asian women. These include organizations such as Apna Ghar ("our home" in Hindi-Urdu), Manavi ("primal women" in Sanskrit), the Nav Nirmaan Foundation, Inc., the New York Asian Women's Center, Raksha ("protection" in several languages), Pragati ("progress"), and Sakhi ("women's friend").

The handful of shelters that are available cannot meet the need of Asian American women, especially limited-English-speaking women, in their regions, let alone the country. All these groups and shelters conduct some form of community education and outreach as part of their prevention activities to address the root causes of domestic violence. Shelters have conducted local advocacy, such as pressuring police departments to hire interpreters or working with them on protocols on handling domestic violence calls in Asian communities. Not until 1997 was the first large national pan-Asian conference convened in California that brought together 400 service providers and activists from across the country. Since then, other conferences have been held, such as one for Koreans in Los Angeles, South Asians in New York, and a pan-Asian conference in Ohio. With such limited capacity, locally based shelters and programs have relied on coalitions such as the National Network on Behalf of Battered Immigrant Women to conduct the statewide and national advocacy needed to address the unique challenges Asian women face, when and if those challenges dovetail with the agenda of these broader coalitions.[5]

Coalition Work

In 2000, as a means to address the lack of a national Asian American battered women's advocacy organization, the San Francisco-based Asian Women's Shelter, the Asian & Pacific Islander American Health Forum, the Family Violence Prevention Fund, and the National Resource Center on Domestic Violence, launched the *Asian and Pacific Islander Domestic Violence Institute (APIDVI)*. The mission of APIDVI is to advocate for policy changes and increased ethnicity specific data collection, facilitate the sharing of service models for battered Asian women and children, and promote national discussions on differing

Asian community perceptions of domestic violence, community responses to the problem and the intersecting cultural values. Since the formation of APIDVI, all the various Asian women's shelters and domestic violence programs have become members. Based on evidence of higher fatality rates among battered Asian women, its first research project is a fatality review of deaths of Asian and Pacific Islander women in major urban centers like Chicago, Santa Clara, San Francisco, and Boston. Its first advocacy project will focus on getting police departments to disaggregate fatality data by ethnicity because most departments simply put Asians under the "Other" category after "White," "Black," and "Hispanic." The APIDVI advocacy will focus on two areas: Welfare Reform and Cultural Competency as they relate to domestic violence. This work will be conducted by working groups consisting of its member organizations and coordinated by APIDVI staff. Initial funding came from the U.S. Department of Health and Human Services.

Transformative Initiatives

An example of work to transform local community attitudes on domestic violence in the Korean community is the SHIMTUH project—a joint project between the Asian Women's Shelter in San Francisco and the Korean Community Center of the East Bay. SHIMTUH has direct service, outreach, and organizing components. It reaches out to the social networks, structures, and institutions in the Korean community to transform cultural norms. Through cultural events, drumming, singing, working with the Korean press, and outreach to indigenous Korean religious institutions, SHIMTUH engages in public dialogue with religious leaders and others to influence more and more spheres in the community. Another example is the Family Violence Prevention Fund's reframing of the concept of "hiya" or shame in the Filipino community. In a poster campaign, the FVPF introduced the concept of "nakakahiya"—a woman should not feel ashamed for having bruises and being beaten, and the community should be ashamed for not helping her.

One example of work among immigrant men is the Tapestri Men's Group, a project of the Refugee's Women's Network, Inc., in Atlanta, Georgia. Tapes-

tri's philosophy is twofold. First, it believes that cultural norms are not immutable and can evolve. Second, it views the violence of men not as an individual pathology amenable to counseling or therapeutic intervention in one-on-one sessions, but rather as a social malaise where a man has learned through modeling at home and in society that the use of violence against women is an accepted way of resolving differences. Thus, Tapestri does not provide anger management because it views men's violence against women not as an angry man out of control, but as a man who chooses to be violent to control his partner.

In the men's groups where Asian, Latino, Caribbean, African, and East European men have participated, the transformative and re-education work takes place not by experts imparting information top down . . . , but through a process where men themselves critically explore, in an atmosphere of mutual respect and horizontal relationships, the antecedents, dynamics, and effects of their violent behaviors, values, and expectations. In the process, men's views of themselves and their roles as partners and fathers are transformed, gender identities are de-constructed and re-constructed, and the men become agents of change in their communities. The Tapestri Men's Group and others like it were created when domestic violence survivors, who did not want to leave their marriages, requested intervention programs for their husbands. As the men participate in the 24-week program, women advocates from Tapestri work with their wives to provide support, ensure that they are not in danger, and monitor the progress being made by the men.

Recommendations for Action

- Address racism, homophobia, and xenophobia within social service and law enforcement agencies that deal with battered Asian American women.

- Increase language access to all services needed by battered women through hiring of interpreters and bilingual staff and creating culturally competent services in police departments, shelters, and counseling and court intervention programs for men.

- Eliminate barriers to public benefits such as the chilling effects of mandatory reporting to the INS, fear of being designated a public charge, and hostile caseworkers.

- Train eligibility caseworkers on the exceptions for battered women, the Family Violence Option in TANF, and the myriad categories of immigrants to correct the widespread erroneous perception that immigrants are no longer eligible for benefits.

- Educate both government agencies and social service providers and immigrant women to understand and utilize the protective provisions in VAWA.

- Repeal the conditional residence status that has trapped women in violent homes and which the passage of VAWA simply will not fix.

- Address and transform cultural norms that accept violence against women as a means of discipline or control. This includes creating programs for both female and male Asian American batterers.

- Conduct studies on relationship violence in queer Asian women communities. Redefine domestic violence theories to include same-gender relationship violence.

NOTES

1. Mainstream shelters are designed in dormitory styles with congregated dining that is alienating to Asian women used to cooking their own foods, feeding their own children, and keeping their children with them most of the time. Additionally, Asian women have a difficult time following mainstream shelters' programs and procedures, such as participating in shelter chores selection, because of their inability to communicate with staff and other residents. They also report feeling very lost when they were forbidden to have any contacts with their mothers, who have traditionally been their source of support.

2. Court sentences that involve serving time and mandatory participation in intervention programs are often insufficient to convey the gravity of the crime to the batterer. In addition, there needs to be culturally relevant sentencing. For example, in the Hmong community, when clan elders resolve domestic violence cases through the mediation process, they may order the husband to hire a shaman for a soul-calling ceremony to heal the wife. When a wife has been abused, the soul leaves her body because it has been mistreated. When the soul is not well, the body is not well. In a soul-calling ceremony, a shaman calls the soul back to the body.

3. VAWA 2000's other provisions allow self-petitioning by women whose abuser husbands die or lose their immigration status or whose husbands have committed bigamy.

4. The seven shelters are the Asian Women's Home in San Jose, the Asian Women's Shelter in San Francisco, the Asian Women United in Minneapolis/St. Paul, the Center for Pacific Asian Families in Los Angeles, the New Moon Shelter in Boston, Apna Ghar in Chicago, and the New York Asian Women's Center. There are also programs within larger shelter programs like the Asian Unit of Interval House in Long Beach/Orange County, CA. In Atlanta, Georgia, the International Women's House serves women who do not speak English, including Asian immigrant women.

5. The National Network is made up of three groups, the Family Violence Prevention Fund, the Immigrant Women Program of NOW Legal Defense Fund (formerly housed at AYUDA, Inc.), and the National Immigration Project of the National Lawyer's Guild.

REFERENCES

Chan, Sue, M.D., "Domestic Violence in Asian and Pacific Islander (API) Communities," compilation of studies, statistics, and data on domestic violence and API's, Asian Health Services.

Family Violence Prevention Fund, January 1999, "Caught at the Public Policy Crossroads: The Impact of Welfare Reform on Battered Immigrant Women."

Perilla, Julia L., "Domestic Violence as a Human Rights Issue: The Case of Immigrant Latinos," reprinted from *Hispanic Journal of Behavioral Sciences*, Vol. 21, No. 2, May 1999, pp. 107–133.

Warrier, Sujata, Ph.D, "(Un)heard Voices: Domestic Violence in the Asian American Community," Family Violence Prevention Fund, produced with a grant from the Violence Against Women Office, Office of Justice Programs, U.S. Department of Justice.

Yoshioka, Marianne, Ph.D., M.S.W.," Asian Family Violence Report: A Study of the Cambodian, Chinese, Korean, South Asian and Vietnamese Communities in Massachusetts," Nov. 2000, Boston, MA.

◆◆◆

THIRTY-NINE

Sexual Violence and American Indian Genocide (1999)

Andy Smith

Native American scholar, writer, and activist **Andrea Smith** is cofounder of INCITE! Women of Color Against Violence, a national organization that utilizes critical dialogue, direct action, and grassroots organizing. She is an award-winning teacher, and has published widely. Her most recent book is *Conquest: Sexual Violence and American Indian Genocide.*

I once attended a conference where a speaker stressed the importance of addressing sexual violence within Native communities. When I returned home, I told a friend of mine, who was a rape survivor, about the talk. She replied, "You mean other Indian women have been raped?" When I said yes, she asked, "Well, why don't we ever talk about it?" Indeed, the silence surrounding sexual violence in Native communities—particularly the sexual assault of adult women—is overwhelming. Under Janet Reno, the Department of Justice poured millions of dollars into tribally-based sexual and domestic violence programs. Although domestic violence programs are proliferating, virtually no tribes have developed comprehensive sexual assault programs.

Native survivors of sexual violence often find no support when they seek healing and justice. When they seek help from non-Indian agencies, they are often told to disassociate themselves from their communities, where their abusers are. The underlying philosophy of the white-dominated anti-rape movement is implicit in Susan Brownmiller's statement: "[Rape] is nothing more or less than a conscious process of intimidation by which all men keep all women in a state of fear."[1] The notion that rape is "nothing more or less" than a tool of patriarchal control fails to consider how rape also serves as a tool of racism and colonialism. At the same time, when Native survivors of sexual violence seek healing within their communities, other community members accuse them of undermining Native sovereignty and being divisive by making their abuse public. According to the Mending the Hoop Technical

Assistance Project in Minnesota, tribally-based sexual assault advocates believe that a major difficulty in developing comprehensive programs to address sexual assault in tribal communities, particularly sexual violence against adult women, is that many community members believe that sexual violence is "traditional." Historical evidence suggests, however, that sexual violence was rare in Native communities prior to colonization, and that it has served as a primary weapon in the U.S. war against Native nations ever since. . . . Far from being traditional, sexual violence is an attack on Native sovereignty itself. As one elder stated at a conference I attended: "As long as we destroy ourselves from inside, we don't have to worry about anyone on the outside."

The Colonial Context of Sexual Violence

Ann Stoler argues that racism is a permanent part of the social fabric: "[R]acism is not an effect but a tactic in the internal fission of society into binary opposition, a means of creating 'biologized' internal enemies, against whom society must defend itself."[2] She notes that in the modern state, it is the constant purification and elimination of racialized enemies that ensures the growth of the national body. "Racism does not merely arise in moments of crisis, in sporadic cleansings. It is internal to the biopolitical state, woven into the web of the social body, threaded through its fabric."[3] Similarly, Kate Shanley notes that Native peoples are a permanent "present absence" in the U.S. colonial imagination, an "absence" that reinforces the conviction that Native peoples are vanishing and that the conquest of native lands is justified.[4] . . . This "absence" is effected through the metaphorical transformation of Native bodies into a pollution from which the colonial body must purify itself. In the 1860s, white Californians described Native people as "the dirtiest lot of human beings on earth." They wear "filthy rags, with their persons unwashed, hair uncombed and swarming with vermin."[5] An 1885 Proctor & Gamble ad for Ivory Soap also illustrates this equation between Indian bodies and dirt:

We were once factious, fierce and wild,
In peaceful arts unreconciled
Our blankets smeared with grease and stains
From buffalo meat and settlers' veins.
Through summer's dust and heat content
From moon to moon unwashed we went.
But IVORY SOAP came like a ray
Of light across our darkened way
And now we're civil, kind and good
And keep the laws as people should.
We wear our linen, lawn and lace
As well as folks with paler face
And now I take, where'er we go
This cake of IVORY SOAP to show
What civilized my squaw and me
And made us clean and fair to see.[6]

In the colonial imagination, Native bodies are also polluted with sexual sin. . . . In 1613, Alexander Whitaker, a minister in Virginia, wrote: "They live naked in bodie, as if their shame of their sinne deserved no covering: Their names are as naked as their bodie: They esteem it a virtue to lie, deceive and steale as their master the divell teacheth them."[7] Furthermore, according to Bernardino de Minaya: "Their [the Indians'] marriages are not a sacrament but a sacrilege. They are idolatrous, libidinous, and commit sodomy. Their chief desire is to eat, drink, worship heathen idols, and commit bestial obscenities."[8]

This understanding of Native peoples as dirty whose sexuality threatens U.S. security was echoed in the comments of one doctor in his attempt to rationalize the mass sterilization of Native women in the 1970s:

People pollute, and too many people crowded too close together cause many of our social and economic problems. These in turn are aggravated by involuntary and irresponsible parenthood. . . . We also have obligations to the society of which we are part. The welfare mess, as it has been called, cries out for solutions, one of which is fertility control.[9]

. . .

Because Indian bodies are considered "dirty," they are sexually violable and "rapable." In patriarchal thinking, only a "pure" body can really be violated. The rape of bodies that are considered inherently impure simply does not count. For instance, women in prostitution have an almost impossible time if they are raped because the dominant society considers a prostituted woman as lacking bodily integrity and violable at all times. Similarly, the history of mutilation of Indian bodies, both living and dead, makes it clear to Indian people that they are not considered to have bodily integrity. President Andrew Jackson, for instance, ordered the mutilation of approximately 800 Muscogee Indian corpses, cutting off their noses and slicing long strips of flesh from their bodies to make bridle reins.[10] Tecumseh's skin was flayed and made into razor-straps.[11] A soldier cut off the testicles of White Antelope to make a tobacco pouch. Colonel John Chivington led an attack against the Cheyenne and Arapahoe in which nearly all the victims were scalped, their fingers, arms, and ears amputated to obtain rings, necklaces, and other jewelry, and their private parts were cut out to be exhibited before the public in Denver.[12] Throughout the history of massacres against Indian people, colonizers attempted not only to defeat Indian people but to eradicate their very identity and humanity. They attempted to transform Indian people from human beings into tobacco pouches, bridle reins, or souvenirs—objects for white people's consumption.

As Stoler explains this process of racialized colonization, "[T]he more 'degenerates' and 'abnormals' [in this case, Native peoples] are eliminated, the lives of those who speak will be stronger, more vigorous, and improved. The enemies are not political adversaries, but those identified as external and internal threats to the population. Racism is the condition that makes it acceptable to put [certain people] to death in a society of normalization."[13] She further notes that "the imperial discourses on sexuality cast white women as the bearers of a racist imperial order."[14] By extension, as bearers of a counter-imperial order, Native women pose a supreme threat to the imperial order. Symbolic and literal control over their bodies is important in the war against Native people, as these examples attest:

When I was in the boat I captured a beautiful Carib woman. . . . I conceived desire to take pleasure. . . . I took a rope and thrashed her well, for which she raised such unheard screams that you would not have believed your ears. Finally we came to an agreement in such a manner that I can tell you that she seemed to have been brought up in a school of harlots.[15]

Two of the best looking of the squaws were lying in such a position, and from the appearance of the genital organs and of their wounds, there can be no doubt that they were first ravished and then shot dead. Nearly all of the dead were mutilated.[16]

One woman, big with child, rushed into the church, clasping the altar and crying for mercy for herself and unborn babe. She was followed, and fell pierced with a dozen lances . . . the child was torn alive from the yet palpitating body of its mother, first plunged into the holy water to be baptized, and immediately its brains were dashed out against a wall.[17]

The Christians attacked them with buffets and beatings. . . . Then they behaved with such temerity and shamelessness that the most powerful ruler of the island had to see his own wife raped by a Christian officer.[18]

I heard one man say that he had cut a woman's private parts out, and had them for exhibition on a stick. I heard another man say that he had cut the fingers off of an Indian, to get the rings off his hand. I also heard of numerous instances in which men had cut out the private parts of females, and stretched them over their saddlebows and some of them over their hats.[19]

Although the era of deliberate, explicit Indian massacres in North America is over, in Latin America the wholesale rape and mutilation of indigenous women's bodies has continued. . . . Many white feminists are correctly outraged by mass rapes in Bosnia, and have organized to instigate a war crimes tribunal against the Serbs. Yet one wonders why the mass rapes of indigenous women in Guatemala, Chiapas, or elsewhere in Latin America have not sparked the same outrage. Feminist legal scholar Catherine MacKinnon argues that in Bosnia, "the world has *never* seen sex used this consciously, this cynically, this elaborately, this openly, this systematically . . . as a means of destroying a whole people."[20] She seems to forget that she only lives on this land because millions of Native people were raped, sexually mutilated and murdered. Is mass rape of European

women "genocide," while mass rape of indigenous women is business as usual? Even in the white feminist imagination, are native women's bodies more rapable than white women's bodies?

The colonization of Native women's bodies continues today. In the 1980s, when I served as a nonviolent witness for the Chippewa spearfishers who were being harassed by white racist mobs, one white harasser carried a sign saying "Save a fish; spear a pregnant squaw." During the 1990 Mohawk crisis in Oka [Quebec], a white mob surrounded an ambulance taking a Native woman off the reservation because she was hemorrhaging after giving birth. She was forced to "spread her legs" to prove it. The police at the scene refused to intervene. An Indian man was arrested for "wearing a disguise" (he was wearing jeans), and was brutally beaten, with his testicles crushed. Two women from Chicago WARN (Women of All Red Nations, the organization I belong to) went to Oka to videotape the crisis. They were arrested and held in custody for eleven hours without being charged, and were told that they could not go to the bathroom unless the male police officers could watch. The place they were held was covered with pornographic magazines.

In 1982, this colonial desire to subjugate Indian women's bodies was quite apparent when Stuart Kasten marketed a new video, "Custer's Revenge," in which players get points each time they, in the character of Custer, rape an Indian woman. The slogan of the game is "When you score, you score." He describes the game as "a fun sequence where the woman is enjoying a sexual act willingly." According to the promotional material:

> You are General Custer. Your dander's up, your pistol's wavin'. You've hog-tied a ravishing Indian maiden and have a chance to rewrite history and even up an old score. Now, the Indian maiden's hands may be tied, but she's not about to take it lying down, by George! Help is on the way. If you're to get revenge you'll have to rise to the challenge, dodge a tribe of flying arrows and protect your flanks against some downright mean and prickly cactus. But if you can stand pat and last past the strings and arrows—You can stand last. Remember? Revenge is sweet.[21]

Ironically, while enslaving women's bodies, colonizers argued that they were actually freeing Native women from the "oppression" they supposedly faced in Native nations. Thomas Jefferson, for example, argued that Native women "are submitted to unjust drudgery. This I believe is the case with every barbarous people. It is civilization alone which replaces women in the enjoyment of their equality."[22] The *Mariposa Gazette* similarly noted that when Indian women were safely under the control of white men, they "are neat, and tidy, and industrious, and soon learn to discharge domestic duties properly and creditably."[23] In 1862, a Native man in Conrow Valley was killed and scalped with his head twisted off; his killers said, "You will not kill any more women and children."[24] Apparently, Native women can only be free while under the dominion of white men, and both Native and white women have to be protected from Indian men, rather than from white men. . . .

. . . Although stereotypes of Native women as beasts of burden for their men prevail, prior to colonization Indian societies were not male-dominated for the most part. Women served as spiritual, political, and military leaders. Many societies were matrilineal and matrilocal. Although there was a division of labor between women and men, women's and men's labor was accorded similar status.[25] Thus, the historical record would suggest, as Paula Gunn Allen argues, that the real roots of feminism should be found in Native societies. . . .

Just as, historically, white colonizers who raped Indian women claimed that Indian men were the real rapists, white men who rape and murder Indian women often make this same claim today. In Minneapolis, a white man, Jesse Coulter, raped, murdered and mutilated several Indian women. He claimed to be Indian, adopting the name Jesse Sittingcrow, and emblazoning an AIM tattoo on his arm.[26] Similarly, Roy Martin, a full-blooded Native man, was charged with sexual assault. The survivor identified the rapist as white, about 25 years old, with a shag haircut. Martin was 35 with hair past his shoulders.[27] Although this case was eventually dismissed, the fact that it even made it to trial indicates the extent to which Native men are seen as the rapists of white women.

Of course, Indian men do commit acts of sexual violence. After years of colonialism and boarding-school experiences, violence has been internalized in Indian communities. However, this view of the Indian man as the "true" rapist serves to obscure who has real power in this racist and patriarchal society. The U.S. is indeed engaged in a "permanent social war" against Native bodies, particularly Native women's bodies, which threaten its legitimacy.[28] Colonizers evidently recognize the wisdom of the Cheyenne saying, "A Nation is not conquered until the hearts of the women [and their bodies as well] are on the ground."

Through this colonization and abuse of their bodies, Indian people have learned to internalize self-hatred. Body image is integrally related to self-esteem. When one's body is not respected, one begins to hate oneself.[29] For example, Anne, a Native boarding-school student, reflects on this process:

> You better not touch yourself. . . . If I looked at somebody . . . lust, sex, and I got scared of those sexual feelings. And I did not know how to handle them. . . . What really confused me was if intercourse was sin, why are people born? . . . It took me a really long time to get over the fact that . . . I've sinned: I had a child.[30]

As her words indicate, when the bodies of Indian people are inherently sinful and dirty, it becomes a sin just to be Indian. Thus, it is not a surprise that Indian people who have survived sexual abuse often say that they no longer wish to be Indian. The Menominee poet Chrystos writes in such a voice in her poem "Old Indian Granny."

You told me about all the Indian women you counsel
who say they don't want to be Indian anymore
because a white man or an Indian one raped them
or killed their brother
or somebody tried to run them over in the street
or insulted them or all of it
our daily bread of hate
Sometimes I don't want to be Indian either
But I've never said so out loud before
Since I'm so proud and political
I have to deny it now
Far more than being hungry
having no place to live or dance
no decent job no home to offer a Granny
It's knowing with each invisible breath
that if you don't make something pretty
they can hang on their walls or wear around their
    necks
you might as well be dead.[31]

The fact that many Native peoples will argue that sexual violence is "traditional" indicates the extent to which our communities have internalized self-hatred. . . . Then, as Michael Taussig notes, Native peoples are portrayed by the dominant culture as inherently violent, self-destructive and dysfunctional. For example, in 1990, Mike Whelan made the following statement at a zoning hearing in South Dakota, calling for the denial of a permit for a shelter to serve Indian women who have been battered:

> Indian Culture as I view it, is presently so mongrelized as to be a mix of dependency on the Federal Government and a primitive society wholly on the outside of the mainstream of western civilization and thought. The Native American Culture as we know it now, not as it formerly existed, is a culture of hopelessness, godlessness, of joblessness, and lawlessness. . . . Alcoholism, social disease, child abuse, and poverty are the hallmarks of this so-called culture that you seek to promote, and I would suggest to you that the brave men of the ghost dance would hang their heads in shame at what you now pass off as that culture. . . . I think that the Indian way of life as you call it, to me means cigarette burns in arms of children, double-checking the locks on my cars, keeping a loaded shotgun by my door, and car bodies and beer cans on the front lawn. . . . This is not a matter of race, it is a matter of keeping our community and neighborhood away from that evil that you and your ideas promote.[32]

Taussig comments on the irony of this logic: "Men are conquered not by invasion but by themselves. It is a strange sentiment, is it not, when faced with so much brutal evidence of invasion."[33]

Completing the destruction of a people involves the destruction of the integrity of their culture and spirituality that forms the matrix of Native women's resistance to sexual colonization. Native counselors generally agree that a strong cultural and spiritual identity is essential if Native people are to heal from abuse. This is because Native women's healing entails healing not only from any personal abuse she has suffered, but also from the patterned history of abuse against her family, her nation, and the environment in which she lives.[34] Because Indian spiritual traditions are holistic, they have the ability to restore survivors of abuse to the community, and to restore their bodies to wholeness. That is why the most effective programs for healing revolve around reviving indigenous spiritual traditions.

In the colonial discourse, however, Native spiritual traditions become yet another site for the commodification of Indian women's bodies. As part of the genocidal process, Indian cultures lose the means to restore wholeness and become objects of consumerism for the dominant culture. Haunani Kay Trask, a Native Hawai'ian activist, describes this process as "cultural prostitution." "Prostitution, in this context, refers to the entire institution which defines a woman (and by extension the 'female') as an object of degraded and victimized sexual value for use and exchange through the medium of money. . . . My purpose is not to exact detail or fashion a model but to convey the utter degradation of our culture and our people under corporate tourism by employing 'prostitution' as an analytical category. . . . The point, of course, is that everything in Hawai'i can be yours, that is, you the tourist, the non-tourist, the visitor. The place, the people, the culture, even our identity as a 'Native' people is for sale. Thus, Hawai'i, like a lovely woman, is there for the taking."[35] . . .

Meanwhile, the colonizing religion [of Native peoples], Christianity, which is supposed to "save" Native women from allegedly sexually exploitative traditional practices, has only made them more vulnerable to sexual violence. The large-scale introduction of sexual violence in Native communities is largely a result of the Christian boarding-school system, which began in the 1600s under Jesuit priests along the St. Lawrence River. The system was more formalized in 1870 when Congress set aside funds to erect school facilities to be run by churches and missionary societies.[36] Attendance was mandatory and children were forcibly taken from their homes for the majority of the year. They were forced to practice Christianity (native traditions were prohibited) and speak English only.[37] Children were subjected to constant physical and sexual abuse. Irene Mack Pyawasit, a former boarding-school resident from the Menominee reservation, testifies to her experience, which is typical of many:

> The government employees that they put into the schools had families, but still there were an awful lot of Indian girls turning up pregnant. Because the employees were having a lot of fun, and they would force a girl into a situation, and the girl wouldn't always be believed. Then, because she came up pregnant, she would be sent home in disgrace. Some boy would be

blamed for it, never the government employee. He was always scot-free. And no matter what the girl said, she was never believed.[38]

Even when teachers were charged with abuse, boarding schools refused to investigate. In the case of just one teacher, John Boone, at the Hopi school, FBI investigations found that he had sexually abused over 142 children, but the school principal had not investigated any allegations of abuse.[39] Despite the epidemic of sexual abuse in boarding schools, the Bureau of Indian Affairs did not issue a policy on reporting sexual abuse until 1987, and did not issue a policy to strengthen the background checks of potential teachers until 1989.[40]

Although all Native people did not view their boarding-school experiences as negative, it appears that abuse became endemic in Indian families after the establishment of boarding schools in Native communities. Randy Fred, a former boarding-school student, says that children in his school began to mimic the abuse they were experiencing.[41] After Father Harold McIntee from St. Joseph's residential school on the Alkali Lake reserve was convicted of sexual abuse, two of his victims were later convicted of sexual abuse charges.[42]

Anti-Colonial Responses to Sexual Violence

The struggle for Native sovereignty and the struggle against sexual violence cannot be separated. Conceptualizing sexual violence as a tool of genocide and colonialism leads to specific strategies for combatting it. Currently, the rape crisis movement has called for strengthening the criminal justice system as the primary means to end sexual violence. Rape crisis centers receive much state funding, and, consequently, their strategies tend to be state-friendly: hire more police, give longer sentences to rapists, etc. There is a contradiction, however, in relying upon the state to solve the problems it is responsible for creating. Native people *per capita* are the most arrested, most incarcerated, and most victimized by police brutality of any ethnic group in the country.[43] Given the oppression Native people face within the criminal justice system, many communities are developing their own programs for addressing criminal behavior based on traditional ways of regulating their

societies. However, as James and Elsie B. Zion note, Native domestic violence advocates are often reluctant to pursue traditional alternatives to incarceration for addressing violence against women.[44] Survivors of domestic and sexual violence programs are often pressured to "forgive and forget" in tribal mediation programs that focus more on maintaining family and tribal unity than on providing justice and safety for women. In his study of traditional approaches for addressing sexual/domestic violence on First Nations reserves in Canada, Rupert Ross notes that these approaches are often very successful in addressing child sexual abuse where communities are less likely to blame the victim for the assault. In such cases, the community makes a pro-active effort in holding perpetrators accountable so that incarceration is often unnecessary. When a crime is reported, the working team that deals with sexual violence talks to the perpetrator and gives him the option of participating in the program. The perpetrator must first confess his guilt and then follow a healing contract, or go to jail. The perpetrator can decline to participate in the program and go through the normal routes in the criminal justice system. Everyone affected by the crime (victim, perpetrator, family, friends, and the working team) is involved in developing the healing contract. Everyone also holds the perpetrator to his contract. One Tlingit man noted that this approach was often more difficult than going to jail.

> First one must deal with the shock and then the dismay on your neighbors' faces. One must live with the daily humiliation, and at the same time seek forgiveness not just from victims, but from the community as a whole. . . . [A prison sentence] removes the offender from the daily accountability, and may not do anything towards rehabilitation, and for many may actually be an easier disposition than staying in the community.[45]

Along similar lines, Elizabeth Barker notes that the problem with the criminal justice system is that it diverts accountability from the community to players in the criminal justice system. Perpetrators are taken away from their community and are further limited from developing ethical relationships within a community context.[46] Ross notes: "In reality, rather than making the community a safer place, the threat of jail places the community more at risk."[47] Since the Hollow Lake reserve adopted this approach, 48 offenders have been identified. Only five chose to go to jail, and only two who entered the program have repeated crimes (one of the re-offenders went through the program again and has not re-offended since). However, Ross notes, these approaches often break down in cases where the victim is an adult woman because community members are more likely to blame her instead of the perpetrator for the assault.[48]

Many Native domestic violence advocates I have interviewed note similar problems in applying traditional methods of justice to cases of sexual assault and domestic violence. One advocate from a tribally-based program in the Plains area contends that traditional approaches are important for addressing violence against women, but they are insufficient. To be effective they must be backed up by the threat of incarceration. She notes that medicine men have come to her program saying, "We have worked with this offender and we have not been successful in changing him. He needs to join your batterers' program." Traditional approaches to justice presume that the community will hold a perpetrator accountable for his crime. However, in cases of violence against adult women, community members often do not regard this violence as a crime and will not hold the offender accountable. Before such approaches can be effective, we must implement community education programs that will change community attitudes about these issues.

Another advocate from a reservation in the Midwest argues that traditional alternatives to incarceration might be more harsh than incarceration. Many Native people presume that traditional modes of justice focused on conflict resolution. In fact, she argues, penalties for societal infractions were not lenient. They included banishment, shaming, reparations, and sometimes death. This advocate was involved in an attempt to revise tribal codes by reincorporating traditional practices, but she found that it was difficult to determine what these practices were and how they could be made useful today. For example, some practices, such as banishment, would not have the same impact today. Prior to colonization, Native communities were so close-knit and interdependent that banishment was often the equivalent of a death sentence. Today, however, Native peoples can simply leave home and join the dominant society. In addition, the elders with whom she consulted admitted that their memories of traditional penal systems were tainted with the experience of being in boarding school.

Since incarceration is understood as punishment, this advocate believes that it is the most appropriate way to address sexual violence. She argues that if a Native man rapes someone, he subscribes to white values rather than Native values because rape is not an Indian tradition. If he follows white values, then he should suffer the white way of punishment.

However, there are a number of difficulties in pursuing incarceration as the solution for addressing sexual assault. First, so few rapes are reported that the criminal justice system rarely has the opportunity to address the problem. Among tribal programs I have investigated, an average of about two cases of rape are reported each year. Because rape is a major crime, rape cases are generally handed to the State's Attorney, who then declines the vast majority of cases. By the time tribal law-enforcement programs even see rape cases, a year might have passed since the assault, making it difficult for them to prosecute. Also, because rape is covered by the Major Crimes Act, many tribes have not developed codes to address it as they have for domestic violence. One advocate who conducted a training for southwestern tribes on sexual assault says that the participants said they did not need to develop codes because the "Feds will take care of rape cases." She asked how many rape cases had been federally prosecuted, and the participants discovered that not one case of rape had ever reached the federal courts. In addition, there is inadequate jail space in many tribal communities. When the tribal jail is full, the tribe has to pay the surrounding county to house its prisoners. Given financial constraints, tribes are reluctant to house prisoners for any length of time.

But perhaps most importantly, as sociologist Luana Ross (Salish) notes, incarceration has been largely ineffective in reducing crime rates in the dominant society, much less Native communities. "The white criminal justice system does not work for white people; what makes us think it's going to work for us?" she asks.

> The criminal justice system in the United States needs a new approach. Of all the countries in the world, we are the leader in incarceration rates. . . . Society would profit if the criminal justice system employed restorative justice. . . . Most prisons in the United States are, by design, what a former prisoner termed "the devil's house." Social environments of this sort can only produce dehumanizing conditions.[49]

As a number of studies have demonstrated, more prisons and more police do not lead to lower crime rates.[50] For instance, the Rand Corporation found that California's three-strikes legislation, which requires life sentences for three-time convicted felons, did not reduce the rate of "murders, rapes, and robberies that many people believe to be the law's principal targets."[51] Changes in crime rate often have more to do with fluctuations in employment rates than with increased police surveillance or increased incarceration rates.[52] Steven Walker concludes: "Because no clear link exists between incarceration and crime rates, and because gross incapacitation locks up many low-rate offenders at a great dollar cost to society, we conclude as follows: gross incapacitation is not an effective policy for reducing serious crime."[53] Similarly, criminologist Elliot Currie found that "the *best* face put on the impact of massive prison increases, in a study routinely used by prison supporters to prove that 'prison works,' shows that prison growth seems not to have 'worked' at all for homicide or assault, barely if at all for rape. . . . "[54]

The premise of the justice system is that most people are law-abiding except for "deviants" who do not follow the law. However, given the epidemic rates of sexual and domestic violence . . . , it is clear that most men are implicated in our rape culture. It is not likely that we can send all of these men to jail. As Fay Koop argues, addressing rape through the justice system simply furthers the myth that rape/domestic violence is caused by a few bad men, rather than seeing most men implicated in such violence.[55] Thus, relying upon the criminal justice system to end violence against women may strengthen the colonial apparatus in tribal communities that furthers violence while providing nothing more than the illusion of safety to survivors of sexual and domestic violence. . . .

Sexual violence is a fundamental attack on Indian sovereignty, and both Native and non-Native communities are challenged to develop programs that address sexual violence from an anti-colonial, anti-racist framework so that we don't attempt to eradicate acts of personal violence by strengthening the apparatus of state violence. Nothing less than a holistic approach towards eradicating sexual violence can be successful. As Ines Hernandez-Avila states:

We must imagine a world without rape. But I cannot imagine a world without rape, a world without misogyny, without imagining a world without racism, classism, sexism, homophobia, ageism, historical amnesia and other forms and manifestations of violence directed against those communities that are seen to be "asking for it." Even the Earth is presumably "asking for it." . . . What do I imagine then? From my own Native American perspective, I see a world where sovereign indigenous peoples continue to plunge our memories to come back to our originality, to live in dignity and carry on our resuscitated and ever-transforming cultures and traditions with liberty. . . . I see a world where native women find strength and continuance in the remembrance of who we really were and are . . . a world where more and more native men find the courage to recognize and honor—that they and the women of their families and communities have the capacity to be profoundly vital and creative human beings.[56]

NOTES

1. Susan Brownmiller, *Against our will* (Toronto: Bantam Books, 1986), p. 5.

2. Ann Stoler, *Race and the education of desire* (Durham, N.C.: Duke University Press, 1997), p. 59.

3. Ibid., p. 59.

4. Lecture, Indigenous Intellectual Sovereignties Conference. UC Davis, April 1998.

5. James Rawls, *Indians of California: The changing image* (Norman: University of Oklahoma Press, 1984), p. 195.

6. Andre Lopez, *Pagans in our midst* (Mohawk Nation: Akwesasne Notes), p. 119.

7. Robert Berkhofer, *The White Man's Indian* (New York: Vintage, 1978), p. 19.

8. David Stannard, *American Holocaust: Columbus and the conquest of the New World* (New York: Oxford University Press, 1992), p. 211.

9. Oklahoma: Sterilization of native women charged to I.H.S., in *Akwesasne Notes*, mid Winter, p. 30.

10. Stannard, *American Holocaust*, p.121.

11. David Wrone and Russell Nelson (eds.), *Who's the savage? A documentary history of the mistreatment of the Native North Americans* (Malabar: Robert Krieger Publishing, 1982), p. 82. Quote William James, *A full and correct account of the military occurrences of the late war between Great Britain and the United States of America* (2 vols., London: printed by the author, 1818), vol. 1, pp. 293–296.

12. John Terrell, *Land grab: The truth about the "winning of the West"* (New York: Doubleday, 1972), p. 13.

13. Stoler, p. 85.

14. Ibid., p. 35.

15. From Cuneo, an Italian nobleman, quoted in Kirkpatrick Sale, *The conquest of paradise: Christopher Columbus and the Columbian legacy* (New York: Knopf, 1990), p. 140.

16. Wrone and Nelson, *Who's the savage?* p. 123. Cite U.S. Commissioner of Indian Affairs, *Annual Report for 1871* (Washington, D.C.: Government Printing Office, 1871), pp. 487–488.

17. Ibid., p. 97. Cite LeRoy R. Haven (ed.), *Ruxton of the Rockies* (Norman: University of Oklahoma Press, 1950), pp. 46–149.

18. Las Casas, p. 33.

19. *The Sand Creek Massacre: A documentary history*, pp. 129–130. Quotes Lieutenant James D. Cannon from "Report of the Secretary of War," 39th Congress, Second Session, Senate Executive Document 26, Washington, D.C., 1867. New York: Sol Lewis, 1973.

20. Catherine MacKinnon, Turning rape into pornography: Postmodern genocide, in *Ms. Magazine*, 4, no. 1, p. 27 (emphasis added).

21. Undated promotional material from Public Relations: Mahoney/Wasserman and Associates, Los Angeles, Calif.

22. Quoted in Roy Harvey Pearce, *Savagism and civilization* (Baltimore: Johns Hopkins Press, 1965), p. 93.

23. Robert Heizer (ed.), *The destruction of California Indians* (Lincoln: University of Nebraska Press, 1993), p. 284.

24. James Rawls, *Indians of California*, p. 182.

25. See Annette Jaimes and Theresa Halsey, American Indian women: At the center of indigenous resistance in North America, in Annette Jaimes (ed.), *The state of Native America: Genocide, colonization, and resistance* (Boston: South End Press, 1992), pp. 311–344.

26. Mark Brunswick and Paul Klauda, Possible suspect in serial killings jailed in N. Mexico, in *Minneapolis Star and Tribune*, May 28, 1987, p. 1A.

27. Indian man being tried for rape with no evidence, in *Fargo Forum*, January 9, 1995.

28. Stoler, p. 69.

29. For further discussion on the relationship between bodily abuse and self-esteem, see *The courage to heal: A guide for women survivors of child sexual abuse*, edited by Ellen Bass and Laura Davis (New York: Harper & Row, 1988), esp. pp. 207–222; and Bonnie Burstow, *Radical feminist therapy* (London: Sage, 1992), esp. pp. 187–234.

30. Quoted in Celia Haig-Brown, *Resistance and renewal* (Vancouver: Tilacum, 1988), p. 108.

31. Chrystos, *Fugitive Colors* (Vancouver: Press Gang, 1995), p. 41.

32. Native American Women's Health and Education Resource Center, *Discrimination and the double whammy* (Lake Andes, S. Dak.: Native American Women's Health and Education Resource Center, 1990), pp. 2–3.

33. Michael Taussig, *Shamanism, colonialism and the wild man* (Chicago: University of Chicago Press, 1987), p. 20.

34. Justine Smith (Cherokee), personal conversation, February 17, 1994.

35. Haunani Kay Trask, *From a native daughter: Colonialism and sovereignty in Hawai'i* (Monroe, Maine: Common Courage Press, 1993) pp. 185–194.

36. Jorge Noriega, American Indian education in the United States: Indoctrination for subordination to colonialism, in *State of Native America*, p. 380.

37. Frederick Binder and David M. Reimers (eds.), *The way we lived* (Lexington, Mass.: D. C. Heath, 1982), p. 59. Quotes U.S. Bureau of Indian Affairs, "Rules for Schools," Annual Report of the Commissioner of Indian Affairs, 1890, Washington, D.C., pp. cxlvi, cl–clii.

38. Fran Leeper Buss, *Dignity: Lower income women tell of their lives and struggles* (Ann Arbor: University of Michigan Press, 1985), p. 156. For further accounts of the widespread nature of sexual and other abuse in boarding schools, see Native Horizons Treatment Center, *Sexual abuse handbook* (Hagersville, Ont.), pp. 61–68; The end of silence, *Maclean's*, vol. 105, no. 37, September 14, 1992, pp. 14, 16; Jim deNomie, American Indian boarding schools: Elders remember, in *Aging News*, Winter 1990–91, pp. 2–6; David Wrone and Russell Nelson, *Who's the savage?* pp. 152–154, cite U.S. Congress, Senate, Subcommittee on Indian Affairs, *Survey of the conditions of the Indians in the United States*, Hearings before a subcommittee of the Committee on Indian Affairs, Senate, SR 79, 70th Congress, 2d session, 1929, pp. 428–429, 1021–1023, 2833–2835.

39. Goodbye BIA, Hello New Federalism, in *American Eagle*, vol. 2, no. 6, December 1994, p. 19. After the allegations of abuse became public, the BIA merely provided a counselor for the abused children who used his sessions with them to write a book.

40. Child sexual abuse in federal schools, in *The Ojibwe News*, January 17, 1990, p. 8.

41. Celia Haig-Brown, *Resistance and renewal*, pp. 14–15.

42. Native Horizons Treatment Center, *Sexual abuse handbook*, p. 66. Quotes *The Province*, July 19, 1989, and *Vancouver Sun*, March 17, 1990.

43. Troy Armstrong, Michael Guilfoyle, and Ada Pecos Melton, Native American delinquency: An overview of prevalence, causes, and correlates, in Marianne O. Nielsen and Robert A. Silverman (eds.), *Native Americans, crime, and justice* (Boulder, Colo.: Westview Press, 1996), p. 81.

44. James Zion and Elsie Zion, Hazho's Sokee'—Stay together nicely: Domestic violence under Navajo common law, in Nielsen and Silverman (eds.), *Native Americans, crime, and justice*, p. 106.

45. Rupert Ross, *Return to the teachings* (London: Penguin Books, 1997), p. 18.

46. Elizabeth Barker, The paradox of punishment in light of the anticipatory role of abolitionism, in Herman Bianchi and Rene van Swaaningern (eds.), *Abolitionism* (Amsterdam: Free University Press, 1986), p. 91.

47. Ross, *Return to the teachings*, p. 38.

48. Rupert Ross, Leaving our white eyes behind: The sentencing of native accused, in Nielsen and Silverman (eds.), *Native Americans, crime, and justice*, p. 168.

49. Luana Ross, *Inventing the savage: The social construction of Native American criminality* (Austin: University of Texas Press, 1998).

50. Steven Donziger, *The real war on crime* (New York: HarperCollins, 1996), p. 42, 162; Samuel Walker, *Sense and nonsense about crime and drugs* (Belmont, Calif.: Wadsworth, 1998); Elliott Currie, *Crime and punishment in America* (New York: Metropolitan Books, 1998).

51. Quoted in Walker, *Sense and nonsense about crime and drugs*, p. 139.

52. Steve Box and Chris Hale, Economic crisis and the rising prisoner population in England and Wales, in *Crime and social justice*, 1982, vol. 17, pp. 20–35. Mark Colvin, Controlling the surplus population: The latent functions of imprisonment and welfare in late U.S. capitalism, in

B. D. MacLean (ed), *The political economy of crime* (Scarborough: Prentice-Hall Canada, 1986). Ivan Jankovic, Labour market and imprisonment, in *Crime and social justice*, 1977, vol. 8 pp. 17–31.

53. Walker, *Sense and nonsense about crime and drugs*, p. 130.

54. Currie, *Crime and punishment in America*, p. 59.

55. Fay Honey Koop, On radical feminism and abolition, in *We who would take no prisoners: Selections from the Fifth International Conference on Penal Abolition* (Vancouver: Collective Press, 1993), p. 592.

56. Ines Hernandez-Avila, In praise of insubordination, or what makes a good woman go bad? In Emilie Buchwald, Pamela R. Fletcher, and Martha Roth (eds.), *Transforming a rape culture* (Minneapolis: Milkweed, 1993), pp. 388–389.

FORTY

◆◆◆

My Vagina Was My Village (1998)

Eve Ensler

Eve Ensler is a playwright and performer, known worldwide for *The Vagina Monologues*, based on interviews with hundreds of women. Her numerous plays have won many honors, including a Guggenheim Fellowship Award in Playwriting. She is a founder of V-Day, a global movement to stop violence against women and girls.

My vagina was green, water soft pink fields, cow mooing sun resting sweet boyfriend touching lightly with soft piece of blond straw.

There is something between my legs. I do not know what it is. I do not know where it is. I do not touch. Not now. Not anymore. Not since.

My vagina was chatty, can't wait, so much, so much saying, words talking, can't quit trying, can't quit saying, oh yes, oh yes.

Not since I dream there's a dead animal sewn in down there with thick black fishing line. And the bad dead animal smell cannot be removed. And its throat is slit and it bleeds through all my summer dresses.

My vagina singing all girl songs, all goat bells ringing songs, all wild autumn field songs, vagina songs, vagina home songs.

Not since the soldiers put a long thick rifle inside me. So cold, the steel rod canceling my heart. Don't know

whether they're going to fire it or shove it through my spinning brain. Six of them, monstrous doctors with black masks shoving bottles up me too. There were sticks, and the end of a broom.

My vagina swimming river water, clean spilling water over sun-baked stones over stone clit, clit stones over and over.

Not since I heard the skin tear and made lemon screeching sounds, not since a piece of my vagina came off in my hand, a part of the lip, now one side of the lip is completely gone.

My vagina. A live wet water village. My vagina my hometown.

Not since they took turns for seven days smelling like feces and smoked meat, they left their dirty sperm inside me. I became a river of poison and pus and all the crops died, and the fish.

My vagina a live wet water village.
They invaded it. Butchered it and burned it
    down.
I do not touch now.
Do not visit.
I live someplace else now.
I don't know where that is.

7

♦♦♦

Relationships, Families, and Households

Losing a close friend, asking for support from family and friends at difficult times, falling in love, moving in with a roommate or partner, holding your newborn baby for the first time, breaking up with a partner of many years, struggling to understand a teenage son or daughter, and helping your mother to die with dignity and in peace are commonplace life events. These ties between us, as human beings, define the very texture of our personal lives. They are a source of much happiness, affirmation, and personal growth as well as frustration, misunderstanding, anxiety, and, sometimes, misery. This chapter looks at personal relationships—between women and men, women and women, parents and children—and the ways in which an idealized notion of family masks the reality of family life for many people in the United States. We argue that families—however they are defined—need to be able to care for their members and that specific forms are much less important than the quality of the relationships between people.

Defining Ourselves Through Connections with Others

As suggested in Chapter 2, personal and family relationships are central to individual development, the definition of self, and the ongoing development of our identities. This involves relying on others when we are very young and later negotiating with them for material care, nurturance, and security; defining our own voice, space, independence, and sense of closeness to others; and learning about ourselves, our family and cultural heritage, ideas of right and wrong, practical aspects of life, and how to negotiate the world outside the home. In the family we learn about socially defined **gender roles:** what it means to be a daughter, brother, wife, or father, and what is expected of us. Family resources, including material possessions, emotional bonds, cultural connections and language, and status in the wider community, are also important for the experiences and opportunities they offer children.

How we are treated by parents and siblings and our observations of adult relationships during childhood provide the early foundation for our own adult relationships. Friends and family members may offer rules for dating etiquette. Magazine features and advice columns coach us in how to catch a man (or woman, in the case of lesbian magazines) and how to keep him or her happy once we have. Jaclyn Geller (2001, p. 10), who teaches writing and literature, cites a "plethora of dating books" published in the 1980s and '90s by women for a mass women's readership. A sampling of titles includes *How to Get a Man to Make a Commitment or Know When He Never Will* (Barnes and Clarke 1986), *If I'm So Wonderful Why Am I Still Single? Ten Strategies That Will Change Your Love Life Forever* (Page 1988), *The Savvy Woman's Success Bible: How to Find the Right Job, the Right Man, and the Right Life* (Santi-Flaherty 1997), *How to Get Married After Thirty-five: The Game Plan for Love* (Rosenberg 1988), *He's Not All That! How to Attract the Good Guys* (Carle 2000), and *Date Like a Man: What Men Know about Dating and Are Afraid You'll Find Out* (Moore and Gould 2001). The ups and downs of personal relationships are the material of countless magazines, novels, movies, pop music, talk shows, reality TV shows (*Who Wants to Marry a Millionaire?*), and sitcoms that increasingly include gay and lesbian characters (Reading 25). Many women value themselves in terms of whether they can attract and hold a partner. Whole sections of bookstores are given over to books and manuals that analyze relationship problems and teach "relationship skills"; counselors and therapists make a living helping us sort out our personal lives. Regardless of sexual orientation, we are all socialized in a heterosexual and heterosexist world, as argued by Adrienne Rich (1986a; see Ingraham 2004).

Marriage, Domestic Partnerships, and Personal Relationships

Young people in the United States currently face fundamental contradictions concerning intimate relationships, marriage, and family life. Marriage is highly romanticized: The partners marry for love and are expected to live happily ever after. Love

marriages are a relatively recent phenomenon. Although most families in the United States no longer arrange a daughter's marriage, they usually have clear expectations of the kind of man they want her to fall in love with. The ideal of marriage as a committed partnership seems to hold across sexual orientation, with women looking for Mr. or Ms. Right. Marriage and motherhood are often thought to be an essential part of a woman's life, the status to strive for, even if she chooses to keep her own name or rarely uses the title Mrs. People may not refer to unmarried women as "old maids" or "on the shelf" as much as in the past, but there is often still a stigma attached to being single in many cultural groups if a woman remains unmarried after a certain age.

Women marry for many reasons, following cultural and religious precepts. They may believe that marriage will make their relationship more secure or provide a stronger foundation for their children. There are macro-level material benefits in terms of taxes, health insurance, pension rights, ease of inheritance, and immigration status. In 1997, the U.S. General Accounting Office found no less than 1,049 federal laws in which benefits, rights, and privileges are contingent on marital status. At the micro and meso levels marriage provides recognition, validation, and a sense of personal empowerment. It is the conventional and respected way of publicly affirming one's commitment to a partner and being supported in this commitment by family and friends, as well as societal institutions. However, under the excitement and romance of the wedding and despite the fact that many partnerships are thriving, marriage as an institution is taking a buffeting, mainly because of changes in the economy and changing ideas of women's role in society (Reading 46; also Coontz 1997; Risman 1998; Skolnick 1991).

Women on welfare are being urged into marriage, however. Given that two-parent families have higher incomes than single parents, the framers of this policy reason that marriage will lift single mothers out of poverty, and the federal government has made millions of dollars available to states for marriage promotion programs. The 1996 Personal Responsibility and Work Opportunity Reconciliation Act that provides for Temporary Assistance to Needy Families (TANF) declares that "marriage is the foundation of a successful society" (quoted in Mink 2002). TANF eligibility rules "can include mandatory enrollment in marriage classes and couples counseling" (Mink 2002). Incentives can be paid to mothers who marry. Moreover, states that reduce births to unmarried women without resorting to abortions can receive "illegitimacy bonuses." Mothers receiving welfare are subject to severe bureaucratic intrusion into their personal lives and their ability to make decisions for themselves and their families. They are required to disclose the identity of their child's father and to pursue a child support order against him, regardless of whether they want the men in their lives.

Contradictions Surrounding the Institution of Marriage

As marriage has become less necessary for many women, the wedding industry has grown enormously (Geller 2001; Ingraham 1999). Weddings are a mainstay of popular culture. A very small sampling of successful wedding films includes *Four Weddings and a Funeral, Monsoon Wedding, My Big Fat Greek Wedding, The Wedding Banquet,* and *The Wedding Singer.* TV shows also include weddings, especially as the climax of a series. Weddings of movie stars, public figures, and royalty are featured in media photo spreads that make use of the "fairy tale formula familiar to many—especially women—since early childhood" (Ingraham 1999, p. 127). Magazines like *Bride's,* wedding experts and managers, bridal-gown designers, florists, jewelers, photographers, and stationery specialists are all part of a highly profitable wedding industry. The average U.S. wedding has 168 guests and costs $22,360 (*Mother Jones* 2005, p. 24). Note that this current emphasis on weddings comes at a time when the institution of heterosexuality is under pressure from feminists and the lesbian, gay, bisexual, and transgender movement. Autobiographical writings on marriage by heterosexual women reflect these contradictions, and also affirm the authors' decisions to marry (Cohen 2001; Corral and Miya-Jervis 2001; Nissinen 2000).

Compared with their mothers or grandmothers, fewer U.S. women are marrying, and many of those who do are marrying later, though they may be involved in committed relationships that last longer than many marriages. In 2003, 75 percent of women between the ages of 20 and 24, and 40 percent aged

between 25 and 29 had never married. From 1970 to 2003, the proportion of women who never married went up from 55 percent to 75 percent for women aged 20 to 24; doubled for those aged 25 to 29 (from 19 percent to 40 percent); and more than doubled for women aged 30 to 34 (from 9 percent to 22 percent) (U.S. Bureau of the Census 2004). Though some research suggests that the vast majority of young people want to marry, a growing number of them see marriage as financially unattainable. For others it may be a longer-term goal. Middle-class women are putting off marriage as well as childbearing. Sociologists Kathryn Edin and Maria Kefalas found that some low-income women choose to have children while they are young as a way of achieving one of their life goals. They hope for marriage sometime in the future when they have more economic stability (Edin and Kefalas 2005).

Others oppose marriage as the institutionalization of social and economic inequalities between men and women. As Naomi Wolf notes in Reading 23, under English and subsequently U.S. law, a husband and wife were one person in law; married women and children were literally the property of their husbands and fathers. Not for nothing was it called wed*lock.* Jaclyn Geller (2001, Chapter 1) gives a detailed history of marriage as a patriarchal institution between fundamentally unequal partners. She views marriage as the paradigmatic institution that makes heterosexuality appear natural and "normal," and as a heterosexual woman she vehemently opposes it. Sociologist Pepper Schwartz (1994) advocates peer marriage—a marriage of equal companions who collaborate to produce "profound intimacy and mutual respect" (p. 2), a model that many young women embrace.

Personal Relationships: Living in Different Worlds?

Other commentators and theorists assume a basic inequality between men and women in personal relationships, though they do not critique the institution of heterosexuality. Therapist John Gray, the author of several best-sellers, including *Men Are from Mars, Women Are from Venus* (1992), argues that men and women are socialized differently and have different styles of communication. He assumes that women as a group are naturally giving and caring

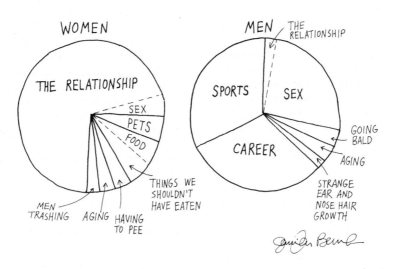

THOUGHT FREQUENCY AS PIE CHARTS

and that men as a group are "wired up" to be providers, an assumption we reject, favoring a social constructionist view of gender as something learned rather than innate (see Chapter 1). Sociolinguist Deborah Tannen (1990) bases her work on the premise that boys and girls grow up in essentially different cultures. She analyzes everyday conversations between men and women to make sense of the "seemingly senseless misunderstandings that haunt our relationships" (p. 13). She argues that, for men, conversations are negotiations about independence; for women they are about connection and closeness. Partners in heterosexual relationships, she notes, are "living with asymmetry," and each can benefit from learning the other's conversational styles and needs (p. 287).

Sexuality is one of the few recognized ways in this society for people to make intimate connections, especially for men, who are not socialized to express emotions easily. In her groundbreaking research into men's and women's attitudes to sexuality and love, Shere Hite (1994) found that for her male respondents, dating and marriage are primarily about sex and that they often shop around for varied sexual experiences. For Hite's women respondents, expressing emotion through sexual intimacy and setting up a home were usually much more important than they were for men. Hite attributes

much of the frustration in personal relationships to these very different approaches. She argues that many women give up on their hope for an emotionally satisfying relationship and settle for companionability with a male partner, while devoting much of their emotional energy elsewhere: to their children, work, or other interests. At the same time, she sees women as "revolutionary agents of change" in relationships, working with men to renegotiate this intimate part of their lives. Naomi Wolf's discussion of radical heterosexuality (Chapter 4) is also relevant here.

Personal relationships always include an element of power, though in more **egalitarian** relationships this shifts back and forth. Social psychologist Hilary Lips (1991) describes this power imbalance in terms of "the principle of least interest" (p. 57), a concept taken from social exchange theory. The person who has the least interest in a relationship—in a heterosexual relationship, often the man—has the most power in it. The least-interested person's moods, wants, and needs will tend to be dominant. This principle is also applicable at the macro level. As a group, women learn that it is our job to catch a man. In dating relationships we often assume the principle of greatest interest, the place of least power. This approach is also useful in thinking about LGBT relationships: does the principle of least interest operate among same-sex couples, and if so, how?

Gay Marriage and Domestic Partnership

Through committed long-term partnerships, concerted lobbying, major national demonstrations, and direct action, lesbians and gay men have emphasized the validity of their families. More gay and lesbian couples are celebrating their relationships in commitment ceremonies, and the *New York Times,* for example, publishes these announcements together with wedding announcements. Demands for gay marriage in the interests of equal treatment for lesbians, gay men, and heterosexual couples provide an interesting counterweight to feminist critiques of marriage as inherently patriarchal. In 1996 the U.S. Congress passed an anti–gay marriage bill, the Defense of Marriage Act, that excludes same-sex couples from receiving federal protections and rights of marriage. Even if states allowed gay marriage, the Defense of Marriage Act would block gay partners from receiving federal benefits. Not all lesbians or gay men want to marry, understanding that "legalizing gay and lesbian marriage will not 'dismantle the legal structure of gender in every marriage'" (Polikoff 1993; also Reading 41 and Gomez 2000).

Lesbians and gay men, together with heterosexual couples who have chosen not to marry, have campaigned for the benefits of "domestic partnership"—to be covered by a partner's health insurance, for example, or to be able to draw the partner's pension if he or she dies. As of December 2003, 200 of the Fortune 500 companies offered domestic-partnership health benefits for same-sex partners, including AT&T, Chase Manhattan Bank, Chevron, Costco Wholesale, Mobil, Microsoft, Viacom, and Wells Fargo (Human Rights Campaign Foundation 2004). The list of state and local governments and academic institutions offering domestic-partnership benefits continues to grow. 2004 saw a flurry of same-sex weddings in Massachusetts, the only state that issues marriage licenses to same-sex couples. San Francisco Mayor Gavin Newsom authorized same-sex weddings in February, but the California Supreme Court banned this later in the year. This issue will continue to be contentious and contested. Advocates argue that mixed-sex marriage laws are discriminatory and unjust, denying same-sex couples the many legal, economic, and social benefits that privilege heterosexual marriages. Some suggest that same-sex marriage, without traditional gender roles, can provide a more equitable model of marriage in the wider society. Some opponents contend that same-sex marriage defiles the sanctity of heterosexual marriage and heterosexual families (see Reading 46). Amy Gluckman (2004) opposes same-sex marriage as a privatized solution for basic supports such as medical insurance and pension plans that should be provided universally. In Reading 41, Paula Ettelbrick argues against marriage for gay men and lesbians and contends that the goals of gay liberation must be much broader than the right to marry. Political science professor Mary Shanley (2004), also questions the whole institution of marriage that same-sex couples seek to enter and propose other arrangements that would offer personal freedoms and supports for committed relationships—gay or straight—such as civil unions, universal care-giving partnerships, "nonconjugal relationships of economic and emotional interdependency," and polyamorous relationships (Shanley 2004, p. 112).

As of August 2005, New Jersey, New Mexico, New York, Rhode Island, and the District of Columbia have no explicit provisions prohibiting marriages between individuals of the same sex. Vermont and Connecticut have statewide laws that provide state-level spousal rights to same-sex couples within the state, as civil unions; Hawai'i, Maine, and New Jersey have statewide laws that provide some spousal rights to unmarried couples; California has a statewide law that provides almost all state-level spousal rights to unmarried couples who register domestic partnerships (Human Rights Campaign Foundation 2005).

College-educated women in their twenties, thirties, and forties have grown up with much more public discussion of women's rights than did their mothers and with expanded opportunities for education and professional work. Those who work in corporate or professional positions have more financial security in their own right than did middle-class housewives of the 1950s, for example, and are less interested in what sociologist Judith Stacey (1996) calls "the patriarchal bargain." Older women, born in the 1920s and brought up during the Great Depression of the 1930s, often valued material security with a man who would be a good provider above emotional closeness or sexual satisfaction. Nowadays, many women expect much more intimacy in personal relationships than did their mothers, which places increased pressure on marriage and intimate relationships.

As we grow as individuals, our personal relationships may also develop in ways that continue to sustain us. Sometimes they cannot support our changing needs and concerns, and we may have to make the difficult decision to leave. Making a marriage or committed relationship "work" involves some combination of loving care, responsibility, communication, patience, humor, and luck. Material circumstances may have a significant impact, especially over the longer term. Having money, food, personal security, a home, reliable and affordable child care, and additional care for elderly relatives; being willing and able to move for a job or a chance to study; and having good health are examples of favorable circumstances. Negative factors that especially affect young African American women and Latinas are the high unemployment rates for men of color and the fact that roughly 30 percent of young African American and Latino men between 18 and 25 are caught up in the criminal justice system.

The couple may look to each other as friends, partners, and lovers and expect that together they can provide for each other's material and emotional needs and fulfill their dreams. In addition to experiencing the joy and satisfaction of sharing life on a daily basis, the partnership may also bear the brunt of work pressures, money worries, changing gender roles, or stress from a violent community, as well as difficulties due to personal misunderstandings, different priorities, or differing views of what it means to be a husband or a wife.

Half of U.S. marriages end in divorce, usually initiated by women, for reasons of incompatibility, infidelity, mistreatment, economic problems, or sexual problems (Kurz 1995). Many women experience the breakup with a mixture of fear, excitement, relief, and a sense of failure. Most divorced or widowed men marry within a year of the end of their previous relationship, often marrying women younger than themselves. Women wait longer to remarry, and fewer do. The majority of older men are married, while the majority of older women are widows. Being old and alone is something that women often fear, though some older women feel

good about their relative autonomy, especially if they are comfortable financially and have support from family members or friends, as mentioned in Chapter 3.

Motherhood and Parenting

Because women are daughters, we all have some perspective on motherhood through the experience of our own mothers or other women who mothered us. Many people regard motherhood as the ultimate female experience and disapprove of women who do not want to be mothers, especially if they are married. Magazines and advertising images invariably show happy, smiling mothers who dote on their children and buy them their favorite foods, cute clothes, toys, videos, CDs, and so forth.

Like marriage, motherhood is also undergoing change. Generally, women in more affluent families have fewer children, across all racial groups. Roughly a third of all babies born in the United States are to unmarried women. Percentages vary considerably by race. Far fewer Chinese American and Japanese American mothers are unmarried (9 percent and 10 percent, respectively), compared to Native American and Puerto Rican women (59 percent) (U.S. Census Bureau 2004, Table 78). More African American and Native American women are likely to have a child die in infancy, compared to White women, Latinas, and Asian Americans. Sharon Olds, Carol Gill and Larry Voss, and Ann Filemyr describe varied experiences of parenting (Readings 42, 43, 44, respectively). Rachel Aber Schlesinger (Reading 45) writes about the geographical and cultural contexts that have shaped the lives of Jewish grandmothers who migrated to North America and about their role in the transmission of culture to their grandchildren, who live in a very different time and place. Shailja Patel (Reading 47) describes how macro-level factors of British imperialism affected her family circumstances and attitudes. In the late nineteenth century, British administrators moved people from one colony to another as needed. Indian men, for example, were taken to Kenya to build railroads and used as a "buffer group" between the British elite and Kenyan Africans. They were allowed to stay on and go into business. By the 1970s, when Kenya gained political independence, many Kenyan Asians were relatively prosperous. They were highly unpopular in newly independent Kenya and ultimately forced to leave, throwing families into personal, economic, and political crisis.

More and more U.S. women are choosing not to have children or are having them later. Over half of all births occur to women in their twenties—the peak childbearing years—but the average age has shifted steadily upward. In 1970, the average age a woman had her first child was 21.4 years compared to 25 years in 2000. Analyzed by race these data show a wide spread: Native American women had the lowest average age at first birth (21.6 years) compared to Japanese and Chinese women (over 30 years) (Mathews and Hamilton 2002). In 2002, 44 percent of all women aged 15–44 had never had a child. In the older age group (40–44 years) this figure was 18 percent in 2002, up from 10 percent in 1976 (Downs 2003). Most of these women are childless on purpose, despite the idea, popularized in the media, that women are controlled by a "biological clock," ticking away the years when conception is possible. Many of these women describe themselves as child-free rather than childless, highlighting that this is a positive choice for them (Bartlett 1994; Ireland 1993; Morrell 1994; Reti 1992; Safe 1996). They challenge the idea that women must have children to be fulfilled; they prefer instead to focus on intimate relationships, friendships, work, travel, community involvements, and connections with other people's children.

Rearing children is hard work, often tedious and repetitive, requiring humor and patience. Many women experience contradictory emotions, including fear, resentment, inadequacy, and anger about motherhood despite societal idealization of it and their own hopes or expectations that they will find it unreservedly fulfilling.

The Social Construction of Motherhood

Adrienne Rich (1986b) has argued that it is not motherhood itself that is oppressive to women, but the way our society constructs motherhood. A contemporary media image of a young mother with immaculate hair and makeup, wearing a chic business suit, briefcase in one hand and toddler in the other, may define an ideal for many young women. But it also sets a standard that is virtually unattainable without causing the mother to come apart at the seams—that is, in the absence of a generous budget for convenience foods, restaurant meals, work clothes, dry cleaning, hairdressing, and good-quality child care. Despite contradictions and challenges, many women are finding joy and affirmation in motherhood (Abbey and O'Reilly 1998; Blakely 1994; Gore and Lavendar 2001; Hays 1996; Jetter, Orleck, and Taylor 1997; Kline 1997; Meyers 2001). In the early 1990s, writer and editor Ariel Gore started the upbeat zine, *Hip Mama*, as her senior project in college; highlights from the first ten years provide hilarious and heart-wrenching essays "from the cutting edge of parenting" (Gore 2004).

Motherhood has been defined differently at different times. During World War II, for example, when women were needed to work in munitions factories and shipyards in place of men drafted overseas, companies often provided housing, canteens, and child care to support these working women (Hayden 1981). After the war women were no longer needed in these jobs, and such facilities were largely discontinued. Psychologists began to talk about the central importance of a mother's care for the healthy physical and emotional development of children (Bowlby 1963). Invoking the notion of maternal instinct, some asserted that a mother's care is qualitatively different from that of others and that only a mother's love will do. Mothers who are not sufficiently "present" can be blamed for their children's problems. Ironically, mothers who are too present, said to be overidentified with their children and a source of negative pressure, are also blamed.

Blame It on the Mother

Mothers have been blamed for damaging their children psychologically, for bringing up children in poverty, for being lesbians, for marrying the wrong men, for divorce, for having children too young, for working outside the home, and for not working outside the home (Ladd-Taylor and Umansky 1998). In 2000, 55 percent of women with infants under a year old were in the workforce, down from 59 percent in 1998. This represents the first decline in 25 years. The drop is primarily among women who are White, married, over 30, and educated (Gardner 2001). According to the

BABY BLUES

Department of Labor Women's Bureau (2005), 70 percent of mothers with children under 18 are in full-time work; 62 percent of mothers with children under 6 years of age are employed full-time. According to syndicated columnist Ellen Goodman (1999), "the cultural consensus still says that professional mothers should be home with the kids while welfare mothers should be out working." Psychologist Elizabeth Harvey's (1999) research on children aged 3 to 12 showed that those whose mothers were in the paid workforce during the first three years were *not* significantly different in terms of behavior, cognitive development, self-esteem, and academic achievement compared with those whose mothers were at home. Any slight differences disappeared by the time the children were of school age.

Despite the fact that so many mothers of young children are in the paid workforce today, working mothers, especially women of color, risk being called unfit and perhaps losing their children to foster homes or state agencies if they do not maintain some conventionally approved standard of family life. This is particularly true for mothers receiving TANF. States can sanction women and drop them from welfare rolls if they do not meet work requirements, do not disclose the identity of their child's father, or refuse to pursue child support orders. The states are entitled to use welfare money to determine whether children of sanctioned mothers are at risk of child abuse and neglect (Mink 2002). Throughout the 1990s, a series of news reports describing low-quality child-care facilities, including some cases in which children were said to have been sexually abused, contributed to the anxiety of working mothers.

The ideology of motherhood has been a persistent rationale for the unequal treatment of women in terms of access to education and well-paid, professional work, though it did not impede the employment of African American women, for example, as domestics and nannies in White people's homes or of White working-class women in factories. Not all of today's older women were able to choose whether or not to stay out of the paid workforce when their children were young. We take up the issue of juggling home and paid work in the next chapter.

Most women spend seventeen years of their lives, on average, taking care of children and eighteen years looking after their elderly parents or their husband's parents (Gould 1997). These periods overlap, usually when the children are in their teens. An additional factor complicating daily life is the high divorce rate, which means that parents and stepparents are involved in ongoing negotiations over shared child-care arrangements—often a source of hostility and stress. Women always suffer a serious drop in their standard of living immediately after divorce—hence the saying, "Poverty is only a divorce away"—whereas men's standard of living goes up (Peterson 1996). Usually mothers retain custody of the children even though fathers may see them on weekends or during school vacations. Roughly 50 percent of divorced fathers pay child support. Those who do not pay are often unemployed or in low-wage jobs. Children are affected emotionally and educationally by the ups and downs of parents' marital difficulties. Though a divorce may bring some resolution, children may have to adjust to a new home, school, neighborhood, a lowered standard of living, or a whole new family setup complete with stepparent, and stepbrothers or sisters. Most children suffer emotionally as a result of divorce but recover their equilibrium (Stewart et al. 1997), and the large majority of children of divorced parents grow up socially and psychologically well-adjusted (Hetherington and Clingempeel 1992; Hetherington and Kelly 2002).

The Ideal Nuclear Family

The family is a key social institution in which children are nurtured and socialized. In much public debate and political rhetoric, the family is touted as the centerpiece of American life. This idealized family, immortalized in the 1950s TV show *Leave It to Beaver,* consists of a heterosexual couple, married for life, with two or three children. The father is the provider while the wife/mother spends her days running the home. This is the family that is regularly portrayed in ads for such things as food, cars, cleaning products, or life insurance, which rely on our recognizing—if not identifying with—this symbol of togetherness and care. It is also invoked by conservative politicians who hearken back to so-called traditional family values. The copious academic and popular literature on the family emphasizes change—some say breakdown—in family life (Coontz 1992, 1997; Mintz and Kellogg 1988; Risman 1998; Skolnick 1991). Conservative politicians and religious leaders attribute many social problems to "broken homes," so-called dysfunctional families, and moral decline, citing divorce rates, teen pregnancy rates, numbers of single-parent families, large numbers of mothers in the paid workforce, a lack of Christian values, and violence (Reading 46). In a *New York Times* article on single mothers, the steady increase in the rate of births to unmarried women since 1952 was called "a predictable metaphor for the fraying of America's collective moral fiber" (Usdansky 1996). Note that this formulation employs a moral framework and implies moral and personal solutions mainly focused on the micro and meso levels. By contrast, from a socioeconomic perspective, changes in U.S. families are attributed to economic changes that have caused manufacturing jobs to be automated or moved overseas, a lack of adequate support for people in poverty, changing

Family Violence

- Up to 50 percent of all homeless women and children in this country are fleeing domestic violence.

- Approximately 1 out of every 25 elder persons is victimized annually. Of those who experience domestic elder abuse, 37 percent are neglected and 26 percent are physically abused. Of those who perpetrate the abuse, 30 percent are adult children of the abused person.

- As violence against women becomes more severe and more frequent in the home, children experience an increase in physical violence by the male batterer.

- Sixty-two percent of sons over the age of 14 were injured when they attempted to protect their mothers from attacks by abusive male partners. Women are 10 times more likely than men to be victims of violent crime in intimate relationships.

Source: National Coalition Against Domestic Violence (www.ncadv.org/resources/statistics_74.html).

economic stresses on personal and family relationships, increased levels of incarceration, and so forth.

Although this mythic family makes up only a small proportion of U.S. families, the prevalence of this ideal image has a strong ideological impact. It serves to both mask and delegitimize the real diversity of family forms and gives no hint of the incidence of family violence, or conflicts between work and caring for children. Sociologist Stephanie Coontz (1997) argues that nostalgia for the so-called traditional family is based on myths. Specifically, the post–World War II White, middle-class family was the product of a particular set of circumstances that were short-lived:

Fewer women remained childless during the 1950s than in any decade since the late nineteenth century. The timing and spacing of children became far more compressed, so that young mothers were likely to have two or more children in diapers at once. . . . At the same time, again for the first time in 100 years, the educational gap between middle-class women and men increased, while job segregation for working men and women seems to have peaked. . . . The result was that family life and gender roles became much more predictable, orderly, and settled in the 1950s than they were either twenty years earlier or would be twenty years later.

(p. 36)

Coontz (1997) argues that holding onto these nostalgic ideas creates problems for contemporary families. "The *lag* in adjusting values, behaviors, and institutions to new realities" can make for marital dissatisfaction and divorce, as well as inappropriate policy decisions (p. 109). Over the past three decades many women and men have been involved in some renegotiation of gender roles in relation to child care and other household responsibilities, a topic we discuss in more detail in the next chapter.

Pam and Lisa Liberty-Bibbens with McKenzie and Brennan

U.S. Families: Cultural and Historical Variations

The idealized family is assumed to provide a secure home for its members, what historian Christopher Lasch (1977) has called "a haven in a heartless world." For some this is generally true. For many women and children—in heterosexual and lesbian families—home is not a safe place but one where they experience emotional or physical violence through beatings, threats, or sexual abuse, as discussed in the previous chapter.

The ideal family, with its rigid gender-based division of labor, has always applied more to White families than to families of color. As cultural critic, teacher, and writer bell hooks (1984a) argues, many women of color and working-class White women have always had to work outside the home. Children are raised in multigenerational families, by divorced parents who have remarried, by adoptive parents, single parents (usually mothers), or grandparents. Eleanor Palo Stoller and Rose Campbell Gibson (1994) note that "when children are orphaned, when parents are ill or at work, or biological mothers are too young to care for their children alone other women take on childcare, sometimes temporarily, sometimes permanently" (p. 162). Sociologist Barbara Omolade (1986)

describes strong female-centered networks linking African American families and households, in which single mothers support one another in creating stable homes for their children. She challenges official characterization of this kind of family as "dysfunctional." Anthropologist Leith Mullings (1997) notes that women-headed households are an international phenomenon, shaped by global as well as local processes like the movement of jobs from industrialized to developing nations. In some families, one or both parents may have a disability, as described by Carol Gill and Larry Voss (Reading 43). Other families are split between countries through work, immigration, and war. Women leave their homes in the Philippines, for example, to work as caregivers for families in countries of the global North. These mothers are able to support their own children financially but rarely see them (Reading 55).

Single women (not all of whom are lesbians) have children through alternative insemination. Lesbians and gay men have established networks of friends who function like family. Some have children from earlier, heterosexual relationships; other gay and lesbian couples are fostering or adopting children (Drucker 1998; Goss and Strongheart 1997; Howey and Samuels 2000; Moraga 1997; Wells 2000). According to the Family Pride Coalition, an umbrella organization for gay and lesbian family support groups, at least 2 million gay and lesbian parents in the United States are raising between 3 million and 5 million children, most of them children of heterosexual marriages. The National Adoption Information Clearinghouse, a federal agency, puts the figures much higher—between 2.5 million and 8 million gay and lesbian parents, and 6 million to 14 million children (Lowy 1999). In Reading 44, journalist, teacher, and poet Ann Filemyr describes "loving across the boundary," as a White woman in partnership with Essie, a woman of color, and comments that "by sharing our lives, our daily survival, our dreams and aspirations, I have been widened and deepened." Their family includes Essie's son and her grandmother. Filemyr makes insightful connections between their personal experiences, other people's reactions to their multiracial household, and the impact of racism and heterosexism on their lives.

Besides providing for the care and socialization of children, families in the United States historically were also productive units. Before the onset of industrialization, work and home were not separated, as happened under the factory system, and women were not housewives but workers. Housework was directly productive in a home-based economy. In addition, women produced goods for sale—dyed cloth, finished garments, lace, netting, rope, furniture, and homemade remedies. Enslaved African women were involved in such production for their owners and sometimes also for their own families. Native American women were similarly involved in productive work for their family and community. Under such a family system both parents could integrate child care with their daily tasks, tasks in which children also participated. Indeed, childhood was a different phenomenon, with an emphasis on learning skills and responsibilities as part of a community, rather than on play or schooling.

Many shopkeeping and restaurant-owning families today—some of them recent immigrants, others the children or grandchildren of immigrants—continue to blend work and home.

Immigration and the Family

Chinese immigrant life in the United States was very different from these earlier family experiences. At first only Chinese men were allowed to enter the United States—to build roads and railroads, for example—creating a community of bachelors. Later, Chinese women were also permitted entry,

and the Chinatowns of several major cities began to echo with children's voices for the first time.

Since 1952, U.S. immigration law and policy have allowed family members to join relatives in this country. This can be a lengthy process, and many families are split between the United States and their native countries. Men and women who migrate to this country often leave their children back home until they have gained a foothold here. Others send their children, especially teenagers, to the "old country" to keep them from the problems of life in the United States, as mentioned by Surina Khan (Reading 26). Some recent Chinese immigrant women, who work long hours for low pay in New York garment factories, are sending their infants back to China to be cared for by family members (Sengupta 1999). They lack affordable child care and the support of an extended family. The children are U.S. citizens by birth and are expected to return to this country when they are school age.

Women who are recent immigrants may be more affected by the customs of their home country, though younger immigrant women see coming to the United States partly in terms of greater personal freedom, as do many young women born here to immigrant parents. Differing aspirations and expectations for careers, marriage, and family life between mothers and daughters may lead to tensions between the generations, as exemplified in Amy Tan's novel *The Joy Luck Club* (1989), and by Surina Khan (Reading 26). According to Stoller and Gibson (1994), many older Asian American women suffer both economic hardship and cultural isolation in this country. Recent elderly immigrants are also affected by cultural isolation, especially if they do not know English and their children and grandchildren are keen to become acculturated. First-generation immigrants who hold traditional views of family obligations, for example, may be disappointed by the treatment they receive from their Americanized children and grandchildren.

Feminist Perspectives on Marriage, Motherhood, and the Family

Marriage and family life are so much a part of our everyday lives, that many of us rarely stop to think much about them. Feminists often challenge commonplace beliefs about these bedrock social institutions that people may not even know they hold.

Challenging the Private/Public Dichotomy

A core idea in much U.S. political thought is that there is a dichotomy between the private and personal (dating, marriage, sexual habits, who does the housework, relationships between parents and children) and the public (religion, law, business). According to this view, these two spheres affect each other but are governed by different rules, attitudes, and behavior. The family, for example, is the place where love, caring, and sensitivity are assumed to come first. How a man treats his wife or children, then, is a private matter. A key aspect of much feminist theorizing and activism has been to challenge this public versus private dichotomy and to explain the family as a site of patriarchal power summed up in the saying "The working man's home is his castle." Every man may not be the most powerful person in the family, yet this is a culturally accepted idea. Such power may operate in relatively trivial ways—as, for example, when Mom and the kids cater to Dad's preferences in food or TV shows as a way of avoiding a confrontation. Usually, as the main wage earner and "head" of the family, men command loyalty, respect, and obedience. Some resort to violence or sexual abuse, as mentioned earlier. White, middle-class feminists like Betty Friedan (1963), who wrote about her dissatisfactions with suburban life and the boredom of being a full-time homemaker, which she described as "the problem which has no name," identify motherhood as a major obstacle to women's fulfillment. By contrast, working-class women—White women and women of color—name a lack of well-paying jobs, a lack of skills or education, and racism, not motherhood, as obstacles to their liberation.

Given the lower status of women in society, Jaclyn Geller (2001) points to marriage as a legal contract between unequal parties. As political scientist Susan Moller Okin (1989) notes, the much-repeated slogan "the personal is the political" is "the central message of feminist critiques of the public/private dichotomy" (p. 124). She lists four ways in which the family is a political entity:

1. Power is always an element of family relationships.
2. This domestic sphere is governed by external rules—for example, those concerning marriage and divorce, marital rape, or child custody.

3. It is in the family that much of our early socialization takes place and that we learn gender roles.
4. The division of labor within the family raises practical and psychological barriers against women in all other spheres of life.

(pp. 128–33)

Mothering and Maternal Thinking

In the late 1970s and early 1980s, feminist writing about motherhood increased enormously with an emphasis on the daily experience of mothering (Lazarre 1976; Rich 1976) and the symbolic meaning of motherhood (Chodorow 1978; Dinnerstein 1976). Adrienne Rich (1986b) advocated thinking of pregnancy and childbirth, a short-term condition, quite separately from child rearing, a much-longer-term responsibility. Psychologists Nancy Chodorow and Dorothy Dinnerstein both advocated shared parenting as essential to undermining rigid gender roles, under which many men are cut off, practically and emotionally, from the organic and emotional concerns of children and dissociated from life processes. Two decades later, sociologists Pepper Schwartz (1994) and Barbara Risman (1998) made similar arguments.

Historian Laurie Umansky (1996) notes that maternalist rhetoric and imagery were central to much 1980s ecofeminism and women's peace activism. Examples include the Unity Statement of the Women's Pentagon Action (Reading 70, Chapter 11). Philosopher Sara Ruddick (1989) argued, further, that the experience and the work of mothering (whether by women or men) has the potential to generate principles of "maternal thinking" based on the desire to preserve life and foster growth. Such principles could serve as a blueprint for human interaction that would involve genuine peace and security. Responsible mothering has also led women to organize for better working conditions, improvements in welfare programs, and environmental justice (Jetter, Orleck, and Taylor 1997). Anthropologist Leith Mullings (1997) describes the transformative work of African American women she interviewed in New York in raising children and sustaining their households and communities as single parents. Sociologist Nancy Naples (1998, p. 113) uses the term "activist mothering" to explain the ways women community workers blend mothering, paid and unpaid labor, and political activism.

The Family and the Economic System

Other feminist theorists see the family as part of the economic system and emphasize its role in the **reproduction of labor** (Benston 1969; Dalla Costa and James 1972; Mitchell 1971; Zaretsky 1976). In this highly unsentimental view, marriage is compared to prostitution, whereby women trade sex for economic and social support. The family is deemed important for society because it is responsible for producing, nurturing, and socializing the next generation of workers and citizens, the place where children first learn to be "social animals." This includes basic skills like language and potty training and social skills like cooperation and negotiation with others or abiding by rules. Women's unpaid domestic work and child care, though not considered productive work, directly benefit the state and employers by turning out functioning members of society. The family also cares for its adult members by providing meals and clean clothes, as well as rest, relaxation, love, and sexual intimacy, so that they are ready to face another working day— another aspect of the reproduction of labor. Similarly, it cares for people who are not in the workforce, those with disabilities, the elderly, or the chronically ill. Still other theorists explain the family in terms of patriarchal power linked to a capitalist system of economic relations, with much discussion of exactly how these two systems are connected and how the gendered division of labor within the family first came about (Hartmann 1981; Jaggar 1983; Young 1980).

Policy Implications and Implementation

Many feminist scholars, policy makers, and activists have followed through on their analyses of women's roles in the family by taking steps to implement the policies they advocate. They have set up crisis lines and shelters for battered women and children across the country and made family violence and childhood sexual abuse public issues, as discussed in the previous chapter. They have argued for shared parental responsibility for child care, payment of child support, and redrawing the terms of divorce such that both postdivorce households would have the same standard of living. Above all, feminists have campaigned for good-quality child care subsidized by government and employers, on-site at big workplaces, and they have organized community child-care facilities and informal networks of parents who share child care. Although some of these efforts have been successful, there is still a great deal to be accomplished if women are not to be penalized for having children, an issue we discuss in Chapter 8.

Although policy makers and politicians often declare that children are the nation's future and greatest resource, parents are given little practical help in caring for them. Susan Moller Okin (1989) notes that so few U.S. politicians have raised children that it seems almost a qualification for political office not to have done so. The editors of *Mothering* magazine pulled no punches when they asked:

> Why is the United States the only industrial democracy in the world that provides no universal pre- or postnatal care, no universal health coverage; . . . has no national standards for child care; makes no provision to encourage at-home care in the early years of life; . . . has no explicit family policies such as child allowances and housing subsidies for all families?
> *(Brennan, Winklepleck, and MacNee 1994, p. 424)*

At the same time, former first lady Hillary Rodham Clinton (1996), adopting an African proverb, argued that "it takes a village to raise a child." Most European countries have instituted family policies with provisions for health care, child allowances, child care, prenatal care, parental leave, and services for the elderly. In the United States, family policy is an unfamiliar term and the few policies that support families, like welfare, unemployment assistance, and tax relief, are inadequate and uncoordinated (Albelda and Tilly 1997; Mason, Skolnick, and Sugarman 1998).

Toward a Redefinition of Family Values

The meaning of family and "family values" varies according to one's cultural and political framework. Carol Gill and Larry Voss describe their experience of egalitarian relationships and shared parenting, and the importance of teaching children nonsexist, antiracist, anticlassist attitudes (Reading 43). Ann Filemyr emphasizes the breadth of her chosen family as well as her biological family (Reading 44). As part of an interracial household, she notes also that she, her partner Essie, and Essie's son walk out of their home into different worlds. Margaret Lamberts Bendroth traces the history behind the "pro-family" position promoted by Protestant fundamentalists at micro, meso, and macro levels (Reading 46). On the basis of the data we cite in this chapter, we argue that elevating the ideal of the nuclear, two-parent family is a major contradiction in contemporary U.S. society. Regardless of its form, we believe that the family should

> care for family members, emotionally and materially;
>
> promote egalitarian relationships among the adults, who should not abuse their power over children;
>
> share parenting between men and women so that it is not the province of either gender;
>
> do away with a gendered division of labor;
>
> teach children nonsexist, antiracist, anticlassist attitudes and behavior and the values of caring and connectedness to others;
>
> pass on cultural heritage; and
>
> influence the wider community.

For personal relationships to be more egalitarian, as far as possible the partners should have shared values or compatible nonnegotiables, have some compatible sense of why they are together, and share power in the relationship. They also need to be committed to a clear communication process and be willing to work through difficulties with honesty and openness. If the relationship is to last, it must be flexible and able to change over time so that both partners can grow individually as well as together. Few of us have much experience to guide us. Indeed, most people have experienced and observed unequal relationships—at home, in school, and in the wider community.

Susan Moller Okin (1989) argues that for society to be just, all social institutions must be just, including the family. We argue that the family must be a source of security for its members, an element in constructing a secure and sustainable future. A sustainable future means that we, in the present generation, must consider how our actions will affect people of future generations. A useful reference here is the Native American "seventh generation" principle: The community is responsible for those not yet born, and because of this, whatever actions are taken in the present must not jeopardize the possibility of well-being seven generations to come. How would we have to restructure our relationships as well as other social institutions in order to honor that principle?

Questions for Reflection

In reading and discussing this chapter, consider these questions:

1. What do you expect/hope for in an intimate relationship?

2. Are you in love now? How can you tell?

3. How does power manifest itself in your relationships with family members, friends, dates, or lovers?

4. Do you think intimate relationships should be monogamous? Why or why not?

5. Do you have friends or dates with people from a racial/ethnic/cultural group different from your own? If so, how did you meet? How have your differences been a factor in your friendship or relationship?

6. How do you define family? Whom do you consider family in your own life?

7. How do macro-level institutions—in particular the government, media, and organized religion—shape people's relationships and family lives?

8. What is at stake with regard to same-sex marriage? Where do you stand on this issue? Why?

9. If women are to have more equal treatment within the family, what kinds of changes in male attitudes and behavior will be needed also? How might this happen?

10. What changes are necessary to involve more men in parenting? Look at the micro, meso, macro, and global levels of analysis.

◆◆◆

Finding Out More on the Web

1. Visit the following Web sites for more information:

   Indiebride: **www.indiebride.com**

   Alternatives to Marriage Project: **www.unmarried.org**

   The Freedom to Marry Coalition of Massachusetts: **www.ftmmass.org**

   The Religious Coalition for the Freedom to Marry: **www.rcfm.org**

   Southerners on New Ground: **www.southnewground.org**

2. Find out more about the Defense of Marriage Act (1996). What assumptions about marriage and the institution of heterosexuality is it based on?

3. Find out about family policies in western European countries (especially Denmark, Germany, the Netherlands, and Sweden). Why do these countries provide better supports for families than the United States?

◆◆◆

Taking Action

1. Talk with your peers—women and men—about your nonnegotiables in a personal relationship. What are you willing to compromise on? Why?

2. Talk with your mother or grandmother (or women their age) about their experiences of marriage, motherhood, and family. What choices have they made in their lives in this regard? What options did they have?

3. Look critically at the way women are portrayed in relationships and the family in magazines, ads, movies, and TV shows. What is being promoted through these media?

FORTY-ONE

◆◆◆

Since When Is Marriage a Path to Liberation? (1989)

Paula Ettelbrick

Lawyer, educator, and civil rights activist **Paula L. Ettelbrick** is the Executive Director of the International Gay and Lesbian Human Rights Commission. She has written and lectured extensively on the civil and constitutional rights of lesbians and gay men.

"Marriage is a great institution, if you like living in institutions," according to a bit of T-shirt philosophy I saw recently. Certainly, marriage is an institution. It is one of the most venerable, impenetrable institutions in modern society. Marriage provides the ultimate form of acceptance for personal intimate relationships in our society, and gives those who marry an insider status of the most powerful kind.

Steeped in a patriarchal system that looks to ownership, property, and dominance of men over women as its basis, the institution of marriage long has been the focus of radical feminist revulsion. Marriage defines certain relationships as more valid than all others. Lesbian and gay relationships, being neither legally sanctioned or commingled by blood, are always at the bottom of the heap of social acceptance and importance.

Given the imprimatur of social and personal approval which marriage provides, it is not surprising that some lesbians and gay men among us would look to legal marriage for self-affirmation. After all, those who marry can be instantaneously transformed from "outsiders" to "insiders," and we have a desperate need to become insiders.

It could make us feel OK about ourselves, perhaps even relieve some of the internalized homophobia that we all know so well. Society will then celebrate the birth of our children and mourn the death of our spouses. It would be easier to get health insurance for our spouses, family memberships to the local museum, and a right to inherit our spouse's cherished collection of lesbian mystery novels even if she failed to draft a will. Never again would she have to go to a family reunion and debate about the correct term for introducing our lover/partner/significant other to Aunt Flora. Everything would be quite easy and very nice.

So why does this unlikely event so deeply disturb me? For two major reasons. First, marriage will not liberate us as lesbians and gay men. In fact, it will constrain us, make us more invisible, force our assimilation into the mainstream, and undermine the goals of gay liberation. Second, attaining the right to marry will not transform our society from one that makes narrow, but dramatic, distinctions between those who are married and those who are not married to one that respects and encourages choice of relationships and family diversity. Marriage runs counter to two of the primary goals of the lesbian and gay movement: the affirmation of gay identity and culture; and the validation of many forms of relationships.

When analyzed from the standpoint of civil rights, certainly lesbians and gay men should have a right to marry. But obtaining a right does not always result in justice. White male firefighters in Birmingham, Alabama have been fighting for their "rights" to retain their jobs by overturning the city's affirmative action guidelines. If their "rights" prevail, the courts will have failed in rendering justice. The "right" fought for by the white male firefighters, as well as those who advocate strongly for the "rights" to legal marriage for gay people, will result, at best, in limited or narrowed "justice" for those closest to power at the expense of those who have been historically marginalized.

The fight for justice has as its goal the realignment of power imbalances among individuals and classes of people in society. A pure "rights" analysis often fails to incorporate a broader understanding of the underlying inequities that operate to deny justice to a fuller range of people and groups. In setting our priorities as a community, we must combine the concept of both rights and justice. At this point in time, making legal marriage for lesbian and gay couples a priority would set an agenda of gaining rights for a few, but would do nothing to correct the power imbalances between those who are married (whether gay or straight) and those who are not. Thus, justice would not be gained.

Justice for gay men and lesbians will be achieved only when we are accepted and supported in this society *despite* our differences from the dominant culture and the choices we make regarding our relationships. Being queer is more than setting up house, sleeping with a person of the same gender, and seeking state approval for doing so. It is an identity, a culture with many variations. It is a way of dealing with the world by diminishing the constraints of gender roles which have for so long kept women and gay people oppressed and invisible. Being queer means pushing the parameters of sex, sexuality, and family, and in the process transforming the very fabric of society. Gay liberation is inexorably linked to women's liberation. Each is essential to the other.

The moment we argue, as some among us insist on doing, that we should be treated as equals because we are really just like married couples and hold the same values to be true, we undermine the very purpose of our movement and begin the dangerous process of silencing our different voices. As a lesbian, I am fundamentally different from non-lesbian women. That's the point. Marriage, as it exists today, is antithetical to my liberation as a lesbian and as a woman because it mainstreams my life and voice. I do not want to be known as "Mrs.

Attached-To-Somebody-Else." Nor do I want to give the state the power to regulate my primary relationship.

Yet, the concept of equality in our legal system does not support differences, it only supports sameness. The very standard for equal protection is that people who are similarly situated must be treated equally. To make an argument for equal protection, we will be required to claim that gay and lesbian relationships are the same as straight relationships. To gain the right, we must compare ourselves to married couples. The law looks to the insiders as the norm, regardless of how flawed or unjust their institutions, and requires that those seeking the law's equal protection situate themselves in a similar posture to those who are already protected. In arguing for the right to legal marriage, lesbians and gay men would be forced to claim that we are just like heterosexual couples, have the same goals and purposes, and vow to structure our lives similarly. The law provides no room to argue that we are different, but are nonetheless entitled to equal protection.

The thought of emphasizing our sameness to married heterosexuals in order to obtain this "right" terrifies me. It rips away the very heart and soul of what I believe it is to be a lesbian in this world. It robs me of the opportunity to make a difference. We end up mimicking all that is bad about the institution of marriage in our effort to appear to be the same as straight couples.

By looking to our sameness and de-emphasizing our differences, we don't even place ourselves in a position of power that would allow us to transform marriage from an institution that emphasizes property and state regulation of relationships to an institution which recognizes one of many types of valid and respected relationships. Until the constitution is interpreted to respect and encourage differences, pursuing the legalization of same-sex marriage would be leading our movement into a trap; we would be demanding access to the very institution which, in its current form, would undermine *our* movement to recognize many different kinds of relationships. We would be perpetuating the elevation of married relationships and of "couples" in general, and further eclipsing other relationships of choice.

Ironically, gay marriage, instead of liberating gay sex and sexuality, would further outlaw all gay and lesbian sex which is not performed in a marital context. Just as sexually active non-married women face stigma and double standards around sex and sexual activity, so too would non-married gay people. The only legitimate gay sex would be that which is cloaked in and regulated by marriage. Its legitimacy would stem not from an acceptance of gay sexuality, but because the Supreme Court and society in general fiercely protect the privacy of marital relationships. Lesbians and gay men who did not seek the state's stamp of approval would clearly face increased sexual oppression.

Undoubtedly, whether we admit it or not, we all need to be accepted by the broader society. That motivation fuels our work to eliminate discrimination in the workplace and elsewhere, fight for custody of our children, create our own families, and so on. The growing discussion about the right to marry may be explained in part by this need for acceptance. Those closer to the norm or to power in this country are more likely to see marriage as a principle of freedom and equality. Those who are more acceptable to the mainstream because of race, gender, and economic status are more likely to want the right to marry. It is the final acceptance, the ultimate affirmation of identity.

On the other hand, more marginal members of the lesbian and gay community (women, people of color, working class and poor) are less likely to see marriage as having relevance to our struggles for survival. After all, what good is the affirmation of our relationships (that is, marital relationships) if we are rejected as women, black, or working class?

The path to acceptance is much more complicated for many of us. For instance, if we choose legal marriage, we may enjoy the right to add our spouse to our health insurance policy at work, since most employment policies are defined by one's marital status, not family relationship. However, that choice assumes that we have a job *and* that our employer provides us with health benefits. For women, particularly women of color who tend to occupy the low-paying jobs that do not provide healthcare benefits at all, it will not matter one bit if they are able to marry their women partners. The opportunity to marry will neither get them the health benefits nor transform them from outsider to insider.

Of course, a white man who marries another white man who has a full-time job with benefits will certainly be able to share in those benefits and overcome the only obstacle left to full societal assimilation—the goal of many in his class. In other words, gay marriage will not topple the system that allows only the privileged few to obtain decent health care. Nor will it close the privilege gap between those who are married and those who are not.

Marriage creates a two-tier system that allows the state to regulate relationships. It has become a facile mechanism for employers to dole out benefits, for businesses to provide special deals and incentives, and for the law to make distinctions in distributing meager public funds. None of these entities bothers to consider the relationship among people; the love, respect, and need to protect that exists among all kinds of family members. Rather, a simple certificate of the state, regardless of whether the spouses love, respect, or even see each other on a regular basis, dominates and is supported. None of this dynamic will change if gay men and lesbians are given the option of marriage.

Gay marriage will not help us address the systemic abuses inherent in a society that does not provide decent health care to all of its citizens, a right that should not depend on whether the individual (1) has sufficient resources to afford health care or health insurance, (2) is working and receives health insurance as part of compensation, or (3) is married to a partner who is working and has health coverage which is extended to spouses. It will not address the underlying unfairness that allows businesses to provide discounted services or goods to families and couples—who are defined to include straight, married people and their children, but not domestic partners.

Nor will it address the pain and anguish of an unmarried lesbian who receives word of her partner's accident, rushes to the hospital and is prohibited from entering the intensive ward or obtaining information about her condition solely because she is not a spouse or family member. Likewise, marriage will not help the gay victim of domestic violence who, because he chose not to marry, finds no protection under the law to keep his violent lover away.

If the laws change tomorrow and lesbians and gay men were allowed to marry, where would we find the incentive to continue the progressive movement we have started that is pushing for societal and legal recognition of all kinds of family relationships? To create other options and alternatives? To find a place in the law for the elderly couple who, for companionship and economic reasons, live together but do not marry? To recognize the right of a long-time, but unmarried, gay partner to stay in his rent-controlled apartment after the death of his lover, the only named tenant on the lease? To recognize the family relationship of the lesbian couple and the two gay men who are jointly sharing child-raising responsibilities? To get the law to acknowledge that we may have more than one relationship worthy of legal protection?

Marriage for lesbians and gay men still will not provide a real choice unless we continue the work our community has begun to spread the privilege around to other relationships. We must first break the tradition of piling benefits and privileges on to those who are married, while ignoring the real life needs of those who are not. Only when we de-institutionalize marriage and bridge the economic and privilege gap between the married and the un-married will each of us have a true choice. Otherwise, our choice not to marry will continue to lack legal protection and societal respect.

The lesbian and gay community has laid the groundwork for revolutionizing society's views of family. The domestic partnership movement has been an important part of this progress insofar as it validates non-marital relationships. Because it is not limited to sexual or romantic relationships, domestic partnership provides an important opportunity for many who are not related by blood or marriage to claim certain minimal protections.

It is crucial, though, that we avoid the pitfall of framing the push for legal recognition of domestic partners (those who share a primary residence and financial responsibilities for each other) as a stepping stone to marriage. We must keep our eyes on the goals of providing true alternatives to marriage and of radically reordering society's views of family.

The goals of lesbian and gay liberation must simply be broader than the right to marry. Gay and lesbian marriages may minimally transform the institution of marriage by diluting its traditional patriarchal dynamic, but they will not transform society. They will not demolish the two-tier system of the "haves" and the "have-nots." We must not fool ourselves into believing that marriage will make it acceptable to be gay or lesbian. We will be liberated only when we are respected and accepted for our differences and the diversity we provide to this society. Marriage is not a path to that liberation.

FORTY-TWO

♦♦♦

35/10 (1987)

Sharon Olds

Sharon Olds is the author of eight volumes of poetry. Winner of fellowships and awards including the 1983 Lamont Poetry Prize and the National Book Critics Circle Award, she is Professor of English at New York University and also teaches a workshop program for the Goldwater Hospital in New York.

Brushing out my daughter's dark
silken hair before the mirror
I see the grey gleaming on my head,
the silver-haired servant behind her. Why is it
just as we begin to go
they begin to arrive, the fold in my neck

clarifying as the fine bones of her
hips sharpen? As my skin shows
its dry pitting, she opens like a small
pale flower on the tip of a cactus;
as my last chances to bear a child
are falling through my body, the duds among
    them,
her full purse of eggs, round and
firm as hard-boiled yolks, is about
to snap its clasp. I brush her tangled
fragrant hair at bedtime. It's an old
story—the oldest we have on our planet—
the story of replacement.

♦♦♦

FORTY-THREE

Shattering Two Molds (1994)

Feminist Parents with Disabilities

Carol J. Gill and Larry A. Voss

Carol J. Gill is Director of Graduate Studies in the Department of Disability and Human Development at the University of Illinois (Chicago), where she also directs the Chicago Center for Disability Research. She writes frequently on issues of disability culture, identity, health, and ethics.

Larry Voss is a researcher in the Department of Disability and Human Development at the University of Illinois (Chicago), engaged in research, training, and community service projects in the social sciences, emphasizing a disability studies approach.

We are two persons with extensive physical disabilities who have raised a nondisabled son. Countering the stereotype of people with disabilities as childlike, fragile, and suffering, we have nurtured and, we believe, nurtured powerfully. With won-der and relief, we have watched our child's development into a generous, emotionally open, strong, and socially responsible adult. It was not a snap. All three of us waged a long struggle against society's devaluation of human difference to get to this place.

Our war against ableist beliefs began in childhood when we acquired our disabilities in the 1950 polio epidemic. We used braces and wheelchairs and would have had little problem attending our neighborhood school if not for architecture and its real foundation: attitudes. In those days before the disability rights movement, we were barred from mainstream life. No ramps or elevators were installed to ensure our access. Instead, we were bussed miles each day to a "special" school with similarly displaced children.

Undoubtedly, these experiences laid the groundwork for our acceptance of a feminist perspective.

We acquired a deep suspicion of unequal treatment and stereotyping in any form. In high school, we identified with the civil rights struggle. In college, our rejection of sexism took definite shape. For Carol, the conscious decision to participate in the women's movement grew from classroom discussion of the work of Greer, Friedan, and Steinem. For Larry, it grew out of heated ideological debates between men and women in radical student collectives during the antiwar movement.

When Larry married a woman from this movement (his first marriage), he found daily life to be a mixture of new and traditional gender roles. During most of the marriage, his partner, who was not disabled, worked as an intensive care nurse while Larry completed his education. Although they shared household duties according to preferences as well as Larry's disability limitations, it was expected that his partner would cook and perform "housewife" chores after coming home from her job.

The decision to have a baby, on the other hand, was planned to be as joint a venture as possible. Larry remained by his wife's side during her prenatal exams and, long before it was accepted practice, he participated in the birth of his son in the hospital delivery room. He remembers this experience as ecstasy and agony—the incomparable joy of watching his child's birth and his sense of helpless horror as the emerging head made an audible tear in his wife's tissues. That painful moment registered clearly in Larry's consciousness—a factor, perhaps, in his later diligence in shouldering childcare duties.

Larry, in fact, became the primary parent. As is true of most children of disabled parents, Brian had little trouble adapting to his father's wheelchair and unconventional strategies for accomplishing daily tasks. When Larry's marriage foundered, he had no intention of parting with his son, then a toddler. Although it was rare for men to get custody of children in divorces, and even rarer for disabled persons, Larry fought to keep Brian with him and won.

Single parenthood was a rich and difficult time for them. Although Larry's sister and mother helped baby-sit, he experienced the loneliness and weight of responsibility that many single parents face. Additionally, there were unique physical and social difficulties. Unemployed and without child support, Larry could afford neither personal assistance nor adequate accessible housing. Consequently, errands such as grocery shopping became all-day feats of endurance. After driving home from the store, he would be forced to leave his wheelchair at the top of the stairs, crawl down the steps several times to his basement apartment and up again, hauling each bag of groceries followed by the baby, and then drag his wheelchair down the steps so he could get back into it and put groceries away!

Even more exhausting were the social hurdles. Strangers as well as family members challenged Larry's decision to keep his child, citing both gender- and disability-based concerns. Brian's first teachers suggested he was being shortchanged by not having a mother or nondisabled parent. (Brian's biological mother moved out of state and maintained very limited contact with him.) Neighborhood children teased or grilled him about his "wheelchair father" and asked why he had no mother. People who knew nothing about Larry's parenting skills would cluck over Brian's misfortune and tell him that having a "crippled daddy" was his cross to bear.

Although we—Carol and Larry—knew each other superficially while attending the same "special" high school, our paths did not cross again until a mutual friend brought us together at the time of Larry's divorce. After several years of intense and romantic friendship, we married.

At first, Brian was thrilled about Carol joining the family. Even before the wedding, which took place when he was seven, he insisted on calling her "Mom." But once it was official, he was ambivalent. Due both to her disability and her feminism, Brian's "new mother" was anything but the traditional nurturing figure people had told him he needed. She was physically incapable of performing many of the cooking and household chores mothers were supposed to do. She was not conventionally pretty. She was unexpectedly strong in communicating her ideas and affecting household decisions. She was even unwilling to change her name when she got married.

Not that Brian had been raised to be sexist. He had a father who baked cookies, cared for a home, brushed his lover's hair, and became an elementary school teacher. He also knew Larry's fondness for baseball, tools, and macho action movies. Father and son openly shared hugs and kisses between bouts of arm wrestling. Larry's philosophy of child-rearing, like his philosophy of education, stressed openness. He had always been pleased that Brian's early years were fairly non-sex-typed. He had let the toddler's strawberry blond hair grow to shoulder length undaunted by family predictions of gender confusion. He admired Brian's eclectic taste in toy trucks and stuffed animals as well as his drawings of kittens, nudes, Army tanks, Spiderman and posies.

But despite Larry's efforts to raise a child liberated from all the "isms," Brian was exposed to and affected by the sexism and ableism (not to mention racism, ethnocentrism, and heterosexism) of the surrounding culture. Dealing with this in addition to the typical tensions of stepparenting introduced a great deal of struggle into our family life.

It is hard for us to separate where our parenting was guided by feminism or by our experience and values as disabled persons. We believe in both notions of a women's culture and a disabled people's culture. Further, we believe the overlap of cultural values in the two communities is significant. Both feminist analysis and the disability independent living philosophy embrace values of interdependence, cooperative problem-solving, flexibility/adaptability, and the importance of relationships in contrast to traditional male values of autonomy, performance, competition, dominance, and acquisition.

By necessity, a guiding principle of our partnership has always been unfettered cooperation. There has been no "women's work" or "men's work." From the start, we negotiated most tasks of life by deciding who could do it, who was good at it, who wanted to do it, who had time, who needed help, etc. Larry's arm strength meant he had kitchen duty. Carol's greater physical limitations meant she organized the lists and schedules. In our professional jobs, we alternated being the major breadwinner. Everything from lovemaking to getting out of the car was an exercise in cooperation and respect—an orchestration of timing, assistance, and down-to-earth tolerance.

Our parenting was similarly orchestrated. As the only one who could drive, Larry did the carpooling. Carol's math acuity made her the homework authority. Larry did more of the "hands-on" parenting jobs: cuddling, restraining, washing, roughhousing. Carol nurtured by storytelling, instructing, reprimanding, discussing, and watching endlessly ("Mom, watch this!").

We both did an enormous amount of talking. Larry explained and lectured. Carol questioned motivations and articulated feelings. We even entered family counseling during several difficult times to talk some more. Reflecting back on it, we realize one of the central themes of all this talking was nurturance: caring for and being responsible for people, animals, plants, and the environment. Larry encouraged empathy in Brian through questions like "How do you think you would feel if that happened to you?" Carol nudged Brian to write notes and make gifts for family members. We gave him regular chores to do for the family and engaged him in many rescues of abandoned and injured stray animals.

Another major theme was prejudice and unfairness. Disability rights and women's rights were frequent topics in our household. Carol often directed Brian's attention to surrounding events, attitudes, and images that contributed to women's oppression, e.g., *Playboy*, sadistic images in rock videos, crude jokes. Most of the time, Brian would roll his eyes and protest that Carol could find sexism in anything. Larry usually backed her up but sometimes he lightened the tension by joining Brian in teasing Carol about her unwillingness to take her menfolk's last name. This was a family joke that ironically conveyed both affection and respect for Carol and got everyone to smile.

We also did a lot of the standard things most people do to raise a nonsexist son, from respecting his need to cry, to encouraging his interests and talents regardless of their traditional "gender appropriateness." Again, this lent a certain eclecticism to Brian's activities, which included sports, cooking, ceramics, drawing, music, reading, swimming and surfing, collecting, etc. On both feminist and pacifist grounds, we tried to avoid the most destructive "macho" stuff. For example, at his request, we enrolled Brian in a karate class. But when we discovered the instructor tested each boy's mettle by getting the class to take turns punching him in the stomach, Larry pronounced it barbaric and encouraged Brian to drop out, which he did. We also kept Brian out of formal team sports run by zealous competitive coaches and pressured him not to join the military when the gung-ho recruiters tried to nab him in high school.

Although we often held little hope that our battle against the "isms" was making an impact, like other parents, we now see that children do pay attention. Brian is now 22 and spontaneously uses words like "sexism" when critiquing the world. He is also our only relative who consistently uses

Carol's proper name in introductions and addressing mail. He is comfortable in the friendship of both men and women. He loves sports and still hugs his childhood stuffed dog when he's sick. He has argued for the rights of women, people with disabilities, and other minorities.

Brian has shared his life for four years with a woman who also has strong goals and opinions. They have found a way to support each other, argue, and give space as needed. Like us, they are lover, companion, and family—equals. Seeing them interact is the great payoff to all our years of struggle. We enjoy watching our son laundering his partner's delicate sweaters or lovingly constructing her sandwiches. We listen to him express the depth of his feelings and respect for her. (Yes, he is a talker like his parents!) They have negotiated their course with cooperation, nurturance, and concern about unfairness. They want to have a family, they want to protect the earth.

When we told Brian about writing this piece, we asked his permission to tell the story of our family. He was enthusiastic and helped us reminisce about the past. One of his recollections confirmed how much he had been affected by the equity in his parents' relationship. He told us that sometimes as a child when he would answer the family telephone, callers would ask to speak to the "head of the house." Brian remembers his natural response to this request was to ask "Which one?" Then he and the caller would have a confusing discussion about which parent was needed on the phone. He said it was always simpler when only one of us was home because then the choice was clear: he would just summon whichever "head of the house" happened to be present!

◆◆◆

Loving Across the Boundary (1995)

Ann Filemyr

Writer and teacher **Ann Filemyr** is the Dean of the Center for Arts and Cultural Studies at the Institute of American Indian Arts in Santa Fe, New Mexico. Her poems have been twice nominated for a Pushcart Prize in Poetry. Her current research is on ecology, feminism, and the intersection of nature, culture, and identity.

Nubian, our puppy, scratches and whines at the bedroom door. Essie sits bolt upright in bed crying out: "What time is it?" Groggy, I squint at the clock, "Almost seven—"

"Granny was supposed to wake us up at six!"

"Maybe she forgot—" I hustle into my bathrobe at the insistent scratching on the door, "I've got to let Nubi out—"

"Granny never forgets to wake us," Essie mutters under her breath as she scrambles out of the tangled sheets.

I race down the stairs, "Granny! GRANNY!"

I find her body on the cold kitchen floor, but she is gone. I can feel her spirit lifting up and out into the golden morning light filtering through the grand old maples that surround the farmhouse. Despite the utter peace in the room, I panic.

"Essie! Essie Carol!" I scream up the stairs to my partner.

Granny's breath is gone, but her body remains. A line from the book *Daughters of Copper Woman* circles through my mind, "*And she left her bag of bones on the beach. . . .*" Sun crowds the kitchen and the golden maple leaves gleam in October light. Essie flies barefoot across cold linoleum, cradling Granny in her arms, the first sob rising in our throats. . . .

Granny had made her bed that morning. She was dressed and ready for her Monday morning walk. But instead of the familiar stroll, Granny had traveled where we could not follow. We shared a long, sad look. Essie's face crumpled in pain. . . .

In the hospital emergency room we wept, our heads bent over Granny's body. Stroking back her wavy black hair (even at 79 her hair had not turned white) we sighed and pleaded. Two years earlier in ICU the doctors had told us she was gone. Her heart would not hold a steady beat. They pointed to the monitor above her unconscious body to show us the erratic yellow line, the uneven blip across the screen. Only the machines kept her breathing. We said no. It was her second heart failure in three months that winter of 1991, but we had plans for our shared lives—Granny, Essie and me. We were anticipating spring. . . .

Granny regained her strength that time. But that was March 1991 and this was October 1993. The doctor nodded to us and spoke with her strong Pakistani accent, "She looks happy. She had a long life. She would die one day." Then she left us alone, but the nurse on duty asked us a million questions about "the body"—about funeral arrangements—about donating organs—about contacting "the family"—we could not respond.

We *are* the family—an elder with her two granddaughters. This is our story of love, though now we are the body of women weeping. Granny was ours to care for, we had taken her into our daily lives because we loved her, and now she is sleeping, and we cannot wake her.

Skin color marked Essie as the one who belonged to Granny. The nurse nodded and smiled at me, "It's so nice of you to stand by your friend at a time like this."

Where else would I be? Granny was my grandmother, too. She loved me like no one else in my life: she loved me fiercely. She knew I had stepped across the line in North America which is drawn across the center of our faces to keep us separate— to keep the great grandchildren of slavekeepers from the great grandchildren of slaves. When she met me as Essie's "friend" twelve years earlier, she had watched me closely, but then she accepted me into her household and into her family. As the elder, her acceptance meant acceptance. She recognized my love for her granddaughter and would say to me, "People talk, but you hold your head up. You walk tall. The Lord sees what you're doing for my granddaughter, how you help her with her son. He sees how you stick together and help each other out." As far as Granny was concerned it was the *quality of our caring* not our sexuality that mattered. In this she was far wiser than most.

For the past three years we had lived together in Yellow Springs, sharing meals and dishes. She would sometimes pull out her old photo albums and tell her stories, laughing at memories of wild times out dancing with her friends in the juke joint

or riding horses with her cousin on her father's ranch or traveling cross country in the rig with her husband and his magical black cat when he worked as a truckdriver. Rich, warm memories, and I would sip my coffee and imagine her days and nights. What sustained her? Love—no doubt. Love and greens and cornbread—good food. That's what she craved. And the kitchen was her favorite room next to her bedroom.

She had been raised in the fields and farms of the south. When I was deciding whether or not to take the job in Ohio, Granny was part of the decision-making process. Moving back to the country after four decades in the city felt like coming full circle to her. She said she wanted to come with us. And it was here in Ohio that Granny and I had the luxury of time together to make our own relationship to each other. She would talk to me about "the things white folks do—" how they tend to "put themselves first like they better than other folks—" how foolish they looked on the TV talk shows "tellin' all their business—" or how much she had enjoyed some of the white friends she and her husband once had.

She spoke her mind without embarrassment or apology. I listened. She had survived the jim crow laws of the south. She had survived segregation and desegregation. She kept a gun under her pillow she called "Ole Betsy" in case someone would try to break in or "mess with her." Granny paid attention to details as a matter of survival. She prided herself on the subtle things she observed in watching how people acted and how they treated one another. She would interpret everything: tone of voice, a simple gesture, the hunch of someone's shoulders. She always knew when someone felt sad or tired. You didn't have to say anything. She comforted. She sympathized. She was extremely skilled at making others feel loved, feel noticed, feel good about themselves. But if Essie had not been in my life it is doubtful that I would have ever known this remarkable woman, her namesake, Essie (Granny) Hall.

When I moved in with Essie in 1982, my nomadic tendencies were pulling at me, urging me to convince Essie that it was a perfect time for us to relocate to another city. I had lived in Milwaukee for two and a half years, for me that was long enough. I'd found a new love, an important someone in my life. It seemed like the perfect time to move on with my new partner. But Essie's life was described and defined by different currents. She had roots. She had family. She told me, "I will be here as long as Granny needs me." I was shocked. My feet carried me freely; I fought against family attachments. Was this difference cultural? Personal? Both? But now I have grown to respect and appreciate this way of being, this way of belonging. Is it a middle-class white cultural tendency to break free, to move on, to move up, to move out? Certainly the bonds of family and of commitment were far stronger for Essie than for me. One of the greatest gifts in my life has been that she shared her son and grandmother with me.

I wanted to tell the emergency room nurse all of this. I held Essie Carol in my arms as she cried. I wanted to scream, "Here we are, can't you see us? Lovers and partners holding each other in a time of crisis—What do you need for proof?". . .

Sunday mornings Granny listened to gospel preachers on her old radio, rocking and clapping to the music. When we weren't home, she'd get up and dance through the rooms of the house, tears flowing freely as she sang out loud. We'd catch her and tease her. Once Granny hung a plastic Jesus in the bathroom; he had his hands folded in prayer and flowing blonde locks thrown back over his shoulders. Essie groaned, "A white man on the bathroom wall!" She took it down and tried to explain to Granny everybody did not worship the same way she did.

We were not only a multiracial household, but one that held different spiritual beliefs. Essie followed a path she had first been introduced to by Granny's mother, her great-grandmother, Caroline Kelly Wright, affectionately known as Ma. Ma wore her hair in long braids and had been called "the little Indian" most of her life. She had married a freed African slave, but she herself was Blackfoot. Ma smoked a pipe and prayed to the sun. Essie remembered as a child the whole family would gather in Ma's bedroom facing East. The dawn's pale light would begin to appear through the open window only a few city blocks from the enormous freshwater ocean called Lake Michigan. Everyone listened as Ma prayed aloud over the family, telling all secrets, opening up all stories, praying to Creator to provide answers, to help guide them to find their purpose in life and hold to it, to be strong. Everything was said on these Sunday mornings and tears fell as Ma blew her smoke toward the light of the rising sun.

Ma had delivered Essie during a wild January blizzard. Ma was a midwife, herbalist, neighborhood dream interpreter, the community sage and soothsayer. If the term had been as popular then as it is now, Ma would have been honored as a shaman. Essie remembers the Baptist preacher visiting their house and saying to Ma, "I'll pray for you, Miz Caroline," and Ma responding, "You can't pray for me, but I can pray for you."

At the age of eight after a preacher had singled her out to stand up and read the Bible as a punishment for something she hadn't even done, Essie told her great-grandmother that she did not want to attend church anymore. Ma agreed. So Essie had little patience for Granny's Christianity. She was especially offended by refrains such as the "Good Master" and would try to point out to Granny how Black Christian faith was a result of slavery, the product of an enforced cultural genocide. Essie would try to "educate" Granny about the ways slaves were punished for trying to hold on to older beliefs, such as the care and worship of the ancestors or relating to land and nature as an expression of the Sacred. Of course this didn't work, and I would try to negotiate peace settlements between the two generations, between the two Essies, between the centuries, between the ancestors and the youth. Neither one of them really listened to me. I would take the younger Essie aside and tell her, "Leave Granny alone. You're not going to change her." And the younger Essie would retort, "But she's trying to change me!". . .

[A]t the funeral the man in the black suit did his best. He tried to save us. He opened the doors of the church and urged us to enter. He forgot about the corpse in the casket behind him, and he called the stray flock home. White men and Black men held each other in the back row. White women held Black women in the front row. And in between were all shades of brown and pink, young and old, from four-week-old Jade, the last baby Granny had blessed, to Mrs. Cooper, Granny's phone buddy. They had spoken every day on the phone for a year. Granny adored "Cooper" as she called her, though they had never met in person. Here we sat in rows before an open casket: all colors, ages, sexualities, brought together by a mutual love for an exceptional person. As some of Essie's family members called out urgently, encouraging the preacher with *Amen* and *Yes, Lord* others ignored the eulogy, attending to their own prayers.

At the funeral we sat side by side in the front row in dark blue dresses. Essie's sister and son sat on the other side of her. We wept and held each other's hands. If Granny loved us for who we were, then we weren't going to hide our feelings here. Certainly there were disapproving glances from some family members, but not all. During the decade we lived in Milwaukee, we had shared childcare and holidays, made it through illnesses and the deaths of other beloved family members—what else qualifies someone as family? Yet despite this, I knew there were those who despised my presence for what I represented was the alien. I was the lesbian, and I was white. For some my presence was an inexcusable reminder of Essie's betrayal. She had chosen to be different, and I was the visible reminder of her difference. For some this was a mockery of all they valued, but she did not belong to them so they could control her identity. Granny knew this, and Granny loved her because she had the strength to be herself.

My family is liberal Democrat, yet my mother once said to me that my choice to love other women would make my life more difficult. She wanted to discourage me from considering it. She said, *I would tell you the same thing if you told me you loved a Black man.* I was then nineteen. It struck me as curious that to love someone of the same sex was to violate the same taboo as to love someone across the color line. In the end I chose to do both. Does this make me a rebel? Certainly if my attraction was based initially on the outlaw quality of it, that thrill would not have been enough to sustain the trauma of crossing the color line in order to share love. The rebellious young woman that I may have been could not make sense of the other story, the story of her darker-skinned sister, without a willingness to question everything I had been raised to accept as "normal," without an active analysis of the politics of racial subjugation and institutionalized white male supremacy. And without personal determination, courage, a refusal to be shamed, a sheer stubbornness based on our assumption that our lives held unquestionable worth as women, as women together, as women of different colors together, despite the position of the dominant culture—and even at times the position of the women's community—to diminish and deny us, we would not have been able to make a life together.

I have participated in and been witness to a side of American life that I would never have glimpsed if Essie had not been my partner. The peculiar and systematic practice of racial division in this country has been brought into sharp focus through many painful but revealing experiences. By sharing our lives, our daily survival, our dreams and aspirations, I have been widened and deepened. It has made me much more conscious of the privileges of being white in a society rigidly structured by the artificiality of "race."

One of the first awakenings came near the beginning of our relationship when her son came home with a note from the school librarian that said, "Your overdue books will cost 45 cents in fines. Irresponsible handling of school property can lead to problems later including prison." I was shocked—threatening a nine-year-old boy with prison because of overdue books? I couldn't imagine what that librarian was thinking. Did she send these letters home with little white boys and girls? I wanted to call the school and confront her. Essie stopped me by telling me a number of equally horrifying stories about this school so we agreed to take Michael out.

We decided that Michael, who had been staying with Granny and Daddy Son and attending the school near their home during the week, should move in full-time with us. Essie worked first shift at the hospital, and I was a graduate student at the university. She left for work at 6 A.M., and I caught the North Avenue bus at 9:30. I would be able to help Michael get to school before I left for the day. We decided to enroll Michael in our neighborhood school.

The neighborhood we lived in was one of the few mixed neighborhoods in the city. It formed a border between the rundown urban center and the suburbs on the west side. The neighborhood school was across an invisible boundary, a line I did not see but would grow to understand. Somewhere between our house and this building, a distance of approximately six blocks, was a color line. A whites-only-no-Blacks-need-applys distinctly drawn and doggedly patrolled. We scheduled a visit with the principal, and when both of us appeared the next morning, we observed a curious reaction. Though polite, she was absolutely flustered.

She could not determine who to direct her comments to. She looked from Essie's closely cropped black hair to my long loose wavy hair, from cream skin to chocolate skin, and stammered, "Who—who is the mother?"

"I am," said Essie.

"I'm sorry," was the reply. "We have already reached our quota of Black students in this school."

"Quota? We live in this neighborhood," I replied. "This is not a question of bussing a child in. He lives here."

She peered at the form we had filled out with our address on it. Then responded coldly, "We are full."

"That's ridiculous," I objected.

"Are you telling me that my child is not welcome to attend the fourth grade in your school?" Essie asked icily.

"We simply don't have room."

Essie stood up and walked out of the room without another word. I wanted to scream. I wanted to force the principal to change her mind, her politics, her preoccupation with the boundaries defined by color. I sat there staring at her. She refused to meet my eyes. I said slowly, "This will be reported to the Superintendent and to the school board," and walked out following Essie to the car.

We scheduled a meeting at the school administration to register a formal complaint and find Michael another school. I was furious. We were taxpayers. These are public schools. How can he be refused entrance? How can a child be denied because of some quota determined by an administrator somewhere? I was naive in matters of race.

I would have to say all white people are naive about the persistence of the color line. We prefer naiveté—in fact we insist on it. If we, as white people, actually faced the entrenched injustice of our socioeconomic system and our cultural arrogance, we might suffer tears, we might suffer the enormous weight of history, we might face the iceberg of guilt which is the underside of privilege. We might begin to glimpse our losses, our estrangement from others, our intense fear as the result of a social system that places us in the precarious position of the top. We might be moved to call out and protest the cruelty that passes for normal behavior in our daily lives, in our cities, and on our streets. . . .

Nothing in my life, my education, my reading, my upbringing, prepared me to straddle the color-line with Essie under the Reagan years in Milwaukee, a post-industrial city suffering economic decline and social collapse. The rigidly entrenched division of social power by race and the enormously draining limitations we faced on a daily basis began to tear at the fabric of our daily survival. I began to experience a kind of rage that left me feeling as sharp as broken glass. I was in this inner state when we finally arrived in the long quiet corridors of the central administration of Milwaukee Public Schools.

We were ushered into an office with a man in a suit sitting behind a desk. He could have been an insurance salesman, a loan officer, or any other briefcase-carrying decision-making tall white man in a position of power and control. We were two women of small build and modest dress, but we were carrying the larger presence—righteous anger. We sat down. I leaned across his desk and challenged him to explain to us why Michael had been refused admittance into the school of our choice. He back-pedaled. He avoided. He dodged. Essie suddenly said, "I am finished. I am taking my child out of school," and stood up.

I snapped my notebook closed, signaling the end of the conversation. The man had never asked me who I was. Did he assume I was a social worker? a family member? a friend? a lawyer? a journalist? Had it even crossed his mind that he was looking at a pair of lovers, at a family, at the two acting parents of this child? For the first time he looked worried, "I am sure we can find an appropriate school for your son. Tell me his interests. We'll place him in one of our specialty schools."

We hesitated.

"I'll personally handle his registration," he seemed to be pleading with us. He looked from Essie to me wondering who his appeal would reach first.

We settled on a school with a square of wild prairie, the environmental science specialty school. It was a half hour bus ride from our home. Michael liked the school, but we did not feel completely victorious. How could we? Though we had challenged the system, these policies and practices which place undue emphasis on the color of a child's skin had not been changed. The school system simply accommodated us, perhaps fearing our potential to cause widespread dissent by giving voice to the intense dissatisfaction of the

African American community with the public school system. We compromised—perhaps exhausted by the constant fight against feeling invisible and powerless. It was not just that Michael was Black. It was also that his family consisted of a white woman and a Black woman, and regardless of our commitment to him, we were not perceived as a valid family unit though we functioned as a family. . . .

It is heartbreaking to raise an African American boy in the U.S. From an early age he is taught that others fear him. He is taught that he is less than. He is taught that his future is defined by certain streets in certain neighborhoods, or that the only way out is through musical or athletic achievement. Michael played basketball and football. He wrote raps and performed them to the punctuated beat of electronic keyboards and drum machines. When it was fashionable, he would breakdance on the living-room floor. He had a few good years in school, but by and large school did not satisfy his quest for knowledge, nor did it provide him with creative avenues for self-expression. . . .

There were so many things I could not do for Michael. I could not clothe him in transparent skin to prevent him from being prejudged by color-conscious teachers who would label him inferior. I could not surround him with safety on the street corner where he waited for his school bus. One grisly morning in November he came home shaking. He and a small boy had been shot at while waiting on a familiar corner two blocks from the house. It was 7:30 A.M. While he was preparing to attend school, boys his age were shooting guns out of car windows hoping to kill somebody in order to get into a gang so they could make money.

On that gray morning, the capitalist notion of success as the acquisition of material wealth appeared for what it is: an absolute perversion of human dignity. Yet white American culture persists in holding material affluence as the highest symbol of achievement. The way this plays out in the lives of people of color and those who love them can be summed up in one word: cruelty. We suffer for a lack of basic resources because of the hoarding, the feverish consumerism, and the complete lack of concern by people who have more than they will ever possibly need. Fashion crimes, ganking [gang violence targeting rival gang members or other

young people], children beating and killing other children to acquire the stingy symbols of status in a society devoid of real meaning—this is what happens on the city streets of the richest nation in the world.

I could not keep Michael from the bullets. I could not move him out into the suburbs where another kind of violence would confront him daily, those who would question his presence and limit his right to move freely from one house to the next. I could not close his eyes to the terror he would see in his friends when death visited among them. I could not hold him against the rage he held inside. A rage that thundered through the house pulverizing everything in its path, terrifying me, tearing at his mother.

What could we say to him about how to live on the mean streets of a bully nation? We did not live on those same streets even though we lived in the same neighborhood. His experience, my experience, his mother's experience—we walked out of the front door into three separate worlds. Worlds we did not define or control except in how we would respond to them. Michael watched the hours I spent typing, writing, scratching out, rewriting. He watched the transformations his mother carried out with color on canvas, making lumps of cold clay into warm red altar bowls with her naked hands. He saw that we took our pain and rage, our grinding frustration and radiant hope, and made something out of it that gave us strength. Michael is still writing, making music, performing in his own music videos. He sees himself as an artist as we see ourselves; this is the thing that has carried us through.

The Westside where we bought a home had always been a working class neighborhood where people invested in their sturdy brick and wood frame houses planting roses in their green squares of grass. The neighborhood had been built in the teens and twenties by German immigrants who took a certain pride in quality. These homes had fireplaces and stained-glass windows, beautifully crafted built-in bookshelves and beveled mirrors. Only a few generations earlier, there was safety and prosperity here. Waves of immigrants—Greek, Polish, Hasidic Jews, African Americans coming North to work in the factories, shared these streets. I can remember walking into the corner bakery and the Greek woman behind the counter asked Essie and I if we were sisters. It was possible there at that time. Blood was shared. Love between the races happened. We laughed and nodded, "Yes—yes, we're sisters." In these moments we utterly and joyfully belonged together.

My friends who lived on the Eastside of the city rarely came to visit after I moved in with Essie. It was as if I had moved to the other side of the moon. . . . I trusted white women less and less as friends because they could not be counted on when things got tough. They tended to retreat. Race issues are ugly and hard, but if white women who want to fight male supremacy can't stand up to their own fears around the issue of color and simultaneously fight white supremacy, how can they really undertake the work of women's liberation? Certainly without an analysis and willingness to deal with race, there is no depth to the commitment. It is simply a get-ahead strategy for a particular middle class white female minority. Today I feel there is a greater commitment to address issues of racism within the feminist movement, but most of the voices I hear are still women of color. . . .

White women are conditioned to stay put, even rebellious daughters who love other women rarely cross the road that divides the races. Any woman who engages in a serious relationship— as friend or family, as lover, or mother to daughter— with a woman of a different shade of skin will find this relationship demanding a deeper vulnerability than any other as long as race relationships continue to be fraught with tension. But if we settle for a divided nation, we settle for social rigidity and police brutality, we settle for ignorance and stereotypes, we settle for emptiness and fear.

I am still learning how to confront racism when I see it, how to educate my friends without alienating them, how to ask for what I need in terms of support. It has been a rare occurrence, but a joyful one, for us to find other mixed-race lesbian couples. When we begin to talk about how difficult it is, we discover certain patterns and find solace that we are not alone. But why should we suffer for being ourselves and finding ourselves in the borderless culture between races, in the undefined space where wakefulness is necessary for survival, where honest communication and self-reflection must replace the simple recipes of romance. . . .

Few of us born in the Americas can trace our bloodline with impunity. So many of our ancestors have been erased or invented as need be. I know very few family names that have not gone without at least one attempt at revision—to anglicize it—simplify it—discard the ethnic or cultural baggage of a *ski* or *stein* or other markers of race/ethnic identity. One who is raised as part of an unwanted people will shift the identity to become acceptable. Note the number of Chippewa and Menominee people in Wisconsin with French last names. One Chippewa man explained to me how in every neighborhood his family adopted another identity: Mexican when living on the Southside, French on the Eastside. Only back up on the reservation could they say aloud their true names. . . .

How many of us are of African descent? Slavery was challenged in part because of the enormous outcry against the "white slave children." Children of enslaved African women who were the result of forced sex with slavemasters ended up on the auction block. Some of these children looked just like the "free" children of "free" European-American mothers. Obviously there was a tremendous outcry resulting from the confusion that the rationale for chattel slavery was based on a strict hierarchy of skin color as the basis of privilege. How could they justify selling these children that by all appearances looked white even if the mother was a light-skinned African American slave? White men in the South parented children on both sides of the yard: women they took as wives, and women who worked the fields. The brown and pale children were half-brothers and half-sisters related by blood through the father. This simple truth was denied, and these children were taught to never consider themselves as one family. There is no doubt that many of us have relatives we never considered before. Part of my work has been beginning to claim these unnamed Ancestors as family.

The day after I wrote that paragraph, I visited my parents. It was a week before Christmas, and I was planning to spend the day with my two grandmothers and my parents. . . . While in my parents' home, I asked about an old photo album that I remembered from childhood. My mother commented that it had recently surfaced from the jumble of daily life and brought it into the kitchen. Tintypes and daguerreotypes, family photographs spanning 1850–1900. Fifty years of Walkers, my mother's father's family.

That night, back in the city, stretched across the guest bed at a friend's house, I slowly turned the pages. There are my Ancestors, among the first generation here from the British Isles. Aunt Mary and Uncle Tom Walker. By pulling the photographs out and inspecting the little leather and brass book, I discovered they settled in Clinton and Seaforth, Ontario. I knew these relatives had lived in Canada, but hadn't known they lived between Lakes Huron, Erie and Ontario! All of the faces were unfamiliar, stiff, caught in frozen poses over a century ago. A few of the photographs I remembered from my childhood, especially the sad-faced child in the unusual robe with straight cropped black hair and Asian eyes. For the first time it occurred to me that this could be the face of a native child—not European at all! Who is this child? Then a particularly striking face caught my attention. A young woman gazed confidently, intently, at what? Her hair hung around her wide face and high cheekbones in thick black ringlets, her full lips barely open, her strong chin—this is a woman of African descent. Who is she to me? She wore a gold hoop earring and a checkered bow over a satin dress. With one arm resting against an upholstered pillow, she posed proudly. Why had I never heard of her before?. . .

No one in my family seems to know much about these faces, these people, these lives, and how they relate to us. . . . If I am supposed to be a proud daughter of the colonizing English and the migrating Irish, why can't I also be a proud daughter of the Anishinabeg or Haudenausaunee, two of the indigenous peoples of this Great Lakes region, as well as a proud daughter of the African Diaspora? In America the idea of Europe was created, as if my English Ancestors weren't trying to dominate my Irish Ancestors. Why can't we talk about our truly diverse heritages? Nothing has been passed down in my family of these darker-skinned faces in my family's picture album. Is the refusal to see ourselves as something other than Northern European based in a fearful grasping after shreds of white-skinned privilege? What do we lose if we acknowledge our connection? What do we gain?

Granny kept a photo album. The pictures were important. Some were tattered and worn out, but they mattered. They held the faces of relatives—cousins, aunts, sisters—men in fine hats and women in silk dresses looking into the camera, into the future. In the album is a small square black and white snapshot of two plump white babies seated outdoors on a stuffed armchair. The Kelly boys. Irish. Part of the family. Essie remembers her great-grandmother telling her children, grandchildren and great-grandchildren, "These are your cousins." I bet those white boys don't show the dark faces of their cousins to their kin. . . .

The tight little boxes of identity defined by our society keep the building blocks of political and economic power in place. How can we gender-bend, race-cross, nature-bond, and love ourselves in our plurality enough to rebel against the deadening crush of conformity? Is it a crisis of the imagination which prevents us from extending compassion beyond the boundaries of limited personal experience to listen *and be moved to action* by stories of injustice others suffer. How can we extend the boundaries of our own identities so that they include "the other"? If we have any hope for the future of life, how can we expand our sense of self to include other people as well as beings in nature? The structure of our society is articulated by separation and difference. How do we challenge this by living according to a sense of connection not alienation?

For us, for Essie and I, the greatest challenge has been inventing ourselves as we went along for we could not find a path to follow. Where are our foremothers? Light and Dark women who held each other's hands through childbirth and child-raising? Who stood side by side and loved each other refusing to budge despite everybody's objections? Who pooled their measly resources together to make sure there was food and heat and light enough for everyone's needs? I want to know them. I want to hear their stories. I'll tell them mine. . . .

Despite the absence of role models, we share specific Ancestors, disembodied presences gliding through our lives like a sudden breeze teasing the candle flame on the altar; secret-keepers who come under guard of moonlight, carrying apple baskets full of fresh fruit which they drop into our sleeping; we wake up before dawn with the sweet taste on our lips of good dreams and lucky numbers. We have our shared Ancestors to thank, and we are fortunate to count Granny among them.

◆◆◆

Personal Reflections on Being a Grandmother (1997)
L'Chol Dor Va Dor

Rachel Aber Schlesinger[1]

Born in Germany, **Rachel Aber Schlesinger** came to the United States as a child and is now Associate Professor in the Division of Social Sciences at York University, Toronto. Her interests include the experiences of Jewish women, change in Jewish families, and the role of grandparents.

My Grandmother

My maternal grandmother lived with us. I learned from her that grandmothers have great power. They represent a relationship that, like a parent's, demands respect and provides love but is different. *Omamma* was a "queen," she kept religious standards high, passed on a sense of family history, and

told wonderful stories. She helped give us a sense of who we were and what we stood for. Our family had religious and family traditions. We were a matriarchal family. The men were important and respected, but the names and the stories were those of the mothers.

The family stories began with my great-grandparents, the rabbi and *rebbitzin* of Luebeck. They had twelve children. My great-grandmother greeted the birth of each child, and indeed every family

[1] I was able to carry out this research with the help of a grant from Canada Multicultural Department and the Centre of Jewish Studies at York University. I want to thank Sarah Taieb Carlen for conducting some of the interviews with Sephardi women in French, and for her help with this project.

occasion with a poem, a *Tischlied*. In quiet moments she wrote a book of poetry for the young Jewish bride, stressing the family and religious roles of Jewish women. This book of poems was still given to my older cousin upon marriage. Before the Second World War, the lives of these women and the poems held commonly understood meanings.

My grandmother was the oldest of eight daughters. In her later years she wrote her memoirs. Even in this religious family the important items that she remembered were elegant balls, clothes, and meeting her husband. She lived in the age of romance, and saw her early years in these terms. She was also deeply religious and supervised the early religious teachings of her grandchildren.

Tragically, she was widowed as a young woman. Her life in Germany was devoted to social service activities; her home was filled with interesting people. Upon her death I found correspondence from Bertha Pappenheim dealing with rescue activities for Jewish women and children. Omamma spoke English well and came to America by way of Portugal in the 1940s. Once here, she divided her time between living with her two surviving children, my mother and my uncle. She did small jobs, was a companion to others, and baby-sat, yet this work never diminished her queenly status in her eyes or in the eyes of others.

My Mother as Grandmother

I was able to understand my mother in her role as a grandparent because of the influence of my grandmother. Both women were unique; daughters and wives of distinguished rabbis, they had a strong sense of self, of Jewish values, and of family *Yehus*.

Mutti's world changed with the Nazi era. My mother's stories were told not to her children who experienced the events she recounted, but to her grandchildren. Since I was the youngest of her children I didn't remember these experiences, but my children told me Mutti's stories. Here is one of the stories.

On *Krystallnacht* in November 1938, the synagogue in Bremen was destroyed and my father, the rabbi, was taken to a concentration camp. My mother, known by Jew and non-Jew in this middle-sized port city, worked for his release and that of the other men taken that night. Each day, as the story goes, she went with her three daughters to the

Gestapo headquarters to ask when the men would be released. One day she was told that they would be sent home on a midnight train, but she did not know which night. Every night, at midnight, she walked to the railway station to see if my father would be coming on that train. Every night, she heard footsteps behind her as a Gestapo officer followed her through dingy parts of town. That did not deter her.

Weeks later, after this routine was followed each night, my father did indeed arrive on a train. Mutti turned around at the station. The footsteps behind her had stopped. She looked up to see the Gestapo officer salute her and my father. He had been following her each night for her protection. That is the kind of devotion my beautiful mother inspired.

Mutti believed in the power of the individual, and the vital role of the woman in the family and in the community. She was a deeply committed Jew. Her religion, her vocation, and her belief system were holistic. I know that her grandchildren loved her, respected her, and understood her. My son told me, "Mutti was unusual. She really believed in what she believed in!"

My Own Experience

Now I am a grandmother. I am a living ancestor! My stories will be different, I live in another land, in another time. I wonder if any of us can transmit to our children's children the tastes, the smells, the environment, the understanding of the values that shaped us.

What do I want to pass on to my grandchildren? I find it easier to ask "how," than to pinpoint "what" it is I want to transmit. Like my grandmother I tell stories, sing songs, and recount family history. If my sisters and I have pictures, we put them on the walls. We use the ability to name to perpetuate memories and names. Those of us who were born in other countries speak in our mother tongue. We use language to recall roots. We model our religious practices and holiday observances. We convey our oral traditions in the kitchens of our homes. As our grandchildren get older, we share secrets often not told to our own children.

The bond between grandchild and grandparents may be the strongest, and of the longest duration, next to the parent bond. Can grandparents transmit values, or is this too difficult due to the age gap between the first and third generation, differences in life experiences, and competition from outside agents of socialization?

Immigrant Grandmothers

For the past few years I have been talking with Jewish grandmothers, asking them about their perceptions of being a grandparent and transmitting their own values to their grandchildren. Let me introduce some of the women who shared their thoughts on this question.

Sephardi Grandmothers

Sara comes from Morocco. There is a big difference between her world and that of her grandmother. Her grandmother was married at twelve years of age and was only fifteen when Sara's mother was born. The role of women in her community was important. Sara recounts that it was often the woman who urged the family to leave, either for Israel, France, or Canada. In Morocco, women lived in separate spheres, yet had valued roles. With the shift to a new country, their roles changed. The family changed from being a large, extended family living with each other to having members dispersed. Sara's family life is strongly linked to religious observance. "If you can't cook, you can't fulfill your religious obligations."

Leaving Morocco meant leaving cultural roles behind. "My grandmother's religious views and her ways will be acknowledged in her home, but maybe not in ours. This means that while we have memory, we may not have continuity of culture." In order for a culture to survive, it must be practiced. It is not good enough to talk of the "old days," if they are not followed today.

Lena, born in Morocco, adds: "Family traditions . . . are very important. They are mostly French traditions, like table manners, classical music, French literature. Yes, in my country, it was our way." She talks about a way of life that combines Jewish and secular culture, a civilized worldview, formed by Continental culture in an Arabic environment, far removed from her present North Toronto setting.

Pina says, "I want to give them an idea of the way we lived. My father taught me wisdom; my mother's family had been in Iraq for millennia, maybe since Abraham."

Nadia, who comes from Turkey adds: "I have to tell them about our life. . . . Here, there is no Turkish atmosphere, no Turkish synagogue, no Turkish bath, no Turkish schools . . . so I have to talk about our way of life, and it is not always possible to imagine. It's like a dream."

Values grow out of a culture. These Sephardi grandmothers want to pass on respect and obedience to elders, for "they know more than us, they have a whole life behind them. Respect, it's like breathing. It comes naturally; we are born with it" (Mrs. C).

Ashkenazi Grandmothers

While Jews from Eastern Europe also had close associations with their home countries, when they talk of bringing grandchildren "home" it is to teach them what can happen to Jewish communities. It is to put the Holocaust into personal terms. Or it is to put the Russian experience into perspective.

Ada is under five feet tall, and she is a survivor—of the Holocaust, of displaced-person camps, of migrations to several countries, before settling in Canada twenty years ago. She spoke in optimistic terms about her life.

For her, her grandchildren are a miracle, the remnants of a family that is once again extended. She feels the need to transmit memories, and has taken her five grandchildren to Poland, to see the *Camps*, to show them what she has survived. She tells them how she picked up her life after the war. She returned to Poland after the war, met her husband, lived in Israel, then came to Canada.

She wants to perpetuate language, not Polish but Hebrew, and speaks it with her grandchildren. Ada models her values, she still volunteers time as a nurse's aide, and together with her husband, remains active in the community. She lives within walking distance of her children.

She finds it difficult to convey her Jewish values. "One son-in-law does not speak Hebrew; he is a Canadian, and cannot even understand the feelings of being a survivor. He tells me I spoil the children."

Mrs. Z came to Canada seven years ago; she focuses on her Lithuanian experiences. Her grandchildren do not understand why she chose to remain in a Communist country. Indeed, she had a high position in the government. She was eventually able to connect with her grandchildren by telling them about her experiences in the underground during the Second World War. She still has difficulties, since her children in Canada became "very Jewish, and I don't understand this. It was not my way."

These women are survivors—of their generation, of the Holocaust, of war. They can no longer return for a visit with their grandchildren; their world died. Many return to visit the death camps, but some women do not want their grandchildren to associate the Jewish life of their own youth only with death and destruction.

Domestic Religion, Food, and Practice

In our families we model our beliefs, talk about them, emphasize what's important. Religious observance is an area we articulate, often in loud, judgmental terms. The grandmothers speak of learning, religious rituals, and observance.

Religion is often viewed from the perspective of the kitchen. Cooking for holidays, talking in the kitchen, passing on *kashrut* by doing, not by reading; these are all examples of transmitting values. Recipes are handed over from generation to generation; they are part of the oral tradition. This too is religious commentary.

In terms of religious observances and even foods, the Sephardi feel a degree of cognitive dissonance. The foods they ate at home are not common in Canada. Ashkenazi families can find familiar kosher or kosher-style foods in supermarkets; the Sephardi cannot.

Mrs. W. had been unable to follow her religion in her home country. "In Latvia I couldn't be religious. Here I want to be, but my husband is still afraid. My granddaughter helps me."

Grandmothers feel that they have contributions to make to the family in terms of ideas, responsibilities, child care, and even financial assistance. Many of them hope that they are role models, as indeed their grandparents had been to them. It is important to them to be seen as representing the old culture, providing continuity of family traditions, while still being close to their grandchildren. They articulate the values of a Jewish education, family closeness and the concept of *Shalom Bayit*. They feel a sense of responsibility to ensure this for the next generation.

These grandmothers reflected a wistfulness for times past. Singing together reminds them of their own childhood. The first contacts with a new grandchild are often through singing songs in grandmother's mother tongue. They hope their grandchildren will respect them as older persons, by means of their behavior, such as good manners. They report that their grandchildren do respect their views and opinions, often coming to them before going to parents to ask for advice.

Roadblocks

Some fear they do not have a place in their grandchildren's lives now, but hope this will develop with time. Factors that impede communication and closeness include physical location, distance, family mobility, and family fragmentation.

Grandparents often have less formal education than their children or grandchildren, and some feel that this educational gap creates barriers. Others report feeling "inferior," "not modern enough." They feel inadequate because they can only transmit what is most common to their own life and experience, for example the customs, traditions, and history of their country of origin. Yet their children and grandchildren may not have a frame of reference for the information grandmothers wish to impart. So much is lost, replaced by strange new ways. Grandparents try to fit their culture into a new setting, and that is often a difficult task.

Even the words we use have changed. In Jewish tradition an older person was a *zakena*, a person of wisdom. In modern Hebrew, the terms *Saba* and *Safta* are used to denote grandparents, the father of my father; what has happened to the concept of wisdom?

Some Reflections

Some of the grandmothers felt frustrated, partly because the changes that have taken place during their lifetimes make it difficult to transmit a sense of what was. Their own world has been transformed through transitions.

Family roles have changed and older women see their status as lower in Canada than it might have been in the old society. The pattern of immigration itself has weakened family links. The new buzz-word of "individualization" undermines the sense of family and of community as well as woman's and grand-mother's role in the family. Grandmothers no longer occupy the same physical space as their children and grandchildren, and they fear that their domestic religion is out of their hands. Today's grandmother may really have little influence in conveying her concept of Jewish culture. A way of life has altered in a short span of time.

The grandmothers I interviewed examined the concepts of societal changes and ideological shifts. The Sephardi women spoke of open community life; some of the Eastern Europeans had belonged to the *Bund* and grown up on socialism. One needs to question if it is possible to have cultural transmission when the culture and politics have changed so drastically.

Are Jewish grandmothers different? Perhaps. This generation of women gives great importance to perpetuating the Jewish people. Older grandparents today are a generation who experienced migrations, displacements, and the Holocaust. We cherish the ability to have given birth, to survive as a people. We worry about the Jewishness of our children and grandchildren. We do have values to pass on—from generation to generation.

Can I transmit a sense of family to my grandchildren? Hopefully, yes. I can provide the smells of *hallah* baking; I can surround them with pictures of family members, of places and events. I can record voices for them to listen to; I can even use videos to pinpoint places and people. Modern technology helps, but being there, talking, being willing to listen, trying to explain our perspective, and respecting our own children and grandchildren may be the keys to future communications and continuity. Our grandchildren are not mind readers; contact, open communication, and understanding are also necessary ingredients in a relationship.

It is harder to impart religious values for eventually we each must find our own path and follow it for a time. We too change and may change our perspectives. That is what we can try to pass on—the ability to see and judge for oneself.

What do I want to communicate? I want healthy, thoughtful, creative, and caring family members—the rest is commentary.

L'chol Dor Va Dor, from generation to generation. My grandmother once told me, "listen carefully to what I will tell you . . . then you will tell this story to your children, and they will tell it to their grandchildren."

But will the story lose its meaning? My grandmother's and mother's stories were unique, coming from urgent times and far away places. I am part of the quiet generation. While I was born in Germany and raised by European parents, I grew up in North America. I need to add my own stories to those of the women in my family.

We are links in a long chain—which of the stories will our great-grandchildren repeat?

◆◆◆

Fundamentalism and the Family (1998)

Gender, Culture, and the American Profamily Movement

Margaret Lamberts Bendroth

Margaret Lamberts Bendroth, a longtime educator in the fields of religion and women's history, is currently the Executive Director of the American Congregational Association in Boston. A prolific writer, she won the Choice Award for Outstanding Book of 2002 for *Women and Twentieth-Century Protestantism.*

. . . Among the religious and political groups that scholars have labeled "fundamentalist," the rhetoric of family decline has served to focus a range of objections to modernity. . . . In the United States over the past twenty years, the family has become a key issue in the moral and political agenda of the broad conservative coalition known as the "religious right."[1]

. . . Since the mid-1970s, the "family values" debate has brought millions of politically uninvolved, conservative Protestants into the voting booth. Over the past two decades, the profamily agenda has expanded to include abortion, homosexuality, and the Equal Rights Amendment (ERA), as well as school board politics and parental rights legislation. These issues first pushed conservative Protestants into the national political arena, and have proved a lucrative fund-raising and vote-getting tool ever since.[2]

This article traces the process by which the family became the moral terrain of religious conservatives. . . . Relatively little of the historical literature on American fundamentalism, which tends to focus on theology and denominational politics, explains why sexuality and family issues have become such an overriding concern among present-day evangelicals. . . . Any examination of the evangelical profamily movement must consider its religious origins; behind the political organizing, which has met with much media attention, specific theological convictions consistently have motivated its leadership as well as the rank and file. . . .[3]

The historical origins of the modern profamily movement also serve as a barometer of change in the cultural role of religion and family life. American Protestant fundamentalism was around for a long time before it took up the family as a theological, much less political, concern. In the late-nineteenth and early-twentieth centuries, gender issues were central to the movement's identity and progress; however, this did not result in a full-fledged agenda to shore up the traditional family.[4] That change came fairly recently, beginning in the years following World War II and accelerating in the late 1970s. The timing and content of this transition are important, having as much to do with the evolving nature of the modern family as with the developing shape of religion in American society. More specifically, the shift reflects the transformation of erstwhile "fundamentalists" into a new group calling themselves "neo-evangelicals."

In American religious history, these two conservative Protestant types—fundamentalist and neo-evangelical (or, simply, evangelical)—are significantly different in theology and social attitudes, and it is worth the trouble to track the discontinuities, especially in regard to women and the family. Early-twentieth-century fundamentalists, as precursors of the modern evangelical movement, said little about the family and, for practical and theological reasons, valued it less. But with the emergence of a neoevangelical movement out of fundamentalism in the 1940s and 1950s, the family became a central metaphor. The difference in rhetoric about the family before and after World War II is a response to contradictory tugs toward separatism and cultural compromise. The need to be left alone and the fear of being ignored has been a tension within the conservative wing of American Protestantism for the past hundred years. Rather than an example of rising militancy among American religious conservatives, the profamily movement (and perhaps its political agenda) illustrates its losing battle against modernity; the military metaphors are more an index of secularization than of true religious radicalism.

Fundamentalism and American Culture

. . . The pluralistic array of denominations and sects, which has characterized American religion since the seventeenth century, has proven remarkably tolerant of strangers.[5] Yet, fundamentalists became outsiders through a complex historical process. The movement arose in the late-nineteenth century among Protestants who found themselves intellectually and spiritually—but not economically or politically—disenfranchised from white, middle-class culture. Their discontent centered around the increasingly this-worldly cast of religion in the Gilded Age, and with the rising skepticism in universities and theological seminaries concerning the staples of the faith, including the infallibility of the Bible.[6]

Fundamentalism began as a faith designed to stir lethargic churchgoers into action. It sought to keep all that was best about the "old-time religion"—a commitment to revivalism, personal conversion, and veneration of the Bible as a source of spiritual inspiration and propositional truth—but, in other ways, fundamentalism drew in the boundaries of Protestant orthodoxy more tightly than ever before. This was especially true around matters of biblical interpretation, where fundamentalists insisted on an inerrant scripture (without factual or scientific error). Fundamentalist eschatology, or study of the "last days," was apocalyptic and premillennial, and focused on biblical passages that predicted a sudden, cataclysmic Second Coming of Christ. These were doctrines calculated to serve as a spiritual antidote to lukewarm piety and theological compromise—although also fated to expose fundamentalist belief to ridicule and caricature by a skeptical American public.[7]

. . . Almost from its inception, the movement took an ambivalent stance toward American culture as both "Babylon" and "Zion," a place of wickedness and land uniquely blessed by God. After fundamentalists lost their hold in the Protestant denominations during the 1920s, the movement flourished in less public venues, but retained its complex sense of mission. Throughout the 1930s and 1940s, fundamentalists never gave up hoping to redeem the nation from corruption, even as they waited impatiently for its downfall.[8] In the American context, therefore, fundamentalism emerged as a mass of contradictions that over the years have proved vexing to outsiders. It was at once antiauthoritarian and obsessed with order; it was fervently apocalyptic, sometimes to the point of otherworldliness, and at the same time enmeshed in American middle-class culture. It was critical of American society, especially its rampant consumerism and pursuit of individual pleasure, yet temperamentally conservative and suspicious of radical change. . . .

New Victorians?

Fundamentalist ambivalence about the family owes much to the movement's origins. It emerged in the late-nineteenth and early-twentieth centuries as a reaction against Victorian social and religious conventions, and the domestic ideal in particular. As defined in popular literature, sermons, and music, and by household furnishings, the domestic ideal raised the respectable middle-class family as a civilizing, Christianizing force above all others.[9] Proponents of Victorian domesticity, a central metaphor of white, middle-class Protestantism, elevated the home to near sacramental status and enshrined woman as its saintly protector.

Early fundamentalists despised such sentimentality, especially when it all but absolved women of original sin. In the opening decades of the twentieth century, the masculine rhetoric of American politics

filtered across American Protestantism, and served as a rallying cry in churches where women had long held numerical majorities.[10] Fundamentalists participated enthusiastically in the trend; by the 1920s, they employed aggressive discourse, and identified the cause of orthodoxy as primarily a masculine endeavor. The leading fundamentalist periodical *Bible Champion,* for example, declared it "manly" to follow Christ, upheld the Bible as "virile literature" and praised Christ himself as "the most manly of men." Indeed, in 1946, Baptist preacher and evangelist John R. Rice condemned the alleged religious superiority of women as a "lie out of hell" and the alleged religious inferiority of men as a "wicked, hellish, ungodly, satanic teaching."[11]

The Victorian domestic ideal did not suit the intense piety that characterized fundamentalism. Emphasis on self-denial and duty demanded a vigorous "emptying of self" to allow for divine infusion. Any competing loyalty, including a human relationship, that stood in the way to complete consecration to God could block the Holy Spirit's power in the believer's life. Fundamentalists saw the Victorian veneration of home and family as a subtle form of idolatry.[12]

Fundamentalism's yearning for religious revival also fed ambivalence about family obligations. Popular fundamentalist revivalists usually offered standard talk about the "old-fashioned family" and the need for Christian homes. Yet their own lives were an ironic counterpoint, since their careers necessitated constant travel away from their wives and children. In a letter written shortly after his wife had suffered what was to be a fatal heart attack, evangelist Harry A. Ironside confessed to a friend that "I do wish I did not have to be away so much while she is ill, but that is one of the trials of the path which one must enter while seeking to minister Christ to others. I often feel," Ironside admitted, "'like saying with the bride in the Song of Solomon,'They made me the keeper of the vineyards, but my own vineyard I have not kept.'"[13] People who believed they were living in the shadow of the Second Coming could not let the ties of sentiment overtake religious duty.

Fundamentalists were not the only American Protestants who were ambivalent about Victorian domesticity, but they were among the few with systematic theological reasons for doing so. Leading premillennialist James H. Brookes, for example, declared that the true believer should "take no part in the trifles and contentions that are going on around him . . . [for he] is no longer at home in the world and he will never be at home until he is with the Lord." Contemporary premillennialist Elizabeth Needham described the world as a "leprous house," advising Christians to keep themselves "unspotted from its contagion" and to live in "wholesome loathing" of its diseased and poisoned air.[14]

By the end of the nineteenth century, male fundamentalist leaders were careful to distinguish their vigorous piety from the sentimentalized conventions of "feminized" religion. This was hardly simple, given that fundamentalist institutions were, like the rest of American religion, predominantly female. But few male leaders acknowledged that touting masculine religion to largely female congregations was at best contradictory, and few women within fundamentalist ranks openly objected to such rhetoric. In the late-nineteenth century, fundamentalism defined itself within the conventions of masculine individualism. Like previous generations of Christian zealots, martyrs, and monastics, many early fundamentalist male leaders adopted Christ's lonely example as a model of holiness. Individualists all, they rejected the conflation of godliness with the middle-class family, and along with it the pious notion that the outside world was an extension of the home, waiting to be "domesticated" by middle-class, white women. The world was a source of temptation and compromise to the Christian seeking to choose the hardest, and truest, path.

Fundamentalist Families

Not surprisingly, fundamentalists in the 1930s and 1940s produced little constructive literature on family life. They viewed the family's role as didactic and defensive, a fortress to be guarded or a sanctuary from "the burden of the battle."[15] From time to time, fundamentalists joined the chorus of worry in Protestant circles and the culture at large, predicting the family's imminent demise. But given that such diatribes have been a standard element of religious publishing in America since its inception, their pessimism about the family was hardly a defining characteristic.

Fundamentalist unease with the family fed into conflicting attitudes about sex. Although often caricatured as terrified of their libidos, fundamentalists in the 1930s and 1940s discussed them far more often than did other mid-twentieth-century Protestants. Advice columns in fundamentalist periodicals frequently warned against the widely believed dangers of sex and obliquely counseled forms of sublimation for healthy, young, single people. But not all fundamentalist leaders were models of restraint. Revivalists from Aimee Semple McPherson to Billy Sunday traded upon a certain amount of sex appeal to gather crowds, and from the platform discussed with startling frankness the specifics of birth control and sex edcuation.[16]

Fundamentalists also said little about religious nurture in the home. Rejecting popular child-rearing advice manuals, they held the line on principles of order and discipline, displaying and almost visceral dislike of psychological experts and their nurturant, relational language. Rice, author of one of the few acceptable fundamentalist manuals on child rearing, dismissed "that foolish theory that love can rule adequately without any punishment for sin." Such sentiment, he scoffed, "denies every fundamental doctrine of the Bible."[17] In the 1940s, fundamentalist writers stood at considerable cultural distance from most middle-class, white Americans, at least on family matters. Most viewed the disparity as a point of pride, a measure of their righteous separation from immorality and disorder. Not only did fundamentalist writers decry the absence of moral authority in "modernist" homes, they doubted the possibility of love and joy. "How empty and cheerless a home without Christ must be!" one writer observed in 1945, guessing that "what happiness there is rests only upon a physical and material basis."[18]

Another measure of separatism for fundamentalists by the end of World War II concerned women's role in the family. To this point, most discussions about women had been in terms of their role in the church and what duties the scriptures warranted. However, this dialogue gave way to one where fundamentalists attempted to codify women's familial role along submissive lines. In strict, hierarchical language—terminology generally missing from fundamentalist discussions of women's roles before the 1940s—writers insisted that the "scriptural home" placed men at the top of a ladder of command.[19] The consistently embattled tone of this writing suggests that fundamentalists adopted this ethic with difficulty, and that its standards of feminine submission had never been normative for the movement as a whole. Still, the growing emphasis on hierarchy and obedience was not minor doctrine, despite its late emergence; by the 1960s and 1970s, many religious conservatives wrote about wifely submission as if it was, and always had been, a central article of Christian faith.

Fundamentalist rhetoric stood in contrast to upbeat discussions about the family among mainline and liberal Protestants. For these culturally dominant Christians, the family was a major concern throughout the first half of the twentieth century. They had their own theological warrant for such an emphasis, beginning with the theology of Christian nurture in the writings of Horace Bushnell in the mid-nineteenth century. Bushnell, a Congregational theologian, emphasized the unfolding of religion in the children of Christian families as a corrective to the stress on dramatic adult conversions that were a feature of religious revivals. His views, scientifically amplified by educational philosopher John Dewey, became institutionalized among religious educators and parents in the early-twentieth century. Writings on the family within the large, white, Protestant denominations—primarily Methodist, Northern Baptist, Presbyterian, and Congregationalist—also tracked the rise of an expressive ideal of family life, then gaining currency in American middle-class culture. The modern family, whether described by pediatrician Dr. Benjamin Spock or a Presbyterian education curriculum, was idealized as a nurturing haven for individuals beset by the impersonal push and shove of the outside world.[20]

From Fundamentalist to Neoevangelical

By the postwar era, the American middle-class family ideal was vastly different from its early-twentieth-century form. Now the emphasis was on the quality of relationships among parents and children, replacing Victorian language of order and duty with a new ethic of individual self-expression. The home became a site for leisure pursuits and interpersonal companionship, rather than a place of economic production. Even the terminology changed, as the postwar generation of psychological care givers spoke less of "the home"—a social institution with

an overarching moral reality of its own—and more about "the family"—meeting the emotional and psychological needs of human beings within an ever-changing set of interpersonal relationships. This shift, which had been under way since the turn of the century, locked in place with the postwar explosion of economic prosperity and suburban living of the baby boom generation.[21]

By the 1950s, the home no longer served as a citadel of defense against worldliness, even for the most determined fundamentalist. For over two decades, the world had been coming into the home on a regular basis, first through radio and then television. In the 1930s, fundamentalists embraced radio with initial reluctance and then enthusiasm as they recognized its potential for evangelistic outreach. In the late 1940s and early 1950s, the same conversation went on about television, but with an air of inevitability. "The boast of one network," a fundamentalist pastor wrote in 1955, "is that it 'brings the world right into your home.' Who wants the world as we know it in our homes?" Yet, like most American families, the majority of fundamentalists could not resist the television invasion, despite its dubious moral effects on home and family life.[22]

However, by the late 1950s, mainline Protestants, much more than fundamentalists, were losing faith in the Christian family. Members of these predominantly white, middle-class churches typified the new relational family, with its emphases on cooperation, togetherness, and democratic relationships. Church leaders struggled to adapt religious education curriculum to meet the set of needs these cultural changes demanded. "Religious illiteracy" among parents was so widespread even in the churchgoing 1950s, denominational officials reported, that the home no longer could be counted on to provide religious nurture. The rising specter of middle-class divorce, as well as charges of excessive "familism" among churches in "suburban captivity," discouraged promises that by praying together Christian families would stay together. In the late 1950s and early 1960s, conversations about the home began to shift from matters around child rearing and religious nurture into a series of debates about family—related issues, beginning with divorce and then spiraling on to birth control, abortion, and homosexuality.[23]

Neoevangelicals quickly advanced into the unoccupied territory, momentarily casting aside skepticism their fundamentalist forebears might have demanded. Since World War II, some fundamentalists have moved toward the centers of social power. Weary of their cultural marginalization, such neoevangelical leaders as Harold John Ockenga and Carl F. H. Henry urged a return to biblical scholarship and intellectual engagement. Their call to action spurred the hopes of those who believed that only a religious revival would save the nation from calamity, and met with increasing success in the postwar years. Billy Graham, who had been raised a fundamentalist, mounted televised evangelistic crusades that reached a cross section of Americans and brought him into the corridors of the White House.[24]

. . . By the 1960s and 1970s, "evangelicals talked about the family with about the same regularity and with nearly the same passion with which the fundamentalists had discussed the Second Advent."[25] For the first time in a long time, religious conservatives—including erstwhile fundamentalists as well as such other conservative groups as Southern Baptists, Mormons, Orthodox Jews, and many Catholics—and secular, middle-class Americans were in hailing distances on matters concerning women and the family.[26] Neoevangelicals spoke an inherited fundamentalist language of crisis and doom, emphasizing the need for order and obedience. But in discussing the family, they clearly had uncovered a topic which all but guaranteed them an appreciative audience and a spot closer in from the margins of American society.

Before the ERA [Equal Rights Amendment] became a polarizing symbol for conservatives, evangelicals' enthusiasm for the cultural mainstream allowed a certain amount of openness toward feminism, at least for a time. In the early 1960s, *Eternity* magazine published pro-ERA editorials, and, by the early 1970s, its more conservative counterpart, *Christianity Today*, cautiously followed. To be sure, both magazines regularly received a flood of angry letters against feminism, but the editorial bent remained constant in favor of equal rights as a minimum standard, until the mid-1970s.[27]

Disputes over women's roles continued for decades, as the winds of feminism clashed head-on with biblical texts on female submission. American Protestants had long debated the meaning and implication of these texts, and, failing to arrive at a consensus, generally agreed to disagree. In the 1970s, however, evangelical scholars and activists

took up the debate with renewed passion for both sides of the issue. In the early 1970s, a small, left-wing, evangelical movement organized the Daughters of Sarah to uphold a generous interpretation of the texts. Other evangelicals, troubled by any attempt to "explain away" the words of scripture, sought to apply the command for submission in a nuanced, egalitarian manner. As the controversy continued, it became more than an arcane discussion of biblical literature; a liberal or conservative perspective on the role of women was a powerful means of marking one's stance toward secular culture, and the feminist movement in particular.[28]

As evangelicals geared up for cultural conquest, they slowly but inexorably surrendered territory. By the 1960s, it was impossible, even for erstwhile fundamentalists, to talk about "the family" without falling into the relational language they once had despised. In 1961, even S. Maxwell Coder, dean of the fundamentalist enclave, the Moody Bible Institute, agreed that reading the Bible in the home could help alleviate the "mental stress" of modern living.[29] Overlooking the disdain of their fundamentalist forebears for secular child-rearing professionals, neoevangelicals began to produce their own parental advice experts, each one better than the last at speaking the nurturant language of middle-class parenting.[30]

The authoritarian advice in some manuals masked their gradual appropriation of a more relational approach. In the 1970s, Bill Gothard's popular Youth Conflicts seminars taught a rigid model of "chain of command," beginning with God and moving downward through fathers, mothers, and children. Despite his use of military metaphors, Gothard's insistence on divine authority did not negate the importance of personality development and relationship skills. Families who used Gothard's methods reported they found personal peace in its moral certainties, and a measure of "relief" from dealing with life's ambiguities.[31]

Gothard's heir, and undisputed leader of the new evangelical family movement, was James C. Dobson, a Nazarene minister's son with a Ph.D. in child development from the University of Southern California. In the late 1970s, Dobson's folksy wisdom and no-nonsense approach to discipline won him almost instantaneous success. By the early 1980s, his first book, *Dare to Discipline*, had sold over 1.2 million copies and his seven-part film series entitled "Focus on the Family" had reached over 10 million viewers. Dobson's weekly radio broadcast, which began in 1977 with forty-three radio stations, grew to over four hundred by 1982.[32]

As successors of fundamentalist John Rice during the 1960s and 1970s, Bill Gothard and James Dobson proved remarkably adept at negotiating between the old fundamentalist-style authoritarianism and the increasingly relational ethos of child rearing. Dobson in particular attracted a middle-class audience of evangelical parents who for religious reasons were not comfortable with the "child-centered" philosophies of such secular authorities as Haim Ginott (Parent Effectiveness Training) and Dr. Spock. Dobson's emphasis on discipline and parental authority led some observers to misread him as an advocate of corporal punishment; in fact, Dobson rarely advocated spanking (although he did not rule it out), preferring to emphasize responsibility and mutual respect among parents and children.[33]

Dobson's success is not surprising. By the late 1970s, evangelicals were hardly a sectarian group out to punish their children into conformity. Although at one time, self-defined evangelicals and fundamentalists were lower on the economic and educational ladder than more liberal Protestants, the gap closed quickly in the 1970s. The evangelicals whom sociologist James Davidson Hunter studied in the mid-1980s were in some instances almost impossible to distinguish by income or education—and in many cases by social attitudes—from their secular, white, middle-class neighbors.[34]

Pressed to locate differences between believer and nonbeliever, the evangelical family literature of the 1960s and 1970s made much of the disparities between a "Christian" family and its secular counterparts. They picked up the older fundamentalist discussions of the home as a hierarchically ordered religious fortress, and reworked it into the secular optimistic language of human potential and psychological "adjustment." . . . Husbands and wives who followed God's directions for their life together could expect happiness; those who chose otherwise risked everything. As popular author Larry Christiansen warned, "If we accept a prescription for marriage completely dependent upon the belief structure of secular humanism, then we must be prepared that the result will be something other than Christian family life.". . . [35]

Such confidence is a bit breathtaking, given the moral complexity of family life in the 1980s and 1990s. The definition of the "family" was becoming a matter of dispute in American culture, in view of rising numbers of divorced, single-parent, blended and reblended, and same-sex households scattered across the population. Perhaps, in some cases, the single-minded simplicity of advice manuals like Christiansen's found readers weary of complexity. But, one need not delve into their motives, when the fundamentalist roots of neoevangelical literature on the family are obvious. Hidden within the relational language of the 1960s and 1970s are the truths—respect for authority and necessity of obedience—that have framed fundamentalist discussions of the family since the 1930s and 1940s.

Profamily Politics

As political and religious analysts have told the story over the past decade, evangelical, profamily politics galvanized around key issues. The list usually includes the 1962 and 1963 Supreme Court decisions banning prayer and Bible reading in public schools; the 1973 *Roe v. Wade* abortion decision; the rise of the Moral Majority in the late 1970s; the raucous 1980 White House Conference on Families; and Ronald Reagan's election as an antiabortion, profamily presidential candidate later that fall. By the early 1980s, as conservative think tanks and political action lobbies met on Capitol Hill in Washington, D.C., the agenda for the religious right seemed clear: Behind all the talk and activity about abortion, homosexuality, public schools, and sex education was a single-minded crusade to protect the moral future of the traditional family through fund-raising and electoral campaigning.[36] Small wonder that in 1991, Hunter tagged the family as the "most conspicuous field of battle" and "most decisive battleground" in the ongoing "culture wars" in American society.[37]

Journalists, academics, and politicians struggled to find an explanation for it all, their opinions forming as quickly as lobbyists descended on Capitol Hill. Some saw the religious right as resurgent traditionalism—an antifeminist backlash or a neo-Victorian morality movement—while others argued it was dangerously new— . . . or part of a larger "fundamentalist" uprising against modern culture. The analyses contained elements of truth, but proved difficult to apply to the rapidly diversifying mix of evangelical Protestants and conservative Catholics on Capitol Hill. By the mid-1980s, the "religious right" label included such large numbers and so many types of evangelicals, as well as Catholics, that it obscured more than it promised to elucidate. Although often dubbed "fundamentalist" by the media, the new profamily movement was far more, incorporating an array of newly politicized conservatives, everyone from Sun Belt Southern Baptists to "megachurch" Californians, pre-Vatican II Catholics, and the charismatic, Pentecostal followers of television evangelists Jim Bakker and Pat Robertson.

Charting the present and future of the religious right will be a longterm project for journalists and academics, although at this point little has been written about the movement's past. Historians have only begun to sort through the narrative of twentieth-century religious history, and much of the literature on American Protestant fundamentalism disassociates the movement from the more recent religious right, or is bogged down in disputes about the theological ancestry of present-day evangelicals. . . . But even a brief historical survey yields conclusions about the meaning of religious right politics today. First is the ongoing difficulty in politicizing American fundamentalism, a movement devoted to spiritual, evangelistic ends for much of its twentieth-century history. Political lobbying on behalf of a social gospel has been the province of liberal and mainline Protestants—people with a long-standing theological stake in redeeming American culture.[38] Indeed, television evangelist Jerry Falwell's much-publicized Moral Majority was almost as controversial in doctrinaire fundamentalist circles as it was in the secular media. Fundamentalist educator Bob Jones III dubbed Falwell "the most dangerous man in America" for trading in his separatist credentials for a seat at the table of Washington, D.C., insiders.[39]

A second historical oddity about the religious right is the centrality of the family in its moral and political agenda. As I have argued, the family was the province of more theologically liberal Protestants for most of the twentieth century; even sexuality issues associated with the family—abortion, homosexuality, and premarital and extramarital sex—alarmed mainline Protestants far earlier than they did fundamentalists and conservative evangelicals. Indeed, until the 1960s, "left-wing" Protestants were most likely to mount a political, profamily movement, if the times called for such—not fundamentalists or evangelicals.

Why a politically and theologically conservative evangelical profamily movement? One reason for the politicization of family issues in the 1970s and 1980s is the religious realignment occurring during this time. After the 1960s, membership in mainline and liberal denominations declined precipitously, while conservative evangelical churches boomed. By the late 1980s, the trends were so obvious that the term mainline was an embarrassing misnomer.[40]

The profamily movement emerged when religious conservatives were beginning to feel a sense of cultural power in the wake of Southern Baptist Jimmy Carter's presidential election; *Time* dubbed 1976 the "year of the evangelical." One sign of success was their new role as leading advocates for the American middle-class family. By the early 1970s, evangelicals had constructed a media empire around the family and related issues of gender roles, child discipline, and the moral hazards of adultery and divorce.

The efficacy of the profamily movement is testimony to the emotions that its moral agenda provoked among grassroots religious conservatives. Well before the Christian Coalition emerged in the national media, a dedicated group of neoevangelical leaders discovered that family matters resonated with churchgoers, providing clear lines between the godly and the unrighteous. Such issues allowed preachers to invoke personal and social morality; and they laid down moral boundaries that differentiated believers from nonbelievers, without rendering religion socially irrelevant. Opposing abortion, divorce, homosexuality, or teenage pregnancy permitted evangelical leaders to evoke a separatist, fundamentalist past and speak a prophetic word to present-day American culture. They could be distinctively "Christian" individuals and modern, late-twentieth-century people.

The politicization of abortion among conservative evangelicals provides an example of this ongoing tension. Before the late 1970s, few evangelicals worried about abortion, perceiving it primarily as a "Catholic issue." Indeed, in 1973, the Southern Baptist Convention endorsed *Roe v. Wade* because it facilitated greater separation between church and state, a long-standing Baptist emphasis.[41] In 1979, however, two respected evangelical leaders, Francis A. Schaeffer and C. Everett Koop, published a book and produced a film series (both with the same title) aimed at stirring conservative Protestants to action. As the 1980 presidential election approached, *Whatever Happened to the Human Race* made its way through the evangelical subculture, arguing that the new acceptance for abortion, as well as euthanasia and infanticide, placed Christians in direct opposition to the secular world. The polarities of the argument, and its sense of moral emergency, made abortion a center of conflict with secular American society. It also opened an imperative for political action. The topic of abortion became a touchstone for a list of moral ills, including homosexuality, pornography, and extramarital sex—all of which evangelicals traced to the spread of what they termed "secular humanism." Evangelicals came to understand that "legal abortion must be stopped not only because it was wrong, morally and biblically wrong, but also because it was part of a hostile campaign to impose liberal ideas upon an unwilling Christian populace." Political organization was the logical recourse, a step vindicated by Reagan's victory in 1980.[42]

Despite the gathering success of the prolife movement among evangelicals, their leaders continued to scout for signs of moral compromise. In 1984, Schaeffer, a staunch fundamentalist Presbyterian during the 1930s and one of the most respected moral leaders of the neoevangelical revival in the 1960s and 1970s, published a follow-up book entitled *The Great Evangelical Disaster*. His son Franky Schaeffer, a filmmaker, produced the accompanying documentary. Together they presented a popular jeremiad against the "post-Christian" spirit of the age—signified most deeply in the feminist movement—and against all evangelicals who embraced it. "Sixty years ago could we have imagined that unborn children would be killed by the millions here in our own country?" the elder Schaeffer demanded. "Or that we would have no freedom of speech when it comes to speaking of God and biblical truth in our public schools? Or that every form of sexual perversion would be promoted by the en-

tertainment media? Or that marriage, raising children, and family life would be objects of attack? Sadly," Schaeffer concluded, "we must say that very few Christians have understood the battle we are in," one of "cosmic proportions." Significantly, *The Great Evangelical Disaster* closed with a passionate diatribe against liberal feminism and a defense of the "biblical pattern" for male and female relationships, spurring a new round of controversy within the evangelical camp about feminism and gender roles.[43]

Events of the past two decades suggest that abortion has served a largely effective "boundary issue," separating the ranks of American evangelicals from the secular world. Opposition to abortion has become a fairly accurate measure of one's separation from "worldliness" and loyalty to evangelical institutions. It has operated as a shorthand protest against a range of moral ills that threatened the sanctity of family life, including undisciplined sexuality, loss of parental control, and (except in the case of a Human Life Amendment to the U.S. Constitution) unwarranted government intrusion.

Conclusion

. . . For fundamentalists in the early part of the twentieth century, the family was a worldly metaphor of personal compromise and secular burdens. And while they often joined the chorus of worry about middle-class morality, they were content to let other Protestants, more entangled with secular obligations, lead in its defense. All this changed rapidly after World War II, but many of the basics of fundamentalist piety about the family—the defensive imagery and emphasis on authority—emerged as the scaffold for the new family movement among evangelicals in the 1960s and 1970s. The more recent phase of the profamily movement has lacked the intellectual and cultural resources necessary for broad social leadership—especially through such a moral and political tangle as the family has become in the late-twentieth century. Some of the moral absolutism comes down to cultural inexperience, reflecting the intellectual and moral shallowness of fundamentalist and evangelical engagement with American society.[44]

The persistent mixture of cultural triumphalism and despair in evangelical profamily politics has proven a durable combination. Having recaptured territory that fundamentalists largely had abandoned, modern-day evangelicals are not likely to renounce it without a struggle, as the movement's militant rhetoric continually testifies. At the same time, however, the overall trajectory of the evangelical profamily movement has been toward a broader cultural acceptance and leadership. Evangelicals are "modern" people, quick to adopt technologies or modes of expression they judge useful. While they may see themselves as Babylonian exiles, lost in a culture headed for ruin, they are not likely to abandon it to destruction. . . .

NOTES

The author wishes to thank the Pew Charitable Trusts for support of the research and writing of this article, and the editors (Winter 1999) of the *Journal of Women's History*, Nikki R. Keddie and Jasamin Rostam-Kolayi, and Virginia Brereton, Michael Hamilton, and David Watt for helpful criticisms.

1. Martin Riesebrodt, *Pious Passion: The Emergence of Modern Fundamentalism in the United States and Iran,* trans. Don Reneau (Berkeley: University of California Press, 1993); and Helen Hardacre, "The Impact of Fundamentalism on Women, the Family, and Interpersonal Relationships," in *Fundamentalisms and Society,* ed. Martin E. Marty and R. Scott Appleby (Chicago: University of Chicago Press, 1993), 129–50.

2. William Martin, *With God on Our Side: The Rise of the Religious Right in America* (New York: Broadway Books, 1996); and James Davidson Hunter, *Culture Wars: The Struggle to Define America* (New York: Basic Books, 1991).

3. John C. Green, James L. Gevth, Corwin E. Smidt, and Lyman Kellstedt, eds. *Religion and the Culture Wars: Dispatches from the Front* (Lanham, Md: Rowan and Little Fiedd. 1996).

4. Betty DeBerg, *Ungodly Women: Gender and the First Wave of American Fundamentalism* (Minneapolis: Fortress Press, 1990); and Margaret Lamberts Bendroth, *Fundamentalism and Gender, 1875 to the Present* (New Haven, Conn.: Yale University Press, 1993).

5. On pluralism, see R. Stephen Warner, "Work in Progress toward a New Paradigm for the Sociological Study of Religion in the United States," *American Journal of Sociology* 98 (March 1993): 1044–93; and R. Lawrence Moore, *Religious Outsiders and the Making of Americans* (New York: Oxford University Press, 1986).

6. The best source is George Marsden, *Fundamentalism and American Culture: The Shaping of Twentieth-Century Evangelicalism, 1870–1925* (New York: Oxford University Press, 1980).

7. Timothy Weber, *Living in the Shadow of the Second Coming: American Premillennialism, 1875–1982* (Chicago: University of Chicago Press, 1987).

8. The story of the latter stage is told in Joel Carpenter's *Revive Us Again: The Reawakening of American Fundamentalism* (New York: Oxford University Press, 1997).

9. Colleen McDannell, *The Christian Home in Victorian America, 1840–1900* (Bloomington: Indiana University Press, 1986).

10. Gail Bederman, "'The Women Have Had Charge of the Church Work Long Enough': The Men and Religion Forward Movement of 1911–1912 and the Masculinization of Middle-Class Protestantism," *American Quarterly* 41 (September 1989): 43265.

11. Margaret Lamberts Bendroth, *Fundamentalism and Gender,* quotations on 3, 65.

12. See, for example, Charles Trumbull, "Have You Surrendered All?" in *The Victorious Christ* (Philadelphia: Sunday School Times Company, 1923), 106. Christine Heyrman describes a similar reaction among evangelicals within the antebellum South in *Southern Cross: The Beginnings of the Bible Belt* (New York: Knopf, 1997).

13. Harry A. Ironside's letter quoted in E. Schuyler English, *H. A. Ironside: Ordained of the Lord* (New York: Loizeaux Bros., 1946), 192.

14. James H. Brookes, "At Home with the Lord," *Truth, or Testimony for Christ* 5, (December 1876): and Elizabeth Needham, "Leprosy in Houses," *Truth, or Testimony for Christ* 8 (August 1882): 418. See also Margaret Lamberts Bendroth, *Fundamentalism and Gender,* chap. 2.

15. L. W. S., "The Christian Home," *Presbyterian Guardian* 7 (January 1940): 73.

16. Edith L. Blumhofer, *Aimee Semple McPherson: Everybody's Sister* (Grand Rapids, Mich.: Eerdmans, 1993); and William McLoughlin, *Billy Sunday Was His Real Name* (Chicago: University of Chicago Press, 1995). "I would rather have my children taught sex hygiene than Greek and Latin," Billy Sunday told an audience of women in 1917. See Billy Sunday, "Sunday's Sermon 'For Women Only,'" *Boston Globe,* 12 January 1917, 9.

17. John R. Rice, "Whipping Children," *Sword of the Lord,* 11 May 1945, 3. See also John R. Rice, *The Home, Courtship, Marriage, and Children* (Wheaton, Ill.: Sword of the Lord Publishing, 1945).

18. "Making the Home Christian," *Northwestern Pilot* 25 (October 1945): 26.

19. Charles C. Ryrie, "Is Your Home Scriptural?" *Bibliotheca Sacra* 109 (October–December 1952): 346–52.

20. See Horace Bushnell, *Christian Nurture* (1861, reprint, Cleveland, Ohio: Pilgrim Press, 1994); Stephen A. Schmidt, *History of the Religious Education Association*

(Birmingham, Ala.: Religious Education Press, 1983); and Elaine Tyler May, "Myths and Realities of the American Family," *A History of Private Life: Riddles of Identity in Modern Times,* ed. Antoine Prost and Gerard Vincent (Cambridge, Mass.: Harvard University Press, 1991), 539–92.

21. Elaine Tyler May, *Homeward Bound: American Families in the Cold War Era* (New York: HarperCollins, 1988).

22. Robert W. Battles, "What about Television?" *Sunday School Times,* November 26, 1955, 941–42. See also Margaret Lamberts Bendroth, "Fundamentalism and the Media, 1930–1990," *Religion and Mass Media: Audiences and Adaptations,* ed. Daniel Stout and Judith Buddenbaum (Thousand Oaks, Calif.: Sage Publications, 1996), 74–84.

23. Dennison Nash and Peter Berger, "The Child, the Family, and the 'Religious Revival' in Suburbia," *Journal for the Scientific Study of Religion* 1–2 (October–April 1961–1963): 85–93. For the story of one particular denomination, see William B. Kennedy, "Neo-Orthodoxy Goes to Sunday School." *Journal of Presbyterian History* 58 (winter 1990): 326–71.

24. Marsden, *Reforming Fundamentalism:* and William Martin, *A Prophet with Honor: The Billy Graham Story* (New York: William Morrow, 1991).

25. David Harrington Watt, *A Transforming Faith: Explorations of Twentieth-Century American Evangelicalism* (New Brunswick, N.J.: Rutgers University Press, 1991), 85.

26. See Phyllis Airhart and Margaret Lamberts Bendroth, eds., *Faith Traditions and the Family* (Louisville, Ky.: Westminster/John Knox Press, 1996).

27. See, for example, JoAnn Menkus, "Women: How Far Will They Go?" *Eternity* 21 (June 1970): 34; "Antifeminism: Are You Guilty?" *Eternity* 21 (September 1970): 7; "That Women's Rights Amendment," *Christianity Today* 14 (6 November 1970): 134; and Ruth Schmidt, "Second-Class Citizenship in the Kingdom of God," *Christianity Today* 14 (1 January 1971): 321–22.

28. Literature on this subject abounds. See, for example, Watt, *Transforming Faith,* 93–136; Judith Stacey, *Brave New Families: Stories of Domestic Upheaval in Late Twentieth Century America* (New York: Basic Books, 1991), 41–174; and Mark Chaves, *Ordaining Women: Culture and Conflict in Religious Organizations* (Cambridge, Mass.: Harvard University Press, 1997).

29. S. Maxwell Coder, "The Christian Family and the Word of God," *Moody Monthly* 61 (August 1961): 15–16.

30. See Diane Chico Kessler, *Parents and the Experts: Can Christian Parents Accept the Experts' Advice?* (Valley Forge, Penn.: Judson Press, 1974).

31. Wilfred Bockelman, *Bill Gothard: The Man and His Ministry: An Evaluation* (Santa Barbara, Calif.: Quill Publications, 1976). See also Bill Gothard, Jr., "The Chain of Command," *Faith for the Family* 3 (March/April 1975): 11–12. For a similar testimony, see Nancy Ammerman, *Bible Believers: Fundamentalists in the Modern World* (New Brunswick, N.J.: Rutgers University Press, 1987).

32. Rodney Clapp, "Meet James Dobson, His Father's Son," *Christianity Today* 22 (7 May 1982): 14; and "Focus at Fifteen," *Focus on the Family Magazine* 16 (March 1992): 10.

33. See, for example, Philip Greven, *Spare the Child: The Religious Roots of Punishment and the Psychological Impact of Physical Abuse* (New York: Vintage Books, 1990); and Donald E. Sloat, *Growing Up Holy and Wholly: Understanding and Hope for Adult Children of Evangelicals* (Brentwood, Tenn.: Wolgemuth and Hyatt, 1990).

34. James Davidson Hunter, *Evangelicalism: The Coming Generation* (Chicago: University of Chicago Press, 1987).

35. Larry Christiansen and Nordis Christiansen, *The Christian Couple* (Minneapolis: Bethany Fellowship, 1977), 21–22.

36. Martin, *With God on Our Side;* and Michael Lienesch, *Redeeming America: Piety and Politics in the New Christian Right* (Chapel Hill: University of North Carolina Press, 1993).

37. Hunter, *Culture Wars* (New York: Basic Books, 1999), 176.

38. William McGuire King, "The Reform Establishment and the Ambiguities of Influence," *Between the Times: The Travail of the Protestant Establishment in America, 1900–1960,* ed. William R. Hutchison (Cambridge, Mass.: Harvard University Press, 1989), 122–40.

39. James Guth, "The Politics of the Christian Right," *Religion and the Culture Wars,* 9–29.

40. Robert Wuthnow, *The Restructuring of American Religion: Society and Faith since World War II* (Princeton, N.J.: Princeton University Press, 1988).

41. Cynthia Gorney, *Articles of Faith: A Frontline History of the Abortion Wars* (New York: Simon and Schuster, 1998), 340–42.

42. Ibid, 343. See also Elizabeth Mensch and Alan Freeman, *The Politics of Virtue: Is Abortion Debatable?* (Durham, N.C.: Duke University Press, 1993); and Kristin Luker, *Abortion and the Politics of Motherhood* (Berkeley: University of California Press, 1984).

43. Francis A. Schaeffer, *The Great Evangelical Disaster* (Westchester, Ill.: Crossway Books, 1984), 23. See, for example, "The Danvers Statement" (paid advertisement, sponsored by the Council on Biblical Manhood and Womanhood) *Christianity Today* 32.

44. See, for example, Mark Noll, *The Scandal of the Evangelical Mind* (Grand Rapids, Mich.: Eerdmans, 1994).

FORTY-SEVEN

Shilling Love (2004)

Shailja Patel

Shailja Patel is a Kenyan Indian American poet. She has appeared at the Lincoln Center (N.Y.), and venues across the United States and Europe, and has presented excerpts from her one-woman show, *Migritude,* in Vienna and Nairobi. Her work is featured in the International Museum of Women in San Francisco. www.shailja.com

One

They never said / they loved us

Those words were not / in any language / spoken by my parents

I love you honey was the dribbled caramel / of Hollywood movies / Dallas / Dynasty / where hot water gushed / at the touch of gleaming taps / electricity surged / 24 hours aday / through skyscrapers banquets obscene as pornography / were mere backdrops / where emotions had no consequences words / cost nothing meant nothing would never / have to be redeemed

My parents / didn't speak / that / language

1975 / 15 Kenyan shillings to the British pound / my mother speaks battle

Storms the bastions of Nairobi's / most exclusive prep schools / shoots our cowering / six-year-old bodies like cannonballs / into the all-white classrooms / scales the ramparts of class distinction / around Loreto convent / where the president / sends his daughter / the government ministers, foreign diplomats / send their daughters / because my mother's daughters / will / have world-class educations

She falls / regroups / falls and re-groups / in endless assaults on visa officials / who sneer behind their bulletproof windows / at US and British consulates / my mother the general / arms her daughters / to take on every citadel

1977 / 20 Kenyan shillings to the British pound / my father speaks / stoic endurance / he began at 16 the brutal apprenticeship / of a man who takes care of his own / relinquished dreams of / fighter pilot rally driver for the daily crucifixion / of wringing profit from a small business / my father the foot soldier, bound to an honour / deeper than any currency / *you must / finish what you start you must / march until you drop you must / give you life for those / you bring into the world*

I try to explain love / in shillings / to those who've never gauged / who gets to leave who has to stay / who breaks free and what they pay / those who've never measured love / by every rung of the ladder / from survival / to choice

A force as grim and determined / as a boot up the backside / a spur that draws blood / a mountaineer's rope / that yanks / relentlessly / up

My parents never say / they love us / they save and count / count and save / the shilling falls against the pound / college fees for overseas students / rise like flood tides / love is a luxury / priced in hard currency / ringed by tariffs / and we devour prospectuses / of ivied buildings smooth lawns vast / libraries the way Jehovah's witnesses / gobble visions of paradise / because we know we'll have to be / twice as good three times as fast four times as driven / with angels powers and principalities on our side just / to get / on / the / plane

Thirty shillings to the pound forty shillings to the pound / my parents fight over money late in the night / my father pounds the walls and yells / *I can't—it's impossible—what do you think I am?* / My mother propels us through school tuition exams applications / locks us into rooms to study / keeps an iron grip on the bank books

1982 / gunfire / in the streets of Nairobi / military coup leaders / thunder over the radio / Asian businesses wrecked and looted Asian women raped / after / the government / regains control / we whisper what the coup leaders planned

Round up all the Asians at gunpoint / in the national stadium / strip them of whatever / they carry / march them 30 miles / elders in wheelchairs / babies in arms / march them 30 miles to the airport / pack them onto any planes / of any foreign airline / tell the pilots / down the rifle barrels / *leave* / *we don't care where you take them* / *leave*

I learn like a stone in my gut that / third-generation Asian Kenyan will never / be Kenyan enough / all my patriotic fervor / will never turn my skin black / as yet another western country / drops a portcullis / of immigration spikes / my mother straps my shoulders back with a belt / to teach me / to stand up straight

50 Kenyan shillings to the pound / we cry from meltdown pressure / of exam after exam where second place in never good enough / they snap / faces taut with fear / *you can't be soft* / *you have to fight* / *or the world will eat you up*

75 Kenyan shillings to the pound / they hug us / tearless stoic at airports / as we board planes for icy alien England / cram instructions into our pockets like talismans / *Eat proper meals so you don't get sick* / *cover your ears against the cold* / *avoid those muffathias* / *the students without purpose or values* / *learn and study* / *succeed* / *learn and study* / *suceed* / *remember remember remember the cost of your life*

they never say / they love us

Two

I watch how I love / I admonish exhort / like a Himalayan guide I / rope my chosen ones / yank them remorselessly up / when they don't even want to be / on the frigging mountain

like a vigilante squad I / scan dark streets for threats I / strategize for war and famine I / slide steel down spines

I watch heat / steam off my skin / when Westerners drop / *I love you*'s into conversation / like blueberries hitting / soft / muffin / dough / I convert it to shillings / and I wince

December 2000 / 120 shillings to the British pound / 90 Kenyan shillings to the US dollar / my sister Sneha and I / wait for our parents / at SFO's international terminal /

Four hours after / their plane landed / they have not emerged

And we know with the hopeless rage / of third-world citizens / African passport holders / that the sum of their lives and labour / dreams and sacrifice / was measured sifted weighted found / wanting / by the INS

Somewhere deep in the airport's underbelly / in a room rank with fear and despair / my parents / who have travelled / 27 hours / across three continents / to see their children / are interrogated / by immigration officials

My father the footsoldier / numb with exhaustion / is throwing away / all the years / with reckless resolve / telling them / *take the passports* / *take them* / *stamp them* / *no readmission EVER* / *just let me out to see my daughters*

My mother the general / dizzy with desperation / cuts him off shouts his down / demands *listen to me I'm the one* / *who filled in the visa forms* / in her mind her lip curls she thinks / *these Americans* / *call themselves so advanced so* / *modern but still* / *in the year 2000* / *they think it must be the husband in charge* / *they won't let the wife speak*

On her face a lifetime / of battle-honed skill and charm / turns like a heat lamp / onto the INS man until he / stretches / yawns / relents / he's tired / it's late / he wants his dinner / and my parents / trained from birth / to offer Indian / hospitality / open their bags and give their sandwiches / to this man / who would have sent them back / without a thought

Sneha and I / in the darkened lobby / watch the
  empty exit way / our whole American /
  dream-bought-with-their-lives / hisses mockery around our rigid bodies / we swallow sobs
  because / they raised us to be tough / they
  raised us to be fighters and into that / clenched
  haze / of not / crying

here they come

hunched / over their luggage carts our tiny /
  fierce / fragile / dogged / indomitable parents

Hugged tight they stink / of 31 hours in transit /
  hugged tighter we all stink / with the bravado
  of all the years / pain bitten down on gargan-
  tuan hopes / holding on through near-
  disasters / never ever / giving in / to softness

The stench rises off us / unbearable / of what /
  was never said

Something / is bursting the walls of my arteries
  something / is pounding its way up my throat
  like a volcano / rising / finally / I understand /
  why I'm a poet

Because I was born to a law / that states / before
  you claim a word you steep it / in terror and
  shit / in hope and joy and grief / in labour endurance vision costed out / in decades of your
  life / you have to sweat and curse it / pray
  and keen it / crawl and bleed it / with the very
  marrow / of your bones / you have to earn /
  its / meaning

8

◆◆◆

Work, Wages, and Welfare

Virtually all women in the world work. They are farmers, artists, craft workers, factory workers, businesswomen, maids, baby-sitters, engineers, secretaries, soldiers, teachers, nurses, sex workers, journalists, bus drivers, lawyers, therapists, waitpersons, prison guards, doctors, cashiers, airline pilots, executives, sales staff, professors, carpenters, dishwashers, filmmakers, mail carriers, dancers, homemakers, mothers, and wives. Many find satisfaction and challenge, even enjoyment, in their work; for others it is a necessary drudgery. This chapter looks at women's experiences of work in the United States, women's wages, and income supports for women without paid work. We argue that economic security is fundamental to women's well-being and the security of our families and communities.

Defining Women's Work

According to dictionary definitions, the English word *economy* comes from two Greek words: *oikos*, meaning "house," and *nemo*, meaning "to manage."

Thus, economy can be understood as managing the affairs of the household, and beyond the household, of the wider society. Modern-day professional economists make a distinction between "productive" and "unproductive" work, however, which is not implied in this original definition. So-called productive work is done for money; work not done for money is defined as unproductive (Waring 1988). This distinction is central to the bind that many women experience in juggling their daily lives. By this analysis, a woman who spends her day making meals for her family, doing laundry, finding the schoolbooks and football shoes, packing school lunches, making beds, washing the kitchen floor, remembering her mother-in-law's birthday, changing diapers, waiting in for the TV repair person, taking the toddler to the park, walking the dog, meeting the older children after school, going to the doctor's office with her mother, making calls about an upcoming PTA meeting, changing the cat litter, paying bills, and balancing her checkbook is not involved in productive work. A United Nations study released in Nairobi, Kenya, in 1985 at the end

Although in recent years some women have broken into professions and jobs that were once the preserve of men, most paid jobs in the United States are divided along gender lines, and women are greatly overrepresented in low-paying jobs. Most women in the workforce do "women's work" in service and administrative support jobs, as secretaries, waitresses, and health aides. They work in day-care centers, elder-care facilities, garment factories, food processing, retail stores, restaurants, laundries, and other women's homes. In addition to earning low wages, such workers are often treated as expendable by employers, as Hattie Gossett points out in Reading 48. Women in professional jobs tend to be elementary school teachers, social workers, nurses, and health-care workers. There is an emphasis on caring for and serving others in many of these jobs; some may also require being on display and meeting dominant beauty standards. As syndicated columnist Cynthia Tucker (1996) remarked, "You do not have to look to Venus or Mars to find the difference in men and women. Just look at their paychecks" (p. 3).

In the idealized nuclear family described in Chapter 7, middle-class White women were not expected to be wage earners. Despite the fact that they were responsible for all the tasks involved in maintaining a home and taking care of a family, many said of themselves, "I don't work; I'm just a housewife." By contrast, women on welfare are thought lazy or work-shy if they concentrate on looking after their children and do not participate in the paid workforce.

of the International Decade on Women (1975–85) stated that women do 75 percent of the world's work; they earn 10 percent of the world's wages and own 1 percent of the world's property. Worldwide, most of women's work is unpaid and officially unproductive.

Anthropologist Leith Mullings (1997) distinguishes four kinds of women's work: paid work in the formal sector; reproductive work, including housework and raising children as well as paid work taking care of children, the elderly, and the sick; work in the informal sector, which may be paid under the table or in favors returned; and transformational work, volunteering in community organizations, professional groups, and clubs of all kinds. One effect of the gendered division of labor in the home has been a similar distinction between women's work and men's work in the paid workforce.

Women in the U.S. Workforce

Before wage labor developed, several economic systems coexisted in this country. Economist Teresa Amott (1993) identifies

> family farming, the *hacienda* system of large ranches in the Southwest, plantation slavery in the South, the economies of the different Native American nations, and the early capitalist industrial enterprises.   *(p. 15)*

She notes that race and ethnicity were central in determining who was assigned to each of these labor systems; gender and class determined what work people performed. Significant inequalities in women's work opportunities may mask economic interconnections among women:

> In a very real sense, the lives of any one group of women have been dependent upon the lives of others. . . . Unfortunately the ties which have joined us have rarely been mutual, equal, or cooperative; instead, our interdependence has been characterized by domination and exploitation. American Indian women's lost lands were the basis for European immigrant wealth. The domestic work of African American and poor European immigrant women, along with the labors of their husbands, sons, and daughters in factories, underwrote the lavish lifestyles of upper-class European American women. The riches enjoyed by the wives and children of Mexican American *hacienda* owners were created by the poverty of displaced and landless Indians and Chicanas. And U.S. political and economic domination of the Philippines and Puerto Rico allowed U.S. women to maintain higher standards of living, and encouraged the migration of impoverished Filipina and Puerto Rican women to U.S. shores.
>
> *(Amott and Matthaei 1996, p. 3)*

The economy of the United States has changed fundamentally because of automation in manufacturing and office work and the movement of jobs overseas. Many U.S. companies have laid off workers, sometimes by the thousands, as they scramble to downsize their operations as a way to cut costs and maintain, or even increase, profits. Innovations such as ATMs, voice mail, salad bars, and self-service gas stations, to name a few everyday examples, all mean fewer jobs. One result has been a growing inequality in earnings between people in professional and technical positions and those without college education who are working low-income jobs. Despite the influx of relatively inexpensive consumer goods into the United States, especially clothing and electronic items from "global factories" around the world, it has become much harder for many families to make ends meet. Several factors have made it imperative that more and more women are income earners. Rents and housing payments, health insurance, and the cost

of college tuition, for example, have increased. Much manufacturing, such as car assembly and related engineering work, which was relatively well paid and largely done by men, has been automated or moved out of the United States. Divorce rates are high, and many fathers pay little or no child support.

According to the U.S. Department of Labor, Women's Bureau (2005), 60 percent of U.S. women were in the paid labor force in 2004, and women made up 46 percent of all workers that year. Most women work full-time, with only 26 percent in part-time jobs. More than two-thirds of all part-time workers (70 percent) are women. Withorn (1999) notes that this is often a "devil's bargain," because wages are low and there are no benefits, but women take these jobs because they need flexibility in their lives to look after children or aging parents. The labor market is structured so that the best positions are reserved

> for those adults who have someone on call to handle the life needs of an always-available worker. Economist Randy Albelda calls these positions "jobs with wives."
>
> *(Withorn 1999, p. 9)*

Seventy percent of U.S. women with children under 18 are in paid employment. Black mothers are more likely to be in the paid workforce than White or Latina mothers. Although 26 percent of families with children under age 18 were maintained solely by women in 2000, there is a wide disparity based on race. Forty-seven percent of Black families, 24 percent of Latino families, and 14 percent of White families were maintained by women.

Women's Wages: The Effects of Gender, Race, Class, Disability, and Education

The best-paid jobs for women are as lawyers, physicians, pharmacists, engineers, computer analysts, and scientists, but many more women earn the minimum wage. Ida Castro, former acting director of the Women's Bureau of the U.S. Department of Labor, commented that "society needs to really look critically at the value given to work performed predominantly by women," and cites child-care workers, home-care attendants, and

Economic Inequalities

- In 1999 the wealth held by the world's 475 billionaires was greater than the combined income of the poorest half of all the people in the world (Bigelow and Peterson 2002, p. 16).

- In 2005, the top 10 percent of U.S. citizens received a total income equal to that of the poorest 2.2 billion people in the rest of the world (*Dollars and Sense* 2005, p. 14).

- The average CEO in the United States makes about 149 times the average factory worker's pay.

- In 2002, 34.6 million people in the United States—nearly one in eight—lived in poverty (Proctor and Dalaker 2003). For children, the poverty rate was 16.7 percent, significantly higher than the population as a whole. Child poverty in the United States is two to three times higher than that of most other Western industrialized countries.

- Every day in the United States, 2,385 babies are born into poverty (Children's Defense Fund 2004).

- Nike CEO Philip Knight's stock in the company is estimated at $4.5 billion; Michael Jordan has a $20 million endorsement deal; a pair of Air Jordans retails generally around $135. The approximate cost of making one pair of Nike running shoes is $5. Women workers in Indonesia who make Nikes earn $1.10 per day (Bigelow and Peterson 2002, p. 151).

- The richest 20 percent of the world's population consumes 86 percent of the world's resources (Bigelow and Peterson 2002, p. 107).

The annual average earnings for full-time workers in 2003 were as follows:

	Earnings	Wage Ratio
All women	30,724	
White women	31,169	75.6
Black women	26,965	65.4
Latinas	22,363	54.3
All men	40,668	
White men	41,211	100
Black men	32,241	78.2
Latinos	26,083	63.3

[Source: De Navas-Walt, Proctor, and Mills (2004)]

Among women in 2003, a college graduate earned more than $38,000, compared with nearly $22,000 for a high school graduate. Investigative journalist Barbara Ehrenreich (2001) called attention to the daily grind experienced by many working women in her firsthand account of low-wage women's work. She worked as a waitress and motel housekeeper in Florida, a cleaning woman and nursing-home aide in Maine, and a Wal-Mart sales clerk in Minnesota. She undertook this project as an experiment to see if she could subsist on her own as a full-time employee, paying for rent and food, while working these kinds of jobs. She admires many of the women she worked with and can readily understand that they are too overwhelmed by everyday existence to be able to improve their prospects. For a woman to go back to school or to find a union job with better pay and benefits she needs access to information, transportation, and the time and "headspace" to explore alternatives. Ehrenreich's coworkers did not have any of these. Her absorbing and insightful account, published by a mainstream publisher and widely reviewed, has brought home the everyday experiences of many working women to middle-class readers.

Working wives contribute significantly to household income. According to the U.S. Bureau of the Census (2000), the average income of married couples with both partners in the paid workforce was $69,463. In families where the wife was not earning, the average income was $39,735. On divorce, the income of a mother and her children

nursing-home workers as persons who earn the minimum wage but do the vitally important work of looking after children and older people (Angwin 1996; Folbre 2001). In 2005 women on average earned seventy-five cents for every dollar that men earned on average. This gap has slowly narrowed in the past two decades, partly because women's wages have improved but also because men's wages have fallen.

usually drops drastically from its predivorce level. More than 75 percent of divorced mothers with custody of their children are employed. Many fathers (more than 50 percent by some estimates) pay little or no child support. The average annual income of families maintained by women was $25,794 in 2000. White single mothers earn more than Black and Latina single mothers, on average. Bear in mind that averages always conceal extremes. Many women and men earn less than the average figures cited above and less than the official **poverty level,** which in 2005 was $16,090 for a family of three (Poverty Guidelines 2005). The federal poverty guideline does not take into account regional differences in the cost of living, and it does not include many basic needs such as housing, transportation, child care, and health care. Some advocates have campaigned for a "living wage" that more adequately reflects the cost of living. Others use a "self-sufficiency standard" that varies from state to state and "provides a measure of income needed to live at a basic level . . . without public or private assistance" (Women's Foundation 2002).

The more education a woman has the more likely she is to be employed. The close relationship between educational attainment and higher wage levels is expected to continue in many jobs, often linked to developments in computer technology. In Reading 50 Shireen Lee acknowledges the barriers for women in technical and computer-based fields. She is optimistic about the opportunities, however, especially as more women are educated for this work. She cites the creation of women-owned high-tech businesses, virtual organizing, and the benefits of women's mentoring as factors that are changing the job market for women and encourages women to enter these fields. Workers need to keep skills up-to-date, which requires access to opportunities to keep learning and a willingness and ability to do so. A lack of educational qualifications is a key obstacle for women on welfare who need greater educational opportunity if they are to acquire meaningful work that pays sustainable wages. Women receiving welfare used to be able to attend college and many were able to move out of poverty as a result, including Congresswoman Barbara Lee who graduated from Mills College (Oakland). The 1996 Personal Responsibility and Work Opportunity Reconciliation Act only allows short-term vocational training or "job readiness education" as work activity, not preparation for professional work. Several scholars and activists advocate for changes in this policy and for more academic institutions, community agencies, and foundations to provide the necessary academic, financial, and social support for poor women's education (see, e.g., Adair 2004; Adair and Dahlberg 2003; Martinson and Strawn 2003; Marx 2002). Nolita Clark and Shannon Stanfield describe their experiences as students in the Hamilton College (Clinton, N.Y.) ACCESS Project, one of the few college programs for women on welfare (Reading 53).

Even with a college education, however, and equivalent work experience and skills, women are far less likely than men to get to the top of their professions or corporations. They are halted by unseen barriers, such as men's negative attitudes to senior women and low perceptions of their abilities, motivation, training, and skills. This barrier has been called a **glass ceiling.** Women can see what the senior positions in their company or their field look like, but few women reach them (Morrison et al. 1992). The Federal Glass Ceiling Commission, appointed by President George Bush, reported in 1995 that in the top Fortune 1000 industrial and 500 service companies 95 percent of senior-level managers were men and, of this number, 97 percent were White (Redwood 1996, p. 2). In 2002, women held 15.7 percent of corporate officer positions in Fortune 500 companies (Catalyst 2002). Women of color held 1.6 percent of positions with corporate-wide responsibility at the 429 companies reporting these data (Hua 2002).

Discrimination Against Working Women: Sexual Harassment, Age, and Disability

The segmented labor market described above is reproduced through micro-, meso-, and macro-level factors. These include unequitable educational opportunities for women, especially women of color; social attitudes and assumptions regarding women's skills, abilities, ambitions, and family responsibilities; and discriminatory practices—many of them subtle—in decisions about hiring, firing, and promotion, as well as the day-to-day organization of work. Reading 49 refers to different assumptions about women workers compared with men workers.

Sexual Harassment   Sexual harassment is a serious problem for many working women. It is defined by the federal Equal Opportunity Commission guide lines as

> unwelcome sexual advances, requests for sexual favors and other verbal or physical conduct of a sexual nature when
>
> 1. submission to such conduct is made either explicitly or implicitly a term or condition of employment;
> 2. submission to or rejection of such conduct by an individual is used as the basis for employment decisions affecting such individual; or
> 3. such conduct has the purpose or effect of unreasonably interfering with an individual's work performance or creating an intimidating, hostile or offensive working environment.

Sexual harassment at work can include verbal abuse, visual abuse, physical abuse, and rape and is against the law. In 1986 the first case concerning sexual harassment (*Meritor Savings Bank v. Vinson*) reached the Supreme Court and established that sexual harassment includes the creation of a hostile or abusive work environment. The Court also held that the appropriate question is not whether the victim tolerated the harassment "voluntarily" but whether it was "unwelcome." The testimony of Anita Hill in November 1991 before a Senate Judiciary Committee considering the confirmation of Clarence Thomas to the Supreme Court made this issue a lead story for virtually every TV talk show, magazine, and newspaper in the country (Morrison 1992). As women talked about their experiences of sexual harassment, its very widespread nature was publicly acknowledged. Employers hastily set up workshops and seminars for their staffs, mindful of the costs of losing sexual harassment lawsuits. Public figures who were sued for sexual harassment in the mid-1990s included President Bill Clinton and Senator Bob Packwood, who was forced by his Republican colleagues to resign his Senate seat. It is important to note that the federal law against sexual harassment applies only to behavior in the workplace or in schools, not to sexual intimidation and abuse in other situations. Daphne Patai (1998) goes so far as to claim that "the mere allegation of 'sexual harassment' now provides women with an extraordinarily effective weapon to wield against men." However, the Supreme Court strengthened protections against sexual harassment in 1998 (Mason 1998), and many women acknowledge the serious difficulties involved in making such allegations.

Age Discrimination   The wage gap between women and men increases with age. One effect of corporate downsizing and layoffs is that a growing number of older, experienced workers are unemployed. They are too young to retire but often considered too old or too expensive to hire. For women over 40, age complicates the job search. It takes longer for such women to find new work than it does men, and their new jobs usually pay less than they were earning before or are part time. There are several myths about older women in the workforce: it is not cost-effective to hire an older woman; she will be hard to train and is likely to have difficulty with new technology; her insurance costs will be higher than for a younger person; and she will not have a strong commitment to work. According to the American Association of Retired Persons (n.d.), none of these myths are borne out by research findings.

Discrimination Against Women with Disabilities
Women with disabilities also have difficulty getting work. They are generally stereotyped as dependent, passive, and incompetent, qualities that are also often attributed to women in general. More African American women and Latinas report a work disability, a disabling condition that makes them unable to work outside the home, than do White women. Work disabilities are more prevalent among older women. At the same time, many women with disabilities that keep them out of the paid workforce do their own cooking, laundry, and housekeeping. Increasing numbers of students with disabilities are going to college. They tend to be older, married, financially independent, and/or veterans. In 2000, 9 percent of first-year college students reported having some kind of disability (University of Minnesota 2001).

Women with disabilities generally have lower educational attainment than nondisabled women, which bars them from entering higher-paying professional work. They may have missed a lot of school as children or may not have been provided

with relevant special education programs. Vocational schools and rehabilitation programs for women who suffer a disability after completing their education also tend to channel them into dependent roles within the family or to low-paying "women's work" in the labor force. Added to these limitations are the prejudices and ignorance of employers and coworkers and the ableist attitudes of this culture. Women with disabilities may also have to make "significant and sometimes costly special arrangements" (Mudrick 1988, p. 246) to maintain their employment, such as transportation or extra help at home. Lisa Schur (2004), professor of labor studies, argues that high schools and colleges need to assist young women with disabilities in making the transition from school to work; advocates and self-help organizations should offer employment counseling to help women with disabilities find jobs; and women with disabilities need to be actively involved in developing programs to improve their job prospects.

Balancing Home and Work

In general, U.S. workplaces are still structured on the assumption that men are the breadwinners and women are the homemakers, despite the fact that more U.S. women are in the paid workforce than ever before, including 70 percent of mothers. Jug-

gling the conflicting demands of paid work and family responsibilities is a defining life experience for many women (Barnett and Rivers 1996; Crittenden 2001; Douglas and Michaels 2004; Folbre 2001; Gould 1997; Hochschild 1989, 1997; Peters 1997; Williams 2000). In Reading 51, journalist and writer Ann Crittenden calculates what her decision to leave her job at the *New York Times* for parenting cost her in lost earnings. She estimates that, in her case, this discriminatory "mommy tax" amounted to "between $600,000 and $700,000, not counting the loss of a pension." She argues for new laws and policies to prevent discrimination against people with caregiving responsibilities as a way to improve a mother's lifetime earnings.

Flextime, Part-Time Work, Home Working, and the Mommy Track   Mothers may try to find a job with hours that are compatible with children's school schedules. This might mean working jobs that allow some flexible scheduling, seeking part-time work, or working at home—whether sewing, minding children, or "telecommuting." Thanks to innovations like fax-modems, electronic mail, and pagers, home working is currently touted for professional and corporate workers as a way to work flexible hours with greater personal freedom and no stressful commute, as argued by Shireen Lee (Reading 50). This may alleviate the problem of child care for some professional families and greatly help the commuter marriage, but for garment workers and child-care providers, who account for the majority of home workers, the pay is poor and there are no benefits. Garment workers on piece-work rates put in long hours, often working into the night. They are also isolated from one another, which makes it much more difficult to improve their pay through collective bargaining.

Another solution to the problem for professional women, put forward in the late 1980s, was that firms adopt a "mommy track." Professional women who wanted career advancement comparable to that of men either would not have children or would somehow manage their lives so as to combine having children with working long hours, attending out-of-town meetings, taking little vacation time, and doing whatever the job demanded. Otherwise, they could "opt" for the mommy track and be recompensed accordingly. Law professor and legal scholar Joan Williams (2000) argues that professional women knew full well that this would mean being marginalized in their careers, and all but a few avoided the mommy track like the plague. Rather, she advocates "deconstructing the ideal-worker norm" and completely rethinking the divide between unpaid caring work and work in the paid workforce.

Child Care   Child care is a family's fourth highest expense, after housing, food, and taxes. For some women who want to work, the cost of child care is prohibitive, even if they can find suitable child-care providers. Federal and state governments, employers, and labor unions offer some assistance to child-care providers and parents in the form of tax credits, grants to child-care programs, on-site care, provisions for child care as part of a benefits package, flextime, and leave for family emergencies, such as sickness. Taken overall, these provisions are woefully inadequate. It is particularly difficult to obtain child care for the hours before and after school and during school vacations. Head Start programs, for example, which offer preschool education to low-income children, are usually available only for a half day and only one in seven children eligible for federal child-care assistance gets help (Children's Defense Fund 2005). The Family and Medical Leave Act of 1993 provides for leave in family emergen-

cies like the birth of a child or illness of a family member, but it covers only firms with fifty or more workers, and the leave is unpaid. Moreover, a worker must have been with the employer for one year to qualify. Over 50 million people have taken leave under the Family and Medical Leave Act in the past twelve years, 50 percent for ten days or less; 58 percent of them are women (National Partnership for Women and Families 2005). Many people are forced to forgo taking such leave because they cannot afford to lose a paycheck. Family advocates are pressing for family leave to be paid. Opponents seek to limit the provisions of the current law on the argument that it is being abused and costing employers in production and worker morale (Armour 2005).

Another aspect of this issue is the working conditions for child-care workers, the vast majority of whom are women who work in their own homes, other women's homes, or at child-care centers and preschool programs. Although parents often struggle to afford child care, child-care workers are poorly paid and, typically, have no health insurance or retirement plans. Child-care workers, on average, earn less than animal caretakers, parking-lot attendants, and garbage collectors. Low pay and difficult working conditions mean that turnover among these workers is high. This situation says a lot about how our society values caring for children (Folbre 2001).

Several scholars point to a "crisis of care" in the United States and other wealthy countries. High numbers of women from countries of the global South, like the Philippines, El Salvador, and the Dominican Republic, are caring for children, elderly people, and sick people here (Cancian et al. 2002; Ehrenreich and Hochschild 2003; Hondagneu-Sotelo 2001; Parreñas 2001; Tuominen 2003; Uttal 2002). In Reading 55, Rhacel Salazar Parreñas analyzes the situation of children in the Philippines whose parents are working overseas. Feminist ethicist Gloria Albrecht (2004, p. 139), professor of religious studies, argues: "how a society organizes the necessary work of social reproduction (access to basic needs, the care of dependent persons, nurturance and socialization) in relationship to the work of material production is a matter of social justice." The data presented in this chapter attest to what Albrecht (2004, p. 139) calls the "unjust pattern that this relationship takes in the United States."

The Second Shift Women employed outside the home still carry the main responsibility for housework and raising children and have very little time for themselves. Although this is particularly acute for single parents, many women living with men also do more housework and child care than their partners (Bianchi et al. 2002; Mainardi 1992). Undoubtedly, this pattern varies among couples and perhaps also at different stages in their lives. Sociologist Arlie Hochschild (1989) estimated that women in the labor force work a **second shift** of at least 15 hours a week more than men, or an extra month of 24-hour days over a year, and argues that men need to do more in the home. Suzanne Bianchi et al. (2002) report significant changes in the gender division of household labor since the 1960s, with men taking on more responsibilities as

Pro-family Policies for the United States

- Provide financial support for full-time child care.
- Create more jobs and stop assuming job-holders have a wife at home.
- Raise wages to a "living wage" level. Mandate equal pay for comparable work.
- Provide financial support to cover housing and health costs—the two major "family budget busters."
- Expand the safety net—through unemployment insurance, temporary disability insurance, or welfare payments.
- Provide affordable and accessible education and training for all.
- Promote community-based economic development.
- Introduce a fairer tax structure that benefits people in the lower tax brackets.

Source: Albelda and Tilly 1997, pp. 147–64.

a result of wives devoting more time to waged work and "changed attitudes about what is expected, reasonable and fair for men to contribute to the maintenance of their home" (p. 184). Nowadays, much less housework is done. Families rely more on the service economy, for example, for take-out meals, and they do less cleaning and far less ironing. A 2003 time-use survey undertaken by the U.S. Department of Labor shows that "the average working woman spends more than twice as much time on household chores and child care than the average working man." On average, the men interviewed spent about one hour a day more at their jobs than the women in the sample and thirty-six minutes more per day in leisure activities and sports (Gold, Mughal, and Kort 2004/2005, p. 19). In households where men are present, housework is often still divided along gendered lines. Husbands and fathers take care of the car, do yard work and household repairs, and take out the trash. Women usually have major responsibility for food shopping, meals, laundry, and child care. These tasks have to be done every day and take more time and emotional energy than "men's" tasks. Women and men in managerial and professional positions, as well as people in lower-paid work are under pressure to work longer hours, with added strains on family life. Upper-middle-class households hire help in the home—cleaners, nannies, maids, and caregivers for the elderly—which helps to free such women from the time crunch and stress of balancing home and work. These domestic workers are usually paid low wages without benefits. In seeking greater freedom for themselves, upper-middle-class women thus find themselves perpetuating poor working conditions for poorer women (see, e. g., Cancian et al. 2002; Hondagneu-Sotelo 2001; Parreñas 2001; Tuominen 2003; Uttal 2002).

Organized Labor and Collective Action

Historically, the male-dominated labor movement has been weak in pressing for changes that would benefit women workers, and women have not been taken seriously as labor leaders. Some male workers were hostile to women in the workforce, fearing for their own jobs and their authority as breadwinners. In support of women in unions, the Coalition of Labor Union Women (CLUW) has four main goals: to organize the unorganized, to promote affirmative action in the workplace, to stimulate political action and legislation on women's issues, and to increase the participation of women in their unions. The coalition emphasizes such issues as equal pay, child care, universal access to health care, and reproductive freedom. It aims to educate working women about their rights, to provide training in dealing with management, and to prepare women for union leadership positions.

Workers usually make significant gains in wage levels and working conditions when they are members of a labor union. In 2003 women union members earned 33 percent more than nonunion women, and the differential is higher for African Americans (36 percent) and Latinas (49 percent) (U.S. Department of Labor. Bureau of Labor Statistics 2004). Union workers are also more likely to have health and pension benefits. Women are now

joining unions at a faster rate than men, particularly the hotel workers (HERE), service employees (SEIU), garment workers (UNITE), public employees (AFSCME), and communications workers (CWA). The United Farm Workers of America (UFW), founded by Cesar Chavez and Dolores Huerta, has pressured growers to sign union contracts to improve the pay and working conditions of its members—women and men—many of whom are migrant workers and immigrants to the United States whose health is continually compromised by chemical pesticides (Reading 34; Ferriss and Sandoval 1997).

The majority of women in the U.S. workforce are not union members. This is partly due to the decline of unions nationally in recent decades. Also, many women work in jobs that are hard to unionize, such as retailing or the fast-food business, where they are scattered at many separate locations.

The nation's largest employer, Wal-Mart, is fiercely anti-union. In 2001 seven women initiated a discrimination suit, *Dukes v. Wal-Mart,* "charging that Wal-Mart Stores Inc. ... has a pervasive and conscious pattern of discrimination against women" (Cox 2001a). In June 2004 this became the largest class-action sex-discrimination suit ever, and could involve 1.6 million present and former employees. Wal-Mart's stringent cost cutting—of prices, wages, and operating costs—has become legendary and is redefining corporate practice, summed up in the phrase: the "Wal-Mart-ing" of the economy. Journalist Liza Featherstone (2004) notes that Wal-Mart has "profoundly altered labor politics, deploying ever more creative and ruthless tactics to suppress the right to organize, while driving down wages and benefits in the retail industry and beyond." Increasingly Wal-Mart's competitors are adopting the Wal-Mart model, making Wal-Mart not just an industry leader but an economy leader.

The Working Poor   Organized labor calls attention to low wages. According to *Business Week* (2004), 63 percent of U.S. families below the federal poverty line have one or more workers. More women than men make up the working poor, and women of color are more than twice as likely to be poor compared with White women. Twenty percent of children under the age of six are living in poverty. Ten percent of people with significant disabilities working full-time fell below the poverty line. In public debate, poor people are usually assumed to be on welfare, masking the reality of life for the many working poor. This includes legal immigrants, who often start off at the bottom of the employment hierarchy. Some people with very low incomes are working minimum-wage jobs, and others work part-time or seasonally. They may be involved in the informal economy as maids, baby-sitters, or gardeners, for example, doing home work for the garment trade, fixing cars, carrying and selling small amounts of drugs, getting money for sex, selling roses at off-ramps.

Others work in sweatshops, discussed in the next chapter, which are also unregulated in terms of wages, hours, and conditions of work. These are on the rise in many major U.S. cities and often employ undocumented workers. Media exposés of clothing companies whose subcontractors operate sweatshops, including The Gap, Macy's, and Mervyn's, brought this issue to public attention. The Union of Needletrades, Industrial and Textile Employees (UNITE) has organized demonstrations outside department stores to encourage shoppers to boycott brands that use sweatshop labor. In 1996 Asian Immigrant Women Advocates, after a three-year campaign, won a significant agreement from garment manufacturer Jessica McClintock to improve labor practices, and such organizing efforts continue.

Affirmative Action   Labor unions, as well as many women's organizations and civil rights organizations, also support affirmative action in employment, introduced as part of the Civil Rights Act of 1964 to improve job possibilities for White women and people of color, whose opportunities in education, job training, and hiring are not equal to those of White men. Affirmative action is not a quota system, as is often claimed; it is not reverse discrimination; and it is not a system for hiring unqualified people. The need for and desirability of affirmative action policies—which have benefited White women more than any other group—were called into question increasingly in the 1990s. The affirmative action policy for state agencies in California was overturned in a ballot initiative in 1996, and in 1998 the University of California banned affirmative action in student admissions. Also in 1998, Washington State voters supported a ban on all state affirmative action programs for all women and

men of color in education, contracting, and employment. In 2002 the Association of American Colleges and Universities affirmed its commitment to affirmative action "as the major strategy for achieving equal opportunity" (AACU 2002). In 2003, the U.S. Supreme Court upheld the right to affirmative action in higher education in lawsuits concerning the University of Michigan undergraduate program and University of Michigan law school. The judges argued that affirmative action provides for a "compelling state interest" in diversity at all levels of society.

Challenges of the Global Economy   A great challenge for U.S. workers, including organized labor, is the continued impact of the globalization of the economy on the availability of work, wage rates, working conditions in the United States, and continued pressure for immigration into this country, as discussed in Chapter 9. As capital becomes increasingly international in its movements, labor will need to become increasingly international in its strategies. This country has a vital tradition of labor organizing, including actions in support of workers in other countries. Although circumstances have changed, there is much to be learned from this history that can be applied today (Cobble 1993; Louie 2001; Milkman 1985, 2000; O'Farrell and Kornbluh 1996).

Pensions, Disability Payments, and Welfare

For women who cannot work because of illness, age, or disability, for those who are made redundant or who cannot leave their children, there is a complex patchwork of income-support measures and means-tested allowances provided by federal and state governments and private pension plans. Community organizations, particularly religious organizations, also provide much-needed informal support to poor people, especially food, clothing, and financial help with schooling. Before the Great Depression of the 1930s, when the economy collapsed and many thousands were suddenly destitute, there was a commonly held belief that poverty was due to laziness and that there was plenty of work available for those willing to roll up their sleeves and get on with it. But the severity of the collapse, which put so many people on bread lines, desperate to feed their families, called for government intervention in the labor market to protect people from the worst effects of the booms and slumps inherent in the economy. This provided the impetus and the political justification for the establishment of Social Security and Medicare programs under the Social Security Act of 1935.

These programs are based on people's relationship to work and are rooted in the principle of the work ethic. Older people can claim pensions because they have already done their share and paid into the Social Security fund during their working lives; people with disabilities may be excused if they are not able to work as long or as vigorously as nondisabled people; those who are laid off because of plant closures or other company changes can usually claim unemployment benefits for a few months while they look for other jobs. Such people are considered "deserving" in contrast to the "undeserving," meaning those who are young and able-bodied but who "simply don't want to work," as is often said nowadays, no less than in the 1930s. This distinction underlies two kinds of benefits: one is based on the concept of social insurance, which allows individuals to draw from an insurance fund to which they have contributed during their working lives; the other is based on the concept of public assistance, under which the needy are given "means-tested" allowances.

Significantly for women today, this Social Security legislation was designed to assist the ideal nuclear family, where the male head of the household was in regular, full-time, paid employment until his death or retirement, and his wife was a full-time homemaker. Seventy years later most U.S. families are not of this type, and most women's benefits are adversely affected because their employment histories, upon which payments are calculated, are not the same as men's.

Pensions and Disability Payments

Retirement pensions are a crucial source of income for older people, but women generally receive significantly lower pension payments than men (Cox 2001b). Pensions are based on wage levels while the person was working and on the number of years in employment. This assumes that only paid work is productive work, so no amount of housekeeping or

caring for children and elderly relatives will count. As mentioned earlier, women generally earn lower wages than men and are more likely to work part-time and to move in and out of the workforce as they balance paid work with raising children and family responsibilities. Currently, few part-time jobs provide health insurance or a pension plan. When women retire, many have to rely on a Social Security pension that will be lower than that for most men, because women were not able to contribute as much to it during their working lives. For divorced women this is particularly serious. Many have not planned independently for retirement (Uchitelle 2001). Financial concerns for older women are further aggravated by the fact that women tend to live longer than men, so their retirement assets must be spread over a longer period of time. At least 40 percent of U.S. women aged 65 and over, and 60 percent of African American women and Latinas in this age group, are entirely dependent on Social Security (Bethel 2005).

Because work and retirement are defined according to the labor market experiences of White middle-class men, this penalizes not only many women but also men of color and people with disabilities. Poor women and men of color often have to piece together an income, depending on seasonal or part-time work, sometimes working informally for cash or favors returned. These factors make them less able to retire completely from paid work when they are older.

A new stereotype of affluent older people in ads for cruises, cars, vitamins, health insurance, and hearing aids suggests that older people are physically fit and enjoying their retirement. This is a welcome change from negative images of elderly people, but it deflects attention from those who are poor. The poverty rate for elderly women was 13 percent, compared to 7 percent among men. For unmarried elderly women it was 19 percent (Social Security Administration 2001). For elderly African Americans living alone the poverty rate increases to 60 percent. Elderly Native Americans as a group have the lowest incomes and the worst housing in the country. At the same time, many older people provide valuable services for themselves and others: participating in community organizations, helping family and friends, looking after children, maintaining and repairing their homes, and doing daily cooking, cleaning, and other housework. Eleanor

Palo Stoller and Rose Campbell Gibson (1994) point out that the advantages of a job with good pay and benefits, a comfortable home, and stimulating opportunities tend to accumulate across the life course. Similarly, disadvantages may also accumulate, producing large differences in economic resources, and often also in health, in old age (p. 107).

The country's elderly population will rise dramatically in the next decade or so as baby boomers reach retirement age. There is concern over the future of the Social Security system, as a larger number of people will be drawing pensions than will be paying into it. Some, claiming that Social Security will become bankrupt, with nothing left for those who are now young, have gone so far as to call for its privatization. Others argue that Social Security can be fixed with relatively modest increases in contributions in the short term, rather than by wholesale privatization. Sixty percent of Social Security beneficiaries are women, and Social Security is the major source of retirement income for the majority of them. Social Security benefits are guaranteed for life, which is important because of women's longer life span. In 2005, President Bush traveled the country promoting plans to change Social Security by allowing younger people to invest in individual private retirement accounts. Organizations like the American Association for Retired Persons, Gray Panthers, Institute for Women's Policy Research, National Women's Law Center, and OWL: Older Women's League have all posted materials to their Web sites explaining the crucial importance of Social Security, especially for women, and suggesting small changes that can keep the system viable.

Women with disabilities also receive less from public income support than do men with disabilities. As a result, fewer women with disabilities are able to claim Social Security Disability Insurance (DI), which was designed with the needs of working men in mind, and must rely on the Supplemental Security Income program (SSI), which is subject to a means test for eligibility and greater bureaucratic scrutiny, often demeaning. Some disabled elderly people may choose disability benefits over Social Security pensions, depending on their work histories. The future of income support for people with disabilities is likely to be influenced by two opposing trends: the growing political clout of the disability rights movement and the desire of many politicians to cut government spending.

Welfare

The issue of government support for poor families became especially controversial in the mid-1990s. In 1996, Aid to Families with Dependent Children (AFDC) was replaced by block grants for Temporary Assistance for Needy Families (TANF), as Title I of the Personal Responsibility and Work Opportunity Reconciliation Act. This was signed into law by President Clinton against opposition from many welfare rights organizations and advocates for poor women and children, such as the National Welfare Rights Union, the Children's Defense Fund, and local campaigns like Survivors Inc. (Roxbury, Mass.), the Coalition for Basic Human Needs (Cambridge, Mass.), and Women of Color Resource Center (Oakland, Calif.). Gwendolyn Mink (1998) roundly criticizes feminist organizations and feminist policy makers for not opposing welfare reform more forcefully. The new law ended federal entitlement to assistance dating back to the Social Security Act of 1935.

TANF is a work-based temporary assistance program. States are required by the federal government to set the following conditions for TANF payments: time limits of two years or less, a five-year lifetime limit on benefits, and a work requirement whereby welfare recipients have to spend at least thirty hours a week in "work experience." This rarely includes basic education, college classes, or training not related to a specific job (see Reading 53). States have flexibility to provide other benefits, such as health care, transportation, or child-care subsidies to cushion the transition from welfare to work. Former welfare recipients are pitted against other low-paid workers, some of whom have been displaced by "workfare 'trainees' working off their welfare grant at less than minimum-wage equivalents" (Cooper 1997, p. 12). They also need affordable child care, a major obstacle for most working mothers. The advantage of workfare trainees to employers is that TANF—in place of wages—is paid out of state funds.

Welfare rolls dropped by more than 50 percent from 4.4 million families in 1996 to 2 million in 2003 (Hays 2004), and government officials claimed welfare reform a great success. In Wisconsin, early efforts to establish what had happened to former welfare recipients found that 38 percent were unemployed (*Los Angeles Times* 1999, p. A21). Studies from 21 states found that those who got jobs did not leave poverty in most cases (Associated Press, May 12,

1999); all jobs obtained by former welfare recipients were low-paying, and many were short-term (Havemann 1999). Critics of welfare reform argued that the changes had reduced the numbers on welfare but had done nothing to end poverty (Hays 2004; Mink 2002).

Myths about welfare recipients are central to the public discourse on this issue, stigmatizing those who need to rely on assistance and serving to erode the possibility of empathy by those who are better-off for those who are poor. The mass media give prominence to stories about welfare "cheats." The prevailing image of a welfare mother is a Black woman with a large family. Proponents of welfare reform justified cuts in welfare programs on the grounds that this would help to reduce the federal budget deficit. Welfare payments accounted for only approximately 1 percent of the federal budget and 2 to 3 percent of states' budgets. Congress reauthorized more onerous welfare provisions in 2003 with an increased work requirement of up to forty hours in most cases and a stronger emphasis on marriage incentive programs. Women's studies professor Gwendolyn Mink (2002) argues that single mothers are poor because "their family caregiving work is unremunerated, not because they do not work or are not married." She notes that some feminists have begun to resist welfare's moral discipline and to redefine welfare as caregivers' income. Several welfare-rights organizations advocate this position, including the Women's Committee of One Hundred, Every Mother Is a Working Mother Network, Quality Homecare Coalition (Los Angeles), and Welfare Warriors (Wisconsin). On December 31, 2002, thousands of poor families reached their five-year lifetime limit for TANF. Moreover, TANF rates are too low to live on, which forces recipients to supplement their welfare checks in some way—by getting money from family and friends or by doing unreported work. Not reporting additional income to the welfare office may make women liable for criminal charges for perjury or fraud. Law professor Kaaryn Gustafson (2005, p. 2) argues that poor families are penalized through "completely inadequate levels of support, through public shaming, and through intrusive administrative forays into their personal lives that none but the truly needy would tolerate." Gustafson shows how the penalizing of welfare recipients "has shifted from the metaphorical to the literal" and become much

harsher in recent years. Law enforcement officials are allowed access to information contained in aid recipients' files. No one who is wanted by law enforcement officials for a felony or for violating the terms of parole or probation—which may be as little as missing a meeting—can receive any government benefits. Anyone found guilty of a drug-related felony is banned from receiving benefits for life. States can require drug tests, fingerprints, and photographs for those applying for benefits. Women who give birth to a child while on welfare are denied a financial increase despite the fact that they have another child to care for.

It is important to note here that many people in this society receive some kind of government support, be it through income-tax deductions for homeowners, medical benefits for those in the military, tax breaks for corporations, agricultural subsidies to farmers, government bailouts to savings and loans companies, or government funding for high-tech military-related research conducted by universities and private firms. This is often not mentioned in discussions of welfare, but it should be.

Feminist Approaches to Women's Work and Income

Comparable Worth

Feminist researchers and policy analysts have been concerned with women's overall working conditions and women's labor history (Amott 1993; Amott and Matthaei 1996; Bergmann 1986; Jones 1985; Kessler-Harris 1990, 2001; Zavella 1987). They have questioned why the job market is segregated along gender lines and have challenged traditional inequities in pay between women and men. These may be partly explained by differences in education, qualifications, and work experience, but part of this wage gap is simply attributable to gender. This has led to detailed discussion of the **comparable worth** of women's jobs when considered next to men's jobs requiring comparable levels of skill and knowledge. Why is it, for example, that secretaries or child-care workers, who are virtually all women, earn so much less than truck drivers or mail carriers, who are mainly men? What do wage rates say about the importance of a job to the wider society? What is being rewarded? Advocates for comparable worth have urged employers to evaluate employees without regard to gender, race, or class, but in terms of knowledge and skills needed to perform the job, mental demands or decision making involved in the job, accountability or the degree of supervision involved, and working conditions, such as how physically safe the job is. Such calculations reveal many discrepancies in current rates of pay between women's work and men's work. Indeed, if pursued, this line of argument opens up the thorny question of how to justify wage differentials at all.

Feminization of Poverty

Feminist researchers have also pointed to the **feminization of poverty** (Abramovitz 1996; Dujon and Withorn 1996; Sidel 1996). The two poorest groups in the United States are women raising children alone and women over sixty-five living alone. *Poverty* is a complex term with economic, emotional, and cultural dimensions. One may be materially well-off but emotionally impoverished, for example, and vice versa. Poverty also needs to be thought about in the context of costs—for housing, food, transportation, health care, child care, and clothes needed to go to work—hence the value of a self-sufficiency standard. Poverty is also linked to social expectations of this materialist culture. Many poor children in the United States clamor for Nikes, for example, in response to high-pressure advertising campaigns.

Impact of Class

A key concept in any discussion of work, income, and wealth is class. In Reading 52, Veronica Chambers discusses the micro-, meso-, and macro-level factors that have shaped the experiences of professional African American women to whom "much has been given" and "much is expected" in terms of success and support for family members and community members. Nolita Clark and Shannon Stanfield discuss the significance of educational opportunities for low-income single parents based on their experiences as students enrolled in the ACCESS project at Hamilton College (N.Y.) (Reading 53). This unique program "assists low-income parents . . . to move from welfare and low-wage work to meaningful career employment . . . through higher education." Current welfare policy only counts "job

readiness" education as work activity, and allows a mere three months of vocational training during a two-year period (see Adair and Dahlberg 2003).

In the United States today, most people describe themselves as "middle class," a term that includes a very wide range of incomes, occupations, levels of security, and life situations. Indicators of class include income, occupation, education, culture and language, neighborhood, clothes, cars, and, particularly important, unearned wealth. As noted in Chapter 2, some people raised in a working-class community may have a middle-class education and occupation later in life and a somewhat mixed class identity as a result. A woman's class position is usually linked to that of her father and husband. For Marxists, a person's class is defined in relation to the process of economic production—whether she or he has to work for a living. There is currently no politically accepted way for most people to make a livelihood except by working for it, and in this society work, in addition to being an economic necessity, carries strong moral overtones. Note that this same principle is not applied to those among the very rich who live on trust funds or corporate profits.

In much public debate in the United States, class is more of a psychological concept—what we think and feel about our class position—than an economic one. Poverty is often explained as resulting from individual low self-esteem, laziness, or dysfunctional families, as we pointed out in Chapter 1. In public discourse on inequality, race is invariably emphasized at the expense of class. Government census data, for example, are analyzed for racial differences much more than for class differences, which gives the impression that race is the most salient disparity among people. In practice race and class overlap, but greater attention to class differences would show different patterns of inequality. It would also show more similarities and more of a basis for alliances between people of color and White people who are economically disadvantaged. Feminist theorists who emphasize class usually work within a Marxist or socialist tradition (Dalla Costa and James 1972; Hartmann 1981; Jaggar 1983; Mies 1986). Scholar and activist Johanna Brenner (2001) argues that working-class women need to organize themselves against sexism and class exploitation—as many are doing through unions or other community-based projects (Louie 2001; Mullings 1997; Naples 1997, 1998).

Policy Implications and Activist Projects

Feminists have tackled the issue of women and work from many angles. In addition to advocating for comparable worth in wage rates, they have encouraged women to return to school to improve their educational qualifications, opposed sexual harassment on the job, campaigned for decent, affordable child-care arrangements, exposed the dangers of occupational injury and the health hazards of toxic work environments, and advocated for women in senior positions in all fields, and that math, science, and computer education be more available and effective for girls. Examples of such organizations include the Institute for Women's Policy Research (Washington, D.C.), the National Organization for Women (Washington, D.C.), 9 to 5 National Organization of Working Women (with chapters in several states), and the Women's Economic Agenda Project (Oakland, Calif.). The "Take Our Daughters to Work Day" initiated by the Ms. Foundation, for example, exposes girls to jobs they may know little about and provides role models for them, which can have a powerful impact. Several organizations have worked to open up opportunities for women to enter well-paying trades such as carpentry and construction, including Hard Hatted Women (Cleveland, Ohio), Women in the Building Trades (Jamaica Plain, Mass.), Minnesota Women in the Trades, and Northern New England Tradeswomen (Essex Junction, Vt.). Many local groups help women to start small businesses, utilizing existing skills. The Women's Bean Project (Denver), Tierra Wools (Los Ojos, N. Mex.), and the Navaho Weaving Project (Kykotsmovi, Ariz.) are group projects that promote self-sufficiency.

Promoting Greater Economic Security for Women

A lack of jobs, low wages, low educational attainment, having children, and divorce all work against women's economic security and keep many women in poverty, dependent on men, or both. As we concluded in Chapter 7, an aspect of security and sustainability for family relationships involves equal opportunities and responsibilities for parenting, which in turn means a redefinition of work. Yet if current trends continue, many young people in the United States—especially young people of color—will never be in regular, full-time employment in their lives. Politicians and businesses promote almost any venture—building convention centers, ballparks, jails, and prisons and maintaining obsolete military bases—on the argument that it will create jobs. Changes in the economy force us to confront some fundamental contradictions that affect women's work and the way work is thought about generally:

> What should count as work?
>
> Does the distinction between "productive" and "unproductive" work make sense?
>
> How should work be rewarded?
>
> How should those without paid work, many of them women, be supported?
>
> How can the current inequalities between haves and have-nots be justified?
>
> Is the work ethic useful? Should it be redefined?
>
> Is materialism the mark of success?

Years ago, pushed by the impact of the Great Depression of the 1930s, social commentators saw great potential for human development promised by (then) new technologies like telephones, Dictaphones, and washing machines, by means of which people could provide for their needs in a relatively short time each week. The British philosopher Bertrand Russell (1935), for example, favored such "idleness" as an opportunity to become more fully human, to develop oneself in many dimensions of life. Recognizing that this could not happen if material living standards had to keep rising, he put forth a modest notion of what people "need." He also understood that these kinds of changes would require political imagination and will.

Questions for Reflection

As you read and discuss this chapter, think about these questions:

1. What are your experiences of work?

2. What have you learned through working? About yourself? About other people's lives? About the wider society? How did you learn it? Who were your teachers?

3. What have you wanted to change in your work situations? What would it take to make these changes? What recourse do you have as a worker to improve your conditions of work?

4. How might pension policies be changed to reflect the range of productivity of women across the life course?

Finding Out More on the Web

1. Consult these Web sites for more information on the wage gap, poverty levels, and welfare reform in your state and nationally:

   9 to 5 National Association of Working Women: **www.9to5.org**

   Children's Defense Fund: **www.childrensdefense.org**

   Coalition of Labor Union Women: **www.cluw.org**

   Institute for Women's Policy Research: **www.iwpr.org**

   National Jobs for All Coalition: **www.njfac.org/jobnews.html**

   Economic Success Clearinghouse: **www.financeproject.org/irc/win.asp**

2. Compare the very low amounts the government spends on welfare with other federal expenditures. See:

   National Priorities Project: **www.nationalpriorities.org**

   War Resisters League: **www.warresisters.org/piechart.htm**

♦♦♦

Taking Action

1. Draw up a detailed budget of your needs, expenses, income, and savings. What did you learn by doing this?

2. Discuss work experiences with your mother or grandmother (or women of their ages). What opportunities did they have? What choices did they make? What similarities and differences do you notice between your own life and theirs at the same age?

3. Analyze representations of women workers in ads, news reports, TV shows, and movies.

FORTY-EIGHT

the cleaning woman/labor relations #4 (1988)

Hattie Gossett

Hattie Gossett is a widely published poet, educator, spoken word artist, and musician. She is the winner of many awards including the New School University's Distinguished Artist-in-Residence Award. She performs her poetry and teaches workshops on writing, Black literature, and Black music.

the doctors knew.

the lab people knew.

the secretaries knew.

the volunteers knew.

the patients knew.

the clinic was moving to a new spot and would be closed for a while and everybody knew ahead of time.

everybody except the cleaning woman.

she only found out on closing day.

i dont know why no one thought to tell you before this the woman doctor said to the cleaning woman over the phone annoyance all up in her voice at being asked by the cleaning woman why they hadnt given her an earlier notice.

i dont know why no one thought to tell you. anyway i have patients now and have no time for you.

it was the cleaning womans dime so she went for broke. but i am dependent on the salary you pay me and now suddenly it wont be there she protested. wouldnt it be fair to give me some kind of severance pay?

severance pay! shrieked the woman doctor. look she snapped you havent been with us that long. only a few weeks. besides i have help at home you know and i . . .

its like this the cleaning woman interrupted not wanting to hear about the doctors help at home (at least not what the doctor was going to say) when you work for a salary you need some kind of reasonable notice when its going to be discontinued so you can prepare yourself. how would you like it if you were in my place?

the woman doctor then tried to offer the cleaning woman a job in the new clinic plus a job in her own new private office but neither of these jobs would start for some weeks. she never did say how she would feel being in the cleaning womans place. the cleaning woman realized she was dealing with people who really didnt care about her. as far as they were concerned she could starve for those few weeks. she wondered how long you would have to work for these people before it was long enough for them to tell you at least 2weeks ahead of time that they were closing. how long is long enough?

forget it the cleaning woman told the woman doctor. she was pissed. she didnt like knowing that she was being shafted and that there wasnt anything she could do. when do you want me to bring back your keys? because she cleaned at night or very early in the morning she had keys to the clinic.

as soon as the woman doctor said anytime in a somewhat startled voice the cleaning woman hung up. she didnt slam down the phone. she put it down gently. but she didnt say goodbye or have a nice day.

damn the cleaning woman said to herself after she had hung up. here these people are supposed to be progressive and look at how they act. here they are running an alternative clinic for lesbians and gays and straights and yet they treat their help just as bad as the american medical association fools treat theirs. are they really an alternative she asked herself.

sure they treat their help bad herself answered laughingly.

the cleaning woman looked up a little surprised because she hadnt heard herself come in. now herself sat down and started eating some of the cleaning womans freshly sliced pineapple.

what do you mean girlfriend the cleaning woman asked herself.

have you forgotten that every sister aint a sister and every brother aint a brother herself began. where did you get this pineapple? its really sweet and fresh.

come on now. dont play games. tell me what you mean the cleaning woman said.

look herself said. some of these sisters and brothers aint nothing but secondhand reprints out of the bidness as usual catalogue in spite of all their tongue flapping to the contrary. and these secondhand reprints can be worse than the originals. like they have to prove that they know how to abuse people even more coldheartedly than the originals do. its getting harder and harder to tell the real alternatives from the rank rapscallions. of course everybody else on the staff knew that the gig was moving but you. in their book you aint nothing no way.

what could the cleaning woman say?

herself was right once again and the cleaning woman tried to tell herself this but that girl didnt hear anything cuz she had already tipped on out taking the last piece of pineapple with her.

so the cleaning woman laughed for a minute. then she stopped brooding over those fools at the clinic.

she got on the phone and started lining up some more work.

later she sat down and wrote this story which she put in the envelope with the clinic keys. she wrote the woman doctors name on the front of the envelope cuz she wanted to be sure the woman doctor would be able to share the story. at the bottom of the story the cleaning woman put not to be copied or reproduced by any means without written permission from the author.

cuz one monkey sho nuff dont stop no show.

He Works, She Works, but What Different Impressions They Make (1980)

Natasha Josefowitz

Natasha Josefowitz is a noted columnist, speaker, and author of many books. Her efforts on behalf of women have earned her numerous awards, including The Living Legacy Award from the Women's International Center, and the Women Helping Women Award from Soroptimist International, a worldwide organization for women in management and professions, working through service projects to advance human rights and the status of women.

Have you ever found yourself up against the old double standard at work? Then you know how annoying it can be and how alone you can feel. Supervisors and coworkers still judge us by old stereotypes that say women are emotional, disorganized, and inefficient. Here are some of the most glaring examples of the typical office double standard.

The family picture is on HIS desk:
Ah, a solid, responsible family man.

HIS desk is cluttered:
He's obviously a hard worker and busy man.

HE'S talking with coworkers:
He must be discussing the latest deal.

HE'S not at his desk:
He must be at a meeting.

HE'S having lunch with the boss:
He's on his way up.

HE'S getting married.
He'll get more settled.

HE'S having a baby:
He'll need a raise.

HE'S leaving for a better job:
He recognizes a good opportunity.

HE'S aggressive.

HE'S careful.

HE loses his temper.

HE'S depressed.

HE follows through.

HE'S firm.

HE makes wise judgments.

HE is a man of the world.

HE isn't afraid to say what he thinks.

HE exercises authority.

HE'S discreet.

HE'S a stern taskmaster.

The family picture is on HER desk:
Hmm, her family will come before her career.

HER desk is cluttered:
She's obviously a disorganized scatterbrain.

SHE'S talking with coworkers:
She must be gossiping.

SHE'S not at her desk:
She must be in the ladies' room.

SHE'S having lunch with the boss:
They must be having an affair.

SHE'S getting married:
She'll get pregnant and leave.

SHE'S having a baby:
She'll cost the company money in maternity benefits.

SHE'S leaving for a better job:
Women are undependable.

SHE'S pushy.

SHE'S picky.

SHE'S bitchy.

SHE'S moody.

SHE doesn't know when to quit.

SHE'S stubborn.

SHE reveals her prejudices.

SHE'S been around.

SHE'S opinionated.

SHE'S tyrannical.

SHE'S secretive.

SHE'S difficult to work for.

FIFTY

The New Girls Network (2004)
Women, Technology, and Feminism

Shireen Lee

Shireen Lee has developed after-school education, employment, and leadership programs for young women. She was one of the founding members and Co-Chair of the Youth Caucus of the United Nations Commission on the Status of Women (UN CSW).

. . . "Imagine," writes Anita Borg, president of the nonprofit Institute for Women and Technology, "a world in which information technology (IT) was used to its highest potential, being an engine for an efficient, ecological economy and providing new opportunities for more people based on more available knowledge. Imagine a political system based on open access to information, better education, more communication, and equal participation. Imagine connecting people around the world in the spirit of positive internationalism, where social goals such as universal literacy, basic education, and health care are achieved."[1]

Technology could help us reimagine societies, communities, and futures that move beyond the binaries—white-black; male-female; straight-gay; First World–Third World; future-past; technological-organic; work-play—of our contemporary world. As they achieve certain credentials in technology, women are participating in these reimaginings. But there continue to be barriers to women getting the right credentials, and to the careers where they can use them.

I grew up in Malaysia, where single-sex education is the norm. I benefited from being able to develop intellectually and physically in an environment free from the consuming social pressures of girl-boy interaction. Throughout my schooling I focused on math and science, and excelled. It seemed natural that I would become an engineer.

In Canada, where I attended college, graduating engineers are each presented with an iron ring in a secret ceremony designed by Rudyard Kipling and dating back to 1922. Engineers wear their rings on the little fingers of their working hands after taking an oath of ethics. At the age of twenty-three, I took off my iron ring when I stopped working at oil refineries, but I did not turn my back on technology.

An Environmental Scan

In 2001, the Bureau of Labor Statistics projected that between 2000 and 2010, eight of the ten fastest-growing occupations would be computer related, with computer engineers topping the list.[2] Yet according to the National Council for Research on Women, women's share of bachelor's degrees in computer science dropped to fewer than 20 percent in 1999, after having reached a high of 37 percent in 1984.[3] A look at these numbers from the supply side suggests that the gap between male and female participation in the technology workforce, instead of closing, will actually widen in the near future. We are simply not graduating enough women to fill tomorrow's technological jobs: information technologists, computer applications specialists, games programmers, code writers in software development, and systems programmers, among others. The Information Technology Association of America predicts that, by 2010, 60 percent of American jobs will require technological skills.[4] Contrast this demand with the following current statistics: women leave engineering jobs—ranging from electrical and mechanical engineering positions to computer-related engineering jobs, such as hardware engineering—at double the rate of men,[5] and women are more likely to leave technological occupations altogether.[6]

The mantra of second wave feminists was "Let us in!" Their success opened the doors to educational opportunities and brought women into schools and the workforce in unprecedented numbers. The women of that generation butted up against centuries-old traditions of patriarchal governance and belief systems to gain financial and reproductive independence. What does the world look like today for the daughters of those 1970s feminists?

Gender and racial discrimination at the end of the twentieth and beginning of the twenty-first century is subtle yet still pervasive. It stems largely from unconscious ways of thinking that have been socialized into all of us, men and women alike. In the realm of technology, its influence spans the pipeline from girls in school to women in the job market.

The Education-Career Discontinuity

Back in 1992, the American Association of University Women (AAUW) published *The AAUW Report: How Schools Short-change Girls*, which claimed that there was a dearth of women in technology careers because girls were not taking math and science classes in school.[7] The approach to the problem at the time can be summed up as follows: If we can get girls to take the classes and excel in them, they will naturally choose corresponding careers. . . .

[Patricia] Campbell and Beatriz Chu Clewell, leading researchers in the field, tell us that girls, particularly those in the middle-class socioeconomic sphere, are now taking math and science classes in the same numbers as boys, and in some cases excelling in them. But they are *still* not choosing technology careers to the extent anticipated ten years ago. Girls do not seem to be making the link between math and science education and technology careers.[8] Campbell believes that many girls place greater importance than do boys on making a positive difference in the larger world. Girls apparently do not see the connection between technology jobs, which tend to be highly specialized and solitary endeavors, and changing the world. Katie Wheeler, executive director of the Girls' Coalition of Greater Boston, a consortium of nonprofits, funders, and researchers interested in girls' issues, agrees. "Girls perceive technology and the hard sciences like physics as not involving people. They don't see in technology the potential to help people in the world. That's why most girls and women end up in the life sciences like biology rather than in high tech."[9] Compounding an already unfavorable situation, research by the Congressional Commission on the Advancement of Women and Minorities in Science, Engineering and Technology Development (CAWMSET) confirms what most people already suspect. Many girls do not see themselves reflected in the role models, men *or* women, in technology careers. The general image of technology workers and engineers as unusually intelligent, socially inept, and absent-minded "geeks" or "nerds" is often a deterrent.[10]

For low-income young people of color, especially African-Americans, Latinos and Latinas, and Native Americans, the question of gender is moot—among them the overriding barrier is economic. Lack of educational resources in inner-city

schools, where the majority of students are blacks and Latinos and Latinas, affect participation and achievement in math and science for both girls *and* boys.[11] In Massachusetts, for example, tenth graders are required to take the Massachusetts Comprehensive Assessment System test, or MCAS, in a variety of subjects, including math and science. In low-income areas such as Springfield, Holyoke, and sections of Boston where a majority of the students are of color, the rate of failure is startling. In Springfield, in the year 2000, 94 percent of tenth-grade Latinos and Latinas and 91 percent of black students failed the math section; in Holyoke, 95 percent of Latinos and Latinas failed; and in Boston, 86 percent of Latinos and Latinas failed, as did 82 percent of black students. Deficient inner-city public school systems make it almost impossible for students to consider fields in technology because they aren't even getting the basic education needed to participate fully in society. Many women and girls of color must fight prejudices against their race, gender, and class that keep them from entering any number of career fields.

Yet there is hope. Many companies that seek to promote ethnic and racial diversity in the workplace have begun to fund training programs which benefit people of color. These programs may not have an impact on a large scale, but they are making a difference in particular neighborhoods. In Washington, D.C., Edgewood Terrace, an 884-unit apartment complex, was once so crime-ridden. . . . After the Community Preservation and Development Corporation, a nonprofit organization, began work to make Edgewood a better place to live, good things started to happen. It created EdgeNet, an intranet-style system that networks users together and hopes to help residents gain computer literacy. The Gateway @ Edgewood Terrace, a CPDC computer learning center that has more that sixty workstations and four networked labs, began to help residents get logged on. In addition, the Gateway center offers classes in computer skills and applications and will offer network management and beginning Microsoft Certified Systems Engineers courses.[12]

Feminism has opened doors for those women who do not have to contend with race and class barriers, especially in fields such as medicine and law. In spring 2001, *The New York Times* reported that for the first time, incoming female students would outnumber male students in law schools across the country.[13] In engineering, however, men dominate:

of all engineering bachelor's degrees awarded in 2000, 47,320 went to men and only 12,216 to women.[14] According to Campbell's research, even in colleges with the strongest outreach and support for women engineering students, enrollment of incoming female students has plateaued at about 20 percent over the last few years.[15] A similar pattern is evident in the workforce. In an article in the *San Francisco Chronicle*, Karen Calo, vice president of human resources for the IBM Software Group in New York, observed that although women now make up 30 percent of lawyers and doctors, fewer than 10 percent of engineers are women.[16] Even fewer are women of color. Technology is still very much a pale male profession.

Subtle Messages, Major Barriers

A historical lack of women in technology careers has resulted in work cultures that have developed without them. According to Sokunthear Sy, a young female engineer at Accenture (formerly Andersen Consulting), there are more informal support structures for men. Male-dominated work environments do a poor job of retaining women once they begin working in industry. "Subtle things like golfing that happen socially because that's the thing to do . . . [to] hang out after hours. Most women don't golf. And women with families can't hang out. Relationships that form outside of work influence decisions at work especially when reviews come around."[17] A . . . survey by Women of Silicon Valley, a joint project of the Community Foundation of Silicon Valley and the strategic advising group Collaborative Economics, confirms that 41 percent of women who work in technology, compared with only 23 percent of women not in technology jobs, feel that they have to "fit into a masculine workplace" to advance.[18]

The subtle messages that women don't belong extends even to seemingly trivial elements, like clothing. As a chemical engineer I had to visit oil refineries several days a week. Attire mandated by safety regulations included steel-toe boots and Nomex fire-resistant overalls, which back then came only in men's sizes. On my first day of work I was forced to show up in boots that were two sizes too big and overalls with sleeves and pant legs rolled up multiple times. I looked like I was playing dress up in my father's clothes—not the image that one wants to project walking into a control room that is 100 percent male workers. . . .

Today overt gender discrimination in schools and the workplace is rarely tolerated, so most people, both male and female, believe that women are on equal footing with men. After-school and mentoring programs to support girls and women in technology are thus often viewed by girls, women, and their male peers as remedial. Sy maintains that "there is a fear that if you get involved in specialized groups, people will think, Oh, you need extra help. You can't do it on your own. For example, if you are in a women's mentoring group and you get promoted, people will say that's why."[19] Support programs can reinforce the stereotype that women are not as capable as men and need a leg up.

Programs targeted at groups that have historically been discriminated against, such as students of color in universities, or women in technology careers, serve to move us along a path of greater equity. It is not the *programs* themselves that need to be eliminated but rather people's *perceptions* of them. Contrast the opposition to affirmative action programs for women and people of color with the G.I. Bill, which provided higher education grants to veterans. The G.I. Bill, after all, can be viewed as a national, federally initiated affirmative action program—benefiting mainly young white men. According to Michael Haydock in an article for *American History,* "By the time the last American World War II veteran was graduated in 1956, the United States was richer by 450,000 engineers, 238,000 teachers, 91,000 scientists, 67,000 doctors, 22,000 dentists."[20] Would the country also benefit from similar increases of women and/or people of color in these professions? This point seems particularly salient in the high-tech sector, where, according to CAWMSET, the demand for skilled American workers will continue to outstrip supply.[21] With the G.I. Bill as a model, one can imagine a grants program that could provide badly needed science and math resources for low-income girls and young women of color in urban public schools. Think of the possibilities—if political will is forthcoming.

Redefining Our Position: Women as Technology Innovators

The challenges facing women in technology fields are nothing new. Most commentary on women and technology—academic and otherwise—makes this clear. However, the focus is often on what women are *not* doing. That vantage point perpetuates a deficit model—women seem perpetually to fall short of expectations. Such an approach can become a self-fulfilling prophecy.

The spotlight rarely shines on what women are doing *right*. They are redefining their involvement with technology and using technology to empower and advance themselves and other women. Problems still exist, but there are many women who have adapted to their environment and found ways to succeed.

Nowhere is this more apparent than in the high-tech sector. Here are the numbers we typically see: There are just three female CEOs among the Fortune 500 and only seven in the Fortune 1000; women hold only 4 percent of the top management positions in Fortune 500 companies.[22] No surprise. What the media usually don't tell us is that women account for 45 percent of the highest ranking corporate officers in Internet companies, and 6 percent of Internet companies financed by venture capital firms in 1999 have female CEOs.[23]

. . . Rather than butting heads with patriarchal corporate America, women are using a different leverage point—smaller, newer companies. That these startling statistics show up in the high-tech sector, an industry that burst into prominence after the feminist era of the 1970s, is probably no accident. High-tech has become the nexus for minirevolutions—linking women's leadership in small businesses and global women's activism to create a new form of feminist activism.

Women Business Owners: Today's Feminists

Women is general are no longer just banging on the doors of corporations saying, "Let us in!" We are taking matters into our own hands and creating new centers of power. Women are starting their own businesses in unprecedented numbers. . . . As of 1996, one in eight women-owned firms in the United States was owned by a woman of color, and the number of these firms has increased three times faster than the overall rate of business growth in the past ten years.[24] What about younger women? Ta'chelle Herron . . . is a twenty-one-year-old woman of color, a product of the urban public school system. She insists that

women *can* use technology for their advancement. "Start your own business! Once you learn the fundamentals of how the systems work, you can switch that around and use it for yourself—to make money. I started my own graphic design business."[25] A 2001 survey on women in Silicon Valley confirms this trend. It found that many women in technology are leaving the corporate workplace. About 10 percent of women in Silicon Valley are independent contractors, and another 20 percent said they planned to start their own businesses in the next three years.[26] The U.S. Small Business Administration tells us that women now own a staggering 9 million companies—38 percent of all U.S. enterprises. They employ over 27.5 million people.[27]

Further, women are breaking down the binaries associated with pleasure and work, activism and work; they are living their activism in ways that they find fulfilling. Feminism, once synonymous with marching in the streets, is now part of the economic engine of the country. Thanks in part to what those marching women accomplished, contemporary women are making change from within institutions. Looking at her peers, Rebecca Tadikonda, a twenty-eight-year-old recent MBA graduate from Stanford University, observes, "Amongst high-tech start-ups where there is a woman CEO or where there are more women on the management team, there are more women in the company overall. If there aren't women or if there are fewer women on the management team, there are fewer women in the company overall."[28] This point seems consistent with recent research by the Stanford Graduate School of Business. According to the report, "Gender and the Organization-Building Process in Young, High-Tech Firms," women's early representation in core scientific and technical roles has decisive consequences for how emerging companies evolve.[29] This presence in turn could have positive implications for the development of women-friendly workplace cultures. . . . Increasing numbers of women in leadership positions in high-tech companies will inevitably offer a more diverse array of role models for young girls and help them see that people in technology careers can be like them. Whether they are conscious of it or not, women leaders are also acting as activists and role models by paving the way for other women. . . .

The High-Tech Sector

Women in the high-tech sector in particular are reimagining the possibilities for work, activism, empowerment, technology, and our future. . . .

The Women's Technology Cluster is an incubator for women-owned high-tech start-ups in San Francisco. Founded by Catherine Muther, a feminist and former head of marketing for Cisco Systems, the cluster provides its companies with a cadre of advisers, partners, and peers who can make connections to funding and other resources. Built into this business model is a unique giveback component. Each business that enters the Women's Technology Cluster commits a small percentage of its equity to the charitable Venture Philanthropy Fund, which over time assists female entrepreneurs and helps sustain other women-owned companies in the cluster. This new collaborative business model embodies the feminist ideals of philanthropy and social equity. Hillary Clinton, in a tongue-in-cheek poke at the "old boys network," dubbed this movement the "new girls network."[30]

Despite their potential, women-owned high-tech start-ups still have a notoriously difficult time raising venture capital, a key source of funding for new companies. Venture capitalists provide financial backing and management assistance to new, fast-growing businesses. Unlike banks, which give loans that have to be repaid as debt, venture capitalists get a portion of the company that they invest in. In 1999 women-led companies received less than 5 percent of the $36 billion invested by venture capitalists.[31] This is not surprising since venture capitalists typically review proposals submitted by people whom they know, whom they know of, or who are like them—the old boys network in action.

In response, women have once again mobilized. In 2000, the National Women's Business Council launched Springboard, an annual series of forums to help women gain access to venture capital. In cities across the country, specially selected groups of women-led companies were coached to present their business plans to hundreds of corporate, individual, and venture investors during daylong events. In just one year Springboard companies raised a total of $450 million in venture capital.[32] According to Denise Brosseau, president of the Forum for Women Entrepreneurs, which cosponsored two Springboard forums in the San Francisco Bay Area, the long-term goal of showcasing women entrepreneurs is to put them on the venture capital map—essentially to give them a jump start into the venture capitalists' network.[33]

In 1994 there was another development just as ground-breaking as Springboard, perhaps even more so. Inroads Capital Partners started the first-ever venture capital fund targeting women entrepreneurs. Today four other funds—Women's Growth Capital Fund, Milepost Ventures (formerly Viridian Capital), Fund Isabella, and Axxon Capital—have followed suit.[34] These funds, all managed *and* founded by women, focus investments on early-stage companies that are led, founded, or owned by women, as well as companies that sell products or services catering primarily to women. Willa Seldon, cofounder and general partner of Milepost Ventures, recalls, "When we first started our fund, a number of people said, 'Why would you even think about doing that?'" Seldon and her peers must feel an enormous sense of satisfaction (and validation) since increasing visibility for women entrepreneurs has translated into real dollars. "There is direct investment [by VC firms] of course," she continues. "But it usually ends up being more after you take into account angel investors [wealthy individuals—women or men—who invest directly in start-up companies, business incubators for women, and additional resources like educational workshops]. Women VC firms have driven larger community backing."[35]

Full participation in a capitalist society is contingent upon private ownership—of money, property, and assets. The relationship is straightforward: ownership grants participation. This is a dynamic from which women have historically been, for the most part, excluded. In the past, legislation curtailed women's rights to ownership of property. Even since (white) American women received legal rights to personal property in the nineteenth century, their participation has been restricted by a culture that views men as the purveyors of monetary and economic matters. Many women continue to face limitations on their ability to participate fully in capitalist society.[36] Yet women with money who invest in women-owned businesses are supporting women's empowerment on many levels. Women can take charge of their own assets. They can invest with an eye toward empowering other women who are in turn starting their own businesses. All these women have the potential to be role models and philanthropists (not merely earners) for the next generation of women.

Virtual Organizing, Global Activism

After I left engineering, I joined a group of women who use technology for feminist empowerment. I bought a one-way train ticket from Toronto to San Francisco to help start a nonprofit organization for girls. Five years later, while I am fully immersed in local, national, and international advocacy for girls and young women, technology remains an integral part of my work, but like other women, I have redefined my involvement with it. Now, as one of the cofounders of the Youth Caucus of the United Nations Commission on the Status of Women, I use Internet technologies to fight for women's rights. In a sense, I have come full circle. I left a job in technology because there was no gender awareness or sensitivity there, and I now use the Internet to organize young women activists from around the world.

The Internet has revolutionized the way we organize. While e-mail, websites, Listservs, search engines, and newsgroups have improved communications for all groups, they have been particularly effective in serving a women's political agenda. All over the world, women's groups tend to be small, helping communities on a local, grassroots level. Historically they have worked in isolation, having little communication with one another. . . . As access to the Internet worldwide has grown exponentially, this circumstance has changed drastically. Even in poor rural communities women may now have access to a computer with an online connection, albeit not with the frequency that we take for granted in the United States. Nonetheless, even sporadic access has globally facilitated information-sharing and coalition-building among women's groups in unprecedented numbers. Through Listservs that help build online communities, young women activists from Nigeria and Bosnia share learning about peer education models in HIV-AIDS prevention, and youth activists from Kenya and India exchange information about the state of girls' and young women's education in their countries.

The Internet offers possibilities for inclusion, diversity, and transparency that feminists have always aspired to but have sometimes had difficulty achieving. New technologies have sped up our communications, allowed us to share information on a grand scale, and given an immediacy to what we do. My favorite image of these new practices remains the computer room set up for the thousands of women's activists who converged on the UN in June 2000 for the Special Session of the General Assembly, also known as Beijing + 5. At each of the twenty or so computer terminals sat a women's rights activist from a different country e-mailing the latest information about the negotiations in New York back to her colleagues at home while hearing feedback on lobbying strategy from the dozens of activists from her country who could not be at the United Nations. If information is power, then that little room was power central.

The Internet has also changed how we interact with government, making it easier for us to influence legislation, demand accountability, and promote democratic participation. Women who have been reluctant to take a visible role in the women's movement now have the option of being "armchair activists" who can have an impact without leaving their homes or sacrificing anonymity. Rebecca Tadikonda epitomizes this new breed of women's activist. "I got an e-mail from a friend of mine about [the appointment of Attorney General John] Ashcroft and clicked on to the website," she says. "It only took five minutes—I wouldn't have done it if it was longer. I ended up forwarding the e-mail to a bunch of my women friends. Then I got another activist e-mail from another woman friend that I had forwarded the e-mail to. It creates networks and is an easy and personal way to get people involved in political activism—*especially* if the e-mail comes from someone you know."[37]

The Internet has definitely brought more women into the political process. According to Jennifer Pozner, founder and executive director of Women In Media News (WIMN), a media watchdog group, since President George W. Bush's inauguration, women have been embracing technology as a means of activism like never before. When President Bush reinstated the "global gag rule," which prevents government agencies from giving funds to private family planning programs outside the United States even if the money is not going to be used for abortion, Patt Morrison wrote a column in the *Los Angeles Times* denouncing it. Morrison sent the president a card that read, "President George W. Bush, in honor of President's day, a donation has been made to Planned Parenthood in your name." People began forwarding the column via e-mail, asking that donations to Planned Parenthood be made in Bush's name. The e-mail spread like wildfire, and Planned Parenthood received $500,000.[38]

Toward an Empowered Future

When we think of technology, we often think more of the *use* of technology—using computers, e-mail, cell phones—and less of the *creation* of technology—designing computer software and hardware. The distinction is important because women now relate to technology much differently then men do. Women tend to be users more than creators of technology, whereas men are as much creators as they are users. Women have clearly used technology to their advantage in their activist work and business lives, but they are often shut out from creating the technology. Being good at using technology and adapting it for our political activism and financial independence is a huge step forward. But women must also play an integral part in creating the technology. To ensure that women are not left behind, we must develop ways to educate and graduate more women engineers and computer scientists and facilitate their participation in the workforce. Bridging this gap will ensure that future generations of feminists will not only express their activism from the outside, through existing technology, but also from within, through new technologies that are created with a gender lens and communities of color in mind.

. . .

According to the Institute for Women and Technology, most product designers create products with themselves in mind.[39] As a result, most new products reflect the desires of the single, eighteen-to thirty-five-year-old men who design them. What if women were at the forefront of creating technology? We can imagine a spectrum of changes from the trivial—keyboards to fit women's smaller hands—to products with broad societal consequences. Will women engineers choose to perpetuate the multibillion-dollar military industry that keeps us locked in war games all over the globe? Or will they apply their intelligence and expertise to solving more pressing global problems?

As a movement, young feminists must continue to fight for meaningful representation and participation in the technology workforce and, equally important, continue to create their own workforces. But there is much work to be done. Gender equity in computer access, knowledge, and use cannot be measured solely by how many women send e-mail, surf the Net, or perform basic functions on the computer. The new benchmark should emphasize computer fluency—being able to interpret the information that technology makes available, mastering analytical skills and computer concepts, employing technology proactively, and imagining innovative uses for technology across a wide range of problems and subjects.[40]

NOTES

1. Anita Borg, *Technology, Democracy, and the Future* (Palo Alto, Calif.: Institute for Women and Technology, 2001), http://www.iwt.org/newsletter/nlarticles/techanddemocracy.html.

2. U.S. Department of Labor, Bureau of Labor Statistics, "BLS Releases 2000–2010 Employment Projections," 3 December 2001, http://www.bls.gov/news.release/ecopro.nr0.htm.

3. Mary Thom, *Balancing the Equation: Where Are Women and Girls in Science, Engineering, and Technology?* (New York: National Council for Research on Women, 2001) http://www.ncrw.org/research/iqsci.htm.

4. Patricia B. Campbell and Lesli Hoey, *Saving Babies and the Future of SMET in America* (Washington, D.C.: Congressional Commission on the Advancement of Women and Minorities in Science, Engineering and Technology Development [CAWMSET], 1999).

5. Advocates for Women in Science, Engineering and Mathematics, "AWSEM Gender Equity Facts in Brief," 25 May 2000, http://www.ogi.edu/satacad/awsem.html.

6. Congressional Commission on the Advancement of Women and Minorities in Science, Engineering and Technology Development (CAWMSET), *Land of Plenty: Diversity as America's Competitive Edge in Science, Engineering and Technology* (Arlington, Va.: 2000), 50.

7. American Association of University Women (AAUW) Educational Foundation, *The AAUW Report: How Schools Shortchange Girls* (Washington, D.C. 1992).

8. Patricia B. Campbell and Beatriz Chu Clewell, "Science, Math, and Girls . . . Still a Long Way to Go," *Education Week*, 15 September 1999, 50, 53.

9. Katie Wheeler, interview with the author, 26 April 2001.

10. CAWMSET, *Land of Plenty*, 59.

11. Ibid, 18.

12. Lisa Vaas, "Minorities Are Crossing the Digital Divide—Industry, Government Work to Close the Gap," *PC Week*, 31 January 2000, 65.

13. Anemona Hartocollis, "Ideas and Trends: Women Lawyers; Justice Is Blind. Also, a Lady," *New York Times*, 1 April 2001, late ed., 3.

14. National Science Foundation, "Table 26: Engineering Degrees Awarded by Degree Level and Sex of Recipient: 1966–2000" (Washington, D.C.), http://www.nsf.gov/sbe/srs/nsf02327/pdf/tab26.pdf.

15. Patricia Campbell, interview with the author, 12 December 2000.

16. Karen A. Calo, "Why Women Aren't Becoming Engineers," *San Francisco Chronicle*, 11 April 2001, 23.

17. Sokunthear Sy, interview with the author, 14 December 2000.

18. Laurie J. Flynn, "Compressed Data: Survey on Women's Role in Silicon Valley," *New York Times*, 23 April 2001, C3.

19. Sokunthear Sy, interview with the author, 14 December 2000.

20. Michael D. Haydock, "The GI Bill," *American History* 2, no. 17 (September–October 1996), 31.

21. CAWMSET, *Land of Plenty*, 11.

22. Internet is Great Equalizer for Women," *Employment Review*, February 2001, http://www.employmentreview.com/2001-02/departments/CNjobhunt.asp.

23. Ibid.

24. Center for Women's Business Research, "Key Facts," October 2001, http://www.nfwbo.org/key.html.

25. Ta'chelle Herron, interview with the author, 10 April 2001.

26. Flynn, "Women's Role in Silicon Valley."

27. Small Business Administration, Office of Women's Business Ownership, "Introduction," 18 April 2001, http://www.sbaonline.sba.gov/womeninbusiness/welcome.html.

28. Rebecca Tadikonda, interview with the author, 19 April 2001.

29. James N. Baron, Michael T. Hannan, Greta Hsu, and Ozgecan Kocak, "Gender and the Organization-Building Process in Young, High-Tech Firms," *The New Economic Sociology*, eds. Mauro F. Guillén, Randall Collins, Paula England, and Marshall Meyer (New York: Russell Sage Foundation).

30. D. M. Osborne, "A Network of Her Own," *Inc. Magazine*, September 2000, http://www.inc.com/articles/details/0,3532,CID20125_REG3,00.html.

31. Ibid.

32. Springboard Enterprises, "About Springboard," 2001, http://www.springboard2000.org.

33. Lakshmi Chaudhry, "Springboard for Women's Biz," *Wired Online*, 27 January 2000, http://www.wired.com/news/print/0,1294,33846,00.html.

34. Ibid.

35. Willa Seldon, interview with the author, 13 July 2001.

36. Robin Stern and Melissa Bradley, "Women and Money," *New Capitalist*.

37. Women all over the United States protested the appointment of John Ashcroft as attorney general because of his dismal record on women's issues. Rebecca Tadikonda, interview with the author, 19 April 2001.

38. Robin Clewley, "Women Power Web of Protests," *Wired Online*, 16 April 2001, http://www.wired.com/news/politics/0,1283,43063,00.html.

39. Institute for Women and Technology, http://www.iwt.org/home.html.

40. AAUW Educational Foundation, *Tech-Savvy: Educating Girls in the New Computer Age* (Washington, D.C., 2000), http://www.aauw.org/research/girls_education/techsavvy.cfm.

FIFTY-ONE

◆◆◆

The Mommy Tax (2001)

Ann Crittenden

Ann Crittenden is a former reporter for *The New York Times, Fortune,* and *Newsweek.* Her widely published articles on economics and finances earned her a Pulitzer Prize nomination.

On April 7, 1999, the Independent Women's Forum, a conservative antifeminist organization, held a news conference at the National Press Club in Washington, D.C. Displayed in the corner of the room was a large green "check," made out to feminists, for ninety-eight cents. The point being made was that American women now make ninety-eight cents to a man's dollar and have therefore achieved complete equality in the workplace.

The sheer nerve of this little exercise in misinformation was astonishing. Upon closer examination, it turned out that the women who earn almost as much as men are a rather narrow group: those who are between the ages of twenty-seven and thirty-three and who have never had children.[1] The Independent Women's Forum was comparing young childless women to men and declaring victory for all women, glossing over the real news: that mothers are the most disadvantaged people in the workplace. One could even say that motherhood is

What is the Value of Unpaid Labor?

1. Decide which non-market activities are work, e.g., cooking, cleaning, childcare, yard work, and repairs. If someone else could do these tasks they count as work.

2. Record how much time is spent on these activities.

3. Calculate the money value of that time.

   • Estimate what it would cost to hire someone to do all the jobs performed by a wife and mother—the "housekeeper wage" approach.

   • Estimate the cost of hiring different specialists for the various services, e.g.,

cleaners, cooks, childcare workers, etc.—the "specialist wage" approach.

Both these methods underestimate the value of women's unpaid labor because they are based on the low wage rates for work traditionally done by women rather than the level of a middle manager or social worker.

• Estimate the homemakers' "opportunity costs"—or the amount she would expect to earn outside the home. This gives much higher valuations for women who can command high rates of pay in the workforce.

Source: Crittenden (2001) pp. 79–80.

now the single greatest obstacle left in the path to economic equality for women.

For most companies, the ideal worker is "unencumbered," that is, free of all ties other than those to his job. Anyone who can't devote all his or her energies to paid work is barred from the best jobs and has a permanently lower lifetime income. Not coincidentally, almost all the people in that category happen to be mothers.

The reduced earnings of mothers are, in effect, a heavy personal tax levied on people who care for children, or for any other dependent family members. This levy, a "mommy tax," is easily greater than $1 million in the case of a college-educated woman.[2] For working-class women, there is increasing evidence both in the United States and worldwide that mothers' differential responsibility for children . . . is the most important factor disposing women to poverty.

. . . The much-publicized earnings gap between men and women narrowed dramatically in the 1980s and early 1990s. All a girl had to do was stay young and unencumbered. The sexual egalitarianism evident in so many television sit-coms, from *Friends* to *Seinfeld* to *Ally McBeal*, is rooted in economic reality. Young women don't need a man to pay their bills or take them out, any more than men need a woman to iron their shirts or cook their dinner. Many childless women under the age of thirty-five firmly believe that all of the feminist battles have been won, and as far as they're concerned, they're largely right.

But once a woman has a baby, the egalitarian office party is over. I ought to know.

Million-dollar Babies

After my son was born in 1982, I decided to leave the *New York Times* in order to have more time to be a mother. I recently calculated what that decision cost me financially.

I had worked full-time for approximately twenty years, eight of those at the *Times*. When I left, I had a yearly salary of roughly $50,000, augmented by speaking fees, freelance income, and journalism awards. Had I not had a child, I probably would have worked at least another fifteen years, maybe taking early retirement to pursue other interests. Under this scenario, I would have earned a pension, which I lost by leaving the paper before I had worked the requisite ten years to become vested. (The law has since changed to allow vesting after five years with one employer.)

My annual income after leaving the paper has averaged roughly $15,000, from part-time freelance writing. Very conservatively, I lost between $600,000 and $700,000, not counting the loss of a pension. Without quite realizing what I was doing, I took what I thought would be a relatively short break, assuming it would be easy to get back into journalism after a few years, or to earn a decent income from books and other projects. I was wrong. As it turned out, I sacrificed more than half of my expected lifetime earnings. And in the boom years of the stock market, that money invested in equities would have multiplied like kudzu. As a conservative estimate, it could have generated $50,000 or $60,000 a year in income for my old age.

At the time, I never sat down and made these economic calculations. I never even thought about money in connection with motherhood, or if I did, I assumed my husband would provide all we needed. And had I been asked to weigh my son's childhood against ten or fifteen more years at the *Times*, I doubt whether the monetary loss would have tipped the scales. But still, this seems a high price to pay for doing the right thing.

The mommy tax I paid is fairly typical for an educated middle-class American woman. Economist Shirley Burggraf has calculated that a husband and wife who earn a combined income of $81,500 per year and who are equally capable will lose $1.35 million if they have a child. Most of that lost income is the wages forgone by the primary parent.[3] In a middle-income family, with one parent earning $30,000 per year as a sales representative and the other averaging $15,000 as a part-time computer consultant, the mommy tax will still be more than $600,000. Again, this seems an unreasonable penalty on the decision to raise a child, a decision that contributes to the general good by adding another productive person to the nation.

. . .

Those who care for elderly relatives also discover that their altruism will be heavily penalized. A small survey of individuals who provided informal, unpaid care for family members found that it cost them an average of $659,139 in lost wages, Social Security, and pension benefits over their lifetimes. The subjects reported having to pass up promotions and training opportunities, use up their sick days and vacations, reduce their workload to part-time, and in many cases even quit their paid jobs altogether. This exorbitant "caring tax" is being paid by an increasing number of people, three-quarters of them women.[4]

The mommy tax is obviously highest for well-educated, high-income individuals and lowest for poorly educated people who have less potential income to lose. All else being equal, the younger the mother, and the more children she has, the higher her tax will be, which explains why women are having fewer children, later in life, almost everywhere.

The tax is highest in the Anglo-Saxon countries, where mothers personally bear almost all the costs of caring, and lowest in France and Scandinavia, where paid maternity leaves and public preschools make it easier for mothers to provide care without sacrificing their income.

Most women never think about the mommy tax until they have an encounter with rude reality. Virginia Daley was an interior designer for Aetna Life & Casualty in Hartford, Connecticut. After almost ten years with the company, and consistently good performance reviews, raises, and promotions, Daley was fired in 1993 from her $46,640-a-year job. The dismissal occurred after she had had a baby and then tried to arrange a more flexible work week, in accordance with the company's stated policies.

Not only were her requests for flexibility denied, her workload was actually increased in the wake of a massive corporate downsizing. Already frustrated, Daley was furious to learn in late 1992 that Aetna's chairman Ronald Compton had been awarded a "Good Guy" award from the National Women's Political Caucus for his support of model family-leave programs. (Aetna also consistently made *Working Mother* magazine's annual list of best companies for employed mothers, and in 1992 was touted as one of the *four* "most family-friendly companies" in America by the Families and Work Institute.)

Daley dashed off a memo to Compton, charging that "when it comes to offering flexible family arrangements, Aetna's performance is far from award-winning." The memo concluded that "realistic options for Aetna employees to meet their family obligations without sacrificing their careers are not generally available today. To continue to represent to Aetna employees and the national media that these options are available is unconscionable."

Three months later Daley was terminated, on the grounds of poor performance.

She sued, and the case went to trial in 1997. Aetna maintained that Daley had lost her position because she wasn't able to handle the additional responsibilities that she was assigned after the downsizing (and the baby). The jury essentially agreed with Aetna. It also agreed with the company that Daley was not speaking out on a matter of public concern when she complained that numerous employees were being denied family-friendly schedules. Her memo to Compton was therefore not "protected speech," i.e., an important statement that entitles an employee to protection from retaliation. Daley lost the case, as well as subsequent appeal.

. . .

According to Daley's lawyer, Philip L. Steele, the jury foreman told him after the trial that although the panel was very sympathetic to Daley, its members felt she had probably "overextended" herself. "They believed it was just too hard for a woman to raise little kids and do a good job," Steele told me. "The thinking was, how can a woman do all that, not how could a company do that?"

The decision cost Daley dearly. She calculates that over the next five years following her departure from Aetna, her income as a part-time consultant was from $90,000 to $154,000 lower than if she had stayed at the company. And that doesn't include the loss of Aetna's annual contribution to her 401K retirement plan. "I figure that if I'd stayed at Aetna another ten years," Daley told me, "their contribution to my 401K alone would have been more than $25,000. That could easily become more than six figures by the time I am retirement age. . . . People need to know that once you have a child you'll definitely be poorer."[5]

. . .

The Cost of Being a Mother

A small group of mostly female academic economists has added another twist to the story. Their research reveals that working mothers not only earn less than men, but also less per hour than childless women, even after such differences as education and experience are factored out. The pay gap between mothers and nonmothers under age thirty-five is now larger than the wage gap between young men and women.

. . .

In the United States . . . Jane Waldfogel at Columbia University . . . set out to assess the opportunity cost of motherhood by asking exactly how much of the dramatic wage gains made by women in the 1980s went to women without family responsibilities. How many of the female winners in the 1980s were people like Donna Shalala, Janet Reno, Elizabeth Dole, and Carole Bellamy, the director of UNICEF: childless women whose work patterns were indistinguishable from those of traditional males.

Back in the late 1970s, Waldfogel found, the difference between men's and women's pay was about the same for all women. Nonmothers earned only slightly higher wages. But over the next decade things changed.[6] By 1991, thirty-year-old American women without children were making 90 percent of men's wages, while comparable women with children were making only 70 percent. Even when Waldfogel factored out all the women's differences, the disparity in their incomes remained—something she dubbed the "family wage gap."[7]

Why do working mothers earn so much less than childless women? Academic researchers have worried over this question like a dog over a bone but haven't turned up a single, definitive answer.

Waldfogel argues that the failure of employers to provide paid maternity leaves is one factor that leads to the family wage gap in the United States. This country is one of only six nations in the world that does not require a paid leave. (The others are Australia, New Zealand, Lesotho, Swaziland, and Papua New Guinea.)[8] With no right to a paid leave, many American mothers who want to stay at home with a new baby simply quit their jobs, and this interruption in employment costs them dearly in terms of lost income. Research in Europe reveals that when paid maternity leaves were mandated, the percentage of women remaining employed rose, and women's wages were higher, unless the leaves lasted more than a few months.[9]

In the United States as well, women who are able to take formal paid maternity leave do not suffer the same setback in their wages as comparably placed women who do not have a right to such leaves. . . .

Paid leaves are so valuable because they don't seem to incur the same penalties that employers impose on even the briefest of unpaid career interruptions. A good example is the experience of the 1974 female graduates of the University of Michigan Law School. During their first fifteen years after law school, these women spent an average of only 3.3 months out of the workplace, compared with virtually no time out for their male classmates. More than one-quarter of the women had worked part-time, for an average of 10.1 months over the fifteen years, compared with virtually no part-time work among the men. While working full-time, the women put in only 10 percent fewer hours than full-time men, again not a dramatic difference.

But the penalties for these slight distinctions between the men's and women's work patterns were strikingly harsh. Fifteen years after graduation, the women's average earnings were not 10 percent lower, or even 20 percent lower, than the men's, but almost 40 percent lower. Fewer than one-fifth of the women in law firms who had worked part-time for more than six months had made partner in their firms, while more than four-fifths of the mothers with little or no part-time work had made partner.[10]

Another survey of almost 200 female M.B.A.s found that those who had taken an average of only 8.8 months out of the job market were less likely to reach upper-middle management and earned 17 percent less than comparable women who had never had a gap in their employment.[11]

Working-class women are also heavily penalized for job interruptions, although these are the very women who allegedly "choose" less demanding occupations that enable them to move in and out of the job market without undue wage penalties. The authors of one study concluded that the negative repercussions of taking a little time out of the labor force were still discernible after twenty years.[12] In blue-collar work, seniority decides who is eligible for better jobs, and who is "bumped" in the event of lay-offs. Under current policies, many women lose their seniority forever if they interrupt their employment, as most mothers do. Training programs, required for advancement, often take place after work, excluding the many mothers who can't find child care.[13]

Mandatory overtime is another handicap placed on blue-collar mothers. Some 45 percent of American workers reported in a recent survey that they had to work overtime with little or no notice.[14] . . . Where does that leave a woman who has to be home in time for dinner with the kids? Out of a promotion and maybe out of a job. Increasingly in today's driven workplace, whether she is blue- or white-collar, a woman who goes home when she is supposed to go home is going to endanger her economic well-being.

The fact that many mothers work part-time also explains some of the difference between mothers' and comparable womens' hourly pay. About 65 percent of part-time workers are women, most of whom are mothers.[15] Employers are not required to offer part-time employees equal pay and benefits for equal work. As a result, nonstandard workers earn on average about 40 percent less an hour than full-time workers, and about half of that wage gap persists even for similar workers in similar jobs.

Many bosses privately believe that mothers who work part-time have a "recreational" attitude toward work, as one Maryland businessman assured me. Presumably, this belief makes it easier to justify their exploitation. But the working conditions they face don't sound very much like recreation. A recent survey by Catalyst, a research organization focused on women in business, found

that more than half of the people who had switched to part-time jobs and lower pay reported that their workload stayed the same. Ten percent reported an increase in workload after their income had been reduced. Most of these people were mothers.[16]

Another factor in the family wage gap is the disproportionate number of mothers who operate their own small businesses, a route often taken by women who need flexibility during the child-rearing years. . . . In 1999, women owned 38 percent of all U.S. businesses, compared with only 5 percent in 1972, a remarkable increase that is frequently cited as evidence of women's economic success. One new mother noted that conversations at play groups "center as much on software and modems as they do on teething and ear infections."[17]

Less frequently mentioned is the fact that many of these women-owned businesses are little more than Mom-minus-Pop operations: one woman trying to earn some money on the side, or keep her career alive, during the years when her children have priority. Forty-five percent of women-owned businesses are home-based. And the more than one-third of businesses owned by women in 1996 generated only 16 percent of the sales of all U.S. businesses in that year.[18]

In 1997, although women were starting new businesses at twice the rate of men, they received only 2 percent of institutional venture capital, a principal source of financing for businesses with serious prospects for growth. Almost one-quarter of female business owners financed their operations the same way that they did their shopping: with their credit cards.[19]

Some researchers have suggested that mothers earn less than childless women because they are less productive. This may be true for some mothers who work at home and are subject to frequent interruptions, or for those who are exhausted from having to do most of the domestic chores, or distracted by creaky child-care arrangements. But the claim that mothers have lower productivity than other workers is controversial and unproven. . . .

It's Discrimination, Stupid

It is revealing that those occupations requiring nurturing skills, such as child care, social work, and nursing, are the most systematically underpaid, relative to their educational and skill demands.[20] These are also, of course, the occupations with the highest percentage of females. But men who are primary caregivers also pay a heavy price: a "daddy tax," if you will. This suggests that at least part of the huge tax on mothers' earnings is due to work rules and practices and habits of mind that discriminate against anyone, of either sex, who cannot perform like an "unencumbered" worker. In other words, discrimination against all good parents, male or female.

Surveys have found that wives may adore husbands who share the parenting experience, but employers distinctly do not. A majority of managers believe that part-time schedules and even brief parental leaves are inappropriate for men.[21] When Houston Oiler David Williams missed one Sunday game to be with his wife after the birth of their first child, he was docked $111,111.

A survey of 348 male managers at twenty Fortune 500 companies found that fathers from dual-career families put in an average of *two* fewer hours per week—or about 4 percent less—than men whose wives were at home. That was the only difference between the two groups of men. But the fathers with working wives, who presumably had a few more domestic responsibilities, earned almost 20 percent less. There it is again: a 20 percent family wage gap.[22]

"Face time still matters as much or more than productivity in many companies," Charles Rodgers, a management consultant in Boston, said. Rodgers told me about a man in a high-tech company who regularly came to work two hours early so that he could occasionally leave early for Little League games with his son. He was given a poor performance rating.[23]

. . .

Only eight states currently have laws prohibiting discrimination against parents in the workplace. Examples include taking a primary parent off a career track out of an assumption that the individual couldn't do the work; hiring someone without children over a more qualified person with children; forcing a primary parent to work overtime, or else; and refusing to hire a single parent, though the employer hires single, childless people. In the course of my reporting, I encountered numerous mothers who felt that their employer's refusal to arrange a shorter workweek, particularly after the birth of a second baby, amounted to career-destroying discrimination.

The Second Baby

Cindy DiBiasi, a former reporter for WUSA-TV, a Gannett-owned station in Washington, D.C., is one of the countless mothers who found that the birth of a second baby, and the impossibility of arranging a short workweek to accommodate it, destroyed her career.

DiBiasi is a slim, attractive, dark-haired woman with a brisk air of self-assurance instantly recognizable as the glossy competence displayed every night on the evening news. In 1989, she became the medical reporter for WUSA, a job that she had long coveted. Two days before she was scheduled to begin her new position, DiBiasi discovered that she was pregnant. She hadn't yet signed a contract, and she didn't tell her bosses for seven weeks. But she was able to put her pregnancy to use, producing a series on having a baby, even arranging for a camera crew to be at the hospital when her daughter was born in August of 1990. She remembers being on camera even after her water broke. "They didn't have to worry about me being committed," she commented wryly.

After a ten-week maternity leave, DiBiasi was back on the job from 10:00 A.M. until 6:00 P.M., producing a five-minute live segment for the 4:00 P.M. news show and a taped piece for the 6:00 P.M. news. All went well until just before her child's first birthday, when DiBiasi had to take three days off to visit her sick father in Illinois. A week later, her child's nanny was unable to come to work for two days in a row. DiBiasi was about one hour late on the first day and two hours late on the next. (Her husband took off work on both days to be at home.)

She was subsequently called into her boss's office and told that she would lose vacation time for the days she took to go to Illinois. "I was amazed," she told me. "I asked if it had anything to do with my being late those two days and explained what had happened. I asked if there was a problem with my work. He said no, but he was getting red in the face. . . . A long time ago a female reporter told me that whenever my child got sick, I should always say it was *me* who was sick. I remember thinking, that's bullshit. How could they want me to be dishonest? But now I wasn't so sure.

"I didn't like the feeling I was getting, so I asked for a meeting with the two top executives. They told me that there was a perception that I was not working 'full days.' I reminded them that I was on the air twice a day, every day, and that nights at home I was reading medical journals to keep up in my field. 'How does the desk know that?' they asked.

"Then they mentioned, almost casually, that they might want to take the medical unit in a different direction, but 'that has nothing to do with you or your work,' they assured me.

"At one point one of them said something like 'the problem is that you think you're the only one who has a family.'. . . Now the guy who said this had a son in college, and the other two men with children had stay-at-home wives. I pointed out that I had a *one-year-old*. And that if I had problems dealing with it I'd tell them. They just looked at me, with this blank, flat look."

During the next six months, DiBiasi was asked to do a live segment on the 5:00 P.M. news, along with her pieces for 4:00 P.M. and 6:00 P.M. She agreed, thinking, "As long as I'm not away from my kid any more time, I'll kill myself for them—that'll solve this. . . . Then I found out that I was pregnant again. I realized that I couldn't keep up the pace, so I asked if I could switch to a three-day week, with a prorated salary cut. The news director said he would think about it.

"I worked all the way up to my delivery, which was in June of 1992. I had eight weeks of maternity leave. Two days before I was to go back, I had a call from the assistant news director. 'We really need help on general assignment,' he said. So after I get back, for the next two months I'm doing fires, accidents, you name it, and I'm not getting home at six-thirty anymore. One day they asked me to do a live shoot in Annapolis at the end of the day, and I said I couldn't—it meant I wouldn't get home until nine P.M. My boss said, 'Can't your nanny just stay?'

"I said, 'Number one, no, she can't stay, and number two, if she *could* stay, I don't want to get home that late. If I do that, I won't see my kids at all.'

"He just looked at me. Than he said, 'So, you'll see them tomorrow.'"

DiBiasi's new position was a demotion, but she continued a while longer, getting home late regularly. Finally, she told the desk that there was no way to be general assignment reporter if one had to be at home at 6:30 P.M. She was told she had to continue on general assignment.[24]

The managers at WUSA had put DiBiasi in a job they knew she couldn't do. She hired a lawyer and began the process of suing the station. The important thing, her lawyer told her, was to stay on the job, no matter how bad it got. Otherwise, management could argue that she had left voluntarily. However, the demands of staying on the job, and preparing a case, proved overwhelming.

"I was suppose to be secretly tape-recording all our meetings," DiBiasi said, "and then come home and transcribe the tapes at night. I had the job, I had to deal with the attorney, my husband was traveling a lot, and I had two little babies. . . . I finally had to quit when it all became just too much of an emotional drain. I would have had to sell short everything in my life I care about; there would have been no more essence to me."

DiBiasi also decided not to sue: "I knew that if I pursued this, they would say I wasn't a good reporter. And there is a contradiction in these kinds of suits, because in order to get punitive damages, you have to show *damage;* you have to show that you're a wilting flower who has been hurt by all this. If you're strong, and are determined not to be a victim, they can argue, so what's the problem?"

So, after fifteen years in television reporting, DiBiasi lost a job she loved, a six-figure income, her health insurance, and her economic independence. Slowly, she was also losing public recognition, a newsperson's working capital. All because she had had the temerity to try to work for fewer days a week while her two children were young. For all of her talent, energy, and drive, DiBiasi, like millions of other mothers, was suddenly only a husband away from financial disaster.[25]

As Cindy DiBiasi's story illustrates, the most popular form of family planning in the United States and other wealthy countries—two children, spaced not too far apart—is incompatible with most women's careers. Even if a new mother and her employer can cope with one child, the second baby is often the final straw. The most sympathetic employers can prove surprisingly resistant to the second baby. A well-known feminist economist told me that she had gone to great lengths to bend the rules at her university to accommodate one of her graduate students who had become pregnant. The woman was given a year's extension on her schedule and time out to be with her new infant. Then, just before she was due to come back, she became pregnant again.

My friend, who believed she had been as progressive as was humanly possible, felt betrayed. She thinks the woman was foolish not to realize that the system can only accommodate so much deviation. "you have to play by the rules to some extent, especially when other people have stuck their neck out for you," she said. This professor, by the way, has no children herself, but she does have tenure.

How to Lower the Mommy Tax

Until now, narrowing the gender wage gap in the United States has depended almost entirely on what might be called the "be a man" strategy. Women are told to finish school, find a job, acquire skills, develop seniority, get tenure, make partner, and put children off until the very last minute. The longer a woman postpones family responsibilities, and the longer her "preparental" phase lasts, the higher her lifetime earnings will be.

Ambitious women of the baby-boom generation and younger have by and large tried to be a man in this way. A good example is Susan Pedersen, a historian who achieved tenure at Harvard in the mid-1990s. By that time, she was married and in her late thirties, but she had postponed having children until her academic career was secure. Motherhood was something she wanted very much, she commented during an interview, but it posed a serious threat to her professional dreams and had to be delayed.[26]

As Pedersen's success demonstrates, this strategy does work—for the very small number who are able to pull it off. And women who have their children later in life do have higher lifetime earnings and a wider range of opportunities than younger mothers. The advice dished out by writers like Danielle Crittenden—no relation—an antifeminist ideologue who has urged women to marry and have their babies young, ignores this, along with some other hard truths. Crittenden never tells her readers that young parents tend to separate and divorce much more frequently than older couples, leaving young mothers and children vulnerable to poverty. Large numbers of the women who end up on welfare are there because they have done exactly what she recommends: married and had children young and then been left to support them alone.[27]

But trying to be a man has its own risks. Many baby-boomer women postponed families only to discover that when they wanted to become pregnant, it was too late. . . . And millions of women don't feel that being a man is the way they want to live their lives. . . .

An alternative strategy is followed in countries like France and Sweden, where the government, private employers, and/or husbands share much more of the costs of raising children. This makes it far easier for women to be mothers and to work. In France, for example, families with two preschool-age children receive about $10,000 worth of annual subsidies, including free health care and housing subsidies and excellent free preschools.[28] As a result, child poverty is unusual, and the pay gap between mothers and others is much smaller in France than in the United States. . . .

Whenever Europe is singled out as a model, the usual response is that Americans would never support such generous social policies. But in fact, the United States already does have an extremely generous social welfare state. But unlike the welfare states of western Europe, the American government doesn't protect mothers; it protects soldiers.

Men who postpone or interrupt civilian employment for military service pay a tax on their lifetime earnings that is quite comparable to the mommy tax. White men who were drafted during the Vietnam War, for example, were still earning approximately 15 percent less in the early 1980s than comparable nonveterans.[29] This "warrior wage gap" is strikingly similar to the family wage gap, again indicating that mothers' lower earnings are not entirely attributable to gender discrimination.

But there is unquestionable discrimination in the way the government has responded to the financial sacrifices that soldiers and parents, particularly mothers, make. . . .

To illustrate this double standard, let's look at two men with identical characteristics. One works as a computer technician, is married to a woman in the same occupation, and has two children. He is a conscientious father, making sure to be home for dinner every night, even helping to cook it. He takes his kids to sporting events, attends teacher conferences, and tries to limit his travel and outside commitments.

This man is legitimately worried about what his dedication to family will do to his career. Let's say he does get fewer promotions and over the years earns 15 to 20 percent less than he would have had he not shared the family obligations. We can realistically say that he pays a significant daddy tax.

Now take a man with the same education and imagine that he spends three or four years in military service. He is worried that these years out of his active professional life will affect his economic future, and they might, although his boss believes that his service was good leadership training. But whatever career losses he suffers will be cushioned by the generous thanks that the nation pays to its ex-servicemen. He discovers that his warrior tax is lowered by these benefits, which are available to him even if he never got near a battlefield:

- He can stay in the military for twenty years as a *part-time reservist* and draw half pay for the rest of his life.[30]

- He will get special preference for government jobs. Extra points will be added to whatever civil service exams he may take, and some rules are written so that he will be chosen over closely ranked nonveterans. In government layoffs, he will have extra protection. Unlike mothers or fathers who find that after a few years out of the job market their credentials are downgraded, his are given a major boost by veterans' preferences.

- If he decides to go back to school for more education, he can qualify for thirty-six months of cash payments worth more than $17,000.

- He also qualifies for a government-guaranteed housing loan, financed at interest rates usually half a percentage point below the going market rate.

- He can make use of a hospital system costing the federal government $17 billion a year.

- He will have access to special low auto insurance rates, available only to individuals with some connection to the military. These come in especially handy when his teenage son begins to drive.

- As long as he remains in the military or works on a military base as a civilian, he can enjoy subsidized child care provided by the best day-care system in the country. For only $37 to $98 a week (in 1997), depending on his income, he can enroll his children in infant and toddler care and preschools staffed by expertly trained and licensed teachers. In the private sector, the fees would be two to four times higher, for often inferior care.

None of these benefits is contingent on service in combat. In 1990, 6.3 million of the 27 million veterans eligible for benefits served only during peacetime. Millions of ex-servicemen, who do not even have a hangnail to show for their harrowing experience in uniform, enjoy the same government largesse that flows to the veterans who were once put in the way of danger.

The benefits paid to military veterans are . . . second only to Social Security in terms of government payments to individuals. And they do an excellent job of reducing the warrior tax. The educational benefits in particular help veterans overcome many of the economic disadvantages they suffer by leaving the workplace for a few years.

A congressional study in the early 1990s concluded that the veterans of World War II who took advantage of the G.I. Bill to earn a college degree enjoyed incomes of up to 10 percent more than they might otherwise have earned. Society was also the beneficiary, for the additional taxes paid by the college-educated veterans during their working lives more than paid for the program.[31]

It hardly needs to be said that there is no G.I. Bill, no health care, no subsidized housing, and no job preferences for mothers. As things now stand, millions of women sacrifice their economic independence and risk economic disaster for the sake of raising a child. This says a lot about family values, the nation's priorities, and free riding.

A third way to reduce the mommy tax would be to expand the antidiscrimination laws to cover parents. Joan Williams, a law professor at American University's Washington College of Law, argues that the design of work around masculine norms can be reconceptualized as discrimination. As an example, Williams suggests that if a woman works full-time, with good job evaluations for a significant period, then switches to part-time because of family responsibilities and is paid less per hour than full-time employees doing similar work, she could claim discrimination under the Equal Pay Act. Williams believes that disparate-action suits could also be filed against employers whose policies (including routine and mandatory overtime, promotion tracks, resistance to part-time work) have a disparate impact on women, producing disproportionate numbers of men in top-level positions.[32]

The essential point is that existing laws, and new laws preventing discrimination against people with caregiving responsibilities, could go a very long way toward improving mothers' lifetime earnings.

The Ultimate Mommy Tax: Childlessness

The cost of children has become so high that many American women are not having children at all. One of the most striking findings of Claudia Goldin's survey of white female college graduates is their high degree of childlessness (28 percent).

Now that the baby-boomer generation is middle-aged, it is clear that more than one-quarter of the educated women in that age group will never have children. Indeed, the percentage of all American women who remain childless is also steadily rising, from 8 to 9 percent in the 1950s to 10 percent in 1976 to 17.5 percent in the late 1990s.

Is this rising childlessness by choice? Goldin thinks not. She found that in 1978, while in their twenties, almost half of the college-educated boomers who would remain childless had said that they did want children. Goldin calculated that almost one-fifth of this entire generation (19 percent) of white college graduates was disappointed in not having a child. This is the ultimate price of the "be a man" strategy that has been forced on working women. For women in business, the price is staggering. A recent Catalyst survey of 1,600 M.B.A.s found that only about one-fifth of the women had children, compared with 70 percent of the men.

. . .

Americans have a hard time realizing that such deeply personal choices as when or whether to have a child can be powerfully circumscribed by broader social or economic factors. American women, in particular, are stunningly unaware that their "choices" between a career and a family are much more limited than those of women in many European countries, where policies are much more favorable to mothers and children.

. . .

In sum, an individual woman's decision whether to have a child or not, and whether to stay home or not, is heavily influenced by her country's willingness to help her bear the costs. In . . . the United States, the official message is *caveat mater*, or "mothers beware": you're on your own.

NOTES

1. This calculation was made by economist June O'Neill, using data from the National Longitudinal Survey of Youth. June O'Neill and Solomon Polachek, "Why the Gender Gap in Wages Narrowed in the 1980s," *Journal of Labor Economics* 11 (1993): 205–28. See also June O'Neill, "The Shrinking Pay Gap," *Wall Street Journal*, October 7, 1994.

2. The concept of the mommy tax was inspired by development economist Gita Sen, who has described the extra economic burden borne by women as a "reproduction tax."

3. Burggraf assumes that the more flexible parent's earnings average $25,750 a year, versus $55,750 for the primary breadwinner. She then multiplies $30,000 (the differ-

ence between what the two parents earn) by 45 (the years in a working lifetime) to get the $1.350 million. *The Feminine Economy and Economic Man*, p. 61.

4. The National Alliance for Caregivers estimates that the number of employed people who provide care for elderly family members will grow to 11 to 15.6 million in the first decade of the twenty-first century.

5. *Virginia V. Daley et al. v. Aetna Life & Casualty et al.*, August 12, 1994. Virginia Daley, personal communication, May 1996; Philip L. Steele, personal communication, October 2000.

6. Jane Waldfogel, "Women Working for Less: Family Status and Women's Pay in the US and UK," Malcolm Wiener Center for Social Policy Working Paper D-94-1, Harvard University, 1994.

7. Jane Waldfogel, "Understanding the 'Family Gap' in Pay for Women with Children," *Journal of Economic Perspectives* 12, no. 1 (winter 1998): 137–56. See also Waldfogel, "The Family Gap for Young Women in the United States and Britain," *Journal of Labor Economics* 11 (1998): 505–19.

8. Elizabeth Olson, "U.N. Surveys Paid Leave for Mothers," *New York Times*, February 16, 1998.

9. Christopher J. Ruhm, "The Economic Consequences of Parental Leave Mandates: Lessons from Europe," *Quarterly Journal of Economics* CXIII, no. 1 (1998): 285–317.

10. Wood, Corcoran, and Courant, "Pay Differentials," pp. 417–28.

11. This 1993 study was coauthored by Joy Schneer of Rider University's College of Business Administration and Frieda Reitman, professor emeritus at Pace University's Lubin School of Business.

12. Joyce Jacobsen and Arthur Levin, "The Effects of Intermittent Labor Force Attachment on Female Earnings," *Monthly Labor Review* 118, no. 9 (September 1995): 18.

13. For a good discussion of the obstacles to mothers' employment in relatively well-paying blue-collar work, see Williams, *Unbending Gender*, pp. 76–81.

14. This survey of 1,000 workers was conducted by researchers at the University of Connecticut and Rutgers University, and was reported in the *Wall Street Journal*, May 18, 1999.

15. A survey of more than 2,000 people in four large corporations found that 75 percent of the professionals working part-time were women who were doing so because of child-care obligations. Only 11 percent of the male managers surveyed expected to work part-time at some point in their careers, compared with 36 percent of women managers. *A New Approach to Flexibility: Managing the Work/Time Equation* (New York: Catalyst, 1997), pp. 25–26.

16. See Reed Abelson, "Part-Time Work for Some Adds Up to Full-Time Job," *New York Times*, November 2, 1998.

17. Tracy Thompson, "A War Inside Your Head," *Washington Post Magazine*, February 15, 1998, p. 29.

18. Information on women-owned businesses provided by the National Foundation for Women Business Owners in Washington, D.C., September 2000.

19. Noelle Knox, "Women Entrepreneurs Attract New Financing," *New York Times*, July 26, 1998.

20. See Paula England, George Farkas, Barbara Kilbourne, Kurt Beron, and Dorothea Weir, "Returns to Skill, Compensating Differentials, and Gender Bias: Effects of Occupational Characteristics on Wages of White Women and Men," *American Journal of Sociology* 100, no. 3 (November 1994): 689–719.

21. [One] study found that 63 percent of large employers thought it was inappropriate for a man to take *any* parental leave, and another 17 percent thought it unreasonable unless the leave was limited to two weeks or less. Martin H. Malin, "Fathers and Parental Leave," *Texas Law Review* 72 (1994): 1047, 1089; cited in Williams, *Unbending Gender*, p. 100.

22. This study, by Linda Stroh of Loyola University, was reported by Tamar Lewin, "Fathers Whose Wives Stay Home Earn More and Get Ahead, Studies Find," *New York Times*, October 12, 1994.

23. Charles Rodgers, personal communication, October 1993.

24. Details of this story were provided by Cindi DiBiasi in November of 1995. When I contacted DiBiasi's former boss, Jack Hurley, he said that these conversations "didn't ring a bell." Neither did other tense encounters between the two. Hurley, who is now with the Freedom Forum in Arlington, Virginia, did remember calling DiBiasi to tell her that she was being taken off the medical beat and given general assignment. "The news director felt that Cindy was a stronger street reporter than medical reporter. The new assignment reflected that," he said.

25. Nancy Norman, a videotape editor who worked at Channel Nine while DiBiasi was there, confirmed her story, and told me that "most of the women at Nine stood behind Cindy." Norman herself sued the company for sexual discrimination and was awarded half a million dollars by a jury. She said it was easier for her to sue because she didn't have any kids.

26. Susan Pedersen, personal interview, June 1996.

27. Being a young mother obviously worked for Crittenden, who was affluent enough to have purchased a $1.3-million home in Washington, D.C., while still in her midthirties. But not many mothers enjoy such options.

28. Barbara Bergmann, personal conversation, January 4, 1999.

29. Joshua D. Angrist, "Lifetime Earnings and the Vietnam Era Draft Lottery: Evidence from Social Security Administrative Records," *American Economic Review* 80, no. 3 (June 1990): 313–31.

30. The United States is the only country in the world that offers *full* retirement to military reservists. In 1993 the cost to taxpayers was $1.9 billion. See Congressional Budget Office, *Reducing the Deficit: Spending and Revenue Options,* Washington, D.C., 1995, p. 64.

31. David O'Neill, "Voucher Founding of Training Programs: Evidence from the G.I. Bill," *Journal of Human Resources* 12, no. 4 (fall 1977): 425–45; and Joshua D. Angrist, "The Effects of Veterans' Benefits on Education and Earnings, "*Industrial and Labor Relations Review* 46, no. 4 (July 1993): 637–57.

32. Williams, *Unbending Gender*, pp. 101–10.

◆◆◆

FIFTY-TWO

To Whom Much Is Given, Much Is Expected: Successful Women, Family and Responsibility (2003)

Veronica Chambers

Former editor and writer at *Newsweek* and *New York Times Magazine,* **Veronica Chambers** is also a children's book author. Much of her work, including her award-winning memoir *Mama's Girl* (1996), focuses on stories that reflect her African and Latina heritage.

To whom much is given, much is expected" was both personal and political to young black women in the 1970s. At the time, Walteen Grady-Truely was getting her undergraduate degree at Michigan State University. She remembers two things distinctly:

the culture of black nationalism that permeated her campus and the sense of marriage panic that hung over her heart. "As I reflect over the atmosphere of the 70s, my decisions were overlaid by the sense that the revolution was going to happen tomorrow and that you had to choose sides," says Walteen. "If you didn't make the right choice, you could hurt the whole black community. It wasn't like I could have the luxury of finding myself. I had to choose the right side of the battle lines. . . ."

For those women who came of age right after the civil rights movement, life was a mixture of often contradictory rules. You were supposed to say it loud about being black and proud, but to assert your independence with black men was counterrevolutionary. Education was a key component to uplifting the race, but as Stokely Carmichael so famously put it, "the black woman's place in the movement is prone." Black men could, and would, date white women without losing their place in the black power movement. Yet, black women who chose to date white men were nothing more than self-deluded, voluntary chattel, ignorant of 200 years of rape and slavery.

At six-feet tall, with a short salt-and-pepper afro, Walteen is now in her late 40s. At the time of our first conversation she's recruiting mentors for at-risk teens as the Director of the New York Volunteer for Youth Campaign. She radiates a strong, calming presence. As we sit and talk at a Thai restaurant near her New York City office, she is in the process of divorcing her husband of 15 years. Her smooth, dark skin is unlined, but there is a definite furrow across her brow. She has been taking a memoir-writing course, she tells me, and it has helped her as she tries to assess the choices that she has made in her life; there are pieces of her younger self that she misses and that she hopes to recover.

Walteen spent her teenage years traveling with her family; her father was in the military. She lived in Nigeria for four years, attended a Swiss boarding school for another year, then graduated from a high school in Bangkok. One of the memories that her writing course has brought up is that in Thailand, as a high school senior, she asked a white classmate to the Sadie Hawkins dance. Returning to the United States to go to school, she would never have considered such a possibility. "When I went to college, there was such a strong era of nationalism," she remembers. "I felt that I didn't have the right not to marry a black man. I felt I had a responsibility to have a black child."

"I didn't have the right." "I felt I had a responsibility." Those are powerful words to use when discussing one's personal life. How did she end up shouldering so much guilt? "It's guilt and responsibility," Walteen corrects me. "I think the two things are very much entwined. No one ever told me that I could be true to myself and still carry out that sense of responsibility." Yet she is hardly alone in her generation of women, who allowed the politics of the black power movement to dictate who and how she loved.

Guilt was also a factor in how Walteen chose her life's work. "Oh absolutely!" she says emphatically.

"I believe it is what drove me in almost all my career choices. I chose to go into education. Before that, I wanted to be a lawyer. It was always with an eye towards creating a world where there would be more people like me, where there would be more people who shared a quality educational background, who had the advantage of having access to the whole world, not just the neighborhood."

This was a powerful notion for Walteen, who felt it was her life's work to bridge the gaps between the blacks who were haves and those who were have-nots. Growing up as a middle-class black girl, Walteen remembers complaining to her parents about her sense of isolation. "I didn't have any friends like me," she says. "I wasn't meeting people. My mother used to say, 'Well, I've been lonely all my life.' I guess she thought that was comforting, but it wasn't." Her mother's comments are clearly a painful memory for Walteen. During our most recent interview, she had moved back home to the Poconos where she's an instructor of education and coordinator for the Learning Support Center at the local Penn State campus. She moved so her son could be near his grandmother and attend better schools, but she worries that while he is now thriving academically, he's also suffering from the same loneliness she once did. "I don't think it's new," she says. "But there's a sense that if you're African American and on the cutting edge economically and educationally, there are not going to be other people like you. There are so few of us. I definitely have that feeling and my son has it, too."

Several years earlier, when she worked in Tribeca, she decided to register her son, Romare, at a nearby school. She knew it would be a marked improvement from the school he attended in their Fort Greene neighborhood. In an effort to ease the transition, she made it a point to continue Romare's play dates with his best friend, Rodney. The boys were both ten when Walteen overhead the following conversation. Rodney asked, "So what's your school like?" Romare said, "Oh, it's a school." Rodney paused, then asked, "Well, do you have gunshot holes in your windows?" It's a painful memory for Walteen, whose face, as she tells the story, displays a mixture of shame and hurt. "It just blew me away," she says. "It was almost as if we had to have a choice between having a community of black people and an environment that was very unsafe or having a safer environment physically and no community. It hurts me to see that repeated over and over again." Even in this day and age, a whole new generation of young people are being offered opportunities that aren't afforded the majority. As far as we have come, there is still a talented tenth—with all the weight of responsibility and guilt that comes along with it.

The Talented Tenth

In 1903, the great scholar W. E. B. DuBois published his masterwork, *The Souls of Black Folk*. DuBois's writing was an intellectual, improvisational pastiche of narrative fiction and social criticism, anthropology and state of the union address—it reads like highly developed literary jazz. In it, he famously declared "the problem of the 20th century is the problem of the color line." DuBois would be hailed as a visionary, again and again. His words resonated throughout almost all of the 20th century's great social struggles and tragedies. Whether it was the Turkish massacres of Armenians, the German slaughter of Jews, or the colonizers' ways with the colonized, it's remarkable how we've been driven again and again into war, massacre and upheaval by the power of racial difference. DuBois, who always meant his quote to address a far greater scale than racial politics in the United States, saw it coming.

DuBois's prophecy was marked not only by the eloquence of his words, but also by the breadth of his scope: what ambitious statesman—black or white—would look a hopeful people in the eye and tell them that racism would last not a decade or two, but 100 years? As bold as it was, his proclamation was hardly a news flash. Even Langston Hughes's fictional colored man on the corner, Jesse B. Semple, could have looked at the masses of sharecropping southerners and northern factory workers addled by poor working conditions and minimum pay and declared "Houston, we have a problem." Any uneducated black man or woman could have told you that Lincoln didn't solve the race problem as they cited the tyranny of hapless, random violence that was a constant threat to their lives. In those fragile years, as former slaves and their children tried to construct a place for themselves within the severe constraints of the northern-mandated freedom, *The Souls of Black Folk* could have been merely a preacher yapping at the choir.

DuBois, however, operated like a jazz musician. For the most part, his book wasn't aimed at black folks at all. Like other great race men and women

before him, such as Frederick Douglass and Sojourner Truth, he sweetened the melody for the liberal white audience that he hoped would start swaying in beat to his cause. Yet he knew that blacks were listening and, in order not to lose their attention and support, he would sometimes curve a note in their direction. His theory of the Talented Tenth swung like that. DuBois's Tenth was the segment of the black community who had the wit, social skills and means to uplift the entire race. This Talented Tenth would be the leaders and architects of black achievement in America. Our shining glory.

From the beginning, the theory brewed controversy. At the turn of the century, the problem of entry into the upper echelons of black society was indeed the problem of the color line. Black elites monitored membership in the most prestigious black civic organizations, churches, fraternities and sororities with a paper bag test: anyone darker than a paper bag need not apply. Despite their own intraracism, these people considered themselves sanctioned by birth and skin color to lead the poorer black masses. They beamed with pride at DuBois's notion of the Talented Tenth because surely, they reasoned, he was talking about them.

Conversely, there were those who disagreed vehemently with DuBois. Some of them could care less about the colorism that plagued the black upper classes. These critics simply saw the idea of a Talented Tenth as being inherently divisive and problematic. How could we commit the wealth of our resources and energies to just one-tenth of our community? How could we be sure that once educated and anointed they would uplift our cause? And what happens, generation after generation, to those who are left behind? It's a question that black people struggle with to this day. Cheryl Mills, former deputy White House counsel and current Oxygen Media vice president, put it this way to Lynette Clemetson in a *Newsweek* article: "We're now getting to this place where we have the privilege to decide if we are all going to be on the same bus or whether or not we are going to get off the bus. I think the black community is finding itself now at this crossroads where it has to decide. Are we going to continue to be connected as a community or are the privilege levels and the progress we're seeing going to mean different things for different [people]?"[1]

Take, for example, an anecdote separated from the race issue altogether. Each year, a poor village has ten students that complete the modest lessons taught in its one-room schoolhouse. They pick one young man to continue his education in the big city. They pay for his schooling, his lodging, his expenses—everything, so he can focus on his studies and become a doctor. Obligation, and some might say guilt, would predicate that the young man returns to the village to open a practice, and perhaps one day, a hospital. But who's to say that the young man will? Maybe he will take a job at a research facility; maybe his destiny is not to cure colicky babies and ill farm animals, but to find the cure to some interminable disease. Maybe his aim or intention isn't even as noble as that. Maybe he takes a job with a big city hospital, gets rich and builds himself a big house. What happens to the village then? What good is their investment in the Talented Tenth? Maybe they should have sent two students to college, with partial scholarships each. Maybe they should have truly hedged their bets and sent three.

Shaking Off the Guilt: A Generational Shift

At 31, Angela Kyle feels much less anxious than Walteen Grady-Truely about finding a place in the black community. And she feels none of the guilt. It's the gift that women of Walteen's generation have given to the women of mine: we have the luxury to find ourselves without worrying that our actions are, as Walteen phrased it, "hurting the whole black community." Angela and I meet at the Bel Age Hotel in Los Angeles; she lives nearby in Beverly Hills. Angela is tall and thin with the kind of All-American freshness of a J. Crew model. Today, she's wearing a close-fitting T-shirt, slacks and has a cardigan tied around her hips. Angela's chestnut-colored skin is flawless, without a hint of makeup, and she wears her shoulder-length hair in a fashionable bob. She's just finished her second day in her new job as senior director of business development at Live Planet—a company often in the news because of its two co-founders, Ben Affleck and Matt Damon. The heartthrobs want to bring together old media (film and television) with new media (the Internet) in intriguing, profitable ways.

It's a high-stakes gambit. Other Internet-related companies led by such visionaries as Steven Spielberg and Ron Howard blew through millions of dollars, then failed. Ben and Matt have Hollywood convinced they'll do better. Angela's an anomaly in the office; the executive suite is largely a good young

boys' network from Boston and their early days as struggling actors in L.A. She's an Ivy League graduate, with business degrees from Columbia University and the London School of Economics. She's a young, black woman in a business that could care less about affirmative action or the Talented Tenth or diversity. She's at Live Planet for one reason alone—to make deals and making deals is what she loves.

Angela remembers that growing up, "I lived in a predominantly white neighborhood and went to a predominantly white school. In order to balance the whole white thing, I went to a black church." It's interesting to me that even Angela's language is more flippant, more casual, than Walteen's pained confessions. By the late 1970s and early 1980s, "the whole white thing" was not a big deal at all. "I was really active in church stuff so I had a group of black girls my age," she says. "Then at school, I had white female friends. I never really tried to bridge the two or bring them together, I was comfortable with them being separate."

Later, at Brown University, Angela felt none of the social or political pressures that Walteen experienced at Michigan State. At Brown, she joined a group called OUAP, the Organization of United African Peoples. But this was hardly her social center. "I wanted to be in OUAP," she says. "I wasn't really active, but I was at least present and accounted for." The desire to be simply "present and accounted for" is a seismic shift from Walteen's college years when she felt weighed down by her obligations to the movement. . . . In contrast, Angela describes her experience with black groups at Brown to being similar to the way her Asian friends felt about Asian-American organizations. "We were all aware of what was going on in our respective communities," she says. "But what drove my experience was meeting people that I had things in common with. I was pretty comfortable forging this network of friends that was racially mixed."

Similarly, when Angela talks about her career in business development, race hardly enters the conversation at all. She's not pressured to find a black husband, hasn't even begun to think about kids. "My thought is that right now I can't get married and I can't have kids," she says. "For me, the ultimate success as an adult is career success, getting to the top of something, winning awards. This is the arena in which I feel like I'm making my mark on the world. I know that I can't balance my life with family in any way, shape or form so I haven't really tried."

In Angela's conversation, there are hints of so many things, especially the luxury of young black women today to put career first. . . . There may be so much talk in the public sphere about successful black women and the dearth of highly educated, high-income earning male counterparts, but there seems to be little realization that for women like Angela, marriage and family aren't a priority. She doesn't know or care if there are "enough" black men out there. She's not really looking. It's not that she doesn't value her black girlfriends or that she isn't interested in black men. It's just that right now she's having too much fun and is way too ambitious to worry.

"My friend Suzie was here last weekend," Angela mentions. "She was saying that sometimes it stresses her out to be in a group of all black women. She says that no matter where the conversation starts, be it on the topic of work or family, it always ends on men and how everyone's looking and can't find one. Blah. Blah. Blah. It's not so much that the fantasy of a Prince Charming doesn't apply to me as a black woman. It's more that I'm a workaholic and I have other issues." And on that note, Angela gets up to leave. Her company is throwing a party to announce the winner of a screenplay competition they've been running. It will be one of her first opportunities to get face time with the heads of her company. With a wave, she is off—to gather intelligence, to meet and greet, to make deals.

Even though they live on different sides of the country, I know that Walteen would be proud of Angela. That in some ways, Angela's attitude is something she is striving for herself. Both women represent a vision of DuBois's Talented Tenth, but they embody it in radically different ways. The last time we met, Walteen said that what she has always admired about my generation is that "You've always represented for me the right to have stuff, the right to carve our own space and not just be the banner carrier for the race. You feel a right to be yourself. This is the next level of black liberation: the right to be ourselves, the right to define our own successes. In the '60s, I might have defined success as the right to fight for my people. That was the pinnacle. You are part of a group of women who are enjoying their lives. That's the next frontier."

Who Do We Owe?

If the civil rights act of 1964 was our economic emancipation, the open sesame to access to the education and jobs that would level the playing field,

then it is a relatively recent freedom. One of the markers of the black middle class is that, for the most part, its members are still closely tied to those in real poverty. The women I interviewed spoke of their concern for the black community in general. But they could also each point to a sibling or a cousin or other relatives who were struggling.

To a certain extent, the problem of the villager who goes off to medical school and feels an obligation to his community is one these women can relate to easily. On a Saturday afternoon in Hoboken, I got together with a group of 30-something and 40-something women. The walls of Tracie Howard's living room were painted a warn golden hue that brought to mind the faded gilt of Renaissance Italy. The chandelier was a 1920s Art Deco find and framed photos of family and friends graced the surface of her baby grand piano. Paintings by prominent African-American artists hung on most walls, while a lighted breakfront displayed her collection of three-legged teacups from Limoges, Japan and Italy. In complete defiance of the old paper bag rule, the women were a rainbow mix from fair-skinned to very dark-skinned. All of them were members of the upper middle class and had ventured to Tracie's from their homes in New York City, Westchester and Greenwich, Connecticut.

The women talked animatedly about their passion for mentoring and community service. For them, it's more than doing a good deed. They see themselves in the young people that they are helping, they believe that their actions are improving the lot not of "poor black folks" but of "brothers and sisters." There's a big difference in the way these women speak about community service and the language their white society counterparts use. By doing good, they feel they are also "doing the right thing," as Spike Lee so aptly called it. Furthermore, their charitable efforts keep them in touch with a home they don't want to leave behind.

I probe a little deeper, and each woman admits that while community service is fulfilling, trying to meet the needs of poorer family members is almost always a losing battle. The women in their 40s have come to terms with the economic disparities in their own families. "No guilt," says one of the guests, an investment banker on Wall Street. Her simple declaration is followed by so many "Amens," the room is almost transformed into Sunday church. But these are women in their 40s, who've made the tough choices and don't take any mess off anyone. I found that among my peers, women in our 30s, there's not always the same confidence. We're not always sure that we don't owe the village every penny in our pockets.

Though I'm not a banker or Wall Street broker, my "Amen" was right there with the others. As the first person in my immediate family to graduate from college, I basked in the glow of achievement. I lived the dream deferred. A year after graduation, I was making more money than my mother was. My role as the family money store began. Siblings and other more distant relatives began to pull a guilt trip on me: I'd been "lucky" to get a scholarship, "lucky" to meet whites who mentored me and offered me jobs. They'd not been so lucky in life. Where they lived, life was hard—or had I forgotten?

Looking back, I could say that I was young and easily influenced. But I know that it was more than that. Despite the hefty student loan bill that I pay each month, I would not have been able to attend college at all had it not been for the largesse of a W. E. B. DuBois scholarship that handled a sizeable portion of my tuition every year. My school, Simon's Rock College, is in Great Barrington, Massachusetts: birth home of DuBois. My reading of *The Souls of Black Folk* at the age of 16 had a powerful impact on how I viewed race and its obligations. I would never have called myself part of the Talented Tenth, but I certainly took my place among its platoons of strivers.

When my summa cum laude degree was rewarded with one good job after another, I knew I had to give back. And as my family laid it out for me: charity begins at home. Throughout my 20s, I buckled under the guilt and pressure and gave out thousands of dollars in "loans" that could never, would never, be repaid. Even when lending money meant draining my savings account or giving away the next month's rent, I jumped at the desperate calls in the middle of the night and the wailing darkness of "I have nowhere else to turn." Like many professional black women, I'm hardly wealthy by mainstream American standards. But compared to the poverty of those I love so dearly, the fact that I even had next month's rent in the bank meant that I was rich. Absolutely loaded. "We have extended family who think we're Rockefellers," says Robin Nelson Rice, a former pharmaceutical company executive now living in London. "We're not even Rock, forget Rockefeller! But from their viewpoint, it's 'Oh yes. Somebody comes and cleans your house. I need that job. I could be that. You could pay me that money.'

They're always calculating. 'Oh, the nanny. Do you hear that? They've got a nanny.'"

For Tarin Washington, a 32-year-old finance executive, earning an MBA roused the jealousy of old friends. As one male friend put it, "You think you're better than me because you're successful and moved out of the hood." It had been a bonanza year for Tarin: she'd recently completed her MBA and purchased a home in Connecticut as well as a used luxury model car. She says, "I realized that his perception of my having reached success was just that, perception. I wasn't anywhere near the success that I have planned for myself. I still have a very long way to go. As a matter of fact, I was still living in the 'hood, just in a new development in a different city!" But like a lot of the women I spoke to, poorer relations and friends thought that the purchase of luxury items, an advanced degree and a healthy income meant that all of your problems were solved, forever and ever.

Soon after I graduated from college I read an article in *Money* magazine that struck a similar chord about the expectations of extended family on young black professionals. The headline of the piece was: "Hunting for the First House." The sub-head read: "Home-buying can be a financial and emotional challenge for any couple. As African Americans looking in Chicago's white suburbs, Trish and Larry Harvey faced special hurdles—but overcame them."[2]

The story went on to introduce us to the Harveys, ages 26 and 29. They were "both MBAs, with fast-track jobs and a combined income close to $100,000 a year." But the article showed this couple to be more than materialistic Buppies. Although childless themselves and still so young, they were raising Trish's 16-year-old niece, Raven. And their "carefully calculated budget" included not only money for rent and insurance, food and a vacation fund, but $500 a month toward assisting relatives. Money that, out of politeness, might be called a loan; but money the Harveys never expected to see again.

Who Is Giving? What Is Expected?

I can't remember the first time I heard the phrase, "to whom much is given, much is expected," though I suspect I was still in diapers. Nor can I tell you how often the phrase was repeated throughout my childhood; the number would have to be in the hundreds, if not the thousands. I heard it every Sunday that I attended church and every Saturday when our family went visiting. I heard it from my teachers when I received high grades and heard it, underlined, when I brought home Cs. The parents of my friends uttered it during pep talks after school and old black ladies murmured it in my ear when I respectfully leaned forward to kiss their powdery cheeks. Along with the West Indian equivalent of "Walk good" and the also often-repeated "Each one teach one," "to whom much is given, much is expected," was passed down as more than a platitude. It was the knight's code, a secret moral compass that would guide me should I make it through the woods, into the kingdom of higher education and on to the palaces of good fortune beyond.

Though I did not know it then, the reference is biblical. It's in the New Testament, Luke 12:48: "For unto whomsoever much is given, of him shall be much required: and to whom men have committed much, of him they will ask the more." The first sentence of the verse had been passed down in the black community (no doubt by savvy pastors who found their collection plates to be a little light). The second part of the verse may not have been uttered, but was certainly implied. I know that I'm not alone among middle-class women and men who have had to learn that you aren't a traitor to the people when you turn down a relative or a friend for a loan. I also know that as black women continue to outpace black men educationally and financially, more of the burden of helping falls upon us. We pay for our success not only financially, but emotionally as well.

In the work place, the "much is given, much is expected" motto can be a double-edged sword for successful black women. Clearly, our success provides an opportunity for service. "It's about taking ownership," one 30-something programmer . . . told me. "I love going out on recruiting trips and being able to reach out to young black kids. Even if they don't come and work for my company, I can give them the tools and tips they need to get ahead. I feel like I'm helping people."

At the same time, the expectation can be that our success means we should be ever grateful and behave accordingly. We are dealt our daily share of racism and sexism, yet our class—and the means by which we make our living—predicates that we must often bite our tongue or risk being labeled as "angry," "difficult," or even "racist.". . .

At home, the challenge can be equally painful. One need only look at the hit film *Soul Food*, the story of three sisters and their families in Chicago.

The most successful one is a lawyer named Terry. As portrayed by Vanessa L. Williams, Terry is brittle, caustic and quick to criticize. The message the filmmakers send is that Terry's ambition has drained her soul. She's on her second marriage and, when husband number two commits adultery, it's Terry's fault for working so hard. Her sister Maxine, in contrast, has no loot but a lot of love: she's been married to her husband for 11 years and the two still flirt shamelessly. Maxine has three beautiful kids, while Terry is trying, but childless. Maxine can also cook huge Sunday dinners, steeped in Southern tradition. Terry has no domestic skills, but a seemingly endless ability to write checks. The film sets her up as a bad guy, but I painfully recognized her plight. Who can blame her for being so cranky when she's the one who's got to pay her mother's hospital bills, fund her youngest sisters' business ventures and bail her brother-in-law out of jail? With not so much as a thank you, mind you. It's little wonder that when Terry explodes, she says, "As far as you know, I'm an ATM. It's always Automatically Terry's Money." My generation is getting better at shaking off the guilt, but for those of us who come from families that were born poor and have stayed poor, balancing the weight of expectation is never easy.

What We Owe Ourselves

As chair of the African-American studies program at Princeton University, Valerie A. Smith is a high-profile figure in a high-pressure job. She is the Woodrow Wilson Professor of Literature and the author of many critically acclaimed books, including *Self-Discovery and Authority in Afro-American Narrative* and *Representing Blackness: Issues in Film and Video*. Among certain passionate circles of Afro-Bohemia, she is known as the woman who brought Andrea Lee's *Sarah Phillips* back into print, a novel about race, class and identity that is now taught in hundreds of colleges nationwide. She is smart. She is powerful. But what I hear more than anything about Valerie Smith is that she is physically fit. I mean really fit. I begin to hear a rumor that while she was a professor at UCLA, she would only hold student conferences during her daily hour-and-a-half hike up Runyon Canyon. I hear that she is known for urging her black women colleagues, students and friends not to give so much of themselves that they don't take time for themselves. It's when this last comment drifts back to me that I decide I have to meet her.

We meet for tea, at 4:00 at Sally Lunn's in Princeton, an old-fashioned teashop that looks like a scene out of *Mary Poppins.* I ask Valerie, who is indeed fit and who looks barely old enough to buy alcohol, much less chair a university department, about her fitness journey. "In junior high school and high school, I really wasn't athletic at all," she tells me. "For a variety of reasons. Mostly I was this high-achieving academic kid, who couldn't get into competitive sports. Then I began running in graduate school. There was a group of us who got together and running was a social thing."

. . .

I ask her about the student conferences held during grueling canyon hikes and she laughs out loud. "I'm notorious for that," she says, mischievously. "I'd get my grad students to have conferences with me during my 6:30 A.M. hike. I felt like I was sending a message: channel your anxiety into this exercise. I also felt like this was a way for them to have my full attention. They certainly were not going to get an hour and a half of my time while I was busy in my office." Not only did some of her students begin to

exercise on their own, but a number of them also quit smoking. "They didn't have enough wind to talk, going up those hills," Valerie says with a smile.

. . .

Smith believes that if we are going to continue to thrive as black women we need to take care of not only our minds and our spirits, but our bodies as well. The week before we meet, thousands of black women had mourned the death of the poet June Jordan. She was 65. For me, as for others, it had echoes of the deaths of Audre Lorde, Virginia Hamilton, Sherley Anne Williams. "We're beginning to see how many of our successful sisters are dying young or suffering from chronic illness," says Smith. "We've got to pay attention to what we eat, what we do physically. We take responsibility for so much. We've got to take responsibility for ourselves."

NOTES

1. Lynette Clemetson and Allison Samuels. "We Have the Power." *Newsweek,* September 18, 2000.
2. Bill Sheeline. "Hunting for the First House." *Money,* December 1993.

F I F T Y - T H R E E

◆◆◆

Remarkable Journeys: Poor, Single Mothers Accessing Higher Education (2004)

Nolita Clark and Shannon Stanfield with Vivyan Adair

A philosophy major at Hamilton College, **Nolita Clark** graduate in 2006 and plans to go to law school. **Shannon Stanfield** is a theater major and creative writing minor, graduating in 2007. **Vivyan Adair** is a professor of women's studies at Hamilton College and director of the ACCESS project, a pilot program that assists welfare-eligible parents to earn college degrees. She authored *From Good Ma to Welfare Queen: A Genealogy of the Poor Woman in American Literature, Photography and Culture* and co-edited *Reclaiming Class: Women, poverty and the promise of education in America.*

Individuals and communities accrue enormous social, cultural, and financial benefits when low-income, single mothers are supported in post secondary educational endeavors. As two students

currently enrolled in a unique program at Hamilton College called The ACCESS Project, we understand how higher education has changed our lives and those of our peers. This project is an educational, social service, and career program that assists low-income parents in our efforts to move from welfare and low-wage work to meaningful and secure career employment through the pathway of higher education. On a daily basis, the program supports students academically as well as helps them overcome substantial obstacles such as lack of adequate childcare and transportation, domestic violence, homelessness, hunger, and low self-esteem.

Students in our program represent a broad range of experiences, abilities, strengths, and challenges. Over 85 percent of ACCESS students are single mothers; 83 percent are over 25 years of age and

58 percent are over age 30; 25 percent are physically and/or learning disabled, 48 percent have high school degrees and only 7 percent had parents who ever attended college. All live below the poverty line (95 percent of us also did so as children) and are eligible for welfare. The average number of children in our homes is 2.3 (which mirrors the national average for all families) and varies from students with only one dependent child at home to others with as many as seven children.

As a group we are fairly representative of the larger "welfare recipient" population in our area. Many of us also experience hardships typical of welfare populations in the contemporary U.S. Both as children and as adults, most of the students in our program have lacked medical and dental care, been homeless or evicted, suffered abuse, and perhaps have experienced low self-esteem and depression as a result. It is equally true, however, that once in the ACCESS program we thrive and succeed in school, work, and with our families. For example in 2003–2004, our ACCESS cohort earned a B average in our courses. We earned these grades (that we are very proud of) while caring for and nurturing our children; working and gaining valuable skills, experience, and networking connections; increasing our understanding of and commitment to the workings of our communities and our nation; and moving permanently away from social service supports.

Our individual experiences are typical of both the struggle and determination that have marked our lives and the lives of our colleagues who are all working student parents. Taken together these narratives represent both the breadth and commonalties of our experiences as low-income, single-mother students.

Nolita

I am a single mother and student who will be a senior this fall at Hamilton College. My goal is to finish my degree and go on to complete a law degree so that I can practice corporate and Native American tribal law. Today, my daughter is a healthy, inquisitive and loving four-year-old. Her life, and my own today, is very different from my own childhood, which was one of my primary motivations for enrolling in school initially.

When I was two, I was introduced to a world of violence, abuse, alcoholism, and drug addiction by my married parents. One of my very first memories was my mother being drunk and breaking my arm. My second was being so badly beaten that I was knocked unconscious. For several years, when I went to sleep at night I would wonder how long I would be able to survive in this world and whether there would be any escape from my abusive home. I was eventually removed from my parents and placed into foster care after many years of torment.

Three events have dramatically changed the course of my life. The first was that after dropping out of high school and while pregnant, I enrolled in a Native American school program in Syracuse, New York. There, patient, kind, and encouraging teachers assisted me in earning my GED. This program was also pivotal in allowing me to connect with other Native American people. I belong to the Prairie Band Potawatomi tribe of Mayetta, Kansas, and have always felt close to my people who seem to be fighting many of the same struggles in life that I am.

Second, I gave birth to a daughter who is caring, energetic, and delightful to be around. She loves me very much and looks up to me to provide her with the love and guidance she needs to be successful in life. When she was born, I realized the opportunity I had to give my daughter the very best and encourage her to reach her fullest potential in the world. The fear of my daughter ever experiencing the things I did motivates me every morning to get up and continue on the pathway I have begun for both of us.

Finally in 2001, I entered into the ACCESS Project. With the help of faculty and administrators I have successfully taken classes, learning a great deal about the world, the academy, and myself in the process. Being the single mother of an energetic pre-schooler, a full-time student, and an employee is not easy. During the school year I work about 30 hours a week and on semester breaks I work full time. I generally get about four or five hours of sleep a night and have *never* had a vacation break from school or work. While fellow students at Hamilton talk of their spring breaks and social events, I head off for work required to support my family. In my spare time, I want nothing more than to read and play and talk with my daughter. Life is difficult, and sometimes almost impossible, but we have a goal and day-by-day we know that we will make it. I will be a professional. We will own a home. My daughter will always be safe, cared for and loved, and she will graduate from high school, go to college, and never experience the pain and uncertainty that I have known.

Although I could not have envisioned this life two or three years ago, with the help of fine educators and with the inspiration my daughter provides me, I have begun a new life. I will bring honor to my daughter, my teachers, and my community. We have begun a legacy of change and are excited and secure about our future.

Shannon

I come from what many in our nation proudly refer to as the heartland. I was raised by wonderful parents who have now been married for over fifty years. We lived in rural upstate New York, where my father was a carpenter and my mother stayed at home to raise eight children. Although we never had much money, we were loved and cared for as my parents provided us with models of hard work and decency.

Like my parents before us, college was not in the plans for our futures. Following my father, my four brothers went on to become hardworking carpenters, and like my mother, my three sisters and I planned on becoming wives and mothers. When I married right after high school and followed my husband across the county so that he could pursue his career, I was confident that I was doing the honorable and reasonable thing. Yet, less than seven years later, I found myself alone with two small and rather traumatized babies, after being lied to, abused, and eventually abandoned.

I simply did not know what to do. I had no resources for putting my young family's life back together. Without any savings, with little education or work experience, I found myself at the mercy of the state. When I went to apply for minimal food stamps and medical insurance, the welfare caseworker was explicit and clear. My children and I were "a drain on the taxpayers," and I must go to work immediately. I was ashamed, embarrassed, and humiliated. Of course, I wanted to work and care for my own children, but the pay for the job to which I was assigned barely covered my rent and left nothing for baby diapers, utilities, or transportation. Each morning I would leave my children to trudge off to a job that could never support us.

The only joy I had in life during those years was being with my children late in the evenings and on the weekends when we would color and read together. Art became my therapy and I dreamed that one day I might go to college to study education and art to forge a career in education that might deliver me and my children from an uncertain and violent past. I imagined taking my children with me as I climbed over the walls built by hopelessness.

Today I am enrolled at Hamilton College and we now walk in a place where hope and opportunity abound. College allows me to wash away the stains of my past as I begin to realize my own potential and as I reshape my family's future through knowledge, self-respect, and fulfillment. It is certainly not easy being in school. I study day and night (and have an A average), work 30 hours a week as a teaching assistant, and care for my two beloved children. But it is more than worth it. In school, I study mathematics, English, anthropology, science, philosophy, and art. My children and I continue to study, learn, and grow together. Today, I am an independent, capable, and hardworking mother raising engaged, self-sufficient, and honorable children. We are on a pathway that will change our lives for the betterment of the culture and our community.

Other women in the ACCESS program share similar experiences. They work diligently and strive to learn, grow, and provide good lives for their children. Most of us have struggled, but we use those struggles to focus and increase our resolve to succeed. Our lives of pain and strength, determination and drive stand in stark contrast to the portraits painted by political pundits and welfare reform advocates about our lack of motivation and ability.

We are grateful for the opportunities we have been given but remain frustrated that because of welfare policy so many others—and certainly the neediest among us—are never allowed to even attempt to reach their fullest potential, denied the opportunity to work diligently so that they can hold their heads up with dignity as responsible and successful parents and professionals. Supporting rather than thwarting poor, single mothers like us in our efforts to access and benefit from higher education would serve as a testament to the promise of a truly free nation. It seems far wiser to re-invest in a national ethic that values and rewards hard work, integrity, diligence, and responsibility as the foundation and requirements of success, security, and the pursuit of happiness in the United States today. We are convinced that such an investment would confirm the power and potential of higher education and fulfill the promise of this nation.

9

◆◆◆

Living in a Global Economy

In September 1995 more than thirty thousand women from virtually every country in the world gathered in Huairou, China, to discuss the many issues and problems faced by women and girls around the world and to work together for change. This was the forum for nongovernmental organizations (NGOs) and was the largest meeting of women in history. A two-hour bus ride away, at the official United Nations Fourth World Conference on Women in Beijing, some five thousand delegates discussed what their governments are doing to improve women's lives and negotiated an official U.N. document, the *Platform for Action.*

There were nearly five thousand workshops listed in the NGO Forum schedule. Among the discussions about literacy and the education of women and girls, nutrition and health care for infants and adults, the need for clean water in many parts of the world, the need for jobs or guaranteed livelihood, the plight of millions of refugees, disability rights, violence against women, sexual freedom, solar stoves, and prostitution, to take just a few examples,

one theme was repeated again and again: the effects on women and girls of the globalization of the economy, and the inequality between the rich countries of the world, often located in the Northern Hemisphere, and the poorer countries of the Southern. This seemingly abstract issue affects everyone and underlies many other problems.

To understand the situations and experiences of women in the United States, it is important to know something of women's lives and working conditions worldwide and the ways we all participate in, and are affected by, the global economy. This chapter takes this wider angle of view, with nation as an additional analytical category together with gender, race, and class. The films *The Global Assembly Line* (distributed by New Day Films, www.newday.com) and *Life and Debt* (distributed by New Yorker Films, www.newyorkerfilms.com) are excellent introductions to the topic, and readers are urged to see them, if possible, in conjunction with reading this chapter. Note the significance of gender in the **international division of labor,** and

Workers in a Reebok factory in China

that this is reinforced by inequalities based on race, ethnicity, and nationality.

The Global Factory

In the past forty years or so, electronic communications and air transport have made it increasingly possible for corporations to operate across national boundaries. Now a company based in the United States, such as Nike, Playtex, IBM, or General Motors, can have much of its manufacturing work done overseas—in, for example, Indonesia, China, Mexico, the Philippines, Guatemala, or parts of Europe—by workers who are paid much lower wages than U.S. workers, as shown in the accompanying box (Collins 2003; Enloe 1995; Greider 1997; Kamel 1990; Kamel and Hoffman 1999; Ross 1997). This organization of work results in inexpensive consumer goods for the U.S. market, particularly clothing, toys, household appliances, and electronic equipment. The global assembly line now also includes computer-based services done by women in the Caribbean (Freeman 2000), and computer support to users in North America by women and men in India. Thus, our lives are

dependent on the labor of a myriad of people in a vast global network, marked by complex inequalities that may mask our interconnections, as economist Teresa Amott (1993) noted regarding the U.S. economy (see Chapter 8). We noted the crisis in care work in North America and western Europe in the previous chapter that allows—and requires—women from the Philippines, Central America, and the Dominican Republic, for example, to enter the United States to work in hospitals and nursing homes, and as child care workers and home-health aides in women's homes. These women's labor "serves as the infrastructure on which First World economic expansion depends" (Litt and Zimmerman 2003, p. 157).

Roughly 90 percent of the factory workers in **offshore production** are young women in their late teens and early twenties. Some countries, like the Philippines and China, have established Export Processing Zones (EPZs), where transnational corporations (TNCs) set up factories making products for export to Europe, the U.S., Canada, and Japan. In Mexico this is done through *maquiladoras*—factories that make goods on contract to a "parent" company, as described by María Patricia Fernández-Kelly in Reading 54. There are over 3,000 *maquildoras*

Labor Cost Comparisons in the Textile Industry, 2004–2005

REGION/COUNTRY	AVERAGE HOURLY WAGES & BENEFITS U.S.$, 2004	RATIO TO U.S. COST %
North America (NAFTA)		
Canada	18.61	118
Mexico	2.19	14
United States	15.78	100
South America		
Argentina	2.86	18
Brazil	2.83	18
Colombia	1.97	13
Venezuela	2.85	18
Western Europe		
France	21.03	133
Germany	27.69	175
Greece	11.67	74
Portugal	6.87	89
Switzerland	35.33	224
U.K.	20.17	128
Central and Eastern Europe		
Bulgaria	1.50	10
Czech Republic	3.94	25
Poland	3.80	24
Turkey	2.88	18
Northeast Asia		
China (coastal)	0.76	5
China (inland)	0.48	3
Hong Kong	6.21	39
South Korea	7.10	45
Taiwan	7.58	48
Southeast Asia		
Indonesia	0.55	4
Malaysia	1.18	7
Thailand	1.29	8
Vietnam	0.28	2
South Asia		
Bangladesh	0.28	2
India	0.67	4
Pakistan	0.37	2
Sri Lanka	0.46	3
Middle East and Africa		
Egypt	0.82	5
Israel	9.35	59
Kenya	0.67	4
Mauritius	1.57	10
Morocco	2.56	16
South Africa	3.80	24

Source: Werner International Management Consultants 2005.

in Mexico; the majority are owned by U.S. interests and located within thirty miles of the border.

Even in countries like Mexico, with protective labor and environmental legislation, these regulations are often not strongly—if ever—enforced in relation to the operations of transnational corporations. Thus, workers experience oppressive working conditions and suffer health problems such as stress from trying to make the assigned quotas; illnesses from exposure to glues, solvents, and other toxic chemicals; and lint and dust in textile factories; or poor eyesight from hours spent at microscopes. In addition, women are often subject to sexual harassment by male supervisors. Mexican women workers in *maquiladoras* have been required to undergo a pregnancy test as a condition of employment and have been denied work if they are pregnant (Human Rights Watch 1999b). Company doctors "routinely administer pregnancy tests and distribute birth control pills" (Tooher 1999, p. 39). Levimex, for example, a Tijuana *maquiladora* owned by the Leviton Manufacturing Co., gave contracts to workers for a month, three months, or one year. Each time the contract was renewed, women had to take a pregnancy test. When workers complain and organize to protest such dire conditions, they are often threatened that the plants will close and move elsewhere; indeed, this has sometimes happened. For example, Nike has moved some of its production from South Korea, where women have campaigned for better wages and working conditions, to Indonesia and China, thereby pitting workers in one country against those in another.

Many thousands of U.S. workers have been laid off through automation or the movement of jobs overseas. Fewer and fewer products are made in the United States. With a lack of manufacturing jobs, the job market in the United States is becoming increasingly polarized between professional jobs and low-paying service work—flipping burgers at McDonald's, for example—that offers few, if any, benefits or job security. Rising unemployment, or underemployment—where people are overqualified for the jobs available—has had devastating social and economic effects across the country.

Public attention in the United States is increasingly focused on the poor working conditions of those who make many of the things we buy, espe-

cially the role of sweatshops. The U.S. General Accounting Office defines sweatshops as employers that violate more than one federal or state labor law. Pharis Harvey, executive director of the International Labor Rights Fund, defines a sweatshop as "any workplace where the wages are inadequate, the hours too long, and the working conditions endanger safety or health—whether or not any laws are violated" (Facts on the Global Sweatshop 1997, p. 16). Sweatshops are common in the garment industry and toy manufacturing (Gordon 2005; Louie 2001; Ross 1997). They exist in many countries, including the United States. The U.S. Department of Labor estimates that more than half the country's 22,000 sewing shops violate minimum wage and overtime laws. Many of these workers are employed in cramped factories, often with blocked fire exits, unsanitary bathrooms, and poor ventilation. According to Sarah Wood (1997), "The terms 'sweatshop' and 'sweating' were first used in the nineteenth century to describe a subcontracting system where the middlemen earned their profit from the margin between the amount they received from a contract and the amount they paid their workers. This margin was 'sweated' from the workers," who received minimal wages for excessive hours worked under poor conditions. Nowadays, too, the garment industry is organized in such a way that big-name retailers like Gap, for example, and brand-name manufacturers like Jessica McClintock contract with sewing shops that hire workers to make the finished product, although they do not directly control workers' wages and working conditions (see Figure 9.1). The retailers and manufacturers, in effect, determine wages for garment workers by controlling the price to the contractor.

Supermarkets and stores in countries of the global North source the products they sell from farms and factories worldwide. Wal-Mart, the world's biggest retailer, exemplifies this model. The company buys products from 65,000 suppliers worldwide and sells to over 138 million consumers every week through its 1,300 stores in 10 countries (Oxfam International 2004, p. 4). Companies at the top of global supply chains seek flexibility and the freedom to operate wherever is most beneficial for them. This results in precarious conditions of employment for those at the bottom of the chain—whether in the global South, migrants

Profit to the retailer: $78

The largest member of the food chain; large retail chains set the prices and the styles of garments.

Profit to the manufacturer: $33

Retailers purchase clothing from manufacturers, which design and register product lines and purchase the fabric. They then contract out the actual clothing production.

Profit to the contractor: $13

Receives orders from manufacturers, then often subcontracts the work out. Cutting, dyeing, and sewing clothing can be performed by different contractors.

Cost to the contractor: $33
Material: $20, Misc. Labor: $10, Seamstress: $3

Garment workers cut, stitch, and dye the clothing that consumers buy at the retail stores.

The skirt sells for $157.

You get paid $3.

Who gets the difference, and how do they spend it?

FIGURE 9.1 Markup of $157 skirt. (*Source: Los Angeles Herald Examiner* garment industry investigation.)

to countries in the global North, or people in poor communities within rich countries. Subcontractors in the middle of the chain are pressured for low prices and speedy turnaround. They pass this on to their workers in low wages, stressful quotas, and enforced overtime in the scramble to fill orders (see Figure 9.2).

In 2005, changing global trade rules affected the garment industry with closures and huge job losses in several countries including Cambodia, El Salvador, the Dominican Republic, Lesotho, and Mauritius, and severe uncertainty for workers and midchain suppliers in many others (Earnest 2005). The earlier rules had imposed a quota system that limited manufacturers' access to the U.S. clothing market.

Korean and Taiwanese companies had set up textile factories in Africa and other parts of Asia purely as a way round the quotas, importing all machinery and materials. On January 1, 2005, this agreement expired, opening up the global garment trade to increased competition, with speculation that China will get a much larger market share on account of its low wage rates and increasing technological sophistication. However, there is also benefit in being located nearer to the U.S. market as speed of shipping is a crucial factor in this highly competitive and faddish business.

Despite serious risks to their jobs, workers are organizing for better pay and working conditions. The National Mobilization Against Sweatshops, for example, was formed by the Chinese Staff and Workers' Association and works with women garment workers in New York's Chinatown (Louie 2001). Increased consumer awareness in North America and western Europe has brought about some changes in wages and working conditions for overseas workers, as consumers have attempted to hold corporations accountable for exploitative conditions. A major campaign against Nike starting in 1997, for example, protested inhumane working conditions in plants making Nike shoes in Vietnam and China (Greenhouse 1997; Sanders and Kaptur 1997). In February 1997, North Olmstead, Ohio, a working-class suburb of Cleveland, became the first U.S. city to ban municipal purchases of sweatshop-made products (Facts on the Global Sweatshop 1997, p. 16). In 1999 Duke University students staged a sit-in in the university president's office to ensure that clothing bearing Duke's name is not made in sweatshops. Students from over 100 colleges called on their institutions to honor a strict code of conduct for overseas factories that make goods bearing college names (Featherstone 2002). In response to this public outcry, the U.S. Department of Labor mounted a media campaign focusing on industry "trendsetters," and President Clinton created a task force of industry, labor, and human rights organizations, the Apparel Industry Partnership (Press 1997). The Partnership agreed on a workplace code of conduct, including health and safety measures, no forced labor or child labor (except in certain countries), nondiscriminatory practices, and limited protections for collective bargaining. The agreement, which is voluntary, also includes a sixty-hour work week and minimum wage (rather

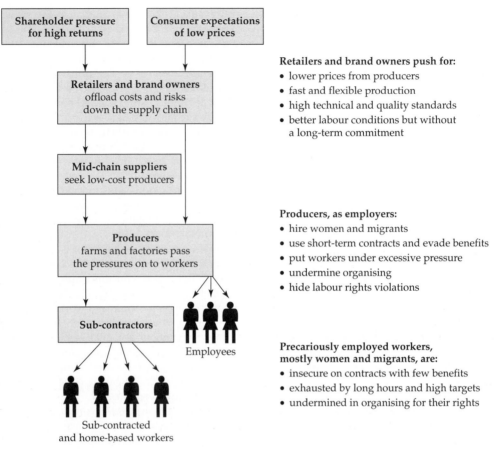

FIGURE 9.2 Supply chain pressures create precarious employment. (*Source:* Oxfam International (2004, 5).)

than living wage) standards (Ross 1997, pp. 293–94). The anti-sweatshop movement won another victory in 2002 when twenty-six major apparel companies (including Gap and Gymboree) settled a lawsuit in favor of workers on the island of Saipan in the western Pacific (Collier 2002). These companies agreed to establish a $20 million fund to pay back wages. The landmark suit, which also included Sears, Nordstrom, Tommy Hilfiger, Calvin Klein, Target, Abercrombie and Fitch, Talbots Inc., J.C. Penney, and Polo Ralph Lauren provided for back wages and damages to workers and established a code of conduct for the treatment of Saipan factory workers, allowing monitors to investigate workers' complaints, and in case of repeated viola-

tions, place manufacturers on probation (Strasburg 2003). The suit was brought by several U.S. groups including the Asian Law Caucus, Global Exchange, and Sweatshop Watch. These activists noted that one problem with winning such a suit is that it may propel manufacturers to move to areas where they can pay even lower wages, such as China. In 2003, in response to the negative impact of global competition on their job security, five women members of Comite Fronterizo de Obrer@s (Border Committee of Women Workers) in Mexico initiated a small-scale clothing production business after being laid off when large *maquiladoras* closed down. This is Maquiladora Dignidad y Justicia (Dignity and Justice Maquiladora Company) which plans to engage in fair trade practices (Hernández and Flory 2005).

The existence of sweatshops and the polarization of the U.S. job market are not random or isolated, however, but an integral part of the global economic system. The driving force is the accumulation of wealth by corporations and individuals. Their **capital**—money and property—is invested in manufacturing, communications, or agriculture, for example. By producing goods, services, and crops, workers earn wages and also increase the wealth of their employers. **Capitalism,** also called the **free market system,** is an economic, political, and cultural system in which the major means of production and distribution are privately held and operated for profit. Labor and nature are seen as resources. In practice there is no "pure" capitalism; rather, the system is a mixture of corporate and government decisions that provide the foundation for business operations. Governments levy taxes that may be used to alleviate poor social conditions. Government and corporate elites share assumptions about what makes the economy successful. In extreme circumstances, governments may sanction the use of police or military force against workers who strike for better pay and working conditions. Governments of some small countries may have operating budgets smaller than those of transnational corporations, a situation that makes control of the corporations difficult. For instance, according to activist and writer Charles Gray (1999) the top three companies in the world—Exxon-Mobil, General Motors, and Ford—each have higher revenues than the national budgets of all but seven countries (United States, Germany, Japan, China, Italy, United Kingdom, and France). Some companies have more revenue than the budgets of their home governments (e.g., Shell/Netherlands and Daewoo/South Korea). It is important to understand the underlying principles of this economic system outlined below.

The Profit Motive

Companies compete with one another to sell their services and products, and they stay in business only as long as it is profitable or while governments are willing to subsidize them, as happens, for example, with agriculture and defense industries in the United States. If enough people can afford to buy gold faucets or to change their cars every six months, these things will be produced regardless of whether ordinary people have an adequate diet or somewhere to live. Women in Malaysia or the Philippines, for example, spend their working lives producing more and more goods for U.S., European, or Japanese markets even if their own daily survival needs are barely met.

Consumerism, Expansionism, and Waste

To expand, companies have to produce more products, develop new products, and find new markets and new needs to supply. The concept of "need" is a tricky one. Many of the things we think we need are not absolute necessities but contrived needs generated by advertising or social pressure. Some needs are also context specific. It is doubtful whether every household in an urban area in the United States with extensive public transportation needs a car, but a car is probably required in a rural area for basic necessities like getting to work, as there is unlikely to be adequate, if any, public transportation. This economic system is intrinsically wasteful. Companies have little or no responsibility to workers left stranded, or for polluted land and water they leave behind when, for example, car assembly plants close down in Detroit or Mattel moves its Barbie doll factory to Malaysia.

The Myth of Progress

There is an assumption that economic growth is the same as "progress"—a much more complex concept with economic, intellectual, social, moral, and spiritual dimensions. This equation often leads people in a highly material society like the United States to value themselves primarily in terms of the money they make and the things they own. At a national level, too, it leads to an emphasis on material success and material security, with support for government policies that facilitate profit making regardless of social costs.

Emphasis on Immediate Costs

The business definition of costs—the immediate costs of raw materials, plant, payroll, and other operating expenses—is a narrow one. It does not

The Village

If we could shrink the earth's population to a village of precisely 100 people, with all the existing human ratios remaining the same, it would look like the following. There would be

57 Asians
21 Europeans
14 from the Western Hemisphere, both north and south
8 Africans

52 would be female
48 would be male

70 would be non-white
30 would be white

70 would be non-Christian
30 would be Christian

89 would be heterosexual
11 would be homosexual

6 people would possess 59 percent of the entire world's wealth and all 6 would be from the United States

80 would live in substandard housing

70 would be unable to read

50 would suffer from malnutrition

1 would be near death; 1 would be near birth

1 (yes, only 1) would have a college education

1 would own a computer

Source: E-mail widely circulated in 2000. A more detailed *State of the Village Report* was compiled by Donella Meadows (1990), Director of the Sustainability Institute (Hartland VT).

take into account longer-term considerations like the effects of production on the environment or workers' well-being. Government regulation of pollution, for example, is frequently resisted by corporations on the grounds that it will increase costs and drive them out of business. In the nineteenth century, European and U. S. factory owners said the same thing about proposals to abolish child labor and reduce working hours to an eight-hour day, both of which were implemented through legislation.

The Global Economy

Complex Inequalities

Our economic system generates profound inequalities within countries—of wealth, material comfort, safety, opportunities, education, social standing, and so on. Members of wealthy elites in Brazil, Saudi Arabia, Indonesia, Turkey, Germany, South Africa, and the United States, to take a few random examples, often have more in common with one another than they do with many of their fellow citizens. Poor people living in Oakland, Detroit, or the south Bronx have rates of illiteracy and infant mortality comparable to those in parts of Africa, Latin America, and the Caribbean. This has led some commentators to talk of "the Third World within the First World" as a way of emphasizing inequalities within countries and drawing connections among poor people worldwide, overwhelmingly people of color.

These inequalities are enhanced in a global economy, which produces inequalities between rich and poor nations. The richest 20 percent of the world's population receives 80 percent of the world's income. Northern industrial countries use 86 percent of the world's resources (Bigelow and Peterson 2002). Workers in one country are pitted against those in another in the corporations' scramble for profits, and this generally erodes their bargaining power. The internationalization and mobility of capital calls for an international labor movement to standardize wages and working conditions. The fact that standards of living and wage rates differ greatly from country to country means that this process of moving work and factories around the world is likely to continue and to become increasingly complex.

Legacies of Colonialism

Current inequalities between countries are often based on older inequalities resulting from colonization. British colonies included India, Ghana, Kenya, Nigeria, Pakistan, and Hong Kong. France had colonial possessions in Algeria, Senegal, Togo, and Vietnam. Although the details varied from place to

What's in a Name?

The various overlapping terms used in the discourse on the global economy offer a convenient shorthand but often obscure as much as they explain.

First World, Second World, Third World

These terms refer to countries that can be roughly grouped together according to their political alliances and economic status. The "First World" refers to North America, western Europe, Australia, New Zealand, and Japan. The "Second World" includes Russia and countries of eastern Europe. The "Third World" includes most of Asia, Latin America, Africa, and the Caribbean. There is an assumption of a hierarchy built into this terminology, with First World countries superior to the rest. Some Native Americans and indigenous peoples in Canada, Latin America, Australia, Aotearoa (New Zealand), and the Pacific Islands use the term "First Nations" to emphasize the fact that their ancestral lands were colonized and settled by Europeans. Some environmentalists use the term "Fourth World" to refer to a scattered collection of small-scale, environmentally sound projects, suggesting an alternative economic and political model. Other commentators use the term "Two-Thirds World" to draw attention to the fact that the majority of the world's population (approximately 68 percent) lives in Asia, Latin America, Africa, and the Caribbean.

Developed, Undeveloped, Underdeveloped, Developing, Maldevelopment

These terms refer to economic development, assuming that all countries will become industrialized like North America and western Europe. Ranging these terms on a continuum from "undeveloped" to "developed" suggests that this process is linear and the best way for a nation to progress. Indeed, economic growth is often assumed to be synonymous with progress. This continuum masks the fact that so-called developing countries have thousands of years of traditional knowledge, and that much of the wealth of developed countries comes from developing countries and is a key reason for their lack of economic development. Vandana Shiva (1988), a researcher, writer, and activist on issues of development and environment from India, emphasizes this connection by using the term "devastated" instead of "underdeveloped" economies. Other commentators speak of "maldevelopment" to refer to exploitation of poorer countries by richer ones.

East/West; North/South

The division between East and West refers to a political and military division between North America and western Europe—the West—countries which, despite differences, stood together against the East—the former Soviet Union and eastern Europe. Clearly this notion of East and West excludes many countries in the Western and Eastern Hemispheres. This distinction also obscures the similarities between these blocs, both highly industrialized with massive military programs. Some writers use the terms North/South to distinguish between rich and poor countries. Rich countries may have their own material wealth and also colonial relationships (currently or in the past) whereby they could extort wealth from others. So-called poor countries often have land, forests, mineral wealth, and people's skills, creativity, knowledge, and hard work. These countries are impoverished because they do not have control over their resources.

place and from one colonial power to another, several factors were central to this process:

- the imposition of legal and political institutions;
- cultural devastation and replacement of language;

- psychological dimensions such as internalized racism; and
- distortions of the economy with dependence on a few agricultural products or raw materials for export.

International Economic Institutions and Trade Agreements

Several groups of countries have joined together, forming trading blocs such as the Economic Community of West African States (ECOWAS) and the European Union (EU), and agreements such as the North American Free Trade Agreement (NAFTA) between Canada, Mexico, and the United States. The goal of these regional institutions is to strengthen the economies of the member countries, although the various countries may not all have the same economic power or influence in the group.

The World Bank

Headquartered in Washington, D.C., the World Bank was set up in 1944 to provide loans for reconstruction after the devastation of World War II and to promote development in countries of the South, where the bank's emphasis has been on major, capital-intensive projects such as roads, dams, hydroelectric schemes, irrigation systems, and the development of large-scale, chemical-dependent, cash-crop production. The bank's investors are the governments of rich countries that make money on the interest on these loans. Because the World Bank assigns voting power in proportion to the capital provided by its shareholders, its decisions are dominated by the governments of the North, and its policies are in line with their concerns.

International Monetary Fund (IMF)

Also based in Washington, the IMF is an international body with 184 member countries. It was founded at the same time as the World Bank to promote international trade and monetary cooperation. It makes loans to governments for development projects and in times of severe budget deficits. France, Germany, Japan, Britain, and the United States have over 50 percent of the votes, which are allocated according to financial contribution to the fund. If member countries borrow from the fund, they must accept a range of conditions, such as structural adjustment programs, and must put export earnings above any other goal for the country's economy.

General Agreement on Tariffs and Trade (GATT)

This trade agreement was started after World War II to regulate international trade. Since its inception, over a hundred nations, responsible for four-fifths of world trade, have participated in the agreement. The latest round of GATT negotiations, which began in 1986, significantly changed the agreement in response to transnational corporations' demand for a reduction of import tariffs, in what consumer activist Ralph Nader (1993) described as "an unprecedented corporate power grab" (p. 1). The changed agreement was adopted by the United States in 1994. Transnational corporations will pay fewer tariffs on the goods they move around the world—data, components, partly finished products, and goods ready for sale. The World Trade Organization (WTO) is the GATT ruling body, established in 1995.

Free Trade Agreements in the Americas

This agreement among the United States, Canada, and Mexico, established in 1994, allows for greater freedom of movement of jobs and products among the three countries. Its proponents argued that these countries needed to collaborate to remain as competitive internationally as the economically powerful European Union and Pacific Rim trading groups. Like GATT, NAFTA was discussed in terms of a liberalization of trade but is in effect a liberalization of capital expansion, serving the interests of transnational corporations against opposition in all three countries from labor, environmentalists, and consumers. The Clinton administration admitted that 75,000 U.S. jobs were lost because of NAFTA. Workers in the Mexico-U.S. border region suffered a sharp drop in their standard of living, "speed-ups" in the labor process, and opposition to labor rights and union organizing (Comité Fronterizo de Obreras—American Friends Service Committee 1999).

Proponents of a plan to expand NAFTA to cover the entire Western Hemisphere in a Free Trade Area of the Americas (FTAA) contend that increased free trade will result in increased prosperity. Opponents argue that workers are likely to lose jobs, and that legislation protecting workers and the environment is likely to be set aside or ruled to be an unlawful limitation on the operations of corporations. Workers, environmentalists, and human rights activists in Brazil, Peru, Paraguay, and Bolivia have organized massive protests against the FTAA, as have "fair trade" activists in the United States (Global Exchange 2002).

In November 2005, concerned citizens from all over Latin America defeated FTAA at the Summit of the Americas meeting in Argentina, and the governments of Argentina, Brazil, Paraguay, Uruguay, and Venezuela opposed FTAA. In the United States there has also been resistance to this plan to expand the NAFTA model, evidenced by congressional opposition to a Central America Free Trade Agreement (CAFTA), which passed by the narrowest of margins, 217 to 215, in a late-night session in July 2005. This provides for a free-trade zone between the United States, Costa Rica, El Salvador, Guatemala, Honduras, Nicaragua, and the Dominican Republic. CAFTA has not been approved by Costa Rica, Nicaragua, or the Dominican Republic due to widespread popular opposition. Guatemala, El Salvador, and Honduras have approved it, bringing in the military to quell protests (Netaid 2005).

World Trade Organization (WTO)

This is an unelected international body over which member nations and their peoples have no democratic control. The WTO allows national governments to challenge each others' laws and regulations as violations of WTO rules against restraints to trade. Cases are decided by a panel of three trade experts. WTO tribunals are secret, binding on member states, and provide no outside appeal or review. Once a WTO ruling is issued, losing countries have a set time to change their law to conform to WTO requirements, pay compensation to the winning country, or face trade sanctions (Working Group on the WTO 1999, p. 5).

In September 1997, a WTO panel ruled that the European Union (EU) was giving preferential access to bananas produced by former colonies in the Caribbean. The United States brought this case against the EU on behalf of the U.S.-based Chiquita Corporation, formerly known as United Fruit. Chiquita produces bananas in Latin America on huge plantations that are notorious for exploiting cheap farm labor and using environmentally damaging techniques. In the Caribbean, banana producers tend to be small-scale farmers who own and work their own small farms, often incurring higher production costs. This was a very divisive case within the WTO because of its economic, social justice, and environmental dimensions. At one point the United States began implementing a threat to impose sanctions on more than $500 million of EU exports, nearly setting off a trade war. The EU eventually said that it would comply with the ruling, subject to negotiation with the United States over the settlement terms (Rethinking Schools 2002). In the shrimp-turtle case, India, Malaysia, Pakistan, and Thailand challenged the U.S. Endangered Species Act that requires domestic and foreign shrimp fishers to catch shrimp by methods that do not kill endangered sea turtles. In 1998 the WTO determined that this law violates WTO rules (Wallach and Sforza 2000; Wallach and Woodall 2004).

Colonial powers extracted raw materials—timber, minerals, and cash crops—which were processed into manufactured goods in the colonial centers for consumption there and for export. During the second half of the twentieth century, virtually all former colonies gained political independence, but they remain linked to their colonizers—politically through organizations like the British Commonwealth and economically through the activities of established firms in operation since colonial times, from the more recent activities of transnational corporations, and by loans from governments and

banks of countries of the global North. Many members of the new political and business elites were educated at prestigious universities in colonial capitals. Whether the handover of political power was relatively smooth or accompanied by turmoil and bloodshed, independent governments have been under pressure to improve living conditions for their populations and have borrowed capital to finance economic development. This combination of circumstances has led many commentators to characterize the continuing economic inequalities between rich and poor countries as **neocolonialism.** The United States is part of this picture because of its colonial relationships with the Philippines, Hawaii (now a state), and Puerto Rico (a commonwealth); the strength of U.S. corporations worldwide; the dominance of U.S. news media and popular culture; the strength of the dollar as an international currency; and the relatively high U.S. shareholding in key international institutions like the World Bank and the International Monetary Fund. They both have their headquarters in the United States and are heavily influenced by U.S. investments and policies.

External Debt

All countries are involved in international trade, buying and selling goods and services. Currently many countries pay more for imports than they earn in exports, leading to external debt, or a balance of payments deficit. For many poor countries in Africa and Latin America, the burden of external debt is catastrophic. Expressed as a percentage of a country's gross national product (GNP—the total value of all goods and services including exports) in 2002, Argentina's external debt was 138.4 percent. For Brazil this was 52.5 percent, Indonesia 80.3 percent, the Philippines 71.4 percent, and Turkey 72.7 percent (World Bank 2004). The United States, too, has a fluctuating budget deficit, now at a high of $412.5 billion compared with a surplus in 2000 (Tanner 2005). Budget deficits are financed with money borrowed from future generations, which makes children worldwide indebted for current loans.

Repayment of Loans   Partly because countries of western Europe and North America have serious balance-of-payments problems themselves, they have pressured other debtor countries to repay loans. Like a person who acquires a second credit card to cover the debt on the first, a country may take out additional loans to cover interest repayments on earlier ones, thus compounding its debt. This situation is complicated by the fact that loans usually have to be repaid in hard currency that can be exchanged on world currency markets: U.S. dollars, Japanese yen, British pounds, French francs, Swiss francs, German marks, and now the euro. To repay the loans, debtor nations have to sell goods and services that richer countries want to buy or that can earn hard currency from poorer countries. These include raw materials (hardwoods, oil, copper, gold, diamonds), cash crops (sugar, tobacco, coffee, tea, tropical fruits and flowers), illegal drugs and drug-producing crops (coca, marijuana, opium poppies), and weapons. Debtor countries may also earn foreign exchange by encouraging their people to work abroad as construction workers or maids or to become mail-order brides (see Reading 56). They may lease land for foreign military bases or trash dumps that take toxic waste from industrialized countries, or they may develop their tourist assets—sunny beaches, beautiful landscapes, and "exotic" young women and children who are recruited into sex tourism.

Structural Adjustment Programs In addition to selling goods and services to offset their external debt, debtor nations have also been under pressure from the World Bank and the IMF to make stringent changes in their economies to qualify for new loans. The aim of such structural adjustment programs is to increase the profitability of the economy. Required measures include

- cutting back government spending on health, education, child care, and social welfare provisions;
- cutting government subsidies and abolishing price controls, particularly on food, fuel, and public transportation;
- adding new taxes, especially on consumer goods, and increasing existing taxes and interest rates;
- selling nationalized industries, or at least a majority of the shares, to private corporations, often from outside the country;
- reducing the number of civil servants on the government payroll;
- improving profitability for corporations through wage controls, tax breaks, loans, and credit, or providing infrastructure by building ports, better roads, or rail transportation;
- devaluing local currency to discourage imports and encourage exports; and
- increasing the output of cash crops, by increasing yields and/or increasing the amount of land in cash crop production.

Though not required to do so by the World Bank, the Reagan, Bush, and Clinton administrations all adopted similar policies for use in the United States, and this has continued under George W. Bush. Such policies are in line with global economic restructuring with the goal of increasing corporate profitability. Examples include the deregulation of air transport and the privatization of public utilities and aspects of the prison industry. Vandana Shiva discusses corporate pressure to privatize water supplies in many countries including the United States (Reading 57). In addition, these administrations restructured government spending by making reductions in the government workforce and cuts in, for example, Medicaid, Medicare, and welfare programs.

Implications of the Debt Crisis for Women Despite women's increased opportunities for paid work in urban areas and export-processing zones in Asia, Latin America, and the Caribbean, the external debt crisis and structural adjustment programs have had a severe impact on women's lives and livelihoods. Addressing the U.N. Commission on the Status of Women in March 1998, Rini Soerojo, the assistant minister of the Ministry of State for the Role of Women, Indonesia, spoke on behalf of 132 developing countries. She emphasized that "the full and effective enjoyment of human rights by women could never be achieved in the absence of sustainable economic growth and a supportive social and international order" (Deen 1998, p. 2). Cuts in social services and health care, often already woefully inadequate, have increased women's responsibilities for child care, health, and family welfare. Cuts in government subsidies for food and other basic items and devaluation of local currencies have reduced women's wages and raised prices, thus doubly reducing their buying power. The emphasis on cash crops for export at the expense of subsistence crops has devastating environmental consequences and makes subsistence agriculture—very often the responsibility of women—much more difficult. Growing cash crops on the flatter land, for instance, pushes subsistence farmers to use steep hillsides for food crops, which is harder work and often less productive and which increases soil erosion. Clearing forests to plant cash crops or raise cattle, as McDonald's did in parts of Central and Latin America, for example, increased soil erosion and reduced the supply of fuel wood, which further added to women's daily burden of work (Dankelman and Davidson 1988; Sen and Grown 1987; Shiva 1988).

Other consequences of the debt crisis include an increase in the number of people seeking work overseas as temporary migrant workers or permanent immigrants; increasing unemployment and underemployment, with growth in the exploitative and unregulated informal sector of the economy (such as sweatshops and low-paid work in homes); an increase in the number of students who have to drop out of school and college because of financial pressures; and a general increase in poverty and hardship. The Philippines, for example, is an impoverished country with external debt that was 71.4 percent of GNP in 2002 (World Bank 2004). It exports people to work in Europe, North America, the Middle East, Hong Kong, and Japan as a way of earning hard currency and considers them national heroes (e.g., Chang 2000; Ehrenreich and Hochschild 2003). Women work as caregivers, assembly-line workers, entertainers; or become - mail-order brides (Perez 2003). Rhacel Salazar Parreñas discusses the impact of this macro-level policy on Philippine families and communities when mothers undertake care work abroad (Reading 55). Ursula Biemann shows the complex pathways of movement for women, including many Filipinas, who enter the global sex trade (Reading 56). Analagous pathways also exist for women doing caring work, sorting them and routing them. Biemann opens the question of whether one can call these movements voluntary and, if so, in what sense, what meanings women ascribe to their decisions, how they understand the constrains within which they live and the opportunities available to them.

Debt Cancellation   Between 1982 and 1990, $160 billion was transferred from Latin America to the developed world in debt repayments (O'Reilly 1991), but this was only the interest on 50 percent of their loans (George 1988). In 1982 Mexico announced that it could not repay its debt, and other countries suspended their repayments throughout the 1980s. In 2001, in the middle of a severe economic recession Argentina stopped making payments on most of its privately held bonds; in 2004 it offered to repay at roughly 35 cents on the dollar, a 65 percent reduction in value, and the biggest sovereign-debt default in history (Davis 2004). Angry investors threatened to withdraw investments, but money managers are involved in

"a relentless search for returns. If Argentina is able to deeply reduce its debt load, it may become a better bet to repay future loans" (Davis 2004). This situation has led to much political and financial debate concerning the legitimacy of debts owed by countries of the South to the North. According to Oxfam International (1998):

> In Africa . . . where one out of every two children doesn't go to school, governments transfer four times more to northern creditors in debt payments than they spend on the health and education of their citizens.

Many activist organizations worldwide support debt cancellation. They argue that much of the money borrowed has benefited only upper-class and professional elites or has gone into armaments, nuclear power plants, or luxuries such as prestige buildings, especially in urban areas. As summed up in the lyrics to *Ode to the International Debt:* "Guns you can't eat/And buildings you can't live/And trinkets you can't wear/It is a debt not owed by the people" (Reagon 1987). In some countries, large sums of money borrowed by governments were kept by corrupt politicians and businesspeople and then reinvested in the lender countries.

It is an inescapable fact that the world's poorest countries are getting poorer and will never be able to pay their international debts. Although this debt is not the only cause of their poverty, it makes their situation significantly worse. With the agreement of the leading industrialized nations, the governing boards of the IMF and World Bank adopted a debt-relief proposal in 1996 for the most heavily indebted countries, mostly in Africa. A few countries benefited under this scheme, but progress has been slow. During the 1990s, people in rich and poor countries took part in major protests against world economic priorities. In June 1999, a worldwide alliance of NGOs and religious groups known as the Jubilee 2000 Coalition presented the leaders of the G-8 (Group of Eight) nations (United States, Japan, Britain, France, Germany, Italy, Canada, and Russia) with a petition signed by 17 million people from rich nations urging debt cancellation (Francis 1999). The G-8 proposed an expansion of the World Bank/IMF debt-relief initiative, and three years later, at its annual meeting in Washington, D.C., in September 2002, the IMF promised that it would announce a dramatic new approach for countries in debt crisis in April 2003. Again in 2005, heads of G-8 nations agreed to eliminate outstanding debts owed to the World Bank, African Development Bank, and the IMF by the eighteen Heavily Indebted Poor Countries (all of them in Africa). Several countries, including Britain, Canada, France, Italy, and Spain have written off some debts owed them by very poor African countries, but, overall, much has been promised and little delivered. In 2005 the Global Call to Action against Poverty, the world's largest anti-poverty coalition of nonprofit organizations, faith-based groups, labor unions, and grassroots movements, continued to pressure the governments of rich countries to address real global imbalances of wealth and power.

Implications of Global Economic Inequalities

Addressing a vast crowd in Havana at the end of a visit to Cuba in January 1996, the late Pope John Paul II criticized unsustainable economic programs imposed by rich countries on the poor and "the resurgence of a certain capitalist neoliberalism that subordinates the human person to blind market forces"; he also deplored the fact that "a small number of countries [are] growing exceedingly rich at the cost of the increasing impoverishment of a great number of other countries" (News Services 1998, p. A1).

In principle, inequality is unjust. Some people's freedom and comfort should not be bought at the expense of other people's oppression, degradation, and poverty. More pragmatically, inequality is a continual source of violence and conflict. On an international level it is one of the main causes of war; on a community level it can lead to alienation, anger, violence, theft, and vandalism.

Connections to U.S. Policy Issues

Two issues of national importance in the United States that are greatly affected by global inequalities are immigration and drugs. Vast differences in living standards between the United States and many other countries are a source of continuing pressure for immigration into this country. These same inequalities also drive the international drug trade, a lucrative earner of hard currency for producer countries as well as for those who procure and sell illegal drugs or launder drug money (Lusane 1991). It is important to understand the global economic forces driving the drug trade and pressures for immigration and to recognize the inadequacy of control measures that do not address underlying causes.

In the following chapter on crime and criminalization, Julia Sudbury discusses the drug trade as a major cause of increased incarceration of women (Reading 63). Here, we consider the issue of immigration, building on the brief history of immigration law and policy included in Chapter 2. The 1990s saw controversial and acrimonious debate in the United States over immigration, along with new legislation, like the 1996 Illegal Immigration Reform and Immigrant Responsibility Act, which aims to control it. Anti-immigration politicians and countless media reports invoked the specter of "alien hordes" poised on the borders, ready to overrun the country, take jobs away from the native born, and drain the welfare system. Wendy Young (1997), director of government relations, Women's Commission for Refugee Women and Children, counters this perception, arguing that undocumented people "typically fill service-sector jobs and are ineligible for most benefits, even though they pay taxes and social security contributions. Moreover, 85% of immigrants come to the United States through legal channels" (p. 9).

At the heart of much of this debate are racism and xenophobia. White people particularly see the country changing demographically with the arrival of more people from Asia, Mexico, and Central and South America. This poses a threat to the dominance of "the Anglo-Saxon part of America's culture" (Holmes 1995b). Such fears provided leverage for a greatly increased Immigration and Naturalization Service budget and tighter border control, especially along the long land border with Mexico, which has been strongly fortified (Ayres 1994). Congress cut government funding for virtually all agencies except the military in the mid-1990s, but the INS budget more than tripled from $1.4 billion in fiscal year 1992 to $4.8 billion in fiscal year 2001 (American Immigration Lawyers Association 2001). Now under the Department of Homeland Security, the former INS has been reorganized into the U.S. Citizenship and Immigration Services, U.S. Immigration and Customs Enforcement, and U.S. Customs and Border Protection.

The distinction between legal and illegal immigrants has been drawn more sharply. The 1986 Immigration Act introduced sanctions against employers, making it illegal to knowingly hire undocumented workers, with fines for those who violate the law. This controversial program was intended to eliminate the "pull" factor of jobs attracting undocumented migrants into the country. Illegal immigrants are hired at low wages by agricultural growers, construction firms, landscaping and cleaning businesses, and the garment industry, for example, as well as by private individuals as maids and baby-sitters. Evidence indicates that employer sanctions have been ineffective; employers are not always prosecuted, and if they are, they tend to consider the relatively small fines as a hazard of doing business. However, as Wendy Young (1997) observed, "Numerous studies have shown that employer sanctions have caused employment discrimination against U.S. citizens and permanent residents who look or sound 'foreign.'" (p. 8).

Increasing numbers of undocumented workers were deported during the early 1990s (Holmes 1995a), and legal immigrants applied for citizenship in record numbers in response to growing controversy over immigration and moves to deny legal immigrants access to government supports. Anti-immigrant rhetoric took on a very different quality after the attacks on the World Trade Center and the Pentagon on September 11, 2001, and the Bush administration's declaration of a long-term "war on terrorism." Distrust and suspicion of foreigners, especially Arabs, South Asians, and "people who look like Muslims," was deployed in support of government policies, as discussed in Chapter 10. Migration policy will continue to be a contentious issue in the United States, particularly in states like California, Florida, New York, and Texas, which have large proportions of immigrants.

International Alliances Among Women

Women's organizations worldwide are concerned with economic issues, including economic development, loans to start small businesses, and other job opportunities for women, as well as the lack of government spending on health care, child care, or care for the elderly. At international feminist meetings and conferences, such as the NGO Forum in September 1995, these global inequalities are central to many discussions. Women from countries of the South invariably challenge those from the North to take up the issue of external debt and structural adjustment with our governments and banks.

Most U.S. feminist organizations focus their work on women's rights in this country, which is understandable, as earlier gains are being eroded. But the separation of domestic and foreign policy masks crucial connections and continuities and can lead to an insularity and parochialism on the part of women in the United States, an important aspect of the ignorance that comes with national privilege. In the context of trade agreements like GATT and NAFTA, Mary McGinn, the North American coordinator for Transnationals Information Exchange, commented, "Unfortunately, most U.S. women's advocacy groups took no position on GATT. But clearly, all women have a lot to lose: expanded freedom for multinational corporations jeopardizes social justice everywhere" (1995, p. 15).

In order to build more effective international campaigns and alliances, women in the North need to learn much more about the effects of corporate and government policies on women in Asia, Africa, Latin America, and the Caribbean, and to understand the connections between these women's situations and our own.

Many women in the United States who attended the NGO Forum spoke to public meetings, religious organizations, women's groups, and school and college classes about their impressions and brought back a heightened understanding of global linkages to their ongoing efforts. The Women of Color Resource Center (Oakland, Calif.), for instance, decided to give priority to the globalization of the economy in its organizing and educational work: "Global economics was at the top of the Beijing agenda; it is now at the top of ours as well" (1996, p. 2). A campaign titled Women's Eyes on the World Bank-U.S., based at Oxfam America (Washington, D.C.), began "to monitor Bank progress toward bringing its lending operations in line with the Beijing Platform" (Williams 1997, p. 1). This is the importance of international gatherings like the

NGO Forum at Huairou or the U.N. *Platform for Action*, which

> criticizes structural adjustment programs; advises cuts in military spending in favor of social spending; urges women's participation at all peace talks and in all decision-making affecting development and environment; confronts violence against women; calls for measuring women's unpaid work; and refers to "the family" in all its various forms.
>
> *(Morgan 1996, p. 20)*

United Nations documents have to be ratified by the governments of individual countries to be accepted as national policy. Even if governments do not ratify them—and the U.S. on several occasions has not—they are still useful for activists in their attempts to hold governments accountable and to show what others have pledged to do for women and girls. Nobel laureate Wangari Maathai, coordinator of the Kenyan Women's Green Belt, comments:

> It's very hard to push governments on issues that affect all aspects of society, let alone those that affect women. But the U.N. document has given us a tool with which to work. Now it's up to the women to push their issues into the boardrooms where political and economic decisions are made by those who did not even bother to come to Beijing.
>
> *(Quoted in Morgan 1996, p. 18)*

The Women's Environment and Development Organization evaluated governments' progress since the 1995 U.N. Conference in Beijing (WEDO 1998) and reported that "over 70 percent of the world's 187 countries have drawn up national action plans or drafts as required by the Beijing Platform" (WEDO press release, March 1, 1998). Sixty-six governments set up national offices for women's affairs, thirty-four of them with the power to initiate legislation. Fifty-eight countries adopted new legislation or policies to address women's rights, particularly concerning violence against women (Latin American and Caribbean countries, China, and New Zealand), female genital mutilation (Egypt), and the trafficking of women and children (Thailand). In March 2005,

women's rights advocates gathered in New York City for the U.N. Commission on the Status of Women meetings (sometimes called Beijing + 10) that reviewed gains made in the decade since the Beijing Conference. At the macroeconomic level it is clear that many women in the United States and abroad have suffered from the effects of free-trade agreements and privatization. As shown by data presented in this chapter and in Chapter 8, the U.S. government has done relatively little to meet the commitments made in Beijing: to ensure women's economic rights and access to economic resources; to work to eliminate occupational segregation and employment discrimination; and to promote harmonization of work and family responsibilities for women and men (Speildoch 2004). Moreover, strong U.S. government support for "free-trade" agreements and militarism, and lack of support for international agencies such as United Nations Population Fund (UNFPA) have increased women's poverty, suffering, and anger in many parts of the world.

The global economic situation has generated new alliances and organizations working across national borders. Examples include STITCH (Support Team International for Textileras), a network of women organizers in the United States and Guatemala, and Comité Fronterizo de Obreras (CFO), or Border Committee of Women Workers, a Mexican worker-controlled organization that works closely with the American Friends Service Committee, a social justice organization. They have won several significant victories, such as winning wages that have been withheld illegally; pressuring companies to implement laws requiring safety equipment and protective clothing; challenging illegal layoffs and dismissals and winning legally mandated severance pay; curbing pollution in communities and factories; teaching workers practical exercises to alleviate repetitive strain injuries; testifying at shareholder meetings to give details of how companies treat their workers; and building the confidence of women workers so that they can stand up for their rights.

Thousands of people, including environmentalists, union members, indigenous people, feminists, and people of many faiths, participated in alternative workshops on economic and environmental issues, as well as protesting the WTO at its third ministerial Conference, in Seattle, November 1999.

This coordinated opposition was successful in stalling the "Seattle round" of talks aimed at further opening up global trade.

Since then, this growing anti-globalization movement has organized mass international protests at IMF, World Bank, and WTO meetings on all continents (Prokosch and Raymond 2002; Starhawk 2002b). Activists from many nations have participated in the World Social Forum, which started in 2001 when 20,000 people from 117 countries came together in Porto Alegre (Brazil) to think and organize in favor of genuine human development, rather than **neoliberal** globalization. The third World Social Forum in 2004 was held in Mumbai (India) and drew over 100,000 people, mainly from Asia. Those scheduled for 2006 and 2007 are to take place in Africa, Asia, and Latin America. The slogan of the World Social Forum is "Another World Is Possible" (see, e.g., Roy 2003, 2004; Solomon 2005). Another international initiative is organized by the International Wages for Housework Campaign and Women's International Network for Wages for Caring Work. Starting in 2000, these groups have organized an annual Global Women's Strike on March 8, International Women's Day, involving women in over 80 countries. The strike draws attention to the fact that virtually all women are workers, though much of the work we do is unwaged. Leaders of women's human rights and religious organizations came together in Chiang Mai, Thailand, in 2004, for an international conference on women and religion. Noting the severe problems of globalization in shaping women's lives and opportunities, they called on religious leaders and institutions to work to advance the well-being of women (Reading 58).

The Seeds of a New Global Economy

In Latin America, the Caribbean, Africa, and Asia, thousands of workers' organizations, environmentalists, feminists, and religious groups are campaigning for better pay and working conditions and for economic development that is environmentally sound (Braidotti et al. 1994; De Oliveira et al. 1991; Leonard 1989), and they are protesting the poverty caused by external debt. Similarly, social and economic justice organizations and networks in countries of the North advocate that we in the United States learn more about the global economy and the impact of global inequalities on people's lives and livelihoods. They also urge us to live more simply: to recycle materials, wear secondhand clothing, barter for things we need, establish collectives and cooperatives, engage in socially responsible shopping and investing, and buy directly from farmers and craftspeople. A number of nonprofit organizations are involved in supporting fair trade between producers and craftspeople in the South and consumers in the North, including Equal Exchange (Cambridge, Mass.), Global Exchange (San Francisco Bay Area), Pachamama (San Rafael, Calif.), Pueblo to People (Houston, Tex.), and Ten Thousand Villages (Akron, Pa.), which all sell through stores and the Internet. Fair trade criteria include paying a fair wage in the local context; providing equal opportunities, especially for the most disadvantaged; engaging in environmentally sustainable practices; providing healthy and safe working conditions; and being open to public accountability. Other projects include dialogue projects linking workers of the North and South, such as North-South Dialogue of the American Friends Service Committee's Latin American/Caribbean Program; campaigns urging a debt amnesty for countries of the South, like Jubilee 2000; campaigns to get institutions to stop buying World Bank bonds; Third World study tours; and direct support through work brigades such as those in Cuba and Nicaragua.

In the 1960s and 1970s, those active in U.S. movements for liberation and civil rights made theoretical and practical connections with anticolonial struggles in such countries as South Africa, Vietnam, Cuba, Angola, and Mozambique. In the twenty-first century, these international linkages are crucial, not merely, as scholar and activist Angela Davis (1997) remarked, "as a matter of inspiration or identification, but as a matter of necessity," because of the impact of the globalization of the economy.

Activists and writers Mary Zepernick (1998a, 1998b) and Virginia Rasmussen (1998) both argue that corporate dominance is not inevitable. In the eighteenth and nineteenth centuries, U.S. city and state governments watched corporations closely and revoked or amended their charters if they harmed the general welfare or exceeded the powers granted them by government. In 1843, for example, the Pennsylvania Legislature declared: "A corporation in law is just what the incorporation act makes it. It is the creature of the law and may be moulded to any shape or for any purpose the Legislature may deem most conducive for the common good" (quoted in Grossman 1998a, p. 1). In 1890 the highest court in New York revoked the charter of the North River Sugar Refining Corporation in a unanimous decision (*People v. North River Sugar Refining Corp.*, 24 N.E. 834.1890). In its judgment, the court noted:

> The judgment sought against the defendant is one of corporate death. The state which created, asks us to destroy, [sic] and the penalty invoked represents the extreme rigor of the law. The life of a corporation, is, indeed, less than that of the humblest citizen. . . . Corporations may, and often do, exceed their authority only where private rights are affected. When these are adjusted all mischief ends and all harm is averted. But where the transgression has a wider scope, and threatens the welfare of the people, they may summon the offender to answer for the abuse of its franchise and the violation of corporate duty. . . . The abstract idea of a corporation, the legal entity . . . is itself a fiction. . . . The state permits in many ways an aggression of capital, but, mindful of the possible dangers to the people, overbalancing the benefits, keeps upon it a restraining hand, and maintains over it prudent supervision.
>
> *(Quoted in Grossman 1998a, p. 2)*

Corporate owners worked hard to change the law and were successful over time. In an 1886 decision, the U.S. Supreme Court declared corporations legal persons. Gradually they were given a long list of civil and political rights, such as free speech, property rights, and the right to define and control investment, production, and the organization of work (Grossman 1998b). They became entitled to the Fourteenth Amendment protection that was added to the Constitution in 1870 to provide due process to freed African Americans (Zepernick 1998b). This resulted in a gradual reversal of the sovereignty of the people over corporations—originally mere legal entities—and an undermining of democracy, for people who are subordinate to corporations are not citizens. Zepernick and Rasmussen note that corporations are *things;* they cannot care or be responsible. The Program on Corporations, Law and Democracy (POCLAD) promotes public discussion of this fundamental contradiction between democracy and corporate control (Ritz 2001). It advocates that city governments, for example, create policies and programs to ensure control over corporations conducting business with the city, as a step toward reclaiming people's power over corporate entities.

This chapter raises key questions about our global economic system. In what ways is this a "free market"? Who pays and at what costs? Who should governments be responsible to? What is needed for this to be a secure and sustainable system?

◆◆◆

Questions for Reflection

In thinking about the issues raised in this chapter, consider these questions:

1. Why does the impact of the globalization of the economy matter to people living in the United States? What does it tell us about structural privilege (which we may not know we have and may not want)? If some of this material is new to you, why do you think you have not learned it before?

2. How does global inequality reinforce sexism, racial prejudice, and institutionalized racism in the United States?

3. How do you define wealth, aside from material possessions? List all the ways you are enriched.

4. Does wealth equal political power? Are rich people always in the **power elite**— the group that influences political and economic decisions in the country? Who makes up the power elite in the United States?

5. How do people in elite positions justify the perpetuation of inequalities to others? To themselves? How are the ideologies of nationalism, racial superiority, male superiority, and class superiority useful here?

Finding Out More on the Web

1. Visit the following Web sites to find out more about organizations that are campaigning against sweatshops and urging Codes of Conduct for corporations:

   CorpWatch: **www.corpwatch.org**

   Sweatshop Watch: **www.sweatshopwatch.org**

2. The following Web sites have information about alternatives to globalization, including fair trade and debt relief:

   Global Exchange: **www.globalexchange.org**

   Global Women's Strike: **www.globalwomenstrike.net**

   Jubilee USA Network: **www.jubileeusa.org**

   Net Aid: **www.netaid.org**

   World Social Forum: **www.forumsocialmundial.org.br**

3. Use your search engine to research organizations concerned with the global sex trade and trafficking such as

   Coalition Against Trafficking in Women (CATW)

   Global Alliance Against Trafficking of Women (GAATW)

   Women's Education, Development, Productivity and Research Organization (WEDPRO)

Taking Action

1. Look at the labels in your clothes and on all products you buy. Where were they made? Look up these countries on a map if you don't know where they are.

2. Do you need all you currently own? List everything you need to sustain life. Which items do you need to buy? Which might you make yourself, share, or barter with others?

3. Find out who manufactures the clothing that bears your college's name, and whether there are sweatshops in your region.

4. Get involved with a campaign that is tackling the issue of sweatshop production or debt relief.

◆◆◆

Maquiladoras (1984)
The View from Inside

María Patricia Fernández-Kelly

A social anthropologist, **María Patricia Fernández-Kelly** teaches in the Department of Sociology and is a Research Associate in the Office of Population Research at Princeton University. Her writing focuses on women and ethnic minorities in the labor force, migration, and economic restructuring. With Lorraine Gray, she co-produced the Emmy award winning documentary, *The Global Assembly Line.*

What is it like to be female, single and eager to find employment at a maquiladora? Shortly after arriving in Ciudad Juárez and after finding stable lodging, I began looking through the pages of newspapers hoping to find a "wanted" ad. My intent was to merge with the clearly visible mass of women who roam the streets of industrial parks of Ciudad Juárez searching for jobs. They are, beyond doubt, a distinctive feature of the city, an effervescent expression of the conditions that prevail in the local job market.

My objectives were straightforward: I was to spend from four to six weeks applying for jobs and obtaining direct experience about the employment policies, recruitment strategies and screening mechanisms used by companies in the process of hiring assembly workers. Special emphasis would be given to the average investment of time and money expended by individual workers in trying to gain access to jobs. In addition, I was to spend an equal amount of time working at a plant, preferably at one involved in the manufacture of apparel.

With this I expected to learn more about working conditions, production quotas and wages at a particular plant. In general, both research stages were planned as exploratory devices that would elicit questions relevant to the research project from the perspective of workers themselves.

In retrospect, it seems odd that the doubt as to whether these goals were feasible or not never entered my design. However, finding a job at a maquiladora is not a self-evident proposition. For many women, actual workers, the task is not an easy one. This is due primarily to the large number of women they must compete with. Especially for those who are older than twenty-five years of age the probability of getting work in a maquiladora is low. At every step of their constant peregrination, women are confronted by a familiar sign at the plants, "No applications available," or by the negative response of a guard or a secretary at the entrance of the factories. But such is the arrogance of the uninformed researcher. I went about the business of looking for a job as if the social milieu had to comply with the intents of my research rather than the reverse. Moreover, I was pressed for time. It was indispensable that I get a job as quickly as possible.

By using newspapers as a source of information for jobs available, I was departing from the common strategy of potential workers in that environment. As my own research would show, the majority of these workers avail themselves of information by word of mouth. They are part of informal networks which include relatives, friends and an occasional acquaintance in the personnel management sector. Most potential workers believe that a personal recommendation from someone already employed at a maquiladora can ease their difficult path.

This belief is well founded. At many plants, managers prefer to hire applicants by direct recommendation of employees who have proven to be dependable and hard-working. For example, at

---

As part of the fieldwork for her study of the *maquiladora* industry in Mexico, anthropologist María Patricia Fernández-Kelly worked in a textile factory in Ciudad Juárez.

Electro Componentes de Mexico, the subsidiary of General Electric and one of the most stable maquiladoras in Juárez, it is established policy not to hire "outsiders." Only those who are introduced personally to the manager are considered to fill up vacancies.

Such a policy is not whimsical. It is the result of evaluations performed on a daily basis during the interactions between company personnel and workers. By resorting to the personal linkage, managers attenuate the dangers of having their factories infiltrated by unreliable workers, independent organizers and "troublemakers." . . .

On the other hand, the resemblance of a personal interest in the individual worker at the moment of hiring enables management to establish a bond often heavily colored by paternalism. From the point of view of workers this is a two-faceted proposition. Some complain of the not unusual practice of superintendents and managers who are prone to demand special services, for example, overtime, in exchange for personal favors: a loan, an exemption from work on a busy day when the presence of the worker at home is required by her children, and so on. As in other similar cases, personal linkages at the workplace can and will be used as subtle mechanisms to exert control.

Workers, in turn, acknowledge a personal debt to the individual who has hired them. In the majority of cases, commitment to the firm is not distinct from the commitment to a particular individual through whom access to employment presumably has been achieved. A job becomes a personal favor granted through the kindness of the personnel manager or the superintendent of a factory. . . .

Only those who are not part of tightly woven informal networks must rely on impersonal ways to find a job. In this situation are recently arrived migrants and older women with children, for whom the attempt to find maquiladora employment may be a new experience after many years spent caring for children and the home. In objective terms my own situation as a newcomer in Ciudad Juárez was not markedly different from that of the former. Both types of women are likely to be found in larger numbers in the apparel manufacturing sector.

This is not a random occurrence. One of the basic propositions in the present work is that differences in manufacturing activity are related to variations in the volume of capital investments. In turn this . . . determines recruitment strategies. Therefore different types of persons are predominately employed in different manufacturing sectors. Ciudad Juárez electronics maquiladoras, for example, tend to employ very young, single women. This is, in effect, a preferred category of potential workers from the point of view of industry.

Workers, on their part, also prefer the electronics sector, which is characterized by the existence of large stable plants, regular wages and certain additional benefits. In contrast, the apparel manufacturing sector is frequently characterized by smaller, less stable shops where working conditions are particularly strenuous. Because of their low levels of capital investment, many of these shops tend to hire personnel on a more or less temporary basis. The lack of even the smallest of commitments to their employees and the need to maintain an elastic work force to survive as capitalist enterprises in a fluctuating international market forces management to observe crude and often ruthless personnel recruitment policies.

One of such firms was Maquiladoras Internacionales. . . .

Attached to the tent-like factory where women work from 7:30 A.M. to 5:00 P.M. from Monday to Friday there is a tiny office. I entered that office wondering whether my appearance or accent would elicit the suspicion of my potential employers. The personnel manager looked me over sternly and told me to fill out a form. I was to return the following morning at seven to take a dexterity test.

I tried to respond to the thirty-five questions contained in the application in an acceptable manner. Most of the items were straightforward: name, age, marital status, place of birth, length of residence in Ciudad Juárez, property assets, previous jobs and income, number of pregnancies, general state of health, and so on. One, however, was unexpected: What is your major aspiration in life? I pondered briefly upon the superfluous character of that inquiry given the general features of the job sought. . . .

The following morning I was scheduled to take an on-the-job test. I assumed that this would consist of a short evaluation of my skills as a seamstress. I was to be proven wrong. At 7 A.M. I knocked at the door of the personnel office where I had filled out the application the day before. But no one was there yet. I peeked into the entrance of the factory in a state of moderate confusion. A dark-haired woman wearing false eyelashes ordered me to go in and promptly led me to my place. Her name was Margarita and she was the supervisor.

I had never been behind an industrial sewing machine of the kind I confronted at this time. That it was old was plain to see; how it worked was difficult to judge. An assortment of diversely cut denim parts was placed on my left side while I listened intently to Margarita's instructions. I was expected to sew patch-pockets on what were to become blue jeans. Obediently, I started to sew. The particulars of "unskilled" labor unfolded before my eyes.

The procedure involved in this operation required perfect coordination of hands, eyes and legs. The left hand was used to select the larger part of material from the batch next to the worker. Upon it, the pocket (swiftly grabbed by the right hand) had to be attached. There were no markers to guide the placement of the pocket on its proper place. This was achieved by experienced workers on a purely visual basis. Once the patch-pocket had been put on its correct position, the two parts had to be directed under a double needle while applying pressure on the machine's pedal with the right foot.

Because the pockets were sewed on with thread of a contrasting color, it was of peak importance to maintain the edge of the pocket perfectly aligned with the needles so as to produce a regular seam and an attractive design. Due to the diamond-like shape of the pocket, it was also indispensable to slightly rotate the materials three times while adjusting pressure on the pedal. Too much pressure inevitably broke the thread or resulted in seams longer than the edge of the pocket. Even the slightest deviation from the needles produced lopsided designs which had to be unsewed and gone over as many times as necessary to achieve an acceptable product. According to the instructions of the supervisor, once trained, I would be expected to sew a pocket every nine to ten seconds. That is, between 360 and 396 pockets every hour, between 2,880 and 3,168 every shift.

For this, velocity was a central consideration. The vast majority of apparel manufacturing maquiladoras operate through a combination of the minimum wage and piecework. At the moment of being hired, workers receive the minimum wage. . . . However, they are responsible for a production quota arrived at by time-clock calculations. Workers receive slight bonus payments when they are able to fulfill their production quotas on a sustained basis throughout the week. In any case they are not allowed to produce less than 80% of their assigned quota without being admonished. And a worker seriously endangers her job when unable to improve her level of productivity.

At Maquiladoras Internacionales a small blackboard indicated the type of weekly bonus received by those able to produce certain percentages of the quota. . . . Managers call this combination of steep production quotas, minimum wages and modest bonuses, "incentive programs."

I started my test at 7:30 A.M. with a sense of embarrassment about my limited skills and disbelief at the speed with which the women in the factory worked. As I continued sewing, the bundle of material on my left was renewed and grew in size, although slowly. I had to repeat the operation many times before the product was considered acceptable. But that is precisely what was troubling about the "test." I was being treated as a new worker while presumably being tested. I had not been issued a contract and, therefore, was not yet incorporated into the Instituto Mexicano del Seguro Social (the National Security System). Nor had I been instructed as to working hours, benefits and system of payment.

I explained to the supervisor that I had recently arrived in the city, alone, and with very little money. Would I be hired? What was the current wage? When would I be given a contract? Margarita listened patiently while helping me unsew one of many defective pockets, and then said, "You are too curious. Don't worry about it. Do your job and things will be all right." I continued to sew aware of the fact that every pocket attached during the "test" was becoming part of the plant's total production.

At 12:30 during the thirty-minute lunch break, I had a chance to better see the factory. Its improvised aura was underscored by the metal folding chairs behind the sewing machines. I had been sitting in one of them during the whole morning, but not until then did I notice that most of them had the well-known emblem of Coca-Cola painted on their backs. I had seen this kind of chair many times in casual parties both in Mexico and in the United States. Had they been bought or were they being rented from the local concessionary? In any event they were not designed in accordance to the strenuous requirements of a factory job, especially one needing the complex bodily movements of sewing. It was therefore necessary for women to bring their own colorful pillows to ameliorate the stress on their buttocks and spines. Later on I was to discover that chronic lumbago was, and is, a frequent condition among factory seamstresses.

My curiosity did not decrease during the next hours, nor were any of my questions answered. At 5 P.M. a bell rang signaling the end of the shift and workers quickly prepared to leave. I marched to the personnel office with the intent of getting more information about a confusing day. But this time my inquiry was less than welcome. Despite my over-shy approach to the personnel manager, his reaction was hostile. Even before he was able to turn the disapproving expression on his face into words, Margarita intervened with energy. She was angry. To the manager she said, "This woman has too many questions: Will she be hired? Is she going to be insured?" And then to me, "I told you already we do piecework here; if you do your job you get a wage, otherwise you don't. That's clear, isn't it? What else do you want? You should be grateful! This plant is giving you a chance to work! What else do you want? Come back tomorrow and be punctual."

This was only the first in a number of application procedures that I underwent. Walking about the industrial parks while following other job-seekers was especially informative. Most women do not engage in this task alone. Rather, they do it in the company of friends or relatives. Small groups of two or three women looking for work may be commonly seen in the circumvicinity of the factories. Also frequent is the experience of very young women, ages between sixteen and seventeen, seen in the company of their mothers. . . .

At the times when shifts begin or end, the industrial parks of Juárez form a powerful visual image as thousands of women arrive in buses, taxi-cabs and *ruteras* while many others exit the factories. During working hours only those seeking jobs may be seen wandering about. Many, but not the

majority, are "older women." They confront special difficulties due both to their age and to the fact that they often support their own children. These are women who, in most cases, enter the labor force after many years dedicated to domestic chores and child-care. The precipitant factor that determines their entry into the labor force is often the desertion by their male companions. The bind they are placed in at that time is well illustrated by the experience of a thirty-one-year-old woman, the mother of six children: "I have been looking for work since my husband left me two months ago. But I haven't had any luck. It must be my age and the fact that I have so many children. Maybe I should lie and say I've only one. But then the rest wouldn't be entitled to medical care once I got the job." Women often look for jobs in order to support their children. But being a mother is frequently the determining factor that prevents them from getting jobs.

In early June, 1978, Camisas de Juárez, a recently formed maquiladora, was starting a second (evening) shift. Until then it had hired approximately 110 workers operating in the morning hours. As it expanded production, a new contingent of workers had to be recruited. Advertisements to that effect appeared in the daily newspapers. I responded to them. So did dozens of other women.

Camisas de Juárez is located in the modern Parque Industrial Bermúdez. On the morning that I arrived with the intent of applying for a job, thirty-seven women had preceded me. Some had arrived as early as 6 A.M. At 10 the door which separated the front lawn from the entrance to the factory had not yet been opened. A guard appeared once in a while to peek at the growing contingent of applicants, but these were given no encouragement to stay on, nor was the door unlocked.

At 10:30 the guard finally opened the door and informed us that only those having personal recommendation letters would be permitted to walk inside. This was the first in a series of formal and informal screening procedures used to reduce the number of potential workers. It was an effective screening device: Thirteen women left immediately, as they did not have the letter of recommendation alluded to by the guard. Others tried to convince him that although they had no personal recommendation, they "knew" someone already employed at the factory. It was through the recommendation of these acquaintances that they had come to apply for a job.

One of them, Xochitl, lacked both a written or verbal recommendation but she insisted. She had with her a diploma issued by a sewing academy. She was hopeful that this would work in her favor. "It is better to have proof that you are qualified to do the job than to have a letter for recommendation, right?" I wondered whether the personnel manager would agree.

Indeed her diploma gave Xochitl claim to a particular skill. But academies such as the one she had attended abound in Ciudad Juárez. For a relatively small sum of money they offer technical and vocational courses which presumably qualify young men and women for skilled work. However, in an environment lacking in employment opportunities, their value is in question. In many cases, maquiladora managers prefer to hire women who have had direct experience on a job or those who are young and inexperienced but who can be trained to suit the needs of a particular firm. As one manager put it to me, "We prefer to hire women who are unspoiled, that is, those who come to us without preconceptions about what industrial work is. Women such as these are easier to shape to our own requirements." . . .

We waited upon the benevolence of the guard who seemed unperturbed by the fluctuating number of women standing by the door. To many of us he was the main obstacle lying between unemployment and getting a job from someone inside the factory in a decision-making position. If only we could get our foot in, maybe there was a chance. . . . The young man dressed in uniform appeared to the expectant women as an arrogant and insensitive figure. I asked him how long he had worked there. With the air of one who feels he has gained mastery over his own fate he answered, "Uy! I've been working here for a very long time, I assure you: almost two years."

To me his words sounded a bit pathetic. But Beatríz and Teresa, two sisters of twenty-three and nineteen years of age, respectively, were not pleased by his attitude. Their patience had been exhausted and their alternating comments were belligerent: "Why must these miserable guards always act this way? It would seem that they've never had to look for a job. Maybe this one thinks he's more important than the owner of the factory. What a bastard!" But their dialogue failed to elicit any response. Guards are accustomed to similar outbursts.

Teresa wanted to know whether I had any sewing experience. "Not much," I told her, "but I used to sew for a lady in my hometown." "Well, then you're very lucky," she said, "because they aren't hiring anyone without experience." The conversation having begun, I proceeded to ask a similar question, "How about you, have you worked before?"

> Yes, both my sister and I used to work in a small shop on Altamirano Street in downtown Juárez. There were about seventy women like us sewing in a very tiny space, about twenty square meters. We sewed pants for the minimum wage, but we had no insurance.
>
> The boss used to bring precut fabric from the United States for us to sew and then he sold the finished products in El Paso. When he was unable to get fabric we were laid-off; sent to rest without pay! Later on he wanted to hire us again but he still didn't want to insure us even though we had worked at the shop for three years.
>
> When I was sixteen I used to cut thread at the shop. Afterwards one of the seamstresses taught me how to operate a small machine and I started doing serious work. Beatríz, my sister, used to sew the pockets on the pants. It's been three months since we left the shop. Right now we are living from the little that my father earns. We are two of nine brothers and sisters (there were twelve of us in total but three died when they were young). My father does what he can but he doesn't have a steady job. Sometimes he does construction work; sometimes he's hired to help paint a house or sells toys at the stadium. You know, odd jobs. He doesn't earn enough to support us.
>
> I am single, thanks be to God, and I do not want to get married. There are enough problems in my life as it is! But my sister married an engineer when she was only fifteen. Now she is unmarried and she has three children to support. They live with us too. Beatríz and I are the oldest in the family, you see, that's why we really have to find a job. . . .

You don't understand; the "econo-me" grew, not the "econo-you."

At that point Beatríz intervened. I asked whether her husband helped support the children. Her answer was unwavering: "No, and I don't want him to give me anything, not a cent, because I don't want him to have any claim or rights over my babies. As long as I can support them, he won't have to interfere." I replied, "But aren't there better jobs outside of maquiladoras? I understand you can make more money working at a *cantina.* Is that true?"

Both of them looked at me suspiciously. Cantinas are an ever present reminder of overt or concealed prostitution. Teresa said,

That is probably true, but what would our parents think? You can't stop people from gossiping, and many of those cantinas are whorehouses. Of course, when you have great need you can't be choosy, right? For some time I worked as a waitress but that didn't last. The supervisor was always chasing me. First he wanted to see me after work. I told him I had a boyfriend, but he insisted. He said I was too young to have a steady boyfriend. Then, when he learned I had some typing skills, he wanted me to be his secretary. I'm not stupid! I knew what he really

wanted; he was always staring at my legs. So I had to leave that job too. I told him I had been rehired at the shop although it wasn't true. He wasn't bad looking, but he was married and had children. . . . Why must men fool around?

At last the guard announced that only those with previous experience would be allowed to fill out applications. Twenty women went into the narrow lobby of Camisas de Juárez, while the rest left in small quiet groups. For those of us who stayed a second waiting period began. One by one we were shown into the office of the personnel manager where we were to take a manual dexterity test. The point was to fit fifty variously colored pegs into fifty similarly colored perforations on a wooden board. This had to be accomplished in the shortest possible time. Clock in hand, the personnel manager told each woman when to begin and when to stop. Some were asked to adjust the pegs by hand, others were given small pliers to do so. Most were unable to complete the test in the allotted time. One by one they came out of the office looking weary and expressing their conviction that they wouldn't be hired.

Later on we were given the familiar application form. Again, I had to ponder what my greatest aspiration in life was. But this time I was curious to know what Xochitl had answered. "Well," she said, "I don't know if my answer is right. Maybe it is wrong. But I tried to be truthful. My greatest aspiration in life is to improve myself and to progress." . . .

After completing the application at Camisas de Juárez there was still another test to take. This one consisted of demonstrating sewing skills on an industrial machine. Again many women expressed doubts and concern after returning to the lobby where other expectant women awaited their turn. In the hours that had been spent together a lively dialogue had ensued. Evidently there was a sense that all of us were united by the common experience of job seeking and by the gnawing anxiety that potential failure entails. Women compared notes and exchanged opinions about the nature and difficulty of their respective tests. They did not offer each other overt reassurance or support, but they made sympathetic comments and hoped that there would be work for all.

At 3:30 P.M., that is, seven hours after the majority of us had arrived at the plant, we were dismissed. We were given no indication that any of us would be hired. Rather, we were told that a telegram would be sent to each address as soon as a decision was made. Most women left disappointed and certain that they would probably not be hired.

Two weeks later, when I had almost given up all hope, the telegram arrived. I was to come to the plant as soon as possible to receive further instructions. Upon my arrival I was given the address of a small clinic in downtown Ciudad Juárez. I was to bring two pictures to the clinic and take a medical examination. Its explicit purpose was to evaluate the physical fitness of potential workers. In reality it was a simple pregnancy test. Maquiladoras do not hire pregnant women, although very often these are among the ones with greater need for employment. . . .

Having been examined at the clinic, I returned to the factory with a sealed envelope containing certification of my physical capacity to work. I was then told to return the following Monday at 3:30 P.M. in order to start work. After what seemed an unduly long and complicated procedure, I was finally being hired as an assembly worker. For the next six weeks I shared the experience of approximately eighty women who had also been recruited to work the evening shift at Camisas de Juárez. Xochitl, Beatríz and Teresa had been hired too.

On weekdays work started at 3:45 P.M. and it ended at 11:30 P.M. At 7:30 P.M. a bell signaled the beginning of a half-hour break during which workers could eat their dinner. Some brought homemade sandwiches, but many bought their food at the factory. Meals generally consisted of a dish of *flautas* or *tostadas* and carbonated drinks. The persistence of inadequate diets causes assembly workers numerous gastric problems. On Saturdays the shift started at 11:30 A.M. and it ended at 9:30 P.M. with a half-hour break. We worked in total forty-eight hours every week and earned the minimum wage, that is, 875 pesos per week; 125 pesos per day; an hourly rate of approximately $0.60. . . .

From the perspective of workers, medical insurance is as important as a decorous wage. This is particularly true in the case of women who have children in their care. Thus, it was not surprising to find out that some new workers at Camisas de Juárez were there mainly because of the *seguro*. María Luisa, a twenty-nine-year-old woman, told me, "I don't have a lot of money, but neither do I have great need to work. My husband owns a small restaurant and we have a fairly good income. But I have four children and one of them is chronically sick. Without insurance medical fees will render us poor. That's the main reason why I am working."

As do the majority of garment maquiladoras, Camisas de Juárez operates by a combination of piecework and the minimum wage. Upon being hired by the plant every worker earns a fixed wage. However, all workers are expected to fulfill production quotas. On the first day at the job I was trained to perform a particular operation. My task was to sew narrow biases around the cuff-openings of men's shirts. As with other operations I had performed before, this one entailed coordination and speed. . . .

As for the production quota, I was expected to complete 162 pairs of sleeves every hour, that is, one every 2.7 seconds, more than 1,200 pairs per shift. It seemed to me that to achieve such a goal would require unworldly skill and velocity. In six weeks as a direct production operator I was to fall short of this goal by almost 50%. But I was a very inexperienced worker. Sandra, who sat next to me during this period, assured me that it could be done. It wasn't easy, but certainly it could be done. . . .

The factory environment was all-embracing, its demands overwhelmed me. Young supervisors walked about the aisles asking for higher productivity and encouraging us to work at greater speed. Periodically their voices could be heard throughout the workplace: "Faster! Faster! Come on, girls, let us hear the sound of those machines!" They were personally responsible before management for the efficiency of the workers under their command.

Esther, who oversaw my labor, had been a nurse prior to her employment in the factory. I was intrigued by her polite manner and her change of jobs. She dressed prettily, seeming a bit out of place amidst the heated humdrum of the sewing machines, the lint and the dispersed fabric that cluttered the plant. She told me it was more profitable to work at a maquiladora than at a clinic or a hospital.

Esther saw her true vocation as that of a nurse, but she had to support an ill and aging father. Her mother had died three years earlier, and although her home was nice and fully owned, she was solely responsible for the family debts. Working at a factory entailed less prestige than working as a nurse, but it offered a better wage. She was now earning almost one thousand pesos a week. As a nurse she had earned only a bit more than half that amount. From her I also learned, for the first time, about the dubious advantages of being a maquiladora supervisor.

As with the others in similar positions, Esther had to stay at the plant long after the shift ended and the workers left. Very often the hours ran until one in the morning. During that time she verified quotas, sorted out production, tried to detect errors and, not seldom, personally unseamed defective garments. With the others she was also responsible for the preparation of shipments and the selection of material for the following day's production. In other words, her supervisory capacities included quality control and some administrative functions.

When productivity levels are not met, when workers fail to arrive punctually or are absent, or when there is trouble in the line, it is the supervisor who is first admonished by management.

Thus, supervisors occupy an intermediary position between the firm and the workers, which is to say that they often find themselves between the devil and the deep blue sea.

As with the factory guard, supervisors and group leaders are frequently seen by workers as solely responsible for their plight at the workplace. Perceived abuses, unfair treatment and excessive demands are thought to be the result of supervisors' whims rather than the creature of a particular system of production. That explains, in part, why workers' grievances are often couched in complaints about the performance of supervisors.

But while supervisors may be seen by workers as close allies of the firms, they stand at the bottom of the administrative hierarchy. They are also the receivers of middle and upper management's dissatisfaction, but they have considerably less power and their sphere of action is very limited. Many line supervisors agree that the complications they face in their jobs are hardly worth the differences in pay. . . .

The Organization of Labor in the Factory

The pressures exerted by supervisors at Camisas de Juárez were hard to ignore. Esther was considerate and encouraging: "You're doing much better now. Soon enough you'll be sewing as fast as the others." But I had doubts, as she was constantly asking me to repair my own defective work, a task which entailed an infinite sense of frustration. I began to skip dinner breaks in order to continue sewing in a feeble attempt to improve my productivity level. I was not alone. Some workers fearful of permanent dismissal also stayed at their sewing machines during the break while the rest went outside to eat and rest. I could understand their behavior; their jobs were at stake. But presumably my situation was different. I had nothing to lose by inefficiency, and yet I felt compelled to do my best. I started pondering upon the subtle mechanisms that dominate will at the workplace and about the shame that overwhelms those who fall short of the goals assigned to them.

The fact is that as the days passed it became increasingly difficult to think of factory work as a stage in a research project. My identity became that of the worker; my immediate objectives those determined by the organization of labor at the plant.

Academic research became an ethereal fiction. Reality was work, as much for me as for the others who labored under the same roof.

These feelings were reinforced by my personal interactions during working hours. I was one link in a rigidly structured chain. My failure to produce speedily had numerous consequences for others operating in the same line and in the factory as a whole. For example, Lucha, my nineteen-year-old companion, was in charge of cutting remnant thread and separating the sleeves five other seamstresses and I sewed. She also made it her business to return to me all those parts which she felt would not meet Esther's approval. According to her she did this in order to spare me further embarrassment. But it was in her interest that I sewed quickly and well; the catch in this matter was that she was unable to meet her quota unless the six seamstresses she assisted met theirs.

Therefore, a careless and slow worker could stand between Lucha and her possibility to get a weekly bonus. The more a seamstress sewed, the more a thread cutter became indispensable. As a consequence, Lucha was extremely interested in seeing improvements in my level of productivity and in the quality of my work. Sometimes her attitude and exhortations verged on the hostile. As far as I was concerned, the accusatory expression on her face was the best work incentive yet devised by the factory. It was not difficult to discern impinging tension. I was not surprised to find out during the weeks spent at Camisas de Juárez that the germ of enmity had bloomed between some seamstresses and their respective thread cutters over matters of work.

Although the relationships between seamstresses and thread cutters were especially delicate, all workers were affected by each other's level of efficiency. Cuffless sleeves could not be attached to shirts. Sleeves could not be sewed to shirts without collars or pockets. Holes and buttons had to be fixed at the end. Unfinished garments could not be cleaned of lint or labeled. In sum, each minute step required a series of preceding operations effectively completed. Delay of one stage inevitably slowed up the whole process.

From the perspective of the workers, labor appeared as the interconnection of efficiently performed individual activities rather than as a structured imposition from above. Managers are nearly invisible, but the flaws of fellow workers are always apparent.

Bonuses exist as seemingly impersonal rewards whose access can be made difficult by a neighbor's laziness or incompetence. As a result, complaints are frequently directed against other workers and supervisors. The organization of labor at any particular plant does not immediately lead to feelings of solidarity.

On the other hand, common experiences at the workplace provide the basis for dialogue and elicit a particular kind of humor. In this there is frequently expressed a longing for relief from the tediousness of industrial work. One of Sandra's favorite topics of conversation was to reflect upon the possibility of marriage. She did so with a witty and self-deprecatory attitude.

She thought that if she could only find a nice man who would be willing to support her, everything in her life would be all right. She didn't mind if he was not young or good-looking, as long as he had plenty of money. Were there men like that left in the world? Of course, with the children it was difficult, not to say impossible, to find such a godsend. Then again, no one kept you from trying. But not at the maquiladora. All of us were female. Not even a lonely engineer was to be found at Camisas de Juárez. One could die of boredom there.

However, the fact that there weren't men around at the plant had its advantages according to Sandra. At many factories men generally occupied supervisory and middle- and upper-management positions. Sandra knew many women who had been seduced and then deserted by engineers and technicians. In other cases, women felt they had to comply with the sexual demands of fellow workers because they believed otherwise they would lose their jobs. Some were just plain stupid. Things were especially difficult for very young women at large plants like RCA. They needed guidance and information to stay out of trouble, but there was no one to advise them. Their families had too many problems to care. . . .

Fortunately, there were the bars and the discotheques. Did I like to go out dancing? She didn't think so; I didn't look like the kind who would. But it was great fun; we should go out together sometime (eventually we did). The Malibú, a popular dancing hall, had good shows. But it was tacky and full of kids. It was better to go to the Max Fim, and especially the Cosmos. The latter was always crowded because everyone liked it so much. Even people from the other side (the United States) came to Juárez just to visit Cosmos. Its décor was inspired by outerspace movies like *Star Wars*. It was full of color and movement and shifting lights. They played the best American disco music. If you were lucky you could meet a U.S. citizen. Maybe he would even want to get married and you could go and live in El Paso. Things like that happen at discotheques. Once a Jordanian soldier in service at Fort Bliss had asked her to marry him the first time they met at Cosmos. But he wanted to return to his country, and she had said no. Cosmos was definitely the best discotheque in Juárez, and Sandra could be found dancing there amidst the deafening sound of music every Saturday evening.

The inexhaustible level of energy of women working at the maquiladoras never ceased to impress me. How could anyone be in the mood for all-night dancing on Saturdays after forty-eight weekly hours of industrial work? I had seen many of these women stretching their muscles late at night, trying to soothe the pain they felt at the waist. After the incessant noise of the sewing machines, how could anyone long for even higher levels of sound? But as Sandra explained to me, life is too short. If you don't go out and have fun, you will come to the end of your days having done nothing but sleep, eat and work. And she didn't call that living. . . .

FIFTY-FIVE

◆◆◆

The Care Crisis in the Philippines (2003)
Children and Transnational Families in the New Global Economy

Rhacel Salazar Parreñas

Rhacel Salazar Parreñas is a professor of Asian American studies at the University of California, Davis. Author of *Servants of Globalization: Women, migration, and domestic work*, her work on migrant workers, immigration, gender, family, and diasporic communities as been published in the *Wall Street Journal* and the *American Prospect*.

A growing crisis of care troubles the world's most developed nations. Even as demand for care has increased, its supply has dwindled. The result is a care deficit,[1] to which women from the Philippines have responded in force. Roughly two-thirds[2] of Filipino migrant workers are women, and their exodus, usually to fill domestic jobs,[3] has generated tremendous social change in the Philippines. When female migrants are mothers, they leave behind their own children, usually in the care of other women. Many Filipino children now grow up in divided households, where geographic separation places children under serious emotional strain. And yet it is impossible to overlook the significance of migrant labor to the Philippine economy. Some 34 to 54 percent of the Filipino population is sustained by remittances from migrant workers.[4]

Women in the Philippines, just like their counterparts in postindustrial nations, suffer from a "stalled revolution." Local gender ideology remains a few steps behind the economic reality, which has produced numerous female-headed, transnational households.[5] Consequently, a far greater degree of anxiety attends the quality of family life for the dependents of migrant mothers than for those of migrant fathers. The dominant gender ideology, after all, holds that a woman's rightful place is in the home, and the households of migrant mothers present a challenge to this view. In response, government officials and journalists denounce migrating mothers, claiming that they have caused the Filipino family to deteriorate, children to be abandoned, and a crisis of care to take root in the Philippines. To end this crisis, critics admonish, these mothers must return. Indeed, in May 1995, Philippine president Fidel Ramos called for initiatives to keep migrant mothers at home. He declared, "We are not against overseas employment of Filipino women. We are against overseas employment at the cost of family solidarity."[6] Migration, Ramos strongly implied, is morally acceptable only when it is undertaken by single, childless women.

The Philippine media reinforce this position by consistently publishing sensationalist reports on the suffering of children in transnational families. These reports tend to vilify migrant mothers, suggesting that their children face more profound problems than do those of migrant fathers; and despite the fact that most of the children in question are left with relatives, journalists tend to refer to them as having been "abandoned." One article reports, "A child's sense of loss appears to be greater when it is the mother who leaves to work abroad."[7] Others link the emigration of mothers to the inadequate child care and unstable family life that eventually lead such children to "drugs, gambling, and drinking."[8] Writes one columnist, "Incest and rapes within blood relatives are alarmingly on the rise not only within Metro Manila but also in the provinces. There are some indications that the absence of mothers who have become OCWs [overseas contract workers] has something to do with the situation."[9] The same columnist elsewhere expresses the popular view that the children of migrants become a burden on the larger society: "Guidance counselors and social welfare agencies can show grim statistics on how many children have turned into liabilities to our society because of absentee parents."[10]

From January to July 2000, I conducted sixty-nine in-depth interviews with young adults who grew up in transnational households in the Philippines. Almost none of these children have yet reunited with their migrant parents. I interviewed thirty children with migrant mothers, twenty-six with migrant fathers, and thirteen with two migrant parents. The children I spoke to certainly had endured emotional hardships; but contrary to the media's dark presentation, they did not all experience their mothers' migration as abandonment. The hardships in their lives were frequently diminished when they received support from extended families and communities, when they enjoyed open communication with their migrant parents, and when they clearly understood the limited financial options that led their parents to migrate in the first place.

To call for the return of migrant mothers is to ignore the fact that the Philippines has grown increasingly dependent on their remittances. To acknowledge this reality could lead the Philippines toward a more egalitarian gender ideology. Casting blame on migrant mothers, however, serves only to divert the society's attention away from these children's needs, finally aggravating their difficulties by stigmatizing their family's choices.

The Philippine media has certainly sensationalized the issue of child welfare in migrating families, but that should not obscure the fact that the Philippines faces a genuine care crisis. Care is now the country's primary export. Remittances—mostly from migrant domestic workers—constitute the economy's largest source of foreign currency, totaling almost $7 billion in 1999.[11] With limited choices in the Philippines, women migrate to help sustain their families financially, but the price is very high. Both mothers and children suffer from family separation, even under the best of circumstances.

Migrant mothers who work as nannies often face the painful prospect of caring for other people's children while being unable to tend to their own. One such mother in Rome, Rosemarie Samaniego,[12] describes this predicament:

> When the girl that I take care of calls her mother "Mama," my heart jumps all the time because my children also call me "Mama." I feel the gap caused by our physical separation especially in the morning, when I pack [her] lunch, because that's what I used to do for my children. . . . I used to do that very same thing for them. I begin thinking that at this hour I should be taking care of my very own children and not someone else's, someone who is not related to me in any way, shape, or form. . . . The work that I do here is done for my family, but the problem is they are not close to me but are far away in the Philippines. Sometimes, you feel the separation and you start to cry. Some days, I just start crying while I am sweeping the floor because I am thinking about my children in the Philippines. Sometimes, when I receive a letter from my children telling me that they are sick, I look up out the window and ask the Lord to look after them and make sure they get better even without me around to care after them. [*Starts crying.*] If I had wings, I would fly home to my children. Just for a moment, to see my children and take care of their needs, help them, then fly back over here to continue my work.

The children of migrant workers also suffer an incalculable loss when a parent disappears overseas.

As Ellen Seneriches,[13] a twenty-one-year-old daughter of a domestic worker in New York, says:

> There are times when you want to talk to her, but she is not there. That is really hard, very difficult. . . . There are times when I want to call her, speak to her, cry to her, and I cannot. It is difficult. The only thing that I can do is write to her. And I cannot cry through the e-mails and sometimes I just want to cry on her shoulder.

Children like Ellen, who was only ten years old when her mother left for New York, often repress their longings to reunite with their mothers. Knowing that their families have few financial options, they are left with no choice but to put their emotional needs aside. Often, they do so knowing that their mothers' care and attention have been diverted to other children. When I asked her how she felt about her mother's wards in New York, Ellen responded:

> Very jealous. I am very, very jealous. There was even a time when she told the children she was caring for that they are very lucky that she was taking care of them, while her children back in the Philippines don't even have a mom to take care of them. It's pathetic, but it's true. We were left alone by ourselves and we had to be responsible at a very young age without a mother. Can you imagine?

Children like Ellen do experience emotional stress when they grow up in transnational households. But it is worth emphasizing that many migrant mothers attempt to sustain ties with their children, and their children often recognize and appreciate these efforts. Although her mother, undocumented in the United States, has not returned once to the Philippines in twelve years, Ellen does not doubt that she has struggled to remain close to her children despite the distance. In fact, although Ellen lives only three hours away from her father, she feels closer to and communicates more frequently with her mother. Says Ellen:

> I realize that my mother loves us very much. Even if she is far away, she would send us her love. She would make us feel like she really loved us. She would do this by always being there. She would just assure us that whenever we have problems to just call her and tell her.

[*Pauses.*] And so I know that it has been more difficult for her than other mothers. She has had to do extra work because she is so far away from us.

Like Ellen's mother, who managed to "be there" despite a vast distance, other migrant mothers do not necessarily "abandon" their traditional duty of nurturing their families. Rather, they provide emotional care and guidance from afar.[14] Ellen even credits her mother for her success in school. Now a second-year medical school student, Ellen graduated at the top of her class in both high school and college. She says that the constant, open communication she shares with her mother provided the key to her success. She reflects:

> We communicate as often as we can, like twice or thrice a week through e-mails. Then she would call us every week. And it is very expensive, I know. . . . My mother and I have a very open relationship. We are like best friends. She would give me advice whenever I had problems. . . . She understands everything I do. She understands why I would act this or that way. She knows me really well. And she is also transparent to me. She always knows when I have problems, and likewise I know when she does. I am closer to her than to my father.

Ellen is clearly not the abandoned child or social liability the Philippine media describe. She not only benefits from sufficient parental support—from both her geographically distant mother and her nearby father—but also exceeds the bar of excellence in schooling. Her story indicates that children of migrant parents can overcome the emotional strains of transnational family life, and that they can enjoy sufficient family support, even from their geographically distant parent.

Of course, her good fortune is not universal. But it does raise questions about how children withstand such geographical strains; whether and how they maintain solid ties with their distant parents; and what circumstances lead some children to feel that those ties have weakened or given out. The Philippine media tend to equate the absence of a child's biological mother with abandonment, which leads to the assumption that all such children, lacking familial support, will become social liabilities.[15]

But I found that positive surrogate parental figures and open communication with the migrant parent, along with acknowledgment of the migrant parent's contribution to the collective mobility of the family, allay many of the emotional insecurities that arise from transnational household arrangements. Children who lack these resources have greater difficulty adjusting.

Extensive research bears out this observation. The Scalabrini Migration Center, a nongovernmental organization for migration research in the Philippines, surveyed 709 elementary-school-age Filipino children in 2000, comparing the experiences of those with a father absent, a mother absent, both parents absent, and both parents present. While the researchers observed that parental absence does prompt feelings of abandonment and loneliness among children, they concluded that "it does not necessarily become an occasion for laziness and unruliness." Rather, if the extended family supports the child and makes him or her aware of the material benefits migration brings, the child may actually be spurred toward greater self-reliance and ambition, despite continued longings for family unity.

Jeek Pereno's life has been defined by those longings. At twenty-five, he is a merchandiser for a large department store in the Philippines. His mother more than adequately provided for her children, managing with her meager wages first as a domestic worker and then as a nurse's aide, to send them $200 a month and even to purchase a house in a fairly exclusive neighborhood in the city center. But Jeek still feels abandoned and insecure in his mother's affection, he believes that growing up without his parents robbed him of the discipline he needed. Like other children of migrant workers, Jeek does not feel that his faraway mother's financial support has been enough. Instead, he wishes she had offered him more guidance, concern, and emotional care.

Jeek was eight years old when his parents relocated to New York and left him, along with his three brothers, in the care of their aunt. Eight years later, Jeek's father passed away, and two of his brothers (the oldest and youngest) joined their mother in New York. Visa complications have prevented Jeek and his other brother from following—but their mother has not once returned to visit them in the Philippines.

When I expressed surprise at this, Jeek solemnly replied: "Never. It will cost too much, she said."

Years of separation breed unfamiliarity among family members, and Jeek does not have the emotional security of knowing that his mother has genuinely tried to lessen that estrangement. For Jeek, only a visit could shore up this security after seventeen years of separation. His mother's weekly phone calls do not suffice. And because he experiences his mother's absence as indifference, he does not feel comfortable communicating with her openly about his unmet needs. The result is repression, which in turn aggravates the resentment he feels. Jeek told me:

> I talk to my mother once in a while. But what happens, whenever she asks how I am doing, I just say okay. It's not like I am really going to tell her that I have problems here. . . . It's not like she can do anything about my problems if I told her about them. Financial problems, yes she can help. But not the other problems, like emotional problems. . . . She will try to give advice, but I am not very interested to talk to her about things like that. . . . Of course, you are still young, you don't really know what is going to happen in the future. Before you realize that your parents left you, you can't do anything about it anymore. You are not in a position to tell them not to leave you. They should have not left us. (*Sobs.*)

I asked Jeek if his mother knew he felt this way. "No," he said, "she doesn't know." Asked if he received emotional support from anyone, Jeek replied, "As much as possible, if I can handle it, I try not to get emotional support from anyone. I just keep everything inside me."

Jeek feels that his mother not only abandoned him but failed to leave him with an adequate surrogate. His aunt had a family and children of her own. Jeek recalled, "While I do know that my aunt loves me and she took care of us to the best of her ability, I am not convinced that it was enough. . . . Because we were not disciplined enough. She let us do whatever we wanted to do." Jeek feels that his education suffered from this lack of discipline, and he greatly regrets not having concentrated on his studies. Having completed only a two-year vocational program in electronics, he doubts his competency to pursue a college degree. At twenty-five, he feels stuck, with only the limited option of turning from one low-paying job to another.

Children who, unlike Jeek, received good surrogate parenting managed to concentrate on their studies and in the end to fare much better. Rudy Montoya, a nineteen-year-old whose mother has done domestic work in Hong Kong for more than twelve years, credits his mother's brother for helping him succeed in high school:

> My uncle is the most influential person in my life. Well, he is in Saudi Arabia now. . . . He would tell me that my mother loves me and not to resent her, and that whatever happens, I should write her. He would encourage me and he would tell me to trust the Lord. And then, I remember in high school, he would push me to study. I learned a lot from him in high school. Showing his love for me, he would help me with my schoolwork. . . . The time that I spent with my uncle was short, but he is the person who helped me grow up to be a better person.

Unlike Jeek's aunt, Rudy's uncle did not have a family of his own. He was able to devote more time to Rudy, instilling discipline in his young charge as well as reassuring him that his mother, who is the sole income provider for her family, did not abandon him. Although his mother has returned to visit him only twice—once when he was in the fourth grade and again two years later—Rudy, who is now a college student, sees his mother as a "good provider" who has made tremendous sacrifices for his sake. This knowledge offers him emotional security, as well as a strong feeling of gratitude. When I asked him about the importance of education, he replied, "I haven't given anything back to my mother for the sacrifices that she has made for me. The least I could do for her is graduate, so that I can find a good job, so that eventually I will be able to help her out, too."

Many children resolve the emotional insecurity of being left by their parents the way that Rudy has: by viewing migration as a sacrifice to be repaid by adult children. Children who believe that their migrant mothers are struggling for the sake of the family's collective mobility, rather than leaving to live the "good life," are less likely to feel abandoned and more likely to accept their mothers' efforts to sustain close relationships from a distance. One such child is Theresa Bascara, an eighteen-year-old college student whose mother has worked as a domestic in Hong Kong since 1984. As she puts it, "[My inspiration is] my mother, because she is the one suffering over there. So the least I can give back to her is doing well in school."

For Ellen Seneriches, the image of her suffering mother compels her to reciprocate. She explained:

> Especially after my mother left, I became more motivated to study harder. I did because my mother was sacrificing a lot and I had to compensate for how hard it is to be away from your children and then crying a lot at night, not knowing what we are doing. She would tell us in voice tapes. She would send us voice tapes every month, twice a month, and we would hear her cry in these tapes.

Having witnessed her mother's suffering even from a distance, Ellen can acknowledge the sacrifices her mother has made and the hardships she has endured in order to be a "good provider" for her family. This knowledge assuaged the resentment Ellen frequently felt when her mother first migrated.

Many of the children I interviewed harbored images of their mothers as martyrs, and they often found comfort in their mother's grief over not being able to nurture them directly. The expectation among such children that they will continue to receive a significant part of their nurturing from their mothers, despite the distance, points to the conservative gender ideology most of them maintain.[16] But whether or not they see their mothers as martyrs, children of migrant women feel best cared for when their mothers make consistent efforts to show parental concern from a distance. As Jeek's and Ellen's stories indicate, open communication with the migrant parent soothes feelings of abandonment; those who enjoy such open channels fare much better than those who lack them. Not only does communication ease children's emotional difficulties; it also fosters a sense of family unity, and it promotes the view that migration is a survival strategy that requires sacrifices from both children and parents for the good of the family.

For daughters of migrant mothers, such sacrifices commonly take the form of assuming some of their absent mothers' responsibilities, including the care of younger siblings. As Ellen told me:

> It was a strategy, and all of us had to sacrifice for it. . . . We all had to adjust, every day of our lives. . . . Imagine waking up without a mother

calling you for breakfast. Then there would be no one to prepare the clothes for my brothers. We are all going to school. . . . I had to wake up earlier. I had to prepare their clothes. I had to wake them up and help them prepare for school. Then I also had to help them with their homework at night. I had to tutor them.

Asked if she resented this extra work, Ellen replied, "No. I saw it as training, a training that helped me become a leader. It makes you more of a leader doing that every day. I guess that is an advantage to me, and to my siblings as well."

Ellen's effort to assist in the household's daily maintenance was another way she reciprocated for her mother's emotional and financial support. Viewing her added work as a positive life lesson, Ellen believes that these responsibilities enabled her to develop leadership skills. Notably, her high school selected her as its first ever female commander for its government-mandated military training corps.

Unlike Jeek, Ellen is secure in her mother's love. She feels that her mother has struggled to "be there"; Jeek feels that his has not. Hence, Ellen has managed to successfully adjust to her household arrangement, while Jeek has not. The continual open communication between Ellen and her mother has had ramifications for their entire family: in return for her mother's sacrifices, Ellen assumed the role of second mother to her younger siblings, visiting them every weekend during her college years in order to spend quality time with them.

In general, eldest daughters of migrant mothers assume substantial familial responsibilities, often becoming substitute mothers for their siblings. Similarly, eldest sons stand in for migrant fathers. Armando Martinez, a twenty-nine-year-old entrepreneur whose father worked in Dubai for six months while he was in high school, related his experiences:

I became a father during those six months. It was like, ugghhh, I made the rules. . . . I was able to see that it was hard if your family is not complete, you feel that there is something missing. . . . It's because the major decisions, sometimes, I was not old enough for them. I was only a teenager, and I was not that strong in my convictions when it came to making

decisions. It was like work that I should not have been responsible for. I still wanted to play. So it was an added burden on my side.

Even when there is a parent left behind, children of migrant workers tend to assume added familial responsibilities, and these responsibilities vary along gender lines. Nonetheless, the weight tends to fall most heavily on children of migrant mothers, who are often left to struggle with the lack of male responsibility for care work in the Philippines. While a great number of children with migrant fathers receive full-time care from stay-at-home mothers, those with migrant mothers do not receive the same amount of care. Their fathers are likely to hold full-time jobs, and they rarely have the time to assume the role of primary caregiver. Of thirty children of migrant mothers I interviewed, only four had stay-at-home fathers. Most fathers passed the caregiving responsibilities on to other relatives, many of whom, like Jeek's aunt, already had families of their own to care for and regarded the children of migrant relatives as an extra burden. Families of migrant fathers are less likely to rely on the care work of extended kin.[17] Among my interviewees, thirteen of twenty-six children with migrant fathers lived with and were cared for primarily by their stay-at-home mothers.

Children of migrant mothers, unlike those of migrant fathers, have the added burden of accepting nontraditional gender roles in their families. The Scalabrini Migration Center reports that these children "tend to be more angry, confused, apathetic, and more afraid than other children."[18] They are caught within an "ideological stall" in the societal acceptance of female-headed transnational households. Because her family does not fit the traditional nuclear household model, Theresa Bascara sees her family as "broken," even though she describes her relationship to her mother as "very close." She says, "A family, I can say, is only whole if your father is the one working and your mother is only staying at home. It's okay if your mother works too, but somewhere close to you."

Some children in transnational families adjust to their household arrangements with greater success than others do. Those who feel that their mothers strive to nurture them as well as to be good providers are more likely to be accepting. The support of extended kin, or perhaps a sense of public accountability for their welfare, also helps children combat feelings of abandonment. Likewise, a more gender-egalitarian value system enables children to appreciate their mothers as good providers, which in turn allows them to see their mothers' migrations as demonstrations of love.

Even if they are well-adjusted, however, children in transnational families still suffer the loss of family intimacy. They are often forced to compensate by accepting commodities, rather than affection, as the most tangible reassurance of their parents' love. By putting family intimacy on hold, children can only wait for the opportunity to spend quality time with their migrant parents. Even when that time comes, it can be painful. As Theresa related:

> When my mother is home, I just sit next to her. I stare at her face, to see the changes in her face, to see how she aged during the years that she was away from us. But when she is about to go back to Hong Kong, it's like my heart is going to burst. I would just cry and cry. I really can't explain the feeling. Sometimes, when my mother is home, preparing to leave for Hong Kong, I would just start crying, because I already start missing her. I ask myself, how many more years will it be until we see each other again?
>
> . . . Telephone calls. That's not enough. You can't hug her, kiss her, feel her, everything. You can't feel her presence. It's just words that you have. What I want is to have my mother close to me, to see her grow older, and when she is sick, you are the one taking care of her and when you are sick, she is the one taking care of you.

Not surprisingly, when asked if they would leave their own children to take jobs as migrant workers, almost all of my respondents answered, "Never." When I asked why not, most said that they would never want their children to go through what they had gone through, or to be denied what they were denied, in their childhoods. Armando Martinez best summed up what children in transnational families lose when he said:

> You just cannot buy the times when your family is together. Isn't that right? Time together is something that money can neither buy nor replace. . . . The first time your baby speaks, you are not there. Other people would experience

that joy. And when your child graduates with honors, you are also not there. . . . Is that right? When your child wins a basketball game, no one will be there to ask him how his game went, how many points he made. Is that right? Your family loses, don't you think?

Children of transnational families repeatedly stress that they lack the pleasure and comfort of daily interaction with their parents. Nonetheless, these children do not necessarily become "delinquent," nor are their families necessarily broken, in the manner the Philippine media depicts. Armando mirrored the opinion of most of the children in my study when he defended transnational families: "Even if [parents] are far away, they are still there. I get that from basketball, specifically zone defense." [He laughed.] "If someone is not there, you just have to adjust. It's like a slight hindrance that you just have to adjust to. Then when they come back, you get a chance to recover. It's like that."

Recognizing that the family is an adaptive unit that responds to external forces, many children make do, even if doing so requires tremendous sacrifices. They give up intimacy and familiarity with their parents. Often, they attempt to make up for their migrant parents' hardships by maintaining close bonds across great distances, even though most of them feel that such bonds could never possibly draw their distant parent close enough. But their efforts are frequently sustained by the belief that such emotional sacrifices are not without meaning—that they are ultimately for the greater good of their families and their future. Jason Halili's mother provided care for elderly persons in Los Angeles for fifteen years. Jason, now twenty-one, reasons, "If she did not leave, I would not be here right now. So it was the hardest route to take, but at the same time, the best route to take."

Transnational families were not always equated with "broken homes" in the Philippine public discourse. Nor did labor migration emerge as a perceived threat to family life before the late 1980s, when the number of migrant women significantly increased. This suggests that changes to the gendered division of family labor may have as much as anything else to do with the Philippine care crisis.

The Philippine public simply assumes that the proliferation of female-headed transnational households will wreak havoc on the lives of children. The Scalabrini Migration Center explains that children of migrant mothers suffer more than those of migrant fathers because child rearing is "a role women are more adept at, are better prepared for, and pay more attention to."[19] The center's study, like the Philippine media, recommends that mothers be kept from migrating. The researchers suggest that "economic programs should be targeted particularly toward the absorption of the female labor force, to facilitate the possibility for mothers to remain in the family."[20] Yet the return migration of mothers is neither a plausible nor a desirable solution. Rather, it implicitly accepts gender inequities in the family, even as it ignores the economic pressures generated by globalization.

As national discourse on the care crisis in the Philippines vilifies migrant women, it also downplays the contributions these women make to the country's economy. Such hand-wringing merely offers the public an opportunity to discipline women morally and to resist reconstituting family life in a manner that reflects the country's increasing dependence on women's foreign remittances. This pattern is not exclusive to the Philippines. As Arjun Appadurai observes, globalization has commonly led to "ideas about gender and modernity that create large female work forces at the same time that cross-national ideologies of 'culture,' 'authenticity,' and national honor put increasing pressure on various communities to morally discipline working women."[21]

The moral disciplining of women, however, hurts those who most need protection. It pathologizes the children of migrants, and it downplays the emotional difficulties that mothers like Rosemarie Samaniego face. Moreover, it ignores the struggles of migrant mothers who attempt to nurture their children from a distance. Vilifying migrant women as bad mothers promotes the view that the return to the nuclear family is the only viable solution to the emotional difficulties of children in transnational families. In so doing, it directs attention away from the special needs of children in transnational families—for instance, the need for community projects that would improve communication among far-flung family members, or for special school programs, the like of which did not exist at my field research site. It's also a strategy that sidelines the agency and adaptability of the children themselves.

To say that children are perfectly capable of adjusting to nontraditional households is not to say that they don't suffer hardships. But the overwhelming public support for keeping migrant mothers at home does have a negative impact on these children's adjustment. Implicit in such views is a rejection of the division of labor in families with migrant mothers, and the message such children receive is that their household arrangements are simply wrong. Moreover, calling for the return migration of women does not necessarily solve the problems plaguing families in the Philippines. Domestic violence and male infidelity, for instance—two social problems the government has never adequately addressed—would still threaten the well-being of children.[22]

Without a doubt, the children of migrant Filipina domestic workers suffer from the extraction of care from the global south to the global north. The plight of these children is a timely and necessary concern for nongovernmental, governmental, and academic groups in the Philippines. Blaming migrant mothers, however, has not helped, and has even hurt, those whose relationships suffer most from the movement of care in the global economy. Advocates for children in transnational families should focus their attention not on calling for a return to the nuclear family but on trying to meet the special needs transnational families possess. One of those needs is for a reconstituted gender ideology in the Philippines; another is for the elimination of legislation that penalizes migrant families in the nations where they work.

If we want to secure quality care for the children of transnational families, gender egalitarian views of child rearing are essential. Such views can be fostered by recognizing the economic contributions women make to their families and by redefining motherhood to include providing for one's family. Gender should be recognized as a fluid social category, and masculinity should be redefined, as the larger society questions the biologically based assumption that only women have an aptitude to provide care. Government officials and the media could then stop vilifying migrant women, redirecting their attention, instead, to men. They could question the lack of male accountability for care work, and they could demand that men, including migrant fathers, take more responsibility for the emotional welfare of their children.

The host societies of migrant Filipina domestic workers should also be held more accountable for their welfare and for that of their families. These women's work allows First World women to enter the paid labor force. As one Dutch employer states, "There are people who would look after children, but other things are more fun. Carers from other countries, if we can use their surplus carers, that's a solution."[23]

Yet, as we've seen, one cannot simply assume that the care leaving disadvantaged nations is surplus care. What is a solution for rich nations creates a problem in poor nations. Mothers like Rosemarie Samaniego and children like Ellen Seneriches and Jeek Pereno bear the brunt of this problem, while the receiving countries and the employing families benefit.

Most receiving countries have yet to recognize the contributions of their migrant care workers. They have consistently ignored these workers' rights and limited their full incorporation into society. The wages of migrant workers are so low that they cannot afford to bring their own families to join them, or to regularly visit their children in the Philippines; relegated to the status of guest workers, they are restricted to the low-wage employment sector, and with very few exceptions, the migration of their spouses and children is also restricted.[24] These arrangements work to the benefit of employers, since migrant care workers can give the best possible care for their employers' families when they are free of care-giving responsibilities to their own families. But there is a dire need to lobby for more inclusive policies, and for employers to develop a sense of accountability for their workers' children. After all, migrant workers significantly help their employers to reduce *their* families' care deficit.

NOTES

1. Arlie Hochschild, "The Culture of Politics: Traditional, Post-modern, Cold Modern, Warm Modern Ideals of Care," *Social Politics*, vol. 2, no. 3 (1995): pp. 331–46.

2. While women made up only 12 percent of the total worker outflow in 1975, this figure grew to 47 percent twelve years later in 1987 and surpassed the number of men by 1995. IBON Facts and Figures, "Filipinos as Global Slaves," vol. 22, nos. 5–6 (March 15–31, 1999), p. 6.

3. Notably, Filipino women. . . also alleviate the care crisis plaguing hospitals and hospices in more developed nations by providing services as professional nurses. At the expense of the quality of professional care in the Philippines, nurses have sought the better wages available outside the country.

4. Gina Mission, "The Breadwinners: Female Migrant Workers," *WIN: Women's International Net Issue* (November 1998): p. 15A.

5. Hochschild and Machung, 1989. By "stalled revolution," Hochschild refers to the fact that the economic contributions of women to the family have not been met with a corresponding increase in male responsibility for household work.

6. Agence France-Presse, "Ramos: Overseas Employment a Threat to Filipino Families," *Philippine Inquirer* (May 26, 1995), p. 11.

7. Perfecto G. Caparas, "OCWs Children: Bearing the Burden of Separation," *Manila Times* (September 30, n.d.), pp. 1–2.

8. Susan Fernandez, "Pamilya ng OFWs maraming hirap" (Many hardships in the families of OFWs), *Abante* (January 27, 1997), p. 5.

9. Lorie Toledo, "Child Sexual Abuse Awareness," *People's Journal* (February 19, 1996), p. 4. Although incest is a social problem in the Philippines, its direct correlation to the emigration of mothers is an unproven speculation.

10. Lorie Toledo, "Overseas job vs. family stability," *People's Journal* (December 15, 1993), p. 4.

11. Bureau of Employment and Labor Statistics, "Remittances from Overseas Filipino Workers by Country of Origin Philippines: 1997–Fourth Quarter 1999," *Pinoy Migrants, Shared Government Information System for Migration*, http://emisd.web.dfa.gov.ph/~pinoymigrants/.

12. Rosemarie Samaniego is a pseudonym. This excerpt is drawn from Rhacel Salazar Parreñas, *Servants of Globalization: Women, Migration, and Domestic Work* (Stanford, Calif.: Stanford University Press, 2001).

13. Ellen Seneriches and the names of the other children whom I quote in this article are all pseudonyms.

14. Pierrette Hondagneu-Sotelo and Ernestine Avila, "'I'm Here, but I'm There': The Meanings of Latina Transnational Motherhood," *Gender and Society*, vol. 11, no. 5 (1997), pp. 548–71.

15. A two-part special report by Caparas, "OCWs Children," which appeared on the front page of the *Manila Times*, summarized the media's incredibly negative view on the plight of children in transnational families. It reported that children suffer from a "psychological toll," "extreme loneliness," "unbearable loss," "strained relations," "incest," and consequently delinquency, as indicated, for instance, by rampant "premature pregnancies." See also Caparas's "OCWs and the Changing Lives of Filipino Families," *Manila Times* (August, 29, n.d.), pp. 1, 5.

16. Similarly, I found that children use the corollary image of the struggling "breadwinner" father to negotiate the emotional strains of their transnational household arrangement.

17. Scalabrini Migration Center (SMC), *Impact of Labor Migration on the Children Left Behind* (Quezon City, Philippines: Scalabrini Migration Center, 2000).

18. SMC, 2000, p. 65.

19. SMC, 2000, p. 57.

20. SMC, 2000, p. 65.

21. Arjun Appadurai, "Globalization and the Research Imagination," *International Social Science Journal,* vol. 160 (June 1999), p. 231.

22. National Commission for the Role of Filipino Women, *Philippine Plan for Gender-Responsive Development,*

1995–2025 (Manila, Philippines: National Commission for the Role of Filipino Women, 1995).

23. Marije Meerman, "The Care Chain," episode 42 of *The New World* (Netherlands: VPRO-TV); www.dnv.vpro.nl/carechain.

24. Policies in various receiving countries restrict the migration of workers' families. Such restrictions can be found both in countries, such as Singapore and Taiwan, that have illiberal policies and in those, like Canada, with liberal policies.

◆◆◆

FIFTY-SIX

Remotely Sensed: A Topography of the Global Sex Trade (2002)

Ursula Biemann

Ursula Biemann is a researcher at the Institute for Theory of Art and Design in Zurich. Her art, writings, and curatorial work focus on media, geography, and gender relations in the economy. Her video essays and installations have been widely shown at international exhibitions and museums including the Museum of Modern Art (MOMA) in New York.

It has become increasingly difficult to find a model of cultural representation that would live up to the complexity of the present discourse of gender and visual culture in the context of globalization. Over the last few years I have recognized the need to locate gender and other categories of identity, such as ethnicity and nationality, within the context of the wider transformations of the public sphere, particularly urban reality. In this endeavour, geography proves to be a useful and attractive arena to articulate questions of the moving subject in relation to space and location. Globalization is a very gendered process: an evergrowing proportion of migrant people looking for work are female. However, beyond a simple feminization of migration we notice that women's labour is being sexualized, that is to say, global processes actually address women directly in their sexuality. The worldwide migration of women into the sex industry or more specifically the burgeoning trafficking in women can be read as a

structural part of pancapitalism. . . . I am using the theoretical framework of geography because it allows for an examination of female migrancy, mobility and routing in relation to specific sites, while at the same time permitting an integration of their psychological and material experience. In other words, I am interested in the practice of linking geo-politics to an understanding of how subjects are produced.

Geography is understood as a visual culture in this context. Satellite media and other geographic information systems are generating profuse quantities of topographic images to be interpreted for scientific, social and military use. Increasingly they make their way into our daily lives, inform the way we think about the world and code our concept of globality. I make it my project to explore how these satellite visions of globality are producing a sexual economy in which it has become thinkable to reorganize women geographically on a global scale.

Countergeographies

Spiralling down from an orbital view the video essay *Remote Sensing* takes an earthly perspective on the topography of the global sex trade. It is a project of countergeography that engages in migration and cross-border circuits, illegal and illicit networks as well as alternative circuits of survival, where women have emerged as key actors. The digital documents generated for the video essay trace the routes and reasons of women who travel across the globe to enter this gigantic Fordism [production line] of service that is the sex industry.

Trafficking hinges on the displacement of women, their costly transportation across topographies from one cultural arrangement to another, from one spatial organization to another, from one abandoned economy to a place of greater accumulations. It is the route that counts. The agents charge money for the vehicle and for the escort who knows the path and the border geography, the contacts and the bribes. Female bodies are the new cargo in these transactions across boundaries that generate massive amounts of footloose capital, abstract global capital that is nevertheless so physical for some. The travel money will go back into bonding women to do unpaid sex work for the trafficking ring. It is a common practice of debt-bondage that places women in the contexts of the historical spaces of the brothel and the colony.

There are numerous structural and political reasons why women move, and are being moved, into the global sex industry. The Mekong region [South East Asia] has traditionally been a burgeoning basin for the trafficking of women who criss-cross borders in all directions. . . . Thailand is no longer just a sending country, but has also become a country of transit and destination. While Thai women migrated in the 1970s to Europe and North America or have been promoted to the higher echelons of the sex industry catering to foreign tourists, there is a need to supply new women and girls to the lower class brothels in Thailand. This market segment draws on the young rural female population in neighbouring countries like Burma, Laos, and Vietnam. China goes through a different predicament. The prolonged period under the one-child policy has caused a major gender disparity in the present generation. Many Chinese men who do not find wives will acquire them abroad. In Taiwan, on the other hand, women prefer a modern life in the city and male farmers have a hard time attracting a wife who wants to live a hardworking rural lifestyle. They also have to import females from the Philippines by the tens of thousands for unpaid agricultural labour and every year 100,000 South East Asian women are shipped into the Japanese entertainment industry, which equals Japan's defence budget in volume.

The commodification and displacement of female bodies in South East Asia generates impressive figures, but my work does not situate itself in the production of factual information. The questions I have to ask myself as an artist and video maker are: How can I dislocate and recontextualize a much belaboured question such as the marketability of women and the objectification of female sexuality? How can a video, rather than simply arguing against capitalism and affirming rigid gender identities, reflect and produce the expansion of the very space in which we write and speak of the feminine? There is a need to investigate the interplay between the symbolization of the feminine and the economic and material reality of women. To reproduce closed, privatized and restricted images of women is confining the feminine further. Some women take the route into sex work voluntarily, others not, it is true, but there is a large grey zone in between these two conditions, a vast field of negotiation, on which I focus my attention. The process of re-signification, which I undertake in my video practice, then, is not only an incessant struggle against the effacement of the diversification and differentiation of the feminine, it is also an analysis of the gendered dynamic inscribed in social and material landscapes. Of course I would like to see the space in which we write our lives, our bodies and sexuality as a heterogeneous one but in the course of creating this space, I am bound to look at the existing technologies and networks of knowledge that operate in delimiting and formalizing it.

Bandana Pattanaik (*Global Alliance Against Traffic in Women, GAATW*): I think seeing them as victims creates a lot of sympathy and therefore people find it easier to accept. If I'll say that I have been forced into prostitution, people say, oh poor thing, let's help her, she is in a really bad situation. But if somebody says I chose to become a prostitute that's very difficult to accept or to understand. Why would you choose to be a prostitute? So many times it's framed in this either/or debate. Either you are a victim or you are an agent. Either you have chosen to be a sex worker or you have been forced into prostitution. And I think there are such large grey areas in between.

While all of my videos to date elaborate on the relations of gender, technology and transnational capitalism, *Remote Sensing* engages maybe most explicitly in a critique of visualizing technologies, particularly the orbital omniscient view of satellite imagery. Taking up a feminist critique that has claimed the importance of the viewing structures and apparatuses for the power relations established by the gaze, there is a need to displace and interrogate the images and to reintroduce a situated way of seeing and knowing. Geographic information systems (GIS) propose an abstract and highly accurate view of the world from the top down. GIS are criticized by feminist scientists for applying binary and mutually exclusive categories that are unable to hold and interpret a great variety of conflicting information. They are also completely unable to think in relational terms and reveal the gendered meaning of data. Cartography is insufficient, then, to map the subjective path of people on the move.

A major objective of *Remote Sensing* is to propose a mode of representation that traces the trajectory of people in a pancapitalist world order wherein the space between departure and arrival is understood as a transnational one, i.e., a potentially subversive space which does not adhere to national rules, but nevertheless a complex material and social space that is formed by economic relations. All this is from a gendered perspective. Remotely gazed at from the orbital perspective, transnational sexuality comes into full sight. In this topography of the global sex trade, the female bodies get sensed and identified, evaluated and re-routed according to their assigned function. The moving women appear as data streams in the video, scans and X-rays portrayed over landscapes passing by, their anatomical and demographic data are recorded, their routes appear in electronic travel schedules on the screen. They are the embodiment of the abstract financial flows that feed the global economy.

Remote Sensing visualizes the multilayered meaning of geography where the mobilization and the sexualization of women is linked to the implementation of new technologies, often in contradictory ways. While the Internet facilitates the migration flow, particularly for women via the bride market, border reinforcement technologies on the other hand hinder and push it into the illegal sector.

Heat and movement sensors, infra-red and roentgen cameras, digital and genetic control mechanisms are developed and put to use along the . . . borders. Parallel to this, European migration politics are quite explicit in their practice of directing migrant women straight into the sex industry without giving them any future option to switch to another trade. For non-European female applicants, the Swiss government only issues "dancers' visas" which hinge on cabaret contracts. The automatic channelling of migrant women into sex work is an index of their status under national rule but it also speaks of the place of sex in that national space where laws protect the flourishing sexual life of male citizens as a privilege and source of power. Two-thirds of the 500,000 women entering Europe's entertainment industry every year are from Eastern post-socialist countries. The social change in these sending countries since the 1990s and the migration politics of the receiving countries both impact the flow of women into the sex trade. Even though the official policy is to fight human trafficking and to help women getting out of the sex trade, the fact is that the number of trafficked women is steadily increasing. Technologies of marginalization always affect women, and particularly economically disadvantaged women, in their sexuality because powerful players like states, scientific complexes, and military institutions tend to create a sexuality that eroticizes hierarchies.

Aida Santos *(Women's Education, Development, Productivity and Research Organization, WEDPRO):* The history of the American involvement in prostitution and trafficking should not be missed. . . . In the 40's the Americans came and established their bases in the Philippines. The presence of the US Army and Navy contributed dramatically to the rise in prostitution and trafficking, in the sense that when you have an institution like twenty-one military bases scattered all over the country in a situation of poverty and where women's status is very low, families are willing to send off their kids to work and the elder daughters are bound by tradition to help their families and send their siblings to school, you've got very rich soil for exploitation. And that's what happened in the former US baselands. The Marines are still coming here for training and when the big carriers dock in the harbour, 10,000 servicemen go on shore. In the small town near the Subic base of Olongapo there are 6000 women registered [to work] in bars.

Since the infrastructure for the entertainment industry was already in place, many of the Rest and Recreation areas created for the US soldiers during the war in Vietnam and Korea have been turned into sites of prostitution and sex tourism. Most of the women who came to the baselands expected to find restaurant jobs, but as it turns out, waitresses do not have a regular salary but work on a commission basis only. Unless they go out with the customers and provide personal entertainment and sexual services, they will not earn a living. Some of the former bases have been transformed into assembly plants for outsourced production paying wages that do not cover their living costs so that many women are bound to gain a complementary income by prostituting. Whether [through] . . . an offspring of military camps or a by-product of Western off-shore operations, women are displaced and drawn into the global economy through sexual labour. Sexual difference becomes a primary structural factor in understanding a migration-bound economy.

Another reason for the trafficking of women is that movements of exile, migration and international business have created the need to supply "familiar" services abroad. So Filipinas are routed to Lagos in Nigeria to cater to Chinese businessmen, Thai women are trafficked to Paris to serve French-born Chinese and Cambodian immigrants, and girls from Nicaragua are dispatched to Southern California to supply camps of Mexican agricultural workers while others are kept in mobile trailer brothels that circulate in the Chicano suburbs of Los Angeles. The clandestine becomes an obscure form of living the locality of culture, a location that remains suspended and transitory. There is no arrival. The existence of these women is marked by a constant mobility, their time is scheduled, their space is confined, civil rights and sexual governance are suspended. The non-status of their existence speaks of a geographic ambivalence, and it is not surprising that these bodies are usually suspended from the cartographic discourse even though they have become an important part of illicit border transactions and underground eco-

nomic circuits and increasingly represent a major source of foreign currency for national households. The video makes an effort to track and register the movement of these women and to infuse meaning into the mapping of their trajectories. Why is it so important to trace their paths through space? I think because these very bodies are in fact the site of numerous conflicts. Clearly, they represent a phantasmatic femininity that has been ruled out from Western consciousness but continues to thrive in the a-national space in which the fleeing temporality of their presence and their non-adherence to a national programme are major criteria. Their service needs to be secured materially but denied in the official ideology. While their civil status is suspended, their figurative representation reveals another phantasm deeply rooted in the bourgeois projections onto permanently seductive postcolonial places. Silk dresses and an Asian gentleness mask the drastic economic imbalance in which the hard bargain between the sexes takes place in capitalist society.

While the powerful players certainly lay the foundation for the global trafficking of women, we have to recognize that most trafficking operations are not conducted by mighty syndicates. They work in small units, relatives or acquaintances who recruit girls in slum neighbourhoods, frequently there are bi-national couples who have good contacts to the source country. Women often feel that these agents are not exploiting them but actually providing a valuable service in their desire to move to richer countries or to the cities for a modern and more exciting life, helping them to trade a slum existence for the glamour of a Bunny Club. And even if they feel lonely and exhausted, they are still able to send money home, not only supporting their family but generating hard cash for their governments.

Siriporn Skrobanek: We respect these women because many are illiterate, cannot speak a word of English but still have a strong will and encounter the whole world. And many of them can survive and struggle in their own way.

The video, *Remotely Sensing,* is available from Women Make Movies (www.wmm.com). A Web site includes images and text: www.geobodies.org/video/sensing/sensing.html

FIFTY-SEVEN

The World Bank, WTO and Corporate Control Over Water (2002)

Vandana Shiva

Vandana Shiva directs the Research Foundation for Science, Technology and Natural Resource Policy in Dehra Dun, India. She is a physicist, ecologist, author, and activist concerned with ecological and economic sustainability, and a winner of the Right Livelihood Award in 1993, an alternative to the Nobel Prize. Her most recent books are *Earth Democracy: Justice, sustainability, and peace,* and *Stolen Harvest: The hijacking of the global food supply.*

Giant water projects, in most cases, benefit the powerful and dispossess the weak. Even when such projects are publicly funded, their beneficiaries are mainly construction companies, industries, and commercial farmers. While privatization is generally couched in rhetoric about the disappearing role of the state, what we actually see is increased state intervention in water policy, subverting community control over water resources. Policies imposed by the World Bank, and trade liberalization rules crafted by the World Trade Organization (WTO), are creating a sweeping culture of corporate-states all over the world.

The World Bank: An Instrument for Corporate Control Over Water

Not only has the World Bank played a major role in the creation of water scarcity and pollution, it is now transforming that scarcity into a market opportunity for water corporations. The World Bank currently has outstanding commitments of about $20 billion in water projects, $4.8 billion of which are for urban water and sanitation, $1.7 billion for rural water schemes, $5.4 billion for irrigation, $1.7 billion for hydropower, and $3 billion for water-related environmental projects.[1] South Asia receives 20 percent of World Bank water loans.

The Bank estimates the potential water market at $1 trillion.[2] After the collapse of the technology stocks, *Fortune* magazine identified the water business as the most profitable industry for investors.[3] . . .

Public-Private Partnerships: International Aid for Water Privatization

Privatization projects funded by the World Bank and other aid agencies are usually labeled "public-private partnerships." The label is powerful, both because of what it suggests and what it hides. It implies public participation, democracy, and accountability. But it disguises the fact that public-private partnership arrangements usually entail public funds being available for the privatization of public goods.

. . .

Public-private partnerships have mushroomed under the guise of attracting private capital and curbing public-sector employment. The World Bank, working on the assumption that the Third World will urbanize by 2025, estimates that $600 billion of investment in infrastructure projects will be required.[4] However, urbanization, like water privatization, is a possible result of World Bank policies, not an inevitable outcome.

Currently, public-private collaborations in water services receive millions of aid dollars. This money is a subsidy for private firms, who bid ferociously for the contracts. In India alone, there are 30 such collaborations in water services.[5] Public-private partnerships in the water business are meant to replace water services as a public service:

> First is the focus on *commercial orientation* through institutional reforms and restructuring. For example, a first step may be restructuring the water and sewage department on a profit center basis. Over time, corporatisation of the utility or separate joint venture companies to manage the water and sewage system will help to bring the necessary commercial orientation.

The second aspect relates to the need for an appropriate regulatory framework. The basic objective of such institutional reform is to move towards a commercial and consumer orientation in service provision. The entire outlook changes from publicly provided free services as a right, to a consumer orientation with access to services.[6]

The erosion of water rights is now a global phenomenon. Since the early 1990s, ambitious, World Bank–driven privatization programs have emerged in Argentina, Chile, Mexico, Malaysia, and Nigeria. The Bank has also introduced privatization of water systems in India. In Chile, it has imposed a loan condition to guarantee a 33 percent profit margin to the French company Suez Lyonnaise des Eaux.[7]

. . .

Privatization arguments have been based largely on the poor performance of public-sector utilities. Government employees are seen as excess staff, responsible for the low productivity of public water agencies.[8] The fact that poor public-sector performance is most often due to the utilities' lack of accountability is hardly taken into account. As it turns out, there is no indication that private companies are any more accountable. . . .

In Chile, Suez Lyonnaise des Eaux insisted on a 35 percent profit.[9] In Casablanca, consumers saw the price of water increase threefold. In Britain, water and sewage bills increased 67 percent between 1989–90 and 1994–95. The rate at which people's services were disconnected rose by 177 percent. In New Zealand, citizens took to the streets to protest the commercialization of water. In South Africa, Johannesburg's water supply was overtaken by Suez Lyonnaise des Eaux. Water soon became unsafe, inaccessible, and unaffordable. Thousands of people were disconnected and cholera infections became rampant.[10]

Despite its unpopularity among local residents worldwide, the rush to privatize water continues unabated. Encumbered by exorbitant debts, countries around the world are forced to privatize water. It is common for the World Bank and IMF to demand water deregulation as part of their lending conditions. Out of the 40 IMF loans disbursed through the International Finance Corporation in 2000, 12 had requirements for partial or full privatization of water supply and insisted

on policy creation to stimulate "full cost recovery" and eliminate subsidies. In order to qualify for loans, African governments increasingly succumb to water privatization pressures. In Ghana, for instance, World Bank and IMF policies forcing the sale of water at market rate required the poor to spend up to 50 percent of their earnings on water purchases.[11]

The WTO and GATS: Trading Away Our Water

The General Agreement on Trade and Tariffs (GATT) was created along with the World Bank and IMF to manage the global economy in the postwar era. The 1944 Bretton Woods Conference gave shape to these institutions and instruments. GATT was intended to become the International Trade Organization in 1948, but the United States blocked the move since the rules of trade favored the South.[12] GATT therefore continued as an agreement until 1995, when the WTO was established on the basis of the agreements made at the Uruguay Round.

Before 1993, GATT dealt only with trade in goods beyond national borders. The Uruguay Round, negotiated between 1986 and 1993, expanded the scope of trade and the power of GATT by adding rules beyond goods and international trade. New rules were introduced on intellectual property, agriculture, and investment. Services were subjected to trade via the General Agreement on Trade in Services (GATS). By the time the WTO formed in 1995, the stage had been set for its unregulated power to override domestic policies and hijack common resources.

While the World Bank is promoting privatization of water through structural adjustment programs and conditions, the WTO is instituting water privatization via free-trade rules embodied in GATS. GATS promotes free-trade in services, including water, food, environment, health, education, research, communication, and transport. The WTO markets GATS as a "bottom up" treaty, citing the freedom of countries to liberalize trade progressively and to deregulate different sectors incrementally. In reality, GATS is a treaty with no reverence for or accountability to national democratic processes. In many cases, governments do not have the liberty to use cultural issues and resources in their WTO negotiations.

GATS not only bypasses government restrictions but also permits companies to sue countries whose domestic policy prevents free-market entry. For instance, in 1996 India passed the Provision of the Panchayats Act, recognizing the local community in tribal areas as the highest forms of authority in matters of culture, resources, and conflict resolution.[13] For the first time since India's independence, village communities (*gram sabhas*) were granted legal acknowledgment as community entities. Village communities retained a number of powers, including the power to approve or reject development plans and programs. *Gram sabhas* were also bestowed with the authority to grant land.

The act accepted the traditions of the people and their cultural identity by honoring their traditional relationship with the natural resources in their homeland. As the law stated, "a state legislation on the panchayats that may be made, shall be in consonance with the customary law, social and religious practices and traditional management practices of community resources."[14] The importance of having control over community resources was recognized not only as an economic necessity but as a touchstone of cultural identity. . . .

The WTO disregards and even subverts hard-won victories such as the Indian Constitution. GATS is a tool to reverse the democratic decentralization to which diverse societies have been aspiring. GATS can challenge measures taken by central, regional, or local governments as well as nongovernmental bodies. Its rules are shaped entirely by corporations without any input from NGOs, local governments, or national governments.

. . .

New Agreements, Old Agenda

The WTO refers to GATS as the "first multilateral agreement on investment." Although a global resistance defeated the Multilateral Agreement on Investment (MAI), the agenda has been resurrected by GATS. A similar free trade treaty is the North American Free Trade Agreement (NAFTA). Under NAFTA, Metalclad, an American waste management company, was able to extort $17 million from the Mexican government in a lawsuit. Metalclad's

hazardous waste treatment and disposal site in the central Mexican state of San Luis Potos was shut down by local officials on the grounds that it was not environmentally sound. Unfortunately, NAFTA allows companies to sue governments for cash compensation if a country implements legislation that "expropriates" the company's future profits. Metalclad invoked this rule in its suit against the Mexican government and eventually won. The intense community opposition to Metalclad's facility was irrelevant.[15]

Corporate trade rights granted by trade agreements such as NAFTA and GATS apply to cases of corporate water ownership and control. NAFTA explicitly lists "waters, including natural or artificial waters and aerated waters," as tradable goods. And of course, as US trade representative Mickey Kantor pointed out in 1993, "when water is traded as a good, all provisions of the agreement governing trade in goods apply."[16]

In 1998, the American company Sun Belt Water sued the Canadian government for $10 billion because the company lost a contract to export water from Canada to California due to a 1991 ban on bulk water export imposed by the government of British Columbia.[17] The company claimed that British Columbia's ban on exports violated the protection of investor rights under NAFTA. The case is still under deliberation. Every level of government—including regional and local—is now forced to adhere to rules that it did not negotiate or agree to. Policy-making is no longer in the hands of local or national governments but in the grip of large multinational corporations. As Jack Lindsay, CEO of Sun Belt, puts it: "Because of NAFTA, we are now stakeholders in the national water policy in Canada."[18]

The Water Giants

Water has become big business for global corporations, which see limitless markets in growing water scarcity and demand. The two major players in the water industry are the French companies Vivendi Environment and Suez Lyonnaise des Eaux, whose empires extend to 120 countries. Vivendi is the water giant, with a turnover of $17.1 billion. Suez had a turnover of $5.1 billion in 1996.[19] Vivendi Environment is the "environmental services" arm of Vivendi Universal, a global media and communications conglomerate involved in television, film, publishing, music, the Internet, and telecommunication.

Vivendi Environment is engaged in water, waste management, energy, and transportation. In 2000, Vivendi Environment was awarded a 43-million-euro contract for a wastewater treatment plan in Berne, Switzerland. Vivendi also has a 50-50 joint venture company called CTSE in the Czech Republic. Total net sales are expected to be 200 million euros. Vivendi's subsidiary, Onyx, owns Waste Management Inc. Vivendi operates waste services in several countries, including Hong Kong and Brazil.

Other water giants include the Spanish company, Aguas de Barcelona, which dominates in Latin America, and the British companies Thames Water, Biwater, and United Utilities. Biwater was established in 1968 and given its name to reflect the company's involvement in both the dirty- and clean-water businesses. Thames is owned by RWE, an electric company whose ventures include water.

Biwater and Thames have operations in Asia, South Africa, and the Americas. In the 1940s, Biwater entered Mexico and the Philippines. By the 1970s, it had contracts in Indonesia, Hong Kong, Iraq, Kenya, and Malawi. By 1992, the Biwater empire had expanded to Malaysia, Germany, and Poland. In 2000, the company, along with a Dutch firm, launched its joint venture company, Cascal. Cascal has contracts in the United Kingdom, Chile, the Philippines, Kazakhstan, Mexico, and South Africa.[20] Another addition to the global water takeover is General Electric, which is working with the World Bank to create an investment fund to privatize power and water worldwide.

The privatization of water services is the first step toward the privatization of all aspects of water. The American water market for water supply and treatment, estimated at $90 billion, is the largest in the world, and Vivendi is investing heavily in order to dominate it. In March 1999, the company purchased US Filter Corporation for more than $6 billion and formed the largest water corporation in North America. Vivendi's projected revenue is $12 billion.[21]

Once the water giants enter the picture, water prices go up. In Subic Bay, the Philippines, Biwater increased water rates by 400 percent.[22] In France, customer fees increased 150 percent but water quality deteriorated; a French government report revealed that more than 5.2 million people received "bacterially unacceptable water."[23] In England, water rates increased by 450 percent and company profits soared by 692 percent—CEO salaries increased by an astonishing 708 percent.[24] Service disconnection increased by 50 percent.[25] Meanwhile, dysentery increased sixfold and the British Medical Association condemned water privatization for its health effects.[26]

In 1998, shortly after Sydney's water was overtaken by Suez Lyonnaise des Eaux, it was contaminated with high levels of *giardia* and *cryptos poridium*.[27] After water testing had been privatized by A&L Labs, in Walkerton, Ontario, seven people, including a baby, died as a result of E. coli.[28] The company treated the test results as "confidential intellectual property" and did not make them public, just as Union Carbide withheld information about the leaked chemicals in its Bhopal, India, plant while thousands were dying.[29] In Argentina, when a Suez Lyonnaise des Eaux subsidiary purchased the state-run water company Obras Sanitarias de la Nación, water rates doubled but water quality degenerated. The company was forced to leave the country when residents refused to pay their bills.[30]

The Great Thirst

In the maquiladoras of Mexico, drinking-water is so scarce that babies and children drink Coca-Cola and Pepsi.[31] Coca-Cola's products sell in 195 countries, generating a revenue of $16 billion. Water scarcity is clearly a source of corporate profits. In an annual report, Coca-Cola proclaims:

> All of us in the Coca-Cola family wake up each morning knowing that every single one of the world's 5.6 billion people will get thirsty that day. If we make it impossible for these 5.6 billion people to escape Coca-Cola, then we assure our future success for many years to come. Doing anything else is not an option.[32]

Companies like Coca-Cola are fully aware that water is the real thirst quencher and are jumping into the bottled water business. Coca-Cola has launched its international label Bon Aqua (Dasani is the American version), and Pepsi has introduced Aquafina. In India, Coca-Cola's water line is called Kinley. In addition to Coca-Cola and Pepsi, there are several other well-known brands such as Perrier, Evian, Naya, Poland Spring, Clearly Canadian, and Purely Alaskan.

In March 1999, in a study of 103 brands of bottled water, the Natural Resources Defense Council found that bottled water was no more safe than tap water.[33] A third of the brands contained arsenic and E. coli and a fourth merely bottled tap water. In India, a study conducted by the Ahmedabad-based Consumer Education and Research Center discovered that only three out the 13 known brands conformed to all bottling specifications.[34] None of the brands was free of bacteria, even though some claimed to be germ-free and 100 percent bacteria-free. Such false and misleading advertising has forced the Indian government to amend its Prevention of Food Adulteration rules to include bottled water. It now differentiates between mineral water obtained from and packaged close to a natural source and treated drinking water.[35]

The consequences of bottled water extend beyond price hikes and unsafe water. Environmental waste is a major cost incurred by the bottling industry. In the 1970s, 300 million gallons of bottled water were sold in non-renewable plastic water containers. By 1998 this number had exceeded 6 billion. In India, the leading bottled water producer Parle Bisleri accounts for 60 percent of the market share. It is expanding its $835 thousand business and hopes to earn $208.8 million by 2002. . . .

Bisleri, Pepsi, and Coke are not the only players in the Indian bottled water market. Britannia Industries and Nestle are also pushing their products, Perrier, San Pellegrino, and Price Life. Britannia markets Evian, which sells at $2 per liter, nearly double the hourly minimum wage. Evian is promoted as "an alternative beverage for lifestyle and fitness needs."[36] More than 500 rich families in India spend approximately $20 to $209 a month on Evian water. The Australian company Auswater Purification Ltd. is promoting its brand, Auswater. Smaller Indian companies like Trupthi, Ganga, Oasis, Dewdrops, Minscot, Florida, Aqua Cool, and Himalayan have also entered the market. These small firms account for 17 percent of the market share.

Global corporations are taking full advantage of the demand for clean water, a demand which has resulted from environmental pollution. Even though the corporations tap clean water resources in nonindustrialized, unpolluted regions, they refer to their bottling practice as "manufacture" of water. . . . The Indian packaged-water market is estimated at $104.4 million, with a growth of 50 to 70 percent per year.[37] In other words, bottled water production is expected to double every two years. Between 1992 and 2000, sales had increased from 95 million liters to 932 million liters.

As quickly as the water market is expanding in India, so is the traditional practice of giving water to the thirsty disappearing. For thousands of years, water was offered as a gift at *piyaos*, roadsides, temples, and marketplaces. Earthen pots known as *ghadas* and *surais* cooled the water during the summer for the thirsty, who would drink from their cupped hands. These pots have been replaced by plastic bottles, and the gift economy has been supplanted by the water market. No longer do all people have a right to quench their thirst; this is a right held exclusively by the rich. Even the president of India laments this misfortune: "The elite guzzle bottles of aerated drinks while the poor have to make do with a handful of muddied water."[38]

In Kerala, the restriction of water to the rich led local organizations to launch a campaign to boycott Coca-Cola. Partly as a protest and partly to develop alternative markets, residents of the coconut-rich state Kerala (Kera means coconut in Malayalam) adopted the slogan "Goodbye Cola, Welcome Tender Coconut."[39] Coconut prices had dropped considerably when WTO rules flooded the region with soya and palm oil. Their low cost and their abundance made coconuts ideal for resisting another global conquest.

Corporations Versus Citizens: Water Wars in Bolivia

Perhaps the most famous tale of corporate greed over water is the story of Cochabamba, Bolivia. In this semidesert region, water is scarce and precious. In 1999, the World Bank recommended privatization of Cochabamba's municipal water supply company, Servicio Municipal del Agua Potable y

Alcantarillado (SEMAPA), through a concession to International Water, a subsidiary of Bechtel.[40] On October 1999, the Drinking Water and Sanitation Law was passed, ending government subsidies and allowing privatization.

In a city where the minimum wage is less than $100 a month, water bills reached $20 a month, nearly the cost of feeding a family of five for two weeks. In January 2000, a citizens' alliance called La Coordinadora de Defensa del Agua y de la Vida (The Coalition in Defense of Water and Life) was formed. The alliance shut down the city for four days through mass mobilization. Within a month, millions of Bolivians marched to Cochabamba, held a general strike, and stopped all transportation.[41] At the gathering, the protesters issued the Cochabamba Declaration, calling for the protection of universal water rights.

The government promised to reverse the price hike but never did. In February 2000, La Coordinadora organized a peaceful march demanding the repeal of the Drinking Water and Sanitation Law, the annulment of ordinances allowing privatization, the termination of the water contract, and the participation of citizens in drafting a water resource law. The citizens' demands . . . were violently rejected. La Coordinora's fundamental critique was directed at the negation of water as a community property. Protesters used slogans like "Water Is God's Gift and Not A Merchandise" and "Water Is Life."

In April 2000, the government tried to silence the water protests through martial law. Activists were arrested, protesters killed, and the media censored. Finally on April 10, 2000, the people won. Aguas del Tunari and Bechtel left Bolivia and the government was forced to revoke its hated water privatization legislation. The water company SEMAPA (along with its debts) was handed over to the workers and the people.[42] In the summer of 2000, La Coordinadora organized public hearings to establish democratic planning and management. The people have taken on the challenge to establish a water democracy, but the water dictators are trying their best to subvert the process. Bechtel is suing Bolivia, and the Bolivian government is harassing and threatening activists of La Coordinadora.[43]

By reclaiming water from corporations and the market, the citizens of Bolivia have illustrated that privatization is not inevitable and that corporate takeover of vital resources can be prevented by people's democratic will.

NOTES

1. www.worldbank.org

2. Maude Barlow, *Blue Gold: The Global Water Crisis and the Commodification of the World's Water Supply* (San Francisco: International Forum on Globalization, 2001), p. 15.

3. *Fortune Magazine*, May 2000

4. Riccardo Petrella, *The Water Manifesto: Arguments for a World Water Control* (London: Zed Books, 2001), p. 20.

5. Vandana Shiva et al. *License to Kill* (New Delhi: Research Foundation for Science, Technology, and Ecology, 2000), pp. 53–58.

6. Meera Mehta, *A Review of Public-Private Partnerships in the Water and Environmental Sanitation Sector in India* (New Delhi: Department for International Development, 1999), p. 7.

7. Barlow, *Blue Gold*, p. 15.

8. Emanuel Idelevitch and Klas Ringkeg, "Private Sector Participation in Water Supply and Sanitation in Latin America" (World Bank, 1995), p. 9.

9. Barlow, *Blue Gold*, p. 18.

10. Ibid.

11. Ghana National Coalition Against the Privatisation of Water, "Water is Not a Commodity" (unpublished document).

12. Ibid.

13. Provisions of the Panchayats (Extension to the Scheduled Areas) Act, 1996, Section 4(b).

14. Ibid., Sec. 4(a).

15. *New York Times*, July 31, 2000.

16. Ibid.

17. Ibid.

18. Quoted in Barlow, *Blue Gold*, p. 36.

19. Petrella, *The Water Manifesto*, p. 68.

20. Ibid.

21. Ibid.

22. Barlow, *Blue Gold*, p. 18.

23. Petrella, *The Water Manifesto*, p. 73.

24. Barlow, *Blue Gold*, p. 16.

25. Ibid.

26. World Development Movement (WDM), "Stop the GATSastrophe," November 2000, www.wdm.org.uk/cambriefs/wto/GATS.htm.

27. Barlow, *Blue Gold*, p. 17.

28. Ibid.

29. This information is based on my personal communication with Dr. Mira Shiva of the Bhopal Medical Relief Group.

30. Petrella, *The Water Manifesto*, p. 68.

31. Barlow, *Blue Gold*, p. 8.

32. "Small is Sustainable," International Society for Ecology and Culture, 2000, p. 1.

33. Barlow, *Blue Gold*, p. 28.

34. Consumer Education Research Center, *Insight* (January/February, 1998).

35. Government of India, PFA Amendment, 2000.

36. *Business Times*, June 26, 2001, p. 10.

37. Ibid.

38. President Narayan's Republic Day speech, 1999.

39. I came across these slogans during a visit to Kerala.

40. Barlow, *Blue Gold*, p. 19.

41. Ibid.

42. Oscar Olivera and Marcela Olivera, "Reclaiming the Water" (unpublished document).

43. Ibid.

FIFTY-EIGHT

◆◆◆

The Chiang Mai Declaration (2004)
Religion and Women: An Agenda for Change

International Committee for the Peace Council

The **International Committee for the Peace Council** is a diverse group of internationally known people of faith. Its mission is to demonstrate that effective interreligious collaboration to make peace is possible. This text was approved at the Peace Council's 2004 annual meeting in Chiang Mai, Thailand, which included a conference held jointly with leaders of international women's organizations.

Preamble:

We, the participants in this conference on women and religion, recognize that contemporary realities have tragic consequences for women's lives. Without a commitment to women's human rights and to the resolution of these tragedies, religions are failing the world. Their own relevance is at stake as they become more and more isolated from the values and needs of their members.

It is urgent that religions address these realities. Religions must be consonant with the cultural evolution in which we are all immersed. Religions must no longer tolerate violence against women. Women are alienated from religions that do. We are committed to working towards change, and we call on others, women and men, to join in this task.

I. Women and Globalization: Problem and Promise

We live in a time of rapid change which provides both challenges and opportunities. This change has profound effects on all our lives.

Our globalized world is ravaged by armed conflict, increasing economic disparity, the feminization of poverty, massive displacement of peoples, violence against women, the pandemic of HIV and AIDS, enduring racism, and extremisms—all of which generate a climate of deep fear and widespread insecurity.

Globalized capitalism has reduced everything to a commodity and everyone to a consumer and commodity. Nowhere is this more evident than in the lives of women:

- Women's and children's bodies are commodified, especially in sexual trafficking.

- Increasingly HIV and AIDS have a woman's face.

- Women and children disproportionately populate the camps of refugees and displaced persons.

- Women make up the greater proportion of exploited laborers.

- Pressures of the globalized economy have led to even greater violence against women and children.

Globalization, however, also bears the promise and possibilities of advancing women's human rights and well-being:

- More women in more places can be gainfully and justly employed.

- Information technology can enable women throughout the world to share strategies, successes, and hope.

II. Women and Religions: Problem and Promise:

Religions at their best celebrate the dignity of each human being and of all life as valuable parts of a sacred whole. They inspire and empower us to compassion and justice.

Religions, however, have not always been at their best. They have collaborated with dehumanizing values of cultural, economic and political powers. Thus they have contributed to the suffering of women:

- They have made women invisible by denying them religious education and excluding them from decision-making.

- They have been silent when patriarchal systems have legitimated the violence, abuse, and exploitation of women by men.

- This silence has been deafening in the face of such atrocities as rape, incest, female genital mutilation, sex selective abortion, and discrimination against sexual minorities.

- They have not recognized the conscience and moral agency of women, especially in relation to their sexuality and reproductive decisions.

But religions can and must do better. They must reclaim their core values of justice, dignity, and compassion and apply these values to women. We reached consensus that:

A. Within the Religions, Women's Religious Literacy Should Be Recognized and Fostered. Women Are:

- Students: Just as education of women is today understood to be critical in transforming the world, so providing women with religious education is critical in transforming religion. Women seek religious education at both basic and advanced levels. They should be welcomed.

- Scholars: In spite of obstacles, women have developed as religious scholars. That scholarship is an essential resource for the overall development of our understanding of religion. It should be promoted.

- Teachers: Male religious leaders and students have much to gain from exposure to women teachers of religion. Unless we work to change men, the ability of religions to progress in sensitivity to women is impossible.

- Leaders: Women should be full participants in the life and institutional leadership of their religious communities. Women are prepared to be decision-makers, and their gifts should be recognized and used to the fullest extent.

B. Within the World:

- Religions should apply their message of peace in order to oppose the daily reality of violence in family and society. There is a contradiction between the message of peace inherent in all religions and the absence of advocacy for peace in the home and society.

- Women are subjects, not objects, in their own lives. The right to choose any role, including motherhood, should be supported socially, economically, and politically.

- Religions should apply the message of social justice to women. The world's religions play a leadership role in seeking social justice, in the environment, against racism, and for the poor. But religions have been largely silent in response to critical issues of women's human rights, in the family and in the work place.

- This is nowhere more evident than in the area of women's sexuality and reproductive health. Given the moral concern about abortion and the range of stances toward it, the view of any particular religious tradition should not be imposed on the consciences of others. Decriminalization of abortion is a minimal response to this reality and a reasonable means of protecting the life and health of women at risk.

Conclusion

Our experience of coming together as women leaders and religious leaders has convinced us that the religious traditions and the aspirations of women are not in opposition. We are not enemies. On the contrary, we share the same commitment to human dignity, social justice, and human rights for all.

We therefore commit ourselves and call on other women and other religious leaders to reach out to each other to enhance mutual understanding, support, and cooperation. This can be done on the regional level to expand the consensus achieved here and at the national level to define concrete, joint activities toward advancing women's human rights and well-being.

We came together as women and men to explore how the positive powers of religion could be engaged to advance the well-being of women. Indeed, we believe that when women and religious traditions collaborate, a powerful force for advancing women's human rights and leadership will be created.

10

♦♦♦

Women, Crime, and Criminalization

The number of women who are serving time in U.S. jails and prisons, on probation, or otherwise caught up in the "correctional" system has increased dramatically in the past twenty years. Criminalization is one of the most dramatic ways in which gender, race, and class position shape women's lives, and it is essential for students of women's studies to understand the processes whereby women become defined as criminals. Many of us are shielded from this reality because incarcerated women are literally locked away, behind bars, and out of sight.

The societal assumptions that justify and reinforce this separation between "inside" and "outside" are that these are bad women, perhaps foolishly involved with criminal men, a little crazy from drink, drugs, or the pain of their lives, but that they must have done something *very wrong* to end up in prison.

This chapter examines the experiences of incarcerated women, processes of criminalization, assumptions about criminality, and theoretical frameworks for understanding the increase in women's imprisonment. In this discussion we draw on points made in previous chapters, particularly concerning violence against women (Chapter 6), women's economic insecurity (Chapter 8), and the effects of economic globalization on women's opportunities (Chapter 9).

This chapter was originally written by Barbara Bloom, MSW, Ph.D., a criminal justice consultant and researcher specializing in the development and evaluation of programs serving girls and women under criminal justice supervision; it has been edited, adapted, and updated by Gwyn Kirk and Margo Okazawa-Rey.

The National Context: "Get Tough on Crime"

The number of people imprisoned in the United States has been growing for the past thirty years. Approximately 330,000 people were in custody in 1972. The incarceration rate increased rapidly during the 1990s mainly due to mandatory minimum sentences for drug offenses introduced in 1986. At the end of 1998 there were 461 people in jails and prisons per 100,000 population. By 2000 this had grown to 699 prisoners per 100,000, the highest rate in the world (The Sentencing Project 2001). By June 2003, more than 2 million people were held in U.S. jails and prisons; over 4 million more were on probation—a period of supervision in the community following a conviction, and 774,588 were on parole—a period of conditional supervised release following a prison term (U.S. Department of Justice 2005a). According to organizer and writer Anannya Bhattacharjee (2002), "The entire apparatus of law enforcement in the United States has expanded dramatically, becoming more punitive, highly integrated, heavily funded, and technologically sophisticated" (p. 1). The criminalization of women must be understood in this pro-punishment context.

In the 1988 presidential election, the Republican candidate George Bush used the case of Willie Horton, a Black inmate from a Massachusetts prison who committed murder while out of prison on the state's furlough program, to establish street crime—burglary, auto theft, mugging, murder, and rape committed by strangers—as one of the most important national issues. This tactic implied that Black men were the ones to fear most. Since then, politicians and the media have reinforced that view by promoting and reporting on legislation such as the "three-strikes-you're-out" law, which requires a life sentence without parole for three-time felons, and by continually publicizing crime stories, particularly high-profile cases such as those involving murder and abduction of children. People are led to believe that no one is safe from street crime anywhere, but especially around African American and Latino men, and that everyone labeled "criminal" is an incorrigible street tough or "gangsta." Contrary to this rhetoric, the facts show that many crime rates have decreased. Violent crime rates reached the lowest level ever recorded in 2003. Robbery and assault rates also declined significantly since 1994 as well as the proportion of serious violent crimes committed by young people (U.S. Department of Justice 2005b). Women are least safe in their own homes or with men they know (as we argued in Chapter 6). Moreover, the greatest economic losses from crime do not happen on the street. According to Alexander Lichtenstein and Michael Kroll (1996), "Society's losses from 'white collar crime' far exceed the economic impact of all burglaries, robberies, larcenies, and auto thefts combined" (p. 20). Nonetheless, high-income criminals who commit such crimes as fraud and embezzlement are not only less likely to be incarcerated but also less likely even to be considered hardened criminals; rather, they may be regarded as people who used bad judgment or went "off track" (Sherrill 1997). The year 2002 saw an unprecedented number of corporate scandals, most notably Enron, but also including Adelphia Communications, Rite Aid, and Martha Stewart. Dozens of corporate executives, financial analysts, regulators, and politicians are criticized for conflicts of interest, and the possibility of fraud. Fewer are investigated and fewer still are convicted.

According to Human Rights Watch (1999a), "get tough on crime" policies, which have enjoyed significant public support, have become the vehicle for abusive policies and constitutional rights violations, documented by international human rights monitors. Although the United States regards itself highly in the area of human rights, "Both federal and state governments have nonetheless resisted applying to the U.S. the standards that, rightly, the U.S. applies elsewhere" (Human Rights Watch 1999a, p. 1). Since the attacks on the World Trade Center and the Pentagon on September 11, 2001, Congress has passed two far-reaching pieces of legislation with regard to civil rights. The Uniting and Strengthening America by Providing Appropriate Tools Required to Intercept and Obstruct Terrorism Act (USA PATRIOT Act) became law on October 26, 2001, and was reauthorized in 2005. It greatly increases the government's powers. It includes measures that

- allow for indefinite detention of noncitizens who are not terrorists on minor visa violations.

- minimize judicial supervision of federal telephone and Internet surveillance by authorities.

- expand the government's powers to conduct secret searches.

- give the Attorney General and the Secretary of State the power to designate domestic groups as terrorist organizations and deport any noncitizens who belong to them.

- give the FBI access to business records about individuals without having to show evidence of a crime.

- lead to large-scale investigation of U.S. citizens for "intelligence" purposes. (American Civil Liberties Union 2002b)

The Homeland Security Act, signed into law on November 25, 20002, involves the creation of a new Department of Homeland Security that includes the functions of the former INS. Among its sweeping provisions, the Act authorizes the collection of data on individuals and groups, including databases that combine personal, governmental and corporate records, including e-mails and Web sites viewed. It also allows more latitude for government advisory committees to meet in secret, if deemed "national-security related" (Chaddock 2002).

Women in the Criminal Justice System

I stood with my forehead pressed as close as possible to the dark, tinted window of my jail cell. The window was long and narrow, the foot-deep wall that framed it made it impossible to stand close. The thick glass blurred everything outside. I squinted and focused, and I concentrated all my attention on the area where my mother said the family would stand and wave. . . . It would be good to see my grandparents and my mother, but it was my daughter I really wanted to see. My daughter who would be two years old in two months.

A couple of minutes passed, and in that small space of time, I rethought my entire life and how it had come to this absurd moment, when I became a twenty-one-year-old girl in jail on a drug charge, a mother who had to wait

for someone to bring my own daughter to glimpse me. I could not rub my hands across her fat, brown cheeks, or plait her curly hair the way I like it.   *(Gaines 1994, p. 1)*

In 2003 over 180,000 women were incarcerated in jails—where people are held before trial and when convicted of a misdemeanor with a sentence of less than one year—and prisons—where people convicted of felony charges and serving more than a one-year sentence are held (Harrison and Karberg 2004). Over 1 million women were on probation or parole, being "supervised" in the community (Glaze 2003).

Historically, women offenders were ignored by researchers and media reports because their numbers were small in comparison with those of men. During the 1990s, however, the rate of growth in women's imprisonment far outstripped that of men's.

There is a growing literature of firsthand accounts that documents women's experiences of incarceration (e.g., Gaines 1994; Lamb and the Women of New York Correctional Facility 2003; Richie 1996; Rierden 1997; Ross 1993; Serna 1992; Stein 1991; Watterson 1996). Shannon Murray (Reading 59) and Marilyn Buck (Reading 60) describe aspects of prison life.

This dramatic increase in the imprisonment of women has been driven primarily by "the war on drugs" and mandatory sentencing for drug offenses, with drug use seen as a criminal matter rather than a public health issue. The majority of female arrests are for drug offenses, such as possession and dealing, and crimes committed to support a drug habit, particularly theft and prostitution, sometimes referred to as drug-related crimes. About half of the women confined in state prisons had been using drugs, alcohol, or both at the time of the offense for which they were incarcerated (Bureau of Justice Statistics 2000). Almost 34 percent of women in state prisons and 72 percent in federal prisons have been convicted of drug-related offenses (Bureau of Justice Statistics 2000). Criminologist Stephanie Bush-Baksette (1999, p. 223) argues that the war on drugs targeted women intentionally. The sentencing guidelines, mandatory nature of the imprisonment laws, focus on first-time offenders, and mandatory minimum sentences for persons with prior felony convictions all brought more women into the criminal justice system and led to a tremendous increase in the number of incarcerated women.

Under current punishment philosophies and practices, women are also increasingly subject to criminalization of noncriminal actions and behaviors. For example, poor and homeless women—many of them mothers—are subject to criminalization as many cities pass ordinances prohibiting begging and sleeping in public places. Another disturbing trend has been the criminalization of HIV-positive women and pregnant drug-addicted women. For example, in 1992, a woman in North Carolina, allegedly HIV-positive, became entangled in the criminal justice system when she went to a public health facility for a pregnancy test. The test was positive, and she was arrested and prosecuted for "failure to follow public health warning." Her crimes were not advising her sexual partners of her HIV status and not using condoms whenever she had sexual intercourse (Cooper 1992; Seigel 1997). Although this may seem an extreme example, it is part of a growing trend. Pregnant women using illegal drugs are characterized as "evil women" and "bad mothers" who are willing to endanger the health of their unborn children in pursuit of drug-induced highs. There also has been a trend to arrest and prosecute these women for "the 'delivery' of controlled substances to their newborns; their alleged mode of 'delivery' to the newborn is through the umbilical cord between birth and the time the cord is cut" (Cooper 1992, p. 11). Law professor Kaaryn Gustafson (2005) notes that welfare rules are becoming more punitive with explicit links to law enforcement, as mentioned in Chapter 8. Law enforcement officials may access information in welfare files. Women wanted by law enforcement officials for a felony or for violating the terms of parole or probation—which may be as little as missing a meeting—cannot receive government benefits. Anyone found guilty of a drug-related felony is banned from receiving benefits for life. States can require drug tests, fingerprints, and photographs for those applying for benefits.

Characteristics of Incarcerated Women

Women prisoners have a host of medical, psychological, and financial problems and needs. Poverty, unemployment, physical and mental illness, substance abuse, homelessness, and a history of sexual abuse often propel women into a revolving cycle of life inside and outside jails and prisons, as described by Shannon Murray (Reading 59). The median age of women in prison is approximately 35 years. The majority of jailed and imprisoned women are high school graduates, but 60 percent of women in state prisons were not working full-time at the time of their arrest. About 37 percent of women had an income of less than $600 per month prior to arrest, and nearly 30 percent received welfare assistance. Nearly 60 percent of women in state prisons report having been physically or sexually abused at least once at some time in their lives prior to incarceration (Bureau of Justice Statistics 2000).

Women in prison are predominantly single heads of households, and 70 percent have children under the age of 18. It is estimated that about 200,000 children under 18 have incarcerated mothers, and that 1.5 million children have a parent behind bars (Mumola 2000). African American children are nearly nine times, and Latino children three times more likely to have a parent in prison than White children (Mumola 2000). Public policy analysts Erika Kates and Paige Ransford (2005) emphasize the criminal justice system's lack of recognition of incarcerated women's role as mothers. They identify a range of factors that prevent regular contact between these mothers and their children: isolated locations of prisons served by poor or nonexistent public transport; restrictive policies governing visits and phone calls; the removal of infants born to women in prison (about 9 percent of women are pregnant when incarcerated); speedy termination of child custody for incarcerated women; restrictive welfare policies that make it difficult for families to be reunited; and women's repeated periods in custody. They outline a Family Connections Policy Framework to support and strengthen relationships between incarcerated women and their children, who are often the key motivating factor for women to try to get their lives back on track, as mentioned by Shannon Murray (Reading 59). The majority of those children live with relatives, primarily grandparents, and approximately 10 percent of them are in foster care, a group home, or other social service agency. Most women in state prisons have a history of prior convictions (65 percent), and 19 percent had been convicted as juveniles (Bureau of Justice Statistics 2000).

Daily Life of Incarcerated Women

- Women prisoners spend on average 17 hours a day in their cells with 1 hour outside for exercise. By contrast, men prisoners spend on average 15 hours a day in their cells with 1.5 hours outside.

- Mothers in prison are less likely to be visited by their children than are fathers because women are sent away to other counties or remote areas of a state more often than men.

- A survey conducted in 38 states revealed that 58 percent of the prisons or jails serve exactly the same diet to pregnant prisoners as to others, and in most cases these meals do not meet the minimum recommended allowances for pregnancy.

- Some women come to prison pregnant; others become pregnant in prison. Few receive prenatal care and many pregnant prisoners suffer a high rate of miscarriage as a result. Congress has banned the use of federal funds for abortion in prison; women who can pay for an abortion themselves may be able to get one at a clinic, but will need to convince prison authorities to get them there. Women who carry their pregnancies to term are often treated inhumanely, denied prompt medical attention, and may be forced to undergo labor and childbirth in shackles (Siegal 1998).

- Health care for prisoners is totally inadequate. It is common practice for prisoners to be denied medical examinations and treatments outright. Incarcerated HIV-infected women have no access to experimental drug trials or the use of new drug protocols. The incidence and spread of HIV/AIDS, hepatitis C, tuberculosis, and other serious communicable diseases is reaching epidemic proportions in many prisons (Lydersen 2001).

- Menstruating women are given small quantities of sanitary products and have to buy more from the commissaries at grossly inflated prices (Lydersen 2001).

- Incarcerated women have specific needs stemming, in part, from the fact that they are responsible for children and that many have experienced sexual or physical violence. They are more likely to be addicted to drugs and to have mental illnesses than incarcerated men. In a National Institute of Justice study of correctional administrators, those in 17 states could name no women's programs that were effective or promising within their jurisdictions. Many of those who could point to existing education or health programs cited the need for more drug-treatment programs and mental health services (National Institute of Justice 1998).

- Sexual abuse of women inmates by male staff is common. This includes insults, harassment, rape, voyeurism in showers and during physical exams, and touching women's breasts and genitals during pat-downs and strip searches (Amnesty International USA 2000).

- The Prison Rape Elimination Act became federal law in 2003, providing for a two-year national data collection process with public hearings, research conducted in prisons, and policy recommendations. It also requires the National Institute of Corrections to take on training and education of officials at all levels of government. The goal is to prevent sexual abuse in prisons and to punish offenders, presumably whether these are fellow inmates or guards. Critics are skeptical that the Department of Justice can carry out meaningful research on such a sensitive subject, and question the need for research, as opposed to changes in policy, on a subject about which so much is already known.

Source: Prison Activist Resource Center 2003 (www.prisonactivist.org/women/), unless otherwise noted.

Incarcerated women use more serious drugs and use them somewhat more frequently than do incarcerated men (Bureau of Justice Statistics 2000). The rate of HIV infection is higher for women prisoners than for men prisoners according to the Bureau of Justice Statistics (2000). Overall, an estimated 3.5 percent of the women report being HIV-positive, compared with 2.2 percent of the men. Nineteen percent of women in New York State prisons are HIV-positive (Honderich 2003, p. 16).

Offenses Committed by Women and Patterns of Arrest

Studies have consistently shown that women generally commit fewer crimes than men and that their offenses tend to be less serious, primarily nonviolent property offenses such as fraud, forgery, and theft, as well as drug offenses (Bloom, Chesney-Lind, and Owen 1994; Honderich 2003). Violent offenses committed by women continue to decline. When women do commit acts of violence, these are usually in self-defense against abusive spouses or partners. Forty-four percent of women who have committed murder have killed their abusive partners (Bureau of Justice Statistics 1999a).

Race and Class Disparities

Most women in the U.S. criminal justice system are marginalized by race and class. Poor women are pushed into the "underground economies" of drugs, prostitution, and theft as a way of supporting themselves and their children. African American women constitute 44 percent of women in jails, 48 percent in state prisons, and 35 percent in federal prisons; Latinas 15 percent of women in jails, 15 percent in state prisons, and 32 percent in federal prisons; White women 36 percent in jails, 33 percent in state prisons, and 29 percent in federal prisons (Bureau of Justice Statistics 2000). Women of color make up 21 percent of the general female population but 67 percent of the state prison population (Bureau of Justice Statistics 2000). According to writers and organizers Jael Silliman and Anannya Bhattacharjee (2002), "For the same offense, Black and Latina women are respectively eight and four times more likely to be incarcerated

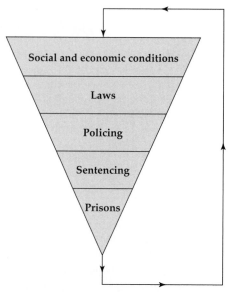

FIGURE 10.1 The Funnel of Injustice (*Source:* Honderich 2003, p. 10.)

than white women" (p. xv). White women are more likely to be placed on probation than women of color.

Many crimes committed on Native American reservations are classified as federal offenses, and lawbreakers are held in federal prisons, usually in remote places long distances away from home and hard to get to by public transportation, two factors that increase the isolation of such prisoners.

Racial bias is a factor in arrests, pretrial treatment, and differential sentencing of women. Professor of criminal justice Coramae Richey Mann (1995) documents disparity in prison sentences by comparing arrest rates with sentencing rates of women offenders in California, Florida, and New York. She found that, in all three states, women of color, particularly African Americans, were disproportionately arrested. The few studies that report race-specific differences indicate more punitive treatment of women of color. Economist Kiaran Honderich (2003) describes this channeling of poor women of color into the criminal justice system in terms of a "funnel of injustice" (see Figure 10.1). In 1996 the issue of differential sentencing for cocaine use surfaced as a public issue. Currently sentences for possession of 500 grams of powder cocaine, mainly used by middle- and upper-middle-class White people, are set at a minimum of five years. Possession of any amount of crack cocaine, mainly used by poor people of color, carries a mandatory minimum sentence of five years.

The "war on drugs," initiated by the Reagan administration in the 1980s, has been aggressively pursued in poor urban neighborhoods, especially poor African American and Latino communities, and in countries of the global South, despite the fact that White people make up the majority of drug users and traffickers. Proponents justified massive government intervention as necessary to quell the drug epidemic, gang violence, and "narco-terrorism." However, critics charged that "Blacks, Latinos, and third world people are suffering the worst excesses of a program that violates . . . civil rights, human rights, and national sovereignty" (Lusane 1991, p. 4). Julia Sudbury takes up this issue in Reading 63.

The declared intention to get rid of drugs and drug-related crime has resulted in the allocation of federal and state funding for more police officers on the streets, more federal law-enforcement officers, and more jails and prisons, rather than for prevention, rehabilitation, and education. Poor women of color have become the main victims of these efforts in two ways: They are trying to hold their families and communities together while so many men of color are incarcerated, and they are increasingly incarcerated themselves. As author, activist, and scholar Clarence Lusane (1991) observes, "The get-tough, mandatory-sentencing laws are forcing judges to send to prison first-time offenders who a short time ago would have gotten only probation or a fine. . . . It is inevitable that women caught selling the smallest amount of drugs will do time" (p. 56). As argued in Chapter 9, the international drug trade must be understood at the global level, as one way producer countries earn hard currency to repay foreign debt. Mandatory minimum prison sentences are not cost effective according to some policy analysts, and appear to have had a negligible effect on the drug trade in this country.

Girls in the Criminal Justice System

When people think of juvenile crime they often think of boys, but roughly two-thirds of incarcerated women were first arrested as juveniles, and about half of them spent time in detention when they were minors (Siegal 1995). Girls are likely to be held in detention for lesser offenses than boys, such as shoplifting, violations of probation and parole, minor public order disturbances, and driving without a license. African American girls are much more likely to be held in detention than White girls or Latinas. There are fewer options for girls as compared with boys in terms of rehabilitation and housing, so girls spend more time in detention awaiting placement. The great majority of girls in the criminal justice system have been physically or sexually abused; many have learning disorders; many use drugs and alcohol (Chesney-Lind 1997). According to journalist Nina Siegal (1995), "Probation officers, counselors, and placement staffers prefer to work with boys because they say girls' problems are more complex and more difficult to address" (p. 16). Girls express more emotional needs than boys. "Middle-class girls with the same problems might end up in therapy, treatment programs, boarding schools, or private hospitals. But girls in Juvenile Hall have fallen through the system's proverbial safety net" (p. 17) or lack of safety net.

Dating from the 1890s, the early juvenile justice system held to the principle of rehabilitation, but the "get tough on crime" policy has meant that many states have changed their approach to an explicitly punitive one. California, for example, has reduced the age at which minors can be tried as adults from 16 to 14 for 24 different crimes. The state has also changed the law on confidentiality so that the names of juvenile offenders can become public knowledge.

Women Political Prisoners

The International Tribunal on Human Rights Violations of Political Prisoners and Prisoners of War in the United States, held in New York City, December 1990, defined a political prisoner as "a person incarcerated for actions carried out in support of legitimate struggles for self-determination or for opposing illegal policies of the United States government" (Bin Wahad 1996, p. 277). A small but significant group of women in federal prisons is there as a result of such political activities, including members of the Puerto Rican Socialist

Party, supporters of Native American sovereignty movements, and participants in Black revolutionary movements in the United States and abroad. Examples include Silvia Baraldini, an Italian citizen, who was given a forty-year sentence, arrested on conspiracy charges arising out of political activities in solidarity with national liberation movements, including assisting in the escape of Black activist Assata Shakur. Like Marilyn Buck, Susan Rosenberg, and Laura Whitehorn, she was active in the women's movement and the anti–Vietnam War movement, and was a supporter of African, African American, and Puerto Rican national liberation movements. According to Elihu Rosenblatt (1996), coordinator at the Prison Activist Resource Center, "Susan Rosenberg was targeted by the FBI for her support of the liberation of Assata Shakur from prison, and her support of the Black Liberation Army. After going underground in the 1980s she was arrested . . . in 1984, convicted of weapons possession, and sentenced to 58 years" (p. 355). From 1986 to 1988, Silvia Baraldini and Susan Rosenberg were held in the "High Security Unit" (HSU), a specially built underground prison for political prisoners in Lexington, Kentucky. Although this sixteen-bed prison housed no more than six women at a time, it became the center of intense scrutiny by national and international human rights organizations, including Amnesty International. As a result of sustained political pressure from activists and the Italian government, Silvia Baraldini was released to Italian authorities in 1999 so that she could return to Italy due to serious complications associated with cancer. Susan Rosenberg and Laura Whitehorn were released in 1999 having served sixteen and fourteen-year sentences respectively. Marilyn Buck is still in prison, serving an eighty-year sentence. In Reading 60, she discusses work in prison.

Since about the mid-1950s, the federal government has operated "counter-insurgency programs," complete with special police forces and lockup facilities, to track, undermine, and destroy left-wing political organizations it deemed radical and militant and to imprison or kill activists. The Federal Bureau of Investigation (FBI) in its Counter Intelligence Programs (COINTELPRO) launched campaigns against the Communist Party in 1954 and, subsequently, against the Socialist Workers Party,

the Puerto Rican independence movement, the Black Power Movement, particularly the Black Panther Party, and the American Indian Movement (AIM) in the 1960s and 1970s (Churchill 1992). Mumia Abu-Jamal, Leonard Peltier, and Geronimo Pratt were all convicted of murder, although they all claim to have been framed by the FBI. Geronimo Pratt was freed in 1997 after over twenty-five years in prison. A judge ruled that the evidence used to convict him had indeed been tampered with, as both Pratt and prison rights activists had argued all along (Booth 1997). Angela Davis, an internationally known scholar and activist, was imprisoned for two years on murder, conspiracy, and kidnapping charges but later acquitted.

Women jailed in the early 1900s for opposition to government policy were suffragists, whose crime was peacefully picketing the White House in their campaign for votes for women. In 1917, for example, hundreds of suffragists, mainly White, middle-class women, organized pickets around the clock. At first they were ignored by the police. By June they began to be arrested, and in August they received thirty-day and sixty-day sentences for obstructing traffic. A number of those who were jailed went on hunger strikes; they were forcibly fed and threatened with transfer to an insane asylum. They were released the following year by order of President Wilson, and the Washington, D.C., Court of Appeals ruled that their arrests, convictions, and imprisonment were illegal (Gluck 1976). This kind of political action was very different from that of revolutionary organizations committed to self-defense and armed struggle if necessary. But, like the sentences of political women prisoners active in the 1970s and '80s, suffragists also received disproportionately long sentences and harsh treatment, clearly intended to discourage this kind of determined opposition to government policy. Activist and writer Julie Browne (1996) notes: "A Ku Klux Klansman, charged with violations of the Neutrality Act and with possessing a boatload of explosives and weapons to be used in an invasion of the Caribbean island of Dominica, received eight years. Yet Linda Evans [charged with bombings claimed by militant left-wing groups], convicted of purchasing four weapons with false ID, was sentenced to forty years—the longest sentence ever imposed for this offense" (p. 285).

Another example of politically motivated incarceration was the internment of thousands of Japanese

Americans in remote camps following the bombing of Pearl Harbor by Japanese troops in 1941, as described by Rita Takahashi in Reading 61. Most of these people were U.S. citizens, living in West Coast states. They were forced to leave their homes, farms, businesses, and other property, and were kept in the camps for the duration of U.S. involvement in World War II. Takahashi comments that although the U.S. constitution "prohibits deprivation of life, liberty, or property without due process of law," these constitutional guarantees "were suspended in this case, and the Government was able to implement this massive program with few questions asked," though there was no evidence that these Japanese Americans were in any way "disloyal" to the United States. In a similar move, authorities arrested some 1,500 men, mostly Arabs, after the attacks of September 11, 2001. In addition, private citizens and various officials have committed acts of violence and harassment against Arab Americans, South Asians, and "people who look like Muslims." In one instance, Samar Kaukab, a U.S. woman of Pakistani descent, was detained at Chicago's O'Hare International Airport in November 2001 and subjected to an unjustified, illegal, and degrading search by airport security personnel. The America Civil Liberties Union filed suit and the matter was settled through a confidential agreement in 2004. In Reading 62, Suad Joseph and Benjamin D'Harlingue present their analysis of negative media coverage of Arabs and Arab Americans, a factor in creating a climate of opinion whereby racial profiling, preemptive arrests and detentions, abuse and humiliation of those detained, and suspension of their constitutional rights can be justified and supported in the name of "national security." In November 2002, a "Special Registration" program required males over 16 years of age from twenty-five mainly Arab and Muslim counties to be fingerprinted, photographed, and questioned about terrorism. This program lasted eighteen months with devastating impact on these communities (Nguyen 2005). Several thousand men were detained and an unknown number deported. As of mid-2004, none of those arrested had been charged or found to have any connection to terrorism (García 2004). Writer Amani Elkassabani includes this incident in her short story "Hanaan's House" (Reading 12). Japanese Americans were among the first to speak out against these detentions, recognizing the similarity with what had happened to their own community sixty years earlier (Kim 2001; Leung and Chow 2002).

Theories of Women and Crime

Until recently there has been a lack of research specifically on women in conflict with the law in the United States. This is partly because far fewer women than men were caught up in the criminal justice system and also because it is difficult for researchers to obtain access to women in prison. Official data collected by the Bureau of Justice are limited and often date back several years by the time they are published, a limitation of the data cited in this chapter.

Early theories of women's criminality either attempted to explain it in individual terms, or used theories developed to explain male criminality and applied them to women. Theories that emphasized individual behavior applied stereotypical assumptions about the "female psyche" that are blatantly sexist and without much evidence to support their claims. They include biological arguments—for example, that women commit crimes as a result of premenstrual syndrome (PMS)—and psychological notions—that "hysterical" women behave criminally, or that women are conniving and manipulative, and so resort to using poison rather than a gun to kill a person. The second type included theories of *social learning* (crime is learned), *social process* (individuals are affected by institutions such as the family, school, and peers), and *social structure* (individuals are shaped by structural inequalities), and *conflict theory*, a specific social structure theory, which generally claims that the law is a weapon of social control used by the powerful against the less powerful (Turk 1995).

An increase in female crime in the 1960s and '70s prompted new theories attributing female criminality to the women's liberation movement. The female offender was identified as its "dark side" (Chesney-Lind 1986). The phenomenon of girls in gangs has also been blamed on the women's movement (Chesney-Lind and Shelden 1992). Sociologist Freda Adler (1975), for example, proposed that women were committing an increasing number of violent crimes because the women's movement had created a liberated, tougher class of women, a view that became known as the "masculinity thesis." Similarly, criminologist Rita Simon (1975) argued that a rise in women's involvement in property crimes, such as theft, embezzlement, and fraud, was due to women entering previously male occupations, such as banking and business, and to their consequent exposure to opportunities for crime that were previously the preserve of men. This is the "opportunity thesis." Neither of these theses is supported by much empirical evidence.

A third theory, the "economic marginalization thesis," posits that it is the absence, rather than the availability, of employment opportunity for women that appears to lead to increases in female crime (Giordano, Kerbel, and Dudley 1981; Naffine 1987). According to this view, most crime committed by women is petty property crime, such as theft, a rational response to poverty and economic insecurity. The increasing numbers of single women supporting dependent children mean that more women may risk the benefits of criminal activity as supplements or alternatives to employment (Rafter 1990). Noting that the majority of female offenders are low-income women who committed non-employment-related crimes, rather than middle- and upper-middle-class professional women who committed employment-related crimes, proponents of economic marginalization theory argue that the feminization of poverty, not women's liberation, is the social trend most relevant to female criminality.

Some feminist scholars view the cause of female crime as originating in male supremacy, and in men's efforts to control women sexually. They attempt to show how physical and sexual victimization of girls and women can be underlying causes of criminal behavior (Chesney-Lind 1995; Owen and Bloom 1995). They argue that the exploitation of women and girls causes some to run away from home or to begin abusing drugs at an early age, which often leads to criminal activity.

Other feminists view gender inequality as stemming from the unequal power of women and men in a capitalist society (Connell 1990; Messerschmidt 1986). They trace the origins of gender differences to the development of private property and male domination over the laws of inheritance, asserting that within the current economic system, men control women economically as well as socially. Such theorists argue that women commit fewer crimes than men because women are isolated in the family and have fewer opportunities to engage in white-collar crimes or street crimes. Because capitalism renders women relatively powerless both in the home and

in the economic arena, any crimes they commit are less serious, nonviolent, self-destructive crimes such as theft, drug possession, and prostitution. Moreover, women's relative powerlessness also increases the likelihood that they will be the target of violent acts, usually by men.

Yet other feminist scholars foreground racism in explaining the disproportionately high incarceration rates for people of color (e.g. Davis 1998; Silliman and Bhattacharjee 2002; Smith 2005). They focus on community experiences of state violence, including the incarceration of people of color, police brutality, and women's struggles to keep their families and communities intact in the face of arrests, harassment, and raids by the police.

In Reading 63, Julia Sudbury takes an intersectional approach to explain the upsurge in women's incarceration. She explores three macro- and global-level factors—the effects of globalization on national economies, the expansion of the prison industry as a profit-making business, and the war on drugs—to account for women's imprisonment. She discusses the experiences of three individual women, one from Canada, one from Colombia, and one from the United States, to illustrate her argument. She critiques feminist criminology on two counts: first, for focusing on women's behavior, assuming a connection between punishment and crime, to explain their incarceration. Rather, Sudbury contends, "we should look at the shifting action of the state as it seeks to control poor communities and populations of color." Secondly, feminist criminologists have focused on gender at the expense of race and class. Advocates, policy makers, and theorists who seek to understand and explain the criminal justice system must, as Sudbury puts it, "engage meaningfully with the significance of race." Following the implications of her analysis, Sudbury assesses three approaches to changing the status quo regarding women's imprisonment: reform, decarceration, and prison abolition.

"Equality with a Vengeance": Is Equal Treatment Fair Treatment?

There is extensive debate among feminist legal scholars about whether equality under the law is necessarily good for women (Chesney-Lind 1995; K. Daly 1994). On the one hand, some argue that the only way to eliminate the discriminatory treatment and oppression that women have experienced in the past is to push for continued equalization under the law. Though equal treatment may hurt women in the short run, in the long run it is the only way to guarantee that women will be treated as equal partners economically and socially. For example, legal scholar and professor of law Catharine MacKinnon (1987) states, "For women to affirm difference, when difference means dominance, as it does with gender, means to affirm the qualities and characteristics of powerlessness" (pp. 38–39). Even legal scholars who do not view women as an oppressed group conclude that women will be victimized by laws created out of "concern and affection" and designed to protect them. Legal scholars Deborah Labelle and Sheryl Pimlott Kubiak (2004) explore how "the legal right to 'substantially equivalent' treatment and facilities for female prisoners was jeopardized by an administrative interpretation of the policy as gender neutral" (p. 417). In the situation they investigated, "female and male prisoners were treated identically—based on the male prisoner model" (p. 418). This meant that no allowances were made for physical contact on prison visits, such as women kissing, hugging, or even touching their children. Male guards were assigned to women's housing units, thus "subjecting women prisoners to twenty-four-hour male supervision—while showering, dressing, and performing basic bodily functions" (p. 419). This compounded incarcerated women's sense of powerlessness, especially as many had been sexually assaulted as girls or as adults. These scholars conclude that equal treatment should not mean gender neutrality, which "is not appropriate in circumstances in which there are real differences in gender socialization and social conditions" (p. 424).

Gender-neutral sentencing reforms have aimed to reduce disparities in sentencing by punishing like crimes in the same way. This emphasis on parity, the utilization of a male standard, and gender-blind mandatory sentencing statutes, particularly for drug-law violations, have all contributed to the rising numbers of women in prison. A Phoenix, Arizona, sheriff proudly boasted, "I don't believe in discrimination," after he established the first female chain gang in the United States, where women, whose work boots are chained together, pick up trash in downtown Phoenix (In Phoenix chain gangs for women 1996). This is what Lahey (1985) has called "equality with a vengeance."

Another effect of the equalization approach has been in the types of facilities women are sentenced to. For example, boot camps have become popular with prison authorities as an alternative to prison for juvenile and adult offenders. New York, for instance, operates a boot camp for women that is modeled on those for men. This includes uniforms, shorn hair, humiliation for behaviors considered to be disrespectful of staff, and other militaristic approaches.

Criminologist Pat Carlen (1989) argues that equality with men in the criminal justice system means more punitive measures applied to women. Instead, she advocates the supervision of women in noncustodial settings in their communities, where they can remain connected with their children and families, and calls for reducing the number of prison beds for women and using nonprison alternatives for all but the most dangerous offenders. She bases her argument on the fact that most women commit nonviolent crimes and are often victims of physical, sexual, and emotional abuse. Therefore, she claims, programs that support women's emotional needs are more appropriate than punitive measures.

The "Prison Industrial Complex"

Some critics describe the expansion and privatization of the prison system, with prison services provided by private firms and prisoners working for corporations, as the "prison industrial complex" (Browne 1996; Davis 1997; Walker 1996). Borrowing from the term "military industrial complex," coined by President Dwight Eisenhower in 1960, the phrase "prison industrial complex" refers to the increasingly interconnected relationship between private corporations, the public prison system, public investment, and public interests. The Corrections Corporation of America manages many prisons in this country. The construction and servicing of prisons and jails have become big business—as argued in Reading 63. Profits are being generated by architecture firms designing prisons, security companies supplying equipment, food distribution companies providing food service, and also, by the direct and indirect exploitation of prisoners. For example, TWA and Best Western (the international motel chain) use prisoners to take calls from customers during times when there is an overflow, such as before holidays and certain vacation periods. Microsoft, Victoria's Secret, and Boeing are also using low-cost prison labor (Parenti 1999), as well as Starbucks and Nintendo (Barnett 2002). This is being done for a number of reasons: It is difficult to attract regular workers for seasonal employment, prisoners do not have to be paid minimum wage or be covered by workers' compensation (a tax employers must pay for regular employees), and they cannot unionize (Lichtenstein and Kroll 1996). In reading 60, Marilyn Buck discusses women's prison work. Telephone companies also profit because people outside jails and prisons are not allowed to call prisoners directly; prisoners are allowed only to call collect, which is one of the most expensive ways of making telephone calls. In August 2005, in *Byrd v. Goord*, a federal trial court ruled in favor of friends and family members of incarcerated prisoners in New York state who are "bearing an unlegislated tax" in inflated phone charges for collect calls to speak with their loved ones (Center for Constitutional Rights 2005). The court ruled that the 60 percent "commission" which the New York State Department of Corrections gets from MCI's profits on the inmate phone system is unconstitutional. However, it upheld two other charges: the restriction of calls to collect only, and the limitations of statewide service to one provider, MCI.

Most state budgets are currently in crisis as a result of economic recession and changes in federal allocations to states. Their colossal investment in new jails and prisons has eaten up a growing portion of states' resources nationwide, in direct competition with other state investments like higher education (see box for details). The enormous costs of mandatory minimum sentences and three-strikes laws have caused many states to reassess their policies and to expand parole and early release, to close prisons and develop alternative sentencing programs—the very reforms that anti-prison advocates want to see (Falk 2003; Miller 2005). Julie Falk (2003) suggests, however, that these changes "are probably temporary, quick-fix solutions that states can and will reverse when the budget crunch eases" (p. 20). Also due to budget constraints, she notes that education, training, and rehabilitation for prisoners have been cut

back severely; overcrowding is getting worse; inmates are being kept in their cells for longer periods to reduce the wage bill for guards; and some prisoners are required to pay for health care as well as room and board. Susan Tucker and Eric Cadora note the failures of what they call "prison fundamentalism" and argue for "justice reinvestment" in poor communities. They challenge the logic of current policy that expects people released from prison with no new skills to return to the same impoverished communities and make a go of their lives (Reading 64). They argue, instead, for investment in poor communities for education, health, job creation, and job training.

Inside/Outside Connections

In Reading 63, Julia Sudbury asks: "Who benefits when more women are imprisoned? What are the processes by which certain actions are labeled criminal and others are not, and how are women channeled into these actions and thus into conflict with the criminal justice system?" This macro-level perspective offers a way to break down the separation between people who find themselves on the "inside" or "outside" of the criminal justice system. It also helps to explain the arrest and detention of whole groups of people such as Japanese Americans in the 1940s, or Arab Americans and South Asian people today.

Women who have never been incarcerated can be allies to incarcerated and formerly incarcerated women by supporting organizations and activities involving former prisoners and advocates. Examples of organizations that support women in prison include Aid to Inmate Mothers (Montgomery, Ala.); California Coalition for Women Prisoners (San Francisco); Chicago Legal Advocacy for Incarcerated Mothers; Legal Services for Prisoners with Children (Oakland); Let's Start (St. Louis, Mo.); and the National Women's Law Center, Women in Prison project (Washington, D.C.). Women on the outside are working with women prisoners in literacy classes, creative writing projects, and theater projects (Fraden 2001; Troustine 2001) such as the Medea Project: Theater for Incarcerated Women (San Francisco) and the Women's Prison Book Project (Minneapolis), or supporting self-help groups run by prisoners, such as Convicted

Comparable Costs: Education, Drug Treatment, and Imprisonment

- Research shows consistently that education is needed to compete in today's workforce and to secure jobs that pay decent wages and benefits. Many people in prison or on probation do not have high school or equivalent level of educational achievement.

- Prisons and higher education compete for budget dollars from a state's General Fund as expenditures that are not mandated by federal requirements nor driven strictly by population like Medicare or K-12 education.

- Throughout the 1980s and 1990s, state spending on prisons, on average, grew at six times the rate of higher-education spending. Forty-five states increased spending on prisons by more than 100 percent; eighteen states by over 200 percent; and the top five (Colorado, Idaho, Oregon, Pennsylvania, and Texas) by over 300 percent (Justice Policy Institute 2002, Table 5). In Maryland, for example, the prison budget increased by $147 million, while the university budget fell by $29 million. In the decade 1988–1998, New York spent $762 million more on corrections while spending on state colleges and universities dropped by $615 million (Justice Policy Institute 2002, p. 3).

- It costs as much or more to send someone to prison as to university. The estimated cost per inmate in California state prisons was $30,929 for fiscal year 2003–2004, or $27,167 in Alameda county jail. Stanford University fees were $40,591 per year, including room, board, books and fees, while U.C. Berkeley (in-state tuition) amounted to $6,730 (Urban Strategies Council 2004).

- Research on the Drug Treatment Alternative-to-Prison Program, carried out in Brooklyn, New York, in the 1990s, showed that participants in this program had lower re-arrest and re-conviction rates compared to those who were incarcerated for similar offenses. Two years after leaving the program, graduates were 67 percent less likely to have been re-convicted as opposed to those in the comparison group two years after leaving prison. Graduates were three-and-a-half times as likely to be employed compared to before their arrest (26 percent were employed on arrest; 92 percent were employed two years after completing the program). These results were achieved at half the average cost of incarceration (National Center for Addiction and Substance Abuse; 2003, p. ii). Despite these findings, for every $100 the state of New York spent on substance abuse in 1998, only $5.81 went to fund prevention, treatment, and research; the rest paid for building and upkeep of prisons, incarceration of drug offenders, and probation and parole services (National Center for Addiction and Substance Abuse, 2003, p. 12).

- Close to half the 2 million people incarcerated in the United States are African American (Justice Policy Institute 2002, p. 8). Between 1980 and 2000, 38 states and all federal prisons added more African American men to prison populations than to enrollment in state colleges and universities (Justice Policy Institute 2002, Table 6). Texas added more than four times the number of African American men to its prison system (54,500) than to its colleges and universities (12,163)—the highest discrepancy nationwide.

Women against Abuse at the California Institution for Women. AIDS awareness programs for people in prison are sponsored by the ACLU National Prison Project (Washington, D.C.) and the AIDS in Prison Project (New York). Women in a maximum-security prison have organized HIV peer education (Members of the AIDS Counseling and Education Program of the Bedford Hills Correctional Facility 1998). Films by and about women who killed abusive partners include *Defending Our Lives* (Cambridge Documentary Films), which tells the story of Battered Women Fighting Back! a group of inmates at a prison in Framingham, Massachusetts. *From One Prison . . .* (Michigan Battered Women's Clemency Project) was produced in collaboration with women at a Michigan prison who are serving life or long-term sentences for killing their batterers.

Advocates press for health care, drug treatment, and educational, therapeutic, and life-skills programs for incarcerated women. They also critique funding priorities of successive administrations that give a higher priority to building jails and prisons than to education, social services, and welfare; they urge a fundamental redirection of these resources. The Rocky Mountain Peace and Justice Center's Prison Moratorium Project (Boulder, Colo.) challenges the idea that prisons can solve social problems based on poverty and inequality. It seeks to halt prison expansion and redirect resources toward the development of alternative sentencing, prevention, and treatment programs, as does the nationwide Critical Resistance network. The nonprofit Justice Policy Institute (2002) argues for repealing mandatory sentencing, reforming drug laws to direct offenders into treatment programs, restructuring sentencing guidelines, and reforming parole practices—where high numbers of parolees currently are returned to custody not for committing new crimes but for technical violations of their parole orders (see Davis 2003; Silliman and Battacharjee 2002; Readings 63 and 64).

Criminalization is a major source of insecurity for poor women and their families, especially African Americans and Latinas. There is a wide gap between organizations working on behalf of women in the criminal justice system and the wider U.S. women's movement reflecting differences in race and class. Data presented in this chapter give grounds for more effective coalition efforts across lines of race and class to address the needs of formerly incarcerated women and those currently in custody.

◆◆◆

Questions for Reflection

As you read and discuss this chapter, consider these questions:

1. Why is there such attention by politicians and the media to street crimes?

2. Where is the prison nearest to where you live? Are men, women, or both incarcerated there? Who are they in terms of class, race, and age?

3. What conditions "outside" would compel a woman to think that a jail or prison is the best place for her to be?

4. Note the official language of "corrections" or the "correctional system." What is being corrected? Why? How? And corrected to what?

◆◆◆

Finding Out More on the Web

1. Research the work of organizations cited in this chapter. How are they working to support women in the criminal justice system? Try to find organizations that are active in your city or state.

2. Use your search engine to find out the financial and human costs each year of white-collar crime in the United States.

3. What is the relationship between state spending on the criminal justice system and spending on higher education in your state?

Taking Action

1. Analyze the way the news media reports crime, or analyze the portrayal of criminals in movies and TV shows. How are women who have committed crimes portrayed? Pay particular attention to issues of race and class.

2. Find out about the daily conditions for women in the jail or prison nearest to you.

3. Find out about activist groups in your area that support incarcerated women. What can you do on behalf of women in prison?

4. The USA PATRIOT Act allows law enforcement agencies access to information on students and to student records. Find out what steps your college or university has taken to provide information under the terms of this act.

FIFTY-NINE

Shannon's Story (1998)

Shannon Murray

I was born in Detroit Lakes, Minnesota, on September 21, 1969. I grew up in the Old Colony projects in South Boston. The neighborhoods in them days were quiet. The parents kept to themselves and the children were well behaved. We would play games like kick ball or Red Rover. There was a huge park across the street from the complex with a playground so there was always something to do.

My family consisted of my mother, my stepfather, my older sister Janine, and my younger brother Robbie. We were a close family that showed a lot of affection for each other. My parents were alcoholics so it was a struggle. We made the best of what we had. We weren't any worse off than other families; in some ways we had more. Somehow my parents managed to send me and my younger brother to Catholic school. In this way I felt more fortunate than others.

My sister and I are American Indians. My mother, stepfather, and brother are Irish. It was hard because my sister and I were often singled out. I've always felt different from everyone else at home and at school.

I first started smoking pot and drinking at the age of 12. By this time, I was more aware of the drug abuse in my neighborhood. The older teens would hang in the hallways smoking pot and drinking. I started to "use" to fit in. It also helped me to escape the feelings I had surrounding my parents' alcoholism.

My first arrest was at the age of 16 for drinking in public. Over the next four years I was able to avoid the arms of the law. I was put into Protective Custody a few times for disorderly conduct. By this time I was drinking and drugging daily. My disease had taken over. I supported my habits by baby-sitting and selling pot. I dropped out of school in the tenth grade because it was getting in the way of me partying the way I wanted to. I had a few jobs here and there but was unable to hold one because they also got in the way of my using.

After I had my daughter Jaquelin at the age of 18, I started smoking coke more and more often. I had used before that but I stopped during my pregnancy, only smoking pot because I was more afraid of the effects coke could have on my baby than the effect of pot.

The cocaine caused me to lose custody of my daughter to my parents and eventually my apartment. I couldn't deal with the pain of losing my daughter so I turned to heroin. This led to many arrests for shoplifting and possession. My first incarceration was at the age of 25. I was to do three months with probation upon my release.

I was scared because of the stories I had heard about jail. I just felt alone and cut off from reality. I kept to myself and didn't get involved with any of the programs except going to the AA meetings for my good time. I was released with the intention of never coming back.

About nine months later I was incarcerated again, this time for a year. I kind of welcomed the incarceration. This time I am taking advantage of the time I have here to learn more about myself. Being here has given me the chance to take a good look at my lifestyle and what I need to change. I am in the Recovery Program here and I have taken classes like Peace at Home, HIV Prevention, Voices Within, Graphic Arts, and I tutor for pre-GED.

It is hard being locked up in a man's prison. I feel there are prejudices against women here at the Suffolk County House of Corrections. We don't have yard privileges except for a caged-in area that we are only allowed access to during the summer months. We aren't allowed to work in the kitchen or anywhere else in the prison except for the two floors which hold female inmates. We are only allowed to go to the other parts of the prison during the night for things like the library or computers.

I think poverty has a lot to do with people being incarcerated. Where there is poverty there is a lot of drug abuse and less access to structured programs. I think prejudice has a lot to do with being incarcerated because there aren't many jobs for minorities and people have to resort to crime to get things they need that you aren't able to at low-paying jobs.

I have learned that I want a better way of life and that I really don't want to come back here. I know I need to lead an honest life if I truly want to stay out of prison. I hope to become a productive person in society by taking on my responsibilities. I am afraid of failing but I know if I pick up by first dealing with my addictions then I won't have to resort to criminal behavior.

◆◆◆

Women in Prison and Work (2004)

Marilyn Buck

Marilyn Buck describes herself as a political prisoner, activist, poet, and artist. Currently serving an eighty-year sentence in the Federal Correctional Institution, Dublin (California), she has completed her bachelors degree in psychology from prison, as well as becoming an accomplished potter. Recipient of the 2001 PEN Prison Writing Program poetry prize, she is involved in cultural and educational activities for women prisoners.

When a woman goes to jail, she is confronted with time—mostly idle time. In many county jails, there is little to do: a few orderly or trustee jobs perhaps, and daily-demanded tasks such as making a meagerly furnished bed. The real work is to learn to maintain one's equanimity and sanity in an insane situation. Insane because the institution, although it exists ostensibly to deprive one of her liberty or to detain her in the belly of the society for the protection of others, does much more. It redefines work, life, and culture.

Labor is a central component in the business of prisons. It has been regarded as a means of punishment as well as of correction; it is seen as both a moralistic coercion and a form of rehabilitation. According to Michel Foucault, the purpose of penal labor is " . . . the constitution of a power relation . . . a schema of individual submission and of adjustment to a productive apparatus."[1] Foucault discounts profit as a motivating factor; however, in the era of the burgeoning prison-industrial complex, profits are enormous.

Because prison labor is firmly established in a power-submission dynamic, it engenders an attitude of rebellion: a moral and ethical response to an immoral situation of coercion and degradation. Involuntary servitude is immoral even though it has been justified by the Catholic and Protestant Reformation churches for centuries.

Work is not always the same as productivity. Work is a measured commodity to order human activity for the benefit, ostensibly of society, but more so for those who own the means of production or have laid claim to all sorts of natural resources: land, minerals, bananas, and human beings. It is extolled on the moral plane to instill habits of order, obedience, and docility.

In its most organized and measurable form, work is generally an exploitation of human labor and creativity to produce value. Even brainwork is likely owned or seized by the person who pays the teacher's, scientist's, or even assembly-line worker's salary.

Productivity, on the other hand, includes paid work, even though it is not necessarily measured, controlled, or owned by a master. Productivity includes working in one's flower gardens, preparing lunch, or playing with children, as well as doing arts and crafts and even writing a journal. It includes pleasure and play and is not always subject to power relations.

A woman's labor, with few exceptions, is extremely alienated, exploited, and grossly underpaid. Women have been socially defined for millennia as the "worker." Few women who enter prison were not already working a lot—as mothers, as employees. Even to be a booster, a drug worker, or a sex worker—although illegal—necessitates the expending of energy transformed into a socially constructed product.

While in jail, before conviction, playing cards, reading harlequin novels (for lack of anything except the ubiquitous bibles), and writing letters can become daily life and work for a female detainee, between the meals and institutional organization. However, in the flash of the booking camera, a prisoner's relation to work is changed. Entering prison strips a woman of her self-worth as a worker who creates value, even though that value has not been socially acknowledged.

Once sentenced, a prisoner moves from jail idleness to prison, where she is informed that she must work or be punished further. As a "new commit" she is "on call" twenty-four hours a day to work for any officer who peremptorily demands her labor. For example, a young Mexican woman was awakened after midnight and told to get up to help buff the floors. She told the officer that she was neither a new commit nor a unit orderly and that she had a job to report to at 7:30 A.M. The officer did not find that fact to be of any importance; she wrote a disciplinary report and sent the woman to the segregation unit in the middle of the night for "refusing an order."

The prisoner resents prison labor. Women work at not rebelling against the officer who demands make-work and elevates her or his own work as valuable because it officially sanctions control over other, criminalized, human beings. The prisoner scorns the officer who says, "Wait," while sitting idly doing nothing in order to reinforce the power relationship and the prisoner's compliance. She suspects that the officer's work is not productive labor, its only product being her submission or humiliation. It is negative productivity—to "unmake" or deconstruct her efficacy as a human being in her own right. Not to work or to do as little as possible of the make-work becomes an act of rebellion; it is an assertion of one's own human dignity and worth.

Nevertheless, women prisoners do submit to prison labor. Most of us come from societies that have been culturally molded and oppressed by the European Christian work ethic in which "idle hands are the devil's workshop." Women work because we feel more productive working, even for "Third World" wages—$0.12 per hour or perhaps even as little as $5.25 per month. Women work not to go crazy, not to have time to think about the world and life from which they were removed to be punished much more than any offense of the law calls for. Working allows one to escape from thinking about the full extent of the punishment, not only to oneself, but also to family, children, friends, and former cowork-ers. We compete for jobs that have clear productive value.

Women work because we are forced to by the prison keepers, under penalty of segregation and loss of privileges that are ordinary assumptions of life in the broader society. We are forced to work in the degrading conditions women all over the world suffer. Additionally, we must be prepared to be patted down by male guards, ostensibly to check to see if we are stealing tools or food. These invasive sexual feels numb us. The possibility that we might lose that low-wage paying job and be thrown into a $5.25 per month make-work job is a greater threat.

Make-work, which makes no pretense of pro-ductive value, reminds us of the depraved nature of such unceasing punishment. The irrationality of prison make-work can be readily observed. Several unit "orderlies"—cleaning women–were ordered to clean the labels off plastic bottles. An adminis-trative official came through the housing unit where these women were working. One woman was not wearing her steel-toed "safety" boots while doing this task. This was an infraction of safety procedures. Consequently, the whole unit was subjected to collective punishment—more than 300 women.

Women work at jobs that earn the prison-industrial complex millions of dollars. Our labor creates profits commensurate with those wrenched out of women working over sewing machines and at word processors in the Caribbean, Latin America, Asia, and Africa.

Women also work because a vast majority must, just to have a pittance to survive on—to buy items of personal hygiene, a candy bar, or most importantly, any materials we might want to use for our own human productivity (such as, for cro-cheting, art, drawing, or ceramics) as well as for telephone calls to our families, children, and friends with whom we desperately seek to main-tain some level of attachment. . . .

Although not to work is an act of resistance, an act of sanity, and even a moral response, women pris-oners do work. We are typical, everyday women who reflect the values of human development but are caught between the concertina wire of repres-sive control and our own human need to be pro-ductive human beings. We face the dilemmas that women, and men, beyond these prison walls face regarding the exploitation and value of our labor, but we have no options in a coercive environment of submission, except further punishment. We are similar to a battered, dominated woman who is locked into her home, subject to every mood of her captor.

Despite the coercive nature of work as disci-pline and punishment, women prisoners continue to expand the horizons of their human productivity. Some women discover resources they did not recog-nize in themselves before imprisonment or which they have developed in response to the repression and punishment we experience daily.

Yet, at those times when we chat among our-selves, there is an underlying recognition that not to work is always an option. Are we willing to pay the price of outright refusal? Mostly not; we have to live here for many long years. A few do refuse. After months, or maybe even years, the keepers may give up on the incorrigible ones; they will turn a blind eye because they know that an individual act of rebellion will not, under usual circumstances, start a work stoppage. As women we work to be useful in our own eyes.

NOTE

1. Michel Foucault, *Discipline and Punish: The Birth of Prison,* 2d ed. (New York: Vintage, 1995), 243.

SIXTY-ONE

◆◆◆

U.S. Concentration Camps and Exclusion Policies (1998)
Impact on Japanese American Women
Rita Takahashi

Rita Takahashi is a Professor of Social Work and Director of the Institute for Multicultural Research and Social Work Practice at San Francisco State University. For the past twenty years she has been conducting life history interviews with seniors in the Japanese American community and plans to make transcripts and tapes of these interviews available through public research libraries and archives.

. . . Under Executive Order 9066, signed by President Franklin Delano Roosevelt on 19 February 1942, people of Japanese ancestry living on the West Coast were excluded from their communities and incarcerated in concentration camps. The government justified its actions on grounds of "military necessity," although more than two-thirds of the incarcerated people were U.S.-born citizens. The camps were initially established and temporarily operated by the U.S. Army, under the name of the Wartime Civil Control Administration (WCCA). Later, jurisdiction was transferred to a newly-created civilian federal agency, the War Relocation Authority (WRA).

U.S. Incarceration Policy for People of Japanese Ancestry

A documented 120,313 persons of Japanese ancestry fell under the jurisdiction of the WRA. Of this number, 112,603 people were forced to leave their homes and enter U.S. concentration camps in seven states—Arizona, Arkansas, California, Colorado, Idaho, Utah, and Wyoming. A third of those incarcerated were classified as resident "aliens," despite the fact that they lived in the United States for many years prior to World War II. Less than one-third of one percent of all evacuated persons of Japanese ancestry (native and foreign-born) had been living in the U.S. for less than ten years.

"Aliens" of Japanese ancestry were "non-citizens" because of discriminatory laws that made them ineligible for naturalized citizenship. At the time of incarceration, 30,619 (80.2 percent) of the first generation "aliens" (known as *Isseis*) had resided in the United States for 23 or more years. Almost all *Isseis* had been residents for more than fifteen years, since the 1924 Immigration Act excluded Japan from further immigration to the United States. Only 345 alien Japanese had resided in the U.S. for less than ten years.

Banished individuals had the choice of moving "voluntarily" to inland states (they had about a three-week period to do so), and approximately 9,000 people did this, to avoid being sent to concentration camps. Approximately 4,000 of these "voluntary resettlers" moved to the eastern half of California. This group was subsequently forced to move again when the Government announced that the entire state of California, not just the western half, was off limits to people of Japanese ancestry. Some 4,889 persons "voluntarily" moved to states outside of California (1,963 to Colorado; 1,519 to Utah; 305 to Idaho; 208 to eastern Washington; 115 to eastern Oregon; and the remainder scattered throughout the United States).

This incarceration policy was consistent with previous discriminatory local, state, and federal policies affecting Asian Americans in the United States. Japanese Americans were targeted, in part because of the economic competition they posed in various states, particularly on the West Coast (California, Oregon, and Washington). Many [state] government officials saw World War II as the perfect opportunity to get rid of Japanese Americans from their states, once and for all. For the U.S. government, under President Roosevelt, the war was a good opportunity to institute its assimilation policy and "Americanization" plan: to disperse persons of Japanese ancestry throughout the U.S., in a deliberate plan to break up the "Little Tokyos" and "Japantowns."

The U.S. Constitution calls for equal protection under the law and prohibits deprivation of life, liberty, or property without "due process of law." These "protective" guarantees were suspended in this case, and the Government was able to implement this massive program with few questions asked. Congress sanctioned the plan and the U.S. Supreme Court failed to challenge its constitutionality. Few dared to oppose such a plan, presented as an urgent necessity to secure a nation under what was rhetorically stated as a dire military threat.

Intelligence Reports Dispute "Military Necessity"

Although military necessity and national security were the stated reason and goal for mass incarceration, decision-making elites knew that there was no threat to U.S. security from Japanese Americans. Top officials had access to years of intelligence reports from a variety of sources, including the Department of State, Department of Justice (through the Federal Bureau of Investigation), Navy Intelligence, and Army Intelligence. In October 1941, Jim Marshall reported:

> For five years or more there has been a constant check on both Issei [first generation immigrants from Japan] and Nisei [second generation, U.S.-born persons of Japanese ancestry]—the consensus among intelligent people is that an overwhelming majority is loyal. The few who are suspect are carefully watched. In event of war, they would be behind bars at once. In case of war, there would be some demand in California for concentration camps into which Japanese and Japanese-Americans would be herded for the duration. Army, Navy or FBI never have suggested officially that such a step would be necessary. . . . Their opinion, based on intensive and continuous investigation, is that the situation is not dangerous and that, whatever happens, there is not likely to be any trouble—with this opinion west coast newspapermen, in touch with the problem for years, agree most unanimously.[1]

In an intelligence report submitted in November 1941 (only three months before President Roosevelt signed Executive Order 9066), Curtis Munson, a Special Representative to the State Department, said that:

> As interview after interview piles up, those bringing in results began to call it the same old tune. . . . There is no Japanese "problem" on the Coast. There will be no armed uprising of Japanese. . . .[2]

Just two days before President Roosevelt signed Executive Order 9066, the Head of the Justice Department, Francis Biddle, encouraged Roosevelt to say something in defense of persons of Japanese ancestry, and wrote, "My last advice from the War Department is that there is no evidence of planned sabotage."[3]

Despite the evidence presented to President Roosevelt—all confirming that there was no threat that warranted *en masse* incarceration—he proceeded with the incarceration policy. He also maintained a consistent pattern of not "setting the record straight" based on intelligence facts.

Experiences of Japanese American Women

All Japanese American women felt the impact of World War II, and the exclusion policy caused major disruptions and upheavals in their lives. It affected their professional careers, impinged on the ways in which they viewed the world, and changed the course and direction of their lives.

Although the exclusion orders affected all women of Japanese ancestry, their specific experiences varied broadly due to many factors, including residence at the time of the exclusion order, age at the time of incarceration (adult or child), the camp that one went into, the job that one was able to get (inside and outside of camp), the college one was admitted to, the degree of cooperation one exhibited toward the concentration camp administrators, and one's status and socioeconomic class.

. . .

The following discussion represents a sampling of five Japanese American women's experiences during World War II derived from interviews conducted by this writer.[4]

Meriko Hoshiyama Mori

A Teenager Left to Fend for Herself After FBI Picked Up Both Parents

Meriko Hoshiyama Mori, born in Hollywood, California, is the only child of Suematsu Hoshiyama (of Niigata-ken, Japan) and Fuki Noguchi Hoshiyama (of Tochig-ken, Japan). Her parents owned a nursery/gardening business in West Los Angeles until World War II. Her mother, who taught at a Japanese language school before the war, was picked up and detained by the Federal Bureau of Investigation (FBI) on 22 February 1942. Fuki Noguchi Hoshiyama was among the few women who were picked up by the FBI (she was later released and sent to Santa Anita Assembly Center, a converted race track). She had the presence of mind to collect the personal thoughts of detainees—other Japanese women who were also picked up by the FBI. These quotations, collected at the time of internment, are hand-written in Japanese.

A few weeks later, in March 1942, Meriko Mori's father, who was the Japanese Language School treasurer, was also picked up by the FBI. Consequently, Meriko Mori was left, by herself, to take care of all the family and business matters. She was only nineteen years of age when both parents were picked up.

As a teenager desperate for help, Meriko Mori went to the social welfare office to get aid. According to Mori, they told her that they could do nothing for her because there were no rules or regulations for cases like hers. Therefore, Mori got no assistance from them. Reflecting back on this experience in a letter dated 10 February 1997, Mori wrote:

> When I was left alone, it was a shock, but perhaps not as great as it might have been because by the time my father was picked up, the FBI had come several times, and did not find him at home, because he was at work. I recall the FBI sitting in the car waiting for him to come home. . . . Although I had said I would be all alone, I recall following them [FBI] to Mr. Hayashida's home a block away where he was picked up. Even now as I write this, tears come to my eyes. It is very difficult to recall unpleasant memories.
>
> My Caucasian neighbors expressed concern and wrote to me in camp. My Japanese neighbors were so concerned [about] their own

families and situation of packing, moving, etc. they expressed concern but did not have the time to be involved in my predicament. If my Aunt Maki and Uncle Iwatsu Hoshiyama did not offer to include me in their family (they had 3 girls and 2 boys), I don't know what I could have done when the welfare department didn't know what to do. To say the least, I was very fortunate and am forever grateful to Maki and Iwatsu Hoshiyama.

When the U.S. entered World War II, Meriko Mori was a sophomore at the University of California at Los Angeles. She was surprised that she was treated like an enemy alien, and angered by her exclusion. In the words of her letter (1997):

> I was angry at the U.S. Government for its treatment of a U.S. citizen, and felt forsaken by my country and lost faith in the U.S. . . . We had lost our freedoms on which the country was founded.

Her studies were disrupted when she had to leave for Manzanar Camp, where she was watched and controlled by the U.S. Army's armed guards. In 1997, she thought about her camp experience, and said, "My memories of Manzanar are [that it was a] very hot or cold desert. I recall many sand storms and walking against the wind backwards." This camp, originally established under the U.S. Army's WCCA, later became a WRA camp. While at Manzanar, Mori earned the top salary of $19 a month for her work as a school teacher. Fifty-five years later, in her 1997 letter, Mori addressed the impact of her experiences:

> These experiences have taught me to be self-reliant, independent, resourceful, and aware of how injustices can be perpetrated on innocent victims who are weak and have no voice. We need to be constantly vigilant.

Kiyo Sato-Viacrucis

A Student Who Left Camp for a Midwest School and Who Returned to Stolen Property

Kiyo Sato-Viacrucis was born in Sacramento, California, the eldest of nine children born to Shinji "John" Sato (from Chiba-ken, Japan) and Tomomi

"Mary" Watanabe Sato (from Aizuwakamatsu, Fukushima-ken). When World War II broke out, the Sato family was farming in the Sacramento area. Having graduated from Sacramento High School in Spring 1941, Kiyo Sato-Viacrucis was attending Sacramento Junior City College at the time of the incarceration orders.

In May 1942, the Sato family was ordered to go to Pinedale Assembly Center, a WCCA facility set up and run by the U.S. Army. Ironically, while her family was sent to a concentration camp, under armed Army guard, her brother was serving in the U.S. Army. He had volunteered after Pearl Harbor was bombed by Japan, and ended up serving for the duration of the war. When Kiyo Sato-Viacrucis volunteered her services to the military, and when she attempted to gain admission into institutions of higher education, she was rejected. Later she wrote to the institutions, saying: "My brother and others are fighting to uphold democratic principles. I cannot understand that an institution of your standing would have such a policy." She was eventually accepted by Western Reserve University in 1945.

After four and one half months at Pinedale, she and her family were shipped, via train and open army truck, to Poston (Arizona) Camp, which was operated by the newly-established civil federal agency, the WRA. Upon her family's arrival in July 1942, the temperature was 127 degrees Fahrenheit. Viewing all the sage brush and experiencing the heat, Kiyo Sato-Viacrucis literally passed out.

Sato-Viacrucis did what she could to leave Poston quickly. After three and one half months, she managed to depart for Hillsdale College in Michigan. Since the college was located in an inland state, she was released only if she would agree to attend this private Baptist college.

After the West Coast was opened to Japanese Americans, Kiyo Sato-Viacrucis was one of the early returnees to Sacramento in 1945. She found that her family's home had been occupied by unknown and unauthorized persons, and that all their stored goods had been stolen. Further, she saw that the Mayhew Japanese Baptist Church (in Sacramento), which had stored the incarcerated Japanese Americans' belongings, had been burned to the ground the night before her return.

The incarceration experience had continuous and long-term impact on excludees. Reflecting on the implications for her and other women, Sato-Viacrucis said, "Partly because of our background, we *nisei* women retreated from a hostile world into our shells like turtles. Even after fifty years, we are afraid to come out and tell what happened." Reminiscing in 1997, fifty-five years after the exclusionary policies and programs, she said:

> *Nisei* [U.S.-born and second generation Japanese American] men were able to go to war and be recognized for their heroic efforts, but we *nisei* women were "war casualties" on two fronts. Not only were we not of the right color for the Navy or Air Force, but we were not acceptable by many institutions of higher learning "due to policy." It was certainly devastating to be rejected by the Navy because of my color, and then by Yale, Johns Hopkins, Western Reserve University schools of nursing, again because of their "policy." It is hard to believe that even our country's most prestigious institutions of higher learning succumbed to social pressure. That is scary. It happened so easily; will it happen again?

Yoshiye Togasaki

A Medical Doctor Who Took Her Practice to the Concentration Camps

Yoshiye Togasaki was born in an upstairs room of the Geary Theater, located in San Francisco. She was the fifth of six children born to Kikumatsu Togasaki (from Ibaraki-ken, Japan) and Shige Kushida Togasaki (from Tokyo). In 1892, her mother had been sent to the United States as an activist in the Women's Christian Temperance Union. This Japanese immigrant woman was a most unique person who did not shy away from publicly expressing her opinions and speaking her mind. She had stood out on the streets of San Francisco, preaching Christian doctrine.

When World War II broke out, Yoshiye Togasaki was already established in her profession as a medical doctor. In those days, women doctors—especially women of color—were a small minority. After her December 1921 graduation from Lowell High School in San Francisco, Togasaki attended the University of California, Berkeley, where she received a bachelor's degree in public health in 1929. With her medical doctor's degree from Johns Hopkins University in June 1935, she took an internship at the Los Angeles General Hospital.

In 1938, Togasaki became chief resident for communicable diseases at the L.A. General Hospital. She remained in this position until just six months before the U.S. entered World War II. At the time of the Pearl Harbor bombing, Togasaki was an assistant to the City of Los Angeles's epidemiologist. Because she knew she would be terminated when the war broke out, she resigned.

Togasaki spent time trying to correct public perceptions about Japanese Americans. Because the President of the Council on Churches harangued persons of Japanese ancestry, Togasaki went directly to him to try to change his belief that Japanese Americans were "untrustworthy." According to Togasaki, his mind was rigidly set.

After the incarceration orders were announced, and when it became clear that Manzanar, California, would be one of the WCCA Assembly Centers, Togasaki volunteered to help set it up. She arrived at the camp on 21 March 1942, and remained there until October 1942. Open trenches and hygienic problems were prevalent throughout the camp. According to Togasaki, she worked sixteen hours a day, dealing with public health and medical matters. For her services, she earned a salary of $16 per month. She managed to get scarce medical supplies, such as vaccines, from friends or associates outside the camp.

Due to overwork, Togasaki became ill, so she went to Tule Lake Camp (also in California) to join her two sisters. Because there were few resources to diagnose and care for her illness, she went to San Francisco's Children's Hospital for diagnosis. This was a rare event, since Japanese Americans were supposed to be excluded from the area. After five or six days at Children's Hospital, Togasaki stayed at the home of a doctor friend in San Francisco. In Togasaki's words, "No one complained that a Japanese American was there."

Togasaki worked as a pediatric doctor at Tule Lake, where she worked with Dr. Pedicord, a retired doctor from the Kentucky mountains who had failed to keep abreast of the latest developments in medicine. He stirred up a lot of antagonism around Tule Lake because of his attitude toward Japanese Americans, whom he viewed as inferior, foreign, and un-American. Considered whistle blowers and antagonists, Togasaki and her two sisters, Kazue (an obstetrician) and Chiye, were transferred to Manzanar in April 1943. Yoshiye Togasaki remained at Manzanar a few months before she left, in July 1943, for a pediatric position at New York's Bellevue Hospital.

Masako Takahashi Hamada

An Excludee Who "Voluntarily" Moved Inland to Idaho

Masako Takahashi Hamada was born in Seattle, Washington, the sixth of seven children born to Kumato Takahashi and Toshi Kato Takahashi, both of Niigata-ken, Japan. After graduating from Garfield High School, she was studying in Seattle when World War II broke out.

During a three-week period in March 1942, Japanese Americans were given the option to "voluntarily" leave their homes in the military exclusion zones (the entire West Coast of the U.S. mainland) and to resettle in an inland state outside the military zones, or be sent to a concentration camp. Masako Takahashi, her mother, and five siblings decided to move and join their oldest brother and his wife in Idaho, where his wife's family [Tamura] resided. Leaving most of their valuable possessions behind, they moved to avoid going into concentration camps. They were among the 305 "voluntary movers" who entered Idaho from the restricted military zones. Another older brother, who was living in Washington at the time of the exclusion, did not move because he was originally unaware of the orders. Consequently, he was incarcerated in a concentration camp.

In the Southern Idaho area where she settled, travel was restricted in certain areas, and "NO JAPS ALLOWED" signs were posted in various businesses, alerting the public that "Japs" would not be served. Of course, it did not matter whether one was a citizen or not; service was denied, regardless. This discriminatory behavior was matched by the Idaho governor's attitude toward Japanese Americans. Governor Chase Clark openly expressed his aversion to any Japanese American migration into the state of Idaho.

Masako Takahashi and her family faced very tough times in the new area. They struggled to make enough money to live, as they encountered new work environments and life situations. They worked for the E. H. Dewey family, who are related to Colonel W. H. Dewey of Silver City, Idaho. Although her goal, at that time, was to be a dress designer, she spent her days working in the fields, hoeing, weeding, and toiling in the hot sun for minimal rewards.

She and her sister (Yuki) went to Chicago to further their education. After the war, she married an Idaho-born Japanese American veteran of World War II, who served with the 442nd Regimental Combat Team, whose motto was "Go for Broke." She remained in Idaho, where she served as a nurse for twenty-five years and where she volunteers her services in Mountain Home, Idaho.

Reflecting upon her experiences in a 3 February 1997 letter, Hamada said, "I hope that such a sad [and] shocking experience will never be repeated again in history. . . . Let us hope that each and every one of us [will] live in peace and harmony."

Tsuru Fukui Takenaka

A Businesswoman Outside the Military Zone Who Faced Government Restrictions

Tsuru Fukui Takenaka was born on 26 August 1900, in Wakayama-ken, Japan. In 1920, after marrying Sennosuke Takenaka in Japan, she came to the United States with her husband who had been working in the U.S. prior to marriage. Upon her arrival in San Francisco, she was detained and quarantined a week by the U.S. immigration authorities at Angel Island. In her words, her immigration detention was "just like jail."

In 1930, she and her husband went to Lovelock, Nevada, and took over the Up-to-Date Laundry

from the Nakamuras. They owned and worked in this hand laundry throughout World War II, and they maintained the business for years thereafter. In fact, Tsuru Takenaka continued to work in the laundry until 1990, when she was 90 years of age. During the years at the laundry, she strenuously worked long hours.

The Takenakas did not have to leave their home and go into concentration camps because they were situated in a non-military exclusion zone. Therefore, the family continued to run the laundry business throughout the war. Although some established customers did not return after the start of World War II, the Takenakas remained busy enough to keep their business going. But the military restrictions, imposed during World War II, affected the Takenakas' free movement. They were restricted to a fifty-mile radius and could not go to the closest large town, Reno. Further, according to Tsuru Takenaka, the Reno mayor was known to harbor anti-Japanese sentiments.

Until after World War II, the Takenaka family was the only Japanese American family in Lovelock, and they did experience some discriminatory treatment. Takenaka's daughter, for example, was not allowed to board a train, and her husband, Sennosuke, was subjected to harassment and "bad" talk when he went to the Persian Hotel and Restaurant in downtown Lovelock.

Final Comments

The World War II experiences of Japanese American women are as varied as the number of people involved. . . . While some women were already established in their profession (e.g., Togasaki), others were just beginning their careers (e.g., Sato-Viacrucis). Some women owned their own businesses in the non-exclusion areas (e.g., Takenaka), while others were employees. All were affected by their residential location. Some living in the military exclusion zones were subjected to FBI raids (e.g., Mori), and most were forced, *en masse,* to go into concentration camps (Mori, Sato-Viacrucis, and Togasaki). With mandatory removal imminent, some chose to move from military exclusion zones prior to being incarcerated in concentration camps (Takahashi Hamada).

Nearly 40 years after this incarceration policy was instituted, the U.S. Commission on Wartime Relocation and Internment of Civilians (CWRIC) was established, in 1980, to "review the facts and circumstances surrounding Executive Order Number 9066 . . . and the impact of such Executive Order on American citizens and permanent resident aliens." The Commission concluded that these policy decisions were shaped by "race prejudice, war hysteria and a failure of political leadership." In summary, "a grave personal injustice was done." Furthermore,

The excluded people suffered enormous damages and losses, both material and intangible. To the disastrous loss of farms, businesses and homes must be added the disruption for many years of careers and professional lives, as well as the long-term loss of income and opportunity. . . .

Following these findings, there were years of debate in the U.S. House of Representatives and in the U.S. Senate concerning compensation to those who had suffered this injustice. After many Congressional sessions, compromises, and legislative drafts, the U.S. House of Representatives passed the Civil Liberties Act on 17 September 1987, by a vote of 243 to 141. The U.S. Senate passed a similar bill on 20 April 1988, also after lengthy discussion, by a vote of 69 to 27. To bring the two congressional versions together, a conference bill was worked out between the U.S. House and U.S. Senate leaders. This conference bill passed in the Senate on 17 July 1988 and in the House on 4 August 1988. President Ronald Reagan signed the Civil Liberties Act of 1988 into law on 10 August 1988.

Because the new law was an authorization bill, there was no provision for actual appropriations of $20,000 payments to each eligible individual. In November 1989, President George Bush signed an authorization bill into law, entitling the U.S. Government to pay up to $500 million each fiscal year, up to a total of $1.25 billion. With this entitlement in

place, the Government was able to begin payments in October 1990.

The redress policy included provisions for a U.S. Government apology for discriminatory wrongs it committed and for individual monetary compensation. The following letter, signed by President George Bush, accompanied each individual redress check:

A monetary sum and words alone cannot restore lost years or erase painful memories; neither can they fully convey our Nation's resolve to rectify injustice and to uphold the rights of individuals. We can never fully right the wrongs of the past. But we can take a clear stand for justice and recognize that serious injustices were done to Japanese Americans during World War II.

In enacting a law calling for restitution and offering a sincere apology, your fellow Americans have, in a very real sense, renewed their traditional commitment to the ideals of freedom, equality, and justice. You and your family have our best wishes for the future.

NOTES

1. Carey McWilliams. *Prejudice: Japanese-Americans: Symbol of Racial Intolerance.* Hamden, CT: Shoe String Press (Reprint), 1971. P. 114.

2. Curtis B. Munson. "Japanese on the West Coast," reprinted in *Hearings before the Joint Committee on the Investigation of the Pearl Harbor Attack* (79th Congress, 1st Session, Part 6). Washington, D.C.: Government Printing Office, January 1946. P. 2686.

3. Bill Hosokawa. *Nisei: The Quiet American.* New York: William Morrow and Company, Inc., 1969. P. 277.

4. Quotes from the five women were taken from interviews conducted by Rita Takahashi or from their letters to her. These women are among 300 Japanese Americans incarcerated during World War II and interviewed by Rita Takahashi between 1991 and 1997.

SIXTY-TWO

Media Representations and the Criminalization of Arab Americans and Muslim Americans (2005)

Suad Joseph and Benjamin D'Harlingue

Suad Joseph is Director of the Middle East/South Asia Studies Program and Professor of Anthropology and Women's Studies at the University of California, Davis. She is General Editor of the *Encyclopedia of Women and Islamic Cultures* and editor of *Gender and Citizenship in the Middle East.*

Ben D'Harlingue is an advanced graduate student in the Graduate Group in Cultural Studies at the University of California, Davis, where he has also taught Introduction to Women and Gender Studies.

Arab Americans and Muslim Americans are heterogeneous peoples from all over the world. They come from different countries, have different histories, belong to different cultures, and use different languages. Arabs, for example, are highly diverse, and include large numbers of Christians and Jews who consider themselves Arab. The total world Arab population is over 300 million (Arab American Anti-Discrimination Committee 2004). By contrast, there are about 1.3 billion Muslims in the world. The majority of Muslims are neither Arab nor Middle Eastern. Over 50 percent of the world's Muslims are from South Asia—India, Pakistan, Bangladesh, and Afghanistan. From the nineteenth century to the middle of the twentieth century, the overwhelming majority of immigrants to the United States from the Arab region were Christian. It was not until the 1960s and 1970s that Muslim immigrants from the Arab world began to outnumber Christian Arab immigrants. The first Muslims in the United States were African slaves. Estimates indicate that 30 to 40 percent of Muslims in the United States are African American; 25 to 30 percent are South Asian Americans; and 12 to 15 percent are Arab American (Ibish 2002).

Despite this wide diversity, however, U.S. media and popular culture tend to portray Arab Americans and Muslim Americans as if they are all the same. This erasure of differences makes it easier for government and the wider society to treat them the same and to make them all, collectively, different from "us." The "us" is the West, the United States—that is, the imagined United States, a white Christian nation that does not include Arabs and Muslims. As Nadine Naber (2000) has argued, Islam has been essentialized and racialized in the U.S., particularly in the politics of citizenship. Persons from Muslim countries and U.S. citizens from Muslim regions are represented in terms of their religion before any of their other multiple identities. Their actions are invariably characterized as "Muslim" regardless of their nature and intent. By prioritizing Islam as their overriding identity, the popular media portray every act of violence or incivility committed by a Muslim as a Muslim act.

In our examination of representations of Arab Americans, Muslim Americans, and Muslims in *New York Times* articles from 2000 to 2004, we found a predominantly negative representation of Islam. In article after article, Islam is presented as reactionary, violent, oppressive, anti-American, and incomprehensible to the "Western mind." Muslim leaders are represented as dangerous fanatics rather than respected spiritual leaders, and Muslim places of worship as sites of insurgencies rather than sites of the sacred. One article captured this image explicitly in its headline, "Seeing Islam as 'Evil' Faith, Evangelicals Seek Converts" (Goodstein 2003). Reporter Laurie Goodstein comments, "At the grass roots of evangelical Christianity, many are now absorbing the antipathy for Islam that emerged last year with the incendiary comments of ministers like Franklin Graham, Jerry Falwell, Pat Robertson and Jerry Vines, the former president of the Southern Baptist Convention. Franklin Graham called Islam 'a very evil and wicked religion,' and Mr. Vines called Muhammad, Islam's founder and prophet, a 'demon-possessed pedophile' '" (Goodstein, 2003, 1).

Samar Kaukab with her ACLU lawyer (see p. 447).

By not questioning these Christian leaders' views of Islam, the reporter, perhaps inadvertently, endorses and reinforces this prevailing negative view.

In the name of the nation and its security, Arab Americans and Muslim Americans have become increasingly racialized and targeted for discriminatory policies and practices by the government. The demonization of Arabs and Muslims reached a new level after 9/11/01 (Abdelkarim 2002, Cainkar 2002, Gonzaga 2002, *Middle East Reports* 2002). The profile of a "terrorist" was made equivalent to "looking" "Middle Eastern" or "Arab" or "Muslim." A U.S. Congressman of Arab background was detained at an airport because he fit this profile (Akram and Johnson 2002). A white, male, Christian U.S. citizen killed a Sikh U.S. citizen because he looked "Arab" or "Muslim," although Sikhs are neither

Arab nor Muslim. Over 1,200 legal residents (mostly Arab and Muslim) were detained without charges or access to attorneys; many were deported without public hearings even though none were found to have direct links with supposedly terrorist organizations (Akram and Johnson 2002, 331). A number of the 5,000 men (mostly Arab and Muslim, 18–33 year olds) were arrested after they responded to an invitation by the Justice Department and the Federal Bureau of Investigation (FBI) for "voluntary" interviews, despite the fact that their visas were in order and they were living in this country legally.

After the bombing of the U.S. federal building in Oklahoma City in 1995, then Attorney General Janet Reno made comments that implied the involvement of Arabs or Muslims in the bombing, as did the media. The FBI focused its investigation on Arabs and Muslims in this country. Congress passed the Anti-Terrorism and Effective Death Penalty Act in 1996, which targets Arab and Muslim U.S. and non-U.S. citizens as suspects of terrorism (Akram and Johnson 2002, 346). Hate crimes against Arab and Muslim U.S. citizens continued well after the identification, arrest, and conviction of white, Christian U.S. citizens responsible for the Oklahoma City terrorist attack.

Yet, when a Christian person acts, their action is not represented as "Christian." Timothy McVey, who bombed the federal building in Oklahoma City, was not described in media reports as committing a Christian act, even though fundamentalist Christianity was part of his worldview. Immediately after the September 11, 2001 bombing of the World Trade Center, the Reverend Jerry Falwell commented that the attacks were the wrath of God brought upon us by gays, lesbians, and feminists. Newspaper reports did not refer to these comments as Christian statements even though Reverend Falwell presents himself as speaking in a Christian voice. The killings of the Ku Klux Klan are not described as Christian although the Christian cross is central to their symbolism. When domestic abuse occurs in Christian homes the media do not look to the Bible to explain domestic abuse. Historians do not try to analyze what it is about Christianity that gives rise to dictators and tyrants such as Hitler, Mussolini, or Franco. In the dominant discourse, however, Muslims are defined by their religion and constructed as "alien," while the normative "we" is defined by economics and politics.

The U.S. government, popular media, TV and radio news, and print journalism often represent Arab Americans and Muslim Americans as uncertain, problematic, or suspect citizens (Joseph 1999). This began long before 9/11/01 (Abraham and Abraham 1983, Aswad 1974, Leonard 2003, Suleiman 1999). In 1914, an immigrant by the name of George Dow was denied U.S. citizenship based on the 1790 statute, which defined citizens as "free white persons" (*Dow v. United States et al.*, No. 1345. 4th Cir. 1915). As a "Syrian of Asiatic birth," (probably a Lebanese Christian), George Dow was not considered to be a "free white person" and therefore ineligible for citizenship. The decision was later appealed and reversed on the basis that Syrians were Semitic, even part Jewish, and therefore white—a clear example of the social construction of race. This case is emblematic of the on-going ambivalence in U.S. citizenship laws and practices towards U.S. citizens of Arab or Muslim origin (Cainkar 1999, Naff 1985, Suleiman 1999). By definition, to be a U.S. citizen was to be white. But, as Mary Ramadan (1996) has pointed out, white was understood to mean not only European but also Christian. Arabs and Muslims are not only "not quite white" as Nadine Naber argued (2000), Muslims are not Christians, and the majority of Arabs are Muslims. Arabs and Muslims are not the same as each other, as argued above, nor with the imagined U.S. white, Christian citizen. Arab and Muslim U.S. citizens embody this contradiction; they continue to be seen as against the grain of the nation (Joseph 1999), as not quite white (Naber 2000, Saliba 1999, Samhan 1999), and, despite legal citizenship, not quite citizens.

Law professors Susan Akram and Kevin Johnson (2002, 337) have observed that " . . . the current treatment of Arabs and Muslims is more extralegal than the internment" of Japanese Americans during World War II (described in Reading 61).

No Executive Order authorizes the treatment of Arabs and Muslims; nor has there been a formal declaration of war. Moreover, nationality, which is more objective and easier to apply than religious and racial classifications, is not used as the exclusive basis for the measures. Rather, the scope of the investigation is broad and amorphous enough to potentially include all Arabs and Muslims, who may be natives of [many] countries.

(Akram and Johnson 2002, 337)

However, the government does have plans for detaining Arab Americans in internment camps as exposed in 1991 by Norman Mineta, then a U.S. Representative and later Secretary of Transportation under President George W. Bush. In an article entitled, "Questioning of Arab-Americans Protested" (Mecoy 1991), a story carried in *The Sacramento Bee* but in few other news media, Mineta "pointed to a 1987 contingency plan the FBI and the Immigration and Naturalization Service drew up to detain Arab-Americans at an internment camp in Oakdale, Louisiana, in the event of war with certain Arab states. Mineta said that plan could still be initiated to 'round up' Arab-Americans" (Mecoy 1991). Moreover, during the 1991 Gulf War, many incidents of violence and harassment were committed against Arab and Muslim U.S. citizens by fellow U.S. citizens in various regions of the country.

Postcolonial theorist Gayatri Spivak showed in her discussion of British rule in India that colonial ideology often seeks to justify colonialist domination as being in the interests of women, constructing imperial intervention in terms of "white men saving brown women from brown men" (Spivak 1988, 297). More recently, anthropologist Lila Abu-Lughod has argued that the U.S. war on terrorism has taken on such a tenor. She points out that First Lady Laura Bush's November 17, 2001 address to the nation linked the "fight against terrorism" to the fight for women's rights, and thus "enlisted women to justify American bombing and intervention in Afghanistan and to make a case for the 'War on Terrorism' of which it was allegedly a part" (Abu-Lughod 2002, 784). Bombing Afghans was thus made to seem as though it was in the service of Muslim women, even though many Afghan women's organizations opposed U.S. intervention. When they cover Arab or Muslim women, U.S. news media tend to represent them as silent, passive, oppressed, inaccessible, and mysterious. The voices of Arab or

Muslim women are rarely represented and most print news sources portray them as in need of rescue. It is inconceivable that women might willingly embrace Islam if one relied on these stories. Abu-Lughod points to the imperial and racist presuppositions of savior discourses: "Projects of saving other women depend on and reinforce a sense of superiority by Westerners, a form of arrogance that deserves to be challenged" (Abu-Lughod 2002, 789). How do discourses about saving Muslim women support forms of state violence such as war and sexism?

The veil (*burka, abayya*) (a pre-Islamic African tradition) and clitoridectomy (a pre-Islamic ritual practiced more in non-Arab than Arab countries and not practiced by the overwhelming majority of Muslims) are pervasively represented as signature Islamic practices in the U.S. press. A *New York Times* article entitled "Behind the Veil: A Muslim Woman Speaks Out" is an example (Simons 2002, A4). The article discusses Ayaan Hirsi Ali's activism against domestic violence, sexual abuse, and genital cutting in Muslim communities in the Netherlands and internationally. The reporter asserts that "[t]he theme of injustice toward Muslim women in Islamic countries has become common in the West." The title of the article stands as a metaphor for practices that the article sympathetically quotes Ali as calling "backwards." According to Lila Abu-Lughod (2002), using the veil as a symbol of sexism elides the complex historical and political dynamics that produce differences amongst women. She stresses that rather than intervene in other communities, it would be better to ask how imperial policies and our social locations as U.S. citizens might contribute to the life conditions of people in other communities and to support demands from within those communities to make women's and men's lives better.

The veil, mobilized as a sign of backwardness or sexism, has underwritten the criminalization of Muslims in the war on terror. In a *New York Times* article entitled "A Little Late, But a Stand Against Hate," Clyde Haberman lauded a group called the Progressive Muslim Union of North America for supposedly acting as a "counterweight to the 'oppressive or dysfunctional practices' that have come to define Islam for many people" (Haberman 2004, B1). "Islam," Haberman asserts, "had become grim, cramped, exclusionary and—no getting

around it—all too often death-embracing." As Haberman reports this group's stand against "treating women as barely human"—implying that sexism is the norm amongst Muslims—he notes: "Not a headscarf or beard was in sight" in the room when he interviewed the group. This narrative implies a link between headscarves, beards, and sexist practices. He also links religiosity to sexism, asserting, "No imam need apply" to this group. Finally, Haberman criticizes the Progressive Muslim Union of North America: "Is it possible to talk about Islam in the post-9/11 world without a single reference to the dread T-word? Nowhere in the group's mission statement or in the members' remarks was terrorism mentioned. Why is that?" For Haberman, whether they are for or against sexism, all Muslims must be suspected of terrorism.

Trinh Minh-ha (1989) has noted that colonialist strategy—through law, policy, military and police activity, and media representations—homogenizes the "other" as a way of creating an oppositional binary that defines the other as enemy. President George W. Bush relied on popularly held stereotypic binaries in his designation of an "axis of evil" which included two Muslim countries, Iraq and Iran, fostering further demonization of Muslims in the U.S. media and popular opinion. The United States is waging a war based on the construction of binary opposites. President Bush's statement, "You are either with us or you are with the terrorists," comes out of a history of control based on the construction of difference.

The impact of the targeting of Arabs and Muslims through media discourse and public policy has been to control both Arab and non-Arab, Muslim and non-Muslim U.S. citizens. Fear mongering has affected the majority of U.S. citizens, particularly people of color, as more repressive measures are implemented in the name of "national security." What is at stake for Arab and Muslim U.S. citizens in the aftermath of 9/11/01 is not simply their home, but the home of all U.S. citizens. The exclusions and inconsistencies of citizenship applied to Arab and Muslim Americans can be used to justify the abuse of the citizenship rights of others. Just as oppression against Native Americans, African Americans, Asian Americans and Latino Americans laid the groundwork for discriminations toward Arab and Muslim Americans, so do the exclusions and inconsistencies practiced toward

Arab and Muslim Americans add bricks to a house heated by fear. Moreover, stereotypical and negative portrayals of Arabs, Arab Americans, and Muslim Americans in the news media are integral to the construction of these diverse people as intrinsically suspect, a key step in the process of their criminalization.

REFERENCES

Abdelkarim, R.Z. 2002. American Muslims and 9/11: A Community Looks Back . . . and to the Future." *Washington Report on Middle East Affairs.* Vol. XXI, No. 7, pp. 82 (Oct. 31).

Abraham, Sameer Y. and Nabeel Abraham, eds. 1983. *Arabs in the New World: Studies on Arab-American Communities.* Detroit: Wayne State University Center for Urban Studies.

Abu-Lughod, Lila. 2002. Do Muslim Women Really Need Saving? Anthropological Reflections on Cultural Relativism and Its Others. *American Anthropologist.* Vol. 104, No. 3, pp. 783–790.

Akram, S. M. and K. Johnson. 2002. Race, Civil Rights, and Immigration Law After September 11, 2001: The Targeting of Arabs and Muslims, *New York University Annual Survey of American Law,* Vol. 58.

American Arab Anti-Discrimination Committee. 2004. *Facts about Arabs and the Arab World.* <http://www.adc.org/index.php?id=248> (accessed: 22 July 2004).

Aswad, Barbara C., ed. 1974. *Arabic Speaking Communities in American Cities.* New York: Center for Immigration Studies.

Cainkar, Louise. 1999. The Deteriorating Ethnic Safety Net Among Arab Immigrants in Chicago. In *Arabs in America: Building a New Future,* edited by Michael Suleiman. Philadelphia: Temple University Press, pp. 192–206.

———. 2002. No Longer Invisible: Arab and Muslim Exclusion After September 11, *Middle East Report* 224 (Fall).

Gonzaga, Russell Reza-Khaliq. 2002. One Nation Under Allah: Islam is the Fastest Growing Religion in America, But it Still Fits the Profile of the "Other." *Colorlines.* Vol 5. No. 3, pp. 27 (Oct 31).

Goodstein, Laurie. 2003. Seeing Islam as "Evil" Faith, Evangelicals Seek Converts, *The New York Times,* Section A, pp. 1, 22, May 27.

Haberman, Clyde. 2004. A Little Late, But a Stand Against Hate, *The New York Times* (Late Edition, East Coast). November 16, p. B1.

Ibish, Hussein. 2002. *Post 9/11 Anti-Arab Discrimination in American Immigration Policy and Practice.* Presented at the Middle East Studies Association Meeting, Washington, D.C., November.

Joseph, Suad. 1999. Against the Grain of the Nation—The Arab. In *Arabs in America: Building a New Future,* edited by Michael Suleiman. Philadelphia: Temple University Press, pp. 257–271.

Leonard, Karen Isaksen. 2003. *Muslims in the United States: The State of Research.* New York: Russell Sage.

Mecoy, Laura 1991. Questioning of Arab-Americans Protested, *The Sacramento Bee.* 24 January, p. A9.

Middle East Report. 2002. Arabs, Muslims and Race in America (Special Issue). No. 224. Fall.

Minh-ha, Trinh. 1989. *Woman, Native, Other: Writing Postcoloniality and Feminism.* Bloomington: Indiana University Press.

Naber, Nadine. 2000. Ambiguous Insiders: An Investigation of Arab American Invisibility, *Ethnic and Racial Studies.* Vol. 23. No. 1 (Jan.), pp. 37–61.

Naff, Alexa. 1985. *Becoming American: The Early Arab Immigrant Experience.* Carbondale, Il.: Southern Illinois University Press.

Ramadan, Mary. 1996. *Anti-Arab Racism and Arab-American Response.* Paper presented at the Association of Arab-American University Graduates Convention. Anaheim, CA., October.

Saliba, Therese. 1999. Resisting Invisibility: Arab Americans in Academia and Activism. In *Arabs in America: Building a New Future* edited by Michael Suleiman. Philadelphia: Temple University Press, pp. 304–319.

Samhan, Helen Hatab. 1999. Not Quite White: Race Classification and the Arab-American Experience. In *Arabs in America: Building a New Future,* edited by Michael Suleiman. Philadelphia: Temple University Press, pp. 209–226.

Simons, Marlise. 2002. Behind the Veil: A Muslim Woman Speaks Out: [Biography], *The New York Times* (Late Edition, East Coast). November 9, p. A4.

Spivak, Gayatri Chakravorty. 1988. Can the Subaltern Speak? In *Marxism and the Interpretation of Culture,* edited by Cary Nelson and Lawrence Grossberg. Urbana: University of Illinois Press, pp. 271–313.

Suleiman, Michael, ed. 1999. *Arabs in America: Building a New Future.* Philadelphia: Temple University Press.

◆◆◆

Women of Color, Globalization, and the Politics of Incarceration (2003)

Julia Sudbury

Scholar and activist **Julia Sudbury** is Professor of Ethnic Studies at Mills College. Editor of *Global Lockdown: Race, Gender and the Prison-Industrial Complex,* her work focuses on women of color, women's activism, globalization and the transnational prison-industrial complex. She held the Canada Research Chair in Social Justice, Equity and Diversity at the University of Toronto (2004–2006).

In November 1999, 40,000 people came together in an explosion of street activism to protest the policies of the World Trade Organization and to highlight the impact of neoliberal globalization on the global south and poor communities in the global north. . . . Labor, environmental, human rights, housing, antiracist, and feminist activists came to Seattle out of a common understanding that problems such as sweatshop working conditions, toxic dumping in black neighborhoods, and cutbacks in welfare, housing, and health care are all rooted in a global capitalist system that values corporate interests and freedoms over human needs for decent wages, shelter, food, and health care. At the Seattle protests, . . . activists used puppets, banners, and flyers to link the struggle against global capital with opposition to the current criminal justice system. Activists challenged police brutality, racial profiling, the death penalty, and the prison industrial complex, arguing that dramatic increases in prison populations have occurred as a result of globalization.

While these connections are being made at the street level, feminist criminologists have had little to say about what connections, if any, may be made between women's imprisonment and the rise of global corporate capital that has occurred in the past two decades. Such an analysis would need to stray beyond the boundaries of what has traditionally been considered within the scope of crim-

inology to examine the broader socioeconomic context of women's criminalization and incarceration. . . . [I] argue that the explosion in women's incarceration is the hidden face of globalization and cannot be understood without reference to three overlapping phenomena. The first is the restructuring of national economies and social welfare provision that has occurred as a result of the globalization of capital. The second . . . is the emergence and subsequent global expansion of what has been labeled a "prison industrial complex" made up of an intricate web of relations between criminal justice institutions, politicians, and . . . corporations. The third is the . . . U.S.-led war on drugs that has crossed national borders to become a global phenomenon.

The Boom in Women's Imprisonment

The past 25 years have witnessed dramatic increases in the use of incarceration in the United States, leading to a prison building boom as federal and state governments rush to keep up with demand for prison beds. Although there are more men in prison than women, the rate of women's imprisonment is spiraling upward at a greater rate than that of men. . . . Similar patterns have occurred in Canada, Europe, and Australasia. In Britain, for example, the number of women in prison doubled between 1985 and 1998. . . .

Statistics that look at gender but not race underrepresent the impact of the prison boom on women of color and indigenous women. In all the countries just mentioned, oppressed racialized groups are disproportionately targeted by the criminal justice system. For example, in the United States, Latinas and African American women make up 60 percent of the prison population. And despite their small numbers in the population, Native

Americans are 10 times more likely than whites to be imprisoned.[1] In New South Wales, Australia, where all women's imprisonment increased by 40 percent in five years, aboriginal women's incarceration increased by 70 percent in only two years.[2] In Canada, aboriginal people comprise 3 percent of the general population and 12 percent of federal prisoners, a figure that increases to over 60 percent in . . . Saskatchewan and Alberta.[3] African Canadians are also disproportionately policed, prosecuted, and incarcerated.[4] Finally, 12 percent of women prisoners in England and Wales are British citizens of African Caribbean descent compared to 1 percent of the general population.[5] In addition, British prisons hold numerous women from West Africa, the Caribbean, and Latin America, either as immigration detainees or serving sentences for drug importation. The crisis of women's prisons can therefore be read as a crisis for women of color and indigenous women worldwide.

Explaining The Prison Boom

How can we explain this explosion in the population of women prisoners? In the 1970s, "emancipation theorists" put forward a possible explanation for an upward trend in women's incarceration. In her influential study, Freda Adler suggested that the women's liberation movement had opened up new opportunities for women, both in the legitimate and in the criminal worlds.[6] Thus women who were now working in white-collar jobs could commit crimes such as fraud and embezzlement, which previously would have been inaccessible to them. Women's liberation was also credited with giving women a more assertive stance and enabling them to engage in violence, burglary, and organized crime, acts that were previously the domain of men.

Subsequent studies challenged Adler's findings; they contested her claim that there had been a rise in women's offending and suggested that any increase could in fact be explained by social factors such as an increase in women's poverty.[7] Despite vigorous challenges to Adler's claims, subsequent work by feminist criminologists has failed to shift the debate around women and crime in two important ways. First, it perpetuates

the commonsense equation between crime and punishment that is at the core of both Adler's work and mainstream criminology. This equation leads us to look to women's behavior for explanations of increases in women's incarceration. If more women are being arrested, prosecuted, and punished, this argument goes, it must be because they are committing more crimes. Sociologists working within a radical framework make a different argument. Rather than looking to women's behavior, we should look at the shifting actions of the state as it seeks to control poor communities and populations of color. Rather than women's criminality, the focus of study should be the role of the state in labeling, prosecuting, and punishing women—that is, women's criminalization. Our search for an explanation for the prison boom must therefore ask: Who benefits when more women are imprisoned? What are the processes by which certain actions are labeled criminal and others are not, and how are women channeled into these actions and thus into conflict with the criminal justice system?

The second limitation of feminist criminology is its unwillingness to engage meaningfully with the significance of race in the criminal justice system, choosing to view women first as gendered beings and only secondly as having a social class, national, or racialized identity. . . . Rather than talking about "woman" as a unitary category, as if all women's experiences were fundamentally the same, feminists of color argue that we must always be explicit about the ways that racism and racial privilege intersect with class location and gender to create unique experiences for diverse women. Intersectionality may produce unexpected outcomes. In some instances, for example, women of color may have as much in common with men of color as they do with middle-class white women. Deploying an intersectional approach to explain women's criminalization therefore requires us to pay as much attention to racial profiling and racialized discrepancies within the criminal justice system as we do to gender disparities. It also requires us to examine the feminization of poverty, the impoverishment and surveillance of communities of color, and global inequalities between third- and first-world nations as causal factors behind the growing criminalization of women.

1. Globalization and the Racialized Feminization of Poverty

. . .

Both urban "ghettos" and small rural towns have been hard hit by the downsizing of manufacturing since the 1970s, suffering high unemployment and a decline in tax revenues. For inner-city residents, especially African Americans and Latinos, these declines have meant underfunded schools, dirty streets, insufficient public housing, and poor health care facilities. Neighborhoods have been taken over by liquor stores, crack houses, and prostitution as supermarkets and department stores relocate to more profitable locations. Women bear the brunt of this social dislocation, because they tend to be the primary caretakers of children and elderly relatives and are responsible for providing adequate food, shelter, medicine, and clothing. For working-class women of color in the inner cities, the globalization of capital translates into few opportunities for a living wage, food and clothing that is expensive and of poor quality, and inadequate day care and schooling for their children.

Rural areas have also been affected by the radical restructuring signaled by globalization. Faced with global commodities markets that set the price for meat, milk, or grain according to the lowest price that can be obtained internationally, small farmers have been unable to compete and have been forced to sell their land or contract to sell their produce to large farming corporations.[8] The emergence of agribusiness as the primary supplier of the nation's food has led to a rise in rural poverty as farm workers, particularly immigrant workers, are forced to work for low wages in insecure, seasonal jobs. Small rural towns that relied on car, munitions, and other industries have also been hit as factories have relocated abroad or closed as a result of a decline in cold war–era military investment. . . .

This newfound mobility has given corporations the ability to pack up and move to a new location if they find that policies and legislation governing workers' rights, wages, and environmental protections are not to their liking. Thus, national governments within the global capitalist economy have seen their policy options narrowed if they wish to remain attractive to corporate capital. The 1990s, therefore, witnessed a shift toward neoliberal policies being pursued by conservative and liberal governments alike. These policies aim to create a liberal environment for corporate profit making and financial speculation. . . .

The global spread of neoliberal social and economic policies is underpinned by two international institutions. The World Trade Organization (WTO) was established as the global headquarters for the drafting and policing of international trading rules. In the past decade, the WTO has come under criticism by activists who claim that by enforcing rules that benefit corporate profit while ignoring the exploitation of child laborers, the use of sweatshops, and environmental destruction by those same corporations, it is complicit in these exploitative practices.[9] The International Monetary Fund (IMF) is an organization with 184 member countries that promotes international monetary exchange and trade and provides loans and economic guidance to impoverished countries. The IMF has been criticized for imposing economic policies on formerly colonized countries that generate immense poverty and suffering. Governments have been forced to cut back public expenditure. In Jamaica, for example, policies introduced since the mid-1980s by the Jamaican Labour Party working closely with the IMF have led to cuts in public-sector employment; the scaling back of local government services in health, and education; increases in the cost of public utilities as state-owned companies are sold to the private sector; and a dramatic decline in real wages. Such cuts hit working-class Jamaican women particularly hard because they carry the burden of caring for children and sick or elderly relatives. This disproportionate impoverishment of third-world women is referred to as the racialized feminization of poverty.

At the same time that the Jamaican state has cut back its role in social welfare, it has stepped up its role in subsidizing foreign and domestic capital. Free trade zones established in Kingston, Montego Bay, and elsewhere offer foreign garment, electronic, and communications companies factory space and equipment, tax exemptions, a cheap female workforce, and for the busy foreign executive, weekends of sun, sea, and sand.[10] Foreign-owned agribusiness and mining companies have also been encouraged, displacing traditional subsistence farming and causing migration from rural areas to the cities, which now account for 50 percent of the Jamaican population. As the economy has shifted, women working in the informal economy as farmers and higglers[11] find themselves unable to keep up with the rising costs of survival. Whereas younger women may find employment in the tourist industry as maids, entertainers, or prostitutes, or within the free trade zones assembling clothes or computers for Western markets, working-class women in their 30s and older have fewer options. Even where these women do find employment, low wages—driven down by multinational corporations in search of ever greater profit margins and kept low by governments unwilling to set a living minimum wage for fear of losing foreign investment—mean that women cannot earn a sufficient income to support their families. The failure of the legal economy to provide adequate means for women's survival then becomes a key incentive for Jamaican women who enter the drug trade as couriers and are subsequently incarcerated in British, Canadian and U.S. prisons. . . .

2. The Prison Industrial Complex

Why has the racialized feminization of poverty under neoliberal globalization led to an explosion in the imprisonment of women? In other words, how can we explain the current state response to the increase in poverty among working-class women and women of color, a response that deploys criminalization and punishment rather than poverty relief or empowerment? Scholars, activists, and former prisoners seeking to explain this problem . . . [rely on] the concept of the prison industrial complex.[12] Joel Dyer argues that three components make up the "perpetual prisoner machine" that transforms criminalized populations in the United States into fodder for the prison system.[13] The first are the large media corporations, like CNN and NBC, that rely on violent and crime-oriented content to grab ratings. The disproportionate airtime dedicated to crime-related news, dramas such as *NYPD Blue* and *Law and Order,* and real-life shows such as *America's Most Wanted* and *Cops* have created a dramatic rise in the fear of crime in the U.S. population at large.[14] These shows provide stereotypical repre-

sentations of communities of color, from the black drug dealer to the Latino "gangbanger," that fuel a racialized fear of crime. The second is the use of market research by politicians to align their platforms with popular views about policy areas. Since the voting population tends to believe that criminal penalties are too soft and that "criminals" are unlikely to serve adequate prison sentences, politicians can win votes by appearing to be "tough on crime." Although Republicans have traditionally positioned themselves as tougher on crime than Democrats, it is only by positioning themselves as equally punitive that liberals can achieve power. Thus the unfounded assumption that building more prisons and jails and incapacitating more people for longer periods will solve deep-rooted social problems, such as drug use, poverty and violence, remains unchallenged by both major parties. . . .

The third component is the intervention of private prison corporations such as Wackenhut Corporation and Corrections Corporation of America, which have generated millions for their shareholders by designing, constructing, financing, and managing prisons, jails, and detention centers. The mutually profitable relationship between private corporations and public criminal justice systems enables politicians to mask the enormous cost of their tough-on-crime policies. Instead of allocating millions for new prison construction in their annual budgets, politicians can simply reallocate revenue funds from welfare, health, or education into contracts with privately run for-profit prisons. . . .

. . . Although the prison industrial complex emerged in the United States, the past 15 years have witnessed its transformation into a transnational phenomenon. . . . U.S.-based prison corporations and their subsidiaries now manage prisons in Britain, Canada, New Zealand, Puerto Rico, Australia, and South Africa; and in all these locations, prison populations are rising. The prison industrial complex incorporates diverse interest groups, all of which stand to profit from the global prison boom. State and national politicians, correctional officer unions, media and corporate executives, and shareholders all benefit in very direct ways from the growth in women's imprisonment.

3. The Global War on Drugs

The third factor implicated in the explosion in women's imprisonment is the global war on drugs. The contemporary war on drugs was announced by U.S. president Ronald Reagan in the early 1980s and formalized in the 1986 Anti Drug Abuse Act. The act made a critical break with the concept of drug users as a medical population in need of treatment and instead targeted them as a criminal population. It also utilized the erroneous assumption that users would be deterred from their habit and dealers and traffickers incapacitated by extensive use of penal sanctions. It was assumed that by removing those involved in the criminalized drug trade from the streets for long periods of time, syndicates would be severely damaged in their ability to get drugs to the streets.[15] Since "liberal" judges could not be trusted to hand down sufficiently severe sentences to deter and incapacitate those involved in the drug trade, the act removed judicial discretion and imposed mandatory minimum sentences.

Thus, treatment programs and community service were effectively barred in cases involving drugs, and sentence length related not to the role of the defendant in the offense, but to the weight and purity of drugs involved. In the United States, African American women and Latinas are disproportionately affected by mandatory minimums for reasons that are both gendered and racialized. The only way a lesser sentence can be given is in cases in which the defendant provides "substantial assistance" in the prosecution of another person. However, women, who tend to be in subordinate positions within drug syndicates and thus have little access to information, are usually unable to make such a deal. The crack-cocaine disparity also feeds the disproportionate impact on women of color. The mandatory minimum sentence for cocaine is one hundred times harsher for crack than for powder cocaine. Thus, being caught with 500 grams of powder cocaine is equivalent to being caught with only 5 grams of crack, itself a derivative of powder cocaine. Since crack is cheaper and has flooded poor inner city neighborhoods, African Americans and Latinos and Latinas receive disproportionate sentences when compared with powder cocaine users and dealers, who are much more likely to be white.

Although the war on drugs has had a dramatic impact on U.S. communities of color, it has reached far beyond U.S. borders. From the mid-1980s, the war on drugs increasingly played a key role in U.S. foreign policy decisions as the Reagan and Bush administrations pushed a U.S. drug agenda on the global community. . . . Whereas the domestic war on drugs is fought primarily by the police beyond the borders of the United States, it has become a military war justifying U.S. military interventions throughout Latin America. By the mid-1990s, Canada, Australia, New Zealand, Taiwan, South and Central America, the Caribbean, and African countries including Nigeria and South Africa were full-fledged partners in the U.S.-driven global war on drugs.

Inside the Transnational Prison Industrial Complex: Three Women's Stories

Accounts of structural economic and political processes are important if we are to understand the reasons behind the boom in women's imprisonment. However, by putting these macrolevel processes in the foreground, we risk losing sight of women's agency. Indeed, in such accounts, women, especially women of color and third-world women, are often reduced to faceless victims while corporations, governments, and supranational bodies such as the IMF and World Bank take center stage. In order to move women of color from the margin to the center, I have chosen to highlight three women's stories. These stories reflect the lives of women incarcerated in three national locations: Britain, Canada, and the United States. Looking beyond the borders of the United States enables us to examine the ways in which globalization, the transnational prison industrial complex, and the global war on drugs lead to the criminalization and incarceration of women of color and third-world women.

Narrative One: Militarization, Displacement, and the War on Drugs

Teresa is a Colombian woman in her early 40s.[16] As a single mother, she struggled to support her three children. Carrying Class A drugs (cocaine) between

Colombia and England enabled her to supplement her meager income. She was arrested at Heathrow airport in England and was given a five-year sentence. . . . She does not know what has become of her three children and has not been able to contact them since she was arrested. Her fear is that they will be homeless since she did not leave any emergency funds for them. Teresa's story challenges us to rethink commonsense ideas about dangerous Latin American "drug traffickers" flooding the United States and Europe with cocaine. In common with many drug "mules" from developing countries, Teresa was pushed into trafficking drugs by desperation. In her words:

> Cargamos drogas porque lo necesitamos; porque tenemos situaciones de financia. Somos de Colombia, de paises del tercer mundo, que son pobres. La situacion en lo que viven, por eso lo hicemos.
>
> We carry drugs because we need to, because we have financial difficulties. We come from Colombia, the third world, which are poor countries. The conditions we live in, that's what pushed us.

Colombia is a country shackled by foreign debt, political and social dislocation, violence, war, and kidnappings. As a leading harvester of the coca leaf, estimated to produce 80 percent of the world's cocaine, Colombia has been a key target of U.S. antidrug interventions. Instead of alleviating horrendous social, political, and economic conditions for women in Latin America, U.S. financial assistance is targeted at building military forces that participate in the war on drugs. These forces have been used to carry out counterinsurgency wars against revolutionary groups like the FARC (Revolutionary Armed Forces of Colombia) and ELN (National Liberation Army) that have spearheaded the struggle for indigenous and poor people's rights. The U.S. military alleges that such groups have received millions of dollars per annum for protecting coca plantations, drug trafficking routes, and airstrips. By identifying these revolutionary groups as "narco-terrorists," the U.S. administration is able to justify providing military expertise and assistance to Colombia, despite its poor human rights record and evidence of collusion between the military and right-wing paramilitary death squads.[17] . . .

In tying aid to military gains against the FARC, the United States finances a four-decade-old civil war in which at least 35,000 people have died and two million have been internally displaced or forced to emigrate. The displacement of peasants and indigenous people is further exacerbated by the use of herbicides and organic toxins that affect large areas of rain forest and groundwater and create health problems for local people in addition to destroying the coca.[18] Women bear the brunt of this atmosphere of violence and instability as displaced landless peasants, as primary caretakers seeking to feed their children, and as spouses of men killed in the fighting. Ironically, the very conditions that pushed Teresa to risk importing Class A drugs are caused in part by the war on drugs. She, like many other foreign nationals in U.S. and European prisons, will be deported after serving a long sentence to a homeland where she has no house, no income, and no social security. In the meantime, she will be replaced by any of the millions of impoverished and desperate women in Latin America, the Caribbean, and Africa who become drug mules each year.

Narrative Two: Racialization, Labeling, and Exclusion

Camille is a 21-year-old African Canadian woman. Camille's mother, an immigrant from Jamaica, brought her up in public housing in the declining West End of Toronto. As a young girl, Camille was in constant conflict with her mother's expectations. She experienced difficulties at school, was labeled as having attention deficit hyperactive disorder (ADHD), and was sent to a school for children with special needs:

> They always told me I was bad, but you know kids. They said I had attention deficit disorder. I went to a couple of behavior schools, after that my mum switched us to Catholic school. I was going there for a while, then grade 2, me and the teacher got into something. I think I hit the teacher. They sent me to another behavior school for a couple of years.

At age 11, Camille was sent by her mother to a group home; this move started a pattern of disruption as she was shuttled between group homes and her mother's apartment. Raising two girls in the racist and often dangerous environment of the inner city, Camille's mother attempted to impress rigid gender roles on her daughters, encouraging them to limit themselves to the domestic sphere. African Caribbean women in Canada are located within a racially gendered capitalist economy in which black femininity is constructed as simultaneously a sign of hard labor and sexual availability.[19] Fearing the racialized sexual subordination of their Canadian-born children, many immigrant women seek to enforce strict sexual mores and harsh discipline. Such attempts can lead to generational conflicts that are sometimes interpreted as a culture gap but in fact arise out of the survival strategies engendered by the experience of migration. Camille resisted her mother's attempts to "protect" her by curtailing her freedom:

> I was a tomboy. Me and my brother always used to do stuff. But then he got older, he didn't want to hang out with me no more. He always got to go outside, and she's always telling me I'm a girl and I can't do this and that. She was always beating me. But I always did my own thing.

On leaving school with few qualifications, Camille found herself unemployed and living with her mother with no source of income. When she was approached by a male friend who asked her if she was interested in earning $5,000 in a week by importing cocaine from Jamaica, she accepted. After being detained by customs at Toronto airport, she was sentenced to two years and four months...

Unlike Teresa, Camille did not have children to support, and her mother paid for her basic needs. However, her situation is indicative of the problems facing young black Canadians who have been failed by an underfunded educational system that is unwilling to deal with the diverse needs of a multiracial population. Rather than places of education, inner-city schools have become locations where young black people are warehoused and, increasingly, policed. Unfamiliar with the Canadian school system, immigrant parents are ill equipped to challenge the labeling of their children as educationally subnormal or

suffering from ADHD. Rather than dealing with working-class black children's needs, schools and child psychiatrists treat difficult behavior as medical problems, thus justifying notions of inherent (racialized) mental incapacity. Camille emerged from the school system with few skills and qualifications into a racially and gender stratified labor market that offers, at best, minimum-wage jobs to young women of color. In the context of a North American youth culture that defines personal value via consumerism, Camille's lack of legitimate access to money, or routes to better earning power, is a significant motivation for her involvement in drug importation.

. . . When funding for prisons and additional policing is squeezed from the budget of a government committed to making tax cuts, further cuts in social spending become inevitable. Youth programs, shelters for women and teens, schools, black community projects, and social workers are all affected. As social workers are forced to raise minimum intervention levels, families with problems that are not considered urgent are left without support. Underfunded social programs are limited to crisis intervention rather than prevention. As schools are forced to operate on limited budgets, the incentive to exclude children who behave in difficult ways is increased. The pattern of Camille's life, dotted with family conflict and violence, school exclusions, and unemployment, is evidence of an absence of appropriate social support. By redirecting tax monies from social programs into the prison industrial complex and by promoting a low-wage, "flexible"[20] labor market, the state exacerbates this trend and ensures that there will be a pool of young women from Ontario's inner-city projects willing to risk their lives by importing drugs.

Narrative Three: Gender Entrapment and the Crack Cocaine Disparity

Kemba Smith was a middle-class African American student at Hampton College, a traditionally black college in Virginia. She became involved with a young man, Khalif Hall, who, unknown to her, was a key figure in a large drug operation. When Hall began to abuse Kemba and threatened to kill her, she did not leave him because she was afraid for her family and herself and because she had become pregnant. Shortly before the drug ring was apprehended, Hall was shot and killed. Kemba pleaded guilty to conspiracy to distribute crack cocaine, but hoped Hall's intimidation would be taken into account. Instead, she was held responsible for the full 255 kilos involved in the offense—although she personally was not found to have handled the drugs—and was sentenced to 24.5 years in prison. Kemba's case has been adopted by activists who oppose the war on drugs, including Families Against Mandatory Minimums, the Kemba Smith Justice Project, and the Million Woman March.[21] . . . The 24.5-year sentence Kemba received is not indicative of a particularly unsympathetic judge but of a series of laws and policies introduced since the mid-1980s that have targeted users and street-level retail sales, highlighting crack cocaine as a particular threat. As Kemba argues:

> While laws should be designed to protect our communities from drug kingpins, instead, low level offenders with little or no involvement in the sale of drugs are being locked up for 15, 25, 30 [years], or 13 life sentences. In fact, I know a 30 year old Black woman, mother of two girls who was sentenced to 13 life sentences.[22]

Under the Anti Drug Abuse Act, Kemba's knowledge of her boyfriend's drug dealing was sufficient for her to receive a mandatory minimum sentence. However, her lack of involvement in the drug ring prevented her from providing information that might have reduced her sentence.

Kemba's case also illustrates what Beth Richie calls the "gender entrapment of battered black women": the high levels of male violence and abuse experienced by African American women entering the criminal justice system.[23] Many women are incarcerated as a direct result of a coercive and violent male figure. The woman's situation may have been caused by involvement in criminal activities, such as prostitution and drug dealing, in which the male is profiting from her; alternatively, her incarceration may be because of self-defense against a violent male partner. Feminist activists have organized around the cases of women incarcerated for killing their abusive part-

ners, but there has been less awareness of the role of male violence—from early childhood sexual abuse to domestic violence—in the lives of women incarcerated for other types of offenses. In this sense, the psychological, physical, and sexual abuse that women are subjected to in prison is just one aspect of a continuum of violence in incarcerated women's lives. Women of color who live in emotionally and economically vulnerable positions in relation to men may be pressured by them to serve as free or cheap labor in the drug business. Although the women's movement has attempted to reduce women's dependence on men, welfare reforms and cutbacks in funding for women's shelters and day care under the Clinton and Bush administrations in the United States have further limited the choices of working-class women in particular. Kemba's case demonstrates that mandatory minimums and heightened police surveillance of communities of color, when combined with women's dependence on and coercion by male family members, create the conditions under which increasing numbers of women of color have been criminalized and turned into fodder for the prison industrial complex. As Kemba argues:

> With the entering of the New Year, I want to give you the gift of vision, to see this system of Modern Day Slavery for what it is. The government gets paid $25,000 a year by you (taxpayers) to house me (us). The more of us that they incarcerate, the more money they get from you to build more prisons. The building of more prisons create more jobs. The federal prison system is comprised of 61% drug offenders, so basically this war on drugs is the reason why the Prison Industrial Complex is a skyrocketing enterprise.[24]

Conclusions and Reflections on Abolitionism

This . . . [article] has described an exponential increase in women's imprisonment internationally and has suggested a new set of questions for feminist researchers and criminologists who wish to explain this phenomenon. . . .

. . .

At a time when increasing numbers of women are being incarcerated, families separated, and communities devastated, any discussion of women, crime, and punishment must end with proposals for change. There are three possible approaches for those wishing to challenge the status quo regarding women's imprisonment: reform, decarceration, and abolition. *Reformers* focus on producing suggestions for change that are practical within the existing system. Feminist reformers have proposed women-centered prison regimes, for example, that require female prison officers, introduce programs on domestic violence and rape, or provide therapists working within a framework of women's empowerment. Feminist reformers have also proposed reforms to the law, legalizing prostitution, for example, or removing status offenses from the criminal law.

There are three problems with reformism. First, . . . reform tends to be incorporated into the prison and used as justification for its expansion. For example, in Canada, demands for women-centered prison regimes led to the construction of five new federal prisons, thus increasing the number of women behind bars. In Britain, the provision of a mother and baby unit led judges to feel more comfortable with sentencing pregnant women to prison. Second, reformers tend to work with the system, thus enabling the stigmatization of those with more radical proposals as idealist and unrealistic. Finally, reformers frequently fail to question why and whether women should be imprisoned in the first place and instead focus on reducing the pains of imprisonment. They are therefore ill equipped to oppose the explosion in women's imprisonment.

The second possibility is *decarceration*. This strategy goes a step further than reform by pushing for laws that will lead to people being released from prison. For example, decarceration strategies emphasize alternative forms of punishment, including fines and community service, as well as rehabilitation and reeducation programs in the free world, such as sex offender training and anger management. . . . A first step toward decarceration is the establishment of a prison moratorium, whereby states are petitioned to pass a resolution preventing the construction of any new prisons. If no new prison beds are made available, the argument goes, officials will have to find other ways to deal with men and women in conflict with the law. Decarceration is an important political strategy that challenges the constant expansion of the prison industrial complex and seeks to reduce the profit motive in prison growth. However, decarceration policies are vulnerable to political swings, and a moratorium can swiftly be reversed.

The third possibility is *abolition*. Prison abolitionists use this term to identify the prison as a fundamentally unjust institution that, like slavery, cannot be reformed.[25] They argue that prisons do not work, fail to reduce crimes, and fail to make vulnerable populations—including women and people of color—safer. Abolitionists also argue that prisons are incapable of rehabilitating people; instead, they brutalize prisoners and return them to their communities ill equipped to survive by legitimate means. Abolitionists point out the huge economic costs of imprisonment, and they argue that public funds could more effectively be spent preventing social problems by creating jobs with a living wage, providing women's shelters, creating youth programs, and developing high-quality education. They also point out the social costs of incarcerating two million people in the United States, with a devastating impact on their families and communities, particularly communities of color.

Abolitionism is the only strategy that requires a fundamental rethinking of the way in which justice is delivered. It requires that we look for the *root causes* of antisocial acts, such as assault, burglary, or domestic violence, and look for alternatives that address these root causes. Abolitionism has not been viewed with great enthusiasm by many feminists, however. After spending years campaigning for the criminal justice system to take rape, domestic violence, and child abuse seriously, many feminists have seen abolitionism as a mechanism that will remove valuable legal protections from women. Feminist abolitionists have dealt with this problem in two ways. First, some have called for the abolition of women's prisons only, arguing that women are imprisoned for very different reasons than men and therefore need different treatment.[26] This argument is, however, unsustainable in the light of calls for equal treatment of women under the law. Second, others have challenged the idea that "the nonsolution of imprisonment" makes women safe and have argued that, in fact, an overreliance on punitive strategies prevents a more fundamental challenge to the patriarchal gender roles—and the institutions that support them—that are at the root of male violence against women.[27]

Reform *in isolation of a broader strategy for social change* serves to legitimize and even expand the prison industrial complex, and decarceration is only a stopgap measure. In contrast, abolitionism . . . offers a radical critique of the punitive approach to women's survival strategies. Abolitionism is the only strategy that removes the profit motive from the criminal justice system and the only approach that challenges the belief that prison works. Although it does not offer an immediate solution, it does provide a *critical framework* within which proposed legislation, campaigns, and activism can be assessed. By working together within an abolitionist framework, scholars, activists, prisoners, and their families are building a movement for lasting social change and for a safe and just global community.[28]

NOTES

1. Patricia Macias Rojas. 1998. Complex Facts, *Colorlines*, Fall.

2. Parliament of New South Wales, Select Committee on the Increase in Prisoner Population, www.parliament. nsw.gov.au, accessed July 4, 2000.

3. Canadian Criminal Justice Association. 2000. *Aboriginal Peoples and the Criminal Justice System*, Ottawa.

4. Commission on System Racism in the Ontario Criminal Justice Sytem. 1994. *Racism Behind Bars*, Toronto: Queens Printers.

5. Mike Elkins, Carly Gray, and Keith Rogers. 2001. *Prison Population Brief: England and Wales April 2001*. London: Home Office Research Development Statistics.

6. Freda Adler, 1975. *Sisters in Crime: The Rise of the New Female Criminal*. New York: McGraw-Hill.

7. Carol Smart. 1979. The New Female Offender: Reality or Myth, *British Journal of Criminology* 19(1): 50–59.

8. William Grieder. 2000. "The Last Farm Crisis," *The Nation*, November 20.

9. Manning Marable. 2000. Seattle and Beyond: Making the Connection in the 21st Century, *Dialogue and Initiative*, Fall.

10. "As Jamaica gets ready to go global and sticks to liberal policies, international investors need look no further than this Caribbean island to find opportunities which they won't regret." Quoted from *Jamaica: Island of Opportunity*, www.vegamedia.com/jamaica/jamaica.html, accessed January 20, 2002.

11. Higglers are traders, often women, who buy and resell cheap clothing, food, and other low-cost products in Jamaica's informal economy.

12. Angela Y. Davis. 1998. Race and Criminalization: Black Americans and the Punishment Industry. In *The Angela Y. Davis Reader*, ed. Joy James. Malden, MA: Blackwell.

13. Joel Dyer. 2000. *The Perpetual Prisoner Machine: How America Profits from Crime*. Boulder, CO: Westview.

14. Mark Fishman and Gray Cavender, eds. 1998. *Entertaining Crime: Television Reality Programs*. New York: Aldine DeGruyter.

15. This has not been the case; instead, criminalization and targeting by law enforcement artificially inflate the price of drugs, so that manufacturing, trafficking, and selling them become immensely profitable and increasingly associated with violence. This mutually profitable relationship between law enforcement and the drug trade has been labeled the "international drug complex" (Hans Van Der Veen. 2000. *The International Drug Complex*. Amsterdam: Center for Drug Research, University of Amsterdam).

16. Pseudonyms have been used to protect the identities of the first two interviewees. The case of Kemba Smith has reached national prominence due to the clemency granted her by president Bill Clinton at the end of his term in office. I have therefore used her real name.

17. Human Rights Groups Criticize Clinton over Aid to Colombian Military. 2000. *San Francisco Chronicle*, August 29.

18. US Sprays Poison in Drug War. 2000. *Observer*, July 2.

19. Dionne Brand. 1999. Black Women and Work: The Impact of Racially Constructed Gender Roles on the Sexual Division of Labour. In *Scratching the Surface: Canadian Anti-Racist Feminist Thought*. ed. Enakshi Dua and Angela Robertson. 1999. Toronto: Women's Press.

20. Corporations prefer a workforce that can be hired and fired according to seasonal fluctuations in demand. This "flexible" workforce is thereby denied stable, permanent employment and adequate compensation for being laid off.

21. For information on the campaigns on behalf of Kemba Smith, see www.geocities.com/CapitolHill/Lobby/8899. These groups were largely responsible for bringing about the pardoning of Kemba Smith in the last days of the Clinton administration in 2000. Kemba has continued to campaign on behalf of the thousands of low-level, drug-involved prisoners who remain incarcerated for obscenely long terms of imprisonment.

22. Kemba Smith, From the Desk of Kemba Smith, www.geocities.com/CapitolHill/Lobby/8899/pen.html, December 13, 1999.

23. Beth Richie. 1996. *Compelled to Crime: The Gender Entrapment of Battered Black Women*. London and New York: Routledge.

24. www.geocities.com/CapitolHill/Lobby/8899.

25. Jim Thomas and Sharon Boehlefeld. 1991. Rethinking Abolitionism: "What Do We Do with Henry?" *Social Justice* 18(3): 239–25.

26. Pat Carlen. 1998. *Sledgehammer: Women's Imprisonment at the Millennium.* Basingstoke and London: MacMillan.

27. Fay Honey Knopp. 1993. On Radical Feminism and Abolition. In *We Who Would Take No Prisoners: Selec-*

tions from the Fifth International Conference on Penal Abolition, ed. Brian D. MacLean and Harold E. Pepinsky, p. 55. Vancouver: Collective Press.

28. Organizations working within this framework include Critical Resistance http://www.criticalresistance.org and the International Conference on Penal Abolition (ICOPA) http://www.interlog.com/~ritten/icopa.html

SIXTY-FOUR

♦♦♦

Justice Reinvestment (2003)

Susan B. Tucker and Eric Cadora

Lawyer and educator **Susan B. Tucker** is the director of the Soros Foundation's After Prison Initiative, a program created to decrease the number of people of color being returned to prison as well as to promote practices that facilitate responsible, lawful citizenship after prison.

Eric Cadora directs the Justice Mapping Center where he oversees the use of geographical analyses to help corrections departments and policy makers understand and address the spatial dimensions of incarceration.

There is no logic to spending a million dollars a year to incarcerate people from one [city] block . . .—over half for non-violent drug offenses—and return them, on average, in less than three years stigmatized, unskilled, and untrained to the same unchanged block. . . .

. . . The Hill in New Haven, Connecticut is a neighborhood where $20 million is spent annually to imprison 387 people. The reality is that almost all these people, like others in prison nationwide, will return to The Hill and other high-incarceration communities. When they return—disproportionately to low-income neighborhoods of color—they will find neighborhoods weakened by their absence and burdened by their return.

A simple but radical question that policymakers are now asking is whether the $20 million spent on prisons make The Hill a safer neighborhood. In a difficult fiscal climate, where city, state, and local officials have an annual $20 million

budget to make communities safe, should they spend it all on prisons? This is the basic question driving justice reinvestment, a fundamental shift in the way we think about public safety in America.

The Failures of Prison Fundamentalism

The goal of justice reinvestment is to redirect some portion of the $54 billion America now spends on prisons to rebuilding the human resources and physical infrastructure—the schools, healthcare facilities, parks, and public spaces—of neighborhoods devastated by high levels of incarceration. Justice reinvestment is, however, more than simply rethinking and redirecting public funds. It is also about devolving accountability and responsibility to the local level. . . .

The principles and particulars of justice reinvestment are driven by the realities of crime and punishment in America today. The war on drugs, three-strikes sentencing schemes, elimination of judicial discretion and parole, and the broad abandonment of rehabilitation have led to an unprecedented level of imprisonment in the U.S.—over 2 million today compared to 200,000 in 1972. The massive number of incarcerated people come from a few neighborhoods across the U.S.—the million-dollar blocks of Brooklyn or the 3 percent of Cleveland neighborhoods that are home to 20 percent of all Ohio prisoners. They are often young people of color convicted of non-violent crimes, poor, undereducated, unemployed, 75 percent drug or alcohol dependent, and 16 percent seriously mentally ill.

A critical component of reinvestment thinking is stopping the debilitating pattern of cyclical imprisonment: 98 percent of these persons will return to the community—630,000 annually—and two-thirds will end up back in prison. One-third of those released return to prison not because of new crimes but because of violations of their parole—missed office appointments, positive drug test results, or breaches of curfew. . . .

From an investment perspective, both our prison and parole/probation systems are business failures. These policies destabilize communities along with the individuals whom they fail to train, treat, or rehabilitate, and whose mental health and substance abuse are often exacerbated by the experience of imprisonment. Recent research by criminologists Todd Clear and Dina Rose indicates that high levels of concentrated incarceration make a neighborhood less safe not more. The "coercive mobility" of cyclical imprisonment disrupts the fragile economic, social, and political bonds that are the basis for informal social control in a community.

The cumulative failure of three decades of prison fundamentalism stands out in sharp relief against the backdrop of today's huge deficits in state budgets. This difficult financial climate is forcing state officials to consider alternatives to increased incarceration, including treatment for the chemically dependent and mentally ill and reformed parole revocation guidelines to restrict the return of low-risk parolees to prison.

From Unproductive Spending to Long Term Investment

Identifying unproductive spending in correction budgets is the first step in the justice reinvestment process; the second step is the segregation and protection of a portion of these funds, and the third step is to reinvest the money into the public safety of high incarceration neighborhoods. . . . [L]egislation in Connecticut earmarking $7.5 million for justice reinvestment in New Haven is a prime example of how this policy can work.

. . . The question should be "What can be done to strengthen the capacity of high incarceration neighborhoods to keep their residents out of prison?" not "Where should we send this individual?"

We advocate taking a geographic approach to public safety that targets money for programs in education, health, job creation, and job training in low-income communities. This includes making parole officers responsible for particular neighborhoods rather than dispersing their caseloads across a wide span. It means that reentry from prison becomes a shared responsibility involving the community, government institutions, and the individual and his or her family. Even if the recent federal reentry initiative of $2 million per state were enough to prepare people leaving prison for employment, the likelihood of successful reentry—without decent jobs in their communities, counseling to identify opportunities, and childcare—will be minimal. Reentry must be a geographically targeted partnership of public and private interests—penal, social services, health providers, and educational institutions. . . .

The solution to public safety must be locally tailored and locally determined. This means a basic shift in the fiscal relations between the state and localities, and with it the devolution of program responsibility and accountability to local government. Under current practice, the state pays for the imprisonment of persons from the city. Dollars and accountability flow out of the neighborhoods. . . .

Under this proposal, local government could reclaim responsibility for dealing with residents who break the law and redeploy the funds that the state would have spent for their incarceration. The localities would have the freedom to spend justice dollars to decrease the risks of crime in the community. They could choose to spend these dollars for job training, drug treatment programs, and preschool programs, as well as incarceration for the dangerous few. . . . The key is making the locality accountable for solving its public safety problems and allowing local governments to reclaim resources. The redirected penal funds could be blended with other government funding streams to focus on local community restoration projects and could be leveraged to attract other public or private investment in housing, employment, or education.

. . . The idea of a civic justice corps is to mobilize people returning home from prison as agents of community restoration. They would join with other community residents to rehabilitate housing and schools, redesign and rebuild parks and playgrounds, and redevelop and rebuild the physical infrastructure and social fabric of their own neighborhoods. But the civic justice corps is only one possible investment in a public safety portfolio. Other investments might include a locally run community loan pool to make micro-loans to create jobs or family development loans for education, debt consolidation, or home ownership and rehabilitation, transportation micro-enterprises for residents commuting outside the neighborhood, a one-stop shop for job counseling and placement services, or geographically targeted hiring incentives for employers.

Role Reversal and the Promise of Reinvestment

Justice reinvestment allocates criminal justice spending to support schools, healthcare, housing, and jobs within the communities most in need of these resources. By doing this, justice reinvestment also increases public safety. The civic justice corps requires workers with training and skills, and prisons should be preparing them. . . . Despite the good intentions of individual parole officers, the system and its conflicting incentives have transformed these parole officers into second-class police officers on the one hand and overburdened, undertrained social workers on the other. But with devolution of parole to the neighborhood and retraining, parole officers could become resources for the restoration of communities and individuals. Instead of harvesting the failures, the incentives could be reversed so that parole officers become partners for public safety.

Finally, with justice reinvestment, the role of the formerly incarcerated will change. . . . Residents of low-income communities of color, now relegated to permanent consumers of correctional services, can—through public reinvestment in individual capacity and community institutions—become builders and restorers of healthy, safe communities.

11

◆◆◆

Women and the Military,
War, and Peace

In the United States most people grow up with pride in this country, its wealth, its power, and its superior position in the world. We learn the Pledge of Allegiance, a sense of patriotism, and that our way of life is worth fighting and perhaps dying for. Most families have at least one member who has served in the military. The United States is number one in the world in terms of military technology, military exports, and military expenditure (Children's Defense Fund 2004). The U.S. military budget is more than that of the next thirteen countries combined (Japan, UK, France, China, Germany, Italy, Saudi Arabia, South Korea, Russia, India, Israel, Turkey, and Brazil) (Stockholm International Peace Research Institute 2005). The largest proportion of our federal budget, $935 billion for fiscal year 2005 or 46 percent, supports current and past military operations, including the upkeep of over four hundred bases and installations at home and over two thousand of

those abroad, the development and maintenance of weapons systems, pensions for retired military personnel, veterans benefits, and interest on the national debt attributable to military spending (War Resisters League 2005). Military operations in Afghanistan and Iraq cost another $5 billion per month. Major companies with household names like Westinghouse, Boeing, and General Electric research and develop weapons systems and military aircraft. War movies are a film industry staple, portraying images of manly heroes. Many best-selling video games involve violent scenarios. "Full Spectrum Warrior," a video game set in an apparently Arab city, was developed with $4 million from the U.S. Army as a training tool for recruits (Ahn and Kirk 2005). The Army also has its own video game, America's Army, as a recruitment tool (www.americasarmy.com). Toy manufacturer Mattel markets a female colleague for G.I. Joe, a helicopter pilot dressed in a jumpsuit and helmet and armed with a 9mm Beretta. Even Barbie is in uniform.

The military shapes our notions of patriotism, heroism, honor, duty, and citizenship. President Clinton's avoidance of military service as a young man was heavily criticized by his detractors in the 1992 and 1996 election campaigns, the suggestion being that this was unpatriotic and not fitting for a president of the United States, who is also the commander in chief of the armed forces. Politically, economically, and culturally, the military is a central U.S. institution. This is more explicit since the attacks on the World Trade Center and Pentagon on September 11, 2001, and the Bush administration's declaration of a long-term "war on terrorism." Under the banner of patriotism, young people decided to enlist in the military and parents were encouraged to support them. Military recruiters are falling behind in their targets as the war in Iraq continues, despite an increased number of recruiters and bigger sign-up bonuses (Harris 2005). The No Child Left Behind Act concerning education also requires high schools to provide the Department of Defense with a directory of all juniors and seniors (names, addresses, and phone numbers) or risk losing federal funding. Parents must be notified; if they object to having their child's information released to military recruiters, the onus is on them to write to the school administration and say so.

As part of the global "war on terrorism" the Bush administration called on the Hollywood film industry to make more pro-war movies. The Walt Disney Corporation distributed a State Department ad nationwide, "Can you trust your neighbor?" that urged people to report any "suspicious" activity to the police. Political scientist Cynthia Enloe shows that many aspects of U.S. culture have become militarized and notes specific ways that culture is deployed in the service of militarism (Reading 65). There are "G.I. Jane Boot Camp" fitness programs. Toy manufacturer Ever Sparkle Inc. has a bombed-out dollhouse where grenades replace salt and pepper shakers, ammunition boxes litter the kitchen, and G.I. Joe, armed with a bazooka, is on the balcony ready for action. High fashions designers are promoting the "military look" and camouflage chic. Backpacks, cell-phone covers, baby clothes, and condoms all come in "cammo."

The Need for Women in the Military

Although the vast majority of U.S. military personnel have always been male, the military has needed and continues to need women's support and participation in many capacities (D'Amico and Weinstein 1999; Enloe 1983; Isakson 1988; Weinstein and White 1997). It needs mothers to believe in the concept of patriotic duty and to encourage their sons, and more recently their daughters, to enlist or at least to support their desire to do so. It needs women nurses to heal the wounded and the traumatized. It needs wives and girlfriends back home, the prize waiting at the end of war or a period of duty overseas, who live with veterans' trauma or who mourn loved ones killed in action. During World War II, White women and women of color symbolized by Rosie the Riveter, were needed for the war effort working in shipyards and munitions factories while men were drafted for active service overseas (Denman and Inniss 1999).

Currently the military needs women to work in electronics and many other industries producing weapons components, machine parts, tools, uniforms, household supplies, and foodstuffs for military contracts. It needs women working in nightclubs, bars, and massage parlors near foreign bases and ports providing R and R, rest and relaxation, for military personnel, or, as it is sometimes called, I and I, intoxication and intercourse (Enloe 1993a, 2000; Sturdevant and Stoltzfus 1992). And the military needs women on active duty, increasingly trained for combat as well as performing more traditional roles in administration, communications, intelligence, or medicine.

Having women in the military to the extent that they are today is a relatively new phenomenon. In 1972 women were only 1.2 percent of military personnel. The following year, after much debate, Congress ended the draft for men, though young men are still required to register for the draft when they turn 18. Many left the services as soon as they could, causing a manpower shortfall that has been made up by recruiting women, especially women of color. In 2004 women were 15 percent of all military personnel (in the Army, Air Force, Navy, Marine Corps, and Coast Guard). Almost half the women in the Army's enlisted ranks were Black (46 percent), compared to 31 percent in the Navy and 28 percent in the Air Force. African American women, Asian American women, Native American women, and

Army Regulations on Hair and Cosmetics

Military uniforms are the subject of detailed regulations and protocols. Uniform committees have long deliberated over appropriate dress for women—seeking to balance the soldier (read male) with the feminine. Nowadays women's uniforms emphasize practicality; they include pants, for example. Maternity uniforms have been introduced for pregnant servicewomen. The emphasis is on uniformity and professionalism, with precise rules governing all aspects of appearance, including fingernails and scrunchies, as shown in this excerpt from Army Regulation 670-1 (AR 670-1) Wear and Appearance of Army Uniforms and Insignia:

(3) Female haircuts will conform to the following standards.

(a) Females will ensure their hair is neatly groomed, that the length and bulk of the hair are not excessive, and that the hair does not present a ragged, unkempt, or extreme appearance. Likewise, trendy styles that result in shaved portions of the scalp (other than the neckline) or designs cut into the hair are prohibited. Females may wear braids and cornrows as long as the braided style is conservative, the braids and cornrows lie snugly on the head, and any hair-holding devices comply with the standards in 1-8a(3)(d) below. Dreadlocks (unkempt, twisted, matted individual parts of hair) are prohibited in uniform or in civilian clothes on duty. Hair will not fall over the eyebrows or extend below the bottom edge of the collar at any time during normal activity or when standing in formation. Long hair that falls naturally below the bottom edge of the collar, to include braids, will be neatly and inconspicuously fastened or pinned, so no free-hanging hair is visible. This includes styles worn with the physical fitness uniform/improved physical fitness uniform (PFU/IPFU).

(b) Styles that are lopsided or distinctly unbalanced are prohibited. Ponytails, pigtails, or braids that are not secured to the head (allowing hair to hang freely), widely spaced individual hanging locks, and other extreme styles that protrude from the head are prohibited. Extensions, weaves, wigs, and hairpieces are authorized; however, these additions must have the same general appearance as the individual's natural hair. Additionally, any wigs, extensions, hairpieces, or weaves must comply with the grooming policies set forth in this paragraph.

(c) Females will ensure that hairstyles do not interfere with proper wear of military headgear and protective masks or equipment at any time [see1-8a(1)(a), above]. When headgear is worn, the hair will not extend below the bottom edge of the front of the headgear, nor will it extend below the bottom edge of the collar.

(d) Hair-holding devices are authorized only for the purpose of securing the hair. Soldiers will not place hair-holding devices in the hair for decorative purposes. All hair-holding devices must be plain and of a color as close to the soldier's hair as is possible or clear. Authorized devices include, but are not limited to, small, plain scrunchies (elastic hair bands covered with material), barrettes, combs, pins, clips, rubber bands, and hair bands. Devices that are conspicuous, excessive, or decorative are prohibited. Some examples of prohibited devices include, but are not limited to, large, lacy scrunchies; beads, bows, or claw clips; clips, pins, or barrettes with butterflies, flowers, sparkles, gems, or scalloped edges; and bows made from hairpieces.

b. Cosmetics.

(1) General. As with hairstyles, the requirement for standards regarding cosmetics is necessary to maintain uniformity and to avoid an extreme or unmilitary appearance. Males are prohibited from wearing cosmetics, to include nail polish. Females are authorized to wear cosmetics with all uniforms, provided they are applied conservatively

and in good taste and complement the uniform. Leaders at all levels must exercise good judgment in the enforcement of this policy.

(a) Females may wear cosmetics if they are conservative and complement the uniform and their complexion. Eccentric, exaggerated, or trendy cosmetic styles and colors, to include makeup designed to cover tattoos, are inappropriate with the uniform and are prohibited. Permanent makeup, such as eyebrow or eyeliner, is authorized as long as the makeup conforms to the standards outlined above.

(b) Females will not wear shades of lipstick and nail polish that distinctly contrast with their complexion, that detract from the uniform, or that are extreme. Some examples of extreme colors include, but are not limited to, purple, gold, blue, black, white, bright (fire-engine) red, khaki, camouflage colors, and fluorescent colors. Soldiers will not apply designs to nails or apply two-tone or multi-tone colors to nails.

Latinas made up 63 percent of enlisted women in the Army, 52 percent in the Navy, and 40 percent in the Air Force. By contrast, 64 percent of women officers in the Army are White, 75 percent of the women officers in the Navy are White, and 76 percent of women officers in the Air Force are White (Women's Research and Education Institute 2002).

The Military as Employer

For many of these women, the military offers much better opportunities than the wider society: jobs with better pay, health care, pensions, and other benefits, as well as the chance for education, travel, and escape from crisis-torn inner cities in the United States. It enhances women's self-esteem and confers the status of first-class citizenship attributed to those who serve their country. Military recruiters emphasize security, professionalism, empowerment, adventure, patriotism, and pride. In noting the benefits of army life in the early 1950s, Jean Grossholtz (Reading 69) includes medical services, expanded opportunities, a ready-made community of women, and a sense of self-worth and accomplishment. Margarethe Cammermeyer served as a military nurse for twenty-six years, in the Army, the Army Reserves, and the National Guard; she was the highest-ranking officer to challenge military policy on homosexuality before being discharged in 1992 on the basis of sexual orientation. Her autobiography emphasizes the professionalism, structure, and discipline she experienced in military life and her keen sense of patriotism and duty (Cammermeyer 1994).

As we argued in Chapter 8, the U.S. labor market has changed markedly over the past three decades or so through automation and the movement of jobs overseas. In addition to a loss of jobs, there are few sources of funding for working-class women's (and men's) education. Government funding for education and many welfare programs was cut back during the 1980s and '90s, but despite the end of the cold war, enormous changes in the former Soviet Union, and cuts in U.S. bases and personnel, the U.S. military budget has been maintained at high levels. Women who enter the military are thus going where the money is. Their very presence, however, exposes serious dilemmas and contradictions for the institution, which we explore in the next section. Another contradiction of this situation is the fact that massive government spending on the military diverts funds that could otherwise be invested in civilian job programs and inner-city communities.

Limitations to Women's Equal Participation in the Military

Support for women's equality within the military is based on a belief in women's right to equal access to education, jobs, promotion, and authority in all aspects of society, and to the benefits of first-class citizenship. Women's rights organizations, such as the National Organization for Women, have campaigned for women to have equal opportunity with men in the military, as have women military personnel, military women's organizations like the Minerva Center (Pasadena, Md.) and the Pallas Athena Network

(New Market, Va.), and key members of Congress like former representative Pat Schroeder, who was on the Armed Services Committee for many years. In 2001, in the military, as in the civilian job market, most enlisted women were doing "women's work," including support and administration (34 percent), health care (15 percent), service and supply (10 percent), and communications and intelligence (10 percent). Among officers this was also true: 41 percent worked in health care, 12 percent as administrators, and 10 percent in supply and logistics (Women's Research and Education Institute 2002).

After years of pressure, women who served in Vietnam were honored with a memorial in Washington, D.C. This advocacy and recognition, together with women's changing position in society, have also affected social attitudes. In 1991, in the Persian Gulf War, for example, military women were featured in headline news stories around the country. Saying good-bye to their families as they prepared to go overseas, they were portrayed as professional soldiers as well as mothers.

Women's equal participation in the military is limited in several ways, however, including limits on combat roles; limited access to some military academies; the effects of a general culture of racism, sexism, and sexual harassment; and the ban on being openly lesbian.

Women in Combat Roles

Women served in the U.S. military during World War II, the Korean War, and the Vietnam War. They were generally designated as auxiliary, according to political scientist Mary Katzenstein (1993), despite the fact that they performed a wider range of tasks than is usually recognized—as transport pilots (Cole 1992), mechanics, drivers, underground reconnaissance, nurses (Camp 1997), and administrators. The influx of women into the military since the mid-1970s and the question of whether to train women for combat have exposed a range of stereotypical attitudes toward women on the part of military commanders, Pentagon planners, and members of Congress, depending on the degree to which they believe that combat is male. From the late 1980s well into the '90s, countless news reports, magazine articles, editorials, and letters to the editor took up this issue.

War-making is increasingly a high-tech, push-button affair, as exemplified in the bombing missions

Are we willing to sacrifice one or two of the children for oil?

of the 1991 Gulf War and the bombing of Kosovo in 1999, of Afghanistan in 2001, and of Iraq in 2003. But old attitudes die hard. Combat roles are dangerous and demanding. Many argue that women are not physically strong enough, are too emotional, and lack discipline or stamina. They will be bad for men's morale, it is said, and will disrupt fighting units because men will be distracted if a woman buddy is hurt or captured. The country is not ready for women coming home in body bags.

Women in the military perform their jobs well. Military planners face a dilemma. They need women to make up the shortfall in personnel; at the same time, they hold sexist or condescending notions about women. Political scientists Francine D'Amico and Laurie Weinstein (1999) comment that the "military must camouflage its reliance on *woman*power in order to maintain its self-image as a quintessentially *masculine* institution" (p. 6). It does this by marginalizing women through sexual harassment, professional disparagement, and distinctions between combatant and noncombatant. What counts as combat in modern warfare is not as simple as it might seem, however, and definitions of "the front" and "the rear" change with developments in military technology. Communications and supply, defined as noncombat areas where women work, are both likely targets of attack.

Media attention on women's participation in the 1991 Persian Gulf War showed that many performed combat roles similar to those of men, and this led to changes in laws and regulations that had previously kept women out of combat assignments (Muir 1993; Peach 1997; Sadler 1997; Skaine 1998). In 1993 the rule barring women from dangerous jobs was changed, though some exceptions were preserved. Women can work on combat ships and jet planes, but not in submarines. Restricting women from combat roles has been a way of limiting their career advancement, as senior positions often require combat experience (Francke 1997; Stiehm 1989). By 1997 women filled only 815 of the 47,544 combat-related jobs that were opened to women in 1993 and 1994 (Study shows few women in combat jobs 1997). In fiscal year 2001, there were 114 active-duty female fighter and bomber pilots, 366 women pilots for other aircraft, and 653 women helicopter pilots. In March 2003, women fought in the war against Iraq, with women among those servicemembers killed or taken prisoner.

Earlier rules banning women from direct combat have shifted during the war against Iraq, where "traditional front lines were virtually obliterated and women were tasked to fill lethal combat roles more routinely than in any conflict in U.S. history" according to *Chicago Tribune* reporter Kirsten Scharnberg (2005). She describes a mission just south of Baghdad where

> a young soldier jumped into the gunner's turret of an armored Humvee and took control of the menacing .50-caliber machine gun. She was 19 years old, weighed barely 100 pounds and had a blond ponytail hanging out from under her Kevlar helmet.
>
> "This is what is different about this war," Lt. Col. Richard Rael, commander of the 515th Corps Support Battalion, said of the scene at the time. "Women are fighting it. Women under my command have confirmed kills. These little wisps of things are stronger than anyone could ever imagine and taking on more than most Americans could ever know."
>
> *(Scharnberg 2005)*

Scharnberg goes on to report that female troops returning from Iraq "appear more prone to post-traumatic stress disorder, or PTSD, than their male counterparts." The Veterans Affairs Department has launched a $6 million study of PTSD among female veterans, the first VA study to focus exclusively on female veterans. A preliminary finding suggests that "female military personnel are far more likely than their male counterparts to have been exposed to

some kind of trauma or multiple traumas before joining the military or being deployed in combat," including physical assault, sexual abuse or rape, a factor that can trigger PTSD (Scharnberg 2005). Research on Vietnam War veterans conducted by psychologist Rachel MacNair (2002) found that troops who had killed—or believed they had killed—suffered significantly higher rates of PTSD than those who had not. A Defense Department study of combat troops returning from Iraq found that many soldiers and Marines suffering from PTSD and readjustment problems were concerned about the stigma attached to appearing weak. They feared "their commanders and fellow troops would treat them differently and lose confidence in them if they sought treatment for their problems" (Scharnberg 2005). This suggests that seeking help may be particularly difficult for women who fought to be assigned positions that were previously closed to them.

Officer Training: Storming the Citadel

In 1975 Congress mandated that the three military academies were to admit women. Researching the experiences of the first women to enter the U.S. Military Academy at West Point, Janice Yoder (1989) noted the severe pressure on these women to do well. They were a highly visible, very small minority, tokens in what had been constructed as an exclusively male institution. They faced tough physical tests designed for men; they were out of the loop in many informal settings and were routinely subjected to sexist notions and behavior by male cadets who did not accept them as peers (Campbell with D'Amico 1999). As a result, for the first four years at least, the dropout rate for women was significantly higher than it was for men, a fact that could be used by policy makers to justify exclusionary practices. Yoder concluded, however, that these women were not competing on equal terms with men, and she argued for changes in evaluation criteria and the overwhelmingly male culture of the Academy, an increase in the number of women entering the Academy, and greater commitment to women's full participation at an institutional level. Since then, women have entered other private military academies like the Citadel and the Virginia Military Institute (VMI) with similarly mixed success. In January 1997, two of the first four women at the Citadel withdrew because of intolerable harassment (Applebome 1997). The other two became the first female cadets to graduate from the Citadel in 1999. Two women also completed their training at the VMI in the same year. In 2002 the first class of Black women graduated from the Citadel.

Sexism and Misogyny

Added to this chilly climate for women are overt sexual harassment and sexual abuse. Many women in the military experience sexual harassment, even though the Department of Defense has had a "specific policy prohibiting sexual harassment of military personnel for over fifteen years," summed up as "zero-tolerance" (Guenter-Schlesinger 1999, p. 195). A 1995 Department of Defense survey reported that 4 percent of all female soldiers said they had been the victim of a completed or attempted rape during their military service, and 61 percent said that they had been sexually harassed in the Army (High 1997). Ninety percent of women in a Veterans Administration study reported harassment, and a third said they had been raped by military personnel (*STAMP Newsletter* 1998/99). Paula Coughlin, a helicopter pilot, went public with her experiences of sexual assault at the 1991 Tailhook naval aviators' convention at the Las Vegas Hilton, where women were subjected to sexual harassment, indecent assault, and indecent exposure. She testified that she endured relentless harassment from colleagues afterward and had since resigned her commission as a Navy lieutenant (Noble 1994). More than eighty other women also filed complaints, and a few also filed civil lawsuits.

After hearing testimony from servicewomen in 1992, a Senate Committee estimated that as many as 60,000 women had been sexually assaulted or raped while serving in the U.S. armed forces. Senator Dennis DeConcini commented, "American women serving in the Gulf were in greater danger of being sexually assaulted by our own troops than by the enemy" (Walker 1992, p. 6). In 1996 this issue surfaced publicly again, when women at the Aberdeen Proving Grounds Ordnance Center in Maryland complained of being sexually harassed and raped by drill sergeants during training. As part of its investigations into these allegations, the Army set up a toll-free hotline, which took four thousand calls in the first week relating to harassment at many military facilities (McKenna 1996/1997). *Time* magazine

reporter Elizabeth Gleick (1996) described this issue as an abuse of power by superiors, threatening "to undermine the thing that many in the military hold sacred: the chain of command" (p. 28). Interviewed for the ABC weekly news program *20/20*, Alan Cranston, former U.S. senator from California, suggested three reasons for the intensity of sexual abuse in the military: men feeling threatened by women coworkers, the general "macho" military culture, and the fact that many military personnel have easy access to guns (Walters and Downs 1996). As the investigation spread, military commanders did their best to attribute any misconduct to "a few bad apples," a comment that military officials also made concerning widespread sexual harassment reported by women cadets at the U.S. Air Force Academy in Colorado Springs in 2003. During an eighteen-month period ending in February 2004, the Department of Defense acknowledged 112 incidents of rape, assault, and other forms of sexual misconduct reported by female soldiers in the Central Command, which includes Iraq and Afghanistan (Shumway 2004). More than 1,000 incidents of sexual misconduct throughout the military were reported in 2003 (Smith 2004). Women who report sexual abuse often find themselves interrogated and intimidated by skeptical officers. Some are disciplined themselves for drinking or wearing civilian clothes at the time of the assaults. Others say they have been given a medical discharge or otherwise "hounded out" of the military (National Women's Law Center 2003; Shumway 2004). Many women simply do not report such incidents.

In the past several years, more women have undertaken scholarly research on sexism as ingrained in military culture (Burke 2004; D'Amico 1998; Guenter-Schlesinger 1999; Morris 1999; Pershing 2003), initiated internal proceedings or lawsuits concerning sexual abuse (Woodman 1997), opened up these issues to a wider audience by writing about their personal experiences (e.g., Dean 1997), and organized to change military protocols, regulations, practices, and culture. Survivors Take Action Against Abuse by Military Personnel (STAMP, Fairborne, Ohio), for example, grew out of women's anger and frustration with the lack of accountability for sexual harassment and abuse of women in the armed forces by their colleagues and superiors. Despite the existence of policies against sexual harassment, and an increase in sensitivity training for military personnel, entrenched military culture blocks the systematic implementation of such policies (Guenter-Schlesinger 1999).

Racism

Although the armed services were officially integrated in 1948, decades before desegregation in the southern states, racism, like sexism, is still a common occurrence in the military between individuals and at an institutional level. The preponderance of women of color in the enlisted ranks also demonstrates the institutionalized racism of the wider society (Hall 1999; Moore 1996). In 1994 a House Armed Services Committee investigation uncovered serious problems with institutionalized racism throughout the armed forces and warned about skinhead and other extremist activity on four military bases visited by investigators. In December 1995, for example, two African American civilians were random victims, shot and killed by three White servicemen, described in press reports as right-wing extremists, from the Army's 82nd Airborne Division at Fort Bragg, North Carolina (Citizen Soldier 1996). In December 1996, two African American airmen at Kelly Air Force Base (Texas) talked to the media about a racist incident in which they were taunted by men wearing pillowcases resembling Ku Klux Klan hoods and said that they were dissatisfied with the Air Force's response to their complaints (2 Black airmen 1996). In 1995 the *New York Times* reported discrimination against African American military personnel in promotion decisions (Military is found 1995). Military statistics generally include Black women as part of the general category of "women in the military," whereas Black service personnel are usually assumed to be Black males. Hall (1999) notes that a 1994 U.S. House Armed Services Committee report found that service members of color perceived racial discrimination in opportunities for career-enhancing assignments or training. This information was not broken down by gender, making it impossible to track discrimination fully. Such limitations in reporting continue.

Sexual Orientation

A final area of limitation for women—and men—in the military concerns sexual orientation. The Pentagon considers homosexuality incompatible with military service, and a series of regulations have precluded lesbians and gay men from serving openly, despite their continuing presence as officers and enlisted personnel (Scott and Stanley 1994; Webber 1993). In Reading 69 Jean Grossholtz pinpoints the contradiction implicit in this policy: The military is based on male bonding, yet homosexuality is banned. Thousands of gay men and lesbians have been discharged over the years in what she refers to as "purges." Research from the Center for the Study of Sexual Minorities in the Military (University of California, Santa Barbara) found that of the 6,300 people discharged between 1998 and 2003 the majority were active duty enlisted personnel in the early stages of their careers (Fouhy 2004). They included linguists, nuclear warfare experts, and other job specialties requiring years of training and expertise. The Army was responsible for 41 percent of these discharges, even though it is down on its recruitment targets and has invoked a "stop loss" order to stop soldiers from retiring or leaving if they are deployed to Iraq or Afghanistan.

During his first presidential election campaign, Bill Clinton promised to lift the ban on gays in the military when he came into office in 1992. Concerted opposition from the Pentagon and many politicians made this impossible, however, and some argue that current policy, summed up as "Don't Ask, Don't Tell, Don't Pursue," is not much different than before. "Homosexual conduct," defined as homosexual activity, trying to marry someone of the same sex, or acknowledging one's homosexuality, is grounds for discharge. A number of lesbians and gay men have challenged this policy in court. Gay rights organizations, like the National Gay and Lesbian Task Force and Gay, Lesbian, and Bisexual Vets of America, continue to raise this issue as an example of lesbians' and gay men's second-class citizenship.

Reports of anti-gay harassment—including verbal abuse, beatings, death threats, and apparent killings—more than doubled in the late 1990s, increasing from 182 violations documented in 1997 to 400 in 1998 (Servicemembers Legal Defense Network 1999a). Military policy expressly forbids such harassment, but in April 1998, five years after the "Don't Ask, Don't Tell, Don't Pursue" policy was introduced, the Pentagon acknowledged that the service branches had not instructed commanders on how to investigate those who make anti-gay threats. The Department of Defense discharged

1,250 service members in 2001 for being lesbian, gay, or bisexual, the largest number of gay discharges in more than a decade (Servicemembers Legal Defense Network 2002). Women were 30 percent of those discharged, though they make up only 15 percent of active duty personnel. In August 1999, the Department of Defense issued its updated policy on gays in the military requiring mandatory training on anti-harassment guidelines for all troops, beginning in boot camp. In March 2000, Pentagon officials conceded that there is a "disturbing" level of gay harassment in the military (Richter 2000) and this continues. The Servicemembers Legal Defense Network (2002) urges Pentagon officials and service members to uphold the Anti-Harassment Action Plan published in 2000, and argues that "forcing lesbian, gay and bisexual service members to hide, lie, evade and deceive their commanders, subordinates, peers, families and friends breaks the bonds of trust among service members essential to unit cohesion" (p. 6).

Military Wives

In Reading 66, Kristin Henderson, a writer who is married to a Navy chaplain, describes the situation of U.S. military wives in North Carolina whose husbands have been deployed to Iraq. She notes the strains on personal relationships and family life, and the wide gaps in the military's family policy that military wives attempt to fill on a voluntary basis as they hold down paid employment and care for their children.

Military wives have been the subject of a number of studies (D'Amico and Weinstein 1999; Enloe 1983, 2000; Weinstein and White 1997). The model military wife is a staunch supporter of her husband's career. She learns to manage the moves from base to base, the disruption of family life, and interruptions in her own work (and, increasingly, she may be in the military herself). Wives and children of military families also suffer abuse at the hands of servicemen husbands and fathers. Researchers attribute this to a combination of factors: the stress of military jobs, family responsibilities, relatively low pay, uncertainty about job security, training for combat, and relative powerlessness at work. Reports of spousal abuse of wives associated with the military rose from 18.6 per thousand in 1990 to 25.6 per thousand in 1996 (U.S. Department of Defense 1996). As is the

case for the estimate of domestic violence in civilian families, this is inevitably a conservative estimate. Rates of domestic violence among military personnel are considerably higher than civilian rates. Anthropologist Catherine Lutz (2004, p. 17) notes that "war always comes home, even when it seems safely exported." "Even in the best of times," she comments, "rates of domestic violence are 3 to 5 times higher in military couples than in comparable civilian ones." This finding is corroborated by Deborah Tucker, executive director of the National Center on Domestic and Sexual Violence, who also co-chaired the Department of Defense Task Force on Domestic Violence (Gettelman 2005; also see Houppert 2005a; 2005b). Women abused by military personnel are often fearful of reporting incidents because of a combination of lack of confidentiality and privacy; limited victim services; lack of training and assistance on the part of military commanders; and disruption caused by moving from base to base.

According to official policy, violence against women and children is not to be condoned or tolerated. However, the message has not been clear and consistent throughout command leadership (Miles Foundation 1999). "The War at Home," which first aired on *60 Minutes* in January 1999 and again in September 2002, helped to make this issue more public and to support victims of military violence. The Miles Foundation (Waterbury, Conn.) and Survivors in Service United have taken up the issue of violence within military families (Hansen 2001). In 2000, President Clinton appointed a Defense Task Force on Domestic Violence, comprising twelve high-ranking military members and twelve civilian members (domestic violence experts and legal practitioners), to assist in improving the military's response to domestic violence. In November 2001, Deputy Secretary of Defense Paul Wolfowitz issued an official memorandum stating that domestic violence will not be tolerated in the military and calling on all commanders to update and standardize education and training programs, to increase protection for victims, to improve coordination between military and civilian agencies that respond to incidents of domestic violence, and to provide information to personnel on local services and resources. Meanwhile, this issue hit the headlines in the summer of 2002 when, within six weeks, the wives of three soldiers who had served in Afghanistan were killed at Fort Bragg (N.C.), allegedly by their husbands. Two of the soldiers killed themselves as well. Three of the four men were in the Special Forces, considered the toughest and most aggressive unit in the Army. The Special Operation command said it would study the stress wartime deployments may be adding to already-shaky marriages. The military announced that soldiers would be screened for psychological problems before they leave Afghanistan and commanders will watch out for symptoms of depression and anxiety among their troops. Also in 2002, a bipartisan effort by elected officials and activists was successful in getting increased funding for domestic violence services in the Defense Appropriation Act for Fiscal Year 2003. Moreover, the Armed Forces Security Act, which became law on December 2, 2002, provides for the enforcement of civilian court protective orders. These case-by-case efforts do not address systemic issues. Catherine Lutz (2004, pp. 17–18) notes that "there is no workplace more supportive of a masculine identity centered in power, control, and violence"; "there is little institutional incentive to rid the service of men who batter, since the military puts its war-making mission above all others"; and "the military attempts to retain soldiers despite their crimes when they see them in terms of training costs that can range from $100,00 to $500,000 per person and more."

The Impact of the U.S. Military on Women Overseas

The worldwide superiority of the United States—in political, economic, and military terms—is sustained by a wide network of U.S. bases, troops, ships, submarines, and aircraft in Europe, Asia, Latin America, the Caribbean, the Pacific, and the Middle East. Since the Bush administration declared war on terrorism after the attacks of September 11, 2001, U.S. bases have been established at thirteen locations in nine countries around Afghanistan, U.S. troops have returned to the Philippines, and there are plans to expand bases into Eastern Europe, Latin America, and Africa. This U.S. presence relies on agreements with each particular government. In return the military may pay rent for the land it occupies. Some local people may be employed directly on the bases; many others work in nearby businesses patronized by U.S. military personnel. We consider four ways that U.S. military policies and bases abroad affect women: through militarized prostitution, through

their responsibility for mixed-race children fathered by U.S. service personnel, through crimes of violence committed by U.S. troops, and through the harmful environmental effects of war and preparations for war.

Militarized Prostitution

As a way of keeping up the morale of their troops, military commanders have long tolerated, and sometimes actively encouraged, women to live outside military camps to support and sexually service the men. With U.S. bases positioned strategically around the globe, especially since World War II, militarized prostitution has required explicit arrangements between the U.S. government and the governments of the Philippines, Japan (Okinawa), Thailand, and South Korea, for example, where many women work in bars and massage parlors, "entertaining" U.S. troops (Enloe 1990, 1993a, 2000; Sturdevant and Stoltzfus 1992). As a way of protecting the men's health, women who work in bars must have regular medical exams, on the assumption that they are the source of sexually transmitted infections (Moon 1997). If the bar women fail such tests, they are quarantined until they pass. They usually earn better money than they can make in other ways, though this may be harder as they grow older. By creating a class of women who are available for sexual servicing, the governments attempt to limit the sexual demands of U.S. military personnel to specific women and specific locations.

Despite the low opinion many local people have of bar women, their work is the linchpin of the subeconomy of the "G.I. towns" adjoining the bases, and many people, including store owners, salespeople, bar owners, restaurateurs, cooks, pimps, procurers, cab drivers, and security men, are in business as a result of their work. Some of the bar women are able to send money to their aging parents or younger siblings, an important part of being a good daughter, especially in countries with few social services or welfare supports. Occupational dangers for the women include psychological violence, rape, and beatings from some of their customers; health risks from contraceptive devices, especially IUDs; abortions; AIDS and other sexually transmitted infections; drug use; and a general lack of respect associated with this stigmatized work. Currently, many women working in bars around U.S. bases in South Korea and Okinawa are recruited from the

Philippines, due to the weakness of the Philippines economy. Korean and Okinawan women used to do this work but as the economies of Korea and Japan have strengthened most Okinawan and Korean women now have other options. Russian women, displaced due to the collapse of the Russian economy in the transition to a capitalist system, also work in bars around U.S. bases overseas. Militarized prostitution is an integral part of the global sex trade (see Reading 56).

Mixed-Race Children Fathered by U.S. Troops

Many bar women and former bar women in Okinawa (Japan), South Korea, the Philippines, and Vietnam have Amerasian children, an often-neglected group. Some of them, born during the Korean War or Vietnam War, are now in their forties and fifties; others are young children born to women recently involved with U.S. troops stationed in South Korea or Okinawa. Most of them have been raised in poverty, further stigmatized by their mothers' occupation and their own mixed heritage. According to Margo Okazawa-Rey (1997), many of the mothers of Amerasian children in South Korea had serious relationships with the children's fathers. Although some marriages take place each year between Korean women and U.S. military personnel in South Korea, most of the men simply leave. They may turn out to be already married in the United States—a fact they had not thought necessary to mention—or they just disappear. Many of the children of these unions have not had much schooling as a result of poverty and intimidation and harassment from their peers. In South Korea, Amerasians whose fathers are African American are more stigmatized than those with White fathers. They may gain some acceptance by doing well in stereotypically Black spheres like sports and music. Some of the girls become bar women like their mothers. A relatively small number of such children are adopted by U.S. families, but this is expensive and not possible for children whose births have not been registered.

Crimes of Violence Against Women

The behavior of U.S. troops in other countries is governed by agreements between the U.S. government and the host government, called Status of Forces Agreements (SOFAs). Usually U.S. military personnel who commit crimes against civilians are dealt with, if at all, through military channels rather than the local courts. In many cases, U.S. troops are not held responsible for crimes they commit. Sometimes they are simply moved to another posting. This is a highly contentious issue, especially for those who do not support the U.S. military presence in their countries. In South Korea, for example, the National Campaign for Eradication of Crime by U.S. Troops in Korea was founded in 1993, growing out of a coalition of women, students, labor activists, religious people, and human rights activists that formed to protest the brutal murder of a young woman, Yoon Kum E, the previous year. The campaign collects information about crimes committed against Korean civilians by U.S. military personnel and cites a South Korean Assembly report that estimated 39,542 such crimes between 1967 and 1987, including murders, brutal rapes, and sexual abuse; incidents of arson, theft, smuggling, fraud, and traffic offenses; an outflow of P.X. (on-base department store) merchandise; and a black market in U.S. goods (Ahn 1996). This situation is not known by many in the United States and is rarely publicized here. This customary silence, however, was broken in the fall of 1995 when a 12-year-old Okinawan girl was abducted and raped by three U.S. military personnel. This incident is one of many; its brutality and the victim's age were important factors in generating renewed outrage at the presence of U.S. bases by many Okinawans. Suzuyo Takazato, cofounder of Okinawa Women Act Against Military Violence, reports on the long history of such incidents in Okinawa (Reading 67; also Fukumura and Matsuoka 2002).

If experiences in Asia are any guide, there are undoubtedly instances of intimidation, sexual abuse, and rape of Iraqi women by U.S. troops. This has, indeed, been alleged in British news reports but not in the United States (L. Harding 2004).

Health Effects of Environmental Contamination

Militaries create more pollution than other institutions, but unlike industry, military pollution is governed by fewer regulations, monitoring programs, and controls (Seager 1993). Routine military operations involve the use of highly carcinogenic materials, including fuels, oils, solvents, and heavy metals, that are regularly released, affecting the land, water, air, and ocean, as well as the health of people living around U.S. bases overseas. Experience in the Philippines, for example, suggests that the U.S. military had not followed its own, admittedly weak, guidelines for the storage and disposal of contaminants. In the mid-1990s, after the U.S. military had evacuated long-term bases in the Philippines, Filipino families were housed at the former Clark Air Force Base where their only water supply was a contaminated well. By 1999, eight women had been diagnosed with breast cancer and nineteen had suffered reproductive problems including miscarriages and stillbirths. A disproportionate number of children suffer rare diseases such as leukemia, congenital heart disease, disorders of the central nervous system, and speech impairments. Some have already died from these effects of military contamination; others are only now beginning to show symptoms (Zamora-Olib 2000). Another example concerns the effects of sustained noise experienced by people living near bases where planes are constantly taking off and landing. Women living around Kadena Air Force Base in Okinawa (Japan), for example, have more low-birth-weight babies than are born in any other part of Japan, attributable to stress caused by noise (Okinawa Prefecture 1998).

The U.S. nuclear weapons industry has also caused long-term environmental devastation in this country and overseas (Birks and Erlich 1989; Lindsay-Poland, and Morgan 1998; Seager 1993; Shulman 1990). In the 1950s and early 1960s the United States military, as well as those of Britain and France, undertook a series of atomic tests in the Pacific that irradiated whole islands and contaminated soil and water for generations to come. The U.S. military conducted tests in Micronesia, which it administered as a United Nations Strategic Trust Territory, supposedly as a step toward the political independence of the islanders. Many Micronesian women have since given birth to children with severe illnesses or disabilities caused by radiation, including some "jellyfish babies" without skeletons who live only a few hours (de Ishtar 1994; Dibblin 1989). Pacific Island women and men have contracted several kinds of cancer as a result of their exposure to high levels of radioactive fallout. Given the long-lasting effects of atomic material in the food chain and people's reproductive systems, these disabilities

and illnesses are likely to last for many generations. Film footage of the U.S. tests, included in newsreels for U.S. audiences, described the islanders as simple people, indeed, as happy savages (O'Rourke 1985). In 1969, some years after the partial Test Ban Treaty (1963), which banned atomic tests in the atmosphere, the United States ended its trusteeship of Micronesia. Henry Kissinger, then secretary of state, was highly dismissive of the indigenous people in his comment, "There's only 90,000 people out there, who gives a damn?" (Women Working for a Nuclear-Free and Independent Pacific 1987).

Many in Pacific Island nations see these atomic—and later nuclear—tests, which France continued until 1996, as imperialist and racist. Various activist organizations are campaigning for a nuclear-free and independent Pacific and see U.S. military bases in Hawaii and Guam, for example, and the activities of the U.S. Pacific fleet as a serious limitation on their sovereignty and self-determination (Trask 1999). Meanwhile, Pacific-island women whose families have been affected by radioactive fallout take the lead in trying to keep their families and devastated communities together.

Women's Opposition to the Military

Early Peace Organizations in the United States

Activist organizations oppose the presence and impact of U.S. military bases in many countries, including those mentioned earlier. This opposition is sometimes based on nationalism, sometimes on arguments for greater self-determination, local control of land and resources, with more sustainable economic development. Women often play a key role in these organizations.

In the United States, too, although many women have supported and continue to support the military in various ways, there is a history of women's opposition to militarism and war with roots in Quakerism and the nineteenth-century suffrage and temperance movements (Alonso 1993; Washburn 1993). Julia Ward Howe, for example, remembered as the author of the Civil War song "The Battle Hymn of the Republic," was involved in the suffrage movement as a way of organizing women for peace. In 1873 she initiated Mothers' Day for Peace on June 2, a day to honor mothers, who, she felt, best understood the suffering caused by war. Women's peace festivals were organized in several U.S. cities, mainly in the Northeast and Midwest, with women speakers who opposed war and military training in schools. The Philadelphia Peace Society was still organizing in this way as late as 1909 (Alonso 1993). Her Mother's Day Proclamation, written in 1870, calls on women to oppose war (Reading 68). During the 1890s many women's organizations had peace committees that were active in the years before U.S. entry into World War I. In 1914 the Women's Peace Party was formed under the leadership of Carrie Chapman Catt and Jane Addams.

Despite difficulties of obtaining passports and wartime travel, over one thousand women from twelve countries, "cutting across national enmities," participated in a Congress of Women in the Hague, Holland, in 1915, calling for an end to the war. The congress sent delegations to meet with heads of state in fourteen countries and influenced press and public opinion (Foster 1989). A second congress at the end of the war proposed an ongoing international organization: the Women's International League for Peace and Freedom (WILPF), which is active in thirty-seven countries today and maintains international offices at the United Nations and in Geneva, Switzerland. Among the participants at the second congress were Mary Church Terrell, a Black labor leader from the United States, and Jeanette Rankin, the first U.S. congresswoman and the only member of Congress to vote against U.S. involvement in both world wars. In the 1950s and again in the 1960s, more U.S. women than men opposed the Korean War and Vietnam War. Women Strike for Peace, founded in 1961 and still active through the 1980s, was initially concerned with the nuclear arms race, as well as the Vietnam War (Swerdlow 1993). These organizations attracted members who were overwhelmingly White and middle class.

Feminist Antimilitarist Perspectives

Women's opposition to militarism draws on a range of theoretical perspectives, which we discuss briefly below. In any particular organization several of these perspectives may provide the basis for activism, but it is useful to look at them separately to clarify different and sometimes contradictory positions.

Women's Peaceful Nature   Although some women —and men—believe that women are "naturally" more peaceful than men, there is no conclusive evidence for this. Differences in socialization, however, from infancy onward, lead to important differences in attitudes, behavior, and responsibilities in caring for others. In U.S. electoral politics since 1980, these differences have been described as creating a "gender gap," under which more women than men oppose high military budgets and environmental destruction and support socially useful government spending (Abzug 1984; Gallagher 1993). Many who oppose the military see the current division of labor in society between men's and women's roles as a fundamental aspect of military systems, whereby men (and now a few women) "protect" women, children, and older people. They ask: Can we afford this dichotomy? Where does it lead? Those who support women's equal access to social institutions argue that everyone should have the opportunity to join the military and take on roles formerly reserved for men. Opponents argue that the abolition of war is dependent on changing this division of labor, with men taking on traditional women's roles and caring for infants and small children, the elderly, and the sick (Dinnerstein 1989; Ruddick 1989).

Maternalism   Some women see their opposition to war mainly in terms of their responsibility to protect and nurture their children; they want to save the lives of both their own children and the children of "enemy" mothers. In the early 1980s, for example, when the U.S. and Soviet militaries were deploying nuclear weapons in Europe, Susan Lamb, who lived near USAF Greenham Common in England, a nuclear base, put it this way:

> I've got two young children, and I've taken responsibility for their passage into adulthood. Everyone tells me they are my responsibility. The government tells me this. It is my responsibility to create a world fit for them to grow up in. I can't say I'm responsible for my children not catching whooping cough and not responsible for doing anything about the threat of annihilation that hangs over them every minute of the day.
>
> *(Quoted in Cook and Kirk 1983, p. 27)*

Human and Financial Costs of War

- Since 1900 there have been more than 250 wars. The civilian casualty rate in World War I was 5 percent, compared to 90 percent of war casualties in 1990, most of whom were women and children. This change is due in part to "deliberate and systematic violence against whole populations" (Swiss and Giller 1993, p. 612).

- There are approximately 50 million up-rooted people around the world due to war—refugees who have sought safety in another country and people displaced within their own country. Between 75 and 80 percent of them are women and children who have lost their homes, farms, and sources of livelihood (UN High Commission for Refugees 2002).

- Women are subjected to widespread sexual abuse in wartime. In the 1990s in Bosnia and Rwanda, rape was a deliberate weapon of war.

- World military expenditure has been increasing since 1998, after an eleven-year period of reductions (1987–98). In 2003 it amounted to an estimated $956 billion, not including supplementary spending as a result of the September 11 attacks on the United States and the subsequent war on terrorism (Stockholm International Peace Research Institute 2005).

- Combat-related and reconstruction costs for the wars against Afghanistan and Iraq have been estimated at approximately $70 billion (2003), over $80 billion (2004), and over $100 billion (2005) (War Resisters League 2005).

- The Department of Defense budget for fiscal year 2006 is $427. Of this, U.S. taxpayers will pay $17.5 billion for nuclear weapons. The same amount of money could pay the salaries of 303,089 elementary school teachers or to build 2,058 new elementary schools. $9.6 billion is allocated for ballistic missile defense; this could provide scholarships for 1,853,209 students at four-year colleges and universities (National Priorities Project, "Federal Budget Trade-offs" www.database. national-priorities.org/tradeoff).

- The cost of one multiple launcher rocket system loaded with ballistic missiles (a long-range self-propelled artillery weapon widely used in the 1991 Persian Gulf War), at $29 million, could have supplied one year's basic rural water and sanitation services for 2 million people in developing countries (Sivard 1996).

- In Cambodia, where one of every 236 people is an amputee; there are as many land mines planted as there are people (estimated 10 million mines and 9.9 million people) (Sivard 1996).

Although this approach can sentimentalize motherhood, it is also powerful because mothers are behaving according to their roles and it is difficult for the state to suppress them. They expose contradictions: that the state, through militarism, does not let them get on with their job of mothering.

Diversion of Military Budgets to Socially Useful Programs   Another argument put forward by peace activists—women and men—concerns government spending. Organizations like Women's Action for New Directions (WAND, Arlington, Mass.) and the Women's International League for Peace and Freedom (WILPF, U.S. Section, Philadelphia) argue

for reductions in military expenditures and redistribution of those funds to provide for social programs that benefit women and their families. Cuts in funding for nuclear weapons, chemical and biological weapons, and U.S. troops, ships, and aircraft carriers around the world, they argue, could fund job-training programs, public housing, education, urban development, environmental cleanup, and AIDS research, for example. They would enable cuts in Medicaid, food stamps, and child nutrition programs to be restored. Former legislative and executive director for WILPF (U.S. section) Jane Midgley (2005) explains the federal budget process; she presents gender-sensitive ways of thinking about government spending and alternative people-centered budgets.

Women's Action for New Directions is organizing nationwide on the issue of the bloated military budget. When tax dollars are diverted from civilian programs like education and health care, where many women are employed, military spending is also at the expense of women's jobs (Anderson 1999). Economist and director of Employment Research Associates Marion Anderson (1999) notes that "every $1 billion transferred from the Pentagon to these civilian expenditures generates a net gain of about 6,800 women's jobs" (p. 248).

The Military as a Sexist and Racist Institution

Opposition to the military also turns on the argument that, by its very nature, the military is profoundly antifeminist and racist and is fundamental to political systems that oppress women and peoples of color. Its ultimate effectiveness depends on people's ability to see reality in oppositional categories: us and them, friends and enemies, kill or be killed (Reardon 1985). To this end it is organized on rigidly hierarchical lines, demanding unquestioning obedience to superiors. Although the military uses women's labor in many ways, as mentioned earlier, it does so strictly on its own terms. The military environment also fosters violence against women. The higher incidence of domestic violence in military families than in nonmilitary families and crimes of violence against women committed near military bases in the United States and overseas are not coincidences but integral aspects of military life and training (Morris 1999). Moreover, rape is used as a weapon of war (Peterson and Runyan 1993; Rayner 1997; Tétreault 1997), as mentioned in Chapter 6 (and Reading 40).

This opposition focuses not only on how the military operates but also on militarism as an underlying system and worldview based on the objectification of "others" as enemies, a culture that celebrates war and killing (Reardon 1985). The Women's Pentagon Action, for example, identified militarism as a cornerstone of the oppression of women and the destruction of the nonhuman world. Thousands of women surrounded the Pentagon in November 1980 and again in 1981. They protested massive military budgets; the fact that militaries cause more ecological destruction than any other institutions; the widespread, everyday culture of violence manifested in war toys, films, and video

games; the connection between violence and sexuality in pornography, rape, battering, and incest; and the connections between militarism and racism. This was no routine demonstration but a highly creative action organized in four stages: mourning, rage, empowerment, and defiance, culminating in the arrest of many women who chose to blockade the doors of the Pentagon (King 1983). The Unity Statement of the Women's Pentagon Action is included as Reading 70.

At an Okinawan rally on violence and human rights violations against girls and women in September 1995, a women's declaration pointed to military training as a systematic process of dehumanization that turns "soldiers into war machines who inflict violence on the Okinawan community, only a chain-link fence away" (Okinawa Women Act against Military Violence 1996, p. 7). These activists see crucial connections between personal violence and international violence, both based on the objectification of others. Political scientist Cynthia Enloe's (1990, 1993b) concept of a constructed militarized masculinity fits in here. Citing the sexual assault of women at the Tailhook meeting of Navy aviators in 1991, the general incidence of sexual assault on military women, men's resistance to women in combat, and fears about openly gay men and lesbians in the military, she argues that the U.S. military is based on very specific notions of "militarized masculinity" (Enloe 1993b). Thus, women in combat roles threaten the manliness of war and the very nature of militarism as male.

Women who oppose militarism have very different perspectives from those who enter the military. They may also have different class positions and more opportunities for education and work. Liberal feminists have criticized feminist peace activists as classist and racist in their condemnation of the military as an employer when working women, especially women of color, have few employment options. While liberal feminists call for women's equality within the military, the Unity Statement of the Women's Pentagon Action argues for equality between men and women but against participation in the military for either sex. Peace activists also argue that the military is no place for gay men and lesbians. Jean Grossholtz (Reading 69) writes that, ironically, it was her involvement in the military, seeing casualties of the Korean War, that changed her views and led her to become a peace activist

DO YOU HAVE A FEMALE *ACTION FIGURE*
THAT SPEAKS OUT AGAINST
DISCRIMINATION AND WAR !?

later in life. Professor of sociology and activist Barbara Omolade (1989) notes the contradictions of militarism for people of color in the United States, many of whom support the military because it provides economic opportunities that are lacking in civilian society. Military personnel of color fight for the United States, a country where they are oppressed. Since World War II, the people they have fought against and are trained to kill are other people of color in various parts of the world—Vietnam, Grenada, Libya, Panama, and Iraq—to take examples from the past several decades.

Globalization and Militarism   Increasingly those who oppose war are linking up with people who oppose the globalization of the economy, understanding that the military system is much broader than war and a core element in the global economy. Colonial expansion and the quest for control of strategic locations and scarce resources have been a major justification and impetus for military intervention for centuries. In the current war on Iraq, a key issue is access to oil supplies. Steven Staples, Chair of the International Network on Disarmament and Globalization (Vancouver, Canada), argues that

> globalization and militarism should be seen as two sides of the same coin. On the one side,

globalization promotes the conditions that lead to unrest, inequality, conflict, and, ultimately war. On the other side, globalization fuels the means to wage war by protecting and promoting the military industries needed to produce sophisticated weaponry. This weaponry, in turn, is used or is threatened to be used to protect the investments of transnational corporations and their shareholders (Staples 2000, p. 18).

Nation-states, militaries, and corporations are increasingly intertwined as military functions are privatized and outsourced (Ferguson and Turnbull 2004). As far back as 1961, President Dwight Eisenhower warned against the power of the "military industrial complex" in a speech on leaving office. Political scientist Spike Peterson has used the term "military industrial congressional academic media complex" to refer to these institutional interconnections which include "revolving-door job opportunities" among the higher echelons of government, military, and corporations. Secretary of State Condoleeza Rice is one of the few women in this loop—formerly a political science professor, administrator, and Provost of Stanford University, she was also on the board of Chevron oil company. Military contractors, like Lockheed Martin and Haliburton, provide substantial campaign contributions and receive government contracts valued in billions of dollars.

As well as employing personnel, the U.S. military provides work for weapons designers, researchers, manufacturers, and salespeople; and companies that produce and sell vehicles, uniforms, foods, and equipment. Governments pay for major weapons systems twice over: public funds underwrite lengthy research and development processes and governments are the sole customers for these weapons. Staples (2000, p. 19) argues that the large U.S. military budget "is for all practical purposes a corporate subsidy" siphoning public money into private hands, and protected under Article XXI of the General Agreement on Tariffs and Trade (GATT), which allows "governments free reign for action taken for national security interests."

The international arms trade, especially trade in smaller arms, is a central part of the global economy because it is an earner of hard currency and a way for many countries to repay foreign debt. Major bombing and missile strikes function like giant bazaars for arms manufacturers as war-tested planes and munitions command a price double or triple that of weapons without such testing. Jostling for contracts to rebuild Iraq was well underway before the war was started, as reported on the business pages and in the financial press.

Redefining Security

Since the attacks of September 11, 2001, and the Bush administration's immediate decision to take military action, many people have questioned whether the military and militarism—as a system of values and operations—can provide human security, as opposed to national security. In Reading 82, Charlotte Bunch, director of the Center for Women's Global Leadership (Rutgers University, N.J.), argues for a redefinition of security based on human rights, for example. American sympathy for the brutal treatment of Afghan women at the hands of the Taliban regime was used to build support for the bombing of Afghanistan in 2001. Prior to this time, successive administrations had not shown much concern for women in Afghanistan. Madeleine Albright, Secretary of State under President Clinton, attempted to take up their cause but did not speak out against U.S. economic sanctions against Iraq in the 1990s, which contributed to the deaths of many thousands of women and children. First Lady Laura Bush assured the nation that bombing Afghanistan would liberate Afghan women, but advocates for Afghan women like Sonali Kolhatkar, founding director of the nonprofit Afghan Women's Mission, argue that this was little more than a cynical ploy to influence U.S. public opinion and mobilize consent for the bombing (Kolhatkar 2004). Anthropologists Lila Abu-Lughod (2002), and Charles Hirschkind and Saba Mahmood (2002) critique cultural relativist assumptions in U.S. public debate some and solidarity events sponsored by established feminist organizations that used the discourse of "saving" Muslim women, reminiscent of colonial and missionary rhetoric. Note that as the First Lady deployed gender arguments seemingly in support of Muslim women, her own gender was also deployed. Similar arguments regarding Iraqi women's liberation were made by President Bush and British Prime Minister Tony Blair in 2003 to justify the bombing of Iraq. Critics have called attention to the fact that Afghan

and Iraqi women desperately need military operations to stop, resources to rebuild their homes and communities, genuine solidarity and support from feminists of other countries, and full involvement in peace-making processes (Heyzer 2005; Kolhatkar 2004, 2005).

This international crisis has given new impetus to feminist understandings of links between U.S. domestic and foreign policy. It generated new energy for established organizations like Women's International League for Peace and Freedom (Philadelphia), Women's Action for New Directions (WAND, Arlington, Mass.), Women in Black (New York and other cities), and Women Against Military Madness (Minneapolis). It has also generated many new groups and networks, including Code Pink (San Francisco and other cities), Mothers Acting Up (Boulder, Colo.), Gather the Women, the Lysistrata Project, Racial Justice 911, and Women United for Peace, all organizing in a decentralized way, often via the Internet. Student groups include Students Taking Action for New Directions (STAND, Atlanta). In November 2002, Code Pink: Women for Peace started a daily peace camp and vigil outside the White House in Washington, D.C., that culminated in a major rally and demonstration against war in Iraq on March 8, 2003, International Women's Day. Also on that day the International Wages for Housework Campaign organized a Global Women's Strike, under the slogan "Invest in Caring, Not Killing," with participating groups from over thirty countries. The Women of Color Resource Center (Oakland, Calif.) held an anti-military fashion show, "Fashion Resistance to Militarism," in 2005, highlighting—and critiquing—the upsurge of "camouflage chic" referred to earlier. On the international level, one thousand women were nominated as a group for the 2005 Nobel Peace Prize. This is a symbolic number to highlight the extent of women's enormous and varied work for peace worldwide and to show that peace is a collaborative effort (www.1000peacewomen.org).

Families for Peaceful Tomorrows came together in 2001 soon after the attacks of September 11, around their belief, "Our grief is not a cry for war." Military Families Speak Out, formed in 2002, is an organization of people who oppose the war in Iraq and who have relatives or loved ones in the military. Gold Star Families for Peace came to prominence in the summer of 2005, when Cindy Sheehan and members of other families who had lost loved ones in the war in Iraq camped outside the Bush family ranch in Crawford (Tex.), asking the president to explain why her son had died. The Central Committee for Conscientious Objectors counsels military personnel who want to leave, and the Youth and Militarism project of the American Friends Service Committee provides information for young people considering enlistment.

Based on data presented in this chapter, we argue that genuine security is not created by militarism. The UN Development Program lists four basic requirements for human security:

- The environment in which we live must be able to sustain human and natural life.

- People's basic survival needs for food, clothing, shelter, health care, and education must be met.

- People's fundamental human dignity, agency, and cultural identities must be honored.

- People and the natural environment must be protected from avoidable harm.

This view includes security for the individual—a major reason why women in the United States are drawn to enlist in the military—but also involves security at the meso, macro, and global levels, as described by Betty Burkes who sees peace in terms of wholeness and celebration (Reading 71; see also Boulding 1990; Reardon 1993).

Questions for Reflection

As you read and discuss this chapter, think about these questions:

1. What purposes does the military serve in this society?

2. Who joins the military? Why?

3. Why has the issue of gays in the military surfaced as an issue of mainstream U.S. politics?

4. What is your idea of security—at all levels of analysis?

5. What can you do to improve your sense of safety/security in different settings?

6. How do you understand the "war on terrorism"?

Finding Out More on the Web

1. Compare the proportion of the federal budget that is spent on education, social services, health, and foreign aid with that spent on the military. How much does your state contribute to the military budget? How much do you contribute? Use the following Web sites:

   Center for Defense Information: **www.cdi.org**

   National Priorities Project: **www.nationalpriorities.org**

   Stockholm International Peace Research Institute: **www.sipri.org**

   War Resisters League: **www.warresisters.org**

2. Find out more about the organizations mentioned in this chapter. What are their strategies and activities?

◆◆◆

Taking Action

1. Think about the ways you usually resolve conflicts or serious differences of opinion with your family, friends and peers, teachers, and employers. What are the dynamics involved in each case? Do you cave in without expressing your opinion? Do you insist that you are right? Does violence play a part in this process? If so, why? What, if anything, do you want to do differently about this in the future?

2. List all the kinds of service you can imagine, as an alternative to military service, that would improve people's security.

3. Analyze the representation of armed conflict and war in the news media or popular culture.

4. Using the information about federal spending you found on the Web, make a budget to provide for genuine security.

5. Research the Women of Color Resource Center's anti-military fashion show (www. coloredgirls.org) and create your own anti-military fashion show on campus or in your community.

SIXTY-FIVE

◆◆◆

Sneak Attack (2002)
The Militarization of U.S. Culture

Cynthia Enloe

Cynthia Enloe is Research Professor in International Development and Women's Studies at Clark University. Her nine books focus on women's roles in globalization and militarization, most recently, *The Curious Feminist: Searching for Women in The New Age of Empire* and *Maneuvers: The International Politics of Militarizing Women's Lives.* She has written for *Ms. Magazine* and *Village Voice,* and serves on the editorial boards of several scholarly journals, including *Signs* and the *International Feminist Journal of Politics.*

Things start to become militarized when their legitimacy depends on their associations with military goals. When something becomes militarized, it appears to rise in value. Militarization is seductive.

But it is really a process of loss. Even though something seems to gain value by adopting an association with military goals, it actually surrenders control and gives up the claim to its own worthiness.

Militarization is a sneaky sort of transformative process. Sometimes it is only in the pursuit of *de*militarization that we become aware of just how far down the road of complete militarization we've gone. Representative Barbara Lee (D.-Calif.) pulled back the curtain in the aftermath of the September 11 attacks when she cast the lone vote against giving George W. Bush carte blanche to wage war. The loneliness of her vote suggested how far the militarization of Congress—and its voters back home—has advanced. In fact, since September 11, publicly criticizing militarization has been widely viewed as an act of disloyalty.

Whole cultures can be militarized. It is a militarized U.S. culture that has made it easier for Bush to wage war without most Americans finding it dangerous to democracy. Our cultural militarization makes war-waging seem like a comforting reconfirmation of our collective security, identity and pride.

Other sectors of U.S. culture have also been militarized:

- **Education.** School board members accept Jr. ROTC programs for their teenagers, and social studies teachers play it safe by avoiding discussions of past sexual misconduct by U.S. soldiers overseas. Many university scientists pursue lucrative Defense Department weapons research contracts.

- **Soldiers' girlfriends and wives.** They've been persuaded that they are "good citizens" if they keep silent about problems in their relationships with male soldiers for the sake of their fighting effectiveness.

- **Beauty.** [In 2002] the Miss America Pageant organizers selected judges with military credentials, including a former Secretary of the Navy and an Air Force captain.

- **Cars.** The Humvee ranks among the more bovine vehicles to clog U.S. highways, yet civilians think they will be feared and admired if they drive them.

Then there is the conundrum of the flag. People who reject militarization may don a flag pin, unaware that doing so may convince those with a militarized view of the U.S. flag that their bias is universally shared, thus deepening the militarization of culture.

The events of post–September 11 have also shown that many Americans today may be militarizing non-U.S. women's lives. It was only after Bush declared "war on terrorists and those countries that harbor them" that the violation of Afghan women's human rights took center stage. Here's the test of whether Afghan women are being militarized: if their well-being is worthy of our concern only because their lack of well-being justifies the U.S.'s bombing of Afghanistan, then we are militarizing Afghan women—as well as our own compassion. We are thereby complicit in the notion that something has worth only if it allows militaries to achieve their missions.

It's important to remember that militarization has its rewards, such as new-found popular support for measures formerly contested. For example, will many Americans now be persuaded that drilling for oil in the Alaskan wilderness is acceptable because it will be framed in terms of "national security"? Will most U.S. citizens now accept government raids on the Social Security trust fund in the name of paying for the war on terrorism?

Women's rights in the U.S. and Afghanistan are in danger if they become mere by-products of some other cause. Militarization, in all its seductiveness and subtlety, deserves to be bedecked with flags wherever it thrives—fluorescent flags of warning.

◆◆◆

The Siege (2004)

Kristin Henderson

Recipient of a Bread Loaf nonfiction fellowship and a nominee for the Pushcart Prize, **Kristin Henderson** is a frequent contributor to the *Washington Post Magazine*. She is the wife of a Navy chaplain and often writes about the military spouse's perspective on deployment, personal relationships, and family life.

Going to war is never easy, but neither is being left behind.

Beth Pratt hunched on a chair in the anonymous, fluorescent-lit exam room of a health clinic on Fort Bragg, N.C. It was a wintry day in early March, she remembers, and her dancer's body drooped with sadness. She picked at the skin around her fingernails.

The nurse practitioner rustled through the door. "So, what brings you in to us today?"

"Oh," said Beth and stopped. Her voice was thin and scratchy. She started again. "I'm having a really hard time with my husband gone." Her husband was deployed to Iraq five months before. "I think I'm really depressed." She started to cry. "I cry like this all the time. And I just want it to stop."

Beth remembers that the nurse practitioner nodded. She was older, with the calm, comforting air of a woman who has raised a whole brood of children and seen it all. She nudged Beth with the usual questions: *Are you feeling any sense of hopelessness or helplessness? Have your sleeping habits changed? Have your eating habits changed? Have you lost weight? How about a change in sexual desire?* Yes, Beth said to each question, struggling to get the word out, yes, yes, yes, and yes, adding to the last, "Actually I don't know, since my husband's not here." And her face crumpled again.

"Honey, have you had any suicidal thoughts?"

Beth didn't say anything. She just nodded.

"Do you have a plan? What are you thinking about?"

"I've been thinking," Beth said softly, "that if I had a gun, I'd shoot myself."

Around the same time, on a back road on Fort Bragg, just a few miles from the health clinic, a gold hand-me-down sedan was doing 70 in a 55-mph zone when the blue and red lights came on behind it, forcing the driver, Marissa Bootes, to stop. It was midnight. The military policeman asked, "Do you know what speed you were going?"

"I have to get to the hospital," Marissa recalls saying. "My daughter woke up screaming that her head hurt. She has a temperature of almost 104; she's burning up. I'm afraid she might have that viral infection that's been going around, that kids have been dying of."

The MP flicked his flashlight over 5-year-old Lexie slumped in her seat. Her hair was wet with sweat, her cheeks flaming, the rest of her skin clammy and pale. The MP frowned, unconvinced. "I hope you're not lying to me."

"Look at me!" said Marissa. "I'm wearing sweats and I've got a sick kid in the back seat. Where else would I be going at 70 miles an hour in the middle of the night?"

He let her go—he just asked her to do him a favor and slow down. Her husband was riding con-

voys in Iraq. Now their kid was sick. She wasn't slowing down for anybody. She hit the accelerator and sped the rest of the way to the Army hospital.

Five hours later, Lexie's temperature was headed back down, and they were dragging home. Before Marissa fell into bed, she says, she faxed the doctor's excuse to her supervisor at the law firm where she worked as a paralegal. She'd landed this job just before her husband was deployed four months earlier, and it was her dream job. But if she tried to drive to those 8 A.M. foreclosure hearings, she might just wrap the company car around a tree. The firm could get someone else to cover the hearings.

At 9, her supervisor was on the phone with one clear message: If those hearings happened without her, she was fired.

Both Marissa Bootes and Beth Pratt are married to lower-level enlisted men in the 82nd Airborne Division. Beth's husband, Pvt. E-2 Luigi Pratt, drove Army trucks on convoys through Iraq's Sunni Triangle. On other convoys along those same roads, Marissa's husband, Spec. Charlie Bootes, manned a Mark-19 fully automatic grenade launcher.

Marissa and Beth have never met. Marissa, 24, grew up in foster homes, has a two-year college degree and is married to her high school sweetheart. On the subject of the war, she had no patience for Americans protesting in the streets; it killed morale, she said, made life harder for soldiers and their families. Beth, 34, had a happy childhood, holds multiple postgraduate degrees and is newly married for the second time, no children. As for the war, she believed it was wrong from the start. The U.N. weapons inspectors, it seemed to her, had been doing just fine. Beth and Marissa didn't have much in common except for this: In the fall of 2003, they both faced the frightening challenge of their husbands' first deployments.

A soldier whose family is struggling with deployment may have a hard time focusing on his or her job. In a combat zone, that's dangerous. Such soldiers may also suffer from low morale and may be less likely to reenlist. "You enlist soldiers," says retired Air Force Lt. Col. Lillie Cannon, who is married to a Fort Bragg Army colonel. "You retain families."

The idea that families are crucial to military readiness is now official policy in an era when, according to a 2002 study by the Military Family Resource Center, half of all service members are married. But families haven't always been a priority at the Pentagon. During Vietnam, when young, single draftees served for two years and got out, only 25 percent were married. If a soldier lived on post with his family, when that soldier went to war, his family had to go live somewhere else.

Outside Fort Bragg in the 1960s, Joanne Hunt lived with her young son in Fayetteville, N.C., in the Dreamland Trailer Court, while her husband served three tours in Vietnam with Army Special Forces. "The place was full of women without husbands," she remembers. "They were all in Vietnam."

Every day, she says, a staff car would come through Dreamland, and the women would watch out their windows to see if it stopped at the trailer of a friend. If it did, they hurried over to comfort her, because her husband wasn't coming home again. They were all the support they had. The loneliness, the sense of isolation from the wider world, could seem unbearable. When Hunt thinks back on the Special Forces wives she knew from that time, she can't remember a single marriage that survived Dreamland. Including her own.

Hunt quotes an old saying: "If the Army wanted you to have a wife, it would have issued you one. In my day, it was true. You had your ID card, you could shop the commissary and go to the hospital, but other than that, while your husband was deployed, the military had no more to do with you."

Military families owe the support they receive today in large part to women like Hunt. In the mid-'70s, as the Army shifted to an all-volunteer force, she participated in a family life symposium, an early effort to improve the Army's support for families. During the '80s, there was a family liaison office up at the Pentagon, and down at the unit level, commanders began organizing their soldiers' spouses into Family Readiness Groups.

The FRG volunteers pass information between the Army unit commander and the families and let families know where to find needed services. The other military services have similar programs, and they all rely on spouses who volunteer to help other spouses adjust to the military or a new duty station, prepare for deployment and then get through it.

For spouses, the initial couple of months of any first deployment are usually the toughest. Then, "families typically adjust and realize, I can take care of this, I can perform these roles," explains Lt. Col. Joseph Pecko, chief of the department of social work at Womack Army Medical Center on Fort Bragg. "A lot of the problems we will see after that is when there is no breather, no respite for the spouse. The family moved here away from loved ones, and they really become isolated."

That's a peacetime deployment. A deployment in wartime raises the stakes. As casualties mounted in Iraq, the chaplains of the 82nd Airborne began to notice a wave of symptoms sweeping through the division's spouses—depression, insomnia, shortness of breath, crying jags—the same symptoms that people often experience after the death of a loved one. It's a common reaction among spouses during a wartime deployment, and it has a name—anticipatory grief.

Fort Bragg and neighboring Pope Air Force Base make up one of the world's biggest military complexes. It alone bustles with more than 45,000 soldiers in the airborne and Special Forces. Before September 11, 2001, on any given day, there were 4,000 or 5,000 soldiers deployed out of Fort Bragg around the world. Two years later, that number had topped 24,000.

Families say goodbye here all the time.

Beth Pratt remembers watching Luigi get his gear together—rain poncho, canteens, gas mask. It was September and it was cold, just before dawn outside his unit's big, brick headquarters. She was seeping tears. He was sweating. Another soldier, passing by, asked Beth, "He's not sick, is he?"

She shook her head. "He's okay. He just sweats when he's nervous."

Beth says Luigi walked her out to her white compact car in the parking lot. "I hate this war," she said. Whenever she said that, her voice took on the tone of a child who's been wronged. "I don't know why we had to go in there in the first place."

Luigi nodded. Then he said: "Uh-oh, they called formation. I got to go." A quick hug and a kiss, as if he were just going down the street, and then he was gone.

While Luigi and the other soldiers in his unit waited for the buses that would take them to the airfield at Pope, Beth says, she drove home to their tiny, rented duplex, where his surfboard leaned in a corner of the living room and her pink pointe shoes hung by their ribbons on the wall next to her drum kit, which she hadn't touched since moving here.

A few hours later, her cell phone rang. It was Camilla Maki, whose husband was a noncommissioned officer in Luigi's platoon. Maki was an FRG volunteer and Beth's contact on the families' phone tree. "Beth, you need to come out here to Green Ramp to see him before he leaves," she said.

Green Ramp was what passed for a waiting terminal at the airfield. Beth wiped her nose with a tissue. "I'm not up to it, really. Anyway, I thought we're not allowed to go to Green Ramp."

"Screw'em," Camilla remembers saying, "come on."

By the time they got to Green Ramp, it was nearly noon and the other wives had been shooed away. Beth peered in the door of the hulking concrete-block building. Men in beige desert camouflage stood and sat on rows and rows of bleachers like drifts of sand, talking, reading, sleeping, killing time.

Someone yelled, "Pratt! Your wife's here!" and several rows over, Luigi jumped up. Beth recalls a surf magazine flapping open in his hand, his grin getting bigger and bigger the closer he came. "Oh my God!" He wrapped her in a bear hug. "You came back!"

She'd given him the magazine while he was packing. She'd written something on every page: I'm so lucky you showed up on my doorstep . . . You make my life complete . . . He'd already read them all. They stood there grinning at each other, his hands resting on her hips, her red-rimmed eyes almost level with his.

Eventually someone yelled: "Pratt! Get over here!" Beth hugged him, but he was wearing his Kevlar vest, and to her he felt awkwardly hard and inhuman. She turned away before he walked out the door to the plane.

A week later, it was Marissa Bootes's turn. The Bootes's prefab starter home is one of many in a neighborhood built right up against a tall, chain-link fence. On the other side of that fence is Fort Bragg. Some days, when Marissa walks out on the back deck, the sky is polka-dotted with parachutes, airborne troopers drifting silently down to the drop zone beyond the pine trees.

The alarm woke Marissa at 4 A.M. She slid out of bed without turning on the light. She says she showered and dressed fast, shoved files into her briefcase as she combed out her wet hair, but before she left the house, she remembers, she sat on the edge of the double bed and watched Charlie sleep.

He was supposed to be gone. Yesterday, at the last minute, the flight was postponed, and she called her supervisor at the law firm to ask if someone could please cover her hearings this morning so she could be there to say goodbye. But she got nowhere with the supervisor, and so here she was, stealing a few last minutes, watching him breathe.

He didn't wake up when she kissed him. "I love you," she whispered.

She recalls walking down the hall to Lexie's room and kissing her, too, before slipping back through the long strands of pink and purple crystals that hung in Lexie's doorway. They were still swaying and clicking when the front door closed.

They'd been High School sweethearts in Erie, Pa., the blond boy-next-door and the daughter of a flower child and a Vietnamese refugee. Back then, Marissa was competing in beauty pageants for Hawaiian Tropic and making plans to go to college and law school. She wanted to work on behalf of neglected children. But then, she found out she was pregnant.

She shifted gears, decided to become a paralegal instead. Charlie worked the graveyard shift at a plastics assembly shop to put her through business college; she worked part time at a gas station, and their families helped watch Lexie during the day.

A few days after September 11, 2001, while the couple was on the couch in their trailer watching TV, Charlie said, "I'm thinking about joining the Army."

Marissa remembers exclaiming, "Oh my God, why would you join now?" But, really, she knew why. They weren't flying a flag, but they'd been talking about how patriotic they felt, like the whole country was in this together. "Is that really what you want to do?"

"I don't know what I want to do," Charlie says he told her. "All I know is, I'm killing myself on third shift. I'm working 70 hours a week and we're still living paycheck to paycheck. We're not going anywhere, Marissa."

They talked about it for a while. Beneath the chassis of the trailer, the wheels were blocked in place. Marissa looked at Charlie. "You're right," she said. "We need to get out of this town and never come back."

Within a year she'd finished school, he'd finished training, and they'd moved to Fayetteville and bought a house. Not long after that, Marissa landed a job with a big law firm out of Charlotte that sent her to county courthouses all over the eastern half of the state. It was high-pressure but high-paying. For the first time in their lives, they didn't have to worry about money.

Beth Pratt's journey toward Fort Bragg began in Minnesota. As soon as she got off the farm where she grew up, she went to college on a scholarship and didn't stop until she had earned degrees in biology, Spanish, nursing and forensic science. About the same time that Marissa was moving to Fayetteville, Beth was at a friend's house in South Florida, falling in love with an easygoing surfer just as he was leaving for basic training. Luigi Pratt, at 30, had joined the Army hoping to get money for college and to help out his immigrant mother with some steady income.

Beth worked as a nurse at a jail clinic. She says she was warned by one of the deputies who had served in the military, "You know he's going to get sent off, right?"

"Yeah," she said, "I know."

"It's not an easy life," she remembers him saying. "I don't know that you're going to like it that much."

She wasn't sure she would, either. But she'd been married before. Her first husband had never made her feel the way Luigi did, like she was a treasure he'd discovered, and she wasn't willing to give that up. So she sold the house she loved in Florida, married the man she loved more, and followed him to Fayetteville, leaving behind her job, her friends, her life.

In Fayetteville, she started knocking on doors, looking for a job in forensics. Nothing opened. She wound up settling for a nursing job in labor and delivery at the Army hospital on Fort Bragg, and she and Luigi began trying to start a family themselves. Within five months, they learned they needed treatment for infertility. Just as they were trying to overcome that blow, Luigi was sent to Iraq.

In the labor and delivery rooms at the Army hospital, a lot of the pregnant women were there with their mothers, sisters or girlfriends. The husbands were overseas—gone to Iraq, Afghanistan, South Korea, Colombia.

Beth worked the overnight shift. Sometimes she'd walk into a delivery room to check on a patient and the TV would be turned to the news. She remembers always doing her best to get out of there before the newscast got around to the latest on the war in Iraq. While some military spouses are addicted to the news, some don't watch at all—it just reinforces the fear.

Sometimes, in the nurse's station, Beth would listen while other nurses talked about the war, about how it was a good thing. She says she felt like asking them, *Where are all those weapons of mass destruction that were supposed to be there?* But she didn't have the nerve to disagree with them out loud, not in an Army hospital. She felt like enough of an outsider as it was.

When she got back home in the morning, she would push a videotape into the VCR and sit on the couch to watch. It was 10 minutes of Luigi surfing, goofing around on the beach, playing with their dog in the living room, taking a shower. "Show me your butt," her voice called, laughing, from behind the camera. Now she couldn't watch without reaching for a tissue.

Military spouses who've been through a deployment always offer one standard piece of advice: Stay busy, but don't forget to take care of yourself. Marissa Bootes took only the first half of that advice. She had been nervous when Charlie left, afraid she wouldn't be able to juggle all the responsibilities without him. But a month into it, she had it all figured out, starting with when and where to cry.

She hadn't cried at all the first two weeks after she kissed him goodbye. Then one day it hit her, the fear that he wouldn't come back. Crying in the car, she'd arrive at a courthouse puffy-eyed and red-nosed; crying at night left her stuffy and headachy and unable to sleep, and sleep was important—it was the only time her fear for him wasn't scratching somewhere at her brain. But in the shower she discovered she could bawl as long and as hard as she wanted and no one would hear, plus the steam kept her nose open and her eyes from getting puffy. So each morning, she says, she'd leave Lexie asleep in the double bed, get her cry out of the way and get on with her day. If later on the fear started to get to her again, she told herself that Charlie was doing work that had to be done, helping the United States fulfill its promise to the Iraqi people and making the world a better place. She found comfort in that.

One night after picking up Lexie from the babysitter, Marissa got back to the house around 9. She loved her new job as a paralegal, loved the challenge of ferreting out titles on foreclosed properties and then managing the real estate auctions on her own. She just wished the hours weren't so long. She says she felt guilty about being away from Lexie so much. She threw the bills from the mailbox onto the pile on the coffee table and charged around to feed the dog, scoop up an armload of dirty clothes from the bathroom floor and crank on the faucet for Lexie's shower.

Nothing happened. She tried the sink. Nothing.

She remembers running out into the cold and circling the house. The yard around the foundation was bone dry, no sign of a burst pipe. It was a mystery, but there was nothing she could do about it till morning. She tucked Lexie into bed and sat down at the computer in the dining room. At midnight, she was still working.

The next morning, wearing her cell phone headset as she raced between counties, she called the water company from the car. "I don't know why my water's shut off," she said. "Is there a problem in the area?"

"Let me check." There was a pause, then, "Uh, you know you didn't pay your bill?"

"But we always pay our bills—" she began. Except it wasn't we who'd always paid them. It was Charlie. Marissa chewed her lip. After he left, she would figure out how to mow the lawn, whacking bushes with a hedge trimmer for the first time in her life. "Baby, I'm amazing!" she told him once when he called, and he agreed. She thought she had figured out his system for paying the bills, too. The water bill was $25. It cost her $60 to get the water reconnected.

It was "Nickel Night," and Broadstreet Cafe and Billiards was thumping. The good music, the hip-hop, started around midnight, and people packed onto the dance floor and around the pool tables and in front of the bars ordering nickel drinks.

Marissa was in the dance pack with her club gear on—shiny silver zippers up and down the legs of her shiny black pants, silver multi-chain belt and, on her feet, her platform dancing shoes. Charlie says he told her to go out and have fun, so here she was. She'd been dancing all night. She never lacked for partners, all of them women. They were the Hooah Wives, one of several online support groups of Fort Bragg wives. "Hoo-*ah*!" That's what soldiers shout in the Army—it means "Good to go!" or "Way to go!" At Broadstreet's that night, there were about a dozen of them. Within a few months they'd number nearly 40, with husbands in units all over the post. They were a variety of ethnicities and religions, some with children, some without, but mostly younger, as young as 18. The group's two den mothers, Jenn Marner and Angela McGriff, were 26

and 33. About one-third of their husbands, including Angela's, were overseas.

Even though Marissa was active in her FRG, this was the group she says she really depended on. One woman's husband called it the cult—they all e-mailed one another obsessively, talked for hours on the phone. Several times a week, one group or another of them hung out in one another's kitchens, hosted coffees, threw impromptu daiquiri parties. Every now and then, they went out dancing with one another.

Marissa worked her way through the crowd back to the table. They were celebrating the birthday of Christine Perry, who liked to introduce herself as "half Korean, like Marissa's half Vietnamese. So, basically, she could do my nails, and I could do her dry cleaning." Christine remembers opening presents, everybody blinding one another with flash photos. When the talk turned to push-up bras, Christine pointed out, matter-of-factly, that she and Marissa didn't need them.

Another woman shouted over the music, "Well *some* of us *do*!" This woman was the kind of person who, when she talked, you could almost see the italics and exclamation points. "But I don't *buy* those damn bras, they're too *expensive*! I use *tube socks*! They give that added *boost*!"

All the Hooah Wives laughed. They laughed harder as the woman made a big show of digging around in her decolletage, as if she were really going to pull out a tube sock. When she actually did, they screamed. She waved it over her head. The guys at the next table were so impressed they sent over a round of drinks.

"Oh my God!" someone hissed, just loud enough to be heard through the music. "Look who just came in."

Someone else said, "Look who she came in *with*." Marissa turned to look. A young woman was leading a guy toward them through the crush. They all knew her, and they all knew her husband was deployed. Marissa's face soured like she'd just chomped the lime in her Corona.

The woman shouted hi and handed a present to Christine. A few voices shouted hi back as if nothing was wrong. Marissa smoked and watched as the two of them made their way around the table to a couple of empty seats beside her. As they sat down, Marissa shouted over the music: "Look, if you're going to cheat on your husband while he's gone, that's your business. But get the hell away from me, 'cause guys talk, and I don't want anybody saying I'm hanging out with you."

Marissa says the woman's eyes widened, her mouth opened slightly. Then the woman got up and pulled the guy away with her into the dancing, sweating crowd.

In a sunny office on Fort Bragg, Maj. James Hartz, a chaplain in forest-green camouflage with a black cross on the lapel, is getting ready to deploy to Korea for a year. Before becoming an ordained minister and then a chaplain, he was an MP. He was a young enlisted soldier once. According to him, they aren't all as accepting as Marissa's husband.

"For some young deployed soldiers," he says, "just the fact that the wife's going to a bar doesn't sit well, the fact that she's out there where she's available. The wives say they only dance with each other, but there are guys there, right? He'll ask, 'Do you talk to them?' And she'll say no. But he's thinking, 'But they're looking at you.' So you can see where this goes in his mind. It plants the seed of doubt."

Over at the Army hospital, social worker Pecko's tough camouflage and harsh haircut are undermined by his eyes, which have seen a lot of other people's pain. "I was deployed nine months in the first Gulf War," he says gently. "After six or seven months, even I was having those thoughts, and my wife and I have a strong, long-term relationship. There was no rational reason. I was just feeling vulnerable."

Beth Pratt knows what that feels like. She recalls someone at work saying, *You know guys always cheat when they're over there.* It stuck in her head. She told herself Luigi hadn't done anything to make her suspicious, but then one evening she was sitting in an FRG meeting, listening to the women next to her compare notes. "My husband calls me every day just about," said one. They were all a lot younger than Beth. "Oh yeah, mine too," said another.

Beth says they asked how often she heard from her husband, like it was some sort of contest. "Well," she remembers saying, knowing she'd already lost, "I heard from him last week—for two minutes. Because the damn satellite telephone didn't work. You know, all the static—how're you doing, shhhhhhh. Yesterday I, shhhhhhh. Missing you, shhhhhhh. Click!"

The other women laughed because they knew what she was talking about. The conversation went on, but after that Beth didn't say much.

When the meeting was over, she went home and had another cry.

"Hey, Baby." Luigi's voice crackled over her cell phone. And then shhhhh-click, the connection went dead.

Beth was in a motel in Myrtle Beach, S.C., hanging out for the weekend with their friend Debbie McKay, who was up from Florida for business. In the minutes after the connection died, Beth told Debbie she was tired of it, she was tired of everything. She didn't know why she got married; it was like they weren't even married anymore. A few minutes later when the phone rang again, and she heard Luigi's relentlessly sunny voice from the other side of the world, she demanded, "Why don't you call me?"

"What do you mean?" he asked.

She was pacing. "Everybody else's husband calls them. Every day, practically. It just makes me wonder if you don't love me anymore."

"Don't—what?" He admits his voice went supernova, and Beth was so startled she stopped pacing. "I *work* all the time!" he yelled. "I don't know what you think I'm doing over here, baby, but I work *all the time*! I barely get to sleep! When can I talk to you? When?" He couldn't believe she'd think he didn't love her, yelled that even when he did find a minute to call her, he couldn't just pick up the phone—he had to stand in a long line, and then after a few minutes the phone would go dead. "You know I love you!" he yelled. "You're the person who keeps me sane!"

Beth was looking at the floor. She'd never heard him raise his voice like that before. She said softly, "I'm sorry." And then, quickly, before the line could go to hell again, she told him she loved him, too.

Afterward, she said to Debbie: "I'm glad he yelled at me. I needed to hear that. All I've been thinking about is the danger he's in when he's out on convoys. I didn't think about how hard he's working."

Debbie said, "I'm just glad you didn't mention you're lying around at the beach." Beth laughed then. But after that fight with Luigi, she decided not to get together with other soldiers' wives anymore. The things they said just made her paranoid.

She had few people she could talk to in Fayetteville. Now she had even fewer.

A short walk up the hill from Downtown, in a quiet neighborhood on a dead-end street, there's a scruffy blue bungalow with a small white, wooden sign in the front yard. "Quaker House," it says above a dove's silhouette. Since the Vietnam war, Quaker House's small, mostly volunteer staff has counseled military personnel who believe they've become conscientious objectors, helping them apply to either get out of the military or shift to noncombatant service.

With her husband in a war zone, Beth had been forced to think about war more than she ever had before. Talking about it with Luigi on the phone, she was starting to think that all wars were pointless, not just this one; so many innocent civilians died. The way she saw it, Saddam Hussein was bad, but there were a lot of bad dictators in the world, and America couldn't go fight all of them. The more she analyzed it, the angrier she got. So, earlier in the deployment, when another wife told Beth about Quaker House, she decided to meet with its director, Chuck Fager. She remembers feeling hopeful that afterward she'd be able to tell Luigi she'd found a way for both of them to act on what they believed. "My husband and I are both opposed to this war," she said to Fager. "Can you help him get out of the Army?"

Fager, gray-bearded and wearing khaki shorts and a T-shirt, slouched in his chair like a melancholy, off-duty Santa. He says he told her, "It's not easy." It's not. Successful applicants have to be able to prove they've changed and now believe the use of violence is always wrong. The process involves a lengthy application and interviews with a psychiatrist, a chaplain and an investigating officer. It's designed to weed out those who want out for political reasons, or are afraid of combat, or have a new spouse who wants them out.

"Chances of success are not good," Fager tells would-be applicants. "People who take this route need to be prepared to take a stand and suffer."

Listening to Fager, Beth knew Luigi wasn't the type to rock the boat. Besides, it was only this war he was opposed to. He said all along that he would be proud to serve in Afghanistan. By the time Beth left two hours later with an armload of application materials, she felt like she was sinking beneath their weight. She had always made her own decisions, controlled her own life, she says. Now she felt like she controlled nothing. She couldn't even help her own husband.

It began to pile up. Five months into the deployment, Beth found herself weeping in an Army health clinic, admitting to a nurse practitioner that if she had a gun she'd shoot herself.

When Beth went to the Health Clinic, she was just hoping to get something to make the pain go away. Within an hour, she had received a prescription for an antidepressant, as well as counseling from a social worker and an appointment to begin regular counseling sessions in town, paid for by the Pentagon. She hadn't known any of those services were available.

The social worker Beth saw was one of five behavioral health care managers on Fort Bragg, one at each of the post's health care facilities. The care managers are part of the Deployment Cycle Support program that was getting underway as Beth and Marissa's husbands took off for Iraq. The Army started developing it in the early 1990s, after one out of every seven service members returning from Desert Storm, according to Department of Defense data, either requested or required evaluation for Gulf War Syndrome (which involves an array of symptoms from chronic fatigue to abdominal pain). And then came the summer of 2002.

That summer, there were five domestic murders connected to Fort Bragg. Three cases involved deployed soldiers just back from Afghanistan who killed their wives; two of those soldiers then killed themselves. All the marriages had apparently been troubled beforehand, and none of the soldiers or their wives had reached out to any of the support programs the Army had available at the time. There's no evidence deployment was directly to blame. But chaplains and social workers report that, after any deployment, most couples pick up where they left off, good or bad.

An Army memo acknowledges that after a wartime deployment, service members and their families may also face "some degree of stress or trauma associated either with the nature of conflict or the disruption of their lives." As many as one in five may also face major depression, anxiety, or post-traumatic stress disorder, according to a report in the July issue of the *New England Journal of Medicine*. And most of those who need help won't seek it out, at least not right away.

Before the murders, the Deployment Cycle Support program was still in development after nearly a decade. The incidents "gave us the impetus for getting this program off the ground," Pecko says. It rolled out within a year. In addition to the care managers and other changes, the program requires all returning soldiers to undergo physical and mental health screening to uncover possible trouble.

However, there are no mandatory mental health surveys for the families. "Families didn't sign the contract; they aren't in the military," points out Jana Lord, coordinator of Army Family Team Building and Army Family Action Plan programs in Europe. "They can't be ordered to do anything, even for their own good."

When families need help and don't know how to get it, military medical personnel, social workers and chaplains can refer those who come to them. The real first responders are the spouse volunteers who lead the FRGs and the other services' family support groups, because they know where to get information. But like all volunteer efforts, some support groups thrive while others wither away. So why does the Pentagon invest so much money in family support services, then rely on a haphazard patchwork of volunteers to spread the word?

"One, it doesn't cost them anything," says Sylvia Kidd, director of family programs for the Association of the United States Army. "And, two, because of tradition, because that is the way it's always been . . . The military freely admits many of the programs wouldn't exist if it weren't for the volunteers working on them."

Besides being free, the use of volunteers has another advantage. They're not perceived as being part of the system. Spouses who need help are more likely to acknowledge it to a fellow spouse, someone like Marissa.

A couple months into the deployment, attrition left Marissa as co-leader of her FRG. Volunteering, working, single-parenting—she was doing it all. She was too busy to feel lonely, and that was how she liked it. She was also too busy to sleep more than four hours a night. She'd forget to eat. She lost 30 pounds in less than two months.

After the deployment's halfway point, at 4:30 on a Friday morning, the phone was ringing. Marissa felt for the handset next to the bed, pulled it over to her ear without lifting her head. It was Charlie. She tried to follow what he was saying because it sounded like it was important, but her eyes kept closing, dark bedroom, warm bed, Lexie's even breathing beside her. And then all of a sudden she heard, "What did I just say?"

"What?"

"If you're falling asleep," he snapped, "I'm going to go."

She was too tired to argue. "Okay."

"Do you know how long I had to stand in line to talk to you?"

"Look, I'm really tired," she said. "I'll talk to you later. Bye."

It wasn't till she woke up a couple hours later that she had the energy to be mad at him for being mad at her. When she complained the next day to some of the Hooah Wives, they say they told her: *Yeah, you work hard, but he's over there getting shot at every day. He calls you in the middle of the night because he needs to hear your voice? Well, you just better suck it up and be there for him.*

A couple of weeks later, Marissa was racing to the hospital with Lexie in the middle of the night and arguing with the MP; the next day she nearly lost her job. By the weekend, Lexie was still under the weather, so Marissa stretched out on the couch with her to just snuggle and watch cartoons. They'd been lying there a while, Marissa remembers, when Lexie said, from out of the blue, "Since Daddy's been gone, we don't get to snuggle and have fun anymore."

For a long, stunned moment, the only thing that moved was the animation on the TV screen. Then Marissa breathed, "You're right," and before she got off the couch that day, she'd made a decision.

She cut back on her work. Over the next couple weeks, her output dropped by a quarter. And then one morning her supervisor called to tell her she needed to do more.

"I can't do more." Marissa was already smoking and typing and wearing the headset, trying to get ready for her hearings that day while she talked. "I can't go back to where I was."

"Well, what you're giving us now isn't enough. I'm going to have to let you go."

"No." Marissa's hands went still. "I'm going to have to quit."

Marissa pulled off the headset. She got up. She remembers feeling defeated, unsure about what to do next—the next hour, the next day, the next month. But when she thought of Lexie, still asleep in the bed, she felt some relief. She lay down on the couch. All around her, the house was suddenly silent and still.

Early last Spring, the crowd of marchers came around the corner from Fayetteville's downtown and on down the hill to the park. They wore blue-jeans and T-shirts, desert camouflage jackets and gothic black. They pushed strollers, carried water bottles and signs and banners— "Bring Them Home

Now"—and an American flag. It was Fayetteville's largest peace rally since the Vietnam War.

The park's band shell was a vast shaded space littered with speakers and microphone stands and drums. Below it, the marchers spread across the grass in the sun. A newsprint program listed speakers and performers—veterans, union members, Hip-Hop Against Racist War, a September 11 family member, and the fourth speaker on the list, "Beth Pratt—military spouse from Fayetteville whose husband is in Iraq."

She'd been invited to speak at the peace rally. Here, at last, was something she could do. A small thing, but something. In the last few weeks, Beth had been feeling steadily better—she'd started attending a church, she'd signed up for a yoga class. When Luigi called, she told him she'd finally picked up her drumsticks again. She says that after she got the invitation to speak at the rally, she asked Luigi if he thought she should do it. "Would it bother you?" she asked.

Over the phone, she had heard him laugh. "Far as I'm concerned, that's what I'm over here for, isn't it? Your freedom of speech?"

Now she walked across the stage and stopped in front of one of the microphones, silhouetted against the crowd. She gripped the pages of her speech and leaned forward.

"My name is Beth Pratt. I'm a nurse, and I grew up in Minnesota."

Her voice boomed over the crowd. She told them it had taken all the courage she had to stand up there and speak for those few minutes. "As far as supporting the troops," she read, "I support my husband one hundred percent, along with all of the other soldiers that are making sacrifices for us. Ending this war and bringing them all home safely would be the best form of support that I can see."

She spoke for just three minutes. When she turned away from the mike, her heartbeat faded out of her ears, and the crowd's roar faded in.

Afterward, as the speeches went on behind her, Beth spoke to reporters from local newspapers and the *New York Times* and to a pudgy man with a cell phone on his hip. He shook Beth's hand. "I'm a producer with NBC," he said. His crew had had some technical difficulties while she was speaking. He wanted her to come over to the camera and tell the rest of the country what she'd just said up there.

Beth frowned and hunched her shoulders. "You mean national TV?" She suddenly looked smaller. She glanced around for a familiar face. "Television. I don't know. I don't know if I should do that."

"What you had to say was very powerful," the producer said, cupping his hands in front of him as if offering a gift. "It's a great opportunity to get your message out there."

She hesitated. "I'm sorry," she said, "I'm just worried about my job. And my husband." As the producer pressed on, she mumbled, "I have to think about it; I don't know." The other reporters exchanged glances. The producer said, "It's right over there; it won't take long." And then Lou Plummer, one of the rally's organizers, shouldered his way into the middle.

"Back off," he barked. A veteran of the National Guard, Plummer looked more like a bouncer than a peace activist. "You don't have to live in this town, but she does. I live here. I know what it's like." As the producer argued with him, another newspaper reporter moved in to ask Beth a few questions.

She didn't do the TV interview, but when she saw her words in print the next day, she liked how it felt; she began wondering what she should do next. She thought about doing something more significant, like joining Doctors Without Borders, an international medical charity, and going overseas. But, in the end, she went no farther than downtown to join the occasional peace vigil. What she wanted was a family with Luigi. She knew it was going to be hard enough to make that happen, she says, without her being gone, too.

Marissa was cleaning out the closets. The Hooah Wives were having a yard sale, and suddenly Marissa had hours to empty her life of junk. She had hours to teach Lexie to ride her two-wheeler. She says she told Charlie about it when he called, described Lexie wobbling off on her own for the first time, and he got quiet. Then Charlie remembers saying, "Seems like you guys are going off someplace without me." She had hours to park herself out on the back deck and smoke and think about that.

And when Charlie called home sounding angry and hollow and tired of being in Iraq, she recalls how she tried to hold him up. "You're providing security," she told him. "If we pulled out now, a lot more people would die; it would be chaos. You guys are over there risking your lives, and it's not for nothing." She poured herself across 6,000 miles. "And I am proud of you."

Online and on the phone with the Hooah Wives, she talked with her friends. "When the man you love is in a life-or-death situation," she said, "it makes you sit down and think about what really matters in your own life." She knew she didn't want to keep doing the kind of paralegal work she could get in Fayetteville. She signed up to go back to college in the fall.

Eventually, Marissa would determine she couldn't afford to go back. In the meantime, she went down to the pack-and-ship store where she used to go every weekend to overnight big packages of legal documents and asked about a job. It paid only $6.50 an hour, but it was part time, and she could get time off whenever she needed it. The woman who ran the place was married to an active-duty soldier, too. She understood that when Charlie came home, the pack-and-ship wouldn't be seeing much of Marissa Bootes for a while.

After seven months in Iraq, first Charlie Bootes and then Luigi Pratt would board planes in Kuwait and fly back around the world to their wives in North Carolina. Both men are scheduled to be deployed again next year, this time to Afghanistan, this time for a year.

Here on Fort Bragg, people constantly say goodbye—but then, most of the time, they get to say welcome home. In Chaplain Hartz's office, there are a couple of institutional office chairs, a box of tissues. A lot of people have sat within the painted cinderblock walls of this room and cried. "You'd like to be able to wave a magic wand," Hartz says, and then his eyes well up. He looks down, and for a long moment he bites his lip. At last he says quietly, "It makes me grateful for my own relationship."

In his first few years as a chaplain, Hartz left his family during three major deployments. "There are benefits," he says. "If the soldier handles it right, his spouse's growth as a person is phenomenal. If the relationship is solid and he's not threatened and he can accept that, and say, Wow, she's more of a woman, she's stronger, she's a better person, and we're a better team. . . ." He leans forward. "The real news is, most of us make it."

S I X T Y - S E V E N

◆◆◆

Report from Okinawa (1997)
Long-Term U.S. Military Presence and Violence Against Women

Suzuyo Takazato

A prominent feminist activist and opinion leader in Okinawa (Japan), **Suzuyo Takazato** is co-facilitator of Okinawa Women Act Against Military Violence, the first women's anti-militarist organization in Okinawa. She has worked as a social worker, particularly concerned with violence against women, and was elected to the Naha City Assembly as an independent candidate for four terms.

In the mid-1990s, thanks to the concerted efforts of women organizers and activists, UN conferences began to address military violence against women in war and armed-conflict situations as a human-rights issue. The Vienna Declaration, adopted at the World Conference on Human Rights, June 1993, focused on mass rape and forced impregnation of women as strategies of "ethnic cleansing" in Bosnia-Herzegovina:

> Violations of the human rights of women in situations of armed conflict are violations of the fundamental principles of international human rights and humanitarian law. In particular, it is essential to effectively engage in addressing all forms of human rights violations, including murder, systematic rape, sexual slavery and forced impregnation. (Vienna Declaration and Program of Action, No. 38)

The Beijing *Platform for Action*, adopted by the UN Fourth World Conference on Women, 1995, built on the Vienna Declaration, stated that "Rape in the conduct of armed conflict constitutes a war crime," and urged the necessity to "take all measures required for the protection of women and children from such acts" and to,

> undertake a full investigation of all acts of violence against women committed during war, including rape, in particular systematic rape, forced prostitution and other forms of indecent assault and sexual slavery, prosecute all criminals responsible for war crimes against women and provide full redress to women victims.
>
> *(Beijing Platform for Action,* article 233*)*

Clearly, cases such as the Japanese military system of sexual slavery during World War II, mass rapes in Bosnia-Herzegovina, and many circumstances of armed conflict are instances in which the violent nature of military power has been directed against women. Today, as in the past, women and children become entangled in wars whenever and wherever armed conflict breaks out.

Military violence against women also occurs in many other situations, such as military occupation, colonial domination, military political control, and even UN military forces' peacekeeping activities. This reality, and policies to address it, are not included in the Beijing *Platform for Action.* Human rights violations which occur as a result of a foreign military presence must be understood and addressed from a gender perspective. Even when women are not at the battle-site, as in Asian countries during the Vietnam War, wherever U.S. troops were stationed or a "Rest and Relaxation" ("R&R") site established, violence against women occurred. This is the case with the long-term U.S. military presence in Okinawa (Japan).

Okinawa's Unique Situation

Okinawa, the southern-most prefecture of Japan, is situated midway between Tokyo and Manila, and has been called the "keystone of the Pacific" by military planners because of its strategic location. Currently, some 59,000 U.S. troops are stationed in Japan, including 12,000 Navy personnel of the Seventh Fleet based at Yokosuka. Seventy-five per cent of the U.S. military presence in Japan is in Okinawa, although Okinawa is only 0.6 per cent of the land area. There are 39 U.S. bases and military installations in Okinawa, roughly 30,000 troops, and 22,500 family members.

Okinawa's situation in regard to U.S. bases differs from other parts of Japan in three ways. In

1945, Okinawa was the site of a fierce, three-month land battle between U.S. and Japanese forces, in which Okinawa citizens became entangled. The Battle of Okinawa resulted in the death of one-fourth of the Okinawan population—more than 200,000 people. The battlefield also became the site of violence against women. Second, the most productive land—where Okinawan people had long secured their livelihood—was requisitioned to build vast U.S. bases. Okinawans, displaced by the battle, were not allowed to return to their land until after the military had selected sites for new bases. Okinawa was under total U.S. military control for 27 years after World War II, during which period the U.S. military in Okinawa was directly involved both in the Korean War and the Vietnam War. Third, administrative control of Okinawa was returned to Japan in 1972 while the Vietnam War was still in process, resulting in continued escalation of U.S. military crime and violence against Okinawan women. Today, 27 years after Okinawa's reversion to Japan, a huge U.S. military presence continues to be located in highly-congested Okinawa, which still serves as the site of U.S. Marine Corps battlefield simulation drills conducted on a regular basis. Many Okinawans oppose this U.S. presence, and are also bitter that successive Japanese governments have allowed Okinawa to bear the major burden of U.S. troops and bases in the country (Japan Coalition on the U.S. Military Bases 1998).

Military Endorsement and Support of Violence Against Women

In general, the extent of military violence against women depends on a number of factors: the attitude of the host government and host country regarding the status of women and respect for their human rights; the legal system that is in place to protect their status; the treaties and agreements between the sending country and the receiving country regarding human rights, and the adequacy of the arrangements to prevent crimes. The larger the economic gap existing between the country deploying the military presence and the country receiving the military presence, the more military personnel look down on women in the host community, view women's sexuality as a commodity to be purchased, and contribute to the growth of military prostitution.

The U.S. military system is overwhelmingly male-dominated, . . . (Enloe 1995; Reardon 1993). Troops engage in daily training exercises to hone their skills in killing and wounding to maintain a constant state of readiness that will enable them to be deployed to a conflict situation on a moment's notice. Military bases in Okinawa are located next to, or within, Okinawan residential areas. U.S. troops are allowed to move freely outside the base, and their violent training overflows into the Okinawa community. The U.S. forces stationed in Okinawa were deployed to the Korean War in the 1950s, the Vietnam War in the 1960s and '70s, and the Persian Gulf War in 1991. The warriors returned to Okinawa on each occasion carrying their pent-up battlefield aggression, which they released on women in the vicinity of military bases.

To promote "morale," U.S. military operations include routine "Rest and Relaxation" sites in Asian countries (Sturdevant and Stoltzfus 1992). Prostitution and rape are the military system's outlets for aggression, and its way of maintaining control and discipline—the target being local women, as well as women in the military or U.S. military families. Prostitution and rape is viewed as a reward—for example, in "R&R"—and serves to bolster a sense of masculinity. After the rape of a 12-year-old Okinawan girl by three U.S. military personnel in 1995 (discussed later in this article), Admiral Richard Macke, Commander of the Asia-Pacific Forces and a veteran of the Vietnam War, declared, "What fools! . . . for the price they paid to rent the car, they could have had a girl" (Schmitt 1995 p. 6Y). He was removed from his position for this remark, a revealing comment on military attitudes to prostitution.

Today, former U.S. military women are denouncing military violence and sexual harassment. Both the U.S. Army and Navy admit the existence of sexual violence within those organizations, including violence in U.S. military families (Kelly 1998).

History of Military Prostitution and Sexual Violence in Okinawa

Between 1943 and 1945, Korean women were brought to Okinawa by the Japanese Imperial Army, and were moved throughout the islands, where they were forced to serve as sexual slaves to Japanese troops stationed in Okinawa to defend the Japanese mainland. There were 130 Japanese military brothels established in Okinawa. Some Okinawan women were also made to serve as Japanese "comfort women."

April, 1945–49: The Battle of Okinawa and the Period of Postwar Chaos

Following the U.S. forces' landing on Okinawa, women were frequently abducted from their homes in areas under U.S. military control, and raped by military personnel. Rapes occurred at random, including the rape of a nine-month-old baby girl (*The Okinawa Times* 1949). Some of these rapes resulted in the impregnation of Okinawan women and the birth of many children, posing a threat to the harmony of postwar Okinawa society. To prevent rape of the civilian population, brothels were established in each local area to service U.S. troops. At the internment camp in Chinen Village, a solitary house was repainted and turned into a U.S. military brothel. According to Okinawan women who laundered U.S. military uniforms they searched the pockets for unused condoms which they returned to the U.S. military before washing the uniforms.

June 1950: Okinawa Bases Become Launching Sites to the Korean War

One portion of land returned by the U.S. military in September 1950 was turned into a brothel area in an attempt to address the frequent rapes perpetuated by soldiers in residential areas and the spread of sexually-transmitted diseases. In an attempt to safeguard U.S. military personnel from sexually-transmitted diseases, women serving U.S. troops were required to undergo periodic checkups. The military established the "A-SIGN" system (with an "Approved" sign awarded to establishments passing the health inspection conducted by U.S. military officials), and the "Off-limits" system (which restricted military personnel from unapproved bars). In the meantime, as Okinawa bases became launching sites to the Korean war, frequent military air crashes and traffic accidents resulted in the deaths of Okinawan citizens.

1965–73: The Vietnam War

B-52's from Kadena Air Base, on the main island of Okinawa, took off for bombing raids over north Vietnam, and Okinawa bases served as personnel deployment, command, training, weapons storage, and "R&R" sites. The brothel areas flourished. Women serviced 20–30 customers a day and were fined for taking time off during their menstrual periods or to care for children or other family members. Women who worked in clubs and bars under a system of controlled prostitution endured heavy debts and sexually-transmitted diseases, as well as suffered brutality at the hands of soldiers returning from Vietnam. Many women working as prostitutes were killed, and many cases of rape-related strangulation occurred. It was said that going to the (outside) toilet alone was a suicidal act, because a woman would likely be raped. According to a survey conducted in 1969, one out of every 50 women was involved in prostitution . . . one out of 30 to 40 for women in their 20s and 30s.

May 1972–1995: The Post-Reversion Period

In 1972, Okinawa reverted to Japan after 27 years of U.S. military administration. In 1973, the U.S. draft system changed from military conscription to voluntary enlistment. At the same time, the Japanese *yen* strengthened against the dollar, and U.S. troops in Japan no longer had superior buying power. During this period, the number of military personnel stationed in Okinawa remained virtually unchanged, although the prostitution areas experienced a sharp decline, as U.S. troops could no longer afford to patronize them. Meanwhile, the number of Okinawan junior-high and high-school girls who were victims of sexual violence increased. Philippine women began working in bars and clubs around military bases in Okinawa, entering Japan on short-term "entertainer" visas. They endured inferior working conditions and severe human rights violations. In fact, in 1983, two Philippine women working in a club near a base burned to death in a fire as a result of unsafe working conditions (*Okinawa Times* 1983). Children fathered by U.S. military personnel and problems related to these men acknowledging paternity and paying child-

support increased during the post-reversion period. For instance, one woman attorney handled 30 of these cases in a two-year period (*Ashabi Shinbun*). In 1991, U.S. bases in Okinawa were once again launching sites for war. This time, U.S. troops were deployed to the Persian Gulf War.

1995–1999: The Rape of a 12-Year-Old Girl

At 8.30 p.m. on September 4, 1995, a 12-year-old girl was returning home from a neighborhood shop in an area near a U.S. base when she was abducted in a car. She was hit and had her eyes and mouth covered. Her body was bound with duct tape. She was raped and then dumped out of the car and left on the side of the road. Her three U.S. military assailants had rented the car inside the military base, purchased duct tape and condoms, and left the base for the purpose of abducting a woman and committing rape. The assailants' statements during their trial made clear their motives for committing the crime. Brothels are drab and reminded them of their poverty-stricken childhoods (personal testimony). Japanese women do not carry weapons such as guns or knives with which to defend themselves, so even if they resist, there is little chance of danger. Japanese people are not able to distinguish U.S. military personnel on the basis of their appearance. Colleagues had committed rape without being caught, so they felt that their victim would not press charges. Thus, they drove around bustling shopping areas and residential neighborhoods for several hours, targeting several women, but failing to accomplish their goal. Finally, they attacked the young girl.

What especially shocked Okinawan citizens was that exactly 40 years before, a six-year-old girl had been abducted, raped, and murdered by U.S. troops (*Ryukyu Shinpo*). This recent incident was merely the latest in a long string of similar incidents that have continued throughout the postwar period. But this case resulted in an outpouring of activity for several reasons. First, the young girl pressed charges. Second, the rape occurred during the Beijing Women's Conference where violence against women was declared a violation of human rights and this inspired confidence in Okinawan women activists returning from Beijing who quickly organized to protest the rape, and U.S. military violence in general. Third, the rape occurred during the 50th-anniversary of the end of the war, a time of reflection concerning Okinawa's 50-year-long military presence. Parents, teachers, and citizens were shocked, and were forced to recognize that the age of the girl made it very clear that such violence reaches out to claim its victims without distinction. Okinawans' perceptions of U.S. military personnel have changed over the years. Nowadays, they move about freely, compared to the Vietnam War period, and are perceived not as military personnel but as American citizens.

Limitations in the Status of Forces Agreement

The stationing of U.S. forces in Okinawa is governed by treaties and agreements between the U.S. and Japanese governments (Status of Forces Agreements). But these agreements treat military crimes lightly, especially crimes against women, and make possible the acceptance of military "R&R" There are several severe limitations to the Status of Forces Agreement from the perspective of Okinawan communities.

No Policy for Preventing the Violation of Women's Human Rights

The freedom of activity of U.S. military forces stationed in Okinawa is guaranteed, but policies to prevent crimes or support victims of crimes committed by U.S. troops has never even been discussed. There is no systematic data on U.S. military crimes. U.S. authorities proclaimed that the rape of the wife or daughter of a U.S. serviceman would result in the death penalty for the assailant. In contrast, punishments for U.S. military crimes were light. In many cases, because the suspect was returned to the U.S., the trial verdict was never known. Until 1972, U.S. military crimes were handled by military courts-martial, and only after Reversion were trials held under the Japanese legal system. During the 27 years of U.S. military control there was no accurate report of the results of military courts-martial. Even today, there is no complete

report of the total number of incidents and how they are dealt with. Some cases are adjudicated through the Japanese courts; while crimes committed inside U.S. bases that result in a court-martial are tried entirely separately.

This situation arose partly due to limitations in Japan's legal system, which judges crimes of rape more lightly than robbery (sentences for robbery result in prison sentences of five to 15 years, while rape results in prison sentences of six months to seven years). Published crime statistics in Okinawa have not itemized rape separately from other felonies like murder, burglary, and arson, another factor which indicates that rape is not taken seriously, and which makes it difficult to organize around this issue. Rape victims are looked down upon by society, and police treatment of rape victims is like enduring a "second rape." Because of women's deeply-rooted mistrust and apprehension toward the Japanese police and the legal system, the number of women reporting a rape represents the tip of the iceberg.

Responsibility for Children Fathered by U.S. Troops Is Not Addressed

The Status of Forces Agreement between the U.S. and Germany makes recommendations concerning the recognition of paternity of a child fathered by U.S. military personnel and the father's responsibility for child support. Whether the father is transferred to a third country or back to the U.S., he can be traced and requested to pay child support. In contrast, there has never been any discussion of this matter in relation to the Status of Forces Agreement between Japan and the U.S.

Do U.S. Citizens Know About the Activities of U.S. Troops in Okinawa?

In the case of the rape of a 12-year-old girl, the U.S. Consul and the U.S. Ambassador in Japan, as representatives of the sending country, issued apologies, followed by the Japanese government. But to what extent are American citizens aware that such crimes occur on a regular basis? For the past 50 years, since the end of World War II, the United States has seen itself as the world's policeman. Even after the end of the Cold War, the U.S. has intervened in regional conflicts throughout the world, and continues to maintain the world's largest military operation. What do U.S. citizens know of military endorsement and support for prostitution and rape? Do they know that crimes committed by U.S. military personnel in Okinawa continue to be treated more lightly than crimes committed by members of the civilian community?

Working to Eliminate U.S. Military Violence Against Women

Okinawan women activists came together to protest the rape of the 12-year-old girl, immediately upon their return from the Beijing Conference, September 1995, a few days after the rape had occurred. Seventy-one women from Okinawa had gone to Beijing to make connections with other Asian women and to share their experiences of living with U.S. bases. Seven of the eleven workshops they presented concerned militarism and peace. Their preparation for the Beijing conference, as well as the inspirational and energizing effect of this momentous gathering, served them well upon their return. They organized a 12-day street vigil in downtown Naha, the capital, drawing worldwide attention to the rape of this girl and, more generally, the many incidents of violence against women by U.S. troops in East Asia. They played a central role in organizing a major demonstration attended by some 85,000 people (out of a total population of one million). They started a new organization, Okinawa Women Act Against Military Violence, to focus on the impact of U.S. military operations on women and children.

Okinawan women are working on this issue in three main ways: developing their own local organizing; uncovering what has happened in the past through conversations, workshops, drama, and historical research; and making international connections through regional and international networks. We have organized vigils, protests, and public demonstrations in Okinawa (Zielenziger 1996). We have sent many petitions and letters to the governments of Okinawa, Japan, and the United States, and have undertaken speaking engagements in Japan, the United States, and as participants in The Hague Appeal for Peace, May 1999 (Burress 1996; Kang

1998). We are engaged in research to ascertain the reality and full extent of military violence against women and the way that cases have been handled. Starting in 1945, we have details of 92 incidents so far, taken from historical records, police reports, newspaper articles, and individual testimony.

When Okinawan women went to the U.S. as part of the American Peace Caravan (Jan–Feb, 1996), the following five demands were issued to U.S. citizens, the U.S. government, and members of Congress:

- We demand the investigation of all past crimes committed by U.S. military personnel in Okinawa, especially those that constitute human rights violations against women and girls;

- We demand the establishment of a concrete plan for the reduction and ultimate removal of all U.S. military personnel from Okinawa, especially the Marines;

- We demand that the U.S. military strengthen its orientation and continuing-education program to sensitize all personnel overseas, and their dependents, to respect and uphold the basic human rights of the citizens of the country in which they are stationed, especially its women and children;

- We demand that the governments of Japan and the United States: (a) implement the *Platform for Action* (*PFA*) approved at the UN Fourth World Conference on Women, (b) revise the Status of Forces Agreement, and (c) reexamine the Japan–U.S. Security Treaty to ensure that these two documents are in accord with the *PFA*;

- We demand that experts on such issues as the violation of women's human rights and the destruction of the environment be dispatched to Okinawa to investigate and evaluate the actual situation existing today.

We appeal to related governments and international agencies to review treaties including the U.S.-Japan Status of Forces Agreement and the new Defense Guidelines, as well as other international agreements, in order to bring them in line with the proposals of the Beijing *Platform for Action* and a gender perspective. We appeal for the revision of laws in order to prevent violence against women and to protect women's and children's human rights.

We are working to promote an international network, support system, and campaign to actualize the goals of the statement approved at the International Conference on Militarism and Human Rights held in Okinawa, May 1997 (Kirk and Okazawa-Rey 1998).

This article originated as a report to the International Conference on Violence against Women in War and Armed Conflict Situations, which reported to the UN Special Rapporteur on Violence Against Women. Tokyo, Oct. 30–Nov. 3, 1997. This article was translated by Carolyn Bowen Francis, and edited by Gwyn Kirk.

REFERENCES

Asahi Shinbun. May 3, 1997: 31.

Burress, C., "Okinawan Base Protesters Bring Cause to Bay Area." *San Francisco Chronicle* 5 Feb. 1996: A15

Enloe, Cynthia. *The Morning After: Sexual Politics at the End of the Cold War.* Berkeley, CA: University of California Press, 1993.

Japan Coalition on the U.S. Military Bases. "It's Time to Bring the U.S. Marines Home!" *New York Times* 23 November 1998: A17.

Kang, Connie, "Okinawans Bring Drive to L.A." *Los Angeles Times* 7 October 1998: A3.

Kelly, R. J. "Assault Reports Distress Pacific's Leading Admiral." *Pacific Stars and Stripes* 13 May 1998: 1.

Kirk, Gwyn and Margo Okazawa-Rey. "Making Connections: Building an East Asia-U.S. Women's Network against U.S. Militarism." *Women and War Reader.* Eds. J. Turpin and L. A. Lorentsen. New York: New York University Press, 1998: 308–322.

Okinawa Times. September 15, 1949.

Okinawa Times. November 12, 1983.

Reardon, Betty A. *Sexism and the War System.* New York: Teachers College Press, Columbia University, 1985.

Ryukyu Shinpo. September 11, 1955.

Schmitt, E., "Admiral's Gaffe Pushes Navy to New Scrutiny of Attitudes." *New York Times* 19 Nov. 1995: 6Y.

Sturdevant, Saundra and Brenda Stoltzfus. *Let the Good Times Roll: Prostitution and the U.S. Military in Asia.* New York: New Press, 1992.

Zielenziger, Michael, "Women Finding a Voice." *San Jose Mercury News* Sept. 12, 1996: 1A.

S I X T Y - E I G H T

◆◆◆

Mother's Day Proclamation—1870 (1870)

Julia Ward Howe

Julia Ward Howe (1819–1910) is known for her Civil War poem *The Battle Hymn of the Republic* championing freedom for all men and women. She published many poems, plays, and travel books, and was active in the women's rights movement, playing a prominent role in several women's suffrage organizations. She saw the devastation of the war through her work with widows and orphans on both sides, and called for women to oppose war in all its forms.

Arise then . . . women of this day!
Arise, all women who have hearts!
Whether your baptism be of water or of tears!
Say firmly:
"We will not have questions answered by irrelevant agencies,

Our husbands will not come to us, reeking with carnage,
For caresses and applause.
Our sons shall not be taken from us to unlearn
All that we have been able to teach them of charity, mercy and patience.
We, the women of one country,
Will be too tender of those of another country
To allow our sons to be trained to injure theirs."

From the voice of a devastated Earth a voice goes up with
Our own. It says: "Disarm! Disarm!
The sword of murder is not the balance of justice."
Blood does not wipe out dishonor,
Nor violence indicate possession.
As men have often forsaken the plough and the anvil

At the summons of war,
Let women now leave all that may be left of
   home
For a great and earnest day of counsel.
Let them meet first, as women, to bewail and
   commemorate the dead.
Let them solemnly take counsel with each other as
   to the means
Whereby the great human family can live in
   peace . . .
Each bearing after his own time the sacred impress,
   not of Caesar,

But of God—
In the name of womanhood and humanity, I
   earnestly ask
That a general congress of women without limit of
   nationality,
May be appointed and held at someplace deemed
   most convenient
And the earliest period consistent with its
   objects,
To promote the alliance of the different nationalities,
The amicable settlement of international questions,
The great and general interests of peace.

S I X T Y - N I N E

◆◆◆

The Search for Peace and Justice (1998)

Notes Toward an Autobiography

Jean Grossholtz

Jean Grossholtz is Professor Emerita of politics and women's studies at Mount Holyoke College. A founding member of Diverse Women for Diversity, she works to educate the public about issues of water contamination and privatization, nuclear weapons and energy, European Union and World Trade Organization proposals, and genetically modified organisms and food.

I was standing in the sunlight on Pennsylvania Avenue watching the passing gays and lesbians, relishing the color, the noise, and the excitement. I saw them coming around the corner, men and women many in uniform carrying signs, "I'm gay and I served." I watched them as they passed, the pride in their faces, the confidence in their step. And suddenly there I was marching, tears streaming down my face, holding the hand of another woman beside me. Here I was, a 65-year-old dedicated peace activist, who had put my body on the line in such out of the way places as the Seneca Army Base, Greenham Common, and Diablo Canyon. I, who had courted federal prison and spent time in many jails for peace, was marching with the military for the rights of gays to serve in an institution I found

distasteful in the extreme. But it was an institution in which I served for four years, nine months, and five days through the Korean War. It was an institution that had meant my personal survival, had honed my political passions to a fine level of anger, had given me a deep and everlasting commitment to end war.

Confused, conflicted, and still a strong lesbian political activist, I walked beside my newfound friend as we traded stories of the purges, the fears, the betrayals by our own and others as we had sought to survive in a hostile environment. I remembered sitting paralyzed in the mess hall while noncommissioned officers who outranked me discussed the dangers of getting too close to the "troops." I knew this was aimed at me. I had just returned from a weekend of love and lust with one of my "troops." It did not matter that I knew some of them were guilty of the same infractions. I was in danger and they were warning me.

It took some time to understand those warnings before I began to hear them. The Lieutenant who made fun of me for walking with my arm around my friend. "Childish," she called it, "high school," not the behavior of a grown woman and a noncommissioned officer. The Captain who mentioned a missing light bulb as a means of casually warning me there was to be a surprise bed check. There were many such warnings as we all did our best to be decent people in an atmosphere of constant betrayal. This way surely madness lies, this occupation of a totally alien space where what one was and wanted to be was denied and hidden and yet ever present.

So there I was marching in the Gay Pride March for a Simple Matter of Justice, reliving those old fears and betrayals, the times I denied, the times I turned my back as others felt the wrath of the Army's purging. This was an important moment. Did I really want to honor the right to serve in this institution? Was I marching for the right of women, of lesbians to join this killing machine?

I had grown up committed to the organization of the working class. I grew up believing in freedom and justice. I read about the strikes of the women textile workers in Lawrence in 1912, and shed real tears when I read of the awful things that happened to strikers. I read of the Pullman Company and their private police and the murdered men at Haymarket in Chicago in 1894. I read of the government's and businessmen's fears of anarchism and the scapegoating of two foreign-born working men, Sacco and Vanzetti. Account after account of those martyred for justice made me understand that capitalism grew in this country at great cost to ordinary people, to the workers whose labor made it all possible. And I dreamed of playing that role, of being the one burnt at the stake or beheaded. Overhearing my father talking with his friends, I learned of the Industrial Workers of the World and their dream of one big union for all the working class. I fell in love with the words of these men and women. Elizabeth Gurley Flynn and Joe Hill and Big Bill Haywood of the Industrial Workers of the World. Nicknamed the Wobblies by some Chinese workers . . . these organizers moved around the country lending their skills to local leadership, integrating grassroots groups, trying to build one big union. Throughout middle school and high school I chased after stories of these grand ideas of equality and justice.

I joined the Army, as did most of the women I met in the Women's Army Corps, to get out of what looked to me a dead-end street. I was 17 years old and going nowhere, with nothing but drinking and living from one shit-level job to the next in my future. I had read enough war novels to know that the men in the Army were not all establishment puppets. I knew some of the people in the Army were the same people who walked the picket lines outside of factories. I did not make the connection between the Army, the state, and the destruction of the IWW. I only knew I had to get somewhere, go somewhere where I would be able to read, to think about these people and their ideas, to find people who used these words this way.

And I had another, deeper, darker secret for leaving my home town, I was a freak. I lusted after women. I did not like boys, could not relate to them except as friends, did not want to marry, or be what the women around me seemed to want. In the small town where I went to high school I was driven crazy by my inability to fit in, to even try, make an attempt. I did not know the words dyke, lesbian. I learned of homosexual and I heard people referring to sick people they called "queer" and I knew that was me. I had hopes and hints there were others like me. When I finally met one such, she was already going into the Army and she convinced me there would be others like us there.

But the driving force was economic. With a high school education all I could do was waitress, wash dishes, work in the laundry, stand all day on an assembly line. I had spent much of my life in small towns or on a farm; I was unused to being cooped up, unused to routine. I drifted from one job to another, failing as a waitress, having a brief happy fling for some months as a short order cook when the male cook got sick. Mostly it was jobs that were killing me, that I could not keep because my anger and despair led me to outraged rebellion. The middle-aged women who stood all day on an assembly line repeating the same movement endlessly hour after hour, having to ask permission to go to the toilet, tried to comfort me. They understood only that we had no choice, that the world offered only this to poor and uneducated people. When I raged they gave me cookies, when I spoke of strikes they laughed. My heart hurting, my body aching, my mind numbed, I would eventually explode at the foreman, the factory superintendent, the product we were making. And I would be fired and move to another factory to repeat the experience.

The Army saved me. Although it led me to some heavy drinking for a time, it also led me to reject that life full force and to see some hope in moving beyond this past to something new. For the first time we had medical care, good food, warm clothes. For many of us our first visit to the dentist. (I credit the Army for the fact that alone of all my siblings I still have real teeth at the age of 67.) I had the first medication for my chronic stomach ulcers that I never had a name for before. We laughed about our uniforms but it was for some of us the first time we were not in danger of being laughed at, criticized for what we wore and how we wore it. We had social services we never thought possible. The Army was the biggest welfare state in the world and it took great care of us. And in the end it gave me the GI Bill and a college education.

We complained and raged against the Army's peculiar ways of trying to break our spirit but all of us secretly gloried in our new wealth and were shamed into lying about our pasts, making up stories that were nowhere near true. We would tell Dick and Jane stories of loving fathers who wore suits and carried briefcases, of mothers smiling and young-looking, of little white houses with shutters and pets. And when one of us would tell the truth of the shopworn mother, the abusive father, the rape by a brother, the fights over money, we would sit together in silence, loving one another and knowing we were all afraid to speak out as she had done, afraid to make ourselves so vulnerable.

I learned that I could be somebody. That I could do all the things they asked of me, that I could stand up against the harshest, most angry of my peers and survive. A lieutenant, angry at me and humiliated because I knew more than she did about what was happening in the world, set me impossible tasks over and over until I was made into a zombie by tiredness and lack of sleep. And I still led my platoon and won good soldier awards. I was a good teacher, a popular leader. I began to see there was a way to have integrity, to be able to live as I really was. Not at first, at first I lied, I passed myself off as what I was not, indeed never wanted to be. I tried on different faces of myself searching for the one that fit. The Army allowed me that space, that time. As long as I did my duty. And that proved easy.

I learned how to act in concert with others. I learned the discipline that group activity required. Much of what the Army thrived on struck me as dumb and not worth paying attention to. The Army demanded total unquestioned obedience. They called it discipline, and punished infractions with idiotic penalties. For example, once, for arguing with an officer, I was sent to remove all the coal from the coal bin, scrub the bin, and put all the coal back. I found this ridiculous. If I thought someone was wrong I needed to say so. Sometimes this worked in my favor and allowed me to blossom, at other times it caused me grief and I paid for my inattention to the Army's rules.

Over time I realized that people liked me, that I was smart, that the Army appreciated me despite all my rebellions. I was sent to Leadership School and the entire unit showed me they thought this was a fine idea, that I was worthy of respect as a leader.

I was sent to Leadership School in Carlisle Barracks, Pennsylvania. There I met some wonderful historians who told us stories of the battles and generals of the Civil War. I fell in love with the history and with the ease which these men told the stories of Grant and Meade and Robert E. Lee and cavalry charges across peach orchids. And then I saw the pictures, the dead strewn across the battlefields. And I remembered Walt Whitman who had become the poet of my liberation, of my becoming.

I learned to teach everything from map-reading to first aid to current events. I grew daily more confident, less confused. I met women who had been to college and we talked of many things. I learned to read the *New York Times,* not knowing then how much it was misshaping and confusing my principled politics of the working class. I was sent to a detachment working with an engineering battalion in the woods of Wisconsin and I became a newspaper editor. Me, the farm girl, editing an Army newspaper. I found myself at the heart of some of the more important activities of the camp.

I learned about war. War had been something I'd read about, something that people became heroes in. And a hero I wanted to be. I did not like the killing. Felt instinctively it was wrong and that nothing would justify it or ever make me take a weapon against another human being. I had grown up with brothers and fathers hunting, hunting for meat for our food. I could not stand the smell of them when they returned—the smell of fresh blood and dead animals. I did not eat the meat they brought so proudly. I did not look at the carcasses as they carved them up and canned the results. Still I wanted to be a hero. I did not altogether reject the idea of armies in battle, of enemies.

After I had been in the Army for a few months, the United States began what they called "a police action" against North Koreans. This reaction started with a movement by North Koreans across the border with South Korea. But 1950 was the height of the Cold War frenzy. Washington was in turmoil over who had "lost" China to the Communists. The inside view in Washington was that the border crossings and troop movements in the North were a precursor of a massive, Soviet-backed invasion. This never happened. Instead the Americans, failing to stop at just policing the border, invaded North Korea and headed for Manchuria. In response, the People's Republic of China entered the war and drove the Americans from the North in a massive and bloody retreat.

A small peacetime army was suddenly increased. Thousands of new recruits were brought in, trained, and sent to Korea. Many died within days of landing at Inch'on. One young man I met from Kansas had lied about his age, entered the Army at 17, was dead on his eighteenth birthday.

As the U.S. Generals pushed to the border, proclaiming victory, the terrible retreats, the terrible killing fields of the North came to haunt us. Pictures of young men, their feet wrapped in blankets, their eyes hollow with horror. "They brought their dead out," the Generals crowed, as if that were a victory. I lay many nights in my cot listening to Taps and remembering the strong young men learning engineering skills in the woods of Wisconsin. I could no longer countenance war. I no longer wanted to be a hero. I wanted to stop war, this war, all wars.

I was transferred from Wisconsin to Fitzsimmons General Hospital in Denver and the wounded came flooding back. As editor of the hospital newspaper, my job was ostensibly to tout the patriotism of these young men. I had considerable freedom until I printed a story about the limited blood supply and then I was put under tighter rein.

As I haunted the wards talking with these men, I came to see what war was really about. I saw that the bravery I had identified with saving one's buddies was really the result of a foolish, meaningless slaughter. The broken bodies of the young men I met in those hospitals were the reverse image of the sweating healthy young men I had seen training in Wisconsin. I knew that I had to organize my life to destroy the idea that war and dying in war was glorious. This blatant disrespect for life was wrong.

The Army taught me that whatever else was true, war was never an answer to any political issue; that politicians and the Generals were not good judges of reality.

But the Army taught me also that I could not love my own kind. For many years I lived in fear and shame. Shame, because what I wanted was so far from what I was supposed to want. Shame, as I saw other WACs seeking private hideouts to live out their realities while maintaining a public posture rejecting that very reality. This option did not appeal to me, it demanded that I think of myself as less than what I was, what I wanted to be. Not being able to talk to each other honestly, not being able to be anything together, they turned to drink. I saw them drinking themselves into an oblivion where shame would be stilled and they could act on their feelings and for some brief moments forget the pain of their unacceptable existence. I could not do this. I felt confused, alienated from those who hated queers and those who would not admit to being queer except when drunk. I was unable to find a center for myself.

As confidence in my own abilities grew, confidence in who I was emerged and I came to understand that the Army's war on homosexuals was wrong, that there was nothing the matter with me that a little healthy acceptance wouldn't cure. I recognized an eerie similarity between the Army's relentless attack on homosexuality, the total rejection of love of your own sex, and the constant insistent bonding with your unit, your buddies. The Army runs on love for your buddies, the willingness to lay down your very life for the group.

The Army's internal war against homosexuality is a warning not to go too far, not to put your faith in individuals but in the unit. And the unit is the Army. Men must be willing to die for the Army, to see their manhood as coming out of the barrel of a gun and its use. It is our national idea of heroism. How many times have we seen U.S. Presidents (Ronald Reagan most especially) visiting caskets in an airplane hangar and declaring these were heroes. Sometimes men who only happened to be at the wrong end of the barracks when a "terrorist" ran his explosive-laden truck into the gate, or when an airplane crashed inadvertently. Heroes simply for being there. No one saw the heroism of the women left as single heads of family back home who still managed to raise their kids and keep them out of poverty in the face of terrible odds. If you put on a uniform you are a hero, you are somebody, you are your nation's finest. Even if you are treated like a pile of shit everywhere you go and are roughed up, discriminated against, called names, within the Army. Such a contradiction—love your buddy like your brother, do not love another man.

The Army's vicious, continuous, almost holy crusade against homosexuals, the periodic purges of the WAC detachments, and the continuous challenges to gay men were all means by which the Army kept its control. Gendered identities made men into soldiers willing to kill for their commanders, and women into either the girl back home or whores. There was no place for anyone who challenged these assumptions. A real man, a soldier, abjures homosexuals even as he learns to put his hope, trust and daily livelihood in his buddies, his unit, his commander. Study what happens to men in battle. Read the war novels by men from every war. They are driven nearly crazy with fear and grief before they can turn to help one another, to express their love physically. How can this clearly "men loving men" organization keep its militaristic pose without undercutting the very thing it is built on?

The Army's relentless pursuit of homosexuals is one way a gendered power structure is kept in place. If women can be competent, active public agents, and men can access that part of themselves which shares the softer, life-enhancing qualities of womanness, what will happen to the killingforce, to the automatic disciplined response to orders?

After I left the Army I watched the madness of the Korean War continue as the United States embarked upon a massive war economy, engaged in a worldwide contest with the "Evil Empire," the Soviet Union. I used the GI Bill to enter college and then went on to graduate school. I studied international relations and political economy. I became a specialist on Southeast Asian politics.

I came to know that the war machines were created not really to be used because that would be the end of the world, but to press the Soviets to spend their resources, to spend to bankruptcy. Meanwhile, American corporations feeding at the military trough developed technology to enter world markets at a great advantage, selling military equipment and technology developed at the taxpayers' expense. This military machine, now released by the fall of the Soviet Union, can be used to secure and guarantee the resources of a new global economic order. From Korea to Vietnam, Grenada, Afghanistan, and Kuwait, the American Army is used to keep imperialism solidly in place. Without the Soviet Army to oppose them, the U.S. military can freely intervene. The global success of the international capitalist economic system is ultimately guaranteed by that military force.

Years after I had left the Army, after I had earned a Ph.D. in Political Science, another American government entered into another war, reminiscent of the Korean War: Vietnam. An area of the world in struggle against colonial rule, a country also divided by international fiat into north and south. And again a U.S.-generated incident and a military response, and once again young men, barely out of basic training, sent to die and Generals chortling about how brave they were, how fine, counting up the numbers they killed as if at a football match.

And I now took to the streets and found myself many times on the opposite side of the Army. Standing holding hands with my colleagues staring into the faces of young men and women frightened by us and worried about their own self-esteem.

I began standing at the gates of Westover Air Base in Massachusetts with a remarkable woman named Frances Crowe. At first we were alone but in time others joined us. Other actions followed, lying in the streets to stop the buses taking the new draftees, blocking the doors of the New York Stock Exchange, surrounding the Pentagon, being dragged to police buses and jails. I learned remarkable strength as we faced our fears of what would happen, of how we would behave when threatened by the police. I sat through endless meetings processing and planning, and nights on church floors with hundreds of others, catching what little sleep we could before an action. I experienced wonderful togetherness in jail cells. And eventually there were the women's peace camps at Seneca and at Greenham Common. Public spaces where women met freely and as equals, seeking a new way of being, a new way of making decisions, a new way of resisting injustice. This it seemed to me was the real beginning of something new, something with hope for a different future.

I have seen women create community; create, without structured authority, large-scale actions and projects. These actions were not without problems and not, in the end, without being somewhat co-opted. But we did create and maintain organized effort, whether to bring attention to Cruise missiles stored at the Seneca Army Base or to keep constant attention on the delivery of Cruise missiles to Greenham. Communities formed, the discipline of consensus decision-making was accepted, and we learned to appreciate ourselves and each other as women. The Women's Peace Camps had their days of glory, of achievement, and to all who came there, something remains, the possibility, maybe only the hope, that another way of living, of making decisions, of sharing in a common life can happen. Those of us who experienced the camps changed our lives. We could hope for an alternative. Even if we had not found it altogether.

Later in New England I joined a wondrous group of women called the Women of Faith. We did monthly actions against the nuclear submarines and their D5 missiles being constructed at Electric Boat in Connecticut. We marched and demonstrated at each launching, sometimes getting arrested, sometimes simply doing guerrilla theater. But each month we did some action. Dancing at the gate one morning at 6:30, we shut down the missile business for 28 minutes and were inordinately proud of it. Another time we invaded their offices, several times we chained ourselves to gates or blockaded entrances.

We would think up our next action while we were waiting arraignment in the holding cell or sitting waiting as part of the support group in the courtroom. The night before the planned action we would meet to make signs, plan the press coverage, assign tasks. We would meet in a church or a private home near our action. For a couple of years we worked together without tension or friction, bringing new women into our group and learning how to talk to the media, handle the jail situation. What broke us up was some of the changes in the military situation and internal disruption caused by one new woman's inability to accept consensus. Until that time we had worked without a slip. Proving that it can be done.

I found some of the same camaraderie, the same sense of belonging to something bigger than one's self, the same willingness to accept others' decisions, as I found in the Army and this time aimed at peace, at justice, and at the creation of political community.

So why was I marching in a parade proclaiming the right of queers to serve in the military? What did I hope to accomplish by this? How did it fit with my peace activism?

I was marching along with hundreds of others to say "Yes, I was there. You can no longer deny my existence. Silencing me and all these others was useless because we know and you know what you are up to. Those of us in uniform are not just robots wound up and set out to kill and be killed at the bidding of the world economic order. We have lives that you do not approve of, we have thoughts and values that reject yours."

So I was marching for all of this, to challenge the Army's gendered system of power, to challenge its failure to honor the love of men and women for each other, to force them to change that reality. Because if they acknowledge the existence of queers in their ranks, in their leadership, and among those who make the decisions that vote them budgets, then they can no longer adhere to that male ideology of exclusion and machoism. Those qualities that have been assigned to women, the experiences and perceptions of women cannot so simply be dismissed. The Army as a male hierarchical institution is weakened.

And I was marching because I wanted to put the lie to all that we have been told was not possible, was dangerous. Contrary to what we are told, I have seen that this country can provide all the necessities of life, housing, food, clothing, health care, and education to hundreds of thousands of people in a very short time. An enormous army was assembled, housed, fed, and clothed in a very short time for the Korean War and again for the Vietnam War. Despite all we have heard of the dangers of the welfare programs and helping people out of trouble, the country did not go bankrupt, those people did not become lazy or valueless. Providing young people with all the necessities of life and good health made them strong and efficient.

Contrary to the claim that we only act out of individual self-interest, I have seen men and women put the good of the community above their own individual wishes. I have seen that men and women can think collectively about how to live together and get a job done. And I have seen them do this despite, not because of, the barbarous discipline.

Equality and justice, my lifelong dreams, are not to be found in fighting, in militarism. Killing people does not bring peace. There are other ways to create common commitments, a willingness to put one's body on the line, the courage to take risks.

It is here we must start to remake the world.

SEVENTY

Unity Statement (1980)

Women's Pentagon Action

In 1980 and 1981, some 2,000 women mainly from the northeastern United States encircled the Pentagon to express their opposition to war through theater and ritual—the **Women's Pentagon Action**. They utilized weaving as a metaphor for women's power against institutions, weaving the doors to the Pentagon shut with brightly colored yarns.

We are gathering at the Pentagon on November 16 because we fear for our lives. We fear for the life of this planet, our Earth, and the life of the children who are our human future.

We are mostly women who come from the northeastern region of our United States. We are city women who know the wreckage and fear of city streets, we are country women who grieve the loss of the small farm and have lived on the poisoned earth. We are young and older, we are married, single, lesbian. We live in different kinds of households: In groups, families, alone, some are single parents.

We work at a variety of jobs. We are students, teachers, factory workers, office workers, lawyers, farmers, doctors, builders, waitresses, weavers, poets, engineers, homeworkers, electricians, artists, blacksmiths. We are all daughters and sisters.

We have come here to mourn and rage and defy the Pentagon because it is the workplace of the imperial power which threatens us all. Every day while we work, study, love, the colonels and generals who are planning our annihilation walk calmly in and out the doors of its five sides. They have accumulated over 30,000 nuclear bombs, at the rate of three to six bombs every day. They are determined to produce the billion-dollar MX missile. They are creating a technology called Stealth—the invisible, unperceivable arsenal. They have revised the cruel old killer, nerve gas. They have proclaimed Directive 59 which asks for "small nuclear wars, prolonged but limited." The Soviet Union works hard to keep up with the United States initiatives. We can destroy each other's cities, towns, schools and children many times over. The United States has sent "advisors," money and arms to El Salvador and Guatemala to enable those juntas to massacre their own people.

The very same men, the same legislative committees that offer trillions of dollars to the Pentagon have brutally cut day care, children's lunches, battered women's shelters. The same men have concocted the Family Protection Act which will mandate the strictly patriarchal family and thrust federal authority into our home life. They are preventing the passage of ERA's simple statement and supporting the Human Life Amendment which will deprive all women of choice and many women of life itself.

We are in the hands of men whose power and wealth have separated them from the reality of daily life and from the imagination. We are right to be afraid.

At the same time, our cities are in ruins, bankrupt; they suffer the devastation of war. Hospitals are closed, our schools deprived of books and teachers. Our Black and Latino youth are without decent work. They will be forced, drafted to become the cannon fodder for the very power that oppresses them. Whatever help the poor receive is cut or withdrawn to feed the Pentagon which needs about $500,000,000 a day for its murderous health. It extracted $157 billion dollars last year from our own tax money, $1,800 from a family of four.

With this wealth our scientists are corrupted; over 40 percent work in government and corporate laboratories that refine the methods for destroying or deforming life. The lands of the Native American people have been turned to radioactive rubble in order to enlarge the nuclear warehouse. The uranium of South Africa, necessary to the nuclear enterprise, enriches the white minority and encourages the vicious system of racist oppression and war.

The President has just decided to produce the neutron bomb, which kills people but leaves property (buildings like this one) intact. There is fear among the people, and that fear, created by the industrial militarists, is used as an excuse to accelerate the arms

race. "We will protect you . . . " they say, but we have never been so endangered, so close to the end of human time.

We women are gathering because life on the precipice is intolerable. We want to know what anger in these men, what fear, which can only be satisfied by destruction, what coldness of heart and ambition drives their days. We want to know because we do not want that dominance which is exploitative and murderous in international relations, and so dangerous to women and children at home—we do not want that sickness transferred by the violent society through the fathers to the sons.

What is it that we women need for our ordinary lives, that we want for ourselves and also for our sisters in new nations and old colonies who suffer the white man's exploitation and too often the oppression of their own countrymen?

We want enough good food, decent housing, communities with clean air and water, good care for our children while we work. We want work that is useful to a sensible society. There is a modest technology to minimize drudgery and restore joy to labor. We are determined to use skills and knowledge from which we have been excluded—like plumbing or engineering or physics or composing. We intend to form women's groups or unions that will demand safe workplaces, free of sexual harassment, equal pay for work of comparable value. We respect the work women have done in caring for the young, their own and others, in maintaining a physical and spiritual shelter against the greedy and militaristic society. In our old age we expect our experience, our skills, to be honored and used.

We want health care which respects and understands our bodies. Physically challenged sisters must have access to gatherings, actions, happy events, work. For this, ramps must be added to stairs and we must become readers, signers, supporting arms. So close, so many, why have we allowed ourselves not to know them?

We want an education for children which tells the true story of our women's lives, which describes the earth as our home to be cherished, to be fed as well as harvested.

We want to be free from violence in our streets and in our houses. One in every three of us will be raped in her lifetime. The pervasive social power of the masculine ideal and the greed of the pornographer have come together to steal our freedom, so that whole neighborhoods and the life of the evening and night have been taken from us. For too many women the dark country road and the city alley have concealed the rapist. We want the night returned: the light of the moon, special in the cycle of our female lives, the stars and the gaiety of the city streets.

We want the right to have or not to have children—we do not want gangs of politicians and medical men to say we must be sterilized for the country's good. We know that this technique is the racists' method for controlling populations. Nor do we want to be prevented from having an abortion when we need one. We think this freedom should be available to poor women as it always has been to the rich. We want to be free to love whomever we choose. We will live with women or with men or we will live alone. We will not allow the oppression of lesbians. One sex or one sexual preference must not dominate another.

We do not want to be drafted into the army. We do not want our young brothers drafted. We want *them* equal with us.

We want to see the pathology of racism ended in our time. It has been the imperial arrogance of white male power that has separated us from the suffering and wisdom of our sisters in Asia, Africa, South America and in our own country. Many North American women look down on the minority nearest them: the Black, the Hispanic, the Jew, the Native American, the Asian, the immigrant. Racism has offered them privilege and convenience; they often fail to see that they themselves have bent to the unnatural authority and violence of men in government, at work, at home. Privilege does not increase knowledge or spirit or understanding. There

can be no peace while one race dominates another, one people, one nation, one sex despises another.

We must not forget the tens of thousands of American women who live much of their lives in cages, away from family, lovers, all the growing-up years of their children. Most of them were born at the intersection of oppressions: people of color, female, poor. Women on the outside have been taught to fear those sisters. We refuse that separation. We need each other's knowledge and anger in our common struggle against the builders of jails and bombs.

We want the uranium left in the earth and the earth given back to the people who tilled it. We want a system of energy which is renewable, which does not take resources out of the earth without returning them. We want those systems to belong to the people and their communities, not to the giant corporations which invariably turn knowledge into weaponry. We want the sham of Atoms for Peace ended, all nuclear plants decommissioned and the construction of new plants stopped. That is another war against the people and the child to be born in fifty years.

We want an end to the arms race. No more bombs. No more amazing inventions for death.

We understand all is connectedness. We know the life and work of animals and plants in seeding, reseeding and in fact simply inhabiting this planet. Their exploitation and the organized destruction of never to be seen again species threatens and sorrows us. The earth nourishes us as we with our bodies will eventually feed it. Through us, our mothers connected the human past to the human future.

With that sense, that ecological right, we oppose the financial connections between the Pentagon and the multinational corporations and banks that the Pentagon serves. Those connections are made of gold and oil. We are made of blood and bone, we are made of the sweet and finite resource, water. We will not allow these violent games to continue. If we are here in our stubborn thousands today, we will certainly return in the hundreds of thousands in the months and years to come.

We know there is a healthy, sensible, loving way to live and we intend to live that way in our neighborhoods and our farms in these United States, and among our sisters and brothers in all the countries of the world.

SEVENTY-ONE

◆◆◆

Full Moon: The Imagery of Wholeness and Celebration (2001)

Betty Burkes

Betty Burkes is a lifelong educator and activist. She has worked as a Montessori pre-school teacher; served as president and long-time board member of Women's International League for Peace and Freedom (U.S. Section); and undertaken peace education projects in Albania, Cambodia, Niger, and Peru with the Hague Appeal for Peace/UN Department of Disarmament Affairs.

Until the last seven or eight months, I would have argued that my most important learning about peacemaking and change has come through relationships with children, either from my own or those in my care. But today I must count the sacred events of the past two months among my most profound teachers: witnessing the heart-breaking-open experience of midwifing a comrade through the process of conscious dying; watching the birth of a child; attending a daughter's ritual transition; and participating in a son's commitment ceremony. These events testify to the essence of politics and feminism in action and to individuals reclaiming authority and power in the context of community.

On the last day of March, my partner Joan, my beloved friend, crossed over into the next world. Exactly one month earlier, on the last day of February, a new life—Isaac Daniel—crossed over into this one. Spending a month with him and his family, singing to him, sitting silently, with him looking deeply into my eyes while I looked deeply into his, feeling peaceful in that moment of recognition was consciousness changing, an insight into the meaning of living peace unfolded. The road to peace, like living and dying, is always under construction. Last weekend, Matthew, Joan's son, stood with Amy under the chupa at a temple in Farmington Hills, Michigan, promising to love and cherish one another in the company of family and friends. They pledged not only to love in the spirit of compassion, but if that promise lost its power to hold them, to separate in the same humility. Tomorrow we will attend daughter Ruth's Bat Mitzvah, a ceremony marking her journey from childhood into womanhood and beyond.

The river of birth, growth, death, and rebirth flowing through the human experience, passages that move in and out of each other, connecting us to one another, tells a story of the persistence and impermanence of life. They highlight the condition of the human impulse to create joyful, productive, creative living environments and relationships. Joan's and my last dance together spun her into a spiral of light and back into the arms of the universe. It pushed me into a contemplative and reflective time, feeling the enormous loss while sensing her amazing liberation. She accepted death as a transformation and a rebirthing process. Our six months of seclusion and uninterrupted care was an unusual articulation of political and feminist activism. Taking charge of my time, deciding that her and my relationship was paramount, resisting pressures from the marketplace doctors and undertakers, assuming authority for determining the details and particulars of her journey from diagnosis to cremation, embracing the wholeness of death, those were profoundly political and feminist actions. Becoming her own expert, she wove a patch of bliss and wholeness into our lives. The world around us, the community to which we belong held us, provided for us, supported Joan's dying and my caretaking.

Individuals claiming power within the context of community is a model for social change and a possible formula for subverting systems of power-over. Living from a community base made our choices possible: to rethink the meaning of time and to reclaim space to be intimate with the sacred changes happening around us, above, below, and within. Magic happened. Being attentive, being with the dying and healing experience transformed us and heightened the sense of our place in the world. We were not alone in our decision to create sacred spaces and to honor the things that we believe the most precious and important about living and non-living. The cycles of earth and all life that lives on within and above are connected and interdependent. One cannot flourish without the other. And each day Joan and I expressed our gratitude, and we made joyful sounds like: "the earth, the air, the fire, the water, / return, return, return, return." And sang "when we return, / They will remain / Wind and rock / Fire and rain." We honored the earth as our mother: "the earth is our mother, / we must take care of her, / the earth is our mother, we must take care of her." For each of the passages that I have mentioned, the community prepared a ritual that spoke to the relatedness: it was our support and deep bond to the person or couple in transition. Creating ritual allows us to envision the possibility of things not ordinarily expected. We have the ability to see and to use our imagination to change reality by changing consciousness. Starhawk calls it "magic," changing consciousness at will (1979, 37). Our culture of estrangement, as we now experience it, would have us believe that magic is impossible. But there was a time in the past—before the burning times and the Inquisition, before the growth of the money economy, before the transatlantic slave trade, before George Washington—when magic was alive and prolific. The past is still alive in the present.

The stillness and silence of Joan's preparations for death offered many hours of reflection and rethinking. It was an opportunity to deepen my commitment to the political and spiritual work that we shared with our local and international community of resistance and resistors. The process was inspiring because it was evidence that what gives life meaning is the journey, not the destination. One of the last things Joan wrote was this:

> The process of dying reminds me why my spiritual self is so important to my political self. Calling in the earth, the air, the fire, the water, and the spirit within is essential grounding for doing political work. Why else do it? To connect with the universe is to be connected with all things, to remember we are not separate, that our actions not only touch each other but those we know not of.

My life is testimony to her observation. Being born an African American is being born with a sense of injustice and a challenge to do something about it. The challenge is one that you can take on in a conscious, intentional way or choose denial, but it never leaves you, like the cycles of life. I took the challenge on politically when I joined the Women's International League for Peace and Freedom (WILPF), a tradition of women acting for peace and justice, uninterrupted since 1915. In April, we celebrated WILPF's eighty-fifth anniversary.

Language is a tricky thing. I did not discover my feminist label or receive support for self-discovery or a sense of my personal power at university. Not until WILPF found me did I discover the language for the values that I grew up living. WILPF is about changing structures, not just practices, creating the intellectual knowledge needed through campaigns and organizing locally, nationally, and internationally to transform those structures that oppress us. It is not about reform or charity. Questioning authority is at the heart of its feminist analysis and politics. Feminist action to subvert the politics of war and peace begins with white women becoming traitors to white privilege and to the domination politics of the white race. An anti-racist agenda must be its core if there is ever to be solidarity among women and effective coalitions that unite us in struggle against suppliers of war and undemocratic governments.

Feminist politics are transformational politics. They offer us the values of sharing power, leading a human life, being responsible to and for one's *sistah* and fellow human beings. Feminist activism acknowledges that the roots of gendered politics are buried in issues of racial, environmental, political, and cultural inequities. It challenges the political-economic structures organized around the principle of male dominance. How we are inextricably linked together for our common good; our survival on this planet is the question that Suzanne Pharr takes on in her book, *In the Time of the Right.*

> Because the voices dominating this country's leadership speak only of the false democracy of the marketplace rather than the democracy of diverse people living in community, we have to find ways to raise new voices that speak to the transformational and educational political work of building a wider, more inclusive community. [Here Pharr quotes Henry Giroux,] "The real challenge of leadership is educating students to live in a multicultural world, to face the challenge of reconciling differences in community, and to address what it means to have a voice in shaping one's future as part of

a broader task of enriching and extending the imperatives of democracy and human rights on both the national and global level."

(1996, 88)

One of the challenges facing a feminist pedagogy, in Departments of Women's Studies, is their home within the patriarchal structures of education which only seek reform, compromise, or structural adjustment. The promise of higher standards of living and solidification with white privilege contributes to thwarting the revolutionary potential of Women's Studies. However, Women's Studies has the rare privilege of having women on the inside, with access to resources and able to employ leadership, power, and education linked to activism. Within WILPF, my local intellectual, political, and spiritual home, we are committed to uprooting and exposing the ills of patriarchy and capitalism. Our commitment to friendship and love makes us feel whole and connected in our work, supplanting the false division between mind and emotion, matter and spirit, the intellectual and the intuitive.

What are we envisioning for the future? Subverting is just the beginning. Without the vision of a culture that is imbued with a feminist agenda, subversion is without life and without spirit. A vision that intertwines economic justice and human rights offers the best possibility of building a strong political base for subverting the gendered politics of war and peace. Every step towards peace must have peace embedded in it. We have to live the vision of the world that we want to create. Taking the lead from Pharr, I frame my thoughts about feminist politics in the context of transformation:

[doing] political work that changes the hearts and minds of people, supports personal and group growth in ways that create healthy, whole people, organizations and communities and is based on a vision of a society where people across lines of race, gender, class and sexuality are supported by institutions and communities to live their best lives.

(1996, 97)

Being born an African American is being born with a history of slavery, rebellion, theft, guilt, genocide, and denial. My personal journey is part of a long tradition of struggle and resistance. I believe that ultimately the political and social transformation of this country was contingent upon the affirmation and vindication of its slave history—an act that would have far-reaching consequences on the global, capitalist institutions in the Western world. There was a direct link between the financial backers of capitalist globalization and the financial houses that managed the transatlantic slave trade. Twentieth- and twenty-first-century global corporatization is the logical extension of the white supremacist, capitalist, patriarchal economic system that engineered the transatlantic slave trade and invented racism to justify it in the sixteenth, seventeenth, and eighteenth centuries.

I am a descendent of slaves who chose to survive during this scarring period of world history. They chose to live. Their choice reminds me daily of my inherited responsibility to the ancient ones and to the unborn generations, a responsibility for subverting, reshaping, and transforming the politics of power that underpin the structures of injustice and war. I was born into a big extended family, learning by example that as individuals we have responsibilities for others and are accountable to the community that values us. Grandma Mamie, the link to our slave past, was a keeper of the family's progress. She grew up with her grandparents, Susan and Jake Christian, emancipated slaves. Through Mamie and her grandparents, we tapped into the heritage of American slavery. She was our window through which we learned about our ingenious and courageous history. Her arms stretched wide to embrace all who came within her reach. She loved us unconditionally and was a buffer to the hostile world that told us we were inferior. Mamie lived by example. She probably never heard the words "feminist intellect," but she was my first real feminist role model. She resisted, she sabotaged the system that never intended for her to survive by non-cooperation. Mamie is my American hero. Her feminism had no label. It was the fabric of her life. One afternoon before she died, a hundred years after she was born, Mamie said to me, "Betty, the way things are is not the way things have to be. You can choose to make a difference."

When I was six-years old, I went to school and entered a world governed by the politics of domination and isolation, racism, and sexism. I was not prepared for the negation and the humiliation that I found there. Even though I persevered, school was a suffering place. My popularity and success was proof to the authorities that the system worked. Unlike my ancestors, I would not have chosen to survive without my father's living example of courageous, philosophical engagement. My dad is my second feminist role model. During those school years, in a hundred different ways, he contradicted the messages of estrangement and judgement from the school culture with affirmations and respect. To him, self-discipline, fairness, conscious living, cooperative and non-competitive learning, community and communication are the substance of life. Racism and sexism are only the shadows. He believed that he could change the world and he did. He chased Jim Crow from the businesses of Malvern, Ohio, and he brought Africa to town through visits from African students from nearby colleges, interrupting the lie that our beginning began in bondage in America. The lessons from that education I never forgot. My dad loved and mentored me through my troubled waters towards healing and understanding as I came to mentor my own daughter when she was called a "dirty little nigger" on the school bus shortly after entering first grade. This event launched my activism and antiracist work.

My years of activism have been an initiation, like a ritual of self-renewal, re-dedicating my life to honoring the survival of the ancient ones who had a vision and faith in the power of the spirit. The transatlantic slave trade was a curse. It was an expression of the white supremacist, capitalist, patriarchal, economic structure that has multiplied its lust for power and global domination beyond reason, reflected in the eyes of hungry and homeless children; weapon-strewn, war-torn landscapes; galloping prison populations; land mine amputees; emaciated refugees; uranium mining; plunder of Indian lands; despoiling of the earth and everything in the universe that it touches.

Nothing short of an organized movement with a feminist perspective and analysis—antiracist, anti-capitalist, and anti-white supremacist—can subvert the gendered politics of war and peace. I believe that transforming society means transforming reality, transforming the intellect. This requires magic, the art of changing consciousness at will. Hope does not lie in avenging the old system but in envisioning a new one, using power to make the world whole. Our challenge is living the changes that we envision will promote peace rather than war. While generating intellectual knowledge in the teaching and research of Women's Studies creates a foundation, repairing ourselves is essential for our survival. The work of women inside the institutions of Women's Studies must collaborate with women and men organizing outside. We must have people who are not just knowledgeable with strong intellects, but people who are courageous enough to take on the work of justice in their personal lives as well as in the world. Feminism is not just about ideas. Our work must also be focused on nurturing the life of the spirit, insisting upon our wholeness and affirming our relational being. We will succeed in building a strong base for transforming the politics of power when, together, we weave a vision that in practice offers a way of life so *alive* it's impossible to resist.

REFERENCES

Pharr, Suzanne. 1996. *In the Time of the Right: Reflections on Liberation.* Oakland, CA: Chardon Press.

Starhawk. 1999. *The Spiral Dance: A Rebirth of the Ancient Religion of the Great Goddess.* San Francisco, CA: HarperCollins.

———. 1997. *Dreaming the Dark: Magic, Sex, and Politics.* Boston: Beacon Press.

12

◆◆◆

Women and the Environment

Place is a fundamental element in our lives whether we live in a spacious suburb, a vibrant—maybe overcrowded—downtown area, an old-established inner-city neighborhood, on a farm, a ranch, or a reservation (Anderson 1991; Barnhill 1999; Williams 1992). Places change over time so that a formerly Polish American or Italian American community may now be home to African Americans or Vietnamese immigrants; a poorer neighborhood may become gentrified as middle-class people move in and push up property values. Neighborhood facilities—churches, temples, synagogues, schools, stores, restaurants, parks, community centers—reflect the interests and concerns of people who live there. The quality of some local services and the physical space also reflect the standing of a particular community in the wider society. In general, middle-class and upper-middle-class communities have better school buildings, more sports facilities, more doctors' offices, and a wider range of stores than poorer neighborhoods. They are also farther from factories, oil refineries, power plants, sawmills, stockyards, railway terminals, highways, garbage dumps, and other sources of pollution, bad smells, and noise.

Many people contribute to safeguarding our physical environment. Federal legislation such as the Clean Air Act and regulatory agencies like the Environmental Protection Agency were established to limit toxic emissions from factories, homes, and vehicles. Cities or counties provide services like potable water, garbage disposal, street cleaning and repair, snow clearance, stop signs and traffic lights, town parks, and recreation centers. National environmental organizations have lobbied for the preservation of wilderness areas as national parks, for the protection of endangered species, and for stronger environmental regulation of industry. Community organizations clear trash from highways and vacant lots, or work in community gardens. Individuals mow lawns, trim trees, sweep the sidewalk, recycle reusable materials, compost organic matter, and buy "green" or environmentally safe products like paper goods from recycled paper or biodegradable soaps and detergents. Important as they are, these efforts cannot keep up with the scale and pace of environmental degradation.

533

Over the past forty years or so, many people in the United States have become increasingly concerned with environmental issues. Hazardous industrial production processes have affected the health of workers and people who live near or downwind of industrial areas. Industrial pollutants, chemical pesticides and fertilizers, and wastes from nuclear power plants and uranium mines are seeping into the groundwater in many parts of the country as exemplified in feature films like *A Civil Action* and *Erin Brockovich*. Homes and schools have been built on land once used for toxic dumps (Gibbs 1995, 1998). Deforestation, global warming, and the disappearance of hundreds of species are also hallmarks of vast environmental destruction worldwide (Worldwatch Institute 2003). Most United States environmental activists probably agree that the greatest threat to environmental security worldwide comes from the waste-producing, industrialized, militarized countries of the North, especially the United States, Canada, Europe, and Japan.

This chapter is concerned with environmental effects on women and with women's activism around environmental issues. It assumes that there is an ethical dimension to living in any location: that we care for the environment for our own sake and for the sake of future generations. As the world has become more integrated, our home places are deeply affected by corporate and governmental decisions often made many miles away and by international agreements and institutions like WTO. As with other topics in this book, environmental issues are experienced at the micro and meso levels, but also have macro- and global-level dimensions. The lenses of gender, race, class, and nation are also essential tools of analysis in this chapter.

In the United States the environmental crisis affects men as well as women, of course, but in terms of environmental health, women and children show the effects of toxic pollution earlier than men do, either because of low body weight or because women's bodies become what some have termed "unhealthy environments" for their babies (Reading 73; Kettel 1996; Nelson 1990; Steingraber 2001). A significant number of babies without brains have been born to women on both sides of the Rio Grande, a river polluted by U.S.-controlled *maquiladora* industries on the Mexican side (Kamel and Hoffman 1999). (Working conditions in these *maquiladoras,* or subassembly plants, are described

in more detail in Chapter 9.) Contact with pesticides has led to poor health for many women farmworkers in the United States and to chronic illnesses or severe disabilities for their children (Chavez 1993; Moses 1993). Several firms have tried to keep women of childbearing age out of the most noxious production processes—often the highest paid—or to insist that they be sterilized, lest women sue them later for fetal damage (Gottlieb 1993). Women who work in computer manufacturing, chicken processing, the dairy industry, and housecleaning are all exposed to chemicals as part of their work, as are manicurists and farm workers.

Children's health is also compromised by environmental factors such as lead in paints and gasoline, air pollution, traffic hazards, and violence that may involve the use of handguns, with significant differences between those living in inner cities and those in suburban neighborhoods (Hamilton 1993; Phoenix 1993). Environmental writer Florence Williams (2005) noted: "If human breast milk came stamped with an ingredients label, it might read . . . 4 percent fat, vitamins A, C, E, and K, lactose, essential minerals, growth hormones, proteins, enzymes and antibodies." In addition, some women also pass traces of DDT, PCBs, dioxin, mercury, lead, benzene, arsenic, or flame retardants to their nursing babies. The Akwesasne Mothers' Milk project in upstate New York, founded by midwife Katsi Cook, was one of the first community projects to explore the toxicity of breast milk in response to Native American mothers' concern that breast-feeding, supposedly the best way to nurture infants, could expose them to pollutants (LaDuke 1999). As biological scientist Sandra Steingraber argues in Reading 73, it is difficult to know how even relatively low chemical levels will affect the development of a fetus or infant. During the sixth month of her pregnancy she studied fetal brain development and, in the excerpt reprinted here, discusses the effects of lead on this highly complex and delicate process. She believes that environmental policy and regulations do not protect our health adequately. She argues for the **precautionary principle,** defined by an international group of scientists, government officials, lawyers, and labor and grassroots environmental activists who met at Wingspread (Racine, Wis.) in January 1998, as follows:

When an activity raises threats of harm to human health or the environment, precautionary measures should be taken even if some cause and effect relationships are not fully established scientifically. In this context the proponent of an activity, rather than the public, should bear the burden of proof.

(Rachel's Environment and Health Weekly 1998, p. 1)

An international covenant banning lead-based paint in 1925, mentioned by Steingraber, was operating on a precautionary principle. But this covenant was not adopted in the United States due to the influence of the lead industry, which dismissed relevant scientific findings as "anti-lead propaganda."

Many household products contain chemicals associated with health hazards. Asian Communities for Reproductive Justice has established POLISH, the Participatory Research, Organizing, and Leadership Initiative for Safety and Health to research the degree to which Asian women and girls and nail salon workers are exposed to toxic chemicals through both personal use and professional occupation. The Environmental Working Group has a Skin Deep project that provides a safety assessment of ingredients in personal care products (www.ewg.org).

Many more women than men are involved in campaigning on behalf of environmental issues at a grassroots level, though women are less active than men concerning environmental issues at the national level (Mohai 1997). We do not see women as somehow closer to nature than men, as is sometimes argued, or as having an essentially nurturing, caring nature. Rather, we see women's environmental activism as an extension of their roles as daughters, wives, and mothers, caring for families and communities. Women have a long-standing history of involvement in community organizing: campaigning against poor housing conditions, high rents, unsafe streets, lead in gasoline, toxic dumps, and so on, described by sociologist Nancy Naples (1998) as "activist mothering." Ideally, taking care of children and other family members should be everyone's responsibility, including government and corporations, and would involve safeguarding and restoring the environment.

In addition to the readings in this chapter, other contributors are also concerned with environmental issues: the health effects of a toxic waste incinerator (Reading 32), possible environmental causes of breast cancer (Reading 34), and the privatization of water supplies worldwide (Reading 57). In Chapter 9

we mention how producing export crops has meant that people in countries of the global South now grow food crops on more marginal land, like steep hillsides, with greater possibility of flooding and soil erosion. Large-scale dams funded by the World Bank have displaced many thousands of small farmers from their land and livelihood. In Chapter 11 we also note the severe, long-term health and environmental effects of military operations, weapons tests, as well as war.

Theoretical and Activist Perspectives

Generally, theories grow out of and inform experience. Women who are concerned about environmental degradation draw on different theoretical and activist perspectives, particularly deep ecology and bioregionalism, ecofeminism, and environmental justice. These are not unitary perspectives, though here we emphasize points of comparison between them rather than their internal variations.

Environmentalism

Over the past forty years, successive U.S. Congresses have passed a number of environmental laws, for example, to improve air and water quality or to protect wilderness areas and endangered species. This is largely due to the work of dedicated environmentalists like Rachel Carson (1962; Dorsey and Thormodsgard 2003; Hynes 1989; Reading 34) and to concerted public education and lobbying by major environmental organizations such as the Sierra Club, the Natural Resources Defense Council, and the Environmental Defense Fund. Limitations of such efforts are that they are slow and invariably compromised by corporate interests. Currently, these hard-earned gains are being rolled back by President Bush's environmental policy that includes the weakening of existing environmental legislation and the role of the Environmental Protection Agency, opening up national forests to commercial interests, allowing exemptions from environmental law for military training and maneuvers, abandoning the international treaty on global warming (the Kyoto Treaty), and an energy plan based heavily on fossil fuels, including the proposal to drill for oil in the Alaska Arctic National Wildlife Refuge.

Deep Ecology and Bioregionalism

Deep ecology is a term coined by Norwegian philosopher Arne Naess and taken up in the United States by ecological philosophers Bill Devall and George Sessions (1985). It is premised on two fundamental principles: self-realization for every being and a "biocentric" equality among species. Many environmental activists in the United States who are drawn to deep ecology are critical of the more mainstream environmental organizations mentioned above, which have a human-centered focus. Earth First! is an activist network that exemplifies principles of deep ecology in practice. It gained public recognition through direct action, particularly in opposition to the logging of old-growth forests in the Pacific Northwest and northern California (J. Davis 1991; Hill 2000; List 1993).

At its worst, deep ecology is sometimes reduced to a rather simplistic view of the world in which nature is "good" and people are "bad." Deep ecologists argue for reducing human population, reducing human interference in the biosphere, and reducing human standards of living. As its name implies, Earth First! has been more interested in saving the earth than in safeguarding the human population. This led to arguments that, for example, if AIDS didn't exist it would have had to be invented, or that starving people in Africa should be left to die so that the human population can be brought back into balance with the carrying capacity of the land (Thropy 1991). Deep ecologists value the preservation of nature in and of itself rather than for any benefit such preservation affords to humans. Nature is often seen in romantic terms: The virgin, feminized wilderness is vulnerable, innocent, and weak, and protecting "her" draws on old macho, militaristic iconography (King 1987). Wilderness is not thought of as the homeland of indigenous people but as a special place where people (at least athletic, nondisabled people) can get close to an "experience" of nature. Critics of U.S. deep ecology oppose its people vs. nature stance and argue, for example, that "if we believe that we are in essence bad for nature we are profoundly separated from the natural world" (Starhawk 2002a, p. 161). Nature is not something far away, to be encountered on weekend hikes or occasional camping trips. Everyone is connected to the natural environment in the most mundane but profound way: through the air we breathe, the water we drink, and the food we eat, as embodied human beings in a continuum of life. Ecofeminist writer and activist Starhawk (2002a) also notes that a "humans-as-blight" view is self-defeating for organizing around environmental issues, as people "don't act effectively out of feeling bad, guilty, wrong, and inauthentic" (p. 161).

In the 1980s and 1990s, people who tried to stop logging, for example, especially in old-growth forests of western states, often found themselves up against loggers who were dependent on timber companies for their livelihood. Feminist and Earth First! strategist and activist Judi Bari, who had been a union organizer, is credited with helping to forge alliances between Earth First!, labor unions, and other social justice organizations. In urban areas, too, industrial jobs are often set against a cleaner environment. Corporations argue that they cannot afford to clean up their operations or that cleaning up would be at the expense of jobs. An alliance between environmentalists and labor organizers is essential. People need a livelihood as well as good environmental conditions, and the two are not mutually exclusive (Goodstein 1999; Pulido 1996; Schwab 1994; Alliance for Sustainable Jobs and the Environment, Portland, Ore.).

A humans-as-nature view prevails within the bioregional movement, which emphasizes decentralization, small-scale projects, agricultural and economic self-sufficiency within bioregions, and a strongly developed attachment to place (Andruss et al. 1990; Berg 1993; Sale 1985). Indigenous people invariably emphasize the importance of connection to the land for their communities, as discussed by lawyer, legal scholar, and Hawaiian sovereignty activist Mililani Trask (Reading 76; also see Allen 1986; LaDuke 1999). This point is taken up by Starhawk (2002a) from the perspective of earth-centered spirituality. Vandana Shiva (2002), director of the Research Foundation on Science, Technology, and Ecology, focuses on "relocalization," as opposed to globalization, which places an enormous economic and environmental burden on countries of the South. She argues that "what can be grown and produced locally should be used locally" rather than exported, and, further, that "relocalization everywhere—in the South and in the North—would conserve resources, generate meaningful work, fulfill basic needs and strengthen democracy" (p. 249; Reading 57). Crucially important for ecofeminists and environmental justice activists is that these localized systems also include a commitment to anti-racist principles, women's liberation, and economic justice.

Ecofeminism

The creation of the term **ecofeminism** is usually attributed to a group of French feminists who founded the Ecology-Feminism Center in 1974, based on their analysis of connections between masculinist social institutions and the destruction of the physical environment (d'Eaubonne 1994). A few years later,

groundbreaking work in the United States by poet and essayist Susan Griffin (1978) and environmental historian Carolyn Merchant (1980) articulated a central insight of ecofeminism, the connection between the domination of women and the domination of nature. These authors pointed to the ways in which Western thought and science has seen nonhuman nature as wild and hostile, so much matter to be mastered and used. Francis Bacon, a seventeenth- century English statesman, philosopher, and champion of modern science, was an early exponent of this view and a powerful influence on the development of Western science. He wrote:

> For you have to but follow and . . . hound nature in her wanderings, and you will be able when you like to lead and drive her afterward to the same place again. . . . Neither ought a man make scruple of entering and penetrating into these holes and corners, when the inquisition of truth is his whole object.
> *(Quoted in Merchant 1980, p. 168)*

In Western thought, nature is often feminized and sexualized through imagery such as "virgin forest," "the rape of the earth," and "penetrating" the wilderness. Shiva (1988) notes that in the Western model of development, *sources,* living things that can reproduce life—whether forests, seeds, or women's bodies—are turned into *resources* to be objectified, controlled, and used. This makes them productive in economic terms. In this view, a forest that is not logged, a river that is not fished, or a hillside that is not mined, is unproductive (Waring 1988). A core point in ecofeminist analysis involves the concept of dualism, where various attributes are thought of in terms of oppositions: culture/nature; mind/body; male/female; civilized/primitive; sacred/profane; subject/object; self/other. Philosopher Val Plumwood (1993) argues that these dualisms are mutually reinforcing and should be thought of as an interlocking set. In each pair, one side is valued over the other. Culture, mind, male, civilized, for example, are valued over nature, body, female, primitive, which are thought of as "other" and inferior. Plumwood argues that dualism is the logic of hierarchical systems of thought—colonialism, racism, sexism, or militarism, which rely on the idea of otherness, enemies, and inferiority to justify superiority and domination. Ecofeminist ideas involve the transcendence of dualistic thought and valuing cultural and ecological diversity. JeeYeun Lee (Reading 5) notes that "ecofeminists challenge our fundamental ideas about living on and with the earth, about our interactions with animals, plants, food, agriculture and industry." Ynestra King (1998) argues that for ecofeminists "Modern Western science and technology . . . capitalism and Eurocentric masculinist culture together pose a threat to the continuation of life on earth" (p. 207; Reading 74). Ecofeminism is intrinsically about intersectionality, and has the potential to link opposition to racism, economic exploitation, militarism, and colonialism with opposition to the domination of women and nature (see Hawthorne 2002; Kirk 1997a, 1997b, 1998; Mies and Shiva 1993; Shiva 1988).

Such a broad approach is open to many interpretations and ideas for activism and organizing. The first ecofeminist conference in the United States, titled "Women for Life on Earth," was held in Amherst, Massachusetts, as a response to the near-meltdown at the Three Mile Island nuclear power plant in 1980, as discussed by ecofeminist writer Ynestra King (Reading 74). One outcome of the conference was the Women's Pentagon Action, a major demonstration against militarism in the early 1980s, mentioned in Chapter 11 (also see Reading 70). Ecofeminism is explored and developed through newsletters and study groups, college courses, animal rights organizing, and long-term women's land projects (see e.g., Adams 1999; Diamond and Orenstein 1990; Gaard 1993; King 1988, 1993b; Sturgeon 1997; Warren 1994, 2000). Some ecofeminist writers and researchers work with local activist groups or contribute to national and international debates. Examples include the National Women's Health Network's research and organizing around industrial and environmental health (Nelson 1990), critiques of reproductive technology and genetic engineering by the Feminist Network of Resistance to Reproductive and Genetic Engineering (Mies and Shiva 1993), and the Committee on Women, Population, and the Environment, which has critiqued simplistic overpopulation arguments that focus only on countries of the South rather than also addressing the overconsumption of the North (Bandarage 1997; Hartmann 1995; Mello 1996; Silliman and King 1999). The Women's Environment and Development Organization (WEDO) coordinated a major international conference in 1991 to work out a women's agenda to take to the U.N. Conference on the Environment and Development in Rio de Janeiro in June 1992. This group was an active participant in the NGO Forum in China in 1995, as we noted in Chapter 9, and at the World Summit on Sustainable Development in Johannesburg, 2002 (WEDO 2002).

Ecofeminist writer Charlene Spretnak (1990) embraces the eclectic nature of U.S. ecofeminism and notes its varied roots in feminist theory, feminist spirituality, and social ecology. This diversity in ecofeminist approaches raises the question of whether there is a sufficiently consistent, intellectually coherent ecofeminist perspective, and many academics claim that there is not. Some women of color argue that, as with such U.S. feminism, ecofeminism emphasizes gender over race and class; others contend that it focuses on abstract ideas about women and nature rather than on practical issues with a material base (Davis 1998; Smith 1997; Taylor 1997). Left-wing radicals, some environmentalists, and many academics reject ecofeminism as synonymous with goddess worship or on the grounds that it assumes women are essentially closer to nature than men. Geographer Joni Seager (1993), for example, has developed a feminist understanding of environmental issues but does not use the term *ecofeminism* to describe her work. At present, U.S. ecofeminism is very much the preserve of writers and scholars, albeit those who are often on the margins of the academy in part-time or temporary positions. Although this may lead to an activism of scholarship—by no means insignificant, as suggested earlier—it does not often connect directly with the reality of daily life for many women organizing around environmental issues (also see Epstein 1993; Kirk 1997; Sachs 1996). We argue that an ecological feminism can, and should, integrate gender, race, class, and nation in its analyses and that its powerful theoretical insights can, and should, translate into practice.

Environmental Justice

The people most affected by poor physical environments in the United States are women and children, particularly from communities of color. Many women of color and poor White women are active in hundreds of local organizations campaigning for healthy living and working conditions in their communities, which are disproportionately affected by

pollution from incinerators, toxic dumps, fertilizers, pesticides, and hazardous working conditions in industry and agriculture (Adamson, Evans, and Stein 2002; Bullard 1990, 1993; Hofrichter 1993; LaDuke 1999; Quintero-Somaini and Quirindongo 2004; Spears 1998; Stein 2004; Szasz 1994). Data show a strong correlation between the distribution of toxic wastes and race, which has been termed **environmental racism** (Lee 1987). The theory of environmental racism and the movement for **environmental justice** draw on concepts of civil rights, under which all citizens have a right to healthy living and working conditions. Organizationally, too, the environmental justice movement has roots in civil rights organizing, as well as in labor unions, Chicano land-grant movements, social justice organizations, and Native American rights organizations. Its tactics include demonstrations and rallies, public education, research and monitoring of toxic sites, preparing and presenting expert testimony to government agencies, reclaiming land through direct action, and maintaining and teaching traditional agricultural practices, crafts, and skills. Examples of local organizations include the Asia Pacific Environmental Network (Oakland, Calif.), the Mothers of East Los Angeles (Pardo 1990), the Newtown Florist Club (Gainesville, GA), the Southwest Network for Environmental and Economic Justice (Albuquerque, N.M., and Austin, Tex.), and West Harlem Environmental Action (New York; see Miller 1993).

Local organizations embrace different issues depending on their memberships and geographic contexts. Some are primarily concerned to stop the location, of toxic waste dumps or incinerators in their neighborhoods, an approach sometimes dubbed the Not-In-My-Back-Yard (NIMBY) syndrome. Most groups are quick to see that it is not enough to keep hazards out of their own neighborhoods if this means that dumps or incinerators will then be located in other poor communities. This has led to coordinated opposition on a local, regional, and national level. The First National People of Color Environmental Leadership Summit in Washington, D.C., in 1991, adopted "Principles of Environmental Justice" included here (Reading 75). Over the next ten years, several major grassroots Networks were formed, such as the African American Environmental Justice Action Network, the Indigenous Environmental Network, and the Farmworkers Network for Economic and Environmental Justice, committed to building a multicultural, multiracial movement.

Besides opposing hazardous conditions, the environmental justice movement also has a powerful reconstructive dimension involving sustainable projects that intertwine ecological, economic, and cultural survival. Examples include Tierra Wools (northern New Mexico), where a workers' cooperative produces high-quality, handwoven rugs and clothing and organically fed lamb from its sheep (Pulido 1993); the Native American White Earth Land Recovery Project in Minnesota, which produces wild rice, maple sugar, berries, and birch bark (LaDuke 1993, 1999); and many inner-city community gardening projects producing vegetables for local consumption (Bagby 1990; Hynes 1996; Warner 1987).

Although very few local environmental issues are exclusively the concern of women, women form the majority of local activists in opposing such hazards as toxic dumps. As noted, women have a history of community organizing. This activism may also be given special impetus if they have sick children or become ill themselves (see Reading 34, Chapter 5, concerning environmental factors and the incidence of breast cancer). Illnesses caused by toxics are sometimes difficult to diagnose and treat because they affect internal organs and the balance of body functioning, and symptoms can be mistaken for those of other conditions. Women have been persistent in raising questions and searching for plausible explanations for such illnesses, sometimes discovering that their communities have been built on contaminated land, as happened at Love Canal, New York, for example, or tracing probable sources of pollution affecting their neighborhoods (Gibbs 1995, 1998; Kaplan 1997). They have publicized their findings and taken on governmental agencies and corporations responsible for contamination. In so doing they are often ridiculed as "hysterical housewives" by officials and reporters and their research trivialized as emotional and unscholarly. By contrast, Nelson (1990), for example, honors this work as kitchen table science. In October 1991, women were 60 percent of the participants at the First National People of Color Environmental Leadership Summit. Many urban gardeners in northern cities are elderly African American women (e.g., Bagby 1990). On the west coast, Latino and Asian immigrants continue the gardening traditions of their homelands. Cindy Chan Saelee describes her mother's garden in Richmond, California, in Reading 72. In rural areas, women work on family subsistence garden plots, planting, harvesting, and processing fruits and vegetables for home use (Sachs 1996). Some know the woods or backcountry areas in great detail, as ethnobotanists, because they go there at different seasons to gather herbs for medicinal purposes. Among Mexican Americans, for example, *curanderas*—traditional healers—continue to work with herbal remedies and acquire their knowledge from older women relatives (Perrone,

Stockel, and Krueger 1989). Others attest to the healing and redemptive power of gardening and caring for plants. Catherine Sneed, for example, founded the Garden Project for prisoners and former prisoners, and comments: "we're not just growing plants—we're growing people" (Sneed 2000, p. 27; see also Gross 1992; Hynes 1996).

When women become involved with environmental justice organizing, they become politicized (Gibbs 1995, 1998; Krauss 1993; Zeff, Love, and Stults 1989). They are caught up in meetings, maybe traveling to other towns and cities and staying away overnight. They spend much more time, and money, on the phone than before. They are quoted in the local papers or on the TV news. They often face new challenges, balancing family responsibilities, perhaps struggling with their husbands' misgivings about their involvement, or facing the tensions of being strong women in male-dominated communities.

Women active in the environmental justice movement generally see themselves and their communities in terms of race and class and "have remained wary of a 'feminist' label" (Gottlieb 1993, p. 234). Indeed, most environmental justice organizations do not draw on a gender analysis, even though many grassroots participants are women. By contrast, ecofeminists have tended to emphasize gender at the expense of race and class, and have been less effective in linking theory and practice in a sustained way. Robert Gottlieb (1993), professor of urban and environmental policy, notes that the U.S. environmental movement as a whole has been unable to respond to the question "What constitutes an agenda and organizing style that incorporates women's experiences?"(p. 234). Given the crucial importance of the environment in a more secure and sustainable world, there is a great need for a theoretical framework that integrates gender, race, class, nation, and environmental issues and that generates broad-based activist efforts.

Connectedness and Sustainability

The writers and activists mentioned in this chapter all work from their sense of relationship and responsibility to maintain or to remake connections between people and the natural world. Together such projects and movements draw on alternative visions and strategies for sustainable living, however small-scale and fragile they might be at present. At root

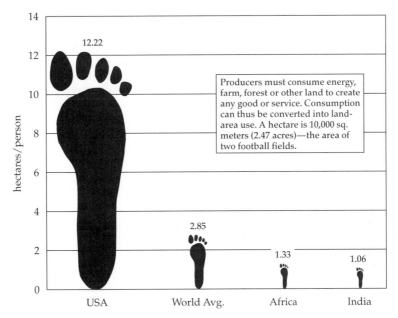

Producers must consume energy, farm, forest or other land to create any good or service. Consumption can thus be converted into land-area use. A hectare is 10,000 sq. meters (2.47 acres)—the area of two football fields.

FIGURE 12.1 Comparative Consumption of Environmental Resources per Person, 2000 (in hectares). (*Source:* Bill Bigelow and Bob Peterson [eds.], *Rethinking Globalization* [Milwaukee, Wis.: Rethinking Schools Press, 2002.] Reprinted by permission of Rethinking Schools Press.)

this is about taking on the current economic system and the systems of power—personal and institutional—that sustain and benefit from it, working to transform relationships of exploitation and oppression.

The idea of sustainability is often invoked but means very different things to different people. For corporate economists, for example, it means sustained economic growth that will yield ongoing profits; for ecologists it involves the maintenance of natural systems—wetlands, forests, wilderness, air and water quality; for environmentalists it means using only renewable resources and generating low or nonaccumulating levels of pollution (Pearce, Markandya, and Barbier 1990). Many concerned with environmental economics note the contradiction between the linear expansionism of capitalist economies and long-term sustainability (Daly and Cobb 1989; Henderson 1991; O'Connor 1994). Scholar and writer Maria Mies (1993) notes that for countries of the South to follow the development model of the industrial North there would need to be two more worlds: one for the necessary natural resources and the other for the waste.

A more sustainable future for both North and South means rethinking current cultural and economic systems and priorities and emphasizing ecologically sound production to meet people's basic needs, as argued by scholar and writer H. Patricia Hynes (Reading 77). She uses the concept **ecological footprint** to refer to the amount of energy, land, water, minerals, and other natural resources required by varying lifestyles and levels of development (see Figure 12.1). A sustainable future implies local control over transnational corporations, reduction of poor countries' foreign debt, and making money available for development that is ecologically sound, as we suggested in Chapter 9. At a local level in the United States it implies support for community gardens, farmers' markets, credit unions, and small-scale worker-owned businesses and markets, mentioned in Chapter 8. It means valuing women's unpaid domestic and caring work, a key aspect of sustaining home and community life (Mellor 1992; Waring 1988). Sociologist Mary Mellor notes that this caring work is geared to biological time. Children need feeding when they are hungry; sick people need care regardless of what time of day it is; gardens need planting in the right season. She argues that, given a gendered division of labor, "women's responsibility for biological time means that men have been able to create a public world that largely ignores it," a world "no longer rooted in the physical reality of human existence" (pp. 258–59). A sustainable future must be based in biological time and will require emotional as well as physical and intellectual labor. Novels provide an effective way of showing the possibilities—positive and negative—of particular philosophies and societal arrangements, and they can help us to imagine different futures (e.g., Butler 1993; Piercy 1976; Starhawk 1993). Environmental artists are working on reclamation and recycling projects that are both practical and beautiful, by using natural materials and natural settings.

To create such a future will also mean changing current definitions of wealth that emphasize materialism and consumerism. A broader notion of wealth includes everything that has the potential to enrich a person and a community, such as health, physical energy and strength, safety and security, time, skills, talents, wisdom, creativity, love, community support, a connection to one's history and cultural heritage, and a sense of belonging. This is not a philosophy of denial or a romanticization of poverty, though it does involve a fundamental **paradigm shift,** or change of worldview, in a country so dominated by material consumption and wealth. Vandana Shiva (2005) calls this process "earth democracy." Writers included in this chapter all implicitly or explicitly argue for a profound change in attitudes, in which human life and the life of the natural world are valued, cared for, and sustained. The Women's Pentagon Action Unity Statement is also relevant here (Reading 70) and Betty Burkes' essay on personal and community connections (Reading 71).

◆◆◆

Questions for Reflection

As you read and discuss this chapter, ask yourself these questions:

1. What does it mean to be part of an interconnected chain of life?

2. What are the main environmental issues in your area?

3. How far are you away from farming—in terms of geographical distance and generations of your family? Are there community gardens in your area?

4. Do you have access to a compost pile or worm box?

5. What are the main illnesses in your area? Are they linked to environmental causes?

6. Think about the practical projects mentioned in this chapter. What resources were used by the people involved? What worldviews are implicit in their actions?

7. What is your vision of a sustainable future?

◆◆◆

Finding Out More on the Web

1. Find out more about the organizations mentioned in this chapter. Evaluate their strategies and activities. The following are women's organizations or those where women are prominent.

   Center for Health, Environment, and Justice: **www.chej.org**

   Committee on Women, Population, and the Environment: **www.cwpe.org**

   Community Food Security Coalition: **www.foodsecurity.org/farm _to_college.html**

Student Environmental Action Coalition: **www.seac.org**

Tierra Wools: **www.tierrawools.com**

White Earth Land Recovery Project: **www.welrp.org**

Women's Environment and Development Organization: **www.wedo.org**

2. In Reading 74, Ynestra King gives data for nuclear warheads and toxic dumps. What are the current figures?

3. In Reading 76, Mililani Trask refers to contamination and destruction of land by military operations at Kahoolawe Island and Johnston Island. What has happened at these places? Find out more about the environmental effects of military activities. A useful place to start is Global Green USA: **www.globalgreen.org.**

4. Find out about pollution in your community at **www.scorecard.org.**

Taking Action

1. Find out about environmental organizations and environmental justice organizations in your area. What are their goals and perspectives? What projects are they currently working on? How could you participate in or support their work?

2. Find out about the people who used to live where you live now. What happened to the Native American people who used to live on this land? Are there other groups who used to live here? How did they support themselves? Why did they move? Where are they now? How are they living now?

3. How big is your ecological footprint? Work out how to make it smaller.

S E V E N T Y - T W O

My Mom's Garden (1998)

Cindy Chan Saelee

Cindy Chan Saelee was part of the Asian Youth Advocates program, organized by Asian Pacific Environmental Network to empower young Laotian women (aged 13–18) in the Richmond (Calif.) area, through political education, peer support, and team-building exercises. This article was published in "Quietly Torn," by and about young Mien American women produced at YO! (Youth Outlook) with support from Pacific News Service.

My mom loves it when it rains—she always says that it's "a little help."

She says that her crops can't grow in our yard because there's not enough water to water the whole garden. The dirt is kind of like sand and it dries up quickly.

My mom had good experiences from the old days in Laos, working on the farm, growing rice, corn, cucumbers, long fat beans. . . . She never had to water the garden there, because the ground was rich, and it was always very moist in the mornings. Back in Thailand and Laos, mothers had to grow their own crops to feed the family. If they didn't, they'd all starve to death!

Now even though they can afford more things, and food, most Iu Mien mothers still like to have their own crops and gardens in their spare time. They love it when their gardens look nice, neat and healthy.

All they need to do is find a place they like, cut down the grass and trees, burn the area and let it dry for a few days before they plant the seeds. It's easy to plant fruits and vegetables—you have to put the seeds in soft dirt and then water it. It saves them a few bucks from having to buy the food.

My mom's garden is behind the garage. There's a small place for parsley, a big place for cucumbers, three different trees—peach and apples trees. It's all planted in a wooden box.

She gets all the seeds from my grandma or she goes and buys it at the store. Peppers, pumpkins, peaches, zucchini, tomatoes, mustard, etc. Some trees are short and some plants are tall.

My mom really likes her garden, especially her apple tree, because she doesn't have to water it as many times as the others. In her free time, she likes to just hang in her garden and water all the plants and vegetables. Every night, before bedtime, she goes back and checks her garden to water it and to make sure that no bugs are trying to eat her plants. If there are, she kills them all with salt.

For me, fun is going out and kicking it, but my mom likes her garden. She puts a lot of effort into making it look neat and good. It's not really easy at first, but you just pick it up and plant your crops. Corn, strawberries, apples, plums, peaches, green vegetables, cucumbers, etc. Imagine all those in a neat garden!

SEVENTY-THREE

◆◆◆

Rose Moon (excerpt, 2001)

Sandra Steingraber

Sandra Steingraber is a biological scientist, award-winning science writer, teacher, cancer survivor, and expert on environmental links between cancer and reproductive health. Author of *Living Downstream: An Ecologist Looks at Cancer and the Environment, Having Faith: An Ecologist's Journey to Motherhood,* and *Post-Diagnosis,* a volume of poetry. She was *Ms. Magazine's* 1997 Woman of the Year, and has held academic appointments at several universities and colleges.

. . . In its narration of life in the womb, the popular literature waxes eloquent over a completely different set of milestones than do the academic texts to which I'm more accustomed. The textbooks devote most of their pages to the complicated early events of organogenesis, with all their origami-like precision. The writing perks up again at the end with the avalanche of hormonal changes that triggers labor and delivery. But the discussion of fetal changes during the second and third trimesters is swift and almost dismissive: growth of body parts, fat deposition, refinement of features. . . .

By contrast, the popular media pass swiftly over the treacherous early months—except to mention morning sickness and symptoms of imminent miscarriage—and hit their rhetorical stride during the months of mid- and late pregnancy. These periodicals dote lovingly on such achievements as growth of the eyebrows (well developed by month six!), the secretion of waxy *vernix* (protects the skin from chapping), and the growth of *lanugo* (fine downy hair that holds the vernix in place). What mother-to-be can resist these endearing details, this special language, which resembles the vocabulary of a Catholic Mass? ("Vernix" is Latin for varnish, "lanugo," for wool.) From the popular books, I learn that a six-month-old fetus is about thirteen inches long and weighs a little more than a pound. I learn that the top of my uterus has risen above my belly button and that the fetus, now pressed directly against the wall of the uterus, is affected by the womb's various squeezings.

. . .

What the popular books and magazines do not talk much about are environmental issues. Even the March of Dimes publication, *Mama,* which is devoted to the prevention of birth defects, does not mention solvents or pesticides or toxic waste sites or Minamata or Vietnam. There is some kind of disconnect between what we know scientifically and what is presented to pregnant women seeking knowledge about prenatal life. At first, I assumed the silence around environmental threats to pregnancy might be explained by the emerging nature of the evidence. Perhaps the writers of public educational materials choose to present only the dangers for which the data are iron-clad and long-standing. All the books and periodicals include a standard discussion of rubella, for example, and urge pregnant smokers to quit.

But the more I read, the more I realize that scientific certainty is not a consistent criterion by which reproductive dangers are presented to pregnant mothers. For example, pregnant women are urged to drink no alcohol. The guidebooks and magazines are unanimous about this. While fetal alcohol syndrome is a well-described and incontrovertible phenomenon . . . no one knows if an occasional glass of wine is harmful. Nevertheless, caution dictates—and again I wholeheartedly agree—that in the absence of information to the contrary, one should assume no safe threshold level. One of the pregnancy books in my collection, *Life Before Birth,* even quotes Voltaire on this issue: "In ignorance, abstain."

Yet this same principle is not applied to nitrates in tap water. Here we assume we *can* set safe thresholds—in this case ten parts per million—even though these thresholds have never been established for fetuses and even though almost nothing is known about transplacental transfer of nitrates or about how nitrate-inactivated hemoglobin in the mother's blood might interfere with oxygen delivery to the fetus. What's more, we allow 4.5 million Americans to drink water with nitrate levels above this arbitrary limit. Four and a half million people surely includes a lot of pregnant women. We also presume we can set safe limits on pesticide residues, solvents, and chlorination byproducts in drinking water—and yet none of these thresholds has ever been demonstrated to protect against fetal damage. In fact, plenty of evidence exists to the contrary. When it comes to environmental hazards, not only do we dispense with the principle of "In ignorance, abstain," we fail to inform pregnant women that the hazards even exist. . . .

The more I read, the more contradictions I see. A recent scientific report summarizing the reproductive effects of chemical contaminants in food reaches a strong conclusion: "The evidence is overwhelming: certain persistent toxic substances impair intellectual capacity, change behavior . . . and compromise reproductive capacity. The people most at risk are children, pregnant women, women of

childbearing age. . . . Particularly at risk are developing embryos and nursing infants."

By comparison one of the most popular guidebooks to pregnancy opens a discussion of this same topic with a complaint about that kind of bad news: "Reports of hazardous chemicals in just about every item in the American diet are enough to scare the appetite out of anyone. . . . Don't be fanatic. Though trying to avoid theoretical hazards in food is a commendable goal, making your life stressful in order to do so is not."

Of course, the don't-worry-be-happy approach does not apply to smoking and drinking; the authors take a very stern, absolutist position on these topics.

I look over at my driver, who's been singing louder and louder.

"Hey, Jeff?"

"Mmm."

"I'm trying to figure something out."

"What's that?" He turns down the radio.

"Not a single one of these pregnancy magazines encourages mothers to find out what the Toxics Release Inventory shows for their own communities."

"You did it though, right?"

"Yeah, I looked it up on the Internet."

"And?"

"And McLean County is one of the top counties in Illinois for airborne releases of reproductive poisons."

I detail for him the results of my research. The biggest emissions of fetal toxicants are hexane from the soybean processing plant and toluene from the auto plant. My list also includes glycol ethers and xylene. All are solvents.

"Jesus," says Jeff.

"I also found out that the university uses six different pesticides on their grounds and fields. So I looked up their toxicology profiles. Two of them are known to cause birth defects in animals." . . .

"So what are you trying to figure out?"

"Two things. One, why is there is no public conversation about environmental threats to pregnancy?"

"What's the other thing?"

I quote Voltaire: "In ignorance, abstain." "Why does abstinence in the face of uncertainty apply only to individual behavior? Why doesn't it apply equally to industry or agriculture?"

"Okay, let me think for a minute." Jeff turns the radio back on. And then turns it off again. "I think the questions overlap. Pregnancy and motherhood are private. We still act like pregnant women are not part of the public world. Their bodies look strange. They seem vulnerable. You are not supposed to upset them. If something is scary or stressful, you shouldn't talk about it."

"But pregnant women are constantly being told what to do. No coffee. No alcohol. No sushi. Stay away from cat feces."

"That's still private. Industry and agriculture are political, public. They exist outside one's own body, outside one's own house. You can't do something immediately about them within the time period of a pregnancy. So it seems unmanageable."

"It's pregnant women who have to live with the consequences of public decisions. We're the ones who will be raising the damaged children. If we don't talk about these things because it's too upsetting, how will it ever change?"

Jeff throws me a look.

"You're the writer. Can you find a language to manage it? Break the taboo?"

Now I have to think for a while.

. . .

Back in our Somerville neighborhood, with its views of Bunker Hill and low-lying, wealthier Cambridge, I forget the expanses of Illinois. Up in our third-floor apartment in this most densely populated city in North America (or so claims the Somerville newspaper on a regular basis), Jeff and I spend a few days bumping into each other and reacquainting ourselves with car alarms and Indian take-out food. In the evenings, we sit out on the balcony and wait for an ocean breeze. The neighbor who shares the balcony with us has planted morning glories and tomatoes, which are already twining up the latticework. In the mornings, I walk the dog to the park, sharing the sidewalk with caravans of strollers pushed by pouty teenagers and muttering grandmothers. I never noticed how many babies lived in my neighborhood. Up and down the block, rhododendrons are blooming in tiny cement yards, and vines of purple wisteria wrap the porches of shingled triple-deckers. Underwear flaps on a hundred clotheslines. From the park's old locust trees hang panicles of fragrant white flowers. It is Somerville's finest season.

With the public library only two blocks away, I resume my research. What interests me now is the sine qua non of pregnancy's sixth month: fetal brain development.

Trying to understand the embryological anatomy of the vertebrate brain nearly unhinged me two decades ago. It was some of the most difficult biology I had ever encountered—and the most beautiful. It was like watching a rose bloom in speeded-up time. Or like spelunking in an uncharted cave. My embryology professor, Dr. Bruce Criley, used to drill us by flashing slides of fetal brain sections on a huge screen while we sat in the darkened lab trying to keep our bearings. "Okay, where are we now?" he would demand, whacking a pointer against an unfamiliar structure. Prosencephalon, rhombencephalon, mesencephalon—ancient-sounding names identified rooms in a continuously morphing cavern.

Both the brain and the spinal cord are made up of the same three layers. The brain then adds a fourth layer when cells migrate from the inside out to form the cortex. It's what happens during and after this migration that is so dazzlingly disorienting. Indeed, in order to explain it all, the language of human brain development borrows its vocabulary from botany, architecture, and geography. There are lumens, islands, aqueducts, and isthmuses. There are ventricles, commissures, and hemispheres. There are roofs and floors, pyramids and pouches. There are furrows called sulci and elevations called gyri. Structures are said to balloon, undulate, condense, fuse, and swell. They pass by, flatten, overgrow, and bury each other. They turn, grow downward, turn again, grow upward.

Some structures are formed from tissues derived from two completely different locations. The pituitary gland, for example, is at the place where an upgrowth from a valley near the mouth meets a downgrowth from the forebrain. Meanwhile, the twelve cranial nerves go forth like apostles to make contact with the far-flung, newly developing eyes, ears, tongue, nose, etc. It was all enough to make us mild-mannered, high-achieving biology majors reel with panic. It also was enough to make us feel, once the lights went on again, that we had just emerged from a secret temple, the likes of which we had never seen before.

On a microscopic scale, the story is a bit simpler—although this may only be because we know so little about what actually goes on at the cellular level. All embryological structures are created through migration. But brain cells travel like spiders, trailing silken threads as they go.

There are two kinds of threads: dendrites and axons. Dendrites are fine and short. They receive messages from other nearby cells. Axons are ropy and long. They send out messages, often over great distances. Of the two, axons develop first. They grow out from the body of the brain cell along a specific pathway and in a specific direction. In this they are guided by proteins called cell adhesion molecules. The dendrites are spun out later. In fact, the peak period of dendrite growth doesn't even begin until late in the third trimester, and it continues until at least a year after birth.

Despite these differences, axons and dendrites have a lot in common. Both types of fibers branch after they elongate so that connections can be made with many other cells. These connecting points—the synapses—continue to increase in number throughout the first two years of life. Both axons and dendrites transmit messages by sending electrochemical signals down their lengths. Sometimes, these signals can also fly between fibers. But in most cases, in order to continue a message from one nerve cell to the next, chemicals have to diffuse across the synaptic space. These are the neurotransmitters, with their role call of familiar names: acetylcholine, dopamine, serotonin.

Fetal brain mysteries abound. Chief among them is the role of the neuroglia, whose name means nerve glue. These are brain cells that do not themselves conduct messages but that apparently exert control over the cells that do. They are far more than glue. In some cases they act as coaches to the neurons' athletes—wrapping their axons in ace-bandage layers of fat and thereby speeding the passage of electricity. They also appear to alter the neurons' diets, for example, by modulating the amount of glucose available. And they provide signals and pathways for migration. In this last capacity, they work in tandem with early-migrating neurons. That is to say, the brain cells that are the first to make the journey to the cortex provide essential cues—along with those of the neuroglia—that help later migrants find their way. But no one knows exactly how these trails are blazed, maps are drawn, and bread crumbs scattered.

Once you understand how the embryonic brain unfolds, chamber after hidden chamber, and how its webs of electricity all get connected up, you can easily see why neurological poisons have such profound effects in utero. Exposures that produce only transient effects in adult brains can lay waste to fetal ones. This happens through a variety of pathways. Neurotoxins can impede synapse formation, disrupt the release of neurotransmitters, or strip off the fatty layers wound around the axons. Neurotoxins can

also slow the outward-bound trekking of migrating fetal brain cells. Because the earliest-maturing brain cells erect a kind of scaffolding to help their younger siblings find their way, a single exposure at the onset of migration can irretrievably alter the brain's architecture. A fetus also lacks the efficient detoxification systems that already-born human beings carry around within their livers, kidneys, and lungs. And, until they are six months old, fetuses and infants lack a blood-brain barrier, which prevents many blood-borne toxins from entering the brain's gray matter.

As if all this weren't enough, fetal brains are made even more vulnerable by lack of fat in the fetal body. The brain is 50 percent fat by dry weight, and after birth, body fat competes with the brain in attracting fat-soluble toxic chemicals. But throughout most of pregnancy, the fetus is lean, plumping up only during the last month or so. In fetuses, toxic chemicals that are fat-soluble—and many of them are—do not have other fat depots in which to be sequestered, and so they have disproportionately greater effects on the brains of fetuses than on the brains of the rest of us.

More than half of the top twenty chemicals reported in the 1997 Toxics Release Inventory are known or suspected neurotoxins. These include solvents, heavy metals, and pesticides. And yet our understanding of brain-damaging chemicals is vague and fragmentary. Part of the problem is that animal testing is of limited use in trying to figure out how a human baby might be affected by exposure to a particular neurotoxin. Humans are born at a much earlier stage of fetal brain development than, for example, monkeys. Rhesus monkeys' brains are closer to their final form when the monkeys are born, and the young are upright and walking before they are two months old, whereas the average age of human walking is thirteen months. Certain structures within rodent brains, on the other hand, are less well developed at birth than ours. For example, cells in the human hippocampus, the seat of memory, are finished being produced at the time of birth, whereas in rodents, they are not formed until well into postnatal life. These kinds of differences between species mean that extrapolating from animal studies to humans is tricky. The windows of vulnerability are different. And obviously, conducting controlled experiments on human embryos and fetuses is not permissible.

Unhappily, plenty of human fetuses have been exposed to brain-damaging chemicals anyway—not through controlled experiments but through unintended exposures. There is much we can learn by studying their various deficits. However, this kind of research did not begin in earnest until the last few decades. According to the old thinking, either a chemical killed the fetus or it didn't. Either a chemical could produce an obvious structural deformity like anencephaly (no brain) or it couldn't. Not until the 1960s and '70s did fetal toxicologists recognize that certain low-level exposures can elicit functional abnormalities in the brain. That is, the brain *looks* fine—it has all the necessary structures— but it doesn't *act* fine. Once researchers tested children who had had low-level exposures to toxicants on cognitive and motor performance, subtle problems became apparent. The same was true for animals. As soon as laboratory testing of neurotoxicants was expanded to include not just birth defects but also behavioral problems (learning, memory, reaction time, the ability to run a maze), myriad other problems became evident. In both cases, researchers began to see that toxicants can affect brain functioning at much lower levels of exposure than they had previously imagined.

Unfortunately, this epiphany in brain research happened long after the establishment of environmental regulations governing toxic chemicals. Many of these regulations are based on pre-World War II assumptions about neurological development, not on the findings of recent studies. When it comes to fetal neurotoxicants, instead of following the admonition "In ignorance, abstain," we adhere to the principle "In ignorance and disregarding emerging science, proceed recklessly."

The sixth month of pregnancy is a joyful one. My round belly elicits smiles and happy comments from postal workers, dog walkers, and fellow subway riders, who compete to be the first to surrender a seat to me.

Meanwhile, the random fetal movements of last month have evolved into a predictable and reassuring choreography. And as the weeks go by, I begin to notice something else about the baby's movements: they are often generated *in response* to something that I do. When I take a warm bath, she begins to squirm and shimmy, as if she were bathing as well. When I curl up to Jeff at night, my belly pressing against his back, she kicks—with enough force that Jeff can feel it, too. If I roll over in bed, she sometimes rolls over. If police cars or fire trucks suddenly

blare down the street, she becomes very still, and I know I won't hear much from her for a while. I pat my belly and try to comfort her. "It's okay, baby; it's just a siren." In these moments, I realize that I am beginning to perceive her as a sentient being—as a child—and myself more and more as her mother.

. . .

A commonly held belief is that natural substances are less toxic to the human body than synthetic ones. Like a lot of folk biology, this idea is both true and misleading at the same time. It all depends on what you mean by "natural."

Consider lead, the element that occupies square number eighty-two in the periodic chart. It is indeed present in the earth's crust. But lead is not really part of nature in the sense that it has no function in the world of living organisms. While abundant in the geological world, it does not naturally inhabit the ecological one. A normal blood lead level in a human being—or any other animal— should be zero. And even in the inanimate world of rocks, the soft, dense, silvery substance we know as lead cannot really be said to exist. Elemental lead has to be roasted and smelted out of other minerals. In this sense, a lead fishing weight is as much a synthetic creation as polyester, plastic wrap, or DDT.

There is no doubt that lead is a remarkable material. Its Latin name *plumbum* (abbreviated Pb by chemists) hints at its usefulness. Think plumbing. Essentially uncorrodible, it has long been used to line water pipes. For the same reason, it has found a place in roofing. Lead salts make excellent pigments, thus lead paint. Tetraethyl lead stops engine knocking, thus leaded gasoline. Lead also has handy electrical properties. Its largest use now is in the manufacture of lead-acid storage batteries, especially the ones used in cars.

Lead is also a formidable destroyer of human brains. This property has been recognized for at least 2,000 years. Once called plumbism, lead poisoning causes capillaries in the brain to erode, resulting in hemorrhage and swelling. Its symptoms include irritability, abdominal spasms, headache, confusion, palsy, and the formation of a black line across the gums. Prenatal transfer of lead across the placenta is also old news. In 1911, women working in the white-lead factories of Newcastle noticed that pregnancy cured plumbism. They were right: by passing lead on to their fetuses, workers lowered their own body burdens and thereby alleviated their symptoms of lead poisoning. Of course, most of their babies died. We now know that lead, once it gains entry into the adult female body, settles into bones and teeth. During the sixth month of pregnancy, when the fetal skeleton hardens, placental hormones free up calcium from the mother's bones and direct it through the placenta. Whatever stores of lead lay in the bones are also mobilized and follow calcium into the fetal body. In this way, a developing baby receives from its mother *her* lifetime lead exposure.

Our understanding about lead's toxicity changed radically in the 1940s. Before then, victims of acute lead poisoning who escaped death were presumed to enjoy a complete recovery. But soon a few observant physicians began to notice that child survivors often suffered from persistent nervous disorders and were failing in school. In the 1960s, behavioral changes were noted in experimental animals exposed to low doses of lead. Then, in the early 1970s, children living near a lead smelter in El Paso, Texas, were found to have lower IQ scores than children living farther away. By the 1980s, studies from around the world documented problems in lead-exposed children who had never exhibited any physical symptoms of acute poisoning. These included short attention spans, aggression, poor language skills, hyperactivity, and delinquency. We now know that lead can decrease mental acuity at levels one sixth those required to trigger physical symptoms. The new thinking is that no safe threshold exists for lead exposure in children or fetuses.

Fetal neurologists have also shed new light on the various ways by which lead wrecks brain development. At levels far lower than required to swell the brain, lead alters the flow of calcium in the synapses, thereby altering neurotransmitter activity. It also prevents dendrites from branching, and it interferes with the wrapping of fat around axons. But it doesn't stop there. Lead affects the adhesion molecules that guide the growth of these axons, thereby altering the architecture of the entire electrical web. It also poisons the energy-generating organelles (mitochondria) within the neuronal bodies and so lowers overall brain metabolism. In laboratory rats, lead inhibits a receptor known to play a key role in learning and memory. The adult brain can fend off some of these problems, thanks both to its blood-brain barrier and to an ability to bind lead to protein and so keep it away from the mitochondria. Fetal brains lack these defenses. This is why early lead exposures have life-changing consequences.

On its surface, the story of lead seems like a story of science triumphing over ignorance. Lead paint was banned in the United States in 1977, the year I graduated from high school, and leaded gas was phased out soon after, finally banned in 1990. With paint and gasoline as the two biggest sources of human lead exposure, the decisions to prohibit—and not just regulate—these products is a shining victory for public health. In their wake, the average blood lead levels in American children have fallen dramatically—75 percent between 1976 and 1991.

But there is another story about lead, told by historians and toxicologists who fought long and hard to banish lead from the human economy. It's a story about the willful suppression of science by industry. It's a story that helps explain why one in twenty American children still suffers from lead poisoning in spite of everything we know. It helps explain why lead, never outlawed for use in cosmetics, can still be found in some lipsticks and hair dyes. And it helps explain why the soil in my neighborhood in Somerville is so full of lead that we are still advised not to grow vegetables in our gardens.

Consider lead paint. Its production was halted in this country in the late 1970s. But in 1925, an international covenant had already banned lead-based paints for interior use in much of the rest of the world. This agreement acknowledged that lead was a neurotoxin and that lead paint in the homes produced lead dust, which is easily ingested when crawling babies put their hands in their mouths or chew on toys. But the United States was not a signatory to this agreement. In fact, the same industry trade group that prevented the United States from adopting the covenant also succeeded in blocking restrictions on lead in plumbing. The lead industry—which owned at least one paint company outright—treated the emerging science on low-level lead poisoning as a public relations problem, dismissing objective research as "anti-lead propaganda."

As has been meticulously documented by two public health historians, Gerald Markowitz and David Rosner, the manufacturers of lead pigments went on the offensive after the 1925 agreement. They reassured the American public that lead fears were unfounded. They even promoted lead paint for use in schools and hospitals. Most wickedly, they employed images of children in advertising. The most famous of these was the Dutch Boy, a cartoon character dreamed up by the National Lead Company. With his requisite haircut, overalls, and wooden shoes, the little Dutch Boy cheerfully sloshed buckets of paint labeled "white lead" in ad campaigns throughout the midcentury. The implicit message was that lead paint was safe for children to handle. . . .

The industry also fought labeling requirements that would warn buyers not to use lead paint on children's toys, furniture, or rooms. Many a nursery was painted with lead by pregnant women eagerly awaiting the birth of their babies. Those questioning the safety of such practices were repeatedly reassured by Lead Industry Associates that a link between lead paint exposure and mental deficiencies has never been proved. And up until the 1970s, this was true—in no small part because the lead industry was the main source of funding for university research on the health effects of lead. Researchers with other opinions and other funding sources were condemned as hysterical and sometimes threatened with legal action. Only when the U.S. government became a major funder of lead research did the case against lead began to mount.

When the truth eventually became undeniable, the industry shifted tactics. Instead of denying lead's powers to damage children's brains, it blamed inner-city poverty and unscrupulous landlords who, the argument went, had allowed paint to peel in their tenement buildings. And the neglected children living there, with nothing better to do, ate it. At one point, recalls a leading toxicologist deeply involved in the lead wars, an industry representative actually suggested that the problem was not that eating lead paint chips made children stupid but rather that stupid children ate paint. All these arguments finally collapsed under the weight of emerging scientific evidence. But decades were wasted in denials, obfuscations, deflections of responsibility, counter-accusations, intimidation of scientists, and attempts to tranquilize a legitimate public concern. The result is that any home built and painted before 1978 probably contains lead paint, and all children and pregnant women living in such buildings continue to face risks from it. And since I live in a century-old building listed on Somerville's historical registry, I am now such a woman. It is a problem that continues to vex landlords and homeowners alike, as removing the lead is expensive and is itself a health

menace. It is a problem that could have been solved in 1925.

Now consider leaded gas. In 1922, General Motors discovered that adding lead to gasoline helped alleviate its tendency to "knock," to burn explosively under high compression. Solving this problem meant that automobile engines could be made bigger, and cars could go faster. Ethanol, which can be distilled from corn, also worked well as an antiknock additive but could not be patented and was therefore not as profitable to the oil companies. In 1923 leaded gas went on sale for the first time. This development immediately attracted the attention of public health officials, who raised urgent questions about the effects of broadcasting lead-laced fumes into public air space. At about the same time, serious health problems began afflicting refinery workers whose jobs involved formulating the lead additive. Several died and many others suffered hallucinations. The tetraethyl lead building at one plant was even nicknamed the House of Butterflies because so many employees who worked in it saw imaginary insects crawling on their bodies.

Then a remarkable thing happened. In 1925, a meeting was convened by the U.S. Surgeon General to address the issue of lead dust. And a moratorium was declared. The sale of leaded gas was banned on the grounds that it might well pose a public health menace. It was a perfect expression of the principle "In ignorance, abstain"—what is now popularly called the precautionary principle. Unfortunately for us all, the moratorium did not hold. After the prohibition took effect, the lead industry funded a quick study that showed no problems with lead exposure. Over the objection that lead was a slow, cumulative poison and that such a study could not possibly reveal the kind of human damage researchers were worried about, the ban was subsequently lifted. The production of leaded gas resumed.

It continued for almost seventy years. By the time it was banned again, this time for good, more than 15.4 billion pounds of lead dust had been released into the environment. Much of this has sifted down into the topsoil. As a metal, lead is not biodegradable and is considered absolutely persistent. In other words, it is not going away anytime soon. It is tracked into homes on the bottoms of shoes. It is absorbed from soil into plant roots. This is why, in high-traffic urban areas such as my neighborhood in Somerville, we cannot grow and eat carrots.

The irony of our gardening situation is that lead in gasoline was finally removed on the basis of a landmark 1979 study showing significant IQ changes among first- and second-graders in response to environmental lead exposures. And the children investigated lived here in Somerville.

Should you ever find yourself in Boston, you may wish to pay a visit to the Old North Church in the North End. It's the one-if-by-land-two-if-by-sea church made famous by Paul Revere. If you go, take a look at the pale violet walls inside the sanctuary. Jeff painted them. Well, he and a crew of men that he supervised. Restoration work and decorative painting are specialties of his; these skills have helped to fund a lot of art projects over the years and paid a lot of rent. Elegant old homes up and down Beacon Hill and on Cambridge's Brattle Street contain his handiwork, as do buildings at Harvard University. Jeff is more at ease with a paintbrush and a sander in his hands than anyone else I have ever met, which is one reason (among others) I fell in love with him.

Now we lie awake on a summery night, reggae drifting into the window from the street below, and discuss whether or not he should continue this work. His blood lead levels are more than double that of the average American male. One physician actually congratulated him for this. Given that his line of work puts him in direct contact with old, lead-based paint, she expected they would be much higher. Jeff is very careful. But even when he changes clothes at the job site and leaves his work pants out on our fire escape, he still comes home covered in dust and paint. He's paying the price for reckless decisions made three generations ago.

But we would like to ensure that our daughter doesn't. Almost nothing is known about how lead exposures in fathers affect their unborn children. "Lower lead levels have not been well studied for their possible effects on the male reproductive system or on pregnancy in the partners of exposed males."

In ignorance, abstain. But can we afford to? With a baby coming? In the end, we decide that Jeff should fold his business. And as soon as the baby is crawling, we'll move out of our apartment. We know there is lead paint under the many layers of latex—our landlord has confirmed it—and we know that painting over lead paint is not considered a safe method of containment. We also know that our neighbors around the corner discovered very high lead levels in the soil in their back yard. Nevertheless, a home lead detector kit has revealed no lead on the surface of our interior walls, in the cupboards, or in the dusty corners behind the radiators. For now, we'll stay put. (It's a decision we later come to question. Blood lead levels are measured in micrograms per deciliter of blood. In children, any number below ten micrograms is considered acceptable. However, pediatric researchers have documented impairments in math, reading, and short-term memory at levels down to five. At nine months, our daughter's blood levels were measured at six micrograms.)

"Don't grow our own root vegetables. Quit a job I like. How come we're always the ones that have to do the abstaining?" Jeff wants to know.

And that is my question exactly. . . .

NOTES

545 Quotation by Voltaire: P. W. Nathanielsz, *Life Before Birth: The Challenges of Fetal Development* (New York: W. H. Freeman, 1996), pp. 158. The literal translation of the original quotation is "Abstain from an action if in doubt as to whether it is right or not" (from "Le Philosophe Ignorant," in *Mélanges de Voltaire* [Paris: Bibliothèque de la Pléiade, Librairie Gallimard, 1961], p. 920). Thanks to Dr. James Matthews, a French scholar, of Illinois Wesleyan University for tracking down the original source.

545 Standards for nitrates in drinking water not shown safe for fetuses: Committee on Environmental Health, American Academy of Pediatrics, *Handbook of Pediatric Environmental Health* (Elk Grove Village, Ill.: AAP, 1999), p. 164; National Research Council, *Nitrate and Nitrite in Drinking Water* (Washington, D.C.: National Academy Press, 1995), p. 2.

545 4.5 million Americans drink water with elevated nitrate levels: AAP, *Handbook of Pediatric Environmental Health*, p. 164.

545 Quote from scientific report: International Joint Commission, *Ninth Biennial Report on Great Lakes Water Quality* (Ottawa, Ont.: International Joint Commission, 1998), p. 10.

545 Quote from popular guidebook: A. Eisenberg et al., *What to Expect When You're Expecting* (New York: Workman, 1996), pp. 129–32.

545 Toxic releases in McLean County: Data on toxic emissions are measured and sent by the industries in question to the U.S. Environmental Protection Agency. These are disseminated on the Internet in a user-friendly format by the Environmental Defense (www.scorecard.org).

545 University's use of pesticides: According to the director of the grounds crew, pesticides used in 1999 include mecoprop and bromoxynil. As of 2001 they are no longer used. Thanks to my student, Sarah Perry, for investigating this issue.

545 34 million pounds of reproductive toxicants released in Illinois in 1997: Toxics Release Inventory (www.scorecard.org).

546 Description of fetal brain development, gross anatomy: B. M. Carlson, *Human Embryology and Developmental Biology*, 2d ed. (St. Louis: Mosby, 1999) pp. 208–48; England, *Life Before Birth*, pp. 51–70.

546–547 Description of fetal brain development, cellular anatomy: D. Bellinger and H. L. Needleman, "The Neurotoxicity of Prenatal Exposure to Lead: Kinetics, Mechanisms, and Expressions," in H. L. Needleman and D. Bellinger, eds., *Prenatal Exposure to Toxicants: Developmental Consequences* (Baltimore: Johns Hopkins University Press, 1994), pp. 89–111; Carlson, *Human Embryology*, pp. 208–48; England, *Life Before Birth*, pp. 51–70; Victor Friedrich, "Wiring of the Growing Brain," presentation at the conference Environmental Issues on Children: Brain, Development, and Behavior, New York Academy of Medicine, New York City, 24 May 1999; Nathanielsz, *Life Before Birth*, pp. 38–42; T. Schettler et al., *In Harm's Way: Toxic Threats to Child Development* (Cambridge: Greater Boston Physicians for Social Responsibility, 2000), pp. 23–28.

547 Neuroglia modulate available glucose: Nathanielsz, *Life Before Birth*, p. 16.

547 Later brain cells follow early-migrating neurons: K. Suzuki and P. M. Martin, "Neurotoxicants and the Developing Brain," in G. J. Harry, ed., *Developmental Neurotoxicology* (Boca Raton: CRC Press, 1994), pp. 9–32.

547 Mechanisms of fetal neurotoxicity: G. J. Harry, "Introduction to Developmental Neurotoxicology," in Harry, *Developmental Neurotoxicology*, pp. 1–7.

547 More than half of TRI chemicals are neurotoxins: U.S. releases of neurotoxins into air, water, wells, and landfills totaled 1.2 billion pounds in 1997. These chemicals include heavy metals such as lead and mercury as well as methanol, ammonia, manganese compounds, chlorine, styrene, glycol ethers, and a variety of solvents, such as toluene and xylene (Schettler, *In Harm's Way*, pp. 103–5).

547 Interspecific differences in brain development: E. M. Faustman et al., "Mechanisms Underlying Children's Susceptibility to Environmental Toxicants," *EHP* 108(2000, sup. 1): 13–21; P. M. Rodier, "Comparative Postnatal Neurologic Development," in Needleman and Bellinger, *Prenatal Exposure to Toxicants*, pp. 3–23.

547–548 When testing expanded to include behavior: Harry, "Introduction to Developmental Neurotoxicology"; H. L. Needleman and P. J. Landrigan, *Raising Children Toxic Free: How to Keep Your Child Safe from Lead, Asbestos, Pesticides and Other Environmental Hazards* (New York: Farrar Straus & Giroux, 1994), pp. 11–15.

548 Historical awareness of lead poisoning: Bellinger and Needleman, "The Neurotoxicity of Prenatal Exposure to Lead: Kinetics, Mechanisms, and Expressions"; Suzuki and Martin, "Neurotoxicants and the Developing Brain."

548–549 Lead's migration into fetal body: Bellinger and Needleman, "The Neurotoxicity of Prenatal Exposure to Lead."

549 Awareness in the 1940s: AAP, *Handbook of Pediatric Environmental Health*, pp. 131–43; H. L. Needleman, "Childhood Lead Poisoning: The Promise and Abandonment of Primary Prevention," *Am. J. of Public Health* 88(1998): 1871–77; Needleman and Landrigan, *Raising Children Toxic Free*, pp. 11–15.

549 Lowering of IQs in El Paso: Described in Needleman and Landrigan, *Raising Children Toxic Free*, pp. 11–15.

549 Studies from around the world: AAP, *Handbook of Pediatric Environmental Health*, pp. 131–43.

549 Lead levels required to affect mental acuity: Suzuki and Martin, "Neurotoxicants and the Developing Brain."

549 Mechanisms by which lead wrecks brain development: Bellinger and Needleman, "The Neurotoxicity of Prenatal Exposure to Lead"; M. K. Nihei et al., "*N*-Methyl-D-Aspartate Receptor Subunit Changes are Associated with Lead-Induced Deficits of Long-Term Potentiation and Spatial Learning," *Neuroscience* 99(2000): 233–42; Suzuki and Martin, "Neurotoxicants and the Developing Brain."

549 Vulnerability of fetus to lead: The elderly are also at risk. As bone demineralizes with age, blood lead levels can rise. In seniors, even slight elevations can have adverse cognitive effects (Bernard Weiss, University of Rochester, personal communication).

549 Life-changing consequences: New research suggests that these consequences include a propensity to violent behavior, as well as a lowered IQ. See, for example, R. Nevin, "How Lead Exposure Relates to Temporal Changes in I.Q., Violent Crime, and Unwed Pregnancy," *Environmental Research* 83(2000): 1–22.

549 Public health triumph of lead bans: AAP, *Handbook of Pediatric Environmental Health*, pp. 131–43.

549 75 percent decline: Nevin, "How Lead Exposure Relates to Temporal Changes."

549 One in twenty children: G. Markowitz and D. Rosner, " 'Cater to the Children': The Role of the Lead Industry in a Public Health Tragedy, 1900–1955," *Am. J. of Public Health*, 90(2000): 36–46.

549 Lead not outlawed in cosmetics: T. Schettler et al., *Generations at Risk: Reproductive Health and the Environment* (Cambridge: MIT Press, 1999), p. 273.

549–550 Lead paint: Markowitz and Rosner, " 'Cater to the Children' "; E. K. Silbergeld, "Protection of the Public Interest, Allegations of Scientific Misconduct, and the Needleman Case," *Am. J. of Public Health* 85(1995): 165–66; Schettler et al., *Generations at Risk*, pp. 52–57.

550 A leading toxicologists remembers: Herbert Needleman, "Environmental Neurotoxins and Attention

Deficit Disorder," presentation at the conference Environmental Issues on Children: Brain, Development, and Behavior, New York Academy of Medicine, New York, N.Y., 24 May 1999.

550 Leaded gas: J. L. Kitman, "The Secret History of Lead," *The Nation* 270(20 March 2000): 11–41; Needleman, "Childhood Lead Poisoning"; H. L. Needleman, "Clamped in a Straitjacket: The Insertion of Lead into Gasoline," *Environmental Research* 74(1997): 95–103; D. Rosner and G. Markowitz, "A 'Gift of God'?: The Public Health Controversy over Leaded Gasoline During the 1920s," *Am. J. of Public Health* 75(1985): 344–52; Silbergeld, "Protection of the Public Interest."

550 1979 study of Somerville children: Needleman, J. Palca, "Lead Researcher Confronts Accusers in Public Hearing," *Science* 256(1992): 437–38.

551 Quote on lower lead levels in men: Schettler et al., *Generations at Risk*, p. 57.

551 Lead-induced impairments: B. P. Lanphear et al., "Cognitive Deficits Associated with Blood Lead Concentrations <10 microg/dL in US Children and Adolescents," *Public Health Reports* 115(2000): 521–29; J. Raloff, "Even Low Lead in Kids has High Cost," *Science News* 159(2001): 277. Furthermore, a 1992 study found that slightly elevated blood lead levels in two-year-olds were associated with deficits in academic performance at age ten (D. C. Bellinger et al., "Low Level Lead Exposure, Intelligence and Academic Achievement: A Long-Term Follow-up Study," *Pediatrics* 90 [1992]: 855–61).

SEVENTY-FOUR

◆◆◆

The Ecofeminist Imperative (1983)

Ynestra King

Ynestra King is a writer and activist focusing on environmental, feminist, and disability issues. Co-author of *Dangerous Intersections: Feminist Perspectives on Population, Environment, and Development,* she has taught at the New School for Social Research and has been a Visiting Scholar at several academic institutions, including Rutgers University and Columbia University.

In the one year since the Conference on Women and Life on Earth (held in Amherst, Massachusetts, in March 1980) our movement has burgeoned. The Conference grew out of hope and fear—out of a fear for life and the awesome powers of destruction arrayed against it and out of a hope—a hope for women's power to resist and create. We came together following the meltdown at Three Mile Island. We talked of our sisters we knew by name and reputation through the mythology of our own movement and of what together we might be, and we decided to call sisters to a conference on Women and Life on Earth.

We are both a beginning and a continuation. We are a beginning for this decade but we continue the work of the many brave and visionary women who have gone before us. There was Ellen Swallow, the founder of ecological science. There was Rachel Carson, who wrote *Silent Spring* [in 1962], sounding a warning about chemicals and pesticides which was not heeded until many years later. There were the women of the Women's Strike for Peace and the Ban the Bomb movements of the fifties, mailing their babies' teeth to Congressmen as a reminder of future generations. And there are the brave women scientists who have spoken out more recently, and the women who have been at the forefront of antinuclear struggles, peace movements, struggles against toxic wastes and for occupational health and safety. There are those who have helped us to imagine the world as it could be: artists, poets, writers and dreamers who have given us new visions of culture, health, technology, community and politics. And there are our sisters the world over, with us in the creation of a planetary movement. We are shaking the world.

Over ten years ago this wave of the feminist movement began. We said then that "the personal is political," that the denial of our selfhood was systemic and political, that masculine society even had a name: "patriarchy."

Many more women now see their oppression as political, not individual. Over the past ten years women have begun to rediscover our history, and to name and work to end violence against women in all its forms, demand equal rights, the right of every woman to decide when and if to bear children, and to express her sexuality freely.

But as we have gained in consciousness and numbers the devastation of the planet has accelerated. Every day brings new disasters, some irrevocable. The story of Love Canal where a school and homes were built on a hazardous waste site is a warning of things to come. Three to six nuclear bombs are produced each day. The Pentagon nuclear arsenal now numbers over 30,000 warheads and it is growing. There are thousands of toxic waste dumps around the country that will not be discovered until observant women notice a common birth defect or sickness in their neighborhood. The coastlines are deteriorating, and the Amazon forest, the source of much of earth's oxygen, is being rapidly defoliated. Each day a whole species of life becomes extinct, never to be seen on this earth.

Ecofeminism is about connectedness and wholeness of theory and practice. It asserts the special strength and integrity of every living thing. For us, the snail darter is to be considered side by side with a community's need for water, the porpoise side by side with appetite for tuna. . . . We are a woman-identified movement, and we believe that we have special work to do in these imperilled times. We see the devastation of the earth and her beings by the corporate warriors, and the threat of nuclear annihilation by the military warriors, as feminist concerns. It is the same masculinist mentality which would deny us our right to our own bodies and our own sexuality, and which depends on multiple systems of dominance and state power to have its way.

At the same time as we have been making the connections between feminism, ecology, and militarism, *the New Right has been making those very same connections.* They are actively opposing women's reproductive freedom, attacking lesbians and gay men, undermining battered women's shelters and efforts to introduce anti-sexist and anti-racist curricula in schools. The Family Protection Act, now being introduced in Congress piecemeal, is explicit about its intention to shore up patriarchal authority in every aspect of our lives. They want to be sure that strong, angry women do not stand in their way, as the carnivorous appetite of the military gobbles up food stamps, Aid for Dependent Children, Medicaid, schools, legal aid and more. We are beginning to have an understanding of ourselves about how these concerns are intertwined and to act on them as we develop an imaginative, transformative women's movement.

Why women? Because our present patriarchy enshrines together the hatred of women and the hatred of nature. In defying this patriarchy we are loyal to future generations and to life and this planet itself. We have a deep and particular understanding of this both through our natures and through our life experience as women.

We have the wisdom to oppose experiments which could permanently alter the genetic materials of future generations. As feminists we believe that human reproduction should be controlled by women not by a male-dominated medical establishment. We insist on the absolute right of a woman to an abortion. We support the life-affirming right of women to choose when and if to bear children.

We oppose war and we recognize its terrible force when we see it, undeclared but all around us. For to us war is the violence against women in all its forms—rape, battering, economic exploitation and intimidation—and it is the racist violence against indigenous peoples here in the U.S. and around the world, and it is the violence against the earth.

We recognize and respect the beauty of cultural diversity as we abhor racism. Racism divides us from our sisters, it lines the pockets of the exploiters and underlies the decimation of whole peoples and their homelands. The imperialism of white, male, western culture has been more destructive to other peoples and cultures than any imperialist power in the history of the world, just as it has brought us to the brink of ecological catastrophe.

We believe that a culture against nature is a culture against women. We know we must get out from under the feet of men as they go about their projects of violence. In pursuing these projects, men deny and dominate both women and nature. It is time to reconstitute our culture in the name of that nature, and of peace and freedom, and it is women who can show the way. We have to be the voice of the invisible, of nature who cannot speak for herself in the political arenas of our society, of the children yet to be born and of the women who are forcibly silenced in our mental institutions and prisons. We have been the keepers of the home, the children and the community. We learn early to observe, attend and nurture. And whether or not we become biological mothers, we use these nurturant powers daily as we go about our ordinary work. No one pays us to do this. If the children are born deformed or go hungry, if the people in homes built on a dumping site or near a nuclear weapons factory have terrible sickness, we are the ones who care for them, take them to the doctor, console survivors and soothe the terrified. And it is women who have begun to confront government agencies, politicians and corporations. As the deadly sludge of our political system encroaches on every aspect of our most intimate lives, all of us know that life cannot go on this way. The political and the personal are joined: the activities of women as feminists and anti-militarists, and the activities of women struggling in our neighborhoods and communities for survival and dignity are the same struggle.

And with the same attentiveness we give consideration to the kinds of jobs people do. Many people in this society are compelled to accept jobs which contribute to the destruction of life. In the workplace women particularly are saddled with menial tasks and meaningless work. We oppose such "jobs" and propose instead that work must involve free self-expression and an execution which is playful, not drudgerous. Demands for full employment which ignore the ecological and social devastation daily wrought in the process of ordinary work are dangerously shortsighted. This technological society offers finally the possibility of a materially abundant society with meaningful work for everyone. It is this potential we must claim for ourselves—that these capacities be used for our needs and desires in an appropriately scaled, ecologically aware manner. To create such a web of life is a precondition for freedom. The creation of work that is not merely a job, or worse yet a perpetuation of the kind of machines which daily destroy both the biosphere and the worker must be a feminist priority. To this end we propose that women begin to use the powers of imagination and creativity we possess as builders, engineers, scientist-alchemists and artists to develop the ways of livelihood and life which fulfil this promise.

In all our workings, we believe in the philosophy of nonviolence—that no person should be make into an "other" to despise, dehumanize and exploit. As women we have been an "other" but we are refusing to be the "other" any longer and we will not make anyone else into an "other." Sexism, racism, class divisions, homophobia and the rape of nature depend on this process of objectification. Men's fear of female sexuality has led them to pile up institutions which limit women's options. These keep us obligated to

man and unaware of alternatives to traditional women's roles and compulsory heterosexuality. It is in the interest of all women to support lesbian women. We oppose anything which presents women from loving each other freely in whatever way we choose.

We are building a feminist resistance movement in the tradition of the militant suffragists of the last wave of feminism, from whom Gandhi and Martin Luther King drew their inspiration. We believe in and practice direct action. By direct action we do not mean activity which is necessarily either legal or illegal, but intentional activity which does not even recognize these governmental sanctions. We mean the creation of a tradition which demands that we act directly, in all matters which concern us, that we do not recognize a higher authority whom we call upon to act for us. If we believe a parking lot should be a garden we might just dig it up and plant a garden. If we believe that there should be vigils of community women against militarism and violence . . . we go out and vigil. If we believe that there should be women's speakouts against violence in every community we will speak. If we believe that women should be safe walking the streets at night we will take back the night.

As ecofeminists the locus of our work is with women in our own communities, in small groups based on personal affinity, shared concerns and a sense of connectedness to our own landscape. But we are joining together regionally, nationally and internationally to confront systems of dominance that go beyond our communities and neighborhoods. Women all over the world are engaging in imaginative direct action to stop the war machine, and to assert our right to our own bodies and our own sexuality and to a poison-free, fruitful earth. Our feminist embrace must come to enfold all these women struggling in our respective communities.

We are the repository of a sensibility which can make a future possible. Feminists must exemplify this in our ideas, our relationships to each other, our culture, politics and actions. It is by necessity that we are feminist utopians. We look backwards to women-centered societies based on respect for life and life cycles. We look forward to new possibilities of reconstituting a culture which is non-hierarchical, which has not only the primitive respect for life and sense of interconnectedness but also those modern technologies which further peace and liberation. Peace is more than the absence of war, as freedom is more than the absence of co-ercion. They mean more than putting down the gun, taking off the shackles, or even just hearing and remembering. They are both ongoing processes which must be constantly attended to, criticized and expanded upon. Our movement is a process without end, much as life itself is a process without end.

SEVENTY-FIVE

◆◆◆

Principles of Environmental Justice (1991)

The First National People of Color Environmental Leadership Summit

The First National People of Color Environmental Leadership Summit was convened by the United Church of Christ's Commission on Racial Justice and held in Washington, D.C., in 1991. Over 1,000 national and international environmental activists gathered, establishing the "Principles of Environmental Justice."

Preamble

We, the people of color, gathered together at this multinational People of Color Environmental Leadership Summit, to begin to build a national and international movement of all peoples of color to fight the destruction and taking of our lands and communities, do hereby re-establish our spiritual interdependence to the sacredness of our Mother Earth; to respect and celebrate each of our cultures, languages and beliefs about the natural world and our roles in healing ourselves; to ensure environmental justice; to promote economic alternatives which would contribute to the development of environmentally safe livelihoods; and, to secure our political, economic and cultural liberation that has been denied for over 500 years of colonization and oppression, resulting in the poisoning of our communities and land and the genocide of our peoples, do affirm and adopt these Principles of Environmental Justice:

1. *Environmental justice* affirms the sacredness of Mother Earth, ecological unity and the interdependence of all species, and the right to be free from ecological destruction.

2. *Environmental justice* demands that public policy be based on mutual respect and justice for all peoples, free from any form of discrimination or bias.

3. *Environmental justice* mandates the right to ethical, balanced and responsible uses of land and renewable resources in the interest of a sustainable planet for humans and other living things.

4. *Environmental justice* calls for universal protection from nuclear testing, extraction, production and disposal of toxic/hazardous wastes and poisons and nuclear testing that threaten the fundamental right to clean air, land, water, and food.

5. *Environmental justice* affirms the fundamental right to political, economic, cultural and environmental self-determination of all peoples.

6. *Environmental justice* demands the cessation of the production of all toxins, hazardous wastes, and radioactive materials, and that all past and current producers be held strictly accountable to the people for detoxification and the containment at the point of production.

7. *Environmental justice* demands the right to participate as equal partners at every level of decision-making including needs assessment, planning, implementation, enforcement and evaluation.

8. *Environmental justice* affirms the right of all workers to a safe and healthy work environment, without being forced to choose between an unsafe livelihood and unemployment. It also affirms the right of those who work at home to be free from environmental hazards.

9. *Environmental justice* protects the right of victims of environmental injustice to receive full compensation and reparations for damages as well as quality health care.

10. *Environmental justice* considers governmental acts of environmental injustice a violation of international law, the Universal Declaration on

Human Rights, and the United Nations Convention on Genocide.

11. *Environmental justice* must recognize a special legal and natural relationship of Native Peoples to the U.S. government through treaties, agreements, compacts, and covenants affirming sovereignty and self-determination.

12. *Environmental justice* affirms the need for urban and rural ecological policies to clean up and rebuild our cities and rural areas in balance with nature, honoring the cultural integrity of all our communities, and providing fair access for all to the full range of resources.

13. *Environmental justice* calls for the strict enforcement of principles of informed consent, and a halt to the testing of experimental reproductive and medical procedures and vaccinations on people of color.

14. *Environmental justice* opposes the destructive operations of multi-national corporations.

15. *Environmental justice* opposes military occupation, repression and exploitation of lands, peoples and cultures, and other life forms.

16. *Environmental justice* calls for the education of present and future generations which emphasizes social and environmental issues, based on our experience and an appreciation of our diverse cultural perspectives.

17. *Environmental justice* requires that we, as individuals, make personal and consumer choices to consume as little of Mother Earth's resources and to produce as little waste as possible; and make the conscious decision to challenge and reprioritize our lifestyles to ensure the health of the natural world for present and future generations.

SEVENTY-SIX

◆◆◆

Native Hawaiian Historical and Cultural Perspectives on Environmental Justice (1992)

Mililani Trask

Mililani Trask is an attorney and a founder of Na Koa Ikaika o Ka Lahui Hawaii, an organization working for the Hawaii sovereignty. She has worked with the United Nations to aid indigenous people from around the world seeking independence, and helped author the U.N. Declaration on the Rights of Indigenous Peoples.

When you ask a Hawaiian who they are, their response is "Keiki hanau o ka aina, child that is borne up from the land." I am a Native Hawaiian attorney. I also have the great honor and distinction, and the great burden and responsibility, of being the first elected Kia'Aina of Ka Lahui Hawai'i, the sovereign nation of the Native Hawaiian people, which we created ourselves in 1987.

_____

This paper was presented at the First National People of Color Environmental Leadership Summit, October 24–27, 1991, Washington, D.C.

It's a great pleasure and honor for me to be here to address a group such as yourselves, such a momentous occasion, the first time that the people of color will gather to consider the impacts on our common land base.

I thought I would begin by giving a little bit of history about Hawaii Nei because many people are not aware of the crisis there and the status of the Native Hawaiian people. As we approach the United Nations' celebration of the discoverers, we are celebrating not only the arrival of Columbus but also of Cortez and Captain Cook. In Hawaii Nei we are celebrating 500 years of resilient resistance to the coming of the "discoverers."

In 1778 Captain James Cook sailed into the Hawaiian archipelago. He found there a thriving Native community of 800,000 Native people, living in balance on their lands, completely economically self-sufficient, feeding and clothing themselves off the resources of their own land base. Within one generation, 770,000 of our people were dead—dead from what is called "mai haole, the sickness of the white man," which Cook brought: venereal disease, flu, pox, the same tragic history that occurred on the American continent to Native American Indians and the Native people of Central and South America.

In 1893 the United States Marines dispatched a group of soldiers to the Island of Oahu for the purpose of overthrowing the lawful kingdom of Hawaii Nei. Prior to 1893, Hawaii was welcomed into the world family of nations and maintained over 20 international treaties, including treaties of friendship and peace with the United States. Despite those international laws, revolution was perpetrated against our government, and our lawful government overthrown. In two years we will mark the hundredth anniversary of when we had the right to be self-determining and self-governing.

In 1959, Hawaii was admitted into the Union of the United States of America. There were great debates that occurred in Washington, DC that focused on the fact that people were afraid to incorporate the Territory of Hawaii because it would become the first state in the union in which white people would be a minority of less than 25 percent. That was the reason for the concern when those debates were launched. In 1959, when Hawaii became a state, something happened that did not happen in any other state of the union. In all of the other states, when the U.S. admitted that state into the union, America set aside lands for the Native people of those states, as federal reserves. Today there is a policy that provides that Native Americans should be self-governing, should be allowed to maintain their nations, should be allowed to pass laws, environmental and otherwise, to protect their land base. That did not occur in the State of Hawaii. In the State of Hawaii in 1959, the federal government gave our lands to the state to be held in trust, and gave the Native Hawaiian people, of which there are 200,000, the status of perpetual wardship. We are not allowed to form governments if we are Native Hawaiian; we are not allowed to control our land base. To this day our lands are controlled by state agencies and utilized extensively by the American military complex as part of a plan designed by Hawaii's Senator Daniel Inouye.

In 1987 we decided to exercise our inherent rights to be self-governing. The Hawaii Visitors Bureau declared 1987 the Year of the Hawaiian for a great tourist and media campaign. We took a look at our statistics: 22,000 families on lists waiting for land entitlements since 1920; 30,000 families dead waiting for their Hawaiian homelands awards; 22,000 currently waiting. We thought to ourselves, how are *we* going to celebrate 1987? And we decided that the time had come to convene a constitutional convention to resurrect our nation and to exert our basic and inherent rights, much to the dismay and consternation of the state and the federal government, and certainly to the shock of Senator Inouye.

We have passed a constitution that recognizes the right and the responsibility of Native people to protect their land base and to ensure water quality, because Western laws have been unable to protect the environment. We decided to lift up and resurrect our nation in 1987, passing our constitution, and we are proceeding now to come out, to announce that we are alive and well, and to network with other people.

I have come to announce that a state of emergency exists with regards to the natural environment of the archipelagic lands and waters of Hawaii, and also a state of emergency exists with regards to the survival of the Native people who live there and throughout the Pacific basin. We have many environmental injustices and issues that need to be addressed; most of them have dire global consequences. The expansion of the United States military complex presents substantial threats to our environment.

Right now on the Island of Hawaii and on the Island of Kauai, Senator Inouye is pressing for what he calls the "space-porting initiative," which we all know to be Star Wars. It will distribute large amounts of toxic gases, it will scorch the earth beyond repair and, most importantly and offensive to us, the lands that have been chosen are lands set aside by the Congress in 1920 for the homesteading of Hawaiian people. These are the lands that are pursued on the Island of Hawaii.

Our response to that is "kapu Ka'u." Ka'u is the district; kapu is the Hawaiian way for saying, "It is taboo." We cannot allow desecration of sacred lands, desecration of historic properties that are the cultural inheritance of our people to be converted for the military complex and for the designs of those who would further the interests of war against others. It is an inappropriate use of Native lands.

Other Threats

The United States Navy continues its relentless bombing of Kahoolawe Island. [This was discontinued in 1990, but the land was not returned to the State of Hawaii until 1994.] Not only have they denuded the upper one-third of that island, but as they have blasted away the lands, trees and shrubs, all that silt has come down to the channels between Kahoolawe and Maui Islands, the channels that are the spawning grounds of the whales that migrate every year to Hawaii Nei.

We now have information coming from Lualualie on the Island of Oahu that there is a very high incidence of leukemia and other cancers among the Hawaiian children who live there. We believe that this is due to electromagnetic contamination. In Lualualie the United States military is taking control of 2,000 acres of Hawaiian homelands, lands set aside by the Congress to homestead our people. These lands were taken over and converted for a nuclear and military storage facility. Ten years ago, in 1981, they issued a report saying that there's electromagnetic radiation there. After the report was issued all the military families were moved out of the base, but nobody told the Hawaiian community that lives in the surrounding area. We have taken it to the Western courts, we have been thrown out, because the court ruled that Native Hawaiians are wards of the state and the federal government. Therefore, Native Hawaiians are not allowed standing to sue in the federal courts to protect our trust land assets. We are the only class of Native Americans, and the only class of American citizens, that are not allowed access to the federal court system to seek redress of grievances relating to breach of trust.

Ka Lahui Hawai'i is pleased and proud to join all of the other Pacific Island nations in opposing the federal policy which is being perpetrated by Mr. Bush and Senator Inouye identifying the Pacific region as a national sacrifice area. What is a national sacrifice area? I did some legal research and I found out that national sacrifice areas usually occur on Indian reservations or in black communities. They are areas that the nation identifies primarily for the dumping of toxic wastes. As the Greens celebrate in Europe what they perceive to be an environmental victory in forcing America to remove its nuclear and military wastes from Europe, we in the Pacific region have been told that Johnston Island and other Pacific nations have been targeted for storage and dumping. We will not allow that and we will continue to speak out against it.

Tourist Evils

Tourism and its attendant evils continue to assault our island land base. Hundreds of thousands of tourists come to Hawaii every year. They are seeking a dream of paradise. They drink our water, they contaminate our environment. They are responsible for millions of tons of sewage every year, which is deposited into the Pacific Ocean. And, in addition, they are taking lands from our rural communities.

Tourism perpetuates certain Western concepts of exclusive rights to land. Tourists don't like to see other people on their beaches. Tourists don't like to allow Native people to go and fish in the traditional ways. And, because of toxification of the ocean due to release of sewage in Hawaii, there are many places where you can no longer find the reef fish. You cannot go there and take the opihi, the squid, or take the turtle, because they're gone now. So in the few remaining areas where there are fish, the state and federal governments have imposed public park restrictions to prevent Native people from going there to lay the net and take the fish. If the fish are taken out, what will the tourists see when they put on their snorkels? Native people are not allowed to fish so that tourists can view through their goggles what remains of the few species we have because their own tourist practices destroyed all the rest of the bounty of our fisheries.

Tourists need golf courses; golf courses need tons of pesticides, herbicides and millions of tons of water. Hawaii is an island ecology, we do not get fresh water from flowing streams. All the water that falls from the rain in Hawaii is percolated through the lava of the islands and comes to rest in a central basal lens underneath our island. As the rains percolate down they bring with them all the herbicides and pesticides that have been used for years by agribusiness: King Cane, Dole Pineapple, United States military. Already on the island of Oahu we have had to permanently close two of our drinking wells because of toxification. Nobody in the State of Hawaii or the Hawaii Visitors Bureau is going to tell you that at the present time there are 30 contaminants in the drinking water in the State of Hawaii.

The specter of geothermal development lays heavily upon our lands. For 25 years the United

States and its allies have been developing geothermal energy in Hawaii. It is destroying the last Pacific tropical rain forest on the Island of Hawaii, Wao Kele o Puna Forest, sacred to the lands of Tutu Pele, our Grandmother Pele, who erupts and gives birth to the earth. This is her home, yet this is the place where they are developing geothermal. And as it proceeds, Native people are denied their basic right to worship there. We have taken this case to the United States Supreme Court. It was struck down along with the Native American freedom of religion cases because the court ruled that religious worship in America must be "site-specific." If you take the Akua, if you put God in the building, American courts will understand. But if you take God and say, "The earth is the Lord's and the fullness of it, the Black Hills of South Dakota, the lands and forests of Tutu Pele," American courts do not understand. . . .

International fishing practices, gill netting and drift netting, are genocide in the sea. As a result of these practices, the Native fisheries are diminished and depleted. In some areas our marine fisheries are depleted to the point that we can no longer harvest that resource.

What is the appropriate response to this environmental and human outrage? In Hawaii Nei we have undertaken to address these things through sovereignty and the basic exertion of the rights of Native people to govern and control their own land base. These are political issues, certainly. But they spring from a very ancient source, a source within our heart, a source that all Natives and people of color understand: our relationship in the global context. As Hawaiians say, "Keiki hanau o ka aina, child that is borne up from the land," understanding that there is an innate connection to the earth as the Mother. We are called upon now as the guardians of our sacred lands to rise up in the defense of our Mother. You don't subdivide your Mother, you don't chop her body up, you don't drill, penetrate and pull out her lifeblood. You protect and nurture your Mother. And the Hawaiian value for that is aloha ai'na, love for the land, malama ai'na, care and nurturing for the land. It is reciprocal. It gives back to the Native people. Our people know that the Akua put us here on this earth to be guardians of these sacred lands. It is a God-given responsibility and trust that a sovereign nation must assume if it is to have any integrity. And so we in Ka Lahui have undertaken this struggle. Environmental racism is the enemy. The question is, What is our response? What really is environmental justice? I'll tell you one thing I learned in law school at Santa Clara. Do you know how they perceive and teach justice, the white schools of this country? A blind white woman with her eyes covered up by cloth, holding the scales of justice. And if you look at it, they're not balanced. The Native scale and the environmental scale are outweighed by other priorities.

Well, environmental justice is not a blindfolded white woman. When I saw the woman with the scales of justice in law school, I thought to myself, "You know, if you blindfold yourself the only thing you're going to do is walk into walls." You are not going to resolve anything. And that's where we are with Western law. I know that there are many attorneys here and others who are working on environmental cases. I support them. We have received a great deal of support from attorneys working in environmental law. But do not put your eggs in the basket of the blind white lady. We must try other approaches.

In closing, I would like to say in behalf of myself and the Hawaii delegation that we are very renewed in coming here, and that when we return to Hawaii in two or three days we will have good news to share with our people, that we have come ourselves these many thousands of miles, that we have looked in the faces of people of color, that we have seen there, in their hearts and in their eyes, a light shining, a light of commitment, a light that is filled with capacity and a light that is filled with love for the Mother Earth, a light that is the same that we have in our hearts.

I try to do one thing whenever I finish speaking. I try to leave the podium by telling people what the motto of Ka Lahui Hawaii is, the motto of our nation that we're forming now. I find it to be very applicable to the situations that we are in. We are facing a difficult struggle. Every bit of commitment and energy is needed to save our Mother Earth and to ensure the survival of our people and all of the species of the earth. It is a difficult row to hoe. There is going to be a great deal of strife and a great deal of pain. But we must proceed; we have no alternative. This is the same position that the native people of Hawaii Nei found themselves in 1987 when we committed to resurrecting our national government. And at the time that we passed that constitution we also adopted a motto. It is a motto that I think you might want to live by as we proceed in this environmental war that we are waging. That motto is: "A difficult birth does not make the baby any less beautiful."

◆◆◆

SEVENTY-SEVEN

Consumption (1999)

North American Perspectives

H. Patricia Hynes

Writer, educator, and researcher **H. Patricia Hynes** is Professor of Environmental Health at the Boston University School of Public Health where she works on urban environmental issues, environmental justice, and feminist perspectives on health. She has won numerous awards, including the 2003 National Delta Omega Award for Innovative Curriculum in Public Health.

. . . The consumption of resources by individuals, by governments and ruling elites, by semi-autonomous and secretive institutions such as the military, and by macroeconomic systems is embedded within the matrix of political economy and cultural values [see Figure 1]. Yet consumption . . . has been reduced to a mere empirical, per capita phenomenon, as if it were detached from those structural and ideological forces that result in wealth-building for some and impoverishment and poor health for others. . . .

What, then, is the content of recent North American critiques of consumption and consumerism? What are their strengths and weaknesses? What core elements of a woman-centered analysis can we bring to them?

. . . A handful of analyses and practice-based responses have emerged to characterize, critique, and provide alternatives to consumption patterns and consumerist ideology in industrialized countries. Among the chief prototypes are three approaches: the "demographics of consumption," movements to simplify life and make consumer choices that are less environmentally damaging, and the computation of the ecological footprint.

Demographics of Consumption

Asking the question "How much is enough?" Worldwatch Institute researcher Alan Durning has amassed quite a stunning picture of the explosion in the consumption of consumer goods and services in the United States and worldwide.[1] He traces the origins of "consumer society" in the United States to the 1920s, with the emergence of name brands, the entrée of packaged and processed foods, the rise of the car as the popular symbol of American upward mobility, and the birth of mass marketing through advertising. Consumerism was stymied by the Depression and World War II, but it picked up enormous momentum in the United States after the war and was rapidly disseminated worldwide, under the gospel of development and the democratization of consumerism, to gain markets for expanding U.S. industries. To cite a few supporting statistics on the radical change in post–World War II consumption: People in the United States own, on the average, "twice as many automobiles, drive two and a half times as far, use 21 times as much plastic, and cover 25 times as much distance by air as their parents did in 1950."[2]

Durning's data on the growth in household appliance ownership over time embody the triumph of the central message of mass marketing: Greater purchasing power and growing choice in the marketplace guarantee a better (and happier) life. Popular culture advertising underpins the macroeconomic maxim: An expanding economy—with rising per capita income and consumer spending—is a healthy economy.

Comparing global patterns of consumption leads Durning to a deeper inquiry into the qualitative differences in consumption among peoples in the world. He asks what kinds of resources people consume on a day-to-day basis and structures his answer around a comparison of consumption by diet, transport, and principal type of materials used. The result is three classes of consumption, the latter two being of much sounder environmental quality than the first, which has no sustainable characteristics.

The primary focus of this tripartite view of consumption in the world—emerging from Worldwatch Institute and a number of liberal environmental, economic, and alternative-lifestyle circles in the United States—is the plight of the consumer class in the United States. Economist Juliet Schor points out

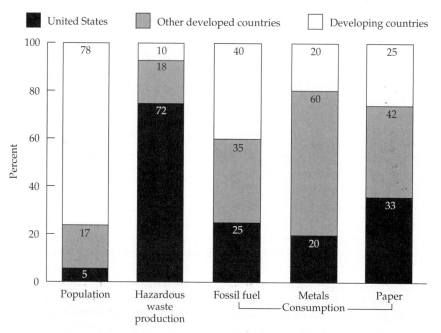

FIGURE 1 Share of Population, Hazardous Waste Production, and Natural Resource Consumption in the United States, Developing, and Developed Regions, 1990s. (*Source:* Natural Resources Defense Council, in Lori S. Ashford, *New Perspectives on Population: Lessons from Cairo. Population Bulletin* [Washington, D.C.: Population Reference Bureau, Inc.], Vol. 50, No. 1 [March 1995], 30.)

that people in the United States work more hours today in their jobs than they did two decades ago, even though we are twice as productive in goods and services as we were in 1948. Why, instead of working more and having less leisure, do we not work less and enjoy more leisure, she queries. Describing the pitfalls of consumerism and the manufacture of discontent that keep middle-class people locked into a work-and-spend cycle, she calls for overcoming consumerism, revaluing leisure, and rethinking the necessity of full-time jobs.[3]

Both Schor and Durning hinge a key part of their prescription—that people rethink and modify their consumerist work- and lifestyles—on the question of happiness. National polls conducted since the 1950s show no increase in the percentage of people who report being "very happy," despite the fact that people now purchase almost twice the number of consumer goods and services they did in the 1950s. Time spent enjoying two of the classic sources of happiness—social relations and

leisure—has diminished as people work more to purchase more nondurable, packaged, rapidly obsolete, nonvital goods and services.

Durning advocates that the consumer class be wary of the estimated 3,000 advertising messages that bombard us per day cultivating consumer taste and needs, and that we climb a few rungs down the consumption ladder by choosing durable goods, public transportation, and low-energy devices. In other words, he points to the consumption patterns of the 3.3 billion "middle consumer class" people in Table 1 as more sound and sustainable for the environment.

Voluntary Simplicity Movement

Arising from these same cultural observations, the voluntary simplicity, or new frugality, movement offers a new road map for those of the consumer class who wish to live better with less . . . this movement was given a high profile by the best-selling

Table 1. World Consumption Classes, 1992

CATEGORY OF CONSUMPTION	CONSUMERS (1.1 BILLION)	MIDDLE (3.3 BILLION)	POOR (1.1 BILLION)
Diet	meat, packaged food, soft drinks	grain, clean water	insufficient grain, unsafe water
Transport	private cars	bicycles, buses	walking
Materials	throwaways	durables	local biomass

Source: Alan Durning, *How Much Is Enough?* (New York: W. W. Norton, 1992), 27.

book *Your Money or Your Life,* a pragmatic self-help approach to living securely on less money in order to spend one's time in more meaningful social, personal, spiritual, and environmentally sustaining ways.[4]

In this movement, people learn to assess their real financial needs (with generous distinctions made between "needs" and "wants"), how to budget and invest to achieve financial independence on a substantially reduced income, and how to calculate the impacts of their lifestyle on the environment through household audits of energy, products, and waste. More than 300,000 people have developed "new road maps" for their future lives, based on core values they have identified in the process of re-thinking what ultimately matters to them. Most reduce their cost of living by 20 percent immediately and, eventually, by even more; many "retire" from careers and full-time jobs to pursue personal and social interests.

If It's Good for the Environment and Good for the Person, What's the Problem?

How can we fault the appeal to happiness and to core values that these critiques of the consumerist culture make? They result in people living "more softly" on the Earth. They reach deeper into a person's self than the green consumer movement, which redirects, but does not necessarily reduce or challenge, consumerism. How many green products are designed for durability and marketed as such? The majority of green product manufacturers employ mass marketing techniques, including the cultivation of "need," and use shallow appeals to feel-good environmentalism to sell their products. Green consumers get locked into seesaw debates over plastic versus paper, for example, never learning that the debate is a foil that deters deeper questions of product durability and necessity. At its best, says Durning, green consumerism outpaces legislation and uses market tactics to reform the market; at its worst, it is "a palliative for the conscience of the consumer class, allowing us to continue business as usual while feeling like we are doing our part."[5]

The primary shortcoming of the "consumer treadmill" critique is that it is socially and politically underdeveloped. Focusing on average per capita consumption, Durning and others make little distinction among the highly disparate economic classes of people within the United States. While our society as a whole is locked into meat, packaged food, soft drinks, and throwaways—with a McDonald's on every corner—the gap between the poorest fifth and richest fifth of the United States begs for an environmental policy that is based on "a hunger and thirst for justice" as well as national concern about global climate change and the decline of personal happiness. The prescriptions to live on less, to get out of the rat race and enjoy more leisure, to examine one's personal values and organize one's life by those values, may not necessarily result in a more equitable or humanistic society. Those who choose voluntary simplicity, durables, and bicycles may live happily and stress-free across town from the angry (or depressed) involuntary poor, with no more empathy, solidarity, or insight into undoing social injustice. (Alternatively, of course, by choosing to live on less, people may end up in less expensive mixed-income neighborhoods, join their

neighborhood associations, and, in so doing, meet and collaborate with the involuntary poor on neighborhood betterment.)

The focus on the cultivation of need by mass marketing and the lack of personal fulfillment, when divorced from an inquiry into the patterns and structures that reward the well-off and punish the poor, creates islands of better-living and more personally satisfied people without necessarily generating a sense of a new social movement or new society. "Twelve-step" programs to break the consumer habit offer good techniques borrowed from self-fulfillment and self-control support-group settings, but they are no substitute for social responses to persistent poverty, to misogyny that sells women as sex to be consumed, to child labor and sweatshops, to the consumption engine of militarism and military spending that siphons the life force out of societies, and to all oppressions of "the other."

Social consciousness within the environmental movement on the other hand, speaks to people's civic and humanistic being, to their quest for a connectedness with others and the earth, to their desire to make the world more just and humane,

Table 2. The Ecological Footprint of the Average Canadian, in Hectares per Capita

	ENERGY	BUILT ENVIRONMENT	AGRICULTURAL LAND	FOREST	TOTAL
Food	0.4		0.9		**1.3**
Housing	0.5	0.1		0.4	**1.0**
Transport	1.0	0.1			**1.1**
Consumer Goods	0.6		0.2	0.2	**1.0**
Resources in Services	0.4				**0.4**
TOTAL	**2.9**	**0.2**	**1.1**	**0.6**	**4.8**

Source: Mathis Wackernagel, *How Big Is Our Ecological Footprint?* (Vancouver: University of British Columbia, 1993), 3.

as well as to the stressed, overworked, and seemingly optionless plight of individuals caught on the work-and-spend treadmill of late-twentieth-century industrial life. Taming consumption through a personal, spiritual quest is part of the answer, but not the whole one.

The Ecological Footprint

The intriguing epithet "ecological footprint" is shorthand for an analysis that more successfully integrates the calculation of consumer impact on the earth with the responsibilities of government, the right of every human to a fair and healthful share of the Earth's resources, and a deep concern for not overloading or degrading global ecosystems.[6] Here, too, the focus is primarily the North American consumer lifestyle and an accounting of its impacts on the environment. However, the goal is to calculate the size of the Canadian and U.S. ecological footprint compared with that of others in lesser-industrialized and nonindustrialized countries and to determine how the oversized North American footprint can be reduced through better regional planning, more ecologically conscious consumption, and the restructuring of industrial technology and economics.

This ecological accounting tool, as geographer Ben Wisner points out so well, inverts "carrying capacity" to ask: Given nearly six billion people in the world, how should we live so as to enable all to live within the limits of the biosphere?[7] The premise of the ecological footprint is that although half the

world lives in cities (and by 2020 an estimated two-thirds of people will), we live in a biosphere much larger than the physical boundaries of our cities and towns when we buy goods that are grown or made from resources outside our municipality or region and when we dispose of our wastes in the global atmosphere and marine environments. The ecological footprint is calculated by translating key categories of human consumption—food, housing, transport, consumer goods and services—into the amount of *productive land* needed to provide these goods and services and to assimilate their resultant waste.

Using assumptions about biomass substitutes for fossil fuels and so on, the authors of this method, Mathis Wackernagel and William Rees, calculate that the amount of land needed to support the average Canadian's present consumption, or ecological footprint, is 4.8 hectares [Table 2].

In their calculations of ecologically productive land, Wackernagel and Rees estimate that an average of 1.6 hectares of land per capita is available worldwide for goods and services. In other words, the average Canadian uses three times as much of the earth's capacity as is available to every person; in other words, the average Canadian's ecological footprint is three times the size it ought to be, since everyone deserves a fair share of the global commons. Correspondingly, the average Indian ecological footprint is 0.4 hectare per person.

The average per capita consumption in Canada, as in every country, is a composite of the consumption of the rich, poor, and middle consumption

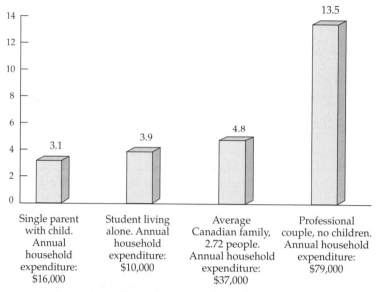

FIGURE 2 Examples of Ecological Footprints of Various Canadian Households, in Hectares per Capita. (*Source:* Mathis Wackernagel, *How Big Is Our Ecological Footprint?* [Vancouver: University of British Columbia, 1993], 3.)

classes. Thus, Figure 2 compares the ecological footprints of various Canadian households in order to show where the extremes of consumption lie and whose consumer lifestyle inordinately appropriates the carrying capacity of the Earth.

Three aspects of this analysis are particularly laudable. First, its starting point is the assumption that every human being has the same claim on nature's productivity and utility. Thus, it is inequitable and undesirable for North Americans to appropriate others' share of the global commons. Second, it promotes an urban and regional planning strategy that would reduce North Americans' footprint on the global environment by reversing sprawl through integrating living, working, and shopping; promoting bike paths and public transportation; and favoring the local economy. Third, it calls for a massive reform of industrial society to free up the ecological space needed by the poor to raise their standard of living, while enabling the well-off to maintain their high material standards.[8] Wackernagel and Rees's recommendations for restructuring industrialism to achieve a smaller ecological footprint on the world include reforms

that are simultaneously being advocated by radical environmental economists:

- Shift taxes from income to consumption and include the full costs of resources and pollution in consumer products through environmental taxes and fees. Including true environmental costs in the full cost of products will motivate industry to make cleaner products and consumers to buy them; it will favor reuse, repair, and reconditioning of products.

- Invest in research into energy- and material-efficient technologies to achieve the "four- to ten-fold reduction in material and energy intensity per unit of economic output" needed in industrial countries to reduce the ecological footprint to a sustainable size.

- Invest the anticipated economic gains from the enhanced efficiency in remediating and restoring critical ecosystems.[9]

Even with a more structural approach to macroeconomic systems and the socially conscious goal of commonweal, certain footprints, in this analysis, remain invisible. Women have much less stake in the global economy than men—by virtue of having little political and economic power, as well as by holding different economic priorities, in many instances, from men. Thus, women have a smaller individual and structural footprint than men and male institutions. The economic and political institution of the military, for example ([which has an] extreme impact on economies, cultures, and ecosystems), arises from patriarchal concepts of power and methods of conflict resolution.

What insights and efforts can a woman-centered analysis bring to the issue of consumption in order to further the goals of redistributing and humanizing our use of natural resources, consumer goods, and services, and of mitigating and reversing our pollution impacts on ecosystems?

Conclusion

. . . Why are more than a billion women and girls consigned to spending hours daily collecting wood and biomass and ingesting smoke when the dissemination of technologies such as more efficient cook stoves and solar cookers would ease their lives; save their health; and conserve woodlands, soil, water, and biomass in critical ecosystems? Authors Kammen and Dove have identified a bias in science against "research on mundane topics" in energy, agriculture, public health, and resource economics. . . .[10] Their analysis of the fallacies that underlie the inattention to labor-, time-, health- and environment-saving technologies is consonant with feminist critiques of science culture and science values.[11] According to the canon of science, the premier scientific work is basic research, uncontaminated by the needs of real people and characterized by objective and detached thought. The potential of "breakthrough discoveries" charges the rarefied atmosphere of science research and relegates revisiting old, unsolved, human-centered problems to second-tier science. In this first-order science, abstract theory, mathematical modeling, speed, distance, and scale are privileged over social benefits, qualitative methods, and the local and small-scale

applications of "mundane" science. In other words, what might be seen as the subjectivizing, sociologizing, and feminizing of science popularizes and banalizes it. . . .

Social goodness and community health, as the "ecological footprint" analysis affirms, are requisites and indices of a sustainable community. In our effort to reduce overconsumption through distinguishing genuine needs and consumerist wants, we must confront the consumption of so-called goods and services that are based on the sexual exploitation of women and girls and are often a consequence of war and environmental degradation, such as prostitution, pornography, and mail-order brides. The impeccable logic of environmental justice—that poor communities of color have been systematically exploited by polluters and industry by reason of race, and suffer disproportionately from poor health—holds for women as well. Like racial justice, a sexual justice that seeks to eliminate the sexual exploitation of women is fundamental to environmental justice, to community health, and to social goodness.

NOTES

1. Alan Durning, *How Much Is Enough?* (New York: W. W. Norton, 1992).

2. Ibid., 30.

3. Juliet Schor, *The Overworked American: The Unexpected Decline of Leisure* (New York: Basic Books, 1991).

4. Joe Dominguez and Vicki Robin, *Your Money or Your Life* (New York: Viking, 1992).

5. Durning, *How Much Is Enough?* op. cit., 125.

6. Mathis Wackernagel and William Rees, *Our Ecological Footprint: Reducing Human Impact on the Earth* (Gabriola Island, British Columbia, and Philadelphia: New Society Publishers, 1996).

7. Ben Wisner, "The Limitations of 'Carrying Capacity,'" *Political Environments* (Winter–Spring 1996), 1, 3–4.

8. Wackernagel and Rees, *Our Ecological Footprint*, op. cit., 144.

9. Ibid., 144–45.

10. Daniel M. Kammen and Michael R. Dove, "The Virtues of Mundane Science," in *Environment*, Vol. 39, No. 6 (July/August 1997), 10–15, 38–41.

11. See Sue V. Rosser, *Female-Friendly Science* (New York: Teacher's College Press, 1990).

13

◆◆◆

Creating Change
Theory, Vision, and Action

In the last one hundred years, women in the United States have won the right to speak out on public issues, to vote, to own property in their own names, the right to divorce, and increased access to higher education and the professions. Developments in birth control have allowed women to have fewer babies, and family size is much smaller than it was in the early years of the twentieth century. Improved health care and better working conditions mean that women now live longer than ever before. Women's wage rates are inching closer to men's. Issues like domestic violence, rape, sexual harassment, and women's sexual freedom are public matters. As a group, women in the United States are more independent—economically and socially—than ever before.

Although women have broken free from many earlier limitations, this book also shows how much still needs to be done. As we argue in previous chapters, many aspects of women's lives are subject to debate and controversy as **contested terrains.** These controversial issues include women's sexuality, reproductive freedom, the nature of marriage and family relationships, the right to livelihood

independent of men, and the right to affordable health care. Gains have been made and also eroded, as conservative politicians aided by conservative religious leaders and media personalities have attempted to turn the clock back.

It is easy to review the details of U.S. women's experiences of discrimination and to come away feeling angry, depressed, hopeless, and disempowered. The interlocking systems that keep women oppressed can seem monolithic and unchangeable. Major U.S. social movements of the past one hundred years—for the rights of working people; the civil rights of peoples of color; women's liberation; disability rights; gay, lesbian, bisexual, and transgender rights—have made significant gains and also seen those gains challenged and attacked.

In this final chapter we consider what is needed to tackle the problems we have identified throughout the book. How can this be done in ways that address underlying causes as well as visible manifestations? More fundamentally, how can women and men build relationships, systems of work, local communities, and a wider world based on sustainability and real security?

569

Each person needs to find meaning in his or her life. Knowing a lot of facts may be an effective way of doing well on tests and getting good grades, but this kind of knowledge does not necessarily provide meaning. Knowing what matters to you means that you can begin to take charge of your own life and begin to direct change. This process involves examining your own life, as suggested through the questions included in each chapter. Unless you do this, you will be absent from your own system of knowledge.

How Does Change Happen?

The process of creating change requires a combination of theoretical insights and understandings, visions of alternatives, and action. This involves using your head, heart, and hands in ways that reinforce one another. The readings in this chapter include a blend of these three aspects, which may involve a spiritual perspective (as in Reading 78 by Christina Leaño). In the book as a whole, several writers draw on their spirituality, or on their values and convictions that women's lives can and should be changed for the better.

Using the Head: Theories for Social Change

As we pointed out in Chapter 1, doing something about an issue or a problem requires us to have a theory, an explanation, of what it is. The theory we create directly shapes what we think ought to be done. Thus *how* we theorize is a key first step in creating change. When people face difficult problems alone, they can draw only on their own insights. Although these are valuable, they are likely to be limited. In talking things over with others, we may discover that they can shed light on things we may have missed, or that they provide a completely different way to think about what we are dealing with. Similarly, if we examine only certain specifics of an issue, examine issues separately, or use a limited analytical framework, we will end up with limited understandings of women's lives. For a fuller picture we need to analyze issues individually and together, looking for commonalities and patterns, recognizing differences, and using frameworks that illuminate as many parts as possible.

This principle has guided our choices in making the selections for this book. Our theoretical ideas, which run through the previous chapters—sometimes explicit, sometimes implicit—are summarized here:

- A social-constructionist perspective allows us to see how social and political forces shape our lives and our sense of ourselves. It encourages us to focus on the specificity of experience and also the diversity of experiences among people. It allows us to see that situations and structures are not fixed for all time but are changeable under the right circumstances.

- How an issue is defined and framed will affect how we think about the problem, where we look for probable causes, our ideas about what ought to be done about it, and who is likely to become involved.

- In analyzing social situations, it is necessary to look at them in terms of micro, meso, macro, and global levels and to understand how these levels affect one another. Strategies for change need to address all of these levels.

- Many women's activist organizations and projects are working on the issues discussed in this book.

- Efforts to create equal opportunities for women and equal access to current institutions have made a difference for many women, but by themselves they cannot achieve a genuinely secure and sustainable world because these are not the goals of most institutions.

Using the Heart: Visions for Social Change

Vision is the second necessary ingredient in creating social change—some idea of a different way of doing things, a different future for humankind, framed by explicit principles around which human relations ought to be organized. Otherwise, as the saying goes, "If you don't know where you're going, any road will get you there."

Visions are about values, drawing from inside ourselves everything we value and daring to think big. The many demands of our busy lives leave most people with little time or opportunity to envision alternatives. In school and college, for example, students are rarely asked to think seriously about their hopes and dreams for a more truly human world in which to live. Much of what we do is guided not by our own visions but in reaction to the expectations of others and outside pressures. Social issues, too, are framed in reactive and negative terms. People talk about "antiracism," for instance, not about what a truly multicultural society would be like.

Some people scorn this step as time-wasting and unrealistic. What matters, they say, is to come up with "realistic" ideas that people feel comfortable with, that businesses will want to invest in, or that fit government programs and guidelines. Tackle something small and specific, something winnable. Don't waste time on grandiose ideas.

Because most of us are not encouraged to envision change, it may take a while to free ourselves from seemingly practical ideas. Our imaginations are often limited to what we know, and that makes it difficult to break out of our cramped daily routines and habits of thought. Envisioning something different also means putting on hold the voice inside your head that says: Are you *crazy?* This will never work! Who do you think you are? Where will you *ever* get the money? Better keep quiet on this one, people will think you're nuts. . . .

Go ahead. Envision the multicultural society, the women's health project, the community play/read/care program for elders and children, the Internet information business run by inner-city teenagers, the women's taxi service, the intimate relationship of your dreams, your blossoming sexuality. Envision it in as much detail as you can. Think it, see it, taste it, smell it, sing it, draw it, and write it down. Share it with others who you think will be sympathetic to it. This is where you're headed. Now all you need is to create the road. The projects we mention throughout this book, like this book itself, all started this way, as somebody's dream.

Using the Hands: Action for Social Change

The third essential ingredient for change is action. Through action, theories and visions are tested, sharpened, and refined to create even more useful theories and more creative visions. In Chapter 1 we referred to philosopher Alan Rosenberg's (1988) distinction between *knowing* and *understanding.* Rosenberg further argues that understanding compels us to action, even though we may not initially want to change our habitual ways of thinking and being. When you understand something, you

> find that [your] world becomes a different world and that [you] must generate a new way to be in the new world. Since each person's way of being in the world is relatively fixed— and serves as protection against the anxieties of the unknown—integration is extremely hard. To give up a world in which one's life makes sense means undergoing great loss. Yet without the readiness to risk that loss we cannot hope to pursue understanding. *(p. 382)*

In previous chapters we mentioned many activist projects, which are all relevant to this discussion. In this chapter, readings by Cynthia Cohen (Reading 79) former director of the Cambridge Oral History Center and writer Allison Wellner (Reading 81) address specific projects. In Reading 80, Vivien Labaton and Dawn Lundy Martin, who are among the founders of the Third Wave Foundation, emphasize the centrality of an integrated, intersectional perspective for many young feminists. They note: "'Woman' as a primary identity category has ceased to be the entry point for much young activist work. Instead, it has become one of the many investigatory means used to affect an infinite number of issues and cultural analyses," including critiques of hip-hop music and theater, creation of independent media, and campaigns opposing oppressive immigration policies, police brutality, sweatshops, militarism, incarceration, and globalization. Here we suggest a range of avenues for trying to implement your visions. Some will be more appropriate than others, depending on your goals and theoretical perspectives. Some of the activities we list below may be impossible for students, who need to concentrate on getting degrees, to participate in. Progressive social change is a long-term project; there will be plenty to do after you graduate (see Naples and Bojar 2002).

- Think of yourself as someone with something valuable to say, who can take the initiative and start something you think is important. Think about what you want to do after college, how to live your values and ideals.

- Express your ideas: talk to others; write 'zines, poems, leaflets, speeches, letters to newspaper editors and politicians; put up flyers or posters;

organize a film series; paint murals, dance, sing, or perform your ideas.

- Be a conscious shopper. Support fair-trade products; boycott products made in sweatshops, for example. Buy directly from farmers' markets or craft producers. Spend your money where it will support your values.

- Support women's organizations, environmental groups, antiracist organizations, or gay/lesbian/bisexual/transgender groups by letting them know you appreciate their work, letting others know these groups exist, attending events, donating money or something the group needs, volunteering your time, proposing ideas for projects, working as an intern for college credit.

- Work for institutional change. Within your family you may want to stop others from telling sexist or racist jokes, create greater understanding between family members, or develop more egalitarian relationships. At school you may want to set up study groups to work together, support teachers who help you, point out glaring gaps in the curriculum or college services to teachers and administrators, challenge racism or sexual harassment.

- Participate in direct action. This includes interrupting, keeping silent, organizing groups of women to walk together at night, defending clinics where abortions are performed, participating in demonstrations and rallies, boycotts, picketing, rent strikes, tax resistance. Whatever the setting, take back the Nike slogan. Just Do It!

- Get involved in grassroots organizing. Meet with others and decide what you can do together to tackle some issue of shared concern.

- Participate in coalitions. Consider joining with other groups on an issue of shared concern so as to be more visible and effective.

- Learn about local and national issues, and let your representatives at city, state, and national levels know your opinions. Urge them to pass appropriate laws and to speak out in public situations and to the media. Use your vote. Help to elect progressive candidates. Support them if they get into office, and hold them accountable to their election promises.

- Learn more about international networks and organizations working on issues that concern you. Consider participating in an international meeting and bringing the knowledge you gain there to your organizing work back home.

A range of supports help us in taking action: a sense of hope and conviction that women's lives can be improved, anger at current inequalities and injustices, reliable allies, well-thought-out strategies, and help from parents, partners, neighbors, friends, children, or total strangers who make a crucial contribution by freeing us so that we can be involved.

Overcoming Blocks to Effective Action

Political action does not always work; that is, a chosen course of action may not achieve our original goals. There are many possible reasons for this: inadequate theoretical understandings and analysis of the issues; choosing inappropriate or ineffective strategies; not following through on the course of action; not being able to get enough people involved for this particular strategy to be effective; wrong timing; the failure of the group to work together well enough; the failure of people whom you thought were allies to come through when needed; and so on. The other major reason, of course, is that the opposition—whether this is your sexist uncle, your boss, the university administration, the city school board, the opposing political party, or the U.S. Congress—was simply more powerful.

Feeling that an action has failed is disheartening and may lead people to give up, assuming that creating change is hopeless. But action *always* accomplishes something, and in this sense it always works. At the very least, activism that does not meet your goals teaches you something important. In hindsight, what may seem like mistakes are actually valuable ways to learn how to be more effective in the future. This is what we called "socially lived" theory in Chapter 1. Always evaluate what you did after some activity or event, personally and with the group. If it worked as you hoped, why did it work? What have you learned as a result? If it did not work, why? What will you do differently next time?

Personal blocks to activism may include practical factors like not having enough time or energy, or needing to focus on some other aspect of life. Emotional blocks include guilt—a paralyzing emotion that keeps us stuck—and cynicism—a frustrated idealism that has turned hopeless and bitter. Anger can be a very useful, high-octane fuel if you can channel it in a constructive direction. Overextending yourself is not a sign of your commitment to your ideals, and trying to do more than you can, under pressure, is one sure way to burn out quickly. Activism for progressive social change needs patience, humor, creativity, a wide range of skills and resources, an ability to talk to other people, a willingness to listen and to change, a willingness to be reflective, refining your ideas, holding onto your visions.

Theorists of social change usually see it as an interplay between actors or agents—individuals and groups—and the social and political structures that form the larger context of our lives and often restrict us. Some emphasize what English professor Ellen Messer-Davidow (1991) calls "agent-centered models of change" that represent powerful people and a passive system (p. 293). This is the view of much political opinion and rhetoric that characterize the U.S. political system as open and responsive to pressure from organized groups. "Social-system models of change represent powerful systems and passive people" (Messer-Davidow 1991, p. 294). This is the view of those who point to the central role money plays in determining who can run for office and, in many cases, who has access to them once they are in power. A third of all eligible voters appear to hold this view, as they are not registered to vote, even though many of these same people may be very active in their churches, synagogues, temples, or other community organizations.

We see a key role for individuals, as change agents, working with others to envision alternatives and bring them into being through collective action: through identity-based politics, feminist movements, electoral politics, and broad-based coalitions and alliances.

Women and Political Activism

Politics involves the use of power. What is it? Who has it? How is it used? Who does it benefit and who is disadvantaged? Sociologists and political scientists define **power** as the ability to influence others. This may be by persuasion, charisma, law, political activism, or coercion (Andersen 2000). As we argue throughout this book, individuals and groups have power and influence based on a range of attributes (race, class, gender, age, education, etc.) that are valued in this society. Many people focus on the ways in which others exert power over us or on the fact that they have more power than we have. We generally pay less attention to the ways in which we have more power than others. This is true especially for members of oppressed groups, such as women and men of color in the United States, where some fundamental aspect of our existence, if not our identity, is predicated on being "the powerless" in many settings.

Poet and essayist Audre Lorde writes of women's personal power (Reading 28, Chapter 4), and several writers in this book refer to the importance of personal empowerment. People exercise power through institutions such as education, religion, corporations, the media, the law, the military, and all aspects of government. Sometimes this happens regardless of individual intent or knowledge of its existence. Power is also expressed in the values and practices of institutions that compel people to think and behave in specific ways. For example, the heterosexist values embedded in our culture and its institutions define the family as a heterosexual couple, legally bound by marriage, and their children. The value and legitimacy attached to this institution is a powerful influence on everyone and is in itself a pressure to marry. Higher education operates out of values that are overwhelmingly Eurocentric, middle class, and masculinist. These values uphold particular ways of learning, certain kinds of discourse, and the use of a specific language. To succeed in college, a student must subscribe to these values, at least in a minimal way.

Power operates at the community, macro, and global levels. Political scientists have focused on formal political organizations, especially the U.S. Congress, where there are relatively few women. As a result, past studies of women's political power have seriously underestimated it. Feminist researchers have pointed out that women's political participation includes active membership in a wide range of local, state, and national organizations including women's clubs and labor unions, working in support of candidates for political office, organizing fund-raising events, circulating petitions, participating in letter-writing and call-in campaigns, as well as voting (see Naples 1997, 1998; West and Blumberg 1990). Several articles in this collection give details of women's organizing: how they draw in participants; strategize about goals, priorities, and activities; and use their knowledge, personal connections, and links to institutions (e.g., Readings 30, 32, 34, 37, 38, 53, 58, 79, 82).

Identity-Based Politics

Throughout this book many writers talk about identity and note significant changes in the way they think about themselves over time. Some mention the difficulties of coming to terms with who they are, the complexities of their contradictory positions, or breaking the silence surrounding taboo subjects, thoughts, and feelings. They also comment that coming to new understandings about themselves and being able to speak from a place of personal identity and self-knowledge is profoundly empowering.

Identity politics is, literally, a politics that puts identity at the center, based on, for example, age, race, ethnicity, or sexual orientation. It usually involves the assumption that this particular characteristic is the most important in the lives of group members and that the group is not differentiated according to other characteristics in any significant way. Identity politics is concerned with wider opportunities—maybe greater visibility and recognition in society, equality, justice, even liberation for ourselves and our group. Our authoritativeness comes from our experience of a shared identity, some common ground of experience that allows a group to say "we." This is the foundation for many student organizations, community groups, religious groups, national networks, and major social movements.

At the same time, identity politics has serious limitations. Groups tend to remain separate, focused on their own issues and concerns, often competing with each other for recognition and resources. The language of identity politics gives voice to people's discrimination and oppression. It does not encourage us to think about identity in a more complex way, as a mix of privilege and disadvantage. In Chapter 2 we introduced the idea that most people occupy multiple positions and that salient aspects of identity may vary significantly depending on the context. An African American graduate student who is about to receive her Ph.D., for example, may be highly respected by her teachers and peers, regardless of their race or hers. A White man walking past her in the street may insult and curse her because she is Black.

Understanding this notion of multiple positionality helps us to see how our personal and group identities are political and how the various identity groups fit together in the wider society. The specific context is crucial. In the public discourse about immigration, for example, there is a fear on the part of White people—usually hinted at rather than stated directly—of being "overrun" by Asians. When the context shifts to a discussion of peoples of color in the United States, however, Asian immigrants and Asian Americans become the "model minority," the standard against which African Americans or Latinos are compared unfavorably. Understanding one's identity involves a recognition of the ways in which one is privileged as well as the ways in which one is disadvantaged, and the contradictions that this raises, as noted by Melanie Kaye/Kantrowitz in Reading 11. With this more nuanced perspective, one not only focuses on the circumstances and concerns of one's own group, but also can use the complexity of one's identity to make connections to other groups. Thus, a White, middle-class woman with a hearing disability can take all of these aspects of her identity and understand her social location in terms of privilege as well as disadvantage. This is important for building effective alliances with others, which we discuss in more detail later. We make a distinction between a narrower identity politics, discussed above, and **identity-based politics,** which has a strong identity component and also a broader view that allows people to make connections to other groups and issues. Melanie Kaye/Kantrowitz (Reading 11) Christina Leaño (Reading 78), and the Combahee River Collective (Reading 3) all exemplify this more connective, identity-based politics.

Feminist Movements

Feminist movements have accomplished enormous change in this country. At the beginning of the twentieth century, suffragists in the United States were nearing the end of a seventy-year-long campaign for women's right to vote, which was finally won in 1920. This campaign had its roots in the nineteenth-century movement for the abolition of slavery. Again in the 1960s, the struggle for racial equality was "midwife to a feminist movement" (Evans 1980, p. 24) as women in the civil rights movement began to look more closely at the ways they were oppressed as women. These two periods are sometimes referred to as feminism's "first wave" and "second wave," respectively, as mentioned in Chapter 1.

Women's organizing since the 1960s has been a powerful force for change at micro, meso, and macro levels, and a transforming experience for those involved (Brenner 1996; F. Davis 1991; DuPlessis and Snitow 1998; Rosen 2000). Women identified sexism in every area of life, including their own personal relationships, traditional gender roles, language, children's play, and symbolic events like the Miss America pageant. They used their own life experience to theorize about patriarchal systems, and they envisioned women's liberation. Some challenged women's exclusion from well-paying jobs in blue-collar trades, higher education, the law, medicine, and the media, as well as seeking to increase pay and improve conditions for jobs based on women's traditional roles. Some organized alternative institutions for women like health centers, publishing projects, music events and recording companies, art, film, writing circles, poetry readings, bookstores, dances, and women-owned land projects. Others campaigned to elect more women to political office at city, state, and federal levels, on the assumption that this would change law and policy to benefit women. Note that these different approaches were based on different theoretical positions, some women seeking equality with men within existing institutions, others wanting to change these structures to be more liberatory for women and men.

Feminist movements have centered on women's supposed shared identity as women. In emphasizing their oppression as women, many White middleclass feminists of the 1960s and '70s glossed over inequalities based on race and class. This assumption of "sisterhood" ignored the experiences of women of color, working-class White women, and White women's racial privilege (Dorothy Allison, Reading 9; also Bunch and Myron 1974; Lorde 1984; Moraga and Anzaldúa 1981; Rich 1986c; Shah 1997; Smith 1983). By contrast, professor of sociology Barbara Omolade's feminist activism grew out of her involvement in the civil rights movement in the mid-1960s when she was just out of college (Omolade 1994). Her mentor and role model was Ella Baker, a courageous and vibrant African American leader, the executive secretary of the Southern Christian Leadership Conference. Omolade notes that Black nationalism provided a powerful liberatory vision for many young African American activists. Women worked hard alongside men, but became critical of and disillusioned with sexism in the civil rights movement and Black power organizations. In the 1970s and '80s, Omolade was involved in various campaigns, drawing on both the sisterhood of Black feminism and the militancy of nationalism.

By the 1990s, the most visible signs of the 1970s women's movements were national organizations like the Fund for a Feminist Majority, the National Abortion Rights Action League (NARAL), the National Organization of Women (NOW), and the National Women's Political Caucus. They were founded by White, middle-class women who have been able to attract the resources and the media coverage that have helped to maintain them over the years. But women's movements were much wider, more diverse, more radical, and more challenging than these organizations (see Baxandall and Gordon 2000). Many women of color, and some White women, have tended to write off second-wave feminism as a White, middle-class movement that is irrelevant to them. Sociologist Becky Thompson (2002) gives a very different account of second-wave feminism from the point of view of women of color and White antiracist women that allows much stronger links between, for example, the Combahee River Collective Statement (Reading 3) and the more contemporary feminism of JeeYeun Lee (Reading 5). (Also see Baxandall 2001; Omolade 1994; Roth 2003; Springer 2005.)

Movements call forth the energies, passions, and visions of many people, often in ways that are life-changing for participants. They inspire and

make space for groundbreaking projects and alternative institutions, as mentioned above. Over time they often generate arguments about strategy and political direction that can lead to more permanent splits. Some women created change through grassroots organizing, providing services and supports that did not exist before. They also provided powerful visions of women's *liberation*. Others focused on the need for laws and public policy to change women's lives, and set their sights on elected office.

Women in Electoral Politics

Women who seek political office invariably do so because they want to make a difference in people's lives, especially for women and children. Those who work hard to support women candidates argue that a critical mass of women in elected office will be able to change public policy and legislation to provide for women's needs. This includes local offices like parent-teacher associations (PTAs), city council seats, statewide offices, and the U.S. Congress. Together with male allies in Congress, women officials and their staff have worked long and hard to pass legislation to ensure better opportunities for women, including, for example, Title IX of the 1972 Education Act, which requires schools and colleges that receive federal funding to provide equal opportunities for male and female students (see the box on page 578 for more details), the Family and Medical Leave Act, and the Violence Against Women Act. They have also worked for improvements in women's wages, the availability of affordable child care, the opening of military combat roles to women, and so forth.

In 1990 women were 5.6 percent of congressional representatives. At the slow rate women's participation was growing, it would be another fifty years before there was equality in state legislatures and at least another three hundred years before there were equal numbers of women and men in Congress. The proportion of women elected to political office has increased since then, though the United States has fewer women in office than many other countries (see Table 13.1). In 2005 women held 81 (15 percent) of the 535 seats in the U.S. Congress: 14 percent of the 100 seats in the Senate and 67 (15.4 percent) of the 435 seats in the House of Representatives. Of the 1,666 women state legislators nationwide, 19 percent were women of color (Center for American Women and Politics 2005). Sociologist Margaret Andersen (2000) notes the impediments that limit women who want to run for political office: voter and media prejudice against women candidates, lack of support from party leaders, lack of access to extensive political networks, and lack of

Table 13.1   Women's Representation in National Legislatures

COUNTRY	% WOMEN IN LOWER OR SINGLE HOUSE	COUNTRY	% WOMEN IN LOWER OR SINGLE HOUSE
Rwanda	48.8	U.K.	19.7
Sweden	45.3	Peru	18.3
Denmark	36.9	Uzbekistan	17.5
Cuba	36.0	Dominican Republic	17.3
Spain	36.0	Panama	16.7
Costa Rica	35.1	Philippines	15.3
Mozambique	34.8	USA	15.2
Germany	32.8	Ireland	13.3
Viet Nam	27.3	South Korea	13.0
Switzerland	25.0	France	12.2
Australia	24.7	Italy	11.5
Mexico	24.2	Ghana	10.9
Tunisia	22.8	Venezuela	9.7
Lithuania	22.0	Malaysia	9.1
Croatia	21.7	India	8.3
Pakistan	21.3	Japan	7.1
Canada	21.1	Algeria	6.2
Nicaragua	20.7	Turkey	4.4
China	20.2	Iran	4.1
Poland	20.2	Kuwait	1.5
North Korea	20.1	Saudi Arabia	0.0

Source: Inter-Parliamentary Union. Women in National Parliaments (as of 31 August 2005) www.ipu.org/wmn-e/classif.htm.

money. At the same time, women seeking office and organizations like Emily's List, the Fund for a Feminist Majority, and the National Women's Political Caucus are working to overcome these limitations (Burrell 1994; Ford 2002; Norris 1997; Thomas and Wilcox 1998; Woods 2000).

As elected officials and as voters, women are more likely than men to hold liberal views and to support the Democratic party. For example, more women than men support gun control, a national health-care system, social programs, tougher sentences for rapists and perpetrators of sexual assault and domestic violence, and workplace equality, as well as issues like women's right to abortion and gay/lesbian rights. This **gender gap** can be significant in two ways: getting more liberal candidates—women and men—elected and giving greater focus to liberal issues once such candidates are in office (Abzug 1984; Gallagher 1993; Norris 1997; Smeal 1984).

By the mid-1990s there were more women in elected positions than ever before. A growing bipartisan Congressional Women's Caucus served as a focus for women's concerns on Capitol Hill. Janet Reno was appointed as the first woman U.S. attorney general in the nation's history, and Madeleine Albright the first woman secretary of state. Bush administration "firsts" include the appointment of Condoleeza Rice as the first woman national security adviser, now Secretary of State. When the 108th Congress convened in January 2003, Nancy Pelosi, the new minority leader of the House, was the first woman to lead either political party and the highest-ranking woman in the 213-year history of Congress.

Title IX

Title IX ("title nine") of the 1972 Education Act is a landmark piece of civil rights legislation requiring educational institutions that receive federal funding to provide equal opportunities for male and female students in academics, athletics, financial assistance, and resources like student health and housing. Indeed, Title IX is a key reason that girls and women have made such gains in higher education, particularly in sports. In 1971, 294,015 girls participated in high school athletics compared to over 2.7 million girls in 2001—an 847 percent increase (U.S. Department of Education, quoted in Nelson 2002, p. 33), and there are now many more opportunities and facilities at the college level also.

A college must meet one of the following three standards to comply with the law. It must have roughly the same proportion of women among its varsity athletes as it has in its undergraduate student body; it must have a "history and continuing practice" of expanding opportunities for women; or it must demonstrate that it is "fully and effectively accommodating the interests and abilities" of its women students (Suggs 2002). Detractors argue that increased resources for women have resulted in fewer opportunities for men, and some athletics departments have achieved parity by cutting opportunities for male students rather than increasing those for women. A General Accounting Office report released in March 2001, however, found a net gain in men's teams from 1982 to 1999, and many more opportunities for men than for women (Nelson 2002). Denise Kiernan (2001) reported that "women receive only 38 percent of all athletic scholarship money, 27 percent of recruiting money and 23 percent of overall athletics budgets." Several Ivy League colleges and state universities have been forced to comply with the law, as women sued them for discrimination.

In 2001 the Department of Education appointed a Commission on Opportunity in Athletics to review the effects of Title IX. Its report, published in February 2003, includes the false assumption that opportunities for women in sports have resulted in fewer opportunities for men. The report recommends legal revisions "to ensure that new sports opportunities for girls and women do not come at the expense of boys' and men's teams" rather than suggesting ways to redirect resources to benefit all athletes (Schemo 2003, p. D1). As of December 2005, there have been no legal revisions. However, in March 2005, with no notice given or public input, the Department of Education Office of Civil Rights (OCR) posted a letter to its Web site clarifying the regulations for compliance. The letter stated that there can be considerable inequality between women's and men's athletic opportunities and a school can still be in compliance unless there is

1. "unmet interest sufficient to sustain a varsity team in the sport(s)";

2. "sufficient ability to sustain an intercollegiate team in the sport(s)"; and

3. "reasonable expectation of intercollegiate competition for a team in the sport(s) within the school's normal competitive region." (OCR 2005).

Schools can gauge students' interest in athletics by conducting an e-mail survey, and can claim that a failure to respond shows a lack of interest in playing sports. This "clarification" does not require schools to look broadly and proactively at whether they are satisfying women's interests in sports. The burden of proof is not on the schools but on students or OCR to show that the institution is discriminating against women.

In March 2005, the U.S. Supreme Court decided that individuals who protest sex discrimination may sue to challenge retaliation if their schools punish them as a result (*Jackson v. Birmingham Board of Education*), a significant re-affirmation of rights provided under Title IX. Moreover, the Court held that for effective enforcement of Title IX retaliation against those who come forward to report discrimination must be prohibited.

More women also hold high office at the state level, whether as governors, attorneys general, state treasurers, chief educational officers, and so on. Whether or not elected women can make a significant difference in political institutions and public policy that is still overwhelmingly dominated by masculinist and corporate interests is the key question.

Many women are on committees concerned with health, education, and social services, and they bring their support for women and knowledge of women's experiences to their work. Those in high positions are doubtless constrained by political considerations. In the Clinton administration, Secretary of State Madeleine Albright, for example, was very vocal about women's oppression in Afghanistan, but, following U.S. government policy, she did not push for an end to economic sanctions against Iraq—a step that would have saved the lives of thousands of people, especially women and children.

Political scientist Michele Swers (2001) reviews data on the effects of women in public office. She found that at the state and national levels women legislators do see women "as a distinct part of their constituency" and "do bring different policy priorities to the legislative agenda, particularly in the area of women's issues" (also see Carroll 2001). There are still too few women in elected office to be able to evaluate their effectiveness fully, and certainly no "critical mass" to change public policy and legislation significantly in favor of women.

In the second half of the nineteenth century, the activism of women, and their male allies, succeeded in winning the vote for women in 1920, and the strength of women's organizing in the 1980s and '90s made it possible for increasing numbers of women to become elected officials. Nevertheless, current public policy and budget priorities, together with a worsening economy, are having disastrous effects on women. Restrictions on the availability of welfare, the erosion of *Roe v. Wade* and affirmative action policies, major tax cuts for the richest citizens, and enormous military spending have all taken resources away from women. Women's organizations and elected officials who seek to improve women's lives currently face a hard road ahead, where a hallmark of success will be holding on to previous gains. This will require strategic thinking, clear focus, hard work, and acts of personal courage, such as that of Congresswoman Barbara Lee, who did not compromise her principles when she voted against authorizing military force in response to the attacks of September 11, in a historic 420-1 House vote on September 14, 2001.

Building Alliances for the Twenty-First Century

We emphasize the importance of alliances across lines of difference for two reasons. First, the many inequalities among women, mentioned throughout this book, often separate us and make it difficult to work together effectively. Those with power over us know this and often exploit differences to pit one group against another. Second, progressive social change is a slow process that needs sustained action over the long haul. Effective alliances, based on a deepening knowledge of others and learning whom to trust over time, are necessary for long-term efforts, in contrast to coalition work, where the important thing is to stand together around a single issue, regardless of other differences. Alliances across lines of difference are both a means and an end. They provide both the process for moving toward, and some experience of, multicultural society. Melanie Kaye/Kantrowitz (Reading 11) and Ann Filemyr (Reading 44) offer insights for alliance building, especially across lines of race and class. Cynthia Cohen (Reading 79) describes a project that brings women together across significant differences.

Some Principles for Alliance Building

Alliances may be personal, campus-wide, city-wide, national, or transnational in scope. Regardless of scale, some basic principles of alliance building include the following points:

- Know who you are, what is important to you, what are your nonnegotiables. Know your strengths and what you bring to a shared venture.

- Decide whether you want to be allies with a particular person or group. What are their values? What are they interested in doing in terms of creating social change? Are they open to the alliance? What is the purpose for coming together? Are you coming together as equals? In solidarity with another group?

- Check out the person or the group as the acquaintance grows. Are they who they say they are? Do you have reason to trust them to be there for you? Judge them by their track records and what actually happens, not by your fears, hopes, or expectations based on previous experiences.

- Commit yourself to communicate. Listen, talk, and listen more. Be committed to the process of communication rather than attached to a specific position. Communication may be through conversations, reading, films, events and meetings, or learning about one another's communities. Work together on projects and support one another's projects. Go into one another's settings as participants, observers, guests. All these activities are part of learning to understand in the sense of folding this knowledge into our own moral frameworks as argued by Alan Rosenberg (1988), mentioned in Chapter 1.

- Share your history. Talk about what has happened to you and to the people of your group.

- Be patient. Wanting to understand, to hear more, to stay connected requires patience from the inside. Allow one another room to explore ideas, make mistakes, be tentative. Hold judgment until you understand what's going on.

- Honesty is the most important thing. Be authentic and ask for authenticity from others. If this is not possible, what is the alliance worth?

- Keep the process "clean." Call one another on bad things if they happen—preferably with grace, teasing maybe, firmly but gently, so that the other person does not lose face. Don't try to disentangle difficulties when it is impossible to do so meaningfully, but don't use externals (too late, too tired, too busy, too many other items on the agenda) to avoid it.

- Be open to being called on your own mistakes, admitting when you're wrong, even if it is embarrassing or makes you feel vulnerable. Tell the other person when his or her opinions and experiences give you new insights and help you to see things differently.

- Do some people in the group take up a lot of time talking about their own concerns? Are they aware of it? How does privilege based on gender, race, class, nation, sexuality, disability, age,

culture, or language play out in this relationship or alliance? Can you talk about it openly?

- What is the "culture" of your group or alliance? What kinds of meetings do you have? What is your decision-making style? If you eat together, what kind of food do you serve? What kind of music do you listen to? Where do you meet? What do you do when you are together? Does everyone in the group feel comfortable with these cultural aspects?

- Work out the boundaries of your responsibilities to one another. What do you want to do for yourself? What do you need others to help with? When? How?

- Look for the common ground. What are the perspectives, experiences, and insights we share?

Overcoming Impediments to Effective Alliances

Many sincere and committed attempts at building alliances have been thwarted, despite the best of intentions. Be aware of several common impediments to creating effective alliances, including the following beliefs and behaviors:

Internalized Oppression   This is a learned mind-set of subservience and inferiority in oppressed peoples. It includes the acceptance of labels, characteristics, prejudices, and perceptions promoted by the dominant society. Specific behaviors include self-hatred and dislike, disrespect for and hatred of others of the same group.

Internalized Domination   This is a mind-set of entitlement and superiority among members of the dominant group. Behaviors such as always speaking first in group discussions, being unconscious of the large amount of physical and social space one takes up, and automatically assuming leadership roles are some manifestations of internalized domination.

Operating from a Politics of Scarcity   This results from a deeply held, sometimes unconscious, belief that there is not enough of anything—material things as well as nonmaterial things like power, positive regard, popularity, friendship, time—and, more important, that however much there is, it will not be shared equally. In this view, inequality is simply a given that cannot be changed. It also justifies individualism and competition.

Subscribing to a Hierarchy of Oppression This involves the placement of one oppressed group in relation to another so that one group's experiences of discrimination, prejudice, and disadvantage are deemed to be worse or better than another's.

Not Knowing One Another's History Ignorance about other persons' backgrounds often results in drawing incorrect conclusions about their experiences. This prevents us from recognizing the complexity of women's experiences and can hide the ways our experiences are both different and similar.

Creating a Secure and Sustainable World

Alliances are central to women's movements in the United States and around the world, as argued by Charlotte Bunch (Reading 82) and Peggy Antrobus (Reading 83). United Nations conferences have provided one avenue for international networking and solidarity (Antrobus 2004). In March 2005, the U.N. Commission on the Status of Women affirmed the Beijing *Platform for Action*, adopted at the Fourth U.N. World Conference on Women held ten years earlier. Delegates reported on the progress—or in many cases, the lack of progress—governments have made to create opportunities for women and to safeguard their health, well-being, and overall security. In contrast to the congratulatory reports of many governments, the New York-based Women's Environment and Development Organization published a scathing report concluding that, in the main, "governments have failed to turn the platform into action, and that, despite well-meaning intentions, many women in all regions are actually worse off than they were ten years ago" (Lederer 2005; WEDO 2005).

Chandra Talpade Mohanty (2003) critiques transnational organizing efforts that reproduce parallel inequalities that define relations between rich and poor nations. As mentioned in Chapter 1, Mohanty embraces transnational multicultural feminism, by which she means a theory and practice that is "noncolonized," and anchored in equality and respect. This would avoid false universalisms and involve ethical and caring dialogue across differences,

divisions, and conflicts. From very different social locations, women would define for themselves a "common context of struggle."

Providing services to women in the United States and reforming existing institutions to make them more responsive to those who are excluded are crucially important in the overall work of progressive social change and have made a difference to generations of women. The challenge for the future is to continue to expand this work. Given the many insecurities of life for women and for men, and the growing threat to the planet itself from increasing industrialization, militarization, and ecological devastation, what sense does it make for women to seek an equal piece of what ecofeminist activist and writer Ynestra King (1993b, p. 76) has called this "rotten and carcinogenic" pie?

Women's movements are shared endeavors. They are many overlapping movements constructed around issues and identities, with links to other progressive movements such as the antiglobalization movement and the antimilitarist movement. Given that corporations control more and more of the world and that women's rights are under serious attack in this country, we need to work together to address interconnected issues: economic survival, reproductive rights, all forms of violence including state violence, criminalization, and incarceration, immigrant rights, and so on, as argued by Labaton and Martin (Reading 80). These vibrant, broad-based efforts draw on our creativity, our emotions, our spirituality, and our sense of justice, strengthening connections between people and communities. There is great accumulated experience and insight about how to work on multi-issue politics, and also much to learn. Grace Lee Boggs, a long-time activist in Detroit, notes that this is both an exciting and a daunting time in human history. She urges: "For our own well-being, for the health and safety of our communities, our cities and our country, we need to accept the awesome responsibility of creating new ways of . . . living" (1994, p. 2).

This book is about U.S. women's lives and the kind of world we need to create for women's empowerment, development, and well-being. This world will be based on notions of genuine security and sustainability. The project of human development—for both women and men—is one that has been in process for a very long time. It is our challenge to take the next steps in this process. How can we settle for anything less?

Activism is not issue-specific
It's a moral posture that, steady state,
*   propels you forward, from one hard*
*   hour to the next.*
Believing that you can do something
*   to make things better, you do*
Something, rather than nothing.

You assume responsibility for the
*   privilege of your abilities.*
You do whatever you can.
You reach beyond yourself in your
*   imagination, and in your wish for*
Understanding, and for change.
You admit the limitations of individual
*   perspectives.*
You trust somebody else.
You do not turn away.   (June Jordan)

Questions for Reflection

As you read and discuss this chapter, think about these questions:

1. What are your assumptions about how people and societies change? What do you think needs changing, if anything?

2. Have you ever been involved in a social-action project or electoral politics? What was your experience like? If you have not, why not?

3. Have you tried to establish and maintain an ongoing relationship, friendship, or working partnership with someone from a background very different from your own? What happened? What did you learn from that experience? What would you do differently, if anything?

4. If you have had such a relationship, why did you become involved in the first place? Was that a good enough reason? Why or why not? If you never have, why not?

5. What do you know about the history of the various groups you are a member of? What do you know about groups that are not your own? How does knowing this history help, and how does not knowing it hinder you in making alliances across lines of difference?

6. What is your vision of a secure and sustainable personal relationship? Community? Society? World?

Finding Out More on the Web

1. Research the work of organizations cited in this chapter. What are their strategies and visions? Who do they speak to? These are additional resources:

   Public Leadership Education Network (PLEN) is a consortium of women's colleges working together to prepare women for public leadership: **www.plen.org**

   Center for Women's Global Leadership (Rutgers University, N.J.) organizes days of international activism against gender violence: **www.cwgl.rutgers.edu**

   Guerilla Girls are a group of women intent on exposing patterns of sexism, racism, and censorship in the art world: **www.guerillagirls.com**

2. In Reading 78, Christina Leaño mentions FACES (Filipino/American Coalition for Environmental Solutions). Find out more about this group's strategies and activities.

3. In Reading 82, Charlotte Bunch mentions the International Criminal Court and the U.N. World Conference Against Racism. What is the significance of these international efforts for women's lives?

4. What is the history of the Equal Rights Amendment? Did your state ratify it when it came up for ratification in the 1970s? What are the arguments for and against an Equal Rights Amendment?

◆◆◆

Taking Action

1. List all the ways you are an activist. Review the suggestions for taking action at the end of each chapter. Commit yourself to continuing to involve yourself in issues that matter to you.

2. Think about how aspects of your identity can help you to make alliances with others. Support campus or community groups that are working together on an issue of shared concern.

3. Where do your elected officials (at the city, state, and national levels) stand on issues that matter to you? What is their voting record on these issues? Write to thank them for supporting issues you care about (if they do), or urge them to change their positions. Present them with information from your course materials or other sources to make a strong case.

4. Many of the issues discussed in this book have implications at the global level. What can you do that will have an impact at that level?

SEVENTY-EIGHT

◆◆◆

Listening to the Voices of My Spiritual Self (2001)

Christina Leaño

Christina Leaño is a Founding Member and Founding Director of Filipino/American Coalition for Environmental Solutions. Since receiving her masters in systematic theology from the Graduate Theological Union in 2004, she has been focused on living her current question of understanding her relationship with her God and deepening her meditation practice.

We are not human beings on a spiritual journey, but spiritual beings on a human journey.

—Pierre Teilhard de Chardin, Jesuit priest and paleontologist (1881–1955)

My whole life has been driven by voices. Tiny, inner, voices that have emerged from some unknown

depths and have guided me (during those times I was willing) to unexpected places. They have taunted me with questions like "What does it mean to be Filipina? Where is God in your life? Why are you doing this social justice work?" until the friction from their words was too uncomfortable to ignore.

During my junior year in college, I was in Kenya participating in a semester abroad program. I was amazed by the vibrancy of the people and the richness of Kenyan culture, yet something inside me was awry. The colorful markets, tropical forests, and reality of daily struggle were foreign and at the same time strangely familiar. I realized that Kenya reminded me of what I had seen in the Philippines during my only visit as a child. This revelation was nudged by one of those prodding voices: "Your experience in Kenya is beautiful. Can you imagine the richness if it were a culture of your own blood? You need not go any further than your own heritage to find cultural treasure. Go, explore that."

This voice spoke from a void within me—this disconnect between my culture and myself. For most of my twenty-one years I did not see myself as a Filipina. Growing up in a white, upper-middle-class suburb and attending a private college preparatory in Florida gave me little opportunity to claim my brownness. There were even times when my color (and my relatives' color) shamed me, as I tried to keep my white friends from seeing our darkness. I had always thought that I was just an average kid with a flat nose and shiny, black hair.

Yet, when that voice emerged within me, I was filled with fear. It was like waking up and realizing that the ground below me was but a mist I was about to slip through. How was it that I did not know my Filipino heritage? What is my history, my culture? Who are my ancestors? Where are my roots? This voice led me from fear toward a hunger that was waiting to be filled. And I realized that I would have to answer those questions before I could move on with my life. How else would I find the ground to walk upon? So I decided that my next destination after college would be the Philippines.

After graduating, I signed up with the Mennonite Central Committee for three years as a volunteer in the Philippines. I chose a Christian organization, because another emerging voice was calling me to explore my spirituality. It frightened the heck out of me, being a "missionary," as I knew the damage that missionaries had done in the Philippines in the past, first during Spanish colonization and then during the American occupation. But there were enough signs—a volunteer placement that fit my exact interests (with the People's Task Force for Bases Cleanup, which dealt with environmental justice issues, the subject of my college thesis) and with people who gave me the support I needed—to show me that my decisions were in line with the Universe's. All I had to do was take a deep breath and trust.

That decision led to a whirlwind of adventure, transformation, and growth. Being in the Philippines gave me an opportunity to learn Tagalog, to get to know tens of cousins, aunts, uncles, grandparents, and to embrace my Filipino-ness that I hardly knew existed. This seed sprouted and bloomed as soon as I swallowed my first drop of Philippine water. Qualities and values that had been passed on to me by my parents—the importance of smooth interpersonal relationships and the centrality of family, faith, and education—were revealed as legacies embedded within the culture. I was Filipina without even realizing it.

Most important, I realized that my identity as a Filipina American was self-defined. I worked in a campaign demanding U.S. responsibility for cleaning up toxic contamination left behind in their former military bases in the Philippines. Thus my passion and desire as a Filipina for justice for the communities around the bases, and my anger at what my government had left behind, provided an opportunity to bridge my two identities. I could use my Filipino heart and my American citizenship for social change in the Philippines that addressed the huge inequities in the hundred-year relationship between the two nations. There was no choosing. I am both.

After two-and-a-half years, I came back to the United States to work in Washington, D.C., as director of a newly launched organization, FACES (Filipino/American Coalition for Environmental Solutions), the U.S. counterpart of the Philippines clean-up campaign. Although there were times of incredible joy and growth, after a year I was overwhelmed with fatigue, sadness, and doubt. I was working too much (isn't 25 too young to burn out?), I was not taking care of my physical, emotional, and spiritual needs, and I was not quite sure why I was doing this social justice work. My good side wanted to assure me that it was because of the enormous injustice resulting from the negligence of the U.S. government. But then there was another side of me, the ego side, which was focused on me trying to make a difference.

Working at FACES, I was still supported by the Mennonite Central Committee and was surrounded by folks who were able to articulate their commitment to social and environmental justice in terms of their faith. They could pull out Bible verses this way and that, while me, with my Catholic non-Bible upbringing, had to tediously search the thin pages for the right lines. How I longed to be able to translate my Catholic faith into a justice-making language.

I also thought that most of my difficulties, such as relating to Congressional aides or public speaking, were rooted in the spiritual. I could not name it, but I sensed that if I was grounded in my faith, tapped into the power of God, I couldn't fail. Most of all, the fatigue and weight of the work I was experiencing felt so wrong. I was depending too much on myself instead of allowing the creative power of God to step in, but how could I let go? That, more than not knowing my ethnic identity, was frightening. But the weeks of crying and being so tired even when I got enough sleep broke me down. My spiritual director labeled my tears "grace," as they provided me an opening to listen to those voices asking me hard questions: "What does it mean to be a child of God? How can you truly ground your social justice work and activism in your faith?"

Next thing I knew, I was flying out to California to study at the Graduate Theological Union in Berkeley. . . . I thought I might be able to take a break from activism while studying, but I have learned that my activism is actually part of my "spiritual practice" and not a distraction from it. I became involved with the San Francisco Bay Area chapter of FACES as co-chair and the work has been non-stop. In the last year and a half, we have marched in rallies, filed a lawsuit against the U.S. military, hosted several cultural events, and given presentations to numerous colleges and organizations.

One of my greatest learnings from studying theology and engaging in movement work is realizing that the great divide between spirituality and activism, contemplation and action, is a false one. My spirituality and contemplation invite me further into my activism, and my activism further into my spirituality and contemplation. Meditation and prayer provide the space for me to get in touch with the suffering of others, to keep myself accountable to the Divine within and around me, and to be honest about my human limitations and needs. Activism allows me to transform the connectedness with others' suffering into action and to live out my beliefs through my relationships with others. Thus, spirituality and activism, contemplation and action are but two sides of the same coin of compassion and love.

It has been quite a journey, and I know there is more to come, thanks to the persistence of those voices. For a while I did not really name them. I now realize that they are the voices of my True Self, the God-self, urging me to follow the map imprinted in my heart, carved by the Life Source herself. To know myself is to peel back all the layers of identity that have been given to me on this earth—as a Filipina, as an American, as a woman, as a lover of justice and peace, and as a Christian—to get to my core as a child of the Universe, the Divine, God. Trusting this process, creating the space, and allowing myself to be led, I have found my true power and a sense of peace. Don't get me wrong, even amidst this happiness, I still seem to be wearing earplugs most of the time, listening to my own beat and rhythm. Thank goodness those voices are loud. May they continue to haunt me, until I claim them as my own.

SEVENTY-NINE

◆◆◆

Common Threads (1994)
Life Stories and the Arts in Educating for Social Change
Cynthia Cohen

Teacher and researcher **Cynthia Cohen** directs the Brandeis Initiative in Intercommunal Coexistence, a program of the university's International Center for Ethics, Justice, and Public Life. Her writings focus on the ethical and aesthetic dimensions of reconciliation. She was founding director of the Oral History Center, Cambridge, Mass.

Introduction

The Oral History Center for Education and Action, (OHC), a community organization . . . located at the Center for Innovation in Urban Education at

Records of the Oral History Center (1978–1998) are housed at Northeastern University: http://www.lib.neu.edu/archives/collect/findaids/m73find.htm.

Northeastern University in Boston, uses oral history methods and the arts for the purpose of strengthening communities. Our work is informed by a strong multicultural and antiracist perspective; it is designed to facilitate the kinds of understanding needed to build alliances across differences.

The OHC's model is based on the idea that everyone has an important story to tell. It emphasizes an attentive quality of listening that can be transformative for both the listener and the teller. It also integrates the arts, in ways that nourish people's imagination, validate diverse cultures, and reach large audiences. The model evolved out of two projects I coordinated under the auspices of The Cambridge Arts Council, in 1980 through 1982: The Cambridge Women's Oral History Project (CWOHP) and the Cambridge Women's Quilt Project (CWQP). This article describes those two projects, as well as others the OHC sponsored during the years when I was its director, from 1982 through 1990.

The Cambridge Women's Oral History Project

In the CWOHP, high school students collected stories from their own and others' cultural communities. We chose the theme "transitions in women's lives" because the young women themselves were undergoing many transitions, and also because it could embrace the experience of women from all groups in the city, including recent immigrants. The young women conducted interviews (mostly in English, but also in Haitian Creole, Portuguese and Spanish), indexed tapes, and created a visual exhibit incorporating photographic portraits, excerpts of oral narrative, and brief biographies. Working with the staff of the project, they created a slide-tape show "Let Life Be Yours: Voices of Cambridge Working Women," which focuses on the theme of work in women's lives. "Let Life Be Yours" asks a question: How have women's cultural and economic backgrounds affected their ability to make choices in their lives? Answers can be found in the women's stories.

Antonia Cruz, a recent immigrant from Puerto Rico: "My father wanted to take me out of school, because it was too expensive, he said.

They were poor, they took me out of school in the fifth grade."

Addie Eskin, a Jewish woman born near Boston: "'What do you mean you have to go to high school, what do you have to go to high school for?' she said. 'Your father is very sick, what do you think, you're gonna go to school and hold your hand out?' And I said, 'Auntie, if I have to wear this middy blouse for the next four years, I'm going to graduate from high school.'"

Henrietta Jackson, a black woman born in Cambridge: "One of the newspapers called Cambridge High and Latin School, and asked the office practice teacher if she had any good student who might want a few hours every day after school in the newspaper office. I was considered one of the fastest typists and I went with two other girls. I was rejected immediately. And she called them and she was practically told they weren't quite ready for a black person. She said that it will be a long time before there won't be this kind of unfair treatment of a person whose only fault is that she happens to have a black face."

Catherine Zirpolo, an Italian woman born in Boston: "1914. I was fortunate, I didn't have to go to work . . . being an only child. . . . When I became of age to go to high school, I wasn't a bit interested in high school. I wanted to be an actress even then. . . ."

When the older women who participated in the Cambridge Women's Oral History Project told stories about the obstacles they faced, they revealed inspiring spiritual strength. The project's political message (i.e., opposing oppression based on race, class and gender) is all the more powerful because their language is personal and accessible, devoid of rhetoric. In evaluation interviews at the end of the project, the young women involved reported that their participation in the project had changed their ideas about older people, about the study of history, and about working with women:

Books are dull, but this way I get enjoyment out of history. . . . Winona and I have had really different lives. She's black and I'm white; I have more opportunities with education, work, and money. She's religious. There's a strength about her, so it's nice to talk to her. She's the kind of inspiring person that makes us want to go out and read and read good books and take it in. She makes you see how somebody can be at peace with things. Part of this is kind of making up for what I couldn't find from my own grandmother.

The people changed my opinions a lot. . . . Older people are pretty active in the community; they have a lot to say, most of them. They are just older, not feeble or anything. I used to see them like stereotypes, as people who sat back and watched the world go by. But they have a big part while it goes by. I never realized that. I got a lot out of seeing women work together. It gives you a sense of self-respect, a sense that I'm a valuable person. You see women working together and taking each other seriously and you know it's there and you know it should be there all the time.

Since its completion in 1984, "Let Life Be Yours" has been translated into Portuguese, Haitian Creole and Spanish. It has been used as the basis for community education programs on women's history, multicultural issues, older people's lives, and oral history methods.

The Cambridge Women's Quilt Project

The Oral History Center's second major project involved sixty women and girls, ranging in age from eight to eighty, working in collaboration with two fabric artists to create images from their lives in fabric. The project was designed as a study of the historical, social and cultural factors that influenced changes in women's lives. Also we intended to reflect on quilt-making: its function in women's lives, and its relationship to oral tradition. Through the project, we were able to enact the very subjects we were studying. For instance, many women and girls found that their participation in the project was itself producing changes in their lives. As has been a part of the American quilting bee tradition historically, participants in the project shared medical and political information, reflected together on their relationships with

boys and men, and gained perspective on the decisions they were facing. They felt themselves becoming part of a community.

The fabric artists supported each woman to create her own image of a story from her own life. One was about braiding a daughter's hair and another about a great-grandmother quilting. Others were about lighting Sabbath candles, dressing up to go to church, riding a donkey in Haiti, making wine in Italy, the dream of walking freely outside at night, hitchhiking throughout Europe and Africa, making life rafts during World War II, giving birth at home, reading alone in one's bedroom, reading to a group of neighborhood children, a childhood picking cotton in the South and a childhood dream of becoming a ballerina.

Our respect for each woman's expression was put to the test when one woman depicted in her quilt patch a child, pants rolled down, being spanked by his parent. When asked to document something important for history, this participant had chosen to represent "a time when parents cared enough about their children to set limits, to punish them when necessary." Other participants were upset by the expression of what they took to be violent: not only the spanking itself, but the humiliation of the child, with his bare bottom exposed. Through discussion, compromise was reached: the patch remained, but restitched with rolled-up pants.

In other ways too, the project created a congruence between the content and methods of our inquiry. For instance, women and girls depicted women weaving rugs, making lace and quilting, and here we were, making a quilt. Several patches honored women as bearers of traditional food ways: a Jamaican aunt carrying fruits home from market on her head, a Mennonite grandmother baking a cherry pie, and an Irish Nana heating tea. As we shared traditional foods and recipes at our potlucks, we were enacting as well as documenting this dimension of women's experience.

A total of 52 fabric images were sewn into two vibrant quilts. Some of the participants tape recorded interviews about the meaning of each patch; these oral narratives were edited into a catalog. Finally, a group of younger women worked with singer/songwriter Betsy Rose to compose a ballad, sung to a traditional Portuguese melody, based on the stories of the quilt patches. The ballad became the audio background for a slide-tape on the making of the quilts.

Informal conversations as well as the more formal sharing of stories in interviews were understood to be an important aspect of the projects. As one participant said,

> People who came were very shy and really, you couldn't see a visible importance about their lives. But once the little quilt square opened it was like they came alive. Everybody was so enthusiastic and one story led to another. . . . Maybe the most important thing about the quilt project was that the women who did it enjoyed each other and talked to each other. . . . There was no performance, and no being performed. Everybody is on stage. Everybody's the song. Everybody's the story teller.

Since their completion in 1982, the quilts have been exhibited in the neighborhoods of the city, at local festivals, and in libraries, stores, churches, schools and cultural and social service organizations. They have traveled to several other New England cities, and as far away as the International Women's Forum in Nairobi, Kenya, and to meetings of the Belize Rural Women's Association in Central America. In one of our most engaging exhibits, viewers of the quilts at the Boston Children's Museum could use nearby computer terminals to call up edited versions of the interview narratives. . . .

Common Threads

As we watched women and girls from different ethnic communities interacting as they sewed the quilts, it became clear that fabric arts were familiar media in which many women felt comfortable expressing themselves. In fact, many of the participants in the quilt project were steeped in the skills and customs of rich fabric traditions such as Portuguese lace-making, Haitian embroidery, African-American appliqué quilting, as well as knitting, crocheting and sewing. Activities using fabric gave women and girls the chance to feel a sense of accomplishment for their skills (generally unacknowledged, even within their own communities), and to learn about one another's lives and cultures.

We used these insights to design Common Threads, an exhibit and series of events which highlighted the stories and work of ten traditional and contemporary fabric artists, each from a different local ethnic community. The exhibit, displayed at a branch of the local library and in the high school, consisted of samples of fabric art such as lace, embroidery, batik, appliqué and crochet, along with the life stories of the women who created the pieces. At several events, members of English-as-a-Second-Language classes and others in the community were invited to bring their own fabric work and other crafts, and to share stories about their lives and their work.

Following the exhibit, the OHC collaborated with several local organizations to sponsor a visit to Cambridge of two Chilean *arpilleristas*, women who use small burlap tapestries to depict the harsh realities of daily life under the dictatorship of Augusto Pinochet. One of the *arpilleristas*, for instance, used a series of her tapestries to document her ten-year search for her son, detained by the military police shortly after Pinochet came to power. Many of the community women who participated in Common Threads and the Cambridge Women's Quilt Project attended a workshop with the *arpilleristas*, making an immediate connection through their common interest in storytelling through fabric. The following year, the OHC built on this awareness by sponsoring our own Stories-in-Fabric workshop, and the resulting tapestries were taken to the International Women's Forum in Nairobi, Kenya.

Because the Common Threads exhibit was temporary, we created a slide-tape show, which explores the social, political, economic and artistic meanings of fabric art in the lives of women. The slide show has been used in educational programs with groups of older people, fabric artists and students of women's history.

Lifelines

In addition to conducting women's oral history projects in community settings, the OHC also collaborated with teachers to adapt its model to a classroom context. Lifelines was a curriculum development project, designed to support fifth through eighth grade and bilingual teachers to incorporate oral history into on-going Social Studies and Language Arts curricula. Two teachers, for example, worked with students on labor history projects. In one case, students created a visual exhibit combining excerpts of interviews with parents and older workers with statistical analyses of the shifting economic base of the city. In the other classroom, students interviewed six women who worked in Cambridge factories during the 1930s and 1940s, and produced an illustrated timeline, visual exhibit, and slide-tape show about the changing patterns of women's work in the Depression, World War II, and the post-war eras. Three Lifelines classes explored topics in family and ethnic studies.

The arts were especially important in a Lifelines project in a Haitian bilingual class. The project was designed specifically to enhance self-esteem. The Haitian students were at the bottom of the social hierarchy at their school. They were teased about their language, their body odor, the possibility of being carriers of AIDS. These assaults on their integrity were sustained while they were struggling to learn a new language, to adjust to separation from members of their families, and often while they were recovering from the political violence and the extreme poverty that had led their families to leave the island whose landscape and culture they still cherished.

Students who had been in the U.S. for just two or three years interviewed Haitian adults who worked in careers of interest to the children. As they began to hear the stories of the adults of their own community validated and celebrated in their classroom, there began an outpouring of expression from them: stories and especially pictures of their lives in Haiti and their bewildering encounters with an American city. With help from a student intern from Harvard, the students created a slide-tape show, "We Are Proud of Who We Are," in which they narrated the stories told them by adults. They also worked with a storyteller to prepare performances of their own narratives. The children's stories and artwork, exhibited in the school corridors, provided contexts for relationship-building between the teachers and administrators in the school's monolingual program and the Haitian children. In subsequent years, students created notecards embellished with their drawings of images from their lives, and sold the cards to raise funds for an eye clinic in Haiti. The entire school participated in that effort, and later a group traveled to Haiti to visit a sister school. Through this project, the students began to realize the possibilities inherent in their own expression, and to understand that they were not only documentors, but makers, of history.

A Passion for Life: Stories and Folk Arts of Palestinian Women

During the same years we were working in collaboration with the Cambridge Public School on Lifelines, one of the women drawn to our Stories-in-Fabric series became involved in the OHC. Her name was Feryal Abbasi Ghnaim, and she worked as a traditional Palestinian embroiderer. Her interests and skills helped define our next major oral history project, A Passion for Life: Stories and Folk Arts of Palestinian and Jewish Women. The project was designed to explore whether stories and folk arts could be used to facilitate communication not just across differences, but across the chasm created by long-standing political conflict and violence.

The project's final exhibition displayed the stories of eight Jewish and Palestinian women, along with objects of folk expression, such as baskets, embroidered dresses, family photographs and cooking utensils. Eighteen public events preceded and accompanied the exhibition; these ranged from sessions of sharing recipes, songs, dance and visual arts, to a theoretical discussion on the role of folk arts in communities in crisis and a workshop on challenging stereotypes of Arab and Jewish people. The members of the project's Directions Committee, which consisted of both Jewish and Palestinian women and others, wrote at the time that we were looking for modes of expression which would invite people in conflict to reach beneath their defenses and their fears, so they could come to recognize each other's humanity:

> In spite of our many differences, we believe there is wisdom in the perspectives of women, who are striving day to day, sometimes under harsh oppression, to create their lives and to recreate culture and community for their children. There is value in the stories of these regular common people who do the mundane but richly detailed work of sowing seeds and harvesting fruits, preparing foods and cleaning homes, fixing remedies and stitching cloth, selling goods and listening to the stories people share when they come together to celebrate, to grieve and to pass on traditions.

The stories and works of art in our exhibition include descriptions of the tragedy of the Palestinian Diaspora and the oppression of Palestinian people under Israeli occupation.

They speak to the terrible persecution which Jewish people have endured throughout history, most horrifyingly manifested in Europe during World War II.

We bring these stories together in one exhibition not to suggest any simple parallels, but to create a vision broad enough to embrace them all. As we listen to stories from both Jewish and Palestinian women, we share feelings of sadness and anger, sometimes outrage. We believe that nothing excuses acts of inhumanity. Has the world not seen enough of families divided, homes and communities destroyed? Have there not been enough precious heirlooms confiscated, people imprisoned, children murdered? How can this fragile fabric of our lives, which we and our mothers and our grandmothers have stitched so carefully—note by note, spoonful by spoonful, caress by caress, story by story—be so brutally torn to shreds?

We engage with this work out of a deep love for our own traditions and an appreciation for the richness of the others'.

We recognize the deep-seated fears of both Palestinian and Jewish people. We are working towards a world in which we all are safe to preserve and develop our cultures. We are inspired by the passion for life which permeates these women's stories and their art: the impulse to create beauty, to nourish children, to take risks, to resist oppression, to celebrate community; and the determination to survive, both physically and spiritually, against forces of brutality and destruction.

Take inspiration from these stories to reach out to each other with openness and respect. Let them motivate you to take a stand for justice and to work for peace.

A Passion for Life proved to be more difficult than we ever could have imagined at the outset. Sometimes it seemed to be little more than a snarl of ethical dilemmas, demanding relationships and intense emotions. At times, both Feryal and I, the project's co-directors, felt pressured by members of our families and communities to withdraw from the project. Key people from both communities chose not to participate, and in a couple of cases, backed out at the last minute. In retrospect, it seems like a miracle that we ever managed to bring the eight women's stories under one roof, even for just a couple of months.

Among the many conflicts we needed to resolve in the course of the project, the most contentious were misunderstandings about language, and our lack of awareness of the meanings and resonances of specific words for members of each other's communities. For many Palestinians, for instance, the word "peace," unless immediately followed by the word "justice," had come to signify a criticism of Palestinian resistance to the Israeli occupation. It was a kind of code, understood by many Jewish people, who had themselves come to perceive the word "justice" as pro-Palestinian. The word "1948" also resonated very differently for members of each community. For Palestinians, 1948 is the year of the *nakba,* or disaster. It is the year of the dispersion, when many Palestinians were dispossessed of their land, the year when the fabric of their lives was permanently rent. Nineteen-forty-eight is the year of the massacre of the citizens of Deir Yessin, a Palestinian village plundered by members of two Jewish right-wing terrorist organizations. Thousands of Palestinians fled from their homes in fear of a repetition of Deir Yessin. For most Jewish people, on the other hand, 1948 marks the creation of the state of Israel, a time of rejoicing in the fulfillment of a dream of a homeland—a symbol that evokes images of security, justice, democracy, and the possibility of a post-holocaust renewal. It isn't just that one group views the history as victors and the other as a people defeated, but that each places the events of the year within a different frame of historical reference.

The most problematic and emotionally charged meanings were encoded in the phrase "the Holocaust." The emotional resonances which surround the memory of the holocaust, the politically motivated abuses of holocaust imagery by both sides, and the disparate meanings which are attached to the word may be among the central barriers to Palestinian-Jewish reconciliation. While most Palestinians and Jews understand each others' readings of the words "peace" and "justice," often they are unaware of the different resonances of references to the holocaust. For most Jews of Eastern European background, the holocaust is a sacred memory. Less than [seventy] years ago, a third of the Jewish people were killed, and this fact still defines communal reality.

What happened in Europe—the systematic obliteration of thousands of communities; the destruction of Yiddishkeit as a living culture; the challenge to Jewish understanding of God, and justice and faith; the magnitude of the suffering and the devastation underscoring the meaning of being homeless in the world—all of this is the context in which contemporary Jews of European heritage came to define their individual and collective identity.

From a Palestinian perspective, "the holocaust" is what they have repeatedly heard as an excuse for the inexcusable brutality and injustice to which they have been subjected. European and American guilt about it was a major factor in turning world opinion to support the Zionist claim to Israel. Palestinian people feel that they are being made to suffer for Europe's crimes, and that somehow the significance of their own suffering diminishes when it is compared to the holocaust. A Palestinian friend once said to me: "Don't put me beside a holocaust survivor; I feel like nothing. How can my suffering compare?"

While Jewish people feel a need to honor the memory of the holocaust by retelling the story and by bearing witness to the tragedy, many Palestinian people are weary of hearing the story. "Why do they have to tell us this story?" asked Feryal. "We are the ones who are suffering now." The documentaries and fictional renditions of the holocaust story on TV often culminate with hopeful references to the new state of Israel, accompanied by images which either demonize Arabs or render their true experience invisible. These are especially painful because of the media's relative silence about Palestinian history and culture, its muteness about Palestinian suffering and legitimate needs for security.

Throughout A Passion for Life, in spite of these misunderstandings of words, there were moments when Palestinian and Jewish people began to understand each other's point of view, to feel each other's suffering, to recognize themselves in each other's aspirations. This happened through hearing each other's stories, and seeing and appreciating each other's artistic work. After hearing the stories of Palestinian women who had become friends, one Jewish woman acknowledged for instance that she had never realized that Jewish people in Israel were living in the actual dwellings which had once belonged to Palestinian families. One Palestinian woman said that although she had known about the holocaust before, she had never truly felt the enormity of it. After seeing Feryal describe the symbols in her embroidery, an older Jewish man, a committed supporter of Israel, commented that he had never realized that Palestinian women were telling stories in their embroidery.

Often, A Passion for Life seemed like an enormous landscape, clouded by terror and confusion. It often seemed that what we were attempting was actually impossible. But, all along, there were moments when the terrain would shift, creating new contours of possibility. These openings, made possible by our caring for each other and by the power of stories and the arts, enlarged our imagination and deepened our yearning for reconciliation. These were the moments that sustained us in our work. Once after a particularly difficult phase of the project, Feryal and I spoke together at a gathering of people from both communities. She showed her beautiful tapestry of a Palestinian woman holding aloft a dove. In its beak is an envelope carrying this message:

> Women of the world: Women love peace to raise their children in, so why don't you make peace your number one goal? I as a Palestinian know intimately that there are two kinds of peace. (1) Peace that is built on the bodies of those brutalized and murdered to silence their calls for their just rights; (2) peace which comes from understanding a people's suffering, sitting down with them to genuinely solve and resolve their problems, so that justice and equality can be the code of the land, not death and suffering.
>
> Why don't we, women, raise our voices high and strong in the service of true peace to preserve our children, our future as human beings? I ask you to support my call for true peace for my people. We are not subhumans. We are people with history and civilization. We are mothers and fathers and children. We have had enough killing and Diaspora. I smuggled my dreams in my hidden wishes and crossed the ocean in hope for peace; for my Palestinian sisters who lost their children in wars and who have been widowed at an early age. I ask you for true peace for my people.

I followed Feryal by reading an excerpt from the extraordinary autobiography of Heda Margolius Kovaly, in which she recounts the events of her life in Prague from 1941 through 1968:

> Three forces carved the landscape of my life. Two of them crushed half the world. The third

was very small and weak, and, actually, invisible. It was a shy little bird hidden in my rib cage an inch or two above my stomach. Sometimes in the most unexpected moments the bird would wake up, lift its head, and flutter its wings in rapture. Then I too would lift my head because, for that short moment, I would know for certain that love and hope are infinitely more powerful than hate and fury, and that, some-where beyond the line of my horizon there was life indestructible, always triumphant.

The first force was Adolf Hitler; the second was Iosif Stalin. They made my life a micro-cosm in which the history of a small country in the heart of Europe was condensed. The little bird, the third force, kept me alive to tell the story.

When I finished reading Kovaly's words, Feryal leaned over and pointed to the dove in her tapestry. "You see," she whispered, "it's the same bird."

EIGHT Y

❖❖❖

Making What Will Become (2004)

Vivien Labaton and Dawn Lundy Martin

Vivien Labaton and **Dawn Lundy Martin** are among the cofounders of the Third Wave Foundation and editors of *The Fire This Time: Young Activists and the New Feminism.*

What Wave?

During the course of our work with the Third Wave Foundation—a national organization that supports young feminists who are doing progressive activism around the country—we are frequently asked by the media, older activists, philanthropic organizations, and others where the next generation of feminist movers and shakers is, what we care about, and whether or not we embody the Generation X myth of apathetic, apolitical slackers that was created for us to live up (or down) to. People wonder who is carry-ing on the legacy of the women's movement, and they look to the same old haunts to find the answers. The problem is, they are looking in the wrong places.

Young feminists in large numbers—both women and men—are doing social justice work all over the country. They are moved to action by social and eco-nomic injustice, the growing divide between rich and poor, contemporary manifestations of colonial-ism, the rapid growth of the prison industrial com-plex, and the deterioration of democracy. They are protesting free trade at meetings of the World Bank, the World Trade Organization, and the International Monetary Fund, in Genoa, Washington, D.C., Quebec City, and other cities all over the world. They are cre-ating independent media that reach people on almost every continent with fresh, corporation-free news. They are creating youth-run organizations that address issues as far-ranging but interconnected as immigration, welfare, education, and queer rights.[1] Growing pockets of young feminist activism across the country (and the world) are building steam with renewed vigor and a broadened vision.

In 1996, though, the landscape of feminist ac-tivism looked very different. Both of us felt uncer-tain about whether we were relevant to any sort of feminist activity; we weren't sure if the feminist movement wanted us, or if we wanted it. As Dawn remembers that time:

When I was twenty-five I felt cast out of femi-nism. Back then, feminism seemed like a physi-cal place, a destination—as in: Last year, I went to feminism, and then I left. My perception was that it was a place for a certain kind of profes-sionalized older activist whom I couldn't relate to. A young, queer, African-American woman, I hunkered down in the progressive feminist-lesbian organization where I worked, and dreamed of something better. Ironically, I was, I believe now, at the very height of my political idealism—more ready than ever to get sweaty for a cause. Yet I didn't feel like an activist at all.

I felt mostly like a paper pusher, a utilitarian arm in a vast but indifferent machine. I had friends just like me. They had taken "assistant" or "associate" positions at traditional feminist organizations but felt, in the end, that the movement, whose philosophies had literally changed their lives, neither wanted nor needed them.

Vivien had just graduated from college and was looking for a job. She recalls:

I was looking for a job that reflected my political perspectives and the range of issues that I was passionate about. What I found instead was that I was forced to pick. I could work at an organization that dealt with abortion rights or I could work at an organization that dealt with racial and economic justice, but I could not do both. Yet I found it impossible to think about abortion rights without thinking about racial and economic justice. It was like being forced to think about my index finger without thinking about my thumb, or my whole hand. I began to believe that we needed a more comprehensive feminism.

Then Dawn and three other young activists—filmmaker Catherine Gund and writers Amy Richards and Rebecca Walker—decided to create an organization that reflected our feminist sensibilities, the Third Wave Foundation. For us, "third wave" feminism simply meant young women and men doing social justice work while using a gender lens. We didn't have any complicated theories about how the third wave differed from previous feminist uprisings. Yet we were aware of the impact we might have on reinventing feminism for future generations of young people who, like us, had at times been burdened by popular misconceptions about the feminist movement.

This reinvention would be both cosmetic and substantive. We wanted to put new faces on the feminist movement. We wanted to make it hot, sexy, and newly revolutionary. No more women's symbol with a fist through the circle, no more recycled-looking mauve paper, and no more images of women who looked nothing like us. Feminism needed an elective surgery—a face-lift, a remodeling—but it also needed an ideological expansion so that it could be more pertinent to contemporary realities and attractive to younger activists. Yes, we were interested

in helping to obliterate media-constructed perceptions of feminism (a militant, irrelevant sect of man-hating dykes), but most of all, we wanted a movement that addressed our races, sexualities, genders, and classes. It would be untrue to suggest that we have achieved all of our lofty goals (few would describe feminism as "sexy"), but we did succeed in carving out a space for a diverse group of younger feminists. They have joined the ongoing dialogue about gender equality and are beginning to revise our definitions of what it means to be a feminist. Is this what it means to be "third wave"?

There have been several efforts to describe what third wave feminism is. Rebecca Walker's 1995 collection of essays *To Be Real: Telling the Truth and Changing the Face of Feminism* "wanted to explore the ways that choices or actions seemingly at odds with mainstream ideas of feminism push us to new definitions and understandings of female empowerment and social change."[2] *Listen Up: Voices from the Next Feminist Generation* (1995), edited by Barbara Findlen, focuses on events of our time and place and how they have shaped young feminist perceptions. The academic collection edited by Leslie Heywood and Jennifer Drake, *Third Wave Agenda* (1997), stakes out a different territory, presenting a "generational perspective, gathering voices of young activists struggling to come to terms with the historical specificity of our feminisms and with the times in which we came of age (the late 1970s through the late 1980s)."[3] Most recently, *Manifesta,* by Jennifer Baumgardner and Amy Richards, attempts to communicate to a new generation of young women the power and possibility of feminism while simultaneously critiquing the old guard's inability to involve young women in the movement. All of these works suggest what it might mean to have another wave of feminism sweep through and *shake shit up,* this one built by that generation of feminist activists born after 1965.

For the most part, however, third wave feminism has been articulated as a generational difference—a reaction against perceptions about feminists that have permeated society, not the movement itself. Many young women's reservations about belonging to the feminist movement are due not to ideological differences but to misconceptions about feminists—that they are separatists, that they are unfashionable, that they burn bras and have lots of cats. Some progressive political young women even shun the term *feminist* as a way to describe their belief systems. Young feminists have shed the media-espoused propaganda about feminists but have taken to heart the criticism from women of color that the second wave was not racially or sexually inclusive enough. The addition of the *third wave* in front of the term *feminism,* for them, is a reclamation—a way to be feminist with a notable difference.

One of the luxuries that our generation has enjoyed is that we've reaped the benefits of all the social justice movements that have come before us; we have come of age in a world that has been shaped by feminism, queer liberation movements, antiracist movements, labor movements, and others. Consequently, many young women and men not only have an understanding of the interconnection of social justice issues but also see them as inextricable from one another.

In 1990 the legal scholar Angela P. Harris wrote, "As feminists begin to attack racism and classism and homophobia, feminism will change from being only about 'women as women' . . . to being about all kinds of oppressions based on seemingly inherent and unalterable characteristics. We need not wait for a unified theory of oppression; that theory can be feminism."[4] Now, in 2004, feminist practices are fulfilling this prediction. By blowing open the idea that class, race, sexuality, and gender are singular entities that exist independently of one another, *The Fire This Time* [edited by Labaton and Martin, 2004] provides a framework for looking at various tendencies toward domination. In this context, feminism offers a central belief system that helps interpret how power imbalances affect our lives. To demand that people focus on one area of concern without recognizing the interconnection of multiple issues would be to demand a level of self-abnegation that does not mirror the way these issues are experienced in our daily lives.

Indeed, young women and men are doing multi-issue work that embodies and reflects the many complications of our global world. If we want to build a feminist world, we must look not only at reproductive rights and equal pay for equal work, but also at the working conditions of women who labor in sweatshops; we must battle sex trafficking as well as the global economic policies that have made sex trafficking a thriving industry and a normative part of the move toward a borderless economy. The feminism that emerges in *The Fire This*

Time shows that there are few issues beyond the movement's reach. It may not be possible to identify a third wave, but we do know that feminist women and men, most thirty-five and under, are making feminism do more work.

Breaking Ranks

Those issues that have traditionally been associated with the feminist movement—reproductive rights, domestic violence, date rape, and equal pay for equal work—are not the only issues that should define it. This is not to suggest, however, that a new set of feminist issues is supplanting the old. Sweatshop labor and police brutality are not new, and the defense of reproductive rights is certainly as necessary as ever. Archetypal feminist issues have been important to women worldwide—and essential to the lives of many of the writers included in this collection. They continue to require our devotion. But we should not become so distracted . . . that we neglect other social justice concerns. The borders of feminism need to be split open, both so that we are freed from ideological rigidity and so that other identity claims of race, sexuality, class, nationality, and geography can move beyond being simply "tolerated" or "included."

Our feminism has roots in past feminist work. Revolutionary writers like Gloria Anzaldúa, Audre Lorde, Cherríe Moraga, Barbara Smith, and other United States Third World feminists have described the intersection of race, sexuality, and gender, and the many ways that these multiple and overlapping identities interact. Similarly, the plan of action that came out of the landmark 1977 Houston Women's Conference, which convened to develop a national agenda for women, focused on many issues, including immigrant rights, Native American rights, lesbian rights, health care, and employment.

Yet the prevailing understanding of feminism has placed a select few issues at the center of what is thought of as feminist activism, neglecting the full range of experiences that inform women's lives. Indeed, one of the major criticisms of mainstream second wave feminism was its inattentiveness to racial, cultural, sexual, and national differences. In this view, feminism found its strength in putting the concerns of First World white women first and framing them as universal, often at the expense of people of color. As Kum-Kum Bhavnani points out,

"The 'sisterhood is global' discourse denied [women of color] the space to assert our differences from white women and masked the power inequalities present within women's movements."[5]

In 1979, when Audre Lorde gave her seminal paper "The Master's Tools Will Never Dismantle the Master's House," at the Second Sex Conference, she chastised organizers for ignoring "Black and Third World women and lesbians." She asked bitingly, "What does it mean when the tools of a racist patriarchy are used to examine the fruits of that same patriarchy?"[6] From their position of marginality, second wave feminists of color and queer feminists formed a critique of the movement and forced the women's movement to include women of color and lesbians in their ranks.

That there is a diversity of women sitting around the decision-making table is progress, but if there is little modification in the selection of issues worthy of feminist concern, then the fact of diversity is moot. *Diversity* has become a popular word, a word so tacitly politically correct that it has lost much of its meaning. It often closes off possibilities rather than opening them up. "We need to diversify our office" means we don't have enough "women," "people of color," "gays and lesbians," "differently-abled," et cetera. Inclusion in this light barely challenges the racist, sexist, homophobic, ability-centric, societal norms. Instead, it reiterates them. Hiring a black or gay worker is something that helps organizations and businesses legitimize their commitment to our friend diversity. Organizations can broaden their appeal [read: get more donations], and businesses can better market their products to the "increasing numbers of Latina/os" and the "growing black middle class." This is not to say that even this kind of diversity should end, but as a culture we must move beyond superficial inclusions.

The feminism of younger activists goes beyond the rhetoric of inclusion. The most significant lesson that we have learned from the second wave . . . is that a feminist movement cannot succeed if it does not challenge power structures of wealth and race. If the model within which one works centralizes whiteness and/or wealth, the poorest and most victimized women in the world will be overlooked. . . . In other words, we see a new movement evolving from one in which there is a dialogue *about* feminism and race to a feminist movement whose conversation *is* race, gender, and globalization.

No Labels, Just Work

Although increasingly young feminists are carving out their own spaces for action (like the Center for Young Women's Development in San Francisco), creating their own organizations (like Sista II Sista in Brooklyn, New York), and defining feminism in their own ways, often our work takes place in organizations that allow broader social justice work to be contextualized as feminist. To notice the next wave of feminism (or however one chooses to label it), one has to look far beyond the National Organization for Women (NOW), the Feminist Majority, or the National Abortion Rights Action League (NARAL). Feminists in their twenties and thirties can also be found at the CAAAV: Organizing Asian Communities, Critical Resistance, and the Center for Third World Organizing; at Internet start-ups and in magazine and book publishing; at bachelorette parties, Gay Pride parades, and vacationing in the Hamptons; in rap music, in independent media, working at fast-food restaurants and on college campuses. From these sites and many more, cutting-edge feminist critiques, analyses, and activisms are expanding the depth and breadth of today's movement.

. . . Some of us boldly claim the term *feminist*; some of us embrace Alice Walker's term *womanist*, which "is to feminist as purple is to lavender";[7] and the not-so-secret truth is, some of us choose not to claim any term at all. And although the narrative we've constructed here is not about what a feminist looks like or what credentials a feminist needs to have, it *is* about pressing hard on the surface of the movement so that a kind of fracture erupts, allowing more young women and men to claim feminism as a framework not just for activism but for living. What some may see as a detrimental fragmentation within the feminist movement, we understand to be a place of power.

If we were to build a feminist movement made up primarily of "feminists" between the ages of eighteen and thirty-five, we would find no single ideological framework from which their activisms emerge. In fact, if we asked ten young feminists what feminism meant to them, we'd likely get ten different answers. We would find, instead, *linked* ideas that incorporate certain second wave feminist tenets: a movement that . . . is situated in discrete and multiple sites. Unlike second wave feminism, which has operated from a monolithic center, multiplicity offers the power of existing insidiously and simultaneously everywhere. "Woman" as a primary identity category has ceased to be the entry point for much young activist work. Instead, it has become one of the many investigatory means used to affect an indefinite number of issues and cultural analyses. . . .

NOTES

1. Sister Outsider, Sista II Sista, Sisters in Action for Power, Third Wave Foundation, Center for Young Women's Development, Young Women United, and the Audre Lorde Project are just a few young-women-led organizations. Many more such projects exist around the country.

2. Rebecca Walker, *To Be Real: Telling the Truth and Changing the Face of Feminism* (New York: Anchor Books, 1995), xxxvi.

3. Jennifer Drake and Leslie Heywood, eds., *Third Wave Agenda: Being Feminist, Doing Feminism* (Minneapolis: University of Minnesota Press, 1997), 2.

4. Angela P. Harris, "Race and Essentialism in Feminist Legal Theory," *Stanford Law Review* 42 (February 1990), 581.

5. Kum-Kum Bhavnani, ed., *Feminism and "Race"* (Oxford and New York: Oxford University Press, 2001), 5.

6. Quoted in ibid., 89.

7. Alice Walker, *In Search of Our Mothers' Gardens* (New York: Harcourt Brace, 1984), xii.

◆◆◆

EIGHTY-ONE

A Chain-Letter Reaction (2004)

Alison Stein Wellner

Alison Stein Wellner is a writer based in New York City whose work focuses on statistical analysis, and workplace and business issues. Former editor of *American Demographics,* her articles have appeared in *Business Week, Christian Science Monitor, Washington Post,* and MotherJones.com.

. . . It was July 2002, and just a few days earlier, the Bush administration had announced that it would not release $34-million appropriated by Congress to sponsor the United Nations Population Fund, an agency of the United Nations that provides reproductive-health programs in more than 140 countries.

Although the agency does not provide abortions, its family-planning activities have long made it a target for anti-abortion activists. Its money was cut off while Ronald Reagan was president and remained so during George H. W. Bush's term, but it was restored under President Bill Clinton. The current Bush administration eliminated federal financing of the agency after the U.S. State Department said that the Population Fund was indirectly supporting coercive abortions and involuntary sterilization programs in China, a charge that the agency denied.

Ms. [Jane] Roberts, a 60-year-old retired teacher and longtime activist for women's issues, was appalled by the administration's decision. She believed that it would have a real human cost—the Population Fund estimates that the money could have prevented two million unwanted pregnancies, 800,000 induced abortions, 77,000 infant and child deaths, and 4,700 maternal deaths worldwide. So she tossed and turned that summer night in her home in Redlands, Calif., trying to figure out what to do.

Suddenly, it came to her: Why not find a way to replace the $34-million that the U.S. government had cut? What if she could, as she put it, create her own "teeny tiny foreign policy" and raise $1 from 34 million people? She felt certain that at least that many people felt as upset about the administration's decision as she did. If she sent an e-mail message out to a few hundred people, she reasoned, and everyone sent it to 10 others, and they sent it to 10 others, and so on, she might be able to touch off a chain effect.

As it turned out, at just about the same time, a total stranger had the same brainstorm. Lois Abraham, 70, a lawyer in Taos, N.M., had been following the Population Fund controversy. She also had the idea to use a chain-style e-mail letter to raise $1 from 34 million people to replace the money. " . . . I was angry," she says. "The e-mail campaign was an idea that germinated from that anger. Doing nothing became unacceptable, and I had received some chain-letter e-mails, some of them more than once, so I knew that it might work."

Two women who had never met, one improbable idea to raise $1 from 34 million people using e-mail: In an era of ever-increasing spam, it sounded like an idea destined to add up to zero. And yet, two years later, Ms. Roberts and Ms. Abraham's brainstorm, or 34 Million Friends of UNFPA, as it has come to be known, has turned into a most successful, if unusual, fund-raising campaign.*

To date, 34 Million Friends of UNFPA has raised nearly $2-million. . . . Moreover, it has helped bolster the United Nations' efforts to improve reproductive-health care in developing countries and offers a number of lessons for fund raisers about what causes a grass-roots campaign to grow.

Ms. Roberts and Ms. Abraham—unaware of each other's existence—independently started the still-unnamed campaign in August 2002. Ms. Roberts began by writing a check to the U.S. Committee for United Nations Population Fund, something that she did every year. In addition to a check for $500, she tucked a dollar bill into the envelope, along with a note that she would be encouraging others to give a dollar too. . . .

Then Ms. Roberts sent e-mail messages to everyone in her many circles: personal friends, acquaintances from environmental and educational groups, national women's organizations, tennis and golf buddies, book-club members. "I really thought this had possibilities," says Ms. Roberts.

Ms. Abraham started by calling the United Nations Population Fund. Her call was fielded by Vernon Mack, chief of the Resource Mobilization Branch. Ms. Abraham described her idea, and wanted to know whether the agency could receive donations from individuals. Up to that point, Mr. Mack says, neither the Population Fund nor the U.S. Committee, which are supported primarily by governments, had tried to raise funds from individuals.

Ms. Abraham "explained to me what she wanted to do," Mr. Mack says, "and I thought to myself, now isn't that interesting? But frankly I didn't think it was going to amount to much." . . .

News of Ms. Abraham's and Ms. Roberts's separate plans surfaced at the next joint weekly meeting held by the United Nations Population Fund and the U.S. Committee, recalls Mari Tikkanen, resource mobilization officer at the Population Fund. Because the two women had uncannily hatched the same idea simultaneously, U.N. officials initially thought that the two women were the same person, Ms. Tikkanen says, despite their different names and locales.

Soon Ms. Roberts and Ms. Abraham were introduced, over the telephone. Ms. Abraham says she was surprised to hear about another person trying to do the same thing as she, and was mostly pleased.

"I did have one worry, and that is probably because I am a control freak," she recalls. "I was very set on the message. To me, it had to be heavy on the cause, light on the politics. That's not because I am not politically engaged—I am—but because I did not want to turn off potential 'friends' who might be Bush partisans but also would support UNFPA and the work it does. My worry was that I might not be able to control the message."

Her worries were unfounded, however. "It turned out that Jane and I naturally complemented one another's efforts and ideas," she says. The retired Ms. Roberts was able to devote time to public speaking, for example, while Ms. Abraham, still working, could not. And the pair were able to reach very different groups of people, adds Ms. Roberts. "Lois has a different network than I do, through her work as an attorney," she says. "Two weeks after she started, her e-mail's going around the World Bank, for goodness sake!"

The e-mail solicitations started to do their work, and the donations came in slowly—at first,

---

*The United Nations Population Fund used to be called the United Nations Fund for Population Activities, or the UNFPA. Although the name has changed, the abbreviation used to describe it has not.

says Ms. Tikkanen, who was tapped to oversee the campaign's logistics. Envelopes with letters and gifts responding to the e-mail messages were routed to her office, and within the next few weeks she coined the name "34 Million Friends."

Then, by early fall 2002, the momentum started to grow. "Our mail unit started bringing buckets of letters, literally," she says. "Soon we were getting four big baskets a day."

It started to dawn on everyone that the 34 Million Friends campaign was taking off. "We never ever expected such incredible response," says Micol Zarb, media officer at the United Nations Population Fund. "There are so many people sending around e-mails to each other. Here's a good cause, sign your name onto this petition," she says. "In the age of the Internet, there's just so much information overload. We never really expected it would spread as quickly as it did, so we had to quickly create a system to respond to all of these envelopes, all of the money, and all of the support. It's a great problem to have."

But it was a problem nonetheless, and Ms. Tikkanen was charged with solving it. First, she had to figure out how to get all of those envelopes opened. She asked Population Fund staff members to volunteer, and they gave their lunch hours, or time after work. She found no shortage of helpers, she says, because most donors included a letter with their donation expressing support for the organization. "It sounds so corny, but reading those letters—really it was so moving, and people were really motivated by it," she says. "In any organization, you're sometimes removed from what you do, so it's good to be reminded."

Ms. Tikkanen designed a system to make sure that the money was properly handled, she says. All envelopes were opened the day they were received, and each was checked by three volunteers. Since the offices lacked a safe, the money was stored in a locked cupboard in Mr. Mack's office.

While the cash-counting system proved adequate, using the team of volunteers turned out to be only a temporary measure. By October 2002, the campaign was starting to get news-media attention. Several prominent newspaper columnists wrote about the campaign, says Ms. Zarb, including Molly Ivins and Ellen Goodman, as did magazines such as *Ms., Marie Claire,* and *O, the Oprah Magazine.* The effect of the coverage was substantial: Before Ms. Ivins's column on the campaign, the Population Fund was receiving 100 letters a day, says Ms. Zarb. After the column ran in October . . . the number increased to 500 letters a day. After Ms. Goodman's column appeared in December, that number jumped to 1,000 daily.

Eventually, about $60,000 a week poured into the United Nations Population Fund and the U.S. Committee headquarters, in thousands of letters. Many donors gave more than $1. "It became clear that we needed to be opening full time," says Ms. Tikkanen.

. . . By May 2003, the campaign had raised its first million dollars, and the U.N. Foundation made another grant to the project—25 cents for every dollar raised, or $250,000. The money was used to pay for Good Works, a consulting company in Boulder, Colo., to take over the day-to-day operations of the campaign, which it did in September.

"This was not something we could have continued to take care of," says Ms. Tikkanen. "We're not set up for that." Even though it was a lot of extra work, she says that she was sorry to see the campaign go: "That year that it lasted here, within us, it was just uplifting for everyone."

Now, two years since the campaign began, it is closing in on the $2-million mark. Ms. Abraham points to the campaign's simplicity and the small amount it requested from donors for its success. "The initial e-mail asked for $1. Just about anyone can do $1," she says. "Since I believe that getting people to focus on the issue was as important as the amount of money they donated, I viewed the small ask as a benefit. Part of the benefit was that we would not be competing for money that people normally give to other causes."

. . . The campaign now focuses, via its Web site (which also accepts online donations), on letting donors know what their gifts have accomplished. For example, using funds from the 34 Million Friends campaign, the Population Fund is providing ambulances to take women to hospitals in Rwanda.

It is also enabling the purchase of 80 motor scooters for midwives, so that they can reach women in remote areas in East Timor. And the money has helped to train 1,000 health assistants in basic emergency obstetric care in Eritrea. Half of the funds raised by the campaign are going toward programs designed to treat obstetric fistula, a pregnancy-related disability, in six countries.

. . . Of course, for Ms. Roberts and Ms. Abraham, the work is far from done. They still have $32-million more before they will hit their goal. So even though the campaign is now administered by Good Works, both women continue to drum up support and interest in the cause. Ms. Roberts, for example, keeps a rigorous speaking schedule on the college circuit, while Ms. Abraham despairs of ever keeping track of all of the e-mail solicitations that she still needs to send.

It's not just about the money, but also about the message that the money is sending, says Ms. Roberts. "I ache to see that total go up," she says. "I want the world to know that we Americans are a generous, good people and that we care. To me, those dollars are sending that message."

E I G H T Y - T W O

◆◆◆

Whose Security? (2002)

Charlotte Bunch

A pioneering organizer for women's rights and human rights, **Charlotte Bunch** is Founder and Executive Director of the Center for Women's Global Leadership at Rutgers University. She has received many fellowships and awards including the 1999 Eleanor Roosevelt Award for Human Rights, and was inducted into the National Women's Hall of Fame in 1996.

When I talk with feminists from other countries, whether from Europe or the Third World, I am repeatedly asked: "Where are the voices of the U.S. women's movement against what the Bush Administration is doing globally, using the excuse of 9/11?"

While I know that many U.S. feminists are concerned about these issues, it is clear that our voices are not being heard much—outside, or even inside, this country. The perception created by the Western media is that virtually all Americans support Bush's militaristic threats, his "you're with us or against us," evil-axis rhetoric, and his unilateralist positions against global treaties from the Kyoto Protocol on the environment to the newly created International Criminal Court. When I mention activities like the weekly Women in Black vigils against U.S. policy in the Middle East held in New York and other cities, or feminists working to change the composition of the U.S. Congress, where only Barbara Lee spoke out . . . immediately after 9/11, they are somewhat relieved.

Yet it is clear that feminists in the United States do not have much impact on U.S. foreign policy, which is military- and corporate-driven. Even though Bush used Afghan women's rights to drum up support for his war, this did not lead to a sustained commitment to Afghan women. It is puzzling to many outside this country how a women's movement that has had such profound influence on U.S. culture and daily life could have so little effect on, or seemingly even concern for, U.S. foreign policy and its impact on women worldwide. The consequences of this failure are disastrous for women in many countries, and they threaten the advances that the global women's movement made in the 1990s.

Current U.S. foreign policy makes it harder to build women's international solidarity in a number of ways. The widespread sympathy that the world offered Americans at the time of 9/11 has given way to anti-Americanism and rage at what the U.S. government is doing in the name of that event. On the day of the attacks, I was still in South Africa following the U.N. World Conference Against Racism held in Durban the week before. People expressed intense concern about what had happened, especially when they learned that I lived in New York. And this was in spite of the great frustration that most felt about the inexcusable disdain for other countries the Bush Administration had just exhibited during the world conference.* But now, resentment and anger at the United States is the overriding sentiment in many other nations. Even some feminist

---

*The U.S. delegation walked out of the conference, objecting to language that linked Zionism and racism, and a proposal for reparations for the descendants of slaves.

colleagues elsewhere tell me that they are now asked how they can really work with Americans, given how little opposition to Bush's foreign policies they see happening here.

This resentment stems in part from the fact that 9/11 is not seen as a defining moment for the rest of the world—at least not in terms of what happened that day. In many places, people have long lived with terrorism, violence, and death on a scale as great as or greater than 9/11. So, while they agree that this was a terrible and shocking event, they consider the U.S. obsession with it, including the assumption that it is the defining moment for everyone, to be self-indulgent and shortsighted.

Of course, September 11 has been a defining event within the United States. But how we understand it in a global context is important. First, we must recognize that our government's responses to it were not inevitable. This event could have taken the country in other directions, including toward greater empathy with what others have suffered, toward more concern for human security and the conditions that give rise to terrorism, and toward recognition of the importance of multilateral institutions in a globally linked world. But that would have required a very different national leadership. Instead, it has become the rationale for an escalation of the regressive Bush agenda domestically and internationally, including more unrestrained exercise of U.S. power and disregard for multilateralism. Other governments have also used the occasion to increase military spending and to erode support for human rights. In that sense, it has become a defining moment because of how it has been used. But the issues highlighted by 9/11 are not new and have been raised by many other events both before and after it.

Indeed, 9/11 has raised the profile of many of the issues feminists were already struggling with globally, such as

- growing global and national economic inequities produced by globalization, structural adjustment, privatization, etc.;

- the rise of extremist expressions of religious and/or nationalist "fundamentalisms" that threaten progress on women's rights around the world (including in the United States) in the name of various religions and cultures;

- the escalation of racist and sexist violence and terrorism in daily life and the growth of sexual and economic exploitation and trafficking of women across the globe;

- an increase in militarism, wars, internal conflicts, and terrorism, which are affecting or targeting civilians and involving more women and children in deadly ways.

Since 9/11 has been used to curtail human rights—including freedom of expression—in the name of "national security," it has added a greater sense of urgency to these concerns, but it has also made it more difficult to address them effectively from a feminist perspective.

Human vs. National Security

The call to redefine security in terms of human and ecological need instead of national sovereignty and borders was advancing pre-9/11 as an alternative to the state-centered concept of "national security," rooted in the military/security/defense domain and academically lodged in the field of international relations. For feminists this has meant raising questions about whose security "national security" defends, and addressing issues like the violence continuum that threatens women's security daily, during war as well as so-called peacetime.

The concept of human security had also advanced through the U.N.—first defined in the U.N. Development Program's 1994 Human Development Report and later taken up by Secretary General Kofi Annan in his Millennium Report in 2000, which spoke of security less as defending territory and more in terms of protecting people.

But efforts to promote the concept of human security—which emerged out of discussions in which women are active, from the peace movement and the debate over development—were set back by 9/11, with the subsequent resurgence of the masculine warrior discourse. The media have been dominated by male "authority" figures, providing a rude reminder that when it comes to issues of terrorism, war, defense, and national security, women, and especially feminists, are still not on the map.

Yet it is women who have been the major target of fundamentalist terrorism, from Algeria to the United States, over the past several decades. And it is mostly feminists who have led the critique of this growing global problem—focusing attention not only on Islamic fundamentalism but on Protestant fundamentalism in the United States, Catholic secret societies like Opus Dei in Latin America, Hindu right-wing fundamentalists in India, and so on.

The events of 9/11 should have generated attempts to address the very real threats to women's human rights posed by fundamentalism, terrorism, and armed conflict in many guises. Instead, the occasion was used to demonize the Islamic Other and to justify further militarization of society and curtailment of civil liberties. Growing militarization, often with U.S. support and arms, has brought an increase in military spending in many other regions, from India and Pakistan to Israel, Colombia, and the Philippines. Meanwhile, the Western donor countries' pledges to support economic development at the U.N. International Conference on Financing for Development in March 2002 fell far short of what would be needed to even begin to fulfill the millennium promises made in 2000 for advancing human security.

Thus, while human security is a promising concept, it is far from being embraced as a replacement for the national security paradigm to which governments remain attached and have made vast commitments.

September 11 and Human Rights

The excuse of 9/11 has been used not only to curtail human rights in the United States—which some here are challenging—but also around the world. The human rights system is in trouble when the U.S. government pulls out of global agreements like the ABM [Anti Ballistic Missile] treaty, aggressively works to undermine new instruments like the International Criminal Court, and says it is not bound by international commitments made by previous administrations, such as the Beijing Women's Conference Platform—parts of which its delegation renounced at the U.N. Commission on the Status of Women in March 2002. All international treaties and human rights conventions depend on the assumption that a country is bound by previous agreements and cannot simply jettison them with every change of administration. This erosion of respect for human rights also appears in the U.S. media, where some mainstream journalists have defended, as a necessary part of the war on terrorism,

the Bush Administration's defiance of international norms regarding political prisoners, and even suggested that the (selective) use of torture may be justified. These are the kinds of arguments put forward by governments that torture and abuse rights and are contrary to the most accepted tenets of human rights.

Indeed, the erosion of the U.S. commitment to human rights helps legitimize the abuses of governments that have never fully accepted or claimed these standards. For while the U.S. government has often been hypocritical in its human rights policies, open disregard for international standards goes a step further and thus strengthens fundamentalist governments and forces that seek to deny human rights in general, and the rights of women in particular.

Ironically, even as public discourse demonizes Islamic fundamentalists, the unholy alliance of the Vatican, Islamic fundamentalists, and right-wing U.S. forces is still working together when it comes to trying to defeat women's human rights. Feminists encountered this alliance in full force at the International Conference on Population and Development in Cairo (1994) and at the World Conference on Women at Beijing (1995), as well as during the five-year reviews of those events in 1999 and 2000. One need only look at the allies of the Bush Administration at the U.N. children's summit in May 2002—such as the Holy See, Sudan, Libya, Iraq, and other gulf states—to understand that this alliance is still functioning globally. We need to closely track the connections among various antifeminist "fundamentalist" forces, not only at the U.N. but in other arenas as well, such as in the making of world health policies, or even in the passage of anti–women's rights national legislation in countries where outside forces have played a key role.

A high-profile example of how the Bush Administration is seeking to weaken the U.N.'s role in protecting human rights was its effort to ensure that the U.N. High Commissioner for Human Rights, Mary Robinson, would not get a second term. She was among the first to frame her response to 9/11 from the perspective of international law, by suggesting that these acts of terrorism be prosecuted internationally as crimes against humanity rather than used as a call to war, but she was quickly sidelined. Because of this, along with her efforts to make the World Conference Against Racism a success in spite of the U.S. contempt for it, the Bush Administration adamantly opposed her reappointment. This opposition dovetailed with that of a number of other governments unhappy with her attention to their human rights abuses. Robinson is only one of the U.N. officials the Bush Administration has targeted in its efforts to purge the institution of its critics and anyone else promoting policies not to its liking.

The Bush Administration's policies post-9/11 have provided cover for other governments, such as China, Pakistan, Russia, and Egypt, to jettison even a rhetorical commitment to certain human rights in the name of fighting terrorism or providing for national security, or for some countries even in Europe it has been an opportunity simply to label issues like racism and violence against women as lower-priority concerns. This has a particular impact on women because it reverses the broadening of the human rights paradigm, which had begun to encompass issues like violence against women and to focus more on socioeconomic rights in the 1980s and '90s.

Women's rights advocates are still seen as the new kids on the human rights block. Feminists only recently won the recognition of women's rights as human rights, and that is now jeopardized even before those rights have been fully accepted and mechanisms for their protection institutionalized. The need to articulate a feminist approach to global security that ensures human rights and human security, and recognizes their interrelationship, is therefore more urgent than ever.

Challenges Ahead for Global Feminism

Women have transformed many aspects of life over the past forty years, and we all live differently because of it. Looking at the world in 2002, however, we have to ask what went wrong: Why have feminists not had a greater impact on global issues? How can we more effectively address current challenges like an increasingly militarized daily life, the rise in the political use of fundamentalism in every religion and region, and the widening economic gap between the haves and have-nots?

Often what American feminists must do to help women elsewhere is not to focus on their governments but to work to change ours so that U.S. policies and corporate forces based here stop harming women elsewhere. To do this, we need to engage in more serious discussion that crosses both the local/global and the activist/academic divides. If we look at women's movements over the past thirty to forty years, their strength has been in very rooted and diverse local bases of action as well as in the development of highly specific research and theory. There has also been rich global dialogue and networking among women across national lines over the past two decades. But in the United States these discourses rarely intersect.

Because the local/national/domestic and the global/international are mostly seen as separate spheres, we often have trouble determining what local actions will have the greatest impact globally. Thus, for example, there has been little interest here in using international human rights treaties like the Convention on the Elimination of All Forms of Discrimination Against Women (CEDAW), to advance domestic issues. There is a tendency not to see the international arena as adding anything to causes at home. But just as women's global networking and international solidarity have helped sustain feminist activists who are isolated in their home countries, U.S. feminists can benefit from the support of women elsewhere, which we will need if we are to challenge what is now openly defended as the American Empire.

Women's activism in the United States must be both local and global to succeed. We must grapple with the dynamic tension between the universality and specificity of our work. Only through such a process can feminists address not only the needs of each situation but also the larger global structures creating many of these conflicts. Then we can move toward an affirmative vision of peace with human rights and human security at its core, rather than continue to clean up after the endless succession of male-determined crises and conflicts. This is our challenge.

EIGHTY-THREE

◆◆◆

The Global Women's Movement: Definitions and Origins (2004)

Peggy Antrobus

Peggy Antrobus is an economist, teacher, researcher, and organizer whose work focuses on women in development. She set up the Women and Development Unit at the University of the West Indies in 1987 and was a founding member of the Caribbean Association for Feminist Research and Action (CAFRA). She was a founding member of DAWN, the network of Third World women promoting Development Alternatives with Women for a New Era, and DAWN's Coordinator (1990–1996).

...This [article] attempts to answer the questions: Is there a global women's movement? How can we understand such a movement? How can it be defined, and what are its characteristics? My conclusion is that there is a global women's movement . . . different from other social movements and . . . defined by diversity, its feminist politics and perspectives, its global reach and its methods of organizing.

Definitions

Many authors admit that this movement does not conform to conventional definitions of a "movement" lacking as it does common objectives, continuity, unity and coordination. Yet this should not surprise us, nor should it be taken as a sign of deficiency. . . . Only a few activists take the view that the objectives of the women's movement are similar to those of labour, human rights and student groups, which seek justice for their members. Many see the objectives of women's groups as broader, seeking changes in relationships that are more varied and complex. At the same time it is sometimes difficult to identify clear objectives; worse, the objectives articulated by some groups seem to contradict those of others. The following quotes from [a] Nigerian case study illustrate the problem:

> The Nigerian women's movement is an unarmed movement. It is non-confrontational. It is a movement for the progressive upliftment

of women for motherhood, nationhood and development.[1]

And again:

> When African women demand equality, we are only asking for our rights not to be tampered with, and the removal of laws that oppress and dehumanize women. We are not asking for equality with our husbands. We accept them as the bosses and heads of the family.[2]

The confusion and contradictions captured in these statements reflect the complexity of a movement that is caught in the tension between what is possible and what is dreamed of, between short-term goals and long-term visions, between expediency and risk-taking, pragmatism and surrender, between the practical and the strategic. Most of all, there is understandable ambivalence surrounding challenging and confronting relationships that are intimate and deeply felt. But the confusion also reflects a lack of clarity about definitions of what groups might be considered part of a "women's movement."

Many activists, including Nigerian activists who identify themselves with a women's movement, would question definitions of the objectives of their movement in terms of the "upliftment of women for motherhood, nationhood and development." They would argue that this instrumentalizes women, while being in complete accord with patriarchal definitions of women's traditional role.

It seems to me that the continuing confusion about what defines women's movements relates not so much to the fact that this movement does not conform to a conventional definition of a movement, but rather to lack of clarity about objectives in contexts that differ widely.

One way of clarifying these apparent contradictions is to recognize two mutually reinforcing tendencies within women's movements—one focused on gender identity (identity politics) and the other concerned with a large project for social transformation. There are two entry points to concerns about a larger social project. One is recognition of the centrality of the care and nurture of human beings to the large social project, and that to address this, given the primacy of women's gendered role in this area, requires addressing gender relations in all the complex interplay of their economic, social, political, cultural and personal dimensions. It also involves locating gender inequality within other forms of inequality that shape and often exacerbate it.

Another entry point is recognition that women cannot be separated from the larger context of their lived experience and that this includes considerations of class, race/ethnicity and geographic location, among other factors. This means that the struggle for women's agency must include engagement in struggles against sources of women's oppression that extend beyond gender.

The larger social project would therefore include transforming social institutions, practices and beliefs so that they address gender relations along with other oppressive relationships, not simply seeking a better place within existing institutions and structures. For this reason, women's movements in countries where the majority of women are marginalized by class, race or ethnicity must be concerned with the larger social project. This is often a point of tension between women's movements in the context of North–South relations, as well as in the context of struggles against oppression on the basis of class, race and ethnicity.

I believe that confusion about definitions of women's movements is also caused by failure to make distinctions between women's organizations as part of a wide spectrum of non-governmental organizations (NGOs) or civil society organizations (CSOs), and those that might be better understood as part of a politically oriented social movement.

Similarly, the term "women's movements" is sometimes used interchangeably with "feminist movements," an error that confuses and misrepresents both feminism and the broad spectrum of women's organizations.

In the final analysis, it seems to me that the identification of feminist politics as the engine of women's movements may help to clarify some of the confusion around women's organizing . . . as well as to focus the answer to the central question: Can women's movements make a difference in the struggle for equity, democracy and sustainability in today's globalized economy? It is the combination of struggles for gender justice with those for economic justice and democracy that enables women's movements to make a difference to the larger social project for transformation of systems and relationships.

An important segment of women's movements is composed of the associations that work to incorporate a feminist perspective into their theoretical, analytical, professional and political work. In academia, most disciplines now have feminist associations—Anthropology, Economics, Political, Social and Natural Sciences and Theology, among others. Moreover, within these disciplines—whether women are organized into feminist associations or not—women in the academies are doing important theoretical and empirical work that deepens our understanding of women's realities and produces the analyses and insights that strengthen the work of activists.

In the professions there are also women's associations—doctors, nurses, midwives, social workers, teachers, lawyers, bankers etc.—that are challenging patriarchal patterns and relationships, raising new questions and changing the practices and methods by which their professions operate.

Many women's organizations, even those that focus on traditional concerns of home and family, are nevertheless important participants in women's movements. Among these are grassroots women's organizations of various kinds—Women's Institutes, Federations of Women, the YWCA, and many worldwide organizations identified with strong advocacy on behalf of women's rights, although they may not describe themselves as feminist.[3]

Finally, a definition of a women's movement must include those individual women who would never join an organization, nor define themselves as feminists, but whose lives and actions nevertheless serve to advance the liberation of women in their community and beyond.

All of these women must be seen as part of, or at least contributing to, women's movements. They are all part of the diversity and richness of a movement that seeks change in the relationships of superiority and inferiority, domination and subordination between women and men in a patriarchal world.

The following statements summarize my own views on women's movements:

- A women's movement is a *political* movement—part of the broad array of social movements concerned with changing social conditions . . .

- A women's movement is grounded in an understanding of women's relations to *social conditions*—an understanding of gender as an important relationship within the broad structure of social relationships of class, race and ethnicity, age and location.

- A women's movement is a *process*, discontinuous, flexible, responding to specific conditions of perceived gender inequality or gender-related injustice. Its focal points may be in women's organizations, but it embraces individual women in various locations who identify with the goals of feminism at a particular point in time.

- Awareness and *rejection of patriarchal privilege* and control are central to the politics of women's movements.

- In most instances, the "movement" is born at the moments in which individual women become aware of *their separateness as women*, their alienation, marginalization, isolation or even abandonment within a broader movement for social justice or social change. In other words, women's struggle for agency within the broader struggle is the catalyst for women's movements.

bell hooks describes this process of *conscientization* thus:

> Our search leads us back to where it all began, to that moment when an individual woman ... who may have thought she was all alone, began a feminist uprising, began to name her practice, indeed began to formulate theory from lived experience.[4]

Women from across the world who identify themselves as part of an international and global women's movement are to be found participating in international meetings organized by feminist associations, networks and organizations such as the International Inter-disciplinary Congress, the Association for Women's Rights and Development (AWID) and UN conferences.[5] They celebrate annual special "days" such as International Women's Day (IWD) on 8 March and International Day Against Violence Against Women on 25 November. They are in constant communication with each other through the Internet, where they sign petitions and statements in solidarity with women around the world, formulate strategies and organize campaigns and meetings.

The movement has important resources:

- resource centers such as the International Women's Tribune Centre (IWTC), set up following the 1975 International Women's Year (IWY) Conference in Mexico City;

- media, such as feminist radio stations like the Costa Rica-based FIRE (Feminist International Radio Endeavor); news services like WINGS (Women's International News Gathering Service) and Women's Feature Services (WFS), supported initially by UNESCO;

- websites;

- publishers and women's presses;

- artists ... —filmmakers, musicians, dancers, painters, writers, poets and playwrights;

- women's funds started by individual philanthropists and organizations that support women's projects, organizations and networks.

Characteristics

Diversity

Experience of the past thirty years points to the pitfall of starting with an assumption of a "global sisterhood," especially when that "sisterhood" is defined by a privileged minority. The emergence of a global movement has indeed depended on the emergence of new and different voices challenging hegemonic tendencies and claiming their own voice and space, and the acceptance of differences within the movements.

Diversity is now recognized as perhaps the most important characteristic of women's movements. Nevertheless, many of the tensions among women in their movements can be related to differences of race/ethnicity, nationality/culture and class, although, as Audre Lorde points out:

> [I]t is not those differences between us that are separating us. It is rather our refusal to recognize [them] and to examine the distortions which result from our misnaming them and their effects upon human behaviour and expectation.[6]

She also reminds us, "There is no such thing as a single-issue struggle because we do not live single-issue lives."[7] Women understand that each of us has multiple identities and that at any point in time one or other may be more important than others. Insistence on focusing on gender in isolation from issues like race, ethnicity and class has often been more divisive than the inclusion of these issues in the agendas of the various movements. It is indeed impossible and even counterproductive to separate the varied forms of oppression because of the systemic links between them. Thus in many countries of the South women have had to confront colonialism, imperialism or racism before they could confront patriarchy.

Feminist Politics

It may be useful to identify feminism as a specific politics, grounded in a consciousness of all the sources of women's subordination, and with a commitment to challenge and change the relationships and structures which perpetuate women's subordinate position, in solidarity with other women. The consciousness of sexism and sexist oppression is the essence of feminist politics, and it is this politics that energizes women's movements, whether or not the word "feminist" is used. It is possible then to identify feminist politics as a specific element within a broader universe of women's organizations, women's movements and other social movements.

Feminists have worked with and within other social movements—especially those on peace, racism, the environment, indigenous peoples and the poor. These initiatives have served both to broaden and redefine the issues of concern to women, as well as to refocus the agendas of these movements.

In addition, there are feminists within institutions and agencies who recognize the ways in which the ideology of patriarchy constrains and diminishes the achievement of laudable goals and objectives, and who engage in the struggle to challenge it.

Feminist politics can also be identified within bureaucratic initiatives and institutional arrangements established for the improvement of the condition and position of women, enabling them to contribute to the movement for gender justice. These include women's bureaus, desks, commissions, special units and gender focal points within mainstream institutions.

Global Reach

Our understanding of the diversity within women's movements that has led us to speak more often of a multiplicity of "movements" would lead many to question the concept of a single global women's movement. However, I would argue, as others have done, that despite the rich diversity of experience, grounded in specific local struggles, women have been able to transcend these to become a movement of global proportions, with a global agenda and perspective.

Here I want to distinguish between an international women's movement and a global women's movement.[8] Although, as Uta Ruppert has pointed out, local or national women's movements have never viewed their activities as "simply crossing the borders of nation states,"[9] I would conceptualize an "international" movement as one in which the national and cultural differences between women were recognizable and paramount. Indeed, this was characteristic of women's movements at the international level in the mid-1970s, at the launching of the UN Decade for Women (1975–85), and to some extent throughout most of the Decade. However, as women established their separate identities along the prevailing axes of North–South, East–West, they discovered commonalities that moved them increasingly towards greater coherence and even common positions in the policy debates around issues of environment, poverty, violence and human rights. At the same time, as these issues became increasingly "global" (as reflected in the themes and agendas of the global conferences of the 1990s), women's movements converged in these global arenas to negotiate and articulate common agendas and positions. As Ruppert puts it:

> The political process of international women's movements has been shaped by the insight that international politics does not simply take place at the inter-nation-state level, but also encompasses multicentric and multilevel processes. Thus the movement's multidimensional political understanding, which is sensitive to differences, almost predestined it to become the most global of social movements of the 1990s.[10]

She goes on to identify:

> [A] second component . . . essential for the women's movement to become an effective global actor, [which] was the movement's shift toward aiming for "globality" as a main objective. Even though there has never been an explicit discourse along these lines, the movement's political practice suggests a conceptual differentiation between three different political approaches on the global level: criticizing and combating globalization as a neoliberal paradigm; utilizing global politics, or rather global governance, as tools for governance under the conditions of globalization; and specifically creating "globality,"[11] which the women's movement has aimed for and worked towards as an important factor in women's global politics.[12]

Methods of Organizing

It is widely understood that a characteristic of a global women's movement is the linking of local to global, the particularities of local experience and struggles to, as Ruppert says, "the political creation and establishment of global norms for world development and global ethics for industrial production, such as (social and gender) justice, sustainability and peace, based on the creation of globally valid fundamental human rights."[13] However, few have related this to the particular methods of feminist organizing.

Although . . . this practice has not been the subject of an explicit discourse, it has nevertheless been based on conscious decisions to involve women from different backgrounds and regions in the search for "globality." These decisions have been the result of an understanding of the ways in which global events, trends and policies impact on local experience, and in particular on the experiences of poor women in the global South.

While Ruppert and others cite women's organizing around the 1992 UN Conference on Environment and Development (UNCED) and the 1993 International Conference on Human Rights as the first signs of this kind of organizing, I would refer to the experience of the network of Third World women, DAWN,[14] in their preparations for the Forum of the 1985 Third World Conference on Women. It was here that a conscious attempt was made to bring together local and regional experiences

as the beginning of a process for the preparation of a platform document for a global event.

. . . The starting point was a meeting at which women were invited to reflect on their experience of development over the course of the Decade for Women—from the perspective of poor women living in the economic South. In this way the final document reflected regional differences, even as it reached for a framework that revealed the linkages between these experiences. This process—which starts with testifying to local, regional, or even individual experiences ("telling our stories," "speaking our truths"), leading to the negotiation of differences and finally to the articulation of a position that attempts to generalize, synthesize or "globalize" the diversity of experience—was repeated in the processes leading to the global conferences on environment, human rights and population. . . .

This methodology, clearly related to that of feminist consciousness-raising and Freirian *conscientization*[15] (combining reflection on personal experience with socio-political analysis to construct and generate global advocacy) has been a powerful tool for the global women's movement. Like *conscientization*, which takes specific realities "on the ground" as the basis for social analysis that can lead to action, it is a *praxis* (process of reflection and action) that has helped to mobilize women to challenge neoliberal and fundamentalist state policies at national and global levels. This praxis has also been a powerful tool in feminist theorizing.

To drive home one of the differences between international women's movements and a global women's movement, I want to compare this feminist method of globalizing to the process of regional meetings and consultations used by the UN in the preparation of their international conferences. The documents that feed into and emerge from these processes have to be screened and sanctioned by governments and, by their very nature, are limited in the degree to which they are able to reflect the realities of women. While the plans and platforms of action that emerge from the conferences contain many recommendations and resolutions that accord with the advocacy of women's movements, they often lack the coherence and clarity of the platforms produced by a movement unrestrained by the conventions of international diplomacy. Moreover, without the vigilance and political activism of women's movements, especially at local or national, but also at global, levels, these recommendations are meaningless to women.

This brings me to another aspect of the links between global and local—the ways in which local actors organize to defend themselves against global threats. Recognizing the relationship between global trends and local realities, women are organizing around the defence of their bodies, their livelihoods and their communities. The word "glocality" has been coined to highlight the ways in which global trends affect local experience. This recognition of a "politics of place" poses new challenges to a global women's movement. While organizing in the defence of "place" has the potential to be the most powerful and effective form of organizing,[16] local groups clearly need information and analysis on the broader policy frameworks that are affecting their lives. A global women's movement also needs links to this level of organizing to retain its relevance and to legitimize its advocacy.

The global women's movement is very aware that action at global level must have resonance at local, national and regional levels if it is to be meaningful to women. In this sense we need to see the global women's movement as made up of many interlocking networks. Many of the global networks have worked to strengthen their links to activities at regional, national and local levels.

A second method of organizing . . . is networking. Some may say that women's movements invented networking! Networking is the method used to make the vertical (local–global) as well as the horizontal (inter-regional as well as issue-specific) links that generate the analysis and the organizing underlying global action.

A third is the linking of the personal to the political, the ways in which gender identification and recognition of common experience can short-circuit difference to create a sense of solidarity. This often makes it easier for women who are strangers to each other to work together.

Symbols and Images

In the final analysis, words may not be enough to enable us to understand the complexity of a global women's movement made up of such a diversity of movements. . . . I have often been struck by the ways in which images and symbols capture the shape and structure of a global women's movement. The images and symbols that come to mind are those of the spiral, the wheel, the pyramid, the web and the patchwork quilt.

A spiral is an open-ended circle. As an adjective it is a "winding about a centre in an enlarging or decreasing continuous cone." As a noun, "a plane or three-dimensional spiral curve" (*Concise Oxford Dictionary*, 1990). In both cases it captures images of continuity and change, depth and expansion—something that is identifiable yet varied.

. . . A spiral is open-ended, continuous, ever enlarging our understanding of events, our perspectives. The global women's movement can be thought of as a spiral, a process that starts at the centre (rather than at the beginning of a line) and works its way outwards, turning, arriving at what might appear to be the same point, but in reality at an expanded understanding of the same event.

A spiral is also dialectic, allowing for the organic growth of a movement of women organizing—a movement in a state of on-going evolution as consciousness expands in the process of exchanges between women, taking us backwards (to rethink and reevaluate old positions) and forwards (to new areas of awareness).

As a number of interlocking networks, a global women's movement might also be likened to pyramids, webs and wheels. In a study of two campaigns, the campaign against breast-milk substitutes in Ghana, and against child labour in the carpet industry in India, the New Economics Foundation (NEF) identified

> three structures for organizing constructive collaboration: the pyramid, the wheel, and the web. Pyramids have a coordinating secretariat who disseminates information through the campaign; wheels have one or more focal points for information exchange, but information also flows directly among the members; in the web, no focal point exist, so information flows to and from all the members in roughly equal quantities.[17]

The pyramid, the wheel and the web underline the fluidity of the global women's movement, comprised as it is of interlocking networks that come together as appropriate, even as each continues to focus on its specific area of interest.

The movement can also be understood as a patchwork quilt, full of colour and different patterns, discontinuous and defying description, but none the less an identifiable entity made up of units that have their own integrity. A quilt, an art form peculiarly developed by women, uses whatever material is available to make something both beautiful and functional. It represents ingenuity, creativity, caring and comfort. A global women's movement can have no better symbol as it seeks to create a world in which people might find beauty, comfort and security.

Origins

Since the concept of a global women's movement conceals the actors who make it possible, I turn now to consider some of the contexts that energized the local struggles out of which a global movement was formed. Reference is often made to "three waves" of the women's movement: the first wave of the late 19th–early 20th century, the second covering the mid-20th century, and the third, the late 20th century. Although these waves are often depicted as distinct, it is instructive to look at the connections between them because, as Gita Sen points out:

> They delineate in an early form potential strengths as well as tensions that characterize the international women's movement right until today. The presence of multiple strands from early on has made for a movement that is broad and capable of addressing a wide range of issues. But the potential tensions between prioritizing economic issues (such as control over resources and property) or women's personal autonomy or bodily integrity existed then and continue to exist now.[18]

Conclusion

It is clear that, despite the lack of clear and common objectives, continuity, unity and coordination, . . . there is nevertheless an identifiable movement enriched by its diversity and complexity, sustained by the depth of its passions and enduring commitment to its causes, and strengthened by the apparent lack of coordination and spontaneity of its strategizing.

Varied experiences highlight the complexity of women's struggles, the interplay between race, class and gender and the need to distinguish between the material and the ideological relations of gender.

There are many roads to the awareness that manifests as involvement in a women's organization or identification as part of a women's movement. There are still more steps towards a feminist consciousness, which would transform involvement in a women's organization into a political struggle for gender equity and equality, often within a broader project for social transformation. Many of the women involved in women's organizations, or movements, were influenced by leftist politics, and discovered their own marginalization within the processes of these struggles. Others began the journey to feminist consciousness through personal experiences; still others through their work experience. A characteristic of many of those involved in women's movements is the process of personal transformation which they undergo as they become aware of gender subordination. At the same time, this essentially individualistic experience seems to engender a connection to the wider universe of injustice in a way that leads to a better understanding of the link between different forms of oppression and builds life-long commitments to the struggle against injustice.

Given these histories, there is no doubt that there is a global women's movement, recognizable in its understanding of how "common difference"[19] links us all in a political struggle for recognition and redistributive justice. Its difference from other social movements lies not only in the absence of homogeneity . . . but in the value it places on diversity, its commitment to solidarity with women everywhere, its feminist politics and its methods of organizing.

. . . as an important global actor in the struggles for a more equitable, humane, sustainable and secure world.

NOTES

1. Interview with representatives of the National Commission for Women, Abuja, 2 February 1993, Amrita Basu (ed.) *The challenge of local feminism: Women's movements in global perspective.* Boulder: Westview Press. (1995), p. 211.

2. Interview with Obiageli Nwankwo, project coordinator, International Federation of Women Lawyers, Enugu, 1993, Basu (1995), p. 212.

3. However, there may be self-defined feminists among their members.

4. bell hooks, 1994. *Teaching to transgress*. New York: Routledge, p. 75.

5. Although UN conferences are also attended by women and organizations that are opposed to advances in women's human rights, as was seen at the Five-Year-Review of the Fourth World Conference on Women, when the call went out from right-wing religion-based organizations for women to come to New York to "defend" women against that "dangerous" document, the Beijing *Platform for Action*.

6. Audre Lorde, *Sister Outsider: Essays and Speeches by Audre Lorde*. Freedom, Calif.: Crossing Press. p. 115.

7. Ibid., p. 138.

8. In thinking about this distinction I have found Uta Ruppert's analysis extremely helpful in M. Braig and S. Wolte (eds.) 2002. *Common ground or mutual exclusion? Women's movements and international relations*. New York: Zed Books.

9. Ibid., p. 148.

10. Ibid., p. 149.

11. Ruppert defines *globality* as "everything global politics or global governance should be based on or directly accompanied by" (ibid., p. 151).

12. Ibid., p. 151.

13. Ibid, p. 151.

14. The Network of Third World women promoting Development Alternatives with Women for a New Era. www.dawn.org.fj.

15. The combination of consciousness and action, "praxis," introduced by Brazilian educator, Paolo Freire, to enable oppressed groups to gain an understanding of the forces impinging on their world, the sources of their oppression.

16. Examples abound. The work of the Chipko movements and of the Self-Employed Women's Association (India) come to mind because they are so well-documented; however, there are examples of this kind of organizing in every region.

17. Jennifer Chapman. 2001. What makes international campaigns effective? Lessons from India and Ghana. In *Global citizen action*, edited by M. Edwards and J. Gaventa, Boulder: Lynne Rienner Publishers, pp. 263–64.

18. Gita Sen. 2003. The politics of the international women's movement. In *Claiming global power: Transnational civil society and global governance*, edited by Srilatha Batliwala and David Brown. Kumarian Press.

19. Gloria Joseph and Jill Lewis. 1986. *Common differences: Conflicts in Black and White feminist perspectives*. Boston: South End Press.

Glossary

GLOSSARY OF TERMS IN COMMON USE

This glossary contains many of the key concepts found in this book. The first time the concept is used in the text it is shown in **bold**. Refer to the definitions here to refresh your memory when you come across the terms again later.

able-bodyism—Attitudes, actions, and institutional practices that subordinate people with disabilities.

adultism—Attitudes, actions, and institutional practices that subordinate young people on the basis of their age.

ageism—Attitudes, actions, and institutional practices that subordinate elderly persons on the basis of their age.

alliance—Working with others, as a result of a deepening understanding of one another's lives, experiences, and goals.

analytical framework—A theoretical perspective that allows one to analyze the causes and implications of a particular issue, rather than simply describing it.

anti-Semitism—Attitudes, actions, and institutional practices that subordinate Jewish people (the term *Semite* is used also to refer to some Arabs).

biological determinism—A general theory holding that a group's biological or genetic makeup shapes its social, political, and economic destiny.

This view is used to justify women's subordination, or the subordination of peoples of color on the argument that they are biologically or genetically different from, and usually inferior to, men or White people.

capitalism—An economic system in which most of the **capital**—property, raw materials, and the means of production (including people's labor)—and goods produced are owned or controlled by individuals or groups—capitalists. The goal of all production is to maximize profit making. Also referred to as **free market system.**

classism—Attitudes, actions, and institutional practices that subordinate working-class and poor people on the basis of their economic condition.

coalition—Usually a short-term collaboration of organizations in which the strategy is to stand together to achieve a specific goal or set of goals around a particular issue, regardless of other differences among the organizations.

commodification—The process of turning people into things, or commodities, for sale; an example is the commodification of women's bodies through advertising and media representations.

comparable worth—A method of evaluating jobs that are traditionally defined as men's work or women's work—in terms of the knowledge and skills required for a particular job; the mental demands or decision making involved; the accountability or degree of supervision involved; and working conditions, such as how physically safe the job is—so as to eliminate inequities in pay based on gender.

conscientization—A methodology for understanding reality, or gaining a "critical consciousness," through group dialogue, critical analysis, and examination of people's experiences and conditions that face them, which leads to action to transform that reality (Freire 1989).

contested terrain—An area of debate or controversy, in which several individuals or groups attempt to impose their own views or meanings on a situation.

criminalization—The process of turning people's circumstances or behaviors into a crime, such as the criminalization of homeless people or mothers with HIV/AIDS.

cultural appropriation—Taking possession of specific aspects of another group's culture in a gratuitous, inauthentic way, as happens, for example, when White people wear their hair in "dreads" or when nonindigenous people use indigenous people's names and symbols or adopt indigenous people's spiritual practices without being taught by indigenous practitioners. A particularly egregious form of cultural appropriation involves using another group's culture to make money. This is routine in the tourist industry, and it also occurs in the "New Age" spirituality movement, for example.

cultural relativism—The view that all "authentic" experience is equally valid and cannot be challenged by others. For example, White-supremacist views of Ku Klux Klan members are seen to be equally as valid as those held by antiracist activists. There are no external standards or principles by which to judge people's attitudes and behaviors.

culture—The values, symbols, means of expression, language, and interests of a group of people. The **dominant culture** includes the values, symbols, means of expression, language, and interests of people in power in this society.

discrimination—Differential treatment against less powerful groups (such as women, the elderly, or people of color) by those in positions of dominance.

ecofeminism—A philosophy that links the domination of women with the domination of nature.

ecological footprint—The amount of land and energy required by various lifestyles and levels of development; calculated by estimating the amount of productive land needed to provide food, housing, transport, and consumer goods and services, and to absorb the waste that results from these processes; expressed in hectares or acres.

environmental racism—The strong correlation between the distribution of environmental pollution, including toxic wastes, and race; the movement for **environmental justice** draws on concepts of civil rights, whereby all citizens have a right to healthy living and working conditions.

essentialism—The view that people have some inherent essence, or characteristics and qualities, that define them. Some people argue, for example, that women are essentially more caring and nurturing than men.

eugenics—The White-supremacist belief that the human race can be "improved" through selective breeding.

feminization of poverty—Women and children constitute the vast majority of poor people in the United States and throughout the world, a result of structural inequalities and discriminatory policies.

fertility rate—The number of children born to women between 15 and 54, considered by official census reports to be the childbearing years.

first-wave feminism—Organizations and projects undertaken by suffragists and women's rights advocates from the 1840s until 1920 when women in the United States won the vote.

free market system—An ideological term used to describe a capitalist economic system with an emphasis on transnational trade and freedom from government regulation. In reality, this system has both government regulation of and support for businesses.

gender bending—Adopting clothing, body language, or behavior that challenges and undermines conventional gender norms and expectations.

gendered division of labor—A division of duties between men and women under which women have the main responsibility for home and nurturing and men are mainly active in the public sphere. Also referred to as **gender roles**.

gender gap—A significant difference between the political attitudes and voting patterns of women and men.

gender socialization—The process of learning the attitudes and behaviors that are considered culturally appropriate for boys or girls.

glass ceiling—An unseen barrier to women's promotion to senior positions in the workplace. Women can see the senior positions in their company or field, but few women reach them because of negative attitudes toward senior women and low perceptions of their abilities and training.

global level of analysis—A term used to describe the connections among people institutions, and issues as viewed from a worldwide perspective.

heterosexism—Attitudes, actions, and institutional practices that subordinate people on the basis of their gay, lesbian, bisexual, or transgender orientation and identification.

imperialism—The process of domination of one nation over other nations that are deemed inferior and to have dependent status for the purpose of exploiting their human and natural resources, to consolidate its power and wealth. An empire is able to draw resources from many nations and to deploy those governments and territories in its interest. Examples include the Roman empire, the British empire, and the current U.S. empire.

identity-based politics—Activism and politics that have a strong identity component but also a broader view that allows people to make connections to other groups and issues.

identity politics—Activism and politics that put identity at the center. It usually involves the assumption that a particular characteristic, such as race, ethnicity, or sexual orientation, is the most important in the lives of group members and that the group is not differentiated according to other characteristics in any significant way.

ideology—Ideas, attitudes, and values that represent the interests of a group of people. The dominant ideology comprises the ideas, attitudes, and values that represent the interests of the dominant group(s). Thus, for example, the ideological role of the idealized nuclear family is to devalue other family forms.

internalized oppression—Attitudes and behavior of some oppressed people that reflect the negative, harmful, stereotypical beliefs of the dominant group directed at them. An example of internalized sexism is the view of some women that they and other women are inferior to men, which causes them to adopt attitudes and behaviors that reinforce the oppression of women.

international division of labor—A division of work between rich and poor countries under which low-waged workers in the global South do assembly, manufacturing, and office work on contract to companies based in the global North.

intersectionality—An integrative perspective that emphasizes the intersection of several attributes, for example, gender, race, class, and nation.

liberal feminism—A philosophy that sees the oppression of women as a denial of equal rights, representation, and access to opportunities.

macro level of analysis—A term used to describe the relationships among issues, individuals, and groups as viewed from a national institutional perspective.

marginality—The situation in which a person has a deep connection to more than one culture, community, or social group but is not completely able to identify with or be accepted by that group as an insider. For example, bisexual, mixed-race/ mixed-culture, and immigrant peoples have connections with separate groups and often find themselves caught between two or more social worlds.

marginalization—Attitudes and behaviors that relegate certain people to the social, political, and economic margins of society by branding them and their interests as inferior, unimportant, or both.

matrix of oppression and resistance—The interconnections among various forms of oppression based on gender, race, class, nation, and so on. These social attributes can be sources of disadvantage as well as privilege. Negative ascriptions and experiences may be the source of people's resistance to oppression.

medicalization—The process of turning life processes, like childbirth or menopause, into medical issues. Thus, menopause becomes an illness to be treated by medical professionals with formal educational qualifications and accreditation. By the same token, experienced midwives are considered unqualified because they lack these credentials.

meso level of analysis—A term used to describe the relationships among issues, individuals, and groups as viewed from a community, or local, perspective.

micro level of analysis—A term used to describe the connections among people and issues as seen from a personal or individual perspective.

militarism—A system and worldview based on the objectification of "others" as enemies, a culture that prepares for, invests in, and celebrates war and killing. This worldview operates through specific political, economic, and military institutions and actions.

militarized masculinity—A masculinity constructed to support militarism, with an emphasis on heroism, physical strength, lack of emotion, and appearance of invulnerability (Enloe 1990, 1993a).

misogyny—Woman-hating attitudes and behavior.

neocolonialism—Continuing economic inequalities between rich and poor countries that originated in colonial relationships.

neoliberal/neoliberalism—economic philosophy and policies that call for the freedom of business to operate with minimal interference from governments, international organizations, or labor unions. Basic tenets include the rule of the market, global free trade, economic deregulation, privatization of government-owned industries (e.g., banks, highways, schools, utilities, postal service), reduction of social welfare spending, and belief in individual responsibility rather than valuing community and the public good. Termed "neo" liberal because it calls for a return to the free-market philosophy that prevailed in the U.S. through the 1800s and early 1900s prior to the enhanced role of government that gained legitimacy during the Depression (1930s), culminating in the "War on Poverty" and other "Great Society" programs of the 1960s.

objectification—Attitudes and behaviors by which people are treated as if they were "things." One example is the objectification of women through advertising images.

objectivity—A form of understanding in which knowledge and meaning are believed to come from outside oneself and are presumably not affected by personal opinion or bias.

offshore production—Factory work or office work performed outside the United States—for example, in Mexico, the Philippines, or Indonesia—that is done for U.S.-based companies.

oppression—Prejudice and discrimination directed toward whole socially recognized groups of people and promoted by the ideologies and practices of all social institutions. The critical elements differentiating oppression from simple prejudice and discrimination are that it is a group phenomenon and that institutional power and authority are used to support prejudices and enforce discriminatory behaviors in systematic ways. Everyone is socialized to participate in oppressive practices, either as direct and indirect perpetrators or passive beneficiaries, or—as with some oppressed peoples—by directing discriminatory behaviors at members of one's own group or another group deemed inferior. See **internalized oppression.**

paradigm shift—A complete change in one's view of the world.

patriarchy—A family, social group, or society in which men hold power and are dominant figures. Patriarchal power in the United States plays out in the family, the economy, the media, religion, law, and electoral politics.

peer marriage—An intentionally egalitarian marriage with an emphasis on partnership, cooperation, and shared roles that are not highly differentiated along gender lines.

postcolonial feminism—A perspective that critiques Western imperialism and imperialist tendencies of Western feminism, and emphasizes historically defined colonial power relations that provide a foundational context for women's lives and struggles for change.

postmodern feminism—A type of feminism that repudiates the broad-brush "universal" theorizing of liberalism, radical feminism, or socialism, and emphasizes the particularity of women's experiences in specific cultural and historical contexts.

poverty level—An income level for individuals and families that officially defines poverty.

power—The ability to influence others, whether through persuasion, charisma, law, political activism, or coercion. Power operates informally and through formal institutions and at all levels (micro, meso, macro, global).

power elite—A relatively small group—not always easily identifiable—of key politicians, senior corporate executives, the very rich, and opinion makers such as key media figures who influence political and economic decisions in the country. Although this group shifts over time, and according to the issue, it is relatively closed.

praxis—Reflection and action upon the world in order to transform it; a key part of socially lived theorizing.

precautionary principle—the view that when an activity raises threats of harm to human health or the environment, precautionary measures should be taken even if some cause and effect relationships are not fully established scientifically. Those proposing the activity should bear the burden of proof rather than the public.

prejudice—A closed-minded prejudging of a person or group as negative or inferior, even without personal knowledge of that person or group, and often contrary to reason or facts; unreasonable, unfair, and hostile attitudes toward people.

privilege—Benefits and power from institutional inequalities. Individuals and groups may be privileged without realizing, recognizing, or even wanting it.

public vs. private dichotomy—The view that distinguishes between the private and personal (dating, marriage, sexual habits, who does the housework, relationships between parents and children) and the public (religion, law, business). Although these two spheres affect each other, according to this view they are governed by different rules, attitudes, and behavior.

racism—Racial prejudice and discrimination that are supported by institutional power and authority. In the United States, racism is based on the ideology of White (European) superiority and is used to the advantage of White people and the disadvantage of peoples of color.

radical feminism—A philosophy that sees the oppression of women in terms of patriarchy, a system of male authority, especially manifested in sexuality, personal relationships, and the family, and carried into the male-dominated world of work, government, religion, media, and law.

reproduction of labor—Unpaid domestic work, usually performed by women, in producing, nurturing, and socializing the next generation of workers and citizens; caring for adult members by providing meals and clean clothes, as well as rest, relaxation, love, and sexual intimacy, so that they are ready to face another working day.

second shift—Responsibilities for household chores and child care after having already done a full day's work outside the home, mostly done by women.

second-wave feminism—Feminist projects and organizations from the late 1960s to the mid-1980s that campaigned for women's equality in all spheres of life and, in some cases, that argued for a complete transformation of patriarchal, capitalist structures. See **liberal feminism, radical feminism, socialist feminism.**

separatism—The process of creating a separate life-space, often for political purposes, such as White lesbian separatists in the 1970s who chose to live in community with other women, to work with women, and to support women's projects. Some people of color may also advocate separatism from White people, institutions, values, and culture, and decide to put their energies only in support of other people of color.

sexism—Attitudes, actions, and institutional practices that subordinate women because of their gender.

situated knowledge—Knowledge and ways of knowing that are specific to a particular historical and cultural context and life experiences.

social constructionism—The view that concepts that appear to be immutable and often solely biological, such as gender, race, and sexual orientation, are defined by human beings and can vary, depending on cultural and historical contexts. On this view, for example, heterosexuality is something learned—socially constructed—not innate. The "normalcy" of heterosexuality is systematically transmitted, and appropriate attitudes and behaviors are learned through childhood socialization, life experiences, and reinforced through institutional norms, policies, and law.

social control—Attitudes, behaviors, and mechanisms that keep people in their place. Overt social controls include laws, fines, imprisonment, and violence. Subtle ones include ostracism and withdrawal of status, affection, and respect.

social institutions—Institutions such as the family, education, the media, organized religion, law, and government.

socialist—Someone who believes that work should be organized for the collective benefit of workers rather than the profit of managers and corporate owners, and that the state should prioritize human needs.

socialist feminism—A view that sees the oppression of women in terms of their subordinate position in a system defined as both patriarchal and capitalist.

social location—The social features of one's identity incorporating individual, community, societal, and global factors such as gender, class, ability, sexual orientation, age, and so on.

speciesism—Attitudes, actions, and institutional practices that subordinate nonhuman species; usually used in discussions of environmental and ecological issues.

standpoint theory—The view that different social and historical situations give rise to very different experiences and theories about those experiences. See **situated knowledge.**

state—Governmental institutions, authority, and control. This includes the machinery of electoral politics, lawmaking, government agencies that execute law and policy, law enforcement agencies, the prison system, and the military.

subjectivity—A form of understanding in which knowledge and meaning are grounded in people's lived experiences; also being the subject rather than an object of theorizing. Since powerless groups have historically been treated as objects of "objective" knowledge production, feminist assertions of subjectivity are also assertions of the previously objectified groups' claims to the subject position (that of actor and agent of action), their ability to create their own knowledge, and, therefore, their agency in knowledge production.

sustainability—The ability of an ecologically sound economy to sustain itself by using renewable resources and generating low or nonaccumulating levels of pollution. A more sustainable future means rethinking and radically changing current production processes, as well as the materialism and consumerism that support excessive production.

theory—An explanation of how things are and why they are the way they are; a theory is based on a set of assumptions, has a perspective, and serves a purpose.

third-wave feminism—Feminist perspectives adopted in the 1990s often by younger women, with an emphasis on personal voice and multiple identities, intersectionality, ambiguity, and contradictions.

References

Abbey, S., and A. O'Reilly, eds. 1998. *Redefining motherhood: Changing identities and patterns.* Toronto: Second Story Press.

Abramovitz, M. 1996. *Regulating the lives of women.* Rev. ed. Boston: South End Press.

Abramson, W., E. Emanuel, V. Gaylord, and M. Hayden. 2000. *Impact: Special issue on violence against women with developmental or other disabilities* 13(3). Minneapolis: The Institute on Community Integration, University of Minnesota. Available online at http://ici.umn.edu/products/impact/133.

Abu-Lughod, Lila. 2002. Do Muslim women really need saving? Anthropological reflections on cultural relativism and its others. *American Anthropologist,* 104(3): 738–790.

Abzug, B. 1984. *Gender gap: Bella Abzug's guide to political power for American women.* Boston: Houghton Mifflin.

Adair, V. 2004. Reclaiming the promise of higher education: Poor single mothers in academe. *On Campus with Women* 33(3–4), Spring/Summer.

———, and S. Dahlberg. 2003. *Reclaiming class: Women, poverty, and the promise of higher education in America.* Philadelphia: Temple University Press.

Adams, C.J. 1999. *The sexual politics of meat: A feminist-vegetarian critical theory.* New York: Continuum. 10th anniversary edn.

Adamson, J., M. M. Evans, and R. Stein, eds. 2002. *The environmental justice reader: Politics, poetics and pedagogy.* Tucson: Arizona University Press.

Adler, F. 1975. *Sisters in crime: The rise of the new female criminal.* New York: McGraw-Hill.

Agosín, Marjorie, ed. 2001. *Women, gender, and human rights: A global perspective.* New Brunswick, N.J.: Rutgers University Press.

Ahn, C., and G. Kirk. 2005. Why war is all the rage. *San Francisco Chronicle,* May 29. D5.

Ahn, I. S. 1996. Great army, great father. In *Great army, great father,* edited by T. H. Yu. Seoul, South Korea: Korean Church Women United.

Aisha. 1991. Changing my perception. *Aché: A Journal for Lesbians of African Descent* 3(3): 28–29.

Alan Guttmacher Institute. 2004. *Sex education: Needs, programs and policies.* New York and Washington, D.C.: Alan Guttmacher Institute.

Albelda, R., and C. Tilly. 1997. *Glass ceilings and bottomless pits: Women's work, women's poverty.* Boston: South End Press.

Albrecht, G.H. 2004. *Hitting Home: Feminist ethics, women's work, and the betrayal of "family values."* New York: Continuum.

Alcoff, L. 1988. Cultural feminism versus post-structuralism: The identity crisis in feminist theory. *Signs: Journal of Women in Culture and Society* 13(3): 405–36.

Allen, P. G. 1986. *The sacred hoop: Recovering the feminine in American Indian traditions.* Boston: Beacon Press.

Allison, D. 1992. *Bastard out of Carolina.* New York: Dutton.

Alonso, H. H. 1993. *Peace as a women's issue: A history of the U.S. movement for world peace and women's rights.* Syracuse, N.Y.: Syracuse University Press.

Alterman, Eric. 2003. *What liberal media? The truth about bias and the news.* New York: Basic Books.

American Association of Retired Persons. N.d. *America's changing work force: Statistics in brief.* Washington, D.C.: American Association of Retired Persons.

American Civil Liberties Union. 2002. *The USA Patriot Act.* Accessed online at http://www.aclu.org on 16 January 2003.

American Heritage Dictionary. 1993. 3d ed. Boston: Houghton Mifflin.

American Immigration Lawyers Association. 2001. *Agency in meltdown: Major problems continue with INS benefits adjudications.* Posted on AILA InfoNet at Doc. No.39ip1001 7 May 2001. Accessed online at http://www.aila.org on 27 December 2002.

American Society of Plastic Surgeons. 2005. Accessed online at www.plasticsurgery.org/public_education/statistical-trends.cfm on 5 July 2005.

Amnesty International USA. 2000. *United States of America: Breaking the chain. The human rights of women prisoners.* New York: Amnesty International USA.

Amott, T. 1993. *Caught in the crisis: Women and the U.S. economy today.* New York: Monthly Review Press.

———, and J. Matthaei. 1996. *Race, gender, and work: A multicultural economic history of women in the United States.* Rev. ed. Boston: South End Press.

Anderlini-D'Onofrio, Serena, ed. 2003. *Women and bisexuality: A global perspective.* New York: Haworth Press.

Andersen, M. 2000. Women, power and politics. Pp. 290–322 in *Thinking about women: Sociological perspectives on sex and gender,* 5th ed. Boston: Allyn and Bacon.

Anderson, L., ed. 1991. *Sisters of the earth: Women's prose and poetry about nature.* New York: Vintage Books.

Anderson, M. 1999. A well-kept secret: How military spending costs women's jobs. Pp. 247–52 in *Gender camouflage,* edited by F. D'Amico and L. Weinstein. New York: New York University Press.

Andre, J. 1988. Stereotypes: Conceptual and normative considerations. In *Racism and sexism: An integrated study,* edited by P. S. Rothenberg. New York: St. Martin's Press.

Andruss, V., C. Plant, J. Plant, and S. Mills. 1990. *Home!: A bioregional reader.* Philadelphia: New Society.

Angwin, J. 1996. Pounding on the glass ceiling. *San Francisco Chronicle,* 24 November, p. C3.

Antrobus, P. 2004. *The global women's movement: Origins, issues and strategies.* New York: Zed Books.

Anzaldúa, G. 1987. *Borderlands la frontera: The new mestiza.* San Francisco: Spinsters/Aunt Lute.

Anzaldúa, G. 2002. Now let us shift . . . the path of conocimiento . . . inner work, and public acts. In *This bridge we call home,* edited by Gloria Anzaldúa and Analouise Keating. New York: Routledge, pp. 540–78.

Applebome, P. 1997. Citadel's president insists coeducation will succeed. *New York Times,* 14 January, p. A1.

Arcana, J. 1994. Abortion is a motherhood issue. Pp. 159–63 in *Mother journeys: Feminists write about mothering,* edited by M. Reddy, M. Roth, and A. Sheldon. Minneapolis: Spinsters Ink.

———. 2005. *What if your mother.* Goshen, Conn.: Chicory Blue Press.

Arditti, R., R. D. Klein, and S. Minden, eds. 1984. *Test-tube women: What future for motherhood?* Boston: Pandora Press.

———, and T. Schreiber. 1998. Breast cancer: The environmental connection—A 1998 update, in *Resist Newsletter.* May/June.

Armour, S. 2005. Family medical leave at center of hot debate. *USA Today.* May 25.

Associated Press. 1999. Most leaving welfare remain poor. *San Francisco Chronicle,* 12 May, p. A6.

Associated Press. 2005. Bush rallies abortion foes in annual protest. *USA Today,* January 25, 2A.

Association of American Colleges and Universities. 2002. *Statement of affirmative action, educational excellence, and higher education's civic mission.* Accessed online at http://www.aacu.org/About/affirmativeaction02.cfm on 21 December 2002.

Avery, B. 1990. Breathing life into ourselves: The evolution of the Black women's health project. Pp. 4–10 in *The Black women's health book,* edited by E. White. Seattle. Seal Press.

Ayres, B. D., Jr. 1994. U.S. crackdown at border stems illegal crossings. *New York Times,* 6 October, pp. A1, A14.

Bagby, R. 1990. Daughter of growing things. Pp. 231–48 in *Reweaving the world: The emergence of ecofeminism,* edited by I. Diamond and G. Orenstein. San Francisco: Sierra Club.

Baird-Windle, P. and E. J. Bader. 2001. *Targets of hatred: Anti-abortion terrorism.* New York: Palgrave.

Baker, B. 1993. The women's convergence for national health care. *The Network News,* July/August, pp. 1, 3.

Baldwin, James. 1984. On being white and other lies, in *Essence* (April).

Bandarage, A. 1997. *Women, population and global crisis: A political-economic analysis.* London and New Jersey: Zed Books.

Barnes, B., and T. Clarke. 1986. *How to get a man to make a commitment or know when he never will.* New York: St. Martin's Press.

Barnett, E. 2002. Prison coffee and games: Starbucks and Nintendo admit their contractor uses prison labor. *Prison Legal News* 13(3): 12–13.

Barnett, R., and C. Rivers. 1996. *She works, he works: How two-income families are happier, healthier, and better-off.* New York: HarperSanFrancisco.

Barnhill, D. L., ed. 1999. *At home on the earth: Becoming native to our place.* Berkeley: University of California Press.

Bart, P., and P. O'Brien. 1993. *Stopping rape: Successful survival strategies.* New York: Teachers College Press.

Bartlett, J. 1994. *Will you be a mother? Women who choose to say no.* London: Virago.

Bass, E., and L. Davis. 1988. *The courage to heal.* New York: Harper & Row.

Baumgardner, J., and A. Richards. 2000. *Manifesta: Young women, feminism, and the future.* New York: Farrar, Straus and Giroux.

Baxandall, R. 2001. Re-visioning the women's liberation movement's narrative: Early second-wave African American feminists. *Feminist Studies* 27(1): 225–45.

———, and L. Gordon, eds. 2000. *Dear sisters: Dispatches from the women's liberation movement.* New York: Basic Books.

Beasley, M., and D. Thomas. 1994. Violence as a human rights issue. Pp. 323–46 in *The public nature of private violence: The discovery of domestic abuse,* edited by M. A. Fineman and R. Mykitiuk. New York: Routledge.

Belenky, M. F., B. M. Clinchy, N. R. Goldberger, and J. M. Tarnle. 1997. *Women's ways of knowing: The development of self, voice, and mind.* 10th anniversary ed. New York: Basic Books.

Bell, D. and R. Klein, eds. 1996. *Radically speaking: Feminism reclaimed.* North Melbourne, Australia: Spinifex Press.

Benard, C., and E. Schlaffer. 1997. "The man in the street": Why he harasses. Pp. 395–98 in *Feminist frontiers IV,* edited by L. Richardson, V. Taylor, and N. Whittier. New York: McGraw-Hill.

Bennett, K. 1992. Feminist bisexuality: A both/and option for an either/or world. Pp. 205–31 in *Closer to home: Bisexuality and feminism,* edited by E. R. Weise. Seattle, Wash.: Seal Press.

Bennett, M., and V. D. Dickerson. 2001. *Recovering the Black female body: Self-representations by African American women.* New Brunswick, N.J.: Rutgers University Press.

Benston, M. 1969. The political economy of women's liberation. *Monthly Review* 21(4): 13–27.

Berg, P. 1993. Growing a life-place politics. In *Radical environmentalism: Philosophy and tactics,* edited by J. List. Belmont, Calif.: Wadsworth.

Bergen, R. K. 1996. *Wife rape: Understanding the response of survivors and service providers.* Thousand Oaks, Calif.: Sage.

Bergmann, B. R. 1986. *The economic emergence of women.* New York: Basic Books.

Bernstein, R., and S. C. Silberman, eds. 1996. *Generation Q.* Los Angeles: Alyson.

Bethel, T. 2005. The gender gyp. *AARP Bulletin Online,* August 9, accessed online at www.aarp.org/bulletin/socialsec/the_gender_gyp on August 9, 2005.

Bhattacharjee, A. 1997. A slippery path: Organizing resistance to violence against women. Pp. 29–45 in *Dragon ladies: Asian American feminists breathe fire,* edited by S. Shah. Boston: South End Press.

———. 2002. Private fists: pubic force: Race, gender, and surveillance. Pp. 1–54 in *Policing the national body: Sex, race, and criminalization,* edited by J. Silliman and A. Bhattacharjee. Cambridge, Mass: South End Press.

Bianchi, S., M. Milkie, L. Sayer, and J. Robinson. 2002. Is anyone doing the housework? Trends in the gender division of household labor. Pp. 174–87 in *Workplace/women's place,* 2d ed., edited by P. Dubeck and D. Dunn. Los Angeles: Roxbury Publishing.

Bigelow, B., and B. Peterson, eds. 2002. *Rethinking globalization: Teaching for justice in an unjust world.* Milwaukee, Wis.: Rethinking Schools.

Bin Wahad, D. 1996. Speaking truth to power: Political prisoners in the United States. In *Criminal injustice: Confronting the prison crisis,* edited by E. Rosenblatt. Boston: South End Press.

Bird, C. 1995. *Lives of ours: Secrets of salty old women.* New York: Houghton Mifflin.

Birks, J., and A. Erlich, eds. 1989. *Hidden dangers: The environmental consequences of preparing for war.* San Francisco: Sierra Club Books.

Black Women's Health Project. 1995. *Reproductive health and African American women. Issue brief.* Washington, D.C.: Black Women's Health Project.

Blakely, M. K. 1994. *American mom: Motherhood, politics, and humble pie.* Chapel Hill, N.C.: Algonquin Books.

Blank, H., ed. 2001. *Zaftig: Well-rounded erotica.* San Francisco: Cleis Press.

Blauner, R. 1972. *Racial oppression in America.* New York: Harper & Row.

Bleier, R. 1984. *Science and gender: A critique of biology and its theories on women.* New York: Pergamon Press.

Bloom, B., M. Chesney-Lind, and B. Owen. 1994. *Women in California prisons: Hidden victims of the war on drugs.* San Francisco: Center on Juvenile and Criminal Justice.

Boggs, G. L. 1994. Fifty years on the left. *The Witness,* May, 8–12.

Bohmer, C., and A. Parrot. 1993. *Sexual assault on campus: The problem and the solution.* New York: Lexington Books/Macmillan.

Bolen, Jean Shinoda. 2003. *Crones don't whine: Concentrated wisdom for juicy women.* Boston: Conari Press.

Bolin, A., and J. Granskog, eds. 2003. *Athletic intruders: Ethnographic research on women, culture, and exercise.* Albany, N.Y.: SUNY Press.

Booth, W. 1997. Ex-Black Panther freed. *Washington Post,* 11 June, p. A1.

Bordo, S. 1993. *Unbearable weight: Feminism, Western culture, and the body.* Berkeley: University of California Press.

Borjesson, Kristina, ed. 2002. *Into the buzzsaw: Leading journalists expose the myth of a free press.* Amherst, N.Y.: Prometheus Books.

Borkovitz, D. K. 1995. Same-sex battering and the backlash. *NCADV Voice,* Summer, 4.

Bornstein, K. 1995. *Gender outlaw: On men, women, and the rest of us.* New York: Vintage/Random House.

———. 1998. *My gender workbook: How to become a real man, a real woman, the real you, or something else entirely.* New York: Routledge.

Boston Women's Health Book Collective. 2005. *Our bodies ourselves: A new edition for a new era.* New York: Simon and Schuster.

———. 1994. *The new ourselves growing older.* New York: Simon & Schuster.

———. 1998. *Our bodies, ourselves for the new century: A book by and for women.* New York: Simon & Schuster.

Boswell, J. 1994. *Same-sex unions in premodern Europe.* New York: Villard Books.

Boulding, E. 1990. *Building a civic culture: Education for an interdependent world.* Syracuse, N.Y.: Syracuse University Press.

Bowlby, J. 1963. *Child care and the growth of love.* Baltimore: Penguin Books.

Boxer, M. 1998. *When women ask the questions: Creating women's studies in America.* Baltimore: Johns Hopkins University Press.

Boylan, J. F. 2003. *She's not there: A life in two genders.* New York: Broadway Books.

Braidotti, R., E. Charkiewicz, S. Häusler, and S. Wieringa. 1994. *Women, the environment and sustainable development: Towards a theoretical synthesis.* London: Zed Books.

Brennan, S., J. Winklepleck, and G. MacNee. 1994. *The resourceful woman.* Detroit: Visible Ink.

Brenner, J. 1996. The best of times, the worst of times: Feminism in the United States. Pp. 17–72 in *Mapping the women's movement,* edited by M. Threlfall. London: Verso Books.

———. 2001. *Women and the politics of class.* New York: Monthly Review Press.

Brice, Carleen. 2003. *Age ain't nothing but a number: Black women explore midlife.* Boston: Beacon Press.

Bright, S. 1994. *Herotica 3.* New York: Plume.

———. ed. 2000. *The best American erotica.* New York: Simon & Schuster.

Brody, J. 2001. Pregnancy prevention, the morning after. *New York Times*, 10 April, p. D8.

Browne, C. 1998. *Women, feminism, and aging*. New York: Springer.

Browne, J. 1996. The labor of doing time. In *Criminal injustice: Confronting the prison crisis*, edited by E. Rosenblatt. Boston: South End Press.

Brownmiller, S. 1975. *Against our will: Men, women, and rape*. New York: Simon & Schuster.

Bruce, C., ed. 2001. *Best bisexual women's erotica*. San Francisco: Cleis Press.

Brumberg, J. J. 1997. *The body project: An intimate history of American girls*. New York: Random House.

Buchwald, E., P. Fletcher, and M. Roth, eds. 2005. *Transforming a rape culture*. Minneapolis: Milkweed. Revised edition.

Bulhan, H. A. 1985. *Frantz Fanon and the psychology of oppression*. New York: Plenum Books.

Bullard, R. D. 1990. *Dumping in Dixie: Race, class, and environmental quality*. Boulder, Colo.: Westview Press.

———. ed. 1993. *Confronting environmental racism: Voices from the grassroots*. Boston: South End Press.

Bullough, V. L., and B. Bullough. 1993. *Cross dressing, sex, and gender*. Philadelphia: University of Pennsylvania Press.

Bunch, C. 1987. *Passionate politics: Essays 1968–1986*. New York: St. Martin's Press.

———, and R. Carillo. 1991. *Gender violence: A human rights and development issue*. New Brunswick, N.J.: Center for Women's Global Leadership, Rutgers University.

———, and N. Myron, eds. 1974. *Class and feminism: A collection of essays from the Furies*. Baltimore: Diana Press.

———, and N. Reilly. 1994. *Demanding accountability: The global campaign and Vienna Tribunal for women's human rights*. New Jersey: Center for Women's Global Leadership, Rutgers University; New York: UNIFEM.

Bureau of Justice Statistics. 1995. *Violence against women: Estimates from the redesigned survey*. Washington, D.C.: U.S. Department of Justice.

———. 1999, December. *Special report: Women offenders*. Washington, D.C.: U.S. Department of Justice.

———. 2000. *Women offenders*. Washington, D.C.: U.S. Department of Justice.

Burke, C. 2004. *Camp all-American, Hanoi Jane, and the high-and-tight: Gender, folklore, and changing military culture*. Boston: Beacon Press.

Burke, P. 1996. *Gender shock: Exploding the myths of male and female*. New York: Anchor Books.

Burnham, Linda. 2001. *The wellspring of Black feminist theory*. Oakland: Women of Color Resource Center. www.coloredgirls.org

Burrell, B. 1994. *A woman's place is in the House: Campaigning for Congress in the feminist era*. Ann Arbor: University of Michigan Press.

Burton, N. 1998. Resistance to prevention: Reconsidering feminist antiviolence rhetoric. Pp. 182–200 in *Violence against women: Philosophical perspectives*, edited by S. French, W. Teays, and L. Purdy. Ithaca, N.Y.: Cornell University Press.

Bush, Melanie E. L. 2004. *Breaking the code of good intentions: Everyday forms of whiteness*. Lanham, Md.: Rowman and Littlefield.

Bush-Baksette, S. R. 1999. The "war on drugs" a war against women? In *Harsh punishment: International experiences of women's imprisonment*, edited by S. Cook and S. Davies. Boston: Northeastern University Press.

Butler, J. 1990. *Gender trouble: Feminism and the subversion of identity*. New York: Routledge, Chapman, & Hall.

Butler, O. 1993. *The parable of the sower*. New York: Warner Books.

Cahn, Susan. 1995. *Coming on strong: Gender and sexuality in twentieth-century women's sport*. Cambridge, Mass.: Harvard University Press.

Califia. P. 2000. *Public sex: The culture of radical sex*. San Francisco: Cleis Press.

Cammermeyer, M. 1994. *Serving in silence*. New York: Viking.

Camp, L. T. 1997. *Lingering fever: A World War II nurse's memoir*. Jefferson, N.C.: McFarland and Co.

Campbell, D., with F. D'Amico. 1999. Lessons on gender integration from the military academies. Pp. 67–79 in *Gender camouflage: Women and the U.S. military*, edited by F. D'Amico and L. Weinstein. New York: New York University Press.

Cancian, F. M., D. Kurz, A. S. London, R. Reviere, and M. C. Tuominen. 2002. *Child care and inequality: Rethinking carework for children and youth*. New York: Routledge.

Caplan, P., ed. 1987. *The cultural construction of sexuality*. London: Tavistock Publications.

Caputi, J., and D. E. H. Russell. 1990. "Femicide": Speaking the unspeakable. *Ms.*, September/October, 34–37.

Carle, G. 2000. *He's not all that!: How to attract the good guys*. New York: Cliff Street Books/HarperCollins.

Carlen, P. 1989. Feminist jurisprudence, or womenwise penology. *Probation Journal* 36(3): 110–14.

Carroll, S. J., ed., 2001. *The impact of women in public office*. Bloomington: Indiana University Press.

Carson, R. 1962. *Silent spring*. Boston: Houghton Mifflin.

Catalyst. 2002. *Census of women corporate officers and top earners of the Fortune 500*. www.catalystwomen.org accessed online on August 6, 2005.

———. 2002. *Fact sheet: Women CEOs*. Accessed online at http://www.catalystwomen.org/press_room/ factsheets/fact_women_ceos.htm on 21 December 2002.

Cavin, S. 1985. *Lesbian origins*. San Francisco: Ism Press.

Center for American Women and Politics. 2001. *Women state legislators: Past, present and future*. New Brunswick, N.J.: CAWP.

Center for Constitutional Rights. 2005. *Federal judge rules on constitutionality of kickback in contract between NY state prisons and MCI,* Center for Constitutional Rights, New York, Press Release, August 30.

Centers for Disease Control and Prevention. 2000. *Tracking the hidden epidemics: Trends in STDs in the United States 2000.* Accessed online at http://www. cdc.gov/nchstp/dstd/stats-Trends/ Trends2000.pdf on 19 November 2002.

———. 2003. *A glance at the HIV/AIDS epidemic.* Accessed online at www.cdc.gov/hiv/PUBS/Facts/ At-a-Glance.htm on July 25, 2005.

———. 2004. Abortion Surveillance-United States, 2001. In *Surveillance Summaries,* Nov. 26. MMWR 2004: 53, no. SS-9.

Chaddock, G. R., 2002. Security act to pervade daily lives. *Christian Science Monitor,* November 21. Accessed online at http://www.csmonitor.com/2002/1121/ p01s03-usju.html on 17 January 2003.

Chalker, R. 1995. Sexual pleasure unscripted. *Ms.,* November/December, 49–52.

Chambers, V. 1995. Betrayal feminism. In *Listen up: Voices from the next feminist generation,* edited by B. Findlen. Seattle, Wash.: Seal Press.

Chang, G. 2000. *Disposable domestics: Immigrant women workers in the global economy.* Cambridge, Mass.: South End Press.

Chapkis, W. 1986. *Beauty secrets: Women and the politics of appearance.* Boston: South End Press.

Chavez, C. 1993. Farm workers at risk. Pp. 163–70 in *Toxic struggles: The theory and practice of environmental justice,* edited by R. Hofrichter. Philadelphia and Gabriola Island, B.C.: New Society Publishers.

Chernin, K. 1985. *The hungry self.* New York: Times Books.

Chesler, P. 1972. *Women and madness.* New York: Avon.

Chesney-Lind, M. 1986. Women and crime: A review of the literature on the female offender. *Signs: Journal of Women in Culture and Society* 12(1): 78–96.

———. 1995. Rethinking women's imprisonment: A critical examination of trends in female incarceration. In *Women, crime, and criminal justice,* edited by B. R. Price and N. Sokoloff. New York: McGraw-Hill.

———. 1997. *The female offender: Girls, women and crime.* Thousand Oaks, Calif.: Sage.

———, and R. G. Shelden. 1992. *Girls, delinquency and juvenile justice.* Pacific Grove, Calif.: Brooks/Cole.

Chiawei O'Hearn, Claudine, ed. 1998. *Half and half: Writers on growing up biracial and bicultural.* New York: Pantheon.

Children's Defense Fund. 2004. Everyday in America. www.childrensdefense.org accessed online, August 6, 2005.

———. 2004. Where America stands. In *The state of America's children yearbook.* Washington, D.C.: Children's Defense Fund.

———. 2005. Child care basics. www.childrensdefense.org accessed online, August 6, 2005.

Chodorow, N. 1978. *Reproduction and mothering: Psychoanalysis and the sociology of gender.* Berkeley: University of California Press.

Churchill, W. 1992. Introduction: The Third World at home. In *Cages of steel: The politics of imprisonment in the United States,* edited by W. Churchill and J. J. Vander Wall. Washington, D.C.: Maisonneuve Press.

Citizen Soldier. 1996. *Newsletter.* New York: Citizen Soldier.

Clare, E. 1999. *Exile and pride.* Cambridge, Mass.: South End Press.

Clinton, H. R. 1996. *It takes a village and other lessons children teach us.* New York: Simon & Schuster.

Cobble, D. S., ed. 1993. *Women and unions: Forging a partnership.* Ithaca, N.Y.: ILR Press.

Cohen, Elliot D., ed. 2005. *News incorporated: Corporate media ownership and its threat to democracy.* Amherst, N.Y.: Prometheus Books.

Cohen, K. 2001. *A walk down the aisle: Notes on a modern wedding.* New York: W. W. Norton.

Cole, J. H. 1992. *Women pilots of World War II.* Salt Lake City: University of Utah Press.

Cole, J., and B. Guy-Sheftall. 2003. *Gender talk: The struggle for women's equality in African American communities.* New York: Ballantine.

Collier, R. 2002. For anti-sweatshop activists, recent settlement is only tip of iceberg. *San Francisco Chronicle,* 29 September, p. A14.

Colligan, S. 2004. Why the intersexed shouldn't be fixed: Insights from queer theory and disability studies. In *Gendering Disability,* edited by B.G. Smith and B. Hutchinson. New Brunswick, N.J.: Rutgers University Press, pp. 45–60.

Collins, J. 2003. *Threads: Gender, labor, and power in the global apparel industry.* Chicago: University of Chicago Press.

Collins, P. H. 1990. *Black feminist thought: Knowledge, consciousness, and the politics of empowerment.* Boston: Unwin Hyman.

———. 2004. *Black sexual politics: African Americans, gender, and the new racism.* New York: Routledge.

Comité Fronterizo de Obreras-American Friends Service Committee. 1999. *Six years of NAFTA: A view from inside the maquiladoras.* Philadelphia: AFSC.

Commonwealth Fund. 1997. *The Commonwealth Fund Survey of the health of adolescent girls: Highlights and methodology.* New York: The Commonwealth Fund.

Connell, R. W. 1990. The state, gender, and sexual politics: Theory and appraisal. *Theory and Society* 19(4): 507–44.

Cook, A., and G. Kirk. 1983. *Greenham women everywhere: Dreams, ideas, and actions from the women's peace movement.* Boston: South End Press.

Coontz, S. 1992. *The way we never were: American families and the nostalgia trap.* New York: Basic Books.

———. 1997. *The way we really are: Coming to terms with America's changing families.* New York: Basic Books.

Cooper, E. 1992. When being ill is illegal: Women and the criminalization of HIV. *Health/PAC Bulletin,* Winter, 10–14.

Cooper, M. 1997. When push comes to shove: Who is welfare reform really helping? *The Nation,* 2 June, 11–15.

Corea, G. 1985. *The mother machine: Reproductive technologies from artificial insemination to artificial wombs.* New York: Harper & Row.

———. 1987. *Man-made women: How reproductive technologies affect women.* Bloomington: Indiana University Press.

Cornell, D., ed. 2000. *Feminism and pornography.* New York: Oxford University Press.

Corral, J. and L. Miya-Jervis. 2001. *Young wives' tales: New adventures in love and partnership.* Seattle: Seal Press.

Cox, M. 2001a. Wal-martyrs: Women take aim at Wal-Mart's glass ceiling by filing the biggest discrimination suit in history. *Ms.,* October/November, 18–20.

———. 2001b. Zero balance: Watch out! Your retirement funds are in more trouble than you think. *Ms.,* February/March, 57–65.

Cox, T. 1999. *Hot sex: How to do it.* New York: Bantam Books.

Crenshaw, K. 1993. The marginalization of sexual violence against Black women. Speech to the National Coalition Against Sexual Assault, 1993 Conference, Chicago. Accessed online at http://www.ncasa.org/marginalization.html.

Crittenden, A. 2001. *The price of motherhood: Why the most important job in the world is still the least valued.* New York: Metropolitan Books.

Croteau, D., and W. Hoynes. 1997. *Media/society: Industries, images, and audiences.* Thousand Oaks, Calif.: Pine Forge Press.

Cruickshank, Margaret. 2003. *Learning to be old: Gender, culture, and aging.* Lanham, Md.: Rowman and Littlefield.

Dalla Costa, M., and S. James. 1972. *The power of women and the subversion of the community.* Bristol, England: Falling Wall Press.

Daly, F. 1994. Perspectives of Native American women on race and gender. In *Challenging racism: Alternatives to genetic explanations,* edited by E. Tobach and B. Risoff. New York: The Feminist Press.

Daly, H. E., and J. B. Cobb Jr. 1989. *For the common good: Redirecting the economy toward community, the environment, and a sustainable future.* Boston: Beacon Press.

Daly, K. 1994. *Gender, crime, and punishment.* New Haven, Conn.: Yale University Press.

Daly, M. 1976. *Gyn/ecology: The metaethics of radical feminism.* Boston: Beacon Press.

D'Amico, F. 1998. Feminist perspectives on women warriors. Pp. 119–25 in *The women and war reader,* edited by L. A. Lorentzen and J. Turpin. New York: New York University Press.

D'Amico, F., and L. Weinstein, eds. 1999. *Gender camouflage: Women and the U.S. military.* New York: New York University Press.

Daniels, C. R. 1993. *At women's expense: State power and the politics of fetal rights.* Cambridge: Harvard University Press.

Dankelman, I., and J. Davidson. 1988. *Women and the environment in the Third World.* London: Earthscan.

Danquah, M. 1998. *Willow weep for me: A Black women's journey through depression.* New York: W. W. Norton.

Darling, M., and J. Tyson. 1999. The state: Friend or foe? Distributive justice issues and African American women. Pp. 214–41 in *Dangerous intersections: Feminist perspectives on population, environment, and development,* edited by J. Silliman and Y. King. Cambridge, Mass.: South End Press.

das Dasgupta, S., and S. DasGupta. 1996. Public face, private space: Asian Indian women and sexuality. Pp. 226–43 in *"Bad girls"/"good girls": Women, sex, and power in the nineties,* edited by N. Bauer Maglin and D. Perry. New Brunswick, N.J.: Rutgers University Press.

Davis, A. 1983. Racism, birth control, and reproductive rights. In *Women, race, and class.* New York: Vintage Books.

———. 1997. A plenary address. Paper presented at conference, Frontline Feminisms: Women, War, and Resistance, 16 January, at University of California, Riverside.

———. 1998. Masked racism: Reflections on the prison industrial complex. *Color Lines,* Fall.

———. 2001. The color of violence against women. *Sojourner: The Women's Forum,* October, 12–13.

———. 2003. *Are prisons obsolete?* New York: Seven Stories Press.

Davis, B. 2004. Will debt move backfire on Argentina? *Asian Wall Street Journal,* November 29, A6.

Davis, F. 1991. *Moving the mountain: The women's movement in America since 1960.* New York: Simon & Schuster.

Davis, J., ed. 1991. *The Earth First! reader: Ten years of radical environmentalism.* Salt Lake City: Peregrine Smith Books.

Dean, D. 1997. *Warriors without weapons: The victimization of military women.* Pasadena, Md.: The Minerva Center.

d'Eaubonne, F. 1994. The time for ecofeminism. In *Ecology,* edited by C. Merchant. Atlantic Highlands, N.J.: Humanities Press.

Deen, T. 1998. Globalisation devastates women, say unions. *InterPress Service,* 4 March.

de Ishtar, Z. 1994. *Daughters of the Pacific.* Melbourne, Australia: Spinifex Press.

D'Emilio, J. 1984. Capitalism and gay identity. Pp. 100–13 in *Powers of desire: The politics of sexuality,* edited by A. Snitow et al. New York: Monthly Review Press.

———, and E. Freedman. 1997. *Intimate matters: A history of sexuality in America.* 2d ed. Chicago: University of Chicago Press.

Denman, J. E., and L. B. Inniss. 1999. No war without women: Defense industries. Pp. 187–99 in *Gender camouflage: Women and the U.S. military,* edited by F. D'Amico and L. Weinstein. New York: New York University Press.

De Navas-Walt, C., B. D. Proctor, and R. J. Mills. 2004. *Income, poverty and health insurance in the United States, 2003.* U.S. Census Bureau. Current Population Reports P60-226, August. Washington, D.C.: U.S. Census Bureau.

De Oliveira, O., T. De Barbieri, I. Arriagada, M. Valenzuela, C. Serrano, and G. Emeagwali. 1991. *Alternatives: The food, energy, and debt crises in relation to women.* Bangalore, India: DAWN.

Devall, B., and G. Sessions. 1985. *Deep ecology: Living as if nature mattered.* Salt Lake City: Smith Books.

Diamond, I., and G. F. Orenstein, eds. 1990. *Reweaving the world: The emergence of ecofeminism.* San Francisco: Sierra Club Books.

Dibblin, J. 1989. *The day of two suns: U.S. nuclear testing and the Pacific Islands.* New York: New Amsterdam Books.

Dicker, Rory, and Alison Piepmeier, eds. 2003. *Catching a wave: Reclaiming feminism for the 21st century.* Boston: Northeastern University Press.

Dickersin, K., and L. Schnaper. 1996. Reinventing medical research. Pp. 57–76 in *Man-made medicine: Women's health, public policy, and reform,* edited by K. L. Moss. Durham, N.C.: Duke University Press.

Digby, T., ed. 1998. *Men doing feminism.* New York: Routledge.

Dinnerstein, D. 1976. *Sexual arrangements and the human malaise.* New York: Harper & Row.

———. 1989. Surviving on earth: Meaning of feminism. In *Healing the wounds,* edited by J. Plant. Philadelphia: New Society Publishers.

Dittrich, L. 1997. Sociocultural factors that influence body image satisfaction in women. Doctoral dissertation, California Institute of Integral Studies, *Dissertation Abstracts International.*

Dollars and Sense. 2005. Rich and poor in the global economy: Interview with Bob Sutcliffe. no 258, March/April, pp. 13–15.

Donchin, A., and L. M. Purdy. 1999. *Embodying bioethics: Recent feminist advances.* Lanham, Md.: Rowman and Littlefield.

Doress-Worters, P., and D. L. Siegal. 1994. *The new ourselves, growing older.* New York: Simon & Schuster.

Dorsey, E., and M. Thormodsgard. 2003. Rachel Carson warned us. *Ms.,* December 2002/January 2003, 43–45.

Douglas, M. 1966. *Purity and danger: An analysis of concepts of pollution and taboo.* London: Routledge and Kegan Paul.

Douglas, S. J., and M. W. Michaels. 2004. *The mommy myth: The idealization of motherhood and how it has undermined women.* New York: Free Press.

Downs, B. 2003. *Fertility of American women, June 2002.* Current Population Reports P20–548. Washington, D.C.: U.S. Census Bureau.

Drucker, J. L. 1998. *Lesbian and gay families speak out: Understanding the joys and challenges of diverse family life.* Cambridge, Mass.: Perseus Publishing.

Duberman M. B., M. Vicinus, and G. Chauncey Jr. 1989. *Hidden from history: Reclaiming the gay and lesbian past.* New York: New American Library.

Ducat, S. J. 2004. *The wimp factor: Gender gaps, holy wars, and the politics of anxious masculinity.* Boston: Beacon Press.

Duff, K. 1993. *The alchemy of illness.* New York: Pantheon.

Duggan, L., and N. Hunter. 1995. *Sex wars: Sexual dissent and political culture.* New York: Routledge.

Dujon, D., and A. Withorn, eds. 1996. *For crying out loud: Women's poverty in the United States.* Boston: South End Press.

Dula, A. 1996. An African American perspective on reproductive freedoms. Panel on Reproduction, Race, and Class at the Third World Congress of Bioethics, Feminist Approaches to Bioethics, November, San Francisco.

DuPlessis, R. B., and A. Snitow, eds. 1998. *The Feminist Memoir Project: Voices from women's liberation.* New York: Three Rivers Press.

Duran, J. 1998. *Philosophies of science/feminist theories.* Boulder, Colo.: Westview Press.

Dworkin, A. 1987. *Intercourse.* New York: Free Press.

———. 1993. *Letters from a war zone.* Chicago: Chicago Review Press.

Dziemianowicz, J. 1992. How we make the stars so beautiful. *McCall's,* July, 105.

Earnest, L. 2005. Made in LA, for now. *Los Angeles Times,* January 16, C1.

Echols, A. 1989. *Daring to be bad: Radical feminism in America 1967–1975.* Minneapolis: University of Minnesota Press.

Edin, K., and M. Kefalas. 2005. *Promises I can keep: Why poor women put motherhood before marriage.* Berkeley: University of California Press.

Edison, L. T., and D. Notkin. 1994. *Women en large: Images of fat nudes.* San Francisco: Books in Focus.

Edut, O., ed. 2000. *Body outlaws: Young women write about body image and identity.* Seattle, Wash.: Seal Press.

———. 2001. Bubbe got back. In *Yentl's revenge: The next wave of Jewish feminism,* edited by Danya Ruttenberg. Seattle: Seal Press, pp. 24–30.

Efon, S. 1997. Tsunami of eating disorders sweeps across Asia. *San Francisco Examiner,* 19 October, p. A27.

Ehrenreich, B. 2001. *Nickel and dimed: On (not) getting by in America*. New York: Henry Holt/Metropolitan Books.

———. 2005. *For her own good: Two centuries of the experts' advice to women*. Garden City, N.Y.: Anchor/Doubleday.

———, and D. English. 1972. *Witches, midwives, and nurses: A history of women healers*. Old Westbury, N.Y.: Feminist Press.

———, E. Hess, and G. Jacobs. 1986. *Remaking love: The feminization of sex*. New York: Anchor/Doubleday.

———, and A. R. Hochschild, eds. 2003. *Global Woman: Nannies, maids, and sex workers in the new economy*. New York: Henry Holt.

Eisenstein, Z. R. 1979. *Capitalism, patriarchy, and the case for socialist feminism*. New York: Monthly Review Press.

———. 1981. *The radical future of liberal feminism*. New York: Longman.

———. 1998. Socialist feminism. Pp. 218–19 in *The reader's companion to U.S. women's history*, edited by W. Mankiller, G. Mink, M. Navarro, B. Smith, and G. Steinem. Boston: Houghton Mifflin.

Ekins, R. 1997. *Male femaling: A grounded theory approach to cross-dressing and sex-changing*. New York: Routledge.

Eng, D. and A. Y. Hom, eds. 1998. *Q & A: Queer in Asian America*. Philadelphia: Temple University.

Enloe, C. 1983. *Does khaki become you? The militarization of women's lives*. Boston: South End Press.

———. 1990. *Bananas, beaches and bases: Making feminist sense of international politics*. Berkeley: University of California Press.

———. 1993a. *The morning after: Sexual politics at the end of the cold war*. Berkeley: University of California Press.

———. 1993b. The right to fight: A feminist Catch-22. *Ms.*, July/August, 84–87.

———. 1995. The globetrotting sneaker, *Ms.*, March/April, pp. 10–15.

———. 2000. *Maneuvers: The international politics of militarizing women's lives*. Berkeley: University of California Press.

Ensler, E. 1998. *The vagina monologues*. New York: Villard/Random House.

Epstein, B. 1993. Ecofeminism and grassroots environmentalism in the United States. Pp. 144–52 in *Toxic struggles: The theory and practice of environmental justice*, edited by R. Hofrichter. Philadelphia and Gabriola Island, B.C.: New Society Publishers.

Erdman, C. 1995. *Nothing to lose: A guide to sane living in a larger body*. San Francisco: HarperSanFrancisco.

Eridani. 1992. Is sexual orientation a secondary sex characteristic? In *Closer to home: Bisexuality and feminism*, edited by E. R. Weise. Seattle, Wash.: Seal Press.

Erlich, J. S. 2003. Grounded in the reality of their lives: Listening to teens who make the abortion decision without involving their parents. *Berkeley Women's Law Journal*, 18: 61–180.

Evans, S. 1980. *Personal politics*. New York: Vintage Books.

Facts on the global sweatshop. 1997. *Rethinking Schools: An Urban Education Journal* 11(4): 16.

Faderman, L. 1981. *Surpassing the love of men: Romantic friendship and love between women from the Renaissance to the present*. New York: William Morrow.

Falk, J. 2003. Fiscal lockdown, *Dollars and Sense*, July/August, pp. 19–23, 45.

Faludi, S. 1991. *Backlash: The undeclared war against women*. New York: Crown.

Family Violence Prevention Fund. 1998. *Domestic violence is a serious, widespread social problem in America: The facts*. Available from the Family Violence Prevention Fund, 383 Rhode Island Ave., San Francisco, CA 94103.

Fausto-Sterling, A. 1993. The five sexes: Why male and female are not enough. *The Sciences*, March/April, 20–24.

———. 2000. *Sexing the body: Gender politics and the construction of sexuality*. New York: Basic Books.

Featherstone, L. 2002. *Students against sweatshops: The making of a movement*. New York, Verso.

———. 2004. Will labor take the Wal-Mart challenge? *The Nation*, June 28.

Feinberg, L. 1996. *Transgender warriors: Making history from Joan of Arc to RuPaul*. Boston: Beacon Press.

———. 1998. *Trans liberation: Beyond pink or blue*. Boston: Beacon Press.

Feldt, G. 2004. *The War on choice: The right wing attack on women's rights and how to fight back*. New York: Bantam.

Feminist Anti-Censorship Task Force. 1992. *Caught looking: Feminism, pornography, and censorship*. East Haven, Conn.: Long River Books.

Ferguson, A. 1989. *Blood at the root: Motherhood, sexuality, and male dominance*. London: Pandora.

Ferguson, K., and P. Turnbull. 2004. Globalizing militaries. In *Rethinking globalism*, edited by M. B. Steger. Lanham, Md.: Rowman and Littlefield, pp. 79–91.

Ferriss, S., and R. Sandoval. 1997. *The fight in the fields: Cesar Chavez and the Farmworkers movement*. New York: Harcourt Brace.

Fiduccia, B. W., and M. Saxton. 1997. Disability feminism: A manifesto. *New Mobility: Disability Culture and Life-style* 8(49): 60–61.

Findlen, B., ed. 1995. *Listen up: Voices from the next feminist generation*. Seattle, Wash.: Seal Press.

Fine, M., and A. Asch, eds. 1988. *Women with disabilities: Essays in psychology, culture and politics*. Philadelphia: Temple University Press.

Fineman, M. A., and R. Mykitiuk, eds. 1994. *The public nature of private violence: The discovery of domestic abuse*. New York: Routledge.

Finger, A. 1990. *Past due: A story of disability, pregnancy, and birth*. Seattle, Wash.: Seal Press.

Firestone, S. 1970. *The dialectics of sex: The case for feminist revolution*. New York: Morrow.

Fisher. B., F. Cullen, and M. Turner. 2000. *The sexual victimization of college women.* Washington, D.C.: U.S. Department of Justice and the National Institute of Justice.

Flanders, L. 1997. *Real majority, media minority: The costs of sidelining women in reporting.* Monroe, Maine: Common Courage Press.

Folbre, N. 2001. *The invisible heart: Economics and family values.* New York: New Press.

Ford, L. E. 2002. *Women and politics: The pursuit of equality.* Boston: Houghton Mifflin.

Foster, C. 1989. *Women for all seasons: The story of W.I.L.P.F.* Athens, Ga.: University of Georgia Press.

Fouhy, B. 2004. Gay, patriotic and banished. *San Francisco Examiner,* June 21, p. 1.

Fox-Genovese, E. 1994. Beyond individualism: The new Puritanism, feminism, and women. *Salmagundi* 101(2): 79–95.

Fraden, R. 2001. *Imagining Medea: Rhodessa Jones and Theater for Incarcerated Women.* Chapel Hill: University of North Carolina Press.

Francis, D. 1999. Rich man's plan seen as stingy. *Christian Science Monitor,* 24 June, p. 6.

Francisco, P. W. 1999. *Telling: A memoir of rape and recovery.* New York: HarperCollins.

Francke, L. B. 1997. *The gender wars in the military.* New York: Simon & Schuster.

Frankenberg, R. 1993. *White women, race matters: The social construction of whiteness.* Minneapolis: University of Minnesota Press.

Fraser, L. 1997. *Losing it: America's obsession with weight and the industry that feeds it.* New York: Dutton.

Freeman, C. 2000. *High tech and high heels in the global economy: Women, work and pink-collar identities in the Caribbean.* Durham: Duke University Press.

Freire, P. 1989. *Pedagogy of the oppressed.* New York: Continuum.

Friedan, B. 1963. *The feminine mystique.* New York: W. W. Norton.

Fries, K., ed. 1997. *Staring back: The disability experience from the inside out.* New York: Plume.

Frieze, I. 2004. *Hurting the one you love: Violence in relationships.* Belmont, Calif.: Wadsworth.

Frye, M. 1992. *Willful virgin: Essays in feminism 1976–1992.* Freedom, Calif.: The Crossing Press.

Fuchs, L. 1990. The reaction of Black Americans to immigration. In *Immigration reconsidered,* edited by V. Yans-McLaughlin. New York: Oxford University Press.

Fukumura, Y., and M. Matsuoka. 2002. Redefining security: Okinawa women's resistance to U.S. militarism. In *Women's activism and globalization: Linking local struggles and transnational politics,* edited by Nancy Naples and Manisha Desai. New York: Routledge, pp. 239–263.

Furman, F. K. 1997. *Facing the mirror: Older women and beauty shop culture.* New York: Routledge.

Fuss, D., ed. 1991. *Inside out: Lesbian theories, gay theories.* New York: Routledge.

Gaard, G., ed. 1993. *Ecofeminism: Women, animals, nature.* Philadelphia: Temple University Press.

Gage, S., L. Richards, and H. Wilmot. 2002. *Queer.* New York: Thunder's Mouth Press.

Gaines, P. 1994. *Laughing in the dark: From colored girl to woman of color—a journey from prison to power.* New York: Anchor Books.

Gallagher, N. W. 1993. The gender gap in popular attitudes toward the use of force. Pp. 23–37 in *Women and the use of military force,* edited by R. Howes and M. Stevenson. Boulder, Colo.: Lynne Rienner Publishers.

Garber, M. 1992. *Vested interests: Cross-dressing and cultural anxiety.* New York: HarperPerennial.

García, A. 2004. White House steps up racial profiling. *War Times,* Summer, p. 3.

Gardner, M. 2001. Mothers who choose to stay home. *Christian Science Monitor,* November 14.

Garner, D. M. 1997. The 1997 body image survey results. *Psychology Today,* January/February, 31–44, 75–84.

Gavey, N., K. McPhillips, and M. Doherty. 2001. "If it's not on, it's not on"—or is it? Discursive constraints on women's condom use. *Gender and Society,* 15(6), December.

Geller, J. 2001. *Here comes the bride: Women, weddings, and the marriage mystique.* New York: Four Walls Eight Windows.

George, S. 1988. Getting your own back: Solving the Third World debt crisis. *New Statesman & Society,* 15 July, 20.

Gettelman, E. 2005. The Pentagon v. abuse: An interview with Deborah Tucker. *Mother Jones,* June 28.

Gibbs, L. 1995. *Dying from dioxin: A citizens' guide to reclaiming our health and rebuilding democracy.* Boston: South End Press.

———. 1998. *Love canal: The story continues.* Gabriola Island, B.C.: New Society Publishers.

Gill, C. 1996. Cultivating common ground: Women with disabilities. Pp. 183–93 in *Man-made medicine: Women's health, public policy, and reform,* edited by K. L. Moss. Durham, N.C.: Duke University Press.

Ginsburg, F. D., and R. Rapp. 1995. *Conceiving the new world order: The global politics of reproduction.* Berkeley: University of California Press.

Ginsburg, L., and M. Taylor. 2002. *What are you hungry for? Women, food, and spirituality.* New York: St. Martin's Press.

Giordano, P., S. Kerbel, and S. Dudley. 1981. The economics of female criminality. Pp. 15–82 in *Women and crime in America,* edited by L. Bowker. New York: Macmillan.

Girshick, L. B. 2002. *Women-to-women sexual violence.* Boston: Northeastern University Press.

Gladstar, R. 1993. *Herbal healing for women: Simple home remedies for women of all ages.* New York: Simon & Schuster.

Glaze, L. E. 2003. Probation and parole in the U.S., 2002. *Bureau of Justice Statistics Bulletin*, August. Washington, DC: U.S. Department of Justice.

Glazer, P. M., and M. P. Glazer. 1998. *The environmental crusaders: Confronting disaster and mobilizing community.* University Park: Pennsylvania State University Press.

Gleick, E. 1996. Scandal in the military. *Time,* 25 November, 28–31.

Global Exchange. 2002. Citizens across the Americas mobilize to fight the FTAA. *Global Exchange Quarterly Newsletter* 52: 3.

Gluck, S. 1976. *From parlor to prison: Five American suffragists talk about their lives.* New York: Vintage Books.

Gluckman, A. 2004. Gay marriage blues. *Dollars and Sense,* 253, May/June: 13.

Gold, J., and S. Villari, eds. 2000. *Just sex: Students rewrite the rules on sex, violence, activism, and equality.* Lanham, Md.: Rowman and Littlefield.

Gold, M., A. Mughal, and M. Kort. 2004/2005. Dispatches national, *Ms.,* XIV (4), Winter.

Goldstein, N., and J. L. Manlowe, eds. 1997. *The gender politics of HIV/AIDS in women.* New York: New York University Press.

Gomez, J. 2000. Otherwise engaged: Marriage is an offer I *can* refuse. *Ms.,* June/July, 67–70.

Goode, E. 2001. Study says 20% of girls report abuse by a date. *New York Times,* 1 August, p. A10.

Goodman, E. 1999. Working moms do no harm. *San Francisco Chronicle,* 4 March, p. A23.

Goodstein, E. 1999. *The trade-off myth: Fact and fiction about jobs and the environment.* Washington, D.C.: Island Press.

Gordon, J. 2005. *Suburban sweatshops: The fight for immigrant rights.* Cambridge, Mass.: Harvard University Press.

Gordon, L. 1988. *Heroes of their own lives: The politics and history of family violence, Boston 1880–1960.* New York: Viking.

———. 1997. Killing in self-defense. *The Nation,* 24 March, 25–28.

Gore, A., and B. Lavendar. 2001. *Breeder: Real life stories from the new generation of mothers.* Seattle, Wash.: Seal Press.

Gore, Ariel. 2004. *The essential* Hip Mama: *Writing from the cutting edge of parenting.* Seattle: Seal Press.

Goss, R. and A. A. S. Strongheart, eds. 1997. *Our families, our values: Snapshots of queer kinship.* New York: Harrington Park Press.

Gottlieb, R. 1993. *Forcing the spring: The transformation of the American environmental movement.* Washington, D.C.: Island Press.

Gould, J. 1997. *Juggling: A memoir of work, family, and feminism.* New York: The Feminist Press.

Grady, D. 2000. Study backs hormone link to cancer for women. *New York Times,* 27 January, p. A17.

Grahn, J. 1984. *Another mother tongue: Gay words, gay worlds.* Boston: Beacon Press.

Gray, C. 1999. *Corporate cash: Few nations can top it.* Eugene, Oreg.: Author.

Gray, J. 1992. *Men are from Mars, women are from Venus: A practical guide for improving communication and getting what you want in your relationships.* New York: HarperCollins.

Greenhouse, S. 1997. Nike shoe plant in Vietnam is called unsafe for workers. *New York Times,* 8 November, p. A1.

Greider, W. 1997. *One world ready or not: The manic logic of global capitalism.* New York: Simon & Schuster.

Griffin, P. 1998. *Strong women, deep closets: Lesbians and homophobia in sport.* Champaign, Ill.: Human Kinetics Publishing.

Griffin, S. 1971. Rape: The all-American crime. *Ramparts* 10(3): 26–35.

———. 1978. *Woman and nature: The roaring inside her.* San Francisco: Harper Colophon.

———. 1999. *What her body thought: A journey into the shadows.* San Francisco: Harper San Francisco.

Gross, J. 1992. A jail garden's harvest: Hope and redemption, *New York Times,* Sept. 3.

Grossholtz, J. 1983. Battered women's shelters and the political economy of sexual violence. Pp. 59–69 in *Families, politics, and public policy: A feminist dialogue on women and the state,* edited by I. Diamond. New York: Longman.

Grossman, R. 1998a. Can corporations be accountable? (Part 1). *Rachel's Environment and Health Weekly,* 30 July, 1–2.

———. 1998b. Can corporations be accountable? (Part 2). *Rachel's Environment and Health Weekly,* 6 August, 1–2.

Guenter-Schlesinger, S. 1999. Persistence of sexual harassment: The impact of military culture on policy implementation. Pp. 195–212 in *Beyond zero tolerance,* edited by M. Katzenstein and J. Reppy. Lanham, Md.: Rowman and Littlefield.

Gullette, M. M. 2004. *Aged by culture.* Chicago: University of Chicago Press.

Gustafson, K. 2005. *To punish the poor: Criminalizing trends in the welfare system.* Oakland: Women of Color Resource Center.

Guy-Sheftall, Beverly, ed. 1995. *Words of fire: An anthology of African-American feminist thought.* New York: The New Press.

Haiken, E. 1997. *Venus envy: A history of cosmetic surgery.* Baltimore: Johns Hopkins University Press.

Haines, S. 1999. *The survivor's guide to sex: How to have an empowered sex life after childhood sexual abuse.* San Francisco: Cleis Press.

Halberstam, J. 2005. *In a queer time and place.* New York: New York University Press.

Hall, G. M. 1999. Intersectionality: A necessary consideration for women of color in the military? Pp. 143–61 in *Beyond zero tolerance,* edited by M. Katzenstein and J. Reppy. Lanham, Md.: Rowman and Littlefield.

Hall, K. Q., ed. 2002. *NWSA Journal,* special issue: Feminist Disability Studies.

Hamer, D., and B. Budge. 1994. *The good, the bad and the gorgeous: Popular culture's romance with lesbianism.* London: Pandora.

Hamilton, C. 1993. Coping with industrial exploitation. In *Confronting environmental racism: Voices from the grassroots,* edited by R. Bullard. Boston: South End Press.

Hamilton, James T. 2004. *All the news that's fit to sell: How the market transforms information into news.* Princeton, N.J.: Princeton University Press.

Hammonds, E. 1995. Missing persons: African American women, AIDS, and the history of disease. Pp. 443–49 in *Words of fire: An anthology of African-American feminist thought,* edited by B. Guy-Sheftall. New York: New Press.

Hansen, C. 2001. A considerable service: An advocate's introduction to domestic violence and the military. *Domestic Violence Report* 6(4): 49, 50, 60–64.

Harding, L. 2004. Focus shifts to jail abuse of women. *Guardian,* May 12.

Harding, S., ed. 2004. *The feminist standpoint theory reader: Intellectual and political controversies.* New York: Routledge.

Harman, B. 1996. Happy ending. Pp. 286–90 in *"Women in the trees": U.S. women's short stories about battering and resistance, 1839–1994,* edited by S. Koppelman. Boston: Beacon Press.

Harne, L., and E. Miller, eds. 1996. *All the rage: Reasserting radical lesbian feminism.* New York: Teachers College Press.

Harris, J., and P. Johnson. 2001. *Tenderheaded: A comb-bending collection of hair stories.* New York: Pocket Books.

Harris, R. 2005. Young blacks shun Army, military says. *St Louis Post Dispatch,* March 15, p. A1.

Harrison, P. M., and J. C. Karberg. 2004. Prison and jail inmates at midyear, 2003. *Bureau of Justice Statistics Bulletin,* May. Washington, D.C.: U.S. Department of Justice.

Hartmann, B. 1995. Dangerous intersections. *Political Environments,* no. 2 (summer): 1–7. Publication of the Committee on Women, Population and the Environment, Hampshire College, Amherst, Mass.

Hartmann, H. 1981. The unhappy marriage of Marxism and feminism: Towards a more progressive union. In *Women and revolution: A discussion of the unhappy marriage of Marxism and feminism,* edited by L. Sargent. Boston: South End Press.

Hartsock, N. 1983. *Money, sex, and power: Toward a feminist historical materialism.* New York: Longman.

Harvey, E. 1999. Short-term and long-term effects of early parental employment on children of the National Longitudinal Survey of Youth. *Developmental Psychology* 35(2): 445–459.

Havemann, J. 1999. Former welfare recipients got more jobs in past 3 years. *San Francisco Chronicle,* 27 May, p. A3.

Hawthorne, S. 2002. *Wild politics: Feminism, globalization, bio/diversity.* Melbourne, Australia: Spinifex.

Hayashi, E. 2005. Military recruiters targeting minority youth. *Los Angeles Times,* April 5.

Hayden, D. 1981. *The grand domestic revolution: A history of feminist designs for American homes, neighborhoods, and cities.* Cambridge, Mass.: MIT Press.

Hays, S. 1996. *The cultural contradictions of motherhood.* New Haven, Conn.: Yale University Press.

———. 2004. *Flat broke with children: Women in the age of welfare reform.* New York: Oxford University Press.

Healey, S. 1997. Confronting ageism: A MUST for mental health. Pp. 368–76 in *In our own words: Readings on the psychology of women and gender,* edited by M. Crawford and R. Unger. New York: McGraw-Hill.

Heise, L. 1989. Crimes of gender. *World Watch,* March/April, 12–21.

———. Pitanguy, and A. Germain. 1994. *Violence against women: The hidden health burden.* World Bank Discussion Papers #255. Washington, D.C.: The World Bank.

Hemmings, C. 2002. *Bisexual spaces: A geography of sexuality and gender.* New York: Routledge.

Henderson, H. 1991. *Paradigms in progress: Life beyond economics.* Indianapolis: Knowledge Systems.

Hennessy, R., and C. Ingraham, eds. 1997. *Materialist feminism: A reader in class, difference, and women's lives.* New York: Routledge.

Henshaw, S. K. 2003. Abortion incidence and services in the United States, 2000. *Family Planning Perspectives,* 35(1), Jan/Feb.

Herman, J. 1992. *Trauma and recovery.* New York: Basic Books.

Hernández, R., and B. Flory. 2005. The label is Justicia! *Quaker Action,* 86(1): 7, Winter

Hesse-Biber, S. J. 1991. Women, weight, and eating disorders: A socio-cultural analysis. *Women's Studies International Forum* 14(3): 173–91.

———. 1996. *Am I thin enough yet?* New York: Oxford University Press.

Hetherington, E. M., and G. Clingempeel. 1992. *Coping with marital transitions: A family systems perspective.* Chicago: Chicago University Press for the Society for Research in Child Development.

Hetherington, E. M., and J. Kelly. 2002. *For better or for worse: Divorce reconsidered.* New York: W. W. Norton.

Heywood, L. 1998. *Bodymakers: A cultural anatomy of women's body building.* New Brunswick, N.J.: Rutgers University Press.

————, and J. Drake. 1997. *Third wave agenda: Being feminist, doing feminism.* Minneapolis: University of Minnesota Press.

————, and S. Dworkin. 2003. *Built to win: The rise of the female athlete as cultural icon.* Minneapolis: University of Minnesota Press.

Heyzer, N. 2005. Seating women at the peace table. In *Stop the next war now,* edited by Medea Benjamin and Jodie Evans. Maui, Hawaii: Inner Ocean Publishing, pp. 167–68.

High, G. 1997. Combating sexual harassment. *Soldiers* 52(2): 4–5.

Hill, J. B. 2000. *The legacy of Luna: The story of a tree, and a woman, and the struggle to save the Redwoods.* San Francisco: Harper San Francisco.

Hirschkind, C., and S. Mahmood. 2002 Feminism, the Taliban, and politics of counterinsurgency. *Anthropological Quarterly* 75(2): 339–54.

History Project. 1998. *Improper Bostonians: Lesbian and gay history from the Puritans to Playland.* Boston: Beacon Press.

Hite, S. 1994. *Women as revolutionary agents of change: The Hite Report and beyond.* Madison: University of Wisconsin Press.

Hochschild, A. R. 1989. *The second shift: Working parents and the revolution at home.* New York: Viking.

————. 1997. *The time bind: When work becomes home and home becomes work.* New York: Henry Holt.

Hofrichter, R., ed. 1993. *Toxic struggles: The theory and practice of environmental justice.* Philadelphia and Gabriola Island, B.C.: New Society Publishers.

Holmes, S. A. 1995a. Ousters of undocumented immigrants set a record. *San Francisco Chronicle,* 28 December, p. A13.

————. 1995b. The strange politics of immigration. *New York Times,* 31 December, p. E3.

Hondagneu-Sotelo, P. 2001. *Doméstica: Immigrant workers cleaning and caring in the shadows of affluence.* Berkeley: University of California Press.

Honderich, K. 2003. *The real cost of prison for women and their children.* Washington, D.C.: The Real Cost of Prisons Project/The Sentencing Project.

hooks, b. 1984a. *Feminist theory: From margin to center.* Boston: South End Press.

————. 1984b. Feminist movement to end violence. Pp. 117–31 in *Feminist theory: From margin to center,* edited by b. hooks. Boston: South End Press.

————. 1993. *Sisters of the yam: Black women and self recovery.* Boston: South End Press.

————. 1994. Seduced by violence no more. Pp. 109–13 in *Outlaw culture: Resisting representations,* edited by b. hooks. New York: Routledge.

————. 2000. *Feminism is for everybody: Passionate politics.* Cambridge, Mass.: South End Press.

Houppert, K. 2005a. Base crime. *Mother Jones,* July/August.

————. 2005b. *Home fires burning: Married to the military—for better or worse.* New York: Ballantine.

Howe, F., ed. 2000. *The politics of women's studies: Testimony from 30 founding mothers.* New York: The Feminist Press at the City University of New York.

Howey, N., and E. Samuels, eds. 2000. *Out of the ordinary: Essays on growing up with gay, lesbian, and transgender parents.* New York: St. Martin's Press.

Hua, V. 2002. Cracks widen in glass ceiling. *San Francisco Chronicle,* 19 November, p. B1.

Hubbard, R. 1989. Science, facts, and feminism. In *Feminism and science,* edited by N. Tuana. Bloomington: Indiana University Press.

————. 1990. *The politics of women's biology.* New Brunswick, N.J.: Rutgers University Press.

Human Rights Campaign Foundation. 2004. *The state of the workplace for lesbian, gay, bisexual, and transgender Americans, 2003.* Washington, D.C.: Human Rights Campaign Foundation.

————. 2005. *Statewide marriage laws.* Washington, D.C.: Human Rights Campaign Foundation.

Human Rights Watch. 1999a. *World report 1999. United States: Human rights developments.* New York: Author.

————. 1999b. No guarantees: Sex discrimination in Mexico's maquiladora sector. Pp. 31–35 in *The maquiladora reader: Cross-border organizing since NAFTA,* edited by R. Kamel and A. Hoffman. Philadelphia: American Friends Service Committee.

Humphrey, S., and A. Kahn. 2000. Fraternities, athletic teams and rape: Importance of identification with a risky group. *Journal of Interpersonal Violence,* 15(12): 1313–22.

Hutchins, L., and L. Kaahumanu. 1991. *Bi any other name: Bisexual people speak out.* Boston: Alyson.

Hynes, H. P. 1989. *The recurring silent spring.* New York: Pergamon Press.

Hynes, P. 1996. *A patch of Eden.* White River Junction, Vt.: Chelsea Green.

Inciardi, J., D. Lockwood, and A. Pottieger. 1993. *Women and crack cocaine.* New York: Macmillan.

Indigo, Susannah. 2000. *Blow jobs and other boring stuff: Teens have casually redefined what used to be called sex.* Accessed online at http://www.salon.com/sex/feature/2000/12/14/teens/print.html on July 21, 2005.

Ingraham, C. 1999. *White weddings; Romancing heterosexuality in popular culture.* New York: Routledge.

————. 2004. *Thinking straight: The power, promise and paradox of heterosexuality.* New York: Routledge.

In Phoenix chain gangs for women. 1996. *New York Times,* 28 August, p. C1.

Institute for Policy Studies and United for a Fair Economy. 2005. *Executive Excess 2005.* Accessed online at www.faireconomy.org/press/2005/EE2005_pr.html.

Ireland, M. S. 1993. *Reconceiving women: Separating motherhood from female identity.* New York: Guilford Press.

Isakson, E., ed. 1988. *Women and the military system.* New York: St. Martin's Press.

Jacob, K. 2002. *Our choices, our lives: Unapologetic writings on abortion.* Minneapolis: Writers Advantage.

Jacobs, R. H. 1993. *Be an outrageous older woman.* 2d ed. Manchester, Conn.: Knowledge, Ideas & Trends.

Jaggar, A. M. 1983. *Feminist politics and human nature.* Totowa, N.J.: Rowman & Allanheld.

———. ed. 1994. *Living with contradictions: Controversies in feminist social ethics.* Boulder, Colo.: Westview Press.

Jaimes, A., and T. Halsey. 1986. American Indian women at the center of indigenous resistance in contemporary North America. Pp. 311–44 in *The state of Native America: Genocide, colonization, and resistance,* edited by A. Jaimes. Boston: South End Press.

Jeffreys, Sheila. 1997. *The idea of prostitution.* North Melbourne, Australia: Spinifex.

———. 2003. *Unpacking queer politics: A lesbian feminist perspective.* New York: Blackwell.

———. 2005. *Beauty and misogyny: Harmful cultural practices in the West.* New York: Routledge.

Jetter, A., A. Orleck, and D. Taylor, eds. 1997. *The politics of motherhood: Activist voices from left to right.* Hanover, N.H.: University Press of New England.

Joffe, C. 1995. *Doctors of conscience: The struggle to provide abortion before and after* Roe v. Wade. Boston: Beacon Press.

Johnson, A. G. 1997. *The gender knot: Unraveling our patriarchal legacy.* Philadelphia: Temple University Press.

Johnson, M. L. 2002. *Jane sexes it up: True confessions of feminist desire.* New York: Four Walls, Eight Windows.

Jones, A. 1980. *Women who kill.* New York: Holt, Rinehart, and Winston.

———. 1994a. Is this power feminism? Living with guns, playing with fire. *Ms.,* June/July, 36–44.

———. 1994b. *Next time, she'll be dead: Battering and how to stop it.* Boston: Beacon Press.

Jones, J. 1985. *Labor of love, labor of sorrow: Black women, work, and the family, from slavery to present.* New York: Vintage Books.

Jong, E. 1998. Ally McBeal and *Time* magazine can't keep the good women down. *New York Observer,* 13 July, p. 19.

Justice Policy Institute. 2002. *Cell blocks or classrooms?* Washington, D.C.: Justice Policy Institute. Accessed online at www.justicepolicy.org/article.php?id=3 on September 2, 2005.

Kadi, J. 1996. *Thinking class: Sketches from a cultural worker.* Boston: South End Press.

Kamel, R. 1990. *The global factory: Analysis and action for a new economic era.* Philadelphia: American Friends Service Committee.

———, and A. Hoffman, eds. 1999. *The maquiladora reader: Cross-border organizing since NAFTA.* Philadelphia: American Friends Service Committee.

Kamen, P. 2000. *Her way: Young women make the sexual revolution.* New York: New York University Press.

Kaplan, L. 1995. *The story of Jane: The legendary underground feminist abortion service.* New York: Pantheon Books.

Kaplan, T. 1997. *Crazy for democracy: Women in grassroots movements.* New York: Routledge.

Kaschak, E., ed. 2002. *Intimate betrayal: Domestic violence in lesbian relationships.* New York: Haworth Press.

Kates, E., and P. Ransford with Carol Cardozo. 2005. *Women in prison in Massachusetts: Maintaining family connections—A research report.* Boston: Center for Women in Politics and Public Policy, McCormack Graduate School of Public Policy, University of Massachusetts.

Katz, J. N. 1995. *The invention of heterosexuality.* New York: Plume.

Katzenstein, M. F. 1993. The right to fight. *Women's Review of Books* 11(2): 30–31.

Katz Rothman, B. 1986. *Tentative pregnancy: Prenatal diagnosis and the future of motherhood.* New York: Viking.

Kaufman, M., C. Silverberg, and F. Odette. 2003. *The ultimate guide to sex and disability: For all of us with disabilities, chronic pain and illness.* San Francisco: Cleis Press.

Kaysen, S. 1994. *Girl interrupted.* New York: Vintage Books.

Kempadoo, K., and J. Doezema, eds. 1998. *Global sex workers: Rights, resistance and redefinition.* New York: Routledge.

Kerr, J., ed. 1993. *Ours by right: Women's rights as human rights.* London: Zed Books.

Kessler-Harris, A. 1990. *A woman's wage: Historical meanings and social consequences.* Lexington: University Press of Kentucky.

———. 2001. *In pursuit of equity: Women, men, and the quest for economic citizenship in 20th-century America.* New York: Oxford University Press.

Kettel, B. 1996. Women, health and the environment, *Social Science Medicine* 42 (10): 1367–79.

Kich, G. K. 1992. The developmental process of asserting a biracial, bicultural identity. Pp. 304–17 in *Racially mixed people in America,* edited by M. P. Root. Newbury Park, Calif.: Sage.

Kiernan, D. 2001. The little law that could. *Ms.,* February/March, 18–25.

Kilbourne, J. 1999. *Deadly persuasion: Why women and girls must fight the addictive power of advertising.* New York: Free Press.

———. 2000. *Can't buy my love: How advertising changes the way we think and feel.* New York: Simon & Schuster.

Kim, E., L. V. Villanueva, and Asian Women United of California. 1989. *Making waves.* Boston: Beacon Press.

Kim, R. 2001. Japanese Americans fight backlash. *San Francisco Chronicle,* October 2.

Kimmel, M. 1993. Clarence, William, Iron Mike, Tailhook, Senator Packwood, Spur Posse, Magic . . . and us.

Pp. 119–38 in *Transforming a rape culture*, edited by E. Buchwald, R. Fletcher, and M. Roth. Minneapolis: Milkweed Editions.

———. 2000. *The gendered society*. New York: Oxford University Press.

———, and M. Messner. 1995. *Men's lives*. 3d ed. Boston: Allyn & Bacon.

Kimmel, M. S., and T. Mosmiller, eds. 1992. *Against the tide: Pro-feminist men in the United States, 1776–1990*. Boston: Beacon Press.

King, Y. 1983. All is connectedness: Notes from the Women's Pentagon Action, USA. In *Keeping the peace*, edited by L. Jones. London: The Women's Press.

———. 1987. Letter to the editor. *The Nation*, 12 December, 702, 730–31.

———. 1988. Ecological feminism, *Z Magazine*, July/August, 124–27.

———. 1993a. The other body. *Ms.*, March/April, 72–75.

———. 1993b. Feminism and ecology. Pp. 76–84 in *Toxic struggles: The theory and practice of environmental justice*, edited by R. Hofrichter. Philadelphia and Gabriola Island, B.C.: New Society Publishers.

———. 1998. Ecofeminism. P. 207 in *The reader's companion to U.S. women's history*, edited by W. Mankiller, G. Mink, M. Navarro, B. Smith, and G. Steinem. Boston: Houghton Mifflin.

Kirk, G. 1997a. Ecofeminism and environmental justice: Bridges across gender, race, and class. *Frontiers: A Journal of Women's Studies* 18(2): 2–20.

———. 1997b. Standing on solid ground: Towards a materialist ecological feminism. In *Materialist feminism: A reader in class, difference, and women's lives*, edited by Rosemary Hennessy and Chrys Ingraham. New York: Routledge, pp. 345–63.

———. 1998. Ecofeminism and Chicano environmental struggles: Bridges across gender and race. Pp. 177–200 in *Chicano culture, ecology, politics: Subversive kin*, edited by D. G. Peña. Tucson: University of Arizona Press.

Klein, R., and L. J. Dumble. 1994. Disempowering midlife women: The science and politics of hormone replacement therapy (HRT). *Women's Studies International Forum* 17(4): 327–43.

Kline, C. B., ed. 1997 *Child of mine: Writers talk about the first year of motherhood*. New York: Hyperion.

Kobrin, Sandy. 2004. More women seek vaginal plastic surgery. *WeNews*, 11/14/04. Accessed at www. womensenews.org/article.cfm?aid=2067, on 7/11/05.

Koedt, A., E. Levine, and A. Rapone, eds. 1973. *Radical feminism*. New York: Quadrangle Books.

Kohl, H. 1992. *From archetype to zeitgeist: Powerful ideas for powerful thinking*. Boston: Little Brown.

Kolhatkar, S. 2004. Afghan women continue to fend for themselves. *Foreign Policy in Focus*, special issue, March.

———. 2005. Freedom through solidarity—the lie of "liberation" in *Stop the next war now*, edited by Medea

Benjamin and Jodie Evans. Maui, Hawaii: Inner Ocean Publishing, pp. 87–89.

Komesaroff, P., P. Rothfield, and J. Daly, eds. 1997. *Reinterpreting menopause: Cultural and philosophical issues*. New York: Routledge.

Koppelman, S., ed. 2004. *"Women in the trees:" U.S. women's short stories about battering and resistance, 1839–2000*. New York: Feminist Press at CUNY.

Koss, M. P. 1988. Hidden rape: Sexual aggression and victimization in a national sample of students in higher education. Pp. 3–25 in *Rape and sexual assault*, expanded edn., edited by A. W. Burgess. New York: Garland.

———, E. T. Dinero, and C. A. Seibel. 1988. Stranger and acquaintance rape: Are there differences in the victim's experience? *Psychology of Women Quarterly* 12: 1–24.

———, L. Goodman, A. Browne, L. Fitzgerald, G. P. Keita, and N. F. Russo. 1994. *No safe haven: Male violence against women at home, at work, and in the community*. Washington, D.C.: American Psychological Association.

Krauss, C. 1993. Blue-collar women and toxic-waste protests: The process of politicization. Pp. 107–17 in *Toxic struggles: The theory and practice of environmental justice*, edited by R. Hofrichter. Philadelphia and Gabriola Island, B.C.: New Society Publishers.

Kreimer, Susan. 2004. Teens getting breast implants for graduation. *WeNews*, 6/6/04. Accessed at www. womensenews.org/article.cfm/dyn/aid/1861, on 7/11/05

Krieger, N., and E. Fee. 1996. Man-made medicine and women's health: The biopolitics of sex/gender and race/ethnicity. Pp. 15–35 in *Man-made medicine: Women's health, public policy, and reform*, edited by K. L. Moss. Durham, N.C.: Duke University Press.

———, and S. Sidney. 1996. Racial discrimination and blood pressure: The CARDIA study of young Black and White adults. *American Journal of Public Health* 86(10): 1370–78.

Kurshan, Nancy. 1996. Behind the walls: The history and current reality of women's imprisonment. In *Criminal injustice: Confronting the prison crisis*, edited by E. Rosenblatt. Cambridge: South End Press.

Kurz, D. 1995. *For richer, for poorer: Mothers confront divorce*. New York: Routledge.

Labelle, D., and Kubiak, S. P. 2004. Balancing gender equity for women prisoners. *Feminist Studies*, 30(2), Summer: 416–26.

Ladd-Taylor, M., and L. Umansky. 1998. *"Bad" mothers: The politics of blame in twentieth-century America*. New York: New York University Press.

LaDuke, W. 1993. A society based on conquest cannot be sustained: Native peoples and the environmental crisis. In *Toxic struggles: The theory and practice of environmental justice*, edited by R. Hofrichter. Philadelphia and Gabriola Island, B.C.: New Society Publishers.

———. 1999. *All our relations: Native struggles for land and life*. Cambridge, Mass.: South End Press.

Lahey, K. 1985. Until women themselves have told all they have to tell. *Osgoode Hall Law Journal* 23(3): 519–41.

Lake, C. 2005. The polls speak: Americans support abortion. *Ms.*, XV(2), Summer: 37, 39.

Lakoff, R. T., and R. L. Scherr. 1984. *Face value*. Boston: Routledge & Kegan Paul.

Lamb, W., and the Women of New York Correctional Facility. 2003. *Couldn't keep it to myself: Testimony from our imprisoned sisters*. New York: ReganBooks.

Lancaster, R. N., and M. di Leonardo, eds. 1997. *The gender/ sexuality reader: Culture, history, political economy*. New York: Routledge.

Larkin, J., and K. Popaleni. 1997. Heterosexual courtship violence and sexual harassment: The private and public control of young women. Pp. 313–26 in *In our own words: Readings on the psychology of women and gender*, edited by M. Crawford and R. Unger. New York: McGraw-Hill.

Lasch, C. 1977. *Haven in a heartless world: The family besieged*. New York: Basic Books.

Lazarre, J. 1976. *The mother knot*. New York: McGraw-Hill.

Lederer. E. 2005. Women said worse off now than 10 years ago. *Associated Press*, March 4.

Lee, C. 1987. *Toxic wastes and race in the United States*. New York: New York Commission for Racial Justice United Church of Christ.

Lefkowitz, B. 1997. *Our guys: The Glen Ridge rape and the secret life of the perfect suburb*. Berkeley: University of California Press.

Lehrman, K. 1993. Off course. *Mother Jones*, September/ October, 45–55.

Leidholdt, D., and J. Raymond. 1990. *The sexual liberals and the attack on feminism*. New York: Pergamon.

Lenskyj, H. 2003. *Out on the field: Gender, sports and sexualities*. Toronto: Women's Press.

Leonard, A., ed. 1989. *SEEDS: Supporting women's work in the Third World*. New York: Feminist Press.

Leong, L. C. P. 2004. Virulent virginity: "Abstinence-only" sex ed programs are putting youth at risk. *Color Lines*, 7(4): 36–37.

Leong, R., ed. 1996. *Asian American sexualities: Dimensions of the gay and lesbian experience*. New York: Routledge.

Lerman, H. 1996. *Pigeonholing women's misery: A history and critical analysis of the psychodiagnosis of women in the twentieth century*. New York: Basic Books.

Le Sueur, M. 1982. *Ripening: Selected work*. 2d ed. New York: Feminist Press at the City University of New York.

Leung, A., and A. Chow. 2002. Mass organizing continues around detainees. *Asian Week*, March 1–7.

Lichtenstein, A. C., and M. A. Kroll. 1996. The fortress economy: The economic role of the U.S. prison system. In *Criminal injustice: Confronting the prison crisis*, edited by E. Rosenblatt. Boston: South End Press.

Light, J. 1996. Rape on the border. *The Progressive*, September, 24.

Lindsay-Poland, J., and N. Morgan. 1998. Overseas Military Bases and Environment. *Foreign Policy in Focus* 3(15): 1–4. Interhemispheric Resource Center and Institute for Policy Studies.

Linton, Simi. 1999. *Claiming disability: Knowledge and identity*. New York: New York University Press.

Lips, H. 1991. *Women, men, and power*. Mountain View, Calif.: Mayfield.

List, P. C., ed. 1993. *Radical environmentalism: Philosophy and tactics*. Belmont, Calif.: Wadsworth.

Litt, J. S., and M. K. Zimmerman. 2003. Global perspectives on gender and carework: An introduction. *Gender and Society*, 17(2): 156–65.

Lobel, K., ed. 1984. *Naming the violence: Speaking out about lesbian battering*. Seattle, Wash.: Seal Press.

Lopez, I. 1997. Agency and constraint: Sterilization and reproductive freedom among Puerto Rican women in New York City. In *Situated Lives: Gender and culture in everyday lives*, edited by L. Lamphere, H. Ragone, and P. Zavella. New York: Routledge, pp. 157–74.

Lorber, J. 1994. *Paradoxes of gender*. New Haven, Conn.: Yale University Press.

Lorde, A. 1984. *Sister outsider*. Freedom, Calif.: The Crossing Press.

———. 1996. *The cancer journals*. San Francisco: Aunt Lute Books.

Los Angeles Times. 1999. 38% of ex-welfare recipients jobless. 15 January, p. A21.

Louie, M. C. Y. 2001. *Sweatshop warriors: Immigrant women workers take on the global factory*. Cambridge, Mass.: South End Press.

Lovejoy, M. 2001. Disturbances in the social body: Differences in body image and eating problems among African American and White women. *Gender and Society* 15(2): 239–61.

Lowy, J. 1999. Gay adoption backlash growing. *San Francisco Examiner*, 7 March, p. A20.

Lublin, N. 1998. *Pandora's box: Feminism confronts reproductive technology*. Lanham, Md.: Rowman and Littlefield.

Luebke, B. F., and M. E. Reilly. 1995. *Women's studies graduates: The first generation*. New York: Teachers College Press.

Lunneborg, P. 1992. *Abortion: A positive decision*. New York: Begin and Garvey.

Lusane, C. 1991. *Pipe dream blues: Racism and the war on drugs*. Boston: South End Press.

Lutz, Catherine. 2004. Living room terrorists. *Women's Review of Books* XXI(5): 17–18.

Lydersen, K. 2001. Bad medicine: For women in prison, health care is either defunct or dangerous. *In These Times* 25(3): 21–23.

Macdonald, B. 1983. *Look me in the eye: Old women, aging, and ageism.* San Francisco: Spinsters Ink.

Mack-Canty, C. 2004. Third-wave feminism and the need to reweave the nature/culture duality. *NWSA Journal* (16)83, Fall: 154–79.

MacKinnon, C. 1987. *Feminism unmodified: Discourse on life and law.* Cambridge, Mass.: Harvard University Press.

———. 1991. From practice to theory, or what is a white woman anyway? *Yale Journal of Law and Feminism* 4(13–22): 1281–1328.

———. 1993. Turning rape into pornography: Postmodern genocide. *Ms.,* June/July, 24–30.

———. 1998. Rape, genocide, and women's human rights. Pp. 43–54 in *Violence against women: Philosophical perspectives,* edited by S. French, W. Teays, and L. Purdy. Ithaca, N.Y.: Cornell University Press.

MacNair, R. 2002. *Perpetration-induced traumatic stress: The psychological consequences of killing,* Westport, Conn.: Praeger.

Maher, F. A., and M. K. T. Tétreault. 1994. *The feminist classroom.* New York: Basic Books.

Mahoney, M. 1994. Victimization or oppression? Women's lives, violence, and agency. Pp. 59–92 in *The public nature of private violence: The discovery of domestic abuse,* edited by M. A. Fineman and R. Mykitiuk. New York: Routledge.

Mainardi, P. 1992. The politics of housework. *Ms.,* May/June, 40–41.

Mainstream. 1997. 15(2): 14–16.

Mairs, N. 1990. Carnal acts. In *Carnal acts: Essays.* Boston: Beacon Press.

———. 1996. *Waist-high in the world: A life among the nondisabled.* Boston: Beacon Press.

Mann, C. R. 1995. Women of color and the criminal justice system. In *The criminal justice system and women,* edited by B. R. Price and N. J. Sokoloff. New York: McGraw-Hill.

Martin, J. A., B. E. Hamilton, P. D. Sutton, S. J. Ventura, F. Menacker, and M. L. Munson. 2003. Births: Final data for 2002. *National Vital Statistics Reports,* 52, 10. Hyattsville, Md.: National Center of Health Statistics.

Martinez, E. 1998. *De colores means all of us: Latina views for a multi-colored century.* Boston: South End Press.

Martinson, K., and J. Strawn. 2003. *Built to last: Why skills matter for long-run success in welfare reform.* Washington, D.C.: Center for Law and Social Policy.

Marx, F. 2002. Grassroots to graduation: low-income women accessing higher education. *Final Report: Evaluation of the Women in Community Development Program, Women's Institute for Housing and Economic Development.* Boston: Center for Research on Women, Wellesley College.

Mason, M. 1998. *USA: Supreme Court strengthens sexual harassment law,* 30 June. Accessed online at http://www.igc.org/igc/wn/hl9806304896/hl1.html.

Mason, M. A., A. Skolnick, and S. Sugarman. 1998. *All our families: New policies for a new century.* New York: Oxford University Press.

Mathews, T. J., and B. E. Hamilton. 2002. Mean age of mother 1970–2000. *National Vital Statistics Reports* 51(1). Washington, D.C.: Department of Health.

———, F. Menacker, and M. MacDorman. 2004. Infant mortality statistics from 2002 period linked birth/infant death data set. *National Vital Statistics Reports* 53(10). Table A. Hyattsville, Md.: National Center for Health Statistics.

McCarthy, C., and W. Crichlow, eds. 1993. *Race, identity, and representation in education.* New York: Routledge.

McChesney, R. W. 2004. *The Problem of the Media: US communications politics in the 21st century.* New York: Monthly Review Press.

McGinn, M. 1995. How GATT puts hard-won victories at risk. *Ms.,* March/April, 15.

McIntosh, P. 1988. *White privilege and male privilege: A personal account of coming to see correspondences through work in women's studies.* Wellesley, Mass.: Center for Research on Women, Wellesley College.

McKenna, T. 1996/1997. Military culture breeds misogyny. *Women Against Military Madness,* December/January, 1.

Meadows, D. 1990. State of the village report, *The Global Citizen,* May 31.

Mello, F. V. 1996. Population and international security in the new world order. *Political Environments,* no. 3 (Winter/Spring): 25–26. Publication of the Committee on Women, Population and the Environment, Hampshire College, Amherst, Mass.

Mellor, M. 1992. *Breaking the boundaries: Towards a feminist green socialism.* London: Virago Press.

Members of the AIDS Counseling and Education Program of the Bedford Hills Correctional Facility. 1998. *Breaking the walls of silence: AIDS and women in a New York State maximum security prison.* Woodstock, N.Y.: Overlook Press.

Merchant, C. 1980. *The death of nature: Ecology and the scientific revolution.* San Francisco: Harper & Row.

Messer-Davidow, E. 1991. Know-how. Pp. 281–309 in *(En)gendering knowledge: Feminists in academe,* edited by J. E. Hartman and E. Messer-Davidow. Knoxville: University of Tennessee Press.

Messerschmidt, J. W. 1986. *Capitalism, patriarchy, and crime: Toward a socialist feminist criminology.* Totowa, N.J.: Rowman and Littlefield.

Messner, M. 1992. *Power at play: Sports and the problem of masculinity.* Boston: Beacon Press.

Meyers, D. T. 2001. The rush to motherhood—pronatalist discourse and women's autonomy. *Signs: Journal of Women in Culture and Society* 26(3): 735–73.

Midgley, J. 2005. *Women and the U.S. budget: Where the money goes and what you can do about it.* Gabriola, B.C.: New Society Publishers.

Mies, M. 1986. *Patriarchy and accumulation on a world scale: Women in the international division of labor.* London: Zed Books.

———. 1993. The need for a new vision: The subsistence perspective. In *Ecofeminism,* edited by M. Mies and V. Shiva. London: Zed Books.

———, and V. Shiva, eds. 1993. *Ecofeminism.* London: Zed Books.

Miles Foundation. 1999. E-mail communication from Christine Hansen, Miles Foundation, to Gwyn Kirk, 11 October 1999.

Military is found less likely to promote Blacks. 1995. *New York Times,* 22 November, p. A20.

Milkman, R., ed. 1985. *Women, work, and protest: A century of U.S. women's labor history.* London: Routledge & Kegan Paul.

———, ed. 2000. *Organizing immigrants: The challenge for unions in contemporary California.* Ithaca, N.Y.: ILR Press.

Miller, P. 1993. *The worst of times: Illegal abortion—survivors, practitioners, coroners, cops, and children of women who died talk about its horrors.* New York: HarperCollins.

Miller, S. 2005. California prison boom ends, signaling a shift in priorities. *Christian Science Monitor,* June 20.

Miller, V. D. 1993. *Building on our past, planning our future: Communities of color and the quest for environmental justice.* Pp. 128–135 in *Toxic Struggles: The theory and practice of environmental justice,* edited by Richard Hofrichter, Philadelphia and Gabriola Is., B.C.: New Society Publishers.

Millett, Kate. 1990. *The loony bin trip.* New York: Simon & Schuster.

Mills, R. J., and S. Bhandari. 2003. Health insurance coverage in the United States: 2002. *Current Population Reports,* Washington, D.C.: U.S. Census Bureau.

Mink, G. 1998. Feminists, welfare reform, and welfare justice. *Social Justice* 25(1): 146–57.

———. 2002. Violating women: Rights abuses in the welfare police state. In *Lost ground: Welfare, poverty, and beyond,* edited by R. Albelda and A. Withorn. Cambridge, Mass.: South End Press, pp. 95–112.

Mintz, S., and S. Kellogg. 1988. *Domestic revolutions: A social history of American family life.* New York: Free Press.

Mitchell, J. 1971. *Woman's estate.* New York: Pantheon.

Mohai, P. 1997. Men, women, and the environment: An examination of the gender gap in environmental concern and activism, pp. 215–39 in *Women working in the environment,* edited by C. Sachs. New York: Taylor and Francis.

Mohanty, C., A. Russo, and L. Torres, eds. 1991. *Third World women and the politics of feminism.* Bloomington: Indiana University Press.

Mohanty, C. T. 2003. *Feminism without borders: Decolonizing theory, practicing solidarity.* Durham, N.C.: Duke University Press.

Moon, K. 1997. *Sex between allies: Military prostitution in U.S.–Korea relations.* New York: Columbia University Press.

Moore, B. 1996. From underrepresentation to overrepresentation: African American women. Pp. 115–35 in *It's our military too! Women and the U.S. military,* edited by J. H. Stiehm. Philadelphia: Temple University Press.

Moore, M., and J. Gould. 2001. *Date like a man: What men know about dating and are afraid you'll find out.* New York: Quill/HarperCollins.

Moraga, C. 1997. *Waiting in the wings: Portrait of a queer motherhood.* Ithaca, N.Y.: Firebrand.

———, and G. Anzaldúa. 1981. *This bridge called my back: Writings by radical women of color.* New York: Kitchen Table/Women of Color Press.

Morell, C. M. 1994. *Unwomanly conduct: The challenge of intentional childlessness.* New York: Routledge.

Morgan, L. M., and M. Michaels. 1999. *Fetal Subjects: Feminist positions.* Philadelphia: University of Pennsylvania Press.

Morgan, R. 1996. Dispatch from Beijing. *Ms.,* January/February, 12–15.

Morgen, S. 2002. *Into our own hands: The women's health movement in the United States, 1969–1990.* Piscataway, N.J.: Rutgers University Press.

Morris, M. 1999. In war and peace: Incidence and implications of rape by military personnel. Pp. 163–94 in *Beyond zero tolerance: Discrimination in military culture,* edited by M. F. Katzenstein and J. Reppy. Lanham, Md.: Rowman and Littlefield.

Morrison, A., R. White, E. Van Velsor, and the Center for Creative Leadership. 1992. *Breaking the glass ceiling: Can women reach the top of America's largest corporations?* Reading, Mass.: Addison-Wesley.

Morrison, T., ed. 1992. *Race-ing, justice, en-gendering power: Essays on Anita Hill, Clarence Thomas, and the construction of reality.* New York: Pantheon.

Morrow, D. 1999. Maker of Norplant reaches settlement in suit over effects. *New York Times,* 27 August, p. A1.

Morrow, L. 1999. Folklore in a box. Pp. 22–26 in *Readings in mass communication: Media literacy and culture,* edited by K. B. Massey, Mountain View, Calif.: Mayfield.

Moses, M. 1993. Farmworkers and pesticides. Pp. 161–78 in *Confronting environmental racism: Voices from the grassroots,* edited by R. Bullard. Boston: South End Press.

Mother Jones. 2005. For Richer or poorer. *Mother Jones* 30(1), Jan.–Feb.: 24–25.

Movement for a New Society. 1983. *Off their backs . . . and on our own two feet.* Philadelphia: New Society Publishers.

Mudrick, N. R. 1988. Disabled women and the public policies of income support. In *Women with disabilities: Essays in psychology, culture, and politics*, edited by M. Fine and A. Asch. Philadelphia: Temple University Press.

Muir, K. 1993. *Arms and the woman.* London: Hodder and Stoughton.

Mullings, L. 1997. *On our own: Race, class, and gender in the lives of African American women.* New York: Routledge.

Mumola, C. J. 2000. *Incarcerated parents and their children.* Bureau of Justice Statistics special report, August. Washington, DC: U.S. Department of Justice.

Muscio, I. 1999. *Cunt: A declaration of independence.* Seattle, Wash.: Seal Press.

Musil, C. M., ed. 1992. *The courage to question: Women's studies and student learning.* Washington, D.C.: Association of American Colleges.

Myers, A., J. Taub, J. F. Morris, and E. D. Rothblun. 1998. Beauty mandates and the appearance obsession: Are lesbians any better off? Pp. 17–25 in *Looking queer: Body image and identity in lesbian, bisexual, gay, and transgender communities*, edited by D. Atkins. New York: Haworth Press.

Nader, R. 1993. *The case against free trade.* San Francisco: Earth Island Press.

Naffine, N. 1987. *Female crime: The construction of women in criminology.* Boston: Allen & Unwin.

Nagel, J. 1997. *Whores and other feminists.* New York: Routledge.

Naidus, B. 1993. *One size does not fit all.* Littleton, Colo.: Aigis Publications.

Naples, N., ed. 1997. *Community activism and feminist politics: Organizing across race, class, and gender.* New York: Routledge.

———. 1998. *Grassroots warriors: Activist mothering, community work, and the war on poverty.* New York: Routledge.

———, and K. Bojar, eds. 2002. *Teaching feminist activism: Strategies from the field.* New York: Routledge.

National Center for Addiction and Substance Abuse. 2003. *Crossing the bridge: An evaluation of the Drug Treatment Alternative-to-Prison Program (DTAP).* New York: NCASA at Columbia University.

National Center for Health Statistics. 2004. *Health, United States 2004.* Hyattsville, Md.: National Center for Health Statistics.

National Clearinghouse on Marital and Date Rape. 1998. Accessed online at http://members.aol.com/ncmdr/index.html.

National Council for Research on Women. 2004. *Missing: Information about women's lives.* New York: NCRW.

National Institute of Justice. 1998. *Women offenders: Programming needs and promising approaches.* Washington, D.C.: U.S. Department of Justice.

National Institute of Justice and Centers for Disease Control and Prevention. 1998. *Prevalence, incidence, and consequences of violence against women: Findings from the National Violence Against Women Survey.* Washington, D.C.: National Institute of Justice and Centers for Disease Control and Prevention.

National Partnership for Women and Families. 2005. FMLA Regulations Threatened. www.nationalpartnership.org accessed online on August 6, 2005.

National Victim Center. 1992. *Rape in America. A report to the nation.* Arlington, Va.: Author.

National Women's Law Center. 2003. *Air Force must face systemic problems to address sexual assaults at Academy*, press release, February 28, accessed online at www.nwlc.org/details.cfm?id=1331&section=newsroom on May 10, 2005.

———. 2004. *Slip-sliding away: The erosion of hard-won gains for women under the Bush administration and an agenda for moving forward.* Washington, D.C.: National Women's Law Center.

Nechas, E., and D. Foley. 1994. *Unequal treatment: What you don't know about how women are mistreated by the medical community.* Philadelphia: Temple University Press.

Nelson, J. 2003. *Women of color and the reproductive rights movement.* New York: New York University Press.

Nelson, L. 1990. The place of women in polluted places. In *Reweaving the world: The emergence of ecofeminism*, edited by I. Diamond and G. Orenstein. San Francisco: Sierra Club Books.

Nelson, M. B. 2002. And now they tell us women don't really like sports? *Ms.*, December 2002/January 2003, 32–36.

Nestle, J., ed. 1992. *The persistent desire: A femme-butch reader.* Los Angeles: Alyson.

Nestle, J., C. Howell, and R. Wilchins. 2002. *Genderqueer: Voices from beyond the sexual binary.* Los Angeles: Alyson Publications.

Netaid. 2005. U.S. approves controversial CAFTA, August 2. Accessed online at www.netaid.org/press/news/ on August 22, 2005.

Neuborne, E. 1994. Cashing in on fear: The NRA targets women. *Ms.*, June/July, pp. 45–50.

Newman, L. 1991. *SomeBody to love: A guide to loving the body you have.* Chicago: Third Side Press.

News Services. 1998. Pope warns against dangers of capitalism. *St. Louis Dispatch*, 26 January, p. A1.

Nguyen, T. 2005. *We are all suspects now.* Boston: Beacon Press.

NiCarthy, G. 1987. *The ones who got away: Women who left abusive partners.* Seattle, Wash.: Seal Press.

———. 2004. *Getting free: You can end abuse and take back your life.* Expanded edition. Seattle, Wash.: Seal Press.

Nissinen, S. 2000. *The conscious bride: Women unveil their true feelings about getting hitched.* Oakland, Calif.: New Harbinger Publications.

Noble, K. 1994. Woman tells of retaliation for complaint on Tailhook. *New York Times*, 5 October, p. A10.

Norris, P., ed. 1997. *Women, media, and politics.* New York: Oxford University Press.

Norsigian, J. 1996. The women's health movement in the United States. Pp. 79–97 in *Man-made medicine: Women's health, public policy, and reform*, edited by K. L. Moss. Durham, N.C.: Duke University Press.

Nowrojee, S., and J. Silliman. 1997. Asian women's health: Organizing a movement. Pp. 73–89 in *Dragon ladies: Asian American feminists breathe fire*, edited by S. Shah. Boston: South End Press.

NWSAction. 2004. Feminist uses of science and technology. College Park, Md.: National Women's Studies Association.

Ochs, Robyn, and Sarah F. Rowley, eds. 2005. *Getting bi: Voices of bisexuals around the world.* Boston: Bisexual Resource Center.

O'Connor, M., ed. 1994. *Is capitalism sustainable? Political economy and the politics of ecology.* New York: Guilford Press.

O'Farrell, B., and J. Kornbluh. 1996. *Rocking the boat: Union women's voices, 1915–1975.* New Brunswick, N.J.: Rutgers University Press.

Office of Civil Rights. 2005. *Additional clarification of intercollegiate athletics policy: Three-part test—Part three.* March 17. Accessed online at www.ed.gov/about/ offices/ list/ocr/docs/title9guidance.additional.html on September 6.

Ogur, B. 1996. Smothering in stereotypes: HIV-positive women. In *Talking gender: Public images, personal journeys, and political critiques*, edited by N. Hewitt, J. O'Barr, and N. Rosebaugh. Chapel Hill: University of North Carolina Press.

Okazawa-Rey, M. 1994. Racial identity development of mixed race persons: An overview. In *Diversity and human service education*, edited by J. Silver-Jones, S. Kerstein, and D. Osher. Council of Standards in Human Service Education Monograph Series, No. 4.

———. 1997. Amerasians in GI town: The legacy of U.S. militarism in South Korea. *Asian Journal of Women's Studies* 3: 1.

———, and G. Kirk. 1996. Military security: Confronting the oxymoron. *CrossRoads* 60: 4–7.

Okin, S. M. 1989. *Justice, gender, and the family.* New York: Basic Books.

Okinawa Prefecture. 1998. *Summary of the second interim report of the Field Study on Public Health around U.S. Bases in Okinawa.* Okinawa, Japan: Research Study Committee of Aircraft Noise Influence to Health.

Okinawa Women Act Against Military Violence. 1996. *An appeal for the recognition of women's human rights.* Naha, Okinawa: Author.

Omolade, B. 1983. Hearts of darkness. In *Powers of desire*, edited by A. Snitow, C. Stansell, and S. Thompson. New York: Monthly Review Press.

———. 1986. *It's a family affair: The real lives of Black single mothers.* New York: Kitchen Table: Women of Color Press.

———. 1989. We speak for the planet. In *Rocking the ship of state: Toward a feminist peace politics*, edited by A. Harris and Y. King. Boulder, Colo.: Westview Press.

———. 1994. Ella's daughters. In *The rising song of African American women.* New York: Routledge.

O'Reilly, B. 1991. Cooling down the world debt bomb. *Fortune*, 20 May, 123.

Orlando, L. 1991. Loving whom we choose. Pp. 223–32 in *Bi any other name: Bisexual people speak out*, edited by L. Hutchins and L. Ka'ahumanu. Boston: Alyson Publications.

O'Rourke, D. 1985. *Half life: A parable for the nuclear age.* Video.

O'Shea, K. 1998. *Women and the death penalty in the United States, 1900–1998.* Westport, Conn.: Praeger.

O'Toole, L., and J. Schiffman. 1997. *Gender violence: Interdisciplinary perspectives.* New York: New York University Press.

Owen, B., and B. Bloom. 1995. Profiling women prisoners. *The Prison Journal* 75(2): 165–85.

Oxfam International. 1998. *Making debt relief work: A test of political will.* Accessed online at http://www. oxfamamerica.org/advocacy/ Test_of_Political_Will.htm.

———. 2004. *Trading away our rights: Women working in global supply chains.* Oxford, UK: Oxfam.

Page, S. 1988. *If I'm so wonderful, why am I still single? Ten strategies that will change your love life forever.* New York: Viking.

Paglia, C. 1990. *Sexual personae: Art and decadence from Nefertiti to Emily Dickinson.* New Haven, Conn.: Yale University Press.

Paley, G. 1998. The illegal days. Pp. 13–20 in *Just as I thought.* New York: Farrar, Straus, Giroux.

Pardo, M. 1990. Mexican American women grassroots community activists: "Mothers of East Los Angeles." *Frontiers: A Journal of Women's Studies* 11(1): 1–7.

Parenti, C. 1999, September. The prison industrial complex: Crisis and control. *Corporate Watch.* San Francisco: Transnational Resource and Action Center.

Parker, S., M. Nichter, C. S. Vuckovic, and C. Ritenbaugh. 1995. Body image and weight concerns among African-American and white adolescent females: Differences that make a difference. *Human Organization* 54: 103–14.

Parreñas, R. S. 2001. *Servants of globalization: Women, migration, and domestic work.* Stanford, Calif.: Stanford University Press.

Patai, D. 1998. *Heterophobia: Sexual harassment and the future of feminism.* Lanham, Md.: Rowman and Littlefield.

Pateman, C. 1988. *The sexual contract.* Stanford, Calif.: Stanford University Press.

Peach, L. J. 1997. Behind the front lines: Feminist battles over combat. Pp. 99–135 in *Wives and warriors: Women and the military in the United States and Canada,* edited by L. Weinstein and C. White. Westport, Conn.: Bergin & Garvey.

Pearce, D., A. Markandya, and E. B. Barbier. 1990. *Blueprint for a Green economy.* London: Earthscan.

Perez, B. E. 2003. Woman warrior meets mail-order bride: Finding an Asian American voice in the women's movement. *Berkeley Women's Law Journal,* 18, pp. 211–36.

Perrone, B., H. H. Stockel, and V. Krueger. 1989. *Medicine women, curanderas, and women doctors.* Norman: University of Oklahoma Press.

Pershing, J. 2003. Why women don't report sexual harassment: A case study of an elite military institution. *Gender Issues,* 21(4): 3–30.

Petchesky, R. 1990. *Abortion and woman's choice: The state, sexuality, and reproductive freedom.* Rev. ed. Boston: Northeastern University Press.

———. 1997. Fetal images: The power of visual culture in the politics of reproduction. Pp. 134–50 in *The gender/sexuality reader,* edited by R. Lancaster and M. di Leonardo. New York: Routledge.

Peters, J. 1997. *When mothers work: Loving our children without sacrificing ourselves.* Reading, Mass.: Addison-Wesley.

Petersen, B. 1991. *Dancing with Daddy: A childhood lost and a life regained.* New York: Bantam Books.

Peterson, R. R. 1996. Re-evaluation of the economic consequences of divorce. *American Sociological Review* 61(3): 528–53.

Peterson, V. S., and A. S. Runyan. 1993. *Global gender issues.* Boulder, Colo.: Westview Press.

Pharr, S. 1988. *Homophobia: A weapon of sexism.* Inverness, Calif.: Chardon Press.

Phillips, L. 2000. *Flirting with danger: Young women reflect on sexuality and domination.* New York: New York University Press.

Phoenix, J. 1993. Getting the lead out of the community. In *Confronting environmental racism,* edited by R. D. Bullard. Boston: South End Press.

Pierce-Baker, C. 1998. *Surviving the silence: Black women's stories of rape.* New York: Norton.

Piercy, M. 1976. *Woman on the edge of time.* New York: Fawcett Crest.

Pitter, L., and A. Stilmayer. 1993. Will the world remember? Can the women forget? *Ms.,* March/April, 19–22.

Plath, S. 1971. *The bell jar.* New York: Harper and Row.

Plumwood, V. 1993. *Feminism and the mastery of nature.* New York: Routledge.

Polikoff, N. 1993. We will get what we ask for: Why legalizing gay and lesbian marriage will not "dismantle the legal structure of gender in every marriage." *Virginia Law Review* 79: 1535–50.

Postman, N., and S. Powers. 1992. *How to watch TV news.* New York: Penguin Books.

Potts, B. 1988. *Witches heal: Lesbian herbal self-sufficiency.* 2d ed. Ann Arbor, Mich.: DuReve Publications.

Poverty Guidelines. 2005. *Federal Register,* February 18, 70(33): 8373–75.

Pratt, M. B. 1984. Identity: Skin blood heart. Pp. 9–63. In E. Bulkin, M. B. Pratt, and B. Smith, *Yours in Struggle: Three feminist perspectives on anti-semitism and racism.* Brooklyn, NY: Long Haul Press.

Press, E. 1997. Breaking the sweats. *The Nation,* 28 April, 5–6.

Prilleltensky, O. 2003. A ramp to motherhood: The experience of mothers with physical disabilities. *Sexuality and Disability,* 21: 21–47.

Prison Activist Resource Center. 1997. *Women in prison.* Fact sheet prepared by Prison Activist Resource Center, Berkeley, Calif.

Proctor, B. D., and J. Dalaker. 2003. *Poverty in the United States: 2002.* Current Population Reports. P60-222. Washington, D.C.: U.S. Census Bureau.

Project for Excellence in Journalism, The. 2005. *The gender gap: Women are still missing as sources for journalists.* Accessed online at www.journalism.org/resources/research/reports/gender/default.asp on 7/5/05.

Prokosch, M., and L. Raymond, eds. 2002. *The global activist's manual: Local ways to change the world.* New York: Thunder's Mouth Press/Nation Books.

Pulido, L. 1993. Sustainable development at Ganados del Valle. In *Confronting environmental racism: Voices from the grassroots,* edited by R. Bullard. Boston: South End Press.

———. 1996. *Environmentalism and economic justice: Two Chicano struggles in the Southwest.* Tucson: University of Arizona Press.

Queen, Carol. 2002. *Real live nude girl: Chronicle of sex positive culture.* San Francisco: Cleis Press.

Quindlen, A. 1994. Feminism continues to grow and reach and affect us all. *Chicago Tribune,* 21 January, sec. 1, p. 21.

Quintero-Somaini, A., and M. Quirindongo. 2004. *Hidden danger: environmental health threats to the Latino community.* New York: Natural Resources Defense Council.

Rachel's Environment and Health Weekly. 1998. The precautionary principle. Feb 19, 586. Accessed online at www.monitor.net/rachel/r586.html on September 4, 2005.

Radical Women. 2001. *The radical women manifesto: Socialist feminism theory, program, and organizational structure.* Seattle: Red Letter Press.

Rafter, N. 1990. *Partial justice: Women, prisons and social control.* New Brunswick, N.J.: Transaction.

Ragone, H., and F. W. Twine, eds. 2000. *Ideologies and technologies of motherhood: Race, class, sexuality and nationalism.* New York: Routledge.

Raine, N. V. 1998. *After silence: Rape and my journey back.* New York: Three Rivers Press.

Rape Abuse Incest National Network. 1999. RAINNews. Accessed online at http://www.rainn.org/news/stat.html.

Raphael, J., and R. Tolman. 1997. *Trapped in poverty, trapped by abuse: New evidence documenting the relationship between domestic violence and welfare.* Project for Research on Welfare, Work, and Domestic Violence. A collaboration between Taylor Institute and University of Michigan Development Center on Poverty, Risk, and Mental Health.

Rasmussen, V. 1998. Rethinking the corporation. *Food and Water Journal,* Fall, 17–21.

Rayner, R. 1997. Women in the warrior culture. *New York Times Magazine,* 22 June, 24–29, 40, 49, 53, 55–56.

Reagan, L. J. 1997. *When abortion was a crime: Women, medicine, and law in the United States 1867–1973.* Berkeley: University of California Press.

Reagon, B. J. 1987. *Ode to the international debt.* Boston: Songtalk.

Reardon, B. A. 1985. *Sexism and the war system.* New York: Teachers College Press.

———. 1993. *Women and peace: Feminist visions of global security.* Albany, N.Y.: SUNY Press.

Redwood, R. 1996. The glass ceiling. *Motion Magazine.* Accessed online at http://www.inmotionmagazine.com/glass.html.

Rennison, C. M. 2002. *Rape and sexual assault: Reporting to police and medical attention, 1992–2000.* Bureau of Justice Statistics, selected findings. Washington, D.C.: U.S. Department of Justice.

———. 2003. *Intimate partner violence, 1993–2001.* Bureau of Justice Statistics, Crime Data Brief. Washington, D.C.: U.S. Department of Justice.

Renzetti, C. M. 1992. *Violent betrayal: Partner abuse in lesbian relationships.* Newbury Park, Calif.: Sage.

Rethinking schools. 2002. *The WTO in action: Case studies.* Accessed online at http://www.rethinkingschools.org/publication/rg/RGWto.shtml on 26 December 2002.

Reti, I., ed. 1992. *Childless by choice: A feminist anthology.* Santa Cruz, Calif.: Her Books.

Rhodes, J. 2005. *Radical feminist writing and critical agency: From manifesto to modern.* Albany, N.Y.: SUNY Press.

Rich, A. 1976. *Of woman born: Motherhood as experience and institution.* New York: W. W. Norton.

———. 1986a. Compulsory heterosexuality and lesbian existence. In *Blood, bread, and poetry.* New York: W. W. Norton.

———. 1986b. *Of woman born: Motherhood as experience and institution.* 10th anniversary ed. New York: W. W. Norton.

———. 1986c. Notes towards a politics of location. Pp. 210–31 in *Blood, bread, and poetry.* New York: W. W. Norton.

Richie, B. 1996. *Compelled to crime: The gender entrapment of battered Black women.* New York: Routledge.

Richter, P. 2000. Armed forces find "disturbing" level of gay harassment. *Los Angeles Times,* 25 March, p. A1.

Rierden, A. 1997. *The Farm: Inside a women's prison.* Amherst: University of Massachusetts Press.

Riley, D. 1988. *Am I that name? Feminism and the category of "women" in history.* Minneapolis: University of Minnesota Press.

Risman, B. J. 1998. *Gender vertigo: American families in transition.* New Haven, Conn.: Yale University Press.

Ristock, J. 2002. *No more secrets: Violence in lesbian relationships.* New York: Routledge.

Ritz, D., ed. 2001. *Defying corporations, defining democracy.* New York: Apex Press.

Roberts, D. 1997. *Killing the Black body: Race, reproduction, and the meaning of liberty.* New York: Pantheon.

Roberts, M. M., and T. Mizuta, eds. 1993. *The reformers: Socialist feminism.* London: Routledge/Thoemmes Press.

Rodríguez, J. M. 2003. *Queer latinidad: Identity practices, discursive spaces.* New York: New York University Press.

Roediger, D. R. 1991. *The wages of whiteness: Race and the making of the American working class.* New York: Verso.

Roiphe, K. 1993. *The morning after: Sex, fear, and feminism.* Boston: Little Brown.

Rooks, N. 1996. *Beauty, culture, and African American women.* New Brunswick, N.J.: Rutgers University Press.

Root, M. P., ed. 1996. *The multiracial experience: Racial borders as the new frontier.* Thousand Oaks, Calif.: Sage.

Rose, Tricia. 2003. *Longing to tell: Black women talk about sexuality and intimacy.* New York: Farrar, Straus & Giroux.

Rosen, R. 2000. *The world split open: How the modern women's movement changed America.* New York: Viking.

Rosenberg, A. 1988. The crisis in knowing and understanding the Holocaust. In *Echoes from the Holocaust: Philosophical reflections on a dark time,* edited by A. Rosenberg and G. E. Meyers. Philadelphia: Temple University Press.

Rosenberg, H. H. 1998. *How to get married after thirty-five: The game plan for love.* New York: HarperCollins.

Rosenblatt, E., ed. 1996. *Criminal injustice: Confronting the prison crisis.* Boston: South End Press.

Rosenblum, B. 1997. Living in an unstable body. Pp. 93–104 in *Staring back: The disability experiences from the inside out,* edited by K. Fries. New York: Penguin/Plume.

Ross, A., ed. 1997. *No sweat: Fashion, free trade, and the rights of garment workers.* New York: Verso.

Ross, L. 1993. Major concerns of imprisoned American Indian and White mothers. In *Gender: Multicultural perspectives,* edited by J. Gonzalez-Calvo. Dubuque, Iowa: Kendall Hunt.

Ross, L. J. 1993. African-American women and abortion: 1800–1970. In *Theorizing black feminisms: The visionary pragmatism of black women*, edited by S. M. James and A. P. A. Busia. New York: Routledge, pp. 141–59.

———, S. L. Brownlee, D. D. Diallo, L. Rodriquez, and the SisterSong Women of Color Reproductive Health Project. 2002. Just choices: Women of color, reproductive health and human rights. Pp. 147–74 in *Policing the national body: Race, gender, and criminalization*, edited by J. Silliman and A. Bhattacharjee. Cambridge, Mass.: South End Press.

Roth, B. 2003. *Separate roads to feminism: Black, Chicana and White feminist movements in America's second wave.* New York: Cambridge University Press.

Rousso, H. 2001. *Strong proud sisters: Girls and young women with disabilities.* Washington, D.C.: Center for Women Policy Studies.

Roy, A. 2003. Confronting empire. In *War Talk.* Cambridge: South End Press, pp. 103–12.

———. 2004. The new American century. *The Nation*, February 9.

Roy, Carole. 2004. *The raging grannies: Wild hats, cheeky songs, and witty actions for a better world.* Montreal: Black Rose Books.

Rubin, G. 1984. Thinking sex: Notes for a radical theory of the politics of sexuality. Pp. 267–319 in *Pleasure and danger: Exploring female sexuality*, edited by C. S. Vance. Boston: Routledge and Kegan Paul.

Ruddick, S. 1989. *Maternal thinking: Toward a politics of peace.* Boston: Beacon Press.

Russell, B. 1935. *In praise of idleness and other essays.* New York: W. W. Norton.

Russell, D. 1995. *Women, madness, and medicine.* Cambridge, England: Polity Press.

Russell, D. E. H. 1975. *The politics of rape: The victim's perspective.* New York: Stein and Day.

———. 1986. *The secret trauma: Incest in the lives of girls and women.* New York: Basic Books.

———. 1990. *Rape in marriage.* Rev. ed. Bloomington: Indiana University Press.

———. 1993. *Making violence sexy: Feminist views on pornography.* New York: Teachers College Press.

Sachs, C. 1996. *Gendered fields: Rural women, agriculture, and environment.* Boulder, Colo.: Westview Press.

Sachs, S. 2000. Sexual abuse reported at an immigration center. *New York Times*, 5 October, p. A20.

Sadler, G. C. 1997. Women in combat: The U.S. military and the impact of the Persian Gulf War. Pp. 79–97 in *Wives and warriors*, edited by L. Weinstein and C. White.

Safe, J. 1996. *Beyond motherhood: Choosing a life without children.* New York: Pocket Books.

Sale, K. 1985. *Dwellers in the land, the bioregional vision.* San Francisco: Sierra Club Books.

Sampson, Rana. 2002. *Acquaintance rape of college students.* Washington, D.C.: U.S. Department of Justice, Office of Community Oriented Policing Services.

Sanday, P. 1990. *Fraternity gang rape: Sex, brotherhood, and privilege on campus.* New York: New York University Press.

Sanders, B., and M. Kaptur. 1997. Just do it, Nike. *The Nation*, 8 December, 6.

Sandoz, J., and J. Winana, eds. 1999. *Whatever it takes: Women on women's sport.* New York: Farrar, Straus, Giroux.

Santi-Flaherty, T. 1997. *The savvy woman's success bible: How to find the right job, the right man, and the right life.* New York: Perigee/Berkeley Publishing Group.

Scharnberg, K. 2005. Female GIs hard hit by war syndrome. *Chicago Tribune*, March 24.

Schemo, D. J. 2003. Women's athletics: Title IX reformers keep men in mind. *New York Times*, 27 February, p. D1.

Scholinski, D. 1997. *The last time I wore a dress.* New York: Riverhead Books.

Schur, L. 2004. Is there still a "double handicap"? Economic, social and political disparities experienced by women with disabilities. In *Gendering disability*, edited by B. G. Smith and B. Hutchison. New Brunswick: Rutgers University Press. pp. 253–71.

Schwab, J. 1994. *Deeper shades of green: The rise of blue-collar and minority environmentalism in America.* San Francisco: Sierra Club Books.

Schwartz, P. 1994. *Love between equals: How peer marriage really works.* New York: Free Press.

Scott, W. J., and S. C. Stanley. 1994. *Gays and lesbians in the military: Issues, concerns, and contrasts.* Hawthorne, N.Y.: Aldine de Gruyter.

Seager, J. 1993. *Earth follies: Coming to feminist terms with the global environmental crisis.* New York: Routledge.

Sedgwick, E. K. 1990. *Epistemology of the closet.* Berkeley: University of California Press.

Segal, L. 1994. *Straight sex: Rethinking the politics of pleasure.* Berkeley: University of California Press.

Segrest, M. 1994. *Memoir of a race traitor.* Boston: South End Press.

Seigel, L. 1997. The pregnancy police fight the war on drugs. Pp. 249–59 in *Crack in America: Demon drugs and social justice*, edited by C. Reinarman and H. G. Levine. Berkeley: University of California Press.

Sen, G., and C. Grown. 1987. *Development, crises, and alternative visions: Third World women's perspectives.* New York: Monthly Review Press.

Sengupta, S. 1999. Squeezed by debt and time, mothers ship babies to China. *New York Times*, 14 September, p. A1.

Sentencing Project, The. 2001. *U.S. continues to be world leader in rate of incarceration.* Washington, D.C.: The Sentencing Project. Accessed online at www.sentencingproject.org on 16 January 2003.

Serna, I. 1992. *Locked down: A woman's life in prison.* Norwich, Vt.: New Victoria Publishers.

Servicemembers Legal Defense Network. 1999a. *Conduct unbecoming. Fifth annual report on "Don't ask, don't tell, don't pursue.*" Accessed online at http://www.sldn.org/scripts/sldn.ixe?page?pr_03_15_99.

———. 1999b. Pentagon fires record number of gays. Accessed online at http://www.sldn.org/scripts/sldn.ixe?page=pr_01_22_99.

———. 2002. *Conduct unbecoming: The eighth annual report on "Don't ask, Don't tell, Don't pursue, Don't harass."* Washington, D.C.: SLDN.

Shah, S., ed. 1997. *Dragon ladies: Asian feminists breathe fire.* Boston: South End Press.

Shanley, M. ed. 2004. *Just marriage.* New York: Oxford University Press.

Shannonhouse, R. 2003. *Out of her mind: Women writing on madness.* New York: Modern Library. Expanded edition.

Sherrill, R. 1997. A year in corporate crime. *The Nation,* 7 April, 11–20.

Shin, A. 1999. Testing Title IX. *Ms.,* April/May, 32–33.

Shiva, V. 1988. *Staying alive: Women, ecology and development.* London: Zed Books.

———. 2002. Relocalization not globalization. Pp. 248–49 in *Rethinking globalization: Teaching for justice in an unjust world,* edited by B. Bigelow and B. Peterson. Milwaukee, Wis.: Rethinking Schools.

———. 2005. *Earth democracy: Justice, sustainability, and peace.* Cambridge: South End Press.

Showalter, E. 1987. *The female malady: Women, madness, and English culture, 1830–1980.* London: Virago.

Shugar, D. R. 1995. *Separatism and women's community.* Lincoln: University of Nebraska Press.

Shulman, S. 1990. Toxic travels: Inside the military's environmental nightmare. *Nuclear Times,* Autumn, 20–32.

Shumway, C. 2004. Violence against female soldiers ignored. *The New Standard,* June 16.

Sidel, R. 1996. *Keeping women and children last: America's war on the poor.* New York: Penguin Books.

Siegal, N. 1995. Girl trouble. *San Francisco Bay Guardian,* 29 November, pp. 16–18.

———. 1998. Women in prison. *Ms.,* September/October, 64–73.

Sigler, H., S. Love, and J. Yood. 1999. *Hollis Sigler's breast cancer journal.* New York: Hudson Hills Press.

Silliman, J., and A. Bhattacharjee, eds. 2002. *Policing the national body: Sex, race, and criminalization.* Cambridge, Mass.: South End Press.

———, M. G. Fried, L. Ross, and E. R. Gutiérrez. 2004. *Undivided rights: Women of color organize for reproductive justice.* Cambridge: South End Press.

———, and Y. King, eds. 1999. *Dangerous intersections: Feminist perspectives on population, environment, and development.* Cambridge, Mass.: South End Press.

Simon, R. 1975. *Women and crime.* Lexington, Mass.: Lexington Books.

Sivard, R. L. 1996. *World military and social expenditures 1996.* 16th ed. Washington, D.C.: World Priorities.

Skaine, R. 1998. *Women at war: Gender issues of Americans in combat.* Jefferson, N.C.: McFarland and Co.

Skolnick, A. 1991. *Embattled paradise: The American family in an age of uncertainty.* New York: Basic Books.

Slater, L. 1998. *Prozac diary.* New York: Random House.

Slugocki, L. A. and E. C. Wilson. 2000. *The erotica project.* San Francisco: Cleis Press.

Smeal, E. 1984. *Why and how women will elect the next president.* New York: Harper & Row.

Smith, A. 1991. To all those who were Indian in a former life. *Ms.,* November/December, 44–45.

———. 1997. Ecofeminism through an anti-colonial framework. Pp. 21–37 in *Ecofeminism: Women, culture, nature,* edited by K. Warren. Bloomington: Indiana University Press.

———. 2001. The color of violence: Violence against women of color. Conference report. *Meridians: Feminism, Race, Transnationalism* 1(2): 65–72.

———. 2002. Better dead than pregnant: The colonization of Native women's reproductive health. Pp. 123–46 in *Policing the national body: Race, gender, and criminalization,* edited by J. Silliman and A. Bhattacharjee. Cambridge, Mass.: South End Press.

———. 2005a. Beyond pro-choice versus pro-life: Women of color and reproductive justice. *NWSA Journal,* 17(1): 119–40.

———. 2005b. *Conquest: Sexual violence and American Indian genocide.* Cambridge: South End Press.

Smith, B. 1998. *The truth that never hurts: Writings on race, gender, freedom.* New Brunswick, N.J.: Rutgers University Press.

Smith, B., ed. 1983. *Home girls: A Black feminist anthology.* New York: Kitchen Table: Women of Color Press.

Smith, B. G., and B. Hutchison, eds. 2004. *Gendering disability.* New Brunswick, N.J.: Rutgers University Press.

Smith, J. 2004. Sexual assaults in army on rise. *Washington Post,* June 3.

Smith, M. 1997. When violence strikes home. *The Nation,* 30 June, 23–24.

Smith, S. 2005. *Women and socialism: Essays on women's liberation.* Chicago: Haymarket Books.

Sneed, C. 2000. Seeds of change, *Yes: A journal of positive futures,* Fall, no. 15.

Snitow, A., C. Stansell, and S. Thompson, eds. 1983. *Powers of desire: The politics of sexuality.* New York: Monthly Review Press.

Solinger, R. 1994. *The abortionist: A woman against the law.* New York: Routledge.

———. 1998. *Abortion wars; A half century of struggle, 1950–2000,* Berkeley: University of California Press.

———. 2000. *Wake up little susie: Single pregnancy and race before Roe v. Wade.* New York: Routledge.

———. 2005. *Pregnancy and power: A short history of reproductive politics in America.* New York: New York University Press.

Solomon, A. 2005. Another World Turns. *The Nation*, Jan 30. Published online at www.thenation.com, accessed August 22, 2005.

Spears, E. G. 1998. *The Newtown story: One community's fight for environmental justice.* Gainesville, GA: Center for Democratic Renewal and Newtown Florist Club.

Spelman, E. V. 1988. *Inessential woman: Problems of exclusion in feminist thought.* Boston: Beacon Press.

Spieldoch, A. 2004. NAFTA Through a gender lens: What "free trade" pacts mean for women. *CounterPunch* accessed at www.counterpunch.org/spieldoch12302004.html on January 9, 2005.

Spretnak, C. 1990. Ecofeminism: Our roots and flowering. In *Reweaving the world: The emergence of ecofeminism,* edited by I. Diamond & G. Orenstein. San Francisco: Sierra Club Books.

Springer, K. 2005. *Living for the revolution: Black feminist organizing, 1968–1980.* Durham: Duke University Press.

Stacey, Jackie. 1993. Untangling feminist theory. Pp. 49–73 in *Thinking feminist: Key concepts in women's studies,* edited by D. Richardson and V. Robinson. New York: Guilford Press.

Stacey, Judith. 1996. *In the name of the family: Rethinking values in the postmodern age.* Boston: Beacon Press.

Stan, Adele. 1995. *Debating sexual correctness.* New York: Delta.

Stanworth, M., ed. 1987. *Reproductive technologies.* Cambridge, England: Cambridge University Press.

Staples, S. 2000. The relationship between globalization and militarism. *Social Justice: A journal of conflict and world change,* 27(4): 18–22.

Starhawk. 1993. *The fifth sacred thing.* New York: Bantam Books.

———. 2002a. Our place in nature. Pp. 160–68 in *Webs of power: Notes from the global uprising.* Gabriola Island, B.C.: New Society Publishers.

———. 2002b. *Webs of power: Notes from the global uprising.* Gabriola Island, B.C.: New Society Publishers.

Steedman, C. 1986. *Landscape for a good woman: A story of two lives.* New Brunswick, N.J.: Rutgers University Press.

Stefan, S. 1994. The protection racket: Rape trauma syndrome, psychiatric labeling, and law. In *Northwestern Law Review,* 88(4): 1271–1345.

Stein, A. 1997. Sisters and queers: The decentering of lesbian feminism. Pp. 378–91 in *The gender sexuality reader,* edited by R. Lancaster and M. di Leonardo. New York: Routledge.

Stein, D., ed. 1991. *From inside: An anthology of writing by incarcerated women.* Minneapolis: Honor Press.

Stein, R., ed. 2004. *New perspectives on environmental justice: Gender, sexuality, and activism,* New Brunswic, N.J.: Rutgers University Press.

Steinem, G. 1983. *Outrageous acts and everyday rebellions.* New York: Holt, Rinehart, & Winston.

Steingraber, S. 2001. *Having faith: An ecologist's journey to motherhood.* Cambridge, Mass.: Perseus Publishing.

Stewart, A., A. Copeland, N. L. Chester, J. Malley, N. Barenbaum. 1997. *Separating together: How divorce transforms families.* New York: Guilford Press.

Stiehm, J. H. 1989. *Arms and the enlisted woman.* Philadelphia: Temple University Press.

Stocker, M., ed. 1991. *Cancer as a women's issue: Scratching the surface.* Chicago: Third Side Press.

Stockholm International Peace Research Institute. 2005. Recent trends in military expenditure. *SIPRI Yearbook 2005.* Stockholm, Sweden: SIPRI.

———. 2005. *The SIPRI Military expenditure database.* Accessed at www.sipri.org on May 25, 2005.

Stoller, E. P., and R. C. Gibson, eds. 1994. *Worlds of difference: Inequality in the aging experience.* Thousand Oaks, Calif.: Pine Forge.

Stonequist, E. V. 1961. *The marginal man: A study in personality and cultural conflict.* New York: Scribner & Sons.

Storr, M., ed. 1999. *Bisexuality: A critical reader.* New York: Routledge.

St. Paige, E. 1999. *Zaftig: The case for curves.* Seattle, Wash.: Darling and Co.

Strasburg, J. 2003. Saipan lawsuit terms OKd. *San Francisco Chronicle,* April 25, B1.

Strossen, N. 2000. *Defending pornography: Free speech, sex, and the fight for women's rights.* New York: New York University Press.

Study shows few women in combat jobs. *San Francisco Chronicle,* 21 October 1997, p. A6.

Sturdevant, S., and B. Stoltzfus. 1992. *Let the good times roll: Prostitution and the U.S. military in Asia.* New York: New Press.

Sturgeon, N. 1997. *Ecofeminist nature: Race, gender, feminist theory and political action.* New York: Routledge.

Suggs, W. 2002. Title IX at 30. *Chronicle of Higher Education,* 21 June, pp. A38–41.

Sullivan, N. 2003. *A critical introduction to queer theory.* New York: New York University Press.

Survivors Take Action Against Abuse by Military Personnel. 1999. *Newsletter 1998/99.* Fairborn, Ohio: Author.

Swerdlow, A. 1993. *Women strike for peace: Traditional motherhood and radical politics in the 1960s.* Chicago: University of Chicago Press.

Swers, M. 2001. Research on women in legislatures: What have we learned, Where are we going? *Women and Politics.* 23: 167–85.

Swiss, S., and J. Giller. 1993. Rape as a crime of war: A medical perspective. *Journal of the American Medical Association* (27): 612–15.

Szasz, A. 1994. *Ecopopulism, toxic waste and the movement for environmental justice.* Minneapolis: University of Minnesota Press.

Takaki, R. 1987. *Strangers from a different shore: Perspectives on race and ethnicity in America.* New York: Oxford University Press.

Takazato, S. 2000. Report from Okinawa: Long-term U.S. military presence and violence against women. *Canadian Women's Studies* 19(4): 42–47.

Tan, A. 1989. *The Joy Luck Club.* New York: G. P. Putnam's Sons.

Tan, C. I. 1997. Building shelter: Asian women and domestic violence. Pp. 108–17 in *Dragon ladies: Asian American feminists breathe fire,* edited by S. Shah. Boston: South End Press.

Tanenbaum, L. 2000. *Growing up female with a bad reputation.* New York: HarperCollins.

Tannen, D. 1990. *You just don't understand: Men and women in conversation.* New York: Morrow.

Tanner, R. 2005. Experts worry mountain of debt will bury U.S., *Chicago Sun-Times,* August 28. Accessed at www.suntimes.com on August 29, 2005.

Tax, M. 1993. Five women who won't be silenced. *The Nation,* 10 May, 624–27.

Taylor, A. J. 1999. High-tech, pop-a-pill culture: "New" forms of social control for Black women. Pp. 242–54 in *Dangerous intersections: Feminist perspectives on population, environment, and development,* edited by J. Silliman and Y. King. Cambridge, Mass.: South End Press.

Taylor, D. E. 1997. Women of color, environmental justice, and ecofeminism. Pp. 38–81 in *Ecofeminism: Women, culture, nature,* edited by K. Warren. Bloomington: Indiana University Press.

Teays, W., and L. Purdy. 2001. *Bioethics, justice, and health care.* Belmont, Calif.: Wadsworth.

Tenenbein, S. 1998. Power, beauty, and dykes. Pp. 155–60 in *Looking queer,* edited by D. Atkins. Binghampton, N.Y.: Harrington Park Press.

Tétreault, M. A. 1997. Accountability or justice? Rape as a war crime. Pp. 427–39 in *Feminist frontiers IV,* edited by L. Richardson, V. Taylor, and N. Whittier. New York: McGraw-Hill.

Thomas, S., and C. Wilcox, eds. 1998. *Women and elective office: Past, present, and future.* New York: Oxford University Press.

Thompson, B. W. 1994. *A hunger so wide and so deep.* Minneapolis: University of Minnesota Press.

Thompson, Becky. 2002. Multiracial feminism: Recasting the chronology of second-wave feminism. *Feminist Studies* 28(2), Summer: 337–60.

Thornhill, R., and C. T. Palmer. 2000. *A natural history of rape: Biological bases of sexual coercion.* Cambridge: MIT Press.

Thropy, M. A. 1991. Overpopulation and industrialism. In *Earth First! reader,* edited by J. Davis. Salt Lake City: Peregrine Smith Books.

Tooher, N. L. 1999. For Mexican women, sexism is a daily battle. Pp. 38–40 in *The maquiladora reader: Cross-border organizing since NAFTA,* edited by R. Kamel and A. Hoffman. Philadelphia: American Friends Service Committee.

Townsend, R., and A. Perkins. 1992. *Bitter fruit: Women's experiences of unplanned pregnancy, abortion, and adoption.* Alameda, Calif.: Hunter House.

Trask, H.-K. 1999. *From a native daughter: Colonialism and sovereignty in Hawai'i.* Rev. ed. Honolulu: University of Hawaii.

Troustine, J. 2001. *Shakespeare behind bars: The power of drama in a women's prison.* New York: St. Martin's Press.

Trujillo, C., ed. 1991. *Chicana lesbians: The girls our mothers warned us about.* Berkeley, Calif.: Third Women Press.

———. 1998. *Living Chicana theory.* Berkeley, Calif.: Third Women Press.

Tuana, N., ed. 1989. *Feminism and science.* Bloomington: Indiana University Press.

Tucker, C. 1996. Women's practical vote for Clinton. *Chicago Tribune,* 9 November, p. 3.

Tuominen, M. C. 2003. *We are not babysitters: Family care providers redefine work and care.* Piscataway, N.J.: Rutgers University Press.

Turk, A. T. 1995. Transformation versus revolutionism and reformism: Policy implications of conflict theory. In *Crime and public policy: Putting theory to work,* edited by H. Barlow. Boulder, Colo.: Westview Press.

2 black airmen allege racial discrimination. 1996. *San Francisco Chronicle,* 4 December, p. A9.

Uchitelle, L. 2001. Lacking pensions, older divorced women remain at work. *New York Times,* 26 June, p. A1.

Umansky, L. 1996. *Motherhood reconceived: Feminism and the legacies of the sixties.* New York: New York University Press.

U.N. High Commissioner for Refugees. 2002. Refugee Women. Accessed online at http://www.worldrefugeeday.info/men2.html on 1 May 2003.

University of Minnesota. 2001. *Information about the Curriculum Transformation and Disability Project.* Accessed online at http://www.crk.umn.edu/people/services/DisabilServ/CTAD.htm on 19 December 2002.

Urban Strategies Council. 2004. *Community Safety and Justice,* special issue, July. Oakland, Calif.: Urban Strategies Council. Accessed online at www.urbanstrategies.org/program/csj/news/2004/2004-07-01.html on September 2, 2005.

U.S. Bureau of Census. 2000. *Statistical Abstract of U.S.* Washington, D.C.: U.S. Bureau of Census.

———. 2004. *Statistical Abstract of U.S.* Washington, D.C.: U.S. Bureau of Census.

U.S. Department of Defense. 1996. *FY 1990–96 spouse and child maltreatment.* Washington, D.C.: U.S. Department of Defense.

U.S. Department of Justice. 1997. *Violence-related injuries treated in hospital emergency departments.* Michael R. Rand. Washington, D.C.: Bureau of Justice Statistics.

———. 2005a. *Almost 6.9 million on probation or parole or incarcerated in U.S. prisons or jails.* Accessed at www.ojp.usdoj.gov/bjs/pub/press/ppus03pr.htm on September 1, 2005.

———. 2005b. *Violent crime rates.* Accessed at www.ojp.usdoj.gov/bjs/gvc.htm accessed on September 1, 2005.

U.S. Department of Labor. Bureau of Labor Statistics. 2004. *BLS News* 04-148. Washington, D.C.: U.S. Department of Labor.

U.S. Department of Labor, Women's Bureau. 2005. *Fact sheets.* Washington, D.C.: U.S. Department of Labor.

———. 2005. *How many people with disabilities are there in the United States?* Washington, D.C.: U.S. Department of Labor. Accessed online at http://www.dol.gov/odep/faqs/people.htm on 12 July 2005.

Usdansky, M. L. 1996. Single motherhood: Stereotypes vs. statistics. *New York Times,* 11 February, p. E4.

Ussher, J. 1991. *Women's madness.* Hemel Hempstead, England: Harvester Wheatsheaf.

Uttal, L. 2002. *Making care work: Employed mothers in the new childcare market.* New Brunswick, N.J.: Rutgers University Press.

Vance, C., ed. 1984. *Pleasure and danger: Exploring female sexuality.* Boston: Routledge and Kegan Paul.

Wade-Gayles, G. 1993. *Pushed back to strength: A Black woman's journey home.* Boston: Beacon Press.

Walker, J. 1996. The prison industrial complex. *RESIST Newsletter* 5(9): 4–6.

Walker, L. 1979. *The battered woman.* New York: Harper & Row.

———. 1984. *The battered woman syndrome.* New York: Springer.

Walker, M. 1992. Sex attacks "rife" on U.S. servicewomen. *London Guardian,* 2 July, p. 6.

Walker, M. U. 1999. *Mother time: Women, aging and ethics.* Lanham, Md.: Rowman and Littlefield.

Walker, R. 1995a. Lusting for freedom. In *Listen up: Voices of the next generation,* edited by Barbara Findlen. Seattle: Seal Press, pp. 95–101.

———. 1995b. *To be real: Telling the truth and changing the face of feminism.* New York: Anchor/Doubleday.

———. 2001. *Black, white, and Jewish: Autobiography of a shifting self.* New York: Riverhead Books.

Wallace-Saunders, Kimberly, ed. 2002. *Skin deep, spirit strong: The Black female body in American culture.* Ann Arbor: University of Michigan Press.

Wallach, L., and M. Sforza. 2000. *The WTO: Five years of reasons to resist corporate globalization.* New York: Seven Stories Press.

———, and P. Woodall. 2004. *Whose trade organization? A comprehensive guide to the World Trade Organization.* New York: New Press.

Walters, B., and H. Downs. 1996. *20/20,* November 15. New York: American Broadcasting Company.

Walters, S. D. 2001. *All the rage: The story of gay visibility in America.* Chicago: Chicago University Press.

Waring, M. 1988. *If women counted: A new feminist economics.* New York: Harper & Row.

Warner, S. B. 1987. *To dwell is to garden: A history of Boston's community gardens.* Boston: Northeastern University Press.

War Resisters League. 2005. *Where your income tax money really goes.* War Resisters League, 339 Lafayette St., New York, NY 10012.

Warren, K. J., ed. 1994. *Ecological feminism.* New York: Routledge.

———. 2000. *Ecofeminist philosophy: A western perspective on what it is and why it matters.* Lanham, Md.: Rowman and Littlefield.

Washburn, P. 1993. Women and the peace movement. Pp. 135–48 in *Women and the use of military force,* edited by R. Howes and M. Stevenson. Boulder, Colo.: Lynne Rienner Publishers.

Wasserman, C. 1992. FMS: The backlash against survivors. *Sojourner: The Women's Forum,* November, 18–20.

Watterson, K. 1996. *Women in prison.* Rev. ed. Boston: Northeastern University Press.

Webber, W. S. 1993. *Lesbians in the military speak out.* Northboro, Mass.: Madwoman Press.

Weedon, C. 1987. *Feminist practice and poststructuralist theory.* New York: Blackwell.

Weinstein, L., and C. White, eds. 1997. *Wives and warriors: Women and the military in the United States and Canada.* Westport, Conn.: Greenwood Press.

Weise, E. R., ed. 1992. *Closer to home: Bisexuality and feminism.* Seattle, Wash.: Seal Press.

Wells, J., ed. 2000. *Home fronts: Controversies in nontraditional parenting.* New York: Alyson Books.

Wendell, S. 1992. Toward a feminist theory of disability. Pp. 63–81 in *Feminist perspectives in medical ethics,* edited by H. B. Holmes and L. M. Purdy. Bloomington: Indiana University Press.

———. 1996. *The rejected body.* New York: Routledge.

Werner International. 2005. *Primary textiles labor cost comparisons.* Winter 2004/2005. Herndon, VA.: Werner International. www.wernertex.com.

West, G., and R. L. Blumberg, eds. 1990. *Women and social protest.* New York: Oxford University Press.

Whisnant, R. and C. Stark. 2004. *Not for sale: Feminists resisting prostitution and pornography.* North Melbourne, Australia: Spinifex.

White, E. 2002. *Fast girls: Teenage tribes and the myth of the slut.* New York: Penguin.

White, E. C. 1985. *Chain, chain, change: For Black women dealing with physical and emotional abuse.* Seattle, Wash.: Seal Press.

———, ed. 1990. *The Black women's health book: Speaking for ourselves.* Seattle, Wash.: Seal Press.

———. 1991. Unhealthy appetites: Large is lovely, unless you're unhappy overeating and unable to lose weight. *Essence,* September, 28.

White, L. 1988. *The obsidian mirror: An adult healing from incest.* Seattle, Wash.: Seal Press.

Wilchins, R. 2002. Gender rights are human rights. In *Genderqueer: Voices from beyond the sexual binary,* edited by J. Nestle, C. Howell, and R. Wilchins. Los Angeles: Alyson Publications.

Wilchins, R. A. 1997. *Read my lips: Sexual subversion and the end of gender.* Ithaca, N.Y.: Firebrand.

Wilkerson, A. 2002. Disability, sex radicalism, and political agency, *NWSA Journal* 14(3), Fall: 33–57. Special issue: Feminist Disability Studies.

Williams, F. 2005. Toxic breast milk? *New York Times Magazine,* 9 Jan. First Person.

Williams, J. 2000. *Unbending gender: Why family and work conflict and what to do about it.* New York: Oxford University Press.

Williams, L., ed. 1997. *Gender equity and the World Bank group: A post-Beijing assessment.* Washington, D.C.: Women's Eyes on the World Bank-U.S.

Williams, T. T. 1992. *Refuge: An unnatural history of family and place.* New York: Vintage.

Wilson, M. 1993. *Crossing the boundary: Black women survive incest.* Seattle, Wash.: Seal Press.

Wingspan Domestic Violence Project. 1998. *Abuse and violence in same-gender relationships: A resource for lesbian, gay, bi, and transgendered communities.* Tucson, Ariz.: Wingspan Domestic Violence Project.

Withorn, A. 1999. Temp work: "A devil's bargain" for women. *Sojourner: The Women's Forum,* October, 9.

Wittig, M. 1992. *The straight mind and other essays.* Boston: Beacon Press.

Wolf, N. 1991. *The beauty myth.* New York: Doubleday.

———. 1993. *Fire with fire: The new female power and how it will change the 21st century.* New York: Random House.

———. 1997. *Promiscuities: The secret struggle for womanhood.* New York: Ballantine.

Women of Color Resource Center. 1996, December. Solicitation letter to donors. Berkeley, Calif.: Women of Color Resource Center.

Women's Environment and Development Organization (WEDO). 1998. *Mapping progress: Assessing implementation of the Beijing Platform.* New York: WEDO.

———. 2002. *Women's action agenda for a healthy and peaceful planet 2015.* New York: WEDO. Available online at http://www.wedo.org.

———. 2005. *Beijing betrayed.* New York: WEDO.

Women's Foundation. 2002. *Failing to make ends meet: The economic status of women in California.* San Francisco: The Women's Foundation.

Women's Research and Education Institute. 2002. *Women in the military.* Washington, D.C.: WREI. Accessed at http://www.wrei.org/projects/wiu/wim/index.htm on 3 January 2003.

Women Working for a Nuclear Free and Independent Pacific, ed. 1987. *Pacific women speak.* Oxford, England: Green Line.

Wood, S. 1997. Blood, sweat, and shears. *Corporate Watch Features,* 22 September. San Francisco: Corporate Watch.

Woodman, S. 1997. An officer and a . . . ? *Ms.,* March/April, 19–22.

Woods, H. 2000. *Stepping up to power: The political journey of American women.* Boulder, Colo.: Westview Press.

Worcester, N. 2004. Hormone replacement therapy: Getting to the heart of the politics of women's health? *NWSA Journal* 16(3), Fall: 56–69.

Working Group on the WTO. 1999. *A citizens' guide to the World Trade Organization.* New York: Apex Press.

World Bank. 2004. *Global debt finance.* Washington, D.C.: World Bank.

World Health Organization. 1946. *Preamble to the Constitution of the World Health Organization,* adopted by the International Health Conference, New York, 19–22 June.

———. 2005. *The World Health Report 2005: Make every mother and child count.* New York: WHO.

Worldwatch Institute. 2003. *State of the world.* Washington, D.C.: Worldwatch Institute.

Yans-McLaughlin, V., ed. 1990. *Immigration reconsidered.* New York: Oxford University Press.

Yen, M. 1989. Refusal to jail immigrant who killed wife stirs outrage. *Washington Post,* 10 April, p. A3.

Yoder, J. 1989. Women at West Point: Lessons for token women in male-dominated occupations. In *Women: A feminist perspective,* edited by J. Freeman. Mountain View, Calif.: Mayfield.

Young, I. 1980. Socialist feminism and the limits of dual systems theory. *Socialist Review,* 10(2–3): 174.

Young, M. E., M. A. Nosek, C. A. Howland, G. Chanpong, and D. H. Rintala. 1997. Prevalence of abuse of women with physical disabilities. *Archives of Physical Medicine and Rehabilitation* 78: S34–S38.

Young, W. A. 1997. Women and immigration. Unpublished manuscript produced for Women's Commission for Refugee Women and Children, Washington, D.C.

Zambrano, M. Z. 1985. *Mejor sola que mal accompanda: For the Latina in an abusive relationship.* Seattle, Wash.: Seal Press.

Zamora-Olib, O. A., ed. 2000. *Inheritors of the earth: The human face of the U.S. military contamination at Clarke Air Base, Pampanga, Philippines.* Quezon City, Philippines: People's Task Force for Bases Cleanup.

Zaretsky, E. 1976. *Capitalism, the family, and personal life.* New York: Harper & Row.

Zavella, P. 1987. *Women's work and Chicano families: Cannery workers of the Santa Clara Valley.* Ithaca, N.Y.: Cornell University.

Zeff, R., M. Love, and K. Stults, eds. 1989. *Empowering ourselves: Women and toxics organizing.* Falls Church, Va.: Citizens Clearinghouse for Hazardous Wastes.

Zepernick, M. 1998a. The sovereign people are stirring. *The Cape Cod Times,* 27 November, p. A15.

———. 1998b. A lesson in democracy. *The Cape Cod Times,* 11 December, p. A15.

Zernike, K. 2003. Many women gleeful at old friend's encore. *New York Times,* March 7, A16.

Zimmerman, L. 2003 (October). Where are the women? The strange case of the missing feminists. When was the last time you saw one on TV? *The Women's Review of Books* XXI(1): 5–6.

Zinn, H. 1995. *People's history of the United States: 1492–present.* Rev. and updated ed. New York: HarperPerennial.

Zita, J., ed. 1997. Special issue: Third wave feminisms. *Hypatia: A Journal of Feminist Philosophy,* vol. 12, no. 3 (Summer).

Credits

Readings and Text Credits

He Works, She Works, but What Different Impressions They Make.

DOROTHY ALLISON, "A Question of Class" by Dorothy Allison, from SISTERS, SEXPERTS, QUEERS by Arlene Stein, copyright © 1993 by Arlene Stein. Used by permission of Dutton Signet, a division of Penguin Putnam Inc.

PEGGY ANTROBUS, Excerpts from "The Global Women's Movement: Definitions and Origins" by Peggy Antrobus from THE GLOBAL WOMEN'S MOVEMENT: Origins, Issues and Strategies, © 2004, pp. 9–25. Reprinted by permission of Zed Books Ltd.

JUDITH ARCANA, "Abortion is a Motherhood Issue" by Judith Arcana.

ASIAN COMMUNITIES FOR REPRODUCTIVE JUSTICE, "Reproductive Justice: Vision, Analysis, and Action for a Stronger Movement" reprinted by permission.

URSULA BIEMANN, "Remotely Sensed: A Topography of the Global Sex Trade" by Ursula Biemann from FEMINIST REVIEW (70) 2002, pp. 75–88. Reprinted by permission of Palgrave Macmillan.

GRACE CAROLINE BRIDGES, "Lisa's Ritual, Age 10" by Grace Caroline Bridges from RESOURCEFUL WOMAN, edited by Shawn Brennan, Julie Winklepeck and G. MacNee. Copyright © 1994. Reprinted by permission of Visible Ink Press.

MARILYN BUCK, "Women in Prison and Work" by Marilyn Buck was originally published in FEMINIST STUDIES, Volume 30, Number 2 (Summer 2004): 451–455, by permission of the publisher, Feminist Studies, Inc.

CHARLOTTE BUNCH, "Whose Security?" by Charlotte Bunch reprinted with permission from the September 23, 2002 issue of THE NATION. For subscription information, call 1-800-333-8536. Portions of each week's Nation magazine can be accessed at http://www.thenation.com.

BETTY BURKES, "Full Moon: The Imagery of Wholeness and Celebration" by Betty Burkes from NWSA JOURNAL, 2001, Vol. 13, no. 2, pp. 74–79. Reprinted by permission of Betty Burkes.

VERONICA CHAMBERS, "To Whom Much is Given, Much is expected: Successful Women, Family, and Responsibility" from HAVING IT ALL? BLACK WOMEN AND SUCCESS by Veronica Chambers, copyright © 2003 by Veronica Chambers. Used by permission of Doubleday, a division of Random House, Inc.

ABRA FORTUNE CHERNIK, "The Body Politic" from LISTEN UP: VOICES FROM THE NEXT FEMINIST GENERATION, edited by Barbara Findlen and published by Seal Press, Seattle, WA. Copyright © 1995 by Barbara Findlen. Used with permission of the publisher.

SANDRA CISNEROS, Copyright © 1996 by Sandra Cisneros. From GODDESS OF THE AMERICAS/LA DIOSA DE LAS

AMERICAS: Writings on the Virgin de Guadalupe, ed. by Ana Castillo. Copyright © 1996 by Ana Castillo. Riverhead Books, New York. Reprinted by permission of Susan Bergholz Literary Services, New York. All rights reserved.

JUDITH ORTIZ COFER, "The Story of My Body" from THE LATIN DELI: PROSE AND POETRY. Copyright © 1993 by Judith Ortiz Cofer. Used by permission of University of Georgia Press.

CYNTHIA COHEN, "Common Threads: Life Stories and Arts in Educating for Social Change" by Cynthia Cohen from NWSA JOURNAL, Vol. 6, No. 2. Reprinted by permission of the author.

COMBAHEE RIVER COLLECTIVE, "A Black Feminist Statement" from THE COMBAHEE RIVER COLLECTIVE STATEMENT in HOME GIRLS: A BLACK FEMINIST ANTHOLOGY. Copyright © 1983 by Barbara Smith. Reprinted by permission of the author and of Kitchen Table: Women of Color Press, P.O. Box 40-4920, Brooklyn, NY 11240-4920.

ANN CRITTENDEN, "The Mommy Tax" (pp. 87–109) from THE PRICE OF MOTHERHOOD by Ann Crittenden, © 2001 by Ann Crittenden. Reprinted by permission of Henry Holt and Company, LLC.

FREDERICA Y. DALY, "Perspectives of Native American Women on Race and Gender" from CHALLENGING RACISM & SEXISM: ALTERNATIVES TO GENETIC EXPLANATIONS, copyright © 1994 by Ethel Tobach and Betty Rosoff, by permission of the Feminist Press at the City University of New York, www.feministpress.org.

AMANI ELKASSABANI, "Hanaan's House" by Amani Elkassabani as appeared in SHATTERING THE STEREOTYPES: Muslim women speak out edited by Fawzia Afzal-Khan, © 2005, pp. 230–243. Reprinted by permission of the author.

CYNTHIA ENLOE, "Sneak Attack: The Militarization of U.S. Culture" by Cynthia Enloe from MS Magazine, December/January 2002. Reprinted by permission of MS Magazine, © 2002.

EVE ENSLER, From THE VAGINA MONOLOGUES by Eve Ensler, copyright © 1998 by Eve Ensler; Foreword copyright © 1998 by Gloria Steinem. Used by permission of Villard Books, a division of Random House, Inc.

PAULA J. ETTELBRICK, "Since When Is Marriage a Path to Liberation?" by Paula J. Ettelbrick. Reprinted by permission of the author.

LESLIE FEINBERG, "We Are All Works in Progress" from TRANS LIBERATION by Leslie Feinberg. Copyright © 1998 by Leslie Feinberg. Reprinted by permission of Beacon Press, Boston.

MARIA P. FERNANDEZ-KELLY, Reprinted by permission from FOR WE ARE SOLD, I AND MY PEOPLE: WOMEN AND INDUSTRY IN MEXICO'S FRONTIER by Maria P. Fernandez-Kelly, the State University of New York Press © 1983, State University of New York. All rights reserved.

Figures, Photo and Cartoon Credits

Name Index

Index

About the Authors

Gwyn Kirk (left) has taught women's studies and sociology at several U.S. academic institutions, including Antioch College where she chaired the women's studies program (1992–1995). She received a Rockefeller Fellowship at the University of Hawaii (2002) and was a Visiting Scholar at the Women's Leadership Institute, Mills College (2001–2003). She shared the Jane Watson Irwin Chair in Women's Studies at Hamilton College with Margo Okazawa-Rey (1999–2001). Her articles on feminism, ecology, militarism, and transnational feminist organizing have appeared in various anthologies and journals including *Berkeley Women's Law Journal, Foreign Policy in Focus, Frontiers, Peace Review,* and *Social Justice.* She writes for popular audiences through activist publications and projects, and op ed pieces. Current research and writing concerns the impact of military operations on the environment and human health. Dr. Kirk is a founder member of the East Asia–U.S.–Puerto Rico Women's Network, started in 1997 by an international group of academics and activists concerned about the negative effects of U.S. military operations on local communities, especially on women, children, and the environment. She has served on the board of Women's Action for New Directions (WAND) Education Fund, a national organization that seeks to redirect excessive military spending to unmet human and environmental needs (2000–2006). Other major publications include *Greenham Women Everywhere: Dreams, Ideas and Actions from the Women's Peace Movement* (1983) co–authored with Alice Cook, and *Urban Planning in a Capitalist Society* (1980). Gwyn Kirk holds a Ph.D. in political sociology from the London School of Economics.

Margo Okazawa-Rey (right) is a Professor in the School of Human and Organizational Development at Fielding University, and Professor Emerita of Social Work at San Francisco State University. She directed the Women's Leadership Institute at Mills College (2002–2005); she was Earl and Edna Stice Feminist Scholar of Social Justice, University of Washington (2004–2005); and has held the Jane Watson Irwin Chair in Women's Studies at Hamilton College and the National Endowment for the Humanities/Jack Gray Chair at the University of Hartford. Professor Okazawa-Rey's articles on transnational feminist praxis, militarism, feminist movements, and critical multicultural education are published in journals such as *Affilia, Social Justice, Peace Review,* and the *Asian Journal of Women's Studies.* She is co–editor of *Beyond Heroes and Holidays: K-12 Anti-Racist, Multicultural Education and Staff Development* (1998), the *Encyclopedia of African American Education* (1996), and *Teachers, Teaching, and Teacher Education* (1987). Professor Okazawa-Rey's scholarship is informed by a lifetime of activism. In the 1970s, she was a member of the Combahee River Collective, a Black feminist group that developed the theory of intersectionality as a basis for feminist praxis. She is a co-founder of the East Asia–U.S.–Puerto Rico Women's Network against Militarism, a transnational project that generates feminist analyses and resistance to U.S. militarism. She has been Research Consultant at the Women's Centre for Legal Aid and Counseling in East Jerusalem, Palestine (2005–2006). Her current research examines the connections between militarism, economic globalization and impacts on women of color. She holds an Ed.D. from Harvard Graduate School of Education.